France

The complete guide, thoroughly up-to-date

Packed with details that will make your trip

The must-see sights, off and on the beaten path

What to see, what to skip

Mix-and-match vacation itineraries

City strolls, countryside adventures

Smart lodging and dining options

Essential local do's and taboos

Transportation tips, distances and directions

Key contacts, savvy travel tips

When to go, what to pack

Clear, accurate, easy-to-use maps

Books to read, videos to watch, background essay

Fodor's Travel Publications, Inc.
New York • Toronto • London • Sydney • Auckland
www.fodors.com/

Fodor's France '98

EDITOR: Natasha Lesser
Editorial Contributors: Rob Andrews, Roberta Beardsley, David Brown, Nancy Coons, Nicole Duplaix, Nigel Fisher, Simon Hewitt, Suzanne Rowan Kelleher, Christina Knight, Alexander Lobrano, Jennifer Paull, Heidi Sarna, Helayne Schiff, M. T. Schwartzman (Gold Guide editor), George Semler, Dinah Spritzer
Editorial Production: Laura M. Kidder
Maps: David Lindroth, *cartographer;* Mapping Specialists Ltd., *cartographers;* Robert Blake, *map editor*
Design: Fabrizio La Rocca, *creative director;* Guido Caroti, *associate art director;* Jolie Novak, *photo editor*
Production/Manufacturing: Mike Costa
Cover Photograph: Suzanne and Nick Geary/Tony Stone Images
Design: Between the Covers

Copyright

ISBN 0-679-03481-1

Special Sales

Fodor's Travel Publications are available at special discounts for bulk purchases for sales promotions or premiums. Special editions, including personalized covers, excerpts of existing guides, and corporate imprints, can be created in large quantities for special needs. For more information, contact your local bookseller or write to Special Markets, Fodor's Travel Publications, 201 East 50th Street, New York, NY 10022. Inquiries from Canada should be directed to your local Canadian bookseller or sent to Random House of Canada, Ltd., Marketing Department, 1265 Aerowood Drive, Mississauga, Ontario L4W 1B9. Inquiries from the United Kingdom should be sent to: Fodor's Travel Publications, 20 Vauxhall Bridge Road, London, England SW1V 2SA.

PRINTED IN THE UNITED STATES OF AMERICA

10 9 8 7 6 5 4 3 2 1

CONTENTS

Maps

ON THE ROAD WITH FODOR'S

WE'RE ALWAYS THRILLED to get letters from readers, especially one like this:

It took us an hour to decide what book to buy and we now know we picked the best one. Your book was wonderful, easy to follow, very accurate, and good on pointing out eating places, informal as well as formal. When we saw other people using your book, we would look at each other and smile.

Our editors and writers are deeply committed to making every Fodor's guide "the best one"—not only accurate but always charming, brimming with sound recommendations and solid ideas, right on the mark in describing restaurants and hotels, and full of fascinating facts that make you view what you've traveled to see in a rich new light.

About Our Writers

Our success in achieving our goals—and in helping to make your trip the best of all possible vacations—is a credit to the hard work of our extraordinary writers and editors.

Roberta Beardsley has lived in Paris for 26 years, enough time to have had at least two lives and many more residences. Seven years near Les Halles has convinced her that where you live has a lot to do with how you spend your evenings. With a little help from her friends, she has scoped out all of *the* best places to see a play, hear some music, or have a drink.

Nancy Coons, who has been based in Europe since 1987, has covered much of northeastern France (and many neighboring countries) for Fodor's. She works from her 300-year-old farmhouse in Lorraine, in launching distance of Luxembourg, Belgium, and Germany. She has written on European culture and food for *The Wall Street Journal, European Travel & Life, Opera News,* and *National Geographic Traveler.*

Nicole Duplaix is a Franco-American citizen of the world, Ph.D. wildlife biologist, author, freelance photojournalist with articles in *National Geographic,* and bon vivant, who has lived on both sides of the Atlantic and is now firmly based in Paris. She has traveled all over the world, but Paris is still her favorite city and Brittany one of her all-time favorite regions. Her ongoing pastimes includes finding the unfindable in Paris for the Web site *Bonjour Paris,* of which she is the executive editor.

Nigel Fisher, the peripatetic writer and knowledgeable publisher of "Voyager International," a newsletter on world travel, updated much of this book. His particular interests are in telling his readers about art, about divine places to stay, and about the most delicious food. Everywhere he goes, he talks to people and makes friends, so he always knows which chefs are striving for the stars and which are resting on their laurels.

Simon Hewitt, who first wrote much of this book, headed to Paris straight from studying French and Art History at Oxford. It was a return to base: His grandmother was French, as are his wife and daughter. He recently moved to Versailles to gain a different perspective on life in and around the French capital. When not contemplating the Sacre-Coeur's aesthetic fallout or the Sun King's bigger-than-life Baroque home, his thoughts often turn to cricket—he is captain of the French national team.

Suzanne Rowan Kelleher traded bagels for croissants when she moved from New York to Paris in 1993. A wayfarer by nature, Suzanne is a travel writer who contributes to *Esquire* and *Travel Holiday.* She has good news about shopping and lodging in Paris: The recession has forced the city to become more value-oriented.

Editor **Natasha Lesser** has lived in Washington, D.C., California, Iowa, Kenya, and France. After exploring every boulevard and back rue in Paris, many a mile of coast in Normandy, and the heights of the French Alps, she has stayed long enough at her desk in New York to pass her knowledge on to you.

Alexander Lobrano has lived in Paris for 10 years, after eating his way through Boston, New York, and London. He writes a weekly dining column for *Paris Time Out* and has reported on French food for many publications, including *Food & Wine* and *Travel & Leisure*. His best meal? Last year at Philippe Detourbe in Paris.

George Semler lives over the border in Spain, but he has skied, hiked, fly-fished, and explored both sides of the Pyrénées for the last quarter of a century. He can say that he's acquainted with each trout in the Pyrénées, of Spanish *and* French persuasion, as well as every wild mushroom and Romanesque chapel. Corsica is his second love and his mountain in the sea.

We'd especially like to thank Marion Fourestier at the French Government Tourist Office in New York.

New This Year

Paris is unforgettable, but there are many other fabulous cities in France that are worth visiting. George Semler has expanded our coverage of Toulouse and added new walking tours. Nancy Coons has created walking tours of Nancy and Strasbourg, and Nigel Fisher has added walking tours for Lyon. For all you nature lovers, we've added more of France's wondrous gorges, canyons, and national parks.

And this year, Fodor's joins Rand McNally, the world's largest commercial mapmaker, to bring you a detailed color map of France. Just detach it along the perforation and drop it in your tote bag.

We're also proud to announce that the American Society of Travel Agents has endorsed Fodor's as its guidebook of choice. ASTA is the world's largest and most influential travel trade association, operating in more than 170 countries, with 27,000 members pledged to adhere to a strict code of ethics reflecting the Society's motto, "Integrity in Travel." ASTA shares Fodor's devotion to providing smart, honest travel information and advice to travelers, and we've long recommended that our readers consult ASTA member agents for the experience and professionalism they bring to the table.

On the Web, check out Fodor's site (www.fodors.com/) for information on major destinations around the world and travel-savvy interactive features. The site also lists the 80-plus radio stations nationwide that carry the *Fodor's Travel Show,* a live call-in program that airs every weekend. Tune in to hear guests discuss their adventures—or call in for answers to your most pressing travel questions.

How to Use This Book

Organization

Up front is the **Gold Guide,** an easy-to-use section divided alphabetically by topic. Under each listing you'll find tips and information that will help you accomplish what you need to in France. You'll also find addresses and telephone numbers of organizations and companies that offer destination-related services and detailed information and publications.

The first chapter, Destination: France helps get you in the mood for your trip. What's Where gets you oriented, New and Noteworthy cues you in on trends and happenings, Pleasures and Pastimes describes the activities and sights that really make France unique, Great Itineraries suggests tours through France as a whole, Fodor's Choice showcases our top picks, and Festivals and Seasonal Events alerts you to special events you'll want to seek out.

Chapters in *France '98* are arranged regionally, beginning with the capital, Paris, and the region around it, the Ile-de-France, then spiraling clockwise around the country from west to east. Each city chapter begins with an Exploring section subdivided by neighborhood; each subsection recommends a walking or driving tour and lists sights in alphabetical order. Each regional chapter is divided by geographical area; within each area, towns are covered in logical geographical order, and attractive stretches of road and minor points of interest between them are indicated by the designation En Route. Throughout, Off the Beaten Path sights appear after the places from which they are most easily accessible. And within town sections, all restaurants and lodgings are grouped together.

To help you decide what to visit in the time you have, all chapters begin with recommended itineraries; you can mix and match those from several chapters to create a complete vacation. The A-to-Z section that ends all chapters covers getting there and getting around. It also provides helpful contacts and resources.

At the end of the book you'll find Portraits, wonderful essays about food, wine, and architecture in France, followed by suggestions for any pretrip research you want to do, from recommended reading to movies on tape with France as a backdrop.

Icons and Symbols

★ Our special recommendations
✕ Restaurant
🏨 Lodging establishment
✕🏨 Lodging establishment whose restaurant warrants a special trip
🦆 Good for kids (rubber duckie)
☞ Sends you to another section of the guide for more information
✉ Address
☎ Telephone number
⏲ Opening and closing times
🎟 Admission prices (those we give apply to adults; substantially reduced fees are almost always available for children, students, and senior citizens)

Numbers in white and black (e.g., ② or ❷) circles that appear on the maps, in the margins, and within the tours correspond to one another.

Dining and Lodging

The restaurants and lodgings we list are the cream of the crop in each price range. Price charts appear in the Pleasures and Pastimes section that follows each chapter introduction.

Hotel Facilities

We always list the facilities that are available—but we don't specify whether they cost extra: When pricing accommodations, always ask what's included. In addition, assume that all rooms have private baths unless otherwise noted.

Assume that hotels operate on the **European Plan** (EP, with no meals) unless we note that they use the **Continental Plan** (CP, with a Continental breakfast daily), **Modified American Plan** (MAP, with breakfast and dinner daily), or the **Full American Plan** (FAP, with all meals).

Restaurant Reservations and Dress Codes

Reservations are always a good idea; we note only when they're essential or when they are not accepted. Book as far ahead as you can, and reconfirm when you get to town. Unless otherwise noted, the restaurants listed are open daily for lunch and dinner. We mention dress only when men are required to wear a jacket or a jacket and tie. Look for an overview of local habits in the Gold Guide.

Credit Cards

The following abbreviations are used: **AE,** American Express; **DC,** Diners Club; **MC,** MasterCard; and **V,** Visa.

Don't Forget to Write

You can use this book in the confidence that all prices and opening times are based on information supplied to us at press time; Fodor's cannot accept responsibility for any errors. Time inevitably brings changes, so always confirm information when it matters—especially if you're making a detour to visit a specific place. In addition, when making reservations be sure to mention if you have a disability or are traveling with children, if you prefer a private bath or a certain type of bed, or if you have specific dietary needs or other concerns.

Were the restaurants we recommended as described? Did our hotel picks exceed your expectations? Did you find a museum we recommended a waste of time? If you have complaints, we'll look into them and revise our entries when the facts warrant it. If you've discovered a special place that we haven't included, we'll pass the information along to our correspondents and have them check it out. So send us your feedback, positive *and* negative: E-mail us at editors@fodors.com (specifying the name of the book on the subject line) or write the France editor at Fodor's, 201 East 50th Street, New York, New York 10022. Have a wonderful trip!

Karen Cure
Editorial Director

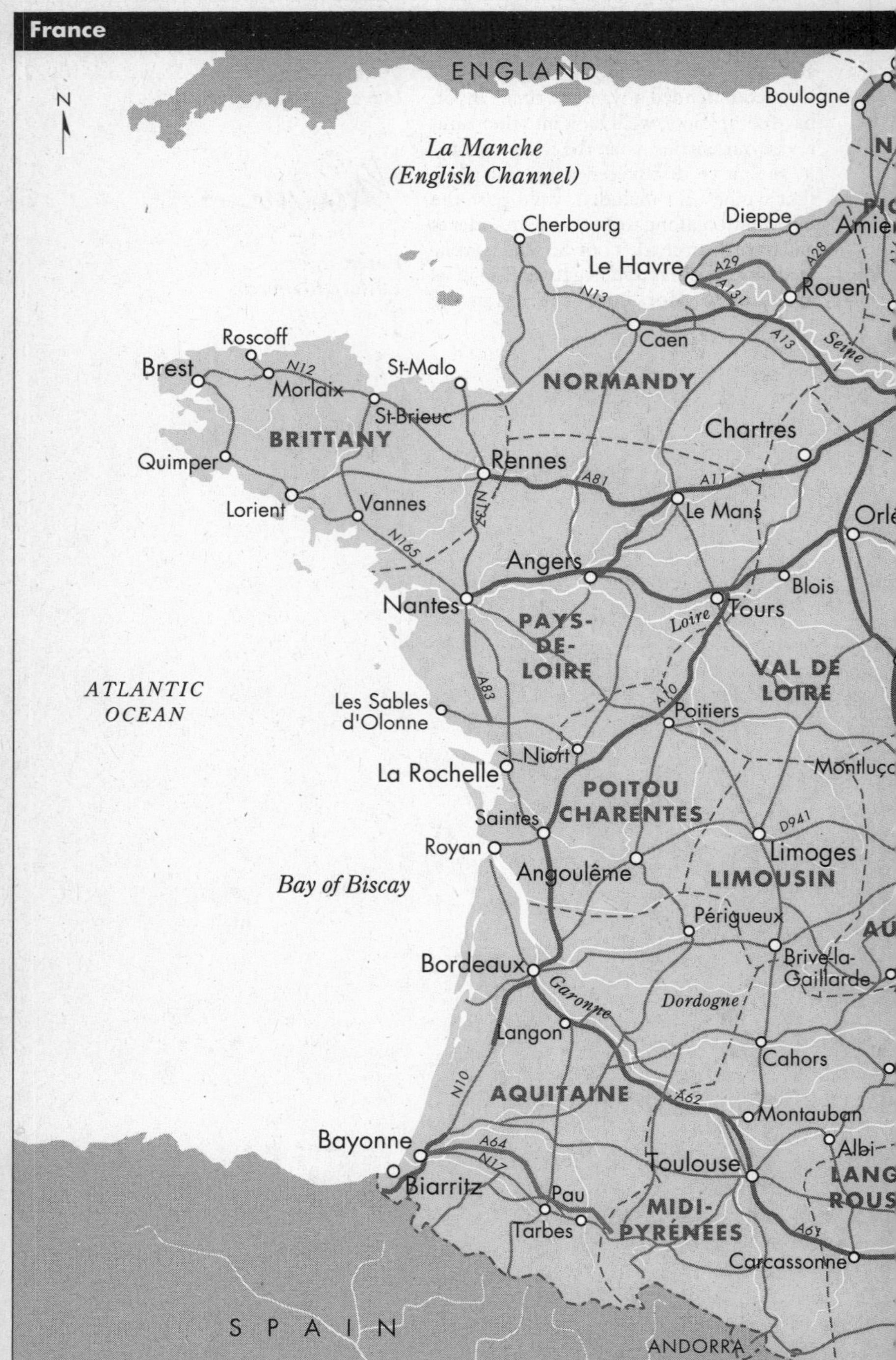
France
ENGLAND
N
La Manche
(English Channel)
Boulogne
Dieppe
Cherbourg
Le Havre
Rouen
Seine
Caen
NORMANDY
Roscoff
Brest
Morlaix
St-Malo
St-Brieuc
BRITTANY
Quimper
Lorient
Vannes
Rennes
Chartres
Le Mans
Angers
Nantes
Blois
Tours
Loire
PAYS-DE-LOIRE
VAL DE LOIRE
ATLANTIC OCEAN
Les Sables d'Olonne
Poitiers
Niort
La Rochelle
Montluçon
POITOU CHARENTES
Saintes
Royan
Limoges
Angoulême
LIMOUSIN
Bay of Biscay
Périgueux
Bordeaux
Brive-la-Gaillarde
Garonne
Dordogne
Langon
Cahors
AQUITAINE
Montauban
Albi
Bayonne
Biarritz
Toulouse
Pau
Tarbes
MIDI-PYRÉNEES
Carcassonne
SPAIN
ANDORRA
N12
N13
N137
N165
A81
A11
A10
A83
A29
A28
A131
A13
D941
N10
A62
A64
N117
A61

Calais
A26/E15
BELGIUM
NORTH
Lille
Arras
PICARDY
Cambrai
miens
St. Quentin
A16
A26
Beauvais
LUXEMBOURG
CHAMPAGNE
ARDENNES
Reims
ILE DE
FRANCE
A4
Metz
ALSACE-
LORRAINE
Paris
Châlons-en-
Champagne
A26
Nancy
Rhine
Strasbourg
GERMANY
Sens
A5
Troyes
A35
A6
Orléans
A31
Colmar
Mulhouse
Auxerre
A6
Belfort
Dijon
Bourges
Beaune
A36
Besançon
Nevers
BURGUNDY
FRANCHE
COMTE
SWITZERLAND
Saône
tluçon
A71
Mâcon
Bourg-en-
Bresse
A40
A72
Clermont-
Ferrand
Lyon
Rhône
ALPES
AUVERGNE
Chambéry
ITALY
Rhône
A7
A49
Le Puy
Aurillac
Grenoble
RHÔNE
VALLEY
A75
Rodez
Montélimar
Gap
Millau
PROVENCE
Sisteron
Avignon
A51
RIVIERA
Nîmes
ANGUEDOC
OUSSILLON
Nice
MONACO
Monte Carlo
Montpellier
Aix-en-Provence
Cannes
A8
Marseille
Narbonne
Toulon
A9
Perpignan
0
50 mi
0
75 km
Mediterranean Sea
Corsica
Corsica
Bastia
Calvi
Corte
Ajaccio
N198
Bonifacio

Europe
Reykjavík
ICELAND
NORWAY
Bergen
SCOTLAND
NORTHERN IRELAND
Edinburgh
North Sea
Skagerrak
Belfast
IRELAND
Irish Sea
DENMARK
Dublin
UNITED KINGDOM
WALES
Hamburg
ENGLAND
NETHERLANDS
Cardiff
Amsterdam
London
The Hague
Rotterdam
ATLANTIC OCEAN
English Channel
Brussels
Bonn
BELGIUM
Frankfurt
Paris
LUXEMBOURG
FRANCE
Zürich
Munich
Bern
SWITZERLAND
Lyon
LIECHTENSTEIN
Milan
Venice
Monte Carlo
Nice
Marseille
MONACO
PORTUGAL
ANDORRA
Florence
Madrid
Lisbon
Barcelona
Corsica
SPAIN
Seville
Granada
Sardinia
Balearic Islands
Tyrrhenian
Gibraltar
Mediterranean Sea
MOROCCO
ALGERIA
TUNISIA
0
400 miles
0
600 km

FINLAND
Gulf of Bothnia
Oslo
SWEDEN
Helsinki
Gulf of Finland
St. Petersburg
Tallinn
Stockholm
ESTONIA
Göteborg
Kattegat
Riga
LATVIA
Moscow
Copenhagen
LITHUANIA
Baltic Sea
Kaunas
RUSSIA
Vilnius
RUSSIA
Kaliningrad
Minsk
Berlin
POLAND
BELARUS
Warsaw
MANY
Kraków
Kiev
Prague
CZECH REPUBLIC
UKRAINE
SLOVAKIA
Vienna
Bratislava
Salzburg
AUSTRIA
Budapest
MOLDOVA
Chişinău
HUNGARY
SLOVENIA
Ljubljana
Zagreb
ROMANIA
CROATIA
Novi Sad
Bucharest
BOSNIA AND HERZEGOVINA
Belgrade
SERBIA
Black Sea
Adriatic Sea
Sarajevo
BULGARIA
MONTENEGRO
Priština
Sofia
Rome
Skopje
Podgorica
F.Y.R. of MACEDONIA
ITALY
Istanbul
Tiranë
Naples
ALBANIA
Ankara
TURKEY
GREECE
Aegean Sea
Ionian Sea
Athens
Sicily
CYPRUS
MALTA
Crete
Mediterranean Sea

SMART TRAVEL TIPS A TO Z

Basic Information on Traveling in France, Savvy Tips to Make Your Trip a Breeze, and Companies and Organizations to Contact

A

AIR TRAVEL

MAJOR AIRLINE OR LOW-COST CARRIER?

Most people choose a flight based on price. Yet there are other issues to consider. Major airlines offer the greatest number of departures; smaller airlines—including regional, low-cost, and no-frill airlines—usually have a more limited number of flights daily. Major airlines have frequent-flyer partners, which allow you to credit mileage earned on one airline to your account with another. Low-cost airlines offer a definite price advantage and fewer restrictions, such as advance-purchase requirements. Safety-wise, low-cost carriers as a group have a good history, but **check the safety record before booking** any low-cost carrier; call the Federal Aviation Administration's Consumer Hotline (☞ Airline Complaints, *below*).

➤ MAJOR AIRLINES: **Air France** (☎ 800/237–2747 in the U.S., ☎ 08–02–80–28–02 in France) to Charles de Gaulle. **American Airlines** (☎ 800/433–7300 in the U.S, ☎ 08–00–23–00–35 in France) to Charles de Gaulle, Orly. **Continental** (☎ 800/231–0856 in the U.S., ☎ 01–42–99–09–09 in France) to Charles de Gaulle. Delta (☎ 800/241–4141 in the U.S., ☎ 01–47–68–92–92 in France) to Charles de Gaulle. **Northwest** (☎ 800/225–2525 in the U.S., ☎ 01–42–66–90–00 in France) to Charles de Gaulle. **TWA** (☎ 800/892–4141 in the U.S., ☎ 01–49–19–20–00 in France) to Charles de Gaulle. **United** (☎ 800/538–2929 in the U.S., ☎ 01–41–40–30–30 in France) to Charles de Gaulle. **USAirways** (☎ 800/428–4322 in the U.S., ☎ 01–49–10–29–00 in France) to Charles de Gaulle.

➤ FROM THE U.K.: **Air France** (☎ 0181/742–6600 in the U.K., ☎ 08–02–80–28–02 in France). **British Airways** (☎ 0345/222–111 in the U.K., ☎ 08–02–80–29–02 in France). **Air U.K.** (☎ 0345/666–777 in the U.K., ☎ 01–44–56–18–08 in France). **British Midland** (☎ 0181/754–7321 or 0345/554–554 in the U.K., ☎ 01–48–62–55–65 in France). **Easyjet** (☎ 0990/292–929 in the U.K., ☎ 04–93–21–48–33 in France) runs scheduled services to Nice from Luton.

➤ SMALLER AIRLINES: **Air Inter-Europe** (☎ 800/237–2747 in the U.S., ☎ 08–03–80–28–02 in France), a subsidiary of Air France, flies all over the country. **Air Liberté** (☎ 01–49–79–09–09) flies from Paris to the Riviera and the southwest region of France.

GET THE LOWEST FARE

The least-expensive airfares to France are priced for round-trip travel. Major airlines usually require that you **book far in advance and stay at least seven days** and no more than 30 to get the lowest fares. Ask about "ultrasaver" fares, which are the cheapest; they must be booked 90 days in advance and are nonrefundable. A little more expensive are "supersaver" fares, which require only a 30-day advance purchase. Remember that penalties for refunds or scheduling changes are stiffer for international tickets, usually about $150. International flights are also sensitive to the season: **plan to fly in the off season** for the cheapest fares. If your destination or home city has more than one gateway, **compare prices to and from different airports.** Also price flights scheduled for off-peak hours, which may be significantly less expensive.

To save money on flights from the United Kingdom and back, **look into an APEX or Super-PEX ticket.** Both sorts should be booked in advance and have certain restrictions, though they can sometimes be purchased right at the airport.

DON'T STOP UNLESS YOU MUST

When you book, **look for nonstop flights** and **remember that "direct" flights stop at least once.** International flights on a country's flag carrier are almost always nonstop; U.S. airlines often fly direct. Try to **avoid connecting flights,** which require a change of plane. Two airlines may jointly operate a connecting flight, so ask if your airline operates every segment—you may find that your preferred carrier flies you only part of the way.

USE AN AGENT

Travel agents, especially those who specialize in finding the lowest fares (☞ Discounts & Deals, *below*), can be especially helpful when booking a plane ticket. When you're quoted a price, **ask your agent if the price is likely to get any lower.** Good agents know the seasonal fluctuations of airfares and can usually anticipate a sale or fare war. However, waiting can be risky: The fare could go *up* as seats become scarce, and you may wait so long that your preferred flight sells out. A wait-and-see strategy works best if your plans are flexible, but if you must arrive and depart on certain dates, don't delay.

TRAVEL PASSES

You can **save on air travel** within Europe if you plan on traveling to and from Paris aboard Air France. As part of their Euro Flyer program, you then can buy between three and nine flight coupons, valid on these airlines' flights to more than 100 European cities. At $120 each, these coupons are a good deal, and the fine print still allows you plenty of freedom.

CHECK WITH CONSOLIDATORS

Consolidators buy tickets for scheduled flights at reduced rates from the airlines then sell them at prices that beat the best fare available directly from the airlines, usually without advance restrictions. Sometimes you can even get your money back if you need to return the ticket. Carefully read the fine print detailing penalties for changes and cancellations, and **confirm your consolidator reservation with the airline.**

➤ CONSOLIDATORS: **United States Air Consolidators Association** (✉ 925 L St., Suite 220, Sacramento, CA 95814, ☎ 916/441–4166, FAX 916/441–3520).

AVOID GETTING BUMPED

Airlines routinely overbook planes, knowing that not everyone with a ticket will show up, but sometimes everyone does. When that happens, airlines ask for volunteers to give up their seats. In return these volunteers usually get a certificate for a free flight and are rebooked on the next flight out. If there are not enough volunteers the airline must choose who will be denied boarding. The first to get bumped are passengers who checked in late and those flying on discounted tickets, **so get to the gate and check in as early as possible,** especially during peak periods.

Always **bring a photo ID to the airport.** You may be asked to show it before you are allowed to check in.

ENJOY THE FLIGHT

For better service, **fly smaller or regional carriers,** which often have higher passenger-satisfaction ratings. Sometimes you'll find leather seats, more legroom, and better food.

For more legroom, **request an emergency-aisle seat**; don't, however, sit in the row in front of the emergency aisle or in front of a bulkhead, where seats may not recline.

If you don't like airline food, **ask for special meals when booking.** These can be vegetarian, low-cholesterol, or kosher, for example.

To avoid jet lag try to maintain a normal routine while traveling. At night **get some sleep.** By day **eat light meals, drink water (not alcohol), and move about the cabin** to stretch your legs.

Some carriers have prohibited smoking throughout their systems; others allow smoking only on certain routes or even certain departures from that route, so **contact your carrier regarding its smoking policy.**

COMPLAIN IF NECESSARY

If your baggage goes astray or your flight goes awry, complain right away. Most carriers require that you file a claim immediately.

➤ AIRLINE COMPLAINTS: U.S. Department of Transportation **Aviation Consumer Protection Division** (✉ C-75, Washington, DC 20590, ☎ 202/366–2220). **FAA Consumer Hotline** (☎ 800/322–7873).

AIRPORTS & TRANSFERS

The major gateways to Paris are Orly and Charles de Gaulle. Flying time is 7½ hours from New York, 9 hours from Chicago, and 11 hours from Los Angeles. Many major airlines also have (less-frequent) flights to Lyon, Nice, Marseille, Bordeaux, and Toulouse.

➤ AIRPORTS: **Orly** (☎ 01–49–75–15–15). **Charles de Gaulle** (☎ 01–48–62–12–12).

B

BARGE TRAVEL

Canal and river trips are popular in France, particularly along the picturesque waterways in Brittany, Burgundy, and the Midi. For further information, contact a travel agent; ask for a "Tourisme Fluvial" brochure in any French tourist office; or one of the companies that organizes barge trips. Also *see* Theme Trips *in* Tour Operators, *below.*

➤ BARGE COMPANIES: **Connoisseur Cruisers** (✉ Halye Nautique, Ile Sauzay, 70100 Gray, ☎ 03–84–65–44–62). **Bourgogne Voies Navigables** (✉ 1 quai de la République, 89000 Auxerre, ☎ 03–86–52–18–99).

BICYCLING

The French are great bicycling enthusiasts—witness the Tour de France—and there are many good bicycling routes in France. For 44 francs a day (55 francs for a 10-gear touring bike) **you can rent a bike from one of 30 train stations;** you need to show your passport and leave a deposit of 1,000 francs or a Visa or MasterCard. Mountain bikes (known as VTT or Vélo Touts Terrains) can be rented from many shops, as well as from some train stations. Bikes may be taken as accompanied luggage from any station in France; some trains in rural areas don't even charge for this. Tourist offices supply details on the more than 200 local shops that rent bikes, or you can get the SNCF brochure "Guide du Train et du Vélo" from any station.

Several good routes are described in detail in the chapters that follow, or contact the Fédération Française de Cyclotourisme for information. The yellow Michelin maps (1:200,000 scale) are fine for roads, but for off-road bicycling you may want to get one of the Institut Géographique National's detailed, large-scale maps. Try their blue series (1:25,000) or orange series (1:50,000). For more bicycling trips, *see* Theme Trips *in* Tour Operators, *below.*

➤ BICYCLING INFORMATION: **Fédération Française de Cyclotourisme** (✉ 8 rue Jean-Marie-Jégo, 75013 Paris, ☎ 01–44–16–88–88). **Institut Géographique National** (✉ IGN, 107 rue La Boétie, 75008 Paris, ☎ 01–42–56–06–68).

BUS TRAVEL

France's excellent train service means that long-distance buses are rare; **regional buses are found mainly where train service is spotty.** Excursions and bus holidays are organized by the SNCF and other tourist organizations. Ask for a brochure at any major travel agent or contact France-Tourisme. Bus tours from the U.K. generally depart from London, for Paris, the Atlantic Coast, Chamonix and the Alps, Grenoble, Lyon, and the Riviera.

➤ TO THE U.K. AND OTHER EUROPEAN COUNTRIES: **Eurolines** (✉ 28 av. Général-de-Gaulle, Bagnolet, ☎ 01–49–72–51–51 in France; ☎ 0171/730–3499 in the U.K.) runs bus trips (via Hovercraft or ferry) from Paris to London and many other European cites.

➤ WITHIN FRANCE: **France-Tourisme** (✉ 1 rue d'Auber, 75009 Paris, ☎ 01–47–42–27–40). **SNCF** (✉ 88 rue St-Lazare, 75009 Paris, ☎ 01–53–25–60–00).

BUSINESS HOURS

BANKS

Banks are open weekdays, generally from 9:30 to 4:30. Most take a one-hour, or even a 90-minute, lunch break. In a pinch, **money can also be exchanged at 24-hour exchange offices or withdrawn from ATM ma-**

chines in Paris and in the larger French cities.

MUSEUMS

Usual opening times are from 9:30 to 5 or 6, but some are only open Sunday afternoons. Many close for lunch (noon–2). Most are closed one day a week (generally Monday or Tuesday) and on national holidays: **check museum hours before you go.**

SHOPS

Large stores in big towns are open from 9 or 9:30 until 7 or 8. Smaller shops often open earlier (8 AM) and close later (8 PM) but take a lengthy lunch break (1–4), particularly in the south of France. Corner groceries, often run by immigrants, frequently stay open until around 10 PM. Some Paris stores are beginning to stay open on Sundays.

C

CAMERAS, CAMCORDERS, & COMPUTERS

Always **keep your film, tape, or computer disks out of the sun.** Carry an extra supply of batteries, and **be prepared to turn on your camera, camcorder, or laptop** to prove to security personnel that the device is real. Always **ask for hand inspection of film,** which becomes clouded after successive exposure to airport x-ray machines, and **keep videotapes and computer disks away from metal detectors.**

➤ PHOTO HELP: **Kodak Information Center** (☎ 800/242–2424). *Kodak Guide to Shooting Great Travel Pictures,* available in bookstores or from **Fodor's Travel Publications** (☎ 800/533–6478; $16.50 plus $4 shipping).

CUSTOMS

Before departing, **register your foreign-made camera or laptop with U.S. Customs** (☞ Customs & Duties, *below*). If your equipment is U.S.-made, call the consulate of the country you'll be visiting to find out whether the device should be registered with local customs upon arrival.

CAR RENTAL

Renting cars in France is expensive—about twice as much as in the United States—as is gas (5.80 francs to 6.80 francs per liter). Rates in Paris begin at about $60 a day and $196 a week for an economy car with air conditioning, a manual transmission, and unlimited mileage. The price doesn't usually take into account the 20.6% VAT tax. You won't need a car in the capital, so **wait to pick up your rental until the day you leave Paris.**

➤ MAJOR AGENCIES: **Alamo** (☎ 800/522–9696, 0800/272–2000 in the U.K.). **Avis** (☎ 800/331–1084, 800/879–2847 in Canada). **Budget** (☎ 800/527–0700, 0800/181181 in the U.K.). **Dollar** (☎ 800/800–4000; 0990/565656 in the U.K., where it is known as Eurodollar). **Hertz** (☎ 800/654–3001, 800/263–0600 in Canada, 0345/555888 in the U.K.). **National InterRent** (☎ 800/227–3876; 0345/222525 in the U.K., where it is known as Europcar InterRent).

➤ LOCAL AGENCIES: **ACAR** (✉ 99 bd. Auguste-Blanqui, 75013 Paris, ☎ 01–45–88–28–38). **Locabest** (✉ 104 bd. Magenta, 75010 Paris, ☎ 01–44–72–08–05). **Rent-A-Car** (✉ 79 rue de Bercy, 75012 Paris, ☎ 01–43–45–98–99).

CUT COSTS

To get the best deal, **book through a travel agent who is willing to shop around.** Also be sure to **make reservations in the U.S. before you leave.** Renting a car from an agency in France, even if it is an American agency, is more expensive than making advanced arrangements from the U.S.

In addition, **ask your travel agent about a company's customer-service record.** How has it responded to late plane arrivals and vehicle mishaps? Are there often lines at the rental counter, and, if you're traveling during a holiday period, does a confirmed reservation guarantee you a car?

Be sure to **look into wholesalers,** companies that do not own fleets but rent in bulk from those that do and often offer better rates than traditional car-rental operations. Prices are best during off-peak periods. Rentals booked through wholesalers must be paid for before you leave the United States.

Also **look into car rental and train travel packages,** these may end up saving you some money and time (☞ Train Travel, *below*).

For a 17-day minimum stay, lease a car from Renault Eurodrive; rates include all taxes, insurance, and unlimited mileage.

➤ LONG-TERM LEASING: **Renault Eurodrive** (☎ 800/221–1052 east; ☎ 800/477–7716 west; and ☎ 800/777–7131 FL and Puerto Rico).

➤ RENTAL WHOLESALERS: **Auto Europe** (☎ 207/842–2000 or 800/223–5555, FAX 800/235–6321). **Europe by Car** (☎ 212/581–3040 or 800/223–1516, FAX 212/246–1458). **DER Travel Services** (✉ Box 1606, Des Plaines, IL 60017, ☎ 800/782–2424, FAX 800/282–7474 for information or 800/860–9944 for brochures). The **Kemwel Group** (☎ 914/835–5555 or 800/678–0678, FAX 914/835–5126).

NEED INSURANCE?

You are generally responsible for any damage to or loss of a rental vehicle. Before you rent, **see what coverage you already have** under the terms of your auto-insurance policy and credit cards.

Collision policies that car-rental companies sell for European rentals typically do not cover stolen vehicles. Before you buy additional coverage for theft, find out if your credit card or auto insurance will cover the loss.

BEWARE SURCHARGES

Before you pick up a car in one city and leave it in another, **ask about drop-off charges or one-way service fees,** which can be substantial. Note, too, that some rental agencies charge extra if you return the car before the time specified on your contract. To avoid a hefty refueling fee, **fill the tank just before you turn in the car,** but be aware that gas stations near the rental outlet may overcharge.

MEET THE REQUIREMENTS

Your own driver's license is acceptable. An International Driver's Permit is a good idea; it's available from the American or Canadian automobile association, or, in the U.K., from the Automobile Association or Royal Automobile Club.

THE CHANNEL TUNNEL

Short of flying, the "Chunnel" is the fastest way to cross the Channel: 35 minutes from Folkestone to Calais, 60 minutes from motorway to motorway, or 3 hours from London's Waterloo Station to Paris's Gare du Nord.

➤ CAR TRANSPORT: **Le Shuttle** (☎ 03–21–00–60–00, in France; ☎ 800/388–3876 in the U.S.; 0990/353535 in the U.K.).

➤ PASSENGER SERVICE: In France, **Eurostar** (☎ 01–42–81–43–27). In the United Kingdom, **Eurostar** (☎ 0345/881881), **InterCity Europe** (✉ Victoria Station, London, ☎ 0171/834–2345, 0171/828–0892 for credit-card bookings). In the United States, **BritRail Travel** (☎ 800/677–8585), **Rail Europe** (☎ 800/942–4866).

CHILDREN & TRAVEL

CHILDREN IN FRANCE

Be sure to plan ahead and **involve your youngsters** as you outline your trip. When packing, include things to keep them busy en route. On sightseeing days try to schedule activities of special interest to your children. If you are renting a car don't forget to **arrange for a car seat** when you reserve. Most hotels in France allow children under a certain age to stay in their parents' room at no extra charge, but others charge them as extra adults; be sure to **ask about the cutoff age for children's discounts.**

FLYING

As a general rule, infants under two not occupying a seat fly at greatly reduced fares and occasionally for free. If your children are two or older **ask about children's airfares.**

In general the adult baggage allowance applies to children paying half or more of the adult fare. When booking, **ask about carry-on allowances for those traveling with infants.** In general, for babies charged 10% of the adult fare you are allowed one carry-on bag and a collapsible stroller, which may have to be checked; you may be limited to less if the flight is full.

According to the FAA it's a good idea to use safety seats aloft for children weighing less than 40 pounds. Airlines, however, can set their own policies: U.S. carriers allow FAA-approved models but usually require that you buy a ticket, even if your child would otherwise ride free, since the seats must be strapped into regular seats. Airline rules vary regarding their use, so it's important to **check your airline's policy about using safety seats during takeoff and landing.** Safety seats cannot obstruct any of the other passengers in the row, so get an appropriate seat assignment as early as possible.

When making your reservation, **request children's meals or a freestanding bassinet** if you need them; the latter are available only to those seated at the bulkhead, where there's enough legroom. Remember, however, that bulkhead seats may not have their own overhead bins, and there's no storage space in front of you—a major inconvenience.

GROUP TRAVEL

If you're planning to take your kids on a tour, look for companies that specialize in family travel.

➤ FAMILY-FRIENDLY TOUR OPERATORS: **Families Welcome!** (✉ 92 N. Main St., Ashland, OR 97520, ☎ 541/482–6121 or 800/326–0724, FAX 541/482–0660). **Grandtravel** (✉ 6900 Wisconsin Ave., Suite 706, Chevy Chase, MD 20815, ☎ 301/986–0790 or 800/247–7651) for people traveling with grandchildren ages 7–17. **Rascals in Paradise** (✉ 650 5th St., Suite 505, San Francisco, CA 94107, ☎ 415/978–9800 or 800/872–7225, FAX 415/442–0289).

LODGING

Some hotel chains offer discounts for families and programs for children. Club Med is particularly family friendly: it has a "Baby Club" (from age four months) at its resort in Chamonix, and "Mini Clubs" (for ages four to six or eight, depending on the resort), and "Kids Clubs" (for ages eight and up during school holidays) at all its resort villages in France except in Val d'Isère. Some clubs are only French-speaking, so check first.

➤ FAMILY-FRIENDLY LODGING: **Club Med** (✉ 40 W. 57th St., New York, NY 10019, ☎ 800/258–2633). **Novotel** (☎ 800/221–4542). **Sofitel hotels** (☎ 800/221–4542).

TRAIN TRAVEL

The SNCF allows children under 4 to travel free (provided they don't occupy a seat) and children 4 to 11 to travel at half fare. The Carte Kiwi (285 francs) allows children under 16 and as many as four accompanying adults to make four journeys at half fare.

Changing compartments for infants are available on all TGVs, although not on all local trains. For more information, *see* Train Travel, *below*.

CONSUMER PROTECTION

Whenever possible, **pay with a major credit card** so you can cancel payment if there's a problem, provided that you can provide documentation. This is a good practice whether you're buying travel arrangements before your trip or shopping at your destination.

If you're doing business with a particular company for the first time, **contact your local Better Business Bureau and the attorney general's offices** in your state and the company's home state, as well. Have any complaints been filed?

Finally, if you're buying a package or tour, always **consider travel insurance** that includes default coverage (☞ Insurance, *below*).

➤ LOCAL BBBs: **Council of Better Business Bureaus** (✉ 4200 Wilson Blvd., Suite 800, Arlington, VA 22203, ☎ 703/276–0100, FAX 703/525–8277).

CUSTOMS & DUTIES

When shopping, **keep receipts** for all of your purchases. Upon reentering the country, **be ready to show customs officials what you've bought.** If you feel a duty is incorrect, appeal the assessment. If you object to the way your clearance was handled, get the inspector's badge number. In either case, first ask to see a supervisor, then write to the port director at the address listed on your receipt. Send a copy of the receipt and other appropriate documentation. If you still don't get satisfaction you can take your case to customs headquarters in Washington.

ENTERING FRANCE

There are two levels of duty-free allowance for travelers entering France: one for goods obtained (tax paid) within another European Union (EU) country and the other for goods obtained anywhere outside the EU or for goods purchased in a duty-free shop within the EU.

In the first category, you may import duty-free: 300 cigarettes or 150 cigarillos or 75 cigars or 400 grams of tobacco; 5 liters of table wine and (1) 1½ liters of alcohol over 22% volume (most spirits), (2) 3 liters of alcohol under 22% by volume (fortified or sparkling wine), or (3) 3 more liters of table wine; 90 milliliters of perfume; 375 milliliters of toilet water; and other goods to the value of 2,400 francs (620 francs for those under 15).

In the second category, you may import duty-free: 200 cigarettes or 100 cigarillos or 50 cigars or 250 grams of tobacco (these allowances are doubled if you live outside Europe); 2 liters of wine and (1) 1 liter of alcohol over 22% volume (most spirits), (2) two liters of alcohol under 22% volume (fortified or sparkling wine), or (3) 2 more liters of table wine; 60 milliliters of perfume; 250 milliliters of toilet water; and other goods to the value of 300 francs (150 francs for those under 15).

ENTERING THE U.S.

You may bring home $400 worth of foreign goods duty-free if you've been out of the country for at least 48 hours and haven't already used the $400 allowance or any part of it in the past 30 days.

Travelers 21 and older may bring back 1 liter of alcohol duty-free. In addition, regardless of your age, you are allowed 200 cigarettes and 100 non-Cuban cigars. (At press time, a federal rule restricting tobacco access to persons 18 years and older did not apply to importation.) Antiques, which the U.S. Customs Service defines as objects more than 100 years old, enter duty-free, as do original works of art done entirely by hand, including paintings, drawings, and sculptures.

You may also send packages home duty-free: up to $200 worth of goods for personal use, with a limit of one parcel per addressee per day (and no alcohol or tobacco products or perfume worth more than $5); label the package PERSONAL USE, and attach a list of its contents and their retail value. Do not label the package UNSOLICITED GIFT, or your duty-free exemption will drop to $100. Mailed items do not affect your duty-free allowance on your return.

➤ INFORMATION: **U.S. Customs Service** (✉ Box 7407, Washington, DC 20044, ☎ 202/927–6724 for inquiries; ✉ Commissioner's Office, 1301 Constitution Ave. NW, Washington, DC 20229 for complaints; ✉ Resource Management, 1301 Constitution Ave. NW, Washington, DC 20229, ☎ 202/927–0540 for registration of equipment).

ENTERING CANADA

If you've been out of Canada for at least seven days you may bring in C$500 worth of goods duty-free. If you've been away for fewer than seven days but more than 48 hours, the duty-free allowance drops to C$200; if your trip lasts 24–48 hours, the allowance is C$50. You may not pool allowances with family members. Goods claimed under the C$500 exemption may follow you by mail; those claimed under the lesser exemptions must accompany you.

Alcohol and tobacco products may be included in the seven-day and 48-hour exemptions but not in the 24-hour exemption. If you meet the age requirements of the province or territory through which you reenter Canada you may bring in, duty-free, 1.14 liters (40 imperial ounces) of wine or liquor *or* 24 12-ounce cans or bottles of beer or ale. If you are 16 or older you may bring in, duty-free, 200 cigarettes and 50 cigars; these items must accompany you.

You may send an unlimited number of gifts worth up to C$60 each duty-free to Canada. Label the package UNSOLICITED GIFT—VALUE UNDER $60. Alcohol and tobacco are excluded.

➤ INFORMATION: **Revenue Canada** (✉ 2265 St. Laurent Blvd. S, Ottawa, Ontario K1G 4K3, ☎ 613/993–0534, 800/461–9999 in Canada).

ENTERING THE U.K.

If your journey was wholly within European Union (EU) countries you needn't pass through customs when you return to the United Kingdom. If you plan to bring back large quantities of alcohol or tobacco, check on EU limits beforehand.

➤ INFORMATION: **HM Customs and Excise** (✉ Dorset House, Stamford St., London SE1 9NG, ☎ 0171/202–4227).

D

DINING

France is two-big-meals-a-day country, with good restaurants around every corner. If you prefer to eat lighter, you can **try a brasserie or a café for rapid, straightforward fare.** French breakfasts are relatively skimpy: good coffee, fruit juice if you request it, bread, butter, and croissants. Although you can have breakfast in hotels, it's a good idea to **eat breakfast in cafés:** It is less expensive and often more enjoyable. Tap water is safe, though not always appetizing (least of all in Paris). There is no need to wear a tie and jacket at most restaurants (unless specified), even fancy ones. For more on what to wear in France, *see* Packing for France, *below.*

DISABILITIES & ACCESSIBILITY

ACCESS IN FRANCE

Though the French government is doing much to ensure that public facilities provide for visitors with disabilities, it still has a long way to go. A number of monuments, hotels, and museums—especially those constructed within the past decade—are equipped with ramps, elevators, and special toilet facilities. Lists of regional hotels include a symbol to indicate which hotels have rooms that are accessible to people using wheelchairs. The SNCF has special cars on some trains that have been reserved exclusively for people using wheelchairs and can arrange for those passengers to be escorted on and off trains and assisted in making connections (the latter service must, however, be requested in advance). Unfortunately, there are very few métro stations that are wheelchair accessible and only some RER stations.

➤ LOCAL RESOURCES: **Association des Paralysés de France** (✉ 17 bd. Auguste-Blanqui, 75013 Paris, ☎ 01–40–78–69–00) for a list of Paris hotels. **Comité Nationale Français de Liaison pour la Réadaptation des Handicapés** (✉ 236-B rue de Tolbiac, 75013 Paris, ☎ 01–53–80–66–66).

TIPS & HINTS

When discussing accessibility with an operator or reservationist, **ask hard questions.** Are there any stairs, inside *or* out? Are there grab bars next to the toilet *and* in the shower/tub? How wide is the doorway to the room? To the bathroom? For the most extensive facilities meeting the latest legal specifications, **opt for newer accommodations,** which are more likely to have been designed with access in mind. Older buildings may offer more limited facilities. Be sure to **discuss your needs before booking.**

➤ COMPLAINTS: **Disability Rights Section** (✉ U.S. Department of Justice, Box 66738, Washington, DC 20035–6738, ☎ 202/514–0301 or 800/514–0301, FAX 202/307–1198, TTY 202/514–0383 or 800/514–0383) for general complaints. **Aviation Consumer Protection Division** (☞ Air Travel, *above*) for airline-related problems. **Civil Rights Office** (✉ U.S. Department of Transportation, Departmental Office of Civil Rights, S-30, 400 7th St. SW, Room 10215, Washington, DC, 20590, ☎ 202/366–4648) for problems with surface transportation.

TRAVEL AGENCIES & TOUR OPERATORS

The Americans with Disabilities Act requires that travel firms serve the needs of all travelers. That said, you should note that some agencies and operators specialize in making travel arrangements for individuals and groups with disabilities.

➤ TRAVELERS WITH MOBILITY PROBLEMS: **Access Adventures** (✉ 206 Chestnut Ridge Rd., Rochester, NY 14624, ☎ 716/889–9096), run by a former physical-rehabilitation counselor. **Accessible Journeys** (✉ 35 W. Sellers Ave., Ridley Park, PA 19078, ☎ 610/521–0339 or 800/846–4537, FAX 610/521–6959), for escorted tours exclusively for travelers with mobility impairments. **Flying Wheels Travel** (✉ 143 W. Bridge St., Box 382, Owatonna, MN 55060, ☎ 507/451–5005 or 800/535–6790), a travel agency specializing in European cruises and tours. **Hinsdale Travel**

Service (✉ 201 E. Ogden Ave., Suite 100, Hinsdale, IL 60521, ☎ 630/325–1335), a travel agency that benefits from the advice of wheelchair traveler Janice Perkins. Wheelchair Journeys (✉ 16979 Redmond Way, Redmond, WA 98052, ☎ 206/885–2210 or 800/313–4751), for general travel arrangements.

➤ TRAVELERS WITH DEVELOPMENTAL DISABILITIES: Sprout (✉ 893 Amsterdam Ave., New York, NY 10025, ☎ 212/222–9575 or 888/222–9575, FAX 212/222–9768).

DISCOUNTS & DEALS

Be a smart shopper and **compare all your options before making a choice.** A plane ticket bought with a promotional coupon may not be cheaper than the least expensive fare from a discount ticket agency. For high-price travel purchases, such as packages or tours, keep in mind that what you get is just as important as what you save. Just because something is cheap doesn't mean it's a bargain.

LOOK IN YOUR WALLET

When you use your credit card to make travel purchases you may get free travel-accident insurance, collision-damage insurance, and medical or legal assistance, depending on the card and the bank that issued it. American Express, MasterCard, and Visa provide one or more of these services, so **get a copy of your credit card's travel-benefits policy.** If you are a member of the American Automobile Association (AAA) or an oil-company-sponsored road-assistance plan, always **ask hotel or car-rental reservationists about auto-club discounts.** Some clubs offer additional discounts on tours, cruises, or admission to attractions. And don't forget that auto-club membership entitles you to free maps and trip-planning services.

DIAL FOR DOLLARS

To save money, **look into "1-800" discount reservations services,** which use their buying power to get a better price on hotels, airline tickets, even car rentals. When booking a room, always **call the hotel's local toll-free number** (if one is available) rather than the central reservations number—you'll often get a better price. Always ask about special packages or corporate rates.

When shopping for the best deal on hotels and car rentals **look for guaranteed exchange rates,** which protect you against a falling dollar. With your rate locked in you won't pay more even if the price goes up in the local currency.

➤ AIRLINE TICKETS: ☎ **800/FLY-4-LESS.**

➤ HOTEL ROOMS: Hotels Plus (☎ 800/235–0909). Hotel Reservations Network (HRN; ☎ 800/964–6835). International Marketing & Travel Concepts (IMTC; ☎ 800/790–4682). Steigenberger Reservation Service (☎ 800/223–5652).

SAVE ON COMBOS

Packages and guided tours can both save you money, but don't confuse the two. When you buy a package your travel remains independent, just as though you had planned and booked the trip yourself. Fly/drive packages, which combine airfare and car rental, are often a good deal. If you **buy a rail/drive pass** you'll save on train tickets and car rentals. All Eurail- and Europass holders get a discount on Eurostar fares through the Channel Tunnel. (☞ Train Travel, *below*).

JOIN A CLUB?

Many companies sell discounts in the form of travel clubs and coupon books, but these cost money. You must use participating advertisers to get a deal, and only after you recoup the initial membership cost or book price do you begin to save. If you plan to use the club or coupons frequently you may save considerably. Before signing up, find out what discounts you get for free.

➤ DISCOUNT CLUBS: Entertainment Travel Editions (✉ Box 1068, Trumbull, CT 06611, ☎ 800/445–4137; $28–$53, depending on destination). Great American Traveler (✉ Box 27965, Salt Lake City, UT 84127, ☎ 800/548–2812; $49.95 per year). Moment's Notice Discount Travel Club (✉ 7301 New Utrecht Ave., Brooklyn, NY 11204, ☎ 718/234–6295; $25 per year, single or family). Privilege Card International (✉ 201 E. Commerce St., Suite 198, Youngstown, OH 44503, ☎ 330/746–5211 or 800/236–9732; $74.95 per year). **Sears's Mature Outlook** (✉ Box 9390, Des Moines, IA 50306, ☎ 800/336–6330; $14.95 per year). **Travelers Advantage** (✉ CUC Travel Service, 3033 S. Parker Rd., Suite 1000, Aurora, CO 80014, ☎ 800/548–1116 or 800/648–4037; $49 per year, single or family). **Worldwide Discount Travel Club** (✉ 1674 Meridian Ave., Miami Beach, FL 33139, ☎ 305/534–2082; $50 per year family, $40 single).

DRIVING

If you plan to drive through France, **get a yellow Michelin map** for each region you'll be visiting. The maps are available from most bookshops and newsagents. For the fastest roads between two points, **look for roads marked *A*** for *autoroutes*. Most are toll roads.

BREAKDOWNS

If your car breaks down on an expressway, **go to a roadside emergency telephone** and call the breakdown service. If you have a breakdown anywhere else, find the nearest garage or contact the police (dial 17).

GAS

Gas is expensive, especially on expressways and in rural areas. When possible, **buy gas before you get on the expressway** and keep an eye on pump prices as you go. These vary enormously; anything from 5.80 to 6.80 francs per liter. The cheapest gas can be found at *hypermarchés* (very large supermarkets). It is possible to go for many miles in the country without passing a gas station—**don't let your tank get too low in rural areas.**

PARKING

Parking is a nightmare in Paris and often difficult in other large towns. Meters and ticket machines (pay and display) are common: Make sure you **have a supply of 1-, 2-, and 5-franc coins.** Parking is free during August in most of Paris, but **be sure to always check the signs before you park, as rules vary.** In smaller towns, parking may be permitted on one side of the street only—alternating every two weeks—so pay attention to signs.

ROADS

France's roads are classified into five types, numbered and prefixed *A, N, D, C,* or *V.* Roads marked *A* (Autoroutes) are expressways. There are excellent links between Paris and most French cities, but poor ones between the provinces (the principal exceptions being A26 from Calais to Reims, A62 between Bordeaux and Toulouse, and A9/A8 the length of the Mediterranean coast). It is often difficult to avoid Paris when crossing France—just **try to steer clear of the rush hours** (7–9:30 AM and 4:30–7:30 PM). A *péage* (toll) must be paid on most expressways: The rate varies but can be steep. The *N* (Route Nationale) roads—which are sometimes divided highways—and *D* (Route Départementale) roads are usually wide and fast, and driving along them can be a real pleasure. Don't be daunted by smaller (*C* and *V*) roads, either. The yellow regional Michelin maps—on sale throughout France—are invaluable.

RULES OF THE ROAD

In France, **you may use your own driver's license,** but you must be able to prove you have third-party insurance. Drive on the right and **yield to drivers coming from the right** if there is no solid white line. You must **wear your seat belt,** and children under 12 may not travel in the front seat. Speed limits are 130 kph (80 mph) on expressways, 110 kph (70 mph) on divided highways, 90 kph (55 mph) on other roads, 50 kph (30 mph) in towns. French drivers break these limits and police dish out hefty on-the-spot fines with equal abandon.

➤ AUTO CLUBS: In the U.S., **American Automobile Association** (AAA, ☎ 800/564–6222). In the U.K., **Automobile Association** (**AA,** ☎ 0990/500600), **Royal Automobile Club** (**RAC;** ☎ 0990/722722 for membership inquiries, 0345/121345 for insurance).

E

ELECTRICITY

To use your U.S.-purchased electric-powered equipment, **bring a converter and adapter.** The electrical current in France is 220 volts, 50 cycles alternating current (AC); wall outlets take continental-type plugs, with two round prongs.

If your appliances are dual-voltage, you'll need only an adapter. Don't use 110-volt outlets, marked FOR SHAVERS ONLY, for high-wattage appliances such as blow-dryers. Most laptops operate equally well on 110 and 220 volts and so require only an adapter.

EMBASSIES

If you need assistance, you can go to your country's embassy. Proof of identity and citizenship are generally required to enter. If your passport has been stolen, get a police report then contact your embassy for assistance.

➤ EMBASSY NUMBERS: **Canada** (✉ 35 av. Montaigne, Paris, 8e ☎ 01–44–43–29–00, métro Franklin D. Roosevelt), open weekdays 8:30–11. **U.K.** (✉ 35 rue du Faubourg-St-Honoré, Paris, 8e, ☎ 01–44–51–31–00, métro Madeleine), open weekdays 9:30–12:30 and 2:30–5. **U.S.** (✉ 2 rue St-Florentin, Paris, 1er, ☎ 01–43–12–22–22 in English or 01–43–12–23–47 in emergencies, métro Concorde), open weekdays 9–3.

EMERGENCIES

Throughout France you can call the ambulance and the police in emergencies. *See* also Emergencies *in* A to Z sections *in* individual chapters for information on regional hospitals.

➤ EMERGENCY NUMBERS: **Ambulance** (☎ 15). **Fire Department** (☎ 18). **Police** (☎ 17).

F

FERRY & HOVERCRAFT TRAVEL

There are a number of ferry and hovercraft routes between the United Kingdom and France. Driving distances from the French ports to Paris are as follows: from Calais, 290 km (180 mi); from Boulogne, 243 km (151 mi); from Dieppe, 193 km (120 mi); from Dunkerque, 257 km (160 mi). The fastest routes to Paris from each port are via the N43, A26, and A1 from Calais and the Channel Tunnel; via the N1 from Boulogne; via the N15 from Le Havre; via the D915 and N1 from Dieppe; and via the A25 and A1 from Dunkerque.

➤ DOVER–CALAIS: **Hoverspeed** (✉ International Hoverport, Marine Parade, Dover CT17 9TG, ☎ 01304/865000; 03–21–46–14–14 in Calais) operates up to 15 crossings a day by Hovercraft and catamaran. The crossings take 35 minutes (Hovercraft) or 55 minutes (catamaran). **P&O European Ferries** (✉ Channel House, Channel View Rd., Dover, Kent CT17 9TJ, ☎ 01304/863000; 03–21–46–10–20 in Calais) has up to 25 sailings a day; the crossing takes about 75 minutes. **Sealink** (✉ Charter House, Park St., Ashford, Kent TN24 8EX, ☎ 01233/646801; 03–21–46–78–30 in Calais) operates up to 25 sailings a day; the crossing takes about 90 minutes.

➤ FOLKESTONE–BOULOGNE: **Hoverspeed** (☎ 03–21–30–27–26 in Boulogne or ☞ Dover–Calais, *above*) is the sole operator on this route, with 10 35-minute crossings a day.

➤ NEWHAVEN–DIEPPE: **Sealink** (☞ Dover–Calais, *above*) has as many as four sailings a day, and the crossing takes four hours.

➤ PORTSMOUTH–LE HAVRE: **P&O European Ferries** (☎ 02–35–19–78–50 in Le Havre or ☞ Dover–Calais, *above*) has up to three sailings a day, and the crossing takes 5½ hours by day, 7½ by night.

➤ RAMSGATE–DUNKERQUE: **Sally Line** (✉ Argyle Centre, York St., Ramsgate, Kent CT11 9DS, ☎ 01843/595522; 03–28–26–70–70 in Dunkerque) has up to six 2½-hour crossings a day.

G

GAY & LESBIAN TRAVEL

The largest gay and lesbian communities, which are in cosmopolitan Paris, are low-key and reserved in public, although active and easily accessible to visitors. Discos and nightclubs are numerous and popular; it takes a serious *couche-tard* (night owl) to keep up with the hip scene (☞ *also* Arts and Nightlife *in* Chapter 2). A number of informative newspapers and magazines that cover the Parisian gay/lesbian scene are available at stores and kiosks in the city: ***Gai Guide, Gai Pied Hebdo, Lesbia,*** and ***Paris Exit.***

➤ GAY & LESBIAN ORGANIZATIONS IN PARIS: **Agora** (✉ 33 bd. Picpus, 12e,

☏ 01-43-42-19-02) provides information on events, meetings, and rallies. **Association des Médecins Gais** (☏ 01-48-05-81-71) and **Ecoute Gaie** (☏ 01-44-93-01-02 after 6 PM) offer advice and information over the phone. **Centre du Christ Libérateur** (✉ 5 rue Crussol, 11e, ☏ 01-48-05-24-48) provides medical care and counseling. **Centre Gai et Lesbien** (✉ 3 rue Keller, 11e, ☏ 01-43-57-21-47) offers a wide range of information on events. **FAACTS** (Free Anglo-American Counseling Treatment Support) at the American Church (✉ quai d'Orsay, 7e) has weekly meetings for people infected or affected by HIV.

➤ TOUR OPERATORS: **Olivia** (✉ 4400 Market St., Oakland, CA 94608, ☏ 510/655-0364 or 800/631-6277), for cruises and resort vacations for lesbians. **R.S.V.P. Travel Productions** (✉ 2800 University Ave. SE, Minneapolis, MN 55414, ☏ 612/379-4697 or 800/328-7787), for cruises and resort vacations for gays.

➤ GAY- AND LESBIAN-FRIENDLY TRAVEL AGENCIES: **Advance Damron** (✉ 1 Greenway Plaza, Suite 800, Houston, TX 77046, ☏ 713/682-2002 or 800/695-0880, FAX 713/888-1010). **Club Travel** (✉ 8739 Santa Monica Blvd., West Hollywood, CA 90069, ☏ 310/358-2200 or 800/429-8747, FAX 310/358-2222). **Islanders/Kennedy Travel** (✉ 183 W. 10th St., New York, NY 10014, ☏ 212/242-3222 or 800/988-1181, FAX 212/929-8530). **Now Voyager** (✉ 4406 18th St., San Francisco, CA 94114, ☏ 415/626-1169 or 800/255-6951, FAX 415/626-8626). **Yellowbrick Road** (✉ 1500 W. Balmoral Ave., Chicago, IL 60640, ☏ 773/561-1800 or 800/642-2488, FAX 773/561-4497). **Skylink Women's Travel** (✉ 3577 Moorland Ave., Santa Rosa, CA 95407, ☏ 707/585-8355 or 800/225-5759, FAX 707/584-5637), serving lesbian travelers.

H

HEALTH

MEDICAL PLANS

No one plans to get sick while traveling, but it happens, so **consider signing up with a medical-assistance company.** Members get doctor referrals, emergency evacuation or repatriation, 24-hour telephone hot lines for medical consultation, cash for emergencies, and other personal and legal assistance. Coverage varies by plan, so **review the benefits carefully.** *See also* Embassies *and* Emergencies, *above.*

➤ MEDICAL-ASSISTANCE COMPANIES: **International SOS Assistance** (✉ Box 11568, Philadelphia, PA 19116, ☏ 215/244-1500 or 800/523-8930; ✉ Box 466, pl. Bonaventure, Montréal, Québec H5A 1C1, ☏ 514/874-7674 or 800/363-0263; ✉ 7 Old Lodge Pl., St. Margarets, Twickenham TW1 1RQ, England, ☏ 0181/744-0033). **MEDEX Assistance Corporation** (✉ Box 5375, Timonium, MD 21094, ☏ 410/453-6300 or 800/537-2029). **Traveler's Emergency Network** (✉ 3100 Tower Blvd., Suite 1000B, Durham, NC 27707, ☏ 919/490-6055 or 800/275-4836, FAX 919/493-8262). **TravMed** (✉ Box 5375, Timonium, MD 21094, ☏ 410/453-6380 or 800/732-5309). **Worldwide Assistance Services** (✉ 1133 15th St. NW, Suite 400, Washington, DC 20005, ☏ 202/331-1609 or 800/821-2828, FAX 202/828-5896).

HIKING

France has many good places to hike and an extensive network of mapped-out Grands Randonnées (GRs or Big Trails) that range from easy to challenging. For details on hiking in France and guides to GRs in specific areas, contact the Club Alpin Français or the Fédération Française de la Randonnée Pédestre, which also publishes good topographical maps. The IGN maps sold in many bookshops are also invaluable (☞ Bicycling, *above*).

➤ HIKING ORGANIZATIONS: **Club Alpin Français** (✉ 24 av. Laumière, 75019 Paris, ☏ 01-53-72-87-00). **Fédération Française de la Randonnée Pédestre** (✉ 64 rue de Gergovie, 75014 Paris, ☏ 01-45-45-31-02).

HOLIDAYS

With 11 national *jours feriés* (holidays) and 5 weeks of paid vacation, the French have their share of repose. In May, there is a holiday nearly every week, so be prepared for stores, banks, and museums to shut their doors for days at a time. Be sure to **call museums, restaurants, and hotels**

in advance to make sure they will be open.

January 1 (New Year's Day); April 13 (Easter Monday); May 1 (Labor Day); May 8 (VE Day); May 21 (Ascension); June 1 (Pentecost Monday); July 14 (Bastille Day); August 15 (Assumption); November 1 (All Saints); November 11 (Armistice); December 25 (Christmas).

I

INSURANCE

Travel insurance is the best way to **protect yourself against financial loss.** The most useful policies are trip-cancellation-and-interruption, default, medical, and comprehensive insurance.

Without insurance you will lose all or most of your money if you cancel your trip, regardless of the reason. It's essential that you **buy trip-cancellation-and-interruption insurance,** particularly if your airline ticket, cruise, or package tour is nonrefundable and cannot be changed. When considering how much coverage you need, look for a policy that will cover the cost of your trip plus the nondiscounted price of a one-way airline ticket, should you need to return home early. Also **consider default or bankruptcy insurance,** which protects you against a supplier's failure to deliver.

Medicare generally does not cover health-care costs outside the United States, nor do many privately issued policies. If your own policy does not cover you outside the United States, **consider buying supplemental medical coverage.** Remember that travel health insurance is different from a medical-assistance plan (☞ Health, *above*).

Citizens of the United Kingdom can buy an annual travel-insurance policy valid for most vacations during the year in which it's purchased. If you are pregnant or have a preexisting medical condition, make sure you're covered.

If you have purchased an expensive vacation, particularly one that involves travel abroad, comprehensive insurance is a must. **Look for comprehensive policies that include trip-delay insurance,** which will protect you in the event that weather problems cause you to miss your flight, tour, or cruise. A few insurers sell waivers for preexisting medical conditions. Companies that offer both features include Access America, Carefree Travel, Travel Insured International, and Travel Guard (☞ *below*).

Always **buy travel insurance directly from the insurance company;** if you buy it from a travel agency or tour operator that goes out of business you probably will not be covered for the agency or operator's default, a major risk. Before you make any purchase, **review your existing health and home-owner's policies** to find out whether they cover expenses incurred while traveling.

➤ TRAVEL INSURERS: In the United States: **Access America** (✉ 6600 W. Broad St., Richmond, VA 23230, ☎ 804/285–3300 or 800/284–8300), **Carefree Travel Insurance** (✉ Box 9366, 100 Garden City Plaza, Garden City, NY 11530, ☎ 516/294–0220 or 800/323–3149), **Near Travel Services** (✉ Box 1339, Calumet City, IL 60409, ☎ 708/868–6700 or 800/654–6700), **Travel Guard International** (✉ 1145 Clark St., Stevens Point, WI 54481, ☎ 715/345–0505 or 800/826–1300), **Travel Insured International** (✉ Box 280568, East Hartford, CT 06128–0568, ☎ 860/528–7663 or 800/243–3174), **Travelex Insurance Services** (✉ 11717 Burt St., Suite 202, Omaha, NE 68154-1500, ☎ 402/445–8637 or 800/228–9792, FAX 800/867–9531), **Wallach & Company** (✉ 107 W. Federal St., Box 480, Middleburg, VA 20118, ☎ 540/687–3166 or 800/237–6615). In Canada: **Mutual of Omaha** (✉ Travel Division, 500 University Ave., Toronto, Ontario M5G 1V8, ☎ 416/598–4083, 800/268–8825 in Canada). In the United Kingdom: **Association of British Insurers** (✉ 51 Gresham St., London EC2V 7HQ, ☎ 0171/600–3333).

L

LANGUAGE

English is widely understood in major tourist areas, and no matter what the area, at least one person in most hotels can explain things to you. It also helps if you **try to master a few**

French words. *See* the French Vocabulary *and* Menu Guide at the back of the book.

LODGING

Hotels are officially classified from one-star to four-star-deluxe. Prices must, by law, be posted at the hotel entrance and should include taxes and service. Rates are always by room, not per person, and you should always **check what bathroom facilities the price includes,** if any. Because replumbing drains is often prohibitive, if not impossible, old hotels may have added bathrooms—often with *douches* (showers), not *baignoires* (tubs)—to the guest rooms, but not toilets. If you want a private bathroom, state your preference for shower or tub—the latter always costing more. Unless otherwise noted, lodging listings in this book include a private bathroom with a shower and tub. When making your reservation, **ask for a *grand lit* if you want a double bed.** The quality of accommodations, particularly in older properties, can vary greatly from room to room; **if you don't like the room you're given, ask to see another.**

Breakfast is not always included in the price, but you are sometimes expected to have it and are occasionally charged for it regardless. In smaller rural hotels you may be expected to have your evening meal at the hotel, too. Negotiating rates has become acceptable in Paris and the provinces. Although you may not be able to reduce the price, you might get an upgrade to a newly redecorated, larger, or deluxe room. Tourist offices in major train stations can reserve hotels for you, and so can tourist offices in most towns.

APARTMENT, HOUSE, & VILLA RENTALS

If you want a home base that's roomy enough for a family and comes with cooking facilities, **consider a furnished rental.** Renting a gîtes ruraux—a furnished cottage, chalet, or apartment—for a week or month can save families and small groups money. There are also more luxurious properties for rent, economical only when your party is large, as well as apartments. Home-exchange directories list rentals, and some services search for a house or apartment for you (even a castle if that's your fancy) and handle the paperwork. Up front registration fees may apply.

➤ GÎTES RENTALS: **Fédération Nationale des Gîtes de France** (✉ 59 rue St-Lazare, 75009 Paris, ☎ 01–49–70–75–75, FAX 01–42–81–28–53) lists gîtes ruraux for rent; indicate the region that interests you or order their annual nationwide guide (115 francs). **French Government Tourist Office** (☞ Visitor Information, *below*) is another source for information about gîtes.

➤ RENTAL AGENTS: **At Home Abroad** (✉ 405 E. 56th St., Suite 6H, New York, NY 10022, ☎ 212/421–9165, FAX 212/752–1591). **At Home in France** (✉ Box 643, Ashland, OR, 97520, ☎ 541/488-9467, FAX 541/488-9468). **Europa-Let/Tropical Inn-Let** (✉ 92 N. Main St., Ashland, OR 97520, ☎ 541/482–5806 or 800/462–4486, FAX 541/482–0660). **Hometours International** (✉ Box 11503, Knoxville, TN 37939, ☎ 423/690–8484 or 800/367–4668). **Interhome** (✉ 124 Little Falls Rd., Fairfield, NJ 07004, ☎ 201/882–6864, FAX 201/808–1742). **Property Rentals International** (✉ 1008 Mansfield Crossing Rd., Richmond, VA 23236, ☎ 804/378–6054 or 800/220–3332, FAX 804/379–2073). **Rental Directories International** (✉ 2044 Rittenhouse Sq., Philadelphia, PA 19103, ☎ 215/985–4001, FAX 215/985–0323). **Rent-a-Home International** (✉ 7200 34th Ave. NW, Seattle, WA 98117, ☎ 206/789–9377 or 800/488–7368, FAX 206/789–9379). **Vacation Home Rentals Worldwide** (✉ 235 Kensington Ave., Norwood, NJ 07648, ☎ 201/767–9393 or 800/633–3284, FAX 201/767–5510). **Villas and Apartments Abroad** (✉ 420 Madison Ave., Suite 1003, New York, NY 10017, ☎ 212/759–1025 or 800/433–3020, FAX 212/755–8316). **Villas International** (✉ 605 Market St., Suite 510, San Francisco, CA 94105, ☎ 415/281–0910 or 800/221–2260, FAX 415/281–0919). **Hideaways International** (✉ 767 Islington St., Portsmouth, NH 03801, ☎ 603/430–4433 or 800/843–4433, FAX 603/430–4444) is a travel club whose members arrange rentals among themselves; yearly membership is $99.

BED & BREAKFASTS

B&Bs, known in France as ***chambres d'hôte* or *gîtes*, are increasingly popular, especially in rural areas.** Check local tourist offices for details or contact Gîtes de France, the national bed-and-breakfast organization that lists places all over the country, from rustic to more luxurious. Often table d'hôte dinners (meals cooked by and eaten with the owners) can be arranged for an extra, fairly nominal fee. Note that in bed-and-breakfasts, unlike hotels, it is more likely that the owners will only speak French. Staying in one may, however, give you more of an opportunity to meet French people.

➤ BED-AND-BREAKFAST INFORMATION: **Maison des Gîtes de France** (✉ 35 rue Godot-de-Mauroy, 75439 Paris, ☎ 01–49–70–75–75).

CAMPING

French campsites have a good reputation for organization and amenities but are crowded in July and August. Many campsites welcome reservations, and in summer, it makes sense to book in advance.

➤ CAMPSITE GUIDE: **Fédération Française de Camping et de Caravaning** (✉ 78 rue de Rivoli, 75004 Paris, ☎ 01–42–72–84–08) publishes a guide to France's campsites; they'll send it to you for 75 francs, plus shipping.

HOME EXCHANGES

If you would like to exchange your home for someone else's, **join a home-exchange organization,** which will send you its updated listings of available exchanges for a year and will include your own listing in at least one of them. Making the arrangements is up to you.

➤ EXCHANGE CLUBS: **HomeLink International** (✉ Box 650, Key West, FL 33041, ☎ 305/294–7766 or 800/638–3841, FAX 305/294–1148) charges $83 per year.

HOTELS

Hotels are officially classified from one-star to four-star-deluxe. France has—but is not dominated by—big hotel chains: Examples in the upper price bracket are Frantel, Holiday Inn, and Novotel. The Best Western, Campanile, Climat de France, and Ibis chains are more moderate. Typically, **chains offer a consistently acceptable standard of modern features** (modern bathrooms, TV, etc.), but tend to lack atmosphere, with some exceptions.

Logis de France hotels are small and inexpensive and can be relied on for comfort, character, and regional cuisine. Look for its distinctive yellow and green sign. The Logis de France paperback guide is widely available in bookshops (100 frs) or from Logis de France.

Relais & Châteaux is a prestigious international group that counts hundreds of converted châteaux and manor houses among its members. Each hotel is distinctively furnished, provides top cuisine, and often has spacious grounds. A booklet listing members is available in bookshops or from Relais & Châteaux.

➤ HOTEL DIRECTORIES: **Best Western** (☎ 800/528–1234 in the U.S.). **Logis de France** (✉ 83 av. d'Italie, 75013 Paris, ☎ 01–45–84–70–00, FAX 01–44–24–08–74; 95 frs). **France-Accueil** (✉ 163 av. d'Italie, 75013 Paris, ☎ 01–45–83–04–22, FAX 01–45–86–49–82). **Relais & Châteaux** (✉ 15 rue Galvani, 75017 Paris, ☎ 01–45–72–96–50, FAX 01–45–72–96–69 or ✉ 11 E. 44th St., Suite 707, New York, NY 10017, ☎ 212/856–0115, ☎ 800/860–4930, or FAX 212/856–0193).

M

MAIL

Letters and postcards to the United States and Canada cost 4.40 francs (about 80¢) for 20 grams. Letters and postcards to the United Kingdom cost 3 francs (about 33p) for up to 20 grams. Letters and postcards within France cost 3 francs. Stamps can be bought in post offices (La Poste) and cafés sporting a red TABAC sign outside.

RECEIVING MAIL

If you're uncertain where you'll be staying, **have mail sent to the local post office,** addressed as "poste restante," or to American Express, but remember that during peak seasons, American Express may refuse to accept mail.

MONEY

The units of currency in France are the franc (fr) and the centime. Bills are in denominations of 500, 200, 100, 50, and 20 francs. Coins are 20, 10, 5, 2, and 1 francs and 50, 20, 10, and 5 centimes. At press time (early 1997), the exchange rate was about 5.5 francs to the U.S. dollar, 4.1 to the Canadian dollar, and 9 to the pound sterling.

ATMS

ATMs are fairly common in larger French cities and are one of the easiest ways to get francs. You may, however, have to look around for Cirrus and Plus locations. Before leaving home, **make sure that your credit cards have been programmed for ATM use in France.** Also, try to get a list of Cirrus or Plus locations from your bank. Note that Discover is generally not accepted in France. Local bank cards do not always work overseas or may access only your checking account; **ask your bank about a MasterCard/Cirrus or Visa debit card,** which works like a bank card but can be used at any ATM displaying a MasterCard/Cirrus or Visa logo. These cards, too, may tap only your checking account; check with your bank about their policy.

➤ ATM LOCATIONS: **Cirrus** (☎ 800/424–7787).

COSTS

The following prices are for Paris; other cities and areas are often cheaper. Note that it is less expensive to eat or drink standing at a café or bar counter than it is to sit at a table. Two prices are listed, *au comptoir* (at the counter) and *à salle* (at a table). Coffee in a bar: 5 francs (standing), 10 francs (seated); beer in a bar: 10 francs (standing), 15 francs (seated); Coca-Cola: 6–10 francs a can; ham sandwich: 15–25 francs; one-mile taxi ride: 35 francs; movie-theater seat: 45 francs (15%–33% cheaper on Monday and Wednesday); foreign newspaper: 10–15 francs.

CURRENCY EXCHANGE

For the most favorable rates, **change money at banks or get money from ATMs.** Although fees charged for ATM transactions may be higher abroad than at home, Cirrus and Plus exchange rates are excellent, because they are based on wholesale rates offered only by major banks. You won't do as well at exchange booths in airports or rail and bus stations, in hotels, in restaurants, or in stores, although you may find their hours more convenient. To avoid lines at airport exchange booths, **get a small amount of local currency before you leave home.**

➤ EXCHANGE SERVICES: **International Currency Express** (☎ 888/842–0880 on the East Coast or 888/278–6628 on the West Coast for telephone orders). **Thomas Cook Currency Services** (☎ 800/287–7362 for locations).

TRAVELER'S CHECKS

Whether or not to buy traveler's checks depends on where you are headed. **Take cash if your trip includes rural areas** and small towns, traveler's checks to cities. If your checks are lost or stolen, they can usually be replaced within 24 hours. To ensure a speedy refund, buy your checks yourself (don't ask someone else to make the purchase). When making a claim for stolen or lost checks, the person who bought the checks should make the call.

O

OUTDOOR ACTIVITIES & SPORTS

France has no shortage of sports facilities. Many seaside resorts are well equipped for water sports, such as windsurfing and waterskiing, and there are public swimming pools in every French town. In winter, the Alps and the somewhat less pricey Pyrénées and Vosges mountains have excellent skiing facilities—both for *ski alpin* (downhill) and *ski de fond* (cross-country).

Bicycling (☞ Bicycling, *above*) and hiking (☞ Hiking, *above*) are popular and, like *équitation* (horseback riding), possible in many rural areas. The many rivers of France offer excellent fishing (check locally for authorization rights) and canoeing. Tennis is phenomenally popular in France, and courts are everywhere: Try to find a typical *terre battue* (clay court) if you can. Golf and squash have caught on; you may be able to find a course or a court not too far away. The French are not so keen on jogging, but you'll have no difficulty locating a suitable local park or avenue. *See* individual chapters for specific outdoor activities and sports listings.

The biggest sporting event in France in 1998 is the World Cup in soccer, to be held in June and July at stadiums throughout France (Paris, St-Denis, Bordeaux, Lens, Lyon, Marseille, Montpellier, Nantes, St-Etienne, and Toulouse). Contact the French Government Tourist Office (☞ Visitor Information, *below*) for information about tickets and matches.

P

PACKING FOR FRANCE

Although you'll usually have no trouble finding a baggage cart at the airport, luggage restrictions on international flights are tight and baggage carts at railroad stations are not always available; **pack light.**

Over the years, **casual dress has become more acceptable,** although Paris is still the world's fashion capital. There is no need to wear a tie and jacket at most restaurants (unless specified), even fancy ones, and jeans are de rigueur at the new Bastille Opéra (a jeans-and-sneakers outfit, however, may raise eyebrows). Shorts are seldom worn in cities—**if you are wearing shorts, you may be denied admission to churches and cathedrals.** More and more people are wearing sneakers, although you may still stand out as a tourist with them on, especially if you wear them when you go out at night. Otherwise, for cities in France, pack as you would for a major American city. For beach resorts, take a cover-up, as wearing bathing suits on the street is frowned upon. Most casinos and nightclubs along the Riviera require jackets and ties.

Most of France is hot in the summer, cool in the winter. Since it rains all year round, **bring a raincoat and umbrella.** You'll need a sweater or warm jacket for the Mediterranean in winter.

If you are staying in budget hotels, **take along soap; many hotels either do not provide it or give you a very limited number.**

Bring an extra pair of eyeglasses or contact lenses in your carry-on luggage, and if you have a health problem, **pack enough medication** to last the entire trip or have your doctor write you a prescription using the drug's generic name, because brand names vary from country to country. It's important that you **don't put prescription drugs or valuables in luggage to be checked**: it might go astray. To avoid problems with customs officials, carry medications in the original packaging. Also, don't forget the addresses of offices that handle refunds of lost traveler's checks.

LUGGAGE

In general, you are entitled to check two bags on flights within the United States and on international flights leaving the United States. A third piece may be brought on board, but it must fit easily under the seat in front of you or in the overhead compartment.

If you are flying between two foreign destinations, note that baggage allowances may be determined not by piece but by weight—generally 88 pounds (40 kilograms) in first class, 66 pounds (30 kilograms) in business class, and 44 pounds (20 kilograms) in economy. If your flight between two cities abroad *connects* with your transatlantic or transpacific flight, the piece method still applies.

Airline liability for baggage is limited to $1,250 per person on flights within the United States. On international flights it amounts to $9.07 per pound or $20 per kilogram for checked baggage (roughly $640 per 70-pound bag) and $400 per passenger for unchecked baggage. Insurance for losses exceeding these amounts can be bought from the airline at check-in for about $10 per $1,000 of coverage; note that this coverage excludes a rather extensive list of items, which is shown on your airline ticket.

Before departure, **itemize your bags' contents** and their worth, and label the bags with your name, address, and phone number. (If you use your home address, cover it so that potential thieves can't see it readily.) Inside each bag, **pack a copy of your itinerary.** At check-in, **make sure that each bag is correctly tagged** with the destination airport's three-letter code. If your bags arrive damaged or fail to arrive at all, file a written report with the airline before leaving the airport.

PASSPORTS & VISAS

Once your travel plans are confirmed, **check the expiration date of your passport.** It's also a good idea to **make photocopies of the data page;** leave one copy with someone at home and keep another with you, separated from your passport. If you lose your passport, promptly call the nearest embassy or consulate and the local police; having a copy of the data page can speed replacement. Remember that **in France, you are required by law to carry identification at all times.**

U.S. CITIZENS

All U.S. citizens, even infants, need only a valid passport to enter France for stays of up to 90 days.

➤ INFORMATION: **Office of Passport Services** (☎ 202/647–0518).

CANADIANS

You need only a valid passport to enter France for stays of up to 90 days.

➤ INFORMATION: **Passport Office** (☎ 819/994–3500 or 800/567–6868).

U.K. CITIZENS

Citizens of the United Kingdom need only a valid passport to enter France for stays of up to 90 days.

➤ INFORMATION: **London Passport Office** (☎ 0990/21010) for fees and documentation requirements and to request an emergency passport.

PRECAUTIONS

Beware of petty theft—purse snatching, pickpocketing, and pilfering from automobiles—throughout France, particularly in Paris and along the Riviera. Use common sense: Avoid pulling out a lot of money in public; wear a handbag with long straps that you can sling across your body, bandolier-style, with a zippered compartment for your money and passport; and don't leave your luggage showing in the car in major cities.

PUBLIC TRANSPORTATION

For information about public transportation in Paris and other major French cities *see* A to Z sections *in* individual chapters.

S

SENIOR-CITIZEN TRAVEL

Older travelers to France can take advantage of many discounts, such as reduced admissions of 20%–50% to museums and movie theaters. Seniors 60 and older should **buy a Carte Vermeil,** which entitles the bearer to discounts on rail travel outside Paris (☞ Train Travel, *below*).

To qualify for age-related discounts, **mention your senior-citizen status up front** when booking hotel reservations (not when checking out) and before you're seated in restaurants (not when paying the bill). Note that discounts may be limited to certain menus, days, or hours. When renting a car, **ask about promotional car-rental discounts,** which can be cheaper than senior-citizen rates.

➤ EDUCATIONAL TRAVEL PROGRAMS: **Elderhostel** (✉ 75 Federal St., 3rd floor, Boston, MA 02110, ☎ 617/426–7788). **Interhostel** (✉ University of New Hampshire, 6 Garrison Ave., Durham, NH 03824, ☎ 603/862–1147 or 800/733–9753, FAX 603/862–1113). **Overseas Adventure Travel** (✉ Grand Circle Corporation, 625 Mt. Auburn St., Cambridge, MA 02138, ☎ 617/876–0533 or 800/221–0814, FAX 617/876–0455).

SHOPPING

Shop **prices are clearly marked** and bargaining isn't a way of life. Still, at outdoor and flea markets and in antiques stores, you can try your luck. If you're thinking of buying several items, you've nothing to lose by cheerfully suggesting to the proprietor, *"Vous me faites un prix?"* ("How about a discount?").

CLOTHING SIZES

To figure out the French equivalent of U.S. clothing and shoe sizes, **do the following, simple calculations.**

To change U.S. men's suit sizes to French suit sizes, add 10 to the U.S. suit size. To change French suit sizes to U.S. suit sizes, subtract 10 from the

French suit size. For example, a U.S. size 42 is a French size 52.

To change U.S. men's collar sizes to French collar sizes, multiply the U.S. collar size by 2 and add 8. To change French collar sizes to U.S. collar sizes, subtract 8 from the French collar size and divide by 2. For example, a U.S. size 15 is a French size 38. A U.S. size 15½ is a French size 39.

French men's shoe sizes vary in their relation to U.S. shoe sizes. A U.S. men's size 6½ is a French size 39; a size 7 is a 39; an 8 is a 40; a 9 is a 41; a 10 is a 42; a 10½ is a 43; and an 11 is a 45.

To change U.S. dress/coat/blouse sizes to French sizes, add 28 to the U.S. size. To change French dress/coat/blouse sizes to U.S. sizes, subtract 28 from the French size. For example, a U.S. women's size 8 is a French size 36.

To change U.S. women's shoe sizes to French shoe sizes, add 32 to the U.S. shoe size. To change French shoe sizes to U.S. shoe sizes, subtract 32 from the French shoe size. For example, a U.S. size 7 is a French size 39.

STUDENTS

In summer, young people from all over Europe and the U.S. congregate in Paris. During the school year, students dominate the Left Bank. Cheap food and lodging are easy to find throughout France, so there's little need to scrounge. In addition, there are student bargains almost everywhere, on train and plane fares, and for movie and museum tickets. To save money, **look into deals available through student-oriented travel agencies.** All you need is an International Student Identity Card.

➤ STUDENT IDS AND SERVICES: **Council on International Educational Exchange** (✉ CIEE, 205 E. 42nd St., 14th floor, New York, NY 10017, ☎ 212/822–2600 or 888/268–6245, FAX 212/822–2699), for mail orders only, in the United States. **Travel Cuts** (✉ 187 College St., Toronto, Ontario M5T 1P7, ☎ 416/979–2406 or 800/667–2887) in Canada.

➤ HOSTELLING: **Hostelling International—American Youth Hostels** (✉ 733 15th St. NW, Suite 840, Washington, DC 20005, ☎ 202/783–6161, FAX 202/783–6171). **Hostelling International—Canada** (✉ 400-205 Catherine St., Ottawa, Ontario K2P 1C3, ☎ 613/237–7884, FAX 613/237–7868). **Youth Hostel Association of England and Wales** (✉ Trevelyan House, 8 St. Stephen's Hill, St. Albans, Hertfordshire AL1 2DY, ☎ 01727/855215 or 01727/845047, FAX 01727/844126). Membership in the U.S., $25; in Canada, C$26.75; in the U.K., £9.30.

➤ STUDENT TOURS: **Contiki Holidays** (✉ 300 Plaza Alicante, Suite 900, Garden Grove, CA 92840, ☎ 714/740–0808 or 800/266–8454, FAX 714/740–0818). **AESU Travel** (✉ 2 Hamill Rd., Suite 248, Baltimore, MD 21210-1807, ☎ 410/323–4416 or 800/638–7640, FAX 410–323–4498).

T

TAXES

All taxes must be included in posted prices in France. The initials TTC (*toutes taxes comprises*—taxes included) sometimes appear on price lists but, strictly speaking, are superfluous. By law, **restaurant and hotel prices must include 20.6% taxes and a service charge.** If they show up as extra charges on your bill, complain.

VALUE-ADDED TAX (VAT)

A number of shops offer VAT refunds to foreign shoppers. You are entitled to an Export Discount of 20.6%, depending on the item purchased, but it is often applicable only if your purchases in the same store reach a minimum of 2,800 francs (for U.K. and EU residents) or 1,200 francs (other residents, including U.S. and Canadian residents). Remember to **ask for the refund, as some stores—especially larger ones—offer the service only upon request.**

TELEPHONES

The country code for France is 33 and the country code for Monaco is 337. All phone numbers in France have a two-digit prefix determined by zone: Paris and the Ile de France, 01; the northwest, 02; the northeast, 03; the southeast, 04; and the southwest, 05. All you need to do to call any region in France is to dial the full 10-digit number.

CALLING FRANCE

To call France from the United States, dial 011 (for all international calls), then dial 33 (the country code), and the number in France, without any inital 0. To call France from the United Kingdom, dial 00–33, then dial the number in France minus any initial 0.

LONG-DISTANCE CALLS

To make a direct international call from France, dial 00 and wait for the tone, then dial the country code (1 for the United States and Canada; 44 for the United Kingdom), area code (minus any initial 0), and number.

Before you go, **find out the local access codes** for your destinations. AT&T, MCI, and Sprint long-distance services make calling home relatively convenient, but you may find the local access number blocked in many hotel rooms. First ask the hotel operator to connect you. If the hotel operator balks, ask for an international operator, or dial the international operator yourself. One way to improve your odds of getting connected to your long-distance carrier is to travel with more than one company's calling card (a hotel may block Sprint, for example, but not MCI). If all else fails, call your phone company collect in the United States or call from a pay phone in the hotel lobby.

➤ ACCESS CODES: **AT&T USADirecct** (☎ 0–800–99–0011; for information, ☎ 800/874–4000). **MCI Call USA** (☎ 0–800–99–0019; for information ☎ 800/444–4444). **Sprint Express** (☎ 0–800–99–0087; for information, ☎ 800/793–1153).

OPERATORS & INFORMATION

To find a number **in France, dial 12 for information.** For international inquiries, dial 00–33 plus the country code.

Another source of information is the Minitel, an on-line network similar to the Internet. You can find one—they look like a small computer terminal—in most post offices, nearly all hotels, and a vast majority of French homes. One Minitel service—available free in many post offices—is an on-line phone book covering the entire country. To use it, dial 3611. When you hear a screeching sound, hit the *appel* (call) key. Type the name you are looking for and hit *envoi* (return). It is also useful for tracking down services: choose *activité* (activity), tap in *piscine* (swimming pool), then Chartres, for example, and it will give you a list of all the pools in Chartres. Go to other lines or pages by hitting the *suite* (next) key. Newer models will connect automatically when you hit the book-icon key. To disconnect, hit *fin* (end).

PAY PHONES

Telephone booths **can almost always be found at post offices, métro stations, and often in cafés.** A local call costs 74 centimes for every three minutes; half-price rates apply weekdays between 9:30 PM and 8 AM, from 1:30 PM Saturday, and all day Sunday.

Most **French pay phones are operated by *télécartes* (phone cards),** which you can buy from post offices, métro stations, and some tabacs (tobacco shops) for a cost of 40 francs for 50 units and 96 francs for 120. Some pay phones accept 1-, 2- and 5-franc coins (1-franc minimum), but the phone card is the most convenient way to make a call.

TIPPING

The French have a clear idea of when they should be tipped. Bills in bars and restaurants include service, but **it is customary to leave some small change** unless you're dissatisfied. The amount of this varies: 30 centimes if you've merely bought a beer, or a few francs after a meal. Tip taxi drivers and hairdressers about 10%. Give ushers in theaters and movie theaters 1 or 2 francs. In some theaters and hotels, coat check attendants may expect nothing (if there is a sign saying POURBOIRE INTERDIT—tips forbidden); otherwise give them 5 francs. Washroom attendants usually get 5 francs, though the sum is often posted.

If you stay in a hotel for more than two or three days, it is customary to leave something for the chambermaid—about 10 francs per day. In expensive hotels you may well call on the services of a baggage porter (bell boy) and hotel porter and possibly the telephone receptionist. All expect a tip: Plan on about 10 francs per item for the baggage boy, but the other tips will depend on how much you've used their services—common sense must guide you here. In hotels that provide room service, give 5 francs to the waiter (this does not apply to breakfast served in your room). If the chambermaid does some pressing or laundering for you, give her 5 francs on top of the charge made.

Gas-station attendants get nothing for gas or oil, and 5 or 10 francs for checking tires. Train and airport porters get a fixed 6–10 francs per bag, but you're better off getting your own baggage cart if you can (a 10-franc coin—refundable—is sometimes necessary). Museum guides should get 5–10 francs after a guided tour, and it is standard practice to tip tour guides (and bus drivers) 10 francs or more after an excursion, depending on its length.

TOUR OPERATORS

Buying **a prepackaged tour or independent vacation can make your trip to France less expensive and more hassle-free.** Because everything is prearranged you'll spend less time planning. Operators that handle several hundred thousand travelers per year can use their purchasing power to give you a good price. Their high volume may also indicate financial stability. But some small companies provide more personalized service; because they tend to specialize, they may also be more knowledgeable about a given area.

A GOOD DEAL?

The more your package or tour includes, the better you can predict the ultimate cost of your vacation. Make sure you know exactly what is covered, and **beware of hidden costs.** Are taxes, tips, and service charges included? Transfers and baggage handling? Entertainment and excursions? These can add up.

If the package or tour you are considering is priced lower than in your wildest dreams, **be skeptical.** Also, **make sure your travel agent knows the accommodations** and other services. Ask about the hotel's location, room size, beds, and whether it has a pool, room service, or programs for children, if you care about these. Has your agent been there in person or sent others you can contact?

BUYER BEWARE

Each year consumers are stranded or lose their money when tour operators—even very large ones with excellent reputations—go out of business. So **check out the operator.** Find out how long the company has been in business, and ask several agents about its reputation. **Don't book unless the firm has a consumer-protection program.**

Members of the National Tour Association and United States Tour Operators Association are required to set aside funds to cover your payments and travel arrangements in case the company defaults. Nonmembers may carry insurance instead. Look for the details, and for the name of an underwriter with a solid reputation, in the operator's brochure. Note: When it comes to tour operators, **don't trust escrow accounts.** Although there are laws governing charter-flight operators, no governmental body prevents tour operators from raiding the till. For more information, *see* Consumer Protection, *above*.

➤ TOUR-OPERATOR RECOMMENDATIONS: **National Tour Association** (✉ NTA, 546 E. Main St., Lexington, KY 40508, ☎ 606/226–4444 or 800/755–8687). **United States Tour Operators Association** (✉ USTOA, 342 Madison Ave., Suite 1522, New York, NY 10173, ☎ 212/599–6599, FAX 212/599–6744).

USING AN AGENT

Travel agents are excellent resources. When shopping for an agent, however, you should **collect brochures from several sources**; some agents' suggestions may be skewed by promotional relationships with tour and package firms that reward them for volume sales. If you have a special interest, **find an agent with expertise in that area** (☞ Travel Agencies, *below*). Don't rely solely on your agent, who may be unaware of small-niche operators. Note that some special-interest travel companies only sell directly to the public and that some large operators only accept bookings made through travel agents.

SINGLE TRAVELERS

Prices for packages and tours are usually quoted per person, based on two sharing a room. If traveling solo, **you may be required to pay the full double-occupancy rate.** Some operators eliminate this surcharge if you agree to be matched with a roommate of the same sex, even if one is not found by departure time.

GROUP TOURS

Among companies that sell tours to France, the following are nationally known, have a proven reputation, and offer plenty of options. The classifications used below represent different price categories, and you'll probably encounter these terms when talking to a travel agent or tour operator. The key difference is usually in accommodations, which run from budget to better, and better-yet to best.

➤ SUPER-DELUXE: **Abercrombie & Kent** (✉ 1520 Kensington Rd., Oak Brook, IL 60521-2141, ☏ 630/954–2944 or 800/323–7308, FAX 630/954–3324). **Travcoa** (✉ Box 2630, 2350 S.E. Bristol St., Newport Beach, CA 92660, ☏ 714/476–2800 or 800/992–2003, FAX 714/476–2538).

➤ DELUXE: **Globus** (✉ 5301 S. Federal Circle, Littleton, CO 80123-2980, ☏ 303/797–2800 or 800/221–0090, FAX 303/347–2080). **Maupintour** (✉ 1515 St. Andrews Dr., Lawrence, KS 66047, ☏ 913/843–1211 or 800/255–4266, FAX 913/843–8351). **Tauck Tours** (✉ Box 5027, 276 Post Rd. W, Westport, CT 06881-5027, ☏ 203/226–6911 or 800/468–2825, FAX 203/221–6828).

➤ FIRST-CLASS: **Brendan Tours** (✉ 15137 Califa St., Van Nuys, CA 91411, ☏ 818/785–9696 or 800/421–8446, FAX 818/902–9876). **Caravan Tours** (✉ 401 N. Michigan Ave., Chicago, IL 60611, ☏ 312/321–9800 or 800/227–2826, FAX 312/321–9845). **Collette Tours** (✉ 162 Middle St., Pawtucket, RI 02860, ☏ 401/728–3805 or 800/832–4656, FAX 401/728–1380). **Trafalgar Tours** (✉ 11 E. 26th St., New York, NY 10010, ☏ 212/689–8977 or 800/854–0103, FAX 800/457–6644).

➤ BUDGET: **Cosmos** (☞ Globus, *above*). **Trafalgar** (☞ *above*).

PACKAGES

Like group tours, independent vacation packages are available from major tour operators and airlines. The companies listed below offer vacation packages in a broad price range.

➤ AIR/HOTEL: **American Airlines Fly AAway Vacations** (☏ 800/321–2121). **Continental Vacations** (☏ 800/634–5555). **Delta Dream Vacations** (☏ 800/872–7786). **DER Tours** (✉ 11933 Wilshire Blvd., Los Angeles, CA 90025, ☏ 310/479–4140 or 800/937–1235). **4th Dimension Tours** (✉ 7101 S.W. 99th Ave., #105, Miami, FL 33173, ☏ 305/279–0014 or 800/644–0438, FAX 305/273–9777). **TWA Getaway Vacations** (☏ 800/438–2929). **United Vacations** (☏ 800/328–6877).

➤ FLY/DRIVE: **American Airlines Fly AAway Vacations** (☏ 800/321–2121). **Delta Dream Vacations** (☏ 800/872–7786). **United Vacations** (☏ 800/328–6877). **Budget World-Class Drive** (☏ 800/527–0700, 0800/181181 in the U.K.) for self-drive itineraries.

➤ FROM THE U.K.: Contact **Cresta Holidays** (✉ Tabley Ct., Victoria St., Altrincham, Cheshire WA14 1EZ, ☏ 0161/926–9999) for hotel and apartment holidays. **Invitation to France** (✉ 4 Alice Ct., 116 Putney Bridge Rd, London SW15 2NQ, ☏ 0181/871–3300) offers chateaux and country-house hotels, and **Thomas Cook** (✉ 45 Berkeley St., London W1A 1EB, ☏ 01733/335–530) offers fly-drive holidays that may include Disneyland Paris.

THEME TRIPS

➤ TRAVEL AGENCIES: **Maison de la France** (☞ Visitor Information, *below*) publishes many brochures on theme trips in France including "In the Footsteps of the Painters of Light in Provence" and "France for the Jewish Traveler." **Travel Contacts** (✉ Box 173, Camberley, GU15 1YE, England, ☏ 011/44/1/27667–7217, FAX 011/44/1/2766–3477) represents over 150 tour operators in Europe.

➤ ADVENTURE: **Adventure Center** (✉ 1311 63rd St., #200, Emeryville, CA 94608, ☏ 510/654–1879 or 800/227–8747, FAX 510/654–4200). **Himalayan Travel** (✉ 110 Prospect

St., Stamford, CT 06901, ☎ 203/359–3711 or 800/225–2380, FAX 203/359–3669). **Mountain Travel-Sobek** (✉ 6420 Fairmount Ave., El Cerrito, CA 94530, ☎ 510/527–8100 or 800/227–2384, FAX 510/525–7710).

➤ ART AND ARCHITECTURE: **Endless Beginnings Tours** (✉ 12650 Sabre Springs Pkwy., Ste. 207-105, San Diego, CA 92128, ☎ 619/679–5374 or 800/822–7855, FAX 619/679–5376). **Esplanade Tours** (✉ 581 Boylston St., Boston, MA 02116, ☎ 617/266–7465 or 800/426–5492, FAX 617/262–9829).

➤ BALLOONING: **Bonaventura Balloon Company** (✉ 133 Wall Rd., Napa, CA 94558, ☎ 707/944–2822 or 800/359–6272, FAX 707/944–2220). **Buddy Bombard European Balloon Adventures** (✉ 855 Donald Ross Rd., Juno Beach, FL 33408, ☎ 561/837–6610 or 800/862–8537, FAX 561/837–6623).

➤ BARGE/RIVER CRUISES: **Abercrombie & Kent** (☞ Group Tours, *above*). **Alden Yacht Charters** (✉ 1909 Alden Landing, Portsmouth, RI 02871, ☎ 401/683–1782 or 800/662–2628, FAX 401/683–3668). **Etoile De Champagne** (✉ 88 Broad St., Boston, MA 02110, ☎ 800/280–1492, FAX 617/426–4689). **European Waterways** (✉ 140 E. 56th St., Ste. 4C, New York, NY 10022, ☎ 212/688–9489 or 800/217–4447, FAX 212/688–3778 or 800/296–4554). **Fenwick & Lang** (✉ 100 W. Harrison, South Tower, Ste., Seattle, WA 98119, ☎ 206/216–2903 or 800/243–6244, FAX 206/216–2973). **French Country Waterways** (✉ Box 2195, Duxbury, MA 02331, ☎ 617/934–2454 or 800/222–1236, FAX 617/934–9048). **KD River Cruises of Europe** (✉ 2500 Westchester Ave., Purchase, NY 10577, ☎ 914/696–3600 or 800/346–6525, FAX 914/696–0833). **Kemwel's Premier Selections** (✉ 106 Calvert St., Harrison, NY 10528, ☎ 914/835–5555 or 800/234–4000, FAX 914/835–5449). **Le Boat** (✉ 10 S. Franklin Turnpike, Ramsey, NJ 07446, ☎ 201/342–1838 or 800/922–0291).

➤ BICYCLING: **Backroads** (✉ 801 Cedar St., Berkeley, CA 94710-1800, ☎ 510/527–1555 or 800/462–2848, FAX 510-527–1444). **Bridges Tours** (✉ 2855 Capital Dr., Eugene, OR 97403, ☎ 541/484–1196, FAX 541/687–9085). **Butterfield & Robinson** (✉ 70 Bond St., Toronto, Ontario, Canada M5B 1X3, ☎ 416/864–1354 or 800/678–1147, FAX 416/864–0541). **Chateaux Bike Tours** (✉ Box 5706, Denver, CO 80217, ☎ 303/393–6910 or 800/678–2453, FAX 303/393–6801). **Classic Adventures** (✉ Box 153, Hamlin, NY 14464-0153, ☎ 716/964–8488 or 800/777–8090, FAX 716/964–7297). **Euro-Bike Tours** (✉ Box 990, De Kalb, IL 60115, ☎ 800/321–6060, FAX 815/758–8851). **Europeds** (✉ 761 Lighthouse Ave., Monterey, CA 93940, ☎ 800/321–9552, FAX 408/655–4501). **Progressive Travels** (✉ 224 W. Galer Ave., Ste. C, Seattle, WA 98119, ☎ 206/285–1987 or 800/245–2229, FAX 206/285–1988). **Uniquely Europe** (✉ 2819 1st Ave., Ste. 280, Seattle, WA 98121-1113, ☎ 206/441–8682 or 800/426–3615, FAX 206/441–8862).

➤ CUSTOMIZED PACKAGES: **Abercrombie & Kent** (☞ Group Tours, *above*). **Alekx Travel** (✉ 519A S. Andrews Ave., Fort Lauderdale, FL 33301, ☎ 954/462–6767, FAX 954/462–8691). **Five Star Touring** (✉ 60 E. 42nd St., #612, New York, NY 10165, ☎ 212/818–9140 or 800/792–7827, FAX 212/818–9142). **The French Experience** (✉ 370 Lexington Ave., Ste. 812, New York, NY 10017, ☎ 212/986–1115).

➤ FOOD AND WINE: **Annemarie Victory Organization** (✉ 136 E. 64th St., New York, NY 10021, ☎ 212/486–0353, FAX 212/751–3149). **Le Cordon Bleu** (✉ 404 Airport Executive Pk., Nanuet, NY 10954, ☎ 800/457–2433). **Cuisine International** (✉ Box 25228, Dallas, TX 75225, ☎ 214/373–1161 or FAX 214/373–1162). **European Culinary Adventures** (✉ 5 Ledgewood Way, Ste.6, Peabody, MA 01960, ☎ 508/535–5738 or 800/852–2625). **Ritz-Escoffier** (in Paris's Ritz hotel, ☎ 800/966–5758).

➤ GOLF: **Golf International** (✉ 275 Madison Ave., New York, NY 10016, ☎ 212/986–9176 or 800/833–1389, FAX 212/986–3720). **ITC Golf Tours** (✉ 4134 Atlantic Ave., #205, Long Beach, CA 90807, ☎ 310/595–6905 or 800/257–4981).

➤ HISTORY: **Herodot Travel** (✉ 775 E. Blithedale, Box 234, Mill Valley, CA 94941, ☎ FAX 415/381–4031).

➤ HOMES AND GARDENS: **Coopersmith's England** (✉ Box 900, Inverness, CA 94937, ☎ 415/669–1914, FAX 415/669–1942).

➤ HORSEBACK RIDING: **Equitour FITS Equestrian** (✉ Box 807, Dubois, WY 82513, ☎ 307/455–3363 or 800/545–0019, FAX 307/455–2354).

➤ HORTICULTURE: **Expo Garden Tours** (✉ 70 Great Oak, Redding, CT 06896, ☎ 203/938–0410 or 800/448–2685, FAX 203/938–0427).

➤ LEARNING: **Smithsonian Study Tours and Seminars** (✉ 1100 Jefferson Dr. SW, Room 3045, MRC 702, Washington, DC 20560, ☎ 202/357–4700, FAX 202/633–9250).

➤ MOTORCYCLE: **Beach's Motorcycle Adventures** (✉ 2763 W. River Pkwy., Grand Island, NY 14072-2053, ☎ 716/773–4960, FAX 716/773–5227).

➤ MUSIC: **Dailey-Thorp Travel** (✉ 330 W. 58th St., #610, New York, NY 10019-1817, ☎ 212/307–1555 or 800/998–4677, FAX 212/974–1420).

➤ NATURAL HISTORY: **Questers** (✉ 381 Park Ave. S, New York, NY 10016, ☎ 212/251–0444 or 800/468–8668, FAX 212/251–0890).

➤ SPAS: **Great Spas of the World** (✉ 630 Fifth Ave., New York, NY 10111, ☎ 212/599–0382 or 800/772–8463, FAX 212/599–0380). **Spa-Finders** (✉ 91 Fifth Ave., #301, New York, NY 10003-3039, ☎ 212/924–6800 or 800/255–7727). **Spa Trek Travel** (✉ 475 Park Ave. S., New York, NY 10016, ☎ 212/779–3480 or 800/272–3480, FAX 212/779–3471).

➤ TENNIS: **Championship Tennis Tours** (✉ 7350 E. Stetson Dr., #106, Scottsdale, AZ 85251, ☎ 602/990–8760 or 800/468–3664, FAX 602/990–8744). **Steve Furgal's International Tennis Tours** (✉ 11828 Rancho Bernardo Rd., #123-305, San Diego, CA 92128, ☎ 619/675–3555 or 800/258–3664).

➤ VILLA RENTALS: **Chez Vous** (✉ 1001 Bridgeway, Ste. 245, Sausalito, CA 94965 ☎ 415/331–2535, FAX 415/331–5296). **Villas International** (✉ 605 Market St., San Francisco, CA 94105, ☎ 415/281–0910 or 800/221–2260, FAX 415/281–0919).

➤ WALKING: **Abercrombie & Kent** (☞ Group Tours, *above*). **Above the Clouds Trekking** (✉ Box 398, Worcester, MA 01602-0398, ☎ 508/799–4499 or 800/233–4499, FAX 508/797–4779). **Backroads** (☞ Bicycling, *above*). **Butterfield & Robinson** (☞ Bicycling, *above*). **Classic Adventures** (☞ Bicycling, *above*). **Country Walkers** (✉ Box 180, Waterbury, VT 05676-0180, ☎ 802/244–1387 or 800/464–9255, FAX 802/244–5661). **Euro-Bike Tours** (✉ Box 990, De Kalb, IL 60115, ☎ 800/321–6060, FAX 815/758–8851). **Mountain Travel-Sobek** (✉ 6420 Fairmount Ave., El Cerrito, CA 94530, ☎ 510/527–8100 or 800/227–2384, FAX 510/525–7710). **Progressive Travels** (☞ Bicycling, *above*). **Uniquely Europe** (☞ Bicycling, *above*). **Wilderness Travel** (✉ 801 Allston Way, Berkeley, CA 94710, ☎ 510/548–0420 or 800/368–2794, FAX 510/548–0347).

➤ YACHT CHARTERS: **Huntley Yacht Vacations** (✉ 210 Preston Rd., Wernersville, PA 19565, ☎ 610/678–2628 or 800/322–9224, FAX 610/670–1767). **Lynn Jachney Charters** (✉ Box 302, Marblehead, MA 01945, 617/639–0787 or 800/223–2050, FAX 617/639–0216). **The Moorings** (✉ 19345 U.S. Hwy. 19 N, 4th floor, Clearwater, FL 34624-3193, ☎ 813/530–5424 or 800/535–7289, FAX 813/530–9474). **Ocean Voyages** (✉ 1709 Bridgeway, Sausalito, CA 94965, ☎ 415/332–4681 or 800/299–4444, FAX 415/332–7460).

TRAIN TRAVEL

The SNCF is generally recognized as Europe's best national rail service: It's fast, punctual, comfortable, and comprehensive. The high-speed TGVs, or Trains à Grande Vitesse (average 255 kph/160 mph on the Lyon/southeast line, 300 kph/190 mph on the Lille and Bordeaux/southwest lines), are the best domestic trains. They operate between Paris and Lille/Calais, Paris and Brussels, Paris and Amsterdam, Paris and Lyon/Switzerland/the Riviera, and Angers/Nantes, and Tours/Poitiers/Bordeaux. As with other main-line trains, a small supplement may be assessed at peak hours. You must **always make a seat reservation for the TGV**—easily obtained at the ticket window or from an automatic machine. Seat reservations are reassuring but seldom necessary on other mainline French trains, except at certain busy holiday times.

If you know what station you'll depart from, you can get a free schedule there (while supplies last), or you can access the new multilingual computerized schedule information network at any Paris station and many provincial ones. You can also make reservations and buy your ticket while at the computer.

If you are traveling from Paris (or any other terminus), **get to the station half an hour before departure** to ensure that you'll have a good seat. The majority of intercity trains in France consist of open-plan cars and are known as *Corail* trains. They are clean and extremely comfortable, even in second class. Trains on regional branch lines are currently being spruced up but lag behind in style and quality. The food in French trains can be good, but it's poor value for the money.

Before boarding, you must **punch your ticket (but not Eurailpass) in one of the orange machines** at the entrance to the platforms, or else the ticket collector will fine you 100 francs on the spot.

It is possible to get from one end of France to the other without traveling overnight. Otherwise you have the choice between high-priced *wagons-lits* (sleeping cars) and affordable *couchettes* (bunks, six to a compartment in second class, four to a compartment in first, with sheets and pillow provided, priced at around 90 francs). Special summer night trains from Paris to Spain and the Riviera, geared to young people, are equipped with disco and bar.

➤ INFORMATION: **SNCF** (✉ 88 rue St-Lazare, 75009 Paris, ☎ 01–45–82–50–50), for information on rail travel in France.

➤ TRAIN-FERRY LINK: **British Rail International** (☎ 0171/834–2345) and **Sealink** (☎ 0233/647047) provide train-ferry travel from the United Kingdom to France.

DISCOUNT PASSES

If France is your only destination in Europe, **consider purchasing a France Rail Pass,** which allows three days of unlimited train travel in a one-month period. Prices begin at $120 for two adults traveling together in second-class and $160 second-class for a solo traveler. First-class rates are $198 for two adults and $160 for a solo traveler. Additional days may be added for $30 a day in either class. Other options include the France Rail 'n Drive Pass (combining rail and rental car), France Rail 'n Fly Pass (rail travel and one air travel journey within France), and the France Fly Rail 'n Drive Pass (a rail, air, and rental-car program all in one).

France is one of 17 countries in which you can **use Eurailpasses,** which provide unlimited first-class rail travel, in all of the participating countries, for the duration of the pass. If you plan to rack up the miles, get a standard pass. These are available for 15 days ($522), 21 days ($678), one month ($838), two months ($1,148), and 3 months ($1,468). If your plans call for only limited train travel, **look into a Europass,** which costs less money than a Eurailpass. Unlike Eurailpasses, however, you get a limited number of travel days, in a limited number of countries, during a specified time period. For example, a two month pass ($316) allows between five and fifteen days of rail travel, but costs $200 less than the least expensive Eurailpass. Keep in mind, however, that the Europass is good only in France, Germany, Italy, Spain, and Switzerland, and the number of countries you can visit is further limited by the type of pass you buy. For example, the basic two-month pass allows you to visit only three of the five participating countries.

In addition to standard Eurailpasses, **ask about special rail-pass plans.** Among these are the Eurail Youthpass (for those under age 26), the Eurail Saverpass (which gives a discount for two or more people traveling together), a Eurail Flexipass (which allows a certain number of travel days within a set period), the Euraildrive Pass and the Europass Drive (which combine travel by train and rental car).

Whichever pass you choose, remember that you must **purchase your pass before you leave** for Europe.

Many travelers assume that rail passes guarantee them seats on the trains they wish to ride. Not so. You need to **book seats ahead even if you are using a rail pass;** seat reservations are required on some European trains, particularly high-speed trains, and are a good idea on trains that may be crowded—particularly in summer on popular routes. You will also need a reservation if you purchase overnight sleeping accommodations.

In France, there are also various train discounts available. When traveling together, **two people (who don't have to be a couple) can save money with the "Prix Découverte à Deux."** Just say you're traveling together when you make a reservation or buy the tickets, and you will get a 25% discount during "périodes bleus" (blue periods; weekdays and not on or near any holidays).

The **Carte Vermeil is a good value if you're over age 60.** There are two options: The first, the Carte Vermeil Quatre Temps, costs 143F and gives you a reduction on 4 trips: 50% off in the blue periods and 20% off during "périodes blanches" (white periods; weekends or on or around holidays). The second, the Carte Vermeil Plein Temps, is 279F and allows you, for one year, 30% reductions on trips in and outside of France.

If you're under 26, you can get a 25% reduction (a valid ID is necessary) on all individual tickets. Or **look into the Carte 12–25** (270F), which offers unlimited 50% reductions for one year (provided that there's space available at that price, otherwise you'll just get the standard 25% discount).

You can **get a discount for children with the Carte Kiwi.** With the card, up to four children under 16 accompanying an adult can get a 50% discount for a full year. It's 285F for four trips and 444F for an unlimited number of trips.

If you don't benefit from any of these reductions and plan on traveling at least 1,000 km (620 mi) round-trip (including several stops), **look into purchasing a Billet Séjour.** This ticket gives you a 25% reduction if you stay over a Sunday and travel only during blue periods.

➤ DISCOUNT PASSES: Eurail- and Europasses are available through travel agents and **Rail Europe** (⊠ 226-230 Westchester Ave., White Plains, NY 10604, ☎ 914/682–5172 or 800/438–7245; ⊠ 2087 Dundas E., Suite 105, Mississauga, Ontario L4X 1M2, ☎ 416/602–4195), **CIT Tours Corp.** (⊠ 342 Madison Ave., Suite 207, New York, NY 10173, ☎ 212/697–2100 or 800/248–8687 or 800/248–7245 in western U.S.), or **DER Tours** (⊠ Box 1606, Des Plaines, IL 60017, ☎ 800/782–2424, FAX 800/282–7474). French rail passes are available at train stations throughout France.

TRANSPORTATION

BY BOAT

Ferries and hovercrafts travel between France and the U.K. (☞ Ferry & Hovercraft Travel, *above*), though the Channel Tunnel (☞ The Channel Tunnel, *above*) has made this route much faster by train.

BY BUS

Long-distance buses are rare because train service is so good; **regional buses are found mainly where train service is spotty.** If you don't want to rent a car and can't get to a place by train, look into excursions and bus tours organized by SNCF and other tourist organizations (☞ Bus Travel, *above*).

BY CAR

Renting **a car gives you greater mobility:** you can access places not reachable by train, drive along back country roads, and come and go whenever you please (without being ruled by the train schedule). But **renting cars in France is expensive**—about twice as much as in the United States—as is gas (☞ Car Rental, *above*). If you would like to combine both car and train travel, consider purchasing a rail/drive package.

BY PLANE

Domestic air travel in France is less expensive than it used to be (though still no bargain at an average of 1,500 francs round-trip) and there are more airline companies flying all over the country. France's domestic airline, Air Inter-Europe (☞ Air Travel, *above*), has flights from Paris to all major cities. For long journeys—from Paris to the Riviera, for instance—**domestic air travel is a time saver, though train travel is always cheaper** and it may be faster when you consider time spent getting to and from the airport.

BY TRAIN

Traveling across France by train is one of the most romantic ways to see the country. High speed TGVs race from place to place and local SNCF lines make connections to towns all over the country (☞ Train Travel, *above*). Train travel **costs depend on a number of factors:** the number of people traveling together, the number of days you are traveling, the distance you are traveling, the time of year you are traveling, and any possible discounts you can get (i.e., based on age or with a rail pass). If you are traveling with a large group or would like to go to out of the way places that the train does not reach, it may be more convenient and economical to rent a car.

TRAVEL AGENCIES

A good travel agent puts your needs first. **Look for an agency that specializes in your destination, has been in business at least five years, and emphasizes customer service.** If you're looking for an agency-organized package or tour, your best bet is to choose an agency that's a member of the National Tour Association or the United States Tour Operator's Association (☞ Tour Operators, *above*).

➤ LOCAL AGENT REFERRALS: **Alliance of Canadian Travel Associations** (✉ Suite 201, 1729 Bank St., Ottawa, Ontario K1V 7Z5, ☎ 613/521–0474, FAX 613/521–0805). **Association of British Travel Agents** (✉ 55–57 Newman St., London W1P 4AH, ☎ 0171/637–2444, FAX 0171/637–0713).

U

U.S. GOVERNMENT

The U.S. government can be an excellent source of inexpensive travel information. When planning your trip, **find out what government materials are available.**

➤ ADVISORIES: **U.S. Department of State American Citizens Services Office** (✉ Room 4811, Washington, DC 20520); enclose a self-addressed, stamped envelope. **Interactive hot line** (☎ 202/647–5225, FAX 202/647–3000). **Computer bulletin board** (☎ 202/647–9225).

➤ PAMPHLETS: **Consumer Information Center** (✉ Consumer Information Catalogue, Pueblo, CO 81009, ☎ 719/948–3334) for a free catalog that includes travel titles.

V

VISITOR INFORMATION

➤ MAISON DE LA FRANCE/FRENCH GOVERNMENT TOURIST OFFICE: **Paris:** (✉ 8 av. de l'Opéra, 75001 Paris, ☎ 01–42–96–10–23). **United States Nationwide** (☎ 900/990–0040; costs 50¢ per minute). **New York City** (✉ 444 Madison Ave., New York, NY 10022, ☎ 212/838–7800). **Chicago** (✉ 676 N. Michigan Ave., Chicago, IL 60611, ☎ 312/751–7800). **Beverly Hills** (✉ 9454 Wilshire Blvd., Beverly Hills, CA 90212, ☎ 310/271–6665, FAX 310/276–2835). **Canada** (✉ 1981 Ave., McGill College, Suite 490, Montréal, Québec H3A 2W9, ☎ 514/288–4264, FAX 514/845–4868; ✉ 30 St. Patrick St., Suite 700, Toronto, Ontario M5T 3A3, ☎ 416/491–7622, FAX 416/979–7587). **U.K.** (✉ 178 Piccadilly, London W1V 0AL, ☎ 0891/244–123, FAX 0171/493–6594). Calls cost 50p per minute peak rate or 45p per minute cheap rate.

➤ LOCAL TOURIST OFFICES: *See* the A to Z sections *in* individual chapters for local tourist office telephone numbers and addresses.

W

WHEN TO GO

June and September are the best months to be in France, as both are free of the midsummer crowds. June offers the advantage of long daylight hours, while cheaper prices and frequent Indian summers, often lasting well into October, make September attractive. Try to avoid the second half of July and all of August, when almost all of France goes on vacation. Huge crowds jam the roads and beaches, and prices are jacked up in resorts. Don't travel on or around July 14 and August 1, 15, and 31.

July and August in southern France can be stifling. Paris can be stuffy in August, too, but it is pleasantly deserted. Many restaurants, theaters, and small shops close, but enough stay open these days to make a low-key, unhurried visit a pleasure. If you want to go to the countryside at this time, stay away from the coast. Hotels and restaurants are less crowded inland.

The ski season in the Alps and Pyrénées lasts from Christmas to Easter; if you can, avoid February, when school holidays mean crowds.

Anytime between March and November will offer you a good chance to soak up the sun on the Riviera. If Paris and the Loire are among your priorities, remember that the weather is unappealing before Easter. If you're dreaming of Paris in the springtime, May is your best bet, not rainy April. But the capital remains a joy during mid-winter, with plenty of things to see and do.

CLIMATE

➤ FORECASTS: **Weather Channel Connection** (☏ 900/932–8437), 95¢ per minute from a Touch-Tone phone.

What follows are average daily maximum and minimum temperatures for Paris and Nice.

PARIS

Jan.	43F	6C	May	68F	20C	Sept.	70F	21C
	34	1		49	10		53	12
Feb.	45F	7C	June	73F	23C	Oct.	60F	16C
	34	1		55	13		46	8
Mar.	54F	12C	July	76F	25C	Nov.	50F	10C
	39	4		58	15		40	5
Apr.	60F	16C	Aug.	75F	24C	Dec.	44F	7C
	43	6		58	15		36	2

NICE

Jan.	55F	13C	May	68F	20C	Sept.	77F	25C
	39	4		55	13		61	16
Feb.	55F	13C	June	75F	24C	Oct.	70F	21C
	41	5		61	16		54	12
Mar.	59F	15C	July	81F	27C	Nov.	63F	17C
	45	7		64	18		46	8
Apr.	64F	18C	Aug.	81F	27C	Dec.	55F	13C
	46	8		64	18		41	5

1 Destination: France

THE BEST OF ALL POSSIBLE WORLDS

FRANCE IS NEITHER TOO HOT nor too cold, neither too wet nor too dry, neither too flat nor too crammed with inconvenient mountains. At any rate, that is what the French say. They think that countries should be hexagonal in shape and about 600 mi across. Spain is too square, Norway is frayed at the edges, l'Angleterre (which is what they usually call Great Britain) is awkwardly surrounded by cold water, Switzerland is landlocked and too small, and the United States is too large (you cross three time zones and then get the same depressing dinner). After God created France, He belatedly realized that He had gone too far: It was too near perfection. "How can I restore the balance?" He asked Himself. Then He saw what to do—He created the French. That is a French story. The French enjoy grumbling about themselves or, rather, about other French people, but in the same breath they admit that there is only one civilized way for people to live, and that is the French way, *la civilisation française*.

My wife and I have lived in France for many years, and we have come to the conclusion that there is something to be said for this view. Our fellow villagers are kind, patient, and friendly, behaving with natural dignity and good manners, like most of the other French people we meet (except Parisians in the rush hour). Visitors to France, particularly Anglo-Saxon visitors, whether they stay a week or a year, will have a better time if they "go native" as far as they find it practicable—and when and where they don't, they should be philosophically aware of the drawbacks of trying to behave as in dear old Birmingham, AL or U.K. (I am using the word "Anglo-Saxon" as the French use it. To them, Louis Armstrong, Robert Burns, James Joyce, and Frank Sinatra are representative Anglo-Saxons; Beowulf and King Alfred have nothing to do with it.)

Let's look at the French timetable. Most of the French are up early, gulping a café au lait and getting to work by 8. By 10, Parisian executives are fuming because their London contacts haven't yet answered the phone (it's only 9 in England). There is no coffee break.

At noon, they are hungry. Work stops for two hours or longer. Museums and small shops close. *Le déjeuner* (called *le dîner* in the country) is a sacred rite. Fast-food outlets have multiplied, but the norm is a proper meal, taking an hour and a half; a surprising number manage to get home for it. However, the increasing number of women at work means that six lunches out of 10 are eaten at restaurants or canteens—substantial, freshly cooked affairs, eaten with serious critical attention. The French grew rich in the '60s: Back in 1920, they each ate nearly three pounds of bread a day—now it is just under a pound, with a corresponding increase in the consumption of meat, fish, and cheese. Less wine is drunk, but more of it is of higher quality.

There is a typical restaurant in our nearest market town (pop. 6,000). It has only one menu: copious hors d'oeuvres, a fish dish or a light meat dish, a more serious meat dish, vegetables in season, a good cheese board, fruit or ice cream. It's always full by 12:30. A couple from San Francisco who stayed in a rented cottage in our village were hardly ever able to use it. They used to get up at 9 and have an Anglo-Saxon sort of breakfast, and so they were hopelessly out of phase with the commercial travelers (up at 6) who form the restaurant's main clientele. You can't start your lunch there at 1:30 or 2, and there are no doggy bags in France. We are in the Midi, where an early start and a siesta are convenient (many of the shops don't reopen until 3:30). However, the couple happily developed the picnic habit: France is God's own country for picnicking, if only you get to the *charcuterie* and the *boulangerie* and the *pâtisserie* well before they close at noon.

Back to work for another four-hour stretch. No tea or coffee break. Are the French mighty toilers? Yes and no. I have conducted oral language examinations in France and in England. The French expect me to keep on examining nonstop from 8 to 12:30 and again from 2 to 6:30. The merciful (lazy?) English think six hours of attentive interviewing per day, with breaks midmorning and mid-afternoon, are all the human mind can stand. French schoolchildren have a much longer day than do Anglo-Saxon ones and have more to learn.

On the other hand, wage earners and schoolchildren have many leisure days. In the '80s, the average industrial worker put in 1,872 hours of work in the United States, 1,750 in Great Britain, but only 1,650 in France. Five weeks' paid vacation is the official minimum, and there are many public holidays. The French have become addicts of leisure in the past two decades. One family in 10 has a second house in the country, where they go on weekends and vacations, causing astounding traffic jams as they flee the cities.

If he finishes his day's work at 6 or 6:30, will our average Frenchman call in at his favorite café for a chat and an aperitif on his way home? Probably not, nowadays. In the past, the café was used as a sort of extra living room for meeting friends or professional contacts, or even for writing novels if you were Jean-Paul Sartre or Simone de Beauvoir. But today an average of two hours and 50 minutes is spent watching television at home, which reduces the time available for social life.

This is sad. The number of cafés has diminished. Fortunately, there are still a lot left, and how convenient they are for the visitor! On the terrace of a French café, you can bask in the sun or enjoy the shade of a multicolor parasol, sipping a cool beer and keeping an eye on life's passing show, while your near and dear toy with Popsicles or write letters. A small black coffee entitles you to spend an hour or two—no hurry.

While we are on the subject: It seems odd to the Anglo-Saxon that in France beer is generally considered a nonalcoholic drink. (Nurses serve it after you give blood.) When you tell the French that some people at home succeed in getting nastily drunk on it, they say, "But they must drink several glasses!" Indeed. A Frenchman will spend half an hour sipping a quarter of a liter. One sees few drunks in France, except in the north, and then very rarely.

I mentioned the aperitif hour to talk not only about cafés but about friendliness. Some people—notably Americans—complain that the French are inhospitable and standoffish. The fact is that they are great respecters of privacy. If the Englishman's home is his castle, the Frenchman's apartment or house is his lair. People simply do not pop into one another's lairs, drinking casual cups of coffee and borrowing half a pound of sugar. They need a neutral place in which to socialize. Britons come somewhere between typical French people and the American middle class. According to Paul Fussell (*Caste Marks*, 1983): "Among the [American] middles there's a convention that erecting a fence or even a tall hedge is an affront."

IT'S DIFFERENT in France. People in the Midi, where we live, just love to talk, and even to listen. But our village neighbors are timid about entering our house. If they want to ask us something, they will wait until we meet, or stay on the doorstep, or phone (from 50 yards away). They penetrate our house, and we penetrate theirs, when specifically invited. That is how they behave among themselves, too. It's not because we are foreigners.

So when do we talk? There are benches everywhere, in the sun and in the shade. The villagers—and we—sit there for hours, chatting. The locals really are interested in you, your habits and tastes, the number and ages of your children, your work, where you come from, and so forth, and are longing to impart a discreet selection of their own personal details. Of course you *may* be invited home. There are no rules about this sort of thing. And if there were, the French would take pleasure in breaking them.

When talking with the French, there are conventions that should be observed if you don't want to be thought a barbarian by people who are unaware of Anglo-Saxon attitudes. You must say *"Bonjour"* followed by *Monsieur, Madame, Mademoiselle, Messieurs, Mesdames,* or *Messieurs-dames* much more often than you would think necessary (on entering a small shop, for instance) and *"Au revoir, Monsieur"* (etc.). Hands are shaken frequently (by colleagues at work, morning and evening, and by the most casual acquaintances). *Bon appétit* can replace *au revoir* shortly before mealtimes. On going through a door, a certain amount of *après-vous*-ing is normal, with *pardon* if you go through first, turning your back. Getting on first-name terms is a sign of much greater intimacy than in England or the United States. Rush-hour Parisian life is more brutal, of course, and, as elsewhere in the world, the driving seat of a car exerts a malign influence. In England, a headlight flash sometimes means "After you"; in France, it means either "After me" or "I am a criminal and I expect you are, too, so watch it, chum, the cops are round the corner."

BACK HOME FROM the café, *le dîner* (called *le souper* in the country) is served around 8, for rich and poor. It's a lighter meal than at midday, with soup replacing hors d'oeuvres. The movies, after a sharp fall as television established itself in every home, have resisted well. Except in Paris, films are dubbed into French, a practice deplored by intellectuals.

Almost all employed people now have a two-day weekend, usually Saturday and Sunday, but Sunday and Monday for many shop workers. Schoolchildren have Wednesday free, but may attend Saturday morning, instead. In recent years, the French have revolutionized their leisure habits: Jogging, swimming, soccer, gymnastics, tennis, and vigorous bicycling (for fun, not transport) are practiced, mainly on weekends, by large numbers of all social classes.

Sunday is a day for enjoying oneself. Though 85% of the population declare themselves Catholics, only 15% of those go to church every week. There is a fairly strong anti-church sentiment among many, even among those who say they are Catholics, but the traditional warfare between priest and primary-school teacher—the one reactionary and the other attached to Republican ideals—is a thing of the past. Divorce, the pill, and legal abortion are widely accepted, even by practicing Catholics.

The great Sunday ritual takes place at noon or soon after. Four out of 10 will visit friends or relations. Sixty percent of families do more cooking on Sundays than on other days. This is also a big day for restaurants that feature a special Sunday menu. Half the French end their Sunday lunch with a fresh fruit tart or some sort of gâteau, which is why the pastry shops are open in the morning and why you see Frenchmen carefully carrying flat cardboard boxes. Then a quarter of the population takes a little siesta.

An essay such as this has to contain rash generalizations. Is there an average French person? Obviously not. There are the rich and the poor, for example. The poor, in France, like champagne, oysters, and foie gras, but they get them less often than do the rich. The same is true of other aspects of life. The gulf between one class and another is not one of tastes and aspirations; rich and poor are in broad agreement on what constitutes a pleasant life. The poor are simply farther away from it than are the rich.

Changing France . . . I was there in 1947, and I said to myself: "How wonderful! But it can't last." On the whole it has. The surge of prosperity in the '60s brought improvements to French life, with some drawbacks (traffic in Paris, for example), but basic traditions die hard. The young ape foreign fashions, with a fast-food/motorcycle/mid-Atlantic pop noise/comic-strip culture, but they grow out of it. Official morality has changed. Contraception used to be forbidden; Paris was famed for its elegant brothels, but women had to go to London for diaphragms and to Switzerland for abortions. All that has gone. In 1988, the rise of AIDS caused a quickly smothered quarrel among bishops about the sinfulness of condoms, which are readily available. *Le topless* is seen on most beaches, and total nakedness on some. But the family remains a powerful, cohesive unit.

What do they think of us? Corresponding to the Anglo-Saxon stereotype that depicts all Frenchmen wearing berets and pointed beards, waving their arms wildly and being saucy with the girls, the French picture Americans as rich, generous, overweight, and likely in world politics or personal relationships to behave like well-meaning bulls in china shops and the English as either tall, silent, inhibited, masochistic, and scrupulously honest or as drunken, sadistic, soccer-watching vandals. Of course nobody really believes any of this, but if you are going to attach a national label to yourself, you might as well be aware of the cliché lurking at the back of the mind.

"Happy as God in France" say the Germans, exaggerating a bit. Anglo-Saxons come in two sorts: Those who love France and those who don't. It's a matter of taste and character. The former find it easy to slip into the French way of life for a week or a month or permanently. The latter are better off in Paris or on the Riviera. But really, the French are canny operators when it comes to enjoying *la douceur de vivre,* the sweetness of life. If you follow their example while in France, you can't go far wrong. (One way to go wrong would be to quote almost any paragraph from this essay to them; at any rate, it will start a vigorously French argument.)

—John P. Harris

Born in England, John P. Harris has lived in a small village in the south of France since 1975. He has written numerous articles for both French and British newspapers and magazines, including the *London Times,* and is the author of *France—A Guide for the Independent Traveler* (Macmillan, London 1987).

NEW AND NOTEWORTHY

Once again France is living with "*cohabitation*"—between Jacques Chirac, the Conservative French president, and Lionel Jospin, the Socialist prime minister who won the early elections in the spring of 1997. Their battle is now to create more jobs in France while maintaining an eye toward the global marketplace and finding common ground with the European Union and the soon-to-be common currency.

The main event in France in 1998 is unquestionably the **World Cup** in Soccer. Thirty-two nations will dispute the title from June 10–July 12, with games in specially renovated and enlarged stadiums across the country (Paris, Bordeaux, Lens, Lyon, Nantes, Marseille, Montpellier, Toulouse, and St-Étienne). A giant new 80,000 all-seater stadium, the **Stade de France,** has been built in St-Denis, a suburb north of Paris, to stage the opening ceremony and final round.

The late François Mitterrand, who did so much to alter the face of Paris during his 14-year presidency, was a keen soccer fan. It is sad that he should miss the World Cup and the completion of two of his most ambitious building projects, in Paris: the **Bibliothèque Nationale François Mitterrand,** the largest, and possibly most spectacular library in the world, rapidly named in his honor; and the postmodern **Cité de la Musique** at La Villette, where a high-tech Music Museum, with a mind-tingling array of 900 instruments that sound as you pass thanks to infrared headphones, opened in 1997.

Exterior cleaning of the **Louvre** is finally over, and so is the replanting and redesigning of the adjacent **Jardin des Tuileries.** The capital's most-visited site, the **Centre Pompidou,** has fallen victim of its own success and will be mostly closed until the year 2000 as it is renovated. Two-wheelers in Paris received a boost with the creation of 32 km (20 mi) of **bicycle lanes** throughout the city. Cars have been banned altogether on Sundays from certain scenic routes, including the banks of the Seine.

Away from Paris, recent events included the long-awaited reopening of the country's largest provincial art museum, the Musée des Beaux-Arts, in **Lille.** In **Abbeville** the decades-long restoration to the lace-like facade of the cathedral-size church of St-Vulfran was finally completed. **Noeux-les-Mines,** near Arras, has made a name for itself as a ski center: A disused coal slag-heap was transformed into a fully equipped artificial ski run. In Alsace, Brittany, and the Basque region there has been a trend toward putting **regional languages** on streets signs along with the French names. In Strasbourg, for instance, the sign for place de la Cathédrale now also reads, "Muenschterplatz."

The disastrous fire in the Channel Tunnel in November 1996 badly undermined confidence in the already debt-plagued system. The **Eurostar** will continue to compete for Paris-London tourism, however, with more aggressive price reductions and attractive travel packages. After several years of railroad developments hogging the transportation limelight, France's **expressway network** has taken to the fast lane: Numerous new autoroutes opened making it easier to avoid snarl-ups for Parisians heading to the provinces. There is also good news for air travel: **Air Inter** has increased the number of domestic flights in France and the result is greater convenience and cheaper fares. In addition, a number of smaller, regionally based competitors have started flying throughout France.

WHAT'S WHERE

Paris

The Eiffel Tower gives you an overview; the Louvre, a good look at the art of the past (with a peek, too, at architecture's present and future). Say a prayer at Notre-Dame, buy a dress you'll love forever, and eat an unforgettable meal anywhere at all. Open your eyes; there's something beautiful or amusing at every step; dawdle around the Latin Quarter, climb up to Montmartre for a peek at Sacré-Coeur, spend a morning at the *marché aux puces* (flea market), and sail down the Seine on the Bateaux Mouches.

Ile-de-France

The green surround of Paris, lushly forested and islanded by meandering rivers, is studded with noble châteaux and their spectacular gardens. Versailles and Fontainebleau, Thoiry, Chantilly, and Maintenon are only a few. From sublime Chartres to Monet's Giverny, then to Disneyland Paris, you can traverse the centuries, all within an hour or so of Paris.

The Loire Valley

Sometimes owned by England, and fought over for centuries, this stretch of the Loire southwest of Paris resounds today with the noise of contented tourists, music festivals, and son-et-lumière spectacles at the extraordinary châteaux. Amboise, Blois, Chenonceau, and Chambord number among the many. Joan of Arc captured Orléans, and here you can learn her history, while at Angers, 208 km (130 mi) downriver, you can visit the fortress and the cathedral, and get to know the wines of Anjou at the Maison du Vin.

Brittany

Nationalistic Brittany, the northwest arm of France, is full of the sound of the sea. It also has massive castles, vast beaches, and prehistoric standing stones. You'll be charmed, as well, by Rennes (medieval, Renaissance, *and* classical buildings), walled St-Malo, Quimper with its pottery, Dinan's old town, and tranquil Nantes. Come to Finistère (land's end) in August for the classic sailboat rally in the Bay of Douarnenez, then visit Ste-Anne-la-Palud during the *pardon,* where you'll see traditional Breton lace *coiffes.*

Normandy

With miles of sandy beaches along the English Channel, Normandy also has folksy seaside towns like Dieppe, Fécamp, Honfleur, and plush resort towns like Trouville, Deauville, and Cabourg. Continue west to reach fabulous Mont-St-Michel, the medieval abbey and village on a rock offshore that's an island at high tide. Inland, you must see Rouen's cathedral and its museums, visit charming Pont-Audemer on a market day, the lace museum in Alençon, and stay a while in Bayeux for the legendary tapestry and the harmonious cathedral. And don't forget camembert and other marvelous cheeses—or your post-dinner calvados.

The North and Champagne

Lille is one of France's liveliest cities—a vibrant return to reality after the moving World War I battlefields and cemeteries near Albert and Arras—and just an hour from Paris by TGV. The new Channel Tunnel, like the traditional ferries, arrives at Calais; head down the Channel coast's uninterrupted stretch of sandy beaches to the elegant resort of Le Touquet. Inland, admire the palace of Compiègne, the mighty castles of Pierrefonds and Sedan, and the awesome cathedrals of Beauvais, Amiens, Noyon, Laon, and Reims—also center of the champagne industry, where bottles snooze in cavernous, chalky cellars. Away to the northeast lie the game-filled forests of the Ardennes.

Alsace-Lorraine and Franche-Comté

In Alsace, France's Germanic eastern corner, the beautiful Route de Vin winds through vineyards and villages among the Vosges foothills, and medieval half-timber houses lend a storybook air. Strasbourg rivals Paris in culture (it's home to the European Parliament), history, and architecture, not to mention haute cuisine (with local foie gras). Nancy, in Lorraine, is home to Baccarat and St-Louis crystal and adds Art Nouveau to its decorative mix. In the Jura, you can visit pretty little towns and buy wooden toys, clocks, and pipes, and even ski.

Burgundy

Drive southeast from Paris to the land of medieval dukes more powerful than kings, noble vineyards, Gothic cathedrals, and fabulous food. Stop first in Troyes (Champagne) to wander the pedestrian streets, see the old churches, timber houses, and museums. Circle the Morvan Forest, stopping in Autun, once a Roman town, and picturesque Vézelay with its basilica, and push on to Dijon, where the Palais des Ducs now houses the wonderful Musée des Beaux-Arts. Be sure to taste the wines at the Marché aux Vins in Beaune, and maybe buy some as you head south, visiting Cluny's Abbey on your way to Mâcon's wine fair in May.

Lyon and the Alps

You can zip down from Paris on the TGV in a couple of hours, and plant yourself in wonderful Lyon while you take in the rest of the region, from the wine villages of Beaujolais to the lakes and marshes of the Dombes and the medieval hilltop village of Pérouges. Then, venture down the Rhône to Vienne for Roman ruins and Renaissance facades and to the river town of Serrières. Pass through Grenoble with its fine museum en route to the Alps. Aix-les-Bains has ruined Roman baths and modern ones, and Annecy has lively Tuesday and Friday markets. Picturesque Talloires and chic Chamonix, with its cable car up the Aiguille du Midi, are two more enticing spots.

The Massif Central and the Auvergne

This unspoiled region, now more easily accessible by autoroute, has volcanoes and ravines, thermal springs, and the dramatic Gorges du Tarn. Visit the exquisite cathedral in the market town of Bourges, elegant Vichy, the museums and cathedral in Clermont-Ferrand, the Parc des Volcans (but not in summer), and wonderful medieval towns and villages like Salers, high-perched Rocamadour, St-Cirq-Lapopie, Figeac, and Ste-Foy.

Provence

Hot, fragrant Provence is full of well-preserved Roman ruins, dozens of produce, flower, and fish markets, and a plethora of outdoor activities to do and see (even bullfighting). Go to Nîmes (in Languedoc) to see the Pont du Gard aqueduct, the amphitheater, the museums, and the beautiful Maison Carré temple. You'll pass through the marshy Camargue en route to Arles, with its Roman arena and theater. Visit Daudet's Moulin in charming Fontvieille, inspect the tiny medieval streets and ancient houses in Les Baux, and stop in Avignon to see the Papal Palace and the famous bridge. Orange has a Roman theater and triumphal arch, and elegant Aix-en-Provence has museums, fountains, and the beautiful Cours Mirabeau boulevard.

The Riviera

Invisible celebrities, pebbly beaches, backed-up traffic, hordes of sunburned bathers—why do people come? Because the medieval hilltop villages (St-Paul-de-Vence, Mougins, Gassin, Vence, Peillon, even touristy Eze), the fields of fragrant flowers that supply the Grasse perfume factories, the wonderful museums, and the lovely, limpid light are still as magnetic as ever. Stylish boutiques, great art, splendid food, exciting nightlife, and spectacular views of crystal bays and cliff-side villas don't hurt either. Nor do the lively, cobbled streets of Nice's old town, the pretty, pastel colors of St-Tropez, or the splendor of Monte Carlo's casino.

Corsica

This island in the Mediterranean, about 160 km (100 mi) southeast of Monaco, is wonderful in spring and fall, and crowded in July and August. You'll need a week to circle it; visit Bastia's old town, explore the mountains along the Scala di Santa Regina, see Corte's citadel, laze on a beach, hear folk songs in Pigna, tour Napoléon's birthplace, Ajaccio, visit fortified Bonifacio, and splurge at the Grand Hôtel de Cala Rossa in the walled town of Porto-Vecchio.

Toulouse, the Midi-Pyrénées, and Roussillon

Sports and nature lovers flock to the southwest corner of France, by the Spanish border, where lively Toulouse, a university town of rosy pink brick, is the cultural star. Fortified Cordes's medieval houses, Albi's huge cathedral, Moissac's fine cloister, and the old Roman town of Lectoure are as appealing. In the Grotte de Niaux you will find marvelous prehistoric paintings in the underground gallery. Relaxing spa towns and wonderful views enliven the Pyrénées' twisting roads, and Carcassonne, within its medieval walls, draws all the world, but should not be missed. And when you see picturesque Collioure's stunning Mediterranean setting you'll know why artists love this region.

The Atlantic Coast

Whatever you want is what you get in the Atlantic Coast region. Castles and châteaux recall medieval battles; Romanesque abbeys and cathedrals echo with history. You may be drawn by the glossy resort of Biarritz, the vast beaches, marshy "Green Venice" in the north, or the Basque villages high in the Pyrénées. Come to elegant Bordeaux in May for the music festival, or any time to sip splendid wines while you indulge in oysters, Périgord truffles, foie gras, and Dordogne caviar.

PLEASURES AND PASTIMES

Art

It is through the eyes of France's artists that many first get to know the country. No wonder people from across the globe come to find Gauguin's bobbing boats at Pont-Aven, Monet's bridge at Giverny, and the gaslit Moulin Rouge of Toulouse-Lautrec—not framed in gilt and hung in a museum, but alive in all their three-dimensional glory. In Arles you can stand on the spot where van Gogh painted and compare his perspective to a placard with his finished work; in Paris you can climb into the garret-atelier where Delacroix created his epic canvases, or wander the redolent streets of Montmartre, once haunted by Renoir, Utrillo, and Modigliani. And, of course, the museums and châteaux hang heavy with masterworks, many of them bringing a telling local insight into French history, culture, and joie de vivre.

Cathedrals

Their extraordinary permanence, their everlasting relevance even in a secular world, and their transcending beauty make the Gothic and Romanesque cathedrals of France a lightning rod if you are in search of the essence of French culture. The product of a peculiarly Gallic mix of mysticism, exquisite taste, and high technology, France's cathedrals provide a thorough grounding in the history of architecture (some say there was nothing new in the art of building between France's Gothic arch and Frank Lloyd Wright's cantilevered slab). Each cathedral imparts its own monumental experience—knee-weakening grandeur, a mighty resonance that touches a chord of awe, and humility in the unbeliever. Even cynics will find satisfaction in the cathedrals' social history—the anonymity of the architects, the solidarity of the artisans, and the astonishing bravery of experiments in suspended stone.

Châteaux

From the humblest feudal ruin to the most delicate Renaissance spires to the grandest of Sun-King spreads, the castles, manor houses, and châteaux-forts of France evoke the history of Europe as no museum can. Standing on castellated ramparts overlooking undulating valleys, it is easy to slip into the role of a feudal lord scrambling to protect his patchwork of holdings from the centralized stronghold of kings and dukes. The lovely landscape takes on a strategic air and you find yourself role playing thus, whether swanning aristocratically over Japanese bridges in the château park or curling a revolutionary lip at the splendid excesses of Versailles. These are, after all, the castles that inspired Sleeping Beauty, Beauty and the Beast, and Snow White, and their fairy-tale magic—rich with history and Disney-free—still holds true.

Cities

Besides being home to the most sophisticated city in the world, France has more to offer than just Paris. Other French cities possess the best of Paris without the staggering crowds, noise, pollution, and traffic. Lyon, Dijon, Bordeaux, Tours, Marseille, and Strasbourg all have strong regional identities (and cuisines), as well as historic *vieilles villes* (old towns), sidewalk cafés, vast farmers' markets, and fine old parks. As for the arts, France's ministry of culture assures that even the country's farthest outreaches have top-notch orchestras, stellar operas, and excellent museums.

Dining

Few countries match France's reputation for good food or offer as many fine restaurants. Eating in France can be a memorable experience, from the simplest picnic lunch of baguette, camembert, and local *jambon* (ham) *sur l'herbe* (on the grass) to the most magnificent haute cuisine in formal splendor. Don't feel guilty if you spend as much of your day in restaurants as in museums and cathedrals, dining is at the heart and soul of French culture. Give yourself over to the leisurely meal; two hours for a three-course menu is par, and you may, after relaxing into the routine, feel pressed at less than three.

L'Esprit Sportif

Though the physically inclined would consider walking across Scotland or bicycling across Holland, they often misconstrue France as a sedentary site where one plods from museum to château to restaurant. But it's possible to have a more active approach: Imagine pedaling past barges on the Saône River or along slender poplars on a *route départmentale* (provincial road); hiking through the dramatic gorges in the Massif Central or over Alpine meadows in the Savoie; or sailing the historic ports of Honfleur or Cap d'Antibes. Experiencing this side of France will take you off the beaten path and into the countryside (and away from those rest stops on the autoroute). As you bike along French country roads or along the extensive network of *Grands Randonnées* (Big Trails) crisscrossing the country, you will have time to tune into the landscape—to study crumbling garden walls, smell the honeysuckle, and chat with a farmer in his *potager* (vegetable garden). Moreover, picnics are more sublime after a day of strenuous activity, and you can gorge without guilt on three-hour dinners when you reach your auberge.

The French Coast

Along the miles of French coast you will find broad-brimmed hats, parasoles, and opaque sunglasses—their modesty and discretion charmingly contradictory in view of—and we mean full view of—the frankly bare flesh that bobbles up and down the kilometers of seashore. And not just the famous *seins nus* (topless women), but the bellies of gastronome *pépés* (grandfathers) as well, swinging low over briefs too brief to mention. Naked children crouch over sand châteaux, their unselfconsciousness a reflection of their elders' own. For the French the summer beach holiday is a sacred ritual, a counterbalance to the winter ski trip—a given, deserved and observed without thought of ozone holes, pollution, or disintegrating beachfront rentals.

To avoid the August stampede, go in June or July. Ironic as it may be, France's most famous coastline possesses the country's worst beaches: Sand along the Riviera is in shorter supply than pebbles. By far the finest French beaches are those facing north (toward the Channel) and west (toward the Atlantic). Many are so vast that you can spread out even at the most popular resorts (like Biarritz, Royan, Dinard, or Le Touquet). Brittany's beaches are the most picturesque.

Shopping

Hunting for treasures in France can be a joy, as well as a frustration, as this proud isolationist country increasingly gives itself over to malls and chain stores. Not to worry: Paris is still the firm fashion capital, but more and more small towns are selling generic goods. You may be surprised to find that the same silk scarf you plan to purchase in France costs less in the mall at home, although it may be more fun to buy. For distinctly French souvenirs, it pays to look to the past: Flea markets and *brocantes* (second-hand shops) sell Art Deco brooches, tiny eaux-de-vie glasses, and evocative old copies of *Paris Match*. And there's always the chance of finding a stray bit of Quimper faience. Another good bet is purchasing regional specialties, though your exports must be legal—madeleines, say, or nougat—as those savory sausages and glass jars of foie gras may be confiscated by customs.

Wine

From the chipped carafe of a coarse *vin de pays* on a local café table to the Gevrey-Chambertin decanted with surgical concentration by a linen-swathed sommelier, wine is indispensable to the French experience. Intricately interlaced with the progress of a well-planned menu (the magical combination of certain foods with the right wines is referred to as a *bon mariage,* or a good marriage), wine can dominate your memory of a fine meal.

FODOR'S CHOICE

Châteaux

★**Chenonceau, Loire Valley.** The most romantic of them all, with arched galleries spanning the Cher, this palace owes its gardens to Catherine de' Medici.

★**Citadelle, Corte, Corsica.** From its spectacular site high over the junction of three rivers, the fortress protects the earlier "Eagle's Nest" château and contains the Musée de la Corse.

★**Hautefort, Périgord.** Part medieval, part Renaissance, vast Hautefort raises an eclectic skyline above its gardens and is full of 17th-century furnishings.

★**Pierrefonds, Champagne.** This huge château, begun in the 12th century, was restored in the 1860s by the fairy-tale imagination of Viollet-le-Duc and the money of Napoléon III.

★**Vaux-le-Vicomte, Ile-de-France.** Louis XIV was so jealous of Nicolas Fouquet's new château that he jailed him on the spot and started work on Versailles to show who was boss. The sumptuous gardens and interior remain unchanged.

★**Versailles, Ile-de-France.** The world's grandest palace has it all: paintings, murals, gold-leafed furniture, the Hall of Mirrors, a landscaped park, a phony village, a giant canal, artful fountains, and shady glades.

★**Vitré, Brittany.** This triangular fortress, with fat, round towers, has stood guard at the gateway to Brittany since the 11th century.

Churches and Abbeys

★**Abbaye de St-Michel de Cuxa, Prades.** With its 10th-century pre-Romanesque arches and its elegant crypt, this abbey is one of the gems of the eastern Pyrénées.

★**Basilique, Vézelay.** This great pilgrim church, part-Romanesque, part-Gothic, gazes serenely over the rolling hills of Burgundy. Marvel at the miniature figures on the carved capitals in the nave.

★**Basilique St-Sauveur, Dinan.** Breton warrior-hero Bertrand du Guesclin's heart lies in the north transept of this church, whose style ranges from Romanesque to Flamboyant Gothic to Renaissance.

★**Cathédrale, Chartres.** Take your binoculars to survey the world's finest collection of medieval stained-glass windows. The mighty, asymmetric spires dominate the flat grainlands for miles around.

★**Cathédrale, Laon.** The hilltop setting—known as the Crowned Mountain—is the most spectacular of any French cathedral, bristling with elegant, openwork towers.

★**Cathédrale Notre-Dame, Amiens.** The colossal cathedral was built in 44 years during the 13th century; note the rose window and humorous carved misericords.

★**Cathédrale St-Étienne, Bourges.** Look for the towers of the cathedral as you approach on N151; inside, note its stained glass and the slender columns rising to an extraordinary height.

★**Église St-Joseph, Le Havre.** Concrete construction at its most spartan yet spectacular is represented in Auguste Perret's 1950s tour de force: part silo, part movie theater, and part rocket.

★**Mont-St-Michel, Normandy.** From its silhouette against the horizon to the abbey and gardens at the peak of the rock, you'll never forget this awe-inspiring sight.

★**Notre-Dame-du-Haut, Ronchamp.** Some say that this free-form chapel is Le Corbusier's masterpiece—utterly individual, yet imbued with peace and calm.

Dining

★**À l'Ami Fritz, Obernai.** The owner-chef serves succulent local specialties and his own wine at this rustic yet chic spot. *$$*

★**L'Assiette Gourmande, Honfleur.** The harbor-front setting on the coast of Normandy gives a hint that seafood is a strong point, but all Gérard Bonnefoy's food is to die for—including the delectable desserts. *$$–$$$*

★**Boyer, Reims.** Chef Gérard Boyer's innovative cuisine and his extensive wine list draw sophisticated diners (and lodgers) to this opulent restaurant in a 19th-century château. *$$$$*

★**Le Brouage, Brouage.** This rustic restaurant (with a few rooms), which serves as the village bar, is just the place to settle the affairs of the world and have a wonderful regional meal. *$*

★**Chez Yvonne, Strasbourg.** This chic yet cozy *weinstübe* (inn) serves classic Alsatian fare and local wines to hip locals and heads of state. *$*

★**Le Coq Gadby, Rennes.** Sample superb seafood dishes and traditional Breton specialities at this restaurant in a 19th-century mansion. *$$–$$$*

★**Le Ferme Campo di Monte, Murato.** The Julliards prepare some of Corsica's best fare at this lovely 350-year-old farmhouse. *$$*

★**Les Feuillants, Céret.** The cuisine at this restaurant, one of best in the area, is yet another manifestation of the town's superb artistic endowment. *$$$*

★**Hôtel Etxemaïté, Larrau.** Dine by the fire on excellent Basque cooking at this restaurant in a country inn. *$$–$$$*

★**Les Magnolias, Plaisance.** Superb, sophisticated regional cooking is created by chef Francis Roussel and served in a wonderfully medieval ambience. *$$*

★**Les Muses, Lyon.** Sit behind enormous statues of the muses on the roof of the opera house while lunching or dining on Philippe Chavent's inspired dishes. *$$*

★**Philippe Detourbe, Paris.** Spectacular contemporary French cuisine is served at this unexpectedly glamourous restaurant. *$$*

★**Pierre Gagnaire, Paris.** Legendary chef Pierre Gagnaire brings together at least three or four different tastes and textures in his sensational dishes. *$$$$*

★**Pigeons Blancs, Cognac.** Chef Jacques Tachet's cooking would be worth a detour even if the handful of rooms weren't charming and reasonable. His three-course carte du jour is a find. *$$*

★**La Terrasse at Juana, Juan-les-Pins.** Chef Christian Morisset is on his way to becoming one of France's top chefs, with his delicious and exquisitely presented seafood dishes. *$$$$*

Lodging

★**Caron de Beaumarchais, Paris.** The theme of this intimate hotel in the heart of the Marais is the work of Caron de Beaumarchais, who wrote *The Marriage of Figaro* in 1778. Rooms reflect the taste of 18th-century French nobility. *$$*

★**Castan, Besançon.** This exquisitely restored 18th-century manor house is just below the Citadelle in the heart of the old town; its rooms are lined with Franche-Comté bibelots and reproduction fabrics. *$$$*

★**Castel-Clara, Belle-Île.** Ask for a room with a view of the sea at this modern hotel perched on a cliff on the lovely island of Belle-Île. *$$–$$$*

★**Champ de Mars, Paris.** Near the rue Cler market, the Eiffel Tower, and Invalides, this comfortable two-star hotel has an attractive, blue and yellow, French country-house style. *$*

★**Château de Camon, Mirepoix.** This medieval castle in the Pyrénées foothills is full of ornate antiques, tapestries, and red velvet—which contrasts nicely with the modern tiled baths and comfortable family-style meals with the charming owner. *$$$*

★**Colombe d'Or, St-Paul-de-Vence.** Once a hangout for the likes of Klee, Picasso, and Utrillo, whose works are still on the walls, this country inn in the hills now draws the rich and famous, for a meal or a stay. *$$$*

★**Costes, Paris.** Jean-Louis and Gilbert Costes's eponymous hotel conjures up the palaces of Napoléon III with sumptuous swags and enough brocade and fringe to blanket the Champs-Elysées. *$$$$*

★**La Cour des Loges, Lyon.** The wonderful atrium lobby is a surprise here, in Old Lyon, but the design of this stylish hotel, carved out of four Renaissance buildings, is an all-round delight. Relax in the tapas bar, and swim in the heated pool. *$$$$*

★ **L'Hostellerie du Vieux Cordes, Cordes.** This old house around a wisteria-draped courtyard is an enchanting place to stay, and not least because of the splendid meals in the opulent crimson dining rooms. *$$*

★ **Hôtels St-Albert et Montaigne, Sarlat-le-Canéda.** These comfortable hotels in the Dordogne on the delightful town square share a good regional restaurant and the services of the pleasant Garrigou family. *$–$$*

★ **Le Maquis, Porticcio, Corsica.** The evocatively named Maquis, by the sea, ranks as one of Corsica's finest *hôtels de charme. $$$–$$$$*

★ **Mas du Langoustier, Île de Porquerolles.** Come by boat or by ferry to this hideaway on the island's westernmost point, where the rooms, the views, and the meals are superb. *$$$*

★ **Palais, Biarritz.** The spacious rooms, vast lawns, and the elegant mirrored dining room overlooking the sea recall the grandeur of the days when Empress Eugénie stayed here. *$$$$*

★ **Les Templiers, Collioure.** No visit is complete without a stay at this cozy hotel filled with over 2,500 original works of art. *$$*

★ **Le Vieux Logis, Les Eyzies-de-Tayac.** A stay at this old stone house, which has a pool and a garden, in the Dordogne is unforgettable; so are the chef's five-course meals. *$$$–$$$$*

Museums

★ **Fondation Maeght, St-Paul-de-Vence.** A small gem of a museum of modern art, it blends its stunning holdings with stylish presentation.

★ **Historial de la Grande Guerre, Péronne.** A spacious, imaginative display of maps, artifacts, newsreels, guns, and nightmarish lithographs rams home the horror of World War I.

★ **Louvre, Paris.** No matter how many times you've visited, be sure to come again; the new construction is stunning.

★ **Musée d'Art Modern, Céret.** This modern art museum has one of the best collections of French and Catalan artists ever assembled outside a major metropolis.

★ **Musée des Arts Décoratifs, Lyon.** You can see the well-displayed furniture, silverware, ceramics, and objects of early Lyonnaise life in a satisfying couple of hours.

★ **Musée Condé, Chantilly.** The château houses a remarkable collection of illuminated manuscripts, tapestries, furniture, paintings, Fouquet miniatures, and stained glass.

★ **Musée Fesch, Ajaccio, Corsica.** Wonderful Italian Old Masters make up the museum's collection.

★ **Musée Ingres, Montauban.** Drawings and paintings by the great French classicist and works from his own collection are housed in this museum in the Bishop's Palace.

★ **Musée Matisse, Le Cateau-Cambrésis.** The Palais Fénelon is now home to paintings, sculpture, and drawings by the town's native son.

★ **Musée de l'Oeuvre Notre-Dame, Strasbourg.** This museum is so much more than just a collection of weathered statues rescued from the cathedral; an effort has been made to create a churchlike atmosphere appropriate for the works of art.

★ **Palais de la Berbie, Albi.** The world's greatest collection of works by Henri de Toulouse-Lautrec are housed in this former fortress with gardens designed by André Le Nôtre.

★ **Palais des Musées, Rennes.** In this large building you will find the Fine Arts Museum, containing one of France's best collections of paintings outside Paris, and the Museum of Brittany, retracing the region's history, period by period.

GREAT ITINERARIES

So, you want to taste France, gaze at its beauty, and inhale its special joie de vivre—all in a one-week to 10-day trip. Let's assume at least that you've seen Paris, and you're ready to venture into the countryside. Here are some itineraries to help you plan your trip. Or create your own route using the suggested itineraries in each chapter.

France for First-Timers

If this is your first time in France, this itinerary will give you a feel for the country's tremendous variety—its Continental heart in the north and its Mediterranean soul in the south. This is the route Parisians used to follow, slowly, surely, heading south to the Mediterranean, feasting and sightseeing along the way.

DURATION➢ 7–10 Days.

THE MAIN ROUTE➢ **Two nights: Vézelay, Saulieu,** or **Beaune.** Visit the medieval basilica and Beaune's Hôtel-Dieu. En route note the virgin forests and the hills and small family-tended vineyards of Burgundy, easing your passage with the memorable *dégustation* (tasting) available free at many of them. Dine in Lyon.

Two to three nights: Avignon and **Provence.** Visit the Roman ruins and medieval towns, the fields of aromatic lavender and of the towering sunflowers that van Gogh painted.

Two to three nights: Cannes and the **Côte d'Azur.** Take a swim in the Mediterranean at one of the trendy (even topless) French beaches. Walk through Eze or another medieval hilltop village. Depending on your inclination, say a prayer at the Matisse Chapel near Vence, or lose your remaining francs at Monte Carlo's Belle Epoque casino.

GETTING AROUND➢ It's best to rent a car in Paris for this itinerary. The TGV speeds through Burgundy and Lyon to the coast, stopping in major cities along the way. You'll have to arrange transport into the countryside or rent a bicycle at the train station.

INFORMATION➢ *See* Chapters 9, 10, 12, and 13.

France for the Family

Sophisticated and suave may be what comes to mind when thinking of France, but there's another side to this varied country: It has a love for children that extends to even the youngest.

DURATION➢ 6–8 Days.

THE MAIN ROUTE➢ **One or two nights: Étretat and Fécamp.** Take a walk on Étretat's cliffs and explore Fécamp's fishing port.

Two nights: Deauville. Visit the casino and the beach. Make an excursion to the charming fishing town of Honfleur.

One night: Baye tapestries and the

Three nights: Brit Michel and make the crepes and e

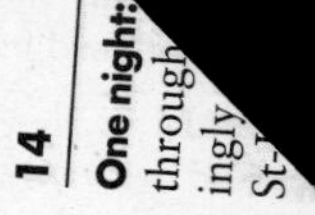

GETTING AROUND➢ Normandy is only a few hours from Paris, although it takes up to five hours to reach its western end. Traveling around Normandy and Brittany is almost impossible without a car.

Trains leave from Gare St-Lazare for Deauville and other Normandy destinations; trains to Brittany leave from Gare Montparnasse.

INFORMATION➢ *See* Chapters 5 and 6.

France for Wine Lovers

French vineyards can be just as spectacular as the wines they produce. This itinerary concentrates on the eastern corridor of France from Champagne to Châteauneuf-du-Pape, if only because the vineyards here are more compact than their counterparts in the Loire Valley and the Cognac and Bordeaux regions.

DURATION➢ 8 Days.

THE MAIN ROUTE➢ **One night: Épernay.** Drive to Reims and visit one of the city-based producers. Take the pretty Route du Vin wine road south along the Montagne de Reims, and pay homage to Dom Pérignon, the blind monk who created champagne, at Hautvillers.

One night: Auxerre. Head south through southern Champagne, via historic Troyes, to Les Riceys, where vertiginous slopes yield France's priciest rosé. Continue southwest to Auxerre via the equally mountainous vineyards of Chablis.

Two nights: Beaune. Visit the pretty wine villages just south of Auxerre. Take the expressway to Dijon to join the short, scenic Route du Vin, lined with some of the world's most famous wine-producing villages, to Beaune. Visit the Marché aux Vins in Beaune for an extensive sampling. The next day make an excursion to the Jura, visiting Arbois and clifftop Château-Chalon.

One night: Villefranche-sur-Saône. Head south along the west bank of the Saône through the vineyards along the Beaujolais Wine Road.

alence. Bypass Lyon and drive (or rather beneath) the increas- steep vineyards of Côte Rotie and oseph. Cross the Rhône at Tain-l'Her- itage near Tournon to admire the famous Hermitage vineyards. Pause at Cornas just before you reach Valence.

One night: Orange. Tour the rocky, sun-baked vineyards of Châteauneuf-du-Pape, just south of Orange, and explore the villages to the east, beneath the towering slopes of Mont Ventoux.

GETTING AROUND➢ Reims is just 90 minutes east of Paris by car. Visiting vineyards and wine villages is impossible without a car (preferably one with a biggish trunk). But go easy on the dégustations.

INFORMATION➢ *See* Chapters 7, 9, 10, and 12.

Outdoor France

France has far more to offer than just museums, palaces, cathedrals, and restaurants. You can enjoy nature at its most varied, with everything from verdant marshlands and sandy beaches to endless pine forests, deep gorges, and towering mountains—all within a few hours' drive.

DURATION➢ 14 Days.

THE MAIN ROUTE➢ **One night: Coulon.** In this sleepy, waterside village you will encounter the Marais Poitevin, nicknamed Green Venice for its tree-lined canals. Explore the banks by bike, rowboat, or foot—or hire a punt, a boat maneuvered with a long wooden pole by a garrulous local guide.

Two nights: La Rochelle. Stroll around the pretty port of La Rochelle, then take a boat trip to any of the neighboring islands—Île de Ré, Île de'Aix, or Île d'Oléron—where you can rent bikes and explore old fortresses. Make an early start south after your second night; walk the ramparts at historic Brouage. Continue via the long sandy beach of the Côte Sauvage—ideal for swimming or sunbathing—to Royan. From here take the *bac* (ferry) across the Gironde estuary. Head south to Lac d'Hourtin, which has excellent canoeing and waterskiing facilities.

One night: Arcachon. You can ride, dive, and play golf at this busy Belle Epoque resort town. Or take a boat into the bay to inspect the nearby oyster beds.

One night: Biarritz. Stop en route at the Dune du Pilat, Europe's highest sand dune. Then meander through the pines of the flat, Landes forest, stopping for a picnic or a game of boules if the fancy takes you. Ritzy Biarritz has cliffs, magnificent beaches, and the coast's best surfing.

One night: Ste-Engrâce. Head east into the foothills of the Pyrénées. The area around Ste-Engrâce is great hiking country, particularly the Gorges de Kakouetta.

Two nights: Lourdes. Drive east to Lourdes. Spend the afternoon at the spa town of Cauterets, then take the chairlift at Pont d'Espagne for a view of the bright blue Lac de Gaube and beyond. The next day, head south along spectacular D921 to Gavarnie to see its famous cirque. Rent a horse or donkey to explore the mountains.

One night: Foix. Head east, via St-Gaudens and St-Girons, to the peaceful town of Foix. The rivers here are excellent for fishing. You might also enjoy a boat trip down the Rivière Souterraine de Labouiche, a mysterious underground river.

One night: Plaisance. Wander through the Limoux vineyards, famous for their sparkling wine. Have lunch in Carcassonne, followed by a walk around the spectacular town walls. Continue north over the scenic Montagne Noire and spend the night at the hotel-restaurant in Plaisance.

Two nights: Ispagnac. Drive up through Millau and spend the next two days exploring the Gorges du Tarn and the Gorges de la Jonte. Both are good places to hike, mountain bike, raft, or canoe.

One night: Clermont-Ferrand or La Grande-Motte. From Ispagnac, you have two choices. Either head north, farther into the Massif Central, taking in spectacular Le Puy-en-Velay on your way to the extinct volcanos (you can survey them from a hot-air balloon at the Puy-du-Dôme) ringing Clermont-Ferrand. Or plunge south toward the bustling city of Montpellier and the nearby Mediterranean resort town of La Grand Motte.

GETTING AROUND➢ The Marais Poitevin is a four-hour drive from Paris (expressway A10 as far as Niort).

INFORMATION➢ *See* Chapters 11, 12, 13, 15, and 16.

Palatial France

The French Revolution ended the old regime, but many of the buildings remain—palaces of local seigneurs and châteaux reserved for the king.

DURATION➢ 5–7 Days.

THE MAIN ROUTE➢ **One to two nights: Versailles** and the **Vallée de Chevreuse.** Visit the châteaux and **Chartres Cathedral.**

Three nights: Tours. Visit Blois, Chambord, Cheverny, and Chenonceau in the Loire Valley.

One night: Fontainebleau and **Vaux-le-Vicomte.**

GETTING AROUND➢ Versailles is a 20-minute drive from downtown Paris (avoid rush hours). The Loire Valley is two hours from the city via A10, or you can take N10 via Chartres to Tours.

The TGV gets to Tours in little more than an hour, and buses run from the train stations to most of the châteaux. You can also rent bicycles at the train stations; the valley is flat and easy to navigate.

INFORMATION➢ *See* Chapters 3 and 4.

FESTIVALS AND SEASONAL EVENTS

France is a festival all year round, with special events taking place throughout the country. For full museum, theater, and concert information, be sure to check the listings in *Pariscope* (which includes reviews in English of the week's main events and new restaurants), *Officiel des Spectacles,* or *Figaroscope,* on arrival in Paris. The *International Herald Tribune* also lists special events in its weekend edition, but not in great detail. The most complete listing of festivals comes in a small pamphlet published by the **Maison de la France** (☞ Visitor Information *in* Gold Guide).

Annual highlights include the Monte Carlo Motor Rally in January, Nice's Carnival in February, the Cannes Film Festival and the French Open Tennis Championships in May, Bastille Day in July, and Paris's Autumn Festival in September.

WINTER

DEC.➢ On the 24th, a Christmas celebration known as the **Shepherd's Festival,** featuring midnight Mass and picturesque "living crèches," is held in Les Baux, Provence. From the end of November through the New Year, Strasbourg mounts its famous **Christmas Market,** with echoes of German gemütlichkeit. **Christmas in Paris** spells celebrations, especially for children, from late December to early January. A giant crèche is set up on the square in front of the Hôtel de Ville (City Hall), and there are automated window displays in the *grands magasins* (department stores) on boulevard Haussmann.

JAN.➢ The **International Circus Festival,** featuring top acts from around the world, and the **Monte Carlo Motor Rally,** one of the motoring world's most venerable races, are held in Monaco. Wine-producing villages throughout France celebrate St-Vincent's Day with festivities on January 22 in honor of their patron saint. The **Tournament St-Vincent,** a colorful Burgundy wine festival, takes place on the third weekend in a different wine village each year. Buy a cup for about 30 francs and then drink as much as you like—or just frolic in the decorated streets. Angoulême hosts the world's biggest and most popular comic-book festival, the **Fête des Bandes Dessinés.**

FEB.➢ The **Carnival de Nice** provides an exotic blend of parades and revelry during the weeks leading up to Lent. Other cities and villages also have their own smaller versions. **The Carnival de Dunkerque** on the weekend before Shrove Tuesday is the most rambunctious street carnival in northern France. The lively four-day **Carnival de Granville** in Normandy also takes place on the weekend before Shrove Tuesday.

SPRING

MAR.➢ The **Salon de Mars,** an art and antiques fair, and the **Salon du Livre,** France's biggest book festival, take place in Paris.

APR.➢ The **Monte Carlo Open Tennis Championships** get under way at the ultraswank Monte Carlo Country Club. The son-et-lumière show at Beaune's Hôtel-Dieu every night from April to mid-November is brilliantly done. The **Foire de Paris** is a giant fair with products, including food, wine, and cheese, and agricultural displays from all over France; it's held at the Porte de Versailles in Paris at the end of the month.

MAY➢ The **Cannes Film Festival** sees two weeks of star-studded events. Classical concert festivals get underway throughout the country. At the end of the month, the **French Open Tennis Championships** are held at Roland Garros Stadium in Paris. Rouen celebrates the national heroine, Joan of Arc, with the **Fête Jeanne d'Arc.**

SUMMER

JUNE➢ From now until September you will find **son-et-lumière** (sound-and-light) shows—historical pageants featuring special lighting effects—at many French châteaux, especially in the Loire Valley. In Paris, there is dancing in the streets during the musical festival, the **Fête de la Musique** on June 21. Strasbourg's **Féte de la Musique** features concerts in the Cathédrale Notre-Dame and various halls. This is a popular time for horse races: The **Prix du Président de la République** is run at the Hippodrome de Vincennes, the **Grand Steeplechase de Paris** is at the Auteuil Racecourse, and the **Grand Prix de Paris,** for equine three-year-olds, is at Longchamp Racecourse. The **24 Heures du Mans,** the famous 24-hour car race, is held in Le Mans.

JULY➢ **Summer arts festival season** gets into full swing, particularly in Provence. Avignon offers a month of top-notch theater, Aix-en-Provence specializes in opera, Carpentras in religious music, Nice holds a big Jazz Festival, and Arles mounts a big photography festival. Northern France's spectacular **Fête de Gayant** (festival of the *giant,* in local patois) is held in Douai on the first Sunday afer July 5. Most important, the **Tour de France,** the world's most famous bicycle race, dominates national attention for three weeks before crossing the finish line on the Champs-Elysées on the last Sunday of the month. On **July 14** all of France celebrates Bastille Day, commemorating the Storming of the Bastille in 1789—the start of the French Revolution. Look out for fireworks, free concerts, and street festivities beginning the evening of the 13th, with the **Bals des Pompiers** (Firemen's Ball) organized by local firemen.

AUG.➢ On **Assumption** (August 15) many towns, notably Chartres and Lisieux, hold religious festivals and processions dedicated to the Virgin Mary. The most famous annual religious festival in Brittany is the ***pardon*** in Ste-Anne-la-Palud, near Quimper, on the last Sunday of August.

AUTUMN

SEPT.➢ The **vendanges,** grape harvests, begin and festivals are held in the country's wine regions. South of Lille, the **Fête d'Ail** in Arleux is a celebration of France's favorite herb, garlic. The **Grande Braderie** turns Lille into one giant street fair on the month's first weekend. Every two even years (in 1998), on the first weekend in September, medieval France is re-created at Dinan's **Fête des Remparts.** The **Fête de Musique de Besançon et Franche-Comté** consists of a series of chamber music concerts in and around Besançon during the month. The **Fête d'Automne,** a major arts and film festival, opens in Paris and continues until December. The world's most stylish antiques fair, the **Paris Biennale,** is held in the capital (even years only). The **Fête des Monuments Historiques,** on the Sunday nearest to September 21, opens the doors of many official and private buildings usually closed to the public.

OCT.➢ The **Prix de l'Arc de Triomphe,** horseracing's most prestigious flat race, is held at Longchamp Racecourse in Paris on the first Sunday of the month. A giant contemporary art exhibition called **FIAC** takes place in Paris early in the month. The weeklong **Paris Indoor Open** attracts the world's top tennis players at the end of the month.

NOV.➢ **Les Trois Glorieuses,** Burgundy's biggest wine festival, features the year's most important wine auction and related merriment in several Burgundy locations. On the third Thursday in November, France—especially Paris—celebrates the arrival of the **Beaujolais Nouveau.** The **Salon des Caves Particulières,** a giant wine fair for independent producers, is held in Paris at the end of the month.

2 Paris

Bearing the marks of 2,000 years of history and a rich cultural heritage, Paris overwhelms, astonishes, and surprises. From the heights of the Arc de Triomphe the city swaggers with the knowledge that it is at the pinnacle of architectural beauty, artistic development, and culinary delight. But on its intimate, winding streets, the city invites unhurried exploration rather than awestruck admiration.

IF THERE'S A PROBLEM WITH A TRIP TO PARIS, it is the embarrassment of riches that faces you. A city of vast, noble perspectives and winding, hidden streets, Paris remains a combination of the pompous and the intimate. Whether you've come looking for sheer physical beauty, cultural and artistic diversions, world-famous dining and shopping, history, or simply local color, you will find it here in abundance.

Pleasures and Pastimes

Cafés

People-watching, some would say, is what Paris is all about; and there's no better place to indulge in this pursuit than the terrace of a sidewalk café. Favored locales include place St-Michel, boulevard du Montparnasse, and place St-Germain-des-Prés, on the Left Bank; and place de l'Opéra, the Champs-Elysées, and Beaubourg, on the Right Bank. But you may enjoy seeking out your own (less expensive) haunts.

Churches

Paris is rich in churches of two architectural styles: the 15th–16th-century overlap of Flamboyant Gothic and Renaissance—at St-Gervais, St-Étienne du Mont, St-Eustache, and St-Séverin—and 17th-century Baroque with domes and two-tiered facades—at Les Invalides, Val de Grâce, and St-Paul–St-Louis. But the city's most enduring religious symbols are medieval—Notre-Dame cathedral and Ste-Chapelle—and 19th-century—Sacré-Coeur and La Madeleine.

Dining

Whether your dream meal is savoring truffle-studded foie gras on Limoges china, or breaking the crust of a steaming cassoulet in a thick crockery bowl, you can find it in Paris. Despite rumblings about lowered standards and increasingly bland fare, Paris remains one of the world's great food capitals. For most visitors, the prospect of eating here is exciting; for many, it's the main reason for a trip.

Museums

Paris has a plethora of museums. Alongside four superstars—the Louvre, the Musée d'Orsay, the Centre Pompidou, and the Cité des Sciences at La Villette—lurk such underestimated delights as the Marmottan (Monets and manuscripts), the Musée de Moyen Age (medieval works of art), and single-artist museums dedicated to the works of Picasso, Rodin, Dalí, and Symbolist Gustave Moreau.

Shopping

Window-shopping is one of Paris's great spectator sports. Tastefully displayed wares—luscious cream-filled éclairs, lacy lingerie, rare artwork, gleaming copper pots—entice the eye and awaken the imagination. Happily, shopping opportunities in Paris are endless and geared to every taste. You can price emerald earrings at Cartier, spend an afternoon browsing through bookstalls along the Seine, buy silk-lined gloves at Dior, tour the high-gloss department stores, or haggle over prices in the sprawling flea markets on the outskirts of town.

EXPLORING PARIS

Updated by Simon Hewitt

A city of vast, noble perspectives and winding, hidden streets, Paris remains a combination of the pompous and the intimate. Whether you've come looking for sheer physical beauty, cultural and artistic diversions, world-famous dining and shopping, history, or simply local color, you will find it here in abundance.

The French capital, for the tourist, is a practical city: It is relatively small as capitals go, with many of its major sites and museums within walking distance of one another. The city is divided into 20 *arrondissements* (districts). The last two digits of the zip code (75002) will tell you the arrondissement (the 2e). Ask a Parisian where she lives, and she'll tell you the number ("in the deuxième or 2nd"). The city's principal tourist axis is less than 6½ km (4 mi) long, running parallel to the north bank of the Seine between the Arc de Triomphe and the Bastille. In fact, the best method of getting to know Paris is on foot, although public transportation—particularly the métro subway system—is excellent. Buy a *Plan de Paris* booklet: a city map-guide with a street-name index that also shows métro stations. Note that all métro stations have a detailed neighborhood map just inside the entrance (☞ Paris A to Z, *below,* for a map of the Paris métro).

Paris owes both its development and much of its visual appeal to the Seine River, which weaves through its heart. Each bank of the Seine has its own personality; the *Rive Droite* (Right Bank), with its spacious boulevards and formal buildings, generally has a more genteel feel than the more carefree *Rive Gauche* (Left Bank) to the south. The historical and geographical heart of the city is Notre-Dame Cathedral on the Ile de la Cité, the larger of the Seine's two islands (the other is the Ile St-Louis).

Our coverage of Paris is divided into eight neighborhood walks. There are several "musts" that you may not want to miss: the Eiffel Tower, the Champs-Elysées, the Louvre, and Notre-Dame. A few monuments and museums close for lunch, between noon and 2, and many are closed on either Monday or Tuesday. Check before you set off. Admission prices listed are for adults, but often there are special rates for students, children, and senior citizens. Don't forget that cafés in Paris are open all day long. They are a great boon if you are weary and in need of a coffee, a beer, or a sandwich, as are *boulangeries* (bakeries).

Numbers in the text correspond to numbers in the margin and on the Paris and Montmartre maps.

Great Itineraries

A visit to Paris will never be quite as simple as a quick look at a few landmarks. Each *quartier* (neighborhood) has its own treasures, and you should be ready to explore—a very pleasant prospect in this most elegant of cities. Outlined here are the main areas to concentrate on depending on the length of your stay. Bear in mind that the amount of time spent visiting monuments—and museums in particular—is not something you can, or would want to, predict with any certainty. Also, to see both the city's large museums and its smaller ones, you probably need at least a week.

IF YOU HAVE 3 DAYS

On your first day, get your bearings—and an overview of the city's attractive waterfront—by taking a trip along the Seine on the Bateaux Mouches (from place de l'Alma) or on the Vedettes de Pont Neuf (from the Square du Vert-Galant). Visit Notre-Dame Cathedral and, if you enjoy medieval architecture, the nearby St-Chapelle on Ile de la Cité, then cross the Seine to the Left Bank and explore the Latin Quarter, using the Panthéon dome as a landmark. End your day in the Luxembourg Gardens, close by. Spend your second day exploring the noble vista between the Arc de Triomphe and the Louvre: Start at the Arc (that way it's all down hill) and work along the Champs-Elysées, across place de la Concorde and the Tuileries Gardens (with the Orangerie and Jeu de Paume museums) to the Louvre. Divide your third day between the Eiffel Tower, the Musée d'Orsay, and Montmartre.

IF YOU HAVE 6 DAYS

Follow the three-day itinerary, then spend one day exploring the Marais and Ile St-Louis, and another combining a visit to the Left Bank's St-Germain and the nearby Invalides. For good shopping and a look at Haussmann's 19th-century Paris, walk down the Right Bank's rue Faubourg St-Honoré and join the Grand Boulevards by the Madeleine church; continue past the Opéra toward place de la République.

IF YOU HAVE 9 DAYS

You can attack the city's "other" museums—the Picasso, Rodin, and Marmottan—after following the six-day itinerary. Check out Montparnasse and some of the attractions on the edge of the city, all reachable by métro: Père Lachaise Cemetery and the Parc de La Villette; the Bois de Boulogne to the west, plus the futuristic area of La Défense; or the Bois de Vincennes to the east. You may also wish to take a day trip to Versailles (☞ Chapter 3).

From the Eiffel Tower to the Louvre

Between the Eiffel Tower and the Louvre lies the grand, opulent Paris of wide avenues and plush hotels. This is an area of dazzling vistas, stellar museums, superb window-shopping, and unbeatable monument-gazing. Fashion shops, jewelers, art galleries, and deluxe hotels proliferate. Local charm is not a feature of this exclusive sector of western Paris; it's beautiful and rich—and a little impersonal. The French moan that it's losing its character, and, as you notice the number of fast-food joints along the most famous street in the city, the Champs-Elysées, you'll know what they mean—though renovation has gone some way to restoring the street's legendary elegance.

The Arc de Triomphe stands foursquare at the top of the Champs-Elysées, site of most French national celebrations. It's the last leg of the Tour de France bicycle race on the third or fourth Sunday in July and the site of vast ceremonies on Bastille Day (July 14) and Armistice Day (November 11). Its trees are often decked with the French *tricolore* and foreign flags to mark visits from heads of state.

A Good Walk

There is no better place to begin than at that iron symbol of Paris, the **Eiffel Tower** ①. The nearer you get, the more evident its colossal bulk becomes—it's far bigger and sturdier than pictures suggest. Beyond is the verdant expanse of the **Champ de Mars** ②, once used as a parade ground, then as site of the World Exhibitions. Landscaped at the start of the century, it frames the distant École Militaire, still in use as a military academy and therefore not open to the public.

Across the Seine from the Eiffel Tower, on the heights of Trocadéro, is the Art Deco **Palais de Chaillot** ③, a cultural center containing numerous museums: an anthropology museum, a museum of French architecture, and a museum of cinema history. If you're in a hurry or have seen enough museums for the day, skip them all and take the métro from here directly to the Arc de Triomphe. Otherwise head down avenue du Président-Wilson to the **Musée d'Art Moderne de la Ville de Paris** ④, with its collection of modern art.

Continue along to bustling place de l'Alma. Down the sloping side-road to the left of the Pont de l'Alma is the embarkation point of the **Bateaux Mouches**, which will take you on a tour of Paris by water. Stylish avenue Montaigne, home to many of the leading Paris fashion houses,

Paris with Arrondissements

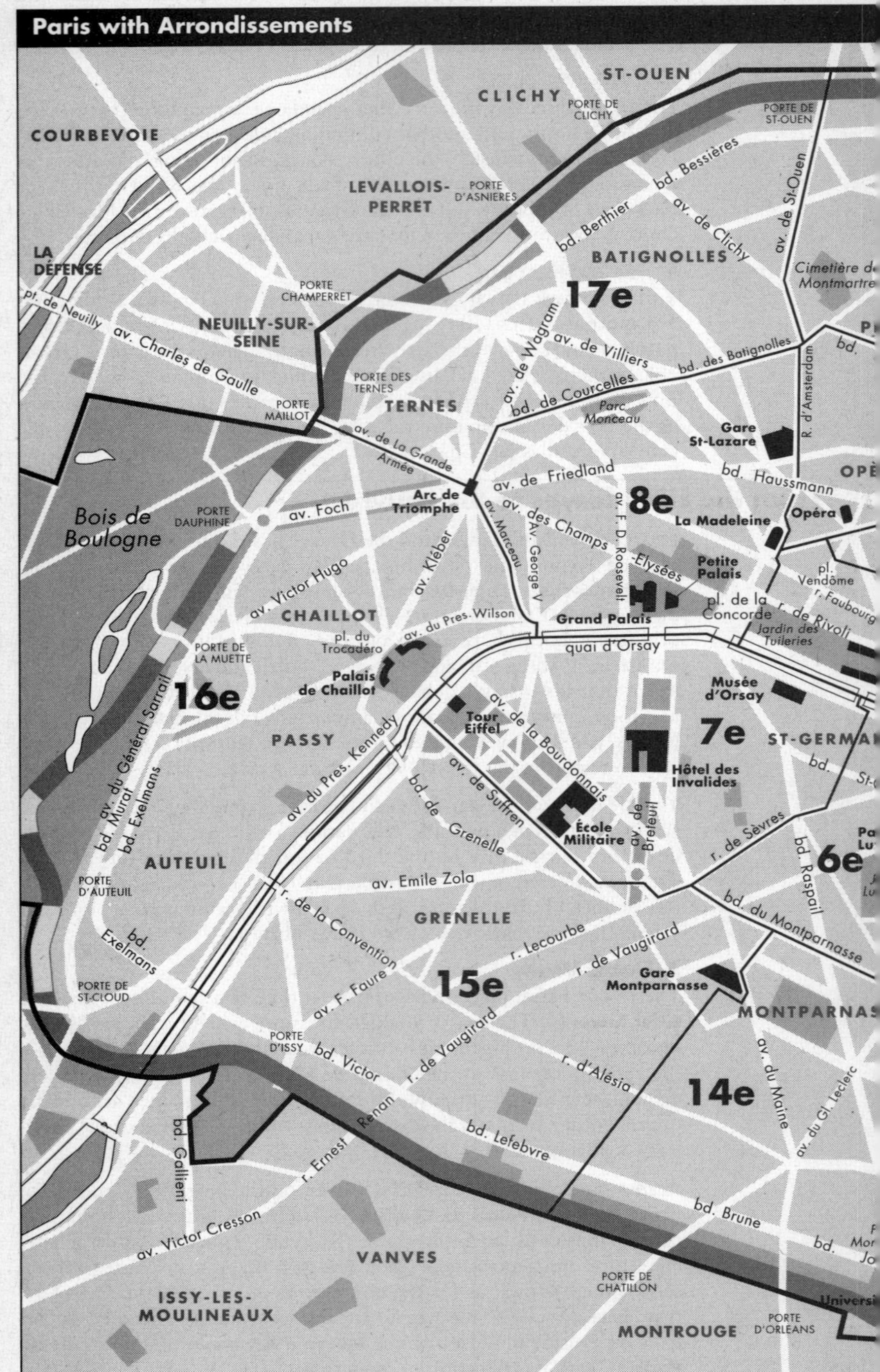

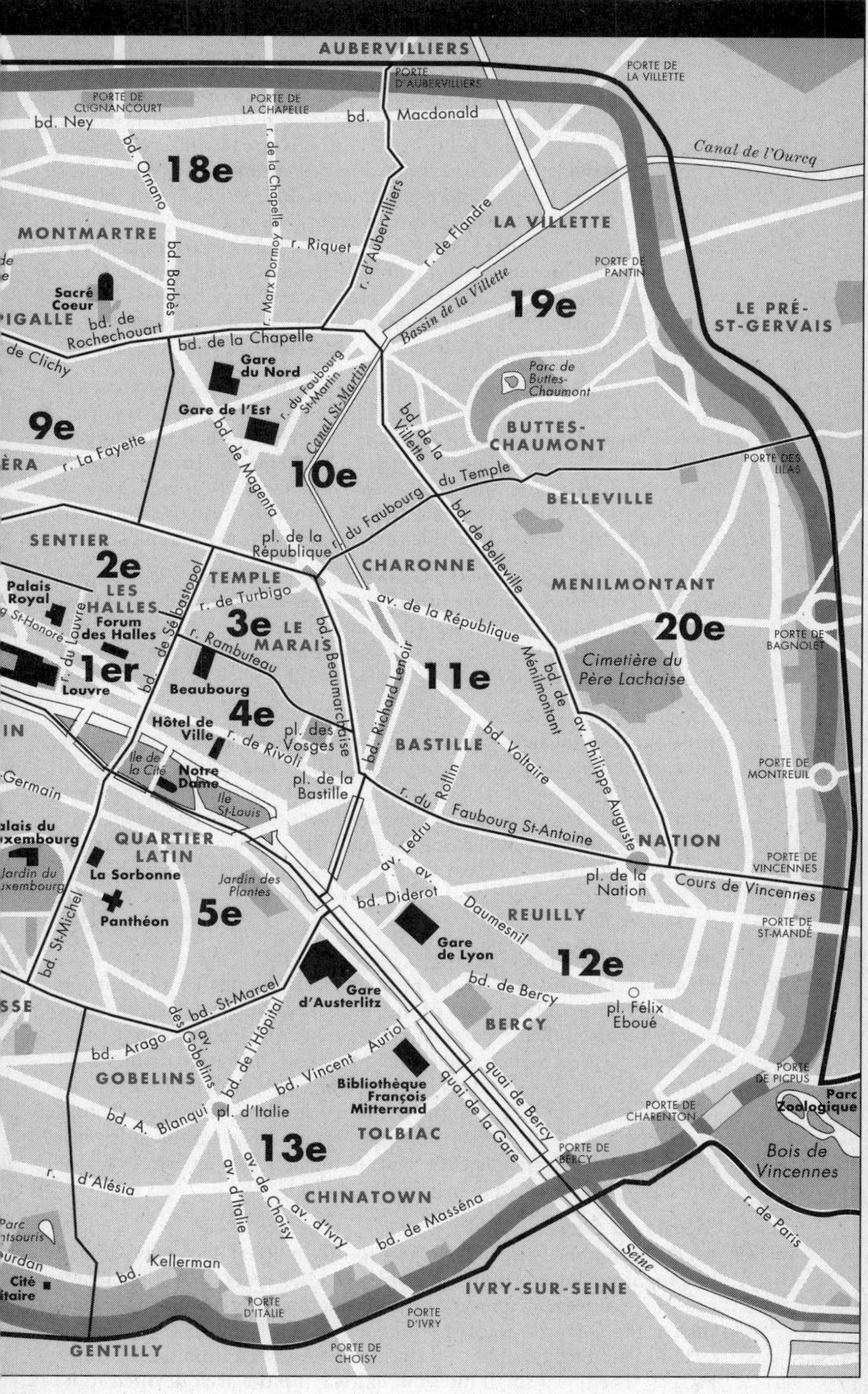
AUBERVILLIERS
PORTE D'AUBERVILLIERS
PORTE DE LA VILLETTE
PORTE DE CLIGNANCOURT
PORTE DE LA CHAPELLE
bd. Ney
bd. Macdonald
Canal de l'Ourcq
bd. Ornano
18e
r. de la Chapelle
r. d'Aubervilliers
r. de Flandre
LA VILLETTE
MONTMARTRE
r. Riquet
r. Marx Dormoy
bd. Barbès
PORTE DE PANTIN
Sacré Coeur
Bassin de la Villette
19e
LE PRÉ-ST-GERVAIS
PIGALLE
bd. de Rochechouart
bd. de la Chapelle
de Clichy
Gare du Nord
r. du Faubourg St-Martin
Canal St-Martin
Parc de Buttes-Chaumont
Gare de l'Est
bd. de la Villette
BUTTES-CHAUMONT
9e
bd. de Magenta
r. La Fayette
10e
PORTE DES LILAS
du Temple
r. du Faubourg
BELLEVILLE
bd. de Belleville
SENTIER
pl. de la République
2e
CHARONNE
MENILMONTANT
TEMPLE
Palais Royal
LES HALLES
r. de Turbigo
bd. de Sébastopol
av. de la République
St-Honoré
Forum des Halles
3e
LE MARAIS
20e
PORTE DE BAGNOLET
r. du Louvre
r. Rambuteau
bd. Beaumarchais
1er
Louvre
r. Richard Lenoir
11e
bd. de Ménilmontant
Cimetière du Père Lachaise
Beaubourg
4e
Hôtel de Ville
pl. des Vosges
BASTILLE
bd. Voltaire
r. de Rivoli
av. Philippe Auguste
PORTE DE MONTREUIL
Ile de la Cité
Notre Dame
pl. de la Bastille
Rollin
Germain
Ile St-Louis
r. du Faubourg St-Antoine
NATION
QUARTIER LATIN
av. Ledru
Palais du Luxembourg
PORTE DE VINCENNES
Jardin du Luxembourg
La Sorbonne
Jardin des Plantes
av. Daumesnil
pl. de la Nation
Cours de Vincennes
bd. Diderot
REUILLY
PORTE DE ST-MANDÉ
Panthéon
5e
bd. St-Michel
Gare de Lyon
12e
Gare d'Austerlitz
bd. de Bercy
bd. St-Marcel
pl. Félix Eboué
BERCY
bd. de l'Hôpital
av. des Gobelins
bd. Arago
bd. Vincent Auriol
quai de Bercy
PORTE DE PICPUS
Parc Zoologique
GOBELINS
Bibliothèque François Mitterrand
quai de la Gare
PORTE DE CHARENTON
bd. A. Blanqui
pl. d'Italie
TOLBIAC
13e
PORTE DE BERCY
Bois de Vincennes
r. d'Alésia
av. d'Italie
av. de Choisy
CHINATOWN
av. d'Ivry
r. de Paris
bd. de Masséna
Seine
bd. Kellerman
IVRY-SUR-SEINE
PORTE D'ITALIE
PORTE D'IVRY
GENTILLY
PORTE DE CHOISY

runs up from place de l'Alma toward the Champs-Elysées. Follow it to the Rond-Point des Champs-Elysées and take a left to reach the Arc de Triomphe, or take avenue Marceau directly from place de l'Alma.

The colossal, 164-foot **Arc de Triomphe** ⑤ sits on place Charles-de-Gaulle, known to Parisians as L'Étoile, or The Star—a reference to the streets that fan out from it. This is Europe's most chaotic traffic circle: Short of a death-defying dash, your only way of getting to the Arc de Triomphe in the middle is to take an underground passage from the far side of the **Champs-Elysées.** The view from the top of the Arc de Triomphe illustrates the star effect of the 12 radiating avenues and enables you to admire the vista down the Champs-Elysées toward place de la Concorde and the distant Louvre. West of the Champs-Elysées, and visible from the Arc de Triomphe, are the **Bois de Boulogne** ⑥, a large park, and the ultramodern arch of **La Défense** ⑦.

Walk down the Champs-Elysées and stop by the main city tourist office, the Office du Tourisme de la Ville de Paris at No. 127 (☞ Visitor Information *in* Paris A to Z, *below*), on the right-hand side as you arrive from L'Étoile. Continue to the Rond-Point and turn right onto the spacious avenue Franklin-D.-Roosevelt. Some 200 yards down is the glass-roofed **Grand Palais** ⑧, which forms an attractive duo with the Petit Palais on the other side of avenue Winston-Churchill.

The leafy lower reaches of the Champs-Elysées, with well-tended gardens off to the left, lead to the broad, airy **place de la Concorde** ⑨. Across place de la Concorde, facing the Champs-Elysées, two smallish buildings stand sentinel to the Jardin des Tuileries. Nearest the rue de Rivoli is the **Musée du Jeu de Paume,** and nearer the Seine is the **Musée de l'Orangerie.**

Stroll through the newly landscaped **Jardin des Tuileries** ⑩ and survey the surrounding cityscape. Manicured lawns and eccentric diagonal hedges lead on toward the Arc du Carrousel, a small relation of the distant Arc de Triomphe. Steps lead down here to the Carrousel du Louvre, a ritzy underground shopping mall. But you'll probably want to stay above ground and cross the paved esplanade, past Louis XIV on his rearing bronze steed, to I. M. Pei's famous glass pyramid entry to the **Louvre** ⑪.

TIMING

This 7-km (4½-mi) walk could be done in a morning or afternoon—if you don't stop and visit any of the shops, monuments, and museums that lie in wait along the way. Chances are you'll need a full day to do justice to this spectacular end of the city. It makes sense to do this walk on one of your first few days in Paris: The city's tourist office is here, and the view from the top of the Arc de Triomphe is like a short course in the city's geography. Sunny weather is a must, when the tour's vistas and photogenic moments are best. At night, head elsewhere in search of Parisian ambience and an affordable meal.

Sights to See

★ ❺ **Arc de Triomphe.** This colossal, 164-foot Triumphal Arch was planned by Napoléon but not finished until 1836, 20 years after Napoléon's rule. It is decorated with some magnificent sculpture by François Rude, such as the *Departure of the Volunteers,* better known as *La Marseillaise,* situated to the right of the arch when viewed from the Champs-Elysées. There is a small museum halfway up the arch devoted to its history. France's Unknown Soldier is buried beneath the archway; the flame is rekindled every evening at 6:30. ✉ *pl. Charles-de-Gaulle,* ☎ *01–43–80–31–31.* 🎫 *32 frs.* ⏲ *Daily 10–5:30; winter, daily 10–5. Métro, RER: Étoile.*

Bateaux Mouches. These popular motorboats set off on their hour-long tours of Paris waters regularly (every half hour in summer) from place de l'Alma. ✉ *pl. de l'Alma,* ☎ *01–40–76–99–99.* 🎫 *40 frs. Métro: Alma-Marceau.*

6 **Bois de Boulogne.** Landscaped by Baron Haussmann in the 1850s, this sprawling, 2,200-acre park, crisscrossed by broad, leafy roads, is in the western fringes of Paris. It has cafés, restaurants, lakes where you can rent boats, waterfalls, a beautiful flower garden, the Parc de Bagatelle, and a delightful children's amusement park, the **Jardin d'Acclimatation** (métro Sablons). Buses traverse the park during the day (service 244 from Porte Maillot), but Le Bois becomes a distinctly adult playground after dark. ✉ *Jardin d'Acclimatation: bd. des Sablons,* ☎ *01–40–67–90–82.* 🎫 *12 frs.* ⏲ *Daily 10–6. Métro: Les Sablons.* ✉ *Parc de Bagatelle: rte. de Sèvres à Neuilly.* 🎫 *10 frs.* ⏲ *Daily 9–5. Métro: Pont de Neuilly.*

Champs-Elysées. The 2-km (1¼-mi) Champs-Elysées was originally laid out in the 1660s by the landscape gardener Le Nôtre as a garden sweeping away from the Tuileries. Explore both its commercial upper half and its verdant lower section. *Métro: George-V, Franklin-D.-Roosevelt.*

2 **Champ de Mars.** This long, formal garden, between the Eiffel Tower and École Militaire, was landscaped at the start of the century. Prior to that it was used as a parade ground and as the site of the World Exhibitions of 1867, 1889, and 1900. *Métro: École Militaire; RER: Champ-de-Mars.*

7 **La Défense.** French planners, with their usual desire to rationalize, ordained that modern high-rise development be banished to the outskirts at La Défense, just west of Paris. The soaring skyscrapers are mainly taken up by offices, with no expense spared in the pursuit of visual ingenuity. The highlight is the giant **Grande Arche de La Défense,** aligned with avenue de la Grande-Armée, the Arc de Triomphe, the Champs-Elysées, and the Louvre. Tubular glass elevators whisk you to the top. ✉ *Parvis de La Défense,* ☎ *01–49–07–27–57.* 🎫 *Arch: 40 frs.* ⏲ *Arch: daily 10–7. Métro: Grande Arche de La Défense; RER: La Défense.*

★ 1 **Eiffel Tower.** Known to the French as La Tour Eiffel (pronounced F.L.), Paris's most famous landmark was built by Gustave Eiffel for the World Exhibition of 1889, the centennial of the French Revolution, and was still in good shape to celebrate its own 100th birthday. Such was Eiffel's engineering wizardry that even in the strongest winds his tower never sways more than 4½ inches. If you're full of energy, stride up the stairs as far as the third deck. If you want to go to the top, you'll have to take the elevator. ✉ *quai Branly,* ☎ *01–44–11–23–23.* 🎫 *By elevator: 2nd floor, 20 frs; 3rd floor, 40 frs; 4th floor, 56 frs. By foot: 2nd and 3rd floors only, 12 frs.* ⏲ *July–Aug., daily 9 AM–midnight; Sept.–June, daily 9 AM–11 PM. Métro: Bir-Hakeim; RER: Champ-de-Mars.*

8 **Grand Palais.** With its curved glass roof, the Grand Palais is unmistakable when approached from either the Seine or the Champs-Elysées and forms an attractive duo with the Petit Palais on the other side of avenue Winston-Churchill. Both were built for the World's Fair of 1900 and, as with the Eiffel Tower, there was never any intention that they would be permanent additions to the city. Unfortunately, the Grand Palais was closed for renovation in 1994 and is unlikely to reopen before 1999. But the Petit Palais contains a permanent collection of French painting and furniture, with splendid canvases by Courbet and

Paris

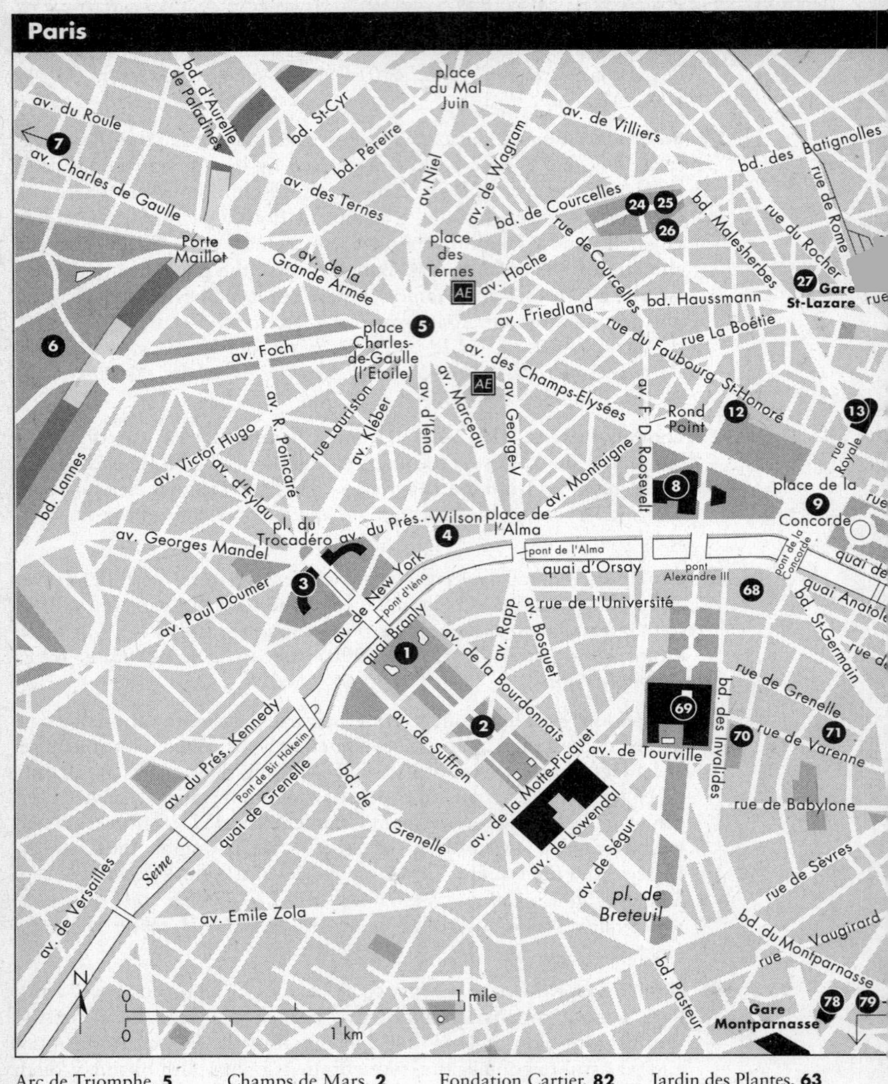

Arc de Triomphe, **5**
Archives Nationales, **45**
Arènes de Lutèce, **65**
Atelier Delacroix, **74**
Bibliothèque François Mitterand, **64**
Bibliothèque Nationale, **18**
Bois de Boulogne, **6**
Bourse, **30**
Bourse du Commerce, **20**
Centre Pompidou (Beaubourg), **43**
Champs de Mars, **2**
Cimetière de Montparnasse, **81**
Cimetière du Père Lachaise, **36**
Comédie Française, **16**
Conservatoire National des Techniques, **32**
La Défense, **7**
École Nationale des Beaux-Arts, **75**
Église de la Madeleine, **13**
Eiffel Tower, **1**
Fondation Cartier, **82**
Forum des Halles, **22**
Grand Palais/Petite Palais, **8**
Hôtel Druout, **29**
Hôtel de Sully, **39**
Hôtel de Ville, **42**
Hôtel des Invalides, **69**
Ile St-Louis, **54**
Institut de France/Hôtel des Monnaies, **76**
Institut du Monde Arabe, **66**
Jardin Atlantique, **80**
Jardin des Plantes, **63**
Jardin des Tuileries, **10**
Jardin du Luxembourg, **77**
Louvre, **11**
Mémorial de la Déportation, **55**
Mosquée, **62**
Musée d'Art Moderne de la Ville de Paris, **4**
Musée Bricard, **46**
Musée Carnavalet, **49**
Musée Cernuschi, **25**
Musée de la Chasse et de la Nature, **44**

Musée Cognacq-Jay, **48**
Musée Maillol, **71**
Musée National du Moyen-Age, **58**
Musée Nissim de Camondo, **26**
Musée d'Orsay, **67**
Musée Picasso, **47**
Musée Rodin, **70**
Notre-Dame, **53**
Notre-Dame de Bonne-Nouvelle, **31**
Opéra Garnier, **28**
Palais Bourbon, **68**
Palais de Chaillot, **3**
Palais de Justice, Conciergerie, and Ste-Chapelle, **52**
Palais de l'Elysée, **12**
Palais-Royal, **17**
Panthéon, **60**
Parc Monceau, **24**
Parc de la Villette, **37**
Place de la Bastille, **38**
Place de Catalogne, **79**
Place de la Concorde, **9**
Place de la République, **35**
Place Vendôme, **14**
Place des Victoires, **19**
Place des Vosges, **50**
Pont Neuf, **51**
St-Augustin, **27**
Ste-Élisabeth, **34**
St-Eustache, **21**
St-Etienne-du-Mont, **61**
St-Germain-des-Prés, **73**
St-Germain-l'Auxerrois, **23**
St-Gervais–St-Protais, **41**
St-Julien-le-Pauvre, **56**
St-Nicolas des Champs, **33**
St-Paul–St-Louis, **40**
St-Roch, **15**
St-Séverin, **57**
St-Sulpice, **72**
La Sorbonne, **59**
Tour Montparnasse, **78**
Val de Grâce, **83**

Bouguereau. ✉ *av. Winston-Churchill,* ☎ *01–42–65–12–73.* 🎫 *27 frs.* ⏲ *Tues.–Sun. 10–5:30. Métro: Champs-Elysées–Clemenceau.*

10 **Jardin des Tuileries.** The recently renovated Tuileries Gardens are typically French: formal and neatly patterned, with statues, rows of trees, and gravel paths. This is a charming place to stroll and survey the surrounding cityscape. *Métro: Tuileries.*

11 **Louvre.** Though it is now a coherent, unified structure, the Louvre—the world's largest museum—is the product of centuries. Originally built by Philippe-Auguste in the 13th century as a fortress, it was not until the reign of pleasure-loving François I, 300 years later, that today's Louvre gradually began to take shape. Through the years, Henri IV (1589–1610), Louis XIII (1610–43), Louis XIV (1643–1715), Napoléon (1804–14), and Napoléon III (1852–70) all contributed to its construction. The recent history of the Louvre centers on I. M. Pei's glass Pyramid, unveiled in March of 1989.

The number-one attraction for most visitors is Leonardo da Vinci's enigmatic Mona Lisa (*La Joconde* to the French); be forewarned that you will find it encased in glass and surrounded by a mob of tourists. The collections are divided into seven sections: Oriental antiquities; Egyptian antiquities; Greek and Roman antiquities; sculpture; paintings, prints, and drawings; furniture; and objets d'art. Don't try to see it all at once; try, instead, to make repeat visits—the admission is reduced on Sunday. Some other highlights of the paintings are *Shepherds in Arcadia,* by Nicolas Poussin (1594–1665); *The Oath of the Horatii,* by Jacques-Louis David (1748–1825); *The Raft of the Medusa,* by Théodore Géricault (1791–1824); and *La Grande Odalisque,* by Jean-Auguste-Dominique Ingres (1780–1867). The *Winged Victory of Samothrace* seems poised for flight at the top of the stairs, and another much-loved piece of sculpture is Michelangelo's pair of *Slaves,* intended for the tomb of Pope Julius II. These can be admired in the Denon Wing, where a new medieval and Renaissance sculpture section is housed partly in the former imperial stables. The French crown jewels (in the objets d'art section of the Richelieu Wing) include the mind-boggling 186-carat Regent diamond. ✉ *Palais du Louvre,* ☎ *01–40–20–53–17.* 🎫 *45 frs; 26 frs after 3 PM and Sun.; free 1st Sun. of the month.* ⏲ *Thurs.–Sun. 9–6, Mon. and Wed. 9 AM–9:45 PM. Some sections open limited days. Métro: Palais-Royal.*

4 **Musée d'Art Moderne de la Ville de Paris.** Both temporary exhibits and a permanent collection of top-quality 20th-century art can be found at the City Museum of Modern Art. It takes over, chronologically speaking, where the Musée d'Orsay (☞ *below*) leaves off: Among the earliest works are Fauve paintings by Vlaminck and Derain, followed by Picasso's early experiments in Cubism. Other highlights include works by Braque, Rouault, Gleizes, Da Silva, Gromaire, and Modigliani. ✉ *11 av. du Président-Wilson,* ☎ *01–53–67–40–00.* 🎫 *27 frs.* ⏲ *Tues.–Sun. 10–5:30, Wed. 10–8:30. Métro: Iéna.*

Musée du Jeu de Paume. The Jeu de Paume Museum, at the entrance to the Tuileries Gardens, is an ultramodern, white-walled showcase for excellent temporary exhibits of bold contemporary art. ✉ *pl. de la Concorde,* ☎ *01–42–60–69–69.* 🎫 *35 frs.* ⏲ *Tues. noon–9:30, Wed.–Fri. noon–7, weekends 10–7. Métro: Concorde.*

Musée de l'Orangerie. Several of Claude Monet's *Water Lily* series head the choice array of early-20th-century paintings in the Orangerie Museum in the Tuileries Gardens. ✉ *pl. de la Concorde,* ☎ *01–42–97–48–16.* 🎫 *28 frs.* ⏲ *Wed.–Mon. 9:45–5:15. Métro: Concorde.*

8 **Palais de Chaillot.** This honey-color, Art Deco culture center facing the Seine, perched atop tumbling gardens with sculpture and fountains, was built in the 1930s. It houses three museums: the **Musée des Monuments Français** (Museum of French Monuments), whose painstaking replicas of statues and archways form an excellent introduction to French medieval architecture; the **Musée du Cinéma Henri-Langlois** (Cinema Museum), tracing the history of motion pictures; and the **Musée de l'Homme** (Museum of Man), whose array of prehistoric artifacts is to serve as the base for a new Primal Art museum to open in 1999. At press time (spring 1997), the **Musée de la Marine** (Maritime Museum), based here for many years, was set to move to an unspecified new location. ✉ *pl. du Trocadéro. Musée du Cinéma:* ☎ *01–45–53–74–39.* 🎫 *30 frs.* ⏲ *Wed.–Mon.; guided tours only, at 10, 11, 2, 3, 4, and 5. Musée de l'Homme:* ☎ *01–44–05–72–72.* 🎫 *30 frs.* ⏲ *Wed.–Mon. 9:45–5. Musée des Monuments:* ☎ *01–44–05–39–10.* 🎫 *21 frs, Sun. 14 frs.* ⏲ *Wed.–Mon. 10–6. Métro: Trocadéro.*

NEED A BREAK? Get a tremendous view of the Eiffel Tower, and a drink or a snack at **Les Monuments** (☎ 01–44–05–90–00), an elegant bar and restaurant in the cinema wing of the Palais de Chaillot.

9 **Place de la Concorde.** This majestic square at the foot of the Champs-Elysées was laid out in the 1770s, but there was nothing in the way of peace or concord about its early years. Between 1793 and 1795 over a thousand victims, including Louis XVI and Marie-Antoinette, were slashed into oblivion at the guillotine. The **Obelisk,** a present from the viceroy of Egypt, was erected in 1833. *Métro: Concorde.*

The Faubourg St-Honoré

The Faubourg St-Honoré, north of the Champs-Elysées and the Tuileries, is synonymous with style—as you will see as you progress from the President's Palace, past a wealth of art galleries, to the monumental Madeleine church and on to stately place Vendôme, home to the Ritz and the world's top jewelers. Leading names in modern fashion are found farther east on place des Victoires, close to what was, for centuries, the gastronomic heart of Paris: Les Halles (pronounced *lay al*), once the city's main market.

Les Halles was closed in 1969 and replaced by a park and a modern shopping mall, the Forum des Halles. The surrounding streets underwent a transformation and are now filled with shops, cafés, and restaurants. The brash modernity of the Forum stands in contrast to the august church of St-Eustache nearby. Similarly, the incongruous black-and-white columns in the classical courtyard of Richelieu's neighboring Palais-Royal present a further case of daring modernity—or architectural vandalism, depending on your point of view.

A Good Walk

Start in front of the most important home in France: the **Palais de l'Elysée** ⑫, or Presidential Palace. Crash barriers and stern policemen keep visitors at bay; in fact, there's more to see in the plethora of art galleries and luxury fashion boutiques that line rue du Faubourg-St-Honoré as you head east. Pass the British Embassy and turn left onto rue Boissy-d'Anglas, then cut right through an archway into Cité Berryer, a restored courtyard with several trendy boutiques. It leads to rue Royale, a classy street lined with jewelry stores. Looming to the left is the **Église de la Madeleine** ⑬, a sturdy neoclassical edifice.

Cross boulevard de la Madeleine and take rue Duphot down to rue St-Honoré, where you'll pass Notre-Dame de l'Assomption, noted for its huge dome and solemn interior. Continue to rue de Castiglione then head left to **place Vendôme** ⑭, one of the world's most opulent squares. Return to rue St-Honoré and follow it to the mighty church of **St-Roch** ⑮.

Take the next right onto rue des Pyramides and cross place des Pyramides, with its gilded statue of Joan of Arc on horseback, to the northernmost wing of the Louvre. Stay on arcaded rue de Rivoli to place du Palais-Royal. On the corner of rue de Richelieu and rue de Rivoli is the **Comédie Française** ⑯, the time-honored setting for performances of classical French drama. To the right of the theater is the unobtrusive entrance to the **Palais-Royal** ⑰; its courtyard is a surprising oasis in the heart of the city.

One block north of here, on rue de Richelieu, is France's original national library, the **Bibliothèque Nationale** ⑱. Rue des Petits-Champs heads east to the circular **place des Victoires** ⑲: That's Louis XIV riding the plunging steed in the center of the square. Head south down rue Croix-des-Petits-Champs, past the nondescript Banque de France on your right, and take the second street on the left to the circular **Bourse du Commerce** ⑳ or Commercial Exchange. Alongside it is the 100-foot-high fluted Colonne de Ruggieri.

You don't need to scale Ruggieri's column to spot the bulky outline of the church of **St-Eustache** ㉑, a curious architectural hybrid of Gothic and classical. The vast site next to St-Eustache is now occupied by a garden, the Jardin des Halles, and the modern **Forum des Halles** ㉒ shopping mall. Rue Berger leads from allée de St-Jean-de-Perse to the square des Innocents, with its handsome Renaissance fountain. Head south along rue St-Denis from the far end of square des Innocents to place du Châtelet, with its theaters, fountain, and the **Tour St-Jacques** looming up to your left. Take a right on quai de la Mégisserie, then a left onto rue du Pont-Neuf. Turn right (rue de l'Arbre-Sec), then left (rue des Prêtres) to reach **St-Germain l'Auxerrois** ㉓, once the French royal family's parish church.

TIMING

With brief visits to churches and monuments, this 5½-km (3½-mi) walk should take three to four hours. On a nice day you may want to linger in the gardens of the Palais-Royal and on a cold day you may want to indulge in an unbelievably thick hot chocolate at the Angélina tearoom.

Sights to See

18 **Bibliothèque Nationale.** France's national library used to contain more than 7 million printed volumes; many have been removed to the giant new Bibliothèque François Mitterrand (☞ *below*). You can admire Robert de Cotte's 18th-century courtyard and peep into the magnificent 19th-century reading room. The collections are on exhibit from time to time in the library's galleries. ✉ *58 rue de Richelieu.* ⊙ *Daily 9–8. Métro: Bourse.*

20 **Bourse du Commerce.** The circular, shallow-domed, 18th-century Commercial Exchange near Les Halles began life as a Corn Exchange; Victor Hugo waggishly likened it to a jockey's cap without the peak. ✉ *rue de Viarmes. Métro or RER: Les Halles.*

16 **Comédie Française.** This theater is the setting for performances of classical French drama, with tragedies by Racine and Corneille and comedies by Molière regularly on the bill. The building itself dates from 1790, but the Comédie Française company was created by that most theatrical of French monarchs, Louis XIV, back in 1680. ✉ *pl. André-Malraux,* ☎ *01–44–58–15–15. Métro: Palais-Royal.*

13 **Église de la Madeleine.** With its rows of uncompromising columns, this sturdy neoclassical edifice—designed in 1814 but not consecrated until 1842—looks more like a Greek temple than a Christian church. In fact, La Madeleine, as it is known, was nearly selected as Paris's first train station (the site of the Gare St-Lazare, just up the road, was chosen instead). Inside, the walls are richly and harmoniously decorated; gold glints through the murk. The portico's majestic Corinthian colonnade supports a gigantic pediment with a frieze of the Last Judgment. ✉ *pl. de la Madeleine.* ⏲ *Mon.–Sat. 7:30–7, Sun. 8–7. Métro: Madeleine.*

22 **Forum des Halles.** Les Halles, the iron-and-glass halls of the central Paris food market, were closed in 1969 and replaced in the late '70s by the Forum des Halles, a modern shopping mall. Unfortunately, much of the plastic, concrete, glass, and mock-marble facade of the multilevel shopping mall, still referred to as "Les Halles," is already showing signs of wear and tear. Nonetheless, if you are a serious shopper, you might want to check it out. ✉ *Main entrance on rue Pierre-Lescot. Métro: Les Halles; RER: Châtelet–Les Halles.*

NEED A BREAK? Founded in 1903, **Angélina** (✉ 226 rue de Rivoli, ☎ 01–42–60–82–00) is an elegant *salon de thé* (tearoom), famous for "L'Africain"—a cup of hot chocolate so thick you'll need a fork to eat it (irresistible even in the summer).

12 **Palais de l'Elysée.** This "palace," where the French president lives, works, and receives official visitors, was originally constructed as a private mansion in 1718 and has housed presidents only since 1873. Although you can catch a glimpse of the palace forecourt and facade through the Faubourg St-Honoré gateway, it is difficult to get much idea of the building's size, or of the extensive gardens that stretch back to the Champs-Elysées. ✉ *55 rue du Faubourg St-Honoré.* ⏲ *Not open to the public. Métro: Miromesnil.*

17 **Palais-Royal.** The buildings of this former palace—royal only in that all-powerful Cardinal Richelieu (1585–1642) magnanimously bequeathed them to Louis XIII—date from the 1630s. Today, the Palais-Royal is home to the French Ministry of Culture, and its buildings are not open to the public. You can, however, visit the colonnaded courtyard with black-and-white striped half-columns and revolving silver spheres that slither around in two fountains—the controversial work of architect Daniel Buren—and the more classical gardens beyond. ✉ *pl. du Palais-Royal. Métro: Palais-Royal.*

14 **Place Vendôme.** With its granite pavement and Second Empire street lamps, Mansart's rhythmic, perfectly proportioned example of 17th-century urban architecture shines in all its golden-stone splendor. The square is a fitting showcase for the deluxe Ritz Hotel and the cluster of jewelry display windows found here. Napoléon had the square's central column made from the melted bronze of 1,200 cannons captured at the battle of Austerlitz in 1805. That's him standing vigilantly at the top. There's parking in an underground lot. *Métro: Opéra.*

19 **Place des Victoires.** This circular square, now home to many of the city's top fashion boutiques, was laid out in 1685 by Jules-Hardouin Mansart in honor of the military victories of Louis XIV. Louis is shown galloping along on a bronze horse in the middle. *Métro: Sentier.*

21 **St-Eustache.** Since the demolition of the 19th-century market halls at the beginning of the '70s, St-Eustache has reemerged as a dominant element on the central Paris skyline. A huge church, it was built as the market people's Right Bank reply to Notre-Dame, though St-Eustache

dates from a couple of hundred years later. With the exception of the feeble west front, added between 1754 and 1788, construction lasted from 1532 to 1637, spanning the decline of the Gothic style and the emergence of the Renaissance. As a consequence, the church is a curious architectural hybrid. ✉ *2 rue du Jour,* ☎ *01–46–27–89–21 for concert information.* ⏲ *Daily 8–7. Métro or RER: Les Halles.*

㉓ **St-Germain l'Auxerrois.** Until 1789, St-Germain was used by the French royal family as their parish church, in the days when the adjacent Louvre was a palace rather than a museum. The facade reveals the influence of 15th-century Flamboyant Gothic style, whereas the fluted columns around the choir, the area surrounding the altar, demonstrate the triumph of classicism. ✉ *pl. du Louvre. Métro: Louvre-Rivoli.*

⑮ **St-Roch.** Designed by Lemercier in 1653 but completed only in the 1730s, this huge church is almost as long as Notre-Dame (138 yards) thanks to Hardouin-Mansart's domed Lady Chapel at the far end. ✉ *rue St-Honoré. Métro: Tuileries.*

Tour St-Jacques. This ornate 170-foot stump tower (now used for meteorological purposes and not open to the public) belonged to a 16th-century church destroyed in 1797. ✉ *pl. du Châtelet. Métro: Châtelet.*

The Grand Boulevards

The focal point of this walk is the uninterrupted avenue that runs in almost a straight line from St-Augustin, the city's grandest Second Empire church, to place de la République, whose very name symbolizes the ultimate downfall of the imperial regime. The avenue's name changes six times along the way, which is why Parisians refer to it, in plural, as the Grand Boulevards.

The makeup of the neighborhoods along the Grand Boulevards changes steadily as you head east from the posh 8e arrondissement toward working-class east Paris. The *Grands Magasins* (Department Stores) at the start of the walk epitomize upscale Paris shopping. They stand on boulevard Haussmann, named in honor of the regional prefect who oversaw the reconstruction of the city in the 1850s and 1860s (☞ A Survey of French Architecture *in* Chapter 17). The opulent Opéra Garnier, just past the Grands Magasins, is the architectural showpiece of the period (often termed the Second Empire and corresponding to the rule of Napoléon III).

A Good Walk

Step through gold-topped iron gates to enter the **Parc Monceau** ㉔, in the tony 8e arrondissement. At the middle of the park, head left to avenue Velasquez past the **Musée Cernuschi** ㉕—home to Chinese art from Neolithic pottery to contemporary paintings—to boulevard Malesherbes. Turn right on boulevard Malesherbes and right again on rue de Monceau to reach the **Musée Nissim de Camondo** ㉖, whose aristocratic interior reflects the upbeat tone of this haughty part of Paris.

Turn left down rue de Téhéran, left along avenue de Messine, and left again on rue de Laborde to get to the innovative iron-and-stone church of **St-Augustin** ㉗. Cross the square in front and turn left along boulevard Haussmann to leafy, intimate square Louis XVI. Some 300 yards further down boulevard Haussmann, you'll find the Grands Magasins: Paris's most renowned department stores. First come the cupolas of Au Printemps, then Galeries Lafayette. Opposite looms the massive bulk of the **Opéra Garnier** ㉘.

Boulevard des Capucines, lined with cinemas and restaurants, heads left from the Opera, becoming boulevard des Italiens before colliding with boulevard Haussmann. A left here down rue Drouot will take you to the **Hôtel Drouot** ㉙, Paris's central auction house. Rue Rossini leads from "Drouot" to rue de la Grange-Batelière. Halfway along on the right is the Passage Jouffroy, one of the many covered galleries that honeycomb the center of Paris. Cross boulevard Montmartre to the passage des Panoramas, leading to rue St-Marc. Turn right, then left down rue Vivienne, to find the foresquare, colonnaded **Bourse** ㉚, the Paris Stock Exchange.

Head east along rue Réaumur, once the heart of the French newspaper industry—stationery shops still abound—and cross rue Montmartre. Take the second left up rue de Cléry: A narrow street that is the exclusive domain of fabric wholesalers. Continue up rue de Cléry as far as rue des Degrés—not a street at all, but a 14-step stairway—then look for the crooked church tower of **Notre-Dame de Bonne-Nouvelle** ㉛, hemmed in by rickety housing that looks straight out of Balzac. The porticoed entrance is around the corner on rue de la Lune, which leads back to the Grands Boulevards, by now going under the name of boulevard de Bonne-Nouvelle.

The Porte St-Denis, a triumphal arch, looms up ahead and, a little farther on, the smaller but similar Porte St-Martin. From here take the rue St-Martin south to the **Conservatoire National des Techniques** ㉜, an industrial museum housed partly in the former church of St-Martin. Current restoration may not end before 1999, so console yourself with a glimpse of the solemn domed forecourt and repair to the leafy square opposite, or to the high, narrow, late Gothic church of **St-Nicolas des Champs** ㉝ across rue Réaumur. Head left on rue de Turbigo, past the cloister ruins and Renaissance gateway that embellish the far side of St-Nicolas. Some 400 yards along on the right is the baroque church of **Ste-Élisabeth** ㉞; shortly after, you reach **place de la République** ㉟. It's a short métro ride from here to the city's most famous cemetery, the **Cimetière du Père Lachaise** ㊱, or to the **Parc de La Villette** ㊲, with its postmodern science and music museums.

TIMING

The distance between Parc Monceau and place de la République is almost 6 km (4 mi), which will probably take you four hours to walk, including coffee breaks and window-shopping. Allot a few additional hours, if not a whole morning or afternoon, to visit the Père Lachaise Cemetery or the Parc de la Villette. Or return to these on another day.

Sights to See

30 **Bourse.** The Paris Stock Exchange, a serene, colonnaded 19th-century building, is a far cry from Wall Street. Take your passport if you want to tour it. ✉ *rue Vivienne.* 🎟 *30 frs.* ⏲ *Guided tours only (in French), weekdays every ½ hr 1:15–4. Métro: Bourse.*

36 **Cimetière du Père Lachaise.** Cemeteries aren't every tourist's idea of the ultimate attraction, but this is the largest and most interesting in Paris. It forms a veritable necropolis with cobbled avenues and tombs competing in pomposity and originality. Leading incumbents include Jim Morrison, Frédéric Chopin, Marcel Proust, Edith Piaf, and Gertrude Stein. Get a map at the entrance and track them down. ✉ *Entrances on rue des Rondeaux, bd. de Ménilmontant, rue de la Réunion.* ⏲ *Daily 8–6 (Oct.–Mar., 8–5). Métro: Gambetta, Philippe-Auguste, Père Lachaise.*

32 **Conservatoire National des Techniques.** The former church and priory of St-Martin des Champs, built between the 11th and 13th centuries, is now part of the National Technical Museum, an industrial museum with a varied collection of models (locomotives, vehicles, and agricultural

machinery), astronomical instruments, and displays on printing, photography, and television. A major renovation may keep the museum shut until 1999. ✉ *292 rue St-Martin,* ☎ *01–40–27–23–31. Métro: Arts et Métiers.*

29 **Hôtel Drouot.** Paris's central auction house offers everything from stamps and toy soldiers to Renoirs and 18th-century commodes. The 16 salesrooms make for fascinating browsing, and there's no obligation to bid. ✉ *9 rue Drouot,* ☎ *01–48–00–20–00.* ⏲ *Viewings Mon.–Sat. 11–noon and 2–6, with auctions starting at 2. Métro: Richelieu-Drouot.*

25 **Musée Cernuschi.** The collection includes Chinese art from Neolithic pottery (3rd century BC) to funeral statuary, painted 8th-century silks, and contemporary paintings, as well as ancient Persian bronze objects. ✉ *7 av. Velasquez,* ☎ *01–45–63–50–75.* 🎟 *17 frs.* ⏲ *Tues.–Sun. 10–5:40. Métro: Monceau.*

26 **Musée Nissim de Camondo.** The elegant decadence of the last days of the regal Ancien Régime is fully reflected in the lavish interior of this aristocratic Parisian mansion, built in the style of Louis XVI. ✉ *63 rue de Monceau,* ☎ *01–45–63–26–32.* 🎟 *27 frs.* ⏲ *Wed.–Sun. 10–noon and 2–5. Métro: Monceau.*

31 **Notre-Dame de Bonne-Nouvelle.** This wide, soberly neoclassical church, built 1823–29, is tucked away off the Grand Boulevards. ✉ *rue de la Lune. Métro: Bonne-Nouvelle.*

28 **Opéra Garnier.** The original Paris Opera, begun in 1862 by Charles Garnier at the behest of Napoléon III, was not completed until 1875, five years after the emperor's abdication. It is said that it typifies Second Empire architecture, which is to say that it is a pompous hodgepodge of styles, imbued with as much subtlety as a Wagnerian cymbal crash. After paying the entry fee, you can stroll around at leisure. The monumental foyer and staircase are impressive and the stage is the largest in the world. Marc Chagall painted the ceiling in 1964. The Opera Museum, containing a few paintings and theatrical mementos, is unremarkable. ✉ *pl. de l'Opéra,* ☎ *01–40–01–22–63.* 🎟 *30 frs.* ⏲ *Daily 10–4:30; closed occasionally for rehearsals; call 01–47–42–57–50 to check. Métro: Opéra.*

NEED A BREAK? There are few grander cafés in Paris than the Belle Epoque **Café de la Paix** (✉ 5 pl. de l'Opéra, ☎ 01–40–07–30–10), once described as "the center of the civilized world."

---

24 **Parc Monceau.** The most picturesque gardens on the Right Bank were laid out as a private park in 1778 and retain some of the fanciful elements then in vogue, including mock ruins and a phony pyramid. The rotunda—known as the Chartres Pavilion—has well-wrought iron gates and was originally a tollhouse. ✉ *Entrances on bd. de Courcelles, av. Velasquez, av. Ruysdaël, av. van Dyck. Métro: Monceau.*

★ 37 **Parc de La Villette.** Until the 1970s this 130-acre site, in an unfashionable corner of northeast Paris commonly known as "La Villette," was home to a cattle market and *abattoir* (slaughterhouse). The site was transformed into an ambitiously landscaped, futuristic park with sweeping lawns, a children's playground, canopied walkways, a cinema, two museums, brightly painted pavilions, and a state-of-the-art concert hall, the **Cité de la Musique** (☞ Nightlife and the Arts, *below*). This giant postmodern musical academy also houses an outstanding museum of music. The former slaughterhouse—the **Grande Halle**—is a magnificent structure whose transformation into an arts center provides an intelligent link with the site's historic past. At the **Géode** cinema, which looks like a huge silver golf ball, films are shown on an enormous, 180-degree-curved screen. The **Cité des Sciences et de l'Industrie,** a science museum, contains dozens of try-it-yourself exhibits that make you feel more participant than onlooker (though most displays are in French only). ⊠ *Cité de la Musique: 221 av. Jean-Jaurès,* ☎ *01–44–84–46–21; Cité des Sciences et de l'Industrie: 30 av. Corentin-Cariou,* ☎ *08–36–68–29–30. Cité des Sciences:* 🎟 *50 frs (planetarium 25 frs), 25 frs after 4* PM. ⏲ *Wed.–Sun. 10–noon and 2–6. Music Museum:* 🎟 *35 frs.* ⏲ *Wed.–Sun. 10–noon and 2–6. Métro: Porte de La Villette, Porte de Pantin.*

35 **Place de la République.** This large, oblong square, laid out by Haussmann 1856–65, is dominated by a matronly, Stalin-size statue symbolizing *The Republic* (1883). "République" has more métro lines than any other station in Paris. *Métro: République.*

27 **St-Augustin.** This domed church was dexterously constructed in the 1860s within the confines of an awkward, V-shape site. It represented a breakthrough in ecclesiastical engineering, insofar as the use of metal pillars and girders obviated the need for exterior buttressing. The dome is bulky but well proportioned and contains some grimy but competent frescoes by the popular 19th-century French artist William Bouguereau. ⊠ *pl. St-Augustin. Métro: St-Augustin.*

34 **Ste-Élisabeth.** This studied essay in Baroque (1628–46) has brightly restored wall paintings and a wide, semicircular apse around the choir. ⊠ *rue du Temple. Métro: Temple.*

33 **St-Nicolas des Champs.** The rounded-arch, fluted Doric capitals in the chancel of this church date from 1560 to 1587, a full century later than the pointed-arch nave (1420–80). ⊠ *rue St-Martin. Métro: Arts-et-Métiers.*

The Marais and the Bastille

The Marais is one of the city's most historic and sought-after residential districts. Renovation is the keynote; well into the '70s, this was one of the city's poorest areas. Regeneration was sparked by the building of the Pompidou Center, arguably Europe's most architecturally whimsical museum. The gracious architecture of the 17th and early 18th centuries, however, sets the tone for the rest of the Marais. Today, most of the Marais's spectacular *hôtels particuliers*—loosely, "mansions," onetime residences of aristocratic families—have been restored; many are now museums. There are trendy boutiques and cafés among the kosher shops in the formerly run-down streets of the Jewish neighborhood around rue des Rosiers. By crisscrossing through the neighborhood along these intimate little streets, you can see it all.

The history of the Marais—the word, incidentally, means marsh or swamp—goes back to when Charles V, king of France in the 14th century, moved his court here from the Ile de la Cité. However, it wasn't until Henri IV laid out place Royale, today the place des Vosges, in the early 17th century, that the Marais became *the* place to live. After the French Revolution, the Marais rapidly became one of the most dissolute areas in Paris, and was spared the attentions of Baron Haussmann, the man who rebuilt so much of Paris in the mid-19th century.

On the eastern edge of the Marais is place de la Bastille, site of the infamous prison stormed on July 14, 1789: An event that came to symbolize the beginning of the French Revolution. Largely in commemoration of the bicentennial of the Revolution, the Bastille area was renovated and became one of the trendiest sections of Paris. Galleries, shops, theaters, cafés, restaurants, and bars now fill formerly decrepit buildings and alleys.

A Good Walk

Make **place de la Bastille** ㊳, which is easily accessible by métro, your gateway into the Marais, to the west. Today the square is dominated by the Colonne de Juillet and the curving glass facade of the modern **Opéra de la Bastille.** The best view of both is to be had from the start of rue St-Antoine. Walk down to the **Hôtel de Sully** ㊴, home to the Caisse Nationale des Monuments Historiques at No. 62. Cross the road and pause at the mighty Baroque church of **St-Paul–St-Louis** ㊵. Take the left-hand side door out of the church into narrow passage St-Paul, then turn right onto rue St-Paul, past the grid of courtyards that make up the Village St-Paul antiques-shops complex. Wind your way through the small streets to the quai de l'Hôtel-de-Ville.

Turn right on quai de l'Hôtel-de-Ville; *bouquinistes* (booksellers) line the Seine to your left. Pause by the Pont Louis-Philippe to admire the dome of the Panthéon floating above the skyline, then take the next right up picturesque rue des Barres to the church of **St-Gervais–St-Protais** ㊶. Beyond the church stands the **Hôtel de Ville** ㊷, the city hall. From the Hôtel de Ville, cross rue de Rivoli and go up rue du Temple. On your right, you'll pass one of the city's most popular department stores, the Bazar de l'Hôtel de Ville, or BHV, as it is known (☞ Shopping, *below*). Take rue de la Verrerie, the first street on your left.

Cross rue du Renard and take the second right past the ornate 16th-century church of St-Merri. Rue St-Martin, full of stores, restaurants, and galleries, leads to the **Centre Pompidou** ㊸. Most of the Center is closed for renovation, but you can still ride to the top in the glass-tubed escalator. The adjacent square Igor-Stravinsky merits a stop for its unusual fountain. Turn left around the back of the Pompidou Center onto rue Beaubourg, then right along rue Rambuteau and the first left onto rue du Temple. Note the Hôtel de St-Aignan at No. 71 and the Hôtel de Montmor at No. 79, both splendid Renaissance mansions. Take a right onto rue des Haudriettes; just off to the left at the next corner is the **Musée de la Chasse et de la Nature** ㊹, the Museum of Hunting and Nature, housed in one of the Marais's most stately mansions. Head right on rue des Archives, crossing rue des Haudriettes, and admire the medieval gateway with two fairy-tale towers, now part of the **Archives Nationales** ㊺, the archives museum entered from rue des Francs-Bourgeois (Street of the Free Citizens) around to the left.

Continue past the Crédit Municipal (the city's grandiose pawnbroking concern), the Dômarais restaurant (housed in a circular 18th-century chamber originally used for auctions), and the church of Notre-Dame des Blancs-Manteaux. A corner-turret signals rue Vieille-du-Temple: Turn left past the palatial Hôtel de Rohan (now part of the Archives Nationales), then right onto rue de la Perle to the **Musée Bricard** ㊻, occupying a mansion as impressive as the assembly of locks and keys within. From here it is a step down rue de Thorigny (opposite) to the palatial 17th-century Hôtel Salé, now the **Musée Picasso** ㊼.

Backtrack along rue de Thorigny and turn left onto rue du Parc-Royal. Halfway down rue Elzévir is the **Musée Cognacq-Jay** ㊽, a must for fans of 18th-century furniture, porcelain, and paintings. Back on rue des Francs-Bourgeois is the **Musée Carnavalet** ㊾, the Paris history museum, in perhaps the swankiest edifice in the Marais. A short walk along rue des Francs-Bourgeois takes you to large, pink-brick **place des Vosges** ㊿, lined with covered arcades. If you want to see more of the Bastille neighborhood, follow rue de Pas-de-la-Mule from the far side of place des Vosges to boulevard Beaumarchais; take a right toward place de la Bastille.

TIMING

This walk is just over 6 km (4 mi) long and will comfortably take a morning or an afternoon. If you choose to spend an hour or two in any of the museums along the way, allow a full day. Be prepared to wait in line at the Picasso Museum. Note that some of the museums don't open until the afternoon and that most shops in the Bastille and the Marais don't open until the late morning.

Sights to See

45 **Archives Nationales.** If you're a serious history buff, you will be fascinated by the thousands of intricate historical documents, dating from the Merovingian period to the 20th century, at the National Archives. ✉ *60 rue des Francs-Bourgeois,* ☎ *01–40–27–62–18.* 🎫 *15 frs.* ⏲ *Wed.–Mon. 1:45–5:45. Métro: Rambuteau.*

43 **Centre Pompidou.** The futuristic, funnel-top Pompidou Center—known to Parisians as Beaubourg, after the surrounding district—was built in the mid-1970s and named in honor of former French president Georges Pompidou (1911–74). The Center was soon attracting over 8 million visitors a year—five times more than intended. Hardly surprising, then, that it was soon showing signs of fatigue: The much-vaunted, gaudily painted service pipes snaking up the exterior needed continual repainting, while the plastic tubing enclosing the exterior escalators was cracked and grimy. In 1996 the government stepped in and took drastic action: shutting the Center until December 1999 and embarking on top-to-bottom renovation. It's still worth passing by, of course. Although the Center is closed for renovation, the escalator up to the roof remains open, with the Parisian skyline unfolding as you are carried through the clear plastic tubes. Inside, some exhibitions will be staged when restoration allows; but the **Musée National d'Art Moderne** (National Museum of Modern Art) will remain closed until the work is completed. ✉ *pl. Georges-Pompidou,* ☎ *01–44–78–12–33.* 🎫 *Building and library entry and escalator ride to the roof: free. Exhibitions: prices vary, check at the main ticket booth on the ground floor.* ⏲ *Mon., Wed.–Fri. noon–10 PM, weekends 10 AM–10 PM. Métro: Rambuteau.*

NEED A BREAK? Stop in for coffee at the high-design **Café Beaubourg** (✉ 43 rue St-Merri, ☎ 01-48-87-63-96), on the corner of place Georges-Pompidou.

39 **Hôtel de Sully.** This late-Renaissance mansion, begun in 1624, has a stately garden and a majestic courtyard with statues, richly carved pediments, and dormer windows. It is the headquarters of the **Caisse Nationale des Monuments Historiques,** responsible for administering France's historic monuments. Guided visits to Paris sites and buildings begin here, though all are conducted in French. ✉ *62 rue St-Antoine,* ☎ *01–44–61–20–00. Métro: St-Paul.*

42 **Hôtel de Ville.** During the Commune of 1871, the Hôtel de Ville was burned to the ground. Today's exuberant building, based closely on the 16th-century Renaissance original, went up between 1874 and 1884. You can't inspect the lavish interior, but head round left to the traffic-free square, with its fountains and forest of street lamps, to admire the exuberant facade. ✉ *pl. de l'Hôtel-de-Ville. Métro: Hôtel-de-Ville.*

46 **Musée Bricard.** The Lock Museum—also called the Musée de la Serrure—is housed in a sober Baroque mansion designed in 1685 by the

architect of Les Invalides, Libéral Bruand, for himself. Anyone with a taste for fine craftsmanship will appreciate the intricacy and ingenuity of many of the locks displayed here. ✉ *1 rue de la Perle,* ☎ *01–42–77–79–62.* 🎟 *30 frs.* ⏲ *Weekdays 2–5. Métro: St-Paul.*

49 **Musée Carnavalet.** Two adjacent mansions in the heart of the Marais house the Carnavelet Museum, the Paris History Museum, with material dating from the city's origins to the present. The museum is full of maps and plans, furniture, and busts and portraits of Parisian worthies down the ages. ✉ *23 rue de Sévigné,* ☎ *01–42–72–21–13.* 🎟 *27 frs.* ⏲ *Tues.–Sun. 10–5:30. Métro: St-Paul.*

NEED A BREAK?

Marais Plus (✉ 20 rue des Francs-Bourgeois, ☎ 01–48–87–01–40), on the corner of rue Elzévir and rue des Francs-Bourgeois, is a delightful, artsy gift shop with a cozy salon de thé at the rear.

44 **Musée de la Chasse et de la Nature.** The Museum of Hunting and Nature is housed in the Hôtel de Guénégaud, designed around 1650 by François Mansart. There is a series of immense 17th- and 18th-century still lifes (notably by Desportes and Oudry) of dead animals and a wide variety of swords, guns, muskets, and stuffed animals. ✉ *60 rue des Archives,* ☎ *01–42–72–86–43.* 🎟 *25 frs.* ⏲ *Wed.–Mon. 10–12:30 and 1:30–5:30. Métro: Rambuteau.*

48 **Musée Cognacq-Jay.** This museum, devoted to the arts of the 18th century, contains outstanding furniture, porcelain, and paintings (notably by Watteau, Boucher, and Tiepolo). ✉ *8 rue Elzévir,* ☎ *01–40–27–07–21.* 🎟 *17 frs.* ⏲ *Tues.–Sun. 10–5:30. Métro: St-Paul.*

47 **Musée Picasso.** The Picasso Museum, housed in the 17th-century Hôtel Salé, contains the paintings, sculptures, drawings, prints, ceramics, and assorted works of art given to the government by Picasso's heirs after the painter's death in 1973 in lieu of death duties. There are works from every period of Picasso's life, as well as works by Cézanne, Miró, Renoir, Braque, Degas, and Matisse. ✉ *5 rue de Thorigny,* ☎ *01–42–71–25–21.* 🎟 *28 frs, Sun. 18 frs.* ⏲ *Thurs.–Mon. 9:30–6. Métro: St-Sébastien.*

Opéra de la Bastille. The state-of-the-art Bastille Opera was erected on the south side of place de la Bastille. Designed by Argentine-born Carlos Ott, it opened July 14, 1989, the bicentennial of the French Revolution. The steep-climbing auditorium seats more than 3,000 and has earned more plaudits than the curving glass facade. ✉ *pl. de la Bastille,* ☎ *01–44–73–13–00. Métro: Bastille.*

38 **Place de la Bastille.** Nothing remains of the infamous Bastille prison destroyed at the beginning of the French Revolution. Until 1988, there was little more to see here than a huge traffic circle and the **Colonne de Juillet**, the July Column (commemorating the overthrow of Charles X in July 1830). As part of the countrywide celebrations for July 1989, the bicentennial of the French Revolution, the Opéra de la Bastille was erected, inspiring substantial redevelopment on the surrounding streets, especially along rue de Lappe and rue de la Roquette. What was formerly a humdrum neighborhood rapidly gained streamlined art galleries, funky jazz clubs, and Spanish-style tapas bars. *Métro: Bastille.*

50 **Place des Vosges.** Laid out by Henri IV at the start of the 17th century, and originally known as place Royale, this square is the oldest in Paris. The two larger buildings on either side were originally the king's and queen's pavilions. The statue in the center is of Louis XIII. With its arcades, symmetrical pink-brick town houses, and trim green garden, bisected in the center by gravel paths and edged with plane trees,

the square achieves harmony and balance. At No. 6 is the Maison de Victor Hugo, where the workaholic French author, famed for *Les Misérables* and *The Hunchback of Notre-Dame,* lived between 1832 and 1848. ⊠ *Maison de Victor Hugo: 6 pl. des Vosges,* ☎ *01–42–72–10–16.* 💵 *27 frs.* ⏲ *Tues.–Sun. 10–5:45. Métro: St-Paul, Chemin-Vert.*

41 **St-Gervais–St-Protais.** This imposing church near the Hôtel de Ville is named after two Roman soldiers martyred by the emperor Nero in the 1st century AD. The church, a riot of Flamboyant-style decoration, went up between 1494 and 1598, making it one of the last Gothic constructions in the country. The facade, constructed between 1616 and 1621, is an early example of French architects' use of the classical orders of decoration on the capitals (topmost sections) of the columns. ⊠ *pl. St-Gervais,* ☎ *01–47–26–78–38 for concert information.* ⏲ *Tues.–Sun. 6:30 AM–8 PM. Métro: Hôtel-de-Ville.*

40 **St-Paul–St-Louis.** The leading Baroque church in the Marais was begun in 1627 by the Jesuits and partly modeled on their Gesu church in Rome. Look out for Delacroix's dramatic *Christ in the Mount of Olives* high up in the transept. ⊠ *rue St-Antoine. Métro: St-Paul.*

The Islands and the Latin Quarter

Of the two islands in the Seine—the Ile St-Louis and the Ile de la Cité—it is the Ile de la Cité that forms the historic heart of Paris. It was here that the earliest inhabitants of Paris, the Gaulish tribe of the Parisii, settled in about 250 BC. They called their little home Lutetia, meaning "settlement surrounded by water." Whereas the Ile St-Louis is today largely residential, the Ile de la Cité remains deeply historic. It has been inhabited for more than 2,000 years and is the site of one of the most beautiful churches in France—the great, brooding cathedral of Notre-Dame. Most of the island's other medieval buildings fell victim to town planner Baron Haussmann's ambitious rebuilding program of the 1860s. Among the rare survivors are the jewel-like Ste-Chapelle, a vision of shimmering stained glass, and the Conciergerie, the former city prison.

South of Ile de la Cité on the Left Bank of the Seine is the bohemian Quartier Latin, with its warren of steep sloping streets, populated largely by Sorbonne students and academics. The name Latin Quarter comes from the university tradition of studying and speaking in Latin, a tradition that disappeared during the Revolution. The university began as a theological school in the Middle Ages and later became the headquarters of the University of Paris; in 1968, the student revolution here had an explosive effect on French politics, resulting in major reforms in the education system.

A grim modern skyscraper at the Jussieu campus, the science division of the University of Paris, reiterates the area's yen for learning, yet fails to outgun the mighty dome of the Panthéon in its challenge for skyline supremacy. Most of the district's appeal is less emphatic: Roman ruins, tumbling street markets, the two oldest trees in Paris, and chance glimpses of Notre-Dame all await your discovery.

A Good Walk

The oldest bridge in Paris, confusingly called the **Pont Neuf** (51), or New Bridge, is built across the western tip of Ile de la Cité. Find your way to the middle of the bridge and the square du Vert-Galant below, with its proud equestrian statue of Henri IV. On the quay side of the square, Vedette motorboats start their tours along the Seine.

Opposite the square, on the other side of the bridge, is place Dauphine, completed the same year as the Pont Neuf (although much altered since). Cross place Dauphine and head left along quai de l'Horloge, named for the oldest clock (*horloge*) in Paris—marking time since 1370 from high up the turreted **Conciergerie,** the prison where Marie-Antoinette was kept during the French Revolution. Then turn left onto boulevard du Palais to reach the imposing **Palais de Justice** ⑤②, the law courts. The real interest here is the medieval **Ste-Chapelle,** tucked away to the left of the main courtyard. The chapel walls, consisting mainly of stained glass, constitute a technical tour de force. Take rue de Lutèce opposite the Palais de Justice, pause at the extensive flower market 150 yards down on the left, then turn right on rue de la Cité to come face to face with the serene, golden facade of **Notre-Dame** ⑤③. This is the geographic and historic heart of Paris, and its dark, solemn interior feels suitably reverential.

Cross the Seine on the Pont St-Louis, at the island's eastern tip, to the **Ile St-Louis** ⑤④, the smaller of the city's two islands. From here, admire the views of Notre-Dame, and the Hôtel de Ville and St-Gervais church on the Right Bank. Just across the bridge is the **Mémorial de la Déportation** ⑤⑤, a starkly moving modern crypt dedicated to the French people who died in Nazi concentration camps. Rue St-Louis-en-l'Ile runs the length of the island, bisecting it in two. Walk down this street and admire the strange, pierced spire of St-Louis-en-l'Ile, then stop off for an ice cream at Berthillon at No. 31.

Cross back to the Ile de la Cité and take the pont au Double across the Seine to square René-Viviani, where you'll find a spectacular view of Notre-Dame. Behind the square lies the church of **St-Julien-le-Pauvre** ⑤⑥, built at the same time as Notre-Dame, and the tiny, elegant streets of the Maubert district. Turn left out of the church and cross rue St-Jacques to the elegantly proportioned church of **St-Séverin** ⑤⑦. The surrounding streets are pedestrian only. Take rue St-Séverin, a right on rue Xavier-Privas, and a left on rue de la Huchette to reach place St-Michel. Gabriel Davioud's grandiose 1860 fountain, depicting St. Michael slaying the dragon, is a popular meeting spot at the nerve center of the Left Bank.

Turn left up boulevard St-Michel and cross boulevard St-Germain. To your left, behind some forbidding railings, lurks a garden with ruins that date from Roman times. These belong to the **Musée National du Moyen-Age** ⑤⑧, the National Museum of the Middle Ages. The entrance is down rue Sommerard, the next street on the left. Cross place Paul-Painlevé in front of the museum up toward **La Sorbonne** ⑤⑨ university, fronted by a small plaza where the Left Bank's student population congregate after lessons. Continue uphill until you are confronted, up rue Soufflot on your left, by the menacing domed bulk of the **Panthéon** ⑥⓪. On the far left corner of place du Panthéon stands **St-Étienne-du-Mont** ⑥①, a church whose facade is a mishmash of architectural styles. Explore the top of quaint rue de la Montagne-Ste-Geneviève alongside, then turn right onto rue Descartes to reach place de la Contrescarpe. This square looks almost provincial during the day as Parisians flock to the daily market on rue Mouffetard.

Pass the old church of St-Médard at the foot of rue Mouffetard, then head left for 250 yards along rue Censier and turn left again into rue Georges-Desplas to find the beautiful white **Mosquée** ⑥②, complete with minaret. Blink twice and you'll be convinced you've left Paris behind. On the far side of the Mosque extends the **Jardin des Plantes** ⑥③, spacious botanical gardens; the first building you'll come to is the **Grande Galerie de l'Évolution,** a museum with a startling collection of stuffed animals, many extinct or endangered. The museums of entomology, paleontology, and mineralogy line one side of the garden; an old-fashioned zoo the other. Further upriver, via quai d'Austerlitz and quai de la Gare, is the new **Bibliothèque François Mitterrand** (64), the French National Library, with its four huge shiny glass towers.

If you forego the distant pleasure of the new library, take the northwest exit from the Jardin des Plantes up rue Lacépède then rue de Navarre to the **Arènes de Lutèce** (65), the remains of a Roman amphitheater. Rue des Arènes and rue Limé lead to place Jussieu and its hideous 1960s concrete campus; there's greater refinement around the corner down rue des Fossés-St-Bernard at the glass-facaded **Institut du Monde Arabe** (66), a center devoted to Arab culture. End your walk here with a cup of mint tea in the rooftop café that overlooks Paris.

TIMING

At just under 6 km (about 3½ mi), this walk can be fitted into a morning or afternoon or serve as the basis for a leisurely day's exploring—given that several sites, notably Notre-Dame and the Musée de Cluny—deserve a lengthy visit. If you're with children, try and do this tour on a Thursday, when the enchanting Grande Galerie d'Évolution stays open till 10 PM. You can easily make a brief excursion to the Bibliothèque François-Mitterrand.

Sights to See

65 **Arènes de Lutèce.** This Roman arena was only discovered in 1869 and has since been excavated and landscaped to reveal parts of the original amphitheater. Designed as a theater and circus, the arena was almost totally destroyed by the barbarians in AD 280, although you can still see part of the stage and tiered seating. ⊠ *Entrances on rue Monge and rue de Navarre.* ⊙ *Daily 8–sunset. Métro: Monge.*

64 **Bibliothèque François Mitterrand.** The last of former president Mitterrand's *grands travaux* (grand building projects) opened in early 1997. The new library subsumes the majority of the collections in the old Bibliothèque Nationale and, with some 11 million volumes between its walls, surpasses the Library of Congress as the largest library in the world. Architect Dominique Perrault's controversial design features four soaring 24-story towers. A vast interior courtyard—resembling a sunken garden—provides breathing space. ⊠ *11 quai François-Mauriac,* ☎ *01–53–79–53–79.* ⊙ *Tues.–Sat. 10–7, Sun. noon–6. Métro: Quai de la Gare.*

Conciergerie. This turreted medieval building by the Seine was originally part of the royal palace on Ile de la Cité. Most people know it, however, as a prison, whence Danton, Robespierre, and Marie-Antoinette were bundled off to the guillotine. You can visit Marie-Antoinette's cell, the guardroom, and the monumental Salle des Gens d'Armes. ⊠ *quai de l'Horloge.* 🎟 *28 frs.* ⊙ *Daily 9:30–6:30; winter, daily 10–5. Métro: Cité.*

Grande Galerie de l'Évolution. This vast, handsome glass-and-iron structure in the Jardin des Plantes was built, like the Eiffel Tower, in 1889 but abandoned in the 1960s. It reopened amid popular acclaim in 1994 and now contains one of the world's finest collections of stuffed animals, including a section devoted to extinct and endangered species. ⊠ *36 rue Geoffroy-St-Hilaire,* ☎ *01–40–79–39–39.* 🎟 *40 frs, 30 frs before 1 PM.* ⊙ *Wed.–Mon. 10–6, Thurs. 10–10. Métro: Monge.*

54 **Ile St-Louis.** The smaller of the two Paris islands displays striking architectural unity, which stems from the efforts of a group of early-17th-

century property speculators led by Christophe Marie. Leading Baroque architect Louis Le Vau (1612–70) was commissioned to erect a series of imposing town houses. *Métro: Pont-Marie.*

66 **Institut du Monde Arabe.** Jean Nouvel's striking 1988 glass-and-steel edifice, the Institute of the Arab World, adroitly fuses Arabic and European styles. Note the 240 shutterlike apertures that open and close to regulate light exposure. Inside, the Institute tries to do for Arab culture what Beaubourg does for modern art, with the help of a sound-and-image center; a vast library and documentation center; and an art museum. The top-floor café provides a good view of Paris. ✉ *1 rue des Fossés-St-Bernard,* ☎ *01–40–51–38–38.* 🎟 *25 frs.* ⏲ *Tues.–Sun. 10–6. Métro: Cardinal-Lemoine.*

👶 63 **Jardin des Plantes.** This enormous swath of greenery contains botanical gardens, the Grande Galerie de l'Évolution (☞ *above*), and three natural history museums: The **Musée Entomologique,** devoted to insects; the **Musée Paléontologique,** to fossils and prehistoric animals; and the **Musée Minéralogique,** to rocks and minerals. There is also an alpine garden, an aquarium, a maze, a number of hothouses, and a small, old-fashioned zoo. ✉ *Entrances on rue Geoffroy-St-Hilaire, rue Buffon.* 🎟 *Museums and zoo 12–25 frs.* ⏲ *Museums: Mon. and Wed.–Fri. 9–11:45 and 1–4:45, weekends 2–4:45; garden daily 7:30–sunset. Zoo: Daily 9–5. Métro: Monge.*

55 **Mémorial de la Déportation.** On the eastern tip of the Ile de la Cité, in what was once the city morgue, lies a starkly moving modern crypt, dedicated to those French men, women, and children who died in Nazi concentration camps. 🎟 *Free.* ⏲ *Daily 9–6; winter, daily 9–dusk. Métro: Maubert-Mutualité.*

62 **Mosquée.** The city mosque was built from 1922 to 1925, complete with arcades and minaret, and decorated in the style of Moorish Spain. The sunken garden and tiled patios are open to the public (the prayer rooms are not) and so are the *hammams,* or Turkish baths. Venture in and sip a restorative cup of sweet mint tea at the café. ✉ *2 pl. du Puits-de-l'Ermite,* ☎ *01–45–35–97–33.* 🎟 *15 frs for guided tour, 65 frs for Turkish baths.* ⏲ *Baths daily 11 AM–8 PM; Fri. and Sun. men only; Mon., Wed., Thurs., and Sat. women only. Guided tours of mosque Sat.–Thurs. 10–noon and 2–5:30. Métro: Monge.*

58 **Musée National du Moyen-Age.** The National Museum of the Middle Ages is housed in the 15th-century Hôtel de Cluny. The mansion has an intricately vaulted chapel and a cloistered courtyard with mullioned windows that originally belonged to monks of the Cluny Abbey in Burgundy, hence the museum's former name, the Musée de Cluny. A stunning array of tapestries heads its vast exhibition of medieval decorative arts. Alongside the mansion are the city's Roman baths and the *Boatmen's Pillar,* Paris's oldest sculpture. ✉ *6 pl. Paul-Painlevé,* ☎ *01–43–25–62–00.* 🎟 *28 frs, Sun. 18 frs.* ⏲ *Wed.–Mon. 9:45–5:45. Métro: Cluny–La Sorbonne.*

★ 53 **Notre-Dame.** Looming above the large, pedestrian place du Parvis is the Notre-Dame cathedral, the most enduring symbol of Paris. Begun in 1163, it was not completed until 1345. The facade seems perfectly proportioned until you notice that the north (left) tower is wider than the south tower. The south tower houses the great bell of Notre-Dame, as tolled by Quasimodo, Victor Hugo's fictional hunchback. The cathedral interior, with its vast proportions, soaring nave, and soft, multicolor light filtering through the stained-glass windows, inspires awe, despite the inevitable throngs of tourists. Visit early in the morning, when the cathedral is at its lightest and least crowded. Window space is limited and filled with shimmering stained glass; the circular rose windows in the transept are particularly delicate. The 387-step climb up the towers is worth the effort for a perfect view of the famous gargoyles and the heart of Paris. ✉ *pl. du Parvis.* 🎫 *Tower 28 frs.* ⏲ *Cathedral 8 AM–7 PM; tower daily (summer) 9:30–12:15 and 2–6, daily (winter) 10–5. Métro: Cité.*

60 **Panthéon.** Originally commissioned as a church by Louis XV, as a mark of gratitude for his recovery from a grave illness in 1744, the Panthéon is now a monument to France's most glorious historical figures, including Voltaire, Zola, Rousseau, and dozens of French statesmen, military heroes, and other thinkers. Germain Soufflot's building was not begun until 1764, or completed until 1790, whereupon godless Revolutionary supremos had its windows blocked and ordered it transformed into the national shrine it is today. ✉ *pl. du Panthéon,* ☎ *01–43–54–34–51.* 🎫 *32 frs.* ⏲ *Daily 10–5:30. Métro: Cardinal-Lemoine; RER: Luxembourg.*

52 **Palais de Justice.** In about 1860, the city law courts were built by Baron Haussmann in his characteristically weighty neoclassical style. You can wander around the buildings, watch the bustle of the lawyers, or attend a court hearing. But the real interest here is the medieval part of the complex, spared by Haussmann: the Conciergerie and Ste-Chapelle (☞ *above* and *below*). ✉ *bd. du Palais. Métro: Cité.*

51 **Pont Neuf.** Crossing the Ile de la Cité, just behind square du Vert-Galant, is the oldest bridge in Paris, confusingly called the New Bridge, or Pont Neuf. It was completed in 1607 and was the first bridge in the city to be built without houses lining either side. *Métro: Pont-Neuf.*

★ **Ste-Chapelle.** The Holy Chapel was built by Louis IX (1226–70), later canonized St-Louis, in the 1240s to house what he believed to be Christ's Crown of Thorns, purchased from Emperor Baldwin of Constantinople. The building's lead-covered wood spire, rebuilt in 1854, rises 246 feet. The somewhat garish lower chapel is less impressive than the upper one, whose walls consist of little else but dazzling 13th-century stained glass. ✉ *In the Palais de Justice,* ☎ *01–43–54–30–09 for concert information.* 🎫 *32 frs.* ⏲ *Daily 9:30–6:30; Oct.–Mar. daily 10–5. Métro: Cité.*

61 **St-Étienne-du-Mont.** The ornate facade of this mainly 16th-century church combines Gothic, Baroque, and Renaissance elements. Inside, the curly, carved rood screen (1525–35), separating nave and chancel, is the only one of its kind in Paris. ✉ *pl. de l'Abbé-Basset. Métro: Cardinal-Lemoine.*

56 **St-Julien-le-Pauvre.** This tiny church was built at the same time as Notre-Dame (1165–1220). The church belongs to a Greek Orthodox order today, but was originally named for St-Julien, bishop of Le Mans, who was nicknamed Le Pauvre (The Poor) after he gave all his money away. ✉ *rue St-Julien-le-Pauvre. Métro: St-Michel.*

57 **St-Séverin.** This unusually wide, Flamboyant Gothic church dominates a Left Bank neighborhood filled with squares and pedestrian streets. Note the splendidly deviant spiraling column in the forest of pillars behind the altar. ✉ *rue des Prêtres St-Séverin.* ⏲ *Weekdays 11–5:30, Sat. 11–10. Métro: St-Michel.*

59 **La Sorbonne.** Named after Robert de Sorbon, a medieval canon who founded a theological college here in 1253, this is one of the oldest universities in Europe. The church and university buildings were restored by Cardinal Richelieu in the 17th century, and the maze of amphitheaters, lecture rooms, and laboratories, and the surrounding courtyards

and narrow streets, retain a hallowed air. You can visit the main courtyard on rue de la Sorbonne and peek into the main lecture hall, a major meeting point during the tumultuous student upheavals of 1968. The square is dominated by the noble university church with cupola and Corinthian columns. Inside is the white marble tomb of that ultimate crafty cleric, Cardinal Richelieu himself. ✉ *rue de la Sorbonne. Métro: Cluny–La Sorbonne.*

From Orsay to St-Germain

This walk covers the Left Bank, from the Musée d'Orsay in the stately 7th arrondissement, to the lively and colorful area around St-Germain-des-Prés in the 6th. In a daringly converted Belle Epoque rail station on the Seine, the Musée d'Orsay houses one of the world's most spectacular arrays of Impressionist paintings. Further along the river, the 18th-century Palais Bourbon, home to the National Assembly, sets the tone for the 7th. Luxurious ministries and embassies—including the Hôtel Matignon, residence of the French prime minister—line the surrounding streets, their majestic scale in total keeping with the Hôtel des Invalides, whose gold-leafed dome climbs heavenward above the regal tomb of Napoléon. The splendid Rodin Museum is only a short walk away.

To the east, away from the splendor of the 7th, the boulevard St-Michel slices the Left Bank in two: on one side, the Latin Quarter (☞ The Islands and Latin Quarter, *above*); on the other, the Faubourg St-Germain, named for St-Germain-des-Prés, the oldest church in Paris. The venerable church tower has long acted as beacon for intellectuals, most famously during the 1950s when Albert Camus, Jean-Paul Sartre, and Simone de Beauvoir ate and drank existentialism in the neighborhood cafés. Today most of the philosophizing is done by tourists, yet a wealth of bookshops, art stores, and antiques galleries ensure that "St-Germain" (as the area is commonly known) retains its highbrow appeal. To the south of St-Germain is the city's most famous and colorful park, the Jardin du Luxembourg.

A Good Walk

Get to the **Musée d'Orsay** ㊿ as early as possible to avoid the crowds who come to see its outstanding collection of art from 1848–1914. A good meeting point is the pedestrian square outside the museum, where huge bronze statues of an elephant and a rhinoceros disprove the idea that the French take their art *too* seriously. Head west along rue de Lille to the **Palais Bourbon** (68), home of the Assemblée Nationale (French Parliament).

Rue de l'Université leads from the Assemblée to the grassy Esplanade des Invalides and an encounter with the **Hôtel des Invalides** (69), founded by Louis XIV to house wounded (or "invalid") veterans. The most impressive dome in Paris towers over the church at the Invalides—the Église du Dôme. From the church, double back along boulevard des Invalides and take rue de Varenne to the Hôtel Biron, better known as the **Musée Rodin** (70), where you can see a fine collection of Auguste Rodin's emotionally charged statues. The quiet, distinguished 18th-century streets between the Rodin Museum and the Parliament are filled with embassies and ministries.

Continue on rue de Varrene to rue du Bac, turn left, then right onto rue de Grenelle, to the **Musée Maillol** (71), dedicated to the work of sculptor Aristide Maillol. Continue on rue de Grenelle past Edme Bouchardon's Fontaine des Quatre Saisons, to the carrefour de la Croix-Rouge, with its mighty bronze Centaur by the contemporary sculptor César. Take rue du Vieux-Colombier to place St-Sulpice, a spacious square ringed with cafés. Looming over the square is the enormous church of **St-Sulpice** (72).

Exit the church, head back across the square, and turn right on rue Bonaparte to reach **St-Germain-des-Prés** (73), Paris's oldest church. Across the cobbled place St-Germain-des-Prés is the café, Les Deux Magots, one of the principal haunts of the intelligentsia after WWII. Two doors down boulevard St-Germain is the Café de Flore, another popular spot with the likes of Jean-Paul Sartre and Simone de Beauvoir after the war. Follow rue de l'Abbaye, alongside the far side of the church, to rue de Furstemberg. The street opens out into a quiet square where you'll find Eugène Delacroix's studio, the **Atelier Delacroix** (74). Take a left on rue Jacob and turn right down rue Bonaparte to the **École Nationale des Beaux-Arts** (75), whose students can often be seen painting and sketching on the nearby quays and bridges.

Continue down to the Seine and turn right along the quai, past the **Institut de France** (76). With its distinctive dome and commanding position overlooking the Pont des Arts—a footbridge affording delightful views of the Louvre and Ile de la Cité—the Institute is one of the city's most impressive waterside sights. Continue along quai de Conti past the **Hôtel des Monnaies,** the national mint. Head up rue Dauphine. It's linked 150 yards up by the open-air passage Dauphine to rue Mazarine, which leads left to the carrefour de Buci, where you can find one of the best morning food markets in Paris. Rue de l'Ancienne-Comédie, so named because it was the first home of the legendary Comédie Française, leads up to busy place de l'Odéon. Cross boulevard St-Germain, and climb rue de l'Odéon to the colonnaded Théâtre de l'Odéon (☞ Nightlife and the Arts, *below*). Behind the theater lies the spacious **Jardin du Luxembourg** (77), one of the most stylish parks in the city.

TIMING

This 6½-km (4-mi) walk could take four hours to a couple of days, depending on how long you spend in the plethora of museums along the way. Aim for an early start—that way you can hit the Musée d'Orsay early, when crowds are smaller, then get to the rue de Buci street market in full swing, in the late afternoon (the stalls are generally closed for lunch until 3 PM). Note that the Hôtel des Invalides is open daily, but Orsay is closed Monday. You might consider returning to one or more museums on another day or night—Orsay is open late on Thursday evening.

Sights to See

74 **Atelier Delacroix.** The studio of artist Eugène Delacroix (1798–1863) contains only a small collection of his sketches and drawings. But those who feel the need to pay homage to France's foremost Romantic painter will want to visit. ✉ *6 rue Furstemberg,* ☎ *01–43–54–04–87.* 🎫 *15 frs, Sun. 10 frs.* ⏲ *Wed.–Mon. 9:45–5:15. Métro: St-Germain-des-Prés.*

75 **École Nationale des Beaux-Arts.** The National Fine Arts College occupies three large mansions near the Seine. The school—today the breeding ground for painters, sculptors, and architects—was once the site of a convent, founded in 1608. Only the church and cloister remained by the time the Beaux-Arts school was established in 1816. Wander into the courtyard and galleries of the school to see the casts and copies of the statues stored here for safekeeping during the Revolution. ✉ *14 rue Bonaparte.* ⏲ *Daily 1–7. Métro: St-Germain-des-Prés.*

NEED A BREAK? The popular **La Palette** café (✉ 43 rue de Seine, ☎ 01–43–26–68–15), on the corner of rue de Seine and rue Callot, has long been a favorite haunt of Beaux-Arts students.

69 **Hôtel des Invalides.** Les Invalides, as it is widely known, is an outstanding monumental Baroque ensemble, designed by Libéral Bruand in the 1670s at the behest of Louis XIV to house wounded, or "invalid," soldiers. Although no more than a handful of old timers live at the Invalides today, the military link remains in the form of the **Musée de l'Armée,** a military museum. The **Musée des Plans-Reliefs,** also housed here, contains a fascinating collection of old scale models of French towns. The 17th-century **Église St-Louis des Invalides** is the Invalides's original ★ church. More impressive is Jules Hardouin-Mansart's **Église du Dôme,** built onto the end of the church of St-Louis, but blocked off from it in 1793. The remains of Napoléon are here. ✉ *51 bis bd. de la Tour-Maubourg,* ☎ *01–44–42–37–67.* ⏲ *Daily 10–6 (Oct.–Mar. 10–5). Métro: Latour-Maubourg.*

Hôtel des Monnaies. Louis XVI transferred the Royal Mint to this imposing mansion in the late 18th century. Although the mint was moved again, to Pessac, near Bordeaux, in 1973, weights and measures, medals, and limited-edition coins are still made here. The **Musée de la Monnaie** (Coin Museum) has an extensive collection of coins, documents, engravings, and paintings. On Tuesday and Friday at 2 PM you can catch the coin metal craftsmen. ✉ *11 quai de Conti.* 🎫 *20 frs, Sun. 15 frs.* ⏲ *Tues., Thurs.–Sun. 1–6, Wed. 1–9. Métro: Pont-Neuf.*

76 **Institut de France.** The Institute is one of France's most revered cultural institutions and its curved, dome-topped facade is one of the Left Bank's most impressive waterside sights. It was built as a college in 1661; at the beginning of the 19th century, Napoléon had it transferred here from the Louvre. The Académie Française, the oldest of the five academies that compose the Institute, was created by Cardinal Richelieu in 1635. Its first major task was to edit the definitive French dictionary (which still isn't finished); it is also charged with safeguarding the purity of the French language. ✉ *pl. de l'Institut. Guided visits reserved for cultural associations only. Métro: Pont-Neuf.*

77 **Jardin du Luxembourg.** The Luxembourg Garden is one of the prettiest of Paris's few large parks. The fountains, ponds, trim hedges, precisely planted rows of trees, and gravel walks are typical of the French fondness for formal gardens. The 17th-century **Palais de Luxembourg,** overlooking the gardens, houses the French Senate; it is not open to the public. It was built, like the surrounding Luxembourg Garden, for Marie de' Medici, widow of Henri IV. It was not completed until 1627 and Marie lived there for just five years before being expelled from France by Cardinal Richelieu in 1632. *Métro: Odéon; RER: Luxembourg.*

71 **Musée Maillol.** Plaster casts and bronzes by Art Deco sculptor Aristide Maillol (1861–1944), whose sleek, stylized nudes adorn the Tuileries, can be admired at this handsome town lovingly restored by his former muse Dina Vierny. ✉ *61 rue de Grenelle,* ☎ *01–42–22–59–58.* 🎫 *40 frs.* ⏲ *Wed.–Mon. 11–6. Métro: Rue du Bac.*

67 **Musée d'Orsay.** In a stylishly converted train station, the Orsay Museum—devoted to the arts (mainly French) spanning the period 1848–1914—is one of the city's most popular museums. The main artistic attraction is the Impressionists: Renoir, Sisley, Pissarro, and Monet are all well represented. The post-Impressionists—Cézanne, van Gogh, Gauguin, and Toulouse-Lautrec—are also on the top floor. On the first floor, you'll find the work of Manet and the delicate nuances of Degas.

Those who prefer more academic paintings should look at Puvis de Chavannes's larger-than-life classical canvases. Those excited by more modern developments should look for the early-20th-century Fauves (meaning wild beasts, the name given them by an outraged critic in 1905)—particularly Matisse, Derain, and Vlaminck. Thought-provoking sculptures lurk at every turn. Two further highlights are the faithfully restored Belle Epoque restaurant and the model of the entire Opéra quarter, displayed beneath a glass floor. ⊠ *1 rue de Bellechasse,* ☎ *01–40–49–48–84.* 🎟 *36 frs, Sun. 24 frs.* ⏲ *Tues.–Sat. 10–6, Thurs. 10–9:30, Sun. 9–6. Métro: Solférino; RER: Musée d'Orsay.*

NEED A BREAK? Find respite from the overwhelming collection of art in the **Musée d'Orsay Café,** behind one of the giant station clocks, close to the Impressionist galleries on the top floor.

70 **Musée Rodin.** The 18th-century Hôtel Biron makes a gracious setting for the sculpture of Auguste Rodin (1840–1917). You'll doubtless recognize the seated *Thinker,* with his elbow resting on his knee, and the passionate *Kiss.* From the second-floor rooms, which contain some fine paintings by Rodin's friend Eugène Carrière (1849–1906), you can see the large garden behind the house. Don't go without visiting the garden: It is exceptional both for its rosebushes (more than 2,000 of them, representing 100 varieties) and for its sculpture. ⊠ *77 rue de Varenne,* ☎ *01–44–18–61–10.* 🎟 *28 frs, Sun. 18 frs.* ⏲ *Easter–Oct., Tues.–Sun. 10–6; Nov.–Easter, Tues.–Sun. 10–5. Métro: Varenne.*

68 **Palais Bourbon.** The most prominent feature of the home of the Assemblée Nationale (French Parliament) is its colonnaded facade, commissioned by Napoléon. ⊠ *pl. du Palais-Bourbon.* ⏲ *During temporary exhibits only. Métro: Assemblée Nationale.*

73 **St-Germain-des-Prés.** Paris's oldest church was first built to shelter a relic of the true cross, brought back from Spain in AD 542. The chancel was enlarged and the church then consecrated by Pope Alexander III in 1163; the tall, sturdy tower—a Left Bank landmark—dates from this period. The church stages superb organ concerts and recitals. ⊠ *pl. St-Germain.* ⏲ *Weekdays 8–7:30; weekends 8–9. Métro: St-Germain-des-Prés.*

72 **St-Sulpice.** Dubbed the Cathedral of the Left Bank, this enormous 17th-century church has entertained some unlikely christenings—the Marquis de Sade's and Charles Baudelaire's, for instance. The 18th-century facade was never finished, and its unequal towers add a playful touch to an otherwise sober design. ⊠ *pl. St-Sulpice. Métro: St-Sulpice.*

Montparnasse

A mile south of the Seine lies the district of Montparnasse, named after Mount Parnassus, the Greek mountain associated with the worship of Apollo and the Muses. Montparnasse's cultural heyday came in the first four decades of the 20th century, when it replaced Montmartre as *the* place for painters and poets to live, and prompted the launch of a string of arty brasseries along the district's main thoroughfare, the broad boulevard du Montparnasse.

The boulevard may lack poetic charm these days, but nightlife stays the pace as bars, clubs, restaurants, and cinemas crackle with energy beneath Europe's second tallest high-rise: the 59-story Tour Montparnasse. While the Tower itself is a typically bland product of the early 1970s, of note only for the view from the top, several more adventurous buildings have risen in its wake: Ricardo Bofil's semicircular Amphithéâtre housing complex, the glass-cubed Cartier center for contemporary art, and the Montparnasse train station with its giant glass facade and designer garden above the tracks.

If you have a deeper feel for history, you may prefer the sumptuous Baroque church of Val-de-Grâce or the quiet earth of Montparnasse cemetery, where Baudelaire, Sartre, Bartholdi (who designed the *Statue of Liberty*), and actress Jean Seberg slumber. After ignoring Hitler's orders to blow up the city, it was in Montparnasse that Governor von Choltitz signed the German surrender in August 1944.

A Good Walk

Walk or take the métro to the Vavin station (only three, short stops from St-Sulpice; *see* From Orsay to St-Germain, *above*), beneath Rodin's 10-foot statue of Balzac, at the corner of boulevards Raspail and Montparnasse. Four cafés, famous since Montparnasse's interwar heyday, are all within a stone's throw on boulevard du Montparnasse: the Café du Dôme at No. 108, La Coupole at No. 102; La Rotonde at No. 105, and La Sélect at No. 99. Head west along boulevard du Montparnasse to **place du 18-Juin-1940.** Towering above it is the **Tour Montparnasse** (78). Behind the skyscraper is the huge, gleaming glass facade of the Gare Montparnasse. Take boulevard Edgar-Quinet to the side of the tower and turn right onto rue de la Gaîté.

Cross avenue du Maine and follow rue Vercingétorix to **place de Catalogne** (79), dominated by the monumental curves of the postmodern Amphithéâtre housing complex. Explore its arcades and circular forecourts, and compare its impersonal grandeur with the cozy charm of Notre-Dame du Travail. As you reemerge from the Amphithéâtre, Pont des Cinq-Martyres leads left over the rail tracks of Montparnasse station. The tracks are hidden beneath a regimented park, the **Jardin Atlantique** (80). Rue Jean-Zay leads from place de Catalogne to the corner of the high-walled **Cimetière de Montparnasse** (81). Enter the cemetery down rue Froidevaux if you wish to pay homage to local and foreign worthies. Rue Froidevaux continues to place Denfert-Rochereau, where you can admire the huge bronze *Lion of Belfort* by Frédéric-Auguste Bartholdi.

Walk up boulevard Raspail, past the eye-catching glass cubicle that houses the **Fondation Cartier** (82). Take the third right onto rue Campagne-Première, a handsome street once inhabited by Picasso, Miró, Kandinsky, and Modigliani. Turn right at the bottom of the street onto boulevard du Montparnasse. At avenue de l'Observatoire stands perhaps the most famous bastion of Left Bank café culture, the Closerie des Lilas. Down avenue de l'Observatoire is the Observatoire de Paris, Louis XIV's astronomical observatory. In the other direction, the tree-lined avenue sweeps past the Fontaine de l'Observatoire. To the right of the fountain, down rue du Val-de-Grâce, is the imposing Baroque dome of the **Val de Grâce** (83) church. Straight ahead is the Jardin du Luxembourg (☞ From Orsay to St-Germain, *above*).

TIMING

The walk around Montparnasse is just under 5 km (3 mi) long and will comfortably take a morning or an afternoon if you choose to check out one of the historic cafés and the cemetery along the way.

Sights to See

81 **Cimetière de Montparnasse.** This cemetery is not picturesque, but it contains many of the quarter's most illustrious residents: Charles Baudelaire, Auguste Bartholdi, Jean-Paul Sartre, Man Ray, Samuel

Beckett, Jean Seberg, and Serge Gainsbourg. ⊠ *Entrances: rue Froidevaux, bd. Edgar-Quinet. Métro: Raspail, Gaîté.*

82 **Fondation Cartier.** Architect Jean Nouvel's eye-catching giant glass cubicle is a suitable setting for the temporary, thought-provoking shows of contemporary art organized here by jewelry giant Cartier. ⊠ *261 bd. Raspail,* ☎ *01–42–18–56–50.* 🎟 *30 frs.* ⏲ *Tues.–Sun. noon–8. Métro: Raspail.*

80 **Jardin Atlantique.** The Atlantic Garden, which opened in 1994, is a small park built over the tracks of Gare Montparnasse, featuring an assortment of trees and plants from countries on the Atlantic Ocean. ⊠ *pont des Cinq-Martyrs-du-Lycée-Buffon. Métro: Gaîté.*

79 **Place de Catalogne.** This square is dominated by Ricardo Boffil's monumental **Amphithéâtre** housing complex, with its chunky reinvention of classical detail; and the turn-of-the-century church of **Notre-Dame du Travail,** which made a powerful statement when it was built. Its riveted iron-and-steel framework was meant to symbolize the work ethos enshrouded in the church's name. *Métro: Gaîté.*

Place du 18-Juin-1940. This square beneath the Tour Montparnasse is named for the date of the radio speech Charles de Gaulle broadcast from London, urging the French to resist the Germans after the Nazi invasion of May 1940. And it was here that German military governor Dietrich von Choltitz surrendered to the Allies in August 1944, ignoring Hitler's orders to destroy the city as he withdrew. A plaque on the wall commemorates the event. ⊠ *Métro: Montparnasse-Bienvenue.*

78 **Tour Montparnasse.** As Europe's second tallest skyscraper, completed in 1973, this 685-foot tower offers a stupendous view of Paris from its open-air roof terrace. If you go to the top-floor bar for drinks, the ride up is free. Fifty-two of the 59 stories are taken up by offices, and a vast commercial complex, including a Galeries Lafayette department store, spreads over the first floor. Banal by day, the tower becomes Montparnasse's neon-lit beacon at night. ⊠ *33 av. du Maine.* 🎟 *42 frs.* ⏲ *Apr.–Sept., daily 9:30 AM–11:30 PM; Oct.–Mar., Sun.–Thurs. 9:30 AM–10:30 PM, Fri.–Sat. 9:30 AM–11 PM. Métro: Montparnasse-Bienvenue.*

83 **Val de Grâce.** This imposing 17th-century Left Bank church, extensively restored in the early 1990s, was commissioned by Anne of Austria and designed by François Mansart. Its powerfully rhythmic two-story facade rivals the Dôme Church at the Invalides as the city's most striking example of Italianate Baroque. ⊠ *1 pl. Alphonse-Laveran. RER: Port-Royal.*

Montmartre

On a dramatic rise above the city is Montmartre, site of the Sacré-Coeur basilica and home to a once-thriving artistic community. Although the fabled nightlife of old Montmartre has fizzled down to some glitzy nightclubs and porn shows, Montmartre still exudes history and Gallic charm.

Windmills once dotted Montmartre (often referred to by Parisians as *La Butte,* meaning "mound"). They were set up here not just because the hill was a good place to catch the wind—at more than 300 feet, it's the highest point in the city—but because Montmartre was covered with wheat fields and quarries right up to the end of the 19th century. Today, only two of the original 20 windmills remain.

Visiting Montmartre means negotiating a lot of steep streets and flights of steps. The crown atop this urban peak, Sacré-Coeur, is something of an architectural oddity. It has been called everything from grotesque to sublime; its silhouette, viewed from afar at dusk or sunrise, looks more like a mosque than a cathedral.

A Good Walk

Set off from **place Blanche** (84): Just off of it, on boulevard de Clichy, is the **Moulin Rouge** (85), the windmill turned dance hall, immortalized by Toulouse-Lautrec. Walk up rue Lepic, to the right of the Moulin Rouge, and wind your way up to the **Moulin de la Galette** (86), atop its leafy hillock opposite rue Tholozé, once a path over the hill. Turn right down rue Tholozé, past Studio 28, the first cinema built expressly for experimental films.

Continue down rue Tholozé to rue des Abbesses, and turn left toward the triangular **place des Abbesses** (87). Follow rue Ravignan as it climbs north, via place Emile-Goudeau, an enchanting little cobbled square, to the **Bateau-Lavoir** (88), or Boat Wash House, at its northern edge. Painters Picasso and Braque had studios in the original building; this drab concrete building was built in its place. Continue up the hill via rue de la Mire to place Jean-Baptiste Clément, where Amedeo Modigliani had a studio.

The upper reaches of rue Lepic lead to rue Norvins, formerly rue des Moulins (Windmill Street). At the end of the street, to the left, is stylish avenue Junot. Continue right past the bars and tourist shops until you reach famous **place du Tertre** (89). Around the corner on rue Poulbot, the **Espace Dali** (90) houses works by Salvador Dali, who once had a studio in the area. Return to place du Tertre. Looming menacingly behind is the scaly white dome of the Basilique du **Sacré-Coeur** (91). The cavernous interior is worth visiting for its golden mosaics; climb to the top of the dome for the view of Paris.

Walk back toward place du Tertre. Turn right onto rue du Mont-Cenis and left onto rue Cortot, site of the **Musée du Vieux Montmartre** (92), which, like the Bateau-Lavoir, once sheltered an illustrious group of painters, writers, and assorted cabaret artists. Another famous Montmartre landmark is at No. 22: the bar-cabaret **Lapin Agile** (93). Opposite the Lapin Agile is the tiny Cimetière St-Vincent where painter Maurice Utrillo is buried.

TIMING

Reserve four to five hours for this 4-km (2½-mi) walk: Many of the streets are steep and slow. Include half an hour each at Sacré-Coeur and the museums (the Dali museum is open daily, but the Montmartre museum is closed Monday).

From Easter through September, Montmartre is besieged by tourists. Two hints to avoid the worst of the rush: Come on a gray day, when Montmartre's sullen-tone facades suffer less than most in the city; or during the afternoon, and return to place du Tertre (maybe via the funicular) by the early evening, once the tourist buses have departed. More festive times of the year are June 24, when fireworks and street concerts are staged around Montmartre, or on the first weekend of October for the revelry that accompanies the wine harvest at the vineyard on rue des Saules.

Sights to See

88 **Bateau-Lavoir.** Montmartre poet Max Jacob coined the name, meaning Boat Wash House, for the original building on this site (which burned down in 1970), saying it resembled a boat and that the warren of artists'

studios within was perpetually paint-splattered and in need of a good hosing down. It was here that Pablo Picasso and Georges Braque made their first bold stabs at the concept of Cubism. The new building also contains art studios, but is the epitome of poured concrete drabness. ✉ *13 pl. Émile-Goudeau. Métro: Abbesses.*

90 **Espace Dali.** Some of Salvador Dali's less familiar works are among the 25 sculptures and 300 prints housed in this museum with an atmosphere that is meant to approximate the surreal experience. ✉ *11 rue Poulbot,* ☎ *01–42–64–40–10.* 🎫 *35 frs.* ⏲ *Daily 10–6; summer, daily 10–8. Métro: Abbesses.*

93 **Lapin Agile.** This bar-cabaret, originally one of the raunchiest haunts in Montmartre, got its curious name—the Nimble Rabbit—when the owner, André Gill, hung up a sign of a laughing rabbit jumping out of a saucepan clutching a bottle of wine. Locals christened it the Lapin à Gill, meaning Gill's Rabbit. When, in 1886, it was sold to cabaret singer Jules Jouy, he called it the Lapin Agile, which has the same pronunciation in French as Lapin à Gill. In 1903 the premises were bought by the most celebrated cabaret entrepreneur of them all, Aristide Bruand, portrayed by Toulouse-Lautrec in a series of famous posters. ✉ *22 rue des Saules,* ☎ *01–46–06–85–87. Métro: Lamarck-Caulaincourt.*

86 **Moulin de la Galette.** This is one of two remaining windmills in Montmartre. It was once the focal point of an open-air cabaret (made famous in a painting by Renoir), and rumor has it that the miller, Debray, was strung up on its sails and spun to death after striving vainly to defend it against invading Cossacks in 1814. Unfortunately, it is privately owned and can only be admired from the street below. ✉ *rue Tholozé. Métro: Abbesses.*

85 **Moulin Rouge.** This world-famous cabaret was built in 1885 as a windmill, then transformed into a dance hall in 1900. Those wild, early days were immortalized by Toulouse-Lautrec in his posters and paintings. It still trades shamelessly on the notion of Paris as a city of sin: If you fancy a Vegas-style night out, this is the place to go. ✉ *82 bd. de Clichy,* ☎ *01–46–06–00–19. Métro: Blanche.*

92 **Musée du Vieux Montmartre.** In its turn-of-the-century heyday, Montmartre's historical museum was home to an illustrious group of painters, writers, and assorted cabaret artists. Foremost among them were Renoir and Maurice Utrillo. The museum also provides a view of the tiny **vineyard**—the only one in Paris—on neighboring rue des Saules. A symbolic 125 gallons of wine are still produced every year. ✉ *12 rue Cortot,* ☎ *01–46–06–61–11.* 🎫 *25 frs.* ⏲ *Tues.–Sun. 11–6. Métro: Lamarck-Caulaincourt.*

87 **Place des Abbesses.** This triangular square is typical of the picturesque, slightly countrified style that has made Montmartre famous. The entrance to the Abbesses métro station, a curving, sensuous mass of delicate iron, is one of the two original Art Nouveau entrance canopies left in Paris. *Métro: Abbesses.*

84 **Place Blanche.** The name—White Square—comes from the clouds of chalky dust that used to be churned up by the carts that carried wheat and crushed flour from the nearby windmills, including the Moulin Rouge. *Métro: Blanche.*

89 **Place du Tertre.** This tumbling square (*tertre* means hillock) regains its village atmosphere only in the winter, when the branches of the plane-trees sketch traceries against the sky. At any other time of year you'll be confronted by crowds of tourists and a swarm of artists clamoring to do your portrait. If one produces an unsolicited portrait, you are

Montmartre

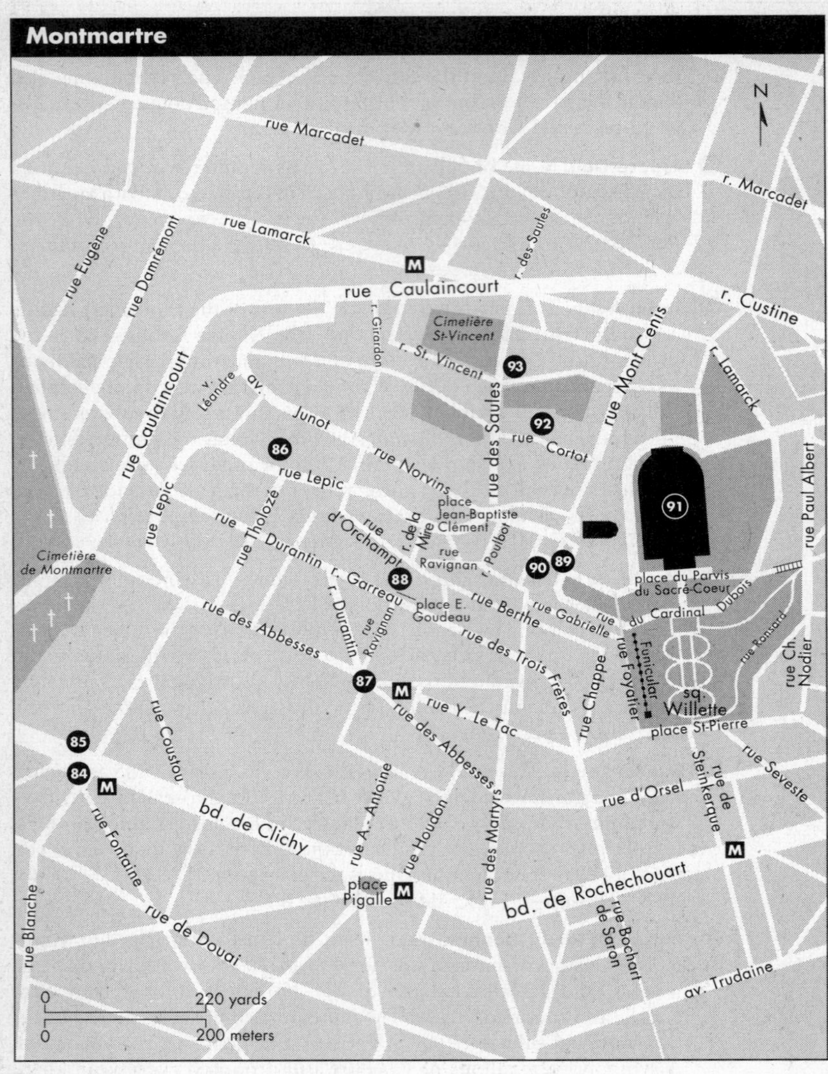

Bateau-Lavoir, **88**
Espace Dali, **90**
Lapin Agile, **93**
Moulin de la Galette, **86**
Moulin Rouge, **85**
Musée du Vieux Montmartre, **92**
Place des Abbesses, **87**
Place Blanche, **84**
Place du Tertre, **89**
Sacré-Coeur, **91**

not obligated to buy it. La Mère Catherine, on one corner of the square, was a favorite with the Russian Cossacks who occupied Paris in 1814. *Métro: Abbesses.*

NEED A BREAK? **Patachou** (✉ 9 pl. du Tertre, ☎ 01–42–51–06–06) sounds the one classy note on place du Tertre, offering exquisite, if expensive, cakes and teas.

91 **Sacré-Coeur.** The Sacred Heart Basilica was erected as a sort of national guilt offering in expiation for the blood shed during the Commune and Franco-Prussian War in 1870–71, and was largely financed by French Catholics fearful of an anticlerical backlash under the new republican regime. The basilica was not consecrated until 1919. Stylistically, the Sacré-Coeur borrows elements from Romanesque and Byzantine models; the effect is strangely disjointed and unsettling. The gloomy, cavernous interior is worth visiting for its golden mosaics; climb to the top of the dome for the view of Paris. ✉ *pl. du Parvis-du-Sacré-Coeur. Métro: Anvers.*

DINING

Updated by Alexander Lobrano

This listing includes restaurants of a variety of styles and price levels, from formal dining rooms serving haute cuisine to cheery bistros offering classical cooking. Generally, Paris restaurants are open from noon to about 2 and from 7:30 or 8 to 10 or 10:30. It's best to make reservations, particularly in summer, although the reviews only state when reservations are absolutely essential. If you want no-smoking seating, make this clear; the mandatory no-smoking area is sometimes limited to a very few tables. Brasseries have longer hours and often serve all day and late into the evening; some are open 24 hours. Assume a restaurant is open every day unless otherwise indicated. Surprisingly, many prestigious restaurants close on Saturday as well as Sunday. July and August are the most common months for annual closings, although Paris in August is no longer the wasteland it used to be.

Most restaurants offer two basic types of menu: à la carte and *prix-fixe* (fixed-price, or *un menu*), which is usually the best value, though choices are limited. Most menus begin with a first course, followed by fish and poultry, then meat; it's rare today that anyone orders something from all three. However, outside of brasseries, wine bars, and other simple places, it's inappropriate to order just one dish, as you'll understand when you see the waiter's expression. The popular *menu dégustation,* with many small courses, allows for a wide sampling of the chef's offerings. In general, consider the season and the daily specials when ordering (for help, *see* the Menu Guide at the end of this book).

Although prices include tax and tip, pocket change left on the table in simple places, or an additional 5% in better restaurants, is appreciated. Places where a jacket and tie are de rigueur are noted. Otherwise, use common sense—jeans and T-shirts are not suitable in Paris restaurants, nor are shorts or running clothes, except in the most casual bistros.

CATEGORY	COST*
$$$$	over 550 frs
$$$	300 frs–550 frs
$$	175 frs–300 frs
$	under 175 frs

**per person for a three-course meal, including 20.6% tax and service but not drinks*

1er Arrondissement

$$ ✕ **Restaurant du Palais-Royal.** Tucked away in the northern corner of the magnificent Palais-Royal garden, this pleasant bistro has a charming terrace and good food. A salad of baby scallops and pleurotus mushrooms in a balsamic vinaigrette are among the interesting contemporary dishes. ✉ *Jardin du Palais-Royal, 110 Galerie Valois,* ☏ *01–40–20–00–27. AE, MC, V. Closed Sun. No lunch Sat. Métro: Palais-Royal.*

$–$$ ✕ **Aux Crus de Bourgogne.** The din of a happy crowd fills this delightful, old-fashioned bistro with bright lights and red-checkered tablecloths. It opened in 1932 and quickly became popular by serving two luxury items—foie gras and cold lobster with homemade mayonnaise—at surprisingly low prices, a tradition that happily continues. ✉ *3 rue Bachaumont,* ☏ *01–42–33–48–24. V. Closed weekends and Aug. Métro: Sentier.*

$ ✕ **Le Moi.** At this superb Vietnamese restaurant, feast on *nems* (deep-fried mini spring rolls) and steamed dumplings. The poultry, beef, or seafood salads are enlivened with fresh Asian herbs like lemongrass and lemon basil. Service is prompt and friendly. ✉ *5 rue Danou,* ☏ *01–47–03–92–05. MC, V. Closed Sun. No lunch Sat. Métro: Opéra.*

2e Arrondissement

$–$$ ★ ✕ **Le Brin de Zinc et Madame.** A bustling old-fashioned bistro with a diverse, lively crowd, Le Brin is ideal for an easygoing night on the town. The decor and the service are a bit rough-and-tumble, but the food is delicious and generously portioned. Salads are huge, fresh, and interesting. Main dishes, such as grilled salmon or roast chicken, are served with sautéed potatoes and vegetables. Tarts are homemade. ✉ *50 rue Montorgueil,* ☏ *01–42–21–10–80. AE, MC, V. No lunch Sun. Métro: Étienne-Marcel.*

3e Arrondissement

$ ✕ **Au Bascou.** Gregarious proprietor Jean-Guy Lousteau enthusiastically shares his knowledge of the wines of southwest France at this fashionable little bistro with mosaics made of broken mirrors. The sturdy, savory cuisine of the Basque country stars on the menu, and the country ham, cod with broccoli puree, and sautéed baby squid are particularly flavorful. ✉ *38 rue Réaumur,* ☏ *01–42–72–69–25. MC, V. Closed weekends. Métro: Arts et Métiers.*

$ ✕ **Chez Omar.** This is the place for couscous, the signature North African dish. Order it with grilled skewered lamb, *merguez* (spicy, red) sausage, a lamb shank, or chicken—portions are generous. The restaurant, in a former turn-of-the-century bistro, is popular with a fashionable crowd. Proprietor Omar Guerida is famously friendly and speaks English. ✉ *47 rue de Bretagne,* ☏ *01–42–72–36–26. MC, V. No lunch Sun. Métro: Filles du Calvaire.*

4e Arrondissement

$$ ✕ **Le Vieux Bistro.** Overlook the touristy location next to Notre-Dame and the corny name, "the old bistro." This place really *is* generations old, and its menu is full of bistro classics, such as beef fillet with marrow, éclairs, and tart Tatin. The decor is nondescript, but the frequently fancy crowd doesn't seem to notice. ✉ *14 rue du Cloître-Notre-Dame,* ☏ *01–43–54–18–95. MC, V. Métro: Hôtel de Ville.*

$ ✕ **Baracane.** The owner of this small, simple place oversees the menu of robust specialties of his native southwest France, including rabbit confit, veal tongue, and pear poached in wine and cassis. The prix-fixe menus make it one of the best values in the Marais. Service is friendly. ✉ *38 rue des Tournelles,* ☏ *01–42–71–43–33. MC, V. Closed Sun. No lunch Sat. Métro: Bastille.*

5e Arrondissement

$$ ✕ **Campagne et Provence.** On the quai across from Notre-Dame, this very pleasant little restaurant with rustic Provençal fabrics and blue grass-cloth wallpaper has a Provençal menu that includes grilled John Dory with preserved fennel, and peppers stuffed with cod and eggplant. In season try the outstanding roasted figs with shortbread and black-currant sauce for dessert. ✉ *25 quai de la Tournelle,* ☏ *01–43–54–05–17. MC, V. Closed Sun. No lunch Sat., Mon. Métro: Maubert-Mutualité.*

$ ★ ✕ **Chantairelle.** Not only is delicious south-central Auvergne cuisine served at this restaurant, but the owners also offer a full regional experience. Hence the decor: recycled barn timbers and essential oils diffusing local scents. The food is hearty and the portions of stuffed cabbage and *potée,* a casserole of pork and vegetables in broth, copious. Have a bottle of Châteauguy, a regional red, and finish up with a blueberry tart. ✉ *17 rue Laplace,* ☏ *01–46–33–18–59. MC, V. Closed Sun. No lunch Sat. Métro: Maubert-Mutualité.*

6e Arrondissement

$$ ✕ **L'Epi Dupin.** Half-timber walls, sisal carpeting, and crisp white table linens are the backdrop for this bistro that draws a loyal clientele. The menu of delicious and reasonably priced French classics is revised regularly and might include mixed green salad garnished with foie gras and fillet of lamb with ratatouille. Bread and pastries are baked on the premises. The prix-fixe menu is an excellent option, and the waiters are friendly. ✉ *11 rue Dupin,* ☏ *01–42–22–64–56. Reservations essential. MC, V. Closed Sun. Métro: Sèvres-Babylone.*

7e Arrondissement

$$$–$$$$ ✕ **Paul Minchelli.** Don't come to this very sleek, chic restaurant expecting elaborate sauces—Minchelli is a minimalist who believes that seasonings should not distract from the taste of his impeccably fresh catch-of-the-day. The baby clams with garlic and fiery *espelette* peppers as well as the sea bass drizzled with lemon and olive oil are just a few of his wonderful dishes. ✉ *54 bd. de La Tour-Maubourg,* ☏ *01–47–05–89–86. MC, V. Closed Sun., Mon. Métro: École Militaire.*

$–$$ ✕ **Au Bon Accueil.** If you want to see what well-heeled Parisians like to eat these days, book a table at this popular bistro as soon as you get to town. The excellent, reasonably priced *cuisine du marché* (daily menu based on what's in the markets) has made it a hit, as have the delicious, homemade desserts. ✉ *14 rue de Montessuy,* ☏ *01–47–05–46–11. Reservations essential. MC, V. Closed Sun. Métro, RER: Pont de l'Alma.*

8e Arrondissement

$$$$ ✕ **Ledoyen.** Chef Ghislaine Arabian has set gastronomic fashion by concentrating on northern French cuisine and creating specialties with beer sauces, such as *coquilles St-Jacques à la bière* (scallops in beer). The elegant restaurant has gilded ceilings and walls, plush armchairs, and tables with candelabra. ✉ *1 av. du Tuit, on the Carré des Champs-Elysées,* ☏ *01–47–42–23–23. Reservations essential. AE, DC, MC, V. Closed weekends. Métro: Place de la Concorde or Champs-Elysées–Clemenceau.*

$$$$ ★ ✕ **Pierre Gagnaire.** Legendary chef Pierre Gagnaire's cooking is at once intellectual and poetic—in a single dish he sensationally brings together at least three or four unexpected tastes and textures. Two intriguing dishes from a recent menu—it changes seasonally—included duck foie gras wrapped in bacon and lacquered like a Chinese duck, and sea bass smothered in herbs with tiny clams. The *Grand Dessert,* a five-course presentation of desserts, is not to be missed. The only drawback is the

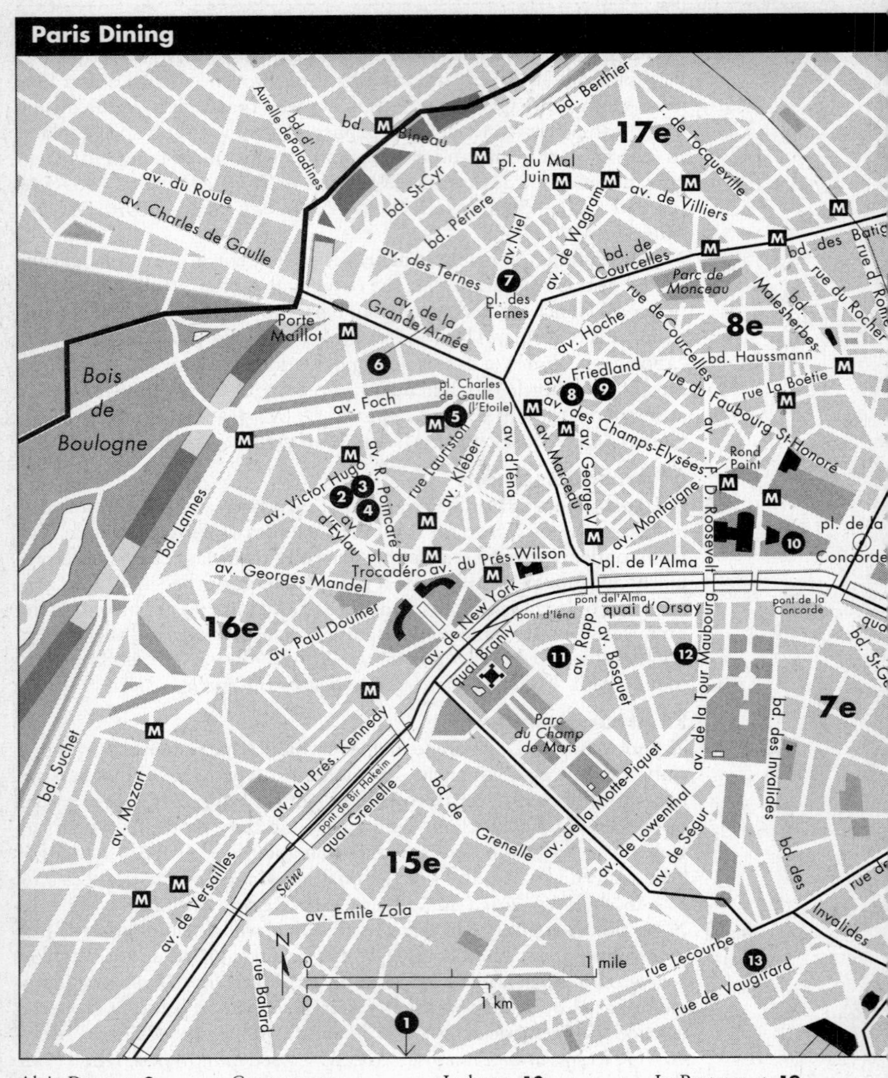

Alain Ducasse, **3**
Au Bascou, **25**
Au Bon Accueil, **11**
Au Trou Gascon, **30**
Aux Crus de Bourgogne, **23**
Baracane, **27**
Le Brin de Zinc et Madame, **24**
Brasserie Flo, **22**
Campagne et Provence, **32**
Chantairelle, **33**
Chardenoux, **28**
Chartier, **18**
Chez Jean, **21**
Chez Michel, **20**
Chez Omar, **26**
La Dinée, **1**
L'Epi Dupin, **15**
Guy Savoy, **7**
Ledoyen, **10**
Le Moi, **17**
Le Petit Rétro, **2**
Le Relais du Parc, **4**
Paul Minchelli, **12**
Philippe DeTourbe, **13**
Pierre Gagnaire, **8**
Prunier, **5**
La Régalade, **14**
Le Restaurant, **19**
Restaurant du Palais-Royal, **16**
Le Square Trousseau, **29**
Taillevent, **9**
Le Terroir, **34**
Le Timgad, **6**
Le Vieux Bistrot, **31**

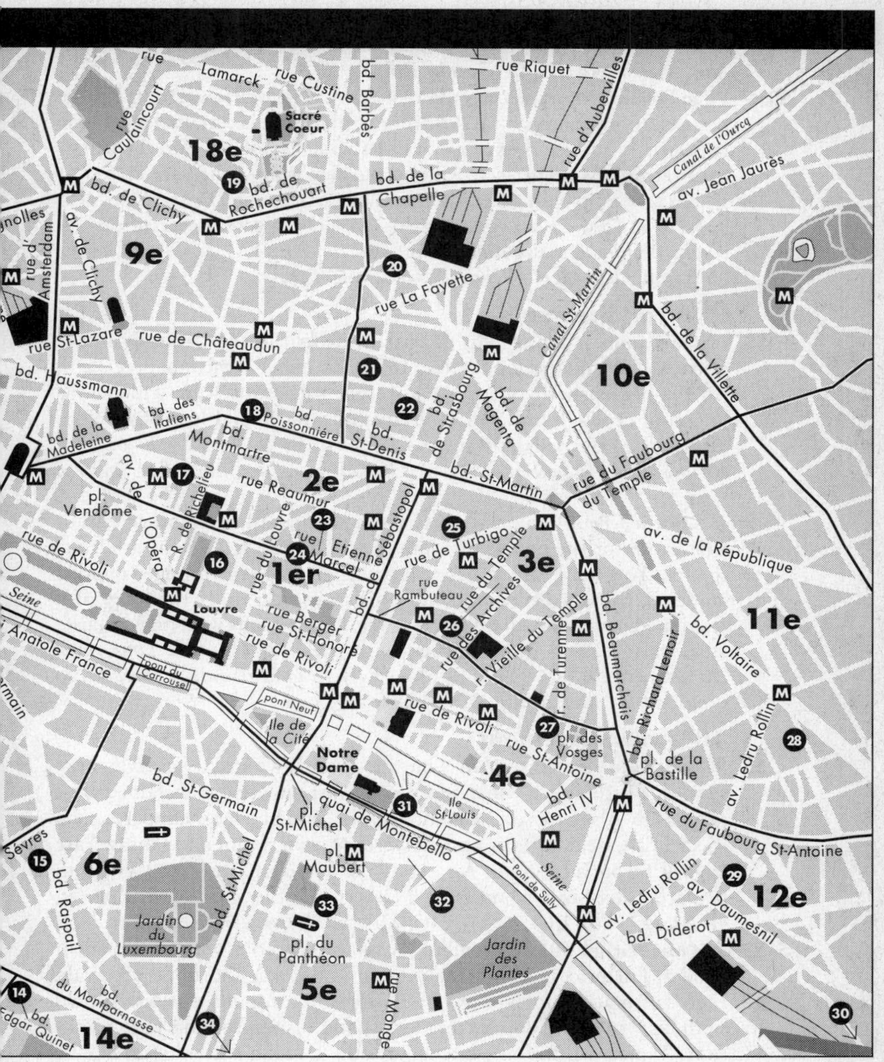
rue Lamarck
rue Custine
bd. Barbès
rue Riquet
rue d'Aubervilles
Canal de l'Ourcq
av. Jean Jaurès
rue Caulaincourt
Sacré Coeur
18e
19
bd. de Rochechouart
bd. de la Chapelle
bd. de Clichy
9e
av. de Clichy
rue d'Amsterdam
20
rue La Fayette
Canal St-Martin
bd. de la Villette
rue St-Lazare
rue de Châteaudun
bd. Haussmann
21
22
10e
bd. des Italiens
18
bd. Poissonnière
bd. St-Denis
bd. de Strasbourg
bd. de Magenta
bd. de la Madeleine
bd. Montmartre
17
av. de l'Opéra
R. de Richelieu
rue Reaumur
2e
bd. St-Martin
rue du Faubourg du Temple
pl. Vendôme
23
25
rue de Turbigo
rue du Temple
3e
av. de la République
rue de Rivoli
16
rue du Louvre
rue Etienne Marcel
24
1er
bd. de Sébastopol
rue Rambuteau
Seine
Louvre
rue Berger
rue St-Honoré
rue de Rivoli
26
rue des Archives
r. Vieille du Temple
r. de Turenne
bd. Beaumarchais
bd. Richard Lenoir
11e
bd. Voltaire
Anatole France
pont du Carrousel
pont Neuf
Ile de la Cité
rue de Rivoli
27
pl. des Vosges
av. Ledru Rollin
28
Notre Dame
rue St-Antoine
4e
pl. de la Bastille
bd. St-Germain
pl. St-Michel
quai de Montebello
31
Ile St-Louis
bd. Henri IV
rue du Faubourg St-Antoine
Sèvres
15
6e
pl. Maubert
Pont de Sully
Seine
29
av. Ledru Rollin
av. Daumesnil
12e
bd. Raspail
bd. St-Michel
Jardin du Luxembourg
33
32
pl. du Panthéon
Jardin des Plantes
bd. Diderot
5e
rue Monge
14
bd. du Montparnasse
bd. Edgar Quinet
14e
34
30

amateurish service and the puzzlingly brief wine list. ✉ *6 rue de Balzac,* ☎ *01–44–35–18–25. Reservations essential. AE, DC, MC, V. Closed Sun. Métro: Charles-de-Gaulle–Étoile.*

$$$$ ✕ **Taillevent.** Many say it's the best restaurant in Paris. Dining in the paneled rooms of this mid-19th-century mansion is certainly a sublime experience. Service is exceptional, the wine list stellar, and the classical French cuisine perfect. Among the signature dishes are cream of watercress soup with caviar and truffled tart of game. Desserts are also superb. ✉ *15 rue Lamennais,* ☎ *01–45–63–39–94. Reservations 3–4 wks in advance essential. Jacket and tie. AE, MC, V. Closed weekends and Aug. Métro: Charles-de-Gaulle–Étoile.*

9e Arrondissement

$$ ✕ **Chez Jean.** Young, stylish Parisians delight in the creativity of the talented chef and the good-value, 165-franc menu at this small, relaxed, off-the-beaten-path place. Some recent selections were a delicious cream of cèpes, John Dory in a crust of potato, and luscious chocolate-and-tea quenelles. ✉ *52 rue Lamartine,* ☎ *01–48–78–62–73. Reservations essential. MC, V. Closed Sun. No lunch Sat. Métro: Cadet.*

$ ✕ **Chartier.** People come to this cavernous turn-of-the-century restaurant more for the bonhomie than the food, which is often rather ordinary. You may find yourself sharing a table with budget-minded students, solitary bachelors, and tourists as you study the long, old-fashioned menu of such favorites as hard-boiled eggs with mayonnaise, steak tartare, and roast chicken with fries. ✉ *7 rue du Faubourg-Montmartre,* ☎ *01–47–70–86–29. Reservations not accepted. No credit cards. Métro: Rue Montmartre.*

10e Arrondissement

$$ ✕ **Brasserie Flo.** This place is hard to find down its passageway near Gare de l'Est, but it's worth the effort. The rich wood and stained glass is typically Alsatian, service is enthusiastic, and brasserie standards such as shellfish, steak tartare, and *choucroute* (sauerkraut and sausage) are savory. Order a carafe of Alsatian wine. It's open until 1:30 AM, with a special night-owl menu from 11 PM. ✉ *7 cour des Petites Écuries,* ☎ *01–47–70–13–59. AE, DC, MC, V. Métro: Château d'Eau.*

$–$$ ✕ **Chez Michel.** If you're willing to go out of your way for excellent food at fair prices, even if the decor and the neighborhood are drab, then this place is for you. Chef Thierry Breton pulls a stylish crowd with his wonderful cuisine du marché and dishes from his native Brittany. Typical of Breton's kitchen are the lasagna stuffed with chèvre cheese and the artichokes and tuna steak with pureed peas. ✉ *10 rue Belzunce,* ☎ *01–44–53–06–20. Reservations essential. MC, V. Closed Sun., Mon. No lunch Sat. Métro: Gare du Nord.*

11e Arrondissement

$$ ✕ **Chardenoux.** A bit off the beaten path but well worth the effort, this cozy neighborhood bistro with etched-glass windows, dark bentwood furniture, and a long zinc bar attracts a cross-section of savvy Parisians. The traditional cooking is first-rate: delicious salads, such as the green beans and foie gras, veal chops with morels, game dishes, savory desserts, and a nicely chosen wine list. ✉ *1 rue Jules-Valles,* ☎ *01–43–71–49–52. AE, V. Closed weekends and Aug. Métro: Charonne.*

12e Arrondissement

$$$ ✕ **Au Trou Gascon.** At this successful Belle Epoque establishment off the place Daumesnil, owner Alain Dutournier serves his version of the cuisine of Gascony—a region of outstanding ham, foie gras, lamb, and poultry—and his classic white-chocolate mousse. ✉ *40 rue Taine,* ☎

01–43–44–34–26. AE, DC, MC, V. Closed weekends, Christmas wk, and Aug. Métro: Daumesnil.

$$ ✕ **Le Square Trousseau.** Since fashion designer Jean-Paul Gaultier moved his headquarters nearby, this charming turn-of-the-century bistro has become very chic. You might see a supermodel or two while dining on the homemade foie gras and tender baby chicken with mustard and bread-crumb crust. The house wine is a good value, especially the Morgon, a fruity red. ✉ *1 rue Antoine Vollon,* ☏ *01–43–44–06–00. MC, V. Métro: Ledru-Rollin.*

13e Arrondissement

$ ✕ **Le Terroir.** A jolly crowd of regulars makes this little bistro festive. The solidly classical menu, based on first-rate ingredients from all over France, offers salads with chicken livers or fresh marinated anchovies, and calves' liver or monkfish with saffron. The pears marinated in wine are excellent for dessert. ✉ *11 bd. Arago,* ☏ *01–47–07–36–99. Closed Sun. No lunch Sat. Métro: Les Gobelins.*

14e Arrondissement

$ ✕ **La Régalade.** This is one of the most talked about restaurants in Paris. The location, in a remote, colorless residential neighborhood, is a nuisance, but Yves Camdeborde's cooking is stunning. Although a veteran of the Crillon, he has kept his prices remarkably low for a three-course feast. Tables are booked far in advance, but service does continue until midnight, and you can often sneak in late in the evening. ✉ *49 av. Jean-Moulin,* ☏ *01–45–45–68–58. Reserve 1 month in advance. MC, V. Closed Sun., Mon., Aug. No lunch Sat. Métro: Alésia.*

15e Arrondissement

$$ ✕ **La Dinée.** Chef Christophe Chabanel's restaurant in this rather remote location is filled noon and night by a crowd of stylish regulars who come to be surprised by his culinary creativity. Signature dishes include fillet of sole with baby shrimp and chicken medallions with peppers in a corn vinaigrette. The dining room, with blue print fabrics and wooden tub chairs, is simple; service is professional. ✉ *85 rue Leblanc,* ☏ *01–45–54–20–49. V. Closed weekends. Métro: Balard.*

$$ ★ ✕ **Philippe Detourbe.** Sample Detourbe's spectacular food at remarkably good prices amidst black lacquer, mirrors, and Burgundy velvet upholstery. The menu of contemporary French cooking changes with every meal and may include smoked salmon filled with cabbage *rémoulade* (creamy dressing) or cod steak with white beans and carmelized endives. Desserts are fantastic. The wine list is brief but well chosen and the service friendly and efficient. ✉ *8 rue Nicolas Charlet,* ☏ *01–42–19–08–59. Reservations essential. MC, V. Closed Sun. No lunch Sat. Métro: Pasteur.*

16e Arrondissement

$$$$ ✕ **Alain Ducasse.** Since he took over from Joel Robuchon, Ducasse has surprised everyone by serving resolutely classical French dishes. One does not feel, however, that this is the pinnacle of French dining, as one did with Robuchon. Ducasse is a marvelous cook, but dishes like a pastry case filled with mushrooms, shrimps, and frog's legs or duckling steamed with anise, satisfy rather than excite. Still you can get a solidly luxurious meal, though you'll have to forgive the robotlike service and the staggeringly expensive menu; the 480-franc lunch menu is your best bet. ✉ *59 av. Raymond-Poincare,* ☏ *01–47–27–12–27. Reservations several months in advance essential. AE, DC, MC, V. Closed Sat., Sun. Métro: Victor Hugo.*

$$–$$$ ✕ **Prunier.** Founded in 1925, this seafood restaurant is one of the best—and surely the prettiest—in Paris. The famous Art Deco mosaics glitter and the white marble counters shine with the impeccably fresh

shellfish displayed like precious jewels. The kitchen not only excels at classic French fish cooking but has added some interesting dishes, like a *Saintongeaise* plate—raw oysters with grilled sausages—eaten in Bordeaux. ✉ *16 av. Victor Hugo,* ☎ *01–44–17–35–85. Reservations essential in upstairs dining room. Jacket and tie. AE, DC, MC, V. Closed Sun., Mon. Métro: Étoile.*

$$ ✕ **Le Relais du Parc.** This bistro-annex is the place to try a lighter version of Alain Ducasse's cooking for less. Two delicious starters—the lobster salad and the baby potatoes with black truffles in a creamy oxtail-stock sauce—make good meals, followed by cheese or dessert. Main courses are also excellent, but the desserts could be better and wine is overpriced. ✉ *55 av. Raymond-Poincare,* ☎ *01–44–05–66–10. Reservations essential. AE, DC, MC, V. Métro: Victor Hugo.*

$ ✕ **Le Petit Rétro.** Two types of clientele—men in expensive suits at noon and well-dressed couples in the evening—frequent this immaculate little bistro with art nouveau tiles and bentwood furniture. You can't go wrong with the daily special, which is written on a chalkboard presented by one of the friendly waitresses. Come when you want a good solid meal, like the perfect *pavé de boeuf* (thick steak) accompanied by au gratin potatoes and some deliciously caramelized braised endive. ✉ *5 rue Mesnil,* ☎ *01–44–05–06–05. MC, V. Closed Sun. No lunch Mon. Métro: Victor Hugo.*

17ᵉ Arrondissement

$$$$ ✕ **Guy Savoy.** Top chef Guy Savoy's other five bistros have not distracted him too much from his handsome luxury restaurant near the Arc de Triomphe. The oysters in aspic, sea bass with spices, and grilled pigeon reveal the magnitude of his talent. His mille-feuille is a contemporary classic. ✉ *18 rue Troyon,* ☎ *01–43–80–40–61. AE, MC, V. Closed Sun. No lunch Sat. Métro: Charles-de-Gaulle–Étoile.*

$$ ✕ **Le Timgad.** For a stylish evening out and a night off from French food, try this elegant, beautifully decorated North African restaurant. Start with a savory *brick* (crispy parchment pastry filled with meat, eggs, or seafood), followed by tasty couscous or succulent *tagine* (meat or poultry that's slowly braised inside a domed pottery casserole). ✉ *21 rue de Brunel,* ☎ *01–45–74–23–70. MC, V. Métro: Argentine.*

18ᵉ Arrondissement

$ ✕ **Le Restaurant.** In tune with the times, chef Yves Pelardeau offers a very good value prix-fixe menu that features his inventive approach to bistro cooking, using Asian and African seasoning to brighten up classical dishes. The menu changes regularly, but dishes like guinea hen with preserved lemon and duckling with figs express his style. Order the less expensive wine of the week. ✉ *32 rue Veron,* ☎ *01–42–23–06–22. AE, MC, V. Closed Mon. Métro: Abbesses.*

LODGING

Updated by Suzanne Rowan Kelleher

The Paris Tourist Office's annual lodging guide lists 1,498 member hotels in the city's 20 arrondissements. The true count, though, is closer to 2,000—some 80,000 rooms in all. Despite the huge choice of hotels here, you should always reserve well in advance.

The criteria when selecting the hotels reviewed below were quality, location, and character. Fewer hotels in outlying arrondissements (the 10th to the 20th) are listed because they are farther from the major sites. Generally, there are more Right Bank hotels offering luxury—or at any rate formality—than there are on the Left Bank, where hotels are often smaller and richer in old-fashioned charm.

As part of a general upgrade of the city's hotels in recent years, scores of lackluster, cheap Paris lodgings have been replaced by good-value establishments in the lower to middle price range. Although air-conditioning has become de rigueur in middle- to higher-priced hotels, it is generally not a prerequisite for comfort. (Paris's hot weather season doesn't usually last long.)

Almost all Paris hotels charge extra for breakfast, with prices ranging from 30 francs to more than 195 francs per person in luxury establishments. For anything more than the standard Continental breakfast of café au lait (coffee with hot milk) and croissants, the price will be higher. A nominal *séjour* (lodging) tax of 7 francs per person, per night is charged to pay for promotion of tourism in Paris.

CATEGORY	COST*
$$$$	over 1,750 frs
$$$	1,000 frs–1,750 frs
$$	600 frs–1,000 frs
$	under 600 frs

**All prices are for a standard double room, including 20.6% tax and service.*

1er Arrondissement

$$$$ ★ 🏨 **Costes.** Jean-Louis and Gilbert Costes have departed from the postmodernism that has been their hallmark. Instead, this sumptuous hotel is in a converted town house that conjures up the palaces of Napoléon III. Every room is swathed in rich garnet and bronze tones and contains a luxurious mélange of patterned fabrics, heavy swags, and enough brocade and fringe to blanket the Champs-Elysées. The bathrooms are truly marvelous affairs. ✉ *239 rue St-Honoré, 75001,* ☎ *01–42–44–50–50,* FAX *01–42–44–50–01. 85 rooms. Restaurant, bar, air-conditioning, in-room modem lines, in-room safes, no-smoking rooms, room service, indoor pool, sauna, exercise room, laundry service. AE, DC, MC, V. Métro: Tuileries.*

$$$$ 🏨 **Meurice.** The Meurice, owned by the Italian CIGA chain, is one of the finest hotels in the city. The Louis XVI–style first-floor salons are sumptuous and the bedrooms, adorned with Persian carpets, opulent. Most bathrooms are done in Florentine marble. Book well in advance to land a room or a suite overlooking the Tuileries Gardens. The hotel's restaurant is fabled. ✉ *228 rue de Rivoli, 75001,* ☎ *01–44–58–10–10,* FAX *01–44–58–10–15. 152 rooms, 28 suites. Restaurant, bar, air-conditioning, no-smoking rooms, room service, laundry service, business services. AE, DC, MC, V. Métro: Tuileries, Concorde.*

$$$$ 🏨 **Ritz.** The Ritz is the crowning gem of the sparkling place Vendôme. Festooned with gilt and ormolu, dripping with crystal chandeliers, and swathed in heavy silk and tapestries, this dazzling hotel, which opened in 1896, is the epitome of fin-de-siècle Paris. Yet it's surprisingly intimate. The lack of a lobby discourages paparazzi and sightseers who might annoy the privileged clientele. Don't miss the famous Hemingway Bar (which the writer claimed to have "liberated" in 1944). ✉ *15 pl. Vendôme, 75001,* ☎ *01–43–16–30–30,* FAX *01–43–16–36–68. 142 rooms, 45 suites. 3 restaurants, 2 bars, air-conditioning, in-room safes, room service, indoor pool, beauty salon, health club, shops, laundry service, meeting rooms, parking (fee). AE, DC, MC, V. Métro: Opéra.*

$$ 🏨 **Britannique.** Open since 1870, the Britannique blends courteous English service with old-fashioned French elegance. It has retained its handsome winding staircase and offers well-appointed, soundproof rooms done in chic, warm tones. During World War I, the hotel served as headquarters for a Quaker mission. ✉ *20 av. Victoria, 75001,* ☎ *01–42–33–74–59,* FAX *01–42–33–82–65. 31 rooms with bath, 9 with shower. Bar, in-room safes. AE, DC, MC, V. Métro: Châtelet.*

Paris Lodging

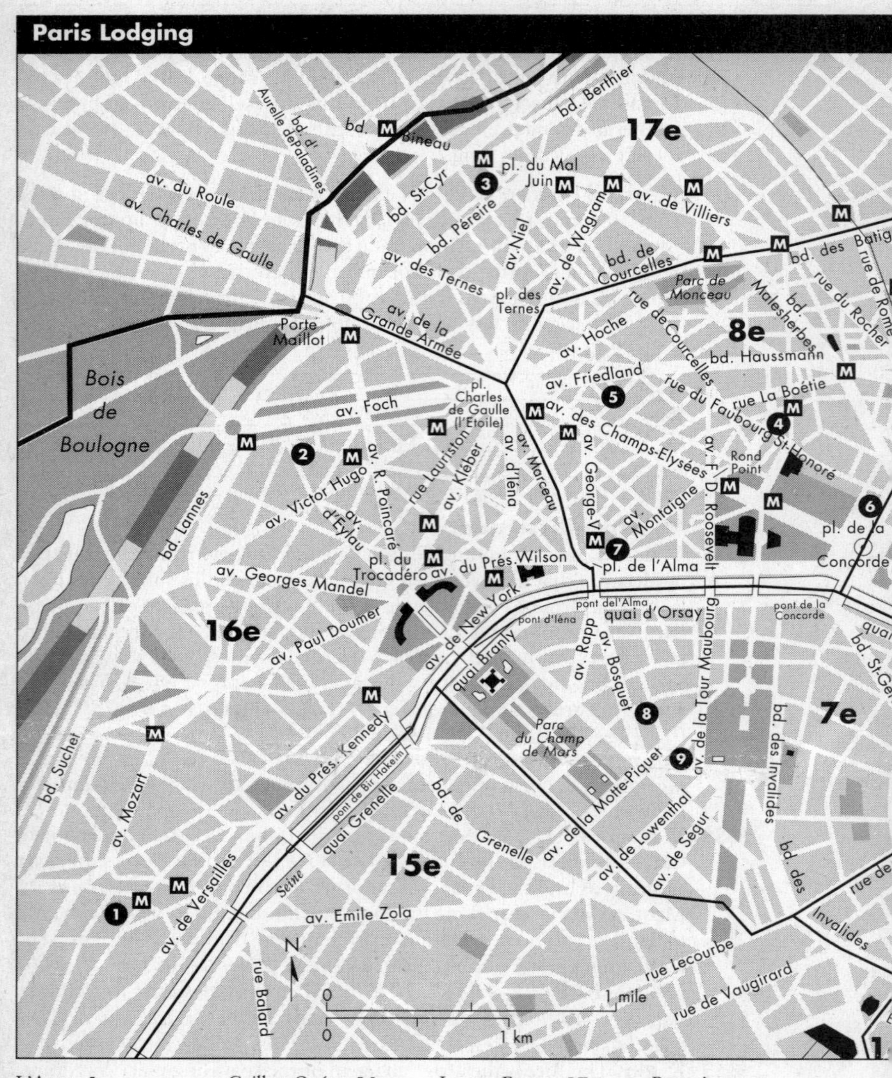

L'Astor, **4**
Atelier Montparnasse, **31**
Britannique, **18**
Caron de Beaumarchais, **19**
Castex, **22**
Champ de Mars, **8**
Costes, **10**
Crillon, **6**
Deux-Iles, **24**
Étoile-Péreire, **3**
Familia, **25**
Gaillon-Opéra, **16**
Grand Hotel Inter-Continental, **13**
Grandes Écoles, **26**
Hôtel de l'Abbaye, **32**
Hôtel de Noailles, **15**
Hôtel du 7e Art, **23**
Istria, **29**
Jardin du Luxembourg, **28**
Lancaster, **5**
Louvre Forum, **17**
Meurice, **11**
Montalembert, **36**
Parc Montsouris, **27**
Le Pavillon Bastille, **21**
Pavillon de la Reine, **20**
Plaza-Athénée, **7**
Queen's Hotel, **1**
Raspail-Montparnasse, **30**
Regyn's Montmartre, **14**
Relais Christine, **35**
Relais St-Germain, **34**
Relais St-Sulpice, **33**
Ritz, **12**
Saint James Paris, **2**
Le Tourville, **9**

18e
Sacré Coeur
rue Lamarck
rue Custine
rue Caulaincourt
bd. Barbès
rue Riquet
rue d'Aubervilliers
Canal de l'Ourcq
av. Jean Jaurès
bd. de Rochechouart
bd. de la Chapelle
bd. de Clichy
av. de Clichy
rue d'Amsterdam
9e
rue La Fayette
rue St-Lazare
rue de Châteaudun
Canal St-Martin
bd. de la Villette
10e
bd. Haussmann
bd. de la Madeleine
bd. des Italiens
bd. Poissonnière
bd. St-Denis
bd. Montmartre
bd. de Strasbourg
bd. de Magenta
rue du Faubourg du Temple
bd. St-Martin
2e
pl. Vendôme
av. de l'Opéra
R. de Richelieu
rue Reaumur
rue du Louvre
rue Etienne Marcel
bd. de Sébastopol
rue de Turbigo
rue du Temple
3e
av. de la République
rue de Rivoli
1er
rue Rambuteau
rue des Archives
Vieille du Temple
Seine
Louvre
rue Berger
rue St-Honoré
rue de Rivoli
r. de Turenne
bd. Beaumarchais
bd. Richard Lenoir
bd. Voltaire
11e
quai Anatole France
pont du Carrousel
Pont Neuf
île de la Cité
rue de Rivoli
rue St-Antoine
pl. des Vosges
pl. de la Bastille
av. Ledru Rollin
Notre Dame
4e
bd. St-Germain
pl. St-Michel
pl. Maubert
quai de la Tournelle
île St-Louis
bd. Henri IV
rue du Faubourg St-Antoine
Sèvres
6e
bd. Raspail
bd. St-Michel
Jardin du Luxembourg
Pont de Sully
Seine
av. Ledru Rollin
av. Daumesnil
12e
bd. Diderot
pl. du Panthéon
Jardin des Plantes
5e
rue Monge
bd. du Montparnasse
bd. Edgar Quinet
14e

$ **Louvre Forum.** This friendly hotel is a find: Smack in the center of town, it offers clean, comfortable, well-equipped rooms (with satellite TV) at extremely reasonable prices. The inexpensive breakfast is served in a homey vaulted cellar. ✉ *25 rue du Bouloi, 75001,* ☎ *01–42–36–54–19,* FAX *01–42–33–66–31. 11 rooms with bath, 16 with shower. Bar. AE, DC, MC, V. Métro: Louvre.*

2e Arrondissement

$$ **Gaillon-Opéra.** One of the most charming in the Opéra neighborhood, this hotel has so much character that you would never guess that it's part of a chain. But Best Western has wonderfully preserved the building's original atmosphere: It still has its old oak beams, stone walls, marble tiles, and leafy patio. ✉ *9 rue Gaillon, 75002,* ☎ *01–47–42–47–74, 800/528–1234 in the U.S.,* FAX *01–47–42–01–23. 26 rooms, 2 suites. Bar, air-conditioning, in-room modem lines, in-room safes, no-smoking rooms, room service, baby-sitting, laundry service. AE, DC, MC, V. Métro: Opéra.*

$$ ★ **Hôtel de Noailles.** With a nod to the work of postmodern designers like André Putnam and Philippe Starck, this new-wave inn is a star among Paris's new crop of well-priced, style-driven boutique hotels. Rooms are individually decorated with funky furnishings and contemporary details; the look is fun and very hip. Breakfast is included in the rate. ✉ *9 rue de Michodière, 75002,* ☎ *01–47–42–92–90,* FAX *01–49–24–92–71. 48 rooms with bath, 5 with shower. In-room safes, no-smoking rooms, laundry service. AE, MC, V. Métro: Opéra.*

3e Arrondissement

$$$$ **Pavillon de la Reine.** This magnificent mansion, reconstructed from original plans, is on the 17th-century place des Vosges. It's filled with Louis XIII–style fireplaces and antiques. Ask for a duplex with French windows overlooking the first of two flower-filled courtyards behind the historic Queen's Pavilion. Breakfast is served in a vaulted cellar. ✉ *28 pl. des Vosges, 75003,* ☎ *01–42–77–96–40, 800/447–7462 in the U.S.,* FAX *01–42–77–63–06. 30 rooms, 25 suites. Bar, air-conditioning, room service, laundry service, free parking. AE, DC, MC, V. Métro: Bastille.*

4e Arrondissement

$$ ★ **Caron de Beaumarchais.** The theme of this intimate jewel is the work of Caron de Beaumarchais, who wrote the *Marriage of Figaro* in 1778. Rooms are faithfully decorated to reflect the taste of 18th-century French nobility, right down to the reproduction wallpapers and upholsteries. Ubiquitous fresh flowers and fluffy bathrobes are a bonus for the price. The fifth- and sixth-floor rooms with balconies are the largest and have beguiling views across Right Bank rooftops. ✉ *12 rue Vieille-du-Temple, 75004,* ☎ *01–42–72–34–12,* FAX *01–42–72–34–63. 17 rooms with bath, 2 with shower. Air-conditioning, in-room safes, laundry service. AE, DC, MC, V. Métro: Hôtel de Ville.*

$$ **Deux-Iles.** This converted 17th-century mansion on the Ile St-Louis has long won plaudits for charm and comfort. Flowers and plants are scattered around the stunning main hall. The delightful rooms, blessed with exposed beams, are small but fresh and airy. Ask for one overlooking the little garden courtyard. In winter, a roaring fire warms the lounge. ✉ *59 rue St-Louis-en-l'Ile, 75004,* ☎ *01–43–26–13–35,* FAX *01–43–29–60–25. 8 rooms with bath, 9 with shower. Air-conditioning, in-room safes, no-smoking rooms, laundry service, meeting rooms. AE, MC, V. Métro: Pont-Marie.*

$ **Castex.** This Marais hotel in a Revolution-era building is a bargain-hunter's dream. Rooms are low on frills but squeaky clean, the owners are extremely friendly, and the prices are rock-bottom, which ensures that the hotel is often booked months ahead by a largely American clientele. There's no elevator, and the only TV is in the ground-floor salon. ✉ *5 rue Castex, 75004,* ☎ *01–42–72–31–52,* FAX *01–42–72–57–91. 4 rooms with bath, 23 with shower. MC, V. Métro: Bastille.*

$ 🏨 **Hôtel du 7e Art.** The theme of this hip Marais hotel fits its name ("Seventh Art" is what the French call filmmaking): Hollywood from the '40s to the '60s. Posters of Cagney, Marilyn, Chaplin, and their contemporaries cover the walls. Rooms are small and spartan, but clean, quiet, and equipped with cable TV. There's no elevator. The clientele is young, trendy, and primarily American. ✉ *20 rue St-Paul, 75004,* ☎ *01–42–77–04–03,* FAX *01–42–77–69–10. 9 rooms with bath, 14 with shower. Bar, breakfast room, in-room safes. AE, DC, MC, V. Métro: St-Paul.*

5e Arrondissement

$$ 🏨 **Jardin du Luxembourg.** Blessed with a charming staff and a smart, stylish look, this hotel, on a calm side street just a block from the Luxembourg Gardens, is one of the most sought-after in the Latin Quarter. Rooms are a bit small (common for this neighborhood) but intelligently furnished and warmly decorated in ocher, rust, and indigo à la provençale. Ask for one with a balcony overlooking the street; the best, No. 25, has dormer windows and a peekaboo view of the Eiffel Tower. ✉ *5 Impasse Royer-Collard, 75005,* ☎ *01–40–46–08–88,* FAX *01–40–46–02–28. 23 rooms with bath, 2 with shower. Bar, air-conditioning, in-room safes. AE, DC, MC, V. Métro: Luxembourg.*

$ 🏨 **Familia.** The hospitable Gaucheron family runs this comfortable hotel with great panache. Paris-theme frescoes, painted by a local art student, adorn the lobby and some of the 30 rooms. The stone walls and tapestries are strictly *à l'ancienne* (antique style). Rooms overlooking the animated Latin Quarter street have double-glazed windows; book ahead for one with a balcony. ✉ *11 rue des Écoles, 75005,* ☎ *01–43–54–55–27,* FAX *01–43–29–61–77. 14 rooms with bath, 16 with shower. Minibars. AE, DC, MC, V. Métro: Cardinal-Lemoine.*

$ 🏨 **Grandes Écoles.** This delightfully intimate place looks and feels like a country cottage dropped smack in the middle of the Latin Quarter. It is off the street and occupies three buildings on a beautiful leafy garden, where breakfast is served in summer. Parquet floors, Louis-Philippe furnishings, lace bedspreads, and the absence of TV all add to the rustic ambience. ✉ *75 rue du Cardinal Lemoine, 75005,* ☎ *01–43–26–79–23,* FAX *01–43–25–28–15. 45 rooms with bath, 6 with shower. No-smoking rooms. MC, V. Métro: Cardinal Lemoine.*

6e Arrondissement

$$$$ 🏨 **Relais Christine.** On a quiet street between the Seine and boulevard St-Germain, this luxurious and popular hotel, occupying 16th-century abbey cloisters, oozes romantic ambience. Rooms are spacious (particularly the duplexes on the upper floors) and well appointed in the old Parisian style; the best have exposed beams and overlook the garden. ✉ *3 rue Christine, 75006,* ☎ *01–43–26–71–80,* FAX *01–43–26–89–38. 35 rooms, 16 suites. Bar, breakfast room, air-conditioning, room service, baby-sitting, laundry service, meeting rooms, free parking. AE, DC, MC, V. Métro: Odéon.*

$$$ ★ 🏨 **Relais St-Germain.** The interior-designer owners of this outstanding hotel in the heart of St-Germain-des-Prés have exquisite taste and a superb respect for tradition and detail. Moreover, the rooms are at least twice the size of what you'll find at other hotels in the area for the same price. Much of the furniture was selected with a knowledgeable eye from the city's *brocantes* (second-hand dealers) and every room has its own, unique treasures. Doubles have separate sitting

areas; four have kitchenettes. Breakfast is included in the rate. ✉ *9 carrefour de l'Odéon, 75006,* ☎ *01–43–29–12–05,* FAX *01–46–33–45–30. 21 rooms, 1 suite. Breakfast room, wine bar, air-conditioning, in-room safes, room service, baby-sitting, laundry service. AE, DC, MC, V. Métro: Odéon.*

$$–$$$ **Hôtel de L'Abbaye.** This delightful hotel near St-Sulpice was a convent in the 18th century. It has a stone-vaulted entrance. The first-floor rooms open onto a flower-filled garden; some of the ones on the top floor have oak beams and alcoves. The four duplexes with private terraces are more expensive. Breakfast is included. ✉ *10 rue Cassette, 75006,* ☎ *01–45–44–38–11,* FAX *01–45–48–07–86. 42 rooms, 4 suites. Bar, breakfast room, air-conditioning, room service. AE, MC, V. Métro: St-Sulpice.*

$$–$$$ **Relais St-Sulpice.** This fashionable little hotel is decorated in a stylish blend of various periods and regions—African artworks line the hallways; Provençal tiles adorn the bathrooms; Chinese engravings wink to Parisians' penchant for the Orient in the 1930s; heavy fabrics drape the windows; and thick, cotton-pique downy comforters envelop wrought-iron beds. There's a sauna downstairs, right off the atrium breakfast salon. Room 11 has a terrific view of St-Sulpice. ✉ *3 rue Garancière, 75006,* ☎ *01–46–33–99–00,* FAX *01–46–33–00–10. 26 rooms. Air-conditioning, in-room modem lines, in-room safes, no-smoking rooms, sauna, meeting rooms, parking (fee). AE, DC, MC, V. Métro: Mabillon, St-Sulpice.*

$$ **Atelier Montparnasse.** This Art Deco–inspired gem of a hotel was designed with style and comfort in mind. Rooms are tastefully decorated and spacious and all the bathrooms feature mosaic reproductions of famous French paintings. The hotel is well situated in Montparnasse within walking distance of the Luxembourg Gardens and St-Germain-des-Prés. ✉ *49 rue Vavin, 75006,* ☎ *01–46–33–60–00,* FAX *01–40–51–04–21. 16 rooms, 1 triple. Bar, room service, laundry service. AE, DC, MC, V. Métro: Vavin.*

7e Arrondissement

$$$–$$$$ **Montalembert.** The Montalembert is one of Paris's most originally voguish boutique hotels. Whether appointed with traditional or contemporary furnishings, rooms are all about simple lines and chic luxury. A host of signature elements were designed especially for the hotel by the world's hippest designers. Ask about special packages if you're staying for more than three nights. ✉ *3 rue de Montalembert, 75007,* ☎ *01–45–49–68–68, 800/447–7462 in the U.S.,* FAX *01–45–49–69–49. 41 rooms and 5 suites with bath, 10 rooms with shower. Restaurant, bar, air-conditioning, in-room safes, room service, in-room VCRs, baby-sitting, laundry service, meeting rooms. AE, DC, MC, V. Métro: Rue du Bac.*

$$–$$$ **Le Tourville.** Here is a rare find: an intimate hotel at more affordable prices. Each room has crisp, virgin-white damask upholstery set against pastel or ocher walls, a smattering of antique bureaus and lamps, and original artwork. Though most doubles are priced at the low end of the $$ category, the four doubles with lovely walk-out terraces nip into the $$$ bracket. Both junior suites have Jacuzzis. The staff couldn't be more helpful. ✉ *16 av. de Tourville, 75007,* ☎ *01–47–05–62–62, 800/528–3549 in the U.S.,* FAX *01–47–05–43–90. 28 rooms, 2 junior suites. Bar, air-conditioning, laundry service. AE, DC, MC, V. Métro: École Militaire.*

$ ★ **Champ de Mars.** Françoise and Stéphane Gourdal's comfortable hotel has rooms done in an attractive blue-and-yellow French country-house style. All are equipped with satellite TV and CNN. The two on the ground floor open onto a leafy courtyard. The neighborhood—near the Eiffel

Tower and Invalides—is also difficult to beat. ✉ *7 rue du Champ de Mars, 75007,* ☎ *01–45–51–52–30,* FAX *01–45–51–64–36. 19 rooms with bath, 6 with shower. AE, MC, V. Métro: École Militaire.*

8e Arrondissement

$$$$ **L'Astor.** Following a top-to-bottom makeover by the elite Westin-Demeure group, L'Astor has been reborn as a bastion of highly stylized, civilized chic. The Art Deco lobby is decked out in boldly patterned armchairs, huge mirrors, and clever ceiling frescoes. Guest rooms are testimonials to the sober Regency style, with weighty marble fireplaces and mahogany furnishings. Several suites have walk-out balconies with superb vistas. The hotel's restaurant is supervised by the celebrated chef Joel Robuchon. ✉ *11 rue d'Astorg, 75008,* ☎ *01–53–05–05–05, 800/228–3000 in the U.S.,* FAX *01–53–05–05–30. 132 rooms, 3 suites. Restaurant, bar, air-conditioning, in-room modem lines, in-room safes, no-smoking rooms, room service, health club, laundry service. AE, DC, MC, V. Métro: Miromesnil, St-Augustin.*

$$$$ **Crillon.** The Crillon, comprising two 18th-century town houses on place de la Concorde, is often called the crème de la crème of Paris's "palace" hotels. Marie-Antoinette took singing lessons here. Rooms are lavishly (some might say overbearingly) decorated with Rococo and Directoire antiques, crystal and gilt wall sconces, and gold fittings. The sheer quantity of marble downstairs—especially in Les Ambassadeurs restaurant—is staggering. ✉ *10 pl. de la Concorde, 75008,* ☎ *01–44–71–15–00,* FAX *01–44–71–15–02. 118 rooms, 45 suites. 2 restaurants, 2 bars, tea shop, air-conditioning, in-room safes, no-smoking rooms, room service, exercise room, meeting rooms. AE, DC, MC, V. Métro: Concorde.*

$$$$ **Lancaster.** The Lancaster—one of Paris's most venerable institutions—has been meticulously transformed into one of the city's most modish, luxury hotels. The new decor seamlessly blends the traditional with the contemporary to evoke an overall feeling of timeless elegance, and every detail speaks of quality. Many of the suites pay homage to the hotel's colorful regulars from Garbo to Huston to Sir Alec Guinness to Marlene Dietrich. ✉ *7 rue de Berri, 75008,* ☎ *01–40–76–40–76, 800/447–7462 in the U.S.,* FAX *01–40–76–40–00. 60 rooms, 8 suites. Restaurant, bar, air-conditioning, in-room safes, room service, in-room VCRs, sauna, exercise room, baby-sitting, laundry service, meeting rooms. AE, DC, MC, V. Métro: George-V.*

$$$$ **Plaza-Athénée.** The Plaza, with its distinctive turn-of-the-century facade, accented with wrought-iron and red awnings, is tucked discreetly among the haute couture houses on avenue Montaigne, just a block from the Champs-Elysées. Rooms, overlooking either the courtyard or the tony, tree-lined avenue, are superb examples of the Louis XV, Louis XVI, or Regency styles. The brand new fitness club affords views of the Eiffel Tower. ✉ *25 av. Montaigne, 75008,* ☎ *01–53–67–66–65, 800/223–6800 in the U.S.,* FAX *01–53–67–66–66. 205 rooms, 65 suites. 2 restaurants, bar, air-conditioning, in-room modem lines, in-room safes, no-smoking rooms, room service, beauty salon, health club, laundry service, meeting rooms. AE, DC, MC, V. Métro: Alma-Marceau.*

9e Arrondissement

$$$$ **Grand Hôtel Inter-Continental.** Open since 1862, Paris's biggest luxury hotel has a facade that seems as long as the Louvre. The grand salon's Art Deco dome and the restaurant's painted ceilings are registered landmarks. The Art Deco rooms are spacious and light. The famed Café de la Paix (☞ The Grand Boulevards, *above*) is one of the city's great people-watching spots. ✉ *2 rue Scribe, 75009,* ☎ *01–40–07–32–32, 800/327–0200 in the U.S.,* FAX *01–42–66–12–51. 514 rooms,*

39 suites. 3 restaurants, 2 bars, air-conditioning, in-room safes, no-smoking rooms, room service, in-room VCRs, sauna, health club, laundry service, meeting rooms. AE, DC, MC, V. Métro: Opéra.

12e Arrondissement

$$ ★ **Le Pavillon Bastille.** Here's a smart address (across from the Opéra Bastille) for savvy travelers who appreciate getting perks for less. The transformation of this 19th-century hôtel particulier into a mod, colorful, high-design hotel garnered architectural awards and a fiercely loyal, hip clientele. The gracious staff pours on the romantic extras (4 PM checkout, fluffy Porthault towels, complimentary minibar) and every detail is pitch perfect. ✉ *65 rue de Lyon, 75012,* ☎ *01–43–43–65–65, 800/233–2552 in the U.S.,* FAX *01–43–43–96–52. 24 rooms, 1 suite. Bar, air-conditioning, in-room safes, minibars, room service. AE, DC, MC, V. Métro: Bastille.*

14e Arrondissement

$$ **Raspail-Montparnasse.** Rooms in this hotel are named after the artists who made Montparnasse the art capital of the world in the '20s and '30s. All are decorated in pastel colors; five offer spectacular panoramic views of Montparnasse and the Eiffel Tower. Most rooms are at the low end of this price category. ✉ *203 bd. Raspail, 75014,* ☎ *01–43–20–62–86,* FAX *01–43–20–50–79. 28 rooms with bath, 10 with shower. Bar, air-conditioning, in-room safes, meeting rooms. AE, DC, MC, V. Métro: Vavin.*

$ **Istria.** This small, charming family-run hotel on a quiet side street was once a Montparnasse artists' hangout. It has a flower-filled courtyard and simple, clean, comfortable rooms with soft pastel-toned Japanese wallpaper. ✉ *29 rue Campagne-Première, 75014,* ☎ *01–43–20–91–82,* FAX *01–43–22–48–45. 4 rooms with bath, 22 with shower. In-room safes, meeting rooms. AE, DC, MC, V. Métro: Raspail.*

$ **Parc Montsouris.** This modest hotel in a 1930s villa is on a quiet residential street next to the lovely Parc Montsouris. Rooms tend to be small, but clean, tastefully furnished, and equipped with satellite TV. Those with showers are very inexpensive. Suites sleep four. ✉ *4 rue du Parc-Montsouris, 75014,* ☎ *01–45–89–09–72,* FAX *01–45–80–92–72. 28 rooms with bath, 7 suites with shower. AE, MC, V. Métro: Montparnasse-Bienvenue.*

16e Arrondissement

$$$$ **Saint James Paris.** Called the "only château-hôtel in Paris," this gracious late-19th-century neoclassical mansion is surrounded by a lush private park. The lavish Art Deco interior was created by jet-set designer André Putnam. Ten rooms on the third floor open onto a winter garden. The restaurant is reserved for guests; in warm weather, meals are served in the garden. The poshest option: booking one of the two duplex gatehouses. ✉ *43 av. Bugeaud, 75016,* ☎ *01–44–05–81–81,* FAX *01–44–05–81–82. 24 rooms, 24 suites. Restaurant, bar, air-conditioning, in-room safes, room service, sauna, health club, baby-sitting, laundry service, meeting rooms, free parking. AE, DC, MC, V. Métro: Porte Dauphine.*

$–$$ **Queen's Hotel.** One of only a handful of hotels in the tony residential district near the Bois de Boulogne, Queen's is a small, comfortable hotel with a high standard of service. Each room focuses on a different 20th-century French artist. The rooms with baths have Jacuzzis. ✉ *4 rue Bastien-Lepage, 75016,* ☎ *01–42–88–89–85,* FAX *01–40–50–67–52. 7 rooms with bath, 16 with shower. Air-conditioning, in-room safes, no-smoking rooms. AE, DC, MC, V. Métro: Michelange-Auteuil.*

17e Arrondissement

$$ **Étoile-Péreire.** Behind a quiet, leafy courtyard in a chic residential district, you will find this unique, intimate hotel, consisting of two parts: a fin-de-siècle building on the street and a 1920s annex overlooking an interior courtyard. Rooms and duplexes are decorated in deep shades of roses or blues with crisp, white damask upholstery. Some of the rooms have air-conditioning. The copious breakfast is legendary, featuring 40 assorted jams and jellies. The bar is always busy in the evening. ✉ *146 bd. Péreire, 75017,* ☎ *01–42–67–60–00,* FAX *01–42–67–02–90. 18 rooms and 5 duplex suites with bath, 3 rooms with shower. Bar, no-smoking rooms, laundry service. AE, DC, MC, V. Métro: Péreire.*

18e Arrondissement

$ **Regyn's Montmartre.** Despite the small rooms, this owner-run hotel has comfortable accommodations. Each floor is dedicated to a Montmartre artist; poetic homages by local writers feature in the hallways. Ask for a room on either of the top two floors for great views of either the Eiffel Tower or Sacré-Coeur. Courteous service and a relaxed atmosphere make this an attractive choice. ✉ *18 pl. des Abbesses, 75018,* ☎ *01–42–54–45–21,* FAX *01–42–23–76–69. 14 rooms with bath, 8 with shower. In-room safes. AE, MC, V. Métro: Abbesses.*

NIGHTLIFE AND THE ARTS

The Arts

Parisians consider their city a bastion of art and culture, and indeed it is. Enormous amounts of government money go into culture, but surprisingly, Paris is not quite on par with New York, London, or Milan for theater, opera, music, or ballet. Nonetheless, Parisian audiences are discerning, so standards are very high. Also, many international companies that you might not see elsewhere perform in Paris. The contemporary dance scene, too, is particularly exciting, as are the plethora of cinemas showing excellent French and American films.

The weekly magazines *Pariscope* (which has an English section), *L'Officiel des Spectacles,* and *Figaroscope* (a supplement to *Le Figaro* newspaper) are published every Wednesday and give detailed entertainment listings. ***Saison de Paris*** is a booklet available at the Paris Tourist Office (☞ Visitor Information *in* Paris A to Z, *below*) or from the Maison de France (☞ Gold Guide). The Paris Tourist Office's **24-hour hot line** in English (☎ 01–49–52–53–56) is another source of information about weekly events.

The best place to buy tickets is at the venue itself; try to purchase in advance, as many of the more popular performances sell out. Also try your hotel or a travel agency, such as **Paris-Vision** (✉ 1 rue Auber, 9e, ☎ 01–40–06–01–00, métro Opéra). Tickets for some events can be bought at the **FNAC** stores—especially Alpha-FNAC (✉ 1–5 rue Pierre Lescot, Forum des Halles, 3rd level down, 1e, ☎ 01–40–41–40–00, métro Châtelet–Les Halles). **Virgin Megastore** (✉ 52 av. des Champs-Elysées, 8e, ☎ 01–44–78–44–08, métro Franklin-D.-Roosevelt) also sells theater and concert tickets. Half-price tickets for many same-day theater performances are available at the **Kiosque Théâtre** (✉ across from 15 pl. de la Madeleine, métro Madeleine), open Tuesday–Saturday, 12:30–8 and Sunday 12:30–6; expect a line. There's another branch inside the Châtelet RER station, open Monday–Saturday.

Classical Music

Paris may not be as richly endowed as New York or London when it comes to music, but the city does have a few good concert halls, and it compensates with a never-ending stream of inexpensive lunchtime and evening concerts in churches, some scheduled as part of the **Festival d'Art Sacré** (☎ 01–44–70–64–10 for information) between mid-November and Christmas.

A varied program of classical and world music concerts are held at the new **Cité de la Musique** (✉ 221 av. Jean-Jaurès, 19e, ☎ 01–44–84–44–84, métro Porte de Pantin). The **Salle Pleyel** (✉ 252 rue du Faubourg-St-Honoré, 8e, ☎ 01–45–61–53–00, métro Ternes) was Paris's principal home of classical music before the new Opéra de la Bastille opened; the Paris Symphony Orchestra and other leading international orchestras still play here regularly. The **Théâtre des Champs-Elysées** (✉ 15 av. Montaigne, 8e, ☎ 01–49–52–50–50, métro Alma-Marceau), an Art Deco temple, hosts concerts and ballet as well as plays.

Churches holding classical concerts—ranging from organ recitals to choral music and orchestral works—include (☞ Exploring, *above,* for addresses): **Notre-Dame, St-Eustache, St-Germain-des-Prés, St-Louis-en-l'Ile, St-Roch,** and **St-Germain l'Auxerrois. Ste-Chapelle** holds particularly outstanding candlelit concerts—make reservations well in advance.

Dance

As a rule, more avant-garde or up-and-coming choreographers can be found in the smaller dance spaces around the Bastille and the Marais and in theaters in the nearby suburbs. Classical ballet can be found in places as varied as the opera house and the sports stadium. Check the weekly guides for listings.

The **Opéra Garnier** (✉ pl. de l'Opéra, 9e, ☎ 01–40–01–17–89, métro Opéra) is home to the well-reputed Paris Ballet, as well as host to major foreign dance troupes and the Paris Opera. The **Palais des Congrès** (✉ pl. de la Porte Maillot, 17e, ☎ 01–40–68–00–05, métro Porte Maillot) is a large, modern hall that presents a classical repertoire to a family audience. The **Palais des Sports** (✉ pl. de la Porte de Versailles, 15e, ☎ 01–44–68–69–70, métro Porte de Versailles), a circular building dating from the 1970s, often stages ballet performances and large-scale spectacles. The **Théâtre de la Ville** (✉ 2 pl. du Châtelet, 4e, métro Châtelet; 31 rue des Abbesses, 18e, métro Abbesses; ☎ 01–42–74–22–77 for both) has a varied international dance program.

Film

Parisians are far more addicted to the cinema as an art form than are Londoners or New Yorkers. There are hundreds of movie theaters in the city, and a number of them, especially in principal tourist areas such as the Champs-Elysées, St-Germain-des-Près, Les Halles, and the Opéra, show first-run films in English. Check the weekly guides for a movie of your choice. Look for the initials "v.o.," which mean *version originale,* i.e., not dubbed. Cinema admission runs from 37 to 51 francs; there are slightly reduced rates on Mondays and, in some cinemas, for morning shows. Most theaters will post two show times: the first is the *séance,* or period of commercials and previews, and sometimes short films. The feature presentation usually starts 10–20 minutes later.

Big-screen fanatics should try the **Grand Rex** (✉ 1 bd. Poissonière, 2e, ☎ 08–36–68–70–23, métro Bonne Nouvelle). The **Max Linder Panorama** (✉ 24 bd. Poissonière, 9e, ☎ 01–48–24–88–88, métro Rue Montmartre) often shows classics on its big screen. The **UGC Ciné Cité Les Halles** (✉ Forum des Halles, Level 3, 1er, ☎ 08–36–68–68–58, métro Les Halles) is the place to see new films on large screens. The Chinese-style **La Pagode** (✉ 57 bis rue de Babylone, 7e, ☎ 01–45–55–48–48, métro François-Xavier) is a national monument and well worth a visit.

The Latin Quarter is the realm of small theaters showing classic and independent films. Showings are often organized around retrospectives (check "Festivals" in weekly guides). **Action Christine Odéon** (✉ 4 rue Christine, 6e, ☎ 01–43–29–11–30, métro Odéon) and **Action Écoles** (✉ 23 rue des Écoles, 5e, ☎ 01–43–25–72–07, métro Maubert-Mutualité) are just two such cinemas in the area.

The **Centre Pompidou** (✉ pl. Georges-Pompidou, 4e, ☎ 01–44–78–12–33, métro Rambuteau) screens many classic and obscure films (during the renovation, films will be shown elsewhere; call for information). The **Cinémathèque Française** (✉ Musée du Cinéma in the Palais de Chaillot, ☎ 01–45–53–74–39, métro Trocadéro) has a reference library, photography collection, and an outstanding assortment of films. Real movie buffs should visit the **Vidéothèque de Paris** (✉ Porte St-Eustache, Forum des Halles, 1er, ☎ 01–40–26–34–30, métro Les Halles), where hundreds of videos are available for viewing and programs of films are organized around themes related to the city of Paris.

Opera

The **Opéra Bastille** (✉ pl. de la Bastille, 11e, ☎ 01–44–73–13–00, métro Bastille) has taken over the role as Paris's main opera house from L'Opéra Garnier (☞ *above*), but many feel it is not living up to its promise of grand opera at affordable prices (which range from 60 to 530 francs). The **Opéra Comique** (✉ 5 rue Favart, 2e, ☎ 01–42–96–12–20, métro Richelieu-Drouot) is a lofty old hall where you'll hear often excellent comic operas and lightweight musical entertainments. Better known as the Théâtre du Châtelet, the **Théâtre Musical de Paris** (✉ pl. du Châtelet, 1er, ☎ 01–40–28–28–40, métro Châtelet) offers opera and ballet for a wider audience, at more reasonable prices.

Theater

A number of theaters line the grand boulevards between Opéra and République, but there is no Paris equivalent to Broadway or the West End. Shows are mostly in French. A fun spot to experience a particularly Parisian form of theater, the *café-théâtre*—a mixture of satirical sketches and variety show riddled with slapstick humor and viewed in a café setting—is at the **Café de la Gare** (✉ 41 rue du Temple, 4e, ☎ 01–42–78–52–51, métro Rambuteau). You need a good grasp of French. The **Comédie-Française** (✉ pl. André-Malraux, 1er, ☎ 01–44–58–15–15, métro Palais-Royal) is a distinguished venue that stages classical drama. The **Théâtre de la Huchette** (✉ 23 rue de la Huchette, 5e, ☎ 01–43–26–38–99, métro St-Michel) should be visited by admirers of Ionesco; this tiny Left Bank theater is where the playwright's short modern plays make a deliberate mess of the French language. **Théâtre de l'Odéon** (✉ pl. de l'Odéon, 6e, ☎ 01–44–41–36–36, métro Odéon) has first-rate companies from the rest of Europe; subtitles (in French) are part of the program.

Nightlife

So you've immersed yourself in culture all day and you want a night out on the town. The hottest spots are around Pigalle—despite its reputation as a seedy red-light district—and the Bastille and Marais areas. The Left Bank has a bit of everything. The Champs-Elysées is making a comeback, though the clientele remains predominantly foreign. On weeknights, people are usually home after closing hours at 2 AM, but weekends mean late-night partying. Take note, though: The last métro runs between 12:30 and 1 AM (you can always take a cab).

Bars and Clubs

More and more, Parisians seem to be bypassing clubs and heading for bars when out on the town. The more upscale Paris *boîtes de nuits* (nightclubs) can be both expensive (1,000 francs for a bottle of gin or whiskey) and hard to get in. But there are an impressive variety of bars—bars serving light food, moody late-night bars, bars with DJs, and bars with live music. The Pigalle area, near Montmartre, is a popular area, despite its reputation as a seedy red-light district. Nightlife is still hopping in and around the Bastille, and the Left Bank has a bit of everything. The Champs-Elysées is making a comeback, though the clientele remains predominantly foreign.

It helps to be famous—or look like a model—to get into **Les Bains** (✉ 7 rue du Bourg-l'Abbé, 3e, ☎ 01–48–87–01–80, métro Étienne-Marcel), a forever-trendy club (closed Monday). **Le Balajo** (✉ 9 rue de Lappe, 11e, ☎ 01–47–00–07–87, métro Bastille) is an old Java ballroom that specializes in salsa and techno; entry is free for women on Thursday. **Buddha Bar** (✉ 8 rue Boissy d'Anglas, 8e, ☎ 01–53–05–90–00, métro Concorde) has a spacious mezzanine bar that overlooks the dining room where cuisines, east and west, meet somewhere in California.

Le Colonial (✉ moored at Port Debilly opposite the Eiffel Tower, 16e, ☎ 01–53–23–98–98, métro Alma) offers a port in a storm for those looking for an alternative to the Pigalle scene. The sizable disco has replaced the first-class cabins. A gin- and tequila-drinking yuppie crowd heads to **Le Dépanneur** (✉ 27 rue Fontaine, 9e ☎ 01–40–16–40–20, métro Blanche). **Keur Samba** (✉ 79 vie La Boétie, 8e, ☎ 01–43–59–03–10, métro St-Philippe-du-Roule) has African decor and rhythms, a tiny dance floor, and an exclusive clientele that stays until dawn.

Le Moloko (✉ 26 rue Fontaine, 9e, ☎ 01–48–74–50–26, métro Blanche) is a popular, smoky, late-night bar with several rooms, a mezzanine, and a small dance floor. **Le Réservoir** (✉ 16 rue de la Forge Royale, 11e, ☎ 01–43–56–39–60, métro Faidherbe-Chaligny), in a yawning space where sewing machines once hummed, has an immense bar and occasional musical guests. **Sanz Sans** (✉ 49 rue du Faubourg St-Antoine, 11e, ☎ 01–44–75–78–78, métro Bastille) has added a new twist to bar life—the "actors" on the upstairs lounge's gilt-framed video screen are really the habitués of the downstairs bar. **Zed Club** (✉ 2 rue des Anglais, 6e, ☎ 01–43–54–93–78, métro Maubert-Mutualité) is a prime rock-and-roll and bebop venue for all ages; it's closed Sunday–Tuesday.

Gay and Lesbian Bars and Clubs

Gay and lesbian bars and clubs are mostly concentrated in the Marais and include some of the most happening addresses in the city. However, trendy clubs fall in and out of favor at lightning speed and one-night discos and tea dances are always popping up, so check the local papers to see what's hot. **Amnésia Café**'s (✉ 42 rue Vieille-du-Temple, 4e, ☎ 01–42–72–16–94, métro Rambuteau) under-lit bar and art deco ceiling paintings attract a young, yuppie gay and lesbian crowd. **Queen** (✉ 102 av. des Champs-Elysées, 8e, ☎ 01–42–89–31–32, métro George V) is one of the hottest nightspots in Paris: Although it's predominantly gay, lesbians and heterosexuals line up to get in, too.

MOSTLY MEN

The oldest gay disco in Paris, **Club 18** (✉ 18 rue de Beaujolais, 1er, ☎ 01–42–97–52–13, métro Pyramides) is as popular and casual as ever, particularly on theme nights. **Quetzal Bar** (✉ 10 rue de la Verrerie, 4e, ☎ 01–48–87–99–07, métro Hôtel-de-Ville) gleams with lots of chrome, blue lighting, and pick-me-up smiles. It's packed and smoky on weekends.

MOSTLY WOMEN

The hub of lesbian nightlife, **La Champmeslé** (✉ 4 rue Chabanais, 2e, ☎ 01–42–96–85–20, métro Bourse) has a dusky back room reserved for women only. **L'Enfer** (✉ 34 rue du Départ, 14e, ☎ 01–42–79–94–94, métro Montparnasse) reserves prime time, Friday and Saturday nights, for a women-only disco crowd. Men get their chance on Thursday and Sunday; Wednesday the doors are open to everyone.

Cabaret

Paris's cabarets are household names—more so abroad than in France, it would seem, judging by the hefty percentage of foreigners present at most shows. You can dine at many of them; prices range from 220 francs (simple admission plus one drink) to more than 800 francs (dinner plus show).

Crazy Horse (✉ 12 av. George V, 8e, ☎ 01–47–23–32–32, métro Alma-Marceau) is one of the best known cabarets, with pretty dancers and raunchy routines: lots of humor and lots fewer clothes. **Folies Bergère** (✉ 32 rue Richer, 9e, ☎ 01–44–79–98–98, métro Cadet), a legend since the days of Manet, has returned to its music hall origins, with the help of ornate costumes and masterful lighting. **Lido** (✉ 116 bis av. des Champs-Elysées, 8e, ☎ 01–40–76–56–10, métro George V) stars the famous Bluebell Girls; the owners claim that no show in Las Vegas can rival it for special effects. That old favorite at the foot of Montmartre, **Moulin Rouge** (✉ pl. Blanche, 18e, ☎ 01–46–06–00–19, métro Blanche), mingles the Doriss Girls, the cancan, and crocodiles in an extravagant spectacle.

Jazz Clubs

Paris is one of the great jazz cities of the world and the French take jazz seriously. For nightly schedules, consult the specialty magazines *Jazz Hot* or *Jazz Magazine*. Nothing gets going till 10 or 11 PM; entry prices vary widely from about 40 francs to over 100 francs.

Mainstream jazz is played in the faded Belle Epoque decor of **Bilboquet** (✉ 13 rue St-Benoît, 6e, ☎ 01–45–48–81–84, métro St-Germain-des-Prés). **Caveau de la Huchette** (✉ 5 rue de la Huchette, 5e, ☎ 01–43–26–65–05, métro St-Michel) is a smoke-filled shrine to the Dixieland beat. **Duc des Lombards** (42 rue des Lombards, 1er, ☎ 01–42–33–22–88, métro Les Halles) is an ill-lit, romantic, bebop venue with decor inspired by the Paris métro. At the Méridien Hotel near Porte Maillot, the **Lionel Hampton Jazz Club** (✉ 81 bd. Gouvion-St-Cyr, 17e, ☎ 01–40–68–30–42, métro Porte Maillot), named for the zingy xylophonist beloved of Parisians, hosts a roster of international jazz players. **New Morning** (✉ 7 rue des Petites-Écuries, 10e, ☎ 01–45–23–51–41, métro Château-d'Eau) is a premier spot for serious fans of avant-garde jazz, as well as folk and world music; decor is spartan, the mood reverential.

Pubs

Paris bars that woo English-speaking clientele with a pub atmosphere and dark beer are becoming increasingly popular with Parisians. **The Cricketers** (✉ 41 rue des Mathurins, 8e, ☎ 01–40–07–01–45, métro St-Augustin), owned by Graham Gooch, the legendary English cricket captain, serves amber ales from Adnams of Essex. **Finnegans Wake** (✉ 42 rue des Boulangers, 5e, ☎ 01–46–34–23–65, métro Jussieu) attracts a mixed Franco-British clientele with Guinness on tap, and Irish music and Gaelic dancing on Thursday night. Near place de la Contrescarpe, **The Mayflower** (✉ 49 rue Descartes, 5e, ☎ 01–43–54–56–47, métro Cardinal Lemoine) is a wood-paneled, leather-benched favorite among Scotchophile Left Bankers, summoned by the sippability of its 101 whiskies.

Rock Clubs

Bataclan (✉ 50 bd. Voltaire, 11e, ☎ 01–47–00–30–12, métro Oberkampf) is a good spot to hear live rock in an intimate setting. **Elysée Montmartre** (✉ 72 bd. Rochechouart, 18e, ☎ 01–44–92–45–45, métro Anvers) dates from Gustave Eiffel, its builder, who, it's hoped, liked a good party. Its following is as diverse as the music.

Wine Bars

Wine bars are a good place to sample a glass (or bottle) of French wine, perhaps with a plate of cheese or charcuterie. Bar owners are often true wine enthusiasts ready to dispense expert advice. Hours can vary widely, so it's best to check ahead; most close around 10 PM. **Aux Bons Crus** (✉ 7 rue des Petits-Champs, 1er, ☎ 01–42–60–06–45, métro Bourse) is a cramped, narrow venue with an authentically Parisian feel. Named after the jolly owner with the widest mustache in town, **Jacques Mélac** (✉ 42 rue Léon-Frot, 11e, ☎ 01–43–70–59–27, métro Charonne) bottles several of his own wines—try the chewy red Lirac. **La Robe et le Palais** (✉ 13 rue des Lavandières-Ste-Opportune, 1er, ☎ 01–45–08–07–41, métro Châtelet) offers over 120 wines from all over France, served *au compteur* (according to the quantity consumed), as well as good, creative light dishes.

OUTDOOR ACTIVITIES AND SPORTS

Bicycling

Paris has been making valiant efforts to become more biker-friendly. Over 32 km (20 mi) of **bicycle lanes** now cross the city, notably along the rue de Rivoli and boulevard St-Germain. Certain roads are banned to cars altogether on Sundays (including the banks of the Seine between the Tuileries and the Eiffel Tower, from 9 AM to 4 PM, and the roads alongside the Canal St-Martin, from noon to 6 PM). With their wide, leafy avenues, the **Bois de Boulogne** (☞ *above*) and the **Bois de Vincennes** (métro Porte Dorée, Château de Vincennes) are good places for biking. Bikes can be rented from the Château de Vincennes métro station (☎ 01–47–66–55–92; 25 francs an hour or 100 francs a day) in the Bois de Vincennes and from Pariscyclo (✉ Rond Point de Jardin d'Acclimation, ☎ 01–47–47–76–50, métro Les Sablons), in the Bois de Boulogne.

The cost for renting a bicycle is around 90–140 francs a day and 160–220 francs a weekend; the 1,000-franc deposit can be left on a credit card. Bicycles are rented at the **Bateaux-Mouches embarkation point** (✉ Pont de l'Alma, 8e, métro Alma-Marceau). Also try **Bicyclub** (✉ 8 pl. Porte de Champerret, 17e, ☎ 01–47–66–55–92, métro Porte de Champerret) and **Paris Vélo** (✉ 2 rue du Fer-à-Moulin, 5e, ☎ 01–43–37–59–22, métro Censier Daubenton).

Health Clubs

Hotels, gyms, and clubs in the city offer one-day or short-term memberships. **Aquaboulevard de Paris** (✉ 4 rue Louis-Armand, 15e, ☎ 01–40–60–10–00, métro Balard) has a gym, Turkish baths, and the city's finest swimming pool, complete with giant slide and wave machine (70 francs per day). **Club Quartier Latin** (✉ 19 rue de Pontoise, 5e, ☎ 01–43–54–82–45, métro Maubert Mutualité) has a 30-meter skylighted pool, a climbing wall, squash courts, and exercise equipment (70 francs per day and 70 francs an hour for squash). **Espace Vit-Halles** (✉ 48 rue Rambuteau, 1er, ☎ 01–42–77–21–71, métro Les Halles) has a broad range of aerobics classes at 90 francs a class, exercise machines, sauna, and steam bath (60 francs per day). The **Vitatop Club** (✉ 8 rue Louis-Armand, 15e, ☎ 01–45–54–79–00, métro Balard), on the top floor of the Sofitel Paris, has a 15-meter pool, sauna, steam room, and Jacuzzi, plus a stunning view of the Paris skyline (180 francs per day).

Jogging

The best inner-city running is in the **Champ-de-Mars,** next to the Eiffel Tower, measuring 2 km (1½ mi) around the perimeter. Shorter and more crowded routes are found in the **Jardin du Luxembourg,** with a 1½-km (about 1-mi) loop just inside the park's fence. The path in the **Jardin des Tuileries** also measures about 1½ km (1 mi). The **Parc Monceau** has a loop of 1 km (⅔ mi). The **Bois de Boulogne,** on the western edge of Paris, has miles of trails through woods and around lakes. The equally bucolic **Bois de Vincennes,** on the eastern side of the city, has a 15-km (9-mi) circuit or a 1½-km (1-mi) loop around the Château de Vincennes itself.

Swimming

The **Piscine des Halles** (✉ pl. de la Rotonde, Forum des Halles, 1er, ☎ 01–42–36–98–44) is a beautiful 50-meter pool. Admission is 24 francs; call for hours. Every arrondissement also has its own pool; ask for the Paris Tourist Office's *Guide du Sport à Paris* for a list of pools near you.

Tennis

There are few tennis courts in Paris, but your best bet is to try the public courts in the **Jardin du Luxembourg.** There is also a large complex of courts at the Polygone sports ground in the **Bois de Vincennes** (a 20-minute walk down route de la Pyramide from the Château de Vincennes métro stop). In addition, there are 11 covered courts (and six squash courts) at **Aquaboulevard** (☞ *above*).

For those who love to watch tennis, Paris stages two of the world's top tournaments. The **French Open** (on clay) takes place during the last week in May and the first week in June, at the bucolic Roland Garros stadium (2 av. Gordon Bennett, 16e, ☎ 01–47–43–48–00) on the eastern edge of the Bois de Boulogne (métro Porte d'Auteuil). The week-long indoor **Paris Open** is at the Palais Omnisports (✉ 8 bd. de Berey, 12e, ☎ 01–44–68–44–68, métro Bercy) at the start of November. Expect to pay between 100 and 300 francs, depending on the day and seat.

SHOPPING

Updated by Suzanne Rowan Kelleher

The shopping opportunities in Paris are endless and geared to every taste. For many, perfume and designer clothing are perhaps the most coveted Parisian souvenirs. However, even on haute couture's home turf, bargains are surprisingly elusive. Foreign visitors, subject to the slings and arrows of international exchange rates, are advised to know prices in their own country before arrival. Even stores that accept currency other than francs will generally give you a lower rate of exchange than banks or exchange offices. You're better off using credit cards, which are widely used. Even the corner newsstand or flea market salesperson is likely to honor plastic for purchases over 100 francs. MasterCard/EuroCard is the most common and preferred card, followed closely by Visa. American Express, Diners Club, and Access are accepted in the larger international stores.

Bargain hunters should watch for the word *soldes* (sales). The two main sale seasons are January and July. While sightseeing, visit the gift shops in Paris's museums, especially the shops in the Louvre, the Musée Carnavalet, the Opéra Garnier, and the Musée des Arts Décoratifs.

Visitors from outside the European Union, aged 15 and over, whose stay in France and/or the EU is less than six months, can benefit from Value Added Tax (VAT) reimbursements, known in France as TVA or *détaxe*. To qualify, non-EU residents must spend at least 2,000 francs in a single store. Refunds vary from 13% to 20.6% and are mailed to you by check or credited to your charge card.

Shopping Areas

Avenue Montaigne

This elegant boulevard is a showcase of international haute-couture houses. Italian moguls Prada and Dolce & Gabbana have joined Chanel, Dior, Nina Ricci, Jil Sander, Guy Laroche, Jean-Louis Scherrer, Emanuel Ungaro, Céline, Valentino, MaxMara, Genny, Krizia, Escada, Thierry Mugler, and Hanae Mori. Here you'll also find accessories by S. T. Dupont, Loewe, Salvatore Ferragamo, and Louis Vuitton. Yves Saint-Laurent and Givenchy are nearby, on avenues Marceau and George-V, respectively, and you'll find Versace on rue François I.

Bastille

Scores of trendy boutiques are clustered between art galleries, bars, and furniture stores in this gentrified neighborhood. Jean-Paul Gaultier has a boutique on rue Faubourg St-Antoine and hot, young newcomer Christophe Lemaire is installed on the rue St-Sabin.

Champs-Elysées

Cafés and movie theaters keep the once-chic Champs-Elysées active 24 hours a day, but the invasion of exchange banks, car showrooms, and fast-food chains has lowered the tone. Four glitzy 20th-century arcade malls (Galerie du Lido, Le Rond-Point, Le Claridge, and Elysées 26) capture most of the retail action.

Left Bank

After decades of clustering on the Right Bank's venerable shopping avenues, the high-fashion houses are now storming the Rive Gauche. Ever since Louis Vuitton, Giorgio Armani, Thierry Mugler, Christian Dior Men, and Romeo Gigli set up Left Bank shops in 1996, anyone who's anyone has rushed to followed suit. (Sonia Rykiel and Yves Saint-Laurent arrived fashionably early in the 1970s). This immensely walkable district between rue de Grenelle and rue de Rennes is also known for its top-quality shoe shops (Maud Frizon, Charles Jourdan, Stéphane Kélian, and Harel).

Les Halles

Most of the narrow pedestrian streets on the former site of Paris's wholesale food market are lined with fast-food joints, sex shops, jeans outlets, and garish souvenir stands, but rue du Jour (featuring MaxMara, Agnès B., and Junior Gaultier boutiques) is an attractive exception. The fabulously quirky Comme des Garçons has shops for both sexes on rue Étienne-Marcel. In the middle of the action is the Forum des Halles, a multilevel underground shopping mall, which used to be a nightmarish mash of noisy teens until it attracted higher-quality merchants and a clutch of promising designers.

Louvre–Palais Royal

The elegant and eclectic shops clustered in the 18th-century arcades of the Palais-Royal sell antiques, toy soldiers, Shiseido cosmetics, dramatic art jewelry from Siki, and even vintage designer dresses. The glossy marble Carrousel du Louvre mall, beneath the Louvre, is lit by an immense inverted glass pyramid. Shops, including Virgin Megastore, the Body Shop, and Esprit, along with a lively international food court, are open on Sunday—still a rare convenience in Paris.

Le Marais

Between the pre-Revolution mansions and tiny kosher food stores that characterize this area are scores of trendy gift shops and clothing stores. Avant-garde designers Azzedine Alaïa, Lolita Lempicka, Issey Miyake, and Romeo Gigli have boutiques within a few blocks of the stately place des Vosges and the Picasso and Carnavalet museums. A growing number of Marais shops are open on Sunday afternoons.

Montparnasse

The bohemian mecca for artists and writers in the '20s and '30s, Montparnasse is better known for bars and restaurants than shops. The commercial center near the train station has a Galeries Lafayette outlet, but it's too charmless to attract many tourists. Rue d'Alésia on the southern fringe of Montparnasse is known for discount clothing shops.

Opéra to La Madeleine

Three major department stores—Au Printemps, Galeries Lafayette, and the British Marks & Spencer (☞ Department Stores, *below*)—define boulevard Haussmann, behind Paris's ornate 19th-century Opéra Garnier. Place de la Madeleine is home to two luxurious food stores, Fauchon and Hédiard. Steps away, on boulevard de la Madeleine, is a classy 75-shop mall, Les Trois Quartiers. Lalique and Baccarat Crystal also have opulent showrooms near the Église de la Madeleine.

Passy–Victor Hugo

The bourgeois and conservative 16e arrondissement attracts predictably classic and upscale retailers, most of whom are centered on rue de Passy and place Victor Hugo. A handful of secondhand shops in this wealthy area offer exceptionally good deals. Réciproque, on rue de la Pompe, is one of the biggest and best discount haunts in Paris.

Place Vendôme and Rue de la Paix

The magnificent 17th-century place Vendôme, home of the Ritz Hotel, and rue de la Paix, leading north from Vendôme, have attracted the world's most elegant jewelers: Cartier, Boucheron, Buccellati, Van Cleef and Arpels, Répossi, Mellerio, Mauboussin, and Mikimoto.

Place des Victoires

This graceful, circular plaza near the Palais-Royal is the playground of cutting-edge fashion icons such as Kenzo, Victoire, and Thierry Mugler. Avant-garde boutiques like Chantal Thomass, Jean-Charles de Castelbajac, Absinthe, and En Attendant les Barbares have fanned into the side streets; Jean-Paul Gaultier's flagship shop is in the nearby Galerie Vivienne arcade. One of the hottest new emporiums to pop up in the neighborhood, Le Shop, at 3 rue d'Argout, rents retail space to hip, up-and-coming designers.

Rue du Faubourg–St-Honoré

The presence of the Elysée Palace and the official residences of the American and British ambassadors means this chic shopping and residential street is well patrolled by the police. The Paris branch of Sotheby's and renowned antiques galleries such as Didier Aaron add artistic flavor. Boutiques include Hermès, Lanvin, Karl Lagerfeld, Réveillon Furs, Louis Feraud, and Christian Lacroix.

Department Stores

Paris's top department stores offer both convenience and style. Most are open Monday through Saturday from about 9:30 AM to 7 PM, and some are open until 10 PM one weekday evening. All six major stores listed below have multilingual guides, international welcome desks, détaxe offices, and restaurants.

Au Bon Marché (✉ 22 rue de Sèvres, 7e, ☎ 01–44–39–80–00, métro Sèvres-Babylone), founded in 1852, is an excellent hunting ground for linens, table settings, and high-quality furniture. The new ground-floor Balthazar men's shop feels like a smart boutique. La Grande Épicerie is one of the largest gourmet groceries in Paris. The basement is a treasure trove for books, classy stationery, and artsy gifts.

Au Printemps (✉ 64 bd. Haussmann, 9e, ☎ 01–42–82–50–00, métro Havre-Caumartin, Opéra, or Auber) has three newly revamped floors of women's fashion featuring hot designers like Helmut Lang, Dolce & Gabbana, and Zara. Free fashion shows are held on Tuesday (all year) and Friday (March–October) at 10 AM under the cupola on the 7th floor of La Mode, the building dedicated to women's and children's fashion. The three-store complex also includes La Maison, for housewares and furniture, and Brummel, a six-floor emporium devoted to menswear.

Bazar de l'Hôtel de Ville (✉ 52–64 rue de Rivoli, 4e, ☎ 01–42–74–90–00, métro Hôtel de Ville), better known as BHV, houses an enormous basement hardware store that sells everything from doorknobs to cement mixers. The fashion offerings are minimal, but BHV is noteworthy for quality household goods, home decor materials, and office supplies.

Galeries Lafayette (✉ 40 bd. Haussmann, 9e, ☎ 01–42–82–34–56, métro Chaussée d'Antin, Opéra, or Havre-Caumartin; Centre Commercial Montparnasse, 15e, ☎ 01–45–38–52–87, métro Montparnasse-Bienvenue) carries nearly 80,000 fashion labels under its roof, including rising stars like Mariot Chanet, Ann Demeulemeester, and Marcel Marongiou. Free fashion shows are held every Wednesday at 11 AM (☎ 01–48–74–02–30 for reservations). Along with the world's largest perfumery, the main store boasts the new "Espace Lafayette Maison," a huge Yves Taralon–designed emporium dedicated to the art of living *à la française* (like the French).

Marks & Spencer (✉ 35 bd. Haussmann, 9e, ☎ 01–47–42–42–91, métro Havre-Caumartin, Auber, or Opéra; 88 rue de Rivoli, 4e, ☎ 01–44–61–08–00, métro Hôtel de Ville) is a British chain chiefly noted for its moderately priced basics (underwear, socks, sleep- and sportswear). Its excellent English grocery and take-out food service are enormously popular with Parisians.

La Samaritaine (✉ 19 rue de la Monnaie, 1er, ☎ 01–40–41–20–20, métro Pont-Neuf or Châtelet), a sprawling five-story complex, carries everything from designer fashions to cuckoo clocks but is especially known for kitchen supplies, housewares, and furniture. Its most famous asset is the rooftop café in Building 2 that offers a marvelous view of Notre-Dame.

Budget

Monoprix or Prisunic are French dime stores—with scores of branches throughout the city—that stock inexpensive everyday items like toothpaste, groceries, toys, typing paper, and bath mats—a little of everything. Both chains carry inexpensive children's clothes of surprisingly good quality.

Tati (✉ central location at 140 rue de Rennes, 6e, ☎ 01–45–48–68–31, métro St-Placide), with outlets throughout the city, is known for its bargain-basement prices and hectic, jumbled sales floors. Shop carefully, as goods—from clothes to kitchen utensils—vary in quality. The store recently introduced a hip "La Rue Est à Nous" line of trendy teen fashions.

English-Language Bookstores

Brentano's (✉ 37 av. de l'Opéra, 2e, ☎ 01–42–61–52–50, métro Opéra) is stocked with everything from classics to children's titles. **Galignani** (✉ 224 rue de Rivoli, 1er, ☎ 01–42–60–76–07, métro Tuileries) is a trove of exquisite art and history books. **Shakespeare & Co.** (✉ 37 rue de la Bûcherie, 5e, ☎ 01–43–26–96–50, métro St-Michel) specializes in expatriate literature. **W. H. Smith** (✉ 248 rue de Rivoli, 1er, ☎ 01–42–60–37–97, métro Concorde) carries an excellent range of travel and language books, cookbooks, and fiction for adults and children.

Shopping Arcades and Markets

Paris's 19th-century commercial arcades, called *passages,* are the forerunners of the modern mall. Glass roofs, decorative pillars, and mosaic floors give the passages great charm. The major arcades are on the Right Bank in central Paris.

Galerie Véro-Dodat (✉ 19 rue Jean-Jacques Rousseau, 1er, métro Les Halles) has painted ceilings and slender copper pillars. The **Galerie Vivienne** (✉ 4 rue des Petits-Champs, 2e, métro Bourse) is home to a range of interesting shops, an excellent tearoom, and a quality wine shop. The **Passage Jouffroy** (✉ 12 bd. Montmartre, 2e, métro Montmartre) is full of shops selling toys, postcards, antique canes, and perfumes. The **Passage des Panoramas** (✉ 11 bd. Montmartre, 2e, métro Montmartre), built in 1800, is the oldest of them all. The **Passage des Pavillons** (✉ 6 rue de Beaujolais, 1er, métro Palais-Royal) is near the Palais-Royal gardens.

Flea Markets

The **Marché aux Puces** on Paris's northern boundary (métro Porte de Clignancourt), which takes place Saturday through Monday, still attracts the crowds, but its once unbeatable prices are now a feature of the past. This century-old labyrinth of alleyways packed with antiques dealers' booths and junk stalls now spreads for over a square mile. Early birds pick up the most worthwhile loot. But be warned—if there's one place in Paris where you need to know how to bargain, this is it!

Food Markets

Paris's open-air food markets are among the city's most colorful attractions. Fruits and vegetables are piled high in vibrant pyramids. The variety of cheeses is always astounding. The lively—sometimes chaotic—atmosphere that reigns in most markets makes them a sight worth seeing even if you don't want or need to buy anything. Every quartier has one, although many are open only a few days each week. Sunday morning, till 1 PM, is usually a good time to go; Monday is the day these markets are likely to be closed.

Many of the better-known markets are in areas you'd visit for sightseeing: **rue de Buci** (6e, métro Odéon; open daily) near St-Germain-des-Prés; **rue Mouffetard** (5e, métro Monge; best on weekends) near the Jardin des Plantes; and **rue Lepic** in Montmartre (18e, métro Blanche or Abbesses; best on weekends). The **Marché d'Aligre** (12e, métro Ledru-Rollin), open Monday mornings and weekends, is a bit farther out, beyond the Bastille on rue d'Aligre; Parisians from all over the city know it and love it, but you won't see many tourists in this less affluent area of town. Foods are mostly ethnic, particularly North African.

PARIS A TO Z

Arriving and Departing

By Bus

Long-distance bus journeys within France are uncommon, which may be why Paris has no central bus depot. But if you are arriving or departing by bus, the leading Paris-based bus company is **Eurolines** (✉ 28 av. du Général-de-Gaulle, Bagnolet, ☎ 01–49–72–51–51) in the near eastern suburbs.

By Car

In a country as highly centralized as France, it is no surprise that expressways converge on the capital from every direction: A1 from the north (225 km/140 mi to Lille); A13 from Normandy (225 km/140 mi to Caen); A4 from the east (499 km/310 mi to Strasbourg); A10 from the southwest (579 km/360 mi to Bordeaux); and A7 from the Alps and Riviera (466 km/290 mi to Lyon). Each connects with the *périphérique*, the beltway, whose exits into the city are named, not numbered.

By Plane

Paris is served by two international airports: Charles de Gaulle, also known as Roissy, 26 km (16 mi) northeast; and Orly, 16 km (10 mi) south. Major carriers, among them TWA, American Airlines, and Air France, fly daily from the United States, while Air France, British Airways, British Midland, and Air U.K. offer regular flights from London. *See* Air Travel *in* the Gold Guide for details.

From Charles de Gaulle, the easiest way to get into Paris is on the **RER-B** line, the suburban express train, beneath Terminal 2. Trains to central Paris (Les Halles, St-Michel, Luxembourg) leave every 15 minutes; the fare is 46 francs, and the journey time is 30 minutes. Note that you have to carry your luggage down up and down from the tracks, and trains can be crowded during rush hour. **Buses** operated by Air France (you need not have flown with the airline) run every 15 minutes between Roissy and western Paris (Porte Maillot and the Arc de Triomphe). The fare is 55 francs, and the journey time is about 40 minutes, though rush-hour traffic may make this a slow and frustrating trip. Additionally, the **Roissybus,** operated by RATP, runs directly between Roissy and rue Scribe by the Opéra every 15 minutes and costs 40 francs. **Taxis** are readily available; the fare will be around 200–250 francs, depending on traffic. For the same price as a taxi for two or more people, **Paris Airports Service** (☎ 01–49–62–78–78, reservations must be made two to three days in advance; MasterCard and Visa are accepted) can meet you on arrival in a private car and drive you to your destination.

From Orly airport, the cheapest way to get to Paris is on the **RER-C** line; there's a free shuttle bus from the terminal building to the train station, and trains leave every 15 minutes. The fare is 30 francs, and the train journey takes about 40 minutes. The **Orlyval** service is a shuttle train that runs direct from each Orly terminal to Antony **RER-B** station every seven minutes. A one-way ticket is 54 francs. **Buses** operated by Air France (you need not have flown with the airline) run every 12 minutes between Orly airport and the Air France air terminal at Les Invalides on the Left Bank; the fare is 40 francs, and the trip can take from 30 minutes to an hour. RATP also runs the **Orlybus** between Denfert-Rochereau métro station and Orly every 15 minutes for 30 francs. A 25-minute **taxi** ride costs 130–180 francs. With reservations, **Paris Airports Service** (☞ *above*) can pick you up at Orly and drive you directly to your destination.

By Train

Paris has five international train stations: Gare du Nord (northern France, northern Europe, and England via Calais or the Channel Tunnel); Gare St-Lazare (Normandy and England via Dieppe); Gare de l'Est (Strasbourg, Luxembourg, Basel, and Central Europe); Gare de Lyon (Lyon, Marseille, the Riviera, Geneva, Italy); Gare d'Austerlitz (Loire Valley, southwest France, Spain). The Gare Montparnasse is used by TGV-*Atlantique* bound for Nantes or Bordeaux.

Getting Around

To help you find your way around, buy a *Plan de Paris par Arrondissement,* a city guide available at most kiosks with separate maps of each district, including the whereabouts of métro stations and an index of street names. Maps of the métro/RER network are available free from any métro station and many hotels. They are also posted on every platform, as are maps of the bus network. Bus routes are also marked at bus stops and on buses. The extensive public transportation system is the best way to get around.

By Bicycle

Despite the recent introduction of bike lanes, bicycling in central Paris is not for the fainthearted. Bicycles can be rented at various locations throughout the city (☞ Outdoor Activities and Sports, *above*).

By Bus

Paris buses are marked with the route number and destination in front, and major stopping places along the sides. Most routes operate from 6 AM to 8:30 PM; some continue until midnight. Ten *Noctambus,* or night buses, operate hourly (1 AM to 6 AM) between Châtelet and various near suburbs. The brown bus shelters, topped by red-and-yellow circular signs, contain timetables and route maps. You can use your métro ticket on the buses; if you have individual tickets (as opposed to weekly or monthly tickets), state your destination and be prepared to punch one or more tickets in the red-and-gray machines on-board the bus.

By Car

Don't use a car in Paris unless you have to. Parking is chronically difficult—and expensive—and traffic, except late at night, is awful.

By Métro

The métro is by far the quickest and most efficient way of getting around. Trains run from 5:30 AM until 1:15 AM (be careful—this means that the famous "last métro" can pass your station anytime after 12:30). Stations are signaled either by a large yellow "M" within a circle or by their distinctive curly, green Art Nouveau railings and archway entrances bearing the full title (Métropolitain). You must know the name of the last station on the line you take, as this appears on all signs. A connection (you can make as many as you like on one ticket) is called a *correspondance.* At junction stations, illuminated orange signs bearing the name of the line terminal appear over the correct corridors for correspondance. Illuminated blue signs marked *sortie* indicate the station exit. In general, the métro is safe, although try to avoid lines 2 and 13 if you're alone late at night. Access to métro platforms is through an automatic ticket barrier. Slide your ticket in and pick it up

Paris Métro

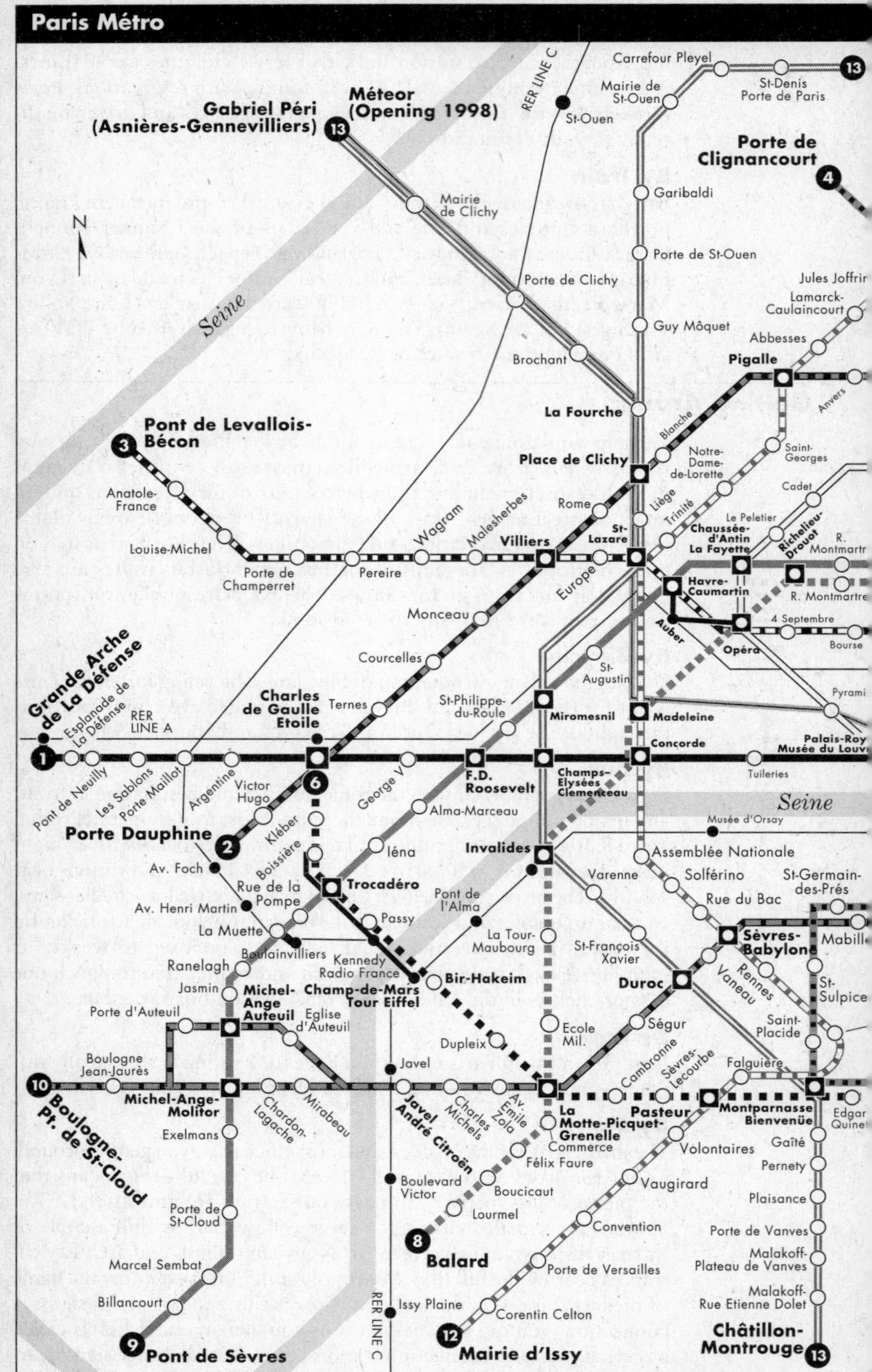

Gabriel Péri (Asnières-Gennevilliers)
Méteor (Opening 1998)
RER LINE C
St-Ouen
Carrefour Pleyel
Mairie de St-Ouen
St-Denis Porte de Paris
Porte de Clignancourt
Garibaldi
Porte de St-Ouen
Mairie de Clichy
Porte de Clichy
Guy Môquet
Jules Joffrin
Lamarck-Caulaincourt
Abbesses
Pigalle
Anvers
Brochant
La Fourche
Seine
Pont de Levallois-Bécon
Anatole-France
Louise-Michel
Porte de Champerret
Pereire
Wagram
Malesherbes
Villiers
Blanche
Place de Clichy
Notre-Dame-de-Lorette
Saint-Georges
Cadet
Rome
Liège
Trinité
St-Lazare
Europe
Chaussée-d'Antin La Fayette
Le Peletier
Richelieu-Drouot
R. Montmartre
Havre-Caumartin
Auber
Opéra
4 Septembre
Bourse
Monceau
Courcelles
Ternes
Grande Arche de La Défense
Esplanade de La Défense
RER LINE A
Charles de Gaulle Etoile
St-Philippe-du-Roule
Miromesnil
St-Augustin
Madeleine
Pyramides
Concorde
Palais-Royal Musée du Louvre
Pont de Neuilly
Les Sablons
Porte Maillot
Argentine
Victor Hugo
George V
F.D. Roosevelt
Champs-Elysées Clemenceau
Tuileries
Alma-Marceau
Musée d'Orsay
Porte Dauphine
Kléber
Boissière
Iéna
Invalides
Assemblée Nationale
Av. Foch
Rue de la Pompe
Trocadéro
Pont de l'Alma
Varenne
Solférino
St-Germain-des-Prés
Av. Henri Martin
Passy
Rue du Bac
La Muette
La Tour-Maubourg
St-François Xavier
Sèvres-Babylone
Mabillon
Boulainvilliers
Kennedy Radio France
Ranelagh
Bir-Hakeim
Rennes
Vaneau
Jasmin
Michel-Ange Auteuil
Champ-de-Mars Tour Eiffel
Duroc
St-Sulpice
Porte d'Auteuil
Eglise d'Auteuil
Ecole Mil.
Ségur
Saint-Placide
Dupleix
Cambronne
Sèvres-Lecourbe
Falguière
Boulogne Jean-Jaurès
Javel
Michel-Ange-Molitor
Chardon-Lagache
Mirabeau
Javel André Citroën
Charles Michels
Av. Emile Zola
La Motte-Picquet-Grenelle
Commerce
Pasteur
Montparnasse Bienvenüe
Edgar Quinet
Boulogne-Pt. de St-Cloud
Exelmans
Félix Faure
Volontaires
Gaîté
Pernety
Boulevard Victor
Boucicault
Vaugirard
Plaisance
Porte de St-Cloud
Lourmel
Convention
Porte de Vanves
Balard
Marcel Sembat
Porte de Versailles
Malakoff-Plateau de Vanves
Billancourt
Issy Plaine
Corentin Celton
Malakoff-Rue Etienne Dolet
Pont de Sèvres
Mairie d'Issy
Châtillon-Montrouge

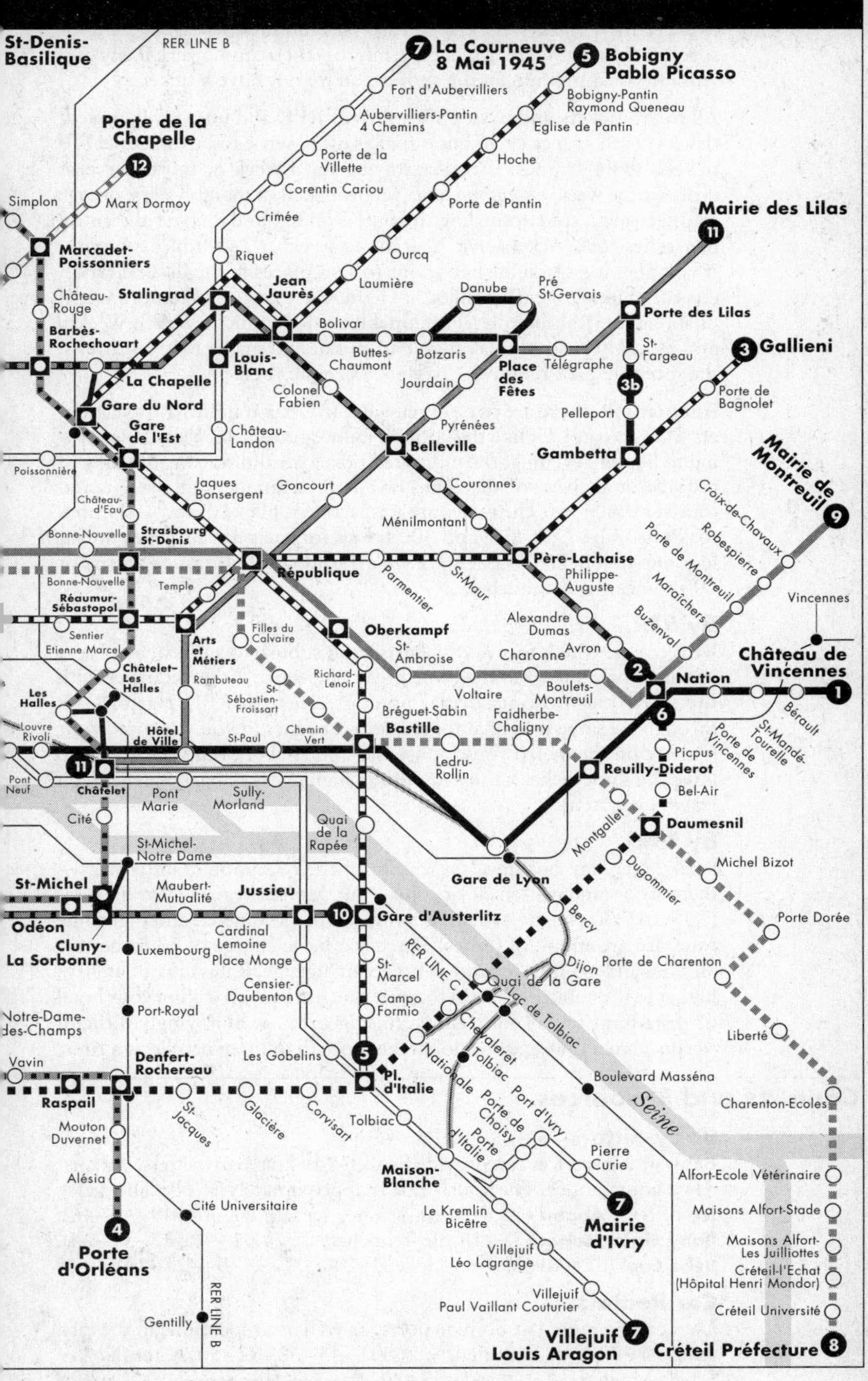
St-Denis-Basilique
RER LINE B
La Courneuve 8 Mai 1945
Bobigny Pablo Picasso
Fort d'Aubervilliers
Bobigny-Pantin Raymond Queneau
Aubervilliers-Pantin 4 Chemins
Eglise de Pantin
Porte de la Chapelle
Porte de la Villette
Hoche
Corentin Cariou
Simplon
Marx Dormoy
Porte de Pantin
Crimée
Mairie des Lilas
Marcadet-Poissonniers
Riquet
Ourcq
Château-Rouge
Stalingrad
Jean Jaurès
Laumière
Danube
Pré St-Gervais
Porte des Lilas
Barbès-Rochechouart
Bolivar
Louis-Blanc
Buttes-Chaumont
Botzaris
Place des Fêtes
Télégraphe
St-Fargeau
Gallieni
La Chapelle
Colonel Fabien
Jourdain
Porte de Bagnolet
Gare du Nord
Gare de l'Est
Pyrénées
Pelleport
Château-Landon
Belleville
Gambetta
Mairie de Montreuil
Poissonnière
Jacques Bonsergent
Goncourt
Couronnes
Croix-de-Chavaux
Château-d'Eau
Ménilmontant
Robespierre
Bonne-Nouvelle
Strasbourg St-Denis
République
Parmentier
St-Maur
Père-Lachaise
Porte de Montreuil
Philippe-Auguste
Maraichers
Vincennes
Temple
Réaumur-Sébastopol
Filles du Calvaire
Oberkampf
Alexandre Dumas
Buzenval
Sentier
Etienne Marcel
Arts et Métiers
St-Ambroise
Charonne
Avron
Château de Vincennes
Châtelet-Les Halles
Rambuteau
Richard-Lenoir
Nation
Les Halles
St-Sébastien-Froissart
Voltaire
Boulets-Montreuil
Louvre Rivoli
Hôtel de Ville
St-Paul
Chemin Vert
Bréguet-Sabin
Bastille
Faidherbe-Chaligny
Bérault
St-Mandé-Tourelle
Porte de Vincennes
Picpus
Reuilly-Diderot
Ledru-Rollin
Pont Neuf
Châtelet
Pont Marie
Sully-Morland
Bel-Air
Cité
Quai de la Rapée
Montgallet
Daumesnil
St-Michel-Notre Dame
Michel Bizot
Gare de Lyon
Dugommier
St-Michel
Maubert-Mutualité
Jussieu
Gare d'Austerlitz
Odéon
Bercy
Porte Dorée
Cluny-La Sorbonne
Luxembourg
Cardinal Lemoine
Place Monge
RER LINE C
Dijon
Porte de Charenton
Quai de la Gare
St-Marcel
Censier-Daubenton
Lac de Tolbiac
Campo Formio
Port-Royal
Notre-Dame-des-Champs
Chevaleret
Liberté
Vavin
Les Gobelins
Nationale
Tolbiac
Denfert-Rochereau
Pl. d'Italie
Port d'Ivry
Boulevard Masséna
Raspail
St-Jacques
Glacière
Corvisart
Porte de Choisy
Charenton-Ecoles
Seine
Mouton Duvernet
Tolbiac
Porte d'Italie
Pierre Curie
Alésia
Maison-Blanche
Alfort-Ecole Vétérinaire
Cité Universitaire
Le Kremlin Bicêtre
Mairie d'Ivry
Maisons Alfort-Stade
Porte d'Orléans
Villejuif Léo Lagrange
Maisons Alfort-Les Juilliottes
Créteil-l'Echat (Hôpital Henri Mondor)
Villejuif Paul Vaillant Couturier
Créteil Université
Gentilly
RER LINE B
Villejuif Louis Aragon
Créteil Préfecture

as it pops up. Keep your ticket during your journey; you will need it to leave the RER system and in case you run into any green-clad inspectors when you are leaving the métro—they can be very nasty and will impose a big fine on the spot if you do not have a ticket.

All métro tickets and passes are valid for RER and bus travel as well; tickets cost 8 francs each, but it makes more sense to buy a *carnet* (10 tickets) for 46 francs. If you're staying for a week or more, the best deals are the weekly *coupon jaune* (yellow ticket) or monthly *carte orange* (orange card), sold according to zone. Zones 1 and 2 cover the entire métro network; tickets cost 72 francs a week or 243 francs a month. If you plan to take suburban trains to visit places in the Ile-de-France, consider a four-zoner (Versailles, St-Germain-en-Laye; 126 francs a week) or six-zoner (Rambouillet, Fontainebleau; 170 francs a week). Weekly and monthly passes are available from rail and major métro stations; the monthly pass requires a passport-size photograph.

Alternatively, there are two-, three-, and five-day unlimited-travel tickets (*Paris Visite*). Unlike the coupon jaune, good from Monday morning to Sunday evening, the unlimited ticket is valid starting any day of the week and gives you discounts on a limited number of museums and tourist attractions. The prices are, respectively, 80, 110, and 170 francs for Paris only; 170, 230, and 300 francs for the suburbs. The equivalent one-day ticket is called *Formule 1* and costs 40 francs (Paris) or 100 francs (with suburbs).

By RER

RER trains, which race across Paris from suburb to suburb, are a sort of supersonic métro and can be great time-savers; they connect with the métro network at several points. Access to RER platforms is through the same type of automatic ticket barrier (if you've started your journey on the métro you can use the same ticket), but you'll need to have the same ticket handy to put through another barrier when you leave the system.

By Taxi

Paris taxis may not have the charm of their London counterparts—there is no standard vehicle or color—but they're cheaper. Daytime rates (7 AM to 7:30 PM) are around 2.80 francs per kilometer, and nighttime rates are around 4.50 francs. There is a basic charge of 13 francs for all rides and a 6-franc charge per piece of luggage. Rates are about 40% higher in the suburbs than in the city. You are best off asking your hotel or restaurant to call for a taxi; cruising cabs are annoyingly difficult to spot. Note that taxis seldom take more than three people at a time.

Contacts and Resources

Baby-Sitters

Baby-sitting services can provide English-speaking baby-sitters with just a few hours notice. The hourly rate is approximately $6 plus an agency fee of $10. **Ababa** (✉ 8 av. du Maine, 15ᵉ, ☎ 01–45–49–46–46). **Baby Sitting Service** (✉ 18 rue Tronchet, 8ᵉ, ☎ 01–46–37–51–24). **Bébé Cool** (✉ 4 rue Faustin-Hélie, 16ᵉ, ☎ 01–45–04–27–14).

Car Rentals

Cars can be rented at both airports, as well as at locations in the city. **Avis** (✉ 60 rue de Ponthieu, 8ᵉ, ☎ 01–45–62–82–50). **Citer** (✉ 113 bd. de Magenta, 13ᵉ, ☎ 01–53–20–04–75). **Europcar** (✉ 202 rue de Rivoli, 1ᵉʳ, ☎ 01–40–15–96–98). **Hertz** (✉ 123 rue Jeanne-d'Arc, 13ᵉ, ☎ 01–45–86–53–33).

Embassies

Canada (✉ 35 av. Montaigne, 8e, ☎ 01–44–43–29–00). **U.K.** (✉ 35 rue du Faubourg-St-Honoré, 8e, ☎ 01–44–51–31–00). **U.S.** (✉ 2 av. Gabriel, 8e, ☎ 01–43–12–22–22).

Emergencies

Ambulance (☎ 15 or 01–45–67–50–50). **Dentist** (☎ 01–43–37–51–00). **Doctor** (☎ 01–43–37–77–77). **Police** (☎ 17). A 24-hour emergency service is available at **American Hospital** (✉ 63 bd. Victor-Hugo, Neuilly, ☎ 01–47–45–71–00). **Hertford British Hospital** (✉ 3 rue Barbès, Levallois-Perret, ☎ 01–47–58–13–12) also has all night emergency service.

Guided Tours

Hour-long boat trips on the Seine are a must for the first-time visitor; the cost is around 50 francs. Some boats serve lunch and dinner (for an additional cost); make reservations in advance. **Bateaux-Mouches** (✉ Pont de l'Alma, 8e, ☎ 01–42–25–96–10, métro Alma-Marceau) boats depart daily 10–noon, 2–7, and 8:30–10:30. **Bateaux Parisiens** (✉ Pont d'Iéna, 7e, ☎ 01–44–11–33–44, métro Trocadéro) depart every half hour in summer and every hour in winter, starting at 10 AM; the last boat departs at at 9 PM (11 PM in summer). **Vedettes du Pont-Neuf** (✉ Depart from the square du Vert Galant, 1er, ☎ 01–46–33–98–38, métro Pont Neuf) depart every half hour 10–noon, 1:30–6:30, and 9 PM–10:30 PM from March to October.

Canauxrama (✉ departures from 5 bis quai de la Loire, 19e, métro Jaurès, or from the Bassin de l'Arsenal, 12e, opposite 50 bd. de la Bastille, métro Bastille, ☎ 01–42–39–15–00) organizes half- and full-day barge tours along the canals of east Paris.

Cityrama (✉ 4 pl. des Pyramides, 1er, ☎ 01–44–55–61–00) and **Paris Vision** (✉ 214 rue de Rivoli, 1er, ☎ 01–42–60–31–25) both organize a number of different tours: two hours on a double-decker bus with live or tape-recorded commentary (English is available) at a cost of about 150 francs; day trips to sights in the Paris region; and theme tours ("Historic Paris," "Modern Paris," "Paris by Night") lasting from 2½ hours to all day and costing 150 to 400 francs (more if admission to a cabaret show is included). For a more intimate—albeit expensive—tour of the city, Cityrama also runs several minibus excursions per day; the bus can take eight people and can pick up or drop off at hotels; the cost is 210 francs for a two-hour tour, 350 francs for three hours. Make reservations through Cityrama or the Tourist Office (☞ *below*). Day trips to sights in the Paris region are also organized by **RATP** (✉ 53 quai des Grands-Augustins, 6e, ☎ 01–40–46–41–41).

Espace Limousines (✉ 18 rue Vignon, 9e, ☎ 01–42–65–63–16) has guides with luxury cars or minibuses (holding up to seven passengers) who will take you around Paris and the environs for a minimum of three hours. Reservations are required, and the cost is about 300 francs per hour.

For sightseeing at your own pace, take **Paris Bus,** a red double-decker with nine pick-up and drop-off points around Paris. Tours start from Trocadéro at 10:20 AM and every 50 minutes until 5. Tickets are good for two days and cost 120 francs.

There are plenty of guided walking tours of specific areas of Paris, often concentrating on a historical or architectural topic. Guides are enthusiastic but not always English-speaking. Charges range from 40–60 francs, and tours last about two hours. Details are published in the weekly magazines *Pariscope* and *L'Officiel des Spectacles* under "Conférences."

You can sometimes make reservations for walking tours organized by the **Caisse Nationale des Monuments Historiques,** Bureau des Visites (⊠ Hôtel de Sully, 62 rue St-Antoine, 4e, ☎ 01–44–61–20–00).

Late-Night Pharmacies

The **Pharmacie Dérhy** (⊠ 84 av. des Champs-Elysées, 8e, ☎ 01–45–62–02–41, métro Georges-V) is open 24 hours a day, 365 days a year. The **Pharmacie Européenne de la Place Clichy** (⊠ 6 pl. Clichy, 9e, ☎ 01–48–74–65–18, métro Place de Clichy) is open 24 hours, seven days a week.

Travel Agencies

Air France (⊠ 119 av. des Champs-Elysées, 8e, ☎ 01–44–08–24–24). **American Express** (⊠ 11 rue Scribe, 9e, ☎ 01–47–77–70–00). **Wagon-Lits** (⊠ 32 rue du Quatre-Septembre, 2e, ☎ 01–42–66–15–80).

Visitor Information

The **Office du Tourisme de la Ville de Paris** (⊠ Paris Tourist Office, 127 av. des Champs-Elysées, 75008, ☎ 01–49–52–53–54; 01–49–52–53–56 for recorded information in English) is open daily 9 AM–8 PM. It has branches at all mainline train stations except Gare St-Lazare.

3 Ile-de-France

Versailles, Chartres, Fontainebleau

The soft light and lush rolling hills of the region around Paris inspired painters and kings alike. Van Gogh took up residence here, as did Louis XIV, who built one of France's most fantastic châteaux at Versailles. Here, too, Gothic architecture reached a pinnacle in the soaring towers of Chartres.

PARIS MAY BE SMALL AS CAPITAL CITIES GO, with just over 2 million inhabitants, but the Ile-de-France, the region around Paris, contains more than 10 million people—one-sixth of France's entire population. That type of statistic conjures up visions of a gray, never-ending suburban sprawl. Nothing could be further from the truth.

Although not actually an *île* (island), the Ile-de-France is figuratively isolated from the rest of France by three rivers—the Seine, the Oise, and the Marne—that weave meandering circles around its periphery. The verdant landscape, within easy reach of the capital, was a strong temptation early on; the region was a favorite retreat of medieval kings and clerics. Castles and palaces went up in the towns of Vincennes, St-Germain-en-Laye, and Provins; abbeys and cathedrals sprang skyward in Chartres, Senlis, and Royaumont.

The Ile-de-France never lost favor with the powerful, partly because its many forests—large chunks of which still stand—harbored sufficient game to ensure a regular kill even for bloated, pampered monarchs. First Fontainebleau, in manageable Renaissance proportions, then Versailles, in minion-crushing, bicep-flexing Baroque excess, reflected the royal desire to transform hunting lodges into palatial residences. Vaux-le-Vicomte, Dampierre, Rambouillet, Maisons-Laffitte, and Chantilly exude almost comparable grandeur.

More recently, another kind of magic kingdom was built in this region: Disneyland Paris. Although it did not meet with instant success, it has finally found its feet. On the whole, however, the architectural impact of the 20th century has been discreet in the Ile-de-France. You may find it disorienting that so many rural backwaters exist within 30 minutes' drive of the capital. The Gallic mania for rational planning—with new developments assigned to restricted areas—has limited the impact of suburban sprawl. Students of modern architecture are served food for thought in such so-called "new towns" as Cergy-Pontoise or St-Quentin-en-Yvelines, and sociologists won't lack material in the concrete ghettos of the "red belt" north of Paris (so called because its working-class population traditionally votes communist), but you can avoid them.

Pleasures and Pastimes

Artists' Residences

Claude Monet's house and garden at Giverny, with its famous lily pond, is a moving visual link to Impressionist painting. In Auvers-sur-Oise, Vincent van Gogh had a final burst of creativity before committing suicide. André Derain lived in Chambourcy; Camille Pissarro at Pontoise; Alfred Sisley at Moret-sur-Loing. Rousseau, Millet, and Corot paved the way for Impressionism with their penchant for outdoor landscape painting at Barbizon.

Châteaux

The majestic château of Versailles, perhaps the most famous palace in the world, is not to be missed. Nor are its splendid neighbors—Fontainebleau, Vaux-le-Vicomte, St-Germain-en-Laye, and Chantilly. And there are another dozen châteaux almost as grand—led by Dampierre, Rambouillet, Maintenon, Maisons-Laffitte, and Thoiry.

Dining

The Ile-de-France's smart restaurants can be just as pricey as their Parisian counterparts. But in smaller towns, and for those prepared to venture off the beaten tourist path, nourishing, well-priced meals are not hard to find. The style of cuisine mirrors that of Paris. "Local delicacies" cited by earnest textbooks—lamb stew, pâté Pantin (pastry filled with meat or fish), or pig's trotters—tend to be obsolete. Instead, look for sumptuous game and asparagus in season in the south of the region, and the soft, creamy cheese of Meaux and Coulommiers to the east. Reservations are a must in summer.

CATEGORY	COST*
$$$$	over 400 frs
$$$	250 frs–400 frs
$$	125 frs–250 frs
$	under 125 frs

**per person for a three-course meal, including tax (20.6%) and tip but not wine*

Forests

Vast tracts of forest around Paris still resist the onset of urbanization. The forests of St-Germain, Rambouillet, Chantilly, and Fontainebleau are the largest and most famous; they are ideal for hiking or biking.

Lodging

In summer, hotel rooms are at a premium and reservations are essential; almost all accommodations in the swankier towns—Versailles, Rambouillet, and Fontainebleau—are on the costly side. Take nothing for granted. Picturesque Senlis, for instance, does not have a single hotel in its historic downtown area.

CATEGORY	COST*
$$$$	over 800 frs
$$$	550 frs–800 frs
$$	300 frs–550 frs
$	under 300 frs

**All prices are for a standard double room for two, including tax (20.6%) and service charge.*

Exploring the Ile-de-France

The region can be covered in a series of loops: west from Paris to Versailles, Chartres, and Giverny; north and east along the Oise Valley via Chantilly to Disneyland; and southeast from Evry to Fontainebleau and Provins.

Numbers in the text correspond to numbers in the margin and on The Ile-de-France, Versailles, and Fontainebleau maps.

Great Itineraries

You could spend weeks visiting the dozens of châteaux and historic towns in the region. But if you don't have that much time, try one of the following shorter itineraries. Spend two to eight days exploring the area or take day trips from Paris—most sites are within easy reach of the capital by car or train.

IF YOU HAVE 2 DAYS

Head west from Paris to nearby **St-Germain-en-Laye** ② and visit either the château or the Prieuré museum. Try to reach **Versailles** ③–⑩ for lunch, then visit the château and the park. The next morning spend more time in Versailles or leave early and visit **Rambouillet** ⑫ or **Maintenon** ⑬ on your way to **Chartres** ⑭; spend half a day exploring the cathedral and the old town.

The Ile-de-France

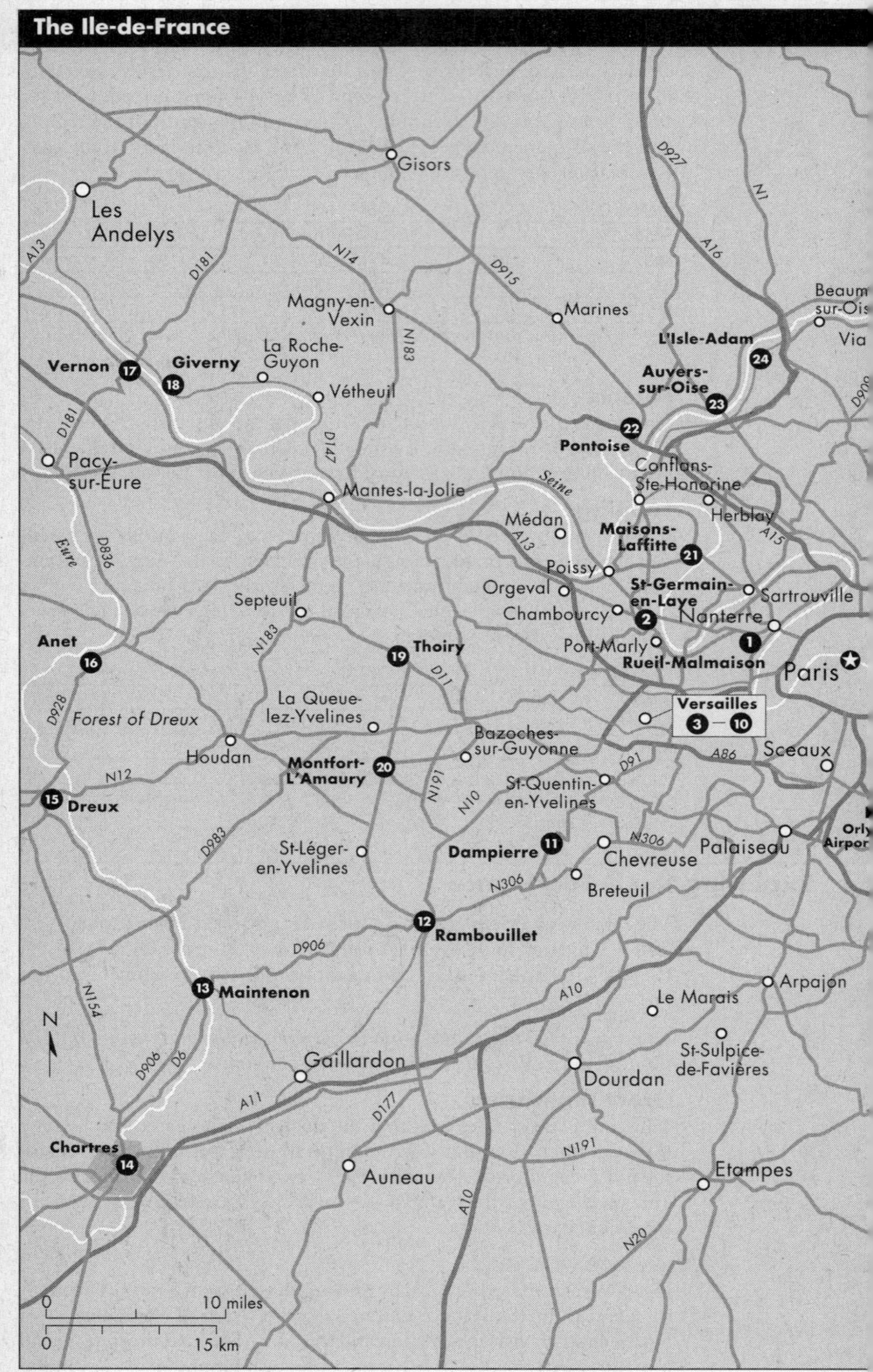

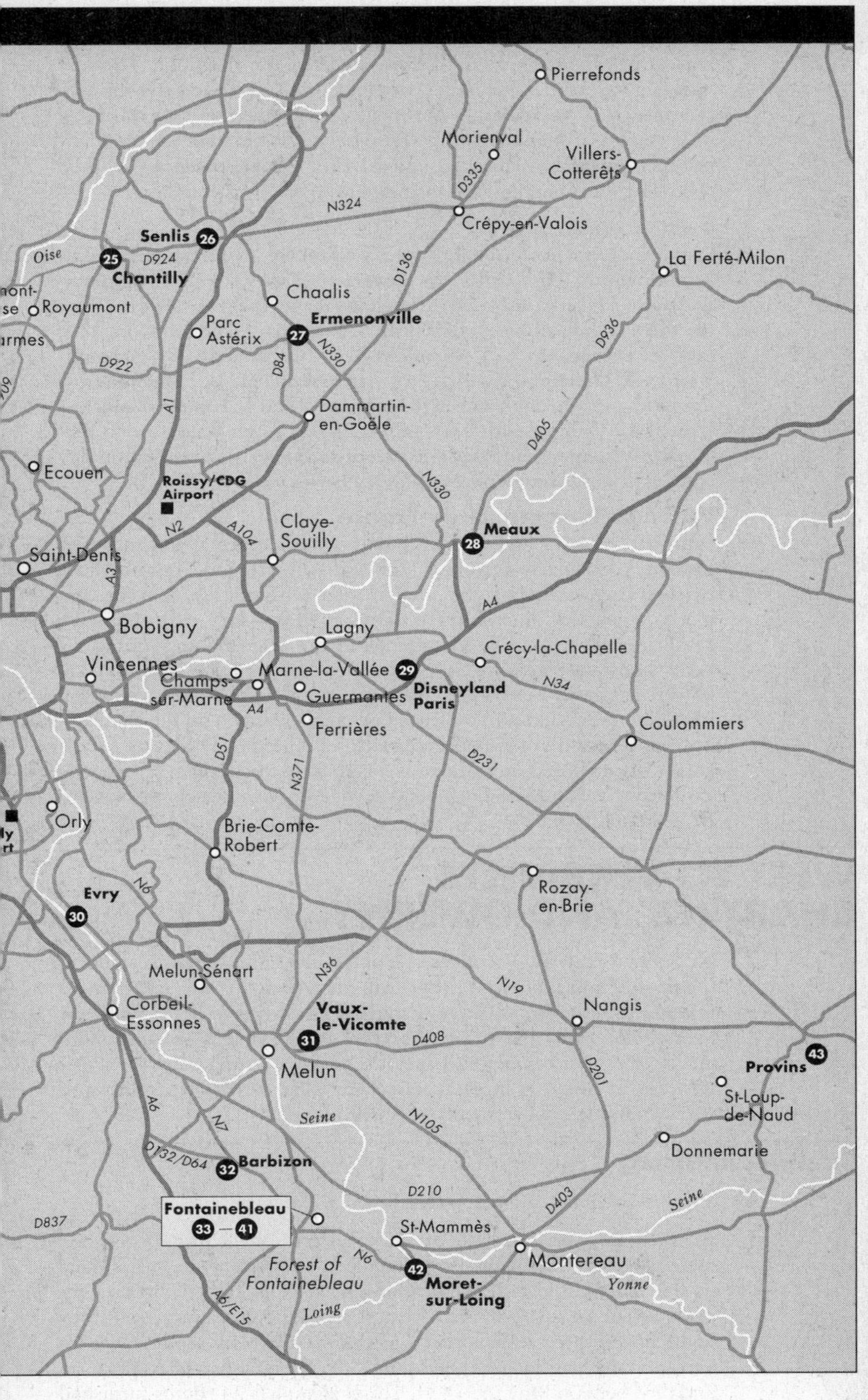
Pierrefonds
Morienval
D335
Villers-Cotterêts
N324
Crépy-en-Valois
Senlis 26
Oise
25 Chantilly
D924
La Ferté-Milon
D136
Royaumont
Chaalis
Ermenonville
Parc Astérix
27
N330
D936
D922
D84
A1
Dammartin-en-Goële
D405
Ecouen
Roissy/CDG Airport
N330
N2
A104
Claye-Souilly
Meaux
28
Saint-Denis
A3
Bobigny
A4
Lagny
Crécy-la-Chapelle
Vincennes
Champs-sur-Marne
Marne-la-Vallée
29
Disneyland Paris
Guermantes
N34
A4
Ferrières
Coulommiers
D51
D231
N371
Orly
Brie-Comte-Robert
Rozay-en-Brie
Evry
N6
30
Melun-Sénart
N36
N19
Nangis
Corbeil-Essonnes
Vaux-le-Vicomte
31
D408
Melun
D201
Provins
43
St-Loup-de-Naud
A6
Seine
N105
N7
Donnemarie
D132/D64
32 Barbizon
D210
D403
Seine
Fontainebleau
33 — 41
D837
St-Mammès
Montereau
N6
Forest of Fontainebleau
42
Moret-sur-Loing
Yonne
Loing
A6/E15

IF YOU HAVE 4 DAYS

Take the expressway north from Paris to **Senlis** ㉖, visit the old town and cathedral, then head to **Chantilly** ㉕ for the afternoon. The next morning follow the Oise Valley, stopping briefly in **Auvers-sur-Oise** ㉓, en route to **Versailles** ③–⑩. Spend the morning of your third day in Versailles or **Rambouillet** ⑫; try to be in **Chartres** ⑭ by early afternoon. Spend the night there and drive to **Fontainebleau** ㉝–㊶ the following morning, perhaps visiting **Barbizon** ㉜ on your way.

IF YOU HAVE 8 DAYS

Spend your first day in **Senlis** ㉖ and **Chantilly** ㉕. On the second day, head down the Oise Valley, via **Auvers-sur-Oise** ㉓ to **St-Germain-en-Laye** ②. Head northwest through the Seine Valley to **Giverny** ⑱ on the third day; spend the night near **Vernon** ⑰. The following day, take the expressway to **Versailles** ③–⑩. On the fifth day, go southwest to **Chartres** ⑭, with a stop in **Rambouillet** ⑫ or **Maintenon** ⑬ if time allows. On day six head to **Barbizon** ㉜ and **Fontainebleau** ㉝–㊶; make it your base for two nights. On day seven make sure to visit **Vaux-le-Vicomte** ㉛ and perhaps **Moret-sur-Loing** ㊷; finish up on day eight at either **Disneyland Paris** ㉙ or **Provins** ㊸.

When to Tour the Ile-de-France

With its extensive forests, the Ile-de-France is especially beautiful in the fall, particularly October. June and July are good months, too, whereas August can be sultry and crowded. On Saturday nights in summer you can see son-et-lumière shows in Moret-sur-Loing and make candlelit visits to Vaux-le-Vicomte. Be aware when making your travel plans that some places are closed one or two days a week: The châteaux of Versailles and Auvers are closed on Monday; the Prieuré museum in St-Germain is closed both Monday and Tuesday; and the châteaux of Chantilly and Fontainebleau are closed Tuesday. Disneyland Paris gets really crowded on summer weekends. So does Giverny (Monet's garden): at its best May–June, but, like Vaux-le-Vicomte, closed November–March.

WEST TO VERSAILLES, CHARTRES, AND GIVERNY

Not only is majestic Versailles one of the most unforgettable sights in the Ile-de-France, but it is also within easy reach of Paris, less than 30 minutes by either train (☞ Arriving and Departing *in* Ile-de-France A to Z, *below*) or car (A13 expressway from Porte d'Auteuil). With neighboring St-Germain-en-Laye, it's also the starting point for a visit to western Ile-de-France, anchored by Chartres to the south and Monet's home at Giverny to the north.

Rueil-Malmaison

❶ *8 km (5 mi) west of Paris on N13 via La Défense.*

Rueil-Malmaison is a slightly dreary western suburb of Paris, but the memory of the legendary pair, Napoléon and Joséphine, still haunts ★ its château. Built in 1622, **La Malmaison** was bought by the future Empress Joséphine in 1799 as a love nest for Napoléon and herself (they had married three years earlier). After the childless Joséphine was divorced by the heir-hungry emperor in 1809, she retired to La Malmaison and died here on May 29, 1814. The château has 24 rooms furnished with exquisite tables, chairs, and sofas of the Napoleonic period; of special note are the library, game room, and dining room. The walls are adorned with works by contemporary artists of the day, such as

Jacques-Louis David, Pierre-Paul Prud'hon, and Baron Gérard. Take time to admire the clothes and hats that belonged to Napoléon and Joséphine, particularly the empress's gowns. Their carriage can be seen in one of the garden pavilions, and another pavilion contains a unique collection of snuffboxes donated by Prince George of Greece. The gardens themselves are delightful, especially the regimented rows of spring tulips. ✉ *15 av. du Château,* ☎ *01–41–29–05–55,* 🎟 *28 frs.* ⏲ *Wed.–Mon. 10–noon and 1:30–5.*

The **Bois Préau,** a smaller mansion dating from the 17th century, is close to La Malmaison (and is included in the same admission ticket). It was acquired by Joséphine in 1810, after her divorce, but was subsequently reconstructed in the 1850s. Today its 10 rooms, complete with furniture and objects from the Empire period, are devoted mainly to souvenirs of Napoléon's exile on the island of St. Helena. ✉ *av. de l'Impératrice,* ☎ *01–47–08–37–67.* 🎟 *15 frs.* ⏲ *Wed.–Mon. 10:30–12:30 and 2–5:30.*

The Ile-de-France was once a wine-producing center—though there's little evidence these days—and one of the few places where the tradition lingers is in the hilly neighboring suburb of Suresnes, where a Fête des Vendanges is staged after the harvest on the first weekend of October.

St-Germain-en-Laye

❷ *8 km (5 mi) west of Rueil-Malmaison on N13, 16 km (10 mi) west of Paris.*

The elegant town of St-Germain-en-Laye, perched on a hill above the Seine and encircled by forest, has lost little of its original cachet, despite the invasion of wealthy Parisians who commute to work on the RER. Those with a bent for the swashbuckling novels of Alexandre Dumas will enjoy the **Château de Monte-Cristo** at Port-Marly on the southern fringe of St-Germain (signposted to your left as you arrive from Rueil-Malmaison). Purists may find that its fanciful exterior, where pilasters, cupolas, and stone carvings compete for attention, has crossed the line from opulence to tastelessness, but—as in the novels, *The Count of Monte-Cristo* and *The Three Musketeers*—swagger, not subtlety, is what counts. Dumas built the château after his books' surging popularity made him rich in the 1840s. Construction costs and lavish partying meant he went broke just as quickly, and he skedaddled to a Belgian exile in 1849. The château contains pictures, Dumas mementos, and the luxurious Moorish Chamber, with spellbinding, interlacing plasterwork executed by Arab craftsmen (lent by the Bey of Tunis) and recently restored by a donation from Moroccan king Hassan II. There's also a miniature version of the Château d'If in Marseilles—scene of the Count of Monte-Cristo's most heroic exploits—in a miniature lake in the château park. ✉ *av. du Président-Kennedy,* ☎ *01–30–61–61–35.* 🎟 *30 frs.* ⏲ *Apr.–Oct., Tues.–Sun. 10–6.*

Next to the RER train station is the stone-and-brick **Château de St-Germain,** with its dry moat and intimidating circular towers; it dates from the 16th and 17th centuries. A royal palace has existed here since the early 12th century, when Louis VI—known as Le Gros (The Fat)—exploited St-Germain's defensive potential in his bid to pacify the Ile-de-France. A hundred years later, Louis IX (St-Louis) added the elegant **Ste-Chapelle,** the château's oldest remaining section. The figures on the tympanum (the inset triangular area over the main door) are believed to be the first known representations of French royalty, portraying Louis with his mother, Blanche de Castille, and other members of his family.

Charles V (1364–80) built a powerful defensive keep in the mid-14th century, but from the 1540s, François I and his successors transformed St-Germain into a palace of more domestic, and less warlike, vocation. Louis XIV was born here, and it was here that his father, Louis XIII, died. Until 1682—when the court moved to Versailles—it remained the country's foremost royal residence outside Paris. Since 1867 the château has housed the impressive **Musée des Antiquités Nationales** (Museum of Ancient History), holding a trove of artifacts, figurines, brooches, and weapons from the Stone Age to the 8th century. ✉ *pl. Charles de Gaulle,* ☎ *01–34–51–53–65.* 🎫 *23 frs, 16 frs on Sun.* 🕙 *Wed.–Mon. 9–5:15.*

★ The quaint **Musée du Prieuré** (Priory Museum) is devoted to the work of the artist Maurice Denis (1870–1943) and his fellow Symbolists and Nabis—painters opposed to the naturalism of their 19th-century Impressionist contemporaries. Denis found the calm of the former Jesuit priory, set above tiered gardens, ideally suited to his spiritual themes which he expressed in stained glass, ceramics, and frescoes, as well as oils. ✉ *2 bis rue Maurice-Denis.* 🎫 *25 frs.* 🕙 *Wed.–Fri. 10–5:30, weekends 10–6:30.*

In the village of Chambourcy, 3 km (2 mi) northwest of St-Germain-en-Laye via N13, you'll find the stately **Maison André-Derain** (André-Derain House). This 17th-century building is where the versatile Derain (1880–1954), best known for his pioneering, hotly colored Fauve paintings, lived from 1935 until his death. You can admire his well-preserved studio and a smattering of his works, and watch a 12-minute film about his career. ✉ *64 Grande Rue,* ☎ *01–30–74–70–04.* 🎫 *20 frs.* 🕙 *Weekends 2–4:30.*

OFF THE BEATEN PATH

MÉDAN – Émile Zola moved to the village of Médan, 11 km (7 mi) northwest of St-Germain-en-Laye, in 1877 after the runaway success of his novel *L'Assommoir.* Until the 1980s Zola's house, overlooking the Seine and the Paris–Le Havre rail line he smokily evokes in *La Bête Humaine,* was used as an orphanage. You can now visit the spacious rooms (including the study where Zola wrote many of his novels) furnished in the surprisingly ostentatious, bourgeois taste of one of France's most rebellious writers, renowned for his defense of the working classes. ✉ *26 rue Pasteur,* ☎ *01-39-75-35-65.* 🎫 *25 frs.* 🕙 *Weekends 2-6.*

Dining and Lodging

$$ ✕ **La Feuillantine.** Friendly service and an imaginative, good-value prix-fixe menu have made this restaurant a success. Gizzard salad, salmon with endive, and herbed chicken fricassee with morels are among the specialties. ✉ *10 rue des Louviers,* ☎ *01–34–51–04–24. MC, V.*

$$ ✕ **La Petite Auberge.** The specialty here is farmhouse-style cooking from the Aveyron region of southwest France. Aged beef is cooked over an open fire, and red wine (Chinon, from the Loire Valley) is drawn straight from the barrel. Game is served in season. ✉ *119 bis rue Léon-Desnoyer,* ☎ *01–34–51–03–99. Jacket required. MC, V. Closed Tues., mid-July–mid-Aug. No lunch Sat.*

$$$–$$$$ ★ 🏨 **La Forestière.** This is St-Germain's most stylish hotel and a member of the deluxe Relais & Châteaux chain. Its forest setting, its 18th-century-style furniture, and its fine restaurant, the Cazaudehore, contribute to a sense of well-being. The restaurant is closed to nonguests on Monday (except holidays). ✉ *1 av. du Président-Kennedy, 78100,* ☎ *01–39–10–38–38,* FAX *01–39–73–73–88. 25 rooms and 5 suites. Restaurant. MC, V.*

Nightlife and the Arts

The giant **Fête des Loges** fair is held in the Forest of St-Germain from July to mid-August.

Versailles

14 km (9 mi) south of St-Germain-en-Laye via N186, 16 km (10 mi) west of Paris.

Paris in the 17th century was a rowdy, rabble-ridden city; Louis XIV hated it. He lost no time in casting his cantankerous royal eye over the Ile-de-France in search of a new power base. Marshy, inhospitable Versailles was the place of his dreams. Down came his father's modest royal hunting lodge and up went a new château. The town itself, with its broad, leafy boulevards, is easily underestimated: Most people are usually exhausted from exploring the palace and park.

★ ❸ The **Château de Versailles** seems monstrous, but it wasn't big enough for the army of 20,000 noblemen, servants, and sycophants who moved in with Louis XIV. A new city—a new capital, in fact—had to be constructed from scratch to accommodate them. Town planners promptly dreamt up vast Baroque mansions and avenues broader than the Champs-Elysées.

It is hardly surprising that Louis XIV's successors felt out of sync with their architectural inheritance. Louis XV transformed the royal apartments into places to live in rather than pose. The hapless Louis XVI cowered in the Petit Trianon in the leafy depths of Versailles's gardens, out of the mighty château's shadow. His queen, Marie-Antoinette, lost her head well before her trip to the guillotine in 1793, pretending to be a peasant shepherdess amid the ersatz rusticity of her oh-so-cute Potemkin hamlet.

You enter the château—built by architects Louis Le Vau and Jules Hardouin-Mansart between 1662 and 1690—through the gilt iron gates from the huge place d'Armes. On the first floor of the château, dead center as you approach across the sprawling cobbled forecourt, is Louis XIV's bedchamber. The two wings were occupied by the royal children and princes of the blood, while courtiers made do in the attics.

One of the palace's trademark sights is the **Galerie des Glaces** (Hall of Mirrors), now fully restored to sparkling glory. It was here, after France's capitulation, that Otto von Bismarck proclaimed the unified German Empire in 1871; and here that the controversial Treaty of Versailles, asserting Germany's responsibility for World War I, was signed in 1919. The **Grands Appartements** (State Rooms) that flank the Hall of Mirrors retain much of their original Baroque decoration: gilt stucco, painted ceilings, and marble sculpture. Perhaps the most extravagant room is the **Salon d'Apollon,** the former throne room, dedicated to the sun god Apollo, Louis XIV's mythical hero. Equally interesting are the **Petits Appartements,** where the royal family and friends lived in (relative) privacy.

In the north wing of the château you'll find the solemn white-and-gold **chapelle** (chapel), completed in 1710; the intimate **Opéra Royal** (opera house), the first oval hall in France, built by J. A. Gabriel for Louis XV in 1770; and, connecting the two, the 17th-century **galleries,** with exhibits retracing the château's history. The south wing contains the majestically proportioned **Galerie des Batailles** (Gallery of Battles), lined with gigantic canvases extolling French military glory. ☎ *01–30–84–74–00.* 🎫 *45 frs.* ⏲ *Tues.–Sun. 9–6:30, 9–5:30 in winter (Ga-*

Cathédrale St-Louis, **8**
Château de Versailles, **3**
Écuries, **7**
Grand Trianon, **4**
Hameau, **6**
Musée Lambinet, **10**
Notre-Dame, **9**
Petit Trianon, **5**

Versailles

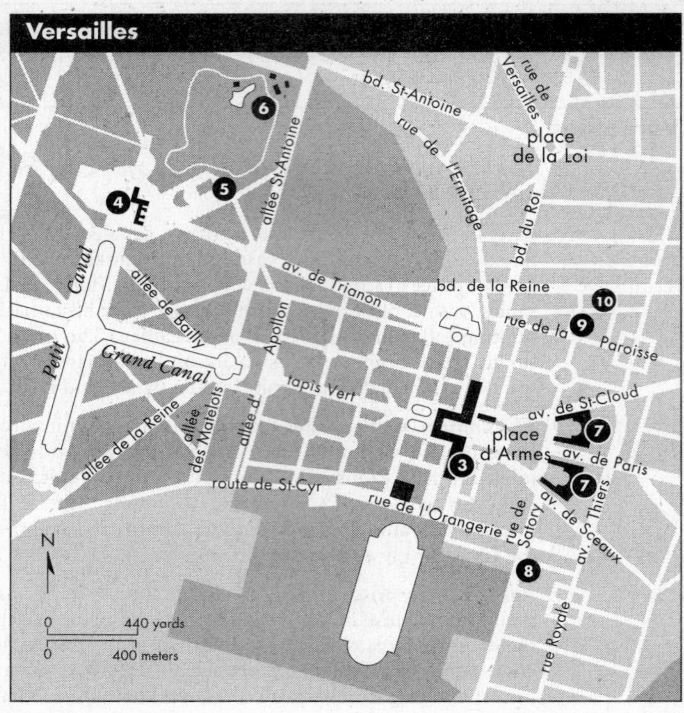

lerie des Glaces 9:45–5; Opéra Royal 9:45–3:30). Tours of Opéra Royal and Petits Appartements every 15 min.

★ After the awesome feast of interior decor, the **park** is an ideal place to catch your breath. The gardens were designed by André Le Nôtre, whose work here represents classical French landscaping at its most formal and sophisticated. The 250-acre grounds include woods, lawns, flower beds, statues, artificial lakes, and fountains galore. The distances are vast—the Trianons themselves are over a mile from the château—so you might like to rent a bike from the Grille de la Reine on boulevard de la Reine (near the Trianon Palace hotel).

The park is at its golden-leafed best in the fall, but is also enticing in summer—especially on Sundays when the fountains are in full flow. They become a spectacle of rare grandeur during the **Fêtes de Nuit,** light-and-fireworks shows in July and September. ☎ *01–39–50–36–22 for details of the Fêtes de Nuit.* 🎫 *25 frs Sun., May–Sept., free other times.* ⏲ *Grounds daily 7–dusk.*

❹ **Grand Trianon,** built by Hardouin-Mansart in 1687, is a scaled-down, pink-marble pleasure palace now occasionally used to entertain visiting heads of state. Most of the time it's open for you to admire its lavish interior and early 19th-century furniture. 🎫 *25 frs.* ⏲ *Oct.–Apr., Tues.–Sun. 10–5:30; May–Sept., Tues.–Sun. 10–6:30.*

❺ The comparatively dainty **Petit Trianon** was built by J. A. Gabriel in 1768. It's a mansion, not a palace—modest by Versailles standards, albeit sumptuously furnished and stuffed with mementos of Marie-Antoinette. Look for her initials wrought into the iron railings of the main staircase. 🎫 *15 frs.* ⏲ *Oct.–Apr., Tues.–Fri. 10–5:30; May–Sept., Tues.–Sun. 10–6:30.*

Beyond the Petit Trianon and across the Petit Lac—which looks more
like a stream, as it describes a wriggly semicircle—is the queen's
6 **Hameau** (hamlet), where Marie-Antoinette lived out her romanticized
dreams of peasant life. With its water mill, genuine lake (Grand Lac),
and pigeon loft, this make-believe village is outrageously pretty.

7 The town of Versailles is majestic. Facing the château are the **Écuries,**
8 royal stables of regal dimensions. The **Cathédrale St-Louis** is an austere edifice with a powerful two-tiered facade; it was built from 1743
to 1754 and contains fine paintings and an organ loft. The sturdy
9 Baroque church of **Notre-Dame** was built from 1684 to 1686 by Jules
Hardouin-Mansart as the parish church for Louis XIV's brand new
town; the Sun King even deigned to lay the foundation stone. Around
the back of Notre-Dame, housed in an imposing 18th-century man-
10 sion, is the wide-ranging **Musée Lambinet,** whose maze of rooms is furnished with paintings, weapons, fans, and porcelain. ✉ *54 bd. de la
Reine,* ☎ *01–39–50–30–32.* 🎟 *25 frs.* ⏲ *Tues.–Sun. 2–6.*

Dining and Lodging

$$$$ ★ ✕ **Les Trois Marches.** The restaurant at the Trianon Palace (☞ *below*) is recognized as one of the best in the Ile-de-France. It's hard to wait after perusing Gérard Vié's menu, including lobster bisque, salmon with fennel, and turbot *galette* (cake). In fine weather you can eat on the huge outdoor terrace. ✉ *1 bd. de la Reine,* ☎ *01–39–50–13–21. Reservations essential. Jacket and tie. Closed Sun., Mon., and Aug. AE, DC, MC, V.*

$$–$$$ ✕ **Brasserie La Fontaine.** If you have neither the time nor the budget to do justice to Gérard Vié's cuisine at Les Trois Marches (☞ *above*), head for his "annex" across the garden. Designed as a true brasserie, with crimson velvet seats and aproned waiters, the restaurant is exceptional when it comes to the zesty simmered snails, pollack roasted with carrots, or chocolate fritters with gingerbread ice. ✉ *1 bd. de la Reine,* ☎ *01–30–84–38–47. AE, MC, V.*

$$ ✕ **Quai No. 1.** Fish and seafood rule supreme amid the sails, barometers, and model ships of this quaintly decked-out restaurant. Home-smoked salmon, and sauerkraut with fish are specialties. Eating à la carte isn't too expensive, and there are good-value prix-fixe menus. ✉ *1 av. de St-Cloud,* ☎ *01–39–50–42–26. MC, V. Closed Mon. No dinner Sun.*

$$$$ 🏨 **Sofitel.** Nestled behind a giant triumphal arch dating from the Sun King's era, this luxury hotel is closer to the old town and château (and a bit cheaper) than the Trianon Palace (☞ *below*). Rooms are spacious and decor subdued to the point of blandness. Prix-fixe menus in the Manèges restaurant start at around 160 francs. ✉ *2 bis av. de Paris, 78000,* ☎ *01–39–53–30–31,* FAX *01–39–53–87–20. 146 rooms and 6 suites. Restaurant, bar, business services. AE, DC, MC, V.*

$$$$ ★ 🏨 **Trianon Palace.** This deluxe hotel, a turn-of-the-century creation of imposing size, is in a huge garden close to the château park. Its once-faded charm was given a thorough overhaul by its new Japanese owners, and the results are spectacular: The health club alone is worth the price of admission. ✉ *1 bd. de la Reine, 78000,* ☎ *01–30–84–38–00,* FAX *01–39–49–00–77. 97 rooms and 32 suites. Restaurant, pool, health club, business services. AE, DC, MC, V.*

$$$ 🏨 **Le Versailles.** This unpretentious modern hotel, close to the château, is warmly recommended if you plan to explore the town on foot. Rooms are comfortable but lack character. ✉ *7 rue Ste-Anne, 78000,* ☎ *01–39–50–64–65,* FAX *01–39–02–37–85. 50 rooms. AE, DC, MC, V.*

$$ 🏨 **Home St-Louis.** The small Home St-Louis is a good, cheap, quiet bet—close to the cathedral and not too far from the château. ✉ *28 rue St-*

Louis, 78000, ☎ 01–39–50–23–55, FAX 01–39–21–62–45. 27 rooms. MC, V.

Nightlife and the Arts

A **music festival,** with concerts and operas in the town and château, runs May–June; call the tourist office (☎ 01–30–97–81–03) for details.

Shopping

Passage de la Geôle (✉ 10 rue Rameau), open Friday–Sunday 9–7, is the site of a good antiques market. **Aux Colonnes** (✉ 14 rue Hoche) is a highly rated *confiserie* (candy shop) with an astounding array of chocolates and candies; it's closed Monday. **Les Délices du Palais** (✉ 4 rue Maréchal-Foch) has everything for the makings of an impromptu picnic (cold cuts, cheese, salads); it's closed Monday. **Eugène Le Gall** (✉ 15 rue Ducis) has a huge choice of cheeses—including one of France's widest selection of goat cheeses; it's closed Sunday afternoon and Monday. The **place du Marché** has an open-air market on Tuesday, Friday, and weekends; there are also four 19th-century timber-roofed halls with smartly presented fish, meat, and spice stalls open every day except Sunday afternoons.

En Route Take the D91 south from Versailles for 14 km (9 mi) to the ruined **Abbaye de Port-Royal-des-Champs,** where France's greatest playwright, Jean Racine, studied in the 1650s. Then turn left along D46 through the glades and folds of the Chevreuse Valley, then right along D906; watch for a left turn 5 km (3 mi) further on, leading to the steep-roofed **Château de Breteuil,** owned by the same family since the 17th century. Interior highlights range from Swedish porcelain to Gobelin tapestries and a richly inlaid Teschen table, encrusted with pearls and precious stones—an 18th-century present from Austrian empress Maria Theresa. The vast wooded park has picnic areas and playgrounds. Life-size wax figures—including English King Edward VII and novelist Marcel Proust (a one-time guest)—lurk in many of the rooms. ☎ *01–30–52–05–02.* 🎫 *Château and grounds: 48 frs; grounds only: 28 frs.* ⏲ *Château: Mon.–Sat. 2:30–6, Sun. 11–6; grounds: daily 10–6.*

Dampierre

⓫ *5 km (3 mi) northwest of Breteuil via D906/D149, 21 km (13 mi) southwest of Versailles via D91.*

The unspoiled village of Dampierre is home to one of the most charming family seats in the Ile-de-France. The stone-and-brick **Château de Dampierre,** surrounded by a moat and set well back from the road, was rebuilt in the 1670s by Hardouin-Mansart for the Duc de Luynes. Much of the interior has kept its 17th-century decoration—portraits, wood paneling, furniture, and works of art. But the main staircase, with its trompe l'oeil murals, and the richly gilded Salle des Fêtes date from the last century. This second floor chamber contains a huge wall painting by the celebrated artist Jean-Auguste Ingres (1780–1867): a mythical evocation of the Age d'Or (Golden Age). The large park was planned by Versailles designer Le Nôtre. ☎ *01–30–52–53–24.* 🎫 *50 frs, grounds only: 32 frs.* ⏲ *Apr.–Oct., Mon.–Sat. 2–6, Sun. 11–noon and 2–6.*

Rambouillet

⓬ *16 km (10 mi) southwest of Dampierre via D91/D906, 32 km (20 mi) southwest of Versailles, 42 km (26 mi) southwest of Paris.*

Haughty Rambouillet, once favored by kings and dukes, is now home to affluent gentry and, occasionally, the French president. The **Château,** surrounded by a magnificent 30,000-acre forest (reason enough for hikers and bikers to plan an excursion this way), is a favored retreat for guests of the state; but usually the château and its grounds are open to the public. Most of the château dates from the early 18th century, but the brawny **Tour François I,** named for the king who died here in 1547, was part of the 14th-century fortified castle that first stood on this site. Highlights include the wood-paneled apartments, especially the **Boudoir de la Comtesse;** the marble-walled **Salle de Marbre,** dating from the Renaissance; and the **Salle de Bains de Napoléon,** (Napoléon's bathroom) adorned with Pompeii-style frescoes. The lakeside facade of the château is a sight of unsuspected serenity, and, as more flowers spill from its balconies, cheerful informality. *28 frs. Wed.–Mon. 10–11:30 and 2–5:30.*

An extensive **park** stretches behind the château; it includes a lake punctuated with small islands. The **Laiterie de la Reine** was built as a dairy for Marie-Antoinette, and has a small temple, grotto, and the shell-lined **Chaumière des Coquillages** (Shell Pavilion). The **Bergerie Nationale** (National Sheepfold) is the site of a more serious agricultural venture: The merino sheep reared here, prized for the quality and yield of their wool, are descendants of beasts imported from Spain by Louis XVI in 1786. *Laiterie 14 frs, Bergerie 21 frs. Laiterie: Wed.–Mon. 10–11:30 and 2–4:30 (until 4 in winter); Bergerie: Fri.–Sun. 2–5 (Oct.–June, Sun. only, 2–5).*

Some 4,000 models and more than 1,300 feet of track make the **Musée Rambolitrain** France's leading model-train museum. There are historic steam engines, old-time stations, and a realistic points and signaling system. *4 pl. Jeanne-d'Arc, 01–34–83–15–93. 20 frs. Wed.–Sun. 10–noon and 2–5:30.*

Dining

$ **Poste.** You can bank on traditional, unpretentious cooking at this former coaching inn right in the center of town. Service is good, as is the selection of prix-fixe menus. Game is a specialty in season. *101 rue du Général de Gaulle, 01–34–83–03–01. AE, MC, V.*

Maintenon

⓭ *23 km (14 mi) southwest of Rambouillet via D906, 65 km (41 mi) southwest of Paris.*

Vestiges of Louis XIV, both atmospheric and architectural, make Maintenon an intriguing stopover on the road to Chartres. The **Château** once belonged to Louis XIV's second wife, Françoise Scarron—better known as Madame de Maintenon—whom he married morganatically in 1684. (As social inferiors, neither she nor her children could claim a royal title.) She had acquired the château as a young widow 10 years earlier, and her private apartments form the hub of the interior visit. A round brick tower (16th century) and square 12th-century keep give the ensemble a muscular dignity at odds with the picturesque back garden, with its lawns, canal, and prim hedges. *pl. Aristide Briand, 02–37–23–00–09. 33 frs. Apr.–Oct., Wed.–Mon. 2–6; Nov.–Mar., weekends 2–5; closed mid-Dec.–late Jan.*

Looming at the back of the château garden and extending through the village from the train station to the D6 are the unlikely ivy-covered arches of a ruined **Aqueduc** (aqueduct), one of the Sun King's most outrageous projects. The original scheme aimed to provide the ornamental lakes in the gardens of Versailles (some 50 km/31 mi away) with water from the River Eure. In 1684, 30,000 men were signed up to construct a three-tiered, 5-km (3-mi) aqueduct as part of the project. Many died of fever in the process, and construction was called off in 1689.

Dining and Lodging

$$$–$$$$ ✕▣ **Château d'Esclimont.** The 16th-century château is well worth seeking out if you wish to eat and sleep like royalty. On luxurious grounds, with lawns, a lake, and a heliport, this member of the Relais & Châteaux chain is a regular target for Parisian power brokers. Rooms are luxuriously furnished in reproduction 18th-century French pieces. The cuisine is sophisticated and varied: Quail, lamb, lobster, and game in season top the menu. Dinner reservations are essential and a jacket and tie are required. ✉ *28700 St-Symphorien-le-Château (19 km/12 mi southeast of Maintenon: take D116 to village of Gaillardon, keep an eye out for church, then turn left),* ☎ *02–37–31–15–15,* FAX *02–37–31–57–91. 48 rooms. Restaurant, pool, 2 tennis courts, fishing. MC, V.*

Chartres

⓮ *19 km (12 mi) southwest of Maintenon via D906, 88 km (55 mi) southwest of Paris.*

Although Chartres is chiefly visited for its magnificent Gothic cathedral with world-famous stained-glass windows, the whole town—with its old houses and picturesque streets—is worth leisurely exploration. Ancient streets tumble down from the cathedral to the River Eure; there is a lovely view of the rooftops beneath the cathedral from rue du Pont-St-Hilaire. Each year on August 15, pilgrims and tourists alike flock here for the **Procession du Voeu de Louis XIII,** a religious procession through the streets, commemorating the French monarchy's vow to serve the Virgin Mary.

★ Worship on the site of the **Cathédrale Notre-Dame** goes back to before the Gallo-Roman period; the crypt contains a well that was the focus of Druid ceremonies. In the late 9th century, Charles II (known as the Bald) presented Chartres with what was believed to be the tunic of the Virgin Mary, a precious relic that attracted hordes of pilgrims. The current cathedral, the sixth church on the spot, dates mainly from the 12th and 13th centuries and was erected after the previous, 11th-century building burned down in 1194. A well-chronicled outburst of religious fervor followed the discovery that the Virgin Mary's relic had miraculously survived unsinged. Reconstruction went ahead at a breathtaking pace. Just 25 years were needed for Chartres cathedral to rise again, and it has remained substantially unchanged ever since.

The lower half of the facade is a survivor of the earlier Romanesque church: This can be seen most clearly in the use of round arches rather than the pointed Gothic type. The **Portail Royal** (Royal Portal) is richly sculpted with scenes from the Life of Christ, and the flanking towers are also Romanesque. The taller of the two spires (380 feet versus 350 feet) was built at the start of the 16th century, after its predecessor was destroyed by fire; its fanciful Flamboyant intricacy contrasts sharply with the stumpy solemnity of its Romanesque counterpart. The **rose window** above the main portal dates from the 13th century, while the three windows below it contain some of the finest examples of 12th-century stained glass in France.

The interior is somber, and your eyes will need time to adjust. The reward: the gemlike richness of the stained glass, with the famous deep "Chartres blue" predominating. The oldest window is arguably the most beautiful: **Notre-Dame de la Belle Verrière,** in the south choir. The cathedral's windows are being gradually cleaned—a lengthy, painstaking process—and the contrast with those still covered in the grime of centuries is staggering. It is well worth taking a pair of binoculars to pick out the details. If you wish to know more about stained-glass techniques and the motifs used, visit the small exhibit in the gallery opposite the north porch. For even more detail, try to arrange a tour (in English) with local institution Malcolm Miller, who has a formidable knowledge of the cathedral's windows. (He leads tours twice a day, Monday through Saturday; the cost is 30 francs. You can reach him at the telephone number below.) The vast black-and-white labyrinth on the floor of the nave is one of the few to have survived from the Middle Ages. The faithful were expected to travel along its entire length (some 300 yards) on their knees.

Guided tours of the **Crypte** (crypt) start from the Maison de la Crypte opposite the south porch. You can also see a 4th-century Gallo-Roman wall and some 12th-century wall paintings. ✉ *16 Cloître Notre-Dame,* ☎ *02–37–21–56–33.* 🎟 *10 frs.* ⏲ *Guided tours of crypt: Easter–Oct., daily at 11, 2:15, 3:30, 4:30, 5:15; Nov.–Easter, daily at 11 and 4.*

The **Musée des Beaux-Arts** (Fine Arts Museum) is in a handsome 18th-century building just behind the cathedral that used to serve as the bishop's palace. Its varied collection includes Renaissance enamels, a portrait of Erasmus by Holbein, tapestries, armor, and some fine, mainly French, paintings of the 17th, 18th, and 19th centuries. There is also a room devoted to the forceful 20th-century land- and snowscapes of Maurice de Vlaminck, who lived in the region. ✉ *29 Cloître Notre-Dame,* ☎ *02–37–36–41–39.* 🎟 *10 frs (20 frs for special exhibitions).* ⏲ *Apr.–Oct., Wed.–Mon. 10–6; Nov.–Mar., Wed.–Mon. 10–noon and 2–5.*

The Gothic church of **St-Pierre** (✉ rue St-Pierre) near the River Eure has magnificent medieval windows from a period (circa 1300) not represented at the cathedral. The oldest stained glass here, portraying Old Testament worthies, are to the right of the choir and date from the late 13th century. Exquisite 17th-century stained glass can be admired at the church of **St-Aignan** (✉ rue des Grenets) around the corner from St-Pierre.

Dining and Lodging

$$$ ✕ **La Vieille Maison.** Occupying a pretty 14th-century building just 100 yards from the cathedral, this restaurant is a fine choice for either lunch or dinner. The setting—on a flower-decked patio—is charming. The menu changes regularly but invariably includes regional specialties, such as asparagus, rich duck pâté, and superb homemade foie gras. Prices, though justified, can be steep, but the 160-franc lunch menu is a good bet. ✉ *5 rue au Lait,* ☎ *02–37–34–10–67. Jacket and tie. AE, MC, V. Closed Mon. No dinner Sun.*

$$ ★ ✕ **Buisson Ardent.** In an attractive, old, oak-beam building almost within sight of the cathedral's south portal, this is a popular restaurant with inexpensive prix-fixe menus (especially good on weekdays) and a choice of imaginative à la carte dishes with delicious sauces. Try the chicken ravioli with leeks or the rolled beef with spinach. Service is

gratifyingly attentive. ✉ *10 rue au Lait,* ☎ *02–37–34–04–66. AE, DC, MC, V. No dinner Sun.*

$$$ **Grand Monarque.** The most popular rooms in this 18th-century coaching-inn are in a separate turn-of-the-century building overlooking a garden. The most atmospheric are tucked away in the attic. There's also a fine restaurant with a varied choice of prix-fixe menus. ✉ *22 pl. des Épars, 28000,* ☎ *02–37–21–00–72,* FAX *02–37–36–34–18. 54 rooms, 52 with bath. Restaurant. AE, DC, MC, V.*

Shopping

Vitrail (stained glass) being the key to Chartres's fame, enthusiasts may want to visit the **Galerie du Vitrail** (✉ 17 rue Cloître Notre-Dame) which specializes in the noble art. Pieces range from small plaques to entire windows, and there are books on the subject in English and French.

Dreux

15 *35 km (22 mi) north of Chartres via N154, 74 km (46 mi) west of Paris.*

Dreux has been a prosperous place since the 16th century, earning the title of Royal Borough in 1556, shortly after completion of the beefy belfry on the main square. The early 19th century conferred lasting glory on the town in the form of the burial chapel of the royal House of Orléans.

In 1816, the Orléans family, France's ruling house from 1830 to 1848, began the construction of a circular chapel-mausoleum on the hill behind the town center. ★ The **Chapelle Royale St-Louis** is built in sugary but not unappealing neo-Gothic style: Superficial ornament rather than structure recalls the medieval style. The magnificently decorated interior can be visited only with a French-speaking guide, but no linguistic explanations are needed to prompt wonder at either the Sèvres-manufactured "stained glass"—thin layers of glass coated with painted enamel (an extremely rare, fragile, and vivid technique)—or the funereal statuary. Some of the **tombs**—an imploring hand reaching through a window to a loved one or an infant wrapped in a cloak of transparent gauze—may evoke morbid sentimentality, but their technical skill and compositional drama belie sculpture's reputation as one of the fustier visual arts. ✉ *2 square d'Aumale,* ☎ *02–37–46–07–06.* *3 frs.* *Daily 9–11:30 and 2:30–6 (4 in winter); closed Jan.*

The church of **St-Pierre,** across the road from the belfry, is an interesting jumble of styles with good stained glass and a 17th-century organ loft. It presents a curious silhouette, with its unfinished classical towers cut off midway. ✉ *pl. Métezeau,* ☎ *02–37–42–06–89.*

Lodging

$$ **Le Beffroi.** This is a modest country hotel, on the historic square that links the church to the belfry; ask for a room with a view. ✉ *12 pl. Métezeau, 28100,* ☎ *02–37–50–02–03,* FAX *02–37–42–07–69. 16 rooms with shower. AE, DC, MC, V.*

OFF THE BEATEN PATH

VERNEUIL-SUR-AVRE – This old market town, 33 km (21 mi) west of Dreux via N12, retains a number of half-timber houses but is mainly of interest for its soaring, richly sculpted belfry, built around 1500. The tower, one of the most eye-catching in France, is visible for miles around.

Anet

16 *16 km (10 mi) north of Dreux via D928, 73 km (46 mi) west of Paris.*

Only picturesque ruins remain of the **Château d'Anet,** begun in 1548 for Henri II's mistress Diane de Poitiers. Her bedchamber can be visited in the Left Wing, the finest surviving section with its 17th-century **Escalier d'Honneur** (Grand Staircase) and tapestries in the **Salle des Gardes** (Guard Room), depicting the adventures of the huntress Diana. The chapel has a 16th-century dome, one of the earliest in France. As you enter the grounds, look up at the tympanum over the gate to admire the cast of Benvenuto Cellini's *Nymph with a Stag* (the original is now in the Louvre). ☎ *02–37–41–90–07.* *36 frs.* *Apr.–Oct., Mon.–Sat. 2:30–6:30, Sun. 10–11:30 and 2:30–6:30.*

Vernon

17 *36 km (22 mi) north of Anet via Pacy-sur-Eure, 76 km (48 mi) northwest of Paris.*

The old town of Vernon, on the Seine, has a medieval church often painted by Impressionist artist Claude Monet, and several fine medieval timber-frame houses (the best, on rue Carnot, houses the tourist office). The church of **Notre-Dame,** across from the tourist office, has an arresting rose-window facade which, like the high nave, dates from the 15th century. Rounded Romanesque arches in the choir, however, attest to the building's 12th-century origins. The church is a fine sight when viewed from behind: Monet liked to paint it from across the Seine.

A few minor Monet canvases, along with other late-19th-century paintings, can be admired in the **Musée Poulain** (town museum). This rambling old mansion is seldom crowded, and the helpful curators are happy to explain local history if you are intrigued by the town's English-sounding name. ✉ *rue du Pont,* ☎ *02–32–21–28–09.* *15 frs.* *Tues.–Sun. 2–6.*

Dining and Lodging

$$$ ★ **Château de Brécourt.** This 17th-century stone-and-brick château, outside of Vernon, has high-pitched roofs, an imposing forecourt, and extensive grounds. Guest room decor follows exuberant turn-of-the-century lines. Even if you're not spending a night here, dine on the inventive food in the august dining room, Le Grand Siècle. Dishes such as lobster mousse and veal with truffles make it a popular spot—and it's even easy to get to from Giverny which is just across the Seine from Vernon. As such châteaux-hotels go, a stay here is a relatively good value. ✉ *27120 Douains (10 km/6 mi south of Vernon along D181),* ☎ *02–32–52–40–50,* FAX *02–32–52–69–65. 24 rooms and 5 suites. Restaurant, pool, tennis court. AE, DC, MC, V.*

Giverny

18 *5 km (3 mi) southeast of Vernon via D5 across the Seine, 72 km (45 mi) northwest of Paris.*

The small village of Giverny, just beyond the official limits of the Ile-de-France, has become a place of pilgrimage for art lovers. It was here that Claude Monet lived for 43 years, until his death in 1926 at the age of 86.

With its pretty pink walls and green shutters, Monet's house, or the ★ **Maison de Claude Monet,** has been lovingly restored, just like the spectacular garden with its famous lily pond. Monet was brought up in Normandy and, like many of the Impressionists, was sold on the soft light of the Seine Valley. After several years at Argenteuil, just north of Paris, he moved downriver to Giverny in 1883 along with his two sons, his mistress Alice Hoschedé (whom he later married), and her six children. By 1890, a prospering Monet was able to buy the house outright.

The house has a warm family feeling that may come as a welcome break after visiting stately French châteaux. Rooms have been restored to Monet's original designs: the kitchen with its blue tiles, the buttercup-yellow dining room, and Monet's bedroom on the second floor. Reproductions of his works, and some of the Japanese prints he avidly collected, crowd the walls. ✉ *84 rue Claude-Monet,* ☎ *02–32–51–94–65.* 🎫 *35 frs.* ⏲ *Apr.–Oct., Tues.–Sun. 10–6.*

Three years after buying his house, Monet purchased another plot of land across the lane to continue his gardening experiments, even di- ★ verting the River Epte to make a pond. The resulting ***jardin*** (garden), with flowers spilling out across the paths, is as cheerful and natural as the house. The famous Japanese bridge and water-lily pond, flanked by a mighty willow and rhododendrons, are across the lane that runs to the side of the house, and can be reached through a tunnel. Images of the bridge and the water lilies during various seasons appear in much of Monet's later work. Looking across the pond, it is easy to conjure up the grizzle-bearded painter dabbing at his canvases—capturing changes in light and a breakdown in form that were to have a major influence on 20th-century art. ✉ *84 rue Claude-Monet,* ☎ *02–32–51–94–65.* 🎫 *35 frs for gardens and home; gardens only: 25 frs.* ⏲ *10–noon and 2–6.*

The spacious, airy **Musée Américain** (American Museum), endowed by Chicago art patrons Daniel and Judith Terra, displays works by American Impressionists who were influenced by—and often studied with—Claude Monet. ✉ *99 rue Claude-Monet,* ☎ *02–32–51–94–65.* 🎫 *35 frs.* ⏲ *Apr.–Oct., Tues.–Sun. 10–6.*

Dining

$$–$$$ ✕ **Moulin de Fourges.** Local connoisseurs find this little mill irresistible. Nestled in verdant countryside, just minutes from the American Impressionist museum, its setting alone is enough to make you ravenous. ✉ *Rue du Moulin, Fourges,* ☎ *02–32–52–12–12. Reservations essential. AE, DC, MC, V. Closed Mon. and Jan.–mid-Feb. No dinner Sun.*

$$ ✕ **Les Jardins de Giverny.** This commendable restaurant, with an old-fashioned dining room that overlooks a rose garden, is close to Monet's house. Enjoy the 130-franc lunch menu or choose from a repertoire of inventive dishes such as foie gras spiked with applejack or scallops with wild mushrooms. ✉ *1 rue Milieu,* ☎ *02–32–21–60–80. AE, V. Closed Mon. and Feb. No dinner Sun.*

En Route The road south of Giverny has difficulty matching the bends of the meandering Seine. Follow signs to Mantes and you'll next encounter the river at the village of **La Roche-Guyon,** dominated by chalky cliffs and a classical château. A few miles farther upriver is the tumbling village of **Vétheuil,** with its 12th-century church. The road (now D147) abandons the riverbank until it reaches **Mantes-la-Jolie,** whose vast 12th-century Notre-Dame church has a twin-towered facade strikingly similar to that of Notre-Dame in Paris. The small, circular windows that ring the east end of the church are an unusual local characteristic, as you may have spotted at Vétheuil.

Thoiry

19 *40 km (25 mi) southeast of Giverny (cross the Seine at Bonnières, then take N13), 17 km (11 mi) southeast of Mantes-la-Jolie via Arnouville, 43 km (27 mi) west of Paris.*

Thoiry is most famous for its 16th-century château with beautiful gardens, wild animal reserve, and gastronomy museum. The village makes an excellent day trip from Paris if you are traveling with children.

Built by Philibert de l'Orme in 1564, the **Château de Thoiry** has a handsome Renaissance facade set off by gardens landscaped in the disciplined French fashion by Le Nôtre, in this case with unexpected justification: The château is positioned directly in line with the sun as it sets in the west at the winter solstice (December 21) and as it rises in the east at the summer solstice (June 21). Heightening the effect, the central part of the château appears to be a transparent arch of light, owing to its huge glass doors and windows.

Owners Vicomte Paul de La Panouse and his American wife, Annabelle, have restored the château and park, opening both to the public. The distinguished history of the La Panouse family—a Comte César even fought in the American Revolution—is retraced in the **Musée des Archives,** where papal bulls and Napoleonic letters mingle with missives from Thomas Jefferson and Benjamin Franklin. The neighboring pantries house a **Musée de la Gastronomie,** whose tempting display of *pièces montées*—virtuoso banquet showpieces—re-create the designs of famed 19th-century chef Antoine Carême. Early recipe books, engravings, and old copper pots are also displayed.

Other highlights of the château interior include the **Grand Staircase,** with its 18th-century Gobelin tapestries; the **Green** and **White salons,** ★ with their antique painted harpsichord and portraits; and the **Salon de la Tapisserie,** with its monumental Don Quixote tapestry bearing the rather gruesome arms (three severed raven's heads) of former owner Machault d'Arnouville. An authentic, homey, faintly faded charm pervades these rooms, especially when fires crackle in their enormous hearths on damp afternoons.

The viscountess is a keen gardener and enjoys experimenting in the less formal **Jardin Anglais** (English Garden), where cricket is played on weekend afternoons during summer, and in her late-flowering **Autumn Garden.** You're allowed to wander at leisure, although it's best not to stray too far from the official footpath through the **parc zoologique** (animal reserve). Note that the parts of the reserve that contain the wilder beasts—deer, zebra, camels, hippos, bears, elephants, and lions—can be visited only by car. The reserve hit the headlines when the first-ever ligrons—a cross between a lion and a tiger—were born here a few years ago. These beasts (bigger than either a lion or a tiger) are now in their second generation and can be seen from the safety of a raised footbridge in the **Tiger Park.** Nearby is a children's play area with a burrow to wriggle through and a huge netted cobweb to bounce around in. ☎ *01–34–87–52–25.* *Château 30 frs. Château, park, and game reserve 99 frs.* *Summer, weekdays 10–6, weekends 10–6:30; winter, daily 10–5.*

Dining and Lodging

$ ✕ **Commerce.** This bar on Thoiry's main street has an attractive upstairs dining room where locals come for hearty weekday lunches. Start with the extensive buffet—pâté, salami, and carrot salad are favorites—followed by a sturdy main course such as steak and chips or beef

Wellington. ✉ *rue de la Porte-St-Martin,* ☎ *01–34–87–40–18. No credit cards. Closed Sat. No dinner.*

$ ✕🏨 **Étoile.** This dowdy hotel-restaurant, just 300 yards from the château along the main street, is more convenient than appealing. Rooms need redecorating, but the restaurant serves a *menu touristique* (special tourist menu) of robust French dishes. ✉ *38 rue de la Porte-St-Martin, 78770* ☎ *01–34–87–40–21,* FAX *01–34–87–49–57. 12 rooms. Restaurant. AE, DC, MC, V. Closed Mon.*

Montfort-L'Amaury

⑳ *13 km (8 mi) south of Thoiry via D76, 42 km (26 mi) west of Paris.*

Montfort-L'Amaury, with its twisting, narrow streets clustered around an old church, is one of the prettiest towns in the Ile-de-France. The bulky Renaissance tower of the church of **St-Pierre** dominates the town square. Note the gargoyles around the far end and, inside, the splendid Renaissance stained glass.

Composer Maurice Ravel lived in Montfort from 1921 until his death in 1937; he composed his famous *Bolero* in 1928 in his "Japanese" garden. His tiny house, now the **Musée Ravel,** has been reconstituted with many of his souvenirs and furnishings (including his piano). ✉ *Le Belvédère, rue Maurice-Ravel,* ☎ *01–34–86–00–89.* 🎫 *21 frs.* ⏲ *Mon.–Thurs. 2–5, weekends 10–noon and 2–5.*

Shortly after moving into his attractive, thatched house 5 km (3 mi) east of Montfort-L'Amaury, politician Jean Monnet, often known as the Father of Europe, is said to have conceived the idea of a European Community in 1950. He lived here until his death in 1979, and was accorded the supreme state accolade of burial in the Paris Panthéon. The **Maison Jean-Monnet,** where Monnet once hobnobbed with world leaders, is now owned by the European Parliament and displays information on the present European Union, Monnet mementos, and a film on his life and ideas—all in 11 different languages, in time-honored Eurocrat tradition. ✉ *Houjarray (take D13 east from Montfort and turn right just before Bazoches-sur-Guyonne),* ☎ *01–34–86–12–43.* 🎫 *Free.* ⏲ *Wed.–Sun. 2–6.*

Lodging

$–$$ ★ 🏨 **Voyageurs.** This small, homey hotel at the bottom of Montfort's cobbled main street, with wood-beam bedrooms, a well-priced restaurant, and a cheerful bar with incongruous but appealing '50s decor, is a handy base for exploring Thoiry, Dreux, or Rambouillet. ✉ *49 rue de Paris, 78490,* ☎ *01–34–86–00–14,* FAX *01–34–86–14–56. 7 rooms with shower. MC, V. Closed mid–late Aug.*

THE OISE VALLEY AND EAST TO DISNEYLAND

This area covers a broad arc beginning north of Paris at Maisons-Laffitte, heading east through the Oise Valley to Chantilly, and continuing southeast through Meaux. Besides being the old stomping grounds for several world-famous artists, the area is now the domain of Disneyland Paris.

Maisons-Laffitte

21 *7 km (4 mi) northeast of St-Germain-en-Laye via D157, 16 km (10 mi) northwest of Paris via N308.*

The riverside suburb of Maisons-Laffitte has an unusually high proportion of elegant villas, many of which were built with profits from the town's famous racecourse and training stables. It is also home to one of France's finest 17th-century properties. The early Baroque ★ **Château de Maisons,** constructed by architect François Mansart from 1642 to 1651, is one of the least-known châteaux in the Ile-de-France. This was not always the case: Sun King Louis XIV came to the house-warming party, and Louis XV, Louis XVI, the 18th-century writer Voltaire, and Napoléon all stayed here. The interior clearly met their exacting standards, thanks to the well-proportioned entrance vestibule with its rich sculpture; the winding **Escalier d'Honneur,** a majestic staircase adorned with paintings and statues; and the royal apartments, above, with their parquet floors and elegant wall paneling. ☎ *01–39–62–01–49.* 🎫 *28 frs.* ⏲ *Daily 10–noon and 1:30–6.*

En Route Take the D308 west into the Forêt de St-Germain, then turn right after 4 km (2½ mi) on N184 to **Conflans-Ste-Honorine,** the capital of France's inland waterway network. Barges arrive from as far afield as the ports of Le Havre and Dunkerque, on the north coast, and are often moored up to six-abreast along the mile-long quayside, near the *conflans* (confluence) of the Rivers Seine and Oise.

Pontoise

22 *8 km (5 mi) north of Conflans-Ste-Honorine via N184/N14, 29 km (19 mi) northwest of Paris via A15.*

A pleasant old town on the banks of the Oise, Pontoise is famous for its link with the Impressionists. The small **Musée Pissarro,** high up in the old town, pays tribute to one of Pontoise's most illustrious past residents: Impressionist painter Camille Pissarro (1830–1903). The collection of prints and drawings is of interest mainly to specialists, but the view across the valley from the museum gardens will appeal to all. ✉ *17 rue du Château,* ☎ *01–30–32–06–75.* 🎫 *Free.* ⏲ *Wed.–Sun. 2–6.*

The **Musée Tavet-Delacour,** housed in a turreted mansion in the center of Pontoise, stages good exhibitions and has a permanent collection that includes landscapes by various local painters and a floor devoted to contemporary art, with intriguing abstract geometric compositions by Otto Freundlich. ✉ *4 rue Lemercier,* ☎ *01–30–38–02–40.* 🎫 *Free.* ⏲ *Wed.–Mon. 10–noon and 2–6.*

Auvers-sur-Oise

23 *7 km (4 mi) east of Pontoise via D4, 33 km (21 mi) northwest of Paris via N328.*

The tranquil Oise River valley, which runs northeast from Pontoise, retains much of the charm that attracted Pissarro, Paul Cézanne, Camille Corot, Charles-François Daubigny, and Berthe Morisot to Auvers-sur-Oise in the second half of the 19th century. But it is the shadow of Vincent van Gogh that haunts every nook and cranny of this pretty riverside village.

Van Gogh moved here from Arles in 1890 to be with his brother, Theo. Little has changed since the summer of 1890, during the last 10 weeks of van Gogh's life, when he painted no fewer than 70 pictures and then shot himself behind the village château. He is buried next to his brother in a simple, ivy-covered grave in the village cemetery. The whole village is peppered with plaques marking the spots that inspired his art; the plaques bear reproductions of his paintings, enabling you to compare his final works with the scenes as they are today. After years of indifference and neglect, his last abode has been turned into a shrine. You can also visit the medieval village church, subject of one of van Gogh's most famous paintings, *L'Église d'Auvers,* and admire Osip Zadkine's powerful modern statue of van Gogh in the village park.

The Auberge Ravoux, the inn where van Gogh stayed, is now the **Maison de van Gogh.** A dingy staircase leads up to the tiny, spartan, wood-floor attic where van Gogh stored some of modern art's most famous pictures under his bed. A short film retraces van Gogh's time at Auvers, and there is a well-stocked souvenir shop. Stop for a drink or for lunch at the ground-floor restaurant. ✉ *8 rue de la Sansonne,* ☎ *01–34–48–07–79.* 🎫 *30 frs.* ⏲ *Tues.–Sun. 10–6.*

The elegant 17th-century village château, set above split-level gar-
★ 🦆 dens, is home to the **Voyage au Temps des Impressionnistes** (Voyage to the Impressionist Era). You'll receive a set of infrared headphones (English available), with commentary that guides you past various tableaux illustrating life in the Impressionist era. Although there are no Impressionist originals—500 reproductions pop up on screens interspersed between the tableaux—some say this is one of France's most imaginative, enjoyable, and innovative museums. Some of the special effects—talking mirrors, computerized cabaret dancing girls, and a simulated train ride past Impressionist landscapes—are worthy of Disney at its best. ✉ *rue de Léry,* ☎ *01–34–48–48–48.* 🎫 *55 frs.* ⏲ *May–Oct., daily 10–8; Nov.–Apr., Tues.–Sun. 10–6:30.*

The landscapist Charles-François Daubigny, a precursor of the Impressionists, lived in Auvers from 1861 until his death in 1878. You can visit the **Atelier Daubigny,** his studio, and admire the remarkable array of mural and roof paintings by Daubigny and fellow artists Camille Corot and Honoré Daumier. ✉ *61 rue Daubigny,* ☎ *01–34–48–03–03.* 🎫 *20 frs.* ⏲ *Tues.–Sun. 2–6:30; closed Nov.–Easter.*

Serious art lovers may want to visit the modest **Musée Daubigny** to admire the drawings, lithographs, and occasional oils by local 19th-century artists, some of which were collected by Daubigny himself. The museum is opposite the Maison de van Gogh, above the tourist office. ✉ *Manoir des Colombières, rue de la Sansonne,* ☎ *01–30–36–80–20.* 🎫 *15 frs.* ⏲ *Wed.–Sun. 2:30–6.*

The small **Musée de l'Absinthe** (Absinthe Museum), near the château, contains publicity posters and other Belle Epoque artifacts evoking the history of absinthe—a forerunner of today's anise-based aperitifs like Ricard and Pernod. Look out for the special spoons used to add sugar to absinthe. Before it was banned in 1915 because of its effects on the nervous system, absinthe was France's national drink. A famous painting by Edgar Degas shows two absinthe drinkers; van Gogh, too, probably downed a few glasses at the Auberge Ravoux (☞ *below*). ✉ *44 rue Callé,* ☎ *01–30–36–83–26.* 🎫 *25 frs.* ⏲ *Oct.–May, weekends 11–6; June–Sept., Wed.–Sun. 11–6.*

Dining

$$ ✕ **Auberge Ravoux.** For total van Gogh immersion, have lunch in the
★ same restaurant he patronized over a hundred years ago. The 140-franc, three-course menu changes regularly, but it's the setting that makes eating here special, with glasswork, lace curtains, and wall decor care-

fully modeled on the original designs. ✉ *52 rue Général-de-Gaulle,* ☎ *01–34–48–05–47. Reservations essential. AE, DC, MC, V.*

L'Isle-Adam

24 *6 km (4 mi) northeast of Auvers-sur-Oise via D4, 35 km (22 mi) north of Paris via N1.*

Residentially exclusive L'Isle-Adam is one of the most picturesque towns in the Ile-de-France. Paris lies just 40 km (25 mi) south, but it could be 100 miles and as many years away. There is a sandy beach along one stretch of the River Oise (via rue de Beaumont); a curious pagodalike folly, the Pavillon Chinois de Cassan; and an unassuming local museum. The **Musée Louis-Senlecq,** on the main street, often stages painting exhibitions and contains numerous attractive works by local landscapists. ✉ *46 Grande Rue,* ☎ *01–34–69–45–44.* *15 frs.* ⏲ *Wed.–Sun. 10–1 and 3–6.*

Dining and Lodging

$$–$$$ **Le Cabouillet.** The riverside Cabouillet aptly reflects the quiet charm of L'Isle-Adam, thanks to its pretty views over the Oise. You can savor these from each of its eight rooms or from the chic restaurant, where the cooking can be inspired (go for the crawfish in Sauternes sauce, if it's on the menu). The restaurant is closed Wednesday. ✉ *5 quai de l'Oise, 95290,* ☎ *01–34–69–00–90,* FAX *01–34–69–33–88. 8 rooms. Restaurant. AE, DC, MC, V. Closed Dec. 25–early Feb.*

En Route From L'Isle-Adam, D922 leads to the small hilltop town of **Beaumont-sur-Oise**—worth a quick peek for its attractive 12th- to 13th-century church of **St-Laurent,** transformed into a cathedral by Émile Zola as the setting for his romantic novel *Le Rêve* (*The Dream*). Some 6 km (4 mi) farther east (via D922 and D909) is the medieval **Abbaye de Royaumont,** founded by Louis IX in 1228. You can visit the only part of the abbey church still standing (the south transept), along with the ivy-clad cloisters, the refectory, and the vaulted kitchens. The monks' dormitories, chapter-house, and library are now part of an international cultural center and seldom open to the public; a music festival (☎ 01–30–35–30–16 for details) is held here in August and September. *22 frs.* ⏲ *Easter–Oct., Wed.–Mon. 10–12:30 and 2–6; Nov.–Easter, weekends 10–12:30 and 2–5.*

Chantilly

25 *10 km (6 mi) northeast of Royaumont via D909, 23 km (14 mi) east of L'Isle-Adam via D4, 37 km (23 mi) north of Paris via N16.*

Romantic Chantilly has a host of attractions: a faux Renaissance château, an eye-popping art collection, splendid Baroque stables, a classy racecourse, and a 16,000-acre forest. Yet it attracts far fewer sightseeing hordes than either Versailles or Fontainebleau.

Although its lavish exterior may be 19th-century Renaissance pastiche, the **Château de Chantilly,** sitting snugly behind an artificial lake, houses ★ the outstanding **Musée Condé,** with illuminated medieval manuscripts, tapestries, furniture, and paintings. The most famous room, the **Santuario,** contains two celebrated works by Italian painter Raphael (1483–1520)—the *Three Ages of Woman* and the *Orleans Virgin*—plus an exquisite ensemble of 15th-century miniatures by the most illustrious French painter of his time, Jean Fouquet (1420–81). Farther on, in the **Cabinet des Livres,** is the Book of Hours of the Duc de Berry, one of the finest medieval manuscripts. Other highlights of this unusual museum are the **Galerie de Psyché,** with 16th-century stained glass and portrait drawings by Flemish artist Jean Clouet II; the **chapelle** (chapel), with sculptures by Jean Goujon and Jacques Sarrazin; and the extensive collection of paintings by 19th-century French artists, headed by Jean-Auguste Ingres. The large **park** behind the château is based on that familiar combination of formal (neatly planned parterres and a mighty straight-banked canal) and romantic eccentricity (the waterfall and the make-believe village that inspired Marie-Antoinette's version at Versailles). ☎ *03–44–57–03–62.* 🎫 *35 frs.* ⏲ *Mar.–Oct., Wed.–Mon. 10–6; Nov.–Feb., 10:30–12:45 and 2–5.*

★ The majestic 18th-century **Grandes Écuries** are the grandest stables in France, and still in use as the **Musée Vivant du Cheval** (Living Museum of the Horse), with a glittering array of carriages and 40 horses and ponies performing dressage exercises. The stables, by the racecourse opposite the château, were designed by Jean Aubert to accommodate 240 horses and 500 hounds in straw-lined comfort, ready for stag and boar hunts in the forests nearby. ✉ *7 rue du Connétable,* ☎ *03–44–57–40–40.* 🎫 *50 frs.* ⏲ *Wed.–Mon. 10:30–5:30.*

OFF THE BEATEN PATH

ÉCOUEN – This small town, 21 km (13 mi) south of Chantilly along N16, is renowned for its Musée de la Renaissance (Renaissance Museum), housed in a turreted château, with a strong collection of 16th- and 17th-century tapestries and furniture from France, Italy, and Holland. ☎ *01–39–90–04–04.* 🎫 *23 frs (16 frs Sun.).* ⏲ *Wed.–Mon. 9:45–12:30 and 2–5:15.*

Dining and Lodging

$$ ✕ **Relais Condé.** Opposite the racecourse, in a building that originally served as an Anglican chapel, is one of the classiest restaurants in Chantilly. Chef Jacques Legrand creates a roster of elegant dishes, including duck with honey and spices and lobster terrine. A reasonably priced menu makes it a suitable lunch spot. There is a good wine list. ✉ *42 av. du Maréchal-Joffre,* ☎ *03–44–57–05–75. Reservations essential. AE, MC, V. Closed Tues.*

$$ ✕ **Relais du Coq Chantant.** This discreet, well-established restaurant attracts a polished clientele of golfers and horse fanciers. Opt for the prix-fixe menu (which changes weekly) to sample a traditional meal based on fowl or rabbit. ✉ *21 rte. de Creil,* ☎ *03–44–57–01–28. Jacket required. AE, DC, MC, V.*

$ ✕ **Capitainerie.** Since the château of Chantilly is a fair walk from the town's main street, it makes sense to have a quick lunch on the spot—at this self-service restaurant in the château's medieval basement, adorned with old kitchen utensils. The buffet is available nonstop from 10:30 through 6:30; you'll find salads, cheeses, and desserts, along with a few hot dishes. ✉ *Château de Chantilly. Reservations not accepted. No credit cards. Closed Tues.*

$$ **Calèche.** Although it's small and underwhelming, and your reception may be somewhat lacking in warmth, this hotel, on the avenue leading from the train station to the château, is cheap and acceptable for a night's stopover. ✉ *3 av. du Maréchal-Joffre, 60500,* ☎ *03–44–57–02–55. 15 rooms, 2 with bath, 13 with shower. MC, V.*

$$ **Campanile.** This functional, modern motel is in quiet, relaxing Les Huit Curés, just outside Chantilly, on the edge of the forest (which compensates for the lack of interior atmosphere). There's a grillroom for straightforward, if unexciting, meals. You can dine outside on the terrace in summer. ✉ *rte. de Creil, 60500 (on N16 toward Creil),* ☎ *03–44–57–39–24,* FAX *03–44–58–10–05. 47 rooms. Grill. MC, V.*

Outdoor Activities and Sports

Chantilly's fabled racecourse comes into its own each June with two of Europe's most prestigious events: the **Prix du Jockey-Club** on the first Sunday of the month, and the **Prix de Diane** the Sunday after.

Senlis

26 *10 km (6 mi) east of Chantilly via D924, 45 km (28 mi) north of Paris via A1.*

Senlis is an exceptionally well-preserved medieval town with crooked, mazelike streets dominated by the svelte, soaring spire of its Gothic cathedral. Two museums—one on hunting and the other centering on fine art and archaeology—are also worth a visit.

The **Cathédrale Notre-Dame,** one of France's oldest and narrowest cathedrals, dates from the second half of the 12th century. The superb ★ spire—arguably the most elegant in France—was added around 1240 and has recently been cleaned and restored. ✉ *pl. de Parvis.*

The **Musée de la Vénerie** (Hunting Museum), across from the cathedral on grounds of the ruined royal castle, is one of France's few full-fledged hunting museums. Displayed are artifacts, prints, and paintings, including excellent works by 18th-century animal portraitist, Jean-Baptiste Oudry. ✉ *Château Royal,* ☎ *03–44–53–00–80.* *14 frs; grounds only: 7 frs.* *Wed. 2–6, Thurs.–Mon. 10–noon and 2–6. Closed mid-Dec.–mid-Jan.*

The town's **Musée d'Art et Archéologie** (Museum of Art and Archaeology), built atop an ancient Gallo-Roman residence, displays some excellent finds, from Gallo-Roman votive objects, unearthed in the neighboring Halatte Forest, to the building's own excavated foundations (found in the basement). Upstairs, the museum presents paintings by—among others—Thomas Couture, Manet's teacher, who lived in Senlis. ✉ *pl. du Parvis-Notre-Dame,* ☎ *03–44–53–06–40.* *14 frs.* *Thurs.–Mon. 9–noon and 1:30–5:30.*

OFF THE BEATEN PATH

PARC ASTÉRIX – Great for kids of all ages, this Gallic theme park, 10 km (6 mi) south of Senlis via the A1 expressway, takes its cue from a French comic-book figure whose adventures are set during the Roman invasion of France 2,000 years ago. Highlights include a mock Gallo-Roman village, a dolphin lake, and a giant roller coaster. ☎ *03–36–68–30–10.* *160 frs.* *Apr.–early Sept., daily 10–6; early Sept.–mid-Oct., Wed. and weekends, 10–6.*

Dining and Lodging

$$ ✕ **Le Bourgeois Gentilhomme.** This cozy, two-floor restaurant in old Senlis serves some interesting dishes: fricassee of burbot with mushrooms and marjoram-scented rabbit with tiny vegetable ravioli, to name just two. ✉ *3 pl. de la Halle,* ☎ *03–44–53–13–22. V. Closed Tues.*

$ **Hostellerie Porte-Bellon.** This is the closest you'll get to spending a night in the historic center of Senlis. A modest yet efficient hotel, the Porte-Bellon is just a five-minute walk from the cathedral and is close to the bus station. ✉ *51 rue Bellon, 60300,* ☎ *03–44–53–03–05,* FAX *03–44–53–29–94. 20 rooms, 14 with bath. Restaurant. MC, V. Closed mid-Dec.–mid-Jan.*

Ermenonville

27 *13 km (8 mi) southeast of Senlis via N330, 43 km (27 mi) northeast of Paris.*

A ruined abbey and children's amusement park, both nearby, add to the appeal of the village of Ermenonville, best known as the final haunt of the 18th-century French philosopher Jean-Jacques Rousseau. The Cistercian **Abbaye de Chaalis,** just off the N330 as you arrive from Senlis, has photogenic 13th-century ruins, a landscaped park that has been restored to its 18th-century appearance, and a château with an eclectic collection of Egyptian antiquities and medieval paintings, together with three rooms displaying manuscripts and other mementos of Jean-Jacques Rousseau. ✉ *Just off N330.* 🎫 *Abbey and park: 30 frs; park only: 12 frs.* ⏲ *Abbey: Mar.–Oct., Mon., Wed.–Fri. 2–6:30, weekends 10:30–12:30 and 2–6:30. Park open year-round, Wed.–Mon. 9–7.*

The **Mer de Sable** playground, opposite the abbey of Chaalis, is a cheerful place for children, with its miniature train, giant slide, small zoo, and curious natural "desert" of sand. ✉ *Parc d'Attractions Jean-Richard,* ☎ *03–44–54–00–96.* 🎫 *69 frs.* ⏲ *Apr., May, and Sept., weekdays 11–6:30, weekends 11–7; June, weekdays 10–6, weekends 11–7; July–Aug., daily 10:30–6:30, Sun. 10:30–7; closed Oct.–Mar.*

The elegant **Parc Jean-Jacques Rousseau,** in the center of Ermenonville, is famous as the initial resting place of the influential writer, who spent the last three months of his life in Ermenonville in 1778 and was buried on the Ile des Peupliers in the middle of the lake. Rousseau's ideas about natural equality made him a hero of the French Revolution, and in 1794 his body was removed to the Panthéon in Paris. A few years later, Napoléon came to Ermenonville to pay homage to Rousseau, saying: "It would have been better for the peace of France if this man had never existed; he paved the way for the French Revolution." When it was pointed out that he could hardly complain about the turn of Revolutionary events, Napoléon is said to have replied: "Time will tell whether it would have been better for peace on earth if Rousseau and I had never lived."

Lodging

$–$$ ★ ✕🏨 **Auberge de la Croix d'Or.** For lunch or an overnight stop in tiny Ermenonville, the Croix d'Or is the place. Its small rooms and homey restaurant have the welcoming feel of a village inn. The attractive park where Jean-Jacques Rousseau was buried is nearby. The restaurant is closed Monday and Sunday dinner, in winter. ✉ *2 rue du Prince-Radziwill, 60950,* ☎ *03–44–54–00–04,* FAX *03–44–54–05–44. 11 rooms with bath or shower. MC, V. Closed mid-Dec.–1st wk Feb.*

Meaux

28 *24 km (15 mi) southeast of Ermenonville via N330, 40 km (25 mi) east of Paris via N3.*

A sturdy cathedral and well-preserved bishop's palace embellish Meaux, a dignified old market-town on the banks of the Marne. An excellent variety of the creamy brie cheese is produced locally. Above the Marne river, the **Cathédrale St-Étienne** took over 300 years to complete, and stylistically is a bit of a hodgepodge. The stonework in the soaring interior becomes increasingly decorative as you approach the west end, culminating in a notable Flamboyant Gothic rose-window. The exterior is somewhat eroded and looks sadly battered—or pleasingly authentic, according to taste. A son-et-lumière with medieval costumes is staged outside the cathedral most weekends in June and July. (Call 01–60–23–40–00 for details.) ✉ *rue St-Étienne.* ⏲ *Daily 8–noon and 2–6.*

The former bishop's palace next to the cathedral, overlooking a trimly patterned garden with remains of the town wall, now houses the **Musée Bossuet.** The museum combines French old masters with a quirky collection of medals commemorating the Paris Commune and Franco-Prussian War. Keen historians will also focus on the documents and mementoes detailing the life of former bishop Jacques Bossuet, a noted 17th-century theologian. ✉ *Ancien Palais Épiscopal,* ☎ *01–64–34–84–45.* 🎫 *15 frs.* ⏲ *Wed.–Mon. 10–noon and 2–6.*

Disneyland Paris

29 *20 km (13 mi) southwest of Meaux via A140 and A4, 38 km (24 mi) east of Paris via A4.*

Disneyland Paris (known originally as Euro Disney) is not what most people travel to France to experience. But if you have a child in tow, the promise of a day there may get you through an afternoon at Versailles or Fontainebleau. If you're a dyed-in-the-wool Disney fan, you'll want to make a beeline for the park to see how it has been molded to appeal to the tastes of Europeans. (Disney's "imagineers" call it their most lovingly detailed park.) And if you've never experienced this particular form of Disney showmanship, you may want to put in an appearance, if only to see what the fuss is all about.

Although great fanfare greeted the opening of Euro Disney, the resort has had its share of troubles: image problems, reports of technical glitches, feuds with neighbors objecting to noisy fireworks, and—worst of all—low attendance levels. In 1994 Disney responded with an about-face: a new name, a tumble in admission prices, and the sale of alcohol in theme-park restaurants. These changes, plus the 10 additional attractions opened since 1992, have helped reverse the slide.

The theme park is made up of five "lands": Main Street U.S.A., Frontierland, Adventureland, Fantasyland, and Discoveryland. The central theme of each land is relentlessly echoed in every detail, from attractions to restaurant menus to souvenirs. The park is circled by a railroad which stops three times along the perimeter.

Main Street U.S.A. goes under the railroad and past shops and restaurants toward the main plaza; the Disney Parades are held here every afternoon and—during holiday periods—every evening.

Top attractions at **Frontierland** are the chilling Phantom Manor, haunted by holographic spooks, and the thrilling runaway mine train of Big Thunder Mountain, a roller coaster that plunges wildly through floods and avalanches in a setting meant to evoke Utah's Monument Valley.

Whiffs of Arabia, Africa, and the West Indies give **Adventureland** its exotic cachet; the spicy meals and snacks served here rank among the best food in the park. Don't miss the Pirates of the Caribbean, an exciting mise en scène populated by eerily human, computer-driven figures, or one of Disney's newest attractions, Indiana Jones and the Temple of Doom, a breathtaking ride that relives some of this luckless hero's most exciting moments.

Fantasyland charms the youngest park goers with familiar cartoon characters from such classic Disney films as *Snow White, Pinocchio,*

Dumbo, and *Peter Pan.* The focal point of Fantasyland, and indeed Disneyland Paris, is Sleeping Beauty's Castle, a 140-foot, bubble-gum pink structure topped with 16 blue- and gold-tipped turrets. Officially known as Le Château de la Belle au Bois Dormant, its design was allegedly inspired by illustrations from a medieval Book of Hours. The castle's dungeon conceals a scaly, green, 2-ton dragon who rumbles in his sleep and occasionally rouses to roar—an impressive feat of engineering, producing an answering chorus of shrieks from younger children.

Discoveryland is a futuristic setting for high-tech Disney entertainment. Robots on roller skates welcome you on your way to Star Tours, a pitching, plunging, sense-confounding ride based on the *Star Wars* films. In Le Visionarium, a simulated space journey is presented by 9-Eye, a staggeringly realistic robot. Space Mountain, Disney's latest attraction, pretends to catapult riders through the Milky Way. ☎ *01–60–30–60–30.* 🎟 *Apr.–Sept. and Christmas period: 195 frs (370 frs for 2-day Passport, 505 frs for 3-day Passport); Oct.–Mar., except Christmas period: 150 frs (285 frs for 2-day Passport, 390 frs for 3-day Passport); includes admission to all individual attractions within the park but not meals. AE, DC, MC, V.* ⏲ *Mid-June–mid-Sept., daily 9 AM–10 PM; mid-Sept.–mid-June, Sun.–Fri. daily 10–6, Sat. 10–8; Dec. 23–Jan. 6, daily 10–8.*

Dining and Lodging

$–$$ ✕ **Disneyland Restaurants.** Disneyland Paris is peppered with places to eat, ranging from snack bars and fast-food joints to five full-service restaurants—all with a distinguishing theme. In addition, Festival Disney (☞ *below*) and Disney hotels have restaurants that are open to the public. But since these are outside the park, it is not recommended that you waste time traveling to them for lunch. Disneyland Paris has relaxed its no-alcohol policy and now serves wine and beer in the park's sit-down restaurants, as well as in the hotels and restaurants outside the park. Eateries serve nonstop as long as the park is open. ☎ *01–60–45–65–40. Sit-down restaurants: AE, DC, MC, V; counter-service restaurants: no credit cards.*

$$–$$$$ 🏨 **Disneyland Hotels.** The resort has 5,000 rooms in six hotels, all a short distance from the park, ranging from the luxurious Disneyland Hotel to the not-so-rustic Camp Davy Crockett. Free transportation to the park is available at every hotel. Several packages that include Disneyland lodging, entertainment, and admission are available through travel agents in Europe. To book your room, contact the Central Reservations Office. ✉ *Centre de Réservations, B.P. 100, 77777 Marne-la-Vallée cedex 4,* ☎ *01–60–30–60–30, 407/934–7639 in the U.S.,* FAX *01–49–30–71–00. All hotels have at least 1 restaurant, bar, and café, indoor swimming pool, sauna, exercise facilities, and free parking. AE, DC, MC, V.*

Nightlife and the Arts

Nocturnal entertainment outside the park centers on **Festival Disney,** a vast pleasure mall designed by architect Frank Gehry. Featured are American-style restaurants (crab shack, diner, deli, steak house), including **Billybob's Country Western Saloon** (☎ 01–60–45–70–79) and **Hurricane's** disco with giant video screen (☎ 01–60–45–70–70). Also in Festival Disney is **Buffalo Bill's Wild West Show** (☎ 01–60–45–71–00 for reservations), a two-hour dinner extravaganza with a menu of sausages, spareribs, and chili; performances by a talented troupe of stunt riders, bronco busters, tribal dancers, and musicians; plus some 50 horses, a dozen buffalo, a bull, and an Annie Oakley–style sharpshooter, with a golden-maned "Buffalo Bill" as emcee. A re-creation of a show that dazzled Parisians a hundred years ago, it's corny but great fun for those who can manage the appropriate suspension of disbelief. There are two shows nightly; the cost is 300 francs.

Outdoor Activities and Sports

A 27-hole **golf course** (☎ 01–60–45–68–04) is open to the public at Disneyland; rental clubs are available, and some special golf packages are available through travel agents.

En Route There are three châteaux just west of Disneyland that merit a stop if you have time. The lavishly furnished **Château de Ferrières** (just off the expressway, 8 km/5 mi west of Disneyland) was built by the Rothschilds in the 19th century; it's open afternoons only, Wednesday–Sunday in summer, Sundays only in winter. The 17th-century **Château de Guermantes** (5 km/3 mi north of Ferrières on D35) has Italianate decor and is open weekends from March through November. The 18th-century **Château de Champs-sur-Marne** (8 km/5 mi west of Guermantes) has gardens with an assortment of ingeniously trimmed hedges; it's open daily except Tuesday.

SOUTHEAST TO FONTAINEBLEAU AND PROVINS

Fontainebleau forms the hub of this heavily wooded southeast region of Ile-de-France. But don't bypass Vaux-le-Vicomte, a masterpiece of 17th-century architecture and garden design; the pretty painters' villages of Barbizon and Moret-sur-Loing; or hilltop Provins, with its well-preserved medieval walls.

Evry

30 *24 km (15 mi) south of Paris via N7.*

One of five "new towns" constructed in the Paris region since the 1960s to house the labor overspill from the capital, Evry has made a determined bid to escape faceless concrete anonymity by building Europe's newest and weirdest cathedral. The **Cathédrale d'Evry,** completed in 1995, is a circular, redbrick building shaped like a drum with the top sliced off, with a ring of trees planted on the roof symbolizing Christ's crown of thorns. The sober interior makes discreet use of different woods and marbles and incorporates high-tech sound and lighting controls that may not surprise Americans but which, by traditionalist European standards, are revolutionary. ✉ *cours Monseigneur-Roméro,* ☎ *01–64–97–85–21.*

Vaux-le-Vicomte

★ 31 *24 km (15 mi) southeast of Evry via N446 to Melun, 5 km (3 mi) northeast of Melun via N36/D215.*

Wonderful proportions and exquisite gardens characterize the stunning **Château de Vaux-le-Vicomte.** Built between 1656 and 1661 for finance minister Nicolas Fouquet, the construction of this château was monstrous even for those days: Entire villages were razed, 18,000 workmen called in, and architect Louis Le Vau, painter Charles Le Brun, and landscape architect André Le Nôtre were hired to prove that Fouquet's refined tastes matched his business acumen. The housewarming party was so lavish that star guest Louis XIV, tetchy at the best of times, threw a jealous fit. He hurled Fouquet in the slammer and promptly began building Versailles to prove just who was boss.

The high-roofed château, partially surrounded by a moat, is set well back from the road behind iron railings topped with sculpted heads. A cobbled avenue stretches up to the entrance and stone steps lead to the entrance hall, which, given the noble scale of the exterior, seems small. There is no grand staircase, either—the stairs are tucked away in the left wing and lead to the private apartments—rooms designed on an intimate scale for daily living. Charles Le Brun's captivating decoration includes the ceiling of the **Chambre du Roi** (Royal Bedchamber), depicting *Time Bearing Truth Heavenward,* framed by stucco work by sculptors François Girardon and Legendre. Along the frieze you can make out small squirrels, the Fouquet family's emblem—even now squirrels are known as *fouquets* in local dialect. But Le Brun's masterwork is the ceiling in the **Salon des Muses,** a brilliant allegorical composition painted in glowing, sensuous colors that surpasses his work at Versailles.

On the ground floor, the impressive **Grand Salon,** with its unusual oval form and 16 caryatid pillars symbolizing the months and seasons, possesses harmony and style despite its unfinished state. In fact, the lack of decoration only points up Le Vau's architectural genius.

In the basement, whose cool, dim rooms were used to store food and wine and house the château's staff, you'll find rotating exhibits about the château's past. Life-size wax figures illustrate the château's history. The **cuisine** (kitchen), a cheerful sight with its gleaming copperware and old menus, is also down here.

Unlike Fontainebleau, Vaux-le-Vicomte is still privately owned and, as such, it doesn't have a perfectly restored interior. But there is no mistaking the grandeur of Le Nôtre's **gardens,** which have been carefully restored. Also visit the **Musée des Équipages** in the stables and inspect a host of carriages and coaches in wonderful condition. ☎ *01–64–14–41–90.* 🎫 *Château and grounds: 56 frs; grounds only: 30 frs; candlelight visits: 75 frs.* ⏲ *Apr.–Oct., daily 10–1, 2–6; Mar. and Nov. 1–11, daily 11–1, 2–5; closed Nov. 12–Feb. Candlelight visits May–Oct., Sat. 8:30 PM–11 PM.*

Dining

$ ✕ **L'Écureuil.** An imposing barn to the right of the château entrance has been transformed into this self-service cafeteria where you can enjoy fine steaks (insist yours is cooked enough), coffee or a snack beneath the ancient rafters of a wood-beam roof. The restaurant is open daily for lunch and tea, and for dinner during candlelit visits. ✉ *Château de Vaux-le-Vicomte. Reservations not accepted. MC, V.*

Barbizon

32 *17 km (11 mi) southwest of Vaux-le-Vicomte via Melun and D64, 50 km (31 mi) southeast of Paris.*

On the western edge of the 62,000-acre Fontainebleau forest, the painters' village of Barbizon retains its atmosphere despite the intrusion of art galleries, souvenir shops, and weekending Parisians. The group of landscape painters known as the Barbizon School—Camille Corot, Jean-François Millet, Narcisse Diaz de la Peña, and Théodore Rousseau, among others—lived here from the 1830s on, paving the way for the Impressionists by their willingness to accept nature on its own terms, rather than use it as an idealized base for carefully structured compositions. In the forest, sealed to one of the famous sandstone rocks, is a bronze medallion by sculptor Henri Chapu which pays homage to Millet and Rousseau.

Corot and company would often repair to the Auberge du Père Ganne after painting; the inn still stands, and is now the **Musée de l'École de Barbizon** (Barbizon School Museum). The museum contains documents of the village as it was in the 19th century as well as a few original works—in addition, the Barbizon artists painted on every available surface, and even now you can see some originals on the walls and in the buffet. ✉ *92 Grande-Rue,* ☎ *01–60–66–22–27.* 🎫 *25 frs.* ⏲ *Wed.–Mon. 10–12:30 and 2–5.*

You can also soak up the arty mood at the **Atelier Jean-François Millet** (Millet's Studio). Though there are no actual Millet works, this studio is where the artist painted some of his most renowned pieces, including *The Gleaners.* ✉ *27 Grande-Rue,* ☎ *01–60–66–21–55.* 🎫 *Free.* ⏲ *Wed.–Mon. 9:30–12:30 and 2–5:30.*

The **Maison-Atelier Théodore Rousseau** was painter Théodore Rousseau's house-cum-studio—in a converted barn. Temporary exhibitions are now staged here. ✉ *55 Grande-Rue,* ☎ *01–60–66–22–38.* 🎫 *25 frs (joint ticket with the Barbizon School Museum,* ☞ above*).* ⏲ *Wed. and Fri.–Mon. 10–12:30 and 2–5.*

Dining and Lodging

$–$$ ✕ **Le Relais.** Large portions of delicious French country specialties are served at this spacious restaurant with a big open fire and paintings and hunting trophies adorning the walls. The choice of prix-fixe menus is good and you can eat on a large terrace, in the shade of lime and chestnut trees. ✉ *2 av. Général-de-Gaulle,* ☎ *01–60–66–40–28. Reservations essential on weekends. MC, V. Closed Wed. No dinner Tues.*

$$ ★ ✕🏨 **Auberge des Alouettes.** This delightful family-run 19th-century inn is on 2 acres of grounds (which the better rooms overlook). The interior has been redecorated in '30s style, but many rooms still have their original oak beams. The popular restaurant (reservations are essential), with its large open terrace, serves light cuisine and barbecued beef in summer. The restaurant is closed Sunday night in winter. ✉ *4 rue Antoine-Barye, 77630,* ☎ *01–60–66–41–98,* FAX *01–60–66–20–69. 22 rooms. Restaurant, tennis court. AE, DC, MC, V.*

Fontainebleau

8 km (5 mi) southeast of Barbizon via N7, 64 km (40 mi) southeast of Paris via A6/N7.

Like Chambord in the Loire Valley or Compiègne to the north, Fontainebleau was a favorite spot for royal hunting parties before it hosted one of France's grandest residences. Begun under the flamboyant Renaissance prince François I, the French contemporary of England's ★ Henry VIII, the **Château de Fontainebleau** was embellished by Italian artists Il Rosso (a pupil of Michelangelo; 1494–1540) and Francesco Primaticcio (1504–70). In fact, they did much more: By introducing the pagan allegories and elegant lines of Mannerism to France, they revolutionized French decorative art. Their extraordinary frescoes and stuccowork can be admired in the Galerie François I and the glorious Salle de Bal (☞ *below*), completed under Henri II, François I's successor. The decorative interlaced initials found throughout the château are also an addition of Henri II; while you might expect to see the royal "H" woven with a "C" (for Catherine de' Medici, his wife), instead you'll find a "D"—indicating his mistress, Diane de Poitiers.

Even Sun King Louis XIV turned his architectural attentions to Fontainebleau, commissioning Hardouin-Mansart to design new pavil-

Cour du Cheval-Blanc, **37**
Cour Henri IV, **35**
Cour Ovale, **34**
Galerie de Diane, **40**
Jardin de Diane, **36**
Musée Napoléon, **38**
Porte du Baptistère, **33**
Salle de Bal, **41**
Salle du Trône, **39**

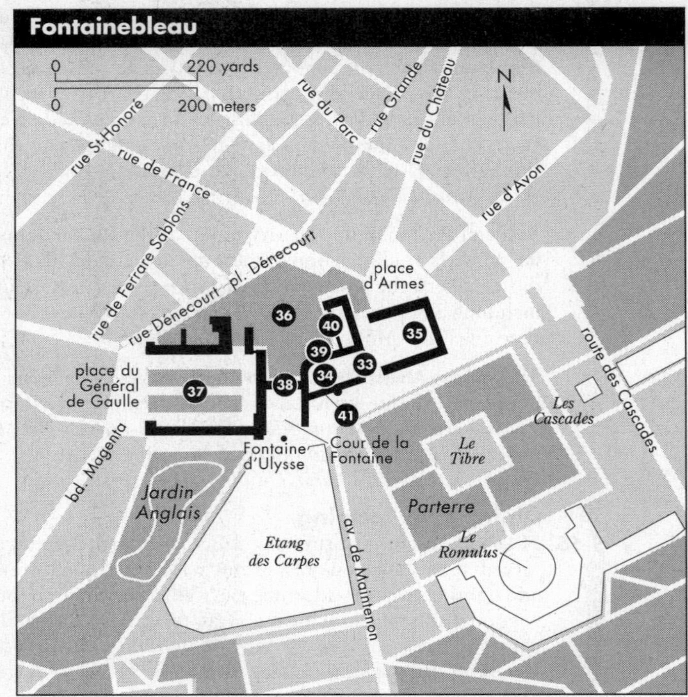

ions and André Le Nôtre to replant the **gardens.** Despite the allure of his main project, Versailles, he and his court returned faithfully each autumn for the hunting season. However, it was Napoléon who made a Versailles, as it were, out of Fontainebleau, by spending lavishly to restore it to its former glory. He held Pope Pius VII prisoner here in 1812 and signed the second church-state concordat here in 1813.

The formal, flowery **Parterre** faces the leafy **Jardin Anglais** (English Garden) across the **Étang des Carpes,** where ancient carp are alleged to swim. Allied soldiers drained the pond in 1915 and ate the fish, and, in the event they missed some, Hitler's hordes did likewise in 1940.

33 The domed **Porte du Baptistère** (Baptism Gateway) is named for the
baptism of the Dauphin—the heir to the throne, later to become Louis
XIII—which took place under the arch of the gateway in 1606. The
34 gateway fronts the **Cour Ovale** (Oval Courtyard), shaped like a flat-
35 tened egg. Opposite the courtyard is the **Cour Henri IV** (Henry IV
Courtyard), a large, severe square built at the same time as the place
36 des Vosges in Paris (1609). Around the corner is the informal **Jardin
de Diane,** with peacocks and a statue of the hunting goddess surrounded by mournful hounds. The palace's most majestic courtyard,
37 the **Cour du Cheval-Blanc** (White Horse Courtyard) contains the famous
horseshoe staircase built by Jean du Cerceau in the early 17th century;
it can be reached from the garden. Here Napoléon bade farewell to
his Old Guard in 1814 before his brief exile on the Mediterranean island of Elba—hence the courtyard's other name, the Cour des Adieux.
Gardens free. Daily 9–dusk.

38 The **Musée Napoléon** contains a lock of his hair, his Légion d'Honneur medal, his imperial uniform, the hat he wore on his return from
39 Elba in 1815, and a bed in which he once slept. There is also a **Salle
du Trône** (Throne Room)—Napoléon spurned the throne-room at Ver-

sailles, a palace he disliked, and established his imperial seat here in the former King's Bedchamber, a room with a suitably majestic decor—and the **Queen's Boudoir,** known as the Room of the Six Maries. The
40 sweeping **Galerie de Diane,** built during the reign of Henri IV (1589–1610), was converted to a library in the 1860s. Other salons boast 17th-century tapestries, marble reliefs by Jacquet de Grenoble, and paintings and frescoes by Primaticcio, Niccolò dell'Abbate, and other members of the Fontainebleau School. The jewel of the interior is the ceremo-
41 nial ballroom—the **Salle de Bal**—nearly 100 feet long, with wood paneling, 16th-century frescoes and gilding, and, reputedly, the first coffered ceiling in France, its intricate pattern echoed by the splendid 19th-century parquet floor. ☎ *01–64–22–27–40.* *32 frs.* ⏲ *Wed.–Mon. 9:30–5.*

Dining and Lodging

$–$$ ✕ **La Route du Beaujolais.** The food is cheap and the atmosphere cheerful at this jolly eatery near the château, where Lyonnais-style cold cuts and bottles of Beaujolais are the mainstays. For something a little more upscale, try the beef fillet with Brie or the braised veal kidney. Prix-fixe meals are priced at 88 and 130 francs. ✉ *3 rue Montebello,* ☎ *01–64–22–27–98. AE, DC, MC, V.*

$$$$ ★ ✕ **Aigle-Noir.** This may be Fontainebleau's costliest hotel, but you can't go wrong if you request one of the rooms overlooking either the garden or the château. They have late 18th- or early 19th-century reproduction furniture, evoking a Napoleonic mood. The restaurant, Le Beauharnais, serves subtle, imaginative cuisine—duck with marjoram is a good choice. There's a tranquil garden for alfresco dining in summer. Reservations are essential and jacket and tie are required. ✉ *27 pl. Napoléon-Bonaparte, 77300,* ☎ *01–64–22–32–65,* FAX *01–64–22–17–33. 56 rooms. Restaurant, pool, sauna, exercise room, convention center. AE, DC, MC, V.*

$$$ **Napoléon.** Opposite the château, this is surely one of the best local properties. Pastel-color rooms have modern furniture and marble baths and look out onto terraces or the indoor garden. The restaurant, La Table des Maréchaux, serves satisfying, deftly prepared classics, and the 130-franc menu is an excellent deal. ✉ *9 rue Grande, 77300,* ☎ *01–64–22–20–39,* FAX *01–64–22–20–87. 57 rooms. Restaurant. AE, DC, MC, V. Closed end of Dec.*

$$ **Londres.** The balconies of this tranquil, family-style hotel with Louis XV decor overlook the château and the Cour des Adieux, where Napoléon bade his troops an emotional farewell. The austere 19th-century facade is a registered landmark. ✉ *1 pl. du Général-de-Gaulle, 77300,* ☎ *01–64–22–20–21,* FAX *01–60–72–39–16. 22 rooms. Restaurant, bar. AE, DC, MC, V. Closed mid-Dec.–early Jan.*

Outdoor Activities and Sports

The forest of Fontainebleau is famed for its fascinating rock formations, where many a novice alpinist first caught the climbing bug. For more information about circuits and organized climbs in the area, contact the **Club Alpin Français** (✉ 24 av. Laumière, 75019 Paris, ☎ 01–42–02–75–94). The forest is also laced with hiking trails; for more information, ask for the *Guide des Sentiers* at the tourist office (☞ Contacts and Resources *in* Ile-de-France A to Z, *below*). Bikes can be rented at the Fontainebleau-Avon train station.

Moret-sur-Loing

42 *10 km (6 mi) southeast of Fontainebleau via N6, 74 km (46 mi) southeast of Paris.*

Close to the confluence of the Rivers Seine and Yonne is the endearing village of Moret-sur-Loing, immortalized by Impressionist painter Alfred Sisley, who lived here for 20 years at 19 rue Montmartre (not open to the public), around the corner from the church. A narrow bridge, one of the oldest in France, leads across the River Loing and provides a view of the village walls, rooftops, and church tower. Those with a sweet tooth, take note: Moret is also renowned for its barley-sugar. A good time to visit the town is on a Saturday evening in summer (mid-June through early September), when 500 locals stage son-et-lumière pageants illustrating the town's history.

Truculent World War I leader Georges Clemenceau (1841–1929), known as The Tiger, is the subject of a cozy museum at **La Grange-Batelière,** the thatched house he used to live in. His taste for Oriental art and his friendship with Impressionist Claude Monet are evoked here. ☎ *01–60–70–51–21. Guided tours only: 35 frs.* ⌚ *Easter–mid-Nov., weekends 3–6.*

En Route From Moret, head north to neighboring St-Mammès, at the confluence of the Loing and Seine rivers, then head east along D39 to **Montereau-Fault-Yonne**—where the Seine meets the great river of northern Burgundy, the Yonne. Montereau was a renowned pottery center until the 1950s, as you will learn at the small Musée de la Faïence (✉ 2 pl. René-Cassin). From Montereau continue along D403, through **Donnemarie** with its huge belfry and past hilltop **St-Loup-de-Naud** with its richly sculpted church portal, to Provins.

Provins

★ 43 *48 km (30 mi) northeast of Moret-sur-Loing, 48 km (30 mi) east of Melun, 80 km (50 mi) southeast of Paris via N19.*

On the hilltop site of a Roman camp, Provins developed into the third most important commercial center in France (after Paris and Rouen) during the Middle Ages. Under the influence of the counts of Champagne, it acquired international renown as a rose-growing center. Climb up to the **Tour de César,** a circular 12th-century keep on a ★ sturdy mound, to admire the panoramic view of the town and its **Remparts,** some of the best-preserved medieval town walls in France. ✉ *rue du Palais.* 🎫 *17 frs.* ⌚ *Daily 10–5.*

Note the incongruous 17th-century classical dome on the 12th-century Gothic church of **St-Quiriace,** beneath the Tour de César. The **Jardin des Brébans,** close to the church, is a pleasant place for a walk. From the garden, rue du Palais leads to place du Châtel, a sloping square with restaurants at the far end.

The 13th-century **Grange aux Dîmes** (Tithe Barn), on rue de Jouy, just off the square, houses a good collection of medieval stone sculptures in its vaulted ground floor. 🎫 *22 frs.* ⌚ *Weekends 2–6.*

In a bid to liven up its image, Provins stages **Soirées Médiévales** (Medieval Evenings) in summer, with pageants and costumes; call the tourist office (☎ 01–64–60–26–26) for details. There is also a **Fête des Moissons** (Harvest Festival) on the last Sunday of August.

Lodging

$$–$$$ **Vieux Remparts.** Old wood beams inside the attractive old building and a cheerful, leafy courtyard make for a cheerful atmosphere.

Rooms are small, but have good light and modern furnishings. ✉ *3 rue Couverte, 77160,* ☎ *01–64–08–94–00,* FAX *01–60–67–77–22. 25 rooms. Restaurant. AE, DC, MC, V.*

ILE-DE-FRANCE A TO Z

Arriving and Departing

By Car

Expressway A13, from the Porte d'Auteuil, links Paris to Versailles. You can get to Chartres on A10 from Porte d'Orléans. For Fontainebleau, take A6 from Porte d'Orléans or, for a more attractive route through the Forest of Sénart and the northern part of the Forest of Fontainebleau, take N6 from Porte de Charenton via Melun. The A4 expressway runs from Paris to Disneyland.

By Plane

Major airports in the Ile-de-France area are **Charles de Gaulle** (☎ 01–48–62–22–80), known as Roissy, 25 km (16 mi) northwest of Paris, and **Orly** (☎ 01–49–75–15–15), 16 km (10 mi) south. Shuttle buses link Disneyland to the airports at Roissy, 56 km (35 mi) away, and Orly, 50 km (31 mi) distant; buses take 45 minutes and run every 45 minutes from Roissy, every 60 minutes from Orly (less frequently in low season), and cost 75 francs.

By Train

Many of the sights mentioned in our exploring text can be reached by train from Paris. Both regional and mainline (Le Mans–bound) trains leave the **Gare Montparnasse** for Chartres; the former also stop at Versailles, Rambouillet, and Maintenon. Gare Montparnasse is also the terminal for trains to Dreux (Granville line) and for the suburban trains that stop at Montfort-L'Amaury, the nearest station to Thoiry.

Some mainline trains from **Gare St-Lazare** stop at Mantes-la-Jolie and Vernon on their way to Rouen and Le Havre. Suburban trains leave the **Gare du Nord** for L'Isle-Adam. Chantilly is on the main northbound line from Gare du Nord (Senlis can be reached by bus from Chantilly) and Provins on a suburban line from **Gare de l'Est.** Fontainebleau—or, rather, neighboring Avon, 2 km (1½ mi) away (there is frequent bus service)—is 45 minutes from **Gare de Lyon.**

St-Germain-en-Laye is a terminal of the **RER-A** (express métro) that tunnels through Paris (main stations at Étoile, Auber, and Les Halles). The RER-A also accesses Maisons-Laffitte and, at the other end, the new suburban station for Disneyland Paris (called Marne-la-Vallée–Chessy), within 100 yards of the entrance to both the theme park and Festival Disney. Journey time is around 40 minutes and trains operate every 10–30 minutes, depending on the time of day. The handiest of Versailles's three train stations is the one reached by the **RER-C** line (main stations at Austerlitz, St-Michel, Invalides, and Champ-de-Mars). Evry can be reached on **RER-D.**

A mainline **TGV** (Trains à Grande Vitesse) station opened at Disneyland in 1994, providing direct access from Lille, Lyon, and, ultimately, London (via the Channel Tunnel) and Brussels.

Getting Around

Although a comprehensive rail network ensures that most towns in the Ile-de-France can make comfortable day trips from Paris, the only way to crisscross the region without returning to the capital is by car.

There is no shortage of expressways or fast highways, but be prepared for delays close to Paris and during the morning and evening rush hours.

Contacts and Resources

Car Rentals

Cars can be rented from agencies in Paris (☞ Contacts and Resources *in* Chapter 2). **Avis** (☎ 01–46–07–82–45). **Europcar** (☎ 01–45–51–21–11). **Hertz** (☎ 01–45–74–97–39).

Emergencies

Ambulance (☎ 15). **Regional hospitals**: Chartres (✉ 34 rue du Dr-Maunoury, ☎ 02–37–30–30–30); Melun (✉ 2 rue Fréteau-de-Pény, ☎ 01–64–71–60–06); and Versailles (✉ 177 rue de Versailles, Le Chesnay, ☎ 01–39–63–91–33). **Hospitals closer to Paris**: American Hospital in Neuilly (✉ 63 bd. Victor-Hugo, ☎ 01–47–45–71–00); and British Hospital in Levallois-Perret (✉ 3 rue Barbès, ☎ 01–47–58–13–12).

Guided Tours

Paris Vision (✉ 214 rue de Rivoli, Paris, 1er, ☎ 01–42–60–31–25) and **Cityrama** (✉ 147 rue St-Honoré, Paris, 1er, ☎ 01–44–55–61–00) run half-day guided trips three times a week to Chartres, Fontainebleau, and Barbizon (with additional departures scheduled in summer) and daily trips to Versailles; the cost ranges from 270–450 francs.

Guided excursions to Giverny are organized by **American Express** (✉ 11 rue Scribe, Paris, 9e, ☎ 01–47–77–77–37) from April through October. The **RATP** (✉ 53 quai des Grands-Augustins, 6e, métro St-Michel, ☎ 01–40–46–41–41) also has guided tours to Giverny.

Alliance Autos (✉ 5 bis av. Foch, St-Mandé, near the Bois de Vincennes, ☎ 01–43–28–20–20) has bilingual guides who will take you on a private tour around the Paris area in luxury cars or a minibus for a minimum of four hours for about 500 francs an hour (call to check details and prices).

Visitor Information

For written inquiries only, contact the **Comité Régional de Tourisme d'Ile-de-France** (✉ 26 av. de l'Opéra, 75001 Paris, ☎ 01–42–60–28–62). Information on Disneyland Paris is available from the **Euro Disneyland Central Reservations Office** (✉ B.P. 100, 77777 Marne-la-Vallée cedex 4, ☎ 01–60–30–60–30). Local tourist offices: **Barbizon** (✉ 55 Grande Rue, ☎ 01–60–66–41–87). **Chartres** (✉ pl. de la Cathédrale, ☎ 02–37–21–50–00). **Fontainebleau** (✉ 31 pl. Napoléon-Bonaparte, ☎ 01–64–22–25–68). **Rambouillet** (✉ 8 pl. de la Libération, ☎ 01–34–83–21–21). **Versailles** (✉ 7 rue des Réservoirs, ☎ 01–39–50–36–22).

4 The Loire Valley

Château Country

Sometimes owned by England, and fought over for centuries, this stretch of the Loire Valley is renowned for its extraordinary châteaux. Ranging from majestic Chambord and Saumur to the palatial Cheverny and Azay-le-Rideau to scenic Chenonceau and Ussé, these châteaux have become almost synonymous with France. At Orléans, too, you can see the country's history: It was here that Joan of Arc had her most rousing successes against the English.

Updated by Simon Hewitt

THE LOIRE IS THE LONGEST RIVER IN FRANCE, originating deep in the heart of the Massif Central and winding its way north and then west for over 960 km (600 mi) before reaching the Atlantic beyond Nantes. Halfway along, just outside the town of Orléans, the river makes a wide, westward bend, gliding languidly through low, rich country known as the Val de Loire—the Loire Valley. In this temperate "garden" region—a 225-km (140-mi) stretch between Orléans and Angers—hundreds of châteaux rise from the rocky banks of the Loire and its tributaries: the rivers Cher, Indre, Vienne, and Loir (with no *e*).

For centuries the Loire River was the area's principal means of transportation and an important barrier against invading armies. Towns arose at strategic bridgeheads, and fortresses—the earliest châteaux—appeared on the slopes of towering hills. The Loire Valley was hotly disputed by France and England during the Middle Ages; it belonged to England (under the Anjou Plantagenet family) between 1154 and 1216 and again during the Hundred Years' War (1337–1453). It was the example of Joan of Arc, the Maid of Orléans (scene of her most stirring victories), that crystallized French efforts to expel the English.

The Loire Valley's golden age came under François I (1515–47), flamboyant contemporary of Henry VIII. His salamander emblem can be seen in many châteaux, including Chambord, the mightiest one. He hired Renaissance craftsmen from Italy and hobnobbed with the aging Leonardo da Vinci, his guest at Amboise. Although the nation's power base shifted to Paris around 1600, aristocrats continued to erect luxurious palaces along the Loire until the end of the 18th century. Since that time, many châteaux—too expensive now for even the wealthiest to maintain—have fallen to the care of the state and are now preserved as cultural and historic monuments.

Pleasures and Pastimes

Châteaux

"Loire" and "château" are almost synonymous; even the word, "château"—part fortress, part palace, part mansion—has no English equivalent. Nearly 20 are described in this chapter, from grandiose Chambord and Saumur to the more intimate Cheverny and Azay-le-Rideau to the incredibly scenic Chenonceau and Ussé. There are genuine castles to admire, too—either preserved in intimidating glory, such as Langeais, Loches, and Angers; or gloriously ruined, like Chinon.

Dining

The Loire region, known as the "garden of France," produces a cornucopia—from beef, poultry, game, and fish to butter, cream, wine, fruit, and vegetables (especially asparagus and mushrooms). It sends its early crops to the best Parisian tables, yet keeps more than enough for local use. Loire wines can be extremely good—and varied. Among the best are Savennières and Cheverny (dry white); Côteaus du Layon and Montlouis (sweet white); Cabernet d'Anjou (rosé); Bourgueil, Chinon, and Saumur-Champigny (red); and Vouvray (white—dry, sweet, or sparkling).

CATEGORY	COST*
$$$$	over 400 frs
$$$	250 frs–400 frs
$$	125 frs–250 frs
$	under 125 frs

**per person for a three-course meal, including tax (20.6%) and tip but not wine*

Lodging

Even before the age of the train, the Loire Valley drew visitors from far and wide. Hundreds of hotels of all kinds have sprung up to accommodate today's travelers. At the higher end of the price scale is the Relais & Châteaux group; some of their best hotels are converted châteaux. At the lower end are the Logis de France hotels: small, traditional inns in towns and villages throughout the region that usually offer terrific value for the money. The Loire Valley is one of the country's most popular vacation destinations, so be sure to make reservations well in advance.

CATEGORY	COST*
$$$$	over 800 frs
$$$	550 frs–800 frs
$$	300 frs–550 frs
$	under 300 frs

**All prices are for a standard double room for two, including tax (20.6%) and service charge.*

Outdoor Activities

Besides the châteaux, the Loire Valley offers a great variety of outdoor activities, from bicycling to picnicking to walking through rolling hills and along riverbanks. The short distances between châteaux and other attractions make bicycling pleasant if you do not want to spend all day pedaling. Bicycles can be rented from many train stations.

Son-et-Lumière

In summer, concerts, music festivals, fairs, and the celebrated son-et-lumière (sound-and-light) extravaganzas held on the grounds of many châteaux abound. Dramatic spectacles that take place after dark, son-et-lumière shows can take the form of historical pageants—with huge casts of people in period costume and caparisoned horses, all floodlit and backed by music and commentary, sometimes in English. They also consist of sound and light shows, with spoken commentary and dialogue but no visible figures, as at Chenonceau. The most magnificent, with more than 100 performers, takes place at Le Lude.

Exploring the Loire Valley

Pick up the Loire River halfway along its voyage from central France to the Atlantic Ocean. Châteaux and vineyards will accompany you throughout your 340-km (210-mi) westbound course from the hilltop wine town of Sancerre to the bustling city of Angers. Lively towns punctuate the route at almost equal distances—Orléans, Blois, Tours, and Saumur—and are useful bases if you're relying on public transportation. Although you may be rushing around to see as many famous châteaux as possible, try to make time to walk through the poppy-covered hills, picnic along the riverbanks, and sample the local wines. If you want an escape from the usual tourist track, explore the lakes and forests of Sologne or wend your way back along the gentle, confusingly named Loir Valley.

Great Itineraries

You need a fortnight to cover the Loire Valley region in its entirety. But even if you don't have that long, you can still see many of the Loire's finest châteaux in three days by concentrating on the area between Blois and Amboise. Five days will give you time to explore these châteaux as well as visit Tours and Angers, two of the region's major cities. In ten days you can follow the Loire from Orléans to Angers.

Numbers in the text correspond to numbers in the margin and on the Loire Valley, Orléans, and Tours maps.

IF YOU HAVE 3 DAYS

Begin in **Blois** ⑮ and move inland through the forest to spend the night at **Chambord** ⑬. The next day take in nearby **Cheverny** ⑭ and return to the river at **Chaumont-sur-Loire** ⑯. Two attractions await just downstream at **Amboise** ⑰: the château and the Clos-Lucé mansion devoted to Leonardo da Vinci. Afterward, take in the Château de Chenonceau (no *x*) in the town of **Chenonceaux** ⑱, for a fitting climax for a visit to this area.

IF YOU HAVE 6 DAYS

Start by following the three-day itinerary through **Blois** ⑮, **Chambord** ⑬, **Cheverny** ⑭, **Chaumont-sur-Loire** ⑯, and **Amboise** ⑰, spending your third night in either **Chenonceaux** ⑱ or the region's major city, **Tours** ⑳–㉔. On day four head west to the attractive châteaux of **Azay-le-Rideau** ㉗, **Ussé** ㉚, and **Chinon** ㉛. The next day continue downstream to the venerable abbey at **Fontevraud** ㉞ and spend the fifth night in **Saumur** ㉟. End up in **Angers** ㊲, a lively city with a dramatic castle and good museums and shops.

IF YOU HAVE 10 DAYS

Stop in **Orléans** ⑦–⑩ on your way west along the Loire, if you are coming from Paris. From there, head to **Blois** ⑮ for the night. Over the next two days, explore **Cheverny** ⑭, **Chambord** ⑬, **Chaumont-sur-Loire** ⑯, **Amboise** ⑰, and **Chenonceaux** ⑱. On day four, detour south to the mighty citadel of **Loches** ⑲, before an overnight stop in **Tours** ⑳–㉔. Take in the reconstituted gardens at **Villandry** ㉕ en route to see the Renaissance pleasure palace at **Azay-le-Rideau** ㉗. The following day head to the château of **Ussé** ㉚ and the castle at **Chinon** ㉛. From Chinon, a short excursion south brings you to the chapel in **Champigny-sur-Veude** ㉜ and the unchanged 17th-century town of **Richelieu** ㉝. Continue west on day eight from Chinon to **Fontevraud** ㉞ and **Saumur** ㉟. Spend the next night in **Angers** ㊲, with a detour to the imposing Château de Serrant if you have time. Finish with a leisurely drive east through the other Loir Valley, from **Le Lude** ㊴ to the historic town of **Vendôme** ㊵.

When to Tour the Loire Valley

The Loire is at its best in May and June, when it still looks like a river; come midsummer, the water level drops, marooning unsightly sandbanks. The valley can be sultry, stuffy, and crowded in July and August, although most of the son-et-lumière shows take place at this time. October is a good off-season option, when all is mist and mellow fruitfulness along the Loire and the mysterious pools of the Sologne, and the trees are turning russet and gold. The fall is also the best time to sample regional specialties such as wild mushrooms and game. On Sundays, try to avoid the main cities, Orléans, Tours, and Angers—most shops are closed.

THE LOIRE VALLEY

Although Orléans is considered the gateway to the Loire—especially if you're coming from Paris—you may want to start exploring this area further east. Take in the hilltop wine town of Sancerre, the hunting and ceramics center of Gien, and the ancient abbey of St-Benoît. A string of fine châteaux dominates the valley west of Orléans—Meung-Sur-Loire, Blois, and Amboise lead the way—but the area's most stunning monuments lie inland: romantic Chenonceau, with its arches half-straddling the River Cher, and colossal Chambord, its forest of chimneys and turrets barely visible above the treetops. Tours, the largest and most central of the cities in the Loire Valley, leads to Ussé and Azay-

The Loire Valley

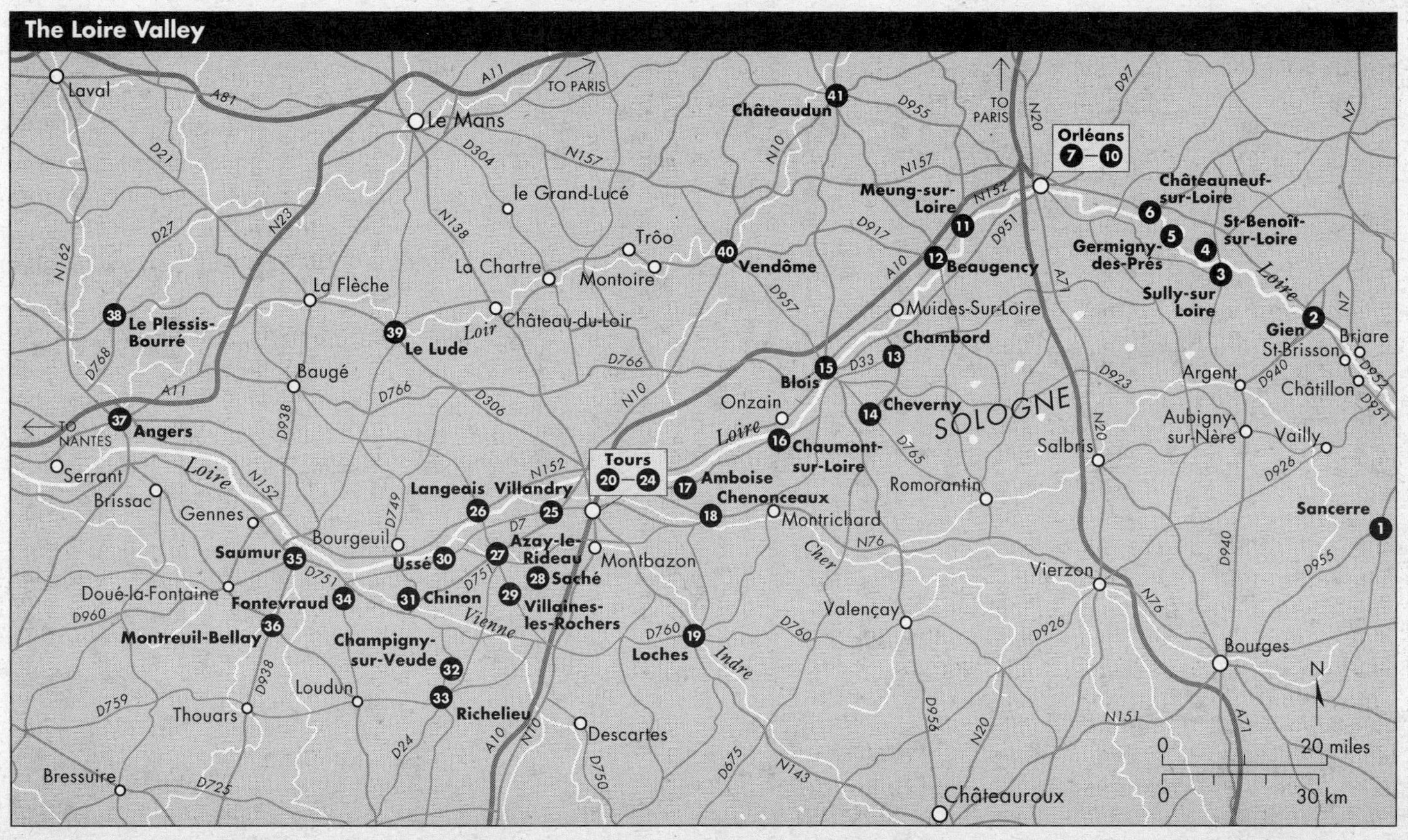

le-Rideau and the more muscular castles of Chinon and Saumur. At Angers you can drive northeast to explore the winding, intimate Loir Valley all the way to Châteaudun, just south of Chartres and the Ile-de-France; or continue along the Loire as far as Nantes, the gateway to Brittany.

Sancerre

❶ *200 km (125 mi) south of Paris via A6 and N7; 120 km (75 mi) southeast of Orléans.*

The hilltop town of Sancerre is a maze of old cobbled streets offering dramatic views of the mountainous vineyards that produce its flinty white wine. Forget about the Loire's reputation for soft pastures and gentle hills: The vineyards of Sancerre (like the town itself) stand on rugged, towering mounds and are among the most scenic in France. The steeply-climbing country roads west of town provide panoramic views. Head for **Chavignol,** just over 3 km (2 mi) away, a wine village with a number of producers who offer sales and tastings. Chavignol is also home to a delicious small round goat cheese, Crottin de Chavignol, that comes soft or hard depending on the time of year.

Nightlife and the Arts

The famous Chavignol goat cheese, and other local cheeses, are celebrated in Sancerre every April during the **Fête du Crottin.**

En Route Head north from Sancerre on D955 and D951 along the west bank of the Loire for 36 km (22 mi) to Châtillon. Stay on D951 and pause to admire the **Pont-Canal de Briare,** a splendid, lamp-lined aqueduct built by Gustave Eiffel in 1890 (the year after his tower) to transport the Canal Latéral de la Loire (Loire Side Canal) across the river. You can walk along the top to admire the view, then have a drink outside the café at the far end of the aqueduct. A few miles further along the west bank of the Loire is the 12th-century castle of **St-Brisson,** whose collection of 13th-century mangonels (giant catapults) is activated by local strongmen every Sunday in summer. The biggest catapult, known as a *couillard,* sends rocks that weigh 20 kilos spinning as high as the castle roof before crashing 150 yards away. From Brisson, continue on to Gien.

Gien

❷ *6 km (4 mi) northwest of St-Brisson; 51 km (32 mi) northwest of Sancerre via D955 and D951; 67 km (42 mi) southeast of Orléans.*

Ceramics and hunting are the twin historical attractions of the pleasant riverside town of Gien. Its redbrick château, completed in 1484, ★ houses the unexpectedly fine **Musée International de la Chasse,** a hunting museum of regal scope. Exhibits trace the various types of hunt—shooting, trapping, fox hunting with hounds—and the display of firearms ranges from harquebuses to rifles. A 13-foot horn (the usual length before a hunting horn is coiled up into its familiar circle) sounds an offbeat note from the ceiling of one room; vast 18th-century hunting pictures by François Desportes and Jean-Baptiste Oudry, dogs and boar to the fore, line the stately hall with its superb beamed roof. ✉ *pl. du Château,* ☎ *02–38–67–69–69.* 🎫 *25 frs.* ⏲ *Apr.–Oct., daily 9:30–6:30; Nov.–Dec. and Mar., Tues.–Sun. 10–noon and 2–5.*

At the **Musée de la Faïencerie** (Earthenware Factory Museum), in an old paste store, admire local Gien earthenware (both old and new), with its distinctive deep blue glaze and golden decoration. Call ahead to arrange a tour of the factory; there's also a shop. ✉ *78 pl. de la Victoire,* ☎ *02–38–67–00–05.* 🎫 *12 frs.* ⏲ *Daily 9–11:45 and 2–5:45.*

Sully-sur-Loire

3 *24 km (15 mi) northwest of Gien via D951; 48 km (30 mi) southeast of Orléans.*

An imposing castle with a park, moat, and spectacular medieval roof makes Sully-sur-Loire worth visiting. The **Château de Sully** dates from the first half of the 14th century. It has a sturdy keep with the finest chestnut roof anywhere along the Loire—a vast structure in the form of an upturned boat, constructed in 1400. The chestnut has the useful property of repelling insects; no sensible spider would spin a web in it. ☎ *02–38–36–36–86.* 🎫 *18 frs.* ⏲ *Daily May–Sept., 9–11:45 and 2–5:45; Oct.–Apr., 10–11:45 and 2–4:45; closed Dec.–Feb.*

St-Benoît-sur-Loire

4 *8 km (5 mi) northwest of Sully-sur-Loire via D60; 40 km (30 mi) southeast of Orléans.*

The highlight of St-Benoît-sur-Loire is its ancient abbey, often called the greatest Romanesque church in France. Village signposts refer to it as "La Basilique."

St-Benoît, or St-Benedict, was the founder of the Benedictine monastic order. In AD 650, a group of monks chose this safe and fertile spot for their new monastery, then returned to Monte Cassino, Italy, to retrieve the bones of St-Benedict with which to bless the site. Despite demands from priests at Monte Cassino for the return of the bones, some of the relics remain here, in the 11th-century **Abbaye St-Benoît.** Following the Hundred Years' War of the 14th and 15th centuries, the monastery fell into a decline, and the Wars of Religion (1562–98) wrought further damage. During the French Revolution, the monks dispersed and all the buildings were destroyed, except the abbey church itself, which became the parish church.

Monastic life here began anew in 1944, when the monks rebuilt their monastery and regained the church for their own use. The pillars of the tower porch are noted for their intricately carved capitals, and the choir floor is an amazing patchwork of many-color marble. Gregorian chants can be heard daily, at mass or vespers, and Sunday services attract worshipers and music lovers from all around. Visitors are welcome to explore the church crypt. ⏲ *Mass and vespers Sun. 11 AM and 6:15 PM, Mon.–Sat. noon and 6:15 PM. Guided English-language tours of the monastic buildings can be arranged; inquire at the monastery shop.*

Germigny-des-Prés

5 *6 km (4 mi) northwest of St-Benoît-sur-Loire via D60; 34 km (21 mi) southeast of Orléans.*

The village of Germigny-des-Prés is famous for its church, one of the oldest in France. Around AD 800, Theodulf, an abbot of St-Benoît, built the tiny **Èlise de Germigny-les-Prés**—a Byzantine arrangement of round arches on square pillars, with indirect light filtering from smaller arches above the central square. The church was carefully restored to its original condition during the last century. Though Theodulf himself brought most of the original mosaics from Italy, only one—covered by plaster and not discovered until 1848—survives. Made of 130,000 cubes of colored glass, it shows the Ark of the Covenant transported by angels with golden halos. The Latin inscription asks us not to forget Theodulf in our prayers. ⊙ *Daily 9–noon and 2–5.*

Châteauneuf-sur-Loire

6 *5 km (3 mi) northwest of Germigny-des-Prés.*

The village of Châteauneuf-sur-Loire has a delightful public park with giant tulip trees, magnolias, weeping willows, and rhododendrons, and is especially beautiful in late May and early June. Little streams on their way to the Loire snake their way across the parkland, past benches, shady copses, and scenic picnic spots. For 12 francs, you can visit the small **Musée de la Marine** in the town hall for a chronicle of the history of navigation on the Loire.

Orléans

125 km (78 mi) south of Paris; 112 km (70 mi) northeast of Tours.

As a natural bridgehead over the Loire, Orléans has long been the focus of hostile confrontations and invasions. In 52 BC Julius Caesar slaughtered its inhabitants and burned it to the ground. Five centuries later, Attila and the Huns did much the same. Next came the Normans; then the Valois kings turned it into a secondary capital. The story of the Hundred Years' War, Joan of Arc, and the Siege of Orléans is widely known. During the Wars of Religion (1562–98), much of the cathedral was destroyed. A century ago, ham-fisted town planners razed many of the city's fine old buildings. Both German and Allied bombs helped finish the job during World War II. Today, however, Orléans is a thriving commercial city; sensitive urban renewal has done much to bring it back to life.

7 The **Cathédrale Ste-Croix** is a riot of pinnacles and gargoyles, both Gothic and pseudo-Gothic, embellished with 18th-century wedding-cake towers. After most of the cathedral was destroyed in the 16th century during the Wars of Religion, Henry IV and his successors rebuilt it. Novelist Marcel Proust (1871–1922) called it France's ugliest church, but most people find it impressive. Inside are vast quantities of stained glass and 18th-century wood carving, plus the modern **Chapelle de Jeanne d'Arc,** with plaques in memory of the British and American war dead. ⊠ *pl. Ste-Croix.* ⊙ *Daily 9–noon and 2–6.*

8 The modern **Musée des Beaux-Arts** (Fine Arts Museum) is across from the cathedral. Take the elevator to the top of the five-story building, then make your way down to see works by such artists as Tintoretto, Velázquez, Watteau, Boucher, Rodin, and Gauguin. The museum's richest collection is its 17th-century French paintings. ⊠ *1 rue Ferdinand-Rabier,* ☎ *02–38–53–39–22.* 🎫 *18 frs.* ⊙ *Wed.–Mon. 10–noon and 2–6.*

9 The **Musée Historique** (Orléans's History Museum) is housed in the **Hôtel Cabu,** a Renaissance mansion restored after World War II. It contains both "fine" and "popular" works of art connected with the town's past, including a remarkable collection of pagan bronzes of animals and dancers. These bronzes were hidden from zealous Christian missionaries in the 4th century and discovered in a sandpit near St-Benoît in 1861. ⊠ *pl. de l'Abbé-Desnoyers,* ☎ *02–38–79–25–60.* 🎫 *15 frs.* ⊙ *Wed.–Mon. 10–noon and 2–6 (until 5 Oct.–Mar.).*

During the 10-day Siege of Orléans in 1429, 17-year-old Joan of Arc
10 stayed on the site of the **Maison de Jeanne d'Arc** (Joan of Arc's House). This faithful reconstruction of the house she knew contains exhibits about her life and costumes and weapons of her time. Several diora-

Cathédrale Ste-Croix, **7**
La Maison de Jeanne-d'Arc, **10**
Musée des Beaux-Arts, **8**
Musée Historique, **9**

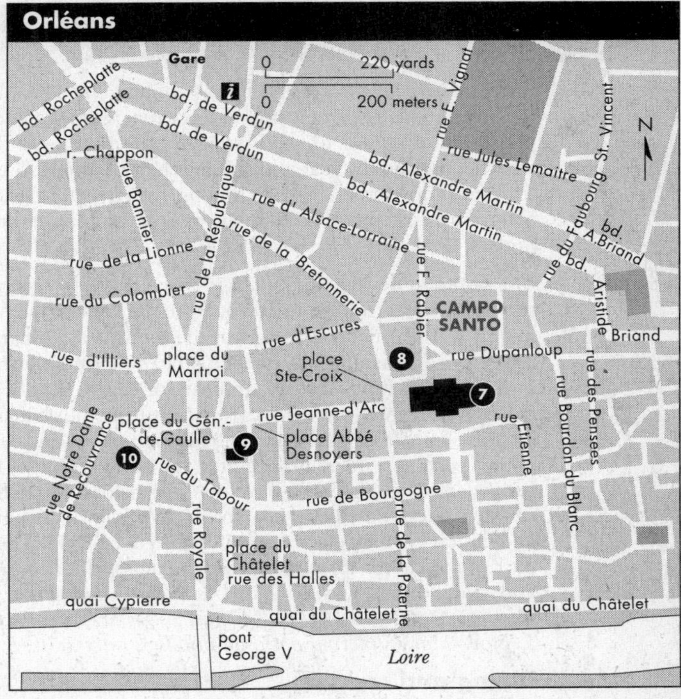

mas modeled by Lucien Harmey recount the main episodes in her life, from the audience at Chinon to the coronation at Reims; her seizure at Compiègne; and the stake at Rouen. ✉ *3 pl. du Général-de-Gaulle,* ☎ *02–38–52–99–89.* 🎫 *12 frs.* ⏲ *May–Oct., Tues.–Sun. 10–noon and 2–6; Nov.–Apr., Tues.–Sun. 2–6 only.*

Dining and Lodging

$$ ✕ **Crémaillère.** Although this bustling restaurant stays open late (orders are taken until 11 PM), service is unflappable. House specialties include ravioli with scallops, bream with smoked ham, and baked apple desserts. ✉ *34 rue Notre-Dame-de-Recouvrance,* ☎ *02–38–53–49–17. AE, DC, MC, V. Closed Sun., Mon., and part of July.*

$$ ✕🏨 **Rivage.** This small, white-walled hotel north of Orléans is a pleasant base for exploring the city. Each of the compact rooms has a little balcony with a view of the tree-lined river; the bathrooms are tiny. There is no elevator. The dining room opens onto a terrace facing the Loire. The menu changes with the season—if you're lucky, chef François Tassain's memorable crayfish, lamb marinated in paprika, and glazed green apple soufflé with apple marmalade will be on the menu. ✉ *635 rue de la Reine-Blanche, 45160 Olivet (5 km/3 mi north of Orléans),* ☎ *02–38–66–02–93,* FAX *02–38–56–31–11. 17 rooms, 11 with shower, 6 with bath. Restaurant, tennis court. AE, DC, MC, V. Closed late Dec.–mid-Jan.*

Nightlife and the Arts

The two-day **Fête de Jeanne d'Arc** (Joan of Arc Festival), on May 7th and 8th, celebrates the heroic Maid of Orléans with a military parade and religious procession.

Meung-sur-Loire

⓫ *16 km (10 mi) southwest of Orléans via N152.*

Intimate Meung-sur-Loire is not as commercial as Amboise or Azay-le-Rideau. The town's most famous citizen was Jehan de Meung, born in 1260 and author of the best-selling *Roman de la Rose* (Geoffrey Chaucer produced a well-known English translation). Give yourself time to wander down rue Jehan-de-Meung, the street that leads off the main square away from the château, to see the marvelous, half-timber houses.

The **Château de Meung** is part 12th-century fortress, part 18th-century residence. From the 12th century to the French Revolution, it served mainly as the official residence of the Bishops of Orléans although, in 1429, Lord Salisbury used it as his headquarters during the Siege of Orléans. (When he was killed in the fray, Lord Talbot took over but could not prevent Joan of Arc from capturing the château.) It was sold after the French Revolution, and had stood empty and derelict for years before private restoration began in the early 1970s. It has since been furnished with a diverse collection of items that range from 12th-century antiques to medieval crossbows, World War II submachine guns, and military helmets from the Middle Ages to 1945. The most unusual part of the château is underground: a network of tunnels, dungeons, and storehouses, with a chapel and torture chamber. ✉ *16 pl. du Martroi,* ☎ *02–38–44–36–47.* 🎫 *32 frs.* ⏲ *Apr.–Oct., daily 9:30–5; Nov.–Mar., Sun. and national holidays only 2:30–5.*

Dining and Lodging

$–$$ ★ ✕🏨 **St-Jacques.** This inn, on Meung's busy main road, is just a five-minute walk from the château and the river. Its family-run restaurant serves excellent fresh food without fuss at deliciously low prices. The reasonably priced menus might include oysters, fillet of duck in a raspberry vinaigrette, lamb or fish, cheese, and dessert. The restaurant is closed Monday. The clean, simple rooms either have a shower or, for 20 francs more, a full bath. ✉ *60 rue du Général-de-Gaulle, 45130,* ☎ *02–38–44–30–39,* FAX *02–38–45–17–02. 12 rooms with bath or shower. AE, MC, V. Restaurant. Closed last 2 wks in Jan.*

Beaugency

⓬ *7 km (4 mi) southwest of Meung.*

A clutch of historic towers and buildings around a 14th-century bridge over the Loire give Beaugency its charm. The buildings include the massive 11th-century **Donjon** (Keep), the Romanesque church of **Notre-Dame,** and the **Tour du Diable** (Devil's Tower) overlooking the river. The **Château Dunois** contains a regional museum with traditional costumes and peasant furniture. ✉ *2 pl. Dunois,* ☎ *02–38–44–55–23.* 🎫 *21 frs.* ⏲ *Wed.–Mon. 10–noon and 2–5.*

Chambord

★ ⓭ *24 km (15 mi) southwest of Beaugency via D925, D951, and D112; 19 km (12 mi) east of Blois; 45 km (28 mi) southwest of Orléans.*

The largest of the Loire châteaux, the **Château de Chambord** is in the middle of a royal game forest with a cluster of buildings—barely a village—across the road. Chambord is the kind of place William Randolph Hearst might have built if he'd had more money. Variously dubbed "megalomaniac" and "an enormous film-set extravaganza," this is one of the most extraordinary structures in Europe.

A few facts about the château set the tone: The facade is 420 feet long, there are 440 rooms and 365 chimneys, and a wall 32 km (20 mi) long encloses the 13,000-acre forest (you can wander through 3,000 acres of it; the rest is reserved for wild boar and other game). Under François I, building began in 1519, a job that took 12 years and required 1,800 workers. His original grandiose idea was to divert the Loire to form a moat, but someone (perhaps his adviser, Leonardo da Vinci) persuaded him to make do with the River Cosson. François I used the château only for short stays; yet when he came, 12,000 horses were required to transport his luggage, servants, and entourage! Later kings also used Chambord as an occasional retreat, and Louis XIV, the Sun King, had Molière perform here. In the 18th century, Louis XV gave the château to Maréchal de Saxe as a reward for his victory over the English and Dutch at Fontenoy (southern Belgium) in 1745. When not besporting himself with wine, women, and song, the marshal stood on the roof to oversee the exercises of his own regiment of 1,000 cavalry. Now, after long neglect—all the original furnishings vanished during the French Revolution—Chambord belongs to the state.

You can wander freely through the vast rooms, filled with a variety of exhibits—not all concerned with Chambord, but interesting nonetheless. The enormous, double-helix staircase looks like a single staircase, but an entire regiment could march up one spiral while a second came down the other, and they would never meet. Also be sure to visit the roof terrace, whose forest of towers, turrets, cupolas, gables, and chimneys was described by 19th-century novelist Henry James as "more like the spires of a city than the salient points of a single building." A short **son-et-lumière** show in French, English, and German, successively, is held on many evenings from mid-May to mid-October; admission is 50 francs. ☎ *02–54–50–40–28.* *40 frs.* ⏲ *July–Aug., daily 9:30–6:30; Sept.–June, daily 9:30–5:15.*

Dining and Lodging

$$ ✕ **St-Michel.** Enjoy simple and comfortable quarters in this revamped country house at the edge of the woods, across from the château. A few of the rooms have spectacular views, the restaurant serves hearty local fare (including game in the fall), and there's a pleasant café-terrace—just the place for contemplation while sipping a drink. ✉ *103 pl. St-Michel, 41250,* ☎ *02–54–20–31–31,* FAX *02–54–20–36–40. 39 rooms, 31 with bath. Restaurant, tennis. MC, V. Closed mid-Nov.–late Dec.*

$$ ★ **Château de Colliers.** Rooms at this 18th-century manor are simply furnished. Bathrooms are country-house style—the tub has a handheld shower head. The Empire Room not only contains marvelous antiques, but it also has a private rooftop terrace with views of the Loire. Dine on a wholesome table d'hôte dinner (make arrangements in advance) in the dining room, with murals on the walls and ceilings. Afternoon tea or an aperitif on the terrace overlooking the Loire is an ideal way to end the day. ✉ *41500 Muides-sur-Loire (6 km/4 mi north of Chambord),* ☎ *02–54–87–50–75,* FAX *02–54–87–03–64. 5 rooms. Pool, tennis court. MC, V. Closed Dec.–mid-Mar.*

Outdoor Activities and Sports

Rent a horse from the former stables of the **Maréchal de Saxe** (✉ château grounds, ☎ 02–54–20–31–01) and ride through the vast national park that surrounds the château.

Cheverny

 *17 km (11 mi) south of Chambord via D112 and D102; 13 km (8 mi) southeast of Blois via D765.*

Cheverny has become synonymous with its restrained, classical château, although the village is officially named Cour-Cheverny.

One of the last in the area to be built, the **Château de Cheverny** was finished in 1634. Its white, elegantly proportioned, classical facade greets you across manicured lawns. The interior—with its painted and gilded rooms, splendid furniture, and rich tapestries depicting the *Labors of Hercules*—is one of the grandest in the Loire region. In the gallery there's a bronze of George Washington alongside a document that bears his signature.

Unfortunately, the gardens are off-limits, as is the orangery, where the Mona Lisa and other masterpieces were hidden during World War II. But you are free to contemplate the antlers of 2,000 stags in the Trophy Room. Hunting, called "venery" in the leaflets, continues vigorously here, with red coats, bugles, and all. In the château's kennels, hordes of hungry hounds lounge about, dreaming of their next kill. Feeding times—*la soupe aux chiens*—are posted on a notice board, and you are welcome to watch the dogs wolf down their dinner. ☏ *02–54–79–96–29.* *32 frs.* *June–mid-Sept., daily 9–6:30; mid-Sept.–mid-June, daily 9:30–noon and 2:15–5.*

Dining

 ✕ **Bernard Robin.** Chef Robin produces fine nouvelle cuisine in his gleaming kitchens, but connoisseurs savor his simpler dishes: carp, game in season, and salmon with beef marrow. The attentive staff brings delicious tidbits to keep you busy between courses. ✉ *1 av. de Chambord, Bracieux (9 km/6 mi northeast of Cour-Cheverny on the road to Chambord),* ☏ *02–54–46–41–22. Reservations essential. Jacket and tie. AE, MC, V. Closed Wed. (except July–Aug.). No dinner Tues.*

OFF THE BEATEN PATH

SOLOGNE – This flat, wooded region, famed for its game, mushrooms, asparagus, and hidden lakes, occupies a vast area of partly drained marshland south of the Loire, between Cour-Cheverny in the west and Gien in the east. With rare exceptions, such as the market town of Romorantin-Lanthenay or the Royal Scottish Stuarts' one- time stronghold of Aubigny-sur-Nère (their 16th-century château is now the town hall), nature—and silence—rule here.

Blois

 *13 km (8 mi) northwest of Cour-Cheverny via D765; 54 km (34 mi) southwest of Orléans; 58 km (36 mi) northeast of Tours.*

Perched on a steep hillside that overlooks the Loire, bustling Blois is a convenient base for exploring the eastern Loire, and is well served by train and expressway. There is a signposted route for a walking tour of the **Vieille Ville** (Old Town)—maps are available from the tourist office. The best view of the town, with its château and numerous church spires rising sharply above the river, is from the Pont Gabriel bridge, on the other side of the Loire.

The massive **Château de Blois** spans several architectural periods and is among the valley's finest. Your ticket entitles you to a guided tour—in English when there are enough visitors who can't understand French—but you are more than welcome to roam around without a guide if you visit between mid-March and August. Before you enter, stand in the courtyard to admire four centuries of architecture. On one side stand the 13th-century hall and tower, the latter offering a stunning view of the town and countryside. The Renaissance begins to flower in the Louis XII wing (built between 1498 and 1503), through which you enter, and comes to full bloom in the François I wing (1515–24). The masterpiece here is the openwork spiral staircase, painstakingly restored. The fourth side consists of the classical Gaston d'Orléans wing (1635–38).

At the bottom of the spiral staircase is a *diaporama,* an audiovisual display that traces the château's history. Upstairs is a series of enormous rooms with tremendous fireplaces, decorated with the gilded porcupine, emblem of Louis XII; the ermine of Anne of Brittany; and, of course, François I's salamander, breathing fire and surrounded by flickering flames. Many rooms have intricate ceilings and carved, gilded paneling; there is even a sad little picture of Mary, Queen of Scots. In the great council room, the Duc de Guise was murdered on the orders of Henri III in 1588. In the **Musée des Beaux-Arts,** in the Louis XII wing, you'll find royal portraits, including Rubens's puffy portrayal of Maria de' Medici as France Personified. Most evenings from April through September, son-et-lumière shows in French and English are staged most. Call the château or the tourist office (☞ The Loire Valley A to Z, *below*) for details; admission is 50 francs. ☎ *02–54–74–16–06.* *35 frs.* ⏲ *Apr.–Aug., daily 9–6; Sept.–Mar., daily 9–noon and 2–5.*

Dining and Lodging

$$$ ✕ **Péniche.** This innovative restaurant is actually a luxurious barge moored on the bank of the Loire. Chef Germain Bosque serves beautifully presented fresh seafood dishes (notably lobsters and oysters). ✉ *promenade du Mail, quai St-Jean,* ☎ *02–54–74–37–23. AE, DC, MC, V.*

$$ ★ ✕ **Rendezvous des Pêcheurs.** This modest restaurant near the Loire has simple decor but offers excellent value for its creative cooking. Chef Eric Reithler studied under Guy Savoy in Paris and has brought inventiveness to his fish and shellfish specialties. ✉ *27 rue du Foix,* ☎ *02–54–74–67–48. MC, V. Closed Mon. dinner, Sun., and Aug.*

$$ ✕ **Médicis.** Rooms at this smart, friendly hotel, about 1 km (½ mi) from the château, are comfortable, air-conditioned, and soundproof. All share a joyous color scheme but are individually furnished. If you wish to splurge, the suite has a whirlpool. The restaurant alone makes a stay here worthwhile. Chef-owner Christian Garanger turns his innovative classical dishes into a presentation—*coquilles St-Jacques* (scallops) with a pear fondue and thin slices of roast hare with black-currant sauce. Service is helpful. The restaurant is closed Sunday dinner off-season. ✉ *2 allée François-Ier, 41000,* ☎ *02–54–43–94–04,* FAX *02–54–42–04–05. 12 rooms, 1 suite. Restaurant, air-conditioning. AE, DC, MC, V. Closed early Jan.*

$$ **Anne de Bretagne.** Although this simple, two-star pension—on a small square across from the cathedral—is nothing to rave about, the rooms, up rather steep stairs, are clean and neat, with bright bedspreads and curtains. The price is a little high for what you get, so you might try the Médicis (☞ *above*) first. There's space to keep your car on the street, which is a plus, and a small bar next door, a congenial spot for a nightcap. ✉ *31 av. du Dr. Jean-Laigret, 41000,* ☎ *02–54–78–05–38,* FAX *02–54–74–37–79. 30 rooms, 5 with bath, 19 with shower, 6 with shower and shared WCs. AE, DC, MC, V. Closed mid-Feb.–mid-Mar.*

Chaumont-sur-Loire

16 *21 km (13 mi) southwest of Blois via D751.*

Chaumont is best known for its sturdy castle with famous stables and magnificent panorama of the Loire. Built between 1465 and 1510, the **Château de Chaumont** was given to Henri II's mistress, Diane de Poitiers, by his wife, Catherine de' Medici, to get her out of the Château de Chenonceau. Benjamin Franklin was a regular visitor here. The interior has been extensively restored but retains less cachet than the majestic stables, where purebreds dined like royalty. ☎ *02–54–20–98–03.* *32 frs.* *Apr.–Sept., daily 9:30–6; Oct.–Mar., daily 10–4:30.*

Dining and Lodging

$$$ ★ **Domaine des Hauts-de-Loire.** Across the river from Chaumont, this exquisite hotel was an 18th-century turreted, vine-covered manor on 180 acres of parkland. Rooms in the main house are furnished with antiques, which creates an aristocratic air; those in the adjacent carriage houses have a mix of old and modern furnishings that harmonize with the exposed brick walls and gabled ceilings. Service is relaxed and unpretentious; the restaurant is first-class, and in 1993 chef Rémy Giraud was justifiably awarded his second Michelin star. The restaurant is closed on Monday. ✉ *rte. d'Herbault, 41150 Onzain,* ☎ *02–54–20–72–57,* FAX *02–54–20–77–32. 28 rooms, 7 suites. Restaurant, tennis court, fishing. AE, DC, MC, V. Closed Nov., Feb.–Mar.*

Amboise

★ 17 *17 km (11 mi) southwest of Chaumont-sur-Loire via D751; 26 km (16 mi) east of Tours.*

Memories of Leonardo da Vinci, a historic château that overlooks the Loire, bustling markets, narrow medieval streets, and plenty of hotels and restaurants make Amboise a superb base.

The **Château d'Amboise** stands on a flattened hill that was originally a Stone Age settlement, fortified in the Iron Age by a ditch and a rampart. An early bridge gave the stronghold strategic importance. In AD 503, Clovis, king of the Franks, met with Alaric, king of the Visigoths, at Amboise. But the 15th and 16th centuries were Amboise's golden age, when the château, enlarged and embellished, became a royal palace. Charles VII stayed here, as did the unfortunate Charles VIII, best remembered for banging his head on a low doorway (you will be shown it) and dying as a result. François I, whose long nose appears in so many château paintings, based his court here. In 1560 his son, François II, settled here with his wife, Mary Stuart (otherwise known as Mary, Queen of Scots), and his mother, Catherine de' Medici. The castle was also the setting for the Amboise Conspiracy, an ill-fated Protestant plot organized against François II; you are shown where the corpses of 1,200 conspirators dangled from the castle walls. Decline and demolition occurred before and after the Revolution; today only about a third of the original building remains.

The château's interior is partly furnished, though not with the original objects; these vanished when the building was converted into a barracks and then a button factory. The great round tower has a spiral ramp rather than a staircase; designed for horsemen, it is wide enough to accommodate a small car. You are free to explore the grounds at your own pace, including the little chapel of St-Hubert with its carvings of the Virgin and Child, Charles VIII, and Anne of Brittany. **Son-et-lumière** pageants take place at the château daily in July and August. ☎ *02–47–57–00–98.* *35 frs; son-et-lumière 30 frs–90 frs.*

Oct.–Mar., daily 9–noon and 2–5; Apr.–June and Sept., daily 9–noon and 2–6:30; July and Aug., daily 9–6:30.

The **Clos Lucé,** up the hill from the château, is a handsome Renaissance manor where Leonardo da Vinci spent the last four years of his life and died in 1519. The basement contains working models built by IBM engineers (using the detailed sketches in his notebooks) of some of da Vinci's extraordinary inventions. Mechanisms on display include three-speed gearboxes, a military tank, a clockwork car, and even a flying machine complete with designs for parachutes. Da Vinci was several centuries ahead of his time. ✉ *2 rue du Clos Lucé,* ☏ *02–47–57–62–88.* *37 frs.* *Sept.–June, daily 9–6; July and Aug., daily 9–7.*

Dining and Lodging

$$$ ✕ **Manoir St-Thomas.** Between the château and the Clos Lucé, this restaurant occupies a fine Renaissance building with an adjacent garden. Chef François Le Coz serves elegant, traditional food, including ravioli *aux huitres* (with oysters and caviar) and *suprême de pintade farci* (stuffed guinea-fowl breast). The list of Touraine wines is enticing. ✉ *1 mail St-Thomas,* ☏ *02–47–57–22–52. Jacket and tie. AE, DC, MC, V. Closed Mon. and mid-Jan.–mid-Mar. No dinner Sun.*

$$–$$$ ✕ **Château de Pray.** This former 13th-century fortress transformed during the Renaissance into a pleasant manor is surrounded by a 25-acre park and a lovely garden. The inside has a cozy, hunting-lodge ambience; the elegantly appointed guest rooms have carved wooden furniture and modern conveniences. One drawback is the hotel's lack of comfortable public spaces. The restaurant has improved greatly under chef Bruno Delagneau, and diners can enjoy a roaring fire and fine views of the river. ✉ *rte. de Chargé, 37530 Chargé (1½/1 mi east of Amboise via D751, on the south bank of the Loire),* ☏ *02–47–57–23–67,* FAX *02–47–57–32–50. 17 rooms, 2 suites. Restaurant. AE, DC, MC, V. Closed Jan.*

$ ★ ✕ **Le Blason.** Behind the château and a five-minute walk from the center of town, this delightful, small hotel is enlivened by its enthusiastic owners. The old building has rooms of different shapes and sizes: No. 229, for example, has exposed beams and a cathedral ceiling; No. 109 is comfortably spacious and has a good view of the square. In the restaurant, superior, reasonably priced fare is served. The menu changes seasonally, but may include roast lamb with garlic and medallions of pork and salmon carpaccio with mustard dressing. ✉ *11 pl. de Richelieu, 37400,* ☏ *02–47–23–22–41,* FAX *02–47–57–56–18. 29 rooms. Restaurant. AE, DC, MC, V.*

$$$ **Choiseul.** Classical elegance and a superb restaurant characterize this Relais & Châteaux hotel on the bank of the Loire, just below the château. The grounds are small but neat. Be sure to visit the caverns where temporary art exhibits are often held. Though rooms are modern, they retain an old and distinctive charm. ✉ *36 quai Charles-Guinot, 37400,* ☏ *02–47–30–45–45,* FAX *02–47–30–46–10. 32 rooms. Restaurant, pool. AE, DC, MC, V. Closed Dec.–Jan.*

En Route Just 3 km (2 mi) south of Amboise on the road to the town of Chenonceaux, pause at the **Pagode de Chanteloup,** an extraordinary 140-foot, seven-story Chinese-style pagoda built for the Duc de Choiseul in 1778.

Chenonceaux

18 *12 km (8 mi) south of Amboise via D81 and D40; 32 km (20 mi) east of Tours.*

The small village of Chenonceaux, on the River Cher, is best known ★ as the site of the **Château de Chenonceau** (without the *x*). From historical figures like Diane de Poitiers, Catherine de' Medici, and Mary, Queen of Scots, to a host of modern travel writers, many have called it the "most romantic" of all the Loire châteaux. Its site, straddling the river, is one of the prettiest and most unusual in France. You could happily spend half a day wandering through the château and grounds. During the peak summer season the château is open—unlike many others—all day. The only drawback is its popularity: If you want to avoid a roomful of English schoolchildren, take a stroll in the grounds and come back when they stop for lunch.

More pleasure palace than fortress, the château was built in 1520 by Thomas Bohier, a wealthy tax collector. When he went bankrupt, it passed to François I. Later, Henri II gave it to his mistress, Diane de Poitiers. After his death, Henri's not-so-understanding widow, Catherine de' Medici, expelled Diane to nearby Chaumont and took back the château. It is to Catherine that we owe the lovely gardens and the handsome, three-story extension whose arches span the River Cher.

Before you go inside, pick up an English leaflet at the gate. Then walk around to the right of the main building to see the harmonious, delicate architecture beyond the formal garden, with the river gliding under the arches. The romantically inclined may want to rent a rowboat and spend an hour drifting. Inside the château are splendid ceilings, colossal fireplaces, authentic furnishings, and paintings by Rubens, del Sarto, and Correggio. As you tour the rooms, be sure to pay your respects to former owner Madame Dupin, tellingly captured in Nattier's charming portrait: Thanks to the great affection she inspired among her proletarian neighbors, the château and its treasures survived the Revolution intact. The château's history is illustrated with wax figures in the **Musée des Cires,** housed in one of the château's outbuildings. Every night from mid-June to mid-September, excellent **son-et-lumière** shows are performed in the illuminated château gardens. ☎ *02–47–23–90–07.* *Château 45 frs; museum 15 frs; son-et-lumière 40 frs.* *Mid-Feb.–mid-Nov., daily 9–5, 6, or 7, depending on the season; mid-Nov.–mid-Feb., daily 9–5.*

OFF THE BEATEN PATH

VALENÇAY – Although 49 km (31 mi) southeast of Chenonceaux, Valençay entices families with its lusciously furnished château, collection of vintage cars, son-et-lumière shows, and eccentric outdoor appeal: The grounds include statues, manicured hedges, peacocks, llamas, and intrepid kangaroos. ☎ *Château: 02–54–00–10–66.* *35 frs. Park only: 10 frs.* *Mid-Mar.–mid-Nov., daily 9–noon and 2–dusk or 8; château and museum closed mid-Nov.–mid-Mar.*

Dining and Lodging

$$–$$$ ★ **Bon Laboureur.** In 1882, this place won Henry James's praise as a simple, rustic inn. Since then, through four generations of the Jeudi family, it has become an elegantly modern hotel. Rooms in the old house are comfortably traditional; those in the former stables are larger and more contemporary; the biggest and most elegant are in the manor house across the street. For honeymooners there is a small separate house. A large garden, with fountains and streams, supplies vegetables and herbs for the kitchen. The food is commendable—try the excellent turbot with hollandaise or the braised rabbit with dried fruits. Make your

dinner reservations early for a table in the original dining room rather than in the annex. ✉ *6 rue du Dr-Bretonneau, 37150,* ☎ *02–47–23–90–02,* FAX *02–47–23–82–01. 36 rooms. Restaurant, pool, bicycles. AE, DC, MC, V. Closed Nov.–mid-Dec.*

Loches

19 *27 km (17 mi) south of Chenonceaux via D40, D80, and D31; 49 km (31 mi) west of Valençay; 39 km (24 mi) southeast of Tours.*

On a rocky spur just beside the River Indre is small, picturesque, medieval Loches. The town is dominated by its **Citadelle.** Unlike Chinon's, which is a ruined shell, much of Loches's defensive walls are well preserved and function as part of the town. At one end is the castle, whose terrace provides a fine view of the roofs and river below and the towers and swallows' nests above; on the other end is the keep.

Inside the **Logis Royaux** (château), on the north end of the citadel, look for the vicious, two-man crossbow that could pierce an oak door at 200 yards. There are some interesting pictures, too, including a copy of the well-known portrait that shows an extremely disgruntled Charles VII and one of his mistresses, Agnes Sorel, poised as a virtuous Virgin Mary (though semi-topless). Her alabaster image decorates her tomb, guarded by angels and lambs. Agnes died in 1450 at age 28, probably poisoned by Charles's son, the future Louis XI. The little chapel was built by Charles VIII for his queen, Anne of Brittany, and is lavishly decorated with sculpted ermine tails, the lady's emblem.

In the **Donjon** (Keep), on the south side of the citadel, one 11th-century tower, half-ruined and roofless, is open for exploration; the others require guided supervision. These towers contain dungeons and will delight anyone who revels in prison cells and torture chambers. ✉ *pl. Charles-VII,* ☎ *02–47–59–01–32.* 🎫 *30 frs.* ⏲ *Jan.–mid-Mar., Thurs.–Tues. 9–noon and 2–5; mid-Mar.–June, daily 9–noon and 2–6; July–Aug., daily 9–6; Sept.–Nov., Thurs.–Tues. 9–noon and 2–5.*

The citadel church of **St-Ours** has a striking roof formed of octagonal pyramids, which dates from the 12th century; a doorway sculpted with owls, monkeys, and mythical beasts; and a baptismal font converted from a Roman altar.

Tours

39 km (24 mi) northwest of Loches via N143; 112 km (70 mi) southwest of Orléans; 240 km (150 mi) southwest of Paris.

The city of Tours has no château—one of France's finest cathedrals more than compensates—but makes an ideal center from which to tour the Loire Valley's attractions by public transportation. Trains from Tours run along the river in both directions, and regular bus services radiate from here; in addition, the city is the starting point for a variety of organized bus excursions (many with English-speaking guides). The formerly small town has mushroomed into a city of a quarter of a million inhabitants, with an ugly modern sprawl of factories, high-rise blocks, and overhead expressway junctions cluttering up the outskirts. But the timber-framed houses in **Le Vieux Tours,** the attractive medieval center around place Plumereau, have been tastefully restored after extensive damage during World War II. Tours is easy to get around by public buses. If you have a car you may prefer to base yourself in any of a dozen smaller towns within a half-hour drive.

★ 20 The **Cathédrale St-Gatien,** built between 1239 and 1484, reveals a mixture of architectural styles. The richly sculpted stonework of its majestic, soaring, two-tower facade betrays the Renaissance influence among local château-trained craftsmen. The stained glass dates from the 13th century (if you have binoculars, bring them). Also take a look at the little tomb with kneeling angels built in memory of Charles VIII and Anne of Brittany's two children. *rue Lavoisier. Daily 8–noon and 2–6.*

What remains of the château is of minor interest, but within it you will
21 find the **Historial de La Touraine**—a group of more than 150 waxwork models that represent historic figures like St-Martin and Joan of Arc, whose deeds helped shape this region for over 15 centuries. There's also a small aquarium next door. *quai d'Orléans, 02–47–61–02–95. Wax museum 35 frs.; aquarium 30 frs. Mid-Sept.–mid-Nov., daily 9–11:30 and 2–6:30; mid-Nov.–mid-Mar., daily 2–5:30; mid-Mar.–mid-June, daily 9–11:30 and 2–6:30; mid-June–mid-Sept., daily 9–6:30.*

22 The **Musée des Beaux-Arts,** in what was once the archbishop's palace, has an eclectic selection of treasures: works by Rubens, Rembrandt, Boucher, Degas, Calder—even Fritz the Elephant, stuffed in 1902. *18 pl. François-Sicard, 02–47–05–68–73. 30 frs. Wed.–Mon. 9–12:45 and 2–6.*

23 Two museums, the **Musée des Vins and the Musée du Compagnonnage** (Wine Museum and Guild Museum), are in and around the cloisters of the 13th-century church of St-Julien, near the Loire. *Compagnonnage* is a sort of apprenticeship-cum-trade-union system, and here you see the masterpieces of the candidates for guild membership: virtuoso craftwork, some of it eccentric (an Eiffel Tower made of slate, for instance, or a varnished noodle château). These stand as evidence of the devotion to craftsmanship that is still an important feature of French life. You are free to visit both the guild and wine museums at your own pace. *8 rue Nationale, 02–47–61–07–93. 25 frs. Wed.–Mon. 9–noon and 2–5.*

24 The **Musée du Gemmail,** in the imposing 19th-century Hôtel Raimbault, contains an unusual collection of three-dimensional, colored-glass window panels. Depicting patterns, figures, and even portraits, the panels are both beautiful and intriguing, since most of the gemlike fragments of glass come from broken bottles. Incidentally, Jean Cocteau coined the word *gemmail* by combining *gemme* (gem) with *émail* (enamel). *7 rue du Mûrier, 02–47–61–01–19. 30 frs. Mar.–mid-Oct., Tues.–Sun. 10–noon and 2:30–6; mid-Oct.–Feb., weekends 10–noon and 2–5:30.*

Dining and Lodging

$$ **Les Tuffeaux.** This restaurant, which faces the château, retains its place as one of Tours's best—without breaking the budget. Chef Gildas Marsollier wins customers with delicious fennel-perfumed salmon, oysters in an egg sauce seasoned with Roquefort, and remarkable desserts. Gentle lighting and a warm, understated decor provide a soothing background. *19 rue Lavoisier, 02–47–47–19–89. MC, V. Closed Sun. No lunch Mon.*

$$$$ **Château d'Artigny.** Built by the Coty perfume tycoon in 1912 as a vast, pseudo–Louis XV house, the ambience of this Relais & Château hotel recalls a perfume ad: Gilt, marble, and plush abound, creating a perfect backdrop for the frequent celebrity guests. The spacious rooms have 18th-century style French furnishings. The nouvelle restaurant is excellent but expensive. You can jog away the calories in the 60-acre park. *rte. d'Azay-le-Rideau, 37250 Montbazon (13 km/8 mi south*

Cathédrale St-Gatien, **20**
Historial de la Touraine, **21**
Musée des Beaux-Arts, **22**
Musée des Vins/Musée du Compagnonnage, **23**
Musée du Gemmail, **24**

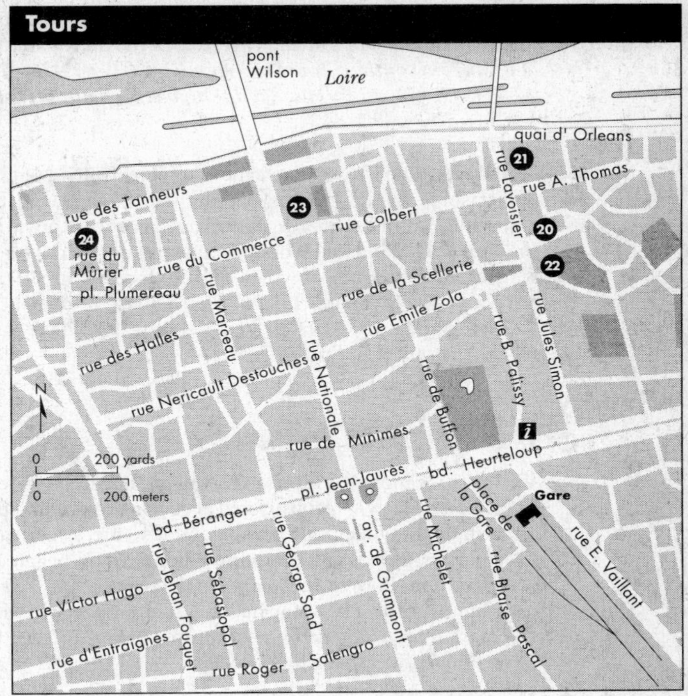

of Tours, west of Montbazon on D17), ☎ *02–47–26–24–24,* FAX *02–47–65–92–79. 55 rooms. Restaurant, pool, tennis court. AE, DC, MC, V. Closed early Jan.*

$$$$ ★ ✕🏨 **Jean Bardet.** Bardet, one of France's top 20 chefs, offers an eight-course *menu dégustation* (tasting menu) and an à la carte menu with oysters poached in muscadet on a puree of watercress and grilled lobster. Reservations are essential. One downside: Both the food and the service can be erratic—not to be expected when the tab for two is close to 1,000 francs. The restaurant is closed Monday. The suites and rooms, though luxurious, are on the exorbitant side. For real style, you can hire Bardet's Rolls Royce Silver Shadow II to take you on a tour of the Loire. ✉ *57 rue Groison, 37000,* ☎ *02–47–41–41–11,* FAX *02–47–51–68–72. 16 rooms, 5 suites. AE, DC, MC, V.*

$$$ ★ ✕🏨 **Domaine de la Tortinière.** Subtle elegance exudes from this little 19th-century château south of Tours. Rooms in the main building convey quiet, rustic luxury; those in the modern annex are less desirable. Some negatives in the old house: the morning gurgle of the water pipes and the sound of doors opening and closing along the corridor. But the beds are so comfy it's a pleasure to be awake in them. Room 15, small but pleasant (680 frs), is quieter. Dinner is a delightful occasion, even if the fare does not quite live up to its reputation. The pigeon in a rich wine sauce and the lobster bisque with a pastry top, though, are excellent. ✉ *10 rte. Ballan, 37250 Veigné (about 12 km/7 mi south of Tours in Veigné),* ☎ *02–47–26–00–19,* FAX *02–47–65–25–70. 21 rooms. Restaurant, pool, tennis court. MC, V. Closed mid-Dec.–Mar.*

$$ ✕🏨 **Moulin Fleuri.** The Indre sweeps by the garden terrace of this converted watermill south of Tours. Chef Alain Chaplin's creative specialties include excellent coquilles St-Jacques, *filet de sandre* (white fish fillet) in a shellfish butter, and *maigret de canard* (duck breast). The restaurant is closed Monday. Rooms vary in price according to size, but even the small ones are bright and cheerful. ✉ *rte. du Ripault, 37250 Veigné (11 km/7 mi south of Tours in Veigné),* ☎ *02–47–26–01–12,* FAX *02–47–34–04–71. 12 rooms, 8 with shower. Restaurant, fishing. AE, MC, V. Closed Feb.*

$$$ ★ **Univers.** The Univers is the best hotel in Tours. Murals in the salon depict some of the famous people who have stayed here: Winston Churchill, Sarah Bernhardt, Maurice Chevalier, Rudyard Kipling, and the Duke of Windsor. Wood panels and soft colors add traditional warmth to the rooms, of which only 10 face the street; the others look onto a flower garden. ✉ *5 bd. Heurteloup, 37000,* ☎ *02–47–05–37–12,* FAX *02–47–61–51–80. 89 rooms, 10 suites. Restaurant, bar, meeting room. AE, DC, MC, V.*

Villandry

25 *16 km (10 mi) west of Tours via D7.*

Villandry is renowned for its extravagant, terraced gardens—the finest in the Loire Valley—reconstituted according to original plans. In 1906, Spanish doctor Joachim Carvalla and his wife, American heiress Ann Coleman, bought the **Château de Villandry** and began a long process of restoration. Both the château and the gardens are from the 16th century, but over the years they had fallen into disrepair. The château has a remarkable gilded ceiling—imported from Toledo, Spain—and a collection of fine Spanish paintings.

★ The **gardens** are unquestionably the main attraction, replanted according to their original, rigorous, geometric design, with zigzagging hedges around flower beds, vegetable plots, and gravel walks. The result is an aristocratic 16th-century *jardin à la française* (French-style garden). Below an avenue of 1,500 precisely pruned lime trees lies an ornamental lake filled with swans: Not a ripple is out of place. The aromatic and medicinal garden, its plots neatly labeled in three languages, is especially appealing. The quietest time to visit is usually during the two-hour French lunch break. ☎ *02–47–50–02–09.* *Château and gardens 45 frs; gardens only 32 frs.* *June–Sept., daily 9–6, gardens 9–8; Oct.–May, daily 9:30–12:30 and 2–5:30, gardens 9–dusk.*

Dining and Lodging

$$ ✕ **Cheval Rouge.** The restaurant in this fine, old-fashioned hotel is popular with locals. They come to eat the surprisingly good classical food—considering its touristy location next to the château—and drink good wine. The best bets are the terrine of foie gras, the calf sweetbreads, and the wood-fired-grill fare. It's closed Monday off-season. Rooms are modern and tidy. ✉ *9 rue de la Mairie, 37510 Villandry,* ☎ *02–47–50–02–07,* FAX *02–47–50–08–77. 20 rooms with bath or shower. Restaurant. MC, V. Closed Nov.–mid-Mar.*

Langeais

26 *8 km (5 mi) west of Villandry.*

Across the Loire from Villandry is the small, old town of Langeais, with a Renaissance church-tower and some 16th-century houses, crushed beneath its massive castle. The **Château de Langeais,** built in the 1460s and never altered, contains a superb collection of fireplaces, tapestries, chests, and beds. Outside, tidy gardens nestle behind sturdy walls and battlements. ☎ *02–47–96–72–60.* *35 frs.* *Easter–Oct., daily 9–6:30; Nov.–Easter, Tues.–Sun. 9–noon and 2–5. Closed Mon.*

Azay-le-Rideau

27 *10 km (6 mi) southeast of Langeais via D57; 24 km (15 mi) southwest of Tours.*

Nestled in a sylvan setting on the banks of the River Indre, the pleasant village of Azay-le-Rideau is famed for its white-walled Renaissance ★ pleasure palace. The 16th-century **Château d'Azay-le-Rideau** was never a serious fortress. It certainly offered no protection to its builder, royal financier Gilles Berthelot, when a financial scandal forced him to flee France shortly after the château's completion in 1529. For centuries, the château passed from one private owner to another and was finally bought by the state in 1905. Though the interior offers an interesting blend of furniture and artwork, you may wish to spend most of your time exploring the enchanting private park, complete with a moatlike lake. Delightful **son-et-lumière** shows are held on the château grounds on summer evenings. ☎ *02–47–45–42–04.* *Château 32 frs; son-et-lumière 50 frs.* *Apr.–Sept., daily 9:30–6; Oct.–Mar., daily 9:30–12:30 and 2–5:30.*

Dining and Lodging

$$ **Grand Monarque.** Just yards from the château, this old hotel has a captive audience—and it tends to show with some pretty offhand service. But the rooms, which vary in size and style, have character; most are simply decorated with an antique or two, and many have exposed beams. The restaurant serves good, traditional food and an extensive selection of Loire wines. The 90-franc lunch menu is a particularly good value. Weekend stays must include dinner. The restaurant is closed Monday lunch and Thursday in winter. ✉ *3 pl. de la République, 37190,* ☎ *02–47–45–40–08,* FAX *02–47–45–46–25. 30 rooms, 27 with bath. Restaurant. AE, DC, MC, V. Closed mid-Dec.–end Jan.*

Outdoor Activities and Sports

Rent bikes from **Leprovost** (✉ 13 rue Carnot, ☎ 02–47–45–40–94) and ride along the River Indre.

Saché

28 *7 km (4 mi) east of Azay-le-Rideau via D17.*

Saché is best known for its associations with the novelist Honoré de Balzac (1799–1850), who lived and wrote in its château. Those who have never read Balzac and don't understand spoken French may find little of interest here; but those who have, and do, will return to the novels with fresh enthusiasm and understanding. The present château, built between the 16th and 18th centuries, is more of a comfortable country house than a fortress. Balzac came here—to stay with his friends, the Margonnes—during the 1830s, both to write and to escape his creditors. The château houses the substantial **Musée Balzac,** whose exhibits range from photographs to original manuscripts to the coffeepot he used to help keep him writing up to 16 hours a day. ☎ *02–47–26–86–50.* *23 frs.* *Feb.–mid-Mar., Thurs.–Tues. 9:30–11:45 and 2:15–4:30; mid-Mar.–Sept., daily 9–noon and 2–6; Oct.–Nov., Thurs.–Tues. 9:30–11:45 and 2:15–4:30.*

Villaines-les-Rochers

29 *6 km (4 mi) southeast of Azay-le-Rideau via D57.*

Local people have been making *osier* (wicker) products for centuries at Villaines. In 1849, when the craft was threatened with extinction, the parish priest persuaded 65 small groups of basket-weavers to form France's first agricultural workers' cooperative. These days craftsmen settle here from all over France—and abroad—attracted by the troglodyte cliff dwellings and back-to-nature lifestyle: The willow-reeds are cultivated in nearby fields and dried in the sun each May, before being transformed into sofas, cat baskets, or babies' rattles (all available at the village shop). A small museum in the **Coopérative de la Vannerie** (Wickerwork Cooperative) tells the cooperative's story. ✉ *1 rue de la Cheneillère,* ☏ *02–47–50–02–09.* 🎫 *7 frs.* ⏲ *Mid-June–mid-Sept., weekend afternoons.*

Ussé

★ ㉚ 14 km (9 mi) west of Azay-le-Rideau via D17 and D7; 36 km (23 mi) southwest of Tours.

As you approach the **Château d'Ussé** (actually in the village of Rigny-Ussé), between the Forest of Chinon and the Loire, an astonishing array of delicate towers and turrets greets you. Literature describes this château as the original Sleeping Beauty castle—the inspiration for Charles Perrault's beloved 17th-century tale. Though parts of the castle are from the 1400s, most of it was completed two centuries later. It is a flamboyant mix of Gothic and Renaissance styles—stylish and romantic, built for fun, not for fighting. Its history supports this playful image: It suffered no bloodbaths—no political conquests or conflicts. And a tablet in the chapel indicates that even the French Revolution passed it by.

After admiring the château's luxurious furnishings and 19th-century French fashion exhibit, climb the spiral stairway to the tower to view the River Indre through the battlements. Here you will also find a waxwork effigy of Sleeping Beauty herself. Before you leave, visit the 16th-century chapel in the garden; its door is decorated with pleasingly sinister skull-and-crossbones carvings. ☏ *02–47–95–54–05.* 🎫 *60 frs.* ⏲ *Mid-Feb.–mid-Nov., daily 9–noon and 2–6.*

Dining

$$ ★ ✕ **Atlantide.** This restaurant is worth seeking out. The small dining room, dressed in white tablecloths, potted plants, and a Grecian statue, has a classic simplicity that allows you to focus on the food. The 105-franc fixed-price three-course menu includes chicken *à la chinoise* (Chinese-style) with a thick mushroom wine sauce, a delicate goat cheese salad, and dessert. ✉ *17 rue Nationale, Avoine (8 km/5 mi southwest of Ussé),* ☏ *02–47–58–81–85. MC, V.*

Chinon

★ ㉛ *13 km (8 mi) southwest of Rigny-Ussé via D7 and D16; 44 km (28 mi) southwest of Tours.*

The town of Chinon—birthplace of author François Rabelais (1494–1553)—is dominated by the towering ruins of its medieval castle perched high above the River Vienne. Though the main tourist office is in the town below, in summer a special annex operates from the castle grounds. Both the village and the château are on steep, cobbled slopes, so wear comfortable walking shoes. The town is a warren of narrow, cobbled streets (some are pedestrian only), lined with half-timber medieval houses.

The vast **Château de Chinon,** a veritable fortress with walls 400 yards long, is from the time of Henry II of England, who died here in 1189 and was buried at Fontevraud. Two centuries later, the castle witnessed an important historic moment: Joan of Arc's recognition of the disguised dauphin, later Charles VII. In the early 17th century, the castle was partially dismantled by Cardinal Richelieu (1585–1642), who used many of its stones to build a new palace 21 km (13 mi) to the south, in Richelieu.

At Chinon, everything except the royal chambers—where there is a small museum—is open to the elements. For a fine view of the region, climb the **Tour Coudray,** where in 1307 leading members of the crusading Knights Templar were imprisoned before being taken to Paris, tried, and burned at the stake. The **Tour de l'Horloge** (Clock Tower), whose bell has sounded the hours since 1399, contains the **Musée Jeanne d'Arc** (Joan of Arc Museum). There are sensational views from the ramparts over Chinon and the Vienne Valley. ☎ *02–47–93–13–45.* 🎫 *Château 27 frs.* ⏲ *mid-Mar.–June and Sept. daily 9–6; July and Aug. daily 9–7; Oct. daily 9–5; Nov.–Dec. and early–mid-Mar., daily 9–noon and 2–5; Jan.–Feb., Thurs.–Tues. 9–noon and 2–5.*

The **Musée du Vin** (Wine Museum), in a vaulted cellar beneath one of Chinon's fine medieval streets, has a fascinating presentation about vine growing and wine and barrel making. English commentary is available, and the admission charge entitles you to a sample of the local product. ✉ *12 rue Voltaire,* ☎ *02–47–93–25–63.* 🎫 *22 frs.* ⏲ *Apr.–Oct., Fri.–Wed. 10–noon and 2–6.*

Dining and Lodging

$$ ★ ✕ **Au Plaisir Gourmand.** Gourmets from all over come to celebrate, and lucky tourists will get a table only if they make reservations (the dining room in this charming old house seats only 30). Chef Jérôme Rigollet uses fresh, local produce inventively. For a real treat, try the Vienne River trout and one of the exceptional local wines. ✉ *2 rue Parmentier,* ☎ *02–47–93–20–48. Reservations essential. Jacket and tie. AE, MC, V. Closed Mon. and mid-Jan.–mid-Feb. No dinner Sun.*

$ ✕ **Jeanne de France.** Local families and swarms of young people patronize this lively little pizzeria in the town's main square. It's a far cry from an American pizza joint, though: Here you can also order jugs of local wine, steaks, and french fries. ✉ *12 pl. Général-de-Gaulle,* ☎ *02–47–93–20–12. Closed Wed., Jan.*

$$$$ ★ ✕🏨 **Château de Marçay.** An efficient staff serves the fashion-conscious guests at this ultra-sophisticated château-hotel outside of Chinon. Rooms in the "pavilion," 50 yards from the main hotel, are pleasantly furnished but have little charm; the more expensive ones in the château have more to offer. Beams and gables add a cozy warmth to the spacious rooms, decorated with antiques. Chef Pascal Bodin serves excellent *carpaccio de canard* (thin slices of marinated cold duck), tournedos of salmon in a Chinon wine sauce, an extensive cheese board (sample the Ste-Marie chèvre), and good wine. ✉ *37500 Marçay (6 km/4 mi south of Chinon),* ☎ *02–47–93–03–47,* FAX *02–47–93–45–33. 35 rooms. Restaurant, pool, tennis court. AE, DC, MC, V. Closed Feb.–mid-Mar.*

$$ ✕🏨 **Gargantua.** This small, quiet hotel in the center of the medieval city was a bailiff's palace in the 15th century. It offers an array of rooms in various sizes and styles; simple good taste prevails throughout. Rooms 7 and 9, with views of the château, are good choices. In the old dining room, delicious local specialties are served—famous omelets and fillet of *barbue* (a white fish) with a marmalade, thyme, and citron sauce. On Friday and Saturday evenings waitresses dress up in medieval costume; in summer you can dine outside and admire Chinon Castle. ✉ *73 rue Voltaire, 37500,* ☎ *02–47–93–04–71. 8 rooms, 4 with bath. AE, DC, MC, V. Closed Wed.*

$$ **Hôtel de France.** Just off Chinon's main square is one of the oldest buildings in town. Built in the 16th century, it was home to many notables until the Revolution, when it became known as the Hôtel de France. Rooms are comfortable, but ask for one of the more recently refurbished ones with a view of the castle. On the ground floor, the restaurant doubles as a bar, a congenial place to regroup your energies for the next adventure. ✉ *47 pl. du Général-de-Gaulle, 37500,* ☎ *02–47–93–33–91,* FAX *02–47–98–37–03. 30 rooms with bath or shower. Restaurant. AE, DC, MC, V.*

Nightlife and the Arts

Chinon stages a **Marché Médiéval** (Medieval Market) during the first weekend of August. The streets are decked with flags and bunting, craftsmen ply their wares, ancient recipes are resurrected, and locals dress up in medieval costumes, with minstrels, jesters, and troubadours on the prowl.

Champigny-sur-Veude

32 *15 km (9 mi) south of Chinon via D749.*

Some of the best Renaissance stained glass in the world is in the village of Champigny-sur-Veude. In the dainty, white-stone ★ **Ste-Chapelle,** the 16th-century windows relate scenes from the Passion, Crucifixion, and the life of the 13th-century French king St-Louis; note the vividness and harmony of the colors, especially the purplish blues. The church was originally part of a château built between 1508 and 1543, but it was razed a century later by order of jealous neighbor Cardinal Richelieu. *25 frs. Apr.–Sept., daily 9–noon and 2–6.*

Richelieu

33 *6 km (4 mi) south of Champigny-sur-Veude.*

The eerie town of Richelieu was founded by Cardinal Richelieu in 1631, along with a megalomaniac château intended to be one of the most lavish in Christendom. The town remains a rare example of rigid, symmetrical, and unspoiled classical town planning, with 28 identical mansions lining the main street. Its bombastic scale and state of preservation are unique; the severe, straight streets have not changed for 350 years, give or take the odd traffic sign. All that's left of the cardinal's vainglorious country retreat, however, are a few outbuildings and parkland.

Fontevraud

34 *20 km (12 mi) northwest of Chinon via D751; 15 km (9 mi) southeast of Saumur.*

The small village of Fontevraud is famous for its large, medieval abbey, of central importance in the history of both England and France. Founded in 1099, the **Abbaye Royale de Fontevraud** had separate churches and living quarters for nuns, monks, lepers, "repentant" female sinners, and the sick. Between 1115 and the French Revolution in 1789, 39 different abbesses—among them a granddaughter of William the Conqueror—directed operations.

The great 12th-century **abbey church,** one of the most eclectic architectural structures in France, contains the tombs of Henry II of England; his wife, Eleanor of Aquitaine; and their son, Richard Coeur de Lion—Richard the Lionhearted. Though their bones were scattered during the Revolution, their effigies remain. Napoléon turned the abbey church into a prison, and so it remained until 1963, when historical restoration work—still under way—began. The **Chapter House,** adjacent to the church, with its collection of 16th-century religious wall paintings (prominent abbesses served as models), is unmistakably Renaissance; the paving stones bear the salamander emblem of François I. Next to the long refectory is the unusual, octagonal **cuisine** (kitchen), topped by 20 scaly-looking stone chimneys led by the **Tour d'Evrault.** ✉ *pl. des Plantagenêtes,* ☎ *02–41–51–71–41.* 🎟 *32 frs.* ⏲ *May–mid-Sept., daily 9–noon and 2–6:30; mid-Sept.–Apr., daily 9:30–noon and 2–5.*

Saumur

★ 35 *15 km (9 mi) northwest of Fontevraud via D947; 65 km (41 mi) west of Tours; 46 km (29 mi) southeast of Angers.*

The ancient town of Saumur, dominated by its mighty, turreted château that perches high above town and river, is an excellent base for exploring the western Loire Valley. It's also known for its flourishing mushroom industry, which produces 100,000 tons per year. The same cool tunnels in which the mushrooms grow also provide an ideal storage place for the local *mousseux* (sparkling wines).

If you arrive in the evening, the sight of the floodlit, elegant, white, 14th-century **Château de Saumur** will take your breath away. Looks familiar? Probably because you've seen it in countless reproductions from the famous *Très Riches Heures* (*Book of Hours*), painted for the Duc de Berri in 1416 (now in the Musée Condé at Chantilly). Inside it's bright and cheerful, with a fairy-tale gateway and plentiful potted flowers. There are two museums here: the **Musée des Arts Décoratifs** (Decorative Arts), with its fine collection of medieval objets d'art and 18th- and 19th-century porcelain, and the **Musée du Cheval** (Horse Museum). Both are included in the guided tour. Afterward, climb the **Tour de Guet** (Watchtower) for an impressive view. ✉ *esplanade du Château,* ☎ *02–41–40–24–40.* 🎟 *35 frs.* ⏲ *July–Sept., daily 9–6:30; Oct. and Apr.–June, daily 9–11:30 and 2–6; Nov.–Mar., Wed.–Mon. 9:30–noon and 2–5:30.*

In the old powder house at the château is the **Musée de la Figurine-Jouet,** a museum with more than 2,000 toy figurines on display. ☎ *02–41–67–39–23.* 🎟 *14 frs.* ⏲ *June and Sept., Wed.–Mon. 2–6; July–Aug., Wed.–Mon. 10–6.*

The **Musée du Champignon** (Mushroom Museum) on the outskirts of Saumur offers an intriguing subterranean tour through fossil-filled caverns where edible fungi are grown. ✉ *rte. de Gennes, St-Hilaire-St-Florent,* ☎ *02–41–50–31–55.* 🎟 *30 frs.* ⏲ *Mid-Feb.–mid-Sept., daily 10–7.*

Dining and Lodging

$$ ✕ **Les Ménestrels.** Chef Christophe Hosselet cooks very acceptable fare in a restored, white-stone, 18th-century mansion that is up against the castle cliff. Specialties include pheasant casserole, fried mushrooms, perch with spring-onion fondue, and beef in a local red wine sauce. ✉ *32–33 quai Mayaud,* ☎ *02–41–67–30–30. AE, DC, MC, V.*

$$$$ ✕🏨 **Prieuré.** This gracious manor west of Saumur is from medieval times but has been tastefully modernized. Rooms are large; the nicest are in the main building; Room 5 overlooks the Loire. Though the garden chalets are luxurious and neatly appointed, they are short on character. In the spacious dining room with a view of the river, crystal and silver clink discreetly. Behind the scenes, chef Jean-Noël Lumineau produces well-executed classics. ✉ *49350 Chênehutte-les-Tuffeaux (8*

km/5 mi west of Saumur on D751 toward Anger), ☎ *02–41–67–90–14,* FAX *02–41–67–92–24. 33 rooms. Restaurant, pool, tennis court. AE, MC, V. Closed Jan.–early Mar.*

$$–$$$ **Loire.** This member of the Best Western chain wins no prizes for charm or friendly service, but it is clean, spacious, and functional. The view of the château from the restaurant is stunning. One drawback: The hotel is across the river from the main part of town, though this makes parking easier. ✉ *rue de Vieux-Pont, 49400,* ☎ *02–41–67–22–42,* FAX *02–41–67–88–80,* ☎ *800/528–1234 (U.S. reservations);* ☎ *0181–541–0033 (U.K. reservations). 44 rooms. AE, DC, MC, V.*

$$ **Anne d'Anjou.** Close to the center of town, this hotel facing the river has a view of the château (floodlit at night) above. Inside the 18th-century building is an astounding staircase, which circles up to the top floor, where there is an impressive mural. Most rooms are simply decorated with old or contemporary furniture and are reasonably priced. Owners Yves and Anne-Marie Touzé will point you to Room 102 (650 frs), with its wood-panel paintings and Empire furnishings. ✉ *32–33 quai Mayaud, 49400 Saumur,* ☎ *02–41–67–30–30,* FAX *02–41–67–51–00. 50 rooms. Restaurant. AE, DC, MC, V.*

Outdoor Activities and Sports

If you want to ride through the rolling hills or take a weeklong equestrian tour of the Loire Valley, head to the **Centre de Tourisme Equestre** (✉ La Metaerer, Trescunault, ☎ 02–41–67–93–28), 3 km (2 mi) from Saumur.

Shopping

Loire wine is not a practical buy—except for instant consumption—but if wine-tasting tours of vineyards inspire you, enterprising wine makers will arrange shipment to the United States. Just southeast of Saumur in Dampierre-sur-Loire, stop in at the **Château de Chaintre** (✉ 54 rue de la Croix-de-Chaintre, ☎ 02–41–52–90–54), where affable Krishna Lester, an English eccentric, produces the region's finest still red and enjoys talking visitors through the production process. For sparkling wine, try **Ackerman** (✉ 19 rue Léopold-Palustre, 49400 St-Hilaire, ☎ 02–41–50–25–33) or **Veuve Amiot** (✉ 21 rue Jean-Ackerman, 49400 St-Hilaire, ☎ 02–41–50–25–24).

Montreuil-Bellay

36 *18 km (11 mi) south of Saumur via N147.*

Montreuil-Bellay is a small riverside town with many 18th- and 19th-century houses, lovely public gardens, and a leafy square next to its castle. The grandiose exterior—majestic towers and pointed roofs—of the 15th-century **Château de Montreuil-Bellay** is as fascinating as its interior. Inside is a fine collection of furniture and tapestries, a fully equipped medieval kitchen, and a chapel adorned with frescoes of angelic musicians. For a memorable view, take a stroll in the gardens; graceful white turrets tower high above the trees and rosebushes and, down below, the little River Thouet winds its lazy way to the Loire. ✉ *pl. des Ormeaux,* ☎ *02–41–52–33–06.* *40 frs.* ⏲ *Apr.–Nov., Wed.–Mon. 10–noon and 2–5:30.*

En Route From Montreuil-Bellay, take D761 northwest to **Doué-la-Fontaine,** 12 km (8 mi) away. The town is home to a zoo, the **Parc Zoologique des Minières** (✉ rte. de Cholet, ☎ 02–41–59–18–58) where deer, emu, and monkeys roam happily, surrounded by golden limestone quarries. It is open May–September, daily 9–7:30, and October–April, daily 10–noon and 2–6; admission is 60 francs. From the zoo, return to D761 to continue to Angers, pausing along the way to admire the towering **Château de Brissac.**

Angers

37 *51 km (28 mi) northwest of Montreuil-Bellay via D761; 10 km (69 mi) west of Tours; 88 km (55 mi) east of Nantes.*

The bustling city of Angers, on the banks of the River Maine just north of the Loire, is famous for its towering castle filled with extraordinary tapestries. But you'll also find a fine Gothic cathedral, a selection of art galleries, and a network of pleasant, traffic-free shopping streets. The town's principal sights lie within a compact square formed by the three main boulevards and the River Maine.

The massive **Château d'Angers,** built by St-Louis (1228–38), glowers over the town from behind turreted moats, now laid out as gardens and overrun with flowers and deer. As you explore the grounds, note the startling contrast between the thick, defensive walls, defended by a drawbridge and 17 massive round towers, and the formal garden, with its delicate, white tufa-stone chapel, erected in the 16th century. For a sweeping view of the city and surrounding countryside, climb one of the castle towers. A well-integrated modern gallery on the castle grounds contains the great ★ **Tenture de l'Apocalypse** (Apocalypse Tapestry), woven in Paris in the 1380s and restored to almost pristine glory in 1996. Measuring 16 feet high and 120 yards long, it shows a series of 70 horrifying and humorous scenes from the Book of Revelation. In one, mountains of fire fall from heaven while boats capsize and men struggle in the water. Another has the beast with seven heads. ✉ *pl. du Président-Kennedy.* ☎ *02–41–87–43–47.* 🎟 *35 frs.* ⏲ *July–Aug., daily 10–7; Sept.–June, daily 9:30–12:30 and 2–5:30.*

The **Cathédrale St-Maurice** is a 12th- and 13th-century Gothic cathedral noted for its curious Romanesque facade and original stained-glass windows; bring binoculars to appreciate both fully. ✉ *pl. Freppel.*

The **Musée des Beaux-Arts,** just south of the cathedral in a house that once sheltered Cesare Borgia and Mary, Queen of Scots, has an impressive collection of Old Masters from the 17th and 18th centuries, including paintings by Raphael, Watteau, Fragonard, and Boucher. ✉ *10 rue du Musée,* ☎ *02–41–88–64–65.* 🎟 *10 frs.* ⏲ *Tues.–Sun. 10–noon and 2–6.*

The **Musée David d'Angers,** in a refurbished, glass-roofed medieval church, has a collection of dramatic sculptures by Jean-Pierre David (1788–1859), the city's favorite son. ✉ *33 rue Toussaint,* ☎ *02–41–87–21–03.* 🎟 *10 frs.* ⏲ *Tues.–Sun. 10–noon and 2–6.*

To learn about the heartwarming liqueur made in Angers since 1849, head to the **Distillerie Cointreau** on the east of the city. The guided visit of the distillery starts with an introductory film, moves through the bottling plant and *alembic* room, with its gleaming copper pot-stills, and ends with a compulsory tasting. ✉ *rue de la Croix-Blanche, St-Barthélémy d'Anjou,* ☎ *02–41–43–25–21.* 🎟 *20 frs.* ⏲ *Tours weekdays June–Sept. every hr at 10, 11, and 2–5, weekends at 3 and 4:30; tours Oct.–May, Mon.–Sat. at 3, Sun. at 3 and 4:30.*

OFF THE BEATEN PATH

CHÂTEAU DE SERRANT – This sumptuous château 17 km (11 mi) southwest of Angers on N23, flanked by stately lawns and a moat, dates from 1546, with additions from the 17th and 18th centuries. The lush, paneled interior is hung with tapestries; the magnificent library is lined with 10,000 books. ☏ *02-41-39-13-01.* 💳 *45 frs.* ⏲ *Apr.–Oct., Wed.–Mon. 9–11:30 and 2–6.*

Dining and Lodging

$$–$$$ ✕ **La Salamandre.** Carefully prepared classical cuisine is served in this restaurant in the Anjou hotel (☞ *below*). Lamb, duck with cranberries, and calamari with crab sauce are just a few of the dishes served amid the Renaissance-style decor and stained-glass windows. Opt for one of the reasonably priced prix-fixe menus. ✉ *1 bd. du Maréchal-Foch,* ☏ *02–41–88–24–82. AE, DC, MC, V.*

$$ ★ ✕ **Toussaint.** Chef Michel Bignon serves nouvelle versions of traditional local dishes, plus fine wines and tasty desserts. Loire River fish with beurre blanc is a particular specialty. There are two dining rooms: The ground floor is less formal; upstairs, the neoclassical room has a better view of the castle. Reserve your table accordingly. ✉ *7 pl. du Président-Kennedy,* ☏ *02–41–87–46–20. Reservations essential. Jacket required. AE, MC, V. Closed Mon. No dinner Sun.*

$ ✕ **La Boucherie.** If you have an appetite for steak and good value, this place is for you. There are various menus with different cuts of beef, but for 55 francs you can get a sirloin, a small salad, crusty bread, and a ¼-liter carafe of wine. Service is friendly, cheerful, and swift. If there is a wait for a table, don't despair: The action is fast; dishes are swept away quickly, and a new paper tablecloth laid in a matter of moments. Tables are close together, and lively conversation adds to the robust atmosphere. ✉ *27 bd. du Maréchal-Foch,* ☏ *02–41–87–27–85. Reservations not accepted. MC, V.*

$ ✕ **California Style.** If you hanker after Texas fare—chili, buffalo wings, spicy burgers—in a party atmosphere with American posters and the young of Angers, make tracks to this small restaurant run by a French couple. It's not a place you'd come to France to visit, but it is a humorous way to satisfy nostalgia! ✉ *13 rue des Poëliers,* ☏ *02–41–87–18–42. No credit cards. No lunch Sun. or Mon.*

$ ✕ **La Treille.** For traditional, simple fare at affordable prices, try this small two-story mom-and-pop restaurant off place Ste-Croix and across from Maison d'Adam, Angers's finest timber house. The prix-fixe menu may start with a *salade au chèvre chaud* (warm goat cheese salad), followed by confit of duck and an apple tart. The upstairs dining room draws a lively crowd; downstairs is quieter. ✉ *12 rue Montault,* ☏ *02–41–88–45–51. MC, V. Closed Sun.*

$$$ 🏨 **Bleu Marine.** You won't find individuality in this standardized chain hotel, but you won't find problems either. Rooms are bright and modern and furnished with a copious amount of Formica. There's a spacious lobby and a good classical restaurant on the ground floor that looks out at Angers's main boulevard. The breakfast buffet is large and splendid. ✉ *18 bd. du Maréchal-Foch, 49000,* ☏ *02–41–87–37–20, 800/888–4747 in the U.S.,* FAX *02–41–87–49–54. 75 rooms. Restaurant, health club. AE, DC, MC, V.*

$$ 🏨 **Hôtel Anjou.** In business since 1850, the Anjou, now part of the Best Western chain, is decorated in a vaguely 18th-century style, including stained-glass windows in the lobby. The spacious rooms have high ceilings, double doors, and modern bathrooms with terry-cloth bathrobes. ✉ *1 bd. du Maréchal-Foch, 49000 Anjou,* ☏ *02–41–88–24–82, 800/528–1324 in the U.S.,* FAX *02–41–87–22–21. 53 rooms. Restaurant. AE, DC, MC, V.*

Nightlife and the Arts

For four weeks beginning in mid-June, the **Fête d'Anjou** (Anjou Festival) enlivens the area around Angers with music, theater, and dance. Call the tourist office (☞ The Loire Valley A to Z, *below*) for details.

Outdoor Activities and Sports

Go canoeing, sailing, fishing, and windsurfing at the **Centre Nautique du Lac de Maine** (✉ av. du Lac-de-Maine, ☎ 02–41–22–32–20), southwest of the city.

Le Plessis-Bourré

38 *20 km (12 mi) north of Angers via D107, off D508 south of Ecuillé.*

The reason to visit Le Plessis-Bourré is to see its Renaissance castle. The **Château du Plessis-Bourré,** built between 1468 and 1473 by Jean Bourré (one of Louis XI's top-ranking civil servants), looks like a traditional grim fortress: The bridge across its moat is nearly 50 yards long. Once you step into the central courtyard, however, the gentler mood of the Renaissance takes over.

What makes this place special is the painted wooden ceiling in the **Salle des Gardes** (Guard Room). Jean Bourré's hobby was alchemy—an ancient branch of chemistry with more than a touch of the occult—and the ceiling's 24 hexagonal panels are covered with scenes that illustrate the craft. Some have overtones of the grotesque dream world of late-medieval Dutch painter Hieronymus Bosch, while others illustrate folktales or proverbs. A few must have been painted just for the fun of it: A topless lady steers a land-yacht with wooden wheels (thought to be an allegory of spirit and matter); people urinate ceremoniously (ammonia was extracted from urine); an emaciated wolf takes a bite out of a startled lady (according to folk legend, the wolf's diet consisted of faithful wives, apparently in short supply); and Thurberesque dogs gambol in between. You may want to ignore the guide's lecture on furniture and spend your time gazing upward. ☎ *02–41–32–06–01.* 🎫 *38 frs.* ⏲ *Sept.–Nov. and Apr.–June, Thurs.–Tues. 10–noon and 2–6.*

Le Lude

39 *62 km (39 mi) east of Le Plessis-Bourré via D74, D766, and D305; 47 km (29 mi) northeast of Saumur; 44 km (28 mi) south of Le Mans.*

One of France's most spectacular son-et-lumière shows takes place in Le Lude in the Loir Valley. The **Château du Lude** comprises three wings. The north, or Louis XII, wing is the earliest, dating from the early 16th century; it houses a ballroom and a spacious, 19th-century library. The François I wing, which faces the park, combines round fortress towers with dainty Renaissance detail, and contains Flemish and Gobelin tapestries and a chimney-piece with the king's carved salamander emblem. The 18th-century Louis XVI wing overlooking the river displays severe, classical symmetry. Interior highlights (guided tours only) include the oval saloon, ornate bedroom, and murals by followers of Raphael. On Friday and Saturday evenings from mid-June to mid-September, more than 130 costumed performers, assisted by fountains ★ and fireworks, take part in Le Lude's **son-et-lumière** pageant chronicling the history of the château and the region from the Hundred Years' War onward. ✉ *pl. François-de-Nicolay,* ☎ *02–43–94–40–54.* 🎫 *30 frs; park only 20 frs; son-et-lumière 85 frs.* ⏲ *Apr.–Sept., 2–6; park 10–noon.*

OFF THE BEATEN PATH

LE MANS – Best known for its 24-hour automobile race in the second half of June, Le Mans (44 km/28 mi north of Le Lude via D307) is a bustling city with Gallo-Roman ramparts, a well-preserved old quarter, and a magnificent cathedral—part Gothic, part Romanesque—perched precariously on a hilltop overlooking the River Sarthe.

En Route Heading east from Le Lude on D305, the gentle **Loir Valley** serves up troglodyte dwellings; the sedate little towns of Château-du-Loir and La Chartre-sur-le-Loir (home to a fine dry white wine, Jasnières); hilltop Trôo with its feudal burial mound; and Montoire, scene of Hitler's meeting with Pétain in 1940.

Vendôme

40 *80 km (50 mi) east of Le Lude via D305 and D917; 32 km (20 mi) northwest of Blois; 70 km (44 mi) west of Orléans.*

The enchanting town of Vendôme may not be on every tourist's itinerary, but its picturesque appeal—the Loir River splits here into numerous arms, creating a canal-like effect—amply merits a visit. Take time to stroll through the narrow streets, and climb up to the gardens of the ruined castle for knockout views of the town center.

★ The Flamboyant Gothic abbey church of **La Trinité,** dominated by a solemn, 12th-century, 262-foot bell tower that served as a model for the elder spire at Chartres, has a dramatic west front with lacy, petal-like stonework by Jean de Beauce. The interior has traces of building from back to the 11th century, and contains amusingly carved choir stalls and fine stained glass. The adjacent cloisters lead to the chapter house, whose wall paintings depict the life of Christ. ✉ *rue de l'Abbaye.*

Châteaudun

41 *45 km (28 mi) northeast of Vendôme via N10; 44 km (28 mi) south of Chartres.*

A medium-size hilltop town, Châteaudun used to be the market center for grain produced in the Beauce. After being destroyed by the Prussians in 1870, the town was largely rebuilt, although some of the 16th- and 17th-century houses between the colossal castle and the 12th-century church of La Madeleine survived.

The **Château de Châteaudun** stands resplendent and impregnable on a steep promontory above the Loir. Although the facade may strike you as decidedly grim, the internal courtyard is overlooked by cheerful, 16th-century buildings. Inside you'll find graceful period furniture and lavish tapestries. The highlight is the Ste-Chapelle (holy chapel), with its collection of 15th-century statues. ✉ *pl. Jehan-du-Dunois,* ☎ *02–37–94–02–90.* 🎫 *32 frs.* ⏲ *Easter–Sept., daily 8–11:45 and 2–6; Oct.–mid-Mar., daily 10–12:30 and 2–5.*

THE LOIRE VALLEY A TO Z

Arriving and Departing

By Car

The Loire Valley is an easy drive from Paris. A10 runs from Paris to Orléans—a distance of 130 km (80 mi)—and on to Tours, with exits at Meung, Blois, and Amboise. After Tours, A10 veers south, toward Poitiers and Bordeaux. A11 links Paris to Angers via Le Mans. Slower but more scenic routes run from the Channel ports down through Normandy into the Loire region.

By Plane

The closest international airports are Paris's Charles-de-Gaulle and Orly.

By Train

Tours and Angers are both served by the super-fast TGV (Trains à Grande Vitesse) from Paris (Gare Montparnasse), and three TGV daily reach Vendôme in 40 minutes. Express trains run every two hours from Paris (Gare d'Austerlitz) to Orléans (usually you must change at Les Aubrais) and Blois. Note that trains for Gien leave from Paris's Gare de Lyon (direction Nevers), and that the nearest station to Sancerre is across the Loire at Tracy.

Getting Around

By Bus

Local bus services are extensive and reliable and are a link between train stations and scenic areas off the river. Inquire at tourist offices for information about routes and timetables.

By Car

By far the easiest way to visit the Loire châteaux is by car; N152 hugs the riverbank and offers excellent sightseeing possibilities. You can arrange to rent a car in all the large towns in the region or at train stations in Orléans, Blois, Tours, or Angers.

By Train

The Loire region's local train network is good, but not great. The main line follows the Loire from Orléans to Blois, Tours, Langeais, Saumur, and Angers, with trains every two hours. There are branch lines from Tours, with less frequent trains, to Loches, Azay-le-Rideau and Chinon, and Vendôme and Châteaudun.

Contacts and Resources

Car Rental

Avis (🖂 6 rue Jean-Moulin, Blois, ☎ 02–54–74–48–15; 🖂 13 rue Sansonnières, Orléans, ☎ 02–38–62–27–04; 🖂 Gare SNCF, Tours, ☎ 02–47–20–53–27). **Hertz** (🖂 5 rue du Dr-Desfray, Blois, ☎ 02–54–74–03–03; 🖂 57 rue Marcel-Tribut, Tours, ☎ 02–47–20–40–24). **Europcar** (🖂 81 rue André-Dessaux, Fleury-les-Aubrais, near Orléans, ☎ 02–33–73–00–40; 🖂 76 rue Bernard-Palissy, Tours, ☎ 02–47–64–47–76).

Emergencies

Ambulance (☎ 15). **Regional hospitals**: Angers (🖂 4 rue Larrey, ☎ 02–41–35–36–37); Orléans (🖂 14 av. de l' Hôpital, ☎ 02–38–51–44–44); Tours (🖂 2 bd. Tonnellé, ☎ 02–47–47–47–47).

Guided Tours

Bus tours for the main châteaux leave daily in summer from Tours, Blois, Angers, Orléans, and Saumur: Ask at the relevant tourist office for latest times and prices. Most châteaux insist that you follow one of their own tours, but try to get a booklet in English before joining the tour, as most are in French. The tourist offices in Tours and Angers also arrange city and regional excursions with **personal guides.**

A **walking tour** sets out from Tours's tourist office every morning at 10 AM from mid-April through October for 40 francs. English-speaking guides will conduct visitors around the historic city of Blois during a walk that starts from the château at 4; the cost is about 30 francs.

Accueil de France (✉ pl. du Président-Kennedy, Angers, ☎ 02–41–87–72–50; ✉ pl. du Maréchal-Leclerc, Blois, ☎ 02–54–74–06–49) organizes numerous tours of the Loire Valley, including car and bus excursions, and even hot-air balloon and boat trips. **Reservations Loisirs Accueil** (✉ 11 pl. du Château, Blois, ☎ 02–54–78–55–50) arranges guided visits to the region's châteaux, as well as balloon and bicycle trips.

Travel Agencies

American Express (✉ 12 pl. du Martroi, Orléans, ☎ 02–38–53–84–54). **Wagons-Lits** (✉ 9 rue Marceau, Tours, ☎ 02–47–20–40–54).

Visitor Information

The Loire region has two area tourist offices, for written inquiries only. For Chinon and points east, contact the **Comité Régional du Tourisme du Centre-de-Loire** (✉ 8 rue Etienne-Dolet, 45050 Orléans). For Fontevraud and points west, contact the **Comité Régional du Tourisme des Pays-de-Loire** (✉ 2 rue de la Loire, 44000 Nantes). Others are as follows: **Amboise** (✉ quai Général-de-Gaulle, ☎ 02–47–57–09–28). **Angers** (✉ 1 pl. du Président-Kennedy, ☎ 02–41–23–15–11). **Blois** (✉ 3 av. du Dr-Jean-Laigret, ☎ 02–54–74–06–49). **Orléans** (✉ pl. Albert-Ier, ☎ 02–38–24–05–05). **Saumur** (✉ pl. de la Bilange, ☎ 02–41–40–20–60). **Tours** (✉ 78 rue Bernard-Palissy, ☎ 02–47–70–37–37).

5 Brittany

St-Malo and the Northern Coast, Nantes and the Atlantic Shore

Thanks to its proximity to Great Britain, its folklore, and its spectacular coastline, Brittany is a favorite destination among English-speaking vacationers. It also has massive castles, prehistoric standing stones, and picturesque medieval towns. The French love the area, too, but don't worry about hordes of tourists—Brittany's vast beaches aren't easily crowded and there are enough châteaux to go around.

Updated by Nicole Duplaix

EVEN THE FRENCH FEEL THEY ARE IN A FOREIGN land when they visit Brittany (Bretagne to the French), the bulbous portion of western France jutting far out into the Atlantic. Cut off from mainstream France, the Bretons are an independent lot who have closer cultural affinities with the Celts across the Channel than with their fellow countrymen. Both Brittany and Cornwall claim Merlin, King Arthur, and the Druids as cult figures; huge Stonehenge-like menhirs and dolmens (prehistoric standing stones) litter the Breton countryside and offshore islands.

Brittany became part of France in 1532, but regional folklore is still very much alive. An annual village *pardon* (a religious festival) will give you a good idea of Breton traditions: Banners and saintly statues are borne in colorful parades, accompanied by hymns, and the whole event is rounded off by food of all kinds. The most famous pardon is held on the last Sunday of August at Ste-Anne-la-Palud, near Quimper. The surrounding Finistère (from *Finis Terrae,* or Land's End) *département* (province), Brittany's westernmost, is renowned for the costumes worn on such occasions—notably the lace bonnets, or *coiffes,* which can tower 15 inches above the wearer's head.

Although Brittany's towns took a mighty hammering from the retreating Nazis in 1944, most have been restored, except for the large concrete-cluttered naval base at Brest. Rennes, the only Breton city with more than 200,000 inhabitants, retains its traditional charm, as do the towns of Dinan, Quimper, St-Malo, and Vannes. Many ancient man-made delights are still found in the region's villages, and castles and cathedrals dot the landscape. Geographically, Brittany remains the land of *Armor* (the sea) and the land of *Argoat* (the forest).

Pleasures and Pastimes

Beaches

Wherever you go in Brittany, the coast is close by: In winter, the frenzied, cliff-bashing Atlantic pounds the shore; in summer, the sprawling beaches and bustling harbors are filled with frolicking bathers and boaters. Dozens of islands, many inhabited and within easy reach of the mainland, dot the coastal waters. The best sandy beaches and a multitude of water sports are found at Dinard, Perros-Guirec, Trégastel-Plage, Douarnenez, Carnac, La Trinité-sur-Mer, and La Baule.

Dining

Not surprisingly, Breton cuisine is dominated by seafood—often lobster, grilled or prepared in a cream sauce. Popular meats include smoked ham and lamb, frequently served with green kidney beans. Fried eel is a traditional dish in Nantes. Brittany is particularly famous for its crepes, served with both sweet and savory fillings. Accompanied by a glass of local cider, they are an ideal light, inexpensive meal.

CATEGORY	COST*
$$$$	over 400 frs
$$$	250 frs–400 frs
$$	125 frs–250 frs
$	under 125 frs

**per person for a three-course meal, including tax (20.6%) and tip but not wine*

Lodging

Brittany has plenty of small, charming, family-run hotels with friendly and personal service, as well as a growing number of luxury hotels and châteaux. Dinard, on the English Channel, and La Baule, on the Atlantic, are the area's two most expensive resorts. In summer, there are large crowds, so make reservations far in advance and reconfirm.

CATEGORY	COST*
$$$$	over 800 frs
$$$	550 frs–800 frs
$$	300 frs–550 frs
$	under 300 frs

**All prices are for a standard double room for two, including tax (20.6%) and service charge.*

Exploring Brittany

Brittany can be divided into two basic areas: the northeast, stretching from Rennes to La Manche (the English Channel), where mighty medieval castles look out over the land and quaint resort towns sit by the sea; and the west coast, extending from Morlaix to Nantes along the Atlantic, where frenzied surf crashes against the cliffs, alternating with sprawling beaches and bustling harbors.

Great Itineraries

If you only have a short amount of time—three days, for instance—concentrate on northeast Brittany. With five days you can explore this area in greater depth, including the capital city of Rennes. In 10 days, you can cover the entire region, if you don't spend too much time in any one place. A car is necessary for getting to the small medieval towns and deserted coastline.

Numbers in the text correspond to numbers in the margin and on the Brittany and Nantes maps.

IF YOU HAVE 3 DAYS

Make either the fortified port of **St-Malo** ⑩ or the medieval town of **Dinan** ⑦ your base for exploring northeast Brittany. Be sure to visit seaside **Dinard** ⑪, ancient **Dol-de-Bretagne** ⑧, Chateaubriand's boyhood home at **Combourg** ⑥, or the 16th-century castle at **La Bourbansais** ⑤, all within a 30-km (20-mi) radius. In addition, the magnificent rock island of **Mont St-Michel** (☞ Chapter 6) is only 50 km (30 mi) away in Normandy.

IF YOU HAVE 5 DAYS

Follow the three-day itinerary, then on the fourth day, stop at the castle at **Montmuran** ④ on your way to **Rennes** ③, the region's capital. Visit the formidable castle in **Vitré** ① and the medieval military town of **Fougères** ② on day five.

IF YOU HAVE 10 DAYS

Make **Rennes** ③ your base for exploring the castles, châteaux, and fortresses at **Vitré** ①, **Fougères** ②, and **Montmuran** ④, making an excursion to the Château de Caradeuc, if you have time. On day three, stop at **La Bourbansais** ⑤, **Combourg** ⑥, or **Dol-de-Bretagne** ⑧ on your way to **Dinan** ⑦ or **St-Malo** ⑩ for the night. Head west the following day on a scenic tour of the coast and spend the night in **Trébeurden** ⑬, on the tip of the Bretonne Corniche. Start early the next day for the quaint streets of **Morlaix** ⑭. Continue west and briefly visit the market town of **St-Pol-de-Léon** ⑮, the fortified château of **Kerjean** ⑯, or the splendid basilica at **Le Folgoët** ⑰. Eat lunch in **Brest** ⑱, a huge modern port town. By late afternoon try to be in **Locronan** ⑳, where sails used to be made for French fleets, so that you can reach picturesque **Douarnenez** ㉒ by evening. On the sixth day, head to **Concarneau** ㉕, France's third largest fishing port. If you have time, be sure to see **Audierne** ㉓, another fishing port, and **Quimper** ㉔, with its lovely river

Brittany

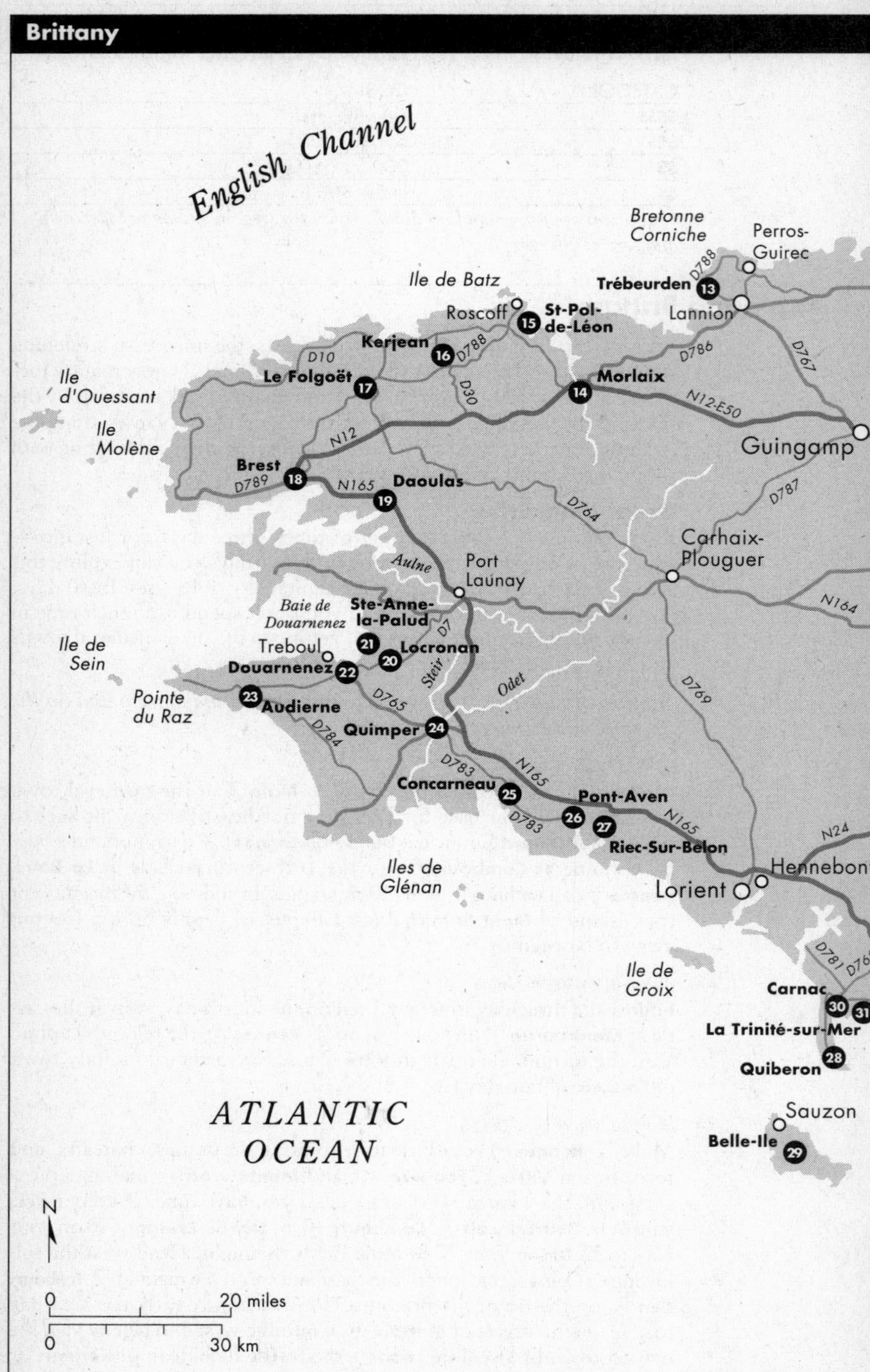
English Channel
Bretonne Corniche
Perros-Guirec
Ile de Batz
Trébeurden 13
D788
Roscoff
St-Pol-de-Léon 15
Lannion
Kerjean 16
D788
D786
D767
D10
Ile d'Ouessant
Le Folgoët 17
D30
Morlaix 14
N12-E50
Ile Molène
N12
Guingamp
Brest 18
D789
N165
Daoulas 19
D764
D787
Carhaix-Plouguer
Aulne
Port Launay
N164
Baie de Douarnenez
Ste-Anne-la-Palud 21
D7
Ile de Sein
Treboul
Locronan 20
Douarnenez 22
Steir
Odet
D769
Pointe du Raz
23 Audierne
D765
D784
Quimper 24
D783
N165
Concarneau 25
Pont-Aven 26
27
D783
N165
Riec-Sur-Belon
N24
Hennebont
Iles de Glénan
Lorient
D781
D768
Ile de Groix
Carnac
30
31
La Trinité-sur-Mer
28
Quiberon
ATLANTIC OCEAN
Sauzon
Belle-Ile 29
N
0
20 miles
0
30 km

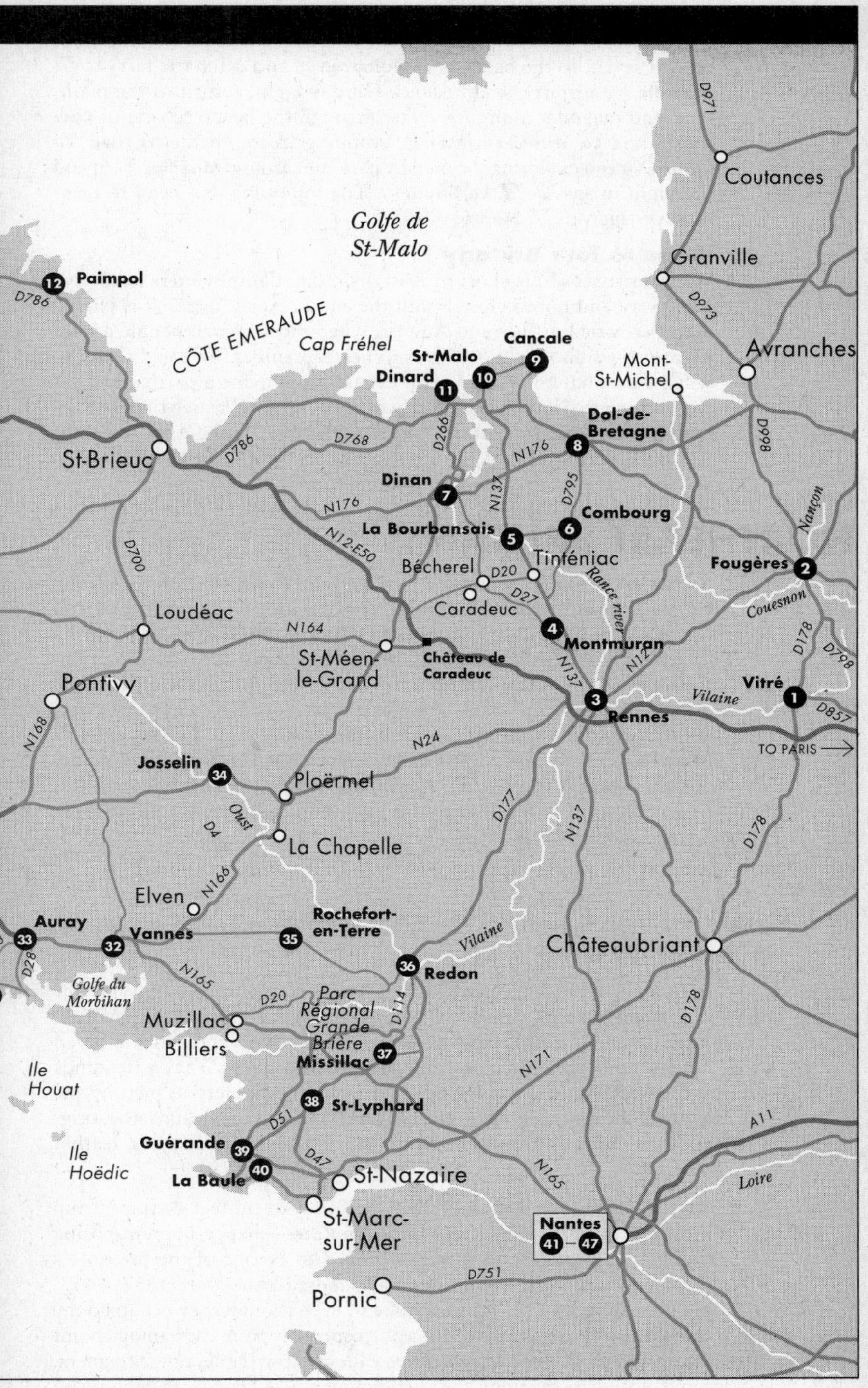

Golfe de St-Malo
Coutances
Granville
D971
D973
Avranches
Mont-St-Michel
Paimpol
D786
CÔTE EMERAUDE
Cap Fréhel
Cancale
St-Malo
Dinard
Dol-de-Bretagne
D998
St-Brieuc
D786
D768
D266
N176
D795
Dinan
N137
Combourg
Nançon
N176
La Bourbansais
Tinténiac
Fougères
N12-E50
Bécherel
D20
Rance river
D700
Caradeuc
D27
Couesnon
Loudéac
N164
Montmuran
D178
D798
St-Méen-le-Grand
Château de Caradeuc
N137
N12
Vitré
Pontivy
Vilaine
Rennes
D857
N168
N24
TO PARIS
Josselin
Ploërmel
D177
N137
D178
Oust
D4
La Chapelle
N166
Elven
Auray
Vannes
Rochefort-en-Terre
Vilaine
Châteaubriant
D28
N165
Redon
Golfe du Morbihan
D20
Parc Régional Grande Brière
D114
D178
Muzillac
Billiers
Missillac
N171
Ile Houat
St-Lyphard
D51
A11
Guérande
Ile Hoëdic
D47
N165
La Baule
St-Nazaire
Loire
St-Marc-sur-Mer
Nantes
D751
Pornic

bank. Get to **Pont-Aven** ㉖ by the end of the day and dine on oysters in nearby **Riec-sur-Belon** ㉗. Drive down the Atlantic seaboard, on day seven, to the beaches of **Quiberon** ㉘ and catch the ferry to **Belle-Île** ㉙, a pretty, small island. On day eight, return to the mainland and meander along the coast through the beach resorts of **Carnac** ㉚ and **La Trinité-sur-Mer** ㉛, stopping in the medieval town of **Vannes** ㉜ and exploring the marshy parkland around **Missillac** ㊲. Spend the night in seaside **La Baule** ㊵. The following day head to tranquil, prosperous **Nantes** ㊶–㊼.

When to Tour Brittany

The tourist season is short in Brittany. Long damp winters keep visitors away and hotels closed until the end of April. Brittany is particularly crowded in July and August, when most French people are on vacation, so choose crowd-free June, September, or early October when autumnal colors and crisp evenings make for a particularly invigorating visit. Late summer, however, is the most festive time in Brittany: The two biggest pardons take place on July 26 (Ste-Anne d'Aurau) and the last Sunday in August (Ste-Anne-la-Palud); the Celtic Festival de Cornouaille, takes place at Quimper in late July.

NORTHEAST BRITTANY

Northeast Brittany extends from the city of Rennes to the coast. The rolling farmland around Rennes is strewn with mighty castles at Vitré, Fougères, and Dinan—remnants of Brittany's important role in efforts to repel French invaders during the Middle Ages and a testimony to the wealth derived from pirate and merchant ships. The beautiful Côte d'Émeraude (Emerald Coast) stretches west from Cancale to St-Brieuc, and the dramatic Côte de Granit Rose (Pink Granite Coast), extends from Paimpol to Trébeurden and the Bretonne Corniche. Follow the coastal routes D786 and D34, winding, narrow roads that total less than 97 km (60 mi) but can take five hours to drive. All along there are spectacular views.

Vitré

❶ *310 km (192 mi) southeast of Paris, 29 km (18 mi) south of Fougéres, 36 km (22 mi) east of Rennes.*

Built high above the Vilaine Valley, Vitré (pronounced vee-*tray*) is one of the age-old gateways to Brittany: There's still a feel of the Middle Ages about its formidable castle, tightly packed and half-timbered houses, remaining ramparts, and dark, narrow alleys. The castle stands at the west end of town, facing narrow, cobbled streets, as picturesque as any in Brittany—rue Poterie, rue d'Embas, and rue Beaudrairie, originally the home of tanners (the name comes from *baudoyers,* leather workers).

First rebuilt in the 14th and 15th centuries to protect Brittany from invasion, the 11th-century **Château de Vitré**—shaped in an imposing triangle with fat, round towers—proved to be one of the province's most successful fortresses: During the Hundred Years' War (1337–1453) the English repeatedly failed to take it, even though they occupied the rest of the town. It is a splendid sight, especially from the vantage point of rue de Fougères across the river valley below. Time, not foreigners, came closest to ravaging the castle, which was heavily, though tastefully, restored during the past century. The **town hall,** however, is an unfortunate 1913 addition to the castle courtyard. You can visit the wing to the left of the entrance, beginning with the **Tour St-Laurent** (tower) and its museum containing 15th- and 16th-century sculptures,

Aubusson tapestries, and engravings. Continue along the walls via **Tour de l'Argenterie**—which contains a macabre collection of stuffed frogs and reptiles preserved in glass jars—to **Tour de l'Oratoire.** 🎫 *21 frs.* ⏲ *Apr.–June, Wed.–Mon. 10–noon and 2–5:30; July–Sept., daily 10–12:30 and 2–6:15; Oct.–Mar., Wed.–Fri. 10–noon and 2–5:30, Mon. 2–5:30.*

Fragments of the town's medieval ramparts include the 15th-century **Tour de la Bridolle** (✉ pl. de la République), five blocks up from the castle. The **Notre-Dame** church (✉ pl. Notre-Dame), with its fine, pinnacled south front, was built in the 15th and 16th centuries.

Dining and Lodging

$$ ✗🏨 **Le Petit Billot.** This friendly hotel, with carved wood paneling and faded pastels, has a delightful, French provincial atmosphere. The restaurant serves good food with a smile: Try the vegetable terrine with a chopped tomato sauce or the fresh grilled mackerel. ✉ *5 pl. du Général-de-Gaulle, 35500,* ☎ *02–99–75–02–10,* FAX *02–99–74–72–96. 22 rooms, 5 with bath. Restaurant. Closed last wk of Dec.*

$ ✗🏨 **Chêne Vert.** One of Vitré's few hotels, Chêne Vert is quintessentially French provincial: creaky stairs, fraying carpets, over-soft mattresses, and less-than-enthusiastic service—with a copious dinner, for next to nothing. But it has some intriguing touches—an enormous model ship on the second floor and zinc-plated walls that submerge the dining room in a mix of art deco and ocean-liner pastiche. It's convenient to D857, just opposite the train station, and 10 minutes from the château. The restaurant is closed Friday for dinner and Saturday, October–May. ✉ *2 pl. du Général-de-Gaulle, 35500,* ☎ *02–99–75–00–58. 22 rooms with bath or shower. Restaurant. Closed mid-Sept.–mid-Oct.*

Fougères

❷ *29 km (18 mi) north of Vitré, 48 km (30 mi) northeast of Rennes.*

For many centuries, Fougères, a traditional cobbling and cider-making center, was a frontier town, valiantly attempting to guard Brittany against attack. One of the reasons for its conspicuous lack of success is the site of its castle: Instead of sitting high up on the hill, it spreads out down in the valley, though the sinuous River Nançon does make an admirable moat. A number of medieval houses line rue de la Pinterie, which leads directly from the castle up to the undistinguished heart of town.

The 13-tower **Château de Fougères,** one of the largest in Europe, covers more than 5 acres. Although largely in ruins, it is an excellent example of the military architecture of the Middle Ages, impressive both inside and out. The thick walls—20 feet across in places—were intended to resist 15th-century artillery fire, but the castle proved vulnerable to surprise attacks and sieges. A visit inside the castle walls reveals three lines of fortification, with the keep at their heart. There are memorable views over Fougères from the **Tour Mélusine** and, in the **Tour Raoul,** a small shoe museum. The second and third stories of the **Tour de Coigny** were transformed into a chapel during the 16th century. ✉ *East end of town on pl. Raoul II,* ☎ *02–99–99–79–59.* 🎫 *22 frs.* ⏲ *Feb.–Mar. and Oct.–Dec., daily 10–noon and 2–5; Apr.–mid-June, daily 9:30–noon and 2–6; mid-June–Sept., daily 9–7.*

The oldest streets are alongside the castle, clustered around the elegant slate spire of **St-Sulpice,** a Flamboyant Gothic church with several fine altarpieces. ✉ *rue de Lusignan.*

In the 1790s Fougères was a center of Royalist resistance to the French Revolution. Much of the action in 19th-century writer Honoré de Balzac's bloodcurdling novel *Les Chouans* takes place hereabouts. The novel's heroine, Marie de Verneuil, had rooms close to the church of **St-Léonard,** which overlooks the Nançon Valley. To get there from the cathedral, follow the river south. Both the footpath leading to the building and church, with its ornate facade and 17th-century tower, have changed little; the garden through which the path leads is known today as the **Jardin Public.** ✉ *rue Porte-St-Léonard.*

Another man who was inspired by the scenery of Fougères was locally born Emmanuel de La Villéon (1858–1944), a little-known Impressionist painter. More than 100 paintings, pastels, watercolors, and drawings—revealing a serene, underestimated talent—are on display at the **Musée La Villéon.** It is in one of the oldest surviving houses (dating from the 16th century) in hilltop Fougères, and to reach it from the Jardin Public, head left past St-Léonard and cross the square into the adjacent rue Nationale. The artist's work ranges from compassionate studies of toiling peasants to pretty landscapes in which soft shades of green melt into hazy blue horizons. ✉ *51 rue Nationale.* 🎫 *8 frs.* ⏲ *Easter–mid-June, weekends, 11–12:30 and 2:30–5; mid-June–mid-Sept., weekdays 10:30–12:30 and 2:30–5:30, weekends and holidays 11–12:30 and 2:30–5.*

Dining and Lodging

$$ ✕🏨 **Les Voyageurs.** The refined cuisine—local duck foie gras or sweetbreads in Madeira sauce—has made this hotel-restaurant a favorite. Be sure to save room for the dessert cart loaded with homemade pastries. The restaurant is closed the last two weeks in August and weekend nights, September to June. Some of the rooms have been pleasantly redecorated in light colors and chintzes: Ask for those. ✉ *10 pl. Gambetta, 35300,* ☎ *02–99–99–08–20,* FAX *02–99–99–08–20. 37 rooms, 17 with bath. Restaurant. Closed mid-Dec.–early Jan.*

Rennes

❸ *348 km (216 mi) west of Paris, 48 km (30 mi) southwest of Fougères, 107 km (66 mi) north of Nantes.*

Rennes (pronounced *ren*) is the traditional capital of Brittany. It has a different flavor from other towns in the region, mainly because of a terrible fire in 1720, which lasted a week and destroyed half the city. The remaining cobbled streets and half-timber, 15th-century houses form an interesting contrast to the classical feel of the cathedral and Jacques Gabriel's disciplined granite buildings, broad avenues, and spacious squares. Many of the 15th- and 16th-century houses in the streets surrounding the cathedral have been converted into shops, boutiques, restaurants, and *crêperies* (crepe houses).

A 19th-century building in classical style that took 57 years to construct, the **Cathédrale St-Pierre** looms above rue de la Monnaie at the west end of the old town, bordered by the River Rance. Stop in to admire its richly decorated interior and outstanding 16th-century Flemish altarpiece. ✉ *pl. St-Pierre.* ⏲ *Mon.–Sat. 8:30–noon and 2–5, Sun. 8:30–noon.*

The **Palais de Justice,** the palatial original home of the Breton Parliament and now the Law Courts, was designed in 1618 by Salomon de Brosse, architect of the Luxembourg Palace in Paris. It was the most important building in Rennes to escape the 1720 fire, but in February 1994, following a massive demonstration by Breton fishermen demanding state subsidies, a disastrous fire broke out at the Parliament building that left it just a charred shell. Much of the art work—though damaged—was saved by firefighters, who arrived at the scene after the building was already engulfed in flames. It was a case of the fire bell that cried "fire" once too often; a faulty bell, which went off regularly for no reason, had led the man on duty to ignore the ringing. As for the cause of the fire itself, rumors abound, and the building is not likely to be restored until 2002. In the meantime, the art treasures are hidden away for safekeeping. ✉ *rue Nationale.*

The **Palais des Musées,** south of the Palais de Justice and left across the quai Émile-Zola, is a huge building containing two museums—the **Musée des Beaux-Arts** and the **Musée de Bretagne.** The Fine Arts Museum on the second floor houses one of the country's best collections of paintings outside Paris, featuring works by Georges de La Tour, Jean-Baptiste Chardin, Camille Corot, Paul Gauguin, and Maurice Utrillo, to name a few. The ground-floor Museum of Brittany retraces the region's history, period by period, by way of costumes, models, porcelain, furniture, coins, statues, and push-button visual displays. ✉ *20 quai Émile-Zola.* *Both museums 20 frs; 1 museum 15 frs.* *Wed.–Mon. 10–noon and 2–6.*

Take a stroll through the lovely **Jardin du Thabor,** east of the Palais des Musées and a five-minute walk via rue Victor-Hugo. It's a large, formal French garden with regimented rows of trees, shrubs, and flowers. There is a notable view of the church of **Notre-Dame-en-St-Mélaine** from the garden. ✉ *rue de Paris.*

Dining and Lodging

$$ ★ ✕ **Palais.** The highly inventive young chef, Marc Tizon, has made this sharp-edged contemporary restaurant one of the best in Rennes. The menu changes with the season and the market, but specialties include roast rabbit and, in winter, fried oysters in crab sauce. ✉ *7 pl. du Parlement de Bretagne,* ☎ *02–99–79–45–01. Dinner reservations essential. Jacket required. AE, DC, MC, V. Closed Mon., Aug. No dinner Sun.*

$ ✕ **Piccadilly Tavern.** Around the corner from the Palais de Justice and next to the Municipal Theater is this oddly named tavern. Its huge, sunny terrace is the perfect place to people-watch while enjoying a half dozen fresh oysters and an aperitif. ✉ *15 Galerie du Théâtre,* ☎ *02–99–78–17–17. V, MC.*

$$–$$$ ★ ✕🏨 **Le Coq Gadby.** A 19th-century mansion with huge fireplaces and antiques sets the stage for this cozy hotel-restaurant. Rooms have a homey atmosphere, with four-poster beds decked out in floral covers; some have fireplaces. French presidents have come here to sample the seafood dishes and traditional Breton specialties—*biscuit de langoustines aux olives noires* (puff pastry filled with langoustines and black olives) and the *frigousse aux trois volailles* (poultry stew). It's a popular place, so reserve ahead; there's no dinner Sunday. ✉ *156 rue d'Entrain, 35300,* ☎ *02–99–38–05–55,* FAX *02–99–38–53–40. 11 rooms. Restaurant. MC, V.*

$$$ 🏨 **Garden Hôtel.** This delightful hotel has an age-old wooden gallery overlooking the sunny inner courtyard where breakfast is served. Rooms are small, but nicely decorated with antiques and bright colors. ✉ *3 rue Duhamel, 35000,* ☎ *02–99–65–45–06,* FAX *02–99–65–02–62. 24 rooms, 8 with bath. Breakfast room. AE, DC, MC, V.*

$$ 🏨 **Central.** This stately, 19th-century hotel is in a quiet, narrow backstreet close to the cathedral. Rooms look out over the street or the courtyard, but the best part about this place is its central location. ✉ *6 rue*

Lanjuinais, 35000, ☎ 02–99–79–12–36, FAX 02–99–79–65–76. 43 rooms with bath or shower. AE, DC, MC, V.

Nightlife and the Arts

Relax with a drink at **Le Pym's** (✉ 27 pl. du Colombier). Dance the night away at **L'Espace** (✉ 45 bd. de la Tour d'Auvergne).

Brittany's principal theater is the **Opéra de Rennes** (✉ pl. de la Mairie, ☎ 02–99–28–55–87). All kinds of performances are staged at the **Théâtre National de Bretagne** (✉ 1 rue St-Hélier, ☎ 02–99–30–88–88).

The first week of July is **Les Tombées de la Nuit** festival, featuring ballet, music, and theater performances staged in old, historical streets and churches; for information (✉ 8 rue du Maréchal Juin, ☎ 02–99–30–38–01). The famous, annual international Rock 'n Roll festival, **Les Transmusicales** (☎ 02–99–31–12–31 for festival information), takes place the second week of December in bars around town and at the Théâtre National de Bretagne (☞ *above*).

Shopping

A lively **street market** is held in and around place des Lices on Saturday morning. **Tidreiz** (✉ pl. du Palais) sells lovely fabrics. **Au Roy d'Ys** (✉ 29 bd. de Magenta) has a particularly large assortment of Breton textiles.

Montmuran

❹ *24 km (15 mi) north of Rennes.*

Montmuran is best known for its castle, once home to one of France's finest knights, Bertrand du Guesclin. Commemorated in countless squares and hostelries across the province, Bertrand du Guesclin was quite a fellow. Cast as the ugly son of a noble family, he became tough and cunning by playing with the peasants. Ashamed of his rough manners, his family kept him hidden from society. However, at the age of 17, he entered a jousting tournament in disguise and successfully unseated several knights. When his identity was discovered, du Guesclin's father proudly brought his son back into the fold. Du Guesclin went on to become one of France's greatest warriors. He was knighted in 1354 and married his second wife in 1372.

An alley of oak and beech trees leads up to the main 17th-century building of Bertrand du Guesclin's **Château,** which is surrounded by a moat and flanked by four towers, two built in the 12th century, two in the 14th. You can visit the towers and a small museum devoted to the castle's history. The château also has two pleasant guest rooms which are open from May to October. Call to reserve. ✉ *35630 Les Ifs,* ☎ *02–99–45–88–88.* 🎫 *20 frs.* ⏲ *Easter–Oct., daily 2–7; Nov.–Easter, weekends 2–6.*

OFF THE BEATEN PATH — **CHÂTEAU DE CARADEUC** – Ambitiously dubbed the Versailles of Brittany, this château, 8 km (5 mi) northwest of Montmuran and 2 km (1 mi) west of the village of Bécherel, is, unfortunately, privately owned and thus not open to the public. As compensation, however, you can explore the surrounding park—Brittany's largest—and admire its statues, flower beds, and leafy alleys. ✉ *rte. de Chateaubriand,* ☎ *02–99–66–77–76.* 🎫 *15 frs.* ⏲ *Apr.–Oct., daily 10–6; Nov.–Mar., weekends 2–6.*

La Bourbansais

❺ *19 km (12 mi) north of Caradeuc, 11 km (7 mi) north of Montmuran, 35 km (22 mi) north of Rennes.*

Venture to La Bourbansais to see its castle. Since it was founded by local lord Jean de Breil in 1583, the **Château de la Bourbansais** has remained in the same family. Its extensive gardens contain a small zoo and a pack of hunting hounds. The buildings were enlarged in the 18th century. The majority of the interior furnishings dates from that period as well, and there's a fine collection of porcelain and tapestries. ☎ *02–99–69–40–07.* ▭ *Castle 40 frs; park 45 frs; castle and park 60 frs.* ⊙ *Castle Apr.–Oct., daily 2–6; Nov.–Mar., weekends 3–4; park daily 2–6.*

Combourg

❻ *11 km (7 mi) east of La Bourbansais, 39 km (24 mi) north of Rennes.*

Combourg is best known as the boyhood home of Romantic writer Viscount Chateaubriand (1768–1848). Chateaubriand grew up in the thick-walled, four-tower **Château de Combourg,** dating mainly from the 14th and 15th centuries. You can visit the Chateaubriand archives and the writer's austere bedroom in the **Tour du Chat** (Cat's Tower). The castle grounds—ponds, woods, and half-tended lawns—are suitably mournful and can seem positively desolate under leaden skies. ☎ *02–99–73–22–95.* ▭ *25 frs, park only 8 frs.* ⊙ *Apr.–June and Sept., Wed.–Mon. 9–noon and 2–5; July–Aug., daily 9–5; Oct., Wed–Mon. 2–4.*

Dinan

★ ❼ *24 km (15 mi) southwest of Dol-de-Bretagne, 52 km (32 mi) north of Rennes.*

Dinan has close links with Brittany's 14th-century anti-English warrior-hero Bertrand du Guesclin (☞ Montmuran, *above*). Du Guesclin won a famous victory here in 1359 and promptly married a local girl, Tiphaine Raguenel. When he died in the siege of Auvergne (central France) in 1380, his body was dispatched home to Dinan. Owing to the great man's popularity, only his heart completed the journey—it rests in the basilica—the rest of him was confiscated by devoted followers in towns along the route.

On place des Merciers, rue de l'Apport, and rue de la Poissonnerie, note the splendid triangular-gable wooden houses. These cobbled streets are so pretty you may think you've stumbled onto a movie set. Rue du Jerzual, which leads down to Dinan's harbor, is also a beautifully preserved medieval street, divided halfway down by the town walls and the massive Porte du Jerzual gateway, and lined with boutiques and crafts shops in 15th- and 16th-century houses. A few restaurants brighten the area around the harbor and boats sail up the River Rance in summer, but the abandoned warehouses mostly bear witness to the town's vanished commercial activity. Above the harbor, near Porte St-Malo, is the leafy promenade des Grands Fossés, the best-preserved section of the town walls, which leads to the castle. The **tourist office** (✉ rue de l'Horloge, ☎ 02–96–39–75–40) is housed in a 16th-century building in the old town.

For a superb view of the town, climb to the top of the medieval clock tower, the **Tour de l'Horloge.** ✉ *rue de l'Horloge.* ▭ *10 frs.* ⊙ *July–Sept., daily 10:45–1:15 and 3–6.*

Breton warrior-hero du Guesclin's heart lies in the north transept of ★ the **Basilique St-Sauveur,** off rue de l'Horloge, one block north of the tourist office. The church's style ranges from the Romanesque south front to the Flamboyant Gothic facade and Renaissance side chapels. The old trees in the **Jardin Anglais** (English Garden), behind the church provide a nice frame. More spectacular views can be found at the bottom of the garden, which looks down the plummeting Rance Valley to the river 250 feet below. ✉ *pl. St-Sauveur.*

The **Château,** at the end of the promenade des Petits Fossés, has a two-story tower, the **Tour du Coëtquen,** and 100-foot 14th-century keep, containing a museum with varied displays of medieval effigies and statues, Breton furniture, and local lace coiffes. ✉ *Porte de Guichet,* ☎ *02–96–39–45–20.* 🎫 *25 frs.* ⏲ *Mar.–May and mid-Sept.–mid Nov., daily 10–11:30 and 2–5:30; June–mid-Sept., daily 10–5:30; mid-Nov.–Feb., Thurs.–Tues. 1:30–5.*

Dining and Lodging

$$ ✕ **La Poudrière.** Under the vaulted ceilings of this restaurant, which is in the cellar of the D'Avaugour hotel (☞ *below*), hearty fare—from *cuisse canard en confite* (duck thigh in its fat) to lobster in a rich wine sauce—is served. ✉ *1 pl. du Champ-Clos,* ☎ *02–96–39–07–49. AE, DC, MC, V.*

$ ✕ **Relais des Corsaires.** Named after the pirates who, it is said, raided Dinan, the Relais is on the banks of the Rance. The mid-range prix-fixe menu provides an ample four-course meal. The welcoming proprietors, Jacques and Barbel Pauwels, also have a more informal grill, Au Petit Corsair, in the 15th-century building next door. ✉ *7 rue du Quai,* ☎ *02–96–39–40–17. AE, DC, MC, V. Closed Jan., Feb.*

$$ ★ 🏨 **D'Avaugour.** This hotel, opposite the castle tower, has a sunny flower garden where breakfast and afternoon tea are served. Most rooms are cozy and look out onto either the garden or the castle. Start the day with the full buffet breakfast. Mme. Quinton is fluent in English and enjoys helping plan day trips. ✉ *1 pl. du Champ-Clos, 22100,* ☎ *02–96–39–07–49,* FAX *02–96–85–43–04. 27 rooms with bath. Restaurant, breakfast room. AE, DC, MC, V.*

$ 🏨 **Arvor.** The cobbled streets of the old town are visible from this comfortably converted 18th-century convent across from the tourist office. Run by the convivial Brigitte Urvoy, it is a good value without frills. ✉ *5 rue A. Pavie, 22100,* ☎ *02–96–39–21–22,* FAX *02–96–39–83–09. 23 rooms with bath or shower. AE, MC, V.*

Nightlife and the Arts

Every two years (next in 1998), on the first weekend in September, medieval France is re-created with a market, parade, jousting tournament, and street music for **La Fête des Remparts,** one of the largest medieval festivals in Europe.

Shopping

The cobbled, sloping **rue de Jerzual** is lined with medieval houses containing shops selling crafts by local wood-carvers, jewelers, leather workers, glass specialists, and silk painters.

Dol-de-Bretagne

8 *17 km (10 mi) north of Combourg, 56 km (35 mi) north of Rennes.*

The ancient town of Dol-de-Bretagne, which still has its original ramparts, looks out from its 60-foot cliffs over Le Marais, a marshy plain stretching across to Mont-St-Michel, 21 km (13 mi) northeast. For extensive views of Le Marais as well as Mont-Dol, a 200-foot granite mound, 3 km (2 mi) north, which is the legendary scene of combat between St. Michael and the devil, walk along the **promenade des Douves,** on the northern part of the original ramparts. Also explore Dol's picturesque main street, **Grand-Rue des Stuarts,** which is lined with medieval houses. The oldest, the Maison des Plaids, at No. 17, has a chunky row of Romanesque arches.

The **Cathédrale St-Samson**—at the end of the Promenade des Douves—is a damp, soaring, fortresslike bulk of granite dating mainly from the 12th to the 14th centuries. This mighty building shows just how influential the bishopric of Dol was in days gone by. The richly sculpted Great Porch, carved wooden choir stalls, and stained glass in the chancel deserve close scrutiny. ✉ *pl. de la Cathédrale.*

During a short, cheerfully guided tour of the small **Musée Historique d'Art Populaire** (Museum of the History of Popular Art), in La Trésorerie off the promenade des Douves, you can see costumes, weapons, and models retracing life in Dol since prehistoric times. The pride of the museum, though, is its assembly of colored wooden religious statues. ✉ *pl. de la Cathédrale,* ☎ *02–99–48–33–46.* 🎟 *20 frs.* ⏲ *Easter–Sept., Wed.–Mon. 9:30–noon and 2–5:30; Oct.–Mar., weekends 2–5:30.*

Dining and Lodging

$$ ✕🏨 **Logis de la Bresche Arthur.** With its crisp outlines, white walls, and glassed-in terrace, this hotel doesn't look as historic as it sounds. But it is cozy. Rooms are functional and inexpensive. Character, smartness, and indulgence are reserved for the restaurant where chef-owner Philipe Martel serves classically inspired roast pigeon with black currant and ginger, and ravioli stuffed with *petits gris* (small snails) in cream sauce. ✉ *36 bd. Deminiac, 35120,* ☎ *02–99–48–01–44,* FAX *02–99–48–16–32. 24 rooms. Restaurant. AE, DC, MC, V. Closed Feb.*

Nightlife and the Arts

On the third Sunday of September, traditional farming tools and methods are on display during **La Fête du Blé Noir** (Black Wheat Feast) at the Musée de la Paysannerie (✉ Baguer Morvan, 4 km/2 mi north of Dol-de-Bretagne, ☎ 02–99–48–04–04).

Cancale

❾ *13 km (8 mi) east of St-Malo, 34 km (21 mi) northeast of Dinan.*

If you enjoy eating oysters, be sure to get to Cancale, a picturesque fishing village renowned for its *bancs d'huîtres* (oyster beds). Sample this delicacy at one of the many quayside restaurants. At the **Musée de l'Huître,** you can learn all about how oysters are farmed. ✉ *Les Parcs St-Kerber, plage de l'Aurore,* ☎ *02–99–89–69–99.* ⏲ *Guided 1-hr tours mid-June–mid-Sept., daily 11 and 3–5; mid-Feb.–mid-June and Oct., daily 3 PM.*

Dining and Lodging

$$$$ ✕🏨 **De Bricourt.** Mont St-Michel is visible from the large stone house where chef Olivier Roellinger grew up and now runs one of the region's best restaurants. Murals, stone fireplaces, and antique tiles create an imposing, yet cozy atmosphere. Local seafood dishes seasoned with exotic spices are the specialty. Don't skip dessert. The restaurant is closed Tuesday and Wednesday in winter. If you wish to stay the night, there are attractive rooms in the main building and the annex. ✉ *1 rue Duguesclin, 35260,* ☎ *02–99–89–64–76,* FAX *02–99–89–88–47. 19 rooms. Restaurant. AE, DC, MC, V.*

$$$$ ✕🏨 **Hôtel Richeux.** One of three hotels in Cancale owned by the Roellingers of De Bricourt, it occupies an imposing turn-of-the-century waterfront mansion built on the ruins of the du Guesclin family's 11th-century château. Request one of the tower rooms, which have stunning views of Mont-St-Michel Bay. Le Coquillage, a small restaurant, closed from mid-November to mid-December, serves local oysters. ✉ *St-Meloir des Ondes, 35350,* ☎ *02–99–89–64–76,* FAX *02–99–89–88–47. 11 rooms. Restaurant. AE, DC, MC, V.*

$$$$ 🏨 **Les Rimains.** The Roellingers' second hotel in Cancale is tucked among towering trees at the end of a rocky point, with the surf directly below. Every room has an ocean view. Breakfast is served in the flower-filled garden. ✉ *1 rue Duguesclin, 35260,* ☎ *02–99–89–64–76,* FAX *02–99–89–88–47. 6 rooms. AE, DC, MC, V. Closed Oct.–Mar.*

St-Malo

★ ⑩ *13 km (8 mi) east of Dinard, 32 km (20 mi) north of Dinan, 69 km (43 mi) north of Rennes.*

One and a half kilometers (1 mile) across the Rance Estuary from Dinard lies the ancient walled town of St-Malo. Although it includes several neighborhoods, people come to see the *intra-muros* (within the walls) section, the fortified town. The stone ramparts of this onetime pirate base have withstood the Atlantic since the 12th century. They were considerably enlarged and modified in the 18th century, and they extend from the castle in St-Malo's northeast corner and circle the old town for a circumference of more than 1½ km (1 mi). The views are stupendous, especially at high tide.

The town itself has proved less resistant: A weeklong fire in 1944, kindled by retreating Nazis, wiped out nearly all the old buildings. Restoration work was more painstaking than brilliant, but the narrow streets and granite houses of the old town were satisfactorily re-created, enabling St-Malo to regain its role as a busy fishing port, seaside resort, and tourist destination. Millions of tourists invade this quaint town, so if you want to avoid crowds, don't come here in summer.

At the edge of the ramparts is the **Château St-Malo,** whose great keep and watchtowers command an impressive view of the harbor and coastline. It houses the **Musée d'Histoire de la Ville,** devoted to local history, and the **Galerie Quic-en-Grogne,** a tower where various episodes and celebrities from St-Malo's past are recalled by way of waxworks. ✉ *Hôtel de Ville. Museums:* ☎ *02–99–40–71–57.* 🎫 *25 frs.* ⏲ *Easter–Sept., Wed.–Mon. 10–noon and 2–6. Château:* ☎ *02–99–40–80–26.* 🎫 *20 frs.* ⏲ *Easter–June and Sept.–Oct., daily 9:30–11:15 and 2–5:15; July–Aug., daily 9:30–11:45 and 2–5:45.*

Five hundred yards offshore is the **Île du Grand Bé,** a small island housing the somber military tomb of Viscount Chateaubriand, who was born in St-Malo. The islet can be reached by a causeway at low tide.

The **Fort National,** also offshore and only accessible by causeway at low tide, is a massive fortress with a dungeon constructed in 1689 by that military-engineering genius Sébastien de Vauban. ☎ *02–99–46–91–25.* 🎫 *10 frs.* ⏲ *Easter–Oct.; call ahead. Hrs and times of ½-hr guided tours depend on the tides.*

North American visitors can pay homage to Jacques Cartier, who set sail from St-Malo in 1535 to discover the St. Lawrence River and found Quebec. Cartier's tomb is in the church of **St-Vincent** (✉ Off Grande-Rue). His statue looks out over the town ramparts, four blocks away, along with that of swashbuckling corsair Robert Surcouf, hero of many daring 18th-century raids on the British navy (he's the one pointing an accusing finger over the waves at England).

Dining and Lodging

$$ ★ ✕ **La Métairie de Beauregard.** It's worth driving to this reasonably priced restaurant in a small manor (from 1653), once the home of a privateer. There's a warm, cozy ambience in the Louis XIII–style dining room. Chef-owner Jacques Gonthier's travels around the world have influenced his classic creations, including crab mille-feuille and John Dory with a cream of prawns. ✉ *35 Bourg St-Étienne (south on N137, then D4 toward Château-Malo),* ☎ *02–99–81–37–06. AE, DC, MC, V. Call ahead off-season.*

$–$$ ✕ **Le Chalut.** Locals and tourists come to this simple, casual, friendly restaurant for fish. You can inspect the night's fare on ice in front and in a large tank in the dining room. Decor is plain—the emphasis is on the food. ✉ *8 rue Corne du Cerf,* ☎ *02–99–56–71–58. Reservations not accepted. MC, V. Closed Jan., 2 wks in Oct. No dinner Sun. off-season.*

$$–$$$ 🏨 **La Digue.** The view of the sea is magnificent from the hotel's terrace and rooms. The largest and most luxurious rooms are pricey, but others are quite reasonable. The bar, also overlooking the water, and the *salon de thé* (tea shop) add to the hotel's charm. ✉ *49 chaussée du Sillon, 35400,* ☎ *02–99–56–09–26,* FAX *02–99–56–41–65. 53 rooms with bath or shower. Bar, tea shop. AE, V. Closed Jan.*

$$ ★ 🏨 **Hôtel Elizabeth.** In a town house built into the ramparts of the city wall, the Elizabeth, near the Porte St-Louis, is a little gem of sophistication in touristy St-Malo. Rooms are generally small but tastefully furnished; rates vary with size. ✉ *rue des Cordeliers, 35400,* ☎ *02–99–56–24–98,* FAX *02–99–56–39–24. 17 rooms. AE, DC, MC, V.*

$$ 🏨 **Jean-Bart.** This clean, quiet hotel next to the ramparts is decorated in cool blues. Beds are comfortable and bathrooms modern, but the rooms, some with views of the sea, are somewhat small. ✉ *12 rue de Chartres, 35400,* ☎ *02–99–40–33–88,* FAX *02–99–40–33–88. 17 rooms. MC, V. Closed mid-Nov.–mid-Feb.*

Nightlife and the Arts

Bar de L'Univers (✉ pl. Chateaubriand) is a nice spot to sip a drink in a pirate's lair setting. **La Belle Époque** (✉ 11 rue de Dinan) is a popular hangout for all ages till the wee hours. **L'Escalier** (✉ rue de la Tour-du-Bonheur) is the place for dancing the night away.

In summer, performances are held at one of Brittany's main playhouses, the **Théâtre Chateaubriand** (✉ 6 rue Groult-St-Georges, ☎ 02–99–40–98–05). On July 14th (Bastille Day) the **Fête du Clos Poulet,** a neighborhood festival with traditional dancing, takes place. August brings a religious music festival, the **Festival de la Musique Sacrée.**

Outdoor Activities and Sports

The **Centre Hippique** (☎ 02–99–81–20–34) is the source for horses. Sailboats can be rented from **Naviloc** (☎ 02–99–82–12–72). The harbor and outside the breakwater are popular sailing spots.

Shopping

A lively **outdoor market** takes place in the streets of old St-Malo every Tuesday and Friday.

Dinard

11 *22 km (14 mi) north of Dinan, 71 km (44 mi) north of Rennes.*

Dinard is the most elegant resort town on this stretch of the Brittany coast. Its picture-book setting on the Rance Estuary opposite the walled city of St-Malo lured the English aristocracy here in droves after it was discovered in the 1850s by an American named Coppinger. What started out as a small fishing port soon became a seaside mecca of lavish turn-of-the-century villas, grand hotels, and a bustling casino. A number of modern establishments punctuate the landscape, but the town still retains something of an Edwardian tone. To make the most of Dinard's beauty, head down to the Pointe de la Vicomte, at the town's southern tip, where the cliffs give panoramic views across the Baie du Prieuré and Rance Estuary, or stroll along the promenade.

When you walk along the **promenade Clair de Lune,** which hugs the seacoast on its way toward the English Channel and passes in front of the small jetty used by boats crossing to St-Malo, it's easy to see why people love this place. The promenade really hits its stride as it rounds the Pointe du Moulinet and heads toward the sandy **Plage du Prieuré,** named after a priory that once stood here. River meets sea in a foaming mass of rock-pounding surf: Be careful as you walk along the slippery path to the calm shelter of the **Plage de l'Écluse,** an inviting sandy beach, bordered by a casino and numerous stylish hotels. The coastal path picks up on the west side of **Plage de l'Écluse,** ringing the Pointe de la Malouine and the Pointe des Étêtés before arriving at the **Plage de St-Enogat.**

At the **Musée de la Mer** (Marine Museum and Aquarium), virtually every known species of Breton bird and sea creature is on display in two rooms and 24 pools. Another room is devoted to the polar expeditions of explorer Jean Charcot, one of the first men to chart the Antarctic. ✉ *Clair de Lune Promenade,* ☎ *02–99–46–13–90.* *15 frs.* *Ascension Day–mid-Sept., daily 10:30–12:30 and 3:30–7:30.*

Nightlife and the Arts

As befitting a fashionable resort, Dinard has a **casino** (✉ bd. Président Wilson, ☎ 02–99–46–15–71).

Outdoor Activities and Sports

Horseback ride at the **Dinard Centre Équestre de la Côte d'Émeraude** (✉ Le Val Porée, ☎ 02–99–46–23–57). Boats can be rented from the **Dinard Yacht Club** (✉ Promenade Clair de Lune, ☎ 02–99–46–14–32). For windsurfing, wander over to the **Wishbone Club** (✉ Digue de l'Écluse, ☎ 02–99–88–15–20).

En Route From Dinard, route D786 follows the coast. To bypass the coastal road, take N12 west to Guingamp and then D767 northwest to Lannion—this will lead you to Trébeurden. If you don't have much time, but do want to drive along the coast, stop at **Cap Fréhel,** the most dramatic site along the coast: Red, gray, and black cliffs rise vertically from the sea. The colors are best in the evening, but at any time of day the sight is formidable. Avoid the seagulls and cormorants and walk down past the small restaurant to the platform for a look at the rocks below. And go up to the lighthouse, whose beam winks at ships more than 100 km (62 mi) away. From Cap Fréhel, D786 continues up to the **Bretonne Corniche,** where you can see the distinctive pink granite rocks eroded into interesting shapes by the sea and wind.

Paimpol

12 *98 km (60 mi) west of St-Malo, 42 km (26 mi) northwest of St-Brieuc, 147 km (91 mi) northwest of Paris.*

Paimpol, on the Bretonne Corniche, is one of the best fishing ports in the area and a good base for exploring this part of the coast. The town is a maze of narrow streets lined with local shops, a number of restaurants, and the inevitable souvenir shops. The harbor is its main focal point: Fishermen used to unload their catch from far-off seas; today, most of the fish is caught in the Channel. From the sharp cliffs you can see the coast's famous pink granite rocks.

Dining and Lodging

$$–$$$ ★ ✕🏨 **Le Repaire de Kerroch.** This delightful hotel overlooking the harbor has spacious rooms, with artfully used odd angles. A favorite, Les Sept Isles, faces the street and has a view of boats. Chef-owner Jean Claude Broc prepares delicious seafood dishes—skate with zesty beurre blanc and sea trout—as well as *lapinereau confite* (young rabbit confit). Be sure to have breakfast so that you can sample the homemade confitures of bananas and green tomatoes. The restaurant is closed on Tuesday and Wednesday, except in July and August. ✉ *29 quai Morand, 22500,* ☎ *02–96–20–50–13,* FAX *02–96–22–07–46. 12 rooms. Restaurant. MC, V. Closed early Jan.–mid-Feb.*

Nightlife and the Arts

La Fête des Terre Neuvas is a celebration of the traditional return from Newfoundland of the Breton fishing fleets on the third Sunday in July. For centuries, but no longer, Breton fishermen sailed to Newfoundland each spring to harvest cod—a long and dangerous journey.

Trébeurden

13 *42 km (26 mi) west of Paimpol, 9 km (6 mi) northwest of Lannion, 47 km (29 mi) northeast of Morlaix.*

A small, pleasant fishing village that has become a summer resort town, Trébeurden makes a good base for exploring Le Castel Peninsula, Trégastel, Ploumanach, and Perros-Guirec. Take a look at the profile of the dramatic rocks off the coast and use your imagination to see Tête de Mort (Death's Head), La Tortoise, Le Sentinel, and Wellington's Hat. The scene changes with the sunlight and the sweep and retreat of the tide, which strands fishing boats among islands that were, only hours before, hidden beneath the sea.

Dining and Lodging

$$$–$$$$ ✕🏨 **Manoir de Lan Kerellec.** The beauty of the Breton coastline is embraced by this Relais & Châteaux hotel. Choose from a range of comfortable accommodations. The restaurant, whose circular dining room has a delightful model of the *Saint Yves* ship suspended from its ceiling, mostly serves seafood, but the roast lamb is also good; it's closed Monday and Tuesday off-season. ✉ *22560 Trébeurden,* ☎ *02–96–23–50–09,* FAX *02–96–23–66–88. 16 rooms, 5 suites. Restaurant, tennis court. AE, DC, MC, V. Closed mid-Nov.–mid-Mar.*

BRITTANY'S WESTERN COAST

Brittany's western coast extends from the town of Morlaix southeast along the Atlantic coast to the city of Nantes at the mouth of the Loire River. The wild, rugged beaches around the little-visited northwestern tip become sandy at Pont-Aven. Inland, the bent trees and craggy rocks make you feel that the sorcerer Merlin is working his magic.

Morlaix

14 *144 km (90 mi) west of St-Malo, 60 km (37 mi) east of Brest, 79 km (49 mi) north of Quimper.*

The town-spanning, 19th-century stone railroad viaduct—300 yards long and 200 feet high—in Morlaix (pronounced mor-*lay*) is an unforgettable sight. The old town is an attractive mix of half-timber houses and low-front shops that rewards unhurried exploration. At its commercial heart is the pedestrian **Grand'Rue,** lined with quaint 15th-century houses. In the adjacent rue du Mur, the three-story, 16th-century **Maison de la Reine Anne** is adorned with statuettes of saints.

Known as the **Musée des Jacobins** because it is housed in a former Jacobin church (note the early 15th-century rose window at one end), the town museum—just off rue d'Aiguillon, parallel to Grand'Rue—has an eclectic collection ranging from religious statues to archaeological finds and modern paintings. ✉ *pl. des Jacobins,* ☎ *02–98–88–68–88.* 🎫 *25 frs.* ⏲ *Apr.–Oct., daily 10–12:30 and 2–6:30; Nov.–Mar., Wed.–Mon. 10–noon and 2–5.*

Every year, 3 million tons of cigars are rolled in the **manufacture de tabac** (cigar factory). Tours can be arranged year-round with advance notice. ✉ *quai de Léon,* ☎ *02–98–88–15–32.*

At the **Brasserie des Deux Rivières** brewery, the beer is brewed according to traditional Breton methods; you can even quaff one on the spot. ✉ *1 pl. de la Madeleine,* ☎ *02–98–63–41–92.* 🎫 *Free.* ⏲ *July and Aug., tours Mon.–Wed. 10:30, 2, and 3:30.*

Dining and Lodging

$–$$ ✕🏨 **Europe.** Though rooms—as in many old hotels—are dreary, this place is convenient. The welcoming, many-mirrored restaurant has a low-cost prix-fixe menu that might include lobster (try the fricassee of Breton lobster with chervil and garlic confit), warm oysters, and smoked salmon. ✉ *1 rue d'Aiguillon, 29210,* ☎ *02–98–62–11–99,* FAX *02–98–88–83–38. 57 rooms, 38 with bath, 3 suites. Restaurant. AE, DC, MC, V.*

St-Pol-de-Léon

15 *10 km (6 mi) northwest of Morlaix.*

St-Pol-de-Léon is a lively market town famous for its cauliflowers and artichokes and dominated by three spires: Two belong to the cathedral, the highest to the chapel.

The pleasingly proportioned **Ancienne Cathédrale** was built between the 13th and 16th centuries and has finely carved 16th-century choir stalls that are worth a trip inside. ✉ *rue Général-Leclerc.*

The **Chapel Notre-Dame du Kreisker,** originally used for meetings by the town council, has a magnificent 250-foot 15th-century granite spire, flanked at each corner by tiny spires known as *fillettes* ("young girls"). It was the prototype for countless bell towers in Brittany. From the top there is a rewarding view across the Bay of Morlaix toward the English Channel. ✉ *rue du Général-Leclerc,* ☎ *02–98–69–01–15.* 🎫 *Tower 5 frs.* ⏲ *Mid-June–mid-Sept., daily 10–noon and 2–5.*

Kerjean

16 *29 km (18 mi) southwest of St-Pol-de-Léon.*

The main reason to come to Kerjean is its castle. With its vast park, ditch, and 40-foot-thick defensive walls, the 15th-century **Château de**

Kerjean looks like a fortress until you see the large windows, tall chimney stacks, and high-pitched roofs of its main buildings. The chapel, kitchens, and main apartments, full of regional furniture, can be visited. Temporary exhibitions are held in the stable wing. Note the old well in the main courtyard. ☎ *02–98–69–93–69.* 🎫 *25 frs.* ⏲ *July–Aug., daily 10–7; Sept. and June, Wed.–Mon. 10–6; Nov.–Dec., Wed. and Sun. 2–5.*

Le Folgoët

17 *16 km (10 mi) west of Kerjean, 24 km (15 mi) northeast of Brest.*

Pilgrims come from afar to attend Le Folgoët's pardon in early September. The sturdy north tower of the splendid **Notre-Dame Basilica** serves as a beacon for the pilgrims coming to drink from the Salaün fountain against the wall behind the church; its water comes from a spring beneath the altar, which can be reached through a sculpted porch. Inside the church is a rare, intricately worked, granite rood screen separating the choir and nave.

Brest

18 *24 km (15 mi) southwest of Le Folgoët, 244 km (151 mi) west of Rennes, 104 km (65 mi) north of Quimper.*

Don't plan to spend much time in the maritime city of Brest; you may even want to bypass the town altogether. Brest's enormous, sheltered bay is strategically positioned close to the Atlantic and the English Channel. World War II left the city in ruins. Postwar reconstruction, resulting in long, straight streets of reinforced concrete, has given latter-day Brest the unenviable reputation of being one of France's ugliest cities. Its waterfront, however, is worth visiting for the few old buildings, castle, and museums, as well as for dramatic views across the bay toward the Plougastel Peninsula. The **Pont de Recouvrance,** which crosses the River Penfeld, is Europe's longest lift-bridge at 95 yards.

Begin your visit at one of the town's oldest monuments, the **Tour Tanguy,** next to the bridge. This bulky, round 14th-century tower, once used as a lookout post, contains a museum of local history with scale models of the Brest of yore. 🎫 *Free.* ⏲ *Oct.–May, Wed.–Sun. 2–6; June–Sept., daily 10–noon and 2–7.*

Brest's medieval **Château de Brest,** across the bridge from the Tour Tanguy, is home to the **Musée de la Marine** (Naval Museum), containing boat models, sculpture, pictures, and naval instruments. A section is devoted to the castle's 700-year history. The dungeons can also be visited. ☎ *02–98–22–12–39.* 🎫 *29 frs.* ⏲ *Wed.–Mon. 9:15–noon and 2–6.*

French, Flemish, and Italian paintings, spanning the period from the 17th to the 20th century, make up the collection at the **Musée Municipal.** ✉ *rue Traverse.* 🎫 *Free.* ⏲ *Mon. and Wed.–Sat. 10–11:45 and 2–6:45, Sun. 2–6:45.*

Maritime technology, fauna, and flora are the themes of the exhibits at the futuristic **Océanopolis** center, overlooking the Moulin Blanc marina. But the biggest attraction is the aquarium—the largest in Europe. ✉ *rue Alain-Colas,* ☎ *02–98–34–40–40.* 🎫 *50 frs.* ⏲ *July–Sept., daily 9:30–6; Oct.–June, daily 9:30–5 (6 on weekends).*

Outdoor Activities and Sports

Rent sailboats from **Centre Nautique** (☎ 02–98–02–11–93).

Nightlife and the Arts

The **Festival des Trois Mers** in July and August is famous for its sacred and choral music performances.

Daoulas

19 *19 km (12 mi) southeast of Brest.*

Stop in Daoulas to admire its 12th-century, still-functioning Romanesque abbey, with cloisters and herbal garden, and the Enclos Paroissial (literally, "parish enclosure," a 16th-century walled garden).

Locronan

20 *46 km (29 mi) south of Daoulas, 17 km (11 mi) north of Quimper.*

Canvas sails for the French fleet were made in the 15th century in the old weaving town of Locronan. Now numerous artists have set up shop here: weavers, potters, painters, and sculptors in summer. Be sure to visit the 15th-century **Church and Chapel of Le Pénity,** dominating the magnificently preserved ensemble of houses and main square.

Dining and Lodging

$–$$ ✕🏨 **Manoir de Moëllien.** This lovely 15th-century manor house, filled with precious antiques, is famous for its local seafood dishes. Sample the *terrine de poisson chaud* (seafood terrine) or the *duo de truites de mer* (poached sea trout). Rooms have terraces overlooking the garden, which makes for a peaceful, country atmosphere. ✉ *Plonevez-Porsay, 28180 (2 km/1 mi north of Locronan),* ☎ *02–98–92–50–40,* FAX *02–98–92–55–21. 10 rooms. Restaurant. AE, DC, MC, V. Closed Jan.–Mar.*

Ste-Anne-la-Palud

21 *49 km (30 mi) southwest of Daoulas, 68 km (42 mi) south of Brest.*

For some fresh sea air and a look at Brittany as it has been for centuries, visit Ste-Anne-la-Palud. As you approach the cliffs and inlets of this resort town, the roads, lined with the stone cottages typical of the area, become blissfully free of cars. The pardon on the last Sunday in August is one of the finest and most authentic age-old religious festivals in Brittany.

Dining and Lodging

$$$–$$$$ ✕🏨 **Hôtel de la Plage.** This former private house sits nestled in a cove on a quiet strip of sandy beach—a remote setting perfect for long, restorative walks. Some of the comfortably furnished rooms face the sea. The hotel, however, has less of a feeling of Brittany than one might want. The food in the restaurant is consistently good, especially the seafood dishes, but not very innovative; reservations are essential and a jacket is required. ✉ *29127 Plonevez-Porzay,* ☎ *02–98–92–50–12,* FAX *02–98–92–56–54. 26 rooms. Restaurant, tennis court, beach. AE, DC, MC, V. Closed mid-Oct.–early Apr.*

Douarnenez

22 *16 km (10 mi) west of Ste-Anne-la-Palud, 10 km (6 mi) west of Locronan, 23 km (14 mi) northwest of Quimper.*

Douarnenez is a quaint old fishing town of quayside paths and zigzagging narrow streets. Boats come in from the Atlantic to unload their catches of mackerel, sardines, and tuna. Just over the Port-Rhu Estuary is Tréboul, a seaside resort town favored by French families.

One of the three town harbors is home to the unique **Port-Musée** (Maritime Port-Museum). Along the wharves, you can visit the workshops of wooden-boat wrights, sail makers, and other old-time craftspeople, then go aboard the historic trawlers, lobster boats, Thames barges, and a former lightship anchored alongside. You can also sail on an antique fishing boat on the second weekend of May. ✉ *quai du Port-Rhu,* ☎ *02–98–92–65–20.* *40 frs June–Sept., 30 frs Oct.–May.* *June–Sept., daily 10–7; Oct.–Dec. and May, Tues.–Sun. 10–12:30 and 2–6.*

Dining and Lodging

$$ ★ **Hôtel Ty Mad.** Artists and writers like Picasso and Breton native Max Jacob frequented this small hotel, in a quiet residential area, in the 1920s. Rooms are not big, but the sea views are great. The delicious dishes, including *terrine de raie à la crème de menthe* (skate pâté with mint sauce) and *lotte flambée à l'estragon* (monkfish flambé with tarragon) are served in the glass-enclosed restaurant. ✉ *plage St-Jean, 29100,* ☎ *02–98–74–00–53,* FAX *02–98–74–15–16. 23 rooms with bath or shower. Restaurant. MC, V. Closed Nov.–Easter.*

Outdoor Activities and Sports

Sailboats can be rented from **Les Voiles d'Iroise** (☎ 02–98–92–74–25), on the bay.

En Route West of Douarnenez, parts of the coast look more like the breezy bluffs of Ireland than France, especially around **Pointe du Raz.** This is the westernmost tip of the country, marked by a dramatic 300-foot drop; the spectacular view is worth the detour. Plan on an hour to walk along the edge of the chasms. The deepest is called **L'Enfer de Plogoff** (the Plogoff Inferno), where the tide rushes in and out with a deafening roar. Go out all the way to the end for broad views of the horizon and coastline and to tremble a while as you become hypnotized by the Raz de Sein, a tidal race whose rip puts fear into everyone's heart.

Audierne

23 *22 km (14 mi) west of Douarnenez, 35 km (22 mi) northwest of Quimper.*

In summer, the small working port of Audierne, where the fishermen come daily bearing the day's catch of langoustines, is a busy pleasure-boat center that is never overcrowded. Most of the visitors are locals, which makes for a nontouristy, welcoming atmosphere.

Dining and Lodging

$$$ ★ **Le Goyen.** In the early morning you can watch the activity in the bustling fishing port from the balcony of your very pretty room (or ultramodern suite) in this modern hotel. In the evening, aperitifs are served while you wait for chef Adolphe Bosser's superb Breton cuisine. Watch the port as you dine on baked turbot with a beef stock sauce, Breton lobster, or aromatic *ris de veau* (veal sweetbread). The restaurant is closed Monday off-season. ✉ *Portside, 29770,* ☎ *02–98–70–08–88,* FAX *02–98–70–18–77. 126 rooms, 3 suites. AE, MC, V. Closed mid-Nov.–mid-Dec.*

Quimper

24 *36 km (22 mi) east of Audierne, 72 km (45 mi) south of Brest, 115 km (71 mi) northwest of Vannes.*

Lively commercial Quimper is the ancient capital of the Cornouaille province, founded, it is said, by King Gradlon 1,500 years ago. Quimper (pronounced cam-*pair*) owes its strange name to its site at the confluence (*kemper* in Breton) of the Rivers Odet and Steir. Stroll along the banks of the Odet and through the old town, with its cathedral. Then walk along the lively shopping street, rue Kéréon and down medieval rue de Guéodet (note the house with caryatids), rue St-Mathieu, and rue du Salle.

The **Cathédrale St-Corentin** is a masterpiece of Gothic architecture and the second-largest cathedral in Brittany (after Dol-de-Bretagne's). Legendary King Gradlon is represented on horseback just below the base of the spires, harmonious mid-19th-century additions to the medieval ensemble. The luminous 15th-century stained glass is particularly striking. Behind the cathedral is the stately **Jardin de l'Évêché** (Bishop's Garden). ✉ *pl. St-Corentin.*

Works by major masters, such as Rubens, Corot, and Picasso, mingle with pretty landscapes from the local Gauguin-inspired Pont-Aven school in the **Musée des Beaux-Arts** (Fine Arts Museum), next to the cathedral. ✉ *40 pl. St-Corentin.* 🎫 *25 frs.* ⏲ *July–Aug., daily 9–7; Sept.–June, Wed.–Mon. 10–noon and 2–6.*

Local furniture, ceramics, and folklore top the bill in the **Musée Départemental** (Breton regional museum) on rue du Roi-Gradlon, adjacent to place St-Corentin. ✉ *1 rue du Roi-Gradlon.* 🎫 *20 frs.* ⏲ *June–Sept., daily 9–6; Oct.–May, Wed.–Mon. 9–noon and 2–5.*

In the mid-18th century, Quimper sprang to nationwide attention as a ceramic manufacturing center when it began producing second-rate imitations of faience, the Rouen ceramics with blue Oriental motifs. Today's more colorful designs, based on floral arrangements and marine fauna, are still often hand-painted. Guided tours are available at the **Musée de la Faïencerie.** ✉ *14 rue Jean Baptiste Bousquet,* ☎ *02–98–90–12–72.* 🎫 *26 frs.* ⏲ *Mid-Apr.–Oct. and school vacations, Mon.–Sat. 10–6.*

Dining

$$ ✕ **Ambroisie.** The decor is modern, with its yellow walls and huge paintings by painter Francis Bacon, and each table has a different setting. But the food remains resolutely old-style Breton, such as *roulade de blé noir au saumon fumé* (rolled wholewheat crepes with smoked salmon) and the *crêpe aux crabes* (crab crepes). ✉ *49 rue Elie Feron,* ☎ *02–98–95–00–02. Reservations essential. AE, MC, V. Closed 1 wk in June and Oct.*

Nightlife and the Arts

The **Celtic Festival de Cornouaille** is held in Quimper in late July (☎ 02–98–55–53–33).

Shopping

Keep an eye out for such typical Breton products as woven and embroidered cloth, brass and wooden goods, puppets, dolls, and locally designed jewelry. When it comes to distinctive Breton folk costumes, Quimper is the best place to look. The streets around the cathedral, especially **rue du Parc,** are full of shops selling the woolen goods (notably thick marine sweaters) in which the region specializes. Faience and a wide selection of hand-painted pottery can be purchased at the **Faïencerie d'Art Breton** (✉ 16 bis rue du Parc).

Concarneau

25 *21 km (13 mi) south of Quimper, 93 km (58 mi) southeast of Brest, 103 km (64 mi) northwest of Vannes.*

Concarneau is the third-largest fishing port in France. A busy industrial town, it has a grain of charm and an abundance of tacky souvenir shops. But it's worth visiting to see its fort in the middle of the harbor. Entered by a quaint drawbridge, the **Ville Close,** the fortified islet in the harbor, was, from early medieval times, regarded as impregnable. The fortifications were further strengthened by the English under John de Montfort during the War of Succession (1341–64). Three hundred years later, Sébastien de Vauban remodeled the ramparts into what you see today: 1 km long (½ mi long) with splendid views across the two harbors on either side. *Ramparts 5 frs. Easter–Sept., daily 10–7:30; Oct.–Easter, daily 10–12 and 2–5.*

The **Musée de la Pêche** (Fishing Museum), close to the drawbridge, has aquariums and exhibits on fishing techniques from around the world. ✉ *rue Vauban,* ☎ *02–98–97–10–20. 30 frs. July–Aug., daily 9:30–7:30; Sept.–June, Tues.–Sun. 10–noon and 2–6.*

Dining

$$–$$$ ✕ **Le Galion.** Nestled in a stone house in the fortified old town, this restaurant, with traditional nautical decor, has a modern, trendy menu. The langoustine fricassee and the *St-Pierre à la rhubarbe* (fish with rhubarb sauce) are excellent. ✉ *rue Guénolé,* ☎ *02–98–97–30–16. MC, V. Closed Mon. Oct.–Easter. No dinner Sun.*

Nightlife and the Arts

During the second half of August you can enjoy the **Fête des Filets Bleus** (Blue Net Festival) in the Ville Close, a weeklong folk celebration in which Bretons in costume swirl and dance to the wail of bagpipes.

Pont-Aven

26 *12 km (7 mi) southeast of Concarneau, 37 km (23 mi) southeast of Quimper, 91 km (56 mi) northwest of Vannes.*

Pont-Aven is a former artists' colony that was Paul Gauguin's headquarters before he headed off to the South Seas. While you're here, visit the museum dedicated to the school, cool off in summer with a boat trip down the estuary from Pont-Aven, or take a walk in the hills among the pastures to the Tremalo chapel, where there is a crucifix attributed to Gauguin. A permanent photography exhibition documents the Pont-Aven School, and works by its participants, are found at the **Musée Municipal.** ✉ *pl. de l'Hôtel de Ville,* ☎ *02–98–06–14–43. 25 frs July–Aug., 20 frs Feb.–June and Sept.–Dec. July–Aug., daily 9:30–7:30; Feb.–June and Sept.–Dec., Tues.–Sun. 10–noon and 2–6.*

Dining and Lodging

$$$ ✕ **La Taupinière.** On the road from Concarneau, in the outskirts of Pont-Aven, you'll find this roadside inn with an attractive garden. The food isn't cheap, but chef Guy Guilloux's fish, crab, crayfish, and Breton ham (grilled over the large, open fire) is worth it. His wine cellar is renowned. ✉ *rte. de Concarneau,* ☎ *02–98–06–03–12. Reservations essential. Jacket required. AE, DC, MC, V. Closed Tues. and mid-Sept.–mid-Oct. No dinner Mon.*

$$$ ✕ **Moulin de Rosmadec.** The Sébilleau's old mill sits in the middle of the rushing, rocky Aven River. You can hear the sound of water gently spilling over the stones beneath your window. In the rustic-looking restaurant, one of the best in France, have lobster or langoustine ravioli, and opt for the prix-fixe menus. Reservations are essential and a jacket is required at the restaurant, closed dinner Sunday and Wednesday, mid-September to mid-June. ✉ *Town center, 29930,* ☎ *02–98–*

06–00–22, FAX *02–98–06–18–00. 4 rooms. Restaurant. MC, V. Closed mid-Nov.–late Nov., Feb.*

$$ ✕🏨 **Roz-Aven.** Built into a rock face on the banks of the River Aven, this efficiently run hotel has simple, clean rooms. The owner, Yann Souffez, speaks excellent English. He describes the furnishings as Louis XVI, but, at best, they appear petit bourgeois. The restaurant has a limited selection of fine prix-fixe menus and wines, priced 20% less than some fancier restaurants. ✉ *11 quai Botrel, 29930,* ☎ *02–98–06–13–06,* FAX *02–98–06–03–89. 24 rooms. Restaurant. MC, V.*

Riec-sur-Belon

27 *16 km (10 mi) east of Pont-Aven down D783, then D24.*

Gourmets will want to make a pilgrimage to Riec-sur-Belon to indulge in the famous oysters.

Dining and Lodging

$–$$ ✕ **Chez Jacky.** This picturesque wharf-side restaurant on the River Belon is the source of some of the country's finest, freshest oysters. ✉ *Rive Droite, Riec-sur-Belon,* ☎ *02–98–06–90–32. MC, V. Closed Mon. and Oct.–Mar.*

$$$$ ✕🏨 **Château de Locquenole.** The château's squat, imposing architecture is countered by the peaceful setting of lawns and woods, through which the River Blavet flows. Design takes a turn for the better inside, with 19th-century furnishings and tapestries. The spacious rooms are similarly decorated; ask for one with a view of the river. Some prefer to stay in the rustic, warm, cozy rooms in the renovated stables at the farm, 3 km (2 mi) away. Marc Angelle, one of France's top chefs, cooks with a keenness of creativity in the restaurant, closed Monday. ✉ *rte. de Port-Louis, 56700 (3 km/2 mi south of Hennebont on D781; 30 km/19 mi south of Pont Aven),* ☎ *02–97–76–29–04,* FAX *02–97–76–39–47. 31 rooms, 4 suites. Restaurant, pool, sauna. AE, DC, MC, V. Closed Jan.–mid-Feb.*

Quiberon

28 *49 km (30 mi) south of Lorient, 46 km (29 mi) west of Vannes.*

Quiberon is a spa town with pearl-like beaches on the eastern side of the 16-km-long (10-mi-long) Presqu'île de Quiberon (the "almost-island" or Quiberon Peninsula), a stretch of rough coastal cliffs and beaches joined to the mainland by a hairbreadth of sand. Its dramatic western coast is dubbed the Côte Sauvage (Wild Coast), a mix of crevices, coves, and rocky grottoes lashed by the sea. A word to the wise: The coast is extremely dangerous and swimming is prohibited. Quiberon's best beach is the Grande Plage (Great Beach), on the protected side of the peninsula. Boats for nearby Belle-Île leave from the harbor of Port-Maria.

Nightlife and the Arts

Quiberon's **casino** (☎ 02–97–50–23–57) has the standard games of chance, as well as shows in summer.

Outdoor Activities and Sports

An 18-km (11-mi) foot path follows the Côte Sauvage, as does the boulevard de la Côte Sauvage, which is perfect for cycling. Bicycles can be rented from **Cyclomar** (✉ 47 pl. Hoche, ☎ 02–97–50–26–00).

Shopping

In a country where gourmandism is virtually a cultural pursuit, **Henri Le Roux** (✉ 18 rue du Port-Maria) has taken the art of chocolatiering to dizzying heights. Check out his delicious displays—created before your very eyes—at his shop near Quiberon Harbor.

Belle-Île

29 *45 mins by boat from Quiberon.*

At 18 km (11 mi) long, Belle-Île is the largest of Brittany's islands. It also lives up to its name: It's beautiful and much less commercialized than Quiberon. Because of the cost and inconvenience of reserving car berths on the ferry, cross over as a pedestrian and rent a car—or, better still, a bicycle—on the island.

The ferry lands at **Le Palais,** where there is a Vauban **citadelle.** From here, head to **Sauzon,** the prettiest fishing harbor, where you can see across to the Quiberon Peninsula and the Gulf of Morbihan to Belle Epoque actress Sarah Bernhardt's summer home. Continue on to the **Grotte de l'Apothicairerie,** which derives its name from the local cormorants' nests, said to resemble apothecary bottles. At **Port Goulphar** is the **grand phare** (big lighthouse). Built in 1835, it rises 275 feet above sea level and has one of the most powerful lights in Europe, visible from 120 km (75 mi) across the Atlantic. If the keeper is available, you may be able to climb to the top.

Dining and Lodging

$$–$$$ ★ ✕☷ **Castel-Clara.** This modern hotel is perched on a cliff overlooking the surf and the narrow Anse de Goulphar bay. Ask for a room with a view. In the bright, airy restaurant, chef Christophe specializes in seafood, literally caught just offshore. The St-Pierre fish baked in sea salt and the grilled sea bream are simple but delicious. ✉ *Port-Goulphar,* ☎ *02–97–31–84–21,* FAX *02–97–31–51–69. 32 rooms, 10 suites. Restaurant, indoor pool, spa, tennis court. MC, V. Closed mid-Nov.–mid-Feb.*

Carnac

★ 30 *17 km (11 mi) north of Quiberon, 32 km (20 mi) south of Lorient, 31 km (19 mi) west of Vannes.*

At the north end of Quiberon Bay, Carnac is famed for its fabulous beaches, but is especially known for its ancient stone monuments. Dating from the Neolithic–early Bronze ages (3500–1800 BC), the origin of Carnac's **megalithic monuments** remains as obscure as those of their English contemporary, Stonehenge, although religious beliefs and astrology were doubtless an influence. The 2,395 menhirs that make up the three **Alignements du Ménec**—Kermario, Kerlescan, and Ménec—are positioned with astounding astronomical accuracy in semicircles and parallel lines over about 1 km (½ mi). There are also smaller-scale dolmen ensembles and three tumuli (mounds or barrows), including the 130-yard-long, 38-foot-high **Tumulus de St-Michel,** topped by a small chapel with views of the rock-strewn countryside. 🎫 *7 frs.* ⏲ *Easter–Oct.; guided tours of tumulus daily Apr.–Sept.*

Nightlife and the Arts

A cosmopolitan crowd goes dancing at **Les Chandelles** (✉ av. de l'Atlantique).

Outdoor Activities and Sports

Horseback riding can be arranged through **Centre Équestre des Menhirs,** (☎ 02–97–55–73–45). Windsurfing equipment can be rented from **De Petigny** (✉ 90 rte. du Pô, ☎ 02–97–52–02–41).

La Trinité-sur-Mer

31 *5 km (3 mi) east of Carnac, 30 km (19 mi) west of Vannes.*

The yachtsman's paradise of La Trinité-sur-Mer is ringed by sandy beaches and oyster beds, and much favored by wealthy, vacationing Parisians. Hundreds of sailboats jam the vast harbor and there are regattas almost daily during the summer. The venerable yacht club counts the most famous record-holders, like Eric Tabarly, among its members. This town is devoted to sailing and famous sailors.

Vannes

32 *25 km (16 mi) east of La Trinité, 115 km (71 mi) southeast of Quimper, 108 km (67 mi) southwest of Rennes.*

Scene of the declaration of unity between France and Brittany in 1532, Vannes is one of the few towns in Brittany to have been spared damage during World War II, so its authentic regional charm remains intact. This also means that the town is packed with tourists in summer. If this doesn't stop you, be sure to walk along the promenade de la Garenne and the ramparts, visit the medieval wash houses and cathedral, browse in the small boutiques and antiques shops in the pedestrian streets around the picturesque place Henri IV, and check out the Cohue, formerly a medieval market hall, now a temporary exhibition center. Scenic boat trips of the Golfe du Morbihan depart from the port.

Inside the **Cathédrale St-Pierre** is a 1537 Renaissance chapel, a Flamboyant Gothic transept portal, and a treasury. ✉ *pl. du Cathédrale.* 🎫 *3 frs.* ⏲ *Treasury mid-June–mid-Sept., Mon.–Sat. 10–noon and 2–6.*

The **Musée Archéologique** (Archaeology Museum) houses a collection of ancient tools and artifacts dating from the Paleolithic to the Middle Ages. ✉ *rue Noé.* ⏲ *Mon.–Sat. 9:30–noon and 2–6,*

OFF THE BEATEN PATH

FORTERESSE DE LARGOËT – The imposing ruins of this fortress, 19 km (12 mi) northeast of Vannes, is in a wooded park near the village of Elven, just off the N166. Its 170-foot 14th-century octagonal keep is the highest in France; its walls are up to 30 feet thick. Alongside is a faithfully restored 15th-century tower. Henry Tudor was held prisoner here before his return to England and the triumphant 1485 military campaign that led to his crowning as Henry VII. Don't miss the magnificent evening son-et-lumière shows from mid-June to mid-September. ✉ *56250 Elven,* ☎ *02-97-53-35-96.* 🎫 *3 frs.* ⏲ *Mid-Jan.–mid-Nov., daily 8–6.*

Dining and Lodging

$$–$$$ ✕ **Règis Mahè.** Step off the train and right into this popular spot, a haven of refinement where seafood reigns supreme. The chef's delicate poached snapper or grilled sea bass garnished with vegetables are so fresh you can still smell the sea air. The prix-fixe menus are your best bet. ✉ *pl. de la Gare,* ☎ *02–97–42–61–41. AE, V. Closed Monday, late Nov., and late Feb. No dinner Sun.*

$$$$ ✕🏨 **Domaine de Rochevilaine.** At sunset on summer evenings, the view of the sea is magnificent. Wealthy Parisians come to this resort in summer to relax; business people come for seminars in winter. Rooms are arranged on two sides of a courtyard, surrounded by terraced gardens; all have modern furnishings, but vary in size; not all face the ocean. Chef Patrice Caillaut's cuisine is excitingly creative, but the prices are somewhat inflated. ✉ *56190 Billiers (20 km/12 mi south of Vannes, at the tip of the Pointe de Pen-lan),* ☎ *02–97–41–61–61,*

FAX 02–97–41–44–85. 36 rooms, 2 suites. Restaurant, pool. AE, DC, MC, V. Closed Feb.–mid-Mar.

$$ ✕🏨 **Image Ste-Anne.** A varied foreign clientele stays in this welcoming hotel in an old, rustic building. The comfortable rooms make the price of a night here seem more than acceptable. Mussels, sole in cider, and duck are featured in the restaurant, which has a very reasonable prix-fixe menu; it's closed dinner Sunday, November–March. ✉ *8 pl. de la Libération, 56000,* ☎ *02–97–63–27–36,* FAX *02–97–40–97–02. 32 rooms with bath or shower. Restaurant. MC, V.*

Auray

33 *20 km (12 mi) west of Vannes, 122 km (76 mi) southwest of Rennes.*

The ancient town of Auray grew up along the banks of the river. Stroll along the narrow cobbled streets in the St-Goustan Quarter. Across the old bridge at the harbor is the **Goélette St-Sauveur,** an old sailing ship tied alongside the quay. In its hold is a sailing museum with many unusual nautical artifacts. ☎ *02–97–40–37–05.* ⊙ *July–Aug., daily 10 AM–noon, Sept.–June by appointment.*

Dining

$$–$$$ ✕ **Clôserie de Kerdrain.** Chef Fernand Corfmat presides over the kitchen in this large Breton house draped in wisteria, where he inventively blends traditional and contemporary cuisine. The *tarte aux légumes et langoustines* (vegetable and langoustine tart) and *ravioles de fruits de mer au jus de homard* (ravioli stuffed with seafood in lobster sauce) are unusual but delicious versions of local recipes. ✉ *20 rue Louis Billet,* ☎ *02–97–56–61–27. AE, DC, MC, V. Closed Mon. mid-Nov.–Mar., last 2 wks of Nov., and 1st 2 wks of Mar. No dinner Sun.*

Nightlife and the Arts

In July, one of the biggest **pardons** in Brittany is held at the sanctuary of Ste-Anne d'Auray (☎ 02–97–57–69–16 for information).

Outdoor Activities and Sports

Take a cruise down the Auray river on the **Vedettes d'Auray** (☎ 02–97–56–59–47) and you'll discover the lovely, 16th-century Château du Plessis-Kaer, and the tiny, tidal fishing port of Bono tucked between the steep banks and the oysters beds of the Pô estuary.

Josselin

34 *24 km (15 mi) north of Largoët, 43 km (27 mi) northeast of Vannes, 78 km (48 mi) west of Rennes.*

The picturesque medieval town of Josselin on the River Oust is known for its castle with two faces. On the side facing the river, the **Château des Rohans** looks like a defensive stronghold with three stout turreted towers linked by austere, near-windowless walls. The landward facade, however, is a riot of intricate pinnacles, gables, and stone ornament, surrounded by gardens. You can visit the library, wood-panel dining room, portrait gallery, and Grand Salon, with its ornate fireplace (only the ground floor is open to the public). 🎫 *22 frs.* ⊙ *July–Aug., daily 10–noon and 2–6; June and Sept., daily 2–6; Apr.–May, Wed. and Sun. 2–6.*

In the former **castle stables** is a 500-strong collection of old dolls. Many are dressed in traditional costume; most date from the 18th century, and one dates from the 17th. 🎫 *22 frs (separate from castle).* ⊙ *June–Sept., daily 10–noon and 2–6; Mar.–May and Oct., Wed. and weekends 2–6.*

OFF THE BEATEN PATH **GUÉHENNO CALVARY** – Eleven kilometers (7 miles) southeast of Josselin along the D778 road is this 16th-century calvary. Its gray granite crosses and statues depict the Crucifixion, and it is the only one in the Morbihan region of Brittany.

Rochefort-en-Terre

35 *45 km (28 mi) southeast of Josselin, 34 km (21 mi) east of Vannes.*

People come to the cheerful old town of Rochefort-en-Terre to see its cozy, ivy-clad medieval castle. The 14th-century **Château de Rochefort-en-Terre** houses a collection of tapestries, armor, chests, furniture, earthenware statuettes, and paintings by Alfred and Trafford Klots, the American artists who lived in the castle and restored it. 🎫 *21 frs.* ⏲ *July–Aug., daily 10–6; Apr.–June and Oct., weekends 10–5:30.*

Redon

36 *25 km (16 mi) southeast of Rochefort-en-Terre, 62 km (39 mi) east of Vannes, 65 km (40 mi) southwest of Rennes.*

The elegant little town of Redon, at the junction of the River Vilaine and the Nantes–Brest canal, was once a busy commercial port. These days the harbor is used exclusively by pleasure boats. On the adjacent quays, stylish 17th–19th-century mansions, with large windows and wrought-iron balconies, look out over the water. Wood-frame medieval houses line the main street, Grande Rue, dominated by the slender spire and magnificent Romanesque tower of the church of St-Sauveur, all that remains of a once-powerful Benedictine abbey.

Missillac and the Parc Régional Grande Brière

37 *22 km (14 mi) south of Redon, 58 km (36 mi) southwest of Vannes.*

Missillac is the gateway to the low-lying marshy area of the Grande Brière Regional Park. Made up of reed marshes and crisscrossed by long, narrow canals, the park is a bird-watcher's delight and is best explored by boat. Boat trips are organized by the **Maison du Parc Naturel Régional de Brière** (✉ Île de Fedrun, St-Joachim, ☎ 02–40–92–68–68) or by **Rando Loisirs en Brière** (☎ 02–40–66–57–32). While you're in Missillac, take a look at the gothic **Château de la Bretesche,** rebuilt in the 16th century with ornate ramparts and a water-filled moat.

St-Lyphard

38 *10 km (6 mi) southwest of Missillac, 16 km (10 mi) northeast of La Baule.*

St-Lyphard is a small village perched on the edge of the Grande Brière Regional Park (☞ *above*). Climb up the church tower for a panoramic view of the Brière marshes. Five kilometers (3 miles) south of St-Lyphard on D51 is the curious **Kerbourg dolmen,** a table-shape megalith.

Guérande

39 *65 km (40 mi) southeast of Vannes, 7 km (4 mi) northwest of La Baule.*

Guérande is a beautiful 15th-century town complete with a tower at each corner and a moat. It's famous for its salt flats.

La Baule

40 *7 km (4 mi) southeast of Guérande, 18 km (11 mi) south of St-Lyphard, 72 km (45 mi) southwest of Vannes.*

One of the most fashionable—and pricey—resorts in France, La Baule has a 5-km (3-mi) seafront promenade lined with hotels. Like Le Touquet and Dinard, it is a 19th-century creation, founded in 1879 to make the most of the excellent sandy beaches that extend around the broad, sheltered bay between Pornichet and Le Pouliguen. A pine forest, planted in 1840, keeps the shifting local sand dunes firmly at bay.

Dining and Lodging

$$$ ✕ **La Marcanderie.** This warm, yellow-walled restaurant with cheerful owners is widely considered the best in town. Potato and scampi tart, lobster salad, monkfish in cider, and scallops in endive top the menu, which starts at 190 francs. ✉ *5 av. d'Agen,* ☎ *02–40–24–03–12. Reservations essential. Jacket and tie. AE, MC, V. Closed Mon. No dinner Sun.*

$$ ✕ **Ferme du Grand Clos.** At this lively restaurant in an old farm house, wafer-thin crepes are served with every imaginable filling, from sweet to savory—mussels, fish, chicken, or chocolate—take your pick. Come early for a table, it's a popular place. ✉ *52 av. de Lattre de Tassigny,* ☎ *02–40–60–03–30. MC, V. Closed Wed. Sept.–June.*

$$ 🏨 **Concorde.** This establishment numbers among the least expensive good hotels in pricey La Baule. It's calm, comfortable, modernized, and a short block from the beach (ask for a room with a sea view). ✉ *1 bis av. de la Concorde, 44500,* ☎ *02–40–60–23–09,* FAX *02–40–42–72–14. 47 rooms with bath or shower. Closed Oct.–Easter.*

$$ 🏨 **Hôtel de la Plage.** One of the few hotels on the beach in St-Marc-sur-Mer, this comfortable place was the setting for Jacques Tati's classic film, *Mr. Hulot's Holiday.* It has been updated since, and *hélas,* the swinging door to the dining room is no longer there. But the view of the sea and the sound of the surf remain. ✉ *37 rue du Commandant Charcot, 44600 St-Marc-sur-Mer (10 km/6 mi south of La Baule),* ☎ *02–40–91–99–01,* FAX *02–40–91–92–00. 33 rooms with bath or shower. Restaurant. V. Closed early–late Jan.*

Nightlife and the Arts

Occasionally you see high stakes on the tables at La Baule's **casino** (☎ 02–40–60–20–23).

Nantes

72 km (45 mi) east of La Baule, 108 km (67 mi) south of Rennes, 114 km (71 mi) southeast of Vannes.

The tranquil, prosperous city of Nantes seems to pursue its existence without too much concern for what's going on elsewhere in France. Cobbled streets surround its castle and cathedral in the town's medieval sector. Across the broad boulevard, cours des 50 Otages, is the 19th-century city. Although Nantes is officially part of the Pays de la Loire, its historic ties with Brittany are embodied in its imposing castle.

Built by the dukes of Brittany, who had no doubt that Nantes belonged
41 in their domain, the **Château des Ducs de Bretagne** is a massive, well-preserved 15th-century fortress with a neatly grassed moat. François II, the duke responsible for building most of it, led a hedonistic existence here, surrounded by ministers, chamberlains, and an army of servants. Numerous monarchs later stayed in the castle, where, in 1598,

Henry IV signed the famous Edict of Nantes advocating religious tolerance.

The **Harnachement**—a separate building inside the castle walls—is home to the **Musée des Salorges** (Naval Museum), devoted principally to the history of seafaring; a separate section outlines the triangular trade that involved transportation of Africans to America to be sold as slaves. As you cross the courtyard to the **Grand Gouvernement** wing, home to the **Musée d'Art Breton Régional** (Regional Folk Art Museum), look for the old well, where the ducal coat of arms is entwined in a magnificent wrought-iron decoration. The **Musée d'Art Populaire** features an array of armor, furniture, 19th-century Breton costumes, and reconstituted interiors illustrating the former life of the Vendée region to the south. ⊠ *Just off rue du Château,* ☎ *02–40–41–56–56.* 🎫 *10 frs, free Sun.* ⊙ *Castle and museums: July–Aug., daily 10–noon and 2–6.; Sept.–June, Wed.–Mon. 10–noon and 2–6.*

42 The **Cathédrale St-Pierre,** opposite the castle, is one of France's last Gothic cathedrals; building began in 1434, well after most other medieval cathedrals had been completed. The facade is ponderous and austere, in contrast to the light, wide, elegant interior, whose vaults rise higher (120 feet) than those of Notre-Dame in Paris. In the transept, notice Michel Colombe's early 16th-century tomb of François II and his wife, Marguerite de Foix, which is one of France's finest examples of funerary sculpture. ⊠ *pl. St-Pierre,* ☎ *02–51–88–95–47.* 🎫 *20 frs.* ⊙ *Crypt: Mon.–Sat. 10–12:30 and 2–6, Sun. 2–6:30.*

A fine collection of paintings from the Renaissance, including works
by Jacopo Tintoretto, Georges de La Tour, Jean-Auguste Ingres, and
43 Gustave Courbet can be found at the **Musée des Beaux-Arts** behind
the Cathédrale St-Pierre, past the 15th-century Porte St-Pierre. ⊠ *10 rue G-Clemenceau,* ☎ *02–40–41–65–65.* 🎫 *20 frs, free Sun.* ⊙ *Mon., Wed.–Sat. 10–noon and 2–6, Sun. 11–6.*

44 Erected in 1843, the **Passage Pommeraye** (⊠ rue Crébillon) is an elegant shopping gallery in the 19th-century part of town. The **Grand**
45 **Théâtre** (⊠ pl. Graslin), down the block from the Passage Pommer-
46 aye, was built in 1783. The 15th-century **Manoir de la Touche** (⊠ rue
Voltaire) was once home to the bishops of Nantes. The mock Ro-
47 manesque **Palais Dobrée,** offsetting the medieval silhouette of the
Manoir de la Touche across the way, was built by arts connoisseur Thomas Dobrée during the past century. Among the treasures within are miniatures, tapestries, medieval manuscripts, and enamels; one room is devoted to the Revolutionary Wars in Vendée. ⊠ *pl. Jean V,* ☎ *02–40–71–03–50.* 🎫 *20 frs, free Sun.* ⊙ *Wed.–Mon. 10–noon and 1:30–5:30.*

Dining and Lodging

$$$ ✕ **Villa Mon Rêve.** This cozy little restaurant is in delightful parkland. Chef Gérard Ryngel concocts elegantly inventive regional fare (the duck or rabbit in muscadet are good choices) and you can sample one of the 45 varieties of muscadet, the local wine, on the wine list. ⊠ *506 rte. des Bords de Loire, Basse-Goulaine (8 km/5 mi east of Nantes),* ☎ *02–40–03–55–50. AE, DC, MC, V. Closed last wk of Oct.*

$$ ✕ **L'Embellie.** Chef Claude Scheiber's cooking at this small, modern
★ bistro is serious and traditional and makes the most of herbs to bring out the natural flavors in the seafood and game dishes. The lunchtime menu is a particularly good value. ⊠ *14 rue Armand-Brossard,* ☎ *02–40–48–20–02. AE, MC, V. Closed Sun., 2nd wk in Aug. No lunch Sat.*

Cathédrale St-Pierre, **42**
Château des Ducs de Bretagne, **41**
Grand Théâtre, **45**
Manoir de la Touche, **46**
Musée des Beaux-Arts, **43**
Palais Dobrée, **47**
Passage Pommeraye, **44**

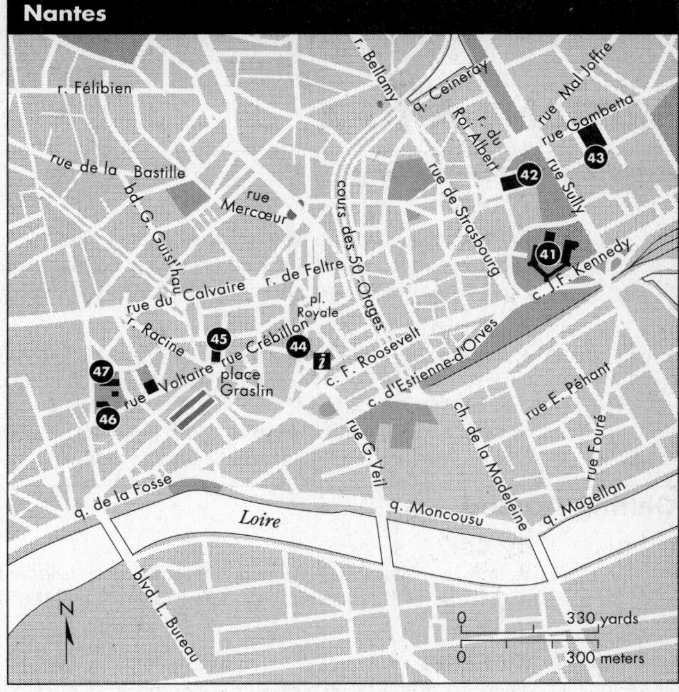

$ ✕ **La Cigale.** Miniature palm trees, gleaming woodwork, colorful enamel tiles, and painted ceilings have led to the official recognition of La Cigale as a *monument historique.* You can savor its Belle Epoque ambience without spending a fortune—the prix-fixe lunch menus are a good value. But the banks of fresh oysters and well-stacked dessert cart may tempt you to order à la carte. ✉ *4 pl. Graslin,* ☎ *02–40–69–76–41. Reservations essential. V.*

$$$ **Hôtel La Pérouse.** Bare parquet floors, plain off-white walls, simple high-tech lighting, and minimal contemporary furnishings make rooms feel spacious. Bathrooms are equally modern and have huge translucent sinks. The amiable staff speaks fluent English. A pedestrian zone full of boutiques and restaurants is right outside the door, and place Royale is less than 10 minutes away. ✉ *3 allée Dusquesne, off cours des 50 Otages, 44000,* ☎ *02–40–89–75–00,* FAX *02–40–89–76–00. 47 rooms. AE, MC, V.*

Nightlife and the Arts

Take a break at the piano bar, **Le Tie Break** (✉ 1 rue des Petites-Écuries), a popular drinking hole. For live jazz, head to the informal **Pub Univers** (✉ 16 rue J. J. Rousseau).

The **Théâtre Graslin** (✉ rue Scribe, ☎ 02–40–69–77–18) is Nantes's principal theater; performance listings are available at the tourist office (✉ pl. du Commerce, ☎ 02–40–47–04–51).

Shopping

The commercial quarter of Nantes stretches from place Royale to place Graslin. For antiques, go to **Cibot** (✉ 7 rue Voltaire). Don't miss chocolate specialist **Georges Gautier** (✉ 9 rue de la Fosse) or his Muscadets Nantais grapes dipped in brandy and covered with chocolate. Since 1803 the Devineau family has been selling wax fruit and vegetables at **Maison Devineau** (✉ 6 pl. Ste-Croix); for 75 francs, you can take home a basket of purple grapes or a cauliflower, as well as handmade candles and wildflower honey.

BRITTANY A TO Z

Arriving and Departing

By Car

Rennes, the gateway to Brittany, is 310 km (193 mi) southwest of Paris. It can be reached in about four hours via Le Mans and the A81/A11 expressways (A11 continues from Le Mans to Nantes).

By Train

There are numerous daily high-speed TGVs (Trains à Grande Vitesse) between Paris (Gare Montparnasse) and both Nantes and Rennes, making this area easily accessible. The trip takes 2–2½ hours to cover the 403 km (250 mi). There is also regular train service up the west coast to Nantes from La Rochelle and Bordeaux.

Getting Around

By Car

Rennes, a strategic base for penetrating Brittany, is linked by good roads to Morlaix and Brest (E50), Quimper (N24/N165), and Vannes (N24/N166).

By Plane

There are domestic airports at Rennes, Brest, Nantes, Morlaix, Dinard, Quimper, and Lorient.

By Train

Some trains from Paris stop at Vitré before forking at Rennes on their way to either Brest (via Morlaix) or Quimper (via Vannes). Change at Rennes for Dol-de-Bretagne and St-Malo; at Dol-de-Bretagne for Dinan and Dinard (bus link); at Morlaix for Roscoff; at Rosporden, 19 km (12 mi) south of Quimper, for Concarneau; and at Auray for Quiberon.

Contacts and Resources

Bicycling

Bikes can be rented at most major train stations.

Car Rental

Avis (✉ pl. de la Gare, La Baule, ☎ 02–40–60–36–28; 3 bd. des Français-Libres, Brest, ☎ 02–98–43–37–73; aéroport, Dinard, ☎ 02–99–46–25–20; 18 bd. de Stalingrad, Nantes, ☎ 02–40–74–07–65; and 8 av. de la Gare, Quimper, ☎ 02–98–90–31–34; or try the national reservations number ☎ 01–46–10–60–60 in Paris).

Guided Tours

Information about organized tours of Brittany is available from the very helpful **Maison de la Bretagne** (✉ Centre Commercial Maine-Montparnasse, 17 rue de l'Arrivée, B.P. 1006, 75737 Paris, ☎ 01–45–38–73–15, FAX 01–43–20–45–07). The **regional tourist offices** in Brest (✉ 8 av. Georges-Clemenceau, ☎ 02–98–44–24–96) and Quimper (✉ pl. de la Résistance, ☎ 02–98–53–04–05) can also provide information about guided tours of Brittany. **France Tourisme** (✉ 3 rue d'Alger, 75001 Paris, ☎ 01–44–50–44–20) organizes three-day tours of Normandy and Brittany from April through October.

Travel Agencies

Wagons-Lits (✉ 22 rue du Calvaire, Nantes, ☎ 02–40–08–29–18; 2 rue Jules-Simon, Rennes, ☎ 02–99–79–45–96).

Visitor Information

The principal regional tourist offices are as follows: **Rennes** (✉ Pont de Nemours, ☎ 02–99–79–01–98). **Brest** (✉ 8 av. Georges-Clemenceau, ☎ 02–98–44–24–96). **Nantes** (✉ pl. du Commerce, ☎ 02–40–47–04–51). Smaller towns also have tourist offices: **Carnac** (✉ 74 av. des Druides, ☎ 02–97–52–13–52). **Concarneau** (✉ quai d'Aiguillon, ☎ 02–98–97–01–44). **Dinan** (✉ 6 rue de l'Horloge, ☎ 02–96–39–75–40). **Dinard** (✉ 2 bd. Féart, ☎ 02–99–46–94–12). **Dol-de-Bretagne** (✉ 3 Grand Rue, ☎ 02–99–48–15–37). **Douarnenez** (✉ 2 rue Dr. Mevel, ☎ 02–98–92–13–35). **La Baule** (✉ 9 pl. de la Victoire, ☎ 02–40–24–34–44). **Morlaix** (✉ pl. des Otages, ☎ 02–98–62–14–94). **Quiberon** (✉ 7 rue de Verdun, ☎ 02–97–50–07–84). **Quimper** (✉ pl. de la Résistance, ☎ 02–98–53–04–05). **St-Malo** (✉ Esplanade St-Vincent, ☎ 02–99–56–64–48). **Vannes** (✉ 1 rue Thiers, ☎ 02–97–47–24–34). **Vitré** (✉ pl. St-Yves, ☎ 02–99–75–04–46).

6 Normandy

Rouen to Mont-St-Michel

On the miles of sandy beaches along the English Channel, you'll find seaside towns such as Dieppe, Fécamp, Honfleur, and Deauville. To the west is Mont-St-Michel, the famous medieval abbey crowning a rock offshore. Inland, Rouen's cathedral and museums, Pont-Audemer's colorful market, and the legendary Bayeux tapestry beckon, as do calvados and marvelous cheeses.

NORMANDY (OR NORMANDIE, as the French spell it), the coastal region northwest of Paris, probably has more associations for English speakers than any other part of France: William the Conqueror, Joan of Arc, and D-Day are household names in English, just as they are in French.

Updated by Simon Hewitt

The area is popular with British vacationers not only because it's right across the Channel, but also because of its countryside: wild, granite cliffs in the west; long, sandy beaches along the coast; wooded valleys in the south; and lush green meadows and apple orchards in the center.

Historic buildings—castles, churches, and monuments—punctuate the Norman countryside. Following the 1066 invasion of England by the Norman duke, William (the Conqueror), Normandy oscillated between English and French control for several centuries. In Rouen, in 1431, Joan of Arc was burned at the stake, marking a turning point in the Hundred Years' War, the last major medieval conflict between the French and the English. The coastline east of the Cotentin Peninsula is lined with the World War II D-Day beaches, where the colossal Allied amphibious landings took place in June 1944. But perhaps Normandy's most celebrated sight is the abbey of Mont-St-Michel, erected on a 264-foot mound of granite cut off from the mainland at high tide; the architectural marvel is the country's most visited spot outside Paris.

Pleasures and Pastimes

Bicycling

The Cotentin Peninsula, jutting out into the English Channel, is suited for easy cycling, particularly the west coast which doesn't get much traffic. The rolling hills of La Suisse Normande, south of Caen, are dotted with little villages and picnic spots connected by country roads that make the area ideal for touring by bike.

The Coast

Normandy has 605 km (375 mi) of coastline bordering the English Channel. There are four major ports—Le Havre, Rouen, Dieppe, and Cherbourg, plus coastal towns with seafaring pasts, such as Honfleur, and former fishing villages like Fécamp. Sandwiched between are beaches and fashionable resort towns—Deauville, Cabourg, and Étretat—where you might find yourself reclining in a deck chair, gin and tonic in hand. The waters are chilly, but you might be tempted to take a dip on a hot, sunny day.

Dining

The Normans are notoriously big eaters: On festive occasions, in the old days, they wouldn't bat an eye at tucking away 24 courses. Between the warm-up and the main course there was a *trou Normand* (Norman hole), a break often lasting several hours, during which lots of calvados (apple brandy) was downed to make room for more food. And Norman food isn't light. Many dishes are cooked with rich cream sauces and with apple flavoring—thus *à la normande* (with cream sauce or apples). Rich local milk makes excellent cheese: Pont-l'Évêque (known since the 13th century) is made in the Pays d'Auge with milk that is still warm and creamy; Livarot (also produced for centuries) uses milk that has stood for a while—don't be put off by its strong smell. The excellent Pavé d'Auge is a firm, square-shape cheese with a strong flavor. Best known of them all is creamy Camembert, a relative newcomer invented by a farmer's wife in the late 18th century. Although

Normandy is not a wine-growing area, it produces excellent hard cider (the best comes from the Vallée d'Auge) and calvados.

Local specialties differ from place to place. Rouen is famous for its *canard à la rouennaise* (duck in blood sauce); Caen, for its *tripes à la mode de Caen* (tripe cooked with carrots in a seasoned cider stock); Mont-St-Michel for *omelettes Mère Poulard* (a secret receipe first made by a local hotel manager in the late 19th century). From the Vallée d'Auge there's *sole dieppoise* (sole poached in a sauce with cream and mussels) and *pré-salé* (lamb from the salt marshes). If you like *boudin noir* (blood sausage), this is the region; for seafood lovers, the coast provides oysters, lobster, and shrimp. In summer, be sure to make reservations at restaurants to assure you can indulge in all these Norman treats.

CATEGORY	COST*
$$$$	over 400 frs
$$$	250 frs–400 frs
$$	125 frs–250 frs
$	under 125 frs

**per person for a three-course meal, including tax (20.6%) and tip but not wine*

Hiking

Gentle rolling countryside makes Normandy ideal for rambling or serious hiking. There are 10 long-distance, signposted itineraries and countless well-indicated footpaths for shorter walks in La Suisse Normande and the Cotentin Peninsula; hostels are found in many of the villages along the trails.

Lodging

Accommodations to suit every taste can be found in Normandy. The beach resort season is very short—July and August only—but weekends are busy most of the year, especially during school holidays. In June and September, lodging is usually available at short notice, and good discounts are given off-season, particularly for stays of more than one night.

CATEGORY	COST*
$$$$	over 800 frs
$$$	550 frs–800 frs
$$	300 frs–550 frs
$	under 300 frs

**All prices are for a standard double room for two, including tax (20.6%) and service charge.*

Exploring Normandy

You won't want to miss medieval Rouen, seaside Deauville, or magnificent Mont-St-Michel. But get away from these popular spots and you can lose yourself along the cliff-lined coast and in the green spaces inland, where the closest thing to a crowd is a farmer with his herd of brown-and-white cows. From Rouen northeast to the coast—the area known as Upper Normandy—medieval castles and abbeys stand guard above the rolling countryside, while resort and fishing towns line the white cliffs of the Côte d'Alabâtre. Popular seaside resorts and the D-Day landing sites occupy the sandy beaches along the Côte Fleurie, and apple orchards and dairy farms cover the countryside in the area known as Lower Normandy. The Cotentin Peninsula to the west juts out into the English Channel. Central Normandy encompasses the peacefully rural, hilly region of La Suisse Normande, along the scenic Orne River.

Numbers in the text correspond to numbers in the margin and on the Normandy, Rouen maps.

Great Itineraries

Without spending too much time in any one place, you can see most of Normandy in about nine days, from the best known spots along the coast to the smaller, rural towns inland. Five days will give you time to meander through the countryside and down the coast. In three days you can just get a feel for the region.

IF YOU HAVE 3 DAYS

Head straight to **Rouen** ②–⑪ and spend a day and a half in the region's cultural capital, then go to **Honfleur** ⑰, the fishing port that caught the Impressionists' eye.

IF YOU HAVE 5 DAYS

Follow the Seine as it snakes through the gentle rolling countryside, on your way from Paris to Rouen. Stop at the formidable fortress at **Les Andelys** ① before going to **Rouen** ②–⑪ for a night and a day. On the third day continue along the Seine Valley on the Route des Abbayes to the abbeys at **Jumièges** ⑫ and **St-Wandrille** ⑬. Cross the Pont de Normandie and spend the night in **Honfleur** ⑰. The next day travel along the Côte Fleurie to the fashionable resort towns of **Deauville-Trouville** ㉕, and **Cabourg** ㉗. By early afternoon try to reach **Caen** ㉘, site of some of World War II's fiercest fighting and home to William the Conqueror's fortress. Spend the night in **Bayeux** ㉙, famous for its medieval tapestry. On the fifth day explore the D-Day landing beaches, **Arromanches** ㉚ and Omaha Beach, then head southwest to **Coutances** ㉛, with its elegant cathedral, and **Granville** ㉜, an old harbor town. Reach the majestic abbey on a rock, **Mont-St-Michel** ㉝, before sundown.

IF YOU HAVE 9 DAYS

Follow the Seine en route from Paris to **Rouen** ②–⑪, with visits to **Les Andelys** ① and Louviers along the way. On the third day wind your way along the Route des Abbayes to the abbeys at **Jumièges** ⑫ and **St-Wandrille** ⑬. Drive north to the port of **Dieppe** ㉑ and stop briefly before heading down the Côte d'Albâtre to the fishing village of **Fécamp** ⑳, and the popular beach town, **Étretat** ⑲. Return south and cross the Pont de Normandie and spend the night in **Honfleur** ⑰. The next day travel along the Côte Fleurie to the seaside resorts, **Deauville-Trouville** ㉕ and **Cabourg** ㉗. Get to **Caen** ㉘ by mid-afternoon for a visit to the "men's" and "women's" abbeys. Stay in medieval **Bayeux** ㉙ overnight. Set aside a day for historic **Arromanches** ㉚ and Omaha Beach. On day seven ramble south through La Suisse Normande's rocky expanse of hills, passing through Thury-Harcourt and **Clécy** ㉞, on the Orne River. Stop for a picnic lunch at the Roche d'Oëtre, a rock with a spectacular view of the countryside. By late afternoon try to be in the spa town of **Bagnoles-de-l'Orne** ㉟. Then drive west, on day nine, to dramatic **Mont-St-Michel** ㉝.

When to Tour Normandy

July and August—when French families vacation—are the busiest months, but also the most activity-filled: Concerts are held every evening at Mont-St-Michel, and the region's most important horse races take place in Deauville in the second half of August. June 6, the anniversary of the Allied invasion, is the most popular time to visit the D-Day beaches. If you're trying to avoid crowds, your best bet is late spring and early autumn, when it is still fairly temperate. Some of the

Normandy

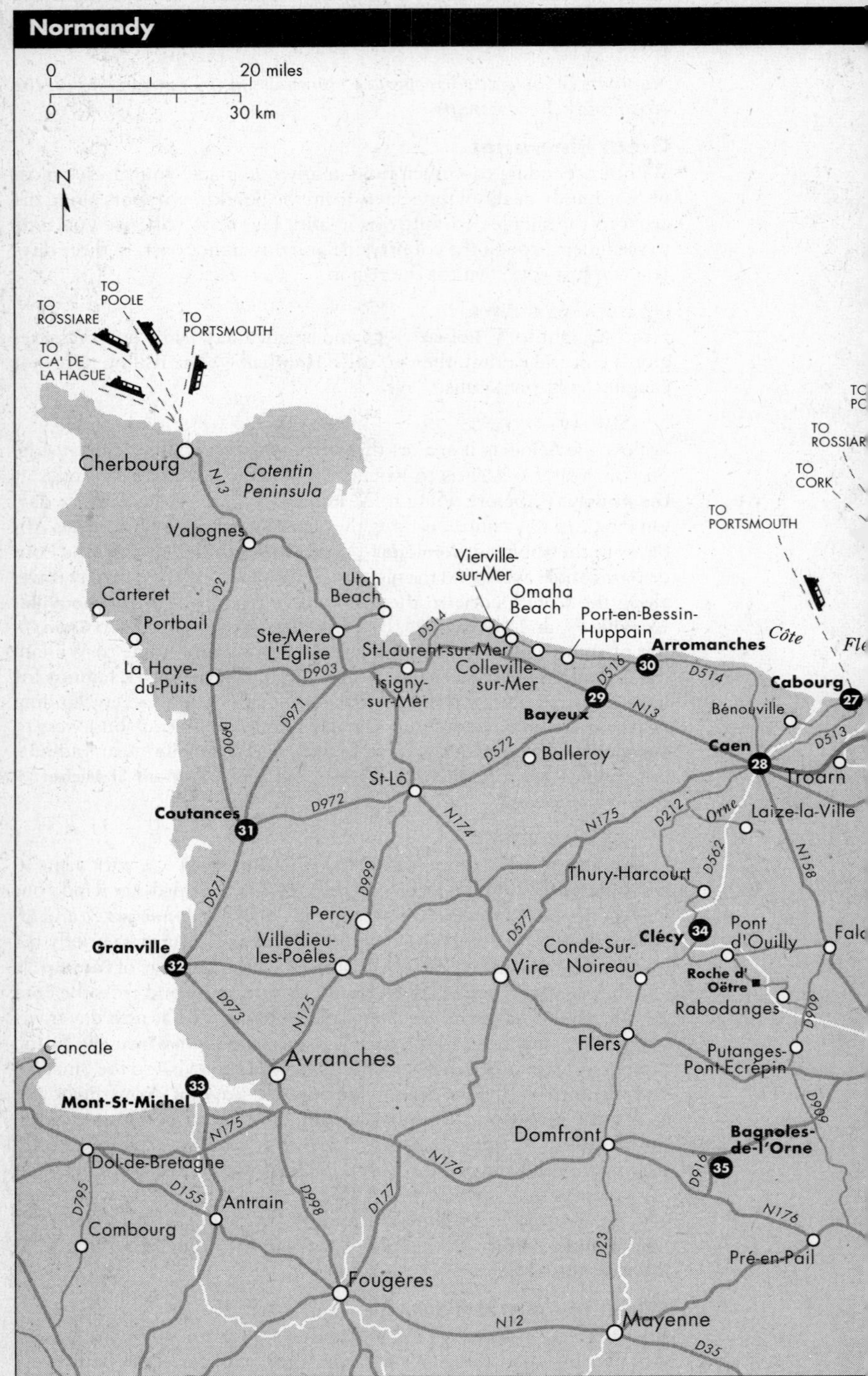
0 20 miles
0 30 km
N
TO POOLE
TO ROSSIARE
TO PORTSMOUTH
TO CA' DE LA HAGUE
Cherbourg
N13
Cotentin Peninsula
Valognes
D2
Carteret
Portbail
Utah Beach
Ste-Mere L'Église
La Haye-du-Puits
D903
D514
Vierville-sur-Mer
Omaha Beach
Port-en-Bessin-Huppain
St-Laurent-sur-Mer
Colleville-sur-Mer
Isigny-sur-Mer
Arromanches
Côte
Fle
D516
D514
TO PORTSMOUTH
TO CORK
TO ROSSIAR
Cabourg
27
30
29
Bayeux
N13
D971
D900
D572
Balleroy
Bénouville
Caen
28
D513
Troarn
St-Lô
Coutances
31
D972
N174
N175
D212
Orne
Laize-la-Ville
D562
N158
D999
Thury-Harcourt
D971
Percy
D577
Clécy
34
Pont d'Ouilly
Falc
Granville
32
Villedieu-les-Poêles
Vire
Conde-Sur-Noireau
Roche d' Oëtre
Rabodanges
D909
D973
N175
Flers
Putanges-Pont-Ecrepin
Cancale
Avranches
33
Mont-St-Michel
N175
Domfront
Bagnoles-de-l'Orne
35
D916
Dol-de-Bretagne
N176
D795
D155
Antrain
D998
D177
N176
Combourg
D23
Pré-en-Pail
Fougères
N12
Mayenne
D35

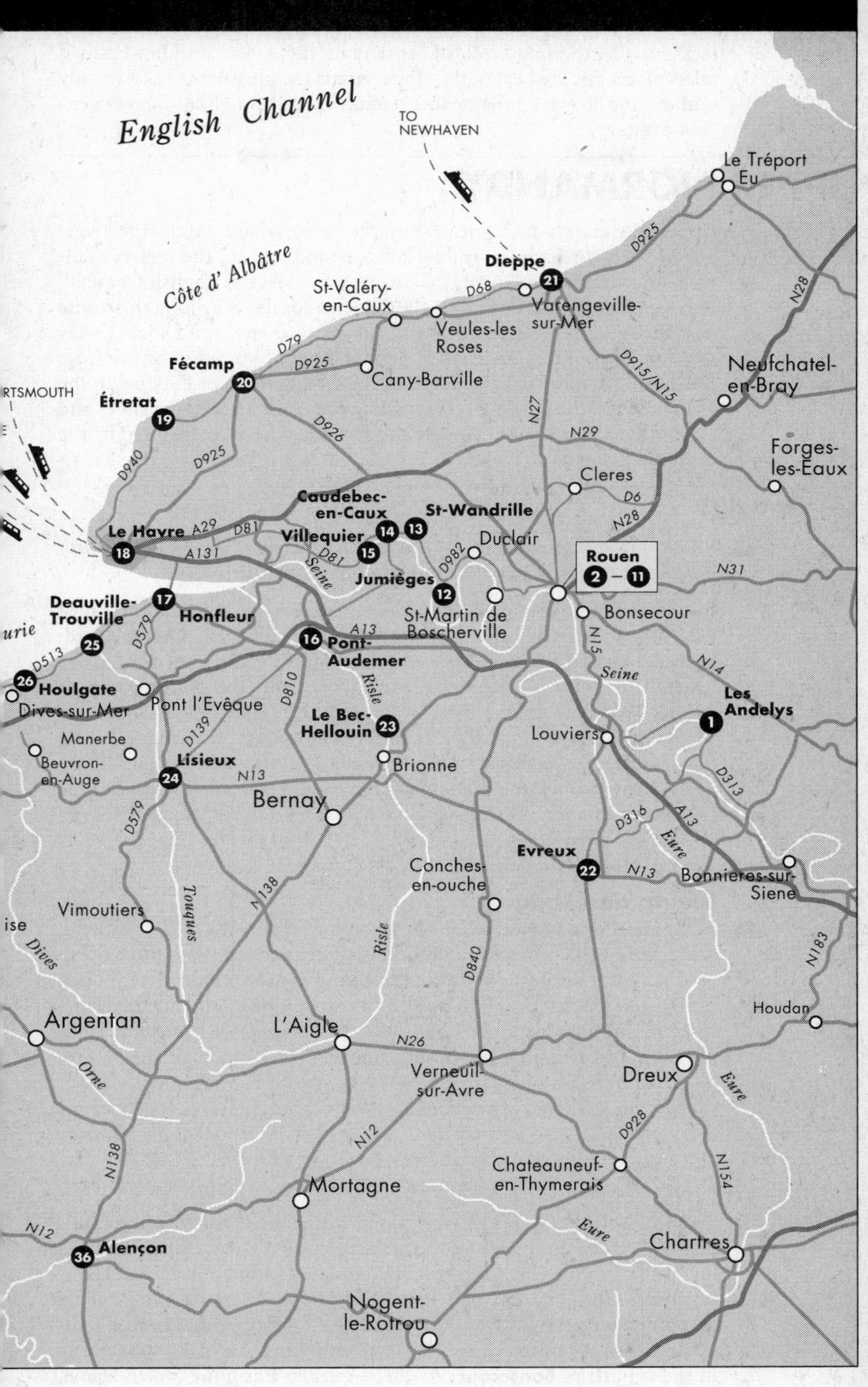
English Channel
TO NEWHAVEN
Côte d' Albâtre
Le Tréport
Eu
Dieppe
21
St-Valéry-en-Caux
Varengeville-sur-Mer
Veules-les Roses
Fécamp
20
Cany-Barville
Neufchatel-en-Bray
Étretat
19
Forges-les-Eaux
Cleres
Caudebec-en-Caux
St-Wandrille
Le Havre
18
Villequier
14
13
15
Duclair
Rouen
2 – 11
Jumièges
12
Deauville-Trouville
17
Honfleur
St-Martin de Boscherville
Bonsecour
25
16
Pont-Audemer
Seine
Risle
26
Houlgate
Dives-sur-Mer
Pont l'Evêque
Les Andelys
1
Le Bec-Hellouin
23
Louviers
Manerbe
Beuvron-en-Auge
Lisieux
24
Brionne
Bernay
Evreux
22
Bonnieres-sur-Siene
Conches-en-ouche
Vimoutiers
Tougues
Dives
Risle
Eure
Houdan
Argentan
L'Aigle
Verneuil-sur-Avre
Dreux
Orne
Chateauneuf-en-Thymerais
Mortagne
Chartres
Alençon
36
Nogent-le-Rotrou
A29
A131
A13
D81
D940
D925
D926
D79
D68
D925
D915/N15
N27
N29
N28
D6
N31
N15
N14
D982
D810
D139
D579
D513
N13
D313
D316
N138
D840
N26
N12
D928
N154
N183
N12
N138

biggest events of the region take place during these seasons: In Rouen, at the end of May, Joan of Arc is celebrated at a festival in her name; in Deauville, the first week of September, the American Film Festival takes place. For the hearty, the winter offers the pleasures of Normandy without the crowds (most places remain open throughout the year, except January).

UPPER NORMANDY

Upper Normandy is delineated by the Seine which winds northwest out of Paris through the rolling hills around Rouen, the region's cultural and commercial capital, on its way to meet the English Channel. Between Rouen and Le Havre, the Seine winds its way along the Route des Abbayes, past ancient abbeys and small towns, amid some lovely scenery. The impressive chalky cliffs and pebbly beaches of the Côte d'Albâtre stretch from Le Havre to the fishing town of Dieppe. In the 19th century, the bathing resorts along the coast attracted writers and artists like Maupassant, Monet, and Braque, who were inspired by the dramatic scenery.

Les Andelys

❶ *88 km (55 mi) northwest of Paris via N14 and D125; 24 km (15 mi) north of Vernon, 40 km (25 mi) southeast of Rouen.*

In one of the most picturesque loops of the Seine, the small town of Les Andelys is set against magnificent chalky cliffs. The **Château Gaillard,** a formidable fortress built by England's King Richard the Lionhearted in 1196, overlooks Les Andelys from the cliff tops, with spectacular views in both directions. Despite its solid defenses, the castle fell to the French in 1204. It suffered considerable damage during the assault, and sections were eventually torn down at the end of the 16th century; only one of its five main towers remains intact, but the location and the ruins bring alive a history long forgotten. ✉ *rue Richard-Coeur-de-Lion,* ☎ *02–32–54–41–93.* 🎫 *15 frs.* ⏲ *Thurs.–Mon. 10–noon and 2–5, Wed. 2–5.*

Dining and Lodging

$$$ ✕🏨 **Hostellerie St-Pierre.** This hotel on the Seine, west of Les Andelys, is the perfect place to stay in the countryside between Paris and Rouen. Room 27 has the best view of the river and French windows that open onto a terrace. Its size, like most others, is modest; all have comfortingly traditional decor. At dinner, sample the *rable de lapin farci* (saddle of rabbit) stuffed with mushrooms in a cider sauce, or the *boudin de poisson* (fish mousse) in beurre blanc. Desserts are generally good, though the *assiette tout chocolat* (all-chocolate plate) is less luscious than expected. ✉ *6 chemin de la Digue, 27430 St-Pierre-du-Vauvray (11 km/7 mi west of Les Andelys),* ☎ *02–32–59–93–29,* FAX *02–32–59–41–93. 14 rooms. Restaurant. MC, V. Closed mid-Nov.–mid-Mar.*

En Route From Andelys, take D313 west along the Seine, through rolling hills and lush green countryside, to the busy market town of **Louviers,** 22 km (14 mi) away. Give yourself an hour to see its old houses and Flamboyant Gothic church, then take N15 north, crossing the Pont de l'Arche, where the Eure and the Seine rivers merge; from here it's another 18 km (11 mi) to Rouen. Just before getting to Rouen, stop briefly in the suburb of **Bonsecours** to check out the **Basilique Notre-Dame,** a fine neo-Gothic church built in 1840 on a hilltop overlooking the Seine.

Rouen

★ *30 km (19 mi) north of Louviers, 40 km (25 mi) northwest of Les Andelys, 132 km (82 mi) northwest of Paris, 86 km (53 mi) east of Le Havre.*

Rouen has a surprising wealth of medieval buildings, despite the fact that a large part of the city was destroyed during World War II and subsequently rebuilt. But even before its massive reconstruction, Rouen had expanded with the development of industries spawned by its increasingly busy port, now the fifth largest in France. Cobblestone streets lined with ancient Norman buildings—like rue d'Amiette, a pedestrians-only street harboring restaurants and small shops—fan out from place St-Maclou, an attractive square surrounded by picturesque half-timber houses. In its more distant past, Rouen gained celebrity when Joan of Arc was burned at the stake here in 1431.

Rouen is known as the City of a Hundred Spires because many of its important edifices are churches. Lording over them all is the magnif-
❷ icent **Cathédrale Notre-Dame.** If you are familiar with the works of Impressionist Claude Monet, you will immediately recognize the cathedral's immense west facade, rendered in an increasingly hazy fashion in his series *Cathédrales de Rouen.* The original 12th-century construction was replaced after a terrible fire in 1200; only the left-hand spire, the **Tour St-Romain** (St. Romanus Tower), survived the flames. The imposing 250-foot steeple on the right, known as the **Tour de Beurre** (Butter Tower), was added in the 15th and 16th centuries and completed in the 17th, when a group of wealthy citizens donated large sums of money for the privilege of eating butter during Lent. Interior highlights include the 13th-century choir, with its pointed arcades; vibrant stained glass depicting the crucified Christ (restored after heavy damage during World War II); and massive stone columns topped by some intriguing carved faces. The first flight of the famous **Escalier de la Librairie** (Booksellers' Stairway), attributed to Guillaume Pontifs (also responsible for most of the 15th-century work seen in the cathedral), rises from a tiny balcony just to the left of the transept. ✉ *pl. de la Cathédrale,* ☎ *02–35–71–00–48.* ⏲ *Mon.–Sat. 8–7, Sun. 8–6.*

❸ The late-Gothic church of **St-Maclou,** across rue de République behind Cathédrale Notre-Dame, bears testimony to the wild excesses of Flamboyant architecture; take time to examine the central and left-hand portals on the main facade, covered with little bronze lion heads and pagan engravings. Inside, note the 16th-century organ, with its Renaissance wood carving, and the fine marble columns. ✉ *pl. St-Maclou,* ☎ *02–35–71–71–72.* ⏲ *Mon.–Sat. 10–noon and 2:30–6, Sun. 3–5:30.*

A former ossuary (a charnel house used for the bodies of plague vic-
❹ tims), the **Aître St-Maclou,** east of place St-Maclou, is one of the last reminders of the plague that devastated Europe during the Middle Ages; these days, it holds Rouen's School of Art and Architecture. French composer Camille Saint-Saëns (1835–1921) is said to have been inspired by the ossuary when he was working on his *Danse Macabre.* The building's massive double frieze is carved with some graphic skulls, bones, and grave-diggers' tools. ✉ *184 rue Martainville.*

❺ A fine example of late Gothic architecture is the **Abbaye St-Ouen** on the square at the end of rue de la République. The stained-glass windows, dating from the 14th to the 16th centuries, are the most spectacular features of the otherwise spare abbey. The church's 19th-century pipe organs have few equals in France. ✉ *pl. du Général-de-Gaulle,*

Abbaye St-Ouen, **5**
Aître St-Maclou, **4**
Cathédrale Notre-Dame, **2**
Église Jeanne d'Arc, **10**
Gros-Horloge, **11**
Musée le Secq des Tournelles, **8**
Musée de la Céramique, **9**
Musée des Beaux-Arts, **7**
St-Godard, **6**
St-Maclou, **3**

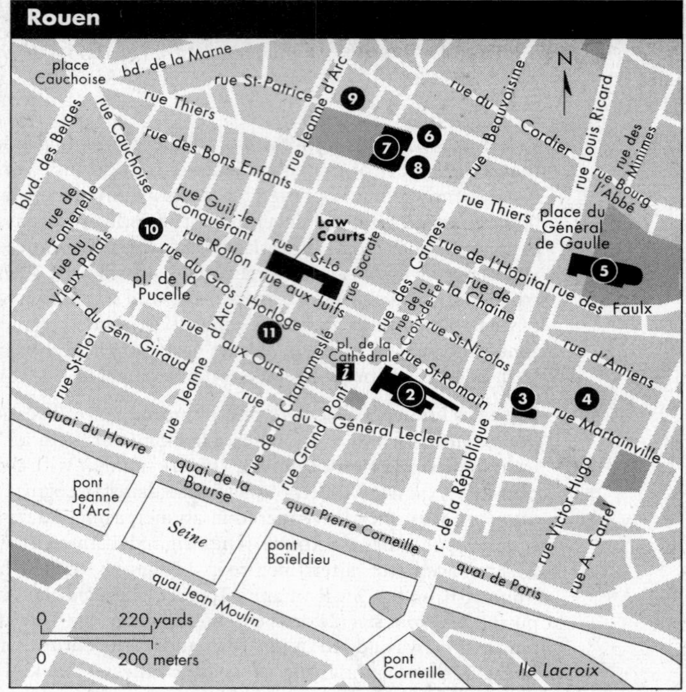

⏲ *Mid-Mar.–Oct., Wed.–Mon. 8–noon and 2–6; Nov.–mid-Dec. and mid-Jan.–mid-Mar., Wed., Sat., and Sun. 10–12:30 and 2–6.*

6 A painted wooden ceiling and fine medieval stained glass, especially the *Tree of Jesse* dating from 1506, distinguish the church of **St-Godard.** ✉ *pl. St-Godard,* ☎ *02–35–71–47–12.*

7 One of Rouen's cultural mainstays is the **Musée des Beaux-Arts** (Fine Arts Museum). It contains a good collection of French paintings from the 17th and 19th centuries, including works by Claude Monet, Alfred Sisley, Auguste Renoir, Eugène Delacroix, and Théodore Chassériau. An entire room is devoted to Rouen-born Théodore Géricault. ✉ *square Verdrel, off rue Thiers,* ☎ *02–35–71–28–40.* 🎫 *20 frs.* ⏲ *Wed.–Mon. 10–6.*

8 The **Musée le Secq des Tournelles** (Wrought Ironwork Museum), behind the Musée des Beaux-Arts, claims to possess the world's finest collection of wrought iron, with exhibits spanning the 3rd through the 19th century. Displays include a range of items used in daily life, accessories, and professional instruments used by surgeons, barbers, carpenters, clock makers, and gardeners. ✉ *square Verdrel,* ☎ *02–35–07–31–74.* 🎫 *13 frs.* ⏲ *Wed.–Mon. 10–1 and 2–6.*

9 A superb array of local faience is housed in the **Musée de la Céramique** (Ceramics Museum), down the road from the Musée des Beaux-Arts. ✉ *rue Faucon,* ☎ *02–35–07–31–74.* 🎫 *13 frs.* ⏲ *Wed.–Mon. 10–1 and 2–6.*

10 Dedicated to Joan of Arc, the modern **Église Jeanne d'Arc** (Joan of Arc Church), a few blocks from rue Thiers, just off rue Jeanne-d'Arc, was built on the spot where she was burned to death in 1431. Not all is spanking new, however: The church incorporates some remarkable 16th-century stained-glass windows taken from the former Église St-Vincent,

destroyed in 1944. ✉ *pl. du Vieux-Marché.* ⏲ *Daily 10–12:15 and 2–6, except Fri. and Sun. mornings.*

11 The name of the pedestrian rue du Gros-Horloge, Rouen's most popular street, comes from the **Gros-Horloge** itself, a giant Renaissance clock. In 1527 the Rouennais had a splendid arch built especially for it, and today its golden face looks out over the street. You can see the clock's inner workings from a 15th-century belfry. Though rue du Gros-Horloge is crammed with boutiques and fast-food joints, a few old houses, dating from the 16th century, remain. Wander through the surrounding old town, a warren of tiny streets lined with more than 700 half-timber houses, many artfully transformed into fashionable shops. ✉ *rue du Gros-Horloge.* 🎫 *Clock 10 frs.* ⏲ *Wed.–Mon. 10–1 and 2–6.*

OFF THE BEATEN PATH

PARC ZOOLOGIQUE DE CLÈRES – This wildlife park in the tiny village of Clères, 22 km (14 mi) north of Rouen via N15 and D155, is home to more than 750 species of birds, plus a motley assortment of free-roaming antelope, deer, kangaroos, and gibbons. ✉ *32 av. du Park, close to D155,* ☎ *02–35–33–23–08.* 🎫 *30 frs.* ⏲ *June–Aug., daily 9–sunset; Mar.–May and Sept.–Nov., daily 9–noon and 3:30–sunset.*

Dining and Lodging

$$$ ★ ✕ **Auberge de la Butte.** Chef Pierre Hervé is renowned for his subtle fish and seafood dishes, including poached oysters wrapped in spinach leaves and fricasseed fillet of sole. The magnificent Norman dining room has exposed beams and half-timber walls adorned with paintings and shining copper pots. This former 18th-century post house, in the suburb of Bonsecour, is well worth seeking out (you'll need a car). ✉ *69 rte. de Paris, Bonsecour (about 3 km/2 mi east of the city center),* ☎ *02–35–80–43–11. Jacket and tie. AE, DC, MC, V. Closed Sun., Mon., late Dec.–early Jan., and Aug.*

$$$ ✕ **La Couronne.** In a 15th-century Norman building, this restaurant is crammed with leather-upholstered chairs and a scattering of sculpture. The traditional Norman cuisine—crayfish salad with foie gras and caviar, duck with orange sauce—makes few modern concessions. ✉ *31 pl. du Vieux-Marché,* ☎ *02–35–71–66–66. Jacket and tie. AE, DC, MC, V.*

$$ ✕ **La Toque d'Or.** This large, bustling bistro next to the market and the Église Jeanne d'Arc has a helpful staff and a huge menu. Excellent specialties include oysters, mussels, and delicious tripe. ✉ *11 pl. du Vieux-Marché,* ☎ *02–35–71–46–29. AE, DC, V.*

$$ ✕🏨 **Hôtel de Dieppe.** Dating from the late 19th century, the Dieppe remains up-to-date thanks to the strong management of four generations of the same family. Staff members are helpful and speak English. The compact rooms are furnished in cheerful, modern style. Street noise can be a problem, though, despite double-glazed windows. The restaurant, Les Quatre Saisons, has a well-earned reputation and serves English-style roasts, as well traditional Norman dishes. ✉ *pl. Bernard-Tissot, 76000,* ☎ *02–35–71–96–00, 800/528–1324 U.S. reservations,* FAX *02–35–89–65–21. 42 rooms. Restaurant, breakfast room. AE, DC, MC, V.*

$$ 🏨 **Mercure Rouen-Centre.** In the jumble of streets near the cathedral—a navigational challenge if you arrive by car—this modern chain hotel has small, comfortable rooms, breezily furnished in pastels. Though not particularly appealing, the location makes this hotel ideal for touring the old streets of the city center; service, too, is efficient. ✉ *7 rue* *de la Croix-de-Fer, 76000,* ☏ *02–35–52–69–52,* FAX *02–35–89–41–46. 125 rooms. Bar. AE, DC, MC, V.*

$–$$ **Hôtel de la Cathédrale.** This hotel is in a medieval building on a narrow pedestrian street behind the cathedral. (Guests can sleep soundly, though: The cathedral bells do not boom out the hour at night.) Rooms are petite, but neat and comfortable. Breakfast is served in the beamed dining room. ✉ *12 rue St-Romain, 76000,* ☏ *02–35–71–57–95,* FAX *02–35–70–15–54. 25 rooms with bath or shower. Breakfast room, parking (fee). MC, V.*

Nightlife and the Arts

The **Fête Jeanne d'Arc** (Joan of Arc Festival) takes place on the Sunday nearest to May 30, with parades, street plays, concerts, and exhibitions. Evening **concerts** and organ recitals are held at St-Maclou in August and at St-Ouen throughout the year; get details from the Rouen Tourist Office (☞ Contacts and Resources *in* Normandy A to Z, *below*). Operas are staged at the **Théâtre des Arts** (☏ 02–35–71–41–36).

Jumièges

12 *24 km (15 mi) west of Rouen: head west on D982 through St-Martin de Boscherville, then turn off left on D143 to get to the Abbaye de Jumièges.*

★ Imposing ruins are all that is left of the once-mighty Benedictine **Abbaye de Jumièges,** founded in 654 by St-Philbert, plundered by Vikings in 841, then rebuilt by William Longswood, Duke of Normandy, around 940, though not consecrated until 1067. The French Revolution forced the evacuation of the remaining 16 monks, whereupon the abbey was auctioned off to a timber merchant, who promptly demolished part of the building to sell the stones. What remains is impressive enough. ✉ *24 rue Guillaume-le-Conquérant,* ☏ *02–35–37–24–02.* 🎫 *32 frs.* ⏲ *Daily 10–noon and 2–6 (until 4 Oct.–Mar.).*

St-Wandrille

13 *14 km (9 mi) north of the Abbaye de Jumièges on D982; 37 km (23 mi) northwest of Rouen.*

The Benedictine **Abbaye de St-Wandrille** is still active today. Founded in the 7th century, the abbey was sacked by the Normans, and rebuilt in the 10th century—although what you see today is an ensemble of styles from the 11th century through the early 18th (mainly the latter). You can hear the monks sing their Gregorian chants at morning Mass if you arrive early (9:25 AM weekdays and 10 AM Sunday and holidays). Be sure to visit the abbey shop down the hill. Everything it sells—from floor polish to spiritual aids—is monk-made. ☏ *02–35–96–23–11.* 🎫 *20 frs.* ⏲ *Guided tour at 3 and 4 weekdays, also 11:30 Sun.*

Caudebec-en-Caux

14 *5 km (3 mi) west of St-Wandrille, 38 km (24 mi) northwest of Rouen.*

The scenic village of Caudebec-en-Caux is a good spot for a walk along the river, maybe stopping for tea at one of the many sidewalk cafés. The village's elaborate 15th-century church was described by effusive French monarch Henri IV (1589–1610) as "the most beautiful chapel in the kingdom."

Villequier

15 *4 km (2 mi) west of Caudebec-en-Caux, 42 km (26 mi) west of Rouen.*

Villequier, another small village along the Seine, has a grim connection for fans of the 19th-century author Victor Hugo. His daughter, Léopoldine, and her husband, Charles Vacquerie, were drowned here in 1843 by the Seine's notorious seasonal tidal wave (these days held at bay by a dam). The **Musée Victor Hugo,** in the mansion where Léopoldine lived, includes the manuscript of Hugo's poem *Contemplations* lamenting her death. ✉ *quai Victor-Hugo,* ☎ *02–35–56–78–31.* *20 frs.* *Wed.–Mon. 10–12:30 and 2–5:30.*

Pont-Audemer

16 *33 km (21 mi) southwest of Caudebec-en-Caux, 50 km (31 mi) west of Rouen.*

Pont-Audemer, on the banks of the River Risle in the heart of calvados country, luckily escaped destruction by warfare and bulldozers. Today, many of its buildings are still as they were in the 16th century when the town made its mark as an important trading center. After taking in the colorful market square, be sure to stroll along impasse St-Ouen and impasse de l'Epée, narrow streets lined with timber-framed medieval houses. Also don't miss the church of **St-Ouen** with its pleasing modern stained-glass windows that blend with richly sculpted medieval stonework. ✉ *rue de la République,* ☎ *02–32–41–12–88.*

Dining and Lodging

$$$ ★ **Belle-Isle sur Risle.** It's hard not to feel like a guest in a private manor here—an impression somehow heightened by a few rough edges. The newer, more modern rooms have wall-to-wall carpeting and department store furniture, but the older ones have rugs on wood floors and assorted traditional furniture gleaned from auctions. Rooms on the first floor have balconies. In the restaurant, young chef Laurent Matuit turns out tasty foie gras blinis, *coquilles St-Jacques* (scallops) with a coulis (thick sauce) of mushrooms, and light pastry tarts with honeyed apples and sorbet. ✉ *112 rte. de Rouen, 27500,* ☎ *02–32–56–96–22,* FAX *02–32–42–88–96. 15 rooms, 4 suites. Restaurant, pool, sauna, tennis court. MC, V.*

$$–$$$ **Auberge du Vieux Puits.** Gustave Flaubert, an early admirer of this hotel in a trellised and beamed cottage, gave it a few lines in his notorious novel *Madame Bovary.* The quiet rooms, furnished with heavy wooden pieces and pretty curtains, overlook the courtyard. The restaurant serves first-rate, rich, innovative Norman cuisine—trout in champagne sauce, calvados sherbet, duckling stew with sour cherries, local cheeses, and fresh fruit tarts. It is closed Monday and Tuesday dinner off-season. Since the inn is primarily a restaurant, you are expected to dine here when you stay overnight. ✉ *6 rue Notre-Dame-du-Pré, 27500,* ☎ *02–32–41–01–48,* FAX *02–32–42–37–28. 7 rooms, 5 with shower. Restaurant. MC, V. Closed mid-Dec.–late Jan.*

$$$ **Le Petit Coq aux Champs.** Rooms at this small luxury hotel in a Norman-style, thatch-roof farmhouse are not large, but they have balconies. No. 39 has two especially comfortable beds, a porthole window, and a good-size bathroom. Though the food isn't particularly exciting, the beamed dining room is cozy and full of antiques. (Meals are not mandatory.) Madame speaks excellent English. ✉ *L'Andrien, 27500 Campigny (take D810 and D29 from Pont-Audemer),* ☎ *02–32–41–*

04–19, FAX *02–32–56–06–25. 12 rooms. Restaurant, pool. AE, DC, MC, V. Closed Jan.*

Honfleur

★ 17 *24 km (15 mi) northwest of Pont-Audemer via N175 and D80; 80 km (50 mi) west of Rouen.*

The colorful port of Honfleur on the Seine estuary has become increasingly crowded since the Pont de Normandie suspension bridge—providing a direct link with Le Havre and Upper Normandy—opened in 1995. The town, full of half-timber houses and cobbled streets, was once an important departure point for maritime expeditions, including the first voyages to Canada in the 15th and 16th centuries. The 17th-century harbor is fronted on one side by two-story stone houses with low, sloping roofs and on the other by tall, narrow houses whose wooden facades are topped by slate roofs.

Soak up the seafaring atmosphere by strolling around the old harbor and paying a visit to the wooden church of **Ste-Catherine** which dominates the harbor's northern corner. It was built by townspeople to show their gratitude for the departure of the English at the end of the Hundred Years' War (1453). ✉ *rue des Logettes,* ☎ *02–31–89–11–83.*

Dining and Lodging

$$$ ✕ **L'Absinthe.** A 17th-century dining room, with stone walls and beamed ceilings, is the magnificent setting for Antoine Ceffrey's masterly seafood and fish creations, such as *barbet* (freshwater cod) prepared with ginger. On sunny days you'll probably want to eat on the sunny terrace. ✉ *10 quai de la Quarantaine,* ☎ *02–31–89–39–00. Jacket and tie. AE, DC, MC, V. Closed 2nd ½ Nov. No dinner Mon.*

$$–$$$ ★ ✕ **L'Assiette Gourmande.** This is one of Honfleur's unsung top restaurants. On the seasonal menu, you might find chef Gérard Bonnefoy's superb coquilles St-Jacques grilled with sautéed asparagus in a raspberry vinaigrette and orange sauce, huge, succulent *noix de St-Jacques* (scallops with hazelnut risotto), or roast lamb from the salt marshes. ✉ *2 quai des Passagers,* ☎ *02–31–89–24–88. Closed Tues. No dinner Mon. off-season.*

$$ ✕ **L'Ancrage.** Massive seafood platters top the bill at this delightful old restaurant that occupies a two-story 17th-century building overlooking the harbor. The cuisine is authentically Norman—simple but good. If you want a change, try the succulent calf sweetbreads. ✉ *12 rue Montpensier,* ☎ *02–31–89–00–70. Reservations essential. MC, V. Closed Wed. and Jan. No dinner Tues.*

$$ ✕ **La Terrasse de l'Assiette.** This restaurant near Ste-Catherine has an excellent prix-fixe menu. The oysters, marinated salmon and haddock, and grilled tuna with tart lemon sauce are uniformly satisfying. The wine list is limited but well priced. ✉ *8 pl. Ste-Catherine,* ☎ *02–31–89–31–33. AE, MC, V. Closed Dec. No dinner Tues. or Sun.*

$$$$ **Ferme St-Siméon.** This 19th-century manor house likes to claim it was the birthplace of Impressionism; its park is said to have inspired Claude Monet and Alfred Sisley. Rooms are decorated in a style that attempts to be opulent: pastel colors and floral wallpaper, antiques and period decor. Those in the converted stables are quieter, but have less character. Be aware, however, that the high prices have more to do with the hotel's reputation than with what it offers. The sophisticated restaurant specializes in fish; the cheese board does justice to the region. ✉ *rue Adolphe-Marais, on D513 to Trouville, 14600,* ☎ *02–31–89–23–61,* FAX *02–31–89–48–48. 22 rooms, 16 suites. Restaurant, pool, tennis court. MC, V.*

$$ ★ **Cheval Blanc.** Alain Petit, the owner of this friendly inn, is a humorous and helpful Frenchman who speaks English excellently. Rooms have fine views of the port; No. 34 is slightly larger, better furnished, and more expensive than the rest, with a small couch, a queen-size bed, gabled ceilings, and a tub with whirlpool-style nozzles. ✉ *2 quai des Passagers, 14600,* ☎ *02–31–81–65–00,* FAX *02–31–89–52–80. 35 rooms, 14 with bath. Breakfast room. MC, V. Closed Jan.*

$$ **Hostellerie Lechat.** This typical 18th-century Norman building stands in a pretty square just behind the harbor. The well-maintained, spacious rooms are filled with French provincial prints—ask for one with a view of Ste-Catherine. Hearty, Norman cuisine is served in the rustic, beamed restaurant, which is closed in January. ✉ *3 pl. Ste-Catherine, 14600,* ☎ *02–31–89–23–85,* FAX *02–31–89–28–61. 23 rooms, 1 suite. Restaurant, bar. AE, DC, MC, V.*

Nightlife and the Arts

The two-day **Fête des Marins** (Marine Festival), including a fishermens' pilgrimage that started in 1861, is held on Pentecost Sunday and Monday. On the Sunday, all the boats in the harbor are decked out in flags and paper roses, and a priest bestows his blessing at high tide. The next day, model boats and local children head a musical procession.

En Route Three kilometers (2 miles) east of Honfleur, you'll see the turnoff to the elegant **Pont de Normandie,** a suspension bridge (toll 32 francs) that crosses the Seine. This is the world's largest cable-stayed bridge, supported by two concrete pylons taller than the Eiffel Tower, and is designed to resist winds of 160 mph. To reach Le Havre, continue west for 16 km (10 mi) on A131.

Le Havre

18 *23 km (14 mi) northwest of Honfleur via the Pont de Normandie; 88 km (55 mi) west of Rouen.*

Le Havre, France's second-largest port (after Marseilles), was bombarded no fewer than 146 times during World War II. Some will find the rebuilt city, with its uncompromising recourse to reinforced concrete and open spaces, bleak and uninviting; others will admire its rational planning and audacious modern architecture. The hilly suburb of Ste-Adresse just to the west, resplendent with its Belle Epoque villas and an old fortress, is also worth a visit for its beach and the fine views of the sea and port.

The **Musée André-Malraux,** the city art museum, is an innovative 1960s building surrounded by a moat. From the outside, this metal-and-glass structure looks in need of repair; inside, however, its spacious, airy design lets daylight flood in. Two local artists are showcased here—Raoul Dufy (1877–1953), with a remarkable collection of his brightly colored oils, watercolors, and sketches on the ground floor; and, upstairs, Eugène Boudin (1824–98), a forerunner of Impressionism, whose compelling beach scenes and landscapes tellingly evoke the Normandy coast and skyline. ✉ *23 bd. Clemenceau,* ☎ *02–35–42–33–97.* *Free.* ⏲ *Wed.–Mon. 10–noon and 2–6.*

★ Perhaps the outstanding postwar building in Le Havre, and one of the most impressive 20th-century churches in France, is the church of **St-Joseph,** built to the plans of Auguste Perret from 1951 to 1957. The 350-foot tower powers into the sky like a fat rocket. The inside is thrilling. No frills here: The 270-foot octagonal lantern towers over the crossing, filled almost to the top with abstract stained glass that hurls colored light over the bare concrete walls. ✉ *bd. François Ier,* ☎ *02–35–42–20–03.*

Lodging

$$ 🏨 **Bordeaux.** The location of this hotel, just one block from the central square, is its main plus—along with its welcoming owners. Like all hotels in Le Havre, prices are high for room size. The small bathrooms have hand-held showers in the tubs. ✉ *147 rue Louis-Brindeau, 76600,* ☎ *02–35–22–69–44,* FAX *02–35–42–09–27. 31 rooms with bath or shower. Parking (fee). MC, V.*

Étretat

★ 19 *28 km (17 mi) north of Le Havre via D940; 88 km (55 mi) northwest of Rouen.*

Although the promenade running the length of the town's pebble beach has been marred by a proliferation of seedy cafés and french-fry stands, this town is justly famous for the magnificent tall rock formations that extend out into the sea. The **Falaises d'Étretat** are white cliffs that are as famous in France as Dover's are in England. At low tide, it is possible to walk through the huge archways formed by the rocks to neighboring beaches. The biggest arch is at the **Falaise d'Aval,** to the south. For a breathtaking view of the whole bay, take the path up to the Falaise d'Aval, from which you can hike for miles across the Manneporte hills . . . or play a round of golf on one of Europe's windiest, and most scenic, courses. Farther south is the appropriately named **Aiguille** (needle), a 300-foot spire of rock jutting into the air just off the coast. To the north towers the **Falaise d'Amont.**

Dining and Lodging

$$ ✕ **Roches Blanches.** The exterior of this family-owned restaurant off the beach is a concrete post–World War II eyesore. But take a table by the window with a view of the cliffs, order the superbly fresh seafood (try the mussels), and you'll be glad you came. ✉ *rue Abbé-Cochet,* ☎ *02–35–27–07–34. Reservations essential Sun. lunch. MC, V. Closed Tues., Wed., Thurs. (Wed. only July–early Sept.), Jan. and Oct.*

$$–$$$ ★ 🏨 **Donjon.** This endearing little château has lovely bay views from a park overlooking town. Rooms, individually furnished with flair, are huge, comfortable, and quiet. Prix-fixe menus and reliable French cuisine—scallops and a seafood platter with lobster—are served in the cozy restaurant. ✉ *chemin de St-Clair, 76790,* ☎ *02–35–27–08–23,* FAX *02–35–29–92–24. 8 rooms, 6 with bath. Restaurant, pool. AE, DC, MC, V.*

Outdoor Activities and Sports

Golfers won't want to miss the chance to play the breathtaking course at the **Golf d'Étretat** (✉ rte. du Havre, ☎ 02–35–27–04–89), 6,072 meters (19,921 feet) long (par 72) across the cliff tops of the Falaise d'Aval; it's closed Tuesday.

Fécamp

20 *17 km (11 mi) northeast of Étretat via D940; 42 km (26 mi) northeast of Le Havre.*

An ancient fishing port on the Côte d'Alabâtre, Fécamp no longer has a commercial fishing fleet, but you can still see lots of boats in the private marina. Before Mont-St-Michel stole the limelight, the town was Normandy's primary place of pilgrimage. The magnificent abbey-church, the **Église de La Trinité** bears witness to Fécamp's religious past. The Benedictine abbey was founded by the Duke of Normandy in the 11th century and became the home of the monastic order of the Précieux Sang et de la Trinité (referring to Christ's blood which supposedly arrived here in the 7th century). ✉ *rue Leroux.*

Fécamp is also the home of the liqueur, Benedictine. The **Palais de la Bénédictine** (Benedictine Palace), seven blocks from La Trinité and across from the tourist office, is housed in a building dating from 1892. A florid mixture of neo-Gothic and Renaissance styles, it's one of Normandy's most popular attractions. You can drop in for a sample—at 12 francs a shot—or browse through the shop selling Benedictine products and souvenirs. ✉ *110 rue Alexandre-le-Grand,* ☎ *02–35–10–26–10.* *27 frs (including tasting).* ⏲ *Easter–mid-Nov., daily 9:30–noon and 2–6; mid-Nov.–Easter, daily 10–1:30 and 3:30–4:30.*

Dining and Lodging

$ ✕ **L'Escalier.** This delightfully simple little restaurant overlooking the harbor serves traditional Norman cuisine. The prix-fixe menus, beginning at 60 francs, consist mainly of fish and seafood dishes. ✉ *101 quai Bérigny,* ☎ *02–35–28–26–79. Reservations essential in summer. DC, MC, V. Closed Mon. and 2 wks in Nov.*

$$$ ✕ **Les Hêtres.** One of the most fashionable chefs in Normandy, Bertrand Warin, runs this restaurant in Ingouville, east of Fécamp. In the elegant dining room, half-timber walls and Louis XIII chairs contrast with sleek, modern furnishings. Large windows look out onto the garden. The restaurant is closed Sunday dinner and Monday; reservations are essential and a jacket and tie are required. There are also four pretty rooms for diners (only) who want to stay the night; they have old wooden furniture and are decorated with engravings. The largest has its own terrace looking onto the garden. ✉ *rue de Fleur, Ingouville, 76460 (28 km/17 mi east of Fécamp),* ☎ *02–35–57–09–30,* FAX *02–35–57–09–31. 4 rooms. Restaurant. MC, V. Closed 1st ½ of Jan., last 2 wks in Aug.*

$$ ★ ✕ **Auberge de la Rouge.** This small auberge is in a little hamlet just south of Fécamp. The menu features a mix of classic and modern dishes, including local specialties; the lobster is good, but the coquilles St-Jacques with herbs and the wild pressed duck are the true temptations. The restaurant is closed Sunday dinner and Monday. Rooms are simply decorated and moderately priced and have modern amenities (TVs). Meals are not mandatory if you stay overnight. ✉ *1 rue du Bois-de-Bocion, St-Léonard, 76400 (1 km/½ mi south of Fécamp),* ☎ *02–35–28–07–59,* FAX *02–35–28–70–55. 8 rooms. Restaurant, minibars. AE, DC, MC, V.*

En Route From Fécamp, take the scenic coastal road (D79), via the quaint harbor of St-Valery-en-Caux. Before you reach Dieppe, look for the tiny hilltop church in **Varengeville-sur-Mer;** the 20th-century painter Georges Braque (1882–1963)—who, with Picasso, is credited with inventing Cubism—is buried in its graveyard. Nearby, visit the **Parc Floral des Moustiers** (Moustiers Flower Park) to admire the colorful collection of rare flowers and giant 100-year-old rhododendrons. ✉ *La Haie des Moustiers,* ☎ *02–35–85–10–02.* *40 frs.* ⏲ *Daily 10–noon and 2–6. Closed Nov.–Mar.*

Dieppe

21 *11 km (7 mi) east of Varengeville-sur-Mer via D75; 64 km (40 mi) northeast of Fécamp; 64 km (40 mi) north of Rouen.*

Bustling Dieppe is part fishing and commercial port, part Norman seaside town, though its days in the fashionable spotlight are past and its hotels have seen better days. It is now mostly a transit stop for the ferries that run from Dieppe three times a day across the Channel to Newhaven, near Brighton. The seafront promenade, boulevard du Maréchal-Foch, separates an immense lawn from an unspoiled pebble beach where, in 1942, many Canadian soldiers were killed during the so-called Jubilee Raid. The town castle surveys the scene from the cliff top.

The 15th-century **Château,** overlooking the Channel at the western end of the bay, contains a museum, well-known for its collection of ivories. In the 17th century, Dieppe imported vast quantities of elephant tusks from Africa and Asia, and as many as 350 craftsmen settled here to work the ivory; their efforts can be seen in the form of ship models, nautical accessories, religious artifacts, and day-to-day objects. The museum also has a room devoted to sketches by Georges Braque. ✉ *square du Canada,* ☎ *02–35–84–19–76.* *13 frs.* ⏲ *Mid-Sept.–mid-June, Wed.–Mon. 10–noon and 2–5 (until 6 Sun.).*

Dining and Lodging

$$ ✕▣ **Windsor.** Of the hotels facing the sea, the Windsor is currently the best kept, with modern rooms, functional furniture, and reasonably sized bathrooms. Request a room with a sea view. The restaurant on the second floor is popular for its panoramic view of the Channel. ✉ *18 bd. de Verdun, 76200,* ☎ *02–35–84–15–23,* FAX *02–35–84–15–23. 50 rooms, 45 with bath or shower. Restaurant. AE, DC, MC, V. Closed Jan.*

Nightlife and the Arts

At night, the **casino** at the Grand Hotel (✉ 3 bd. de Verdun, ☎ 02–35–82–33–60) comes alive with shows and gambling.

Jazz aficionados can enjoy the **Festival Européen de Jazz Traditionnel** (European Traditional Jazz Festival) held in mid-June at Luneray, 8 km (5 mi) southwest of Dieppe. For information, contact the tourist office (☞ Contacts and Resources *in* Normandy A to Z, *below*).

Outdoor Activities and Sports

Bikes can be rented from Dieppe's train station for 44–55 francs a day; the flat terrain around the city is great for biking. For information on routes, check with the tourist office (☞ Contacts and Resources *in* Normandy A to Z, *below*).

LOWER NORMANDY

Lower Normandy encompasses the sandy Côte Fleurie (Flower Coast), stretching from the resorts of Trouville and Deauville to the D-Day landing site of Omaha Beach. Lush green meadows and apple orchards cover the countryside from west of the market town of Lisieux—the heart of calvados country. Some of the fiercest fighting after the World War II D-Day landings took place around Caen and Bayeux, as many monuments and memorials testify. To the south, in the prosperous Pays d'Auge, dairy farms produce the region's famous cheeses. Rising to the west is the fabled Mont-St-Michel.

Évreux

22 *102 km (63 mi) northwest of Paris via A13 and N13; 50 km (31 mi) south of Rouen via N15 and N154.*

From the 5th century on, Évreux, capital of the Eure *département* (administrative region), was ravaged and burnt by a succession of armies—first the Vandals, then the Normans, the English, and various French kings. World War II played its part as well. But the town has been restored and is now embellished by gardens and calm overgrown footpaths.

Évreux's principal historic site is the **Cathédrale Notre-Dame,** in the heart of town just off rue Corbeau. Unfortunately, it was an easy victim of the many fires and raids that took place over the centuries; all that's left of the original 12th-century construction are the nave arcades. The lower parts of the chancel date from 1260, the chapels from the 14th century. Yet it's an outstanding example of Flamboyant Gothic inside and out. Don't miss the choir triforium and transept, the 14th-century stained-glass windows in the apse, or the entrance to the fourth chapel. ✉ *pl. Notre-Dame,* ☎ *02–32–33–06–57.*

Le Bec-Hellouin

23 *46 km (29 mi) northwest of Évreux via N13 and D130; 39 km (24 mi) southwest of Rouen.*

Le Bec-Hellouin is centered around its abbey. Dating from 1034 when the knight Herluin exchanged his charger for a donkey and took up the simple life, the **Abbaye du Bec-Hellouin** was demolished during the French Revolution and the monks driven out. Only the 15th-century **Tour St-Nicolas,** part of the south transept, and the bases of some of the 11th-century pillars remain, together with a 13th-century Gothic door and some statues from the 14th and 15th centuries. ✉ *Abbaye du Bec-Hellouin,* ☎ *02–32–44–86–09.* *25 frs.* *Guided tours only: June–Sept., Wed.–Mon. at 10, 11, 3, 4, 5; Sun. and holidays at 12:15, 3:30, 4, 6; Oct.–May, Wed.–Mon. at 11, 3:15, 4:30; Sun. and holidays at noon, 3, 4.*

Dining and Lodging

$$ ✕ **Auberge de l'Abbaye.** You can find fantastic, traditional Norman cooking at this rustic inn with a classic *colombage* facade (exposed timber in stucco walls). Inside, beamed ceilings and stone walls are hung with ornamental copper pans. The delightfully old-fashioned, small bedrooms are reserved for diners (though you don't have to stay to eat). This restaurant serves an exceptional apple tart. It's closed Monday dinner and Tuesday off-season. ✉ *pl. de l'Église, 27800,* ☎ *02–32–44–86–02,* FAX *02–32–46–32–23. 8 rooms with bath or shower. Restaurant. MC, V. Closed Jan.–Feb.*

Lisieux

24 *47 km (29 mi) west of Le Bec-Hellouin via D130, N138, and N13; 82 km (51 mi) southwest of Rouen.*

Lisieux is the main market town of the prosperous Pays d'Auge, an agricultural region famous for cheeses named after such towns as Camembert, Pont l'Évêque, and Livarot. It is also a land of apple orchards, used for the finest calvados. Although Lisieux emerged relatively unscathed from World War II, it has few historic monuments beyond the 12th- and 13th-century **Cathédrale St-Pierre.** (The tower to the left of the imposing facade is later than it looks—it's a rare example of 17th century neo-Gothic reconstruction.) ✉ *pl. François-Mitterand,* ☎ *02–31–62–09–82.*

The town's fame stems from Ste-Thérèse (1873–97), who came to Lisieux as a child, joined a convent at 15, and spent the last 10 years of her life as a Carmelite nun. Thérèse was canonized in 1925, and in 1954 the **Basilique Ste-Thérèse**—one of the world's largest 20th-century churches, with a huge dome and an interior of colored marble—was built in her honor. From the cathedral, walk up avenue Victor-Hugo and branch left onto avenue Jean-XXIII. A **son-et-lumière** show, running through 2,000 years of history, is presented at the basilica every evening (bar Sunday) at 9:45 from June to September. The **Procession de la Vierge** (Virgin's Procession) is held on August 15. The **Procession de la Fête Ste-Thérèse** takes place on the last Sunday in September. ✉ *av. Jean-XXIII,* ☎ *02–31–78–52–62.* *Son-et-lumière 35 frs.*

En Route Connoisseurs of apple brandy will be keen to explore the **Pays d'Auge** between Lisieux and Beuvron-sur-Auge, 27 km (17 mi) to the west. This is the heart of calvados country: You don't need a fixed itinerary, just follow your nose and the minor roads, keeping an eye out for local farmers selling calvados. From Beuvron, nearby A13 will speed you to Deauville, 40 km (25 mi) away, in about 25 minutes.

Deauville–Trouville

25 *29 km (17 mi) north of Lisieux via D579 and N177; 92 km (57 mi) west of Rouen.*

The twin seaside resorts of Deauville and Trouville are separated by the estuary of the River Touques, and joined by a bridge. While the two towns have distinctly different atmospheres, it's easy (and common) to shuttle between them.

Deauville is a chic watering hole for the French bourgeoisie and would-be fashionable personalities from farther afield, attracted by its racecourse, casino, marina and regattas, palaces and gardens, and, of course, its sandy beach. The **Promenade des Planches**—the boardwalk extending along the seafront and lined with deck chairs, bars, and striped cabanas—is the place for celebrity spotting. With high-price hotels, designer boutiques, and one of the smartest, gilt-edge casinos in Europe, Deauville's fashionable image attracts the wealthy throughout the year.

Although Trouville is now considered an overflow town for its more prestigious neighbor, it became one of France's first seaside resorts when Parisians began flocking here in the mid-19th century. In contrast to Deauville, Trouville is more of a family resort with few pretensions. If you'd like to see a typical French holiday spot rather than look for glamour, stay in Trouville. It, too, has a casino and boardwalk, a bustling fishing port, and a native population that makes it a livelier place out of season than Deauville.

Dining and Lodging

$$$$ **Normandy.** The fashionable and monied from Paris have been attracted to this hotel, with its traditional Norman facade and underground passage to the casino, since it opened in 1912. A luxurious sense of well-being pervades the chandeliers and columns of the public areas. Request a room with a sea view. Breakfast (96 francs) is served around the indoor pool. The gourmet restaurant, La Potinière, and the large dining room both serve mouthwatering variations on Norman cuisine. ✉ *38 rue Jean-Mermoz, 14800 Deauville,* ☎ *02–31–98–66–22, 800/223–5652 for U.S. reservations,* FAX *02–31–98–66–22. 271 rooms. 2 restaurants, pool, sauna. AE, DC, MC, V.*

$$$$ **Royal.** This gigantic five-star hotel, overlooking the sea and close to the casino, is more than a little self-important. Many of the rooms are decorated in traditional, warm colors, with dark wood cabinetry; ask for one facing the sea. Of the two restaurants, L'Étrier has the stronger emphasis on haute cuisine. ✉ *bd. Eugène-Cornuché, 14800 Deauville,* ☎ *02–31–98–66–33, 800/223–5652 for U.S. reserva-*

tions, FAX 02–31–98–66–34. 281 rooms. 2 restaurants, pool, sauna. AE, DC, MC, V. Closed mid-Nov.–early Mar.

$$–$$$ **Beach Hotel.** Although it lacks character, this hotel, one of the newer ones in town, is handy because of its location behind the casino. Print fabrics add color to the pristine white rooms; most rooms overlook the sea or the harbor. Public rooms are designed for the flow of guests who often arrive on package tours, so expect efficiency rather than personal service. ✉ *quai Albert I, 14360 Trouville,* ☎ *02–31–98–12–00,* FAX *02–31–87–30–29. 110 rooms. Restaurant, pool, meeting rooms. AE, DC, MC, V.*

$$ **Continental.** One of Deauville's oldest buildings is now this provincial hotel, four blocks from the sea and within easy walking distance of the town center and downtown Trouville. Rooms are small but simple, pristine, and reasonably priced for Deauville. Breakfast is served in your room. ✉ *1 rue Désiré-le-Hoc, 14800 Deauville,* ☎ *02–31–88–21–06,* FAX *02–31–98–93–67. 48 rooms with bath or shower. AE, DC, MC, V. Closed mid-Nov.–mid-Mar.*

$–$$ **Carmen.** This straightforward, unpretentious little hotel is around the corner from the casino and a block from the sea. Rooms range from plain and inexpensive to comfortable and moderate. The owners, the Bude family, are on hand to advise guests. ✉ *24 rue Carnot, 14360 Trouville,* ☎ *02–31–88–35–43,* FAX *02–31–88–08–03. 18 rooms. Restaurant. AE, DC, MC, V. Closed Jan.–mid-Feb., and 10 days in Oct.*

Nightlife and the Arts

Formal attire is required at Deauville's smart **casino** (✉ bd. Cornuché, ☎ 02–31–13–31–14). Trouville's **casino** is slightly less highbrow than Deauville's (✉ quai Albert I, ☎ 02–31–87–75–00). **Le Revoir** (✉ 14 bis rue Désiré-le-Hoc, Deauville) is the place for dancing. Night owls enjoy the smoky ambience of **Club Melody** (✉ 13 rue Albert-Fracasse, Deauville); it's open until 5 AM.

One of the biggest cultural events on the Norman calendar is the **American Film Festival,** held in Deauville during the first week of September.

Outdoor Activities and Sports

At the **Club Nautique de Deauville** (✉ quai de la Marine, ☎ 02–31–88–38–19), hiring the smallest boat (16 feet) costs just 100 francs, while a day on an 80-foot yacht will set you back about 500 francs per person. Small and large sailing boats may also be rented from the **Club Nautique de Trouville** (✉ Digue des Roches Noires, ☎ 02–31–88–13–59). Deauville becomes Europe's horse capital in August, when breeders jet in from around the world for its yearling auctions and the races at its two attractive **Hippodromes** (racetracks).

Houlgate

26 *14 km (9 mi) southwest of Deauville via D513; 27 km (17 mi) northeast of Caen.*

Cheerful Houlgate, bursting with wood-beamed, striped-brick Belle Epoque villas, is a personable alternative to its pricier neighbors Deauville and Cabourg. The setting is prettier, too, with the steep Falaise des Vaches Noires (Black Cow Cliff) providing a rocky backdrop to the town's enormous sandy beach.

Dining and Lodging

$–$$ ✕ **1900.** Don't be misled by the tacky glass veranda at the front: A wonderful dining room lurks behind, with Art Nouveau lamps and a fine, carved bar almost as old as the regiment of varied-size calvados bottles that parade across the top. Claire is the good-humored *patronne;*

her husband, Alain, is a deft cook with a penchant for fish and seafood. Service from the young trainees, impeccable in their black and white aprons, is discreet and helpful. You can stay the night here, too: Rooms in the modernized annex, 100 yards down the street, are preferable to the slightly dowdy ones in the main building. ✉ *17 rue des Bains, 14510,* ☎ *02–31–28–77–77,* FAX *02–31–28–08–07. 21 rooms, 14 with bath or shower. Restaurant. MC, V.*

En Route As you drive west along the seafront toward Cabourg, pause to visit the center of historic **Dives-sur-Mer,** with its oak-beamed medieval market-hall, rickety square, and chunky Gothic church.

Cabourg

27 *4 km (2 mi) west of Houlgate via D513; 25 km (16 mi) northeast of Caen.*

Cabourg still takes itself seriously and retains a certain frowsy 19th-century elegance. Its streets fan out from a central hub near the seafront where the casino and the Grand Hôtel are situated. Marcel Proust, the early 20th-century novelist, often vacationed here. One of the volumes in his epic *A La Recherche du Temps Perdu* (In Search of Lost Time) paints an evocative picture of life in the resort, named Balbec in the novel; Cabourg responded by naming its magnificent seafront promenade after him.

Lodging

$$$$ **Pullman Grand Hôtel.** This luxurious white-stucco hotel, on the seafront in the heart of town, is connected to the casino and has a lively piano bar in summer. Many rooms have balconies overlooking the sea; Proust used to stay in Room 147. In the restaurant, Le Balbec, you can dine on traditional French cuisine of a high standard but no great sophistication. ✉ *promenade Marcel-Proust, 14390,* ☎ *02–31–91–01–79,* FAX *02–31–24–03–20. 70 rooms. Restaurant, bar. AE, DC, MC, V.*

En Route Take the D514 west from Cabourg toward Caen then, after 13 km (8 mi), turn right to Bénouville across the **Pont Pegasus** (Pegasus Bridge) over the Canal de Caen. Early on June 6, 1944, the British 6th Airborne Division landed by glider and captured the bridge (named for the division's emblem, showing Bellerophon astride his winged horse Pegasus). This proved the first symbolic step toward the liberation of France from Nazi occupation. The original drawbridge—erected in 1935 but replaced by a replica for safety reasons in 1993—was moved 200 yards away in 1997.

Caen

24 km (15 mi) southwest of Cabourg, 120 km (75 mi) west of Rouen, 150 km (94 mi) north of Le Mans.

With its abbeys and castle, Caen, a busy commercial city and the capital of Lower Normandy, is very different from the coastal resorts. William of Normandy ruled from Caen in the 11th century before he conquered England. Nine hundred years later, the two-month Battle of Caen devastated the town in 1944. Much of the city burned in a fire that raged for 11 days, and the downtown area was almost entirely—yet tastefully—rebuilt after the war.

A good place to begin exploring Caen is the **Hôtel d'Escoville,** a stately mansion in the city center, built by a wealthy merchant Nicolas Le Valois d'Escoville in the 1530s. The building was badly damaged during the war but has since been restored; the austere facade conceals an elaborate inner courtyard, reflecting the Italian influence on early Renaissance Norman architecture. The city tourist office is housed here, and has excellent resources. ✉ *pl. St-Pierre,* ☎ *02–31–27–14–14.*

Across the square is the late Gothic church of **St-Pierre,** a riot of ornamental stonework. Looming on a mound ahead of the church is the **Château**—the ruins of William the Conqueror's fortress, built in 1060 and sensitively restored after the war. The castle gardens are a perfect spot for strolling, and the ramparts afford good views of the city. The citadel also contains two museums (☞ *below*) and the medieval **Chapelle St-Georges.**

The **Musée des Beaux-Arts,** within the castle's walls, built an airy new wing in 1994. It's a heavyweight among France's provincial fine art museums; its old master collection includes works by Poussin, Rembrandt, Titian, Tintoretto, van der Weyden, and Paolo Veronese. ✉ *Entrance by the castle gateway,* ☎ *02–31–85–28–63.* 🎫 *25 frs (free Wed.).* ⏲ *Wed.–Mon. 10–6.*

The **Musée de Normandie** (Normandy Museum), also within the castle precincts, is dedicated to regional arts, such as ceramics and sculpture, plus some local archaeological findings. ✉ *Entrance by the castle gateway,* ☎ *02–31–86–06–24.* 🎫 *10 frs (free Wed.).* ⏲ *Wed.–Mon. 10–12:30 and 1:30–6.*

★ Caen's finest church, of cathedral proportions, is part of the **Abbaye aux Hommes** (Men's Abbey), a monastery built by William the Conqueror. The abbey was begun in Romanesque style in 1066 and added to in the 18th century. Note the magnificent yet spare facade of the **St-Étienne** abbey church, whose spareness is enhanced by two 11th-century towers topped by octagonal spires. Inside, what had been William the Conqueror's tomb was destroyed by 16th-century Huguenots during the Wars of Religion. However, the choir still stands; it was the first to be built in Norman Gothic style, and many subsequent choirs were modeled after it. ✉ *pl. Louis-Guillouard,* ☎ *02–31–30–41–00.* 🎫 *Guided tours 10 frs.* ⏲ *Tours daily at 9:30, 11, 2:30, 4.*

The **Abbaye aux Dames** (Women's Abbey) was built by William the Conqueror's wife, Matilda, in 1062. Once a hospital, the abbey now contains the offices of the Regional Council and is not open to the public. But you can visit the squat **Église de la Trinité,** which is a good example of 11th-century Romanesque architecture, though its original spires were replaced by bulky balustrades in the early 18th century. The 11th-century crypt once held Matilda's tomb which was destroyed during the French Revolution. Note the intricate carvings on columns and arches in the chapel. ✉ *pl. Reine-Mathilde,* ☎ *02–31–06–98–98.* 🎫 *Free.* ⏲ *Guided tours daily at 2:30 and 4.*

A good introduction to the Normandy landings of 1944 is available at the stark modern **Mémorial.** At this museum, videos, photos, arms, paintings, and prints detail the Battle of Normandy and the French Liberation within a historical context, from the 1930s to the 1960s. Multimedia screens also depict D-Day and the Battle of Normandy. ✉ *esplanade Dwight-D.-Eisenhower,* ☎ *02–31–06–06–44.* 🎫 *65 frs.* ⏲ *Jan.–June and Sept.–Dec., daily 9–7; July–Aug., daily 9–9.*

Dining and Lodging

$$$ ★ ✕ **Bourride.** On one of Caen's oldest streets, near the castle, this restaurant is one of the region's best, hands-down. Chef Michel Bruneau's specialties include baked *St-Pierre* (whitefish) with green mango, and baby pigeon in a salted bean crust. The small dining room is typically Norman—stone walls, beamed ceilings, and a large fireplace. ✉ *15 rue* *du Vaugueux,* ☎ *02–31–93–50–76. Reservations essential. Jacket and tie. AE, DC, MC, V. Closed Sun., Mon., most of Jan., 2nd ½ of Aug.*

$$$ ✕🏨 **La Pommeraie.** Chef-owner José Aparicio's celebrated restaurant is found in a 17th-century former priory in the small village of Bénouville outside of Caen. The excellent fish and seafood come off without a hitch. Aperitifs and coffee are served in the garden. Diners can stay the night in the 11 expensive rooms (800 francs) in the adjoining hotel, Manoir d'Hastings. ✉ *18 av. de la Côte-de-Nacre, Bénouville (10 km/6 mi northeast of Caen),* ☎ *02–31–44–62–43,* FAX *02–31–44–76–18. Reservations essential. Jacket and tie. AE, DC, MC, V. Closed Sun. night and Mon.; also mid-Nov.–mid-Apr.*

$$–$$$ 🏨 **Relais des Gourmets.** The hotel's comfortable, pastel-color modern rooms are reasonably large, though they vary in size; those with showers cost less (450 francs) than the ones with full baths (580 francs). As icing on the cake, the restaurant is terrific; you can dine in the garden in summer. ✉ *15 rue de la Geôle, 14000,* ☎ *02–31–86–06–01,* FAX *02–31–39–06–00, 0181/541–0033 for U.K. reservations, 800/528–1234 for U.S. reservations. 32 rooms with bath or shower. Restaurant. AE, DC, MC, V.*

$$ 🏨 **Dauphin.** Although it's downtown, Le Dauphin is peaceful and quiet. The building is a former priory dating from the 12th century, but the smallish rooms are briskly modern. Those overlooking the street are soundproof; the ones in back have views of the serene garden courtyard. Service is friendly and efficient, both in the hotel and in the excellent, though rather expensive, restaurant. (The restaurant is closed Saturday.) ✉ *29 rue Gémare, 14000,* ☎ *02–31–86–22–26,* FAX *02–31–86–35–14. 21 rooms with bath or shower. Restaurant. AE, DC, MC, V.*

Shopping

A **marché au puce** (flea market) takes place on Friday morning on place St-Saveur and on Sunday morning on place Courtonne. In June, collectors and dealers flock to Caen's bric-a-brac and **antiques fair.**

Bayeux

29 *28 km (17 mi) northwest of Caen via N13.*

Bayeux, the first town to be liberated during the Battle of Normandy, is steeped in history—home to a Norman-Gothic cathedral, a museum dedicated to the Battle of Normandy, and the world's most celebrated piece of needlework: the Bayeux Tapestry. Bayeux's medieval atmosphere makes it a popular base, especially among British travelers, from which to make day trips to other Normandy hot spots; the tourist office (☞ Contacts and Resources *in* Normandy A to Z, *below*) can help plan sightseeing trips in the area.

★ Really a 225-foot-long embroidered scroll stitched in 1067, the Bayeux Tapestry, known here as the **Tapisserie de la Reine Mathilde,** depicts, in 58 separate scenes, the epic story of William of Normandy's conquest of England in 1066. The tapestry was probably commissioned from Saxon embroiderers by the count of Kent—who was also the bishop of Bayeux—to be displayed in his newly built cathedral, the Cathédrale Notre-Dame (☞ *below*). Despite its age, the tapestry is in remarkably good condition; the extremely detailed, often homey scenes provide an unequaled record of the clothes, weapons, ships, and lifestyles of the day. It's showcased in the **Musée de la Tapisserie** (Tapestry Museum), in an 18th-century building; for 5 francs, you can hire headphones and listen to an English commentary on the tapestry, scene by scene. ✉ *Cen-*

tre Guillaume le Conquérant, 13 bis rue de Nesmond, ☎ *02–31–92–05–48.* 🎫 *37 frs.* ⏲ *May–mid-Sept., daily 9–6:30; mid-Sept.–Apr., daily 9:30–12:30 and 2–6.*

The **Musée Baron-Gérard** contains a fine collection of Bayeux porcelain and lace, ceramics from Rouen, a marvelous collection of apothecary jars from the 17th and 18th centuries, and 16th- to 19th-century furniture and paintings. From the Tapestry Museum head up rue de Nesmond to rue Larchet, turning left into lovely place des Tribuneaux. ✉ *1 rue la Chaîne, pl. des Tribuneaux,* ☎ *02–31–92–14–21.* 🎫 *37 frs (joint ticket from Tapestry Museum).* ⏲ *June–mid-Sept., daily 9–7; mid-Sept.–May, 10–12:30 and 2–6. Closed 2 wks in Jan.*

Bayeux's mightiest edifice, the **Cathédrale Notre-Dame** is a harmonious mixture of Norman and Gothic architecture. Note the portal on the south side of the transept that depicts the assassination of English Archbishop Thomas à Becket in Canterbury Cathedral in 1170, following his opposition to King Henry II's attempts to control the church. ✉ *rue de Bienvenu,* ☎ *02–31–92–01–85.*

At the **Musée de la Bataille de Normandie** (Battle of Normandy Museum) detailed exhibits trace the story of the Battle of Normandy from June 7 to August 22, 1944. The ultramodern museum, sunk partly beneath the level of its surrounding lawns, contains an impressive array of war paraphernalia, including uniforms, weapons, equipment, 150 waxworks, and a film depicting scenes and tactics of the invasion. ✉ *bd. Général-Fabian-Ware,* ☎ *02–31–92–93–41.* 🎫 *30 frs.* ⏲ *May–mid-Sept., daily 9–6:30; mid-Sept.–Apr., daily 10–noon and 2–6.*

Dining and Lodging

$ ✕ **Amaryllis.** This small restaurant's prix-fixe menu doesn't skimp on the number of choices. The three-course dinner, with six choices per course, may include a half dozen oysters, fillet of sole with a cider-based sauce, and pastries for dessert. ✉ *32 rue St-Patrice,* ☎ *02–31–22–47–94. AE, DC, MC, V. Closed Mon., and mid-Dec.–mid-Jan.*

$$$$ ★ ✕🏨 **Château d'Audrieu.** The Hollywood version of a palatial château is fulfilled at this family-owned property. An avenue leads to an imposing, elegant 18th-century facade that sets the tone for what lies within—Old World opulence, with wall sconces, overstuffed chairs, and antiques. Rooms 50 and 51 have gabled ceilings with exposed-wood beams. The restaurant has an extensive wine list, and chef Alain Cornet keeps to a classical repertoire of dishes. The restaurant is closed Monday. ✉ *14250 Audrieu (15 km/9 mi from Bayeux off N13),* ☎ *02–31–80–21–52,* FAX *02–31–80–24–73. 30 rooms. Restaurant, bar, pool, helipad. MC, V. Closed Dec.–Feb.*

$$$–$$$$ ✕🏨 **Chenevière.** This hotel is in a 19th-century grand manor in parkland between Bayeux and the coast. Rooms have modern furnishings, with plain draperies on the floor-to-ceiling windows and flowered bedspreads. The restaurant lives up to its surroundings; Claude Esprabens's roasted scampi with sesame seeds and fresh chanterelles is delicious, as is the warm *escalope de foie gras de canard* (sliced duck liver) with raspberry sauce. Try one of the not-too-sweet desserts, like the goat cheese in puff pastry or the apple stuffed with Camembert. ✉ *Les Escures, 14520 Commes (9 km/5½ mi north of Bayeux via D6),* ☎ *02–31–21–47–96,* FAX *02–31–21–47–98. 19 rooms. Restaurant. AE, DC, MC, V.*

$$–$$$ ✕🏨 **Grand Hôtel du Luxembourg.** The Luxembourg, a Best Western affiliate, has small but adequate rooms; all but two face the courtyard garden. Off-season rates are only slightly higher than at the town's two-star hotels which makes this place a good choice in winter. It's also got one of the town's best restaurants, Les Quatre Saisons. The menu is seasonal; depending on the time of year, you might have a salmon *galette* (cake) or chicken roasted with cider. ✉ *25 rue des Bouchers, 14400,* ☎ *02–31–92–00–04, 800/528–1234 for U.S. reservations,* FAX *02–31–92–54–26. 19 rooms, 3 suites. Restaurant, bar, dance club. AE, DC, MC, V.*

$$ ✕🏨 **Lion d'Or.** The Lion d'Or is a handsome '30s creation in the center of town. Palm trees arch over the garden courtyard and flowers cascade from balcony window boxes. The comfortable rooms are decorated with pretty fabrics. In the chic, apricot-color restaurant, *andouille chaude Bovary*—perhaps Madame's own recipe for hot sausage—is served. ✉ *71 rue St-Jean, 14400,* ☎ *02–31–92–06–90,* FAX *02–31–22–15–64. 22 rooms. Restaurant. AE, DC, MC, V. Closed late Dec.–mid-Jan.*

$$ ★ 🏨 **Manoir du Carel.** Archives suggest that the Manoir du Carel, an ideal spot halfway between Bayeux and the Normandy beaches, was constructed as a fortified manor by an Englishman during the Hundred Years' War. Certainly the narrow slits serving as windows on the tower suggest a defensive stance. Current owner Jacques Aumond offers comfortable rooms with modern furnishings. The cottage on the grounds has a kitchen plus a fireplace which masks a brick oven where, prior to the revolution, villagers had their bread baked. The lounges have turn-of-the-century furniture and are perfect places for a glass of wine before going out to dinner. ✉ *Maisons, 14400 (5 km/3 mi northwest of Bayeaux),* ☎ *02–31–22–37–00,* FAX *02–31–21–57–00. 3 rooms, 1 cottage. Breakfast room.*

Outdoor Activities and Sports

Bicycles are rented at **Family Home** (✉ 39 rue du Général-Dais, ☎ 02–31–92–15–22) for around 50 francs a day. Ask the tourist office for trail information (☞ Contacts and Resources *in* Normandy A to Z, *below*).

The **Rassemblement International de Ballons** (International Balloon Festival, ☎ 02–31–21–62–19 for information) takes place in mid-June at the 17th-century château of Balleroy, 16 km (10 mi) southwest of Bayeux. Hot-air balloons fill the Normandy skies as a fair with dancing, acrobatics and horse-drawn carriages takes place on the château grounds.

Shopping

Handmade lace is a specialty of Bayeux. Although it's expensive, it's exceptional, particularly at the **Conservatoire de la Dentelle** (✉ Hôtel du Doyen, rue Leforestier, ☎ 02–31–92–73–80. ⏲ Daily 9–noon, 2–5).

Arromanches

30 *10 km (6 mi) northeast of Bayeux via D516; 31 km (19 mi) northwest of Caen.*

There's little point in visiting all five sites of the Normandy invasion, since not much remains to mark the furious fighting waged hereabouts. In the bay off of Arromanches, however, some elements of the floating harbor are still visible. Contemplate those seemingly insignificant hunks of concrete protruding from the water, and try to imagine the extraordinary technical feat involved in towing the two floating harbors across the Channel from England. (The other was moored at Omaha Beach but was destroyed on June 19, 1944, by a violent storm.)

The **Musée du Débarquement** (Normandy Landings Museum), on the seafront, has models, mock-ups, and photographs depicting Operation Overlord—the code name for the Invasion of Normandy. Five beachheads (dubbed Utah, Omaha, Gold, Juno, and Sword) were established along the coast to either side of Arromanches. Preparations started in mid-1943, and British shipyards worked furiously through the following winter and spring building two artificial harbors (called Mulberries), boats, and landing equipment. The British troops that landed on Sword, Juno, and Gold on June 6, 1944 quickly pushed inland and joined with parachute regiments that had been dropped behind the German lines. U.S. forces met with far tougher opposition on Omaha and Utah beaches, however, and it took them six days to secure their positions and meet the other Allied forces. From there, they pushed south and west, cutting off the Cotentin Peninsula on June 18 and taking Cherbourg on June 26. Meanwhile, British forces were encountering fierce resistance at Caen and did not take it until July 9; St-Lô was not liberated until July 19. ✉ *pl. du 6-Juin,* ☎ *02–31–22–34–31.* *32 frs.* ⏲ *May–Sept., daily 9–7; Oct.–Apr., daily 9:30–4:30.*

The D-Day Landing Beaches

Along with the nearby villages of St-Laurent-sur-Mer and Vierville-sur-Mer, **Omaha Beach,** 20 km (12 mi) west of Arromanches, saw some of the heaviest fighting during the D-Day invasions. Nearly 10,000 soldiers spearheading the Allied invasion lost their lives here. Most of the 4,659 American casualties on D-Day occurred here, and many of the fallen are buried at the moving **Cimetière du St-Laurent** (St-Laurent Cemetery) above the beach. Stroll around the beach and grassy tops of the dunes in St-Laurent-sur-Mer and you'll see sad remnants of the war—ruined bunkers, rows of trenches, the remains of barbed-wire defenses, and the **Monument du Débarquement** (Monument to the Normandy Landings). In Vierville-sur-Mer, the **Monument to the Members of the U.S. National Guard** who fought in both world wars stands just back from the beach.

From Vierville it is a 45-minute drive around the coast to **Utah Beach,** 48 km (30 mi) away. Unless you are an assiduous student of World War II—or keen to drive up to Cherbourg at the top of the Cotentin Peninsula, where ferries cross the Channel to England—head southwest from Omaha Beach to **Isigny-sur-Mer** (known for its small, tasty oysters), pass through Carentan, with its mighty octagonal church spire, and continue via D971 to Coutances.

Coutances

31 *66 km (41 mi) southwest of Omaha Beach, 64 km (40 mi) southwest of Bayeux via D572 and D972; 76 km (47 mi) south of Cherbourg.*

If you're interested in cathedral architecture, you'll want to stop off in ★ Coutances. Many consider the largely 13th-century **Cathédrale Notre-Dame,** with its famous octagonal lantern rising 135 feet above the nave, to be the most harmonious Gothic building in Normandy. On the outside, especially the facade, note the obsessive use of turrets, spires, slender shafts, and ultra-narrow pointed arches squeezed senseless in their architectural pursuit of vertical takeoff.

Lodging

$ **Moulin Girard.** If you have a hankering for English hospitality, cheerful conversation, and inexpensive accommodations, Roger and Jasmine Albon's inn is the place to head. The main house has three very small rooms and the Norman-style cottage has a two-bedroom suite—for 350 francs, including breakfast, it's ideal for a family or two couples. This is a great base for exploring the area. ✉ *Le Chefresne, 50410 Percy (26 km/16 mi southeast of Coutences; from Villedieu-les-Poêles, take a right on D98 as you enter Percy in the direction of Tessy-sur-Vire, then right on D452 for Le Chefresne),* ☎ FAX *02–33–61–62–06. 3 rooms, 1 suite. No credit cards.*

Granville

32 *30 km (19 mi) south of Coutances via D971; 107 km (67 mi) southwest of Caen.*

Proud locals like to call Granville the "Monaco of the North." It's perched on a rocky outcrop, and has a sea-water therapy center, and . . . the similarities end there. Free of casinos and sequins, Granville instead has a down-to-earth feel. Granite houses cluster around the church in the old town, while the harbor below is full of working boats. There are fine views of the English Channel from the ramparts; catamarans spurt over to Jersey daily in summer. If you drive a few miles down the coast, you'll find sandy beaches and a view of the distant Mont-St-Michel.

Nightlife and the Arts

The rambunctious **Carnaval de Granville** involves four days of parades and festivities, culminating each year on Shrove Tuesday. The **Grand Pardon des Corporations de la Mer,** a *pardon,* or religious festival, devoted to the sea, is celebrated on the last Sunday of July with a military parade, regatta, and platefuls of shellfish.

Outdoor Activities and Sports

Granville is a center for aquatic sports; inquire about sailboat jaunts at the **Centre Régional de Nautisme de Granville** (✉ Anse de Hérel, ☎ 02–33–50–18–95). **Lepesqueux Voile** (✉ 3 rue Clément-Desmaisons, ☎ 02–33–50–18–97) rents boats and yachts for cruising.

Shopping

It is said that every kitchen worth its salt in France buys its pans from **Villedieu-les-Poêles,** 28 km (18 mi) east of Granville. The town is famous for its copperware and shops line the main street, rue Carnot, but you can find smaller outlets, with better buys, on the parallel rue du Dr-Harvard. Tuesday is market day, so parking becomes a bit of a problem.

Mont-St-Michel

★ 33 *44 km (27 mi) south of Granville via D973, N175, and D43; 123 km (77 mi) southwest of Caen, 67 km (42 mi) north of Rennes.*

The dramatic silhouette of Mont-St-Michel against the horizon may well be your most lasting image of Normandy. The abbey's fascination stems not only from its rocky perch a few hundred yards off the coast (it's cut off from the mainland at high tide), but from its legendary origins and the sheer exploit of its construction. The abbey stands at the top of a 264-foot mound of rock; the granite used to build it was transported from the Isles of Chausey (just beyond Mont-St-Michel Bay) and Brittany and laboriously hauled up to the site.

Before you visit this awe-inspiring monument, be warned that the sea that separates the rock from the mainland is extremely dangerous: It's subject to tidal movements that produce a difference of up to 45 feet between low and high tides, and because of the extremely flat bay bed, the water rushes in at an incredible speed. Also, there are patches of quicksand, so walk carefully!

The abbey's construction took more than 500 years, from 1017 to 1521. Legend has it that the Archangel Michael appeared to Aubert, bishop of Avranches, inspiring him to build an oratory on what was then called Mont Tombe. The original church was completed in 1144, but new buildings were added in the 13th century to accommodate the monks, as well as the hordes of pilgrims who flocked here even during the Hundred Years' War, when the region was in English hands. The Romanesque choir was rebuilt in an ornate Gothic style during the 15th and 16th centuries. The abbey's monastic vocation was undermined during the 17th century, when the monks began to flout the strict rules and discipline of their order, drifting into a state of decadence that culminated in the monks' dispersal and the abbey's conversion into a prison, well before the French Revolution. In 1874 the former abbey was handed over to a governmental agency responsible for the preservation of historic monuments; only within the past 20 years have monks been able to live and work here once more.

A causeway—to be replaced eventually by a bridge, thus allowing the bay waters to circulate freely—links Mont-St-Michel to the mainland. Leave your car in the parking lot (10 francs) at the foot of the mount, outside the main gateway. If you are staying the night on Mont-St-Michel, take what you need in a small suitcase; you cannot gain access to your hotel by car.

The island village, with its steep, narrow streets, is best visited out of season, from September to May. The hordes of tourists and souvenir sellers can be stifling in summer, but you can always take refuge in the abbey's gardens. From the ramparts in general and the North Tower in particular there are dramatic views of the bay. Give yourself at least a couple of hours here. However, with the mount's inflated prices you may want to stay elsewhere.

The climb to the abbey is hard going, but it's worth it. Head first for the **Grand Degré,** the steep, narrow staircase on the north side. Once past the ramparts, you'll come to the pink-and-gray granite towers of the **Châtelet** and then to the **Salle des Gardes,** the central point of the abbey. Guided tours start from the **Saut Gautier** terrace (named after a prisoner who jumped to his death from it): You must join one of these groups if you want to see the beautifully wrought **Escalier de Dentelle** (Lace Staircase) inside the church. ☎ *02–33–89–80–00.* *40 frs.* *Mid-May–Sept., daily 9:30–11:30 and 1:30–6; Oct.–mid-May, Wed.–Mon. 9:30–4:30.*

Dining and Lodging

$$$$ **Mère Poulard.** The hotel of the most celebrated restaurant on the mount consists of adjoining houses with small, simple, clean rooms, up three steep flights of narrow stairs. The restaurant's reputation derives partly from Mère Poulard's famous secret omelet recipe and partly from its location, overlooking the bay. The owners trade on a captive market—prices are exorbitant and the menu doesn't accurately reflect what you will pay. Room prices start low, but ratchet upward the bigger they get. Also, you are usually requested to book two meals with the room. Reservations are essential for the restaurant. ✉ *Grand Rue, 50116,* ☎ *02–33–60–14–01,* FAX *02–33–48–52–31. 26 rooms. Restaurant, piano bar. AE, DC, MC, V.*

$$–$$$ **Terrasses Poulard.** Hordes of tourists come to this ensemble of buildings clustered around a small garden in the middle of the mount. ✉ *Grand Rue, opposite the parish church, 50116,* ☎ *02–33–60–14–09,* FAX *02–33–60–37–31. 29 rooms. Restaurant, billiards, library. AE, DC, MC, V.*

$$ ★ **Le Manoir de la Roche Turin.** This small ivy-clad manor house on four acres of parkland is a delightful alternative to the high price of staying on Mont-St-Michel. Rooms are pleasantly old-fashioned, but the bathrooms are modern. The owners, M. and Mme. Barraux, run a comfortable dining room with an open fireplace: The pré-salé lamb is superb. In summer, aperitifs are served in the garden, where there's a view of Mont-St-Michel. The restaurant is closed Monday. ✉ *34 route de la Roche-Turin, 50220 Courtils (9 km/5 mi from Mont-St-Michel),* ☎ *02–33–70–96–55,* FAX *02–33–48–35–20. 11 rooms, 1 suite. Restaurant. MC, V. Closed mid-Nov.–mid-Mar.*

Nightlife and the Arts

Evening concerts are held in the abbey during the **Heures Musicales** (Musical Hours) in July and August.

LA SUISSE NORMANDE

La Suisse Normande (Swiss Normandy), a rocky expanse of hills and gullies south of Caen, has an abundance of natural beauty with few man-made sights. Striking as the scenery is, however, you'll need to exert your powers of imagination to spot much resemblance to the Swiss Alps. The small town of Thury-Harcourt is considered the gateway to La Suisse Normande; it's famous for the beautiful gardens of its ruined castle. Routes D212 and D562 are particularly scenic roads through this region.

Clécy

34 *44 km (28 mi) south of Caen.*

La Suisse Normande's main tourist center is on the Orne River at Clécy. Take the steep roads up to the cliff tops overlooking the river, where there are lovely views of the woods on the other bank.

Dining

$ ✕ **La Potinière.** Stop for a drink or a snack at this great, open-air, riverbank café. Crepes with either sweet or savory fillings are the biggest temptations. ✉ *La Cambronnerie,* ☎ *02–31–69–76–75. Closed Oct.–Apr.*

En Route From Clécy, take D562 south for just over 3 km (2 mi), and turn left at Le Fresne onto D1, which winds its way through the valley of the Noireau to another riverside resort town, **Pont d'Ouilly** (home to a famous pardon on the first Sunday after August 15). Head south along the Orne on D167, veer right at Pont-des-Vers onto D43, and turn left ★ at Rouvrou to reach the **Roche d'Oëtre,** a rock with spectacular views of the craggy hills that give the region its name. Follow the Orne Valley on D301 to the dramatic **Gorges de St-Aubert** (St-Aubert Gorge); park and follow the signs on foot if you want to admire the gorge up close. Continue on D301 to Rabodanges, then go south on D121 to get to the **Barrage de Rabodanges** (Rabodanges Dam), which dams the Orne and forms a small lake. The dam is best admired from the Pont Ste-Croix, 1½ km (1 mi) further on. Cross the lake on the Pont Ste-Croix and continue to the tumbling little town of **Putanges-Pont-Ecrepin,** with its distinctive, pointed church tower. From Putanges, the Orne winds east toward **Argentan,** heavily damaged during the last days of the Battle of Normandy. Rather than follow the river, however, drive south from Putanges, along D909, then D19, to Bagnoles-de-l'Orne, 29 km (19 mi) away.

Bagnoles-de-l'Orne

35 *80 km (50 mi) south of Caen.*

Bagnoles-de-l'Orne, the region's most beautiful spa town, overlooks a forest-fringed lake formed by the River Yée. Forty-five hotels and a casino are only part of what draws people here: From April through October some 20,000 people come to cure their blood-related ailments by soaking in the chemical-laden waters. Indeed, the nickname for Bagnoles-de-l'Orne is the "Capital of Veins."

Dining and Lodging

$$ ★ **Manoir de Lys.** This warm, inviting Norman country house presides over a beautifully landscaped park on the forest's edge. Room size varies—some have French windows that open onto the gardens; others, in the new wing, are slightly larger and have exposed beams. Chef-owner Paul Quinton and his son Franck are winning accolades for their creations, such as lobster tournedos and ravioli with frogs' legs. The Quintons also lead weeklong cooking classes several times a year. The restaurant is closed Sunday night and Monday. ✉ *Croix Gauthier, rte. de Juvigny (2 km/1 mi from the casino), 61140,* ☎ *02–33–37–80–69,* FAX *02–33–30–05–80. 20 rooms. Restaurant, tennis court. AE, MC, V. Closed Jan.–mid-Feb.*

Nightlife and the Arts

Among France's best, the **casino** (✉ 6 av. Robert Cousin, ☎ 02–33–37–84–00) has the usual games, plus a cabaret.

Alençon

36 *48 km (30 mi) southeast of Bagnoles-de-l'Orne, 49 km (31 mi) north of Le Mans.*

Historic Alençon, an attractive town south of the Ecouves Forest on the eastern edge of the Normandie-Maine nature park, has been a lace-making center since 1665. By the end of the 17th century *point d'Alençon* was de rigueur in all fashionable circles.

The **Musée des Beaux-Arts et de la Dentelle** (Museum of Fine Arts and Lace) contains a sophisticated collection of lace from Italy, Flanders, and France, along with paintings from the French school that span the 17th to the 20th century. ✉ *rue Charles-Aveline,* ☎ *02–33–32–40–07.* *17 frs.* *Tues.–Sun. 10–noon and 2–6.*

Shopping

Handmade lace is a rarity and prices are high, but this kind of labor-intensive, superior-quality creation never comes cheap: The **Musée de la Dentelle** (✉ 31 rue du Pont-Neuf, ☎ 02–33–26–27–26) has an excellent selection.

NORMANDY A TO Z

Arriving and Departing

By Boat

A number of ferry companies sail between the U.K. and ports in Normandy. **Brittany Ferries** (☎ 01705/827701 in U.K.; 08–03–82–82–82 in France) travels between Caen (Ouistreham) and Portsmouth, and Poole and Cherbourg. **P&O European Ferries** (☎ 0130/21–0004 in Portsmouth; 02–35–19–78–50 in Le Havre) travels between Le Havre and Portsmouth, and Cherbourg and Portsmouth. **Stena** (☎ 01273/51–6699 in Newhaven; 02–35–06–39–00 in Dieppe) travels between Dieppe and Newhaven, and Cherbourg and Southampton.

By Car

The A13 expressway from Paris slices its way to Rouen in 1½ hours (toll 35 francs) before continuing to Caen (2½ hours) with a fork to Le Havre (A131). N13 continues from Caen to Cherbourg via Bayeux in another two hours.

By Plane

Paris's Charles de Gaulle (Roissy) and Orly airports are international visitors' closest links with the region. **Air Inter** (☞ Air Travel *in* the Gold Guide) flies to Caen, but tickets are expensive. From the U.K., there are regular flights to Caen and Deauville from London, and to Cherbourg from Southampton and the Channel Islands (☞ Air Travel *in* the Gold Guide).

By Train

From Paris (Gare St-Lazare), separate lines head to Upper Normandy (Rouen and Le Havre or Dieppe) and Lower Normandy (Caen via Évreux and Lisieux). If you're thinking about taking the train from Paris to Mont-St-Michel, forget it. Connections are so complicated it will take you all day.

Getting Around

By Car

The 1995 opening of the Pont de Normandie, between Le Havre and Honfleur, has effectively united Upper and Lower Normandy and made driving between the two regions a lot easier. A13/N13, linking Rouen to Caen, Bayeux, and Cherbourg, is the backbone of Normandy: expressway as far as Caen, fast highway thereafter. If you have extra time, taking Normandy's scenic minor roads can be very rewarding.

By Train

Unless you are content to stick to the major towns (Rouen, Le Havre, Dieppe, Caen, Bayeux), visiting Normandy by train may prove frustrating. You can reach several smaller towns (Fécamp, Deauville, Cabourg), and even Mont-St-Michel (sort of—it's a 15-minute taxi ride from Pontorson), on snail-paced branch lines, but the intricacies of what is arguably Europe's most complicated regional timetable will have driven you nuts by the time you get there.

Contacts and Resources

Bike Rental

You can rent bicycles from several major train stations for about 45 francs per day.

Car Rental

Avis (✉ 44 pl. de la Gare, Caen, ☎ 02–31–87–31–84; 24 rue Malouet, Rouen, ☎ 02–35–72–77–50). **Europcar** (✉ 25 cours de la République, Le Havre, ☎ 02–35–25–21–95).

Emergencies

Ambulance (☎ 15). **Regional hospitals:** Caen (✉ av. de la Côte-de-Nacre, ☎ 02–31–06–31–06); Le Havre (✉ 29 av. Pierre-Mendès-France, Montivilliers, ☎ 02–32–73–32–32); Rouen (✉ chemin de la Bretèque, Bois Guillaume, ☎ 02–35–59–40–40).

Guided Tours

Périer Voyages (✉ 130 rue Martainville, 76000 Rouen, ☎ 02–35–98–59–00) arranges custom driving tours with an English-speaking driver. **Viking Voyages** (✉ 16 rue du Général-Giraud, 14000 Caen, ☎ 02–31–27–12–34) specializes in two-day packages by car, with overnight stays in private châteaux, as well as bike trips around the region and "Normandy Antiques" tour by car. The **French Association of Travel Agents** organizes two-day tours of the area from April to October; contact Voyages Beaudelin (✉ 18 rue Ganterie, 76000 Rouen, ☎ 02–35–71–39–46) for details. **Trans Canal** (✉ 13 rond-point de l'Orne, Caen, ☎ 02–31–34–00–00) arranges two-hour cruises on Caen's canal. Wellcome (02–35–07–79–79) organizes tours of the D-Day landing beaches.

Cityrama (✉ 4 pl. des Pyramides, 75001 Paris, ☎ 01–42–60–30–14) organizes one-day bus excursions from Paris to Mont-St-Michel on Saturdays with meals included; the cost is 975 francs. There is also a two-day package that includes the châteaux of the Loire. **Paris-Vision** (✉ 214 rue de Rivoli, 75001 Paris, ☎ 01–42–60–31–25) also runs one-day bus excursions from Paris to Mont-St-Michel on Saturdays, as well as two-day trips to the Loire.

Outdoor Activities and Sports

For information on trails and hiking courses, contact the **Comité Départemental de la Randonnée Pédestre de Seine-Maritime** (✉ B.P. 666, 76008 Rouen, no phone). For information regarding stables, get in touch with **La Ligne d'Équestre de Normandie** (✉ 10 pl. de Demi-Lune, 14039 Caen, ☎ 02–31–84–61–87).

Travel Agencies

American Express (✉ 1–3 pl. Jacques-Lelieur, Rouen, ☎ 02–32–08–19–20; 57 quai Georges V, Le Havre, ☎ 02–32–74–75–76). **Havas** (✉ 25 Grande-Rue, Alençon, ☎ 02–33–32–88–88; 80 rue St-Jean, Caen, ☎ 02–31–86–04–01; 14 pl. Nationale, Dieppe, ☎ 02–35–84–29–16).

Visitor Information

Each of Normandy's five départements has its own central tourist office. **Alençon** (✉ 88 rue St-Blaise, ☎ 02–33–28–88–71) for the Orne. **Caen** (✉ pl. St-Pierre, ☎ 02–31–27–14–14) for Calvados. **Évreux** (✉ bd. Georges-Chauvin, ☎ 02–32–31–51–51) for the Eure. **Rouen** (✉ 25 pl. de la Cathédrale, ☎ 02–32–08–32–40) for the Seine-Maritime. **St-Lô** (✉ rte. Villedieu, ☎ 02–33–05–98–70) for La Manche. Other major Norman towns with tourist offices include: **Bayeux** (✉ Pont St-Jean, ☎ 02–31–92–16–26). **Dieppe** (✉ Pont Ango, ☎ 02–35–84–11–77). **Fécamp** (✉ 113 rue Alexandre-le-Grand, ☎ 02–35–28–51–01). **Le Havre** (✉ 1 pl. de l'Hôtel-de-Ville, ☎ 02–35–21–22–88). **Honfleur** (✉ 9 rue de la Ville, ☎ 02–31–89–23–30).

7 The North and Champagne

Lille, Reims, and the Ardennes

Just an hour from Paris on the TGV (Trains à Grande Vitesse) and right across the English Channel, the North and Champagne harbor many treasures: uninterrupted stretches of sandy beach, moving World War I battlefields, mighty castles, beefy belfries, and awesome cathedrals. Lille, one of France's liveliest cities, is here, as is Reims, the capital of bubbly. To the northeast lies the thick forest of the Ardennes.

Updated by Simon Hewitt

TOO FEW PEOPLE VISIT NORTHERN FRANCE. The crowd-following French flock south each year in search of a suntan. The millions of tourists who buzz through the Channel ports of Calais and Dunkerque make a beeline to Paris. But the Channel Tunnel, perhaps the most ambitious engineering project of the late 20th century, is beginning to change this, making it easier and less expensive for the British to flit across for day and weekend trips.

The north of France is an industrial region, but don't look for slag heaps and smokestacks everywhere; heavy industry is highly centralized. This is a green and pleasant land where wooded, restful landscapes predominate; Lille, the regional capital, has plenty to see. To the southeast, the grapes of Champagne flourish on the steep slopes of the Marne Valley and the Montagne de Reims, really more of a mighty hill than a mountain. Reims is the only city in Champagne, and one of France's richest tourist venues. The kings of France were crowned in its cathedral until 1825, and every age since the Roman period has left an architectural mark. The thriving champagne business has conferred wealth and, sometimes, an arrogant reserve on the region's inhabitants. The down-to-earth folk of the North reserve a warmer welcome.

Pleasures and Pastimes

Beaches

The northern French coast, from Calais to Le Touquet, is one long, sandy beach, known as the Côte d'Opale. It is sometimes short of sun, but not of space or beach sports like *char à voile* (sand sailing), those windsurfing boards on wheels that race along the sands at up to 112 kph (70 mph). The climate is bracing, often windy, but there are wonderful scenic spots along the cliffs south of Calais at Cap Gris Nez and Cap Blanc Nez. Le Touquet is one of France's swankiest coastal resorts towns; Le Crotoy, Wimereux, and Hardelot are more family-oriented.

Champagne

The world's most famous sparkling wine comes from France's northernmost vineyards along the towering Marne Valley between Epernay and Château-Thierry, and on the slopes of the Montagne de Reims, between Epernay and Reims. Champagne firms, in these two towns and in Ay, welcome you into their chalky, mazelike cellars. You can also visit the tomb of Dom Perignon, the inventor of champagne, in Hautvillers. Just follow the Route du Vin south of Reims.

Churches and Cathedrals

Northern France contains many of France's most remarkable Gothic cathedrals: Amiens, the largest; Beauvais, the highest; Noyon, the earliest; Abbeville, the last; Reims, with the most richly sculpted facade; and Laon, with the most towers (and the most spectacular hilltop setting). The region's smaller churches are also admirable—the intricate stonework of Rue and L'Épine; the ruined drama of Mont St-Eloi; the modern stained glass of Mézières; and the Baroque brickwork of Asfeld.

Dining

The cuisine of northern France is robust and hearty. Beer is often used as a base for sauces; french fries and mussels are featured on most menus; vans selling fries and hot dogs are a common sight; and large quantities of mussels and fish, notably herring, are consumed. Smoked ham and, in season, boar and venison are specialties of the Ardennes. Be sure to sample the region's creamy cheeses: the soft, square *Maroilles* with a dark red rind; and the fiery, pyramid-shape *boulette d'Avesnes*. Sweet tooths will enjoy the macaroons and *bêtises de Cambrai* (a minty lollipop). Ham, pigs' feet, gingerbread, and champagne-based mustard are specialties of the Reims area, as is ratafia, a sweet aperitif made from grape juice and brandy. To the north, a glass of *genièvre* (brandy made from juniper berries, which is sometimes added to black coffee to make a *bistouille*) is the classic conclusion to a good meal.

CATEGORY	COST*
$$$$	over 400 frs
$$$	250 frs–400 frs
$$	125 frs–250 frs
$	under 125 frs

**per person for a three-course meal, including tax (20.6%) and tip but not wine*

Lodging

Northern France is overladen with old hotels, often rambling and simple, seldom pretentious. Good value is easier to come by than top quality, except in major cities (Amiens, Lille, and Reims) or at Le Touquet, whose Westminster Hotel numbers among the country's best.

CATEGORY	COST*
$$$$	over 800 frs
$$$	550 frs–800 frs
$$	300 frs–550 frs
$	under 300 frs

**All prices are for a standard double room for two, including tax (20.6%) and service charge.*

War Memorials

Northern France was in the frontline of battle during the world wars and suffered heavily. The city of Reims was shelled incessantly during World War I, and such names as the Somme and Vimy Ridge evoke the bloody, deadlocked battles that raged from 1914 to 1918. Cemeteries and war memorials may not be the most cheerful items on your itinerary, but they do have a melancholy, thought-provoking beauty.

Exploring the North and Champagne

The area known as the North (Nord, in French) stretches from the River Somme up to Calais and the Channel Tunnel, including the vibrant city of Lille. Champagne encompasses Reims and the area northeast of Paris, including southern Picardy and the Ardennes by the Belgian border.

Great Itineraries

With about a week and a half you can cover most of the region, beginning on the coast in Calais and ending in L'Épine. Five days will give you time to explore inland, from Lille to Châlons-en-Champagne. With only three days, concentrate on the most scenic attractions in Picardy and Champagne.

IF YOU HAVE 3 DAYS

Numbers in the text correspond to numbers in the margin and on the North; South Picardy, Champagne, and the Ardennes; Lille; and Reims maps.

Start in **Compiègne** ㉙ at its elegant palace, then head to **Pierrefonds** ㉚ to see its mighty castle. By dinner time, be in the hilltop, cathedral town of 🏨 **Laon** ㉟. After visiting Laon the next morning, drive to 🏨 **Reims** ㊶–㊽ for the afternoon, the night, and maybe part of the third morning. Make the champagne vineyards to the south—on the Montagne de Reims, along the **Route du Vin,** and in the steeply terraced Marne Valley west of **Épernay** ㊾—your next destination.

IF YOU HAVE 5 DAYS

Begin with a day in the vibrant city of **Lille** ③–⑬. The next morning take in stately **Arras** ① and the moving war cemeteries nearby, en route to **Compiègne** ㉙. Devote day three to **Pierrefonds** ㉚ and **Laon** ㉟ and day four to **Reims** ㊶–㊽. Spend your last day touring the Montagne de Reims and the **Route du Vin,** then head east from **Épernay** ㊾ to the historic town of **Châlons-en-Champagne** ㊿.

IF YOU HAVE 9 DAYS

Start in **Calais** ⑱ and venture along the Channel cliffs to **Boulogne-sur-Mer** ⑲. If want to go to the beach, head down the coast to **Le Touquet** ⑳ and rejoin the itinerary at Amiens. If you prefer history and culture, head inland from Boulogne to **Lille** ③–⑬ for the night and following morning. That afternoon go south to **Arras** ①. On day four, cross the **Somme battlefields** via **Albert** ㉕, ending the day in the cathedral city of **Amiens** ㉔. The next day visit **Beauvais** ㉘, home to another cathedral and a fine tapestry museum, then go east to **Compiègne** ㉙. Day six will see you in **Pierrefonds** ㉚ and **Laon** ㉟. On day seven head northeast into the Ardennes to explore historic **Charleville-Mézières** ㊲; stay overnight in **Sedan** ㊳, home to Europe's largest castle. The following morning go to **Reims** ㊶–㊽. On day nine, go to the champagne vineyards south of Reims en route to **Châlons-en-Champagne** ㊿ and the fine hotel-restaurant by the basilica in **L'Épine** (51).

When to Tour the North and Champagne

Compared to many regions of France, the North remains relatively uncrowded in July and August, and the huge Channel beaches have room for everyone. The liveliest time in Lille is the first weekend in September during its three-day street fair, La Grande Braderie. Other local fairs include the Dunkerque Carnival in February and the Giants' Carnival in Douai in July. Make sure to visit Reims and Champagne between May and October; the region's ubiquitous vineyards are a dismal, leafless sight the rest of the year. The wooded Ardennes are attractive in fall, when local game highlights menus.

BETWEEN THE CHANNEL AND THE SOMME

Starting from Arras—easily accessible by expressway and TGV from Paris—this region extends counterclockwise to Lille; northwest to the Channel Coast and down to St-Valery-sur-Somme; then east through the Somme Valley, taking in Amiens, Albert, and many World War I battlefields. Around the city of Arras you can also see many memorials to World War I. Along the coast, you can find mile upon mile of empty, sandy beaches. Unfortunately, Calais and Dunkerque, your first ports of call coming from England, are among the country's ugliest towns. But the old sections of neighboring Boulogne-sur-Mer are far more appealing, as are the narrow streets of ancient Montreuil and the posh avenues of fashionable Le Touquet.

Arras

❶ *178 km (105 mi) north of Paris via A1, 113 km (70 mi) southeast of Calais via A26.*

At first glance you might not guess that Arras, the capital of the historic Artois region between Flanders and Picardy, was badly mauled

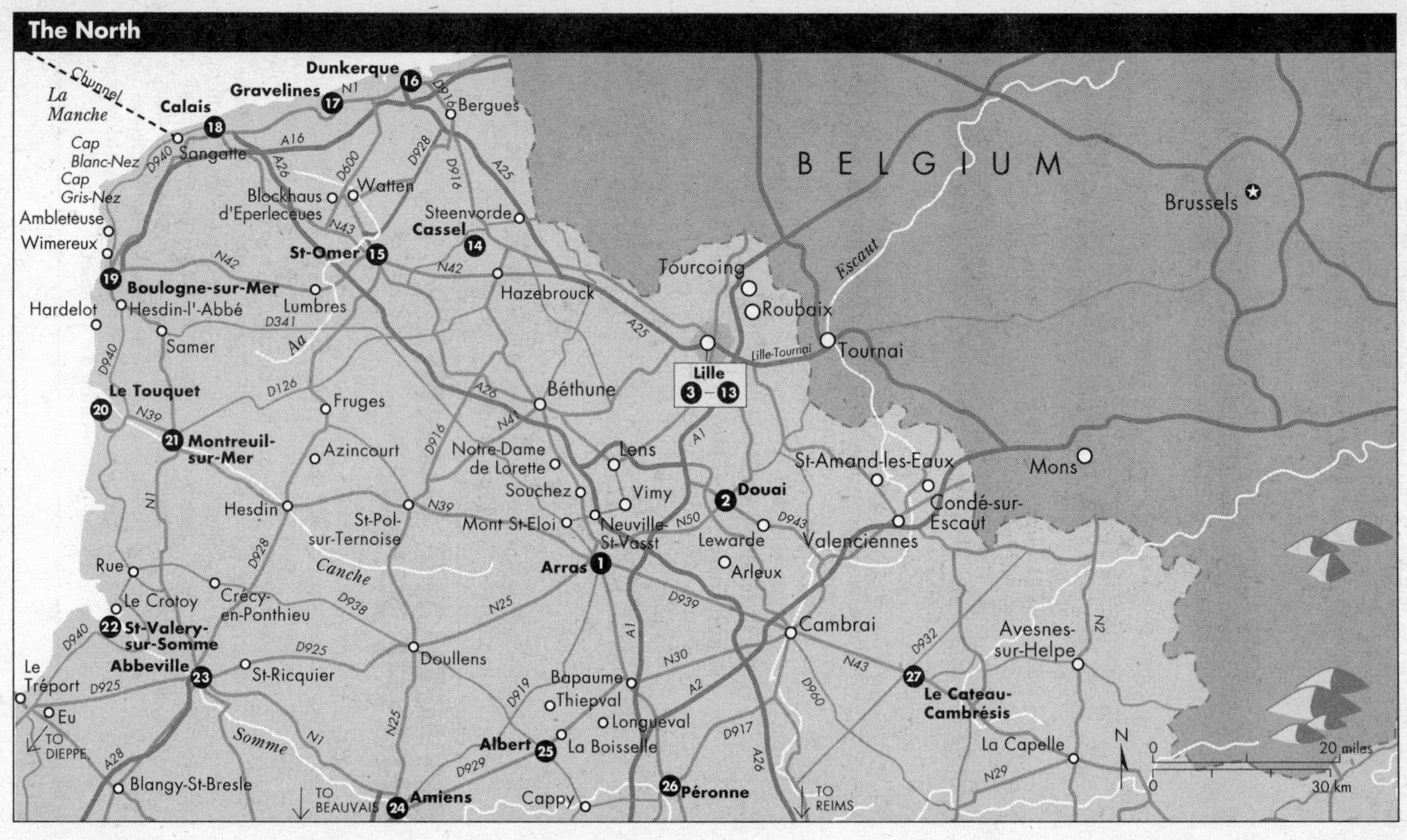

The North
La Manche
Chunnel
Calais 18
Gravelines 17
Dunkerque 16
Bergues
Sangatte
Cap Blanc-Nez
Cap Gris-Nez
Ambleteuse
Wimereux
Blockhaus d'Eperlecques
Watten
Steenvorde
Cassel 14
St-Omer 15
Hazebrouck
19 Boulogne-sur-Mer
Hesdin-l'-Abbé
Lumbres
Hardelot
Samer
Aa
Le Touquet 20
21 Montreuil-sur-Mer
Fruges
Azincourt
Hesdin
St-Pol-sur-Ternoise
Béthune
Notre-Dame de Lorette
Souchez
Mont St-Eloi
Lens
Vimy
Neuville-St-Vaast
Arras 1
Tourcoing
Roubaix
Lille 3–13
Lille-Tournai
Tournai
Escaut
BELGIUM
Brussels
Mons
St-Amand-les-Eaux
Condé-sur-Escaut
Valenciennes
2 Douai
Leward e
Arleux
Cambrai
27 Le Cateau-Cambrésis
Avesnes-sur-Helpe
La Capelle
Rue
Le Crotoy
Crécy-en-Ponthieu
Canche
22 St-Valery-sur-Somme
Abbeville 23
St-Ricquier
Doullens
Le Tréport
Eu
TO DIEPPE
Somme
Blangy-St-Bresle
TO BEAUVAIS
24 Amiens
Cappy
Albert 25
La Boisselle
Longueval
Thiepval
Bapaume
26 Péronne
TO REIMS
A16 A26 A25 A1 A2 A28 A26
N1 N2 N25 N29 N30 N39 N41 N42 N43 N50
D916 D928 D600 D940 D341 D126 D938 D925 D939 D943 D917 D960 D932 D929 D919
N
0 20 miles
0 30 km

South Picardy, Champagne, and the Ardennes

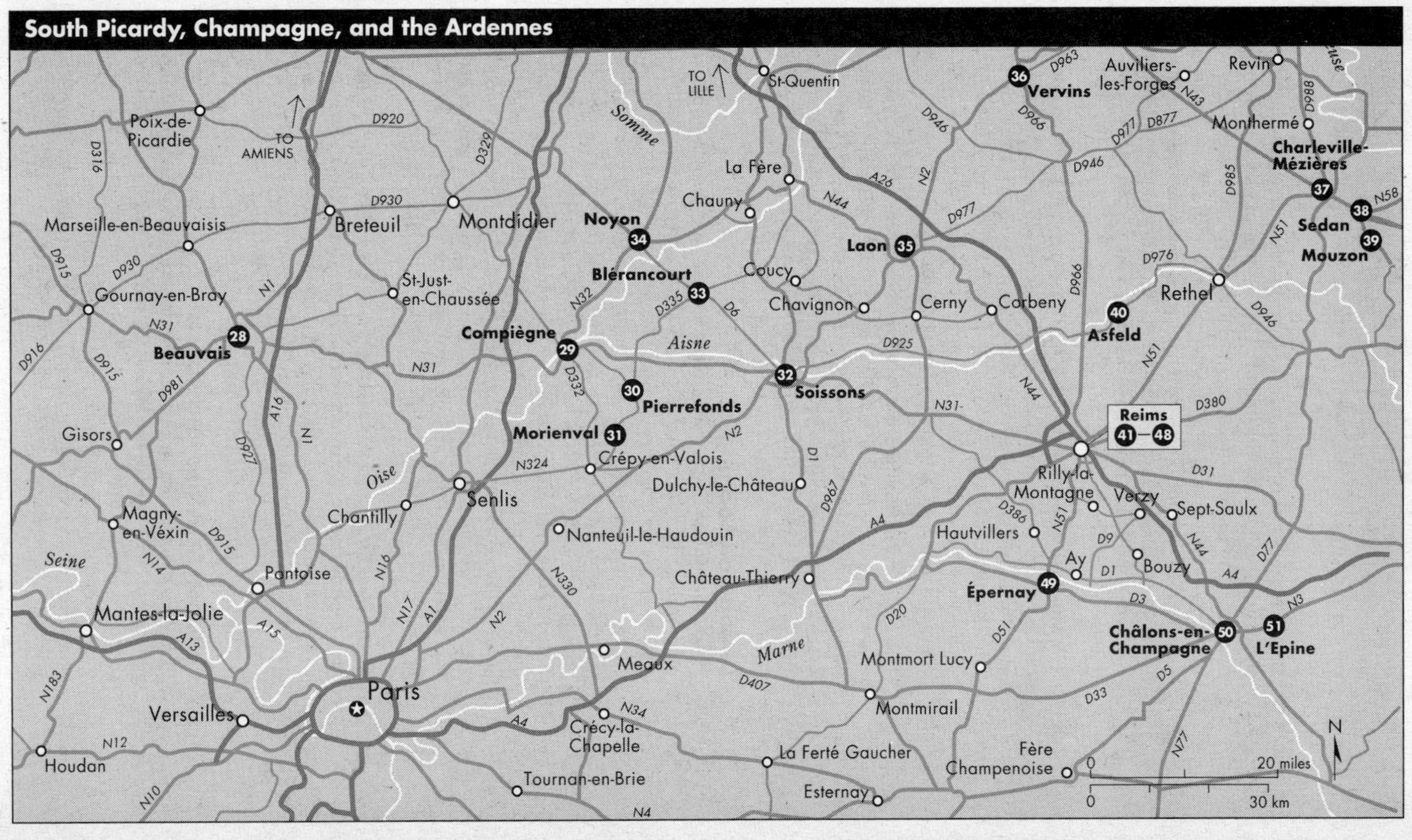

during World War I. But its historic core, with two of the finest squares in the country, has been skillfully restored to its 17th- and 18th-century grandeur, when Arras was an important trading and cloth-making center.

★ **Grand'Place** is one of two main squares in Arras: a grand, harmonious showcase of 17th- and 18th-century Flemish civil architecture. The gabled facades recall those in Belgium and Holland and are a reminder of the unifying influence of the Spanish colonizers of the "Low Lands" during the 17th century. The smaller, arcaded **place des Héros,** separated by a short block from the Grand'Place, is dominated by the richly worked—and much restored—**Hôtel de Ville** (Town Hall), capped by a 240-foot belfry.

The **Musée des Beaux-Arts** (Fine Arts Museum), in an imposing 18th-century former abbey, houses a rich collection of porcelain and paintings, including several major 19th-century French works. ✉ *20 rue Paul-Doumer,* ☎ *03–21–71–26–43.* 🎫 *15 frs.* ⏲ *Apr.–mid-Oct., Wed.–Mon. 10–noon and 2–6; mid-Oct.–Mar., Mon. and Wed.–Fri. 10–noon and 2–5, weekends 10–noon and 2–6.*

The 19th-century **Cathédrale St-Vaast,** behind the Fine Arts Museum, is a white-stone classical building, every bit as vast as its name (pronounced "va") almost suggests. It replaced the previous Gothic cathedral that was destroyed in 1799; though it was half-razed during World War I, restoration was so skillfully done you'd never know. ✉ *rue des Teinturiers.*

Dining and Lodging

$$$ ✕ **La Faisanderie.** This splendid restaurant, in a former stable, serves memorable variations on international fare: *pied de veau* (calf's foot), pike baked with frogs' legs, and cod with local Arleux garlic. A loyal clientele supports its long-standing gastronomic reputation. ✉ *45 Grand'Place,* ☎ *03–21–48–20–76. Reservations essential. Jacket and tie. AE, DC, MC, V. Closed Mon. No dinner Sun.*

$ ✕ **La Rapière.** This lively alternative to its posh neighbor, La Faisanderie, dishes up distinctly local cuisine, including andouillettes and *poule à la bière* (hen in beer), as well as a broad range of specialties like *escalope de veau au Camembert* (thinly slice veal with Camembert) and *foie gras maison* (house foie gras), all in a casual setting. ✉ *44 Grand'-Place,* ☎ *03–21–55–09–92. AE, MC, V. No dinner Sun.*

$$ ★ 🏨 **Univers.** Once an 18th-century monastery, this stylish hotel has a pretty garden and a charming restaurant. Its central location and courtyard and garden views make it a favorite stop. The interior has been modernized, but retains rustic provincial furniture. ✉ *5 pl. de la Croix-Rouge, 62000,* ☎ *03–21–71–34–01,* FAX *03–21–71–41–42. 36 rooms with bath or shower. Restaurant. AE, MC, V.*

Outdoor Activities and Sports

Crazy as it may seem in this least mountainous of regions, the small mining town of **Noeux-les-Mines,** 24 km (15 mi) north of Arras, has made a name for itself recently as France's leading ski center between the Alps and the Channel. Imaginative local councillors have transformed one of the giant *terrils* (slag heaps) into an artificial ski run. ✉ *Loisinord, rue Léon-Blum,* ☎ *03–21–26–84–84.*

The Artois Battlefields

North of Arras are several of the superbly cared-for war cemeteries that count among the most moving sights in northern France, recalling the murderous stalemate that raged locally for much of World War I.

Legend has it that the once-vast abbey of **Mont St-Eloi,** 8 km (5 mi) northwest of Arras via D341—razed during the French Revolution—is connected to Arras by an enormous underground tunnel. Its ghostly towers, peering mournfully over the tiny village and surrounding countryside, are visible for miles around. They were one story higher before World War I, when their lookout potential invited constant bombardment.

With its gentle slopes, trees, and manicured lawns, **La Targette,** 4 km (2½ mi) east of Mont St-Eloi via D49, is one of the most serene and beautiful of all French war cemeteries. Take the main road, D937, to get to the small **Musée de la Guerre 1914–18** (World War I Museum), opposite a stark war memorial in the form of a giant torch. It has a dusty collection of posters, documents, costumes, and weapons.

The road opposite the World War I Museum leads to **Neuville-St-Vaast,** where its Art Deco church is a stately example of 1920s reconstruction. ★ From Neuville, take D55 to **Vimy Ridge,** now a park commemorating a Canadian victory during World War I. With its woods and lush grass, this has become a popular picnic spot—yet the preserved trenches and savagely undulating terrain are harsh reminders of the combat waged here in 1917. The simple, soaring, white-stone Canadian War Memorial, a cleft rectangular tower adorned with female figures in tearful lament, is highly effective. Its base is inscribed with thousands of names of the fallen.

From Vimy, return to Neuville and take D937 north, past the beautiful circular cemetery of the **Cabaret Rouge.** Just north of Souchez is **Notre-Dame de Lorette,** a colossal cemetery standing on a windswept hill 500 feet above the plain. There is a mock-Byzantine church and a huge tower containing a small war museum; from the top there are extensive views of the surrounding countryside. Return to Souchez, follow signs to Liévin, take A21 around **Lens**—whose giant soccer stadium will host games in the 1998 World Cup—then follow A21 to Douai.

Douai

❷ *24 km (15 mi) northeast of Arras via N50, 21 km (13 mi) east of Lens, 35 km (22 mi) south of Lille.*

The industrial town of Douai still has several imposing mansions recalling its 18th-century importance as capital of the French province of Flanders. But it is most noteworthy as the home of northern France's most famous **Beffroi** (Belfry), whose turrets and pinnacles are immortalized in a painting by Camille Corot, now in the Louvre. The sturdy tower, completed in 1410, rises 210 feet from the ground and is topped by a huge weather vane in the form of a Flanders Lion. The peal of bells—62 of them!—sounds the quarter hours with a variety of tunes. Climb the 192 steps to the top for a view of the town and the Scarpe River. ✉ *rue de la Mairie,* ☎ *03–27–87–26–63.* ⏲ *Apr.–Sept., Mon.–Sat. 10–noon and 2:30–5:30, Sun. 2:30–5:30.*

Few herbs are more readily associated with France than *ail* (garlic), and France's unofficial Garlic Capital is **Arleux,** 11 km (7 mi) south of Douai, where a Fête d'Ail (Garlic Festival) is held on the first Sunday of September. Smoked garlic cloves are a local specialty. Just south of Arleux, the ponds and small lakes known as the **Étangs de la Sensée** provide a scenic backdrop for strolls and picnics.

The abandoned mine at **Lewarde,** 7 km (4 mi) east of Douai, has been skillfully converted into the Centre Historique Minier, a museum charting the history of the local coal industry. You can admire beefy machinery, stroll around an interesting photographic exhibit, and take a train ride through reconstructed coal galleries. Wear sturdy shoes and allow 2 hours for the visit. ☎ *03–27–95–82–82.* 🎫 *52 frs.* ⏲ *Apr.–Sept., daily 10–5; Oct.–Mar., daily 10–4.*

Nightlife and the Arts

Giants and processions go together in northern France, most famously during the **Fêtes de Gayant** (Festival of the Giant, in local patois), which has been held in Douai on the first Sunday after July 5 ever since Flanders and France signed a peace treaty in 1530. A family of five giants, over 25 feet tall, are borne through the streets by dozens of invisible porters, pursued by a float with an outsize Wheel of Fortune. At 11 o'clock the city bells ring out and hundreds of pigeons are released from the town hall.

En Route To get a feel for the area between Lewarde and Valenciennes—chosen by Émile Zola as the setting for his epic mining novel *Germinal*—take D13 then D47 northeast from Lewarde to Marchiennes. Continue on D35 to **St-Amand-les-Eaux** to admire its 270-foot, 17th-century Baroque belfry, topped by a cupola, then head northwest to Lille.

Lille

220 km (137 mi) north of Paris, 100 km (63 mi) southeast of Calais, 56 km (35 mi) northeast of Arras, 100 km (62 mi) west of Brussels.

For a big city supposedly reeling from the problems of its main industry, textiles, Lille—the name comes from *l'isle* ("the island") in the Deûle River, where the city began—is remarkably dynamic and attractive. After experiencing Flemish, Austrian, and Spanish rule, Lille passed into French hands for good in 1667. Since the arrival of the TGV in 1994, it is again a European crossroads, a quick trip by train from Paris, London, and Brussels.

3 The shiny glass towers of the new **Euralille** complex, the high-tech commercial center that is Lille's answer to La Défense near Paris, greet travelers arriving at the new TGV station, Lille-Europe. Hotels and shops dominate the complex, and students of modern architecture may find it stimulating. Avenue Le Corbusier links Euralille to the original rail station, still used for non-TGV services and now renamed Lille-Flandres. The station building, originally the Gare du Nord in Paris, was moved brick by brick to Lille in 1866.

4 The sumptuous church of **St-Maurice,** just off place de la Gare, is a large, five-aisle structure built between the 15th and 19th centuries. ✉ *rue de Paris.*

5 The majestic **Porte de Paris,** overlooked by the 340-foot brick tower of the Hôtel de Ville, is a cross between a mansion and a triumphal arch. It was built by Simon Vollant in the 1680s in honor of Louis XIV and was originally part of the city walls. ✉ *rue de Paris.*

6 The **Musée des Beaux-Arts,** the country's largest fine arts museum outside of Paris, was scheduled to reopen in 1997 after renovation. It houses a noteworthy collection of Dutch and Flemish paintings (Anthony Van Dyck, Peter Paul Rubens, Flemish Primitives, and Dutch landscapists) as well as some charmingly understated still lifes by Chardin, works by the Impressionists, a few bombastic 19th-century French painters, and dramatic canvases by El Greco, Goya, Tintoretto, and Paolo Veronese. A ceramics section displays some fine examples of Lille faience (earthenware). ✉ *pl. de la République,* ☎ *03–20–57–01–84, call for hours and admission price.*

Citadelle, **13**
Euralille, **3**
Hospice Comtesse, **11**
Musée des Beaux-Arts, **6**
Notre-Dame de la Treille, **12**
Palais Rihour, **7**
Porte de Paris, **5**
place du Général-de-Gaulle, **8**
St-Maurice, **4**
Vieille Bourse, **9**
Le Vieux Lille, **10**

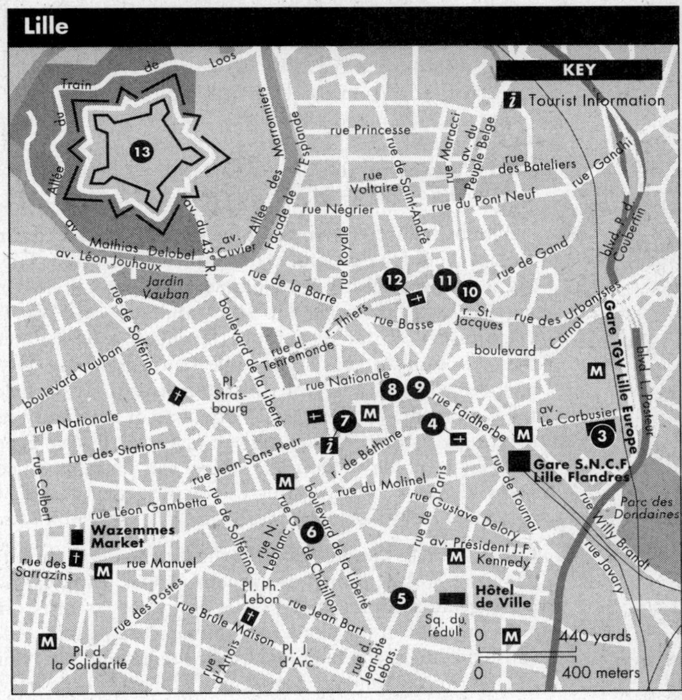

7 The late-15th-century **Palais Rihour** (Rihour Palace), built for Philippe le Bon, duke of Burgundy, is famed for its octagonal turret and staircase with intricate, swirling-pattern brickwork. The city **tourist office** is housed in the vaulted, former guardroom on the ground floor. ✉ *pl. Rihour.*

8 Lille's most famous square, Grand'Place, is next door to place Rihour and is now officially called **place du Général-de-Gaulle** (Charles de Gaulle was born in Lille in 1890). The *Déesse* (Goddess) atop her giant column, clutching a linstock (used to fire a cannon), has dominated the square since 1845; she commemorates Lille's heroic resistance to an Austrian siege in 1792. Other landmarks include the handsome, gabled 1932 facade of *La Voix du Nord* (the main regional newspaper), topped by three gilded statues symbolizing the three historic regions of Flanders, Artois, and Hainaut; and the Furet du Nord, which immodestly claims to be the world's largest bookshop.

9 The elegant **Vieille Bourse,** on one side of Grand'Place, was built in 1653 by Julien Destrées as a commercial exchange to rival those of the Low Countries. Note the bronze busts, sculpted medallions, and ornate stonework of its arcaded quadrangle.

10 **Le Vieux Lille** (Old Lille) dates mainly from the 17th and 18th centuries; its richly sculpted facades, often combining stone facings with pale pink brickwork, have been tastefully restored. Rue de la Grande-Chaussée, quaintly named rue des Chats-Bossus (Street of the Hunchbacked Cats), and rue de la Monnaie wind north from the Vieille Bourse through the heart of the old town. Perhaps the most ornate building, on place Louise-de-Bettignies, is the **Maison de Gilles de la Boë,** built in the 1630s for a rich grocer.

⓫ The **Hospice Comtesse** (Countess Hospital), founded in 1237 by Jeanne de Constantinople, countess of Flanders, as a hospital, was rebuilt in the 15th century after a fire destroyed most of the original building. Local artifacts from the 17th and 18th centuries form the backbone of the museum now housed here, but its star attraction is the **Salle des Malades** (Sick Ward), featuring a majestic wooden ceiling. ✉ *32 rue de la Monnaie,* ☎ *03–20–49–50–90.* *15 frs (5 frs Sat. afternoon and Wed.).* ⏲ *Wed.–Mon. 10–12:30 and 2–6.*

⓬ The bulky church of **Notre-Dame de la Treille** stands on the spot of a medieval church dismantled during the Revolution. The present building was only begun—in a suitably neo-Gothic style—in 1856. Building was halted from 1869 to 1893, and by World War I only the choir was finished. In the meantime, the church was made into a basilica, then the unfinished basilica became a cathedral, none of which did much to speed construction. The roof vaults were only finished in 1973, and the west front, with its dismal expanses of gray concrete, remains despairingly incomplete. Grandiose plans for a new, glass facade seem unlikely to come to fruition, and so this mighty edifice stands like a colossal wreck, admonishing the quaint, cozy streets of old Lille like some latter-day Ozymandias. ✉ *rue des Trois-Mollettes.*

⓭ Lille's gigantic **Citadelle** patrols the northwest of the city from the enchanting Bois de Boulogne gardens, whose leafy walkways alongside photogenic streams attract hordes of strollers, cyclists, and joggers. The colossal walls of the citadel are immaculately preserved, no doubt because the site is still inhabited by the French military (you can only visit the interior on Sunday afternoons). Construction started in the 1660s; of course that genius of military engineering, Sébastien de Vauban, got the commission. Some 60 million bricks were baked in record time—Louis XIV's prime northern outpost needed urgent defending—and the result is a fortified town in its own right. ⏲ *Guided tours only Sun. at 3 PM, Apr.–Oct.: contact tourist office,* ☎ *03–20–21–94–21.*

Dining and Lodging

$$$ ✕ **L'Huîtrière.** Behind a magnificent Art Deco fish shop, you'll find this elegant seafood restaurant serving fresh, local seafood, simply prepared in regional (Flemish) style—turbot hollandaise, *waterzooie* (a mild, creamy fish stew), and, of course, oysters from La Manche (the English Channel). The clientele is chic, well-heeled; the decor luxurious; and prices justifiably high. ✉ *3 rue des Chats-Bossus,* ☎ *03–22–55–43–41. Jacket and tie. AE, DC, MC, V. Closed Aug. No dinner Sun.*

$$ ✕ **Le Hochepot.** Just two blocks from Grand'Place, this cozy, old-fashioned spot serves simple, homey regional food, much of it cooked in (and served with) locally made beer. ✉ *6 pl. Mendès-France,* ☎ *03–20–54–17–59. MC, V. Closed Sun. No lunch Sat.*

$ ✕ **Les Brasseurs.** This dark, wood-paneled brasserie beside Lille-Flandres station brews its own beer on the spot. There are four types—blond (lager), amber, dark (stout), and white (wheat beer)—and *La Palette du Barman* lets you sample all four for 24 francs. Sausages, sauerkraut, steak, and *flammekueches* (crispy pancakes topped with bacon and onions) are served as accompaniment. ✉ *22 pl. de la Gare,* ☎ *03–20–06–46–25. AE, V.*

$$ **Bellevue.** This central, elegant prewar hotel, favored by British travelers, has many large, comfortable Art Deco rooms, impeccably modern baths, and the sort of deferential service you can no longer take for granted. It also has a leather-lined bar. ✉ *5 rue Jean-Roisin, 59800,* ☎ *03–20–57–45–64,* FAX *03–20–40–07–93. 80 rooms with bath or shower. Bar. AE, DC, MC, V.*

Nightlife and the Arts

Le Crypton (✉ 32 pl. Louise-de-Bettignies, ☎ 03–20–06–58–33) is the place to dance the night away. Boogie at **Le Pirogue** (✉ 16 rue Jean-Jacques Rousseau, ☎ 03–20–31–70–82). **La Renardière** (✉ 227 bd. Victor-Hugo, ☎ 03–20–57–03–46), a nightclub, is another bet for a good night out.

Lille is at its liveliest during the first weekend of September, when the **Grande Braderie** summons folk from miles around to what is theoretically a giant street market but has now become a 36-hour party, awash in oceans of beer and swimming with mussels. The mountains of mussel shells along the sidewalks on Monday morning (and the communal headaches) defy belief.

The **Opéra de Lille** (✉ pl. du Théâtre, ☎ 03–20–55–48–61) is one of France's few opera houses; the season runs October–June. The **Orchestre National de Lille** (✉ 3 pl. Mendès-France, ☎ 03–20–54–67–00) is a well-respected symphony orchestra.

Cassel

14 *45 km (28 mi) northwest of Lille via A25 and D948 from Steenvoorde (exit 13).*

At Cassel, the North's ubiquitous image as Le Plat Pays (The Flat Land) is given a nasty jolt by a 580-foot mound towering over the plain like a land-bound Mont-St-Michel. Sailors use it as a landmark from the English Channel—27 km (17 mi) away. **Mont-Cassel** is the highest of a series of outcrops known as the Monts de Flandre, although the 520-foot Mont des Réollets (to the east) runs a close second. There's a wooden windmill at the top. The views from the surrounding gardens extend over higgledy-piggledy roofs to a patchwork quilt of wheat fields. The sloping town square, over 200 yards long, lurches around nearby in search of a ruler. A lively Carnival provides a couple of candidates on Easter Monday: giants Reuze-Papa and Reuze-Maman.

St-Omer

15 *23 km (14 mi) southwest of Cassel via D933, 64 km (40 mi) northwest of Lille.*

St-Omer is not the archetypal northern industrial town. With its yellow-brick buildings it looks different from its neighbors, and an air of 18th-century prosperity hovers about the place.

The **Basilique Notre-Dame,** surrounded by narrow streets at the top end of the main town square, is a large, homely cathedral-size church, whose relatively low ceiling and broad windows with geometric tracery bears testimony to the local influence of the English Perpendicular style during the 15th century. ✉ *rue Henri-Dupuis.*

The **Hôtel Sandelin,** the town museum, is a 1777 mansion containing 18th-century furniture and paintings and, above all, an exceptional collection of porcelain and faience, with over 700 pieces of delftware. ✉ *14 rue Carnot,* ☎ *03–21–38–00–94.* 🎟 *18 frs.* ⏲ *Wed. and weekends 10–noon and 2–6, Thurs. and Fri. 10–noon and 2–5.*

Vestiges of World War I pepper the north of France, but none of them are as grisly as the Nazi specter lurking in the forest near Watten, 13 km (8 mi) north of St-Omer. The **Blockhaus d'Eperlecques,** a bunker of monstrous size and intent, 80 feet high with concrete walls 20 feet thick, was erected in 1943 by 35,000 slave laborers as the secret base for the assembly and launch of the V2 rocket-bomb. So secret, in fact, you can't even see it from the entrance 100 yards away. Yet not secret enough to escape Allied reconnaissance: RAF bombers destroyed the bunker and saved London from being blown to smithereens. Strategic loudspeakers fire out French commentary as you walk around—but the site's message is essentially unspeakable, even if tourist leaflets like to claim that this is where the Space Race began (the V2's creator, Wernher von Braun, defected to the West and helped pioneer the U.S. space program). ✉ *Off D205 west of Watten,* ☎ *03–21–88–44–22.* 🎟 *35 frs.* ⏲ *June–Sept., daily 10–1 and 2–7; Apr., May, Oct., Nov., daily 2–6.*

Dining and Lodging

$$ ✕ **Le Cygne.** *Maigret de canard* (duck breast), not *cygne* (swan), tops three- and four-course menus at Le Cygne, in the old section of St-Omer, near the cathedral. Traditional, regional cuisine holds sway—nothing fancy, but honest fare such as hot duck sausage, smoked salmon with strips of trout, and local Olivier cheeses. ✉ *8 rue Caventou,* ☎ *03–21–98–20–52. MC, V. Closed Tues. and late Dec.–mid-Jan. No lunch Sat.*

$$$ ★ ✕🏨 **Moulin de Mombreux.** Huge cogs and waterwheels, skillfully integrated into the decor, reflect the 18th-century watermill origins of the Moulin, west of St-Omer in Lumbres. Chef Jean-Marc Gaudry cooks up tasty cuisine—poached oysters in fennel, lamb in foie gras sauce, and raspberry soufflé. Silver candlesticks and original wood beams lend the dining room atmosphere. The discreet if unoriginal charm of pastel shades in the rooms is augmented by a spacious breakfast room with large windows and wicker chairs. ✉ *rte. de Bayenghem, 62380 Lumbres (9 km/6 mi from St-Omer),* ☎ *03–21–39–62–44,* FAX *03–21–93–61–34. 30 rooms. Restaurant, breakfast room. AE, DC, MC, V. Closed mid-Dec.–early Jan.*

En Route If you have gone to the Eperlecques Blockhaus, return to Watten, cross the Aa River, and turn right up to the top of **Mont Watten,** where you will find a ruined abbey, an old windmill, and a sweeping panorama of the surrounding forest and countryside. There is another impressive view 8 km (5 mi) farther along the hilltop road D226, at **Merckeghem:** You can sometimes see to Dunkerque and the sea, 24 km (15 mi) away. Continuing north via D928, you will come to the attractive walled town of **Bergues,** partly surrounded by a moat and canals, and home to a **beer festival** at the end of May and the Christmastime **Fête St-Nicolas** on the first Sunday of December.

Dunkerque

16 *9 km (6 mi) north of Bergues via D916, 37 km (23 mi) north of St-Omer, 73 km (46 mi) northwest of Lille.*

For English-speakers, "Dunkirk" conjures up the evacuation of 1940, when 338,000 men escaped the Nazi advance, ferried to safety across the Channel by an impromptu fleet consisting in large part of small private boats. Dunkerque was three-quarters destroyed in World War II but remains the third largest port in France. Some of the historic buildings left are the 14th-century **Leughenaer** (✉ rue de Leughenaer), one of 28 towers that once circled the town; the 16th-century church of **St-Eloi** (✉ rue Clemenceau); and the 190-foot **Beffroi** (✉ opposite the church) built in 1440, with 48 bells that chime every quarter hour.

Nightlife and the Arts

Dunkerque is renowned for its rambunctious three-day **Carnival** ending Shrove Tuesday, when the inhabitants throng the streets in fancy dress and the mayor flings herrings at the crow from the town-hall balcony. The rest of the year you can fling you rancs into the one-armed bandits at the casino in neighboring **Malo-les-Bains** (✉ pl. du Casino, ☎ 03–28–59–18–23).

Gravelines

⓱ *17 km (11 mi) west of Dunkerque via N1.*

The fortified town of Gravelines is noteworthy for its b star-shape ramparts, surrounded by a moat fed from the Als and were the work of Italian engineer Oligiati, at the behest of Both Emperor Charles V in the 1540s. an

Calais

⓲ *44 km (28 mi) southwest of Dunkerque, 40 km (25 mi) north St-Omer.*

Few vestiges remain of the old, once-pretty port of Calais that owed its wealth to the lace industry rather than to the day-trippers who come across the Channel by ferry to shop for tax-free wine and beer. You won't want to stay here long, but there are a few sights to see before dashing off.

You don't need to be a sculpture fanatic to appreciate Auguste Rodin's powerful bronze **Monument des Bourgeois de Calais,** which dominates the Parc St-Pierre by the town hall (whose sturdy brick tower is visible for miles around). The bourgeois in question were townspeople who, in 1347, when Calais fell to English king Edward III after an eight-month siege, offered their lives in exchange for his sparing the town. Edward's queen, Philippa, intervened on their behalf, and the courageous men were saved. Calais, on the other hand, remained in English hands until 1558, and was the last English toehold in France.

The **Musée des Beaux-Arts et de la Dentelle** (Fine Arts and Lace Museum) contains some fine 19th- and 20th-century paintings, Rodin bronzes, local historical displays, and exhibits documenting the Calais lace industry. ✉ *25 rue Richelieu,* ☎ *03–21–46–48–48.* *15 frs (free Wed.).* ⏲ *Wed.–Mon. 10–noon and 2–5:30.*

The much-restored **Notre-Dame** church, where Général de Gaulle was married in 1921, was built by the English in the 14th century. Admire the simple, vertical elegance of the windows and the ornate fan vaulting. ✉ *rue Notre-Dame.*

Napoléon dreamed of it and the Victorians even started digging it, but it was only in May 1994 that the **Channel Tunnel** (Tunnel sous la Manche) was finally inaugurated by Queen Elizabeth II and late president François Mitterrand. Eurostar rail service between Paris and London began in the fall of 1994. Le Shuttle's special double-decker trains for cars run continually and there is no need to book ahead. Drivers arriving from England disembark at Coquelles, 5 km (3 mi) from Calais, where the Centre Information has models, a film, and brochures on the tunnel and the region. ☎ *03–21–00–60–00.* ⏲ *Information Center: May–Sept., daily 10–7; Oct.–Apr., Mon.–Sat. 2–6, Sun. 10–6.*

Dining

Sole Meunière. As its name ("sole fried in butter") suggests, the Sole Meunière is a temple of fish and seafood—not that anything else could expected from a restaurant next to Calais Harbor. Dine amidst the mate-feeling decor of soft grays and pinks. The prix-fixe menus are a go… value. ✉ *1 bd. de la Résistance,* ☎ *03–21–34–43–01. Reservations essential. AE, DC, MC, V. Closed Mon.*

En Route …thwest of Calais, on the D940 coast road, are two points, Cap Blanc-Nez and **Cap Gris-Nez.** Stop at the latter for a bracing stroll along the cliff tops beneath a lighthouse and the ominous outlines of a World War II concrete bunker. On a clear day you may be able to spot the White Cliffs of Dover across the Channel. D940 continues south, winding past **Ambleteuse,** with its small fort built by Vauban in the 1680s. Farther south along D940, just before Boulogne-sur-Meris, is **Wimereux,** a cheerful Belle Epoque resort town.

…logne-sur-Mer

19 *42 km (26 mi) southwest of Calais via D940; 88 km (55 mi) west of Lille.*

Boulogne-sur-Mer, famous for its kippers (smoked herring), is France's largest fishing port. The rebuilt concrete streets around the port are ugly and unpleasant, but the old town on the hill is a different world—pretty, well-kept, and full of character. Perhaps this is why Napoléon chose Boulogne as his base in 1803 while making his fruitless plans to cross the Channel.

The **Colonne de la Grande Armée,** a 160-foot marble column begun in 1804 to commemorate Napoléon's invasion of England, is north of the town just off the road to Calais. The idea was shelved in 1805, an… the Column was only finished 30 years later under Louis-Philippe. T… 263 steps take you to the top and a wide-reaching panoramic vie… the weather is clear, and you're blessed with Napoleonic vision… may be able to make out the distant cliffs of Dover. ✉ *Off th… to Calais,* ☎ *03–21–80–43–69.* *15 frs.* *Nov.–Sept., Thur… 10–noon and 2–5.*

The four main streets of the **Ville Haute** (Upper Town) inter… **Bouillon.** Here you will find the 18th-century brick **Hôtel…** the **Hôtel Desandrouins,** where Napoléon spent man… pondering how to invade Britain. Dominating them all i… **Basilique Notre-Dame,** its distinctive elongated dom… out at sea. Surrounding the basilica are cobbled streets… ramparts, dating from the 13th century and offeri…

Nausicaâ, the Centre National de la Mer (Nati… claims to be Europe's largest marine complex, v… iums containing no fewer than 4,000 fish. Fi… also staged here, and there is a library, large b… ✉ *bd. Ste-Beuve,* ☎ *03–21–30–98–98.…* *weekdays 10–6, weekends 10–7; June–m…*

Dining and Lodging

$$–$$$ ★ ✕ **Liégeoise.** Good, traditional food … keeps this restaurant at the top of B… modern—an eccentric contrast of bl… and the prix-fixe menus are expen… fies the cost with his delicate sa… the *menu poisson,* the list of ava… *21–31–61–15. Reservations … AE, DC, MC, V. Closed We…*

$$ **Cléry.** Extensive lawns … hotel in an 18th-century ch… Enter to find an old wooden sta…

$–$$ … M… be… int…

Rooms vary in price and decor; those in the former stables were converted into light, spacious, and modern spaces. It was at this château that Napoléon decided to abandon his plans to invade England. As you bask in the peace and quiet of the beautiful grounds, you'll understand why. ✉ *62360 Hesdin-l'Abbé, (8 km/5 mi inland from Boulogne, along N1),* ☎ *03–21–83–19–83,* FAX *03–21–87–52–59. 18 rooms with bath or shower. Breakfast room, tennis court. AE, DC, MC, V.*

$$ **Métropole.** This small hotel is handy for ferry passengers, but like most of the Ville Basse (Lower Town), no great architectural shakes. Although no exciting views are to be had from the rather faceless '50s building, the small garden is pleasant for breakfast in summer and rooms are adequately furnished and individually decorated. ✉ *51 rue Thiers, 62200,* ☎ *03–21–31–54–30,* FAX *03–21–30–45–72. 25 rooms with bath or shower. AE, DC, MC, V. Closed late Dec.–early Jan.*

Outdoor Activities and Sports

The coast is a popular spot for speed sailing and sand sailing, particularly at Le Touquet, Hardelot, Dunkerque, Bray-Dunes, and Berck-sur-Mer (it costs about 80 francs per hour). For details, contact the **Drakkars** club (✉ Base Nautique Sud, 62152 Hardelot-Plage, ☎ 03–21–91–81–96), 14 km (9 mi) south of Boulogne.

Le Touquet

★ 20 *28 km (17 mi) south of Boulogne via D940, 95 km (59 mi) west of Arras.*

At the mouth of the Canche estuary, Le Touquet is a superb example of an elegant Victorian seaside resort town. It sprang out of nowhere in the late 19th century, adopting the name Paris-Plage. Mainly because gambling laws were stricter in Victorian England than in France, the English, not the Parisians, were the town's mainstay. A cosmopolitan atmosphere remains, although many French people, attracted by the airy, elegant avenues and invigorating climate, have moved here for good. On one side is a fine sandy beach; on the other, an artificial forest planted in the 1850s. A casino, golf courses, and a racetrack cater to fashionable leisure activities.

Dining and Lodging

$$$ ✕ **Flavio.** Fish is the star at this elegant spot near the casino. Chef Guy Delmotte specializes in lobster and charges whale-size prices for his lobster menu. The other two prix-fixe menus will please most (wine is included in the 220-franc, weekday carte du jour). Cut glass and Oriental carpets add a note of dated glamour. ✉ *1 av. du Verger,* ☎ *03–21–05–10–22. Reservations essential. Jacket and tie. AE, DC, MC, V. Closed Mon. (except July–Aug.) and Jan.*

$$$ ★ **Westminster.** The Westminster's mammoth redbrick facade looks as if it were built just a few years ago; in fact, it dates from the 1930s and, like the rest of the hotel, has been extensively restored. The enormous double rooms are a good value and the bridal suite is the last word in thick-carpeted extravagance. The hotel's brasserie is modestly priced (lunch and dinner); the Pavillon restaurant serves inventive French cuisine. ✉ *av. du Verger, 62520,* ☎ *03–21–05–48–48,* FAX *03–21–05–45–45. 115 rooms. Restaurant, bar, brasserie, indoor pool, hot tub, sauna, squash. AE, DC, MC, V. Closed mid-Jan.–early Feb.*

Outdoor Activities and Sports

Accolade, a water park on the beachfront, has numerous water-sports facilities, half outdoors, half in, including a toboggan run, a large pool with wave machine, and a sauna. ✉ *bd. Thierry-Sabine,* ☎ *03–21–*

05–63–59. 52 frs for 3 hrs, 58 frs for 4 hrs, 64 frs for 5 hrs, 70 frs all day. Mid-Feb.–June and Sept.–Oct., daily 10–6; July–Aug., daily 10–7.

Montreuil-sur-Mer

21 *16 km (10 mi) east of Le Touquet, 80 km (50 mi) west of Arras.*

Despite its seaside-sounding name, Montreuil-sur-Mer is 16 km (10 mi) inland. It was once a port, but the River Canche silted up and left it high and dry. The ancient town has majestic walls and ramparts, as well as a faded, nostalgic charm to which various authors, notably Victor Hugo, have succumbed; an episode of *Les Misérables* is set here.

Wherever citadels and city walls loom on the French horizon, it's a fair bet that Vauban had a hand in their construction. Montreuil is no exception. In about 1690, Vauban supplemented the existing 16th-century towers of the **Citadelle** with an imposing wall, whose grassy banks and mossy flagstones can be explored at leisure. There are extensive views on all sides. ✉ *rue Carnot,* ☎ *03–21–06–10–83. 10 frs. Wed.–Mon. 10–noon and 2–6.*

OFF THE BEATEN PATH **AZINCOURT** – The Battle of Agincourt (Azincourt in French), one of the proudest dates in English history, took place 35 km (22 mi) east of Montreuil in October 1415 when, in boggy conditions, Henry V's well-grouped, lightly clad longbowmen defeated Charles VI's more numerous, but heavily armored, French troops. There's an orientation map and a clearly marked trail.

Dining and Lodging

$$$–$$$$ ★ **Château de Montreuil.** At this manor house facing the citadel, rooms are furnished with 18th- and 19th-century antiques. No. 208 has a large sitting area and a view of the garden. The less expensive rooms, in the converted stables, are also pleasantly furnished, but smaller. Bathrooms are luxurious. Owner Lindsay Germain is English. Her husband Christian is an excellent chef: His forte is bringing out the natural flavor in such dishes as lightly sautéed scallops served with *pompadour* (a variety of potato) and lamb chops with a wine sauce glaze. The restaurant is closed Thursday lunch and Monday. ✉ *4 chaussée des Capucins, 62170,* ☎ *03–21–81–53–04,* FAX *03–21–81–36–43. 12 rooms and 1 suite. Restaurant. Closed mid-Dec.–Feb.*

En Route Driving from Montreuil-sur-Mer to St-Valery-sur-Somme, you will pass the small town of **Rue,** 28 km (17 mi) south. It is known for its extravagantly sculpted **Chapelle du St-Esprit,** with lacelike stonework and stellar-patterned vaulting. Some 6 km (4 mi) south of Rue is the cheerful, unpretentious resort town of **Le Crotoy** on the northern edge of the **Baie de Somme** (Bay of the Somme), where sheep graze peacefully on the salt marshes. Skirt around the bay on D940 to St-Valery-sur-Somme.

St-Valery-sur-Somme

22 *37 km (23 mi) south of Montreuil-sur-Mer via D940, 65 km (41 mi) northwest of Amiens.*

St-Valery-sur-Somme is a pretty fishing (squid and shellfish are specialties) and resort town with a shady seaside promenade, medieval fortifications, and the remains of St-Valery himself. The flint-and-sandstone-checkerboard **Chapelle des Marins** (Mariners' Chapel), an 18th-century chapel at the far end of the town's bay-side promenade (where there are views of the Somme estuary), houses the tomb of St-Valery.

The **Chemin de Fer de la Baie de Somme** (Somme Bay Steam Railway) chugs around the marshy Somme Bay between St-Valery and Le Crotoy. In 1994 the railway acquired the *130T* locomotive used during construction of the Panama Canal, owned by Detroit's Ford Museum until 1977. ✉ *Departs from the port,* ☎ *03–22–26–96–96.* *63 frs.* *July–Aug., Wed.–Mon. 3:30; Apr.–June and Sept., Wed. and weekends only 3:30.*

The **Maison de l'Oiseau** (Bird House), just west of St-Valery on D204 (direction Cayeux-sur-Mer), has a collection of 400 stuffed birds and a video presentation of their local habitats. ✉ *carrefour du Hourdel,* ☎ *03–22–26–93–93.* *30 frs.* *Mar.–Nov., daily 10–6.*

OFF THE BEATEN PATH

EU and LE TRÉPORT – The neighboring towns of Eu and Le Tréport are 24 km (15 mi) southwest of St-Valery, just over the regional boundary in Normandy. Eu, slightly inland, has a stately church and a brick château where King Louis-Philippe once entertained Queen Victoria. Le Tréport has a lively harbor and cliff-top promenade.

Abbeville

23 *20 km (12 mi) southeast of St-Valery-sur-Somme via D40, 43 km (27 mi) northwest of Amiens.*

The historic town of Abbeville was heavily reconstructed after being reduced to rubble in 1940. Its most admirable building is its Gothic church, **St-Vulfran.** Begun in 1488, it was the last cathedral-size church to be constructed in the Gothic style. It was here that, according to 19th-century art historian John Ruskin, Gothic "lay down and died." After decades of restoration, the riotous tracery and ornament of its much-mauled facade have been revived. The tall, elegant nave retains fine medieval stained glass. Work is still in progress on the 17th-century choir. ✉ *rue St-Vulfran.*

Another magnificent church, **St-Riquier** is 9 km (6 mi) northeast of Abbeville via D925 in the village of the same name. Its nave is over 100 yards long and the majestic Flamboyant Gothic facade is dominated by a weighty, richly sculpted tower.

OFF THE BEATEN PATH

CRÉCY-EN-PONTHIEU – This small town, 19 km (12 mi) north of Abbeville, was the scene of a famous English victory during the Hundred Years' War in 1346, when 20,000 Frenchmen perished at the hands of Edward III. North of the town, on D111, is a hillock known as the Moulin Édouard-III, said to be the site of a windmill where Edward surveyed the battlefield. Just southeast of Crécy on D56 is the Croix de Bohême, a cross marking the spot where France's hapless ally John the Blind, King of Bohemia, stumbled into oblivion.

Amiens

24 *43 km (27 mi) southeast of Abbeville via N1, 64 km (40 mi) southwest of Arras.*

Although much of the city counts as a catastrophic example of post–World War I and II reconstruction, Amiens's Gothic cathedral survived unscathed. The waterfront quarter of **St-Leu,** around the cathedral, is a lively spot to explore: It has colorful, restored houses and eclectic shops.

★ By far the largest church in France, the **Cathédrale Notre-Dame** could fit Paris's Notre-Dame inside twice. It may lack the stained glass of Chartres or the sculpture of Reims, but, for architectural harmony, engineering proficiency, and sheer size, it has no peer. The soaring, asymmetrical facade of the cathedral has a notable Flamboyant Gothic rose window and dominates the surrounding nondescript brick streets. Inside, the overwhelming sensation of space is enhanced by the absence of pews in the nave, a return to medieval tradition. There is no stylistic disunity to mar the perspective: Construction took place between 1220 and 1264, a remarkably short period in cathedral-building terms. One of the highlights of your visit is hidden from the eye, at least until you lift up some of the 110 choir stalls and admire the humorous, skillful misericord (seat) carvings executed between 1508 and 1518. A **son-et-lumière**—with some performances in English—takes place in the cathedral from mid-April through mid-October, Tuesday and Thursday through Saturday. ✉ *pl. St-Michel,* ☎ *03–22–92–77–29. Son-et-lumière:* ☎ *03–22–91–83–83 for information.* 🎫 *60 frs.*

The **Hôtel de Berny,** around the corner from the cathedral, is an elegant brick mansion built in 1633, filled with 18th century furniture and tapestries, and objets d'art. ✉ *36 rue Victor-Hugo,* ☎ *03–22–91–81–12.* 🎫 *10 frs.* ⏲ *Tues.–Sun. 10–12:30 and 2–6.*

Jules Verne (1828–1905) lived in Amiens for some 35 years and his former home has become the **Centre de Documentation Jules Verne** (✉ 2 rue Charles-Dubois, ☎ 03–22–45–37–84). It contains some 15,000 documents about Verne's life as well as original furniture and a reconstruction of the writing studio where he created his science fiction classics. True Verne fans might want to visit his dramatically sculpted tomb in the **Cimetière de la Madeleine** (✉ 2 rue de la Poudrière).

The **Hortillonnages,** on the east side of town, are commercial watergardens—more than 700 acres—where vegetables have been grown since Roman times. They're best visited by boat. ✉ *Boats leave from 54 bd. de Beauvillé,* ☎ *03–22–92–12–18.* 🎫 *30 frs.* ⏲ *Apr.–Oct., daily 2–6.*

Dining and Lodging

$$ ✕ **Joséphine.** This unpretentious, good-value restaurant in central Amiens is a reliable choice. Solid fare, decent wines, and rustic decor (a bit on the stodgy side, like the sauces) pull in many foreign customers, notably Brits. ✉ *20 rue Sire-Firmin-Leroux,* ☎ *03–22–91–47–38. AE, MC, V. Closed Mon. and 3rd wk in Aug. No dinner Sun.*

$$ ✕ **Les Marissons.** In the prettiest and oldest section of Amiens, near the cathedral, this restaurant serves creative takes on regional ingredients. Few of the burbot swimming in the Somme could ever have dreamed they would be end up cooked with apricots, for example; rabbit is accompanied by mint and goat cheese, and black currants add tang to the local pigeon. To avoid pricey dining à la carte, order from one of the three prix-fixe menus. ✉ *68 rue des Marissons,* ☎ *03–22–92–96–66. Jacket and tie. AE, DC, MC, V. Closed Sun. No lunch Sat.*

$–$$ 🏨 **La Paix.** This hotel in an old quarter of Amiens was reconstructed after World War II. Convenience, private parking, and a view of a nearby church from some of the rooms offset a certain lack of personality, though the breakfast room tries valiantly to suggest an 18th-century Louis XV salon. Foreign guests are common and English is spoken. ✉ *8 rue de la République, 80000,* ☎ *03–22–91–39–21,* FAX *03–22–92–02–65. 26 rooms, 11 with bath. Breakfast room, free parking. AE, MC, V.*

Nightlife and the Arts

The **Théâtre d'Animation Picard** (✉ 24 rue St-Leu, ☎ 03–22–92–42–06) presents a rare glimpse of the traditional Picardy marionettes, wooden puppets in bright costumes known locally as Chès Cabotans d'Amiens. Shows are performed on weekends in French (daily in August), with plot synopses in English; admission is 50 francs.

Albert

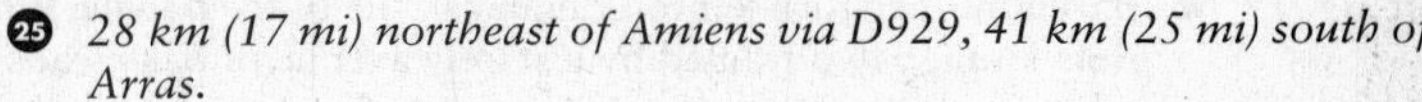

25 *28 km (17 mi) northeast of Amiens via D929, 41 km (25 mi) south of Arras.*

Like nearby Amiens, the dour brick town of Albert stands in the *département* (province) of the Somme—a name forever etched into history as site of one of the bloodiest battles of World War I. On July 1, 1916, whole regiments of Allied soldiers went "over the top" only to be mowed down by a hail of German machine-gun fire. When the front stabilized in late November, the Allies had advanced just 8 km (5 mi). Even now, 80 years later, shells and grenades still rise to the surface of the fields hereabouts; 90 tons of these dormant time bombs are collected and destroyed every year.

The **Musée des Abris** (Trenches Museum) uses photographs, costumes, guns, and sandbags to evoke the soldiers' life in the trenches. The museum is almost entirely underground (wear a sweater) and, by the time you come up for air, you've tunneled your way through to a tranquil park 100 yards from where you started. ✉ *rue Anicet-Godin,* ☎ *03–22–75–16–17.* 🎫 *25 frs.* ⏲ *Mar.–Nov., daily 10–noon and 2–6.*

Looming above the museum is the neo-Byzantine, brick **Basilique Notre-Dame-de-Brébières,** an ostentatious country cousin of churches like Fourvière in Lyon or Sacré-Coeur in Paris. Its wealth derives from a "miraculous" 11th-century statue of the Virgin Mary, still venerated by pilgrims. But it is another miraculous statue of the Virgin—the one on top of the 220-foot tower—that captivates most visitors. When the basilica was nearly reduced to rubble in 1916, this mighty gold Virgin, holding aloft the infant Jesus, was left dangling from the tower at right-angles, as if held in place by a magic thread. Postcards showing this astonishing scene look like primitive examples of trick photography; in fact, they capture one of the most poignant, symbolic images of World War I. ✉ *pl. d'Armes,* ☎ *03–22–75–09–54.*

Dining

$$ ✕ **L'Escale.** This vine-covered restaurant in the tiny village of Cappy, southeast of Albert, is worth seeking out: With its antiques and needlework tablecloths and menu illustrated with poems and old photos, it has the feel of a country cottage. The seasonal, regional dishes (smoked eel, duck, and black pudding) are accompanied by subtle, refined sauces. ✉ *22 chaussée Léon-Blum, Cappy (10 km/6 mi southeast of Albert),* ☎ *03–22–76–02–03. MC, V. No dinner Sun.–Wed.*

The Somme Battlefields

The Battle of the Somme raged from July through November 1916 and left a million dead. During those five futile months, the Allies, including Irish, Canadian, and South African soldiers, progressed about 8 km (5 mi) along the hills above the Ancre River north of Albert.

From Albert, take D929 (direction Bapaume) and stop after 2 km (1 mi) at **La Boisselle,** to inspect the awesome Lochnagar Crater caused by German shellfire. Follow D20 west from La Boisselle, then D50 north, to reach the **Beaumont-Hamel Parc Mémorial,** where a bronze caribou—

emblem of the Newfoundland regiments that fought here—peers mournfully over trenches and undulating, shell-shocked terrain. Backtrack down the hill from the Newfoundland memorial, cross the Ancre River, and head up the hill on the other side. On the left is the **Tour Ulster** (Ulster Tower) commemorating troops from Belfast. A few hundred yards past the Ulster Tower is the village of Thiepval; follow signs to the bombastic brick **British War Memorial,** a disjointed triumphal arch that looks as if it were made of giant Lego blocks. Take D73 to
★ Bazentin, then turn left to Longueval, site of the **Delville Wood Memorial**: A long lawn framed by a stately avenue of oaks leads to an airy, white-stone pentagon, modeled on the Castle of Good Hope in Cape Town. Here giant photographs and etched glass panels evoke the memories of South Africans who fought in the war.

Péronne

26 *15 km (10 mi) southeast of Longueval via D20 and N17, 27 km (17 mi) southeast of Albert, 50 km (31 mi) east of Amiens.*

The small, brick town of Péronne was almost entirely razed in 1916.
★ It is now home to a fine World War I museum, the **Historial de la Grande Guerre.** Tastefully integrated within a ruined brick castle, this spacious modern museum has a thought-provoking variety of exhibits, from TV monitors playing old newsreel to soldiers' uniforms strung out on the floor surrounded by machine guns and a dim roomful of nightmarish war lithographs by Otto Dix. There is a good shop, with books in English, and café with views of a leafy-banked lake. Walk around to the end and you'll find the Somme River, strewn with islands, languidly colliding with its tributary, the Cologne. ✉ *pl. du Château,* ☎ *03–22–83–14–18.* 🎟 *39 frs.* ⏲ *May–Sept., daily 10–6; Oct.–mid-Dec. and mid-Jan.–Apr., Tues.–Sun. 10–5:30.*

Le Cateau-Cambrésis

27 *50 km (31 mi) northeast of Péronne via D6 and D932.*

★ Artist Henri Matisse (1869–1954) was born in Le Cateau. The **Musée Matisse** (Matisse Museum), housed in the Palais Fénelon (former home to the archbishops of Cambrai), contains a number of early oil paintings and sculptures, plus a superb collection of 50 drawings selected by Matisse himself. Call ahead to ask the enthusiastic curator, Dominique Szymusiak, to show you around (her English is excellent). ✉ *Palais Félon,* ☎ *03–27–84–13–15.* 🎟 *16 frs.* ⏲ *Wed.–Sat. and Mon. 10–noon and 2–6, Sun. 10–noon and 2:30–6. Free guided tour Sun. at 3.*

SOUTH PICARDY, CHAMPAGNE, AND THE ARDENNES

As you head east, from Beauvais to Laon, the plains of Picardy gradually give way to rolling, wooded hills, then, closer to the Belgian border, to the rugged Ardennes forests. Farther south, the cheerful villages and vine-covered slopes of Champagne, around Reims, provide a scenic circuit for all with a taste for the world's bubbliest wine. Châlons-en-Champagne, the administrative capital of Champagne country, is easily accessible from Paris, the Channel, and Lorraine (☞ Chapter 8).

Beauvais

28 *60 km (18 mi) south of Amiens via A16; 95 km (59 mi) southwest of Péronne via N17, D930, and N1; 76 km (48 mi) north of Paris.*

Beauvais and its neighbor Amiens have been rivals since the 13th century, when they locked horns over who could build the bigger cathedral. Beauvais lost—gloriously.

★ Bristling with pinnacles and flying buttresses, and soaring like some giant hedgehog above the characterless modern blocks of the town center, is the tallest cathedral in France: the **Cathédrale St-Pierre.** You may have an attack of vertigo just gazing up at its vaults, 153 feet off the ground. Tallest, yes; biggest, no. The choir collapsed in 1284, shortly after completion, and was only rebuilt with the aid of extra pillars. This engineering fiasco proved so costly that the transept was not attempted until the 16th century. It was worth the wait: the transept is an outstanding example of Flamboyant Gothic, and still standing—which is more than can be said for the megalomaniac 450-foot spire erected at the same time. This lasted precisely seven years and, when it came crashing down, the nave was shored up, all remaining funds were hurled at an emergency consolidation program, and Beauvais's dream of having the largest church in Christendom disappeared. Now the cathedral is starting to lean and cracks have appeared in the choir vaults. No such problems bedevil the **Basse Oeuvre** (closed to the public), which juts out impertinently where the nave should have been: It has been there for a thousand years. ⏲ *Daily 9–12:30 and 2–6.*

From 1664 to 1939, Beauvais was one of France's leading tapestry centers; it reached its zenith in the mid-18th century. The modern **Galerie Nationale de la Tapisserie** (National Tapestry Gallery), next to the cathedral, has examples from all periods. ✉ *1 rue St-Pierre,* ☎ *03–44–05–14–28.* 🎫 *25 frs.* ⏲ *Mar.–Oct., Tues.–Sun. 9:30–11:30 and 2:30–6; Nov.–Feb., Tues.–Sun. 10–11:30 and 2:30–4:30.*

The beautiful old Bishop's Palace, now the **Musée Départemental de l'Oise** (Oise Museum), contains a varied collection of paintings, ceramics, and regional furniture. Highlights include an epic canvas of the French Revolution by 19th-century master Thomas Couture, complete with preparatory sketches, and the lovely attic room under the sloping roofs. ✉ *1 rue du Musée,* ☎ *03–44–48–48–48.* 🎫 *16 frs.* ⏲ *Wed.–Mon. 10–noon and 2–6.*

Compiègne

29 *60 km (38 mi) east of Beauvais via N31, 82 km (51 mi) northeast of Paris.*

Compiègne, a bustling town of some 40,000 people, is at the northern limit of the Ile-de-France forest, on the edge of the misty plains of Picardy: prime hunting country, a sure sign that there's a former royal palace in the vicinity. The one here enjoyed its heyday in the mid-19th century under Napoléon III. But the town's place in history looks both farther back—Joan of Arc was captured in battle and held prisoner here, and the 15th-century Hôtel de Ville possesses an exceptional Flamboyant Gothic facade—and farther forward: The World War I armistice was signed in Compiègne Forest on November 11, 1918.

★ The 18th-century **Palais de Compiègne** was restored by Napoléon I and favored for wild weekends by his nephew Napoléon III. The first Napoléon's legacy is more clearly felt: His state apartments have been refurnished, using the original designs for wall hangings and upholstery, and brightly colored silk and damask adorn every room. Much of the elegant mahogany Empire furniture gleams with ormolu, and the chairs sparkle with gold leaf. Napoléon III's furniture looks, in contrast, ponderous and ostentatious. A gently rising, 4-km (2½-mi) vista leads back from the palace, inspired by the park at Schönbrunn in Vienna, where Napoléon I's second wife, empress Marie-Louise, was brought up. Also here is the **Musée de la Voiture** (Car Museum), which has a large collection of carriages, coaches, and old cars, including the *Jamais Contente* ("Never Satisfied"), the first car to reach 100 kph (62 mph). ✉ *pl. du Général de Gaulle,* ☎ *03–44–40–04–37.* *32 frs.* *Wed.–Mon. 9:15–6:15.*

An amazing collection of 85,000 lead soldiers depicting military uniforms through the ages is found in the **Musée de la Figurine** (Figurine Museum). ✉ *28 pl. de l'Hôtel-de-Ville,* ☎ *03–44–40–72–55.* *12 frs.* *Mar.–Oct., Wed.–Sun. 9–noon and 2–6; Nov.–Feb., Wed.–Sun. 9–noon and 2–5.*

Some 7 km (4 mi) east of Compiègne via N31, near Rethondes, is the **Wagon de l'Armistice** (Armistice Rail Car), a replica of the one where the World War I armistice was signed in 1918. In 1940 the Nazis turned the tables and made the French sign their own surrender in the same place—accompanied by Hitler's famous jig for joy—then tugged the car off to Berlin, where it was later destroyed. The car is part of a small museum in a leafy clearing. ✉ *Near Rethondes off of N31,* *10 frs.* *Apr.–Oct., Wed.–Mon. 9–noon and 2–6:30; Nov.–Mar., Wed.–Mon. 9–noon and 2–5:30.*

Dining and Lodging

$$ **Rôtisserie du Chat qui Tourne.** It may have a silly name (The Cat That Turns the Spit), but this hotel is central, cheap, and the epitome of French provincial—rooms have creaky, uneven floors and the prim *patronne,* Madame Robert, appears from nowhere as you cross the threshold with all the officious alacrity of a Paris concierge. Avoid the smaller rooms; others can sleep four and are ideal for families with young children. The restaurant, with its brass lights and plush curtains, tries vainly to resemble an antechamber as blasé waiters putter around failing to be discreet. The cuisine is inventive (scallops in crab sauce, duck with figs), but avoid the skimpy 90-franc lunch menu. ✉ *17 rue Eugène-Floquet, 60200,* ☎ *03–44–40–02–74,* FAX *03–44–40–48–37. 21 rooms with bath or shower. Bar. MC, V.*

Pierrefonds

★ 30 *14 km (9 mi) southeast of Compiègne via D973, 77 km (48 mi) northeast of Paris.*

Dominating the attractive lakeside village of Pierrefonds is its huge medieval castle. Built in the 12th century, the **Château de Pierrefonds** was comprehensively restored in the 1860s to imagined former glory at the behest of upstart emperor Napoléon III. Architect Viollet-le-Duc left a crenellated fortress with a fairy-tale silhouette, although, like the fortified town of Carcassonne which he also restored, Pierrefonds is considered more a construct of what Viollet-le-Duc thought it should have looked like than what it really was. A visit takes in the chapel, barracks, and the majestic keep holding the lord's bedchamber and reception hall. ☎ *03–44–42–72–72.* *32 frs.* *Guided tours only: May–Aug., daily 10–6; Apr. and Sept., daily 10–noon and 2–6; Oct.–Mar., Thurs.–Mon. 10–noon and 2–4:30.*

Dining and Lodging

$$ **Étrangers.** An attractive lakeside terrace, château views, and a welcoming restaurant make this three-story hotel ideal, although it lacks an elevator. American and English guests are frequent. In the restaurant, try the monkfish in blueberries or the slow-cooked veal-kidney casserole. Menus begin at 95 francs. The restaurant is closed Monday from mid-November to mid-March and Sunday dinner. ✉ *10 rue*

Beaudon, 60350, ☎ *03–44–42–80–18,* FAX *03–44–42–86–74. 18 rooms, 10 with bath. Restaurant, horseback riding, bicycles. AE, DC, MC, V.*

Morienval

31 *8 km (5 mi) south of Pierrefonds via D335.*

The village of Morienval is best known for its elegant but relatively modest 11th-century Romanesque church: one of the key buildings in architectural history. In 1122 the relics of St-Annobert were translated to the **Église Notre-Dame,** and the church became a center of pilgrimage. The need for a new ambulatory (so everyone could get a look at the saintly remains) was obvious, but no one knows why the masons at Morienval, when extending the church at the east end behind the altar, hit on the innovative idea of using stone vaults, supported on "ribs" springing diagonally from column to column. Few dispute, however, that this architectural breakthrough, the structural basis of the Gothic style (along with pointed arches), occurred at Morienval about 1135. It was promptly adopted at the great basilica of St-Denis near Paris and swept through northern France during the years that followed. Much of the original church remains, notably the east tower and the columns in the nave, whose astonishing carved capitals feature spirals, stars, masks, and animals.

Soissons

32 *31 km (19 mi) east of Pierrefonds via D335 and N31, 96 km (60 mi) northeast of Paris via N2, 56 km (35 mi) west of Reims.*

Although much damaged in World War I, Soissons commands attention for its two huge churches: one intact, one in ruins.

The Gothic **Cathédrale Notre-Dame** is nearly 130 yards long. The interior, with its pure lines and restrained ornament, creates a more harmonious impression than the asymmetrical, one-tower facade. The most remarkable feature, however, is the rounded, two-story transept, a feature more frequently found in the German Rhineland than in France. ✉ *pl. Fernand-Marquigny.*

The twin-spired facade is all that is left of the abbey church of **St-Jean-des-Vignes,** otherwise destroyed just after the Revolution, with its stones used to restore the cathedral. Ruined or not, St-Jean-des-Vignes remains the most impressive sight in Soissons, its hollow rose-window peering out over the town like the eye of some giant Cyclops. ✉ *cours St-Jean-des-Vignes.*

Blérancourt

33 *23 km (14 mi) northwest of Soissons via D6.*

Blérancourt is home to the **Musée National de la Coopération Franco-Américain** (Museum of French-American Cooperation). Two pavilions and monumental archways are all that remain of the original 17th-century château, demolished during the French Revolution. Anne Morgan founded the museum in 1924. Pictures, sculptures, and documents chart Franco-American relations, with emphasis on the American Revolution and the two world wars. The grounds include gardens and an arboretum. ☎ *03–23–39–60–16.* 🎫 *16 frs.* ⏲ *Wed.–Mon. 10–12:30 and 2–5:30.*

Noyon

34 *14 km (9 mi) northwest of Blérancourt, 37 km (23 mi) northwest of Soissons, 24 km (15 mi) northeast of Compiègne.*

Noyon is a frequently overlooked cathedral town that owed its medieval importance to the cult of 7th-century St. Eloi, patron of blacksmiths and a former town bishop. Its second famous son, the Protestant theologian John Calvin, was born here in 1509. The old streets around the cathedral are at their liveliest during the Saturday morning market.

Constructed between 1150 and 1290, the **Cathédrale St-Eloi** was one of the earliest attempts at what was to become the Gothic cathedral, as is evident in the four-story nave; the intermittent use of rounded as well as pointed arches; and the thin, pointed lancet (as opposed to rose) windows in the austere facade. Pause for a wry smile at the "piazza" in front of the cathedral, with its elegant town houses arranged in a semicircle in bashful imitation of St. Peter's in Rome; then head down the cobbled lane to the left of the facade to admire the timber-fronted, 16th-century library behind the cathedral.

Dining and Lodging

$$ ✕🏨 **St-Eloi.** Conveniently located between the station and the cathedral, this stylish hotel, with its renovated, marble-lined reception area and airy, pastel-shade dining room, belies its forbidding redbrick exterior. The spacious rooms have high ceilings and reproduction furniture; several have garden views. Affordable prix-fixe menus are available in the restaurant, which is closed Sunday dinner and August. ✉ *81 bd. Carnot, 60400,* ☎ *03–44–44–01–49,* FAX *03–44–09–20–90. 17 rooms. Restaurant, bar. MC, V.*

En Route N32 leads east from Noyon to **Chauny,** with its colossal town hall and handsome 1920s buildings. From Chauny, D1 south will take you to **Coucy-le-Château,** a hilltop village whose majestic walls—once punctuated by 28 towers—took a hammering during World War I. From Coucy, drive southeast through Pinon, turning left onto N2 and right along D18, to arrive at the hilltop road separating the valleys of the Aisne and the Ailette, known as the **Chemin des Dames,** the site of a disastrous French offensive in April 1917 that led to futile slaughter and mutiny. Pass through **Cerny-en-Laonnois,** stopping briefly at the French memorial and the dank, dismal **Caverne du Dragon,** used as an arsenal and living quarters by the Germans and now the site of an eerie underground war museum open Wednesday–Monday, 10:30–noon and 2–5:30. At the **Plateau de Californie,** near Craonne, there is a panoramic view of the scene of combat. From Corbeny, take N44 northwest to Laon.

Laon

★ 35 *53 km (33 mi) east of Noyon, 47 km (29 mi) northwest of Reims, 47 km (29 mi) southeast of St-Quentin.*

On a splendid hilltop site, Laon is called the "crowned mountain"—a reference to the forest of towers sprouting from its ancient cathedral. The cathedral and enchanting old town are a must, but strangely, the French ignore Laon as a tourist venue. The medieval ramparts, virtually undisturbed by passing traffic, provide a ready-made itinerary for a tour of old Laon. Panoramic views, sturdy gateways, and intriguing glimpses of the cathedral lurk around every bend.

★ The **Cathédrale Notre-Dame,** constructed between 1160 and 1235, is a superb example of early Gothic. The light interior gives the impression of order and immense length (120 yards in total). The flat east end, an English-inspired feature, is unusual in France. The upper galleries that extend around the building are typical of early Gothic; you can visit them (and the towers) on weekend afternoons with a guide from the tourist office (☞ Contacts and Resources *in* The North and Champagne A to Z, *below*) on the cathedral square. The filigreed elegance of the five remaining towers is audacious and rare: French medieval architects preferred to concentrate on soaring interiors, with just two towers at the west end. Note the sense of movement imparted by Laon's majestic west front; compare it with the more placid, two-dimensional feel of Notre-Dame in Paris. Look, too, for the stone oxen protruding from the towers—a tribute to the stalwart, 12th-century beasts who carted up blocks of stone from quarries far below. ✉ *pl. du Parvis.*

The **Chapelle des Templiers** is a small, well-preserved octagonal 12th-century chapel on the grounds of the **Musée de Laon,** the town museum. The museum has a fine collection of Greek terra-cotta vases. ✉ *32 rue Georges-Ermant,* ☎ *03–23–20–19–87.* 🎫 *Museum 15 frs.* ⏲ *Apr.–Oct., Wed.–Mon. 10–noon and 2–6; Nov.–Mar., Wed.–Mon. 10–noon and 2–5.*

Dining and Lodging

$$ ✕ **La Petite Auberge.** Chef Willy-Marc Zorn dishes up modern, imaginative cuisine at this cozy, 18th-century-style restaurant close to the train station. The hare stew and salmon with pigs' feet are especially good. The recherché, 149- and 199-franc menus are good bets. ✉ *45 bd. Pierre-Brossolette,* ☎ *03–23–23–02–38. AE, DC, MC, V. No lunch Sat. or dinner Sun.*

$$ ✕🏨 **Bannière de France.** In business since 1685, this old-fashioned, uneven-floored hostelry is just five minutes from the cathedral. Madame Lefèvre, the patronne, speaks fluent German and English. Rooms are cozy and quaint. The restaurant's venerable dining room features sturdy cuisine (trout, guinea fowl, lemon sole à la Normande) and good-value, prix-fixe menus. ✉ *11 rue Franklin-Roosevelt, 02000,* ☎ FAX *03–23–23–31–56. 18 rooms, 14 with bath or shower. Restaurant. AE, DC, MC, V. Closed late Dec.–early Jan.*

Vervins

36 *36 km (22 mi) northeast of Laon via N2, 48 km (30 mi) east of St-Quentin.*

Vervins is everybody's idea of a picture-postcard French village. Snugly tucked in behind crumbling ramparts, the town's steep, purplish slate roofs are set off against slender redbrick chimneys. Explore its tumbling cobbled streets and inspect the church of **Notre-Dame,** with its 13th-century choir, wall paintings (notably Jouvenet's vast 1699 *Le Repas Chez Simon*), and 16th-century tower propped up by bulky corner buttressing.

Dining and Lodging

$$$ ✕🏨 **Tour du Roy.** This hotel, in a converted medieval manor house built of stone from the town's ramparts, is run by garrulous Claude Desvignes. While he rattles away amusingly in English, his wife, Annie, holds sway in the kitchen. An excellent cook, she creates classical dishes with an emphasis on local produce and dishes like turbot with sorrel, and *flamiche aux poireaux* (puff pastry tart with cream and leeks). Rooms display the character of the owners: a blend of the traditional and the modern; one of the best has a private roof terrace. ✉ *45 rue du*

Général-Leclerc, 02140, ☏ *03–23–98–00–11,* FAX *03–23–98–00–72. 12 rooms, 3 suites. Restaurant. AE, DC, MC, V. Closed mid-Jan.–mid-Feb.*

En Route Vervins is on the edge of the French Ardennes, the thick forested region along the Belgian border. But you can go further into the Ardennes by heading northeast on D963 via Hirson, Auvillers-les-Forges, and the fortress town of Rocroi, to **Revin,** a small industrial town tucked in between a double bend in the meandering Meuse River. As D1 twines southwest along the tortuous, wooded Meuse River Valley, an imposing row of rolling peaks, the **Dames de Meuse,** looms to the right. Across the river is the 900-foot Roches de Laifour, striking rock formations. Pause at the village of **Monthermé** to stroll through the old streets. From Monthermé, D1 hugs the river past slate quarries and metalworks, through oak and evergreen forest. Due north of Charleville-Mézières are the four spiky quartzite summits of the **Rocher des Quatre Fils Aymon** (Aymon's Four Sons), a steep rock formation rising above Château-Regnault.

Charleville-Mézières

37 *69 km (43 mi) southeast of Vervins, 80 km (50 mi) northeast of Reims.*

Charleville-Mézières, in the Ardennes, was originally two towns separated by a branch of the capricious River Meuse. Mézières, an administrative and military center, has a more regimented feel than folksy Charleville, where a warren of narrow pedestrian streets encircles a large, shambling square. The two towns were officially united in 1966.

With its pink brick, arcades, and steep slate roofs, Charleville's **place Ducale,** designed around 1610 by Clément Métezeau, recalls the place des Vosges in Paris, designed by his elder brother Louis. Place Ducale has no trees or railings to mask the view; its original symmetry, however, has been zapped by rooftop accretions and a 19th-century church and town hall. The square is at its liveliest during the market on Tuesday, Thursday, and Saturday mornings.

The **Vieux Moulin** (Old Mill), a majestic 1626 watermill straddling a branch of the Meuse, hosts temporary art exhibits and a museum devoted to Charleville's most famous son: precocious "punk" poet Arthur Rimbaud. Pictures, souvenirs, and photographs chart his turbulent career, revealing that he fled Charleville at age 17, after writing his masterpiece, "Le Bateau Ivre" ("*The Drunken Boat*"). He died in 1891 in Marseille at age 37 but is buried in Charleville's town cemetery. ✉ *quai Arthur-Rimbaud,* ☏ *03–24–32–44–65.* *10 frs.* ⏲ *Tues.–Sun. 10–noon and 2–6.*

The subtle lighting and spacious, imaginative layout at the **Musée de l'Ardennes** (Ardennes Museum) lend its displays of guns, coins, keys, pottery, and archaeological findings an almost abstract aesthetic appeal. There are also local paintings and a re-created, rustic regional interior. ✉ *31 pl. Ducale,* ☏ *03–24–32–44–60.* *22 frs.* ⏲ *Tues.–Sun. 10–noon and 2–6.*

Le Grand Marionnettiste (The Giant Puppeteer), tucked away between the Musée de l'Ardennes and place Winston Churchill, was commissioned in 1991 by Charleville's International Puppet Institute. It is a surreal spectacle: a huge turquoise frame, topped by a clock and a gold mask peeping out of the roof, with a pair of giant gold legs in the alleyway beneath. Every hour from 10 AM to 9 PM, the red stage curtains slide open to reveal gold hands pulling the strings of a plethora of puppets enacting the local legend of the *Quatre Fils Aymon* (*Aymon's*

Four Sons), after which the rock formations north of town are named. On Saturday at 9:15 PM, all 12 tableaux appear in sequence.

★ In the 16th-century basilica of **Notre-Dame de l'Espérance,** in Mézières, Charles IX married Elizabeth of Austria in 1570. It has a four-square Renaissance tower topped by a fancy 19th-century spire, but the real attraction lies inside. "The church of Mézières is reputed for its stained glass," wrote Victor Hugo in 1838. Alas, the windows he admired have long since been blasted into oblivion during repeated invasions, but today you can admire the most ambitious modern stained glass anywhere in France: an entire church of abstract, geometric designs by René Dürrbach. The overall effect is a breathtaking collision of old and new, one of the most homogeneous displays of stained glass outside Chartres. A guidebook to its biblical symbolism is available from the presbytery. ✉ *av. de St-Julien.*

Dining

$$ ✕ **La Côte à l'Os.** Fish is the specialty here: Sea bass, marinated salmon, and braised pike often figure on the menu. The long, cheerful dining room, decked out with fresh flowers, is popular with locals for its 89-franc, prix-fixe lunch menu. Service is welcoming but low-key. ✉ *11 cours Aristide-Briand,* ☎ *03–24–59–20–16. AE, MC, V.*

Sedan

㊳ *21 km (13 mi) southeast of Charleville-Mézières via A203.*

The fame of Sedan far outweighs its modest size. To English speakers its name has become associated with cars and chairs—accidentally, say sedentary etymologists. In France, Sedan is forever written into the national psyche because here, in 1870, Napoléon III's Second Empire came crashing down as the Prussian army smashed through, taking Napoléon and 83,000 soldiers prisoner, then steaming on toward Paris. Émile Zola captured the mayhem in his epic novel *La Débâcle*.

★ The grim, massive **Château Fort** that dominates Sedan may not be the most impregnable in Europe, but it claims to be the largest. The colossal front, illuminated at night, dominates the town like a Wall of Jericho; the daunting courtyard is hemmed in by bleak walls seven stories high and up to 24 feet thick. The castle was used as a prison during World War II, and you can see why.

Founded in 1424 by the Lords of Sedan, the castle was virtually a town in its own right and could house 4,000 soldiers. Its sturdy walls withstood sieges in 1495 and 1521, when Charles V was forced to seek a truce despite attacking with more than 30,000 men. Elizabeth of Austria stayed here in 1570 before her marriage to Charles IX in Mézières, as did Henri II and Catherine de' Medici, and Henri IV and Maria de' Medici. Sedan became part of France only in 1642; Louis XIV stayed here during the siege of Stenay. Documents relating the castle's history can be examined in the **museum** in the south wing, along with archaeological finds. The castle's **Historium** has tableaux depicting its history, and a self-guided tour with infrared headsets and multilingual commentary. Try to visit at nightfall on Friday, Saturday, or Sunday in summer for a guided tour by torchlight. ☎ *03–24–27–73–75.* 🎫 *45 frs.* ⏲ *Mid-Mar.–mid-Sept., daily 10–6; mid-Sept.–mid-Mar., daily 1:30–5:30.*

In the **Vieille Ville** (Old Town), between the castle and the Meuse, several streets are pedestrians-only, especially around place d'Armes. The square is dominated by the church of **St-Charles,** with its pepper-pot towers. The triangular **place de la Halle** leads into **rue du Ménil,** lined with 17th- and 18th-century houses. **Place Turenne,** by the river, is spoiled by the five skyscrapers that glower down from the hill behind, although from here you can glimpse remnants of the awesome walls and catch a rooftop view of higgledy-piggledy chimneys gushing smoke in a satisfyingly Dickensian manner.

Dining and Lodging

$ ✕🏨 **Europe.** Convenience is the main reason to stay at this modern hotel by the train station, on the outskirts of town. Rooms are clean, comfortable, and soundproof, if a little characterless. The spacious bar is a fine place to unwind with an aperitif before dining on boar or venison (in season) at the hotel restaurant. ✉ *2 pl. de la Gare, 08200,* ☎ *03–24–27–18–71,* FAX *03–24–29–32–00. 24 rooms with bath or shower. Restaurant, bar. MC, V. Closed late Dec.–early Jan.*

OFF THE BEATEN PATH

DOUZY – The small aerodrome in Douzy, 8 km (5 mi) east of Sedan via N43, is home to the Musée des Débuts de l'Aviation (Museum of the Origins of Aviation), devoted, in particular, to the pioneering exploits of Roger Sommer (1877–1965), who edged past Wilbur Wright's previous best to set a flight record of 2 hours, 27 minutes at Châlons-en-Champagne on August 7, 1909. 🎫 *14 frs.* ⏲ *June–Aug., Tues.–Sun. 10–noon and 2–6; May and Sept., Tues.–Sun. 2–6; Apr. and Oct., weekends 2–6.*

Mouzon

39 *9 km (6 mi) south of Douzy via D964; 17 km (11 mi) southeast of Sedan.*

The small village of Mouzon, on the Meuse River, is dwarfed beneath the twin towers of its 13th-century abbey church. With fat, round columns and a second-story gallery, the imposing edifice of the **Église Notre-Dame,** 215 feet long and 70 feet high, is a stylistic successor to the cathedrals of Laon and Notre-Dame in Paris.

The **Musée du Feutre** (Felt Museum) outlines the 8,000-year history of felt, from its immemorial manufacture in Turkey, Afghanistan, and Mongolia to its latter-day use in games, decorations, cars, and pens. ✉ *rue Jean-Claude-Stoltz,* ☎ *03–24–26–19–91.* 🎫 *14 frs.* ⏲ *July–Aug., daily 10–noon and 2–6; June and Sept., daily 2–6; Apr., May, and Oct., weekends 2–6.*

Asfeld

40 *84 km (52 mi) southwest of Mouzon via D19, D30, and D926; 28 km (17 mi) north of Reims.*

The tiny village of Asfeld is home to one of France's most surprising churches. The **Église St-Didier,** designed by Father François Romain for the Count d'Avaux in 1683, is a whimsical essay in Roman Baroque, with curves, cupolas, a rotunda, colonnades, oval side chapels, and hardly a straight line in sight. The ground plan is said to be based on a viola, and the individual bricks are not rectangular but concave or convex. The church would look swell in a tony sector of Rome; in this tiny village it hovers between the sublime and the ridiculous. ☎ *03–24–72–94–97.* ⏲ *Daily 8–7.*

Reims

27 km (17 mi) south of Asfeld via D926, D37, and D274; 144 km (90 mi) east of Paris.

Although most of its historic buildings were flattened in World War I and replaced by drab, modern architecture, Reims sparkles with some of the biggest names in champagne production. The maze of champagne cellars make the city a must, as do the splendid cathedral and the fine arts museum. Several champagne producers organize visits to their cellars, combining video presentations with guided tours of their cavernous, chalk-hewn underground warehouses.

★ 41 Reims's **Cathédrale Notre-Dame** was the age-old setting for the coronations of the French kings. Clovis, king of the Franks in the 6th century, was baptized in an early structure on this site; Joan of Arc led her recalcitrant dauphin here to be crowned King Charles VII; Charles X's coronation, in 1825, was the last. The high, solemn nave is at its best in summer when the light shows up the plain lower walls adorned by 16th-century tapestries relating the life of the Virgin Mary. The east-end windows have stained glass by Marc Chagall. Admire the vista toward the west end, with an interplay of narrow pointed arches.

The glory of Reims's cathedral is its facade: It's so skillfully proportioned that initially you have little idea of its monumental size. Above the north (left) door hovers the *Laughing Angel,* a delightful statue whose famous smile threatens to melt into an acid-rain scowl. Pollution has succeeded war as the ravager of the building's fabric. Restoration is an ongoing process. With the exception of the 15th-century towers, most of the original building went up in the 100 years after 1211. A stroll around the outside reinforces the impression of harmony, discipline, and decorative richness. The east end presents an idyllic sight across well-tended lawns. Spectacular **son-et-lumière** shows are performed both inside (50 francs) and outside (free) the cathedral on evenings in July and August. ✉ *pl. du Cardinal-Luçon.* ⏲ *Daily 7:30–7:30.*

42 The **Palais du Tau** (the former archbishop's palace), alongside the cathedral, houses an impressive display of tapestries and coronation robes, as well as several statues rescued from the cathedral facade before they fell off. The second-floor views of Notre-Dame are terrific. ✉ *2 pl. du Cardinal-Luçon,* ☎ *03–26–47–81–79.* 🎫 *32 frs.* ⏲ *July–Aug., daily 9:30–6:30; mid-Mar.–June and Sept.–mid-Nov., daily 9:30–12:30 and 2–6; mid-Nov.–mid-Mar., weekdays 10–noon and 2–5, weekends 10–noon and 2–6.*

43 The **Musée des Beaux-Arts,** two blocks southwest of the cathedral, has an outstanding collection of paintings: no fewer than 27 Corots, and Jacques-Louis David's celebrated portrait of the Revolutionary polemicist Jean-Paul Marat stabbed in his bath by Charlotte Corday. ✉ *8 rue Chanzy,* ☎ *03–26–47–28–44.* 🎫 *10 frs, or 15 frs for joint ticket with the Salle de Reddition (*☞ below*).* ⏲ *Wed.–Mon. 10–noon and 2–6.*

44 The 11th-century **Basilique St-Rémi,** down rue Chanzy and rue Gambetta, honors the 5th-century saint who gave his name to the city. St-Rémi is nearly as long as the cathedral, and its interior seems to stretch into the endless distance, an impression created by its relative murk and lowness. The airy, four-story Gothic choir contains some fine original 12th-century stained glass. ✉ *53 rue St-Rémi,* ☎ *03–26–85–31–20.*

The tour of the **Taittinger** cellars is the most spectacular. ✉ *9 pl. St-Niçaise,* ☎ *03–26–85–45–35.* ⏲ *Weekdays 9:30–1 and 2–5:30, weekends 9–noon and 2–6. Closed weekends Dec.–Feb.*

46 **Mumm** is one of the few champagne houses to give out free samples after the tour. ✉ *34 rue du Champ-de-Mars,* ☎ *03–26–49–59–70.* ⏲ *Mar.–Oct., daily 9–11 and 2–5.*

47 The **Porte de Mars,** an unlikely but impressive 3rd-century Roman arch adorned by faded bas-reliefs depicting Jupiter, Romulus, and Remus, looms up across from the train station. ✉ *rue de Mars.*

Basilique St-Rémi, **44**
Cathédrale Notre-Dame, **41**
Mumm, **46**
Musée des Beaux-Arts, **43**
Palais du Tau, **42**
Porte Mars, **47**
Salle de Reddition, **48**
Taittinger, **45**

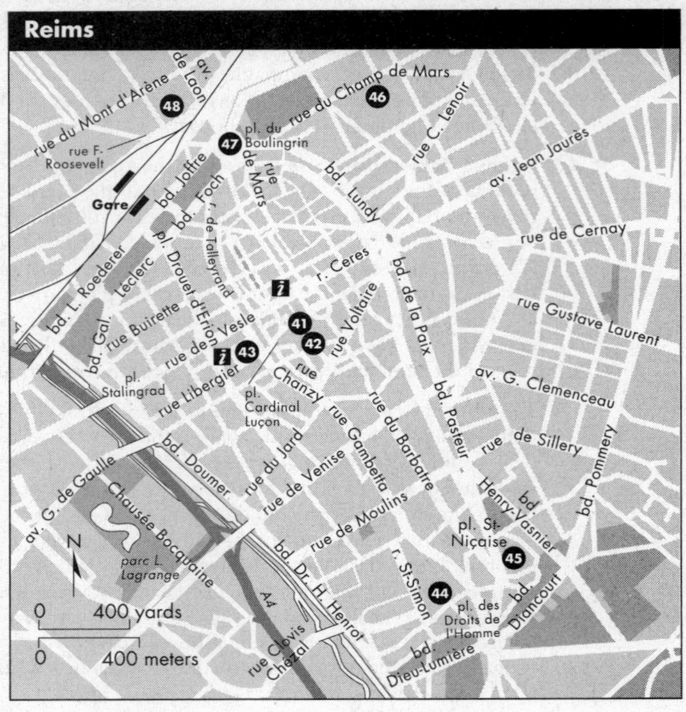

48 The **Salle de Reddition** (Surrender Room), near the train station, also known as the Salle du 8 mai 1945, is a well-preserved, map-covered room used by General Eisenhower as Allied headquarters at the end of World War II. It was here that General Alfred Jodl signed the German surrender at 2:41 AM on May 7, 1945. Fighting officially ceased at midnight the next day. ✉ *12 rue Franklin-Roosevelt,* ☎ *03–26–47–84–19.* 🎫 *10 frs.* ⏲ *Apr.–mid-Nov., Wed.–Mon. 10–noon and 2–6.*

Dining and Lodging

$$ ✕ **Vigneron.** This little brasserie in a 17th-century mansion is cozy and cheerful, with two tiny dining rooms displaying a jumble of champagne-related paraphernalia. The food is delightful as well: relatively cheap, distinctly hearty, and prepared with finesse. Try the pigs' feet or andouillettes slathered with delicious mustard made with champagne. ✉ *pl. Paul-Jamot,* ☎ *03–26–47–00–71. MC, V. Closed Sun., late Dec.–early Jan., and most of Aug. No lunch Sat.*

$$$$ ★ ✕🏨 **Boyer.** Gérard Boyer, one of the country's most highly rated chefs, impresses with creations from wild mushrooms in cream to scallops with endive confit. The extensive wine list pays homage to Reims's champagne heritage. The restaurant is closed Monday and Tuesday lunch; make reservations and wear a jacket and tie. The building is magnificent, too: a late 19th-century château surrounded by an extensive park. The decor is opulent, typified by ornate chandeliers, towering ceilings, and gilt mirrors. There are 19 luxurious suites, with wonderful views. ✉ *Les Crayères, 64 bd. Henri-Vasnier, 51000,* ☎ *03–26–82–80–80,* FAX *03–26–82–65–52. 19 rooms. Restaurant, indoor pool. AE, DC, MC, V. Closed late Dec.–early Jan.*

$$$ ✕🏨 **Paix.** A modern, eight-story hotel, 10 minutes' walk from the cathedral, La Paix has stylish rooms with 18th- and 19th-century reproductions, a pretty garden, and a rather incongruous chapel. Its brasserie-style restaurant serves good, though not inexpensive, cuisine (mainly grilled meats and seafood) and generous breakfasts; it is closed Sunday. ✉ *9 rue de Buirette, 51000,* ☎ *03–26–40–04–08,* FAX *03–26–47–75–04. 105 rooms with bath or shower. Restaurant, bar, pool. AE, DC, MC, V.*

$$–$$$ ✕🏨 **Cheval Blanc.** This hotel, owned for five generations by the hospitable Robert family, is in the small village of Sept-Saulx, southeast of Reims. Rooms are across the road in a parklike setting—with swings for kids and a tennis court—on the small River Vesle. Some rooms are quite small, but opening the French doors onto the garden helps. The newer suites are larger and have modern furnishings. Dinner is elaborate. The salad of escargot and *champignon* (mushroom) is a treat, as is the *pintade* (roast pigeon) with plum sauce. ✉ *rue du Moulin, 51400 Sept-Saulx (20 km/12 mi southeast of Reims, just off D8),* ☎ *03–26–03–90–27,* FAX *03–26–03–97–09. 25 rooms. Restaurant, tennis court, fishing. AE, DC, MC, V. Closed Feb.*

$$ ★ ✕🏨 **Gambetta.** Primarily foreign guests come to this modest, comfortable hotel near the cathedral. The smallish rooms, with modern furnishings and pastel-color walls, have all the creature comforts. The restaurant, Le Vonelly, serves specialties like duck in fig vinegar, fillet of sea bream in a zesty sauce, and a wonderful pear soufflé with strawberry sherbet; it is closed Sunday dinner and Monday. ✉ *9 rue Gambetta, 51000,* ☎ *03–26–47–41–64,* FAX *03–26–47–22–43. 14 rooms. Restaurant. AE, MC, V.*

Route du Vin

9 km (6 mi) south of Reims via N51 and D26

The grapes of Champagne flourish on the steep slopes of the Marne Valley and the Montagne de Reims—more of a forest-topped plateau than a mountain—south of Reims. As you begin to climb the Montagne de Reims, spin off left onto D26: This is the Route du Vin. The "Wine Road" is so named because it winds around the vine-entangled eastern slopes of the Montagne, through pretty wine villages such as **Chigny-les-Roses, Rilly-la-Montagne, Mailly-Champagne, Verzy,** and the aptly named **Bouzy,** where a fashionable but overpriced red wine is produced. **Ay,** along the north bank of the Marne River, was once capital of the champagne vineyards; Henry VIII was a keen tippler of its wines.

To understand how the still wine of King Harry's time became exciting, sparkling champagne, continue west to **Hautvillers.** Here the monk Dom Pérignon (1638–1715), whose blindness enhanced his taste buds and sense of smell, invented champagne as we know it by using corks for stoppers and blending wines from different vineyards. Dom Pérignon's simple tomb-slab, in a damp, dreary Benedictine abbey church (now owned by Moët et Chandon), is a forlorn memorial to the hero of one of the world's most lucrative drink industries. Champagne vineyards extend west from Hautvillers all the way to **Château-Thierry,** 50 km (31 mi) away, as well as along D1, which provides many a scenic overview as it hugs the steeply sloped Marne Valley. Look out for signs that read DÉGUSTATION (tasting).

Épernay

49 *6 km (4 mi) south of Hautvillers, 26 km (16 mi) south of Reims.*

Unlike Reims with its numerous treasures, the town of Épernay, on the south bank of the Marne, appears to live only for champagne. Unfortunately, no relation exists between the fabulous wealth of Épernay's illustrious wine houses and the drab, dreary appearance of the town as a whole. Most of the champagne firms are spaced out along the long, straight avenue de Champagne and, although their names may provoke sighs of wonder, their facades are either functional or overdressy. The attractions are underground, in the cellars.

Of the various champagne houses open to the public, **Mercier** offers the best deal; its sculpted, labyrinthine caves contain one of the world's largest wooden barrels (with a capacity of over 200,000 bottles); you can tour the cellars in the speed and comfort of a small train. A generous glass of champagne is your post-visit reward. ⊠ *75 av. de Champagne,* ☎ *03–26–54–71–11.* 🎟 *Free.* ⏲ *Mar.–Oct., daily 10–noon and 2–5; Nov.–Feb., Mon.–Sat. 10–noon and 2–5.*

Dining and Lodging

$$$ ✕🏨 **La Briqueterie.** Épernay is short on good hotels, so it's worth driving south to Vinay to find this commodious, luxurious, and comfortable hotel in a former manor on large grounds. The spacious rooms are furnished in modern style; ask for one overlooking the garden. In the restaurant, a mix of classical and neoclassical creations are served, including *navarin de turbot et langoustines* (stew of turbot and prawns) and *aiguillettes de pintade* (thin slices of guinea fowl in wine sauce). ⊠ *4 rte. de Sézanne, 51530 Vinay (6 km/4 mi south of Épernay),* ☎ *03–26–59–99–99,* FAX *03–26–59–92–10. 40 rooms. Restaurant, pool, sauna. AE, DC, MC, V. Closed late Dec.*

Nightlife and the Arts

The leading wine festival in the Champagne region is the **Fête St-Vincent** (named for the patron saint of vine growers) on the first weekend after January 22 in Ambonnay, 24 km (15 mi) east of Épernay.

Shopping

Champagne is not the only Épernay specialty. At **La Chocolaterie** (⊠ 9 rue Gallice), Monsieur Thibaut performs confectionery miracles before your eyes. Take home some of his startling array of chocolate goodies or indulge on the spot in the adjoining Salon de Thé, open Tuesday through Saturday.

Châlons-en-Champagne

50 *34 km (21 mi) east of Épernay via N3, 44 km (28 mi) southeast of Reims.*

Strangely enough, the official administrative center of the champagne industry is not Reims or Épernay but Châlons-en-Champagne. Yet this large town is of principal interest to fans of medieval architecture on account of its vast cathedral and smaller church.

The 13th-century **Cathédrale St-Étienne** is a harmonious structure with large nave windows and tidy flying buttresses; the exterior effect is marred only by the bulky 17th-century Baroque west front. ⊠ *rue de la Marne.*

★ With its twin spires, Romanesque nave, and early Gothic choir and vaults, the church of **Notre-Dame-en-Vaux** bears eloquent testimony to Châlons's medieval importance. The small **museum** beside the excavated cloister contains outstanding medieval statuary. ⊠ *rue Nicolas-Durand,* ☎ *03–26–64–03–87.* 🎟 *20 frs.* ⏲ *Apr.–Sept., Wed.–Mon. 10–noon and 2–6; Oct.–Mar., Wed.–Mon. 10–noon and 2–5.*

Dining and Lodging

$$–$$$ ✕🏨 **Angleterre.** Rooms at this stylish venue in central Châlons have elaborate decor and marble bathrooms; those in the back are quietest. The restaurant, in particular, stands apart: Chef Jacky Michel's creations include *blanc de turbot au Champagne* (turbot in champagne), lobster salad in truffle vinaigrette, and *tout-pommes,* a dessert featuring five variations on the humble apple. Breakfast is a superb buffet. ✉ *19 pl. Monseigneur-Tissier, 51000,* ☎ *03–26–68–21–51,* FAX *03–26–70–51–67. 19 rooms with bath or shower. AE, DC, MC, V. Closed mid-July–early Aug., late Dec.–early Jan.*

L'Épine

51 *7 km (4 mi) east of Châlons-en-Champagne via N3.*

The tiny village of L'Épine is dominated by its church. The twin-towered Flamboyant Gothic **Basilique de Notre-Dame de l'Epine** has a magnificent facade of intricate patterns, spires, and an interior that exudes elegance and restraint.

Dining and Lodging

$$$ ★ ✕🏨 **Aux Armes de Champagne.** The highlight of this cozy former coaching inn opposite the basilica is the restaurant, with its renowned champagne list and imaginative, often spectacular cuisine by chef Gilles Blandin. Opt for the 200-franc *menu gastronomique,* or order the delicate rabbit terrine or grilled sole and lobster with artichokes from the à la carte menu. Ask for a table by the window, with a view of the church. Rooms are furnished with solid, traditional reproductions, wall hangings, and thick carpets. No. 21, with wood beams, is especially nice. ✉ *31 av. du Luxembourg, 51460,* ☎ *03–26–69–30–30,* FAX *03–26–66–92–31. 37 rooms. Restaurant, tennis court. AE, DC, MC, V. Closed Jan.*

THE NORTH AND CHAMPAGNE A TO Z

Arriving and Departing

By Car

The A1 expressway from Paris passes close to Compiègne (N32 heads off to Noyon) and Arras (where A26 branches off to Calais) before reaching Lille. Journey time is about 100 minutes to Arras and 2½ hours to Lille. Drivers arriving via the Channel Tunnel disembark at Sangatte, near Calais, and can join the A26 expressway that heads to Arras (75 minutes) and Reims (2½ hours).

By Ferry

A few ferry and hovercraft companies travel between the Northern region of France and the United Kingdom. Companies traveling between Calais and Dover include **Hoverspeed, P&O European Ferries,** and **Sealink.** The sole operator of the route between Boulogne and Folkestone is Hoverspeed. For more information *see* Ferry & Hovercraft Travel *in* the Gold Guide.

By Plane

If you are coming from the U.S. or most other destinations, count on arriving at Paris's Charles-de-Gaulle airport, handily placed on the northbound A1 expressway and the TGV line to Lille. If coming from London, consider the occasional direct flights from Heathrow to Lille-Lesquin and from Gatwick to Beauvais. There is also a domestic airport in Reims; Air Charter (☎ 01–45–60–33–00) has a few flights a week.

By Train

TGV speed from Paris (Gare du Nord) to Lille (256 km/160 mi) in just one hour. A separate TGV service links Paris (Gare du Nord) to Arras (50 minutes) and Dunkerque (2 hours). The Paris–Calais train chugs unhurriedly around the coast, taking nearly three hours to cover 300 km (186 mi) via Amiens. There is also frequent daily service from Paris

(Gare du Nord) to Compiègne and Noyon, as well as to Laon (taking two leisurely hours to cover 140 km/87 mi). Regular trains cover the 175 km (109 mi) from Paris (Gare de l'Est) to Reims in 1½ hours, continuing to Charleville and Sedan. TGV, via the Channel Tunnel, link London to Lille in 2 hours; some stop at Calais.

Getting Around

By Car

A26 heads inland from Calais and St-Omer to Arras (where it intersects with A1), Laon, and Reims, which is directly linked to Paris by A4. N1 follows the railroad around the coast from Belgium and Dunkerque through Calais, Boulogne, Montreuil-sur-Mer, Amiens, and Beauvais to Paris. A new expressway, route A16, is under construction: It will follow the coast from Dunkerque to Abbeville before heading inland to Paris via Amiens and Beauvais. At press time (spring 1997) only the end segments—from Dunkerque to Boulogne and from Amiens to Cergy-Pontoise, near Paris—were completed.

By Train

It is easy to get around this region by train. Most sites can be reached by regular train service, except for the war cemeteries and the Pierrefond château. From Calais, the main line (Grande Ligne) follows the coast. The Lille-Calais regional line (T.E.R.) stops at St-Omer. From Calais, it follows the coast to Boulogne, Montreuil, Etaples (bus link to Le Touquet 6½ km/4 mi away), Abbeville, and Amiens, where a change is needed to reach Beauvais or Reims (via Laon). Trains leave Reims for Épernay, Châlons, and Charleville/Sedan.

Contacts and Resources

Car Rentals

Avis (✉ 36 pl. d'Armes, Calais, ☎ 03–21–34–66–50; Calais car ferry terminal, ☎ 03–21–96–47–65; Calais Hoverport, ☎ 03–21–96–66–52; cour de la Gare, Reims, ☎ 03–26–47–10–08). **Europcar** (✉ 32 pl. de la Gare, Lille, ☎ 03–20–06–18–80). **Hertz** (✉ 5 bd. d'Alsace-Lorraine, Amiens, ☎ 03–22–91–26–24; 10 bd. Daunou, Boulogne, ☎ 03–21–31–53–14).

Emergencies

Ambulance (☎ 15). **Hospitals:** Amiens (✉ pl. Victor-Pauchet, ☎ 03–22–66–80–00); Charleville-Mézières (✉ 28 rue Aubilly, ☎ 03–24–56–70–70); Compiègne (✉ 8 av. Henri-Adnot, ☎ 03–44–23–60–00); Lille (✉ bd. de Belfort, ☎ 03–20–87–48–48); Reims (✉ American Hospital, 47 rue Cognacq-Jay, ☎ 03–26–78–78–78).

Guided Tours

The **Lille Tourist Office** (✉ pl. Rihour, ☎ 03–20–21–94–21) is a mine of information about companies that give bus tours of northern France. **Loisirs-Accueil Nord** (✉ 15 rue du Nouveau-Siècle, Lille, ☎ 03–20–54–88–73) organizes bus trips to Boulogne and Flanders, and can arrange fishing, walking, and beer-tasting tours. **Renaissance du Vieux Boulogne** (✉ rue Bernet, Boulogne-sur-Mer, ☎ 03–21–92–11–52) arranges trips to Boulogne's old town and port for groups of up to four; the cost for two hours is 350 francs.

Travel Agencies

Wagons-Lits (✉ 1 rue Paul-Bert, Calais, ☎ 03–21–34–79–25; and 74 bis rue Nationale, Lille, ☎ 03–20–57–72–45).

Visitor Information

The principal regional tourist offices in Amiens, Lille, and Reims are good sources of information about the region. Other, smaller towns also have their own tourist offices. **Abbeville** (✉ 1 pl. de l'Amiral-Courbet, ☎ 03–22–24–27–92). **Amiens** (✉ 20 pl. Notre-Dame, ☎ 03–22–91–16–16). **Arras** (✉ pl. des Héros, ☎ 03–21–51–26–95). **Beauvais** (✉ 1 rue Beauregard, ☎ 03–44–45–08–18). **Boulogne** (✉ Forum Jean-Noël, quai de la Poste, ☎ 03–21–31–68–38). **Calais** (✉ 12 bd. Clemenceau, ☎ 03–21–96–62–40). **Charleville-Mézières** (✉ 22 pl. Ducale, ☎ 03–24–56–06–08). **Compiègne** (✉ pl. de l'Hôtel-de-Ville, ☎ 03–44–40–01–00). **Laon** (✉ pl. du Parvis, ☎ 03–23–20–28–62). **Lille** (✉ pl. Rihour, ☎ 03–20–21–92–21). **Montreuil-sur-Mer** (✉ pl. Darnétal, ☎ 03–21–06–04–27). **Reims** (✉ 2 rue Guillaume-de-Machault, ☎ 03–26–77–45–25). **Le Touquet** (✉ Palais de l'Europe, pl. de l'Hermitage, ☎ 03–21–05–21–65). **Noyon** (✉ pl. de l'Hôtel-de-Ville, ☎ 03–44–44–21–88). **Pierrefonds** (✉ rue Louis-d'Orléans, ☎ 03–44–42–81–44). **St-Omer** (✉ pl. Paul-Painlevé, ☎ 03–21–98–08–51). **Sedan** (✉ pl. du Château, ☎ 03–24–27–73–73).

8 Alsace-Lorraine and Franche-Comté

Nancy, Strasbourg, and the Jura

In Alsace-Lorraine you can wind along the Route de Vin through vineyards and villages among the Vosges foothills; see medieval, half-timber houses with a storybook air; visit churches that tell Joan of Arc's heroic story; and explore Strasbourg, which rivals Paris in culture, history, architecture, and haute cuisine. Then head southeast to the Franche-Comté, where you can find pretty little towns and hike in the Jura Mountains.

THOUGH ALSACE AND LORRAINE are often linked, the two regions have always had strong individual cultures, cuisines, and architectural styles. Only their recent past ties them together: In 1871, after France's defeat in the Franco-Prussian War, Alsace and Lorraine, sutured together by Bismarck, were ceded to Germany as part of the spoils of war. The region was systematically (but unsuccessfully) Teutonized, and two generations grew up culturally torn—until 1919 when, after World War I, France reclaimed the territory.

Updated by Nancy Coons

But no matter how forcefully the French tout its Frenchness, Alsace's German roots go deeper than the late 19th century, as one look at its storybook medieval architecture will prove. In fact, this strip of flatland and vine-covered hills squeezed between the Rhine and the Vosges mountains was called Prima Germania by the Romans and belonged to the fiercely German Holy Roman Empire for more than 700 years. A heavy German influence is still evident. Regional dialect is widespread; conversations between locals are incomprehensible even to most Frenchmen; town names look German; and the main daily paper, *Les Dernières Nouvelles d'Alsace,* is published in both languages. It seems ironic that France's famous national anthem, the "Marseillaise" (composed by Rouget de Lisle) was first sung in Strasbourg—as the battlesong of the Rhine Army—in 1792.

Lorraine, west of the Vosges, creased by the cheerful Moselle Valley, evolved as decidedly less German than its neighbor. It served French and Burgundian lords as well as the Holy Roman Empire, coming into its own under the powerful dukes of Lorraine in the Middle Ages and the Renaissance. In the Franche-Comté region to the south, the Jura Mountains form a natural border more than 160 km (100 mi) long between France and Switzerland and provide a winter-sports alternative to the Alps. Birthplace of Louis Pasteur and Victor Hugo and home to the celebrated aperitif, Pernod, the Jura is dotted with pretty little towns.

Pleasures and Pastimes

Dining

Alsace cooking tends to be heavy: *choucroute* (sauerkraut served with ham and sausages) and *baeckoffe* (a hearty meat and potato casserole). But there is sophistication, too: Foie gras accompanied by a *vendanges tardives* (late-harvested) glass of Gewürztraminer; and trout and chicken cooked in Riesling, the classic wine of Alsace. Snails and seasonal game are other favorites, as are Muenster cheese, salty *bretzel* loaves, and briochelike *kouglof* bread. Carp fried in bread crumbs is a specialty of southern Alsace. Lorraine, renowned for quiches, is also famous for its dumplings, madeleines, dragées (almond candies), and macaroons. Lorraine shares the Alsatian love of pastry and fruit tarts. Restaurant prices tend to be lower in Lorraine than in Alsace, but only in German-influenced Alsace will you find *weinstübes* (cozy paneled inns serving wine and snacks or meals). Beef and freshwater fish are menu mainstays in the Jura. Hard, flavorsome Comté and Beaufort are the choice local cheeses, along with Morbier, Vacherin, and Cancoillotte. Fondue is a popular winter dish.

CATEGORY	COST*
$$$$	over 400 frs
$$$	250 frs–400 frs
$$	125 frs–250 frs
$	under 125 frs

**per person for a three-course meal, including tax (20.6%) and tip but not wine*

Lodging

Accommodations are easier to find in Lorraine and the Jura than in Alsace, where advance reservations are essential in summer. Alsace is rich in *gîtes*—rented country houses or bed-and-breakfasts. Throughout Alsace, hotels are well scrubbed, with tile bathrooms, good mattresses, and geraniums spilling from every window sill. Lorraine tends to lack the Teutonic comforts of Alsace, subscribing to the more Latin laissez-faire school of innkeeping (concave mattresses, dusty bolsters, creaky floors).

CATEGORY	COST*
$$$$	over 800 frs
$$$	500 frs–800 frs
$$	250 frs–500 frs
$	under 250 frs

**All prices are for a standard double room for two, including tax (20.6%) and service charge.*

Outdoor Activities and Sports

The region is ideal for a variety of outdoor activities: bicycling in the southern part of Lorraine, horseback riding through the forests, fishing in the angler's paradise of Franche-Comté, or hiking in the Vosges and Jura mountains.

Wine and Brew

Some of France's finest white wines are produced in Alsace—Riesling, Gewürztraminer, Pinot Gris, and Muscat, as well as light-red Pinot Noir. Alsace is also a major brewing area—cafés throughout France usually serve Kronenbourg and Kanterbräu blonde beers, as well as the strong gold Fischer, brewed in Strasbourg. Lorraine is renowned for its fruit-based eaux-de-vie, made from cherries (kirsch) or plums (*mirabelle* and *quetsche*). In the Jura, look out for sweet *vin de Paille,* made from raisins, and for the sharp, dry *vin jaune,* made from sauvignon grapes.

Exploring Alsace-Lorraine and Franche-Comté

Begin exploring this region to the west—nearest Paris—where the battlegrounds of Verdun provide a poignant introduction to Lorraine. Linger in the artistic city of Nancy then spear east to Strasbourg (146 km/91 mi east), a city of such historic and cultural importance that it is well worth exploring in depth. From here, tour the rest of Alsace, following the photogenic Route du Vin (Wine Road) to Mulhouse. Finally, head south to Besançon and the spectacular scenery of Franche-Comté and the Jura.

Great Itineraries

You can cover most of the Alsace-Lorraine and Franche-Comté in about nine days. With five days, you can see the northern part of Lorraine, from Verdun to Nancy, and most of Alsace. Three days will give you just enough time to explore Alsace, including the cosmopolitan city of Strasbourg.

Numbers in the text correspond to numbers in the margin and on the Lorraine, Alsace, Franche-Comté, Nancy, and Strasbourg maps.

IF YOU HAVE 3 DAYS

Explore Alsace, beginning with a day and night in the delightful city of **Strasbourg** ㉙–㊶. The next day start out early, south along the Route du Vin to pretty **Obernai** ㊹, the hilltop abbey of **Mont-Ste-Odile** ㊺, the charming villages of **Barr** ㊻, **Andlau** ㊼, and **Dambach-la-Ville** ㊽, and the dramatic castle in **Haut-Koenigsbourg** ㊿. Spend the night in **Riquewihr** (52), which feels like a film set. On day three visit **Ribeauvillé** (51) and the museum towns of **Colmar** (53) and **Mulhouse** (56).

IF YOU HAVE 6 DAYS

Coming from Paris, start at Lorraine's moving battlefields of **Verdun** ⑲, then head east to the cathedral city of **Metz** ㉑. On day two, concentrate on **Nancy** ①–⑱. Another option is to go to Nancy first and take day trips from there. Spend your third evening in **Strasbourg** ㉙–㊶, and your fourth in Ottrot, outside **Obernai** ㊹, or in Mittelbergheim, outside **Barr** ㊻, halfway along the Route du Vin; visit **Mont-Ste-Odile** ㊺ along the way. Take in bustling **Sélestat** ㊾, with its fine churches, on day five, along with **Haut-Koenigsbourg** ㊿ and **Ribeauvillé** (51), ending up in **Riquewihr** (52). On day six head to **Colmar** (53) and **Mulhouse** (56).

IF YOU HAVE 9 DAYS

Begin in **Verdun** ⑲ and **Metz** ㉑, then head south through Lorraine to the crumbling cathedral town of **Toul** ㉔ and Joan of Arc's birthplace at **Domrémy-la-Pucelle** ㉖. Spend day three in **Nancy** ①–⑱. On day four make **Strasbourg** ㉙–㊶ your goal. The next day, follow the Route du Vin to **Obernai** ㊹, **Mont-Ste-Odile** ㊺, and **Barr** ㊻. Continue south to **Sélestat** ㊾, **Haut-Koenigsbourg** ㊿, **Ribeauvillé** (51), and **Riquewihr** (52). Start day seven in **Colmar** (53), with its splendid Unterlinden Museum, then drive down to **Mulhouse** (56), **Belfort** (57), and **Besançon** (60). Explore this historic Franche-Comté town on the morning of day eight, then head to scenic riverside **Ornans** (61) and the waterfall at the Source de la Loue, before wheeling west to the wine town of **Arbois** (67). Use Arbois as a base to explore the grandiose Jura scenery at the Reculée des Planches, the Cirque du Fer-à-Cheval, **Baume-les-Messieurs** (65), and the hilltop village of **Château-Châlon** (66). If time allows, end your tour at the "ideal village" of **Arc-et-Senans** (69).

When to Tour Alsace-Lorraine and Franche-Comté

June and September are warmest and sunniest. Many regional towns and villages, especially the wine villages of Alsace, stage summer festivals; note the spectacular pagan-inspired burning of the three pine trees at Thann (late June), the Flower Carnival at Sélestat (mid-August), and the wine fair at Colmar (first half of August). Some of the region's top sights, however—notably Haut-Koenigsbourg—can be besieged by tourists in July and August, so go early in the morning. Although Lorraine is a lusterless place in winter, the Vosges and Jura mountains make tentative attempts to challenge the Alps as skiing venues—plentiful snow cannot always be guaranteed—while Strasbourg pays tribute to Germanic tradition with a Christmas Fair.

NANCY

For architectural variety, few French cities match Nancy, which is in the heart of Lorraine (146 km/91 mi east of Paris). Medieval ornament, 18th-century grandeur, and Belle Epoque fluidity rub shoulders in a town center that mingles commercial bustle with stately elegance. Its majesty derives from a long history as home to the powerful dukes of

Lorraine

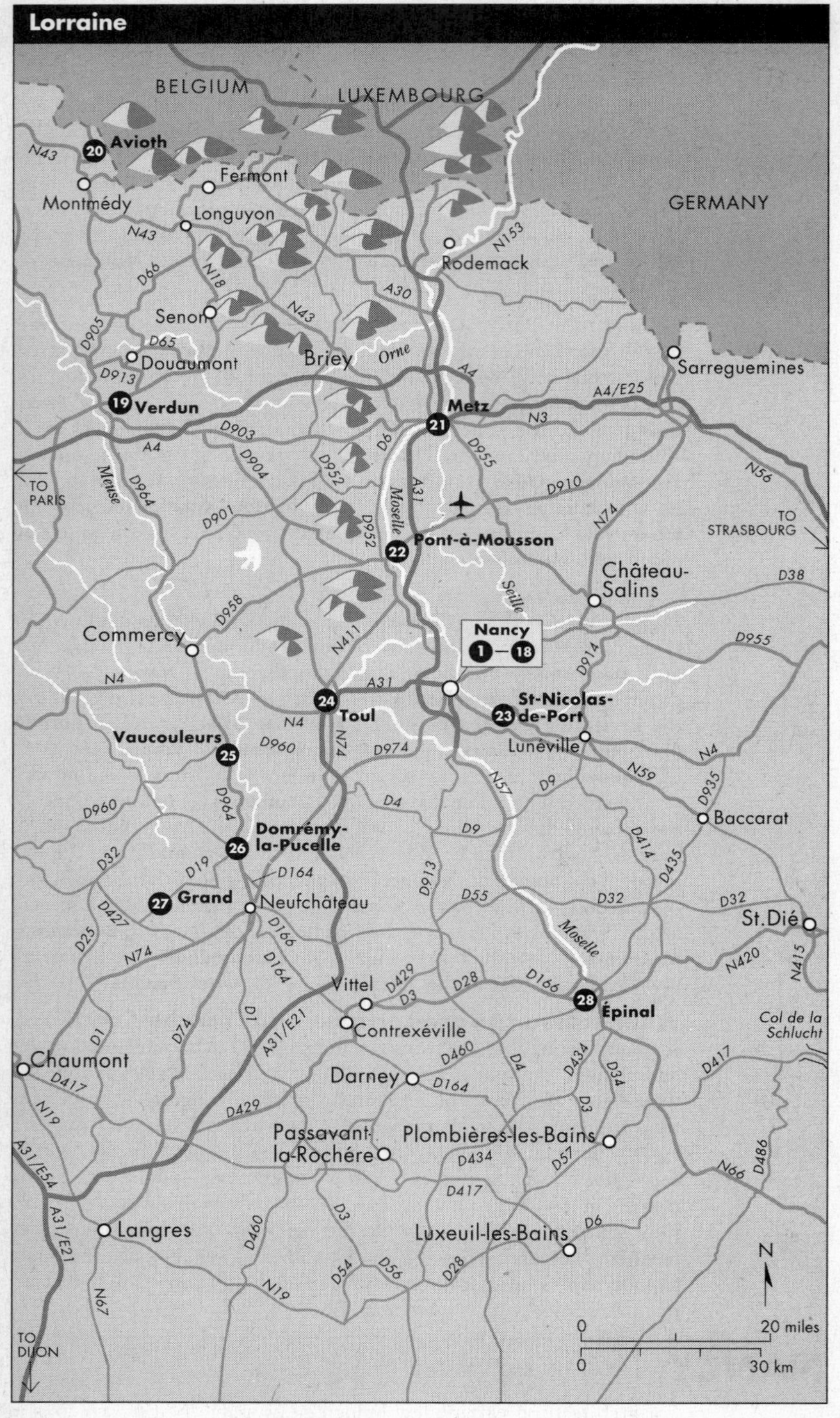
BELGIUM
LUXEMBOURG
GERMANY
Avioth
Fermont
Montmédy
Longuyon
Rodemack
Senon
Douaumont
Briey
Orne
Sarreguemines
Verdun
Metz
TO PARIS
Meuse
Moselle
Pont-à-Mousson
TO STRASBOURG
Château-Salins
Seille
Commercy
Nancy
1 – 18
Toul
St-Nicolas-de-Port
Vaucouleurs
Lunéville
Domrémy-la-Pucelle
Baccarat
Grand
Neufchâteau
St.Dié
Vittel
Épinal
Contrexéville
Col de la Schlucht
Chaumont
Darney
Passavant-la-Rochére
Plombières-les-Bains
Langres
Luxeuil-les-Bains
TO DIJON
N
0
20 miles
0
30 km

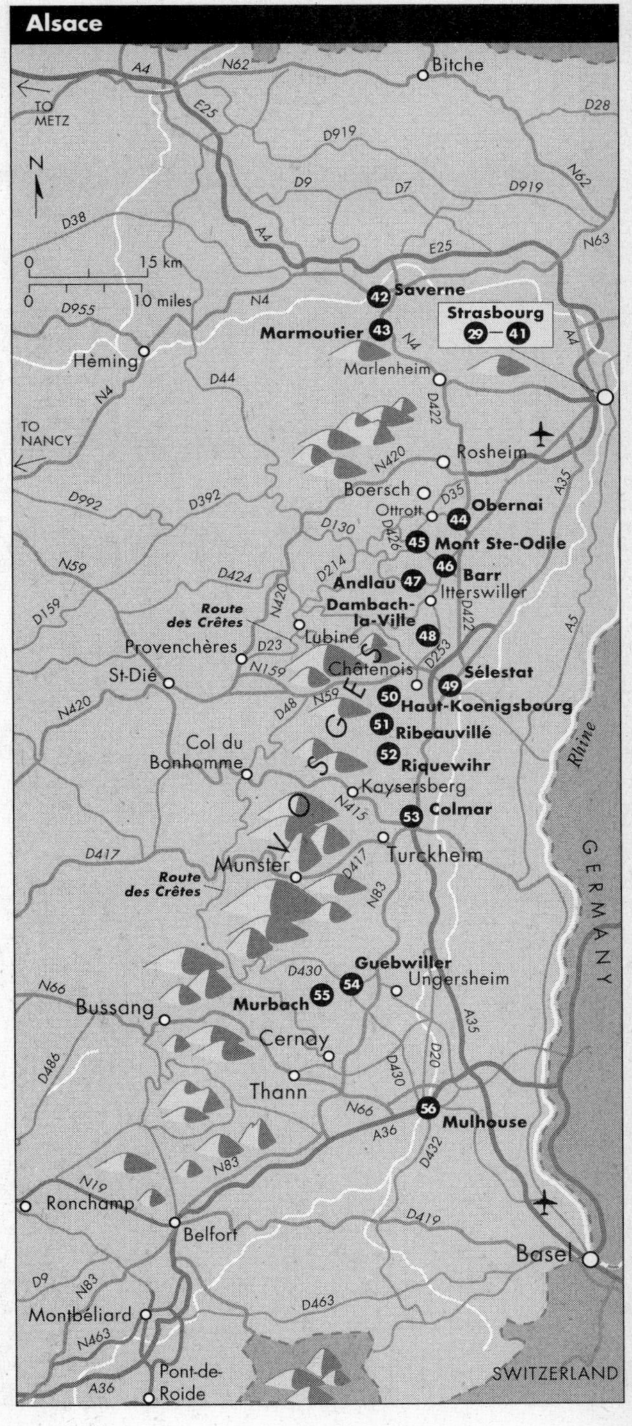
Alsace
Bitche
TO METZ
A4
N62
E25
D28
D919
N62
D9
D7
D919
N
D38
A4
E25
N63
0
15 km
0
10 miles
D955
N4
42 Saverne
Strasbourg
29—41
Marmoutier 43
N4
A4
Hèming
Marlenheim
D44
N4
D422
TO NANCY
N420
Rosheim
D992
D392
Boersch
D35
A35
Ottrott
44 Obernai
D130
D426
45 Mont Ste-Odile
N59
D214
46 Barr
D424
Andlau 47
Itterswiller
N420
D159
Route des Crêtes
Dambach-la-Ville
D422
A5
Lubine
48
Provenchères
D23
N159
Châtenois
D253
St-Dié
49 Sélestat
N420
D48
N59
50 Haut-Koenigsbourg
VOSGES
51 Ribeauvillé
Rhine
Col du Bonhomme
52 Riquewihr
Kaysersberg
N415
53 Colmar
D417
Munster
D417
Turckheim
GERMANY
Route des Crêtes
N83
Guebwiller
D430
54
Ungersheim
N66
Bussang
Murbach 55
A35
Cernay
D486
D430
D20
Thann
N66
56 Mulhouse
A36
D432
N83
N19
Ronchamp
Belfort
D419
Basel
D9
N83
Montbéliard
D463
N463
Pont-de-Roide
A36
SWITZERLAND

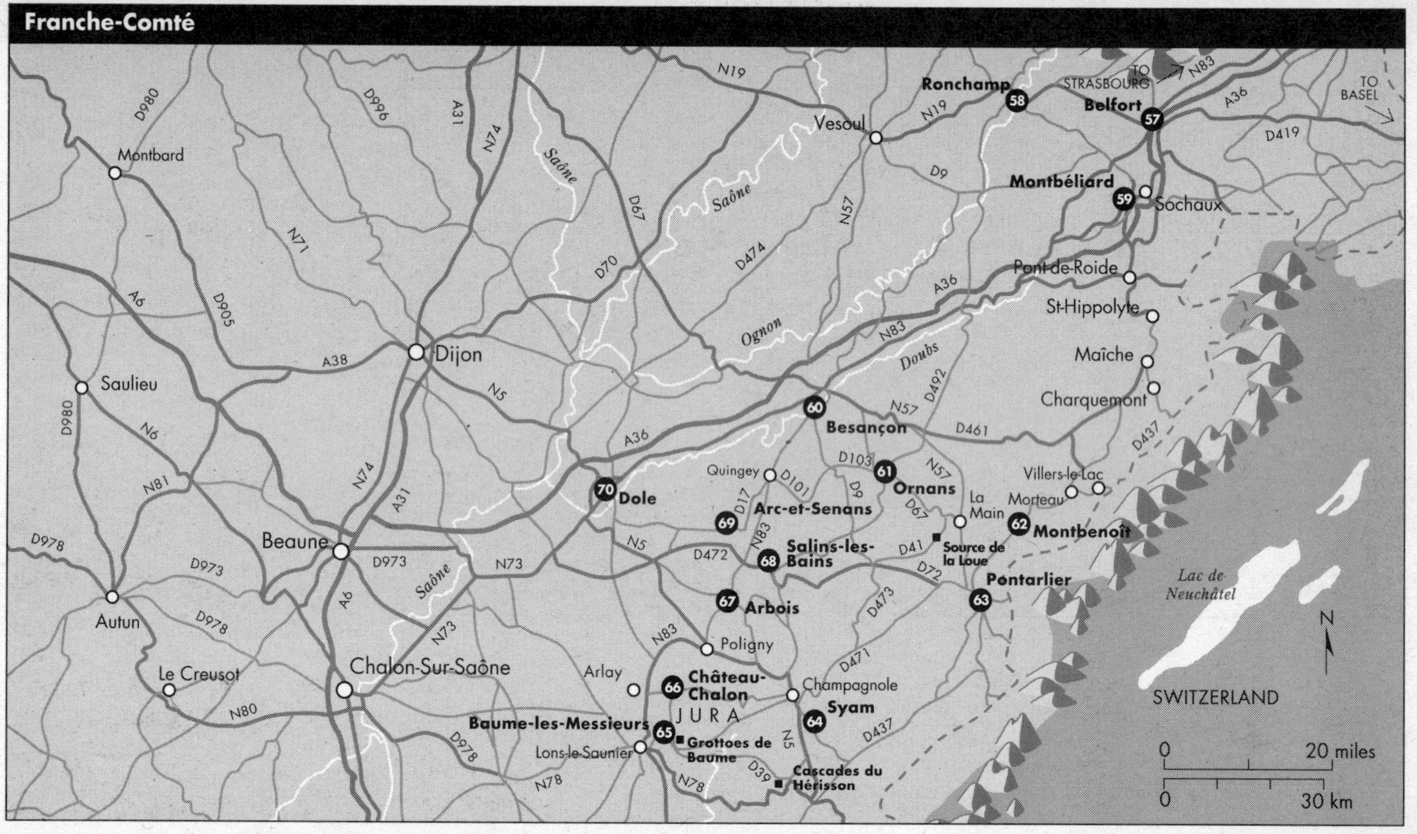
Franche-Comté
TO STRASBOURG
TO BASEL
Ronchamp 58
Belfort 57
Vesoul
Montbéliard 59
Sochaux
Pont-de-Roide
St-Hippolyte
Maîche
Charquemont
Montbard
Dijon
Saulieu
60 Besançon
Quingey
61 Ornans
Villers-le-Lac
Morteau
La Main
62 Montbenoît
70 Dole
69 Arc-et-Senans
Source de la Loue
68 Salins-les-Bains
Pontarlier
63
Beaune
Autun
67 Arbois
Poligny
Le Creusot
Chalon-Sur-Saône
Arlay
66 Château-Chalon
Champagnole
64 Syam
JURA
Baume-les-Messieurs 65
Grottoes de Baume
Lons-le-Saunier
Cascades du Hérisson
Saône
Ognon
Doubs
Lac de Neuchâtel
SWITZERLAND
N
0 20 miles
0 30 km

Lorraine, whose double-barred crosses figure prominently on statues and buildings. Never having fallen under the rule of the Holy Roman Empire or, more recently, the Germans, this Lorraine city retains an eminently Gallic charm.

The Historic Center

Concentrated northeast of the train station, this neighborhood—rich in architectural treasures as well as museums—includes the classical place Stanislas and the shuttered, medieval Vieille Ville (Old Town).

A Good Walk

Begin your walk at the symbolic heart of Nancy, **place Stanislas** ①. On the eastern corner is the **Musée des Beaux-Arts** ②, the art museum. Cross place Stanislas diagonally and head south down rue Maurice Barrès to the Baroque **Cathédrale** ③. On leaving, turn left down rue St-Georges and right up rue des Dominicains, stopping to admire the elegant stonework on No. 57, the Maison des Adams, named for the sculptors who lived in (and decorated) the edifice in the 18th century.

Recross the place Stanislas and go through the monumental Arc de Triomphe, entering into the peaceful **place de la Carrière** ④. At the colonnaded Palais du Gouvernement, former home of the governors of Lorraine, turn right into the vast, formal city park known as **La Pépinière** ⑤. From the park's entrance at the foot of the place de la Carrière, head straight under the arches and into the Vieille Ville. Dominating place de la Carrière is the church of **St-Epvre** ⑥, clearly constructed to make up for the lack of a Gothic cathedral in Nancy.

Head immediately right up the picturesque Grande-Rue, with its antiques shops, bookstores, and artisanal bakeries behind brightly painted facades. On your right, you'll see the **Palais Ducal** ⑦. Here is the main branch of the Musée Historique Lorraine, a marvelous complex that includes the **Convent des Cordeliers** ⑧, with its small, Gothic church and folk arts museum. At the end of Grand-Rue is the **Porte de la Craffe** ⑨, the last of Nancy's medieval fortifications.

TIMING

Depending on how much time you spend in the museums, this walk could take a few hours or a whole day. Note that all the museums are closed on Tuesday.

Sights to See

❸ **Cathédrale.** This vast, frigid edifice was built in the 1740s in a ponderous Baroque style that has none of the ease and grace of the 18th-century place Stanislas. Its most notable interior feature is a murky 19th-century fresco in the dome. The **Trésor** (Treasury) contains minute 10th-century splendors in carved ivory and gold. ✉ *pl. Stanislas.*

❽ ★ **Convent des Cordeliers.** This church structure, just up the street from the Palais Ducal, houses the **Musée des Arts et Traditions Populaires** (Museum of Folk Arts and Traditions). In a series of evocative rural interiors, it shows how local people lived, displaying craftsmen's tools, colorful crockery, and regional furniture stained a rich black-brown with pigs' blood. The dukes of Lorraine are buried in the crypt of the adjoining **Église des Cordeliers,** a Flamboyant Gothic church; the *gisant* (reclining statue) of Philippa de Gueldra, second wife of René II, is a moving example of Renaissance portraiture, executed in limestone in flowing detail. The octagonal Ducal Chapel was begun in 1607 in the classical style, modeled on the Medici Chapel in Florence. ✉ *66 Grande-Rue,* ☏ *03–83–32–18–74.* 🎫 *20 frs.* ⏲ *May–Sept., Wed.–Mon. 10–6; Oct.–Apr., Wed.–Mon. 10–noon and 2–5, Sun. to 6.*

★ ❷ **Musée des Beaux-Arts.** Housed in this splendid building are art treasures of merit equal to the noble white facade. You'll find 19th- and 20th-century paintings by Monet, Manet, Utrillo, and Modigliani; a hefty *Transfiguration* by Rubens; a wealth of Old Masters from the Italian, Dutch, Flemish, and French schools; and impressive glassworks by Nancy-native Antonin Daum. ✉ *pl. Stanislas,* ☎ *03–83–85–30–72.* 🎫 *20 frs (30 frs for joint admission with the Musée de l'École de Nancy;* ☞ below*).* ⏲ *Mon. 2–6; Wed.–Sun. 10:30–6.*

❼ **Palais Ducal.** The Ducal Palace was built in the 13th century and completely restored at the end of the 15th century. The main entrance to the palace, and the **Musée Historique Lorrain,** which it now houses, is 80 yards farther down the street. A spiral stone staircase leads up to the palace's most impressive room, the **Galerie des Cerfs.** Exhibits here (including pictures, armor, and books) recapture the Renaissance mood of the 16th and 17th centuries—one of elegance and merry-making, though not devoid of stern morality: An elaborate series of huge tapestries, *La Condemnation du Banquet,* expounds on the evils of drink and gluttony. ✉ *64 Grande-Rue,* ☎ *03–83–32–18–74.* 🎫 *20 frs.* ⏲ *May–Sept., Wed.–Mon. 10–6; Oct.–Apr., Mon. and Weds.–Sat. 10–noon and 2–5, Sun. to 6.*

❺ **La Pépinière.** This lovely, landscaped city park contains labeled ancient trees, a rose garden, playgrounds, a carousel, and a small zoo. ✉ *Entrance off pl. de la Carrière.*

❹ **Place de la Carrière.** Lined with pollards and handsome 18th-century mansions (another successful collaboration between Stanislas and Héré), this elegant rectangle leads from place Stanislas to the colonnaded facade of the **Palais du Gouvernement,** former home of the governors of Lorraine.

★ ❶ **Place Stanislas.** The severe, gleaming-white classical facades of this imposing square are given a touch of rococo jollity by fancifully wrought gilt-iron railings. The square is named for Stanislas Leszczynski, twice dethroned as King of Poland, but offered the throne of Lorraine by Louis XV (his son-in-law) in 1736. Stanislas left a legacy of spectacular buildings, undertaken between 1751 and 1760 by architect Emmanuel Héré and ironwork-genius Jean Lamour. The sculpture of Stanislas that dominates the square went up in the 1830s when the square was named after him. Framing the exit is the **Arc de Triomphe,** erected in the 1750s to honor Louis XV. The facade features the gods of war and the gods of peace; Louis's portrait is here.

❾ **Porte de la Craffe.** The only remains of Nancy's medieval fortifications looms at one end of Grande-Rue. Built in the 14th and 15th centuries, it served as a prison through the Revolution. The thistle and cross are symbols of Lorraine.

❻ **St-Epvre.** A 275-foot spire towers over this splendid neo-Gothic church rebuilt in the 1860s. Most of the 2,800 square yards of stained glass were created by the Geyling workshop in Vienna; the chandeliers were made in Liège, Belgium; many carvings are the work of Margraff of Munich; the heaviest of the eight bells was cast in Budapest; and the organ, though manufactured by Merklin of Paris, was inaugurated in 1869 by Austrian composer Anton Bruckner. ✉ *pl. de la Carrière.*

Art-Nouveau Nancy

Nancy was a principal source of the revolution in decorative arts that produced Art Nouveau and *Jugendstil* (the German version). Inspired and coordinated by the glass master Émile Gallé, the local movement,

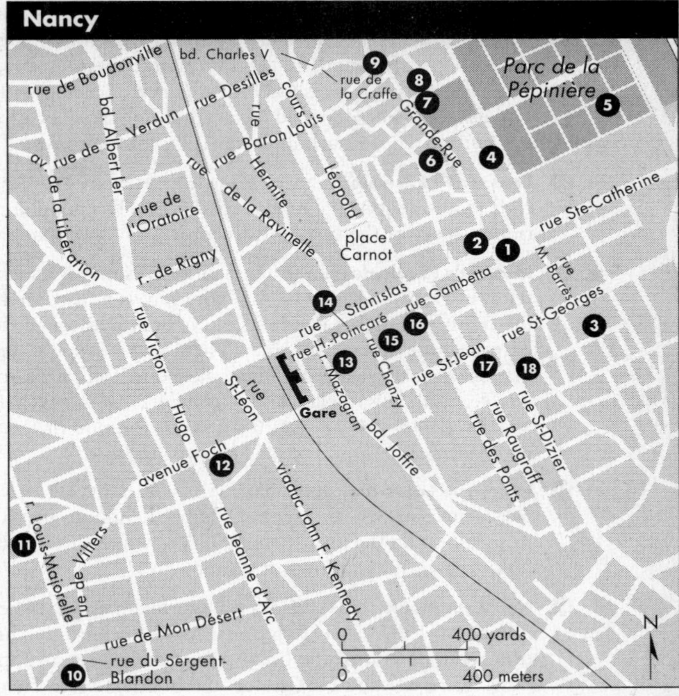

Avenue Foch, **12**
Brasserie l'Excelsior, **13**
Cathédrale, **3**
Convent des Cordeliers, **8**
Musée de l'Ecole de Nancy, **10**
Musée des Beaux-Arts, **2**
No. 1 rue Louis-Majorelle, **11**
No. 2 rue Bénit, **16**
No. 9 rue Chanzy, **15**
No. 40 rue Henri-Poincaré, **14**
Nos. 42-44 rue St-Dizier, **18**
Palais Ducal/ Musée Historique Lorrain, **7**
La Pépinière, **5**
Place de la Carrière, **4**
Place Stanislas, **1**
Porte de la Craffe, **9**
Rue Raugraff, **17**
St-Epvre, **6**

formalized in 1901 as l'École de Nancy, nurtured the floral *pâte de verre* (literally, glass dough) and stained glass works of Antonin Daum, Jacques Gruber, and Émile Gallé; the fluid furniture of Louis Majorelle; and the sinuous architecture of Lucien Weissenburger, Émile André, and Eugène Vallin. Thanks to these artists, Nancy's downtown architecture flows and flowers above the sidewalks like a living garden.

A Good Walk

The **Musée de l'École de Nancy** ⑩ is the best place to immerse yourself in the fanciful style that crept into interiors and exteriors throughout Nancy. To get to the museum from the busy shopping street rue St-Jean (just up rue des Dominicains from place Stanislas), take Bus 5 or 25 uphill; get off at place Pain-Levée. From the museum, turn left up rue du Sergent Blandan and walk about four blocks to **No. 1 rue Louis-Majorelle** ⑪. Cut east to rue de Villers and head up **avenue Foch** ⑫ to admire the colorful structures at No. 71, No. 69, and No. 41. Hike over the viaduc Kennedy and the *gare* (train station), turn left past the department store, Printemps, and follow rue Mazagran to the **Brasserie l'Excelsior** ⑬. Turn right toward **No. 40 rue Henri-Poincaré** ⑭. Turn right and walk past **No. 9 rue Chanzy** ⑮ (now the Banque Nationale de Paris). Head left to find **No. 2 rue Bénit** ⑯ with its ornate metal structure. Head south to rue St-Jean; at the corner of **rue Raugraff** ⑰, you'll spot two bay windows, remnants of stores that were once here. Continue up rue St-Jean and turn right to find **Nos. 42–44 rue St-Dizier** ⑱. Many more Art Nouveau addresses are scattered throughout the city; you can get a detailed map at the tourist office.

TIMING

Allow a full morning to linger in the Musée de l'École de Nancy and then, over an hour and a half or so, wander back circuitously toward the Vieille Ville, stopping to admire Art Nouveau masterworks along the way.

Sights to See

12 **Avenue Foch.** This busy boulevard lined with solid mansions was built for Nancy's affluent 19th-century middle class. At No. 69, the occasional pinnacle suggests Gothic influence on a house built in 1902 by Émile André, who designed the neighboring No. 71 two years later. No. 41, built by Paul Charbonnier in 1905, bears ironwork by Majorelle.

13 **Brasserie l'Excelsior.** This bustling brasserie has a severely rhythmic facade that is invitingly illuminated at night. The popular restaurant continues to evoke the turn of the century. ✉ *5 rue Mazagran.*

★ 10 **Musée de l'École de Nancy.** The School of Nancy Museum, the only museum in France devoted to Art Nouveau, is housed in an airy, turn-of-the-century garden–town house, was built by Eugène Corbin, an early patron of the School of Nancy. There isn't a straight line in the house; pianos ooze, bedsteads undulate; the wood itself, hard and burnished as it is, seems to have melted and reformed. ✉ *36 rue du Sergent-Blandon,* ☎ *03–83–40–14–86.* *20 frs, 30 frs for joint ticket with Musée des Beaux-Arts.* ⏲ *Mon. 2–6, Wed.–Sun. 10:30–6.*

11 **No. 1 rue Louis-Majorelle.** This villa was built in 1902 by Paris architect Henri Sauvage for Majorelle himself. Sinuous metal supports seem to sneak up on the unsuspecting balcony like swaying cobras, leading up to the grand windows of Gruber.

16 **No. 2 rue Bénit.** This elaborately worked metal exoskeleton, the first in Nancy (1901), is as functional as it is beautiful. The fluid decoration reminds you of the building's past as a seed supply store. Windows were worked by Gruber; the builders were Henry-Barthélemy Gutton (architect) and Henri Gutton (engineer); Victor Schertzer conceived the metal frame.

15 **No. 9 rue Chanzy.** Designed by architect Émile André, this lovely structure—now a bank—can be visited during business hours to view the cabinetry of Majorelle, decor of Paul Charbonnier, and stained-glass windows of Gruber.

14 **No. 40 rue Henri-Poincaré.** The Lorraine thistle and brasserie hops weave through this undulating exterior, designed by architects Émile Toussaint and Louis Marchal. Victor Schertzer conceived this metal structure in 1908, after the success of No. 2 rue Bénit. Gruber's windows are enhanced by the curving metalwork of Majorelle.

18 **Nos. 42–44 rue St-Dizier.** Eugène Vallin and Georges Biet left their mark on this graceful 1903 bank structure; its open weekdays 8:30–5:30.

17 **Rue Raugraff.** Once there were two stores here, built in 1901. The bay windows are the last vestiges of the work of Charles Vallin, Émile André, and Eugène Vallin. ✉ *At the corner of rue St-Jean.*

Dining and Lodging

$$$ ★ ✕ **Capucin Gourmand.** Art Nouveau decor and faultless service set the tone at one of Nancy's finest restaurants. Chef Gérard Veissière's menu includes such regional specialties as foie gras, game in casserole, and classic quiche Lorraine. Desserts are superb, the Toul wines admirable. ✉ *31 rue Gambetta,* ☎ *03–83–35–26–98. Reservations essential. Jacket and tie. V. Closed Sun., Mon., and Aug.*

$$ ✕ **Comptoir du Petit Gastrolâtre.** Under the direction of chef Patrick Tanesy, this pleasant, low-key bistro serves sophisticated regional cooking. Recommended dishes include baeckoffe with foie gras, pike roasted with garlic, a delectable fricassee of snails, and gingerbread. ✉ *1 pl. Vaudemont,* ☎ *03–83–35–51–94. MC, V. Closed Sun., Mon.*

$ ★ ✕ **Au P'tit Cuny.** From the Musée des Arts et Traditions Populaires cross the street to sink your teeth into authentic Lorraine cuisine in the form of choucroute, *tête de veau* (veal head), or tangy veal tourte. The beams and collected farm tools comfort the neighborhood's *intellos* (intellectuals) and *bohèmes* (bohemians). ✉ *97–99 Grand-Rue,* ☎ *03–83–32–85–94. MC, V. Closed Sun., Mon.*

$$$ ★ **Grand Hôtel de la Reine.** This hotel is every bit as swanky as the place Stanislas on which it stands; the magnificent 18th-century building is officially classified as a historic monument. Rooms are decorated in a suitably grand Louis XV style; the most luxurious look out onto the square. The costly restaurant, Le Stanislas, serves classic-nouvelle cuisine; the prix-fixe weekday lunch menus are the best value. ✉ *2 pl. Stanislas, 54000,* ☎ *03–83–35–03–01,* FAX *03–83–32–86–04. 51 rooms. Restaurant, bar. AE, DC, MC, V.*

$ **Carnot.** This somewhat generic downtown hotel, with 1950s-style comforts and mostly tiny rooms, is handy to cours Léopold parking and backs up on the old town. Corner rooms are sizable, back rooms quiet. ✉ *4 cours Léopold,* ☎ *03–83–36–59–58,* FAX *03–83–37–00–19. 33 rooms with bath or shower. Breakfast room. MC, V.*

$ **De Guise.** Deep in the shuttered old town, in this formerly noble mansion with a magnificent stone-floor entry, the dramatic sweeping stairs unfortunately wind up to a standard, creaky renovation job. Breakfast on the once-grand main floor and an excellent location make this a good choice for bargain-hunting romantics. ✉ *18 rue de Guise,* ☎ *03–83–32–24–68,* FAX *03–83–35–75–63. 45 rooms. MC, V. Closed 2 wks in Dec. and Aug.*

Nightlife and the Arts

Métro (✉ 1 rue du Général-Hoche, ☎ 03–83–40–25–13) is a popular discotheque. The **Majéstique** (✉ 22 rue St-Dizier, ☎ 03–83–32–83–42) has a bar, dance floor, and occasional live concerts. **Les Caves du Roy** (✉ 9 pl. Stanislas, ☎ 03–83–35–24–14) attracts a young upscale crowd who come to dance.

The **Orchestre Symphonique et Lyrique** (✉ 1 rue Ste-Catherine, ☎ 03–83–85–30–65) is a highly rated classical orchestra.

Shopping

The **Daum** glassworks (✉ 17 rue des Cristalleries, ☎ 03–03–83–30–80–20) sells deluxe crystal and examples of the city's traditional Art Nouveau pâte de verre. **Librairie Lorraine** (✉ 93 Grande Rue, ☎ 03–83–36–79–52), across from the Musée des Arts et Traditions, is an excellent bookstore devoted entirely to Lorraine history and culture.

LORRAINE

Although the present-day decline of the steel and coal industries and the miseries of its small farmers have left parts of Lorraine tarnished and neglected—some might say unspoiled—its rolling countryside is dotted with orchards and crumbling stucco villages, abbeys, fortresses, and historic towns. It is the home of Baccarat and St-Louis crystal and was once a great faïence center; it is also the birthplace of Joan of Arc, Gregorian chant, and Art Nouveau. Majestic Nancy is at its heart. Throughout Lorraine you'll find the statue of the region's patron saint, St-Nicholas—old Saint Nick himself—with three children in a *saloir,* or saltbox. Every December 6th Lorraine schoolchildren reenact the legend: A greedy butcher slaughtered and salted down three children as hams, but when St-Nicholas dropped by his place for a meal, he discovered the deed and brought them back to life.

Verdun

 *66 km (41 mi) west of Metz, 93 km (58 mi) northwest of Nancy, 262 km (164 mi) east of Paris.*

A key strategic site along the Meuse Valley, Verdun is famous, above all, for the 18-month battle between the French and the Germans in World War I. It left more than 700,000 dead and nine villages wiped off the map. Both sides fought with suicidal fury, yet no significant ground was gained or lost. To this day, the scenes of battle are scarred by bomb craters, stunted vegetation, and thousands of unexploded mines and shells, rendering the area permanently uninhabitable.

Verdun's leading World War I memorial is at **Douaumont,** 10 km (6 mi) north. The bizarre, evocative structure—a little like a cross, a lot like a bomb—rears up over an endless sea of graves, its ground-level windows revealing undignified heaps of human bones harvested from the killing fields. Climb to the top of the tower (6 francs) for a view of the cemetery. In the basement a film dwells on the agony of the futile butchery. ☎ *03–29–84–54–81.* 🎟 *Film 15 frs.* ⏲ *Mar.–Apr. and Oct., daily 9–noon and 2–5:30; Nov. daily 9–noon and 2–5; Apr.–June, daily 9–6; July–Aug., daily 9–6:30; Sept., daily 9–noon and 2–6.*

The square, modern **Mémorial de Verdun,** in Fleury-devant-Douaumont, is a World War I museum with emotionally charged texts and video commentary, as well as uniforms, weapons, and the artwork of soldiers (Art Nouveau vases hammered from artillery shells). ☎ *03–29–84–35–34.* 🎟 *20 frs.* ⏲ *Mid-Apr.–Dec., daily 9–6; Feb.–mid-Apr., daily 9–noon and 2–5:30.*

OFF THE BEATEN PATH

MONTMÉDY – When Louis XVI was arrested at Varennes in 1791, he was fleeing by coach toward the refuge of Montmédy, 48 km (30 mi) north of Verdun. The mighty hilltop citadel was redesigned and reinforced by the great military architect Vauban. His signature star-shape fortifications thrust out over the valley, and drivers still enter the tiny upper village over a drawbridge. Once inside, there's not much to see but a sleepy, undeveloped neighborhood.

Dining and Lodging

$$ ★ ✕ **La Tourtière.** This isolated culinary treasure, in the village of Senon, serves fine, simple regional fare, prepared by a sophisticated homegrown chef. The dark-beamed, firelit monks' lodging is an atmospheric backdrop. Sample the wild-mushroom *tourtes* (pies) and home-smoked *pintadeau* (guinea fowl). ✉ *2 pl. Eugène-Antoine, Senon (30 km/19 mi northeast of Verdun),* ☎ *03–29–85–98–30. AE, MC, V. Closed Wed. No dinner Tues.*

$$$ ✕🏨 **Coq Hardi.** This large, steep-roofed, half-timber hotel, built in 1827 on the banks of the Meuse, is furnished in solid regional style. A familylike welcome pervades here and in the large restaurant, where traditional cuisine dominates without stuffiness: foie gras on quail eggs, suckling pig larded with truffles, and strawberry *tarte tatin* (upside down, caramelized tart). ✉ *8 av. de la Victoire, 55100,* ☎ *03–29–86–36–36,* FAX *03–29–86–09–21. 35 rooms with bath or shower. Restaurant. AE, DC, MC, V.*

Avioth

56 km (35 mi) north of Verdun, 149 km (92 mi) northwest of Nancy, 8 km (5 mi) north of Montmédy.

The tiny village of Avioth is most famous for its sumptuous **Basilique d'Avioth.** A miraculous statue of the Virgin was discovered in Avioth in the 11th century, and the faithful poured in for the next 300 years, which explains the basilica's surprising richness. Construction of the church lasted from the late 13th to the early 15th centuries, finishing amid the elaborate stone lace of the Flamboyant Gothic style. The interior contains a 14th-century altar and medieval frescoes on the choir vaults. The *recevresse,* a free-standing Flamboyant tower in front of the main entrance, once held the miraculous statue and received the offerings of pilgrims.

Metz

66 km (41 mi) east of Verdun, 53 km (33 mi) north of Nancy, 160 km (100 mi) northwest of Strasbourg.

Despite its industrial background, Metz, the capital of the Moselle region, is officially classed as one of France's greenest cities: Parks, gardens, and leafy squares abound. At its heart you'll find one of the finest Gothic cathedrals.

At 137 feet from floor to roof, the **Cathédrale St-Étienne** is one of France's highest; and, thanks to nearly 1½ acres of window space, one of the lightest. The narrow 13th- to 14th-century nave channels the eye toward the dramatically raised 16th-century choir, whose walls have given way to huge sheets of richly colored, gemlike glass by masters old and modern, including artist Marc Chagall (1887–1985). The oldest windows—on the right rear wall of the transepts, over the modern organ—date from the 12th century and, in their dark, mosaiclike simplicity, are a stark contrast to the ethereal new stained glass. A pair of symmetrical 290-foot towers flank the nave, marking the division between the two churches merged to form the cathedral. The tower, with a fussy 15th-century pinnacle, houses **Dame Mutte,** an enormous bell cast in 1605 and tolled on momentous occasions. The **Grand Portal** beneath the large rose window was reconstructed by the Germans at the turn of the century; the statues of the prophets include, on the right, *Daniel,* sculpted to resemble Kaiser Wilhelm II (his unmistakable upturned mustachio was shaved off in 1940).

The **Musée d'Art et d'Histoire** (Museum of Art and History), in a 17th-century former convent, has a wide-ranging collection of French and German paintings from the 18th century on; military arms and uniforms; and local finds evoking the city's Gallo-Roman, and medieval past. Religious works of art are stored in the **Grenier de Chèvremont,** a granary built in 1457. An Escherlike labyrinth of stairways excludes wheelchairs, strollers, and poor navigators. ✉ *2 rue du Haut-Poirier,* ☎ *03–87–75–10–18.* 🎫 *20 frs.* 🕒 *Daily 10–noon and 2–5.*

The small, heavily restored church of **St-Pierre-aux-Nonnains** has round stones and rows of red bricks that are thought to date from the 4th century, predating Attila the Hun's sacking of Metz; thus, Metz claims the oldest church in France. The best of the rare Merovingian ornaments salvaged from the 6th-century version of the chapel are displayed in a full reproduction in the Museum of Art and History. ✉ *rue Poncelet.*

Walibi Schtroumpf, a theme park north of Metz, has 30 attractions featuring the cuddly blue dwarves known in English as Smurfs. ✉ *Voie*

Romaine, Maizières-les-Metz (just off A31, 10 km/6 mi north of Metz), ☎ *03–87–51–73–90.* 105 *frs.* Mid-Apr.–May 1, daily 10–6; May and Sept., Wed. and weekends 10–6; June, daily 10–6; July–Aug., daily 10–7.*

Dining and Lodging

$$–$$$ ✕ **La Dinanderie.** Chef Claude Pieriorgi serves inventive cuisine—spicy ragout of local snails and salmon in turnip and bacon cream—for reasonable prices. The intimate restaurant, across the River Moselle from the cathedral, is attractively refurbished in pastels. ✉ *2 rue de Paris,* ☎ *03–87–30–14–40. AE, MC, V. Closed Sun., Mon., mid-Feb., and last 3 wks in July.*

$$ ✕ **À la Ville de Lyon.** Just below the cathedral in a venerable vaulted setting, this charming eatery has a fabulous wine list (30,000 bottles in stock) and a no-nonsense menu. Dishes range from juicy grilled veal kidneys to the ubiquitous local mirabelle soufflé *glacé* (frozen). ✉ *7 rue des Piques,* ☎ *03–87–36–07–01. AE, DC, MC, V. Closed Mon., and most of Aug. No dinner Sun.*

$$ ✕ **La Baraka.** Below the cathedral, this classic French-Moroccan couscous spot with a lively, unstuffy ambience offers a fiery but digestible break from French cooking. If you burned out on couscous in Paris, venture toward *méchoui* (lamb shish kebab) or *tajine,* a meat stew simmered in terra-cotta. ✉ *24 pl. de Chambre,* ☎ *03–87–36–33–92. MC, V. Closed Wed.*

$ ✕ **La Dauphiné.** Stop at this delightful barrel-vaulted tearoom to have *tourte Lorraine* (meat pie), delicious gratin potatoes, or the plat du jour, and a generous slice of fruit tart. Locals claim permanent lunch stations, but there's room upstairs, too. ✉ *8 rue du Chanoine-Collin,* ☎ *03–87–36–03–04. MC, V. Closed Tues.*

$$–$$$ ★ **Royal Bleu Marine.** This fully modernized hotel, taken over and buffed up by the Campanile chain, occupies a sumptuous Belle Epoque building not far from the train station. Rooms come in a choice of styles (old-fashioned luxury versus simpler modernity). All are soundproof. ✉ *23 av. Foch, 57011,* ☎ *03–87–66–81–11,* FAX *03–87–56–13–16. 76 rooms. Restaurant, bar, sauna, exercise room. AE, DC, MC, V.*

Pont-à-Mousson

22 *27 km (17 mi) south of Metz on N57, 27 km (17 mi) northwest of Nancy.*

The name Pont-à-Mousson may ring a bell if you've strolled a few French streets: It adorns most of the manholes in France, all made in the town's foundries along the Moselle river. The town's ornate 15th-century church of **St-Martin** has a host of gravity-defying sculptures and gargoyles. The Baroque **Abbaye des Prémontrés,** begun in 1608, displays sharp contrast between its serene, classical exterior and its flamboyant interior. East of the town, a steep climb leads to the summit of the **Butte de Mousson,** a feudal stronghold where a ruined chapel and fortification walls frame spectacular views over the Moselle Valley.

St-Nicolas-de-Port

23 *20 km (12 mi) southeast of Nancy.*

The small industrial town of St-Nicolas-de-Port is saved from mediocrity by its colossal basilica. Legend has it that a finger of St. Nicholas was brought to the town during the 11th-century Crusades. Holding such a priceless relic, the **Basilique de St-Nicolas-de-Port** (1495–1555) was rapidly besieged by pilgrims (including Joan of Arc who came to ask St-Nicolas's blessings on her famous journey to Orléans). The simplified column capitals and elaborate rib vaulting are shining examples of Flamboyant Gothic enjoying a final fling before the gathering impetus of the Renaissance, as is the 280-foot onion-dome towers, almost symmetrical but, as was the Gothic wont, not quite. Inside, the slender, freestanding 90-foot pillars in the transept are the highest in France.

Toul

24 *23 km (14 mi) west of Nancy.*

The old town of Toul, nestled behind mossy, star-shape ramparts, has been a bishopric since AD 365, and merited visits from the Frankish King Clovis to study the Christian faith; from Charlemagne in passing; and from a young, premilitary Joan of Arc, who was sued in the Toul court for breach of promise when she threw over a beau for the voice of God. In 1700, under Louis XIV, the military engineer Vauban built the thrusting ramparts around the town.

The ramshackle streets of central Toul haven't changed much for centuries—not since the embroidered, twin-tower facade, a Flamboyant Gothic masterpiece, was woven onto the **Cathédrale St-Étienne** in the second half of the 15th century. The cathedral's interior, begun in 1204, is long (321 feet), airy (105 feet high), and more restrained than its exuberant facade. On one side of the cathedral are the 14th-century **cloisters,** and on the other a pleasant **garden** behind the **Hôtel de Ville** (Town Hall), built in 1740 as the Bishop's Palace. ⏲ *Summer, daily 9–6; winter, daily 9–dark.*

The **Musée Municipal** (Town Museum), housed in a former medieval hospital, has a well-preserved *Salle des Malades* (Patient's Ward) dating from the 13th century. Archaeological finds, ceramics, tapestries, and medieval sculpture are on display. ✉ *25 rue Gouvion-St-Cyr,* ☎ *03–83–64–13–38.* 🎟 *17 frs.* ⏲ *Apr.–Oct., Wed.–Mon. 10–noon and 2–6; Nov.–Mar., Wed.–Mon. 2–6.*

The choir of the attractive church of **St-Gengoult** has beautifully preserved 13th-century stained-glass windows. Unfortunately, because of repeated vandalism, it is closed to the public, although attending Sunday Mass (10:30 AM) will reward the devout. The adjoining Flamboyant Gothic **cloisters,** later than those of the cathedral but equally picturesque, stay open at all hours. ✉ *pl. du Marché.*

Dining

$$$ ✕ **Le Dauphin.** The large, flower-laden dining room was once a G.I. canteen, and the setting (in an industrial area 5 km/3 mi from town) has little of the ambience of historic Toul. Yet Christophe Vohmann entices with cooking of great finesse, tapping local farms and forests, as well as the seafood market, to make such dishes as monkfish with bacon and soufflé of dried mirabelles. Prices à la carte run quickly out of hand. ✉ *rte. de Villey-St-Étienne,* ☎ *03–83–43–13–46. Reservations essential. Jacket and tie. AE, MC, V. No dinner Sun.*

Vaucouleurs

25 *24 km (15 mi) southwest of Toul on D960.*

Below the medieval walls and ruins of Robert de Baudricourt's ancient château in the modest market town of Vaucouleurs, you can see the Porte de France, through which Joan of Arc led her armed soldiers to Orléans.

Dining and Lodging

$ ✕ **De la Poste.** On the main street, this simple place has quiet rooms over a pleasant, intimate restaurant. The good regional menu is served noon and night, except Sunday night and Monday. A friendly family cooks, serves the meals, and checks you in. ✉ *12 av. André Maginot, 55140.* ☎ *03–29–89–40–01,* FAX *03–29–89–40–93. 9 rooms. Restaurant. MC, V. Closed end Dec.–Jan.*

Domrémy-la-Pucelle

26 *40 km (25 mi) southwest of Toul, 19 km (12 mi) south of Vaucouleurs.*

Joan of Arc was born in a stone hut in Domrémy-la-Pucelle. You can see it, as well as the church where she was baptized, the figure of Ste-Marguerite she prayed before, and the hillside where she tended sheep and first heard voices telling her to take up arms and save France from the English.

The humble stone-and-stucco **Maison Natale Jean d'Arc** (Joan of Arc Birthplace)—an irregular, slope-roofed former cowshed—has been preserved with some reverence, and an attached museum retells her story. After she heard the voices, Joan walked 19 km (12 mi) to Vaucouleurs (☞ *above*). Dressed and mounted like a man, she led her forces to lift the siege of Orléans, defeated the English, and escorted the unseated Charles VII to Reims, to be crowned king of France. Military missions after Orléans failed—including an attempt to retake Paris—and she was captured at Compiègne. The English turned her over to the Church, which sent her to be tried by the Inquisition for witchcraft and heresy. She was convicted, excommunicated, and burned at the stake in Rouen. ✉ *2 rue de la Basilique,* ☎ *03–29–06–95–86.* *6 frs.* ⌚ *Apr.–Sept., daily 9–12:30 and 2–7; Oct.–Mar., Wed.–Mon. 9:30–12 and 2–5.*

The ornate, late-19th-century **Basilique du Bois-Chenu,** a pleasant walk up a country road from Joan of Arc's birthplace, has enormous painted panels telling her story in glowing pre-Raphaelite tones.

Lodging

$ **Jeanne d'Arc.** Stay next door to Joan of Arc's childhood church and wake to the bells that summoned her voices. Accommodations are considerably less evocative, in jazzy '60s tile and paneling, but bathrooms are spotless and breakfasts (in-room only) generous. ✉ *1 rue Principale, 88630,* ☎ *03–29–06–96–06. 12 rooms. No credit cards. Closed mid-Nov.–Mar.*

Grand

27 *15 km (9 mi) northwest of Domrémy-la-Pucelle: from Domrémy, follow signs down country roads west toward Grand.*

In the tiny, enigmatic architectural treasure of Grand, a spring developed into a center for the worship of the Gallo-Roman sun god Apollo-Grannus. It was important enough to draw the Roman Emperors Caracalla and Constantine. In the upper village there is a marvelously expressive floor mosaic with realistic animal details and an amphitheater that once seated 20,000. Surrounding the mosaic are scraps of exotic stone and relics transported from across two continents, bearing witness to this isolated village's opulent past. ☎ *03–29–06–63–43.* *20 frs for amphitheater and mosaic.* ⌚ *Apr.–Sept., daily 9–noon and 2–7; Oct.–Mar., daily 10–noon and 2–5.*

Épinal

28 *84 km (53 mi) southeast of Domrémy, 69 km (43 mi) south of Nancy, 97 km (61 mi) north of Belfort.*

A printing center since 1735, Épinal, on the Moselle River at the feet of the Vosges, is famous throughout France for boldly colored prints, popular illustrations, and hand-colored stencils. **L'Imagerie Pellerin,** the artisanal workshop, has a slide show tracing the history of local printing. ✉ *42 bis quai de Dogneville,* ☎ *03–29–34–21–87.* *Free. Guided tour with slide show: 25 frs.* *Tours: 10, 11, 3, and 4:30 for 45 mins. Gallery/salesroom open between tours: Mon.–Sat. 8:30–noon and 2–6:30, Sun. 2–6:30.*

On an island in the Moselle in the center of Épinal, the spectacular **Musée Départemental d'Art Ancien et Contemporain** (Museum of Ancient and Contemporary Art) is in a renovated 17th-century hospital, whose classical traces are still visible under a dramatic barrel-vaulted skylight. It contains France's fourth largest collection of contemporary art, as wells as Gallo-Roman artifacts; rural tools, and local faïence; and Old Masters, including some fine drawings and watercolors by Fragonard and Boucher. ✉ *1 pl. Lagarde,* ☎ *03–29–82–20–33.* *30 frs.* *Apr.–Sept., Wed.–Mon. 10–noon and 2–6; Oct.–Mar., Wed.–Mon. 10–noon and 2–5.*

STRASBOURG

Though centered in the heart of Alsace (490 km/304 mi east of Paris) and drawing appealingly on Alsatian gemütlichkeit (friendliness), the city of Strasbourg is a cosmopolitan French cultural center and, in many ways, the unofficial "capital" of Europe. Against an irresistible backdrop of old half-timber houses, waterways, and the colossal single spire of the red sandstone cathedral, Strasbourg is an incongruously sophisticated mix of museums, elite schools (including the notorious hothouse for blooming politicos, the École Nationale d'Administration, or National Administration School), international think tanks, and the European Parliament.

The Romans knew Strasbourg as Argentoratum before it came to be known as Strateburgum, or city of (cross) roads. After centuries as part of the Germanic Holy Roman Empire, the city was united with France in 1681, but retained independence regarding legislation, education, and religion under the honorific title Free Royal City. Since World War II, Strasbourg has become a symbolic city, embodying Franco-German reconciliation and the wider idea of a united Europe. The city center is effectively an island within two arms of the River Ill; most major sites are found here, but the northern districts also contain some fine buildings erected over the last 100 years, culminating in the Palais de l'Europe.

The Historic Heart

This central area, from the cathedral to picturesque Petite France, concentrates on the best of old Strasbourg, with its twisting backstreets, flower-lined courts, tempting shops, and inviting weinstübes.

A Good Walk

Begin at place Gutenberg and head up rue Mercière, lined with souvenir shops. To see a bit of Strasbourg's appealing combination of cozy weinstübes, medieval alleys, and chic shops, turn left up rue des Tailleurs, and head right up the rue des Hallebardes. Duck left up "rue pittoresque" (really rue des Orfevres), then circle right down rue Chaudron and again down rue du Sanglier. Head back right down rue des Hallebardes and cut into place de la Cathédrale, passing the landmark Maison Kammerzell (☞ Dining and Lodging, *below*).

Emerging from this close-packed warren of dark-timber buildings and narrow streets, you'll confront the magnificent **Cathédrale Notre-Dame** ㉙. Turn right from the tower and cross the square to the **Musée de l'Oeuvre Notre-Dame** ㉚, with its collection of statuary. Leaving the museum, turn right and approach the vast neighboring palace, the **Palais Rohan** ㉛. Once the headquarters of the powerful prince-bishops, the Rohans, it now houses the Musée des Arts Décoratifs, the Musée Archéologique, and the Musée des Beaux-Arts.

Once out of the château's entry court, double back left and turn left again, following rue des Rohans to the river. From here you can take a boat tour of the old town (☞ Outdoor Activities and Sports, *below*). Veer away from the water and cross place du Marché du Cochons du Lait (Suckling Pig Market Square) and place de la Grande Boucherie (Grand Slaughterhouse Square) to reach the **Musée Historique** ㉜, with its collection of paintings, weapons, and furniture from Strasbourg. Across the street is the modern glass entrance to the **Ancienne Douane** ㉝, the former customs house, now a vast venue for temporary exhibitions. Cross Pont du Corbeau to cour du Corbeau, a ramshackle 14th-century courtyard whose hostelry once welcomed kings and emperors. Back to the left, fronting the quai, is the **Musée Alsacien** ㉞, where you can get a glimpse of how Alsatian families used to live.

If time and energy allow, strike out toward the picturesque quarter of **Petite France** ㉟. Cross Pont St-Nicolas and follow the riverside promenade west. At Pont St-Martin, take rue des Dentelles to rue du Bain aux Plantes. Explore the alleys, courts, cafés, and shop windows at will as you work your way west. Eventually you will reach the three, monumental **Ponts Couverts** ㊱. Just beyond the bridges lies the grass-roof dam, the **Barrage Vauban** ㊲. Climb to the top; from here you'll see a gleaming glass-framed building, the new **Musée d'Art Moderne** ㊳.

TIMING

Allow at least a full day to see Strasbourg—perhaps visiting the old town and Cathedral in the morning, ending at 12:30 with the mechanical clock, then lunch on a nearby backstreet. The afternoon might allow two museum stops or time to wander through Petite France. Two days would allow more museum time; a third day would allow you to take in the monumental sights at place de la République and the Palais de l'Europe (☞ *below*).

Sights to See

33 **Ancienne Douane.** The airport-hangar scale and flexible walls lend themselves to enormous expositions of Old Master paintings as well as archaeology and history at this former customs house on the Ill River. ✉ *1 rue de Vieux-Marché-aux-Poissons,* ☎ *03–88–52–50–04.* 🎫 *30 frs.* ⏲ *Daily 11–6:30, Thurs. to 10* PM.

37 **Barrage Vauban.** Just beyond the Ponts Couverts is the grass-roof Barrage Dam, built by its namesake in 1682. Climb to the top for a stunning view across the roofs of old Strasbourg. ✉ *Ponts Couverts.* 🎫 *Free.* ⏲ *Nov.–Mar., daily 9–7; Apr.–Oct., daily 9–8.*

★ 29 **Cathédrale Notre-Dame.** Rosy, ornately carved Vosges sandstone masonry covers the facade of this most novel and Germanic of French cathedrals, a triumph of Gothic art completed in 1284. Not content with the outlines of the walls themselves, medieval builders mounted slender, rodlike shafts of stone everywhere. The off-center **spire,** finished

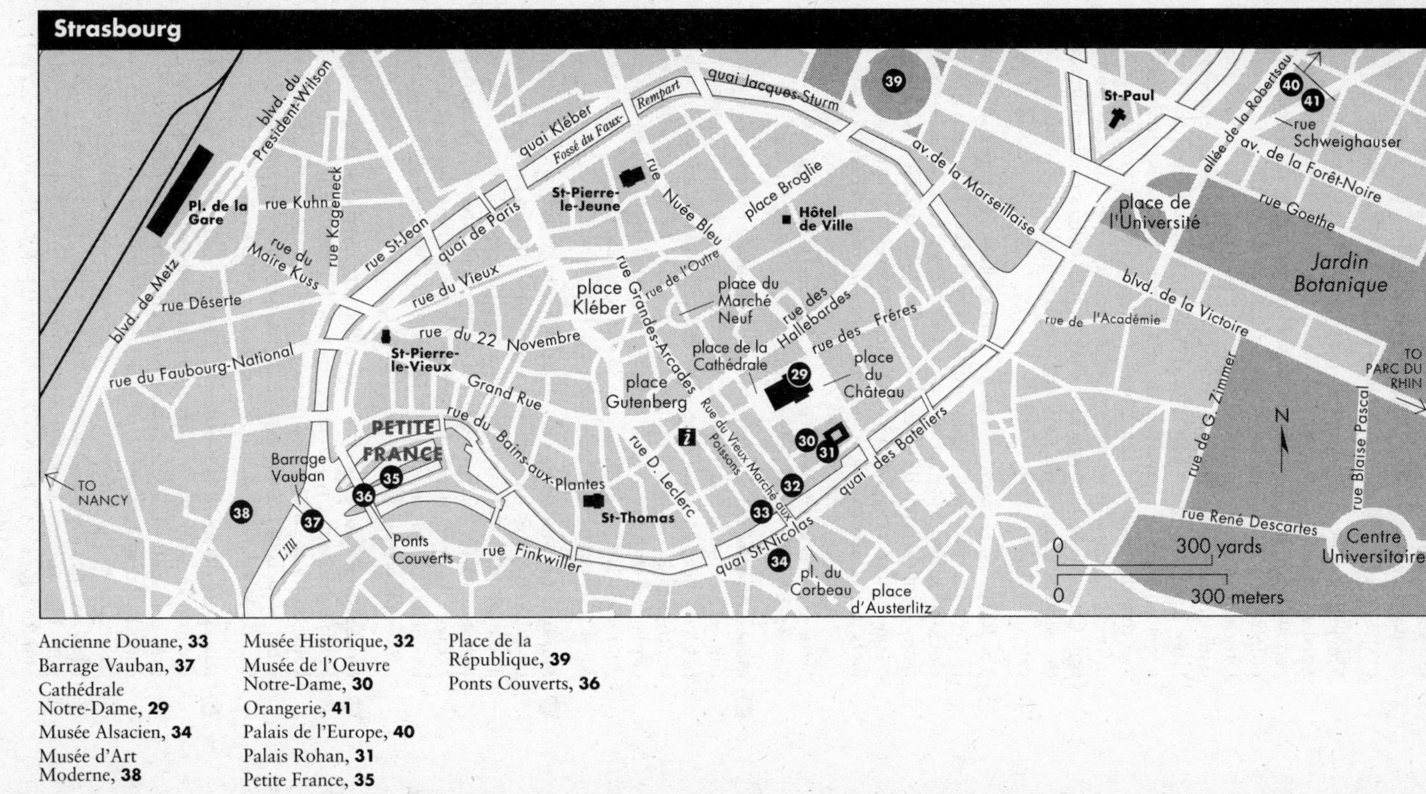

Ancienne Douane, **33**
Barrage Vauban, **37**
Cathédrale Notre-Dame, **29**
Musée Alsacien, **34**
Musée d'Art Moderne, **38**
Musée Historique, **32**
Musée de l'Oeuvre Notre-Dame, **30**
Orangerie, **41**
Palais de l'Europe, **40**
Palais Rohan, **31**
Petite France, **35**
Place de la République, **39**
Ponts Couverts, **36**

in 1439, looks absurdly fragile as it tapers skyward some 466 feet; you can nonetheless climb its 330 steps to the top to take in sweeping views of the city, the Vosges mountains, and the Black Forest.

The interior presents a stark contrast to the facade: It is older (mostly finished by 1275) and the nave's broad windows emphasize the horizontal rather than the vertical. Note Hans Hammer's ornately sculpted pulpit (1484–86), and the richly painted 14th- to 15th-century organ loft that rises from pillar to ceiling. The left side of the nave is flanked with richly colored Gothic windows honoring the early leaders of the Holy Roman Empire–Otto I and II, and Heinrich I and II. The **choir** is not ablaze with stained glass, but framed by chunky masonry. The fact that the choir is raised above the level of the rest of the church reinforces an aura of murky mystical sanctity. The elaborate 16th-century **Chapelle St-Laurent,** to the left of the choir, merits a visit; turn to the right to admire the **Colonne d'Anges** (Angels' Column) an intricate pillar dating from 1230.

The Renaissance machinery of the 16th-century **Horloge Astronomique** (Astronomical Clock) whirs into action at 12:30 PM daily: Macabre clockwork figures enact the story of Christ's Passion. Every evening from April through the end of September, the cathedral is the sight of a son-et-lumière show in French or German (but virtuoso lighting effects translate into any language). ⊠ *pl. de la Cathédrale.* *Clock 5 frs, spire 13 frs, son-et-lumière: 30 frs.* *Clock: daily 12:30 PM, but the line starts at the south door at 11:45 AM; Spire: daylight hrs; performances at 8:15 PM in German and 9:15 PM in French.*

34 **Musée Alsacien.** In this labyrinthine half-timber home, with layers of carved balconies sagging over a cobbled inner courtyard, local interiors have been faithfully reconstituted. The diverse activities of blacksmiths, clog makers, saddlers, and makers of artificial flowers are explained with the help of old-time artisans' tools and equipment. ⊠ *23 quai St-Nicolas,* ☎ *03–88–35–55–36.* *20 frs.* *Wed.–Sat. and Mon. 10–noon and 1:30–6, Sun. 10–5.*

38 **Musée d'Art Moderne.** The Modern Art Museum, opening at the end of 1998, features high-quality temporary expositions of new, esoteric and unsung modern art. Its permanent collection ranges from the Impressionists to postwar abstract painters. Native son Jean Arp, the Dadaist, is prominently featured, as are the drawings and aquarelles of Gustave Doré, also from Alsace. ⊠ *rue Molsheim. Contact tourist office (*☞ below*) for hrs and admission.*

32 **Musée Historique.** This 1588 step-gabled slaughterhouse houses the Local History Museum, which contains a collection of maps, armor, arms, bells, uniforms, traditional dress, printing paraphernalia, and two huge relief models of Strasbourg. ⊠ *2 rue du Vieux-Marché-aux-Poissons,* ☎ *03–88–32–25–63. Call for prices and hrs.*

★ 30 **Musée de l'Oeuvre Notre-Dame.** There is more to this museum than the usual assembly of dilapidated statues rescued from the local cathedral before they fell off. A conscious effort has been made to create a church atmosphere and to provide an appropriate setting for the works of art. Part of one room evokes a narrow, low-roofed cloister. A polished wooden staircase leads to a suite of small passages and large rooms, with Flemish and Upper Rhine paintings, stained glass, gold objects, and furniture. ⊠ *3 pl. du Château,* ☎ *03–88–52–50–00.* *20 frs.* *Tues.–Sat. 10–noon and 1:30–6, Sun. 10–5.*

31 **Palais Rohan.** The exterior of Robert de Cotte's neoclassical building (1732–42) is starkly austere. But the glamour is inside, in Robert le

Lorrain's magnificent ground-floor rooms, led by the great **Salon d'Assemblée** (Assembly Room) and the book- and tapestry-lined **Bibliothèque des Cardinaux** (Cardinals' Library). The library leads to a series of less august rooms that house the **Musée des Arts Décoratifs** (Decorative Arts Museum) and its elaborate display of ceramics. Works by Hannong, a porcelain manufacturer active in Strasbourg from 1721 to 1782, are comprehensively represented; dinner services by other local kilns reveal the influence of Chinese porcelain. The **Musée des Beaux-Arts** (Fine Arts Museum), also in the château, features masterworks of European paintings from Giotto and Memling to El Greco, Rubens, and Goya. Downstairs, the **Musée Archéologique** displays regional archaeological findings. ✉ *2 pl. du Château,* ☎ *03–88–52–50–00.* 🎫 *40 frs all museums; per museum, 20 frs.* ⏲ *Wed.–Sat. and Mon. 10–noon and 1:30–6; Sun. 10–5.*

35 **Petite France.** With its gingerbread half-timber houses that seem to lean precariously over the canals of the Ill, its novel shops, and inviting little restaurants, this is the most charming and magical neighborhood in Strasbourg. Wander up and down the tiny streets that connect rue du Bain aux Plantes and rue des Dentelles to Grand' Rue, and stroll the waterfront promenade.

36 **Ponts Couverts.** These three bridges, distinguished by their three stone towers, were once covered with wooden shelters. Part of the 14th-century ramparts that framed old Strasbourg, they span the Ill as it branches into four fingerlike canals.

Beyond the Ill

If you've seen the center and have time to strike out in new directions, head across the Ill to view two architectural landmarks unrelated to Strasbourg's famous medieval past: place de la République and the European Union's Palais de l'Europe.

A Good Walk

North of the cathedral, walk up rue des Hallebardes and turn left on rue du Dôme. Take a right onto place Broglie and continue up this main thoroughfare across the river to the striking circle of red sandstone buildings on the **place de la République** ㊴. Back at the river, head for a bus stop on avenue de la Marseillaise and take Bus 23 to the **Palais de l'Europe** ㊵ for a guided tour (by appointment, arranged in advance). From here, plunge into the greenery of the **Orangerie** ㊶. Either indulge in a three-hour lunch at the stellar Buerehiesel (☞ Dining and Lodging, *below*) or picnic on a bench.

TIMING

Basing your schedule on your tour appointment at the Palais de l'Europe, allow about a half day for this walk; if need be, you can while away the wait in the Orangerie.

Sights to See

41 **Orangerie.** Like a private backyard to the Eurocrats in the Palais de l'Europe, this delightful park is laden with flowers and punctuated by noble copper beeches. It contains a lake and, close by, a small reserve of rare birds, including flamingos and noisy local storks. ✉ *av. de l'Europe.*

40 **Palais de l'Europe.** Designed by Paris architect Henri Bernard in 1977, this Continental landmark is headquarters to the European Court of Human Rights and the Council of Europe, founded in 1949 and independent of the European Union. It also houses the European Parliament, which participates in legislation of the European Union. A guided tour introduces you to the intricacies of their workings, and may allow

you to eavesdrop on a session. Arrange your tour by telephone in advance; appointments are fixed according to language demands, and usually take place in the afternoon. Note: You must provide a *pièce d'identité* (ID) before entering. ✉ *av. de l'Europe,* ☎ *03–88–41–20–29 information; 03–88–17–20–07 appointments.* 🎫 *Free.* ⏲ *Guided tours by appointment Mon.–Fri.*

39 **Place de la République.** The spacious layout and ponderous architecture of this monumental *cirque* (circle) have nothing in common with the old town, except the local red sandstone. A different hand was at work here—that of occupying Germans, who erected the former Ministry (1902); the Academy of Music (1882–92); and the Palais du Rhin (1883–88). The handsome neo-Gothic church of **St-Paul** and the pseudo-Renaissance **Palais de l'Université,** constructed between 1875 and 1885, also bear the German stamp. Heavy, turn-of-the-century houses, some betraying the whimsical curves of the Art Nouveau style, frame **allée de la Robertsau,** a tree-lined boulevard that would not look out of place in Berlin.

Dining and Lodging

$$$$ ★ ✕ **Buerehiesel.** This lovely Alsatian farmhouse, reconstructed in the Orangerie, warrants a pilgrimage if you are willing to pay for some of the finest cooking in France. Antoine Westermann stands in the upper echelon of chefs while remaining true to the ingredients and specialties of his native Alsace: a fish *matelote* (casserole) in Riesling, and guinea hen with fresh foie gras. European *parlementaires* come on foot; others might come on their knees. ✉ *4 parc de l'Orangerie,* ☎ *03–88–61–62–24. Reservations essential. AE, DC, MC, V. Closed Tues., Wed.*

$$$$ ✕ **Crocodile.** Chef Émile Jung is celebrated throughout the region for his Alsatian dishes prepared with an urbane finesse: truffle turnover, warmed goose liver with apples and ginger, and bitter-chocolate cherry cake. The restaurant's opulent decor makes a sophisticated backdrop for a sensual meal. ✉ *10 rue de l'Outre,* ☎ *03–88–32–13–02. Reservations essential. Jacket and tie. AE, DC, MC, V. Closed Sun., Mon., 2nd wk in July–1st wk in Aug., and Dec. 25–Jan. 1.*

$$ ★ ✕ **Chez Yvonne's Burjerstuewel.** Behind red-checked curtains, you'll find artists, tourists, lovers, and heads of state sitting elbow-to-elbow in this classic weinstübe. They come to savor steaming platters of duck confit on juniper-peppered choucroute or tête de veau in white wine. Warm Alsatian fabrics dress tables and lamps, the china is regional, the photos historic, and the ambience all chic—and no kitsch. ✉ *10 rue du Sanglier,* ☎ *03–88–32–84–15. AE, DC, MC, V. Closed Sun. No lunch Mon.*

$$ ✕ **Maison Kammerzell.** This restaurant glories in its richly carved, half-timber, 15th-century building—probably the most familiar house in Strasbourg. Fight your way through the tourist hordes on the terrace and ground floor to one of the atmospheric rooms above, with their gleaming wooden furniture and stained-glass windows. Foie gras and choucroute are best bets, though you may want to try the chef's pet discovery, choucroute with freshwater fish. Portions are large, but service can be slipshod. ✉ *16 pl. de la Cathédrale,* ☎ *03–88–32–42–14. AE, DC, MC, V.*

$–$$ ✕ **Au Sanglier.** Step off the busy rue des Hallebardes and settle by the fireplace in this dark-timber, lace-clothed old dining room, where you can delve into crisp *jambonneau* (ham shank), trout in white-wine cream sauce, or cheese-crusted onion soup. Wines are local and reasonable, and service familial. ✉ *11 rue du Sanglier,* ☎ *03–88–32–64–58. MC, V. Closed Sun. No lunch Mon.*

Pick up the phone.

Pick up the miles.

Use your MCI Card® to make an international call from virtually anywhere in the world and earn frequent flyer miles on one of seven major airlines.

Enroll in an MCI Airline Partner Program today. In the U.S., call **1-800-FLY-FREE.** Overseas, call MCI collect at **1-916-567-5151.**

1. To use your MCI Card, just dial the WorldPhone access number of the country you're calling from. (For a complete listing of codes, visit www.mci.com.)
2. Dial or give the operator your MCI Card number.
3. Dial or give the number you're calling.

# **Austria** (CC)♦	022-903-012
# **Belarus** (CC)	
From Brest, Vitebsk, Grodno, Minsk	8-800-103
From Gomel and Mogilev regions	8-10-800-103
# **Belgium** (CC)♦	0800-10012
# **Bulgaria**	00800-0001
# **Croatia** (CC)★	99-385-0112
# **Czech Republic** (CC)♦	00-42-000112
# **Denmark** (CC)♦	8001-0022
# **Finland** (CC)♦	08001-102-80
# **France** (CC)♦	0-800-99-0019
# **Germany** (CC)	0130-0012
# **Greece** (CC)♦	00-800-1211
# **Hungary** (CC)♦	00▼800-01411
# **Iceland** (CC)♦	800-9002
# **Ireland** (CC)	1-800-55-1001
# **Italy** (CC)♦	172-1022
# **Kazakhstan** (CC)	8-800-131-4321
# **Liechtenstein** (CC)♦	0800-89-0222
# **Luxembourg**	0800-0112
# **Monaco** (CC)♦	800-90-019
# **Netherlands** (CC)♦	0800-022-91-22
# **Norway** (CC)♦	800-19912
# **Poland** (CC)✣	00-800-111-21-22
# **Portugal** (CC)✣	05-017-1234
Romania (CC)✣	01-800-1800
# **Russia** (CC)✣ ♦	
To call using ROSTELCOM ■	747-3322
For a Russian-speaking operator	747-3320
To call using SOVINTEL ■	960-2222
# **San Marino** (CC)♦	172-1022
# **Slovak Republic** (CC)	00-421-00112
# **Slovenia**	080-8808
# **Spain** (CC)	900-99-0014
# **Sweden** (CC)♦	020-795-922
# **Switzerland** (CC)♦	0800-89-0222
# **Turkey** (CC)♦	00-8001-1177
# **Ukraine** (CC)✣	8▼10-013
# **United Kingdom** (CC)	
To call using BT ■	0800-89-0222
To call using MERCURY ■	0500-89-0222
# **Vatican City** (CC)	172-1022

Is this a great time, or what? :-)

Automation available from most locations. (CC) Country-to-country calling available to/from most international locations. ♦ Public phones may require deposit of coin or phone card for dial tone. ★ Not available from public pay phone. ▼ Wait for second dial tone. ✣ Limited availability. ■ International communications carrier. Limit one bonus program per MCI account. Terms and conditions apply. All airline program rules and conditions apply. Is this a great time or what? is a service mark of MCI.

$ ★ **Au Tire-Bouchon.** Near the cathedral on a small backstreet, this comfortable weinstübe, called "Corkscrew," serves classic choucroute and grilled *quenelles de foie* (liver dumplings), plus lighter options: *salade de Gruyère* (nutty cheese and onion bits in a rich vinaigrette)—and local wines by the carafe. ✉ *5 rue des Tailleurs-de-Pierre,* ☎ *03–88–32–47–86. MC, V. Closed Sun.*

$$$$ **Régent-Contades.** This sleek, modern hotel is in a revamped mansion in a residential, turn-of-the-century district close to the River Ill (ask for a room with a view of St-Paul's). First-class amenities add to the appeal of the spacious rooms. ✉ *8 av. de la Liberté, 67000,* ☎ *03–88–15–05–05,* FAX *03–88–37–13–70. 44 rooms. Bar, sauna. AE, DC, MC, V.*

$$$$ **Régent-Petite France.** Opposite the Ponts Couverts is the newest and smartest of the city's hotels. The outside of the building (originally an ice factory) is almost unchanged—but the inside is resolutely modern, with a spacious marble vestibule. Some rooms overlook the river; all vary considerably in size (and price). Ask to see your's first. Beer-based dishes are a specialty at the Pont Tournant restaurant. ✉ *5 rue des Moulins, 67000 (aim for Pont St-Thomas, opposite St-Thomas church, then head west on quai Finkwiller, before bearing right onto rue des Moulins),* ☎ *03–88–76–43–43,* FAX *03–88–76–43–76. 72 rooms. Restaurant, piano bar. AE, DC, MC, V.*

$$ **Rohan.** Just a block from the cathedral on one of the picturesque pedestrian (read tourist) streets, this gracious old city hotel has sleek, modernized rooms and a welcoming atmosphere. Despite your placement at the heart of old-town action, quarters are surprisingly quiet. ✉ *17–19 rue Maroquin, 67000,* ☎ *03–88–32–85–11,* FAX *03–88–75–65–37. 36 rooms. MC, V.*

$ **Gutenberg.** A 200-year-old mansion is the setting of this hotel, just off place Gutenberg. Several rooms, as well as the reception and breakfast area, have been modernized with a sleek, scrubbed decor, though enough antique oak details remain to remind you of the building's history. ✉ *31 rue des Serruriers, 67000,* ☎ *03–88–32–17–15,* FAX *03–88–75–76–67. 50 rooms, 17 with bath, 27 with shower. Breakfast room. MC, V. Closed 1st wk in Jan.*

Nightlife and the Arts

Le Feeling (✉ 19 rue du Marais-Vert, ☎ 03–88–22–05–58) is a popular dance bar. **Le Bambou** (✉ 366 rte. de la Wantzeneau, ☎ 03–88–41–87–17) is a disco for the young and *branché* (hip).

The annual **Festival de Musique** is held from June to early July at the modern Palais des Congrès and at the cathedral; contact the Amis de la Musique (✉ 24 rue de la Mésange, ☎ 03–88–32–43–10) for more information. The **Opéra du Rhin** (✉ 19 pl. Broglie, ☎ 03–88–75–48–23) has a sizable repertoire. Classical concerts are staged by the **Orchestre Philharmonique** (✉ Palais des Congrès, ☎ 03–88–15–09–09).

Outdoor Activities and Sports

The **Port Autonome de Strasbourg** (☎ 03–88–32–75–25) organizes 75-minute boat tours along the River Ill, leaving from behind the Palais Rohan; the fee is 38 francs.

Shopping

The lively city center is full of specialized shops and boutiques, including chocolate shops and delicatessens selling local foie gras. Watch for warm paisley linens and rustic homespun fabrics, Alsatian pottery, and local wines. Rue des Hallebardes, next to the cathedral; rue des Grandes Arcades, with its shopping mall; and place Kléber form the city's commercial heart.

ALSACE

The Rhine River forms the eastern boundary of both Alsace and France. But the best of Alsace is not found along the Rhine's industrial waterfront. Instead it's nestled in the Ill valley at the base of the Vosges, southwest of cosmopolitan Strasbourg. Northwest is Saverne, and the beginning of the Route du Vin, the great Alsace Wine Road, which winds its way south through the Vosges foothills, fruitful vineyards, and medieval villages that would serve well on a film set for William Tell. Signs for the road help you keep your bearings on the twisty way south, and you'll find limitless opportunity to stop at wineries and sample the local wares. At the industrial town of Mulhouse, you'll leave behind the charms of Alsace and head into the historic wilds of Franche-Comté.

Saverne

42 *37 km (23 mi) northwest of Strasbourg.*

Saverne, gateway to the northern Vosges, has a stately castle with an exuberant rose garden. Built out of red sandstone, the 18th-century **Château des Rohans** is renowned for its majestic north facade, lined by fluted pilasters and a Corinthian colonnade. The right wing houses an interesting museum devoted to archaeology, religious statuary, and local history. Don't miss the **Roseraie,** (Rose Garden) with 1,000 types of rose. ☎ *03–88–91–06–28.* *Château 15 frs.* *Mar.–mid-June, Wed.–Mon. 2–5; mid-June–mid-Sept., Wed.–Mon. 10–12 and 2–6; mid-Sept.–Nov., Wed.–Mon. 2–5; Dec.–Feb., Sun. 2–5.*

Marmoutier

43 *6 km (4 mi) south of Saverne, 41 km (25 mi) northwest of Strasbourg.*

Marmoutier is worth a stop to see its handsome Romanesque **Église Abbatiale** (abbey church). The facade, dating from the 11th and 12th centuries, is pure Lombard Romanesque, built from local Vosges sandstone. Inside, you'll find a handsome 1710 organ, built by Silbermann (organ maker to J. S. Bach).

Obernai

44 *35 km (22 mi) south of Saverne, 27 km (17 mi) southwest of Strasbourg.*

Obernai is a thriving, colorful Renaissance market town with a medieval belfry, a Renaissance well, and a late-19th-century church. Place du Marché, in the heart of town, is dominated by the stout, square 13th-century **Kappellturm Beffroi** (belfry), topped by a pointed steeple flanked at each corner by frilly openwork turrets added in 1597. An elaborate Renaissance well near the belfry, the **Puits à Six-Seaux,** was constructed in the 1570s; its name recalls the six buckets suspended from its metal chains. The twin spires of the parish church of **St-Pierre-St-Paul** compete with the belfry for skyline preeminence. They date, like the rest of the church, from the 1860s, although the 1504 Holy Sepulcher altarpiece in the north transept is a survivor from the previous church, along with some 15th-century stained glass.

Dining and Lodging

$$ ★ ✕🏨 **L'Ami Fritz.** In the center of Ottrott, west of Obernai, this place combines chic, warmth, and a rustic atmosphere. The chef's specialties include succulent *presskopf* (head cheese), tender onion tarts, and seasonal game with traditional chestnut-and-red-cabbage garnish. The weekday lunch menu is a great deal; the restaurant is closed Wednesday. The all-modern hotel is in a separate building 300 yards away. Rooms are spacious, solid, and impeccable. ✉ *8 rue des Châteaux, 67530 Ottrott (about 3 km/2 mi from Obernai),* ☎ *03–88–95–80–81,* FAX *03–88–95–84–85. 17 rooms with bath or shower. Restaurant. AE, DC, MC, V.*

Shopping

Dietrich (✉ 58 and 74 rue du Général-Gouraud, ☎ 03–88–95–57–58), on the town market square, has a varied selection of beautifully crafted household goods.

Mont-Ste-Odile

★ 45 *12 km (8 mi) southwest of Obernai, 42 km (26 mi) southwest of Strasbourg.*

Mont-Ste-Odile, a 2,500-foot mound, has been an important religious and military site for 3,000 years. An eerie 9½-km-long (6-mi-long) *mur païen* (pagan wall), up to 12 feet high and, in parts, several feet thick, rings the summit; its mysterious origins and purpose still baffle archaeologists. The Romans established a settlement here, and at the start of the 8th century, Odile, daughter of Duke Etichon of Obernai, founded a convent on the same spot after recovering her sight while being baptized (she had been born blind). Odile—the patron saint of Alsace—died here in AD 720; her sarcophagus rests in the Chapelle Ste-Odile. The convent still remains, rescued by the bishop of Strasbourg in 1853, after repeated plunder, military vandalism, and the expulsion of its nuns during the French Revolution. Allow time for an arduous switchback drive to the top.

Barr

46 *11 km (7 mi) southeast of Mont Ste-Odile, 8 km (5 mi) south of Obernai, 33 km (20 mi) southwest of Strasbourg.*

Barr is a thriving little town surrounded by vines, with some charming narrow streets (notably rue des Cigognes, rue Neuve, and the tiny rue de l'Essieu), a cheerful Hôtel de Ville, and a decorative arts museum. Most buildings date from after a catastrophic fire of 1678; the only medieval survivor is the Romanesque tower of St-Martin, the Protestant church.

Admire original furniture, local porcelain, earthenware, and pewter at the **Musée de la Folie Marco,** housed in a steep-tiled mansion built by local magistrate Félix Marco in 1763. One section of the museum explains the traditional process of *schlittage*: Sleds, bearing bundles of freshly sawed tree trunks, once slid down forest slopes along a "corduroy road" made of logs. ✉ *30 rue du Dr-Sultzer,* ☎ *03–88–08–94–72.* 🎟 *10 frs.* ⏲ *July–Sept., Wed.–Mon. 10–noon and 2–6; June and Oct., weekends 10–noon and 2–6.*

Dining and Lodging

$$ ✕🏨 **Gilg.** Looking over the tiny medieval village of Mittelbergheim, outside Barr, this historic inn specializes in a pleasant mix of classic and regional cuisine (fish presskopf, frogs' legs in Riesling) with wines from neighboring vineyards, served in a timbered and vaulted wein-

stübe. The restaurant is closed Tuesday dinner and Wednesday. Rooms are more atmospheric than comfortable and the 17th-century stone spiral staircase leading upstairs is best suited to young romantics. ✉ *1 rue Rotland, 67140 Mittelbergheim,* ☎ *03–88–08–91–37,* FAX *03–88–08–45–17. 10 rooms. Restaurant. AE, DC, MC, V. Closed 1st 3 wks of Jan., and late June–early July.*

Andlau

47 *3 km (2 mi) southwest of Barr, 37 km (23 mi) southwest of Strasbourg.*

Andlau has long been known for its magnificent abbey. Built in the 12th century, the **Abbaye d'Andlau** has the richest ensemble of Romanesque sculpture in Alsace. Sculpted vines wind their way around the doorway as a reminder of wine's time-honored importance to the local economy. A statue of a female bear, the abbey mascot—bears used to roam local forests and were bred at the abbey until the 16th century—can be seen in the north transept. Legend has it that Queen Richarde, spurned by her husband Charles the Fat, founded the abbey in AD 887 when an angel enjoined her to construct a church on a site to be shown to her by a female bear.

Dambach-la-Ville

48 *5 km (3 mi) southwest of Andlau, 42 km (26 mi) southwest of Strasbourg. From Andlau, take D253 to the junction with D603; keep right; about 1 km (1//2 mi) later, turn right, then left through Itterswiller before turning right toward Dambach-la-Ville.*

Dambach-la-Ville is a fortified medieval town protected by ramparts and three powerful 13th-century gateways. Dambach is particularly rich in half-timber, high-roof houses from the 17th and 18th centuries, clustered mainly around **place du Marché** and its 16th-century **Hôtel de Ville.**

En Route Just south of Dambach is the imposing **Château d'Ortenburg** on the hilltop to your right, constructed in 1000 by Wernher d'Ortenburg and restored in 1258 by Rodolphe de Habsbourg.

Sélestat

49 *9 km (5 mi) southeast of Dambach, 19 km (12 mi) south of Barr, 47 km (29 mi) southwest of Strasbourg.*

Sélestat, midway between Strasbourg and Colmar, is a lively, historic town with a Romanesque church and a library of medieval manuscripts. The church of **St-Foy** dates from between 1155 and 1190; its Romanesque facade remains largely intact (the spires were added in the 19th century), as does the 140-foot octagonal tower over the crossing. Sadly, the interior was mangled during the centuries, chiefly by the Jesuits; their most inspired legacy is the Baroque pulpit of 1733 illustrating the life of St. Francis Xavier. Note the Romanesque bas-relief next to the baptistry, originally the lid of a sarcophagus. ✉ *pl. du Marché-Vert.*

Among the precious manuscripts on display at the **Bibliothèque Humaniste,** a major library founded in 1452 and installed in the former Halle aux Blés, are a 7th-century lectionary and a 12th-century Book of Miracles. ✉ *1 rue de la Bibliothèque,* ☎ *03–88–92–03–24.* 🎫 *20 frs.* 🕓 *Weekdays 9–noon and 2–6, Sat. 9–noon; July–Aug., also weekends 2–5.*

Nightlife and the Arts

The colorful **Corso Fleuri** (Flower Carnival) takes place on the second Sunday in August, when the town decks itself—and the floats in its vivid parade—with a magnificent display of dahlias.

Haut-Koenigsbourg

50 *12 km (8 mi) west of Sélstat, 59 km (36½ mi) southwest of Strasbourg.*

One of the most popular spots in Alsace is the romantic, crag-top castle in Haut-Koenigsbourg. Originally built as a fortress in the 12th century, the ruins of the **Château du Haut-Koenigsbourg** was presented by the town of Sélestat (or Schelestadt; the German name was used then) to German emperor Wilhelm II in 1901. It looked just as a kaiser thought it should and he restored it with some diligence and no lack of imagination—squaring the main tower's original circle, for instance. The site, panorama, drawbridge, and amply furnished imperial chambers may lack authenticity, but they are undeniably dramatic. ☎ *03–88–92–11–46. Château 36 frs. June–Sept., daily 9–6; Apr.–May, daily 9–noon and 1–6; Oct. and Mar., daily 9–noon and 1–5; Nov.–Feb., daily 9–noon and 1–4.*

Ribeauvillé

51 *14 km (9 mi) southwest of Sélestat, 63 km (39 mi) southwest of Strasbourg.*

The beautifully preserved, half-timber town of Ribeauvillé, surrounded by rolling vineyards and three imposing châteaux, produces some of the best Riesling in Alsace. Its narrow main street, crowded with weinstübes, pottery shops, bakeries, and wine sellers, is bisected by the 13th-century **Tour des Bouchers,** a clock-belfry completed (gargoyles and all) in the 15th century. Storks' nests crown several towers in the village. The Trimbach family has made Riesling and superb Gewürztraminer here since 1626.

Dining and Lodging

$ ✕ **Caveau de l'Ami Fritz.** Tucked into a low-vaulted hall, with glowing fireplace, paisley linens, and polished wood, this simple, casual spot serves good, hot food all day. Full meals include choucroute and game, but there are also soups, salads, mouthwatering onion tarts, and *tarte flambée* (a delicate bacon-and-crème-fraîche pizza). ✉ *1 pl. Ancien Hôpital,* ☎ *03–89–73–68–11. MC, V.*

$$ **De la Tour.** In the center of Ribeauvillé and across from the Tour des Bouchers, this hotel, with an ornate Renaissance fountain outside its front door, is a good choice for experiencing the atmospheric town by night. Rooms and amenities are modern; those on the top floor have exposed timbers and wonderfully ramshackle roof-top views. ✉ *1 rue de la Mairie, 68150,* ☎ *03–89–73–72–73,* FAX *03–89–73–38–74. 35 rooms. Breakfast room, sauna. MC, V.*

Riquewihr

★ 52 *5 km (3 mi) south of Ribeauvillé, 68 km (42 mi) south of Strasbourg.*

Riquewihr is a living museum to the quaint architecture and storybook atmosphere of old Alsace. Its steep main street, ramparts, and winding back alleys have scarcely changed since the 16th century and could easily serve as a film set. The town certainly attracts enough tourists. Overlook the plethora of kitschy souvenir shops and peep into courtyards at massive wine presses, study the woodwork and ornately decorated houses, stand in the narrow old ghetto on the cours des Juifs, or climb up a narrow wooden stair to the ramparts. You would also do well to settle into a weinstübe to sample some of Alsace's famous wines.

Dining and Lodging

$$ ✕🏨 **Sarment d'Or.** This cozy little hotel stands apart for its irreproachable modern comforts tactfully dovetailed with stone, dark timbers, and meter-thick walls. The restaurant downstairs offers firelit romance with its pastry-wrapped pâté, presskopf, and breast of duck in Pinot Noir. It has a reasonable daily menu, despite ambitious à la carte prices, and it's closed Sunday dinner and Monday. ✉ *4 rue du Cerf, 68340,* ☎ *03–89–47–92–85,* FAX *03–89–47–99–23. 17 rooms. Restaurant. MC, V. Closed Jan.*

Colmar

53 *16 km (10 mi) southeast of Riquewihr, 71 km (44 mi) southwest of Strasbourg.*

Much of Colmar's architecture is modern, on account of the destruction of World Wars I and II. But the heart of this proud merchant town is still a web of well-preserved pedestrian streets that fan out from the beefy-towered church of **St-Martin** toward the 15th-century customs house, the twin-turreted **Maison aux Arcades** (1609). Calm canals wind through **La Petite Venise** (Little Venice), an area of bright Alsatian houses with colorful shutters and window boxes south of the center of town. Colmar is also home to the finest art museum in Alsace and was once home to Bartholdi, designer of the Statue of Liberty.

★ The **Musée d'Unterlinden** was once a medieval convent and is now a museum. The star attraction is the ***Retable d'Issenheim*** (Issenheim Altarpiece; 1512–16) by Matthias Grünewald, majestically displayed in the convent's Gothic chapel. Originally painted for the Antoine convent at Issenheim, 32 km (20 mi) south of Colmar, the altarpiece was believed to have miraculous healing powers over ergotism, a widespread disease in the Middle Ages. The enormous work's raw emotional drama and fantasy moves sharply away from the stilted restraint of earlier paintings toward the humanistic realism of the Renaissance. Modern art, stone sculpture, ancient wine presses and barrels, and local crafts cluster around the enchanting 13th-century cloister. ✉ *1 rue Unterlinden,* ☎ *03–89–20–15–50.* 🎫 *30 frs.* ⏲ *Apr.–Oct., daily 9–6; Nov.–Mar., Wed.–Mon. 9–noon and 2–5.*

The **Église des Dominicains** (Dominican Church), southeast of the museum off rue Unterlinden, houses the Flemish-influenced *Madonna of the Rosebush* (1473) by Martin Schongauer (1445–91). This work, stolen from St-Martin's in 1972 and later recovered and hung here, has almost certainly been reduced in size from its original state, but retains enormous impact. The grace and intensity of the Virgin matches that of the Christ child; yet her slender fingers dent the child's soft flesh (and his fingers entwine her curls) with immediate intimacy. Schongauer's text for her crown: *"Me carpes genito tuo o santissima virgo"* ("Choose me also for your child, o holiest Virgin.") ✉ *pl. des Dominicains,* ☎ *03–89–24–46–57.* 🎫 *8 frs.* ⏲ *Mid-Mar.–Dec., daily 10–6.*

The **Maison Pfister,** built in 1537, is the most striking of Colmar's many old dwellings. Note its decorative frescoes and medallions, carved balcony and ground-floor arcades. ✉ *11 rue Mercière.*

The **Musée Bartholdi** is the former home of Frédéric-Auguste Bartholdi (1834–1904), the local sculptor who designed the Statue of Liberty.

✉ *30 rue des Marchands,* ☎ *03–89–41–90–60.* 🎫 *20 frs.* ⏲ *Apr.–Dec., Wed.–Mon. 10–noon and 2–6.*

Dining and Lodging

$$$ ✕ **À l'Echevin.** This restaurant in Le Maréchal hotel (☞ *below*) is atmospheric, if pricey. Meals, served in the garden, along the canal, might include freshwater fish choucroute, frogs' legs soup with truffle juice, and farm-raised pigeon. ✉ *5 pl. des Six-Montagnes-Noires,* ☎ *03–89–41–60–32. MC, V.*

$$ ✕ **Caveau Hansi.** Named for the Rockwell-like illustrator whose beclogged folk-children adorn most of the souvenirs of Alsace, this hypertraditional beamed tavern in the old town serves excellent down-home classics such as choucroute and pot-au-feu, prepared and served with a sophisticated touch despite the waitresses' dirndls. ✉ *23 rue des Marchands,* ☎ *03–89–41–37–84. MC, V. Closed Thurs., and Jan. No dinner Wed.*

$ ✕ **Au Koïfhus.** On a beautiful old-town summer terrace, dive into choucroute, baeckoffe, or tender-crisp tarte flambée without dealing with stuffy service or heavy *additions* (bills). Have another pitcher of Riesling and spend the evening. Indoors, the big, open dining room glows with wood and warm fabric. Reserve in summer for a seat on the lovely square. ✉ *2 pl. de l'Ancienne-Douane,* ☎ *03–89–23–04–90. DC, MC, V. Closed Thurs. and Jan.*

$$$ ★ 🏨 **Le Maréchal.** A maze of corridors connects the three Renaissance town houses that make up this hotel near the Lauch River. Some of the rooms are small, decorated predominantly in light, cheerful colors; some are endearingly rustic, with beams and curvy walls and floors; those in back have good river views. ✉ *5 pl. des Six-Montagnes-Noires, 68000,* ☎ *03–89–41–60–32,* FAX *03–89–24–59–40. 30 rooms. Restaurant. MC, V.*

$$ 🏨 **Colbert.** The convenient location, halfway between the train station and the ancient town center, is a plus. Rooms are well equipped and air-conditioned, if decor is overbright. Ask for a quieter room along rue des Taillandiers. ✉ *2 rue des Trois-Épis, 68000,* ☎ *03–89–41–31–05,* FAX *03–89–23–66–75. 50 rooms with bath or shower. Bar, air-conditioning. AE, MC, V.*

$$ 🏨 **Rapp.** In the old town, just off the Champ de Mars, this solid, modern hotel has business-class comforts, as well as an indoor pool and a sauna. ✉ *1–5 rue Weinemer, 68000,* ☎ *03–89–41–62–10,* FAX *03–89–24–13–58. 42 rooms. Restaurant, breakfast room, weinstübe, indoor pool, sauna. AE, MC, DC, V.*

Nightlife and the Arts

During the first half of August, Colmar celebrates with its annual **Foire Régionale des Vins d'Alsace,** a commercial wine fair in the Parc d'Exposition. Events include folk music and theater performances, and, above all, the tasting and selling of wine.

Guebwiller

54 *26 km (16 mi) southwest of Colmar, 35 km (22 mi) north of Mulhouse, 94 km (58 mi) south of Strasbourg.*

Despite its admirable churches, fine old buildings, and pleasantly authentic feeling, Guebwiller is often overlooked.

The **Église St-Léger** (1180–1280) is one of the most harmonious Romanesque churches in Alsace, though its original choir was replaced by the current Gothic one in 1336. The bare, solemn interior is of less interest than the three-tower exterior. The towers match—almost: The one on the left has small turrets at the base of its steeple, whereas the one on the right is ringed by triangular gables. The octagonal tower over the crossing looms above them both, topped by a seldom-visited stork's nest. The surrounding square is home to a lively weekly market. ✉ *pl. St-Léger.*

The **Église Dominicain** has an unmistakable silhouette thanks to the thin, lacy lantern that sticks out of its roof like an effeminate chimney. Its large, 14th-century nave is adorned with frescoes and contains a fine rood screen. ✉ *rue de l'Hôpital.*

Guebwiller's third and largest church, **Notre-Dame,** possesses a Baroque grandeur that would not be out of keeping in Paris—a reflection of the wealth of the Benedictine abbey at nearby Murbach, whose worldly friars, fed up with country life, opted for the bright lights of Guebwiller in the mid-18th century. The monks—who needed a noble pedigree of four generations to take the cloth—outmaneuvered church authorities by pretending to take temporary exile in Guebwiller while "modernizing" Murbach Abbey, thus circumnavigating the papal permission required before abbeys could move. As a token gesture, the crafty clerics smashed the nave of Murbach Abbey but failed to replace it and refused to budge from their "temporary" home. Instead, they commissioned Louis Beuque to design this new church in Guebwiller (1762–85). The interior is majestic but not overbearing. The gold-and-marble high altar fits in better, perhaps, than does the trick 3-D-effect stucco Assumption (1783), an example of Baroque craftsmanship at its most outlandish. ✉ *rue de la République.*

The **Musée du Florival** occupies one of the 18th-century canon's houses alongside Notre-Dame. It has a fine collection of ceramics designed by Théodore Deck (1823–91), a native of Guebwiller and director of the renowned Sèvres porcelain factory near Paris. It also contains archaeological treasures, artifacts from everyday life, and religious sculpture. ✉ *1 rue du 4-Février,* ☎ *03–89–74–22–89.* *15 frs.* *Mon. and Wed.–Fri. 2–6; weekends 10–noon and 2–6.*

OFF THE BEATEN PATH

ECOMUSÉE DE HAUTE-ALSACE – This open-air museum near Ungersheim, southeast of Guebwiller (via D430), is really a small village created from scratch in 1980, including 65 historic peasant houses and buildings typical of the region. An entire sawmill demonstrates its conversion from waterwheel to dynamo; an aviary swarms with honeybees; apples are pressed and cider tasted; and pigs are slopped. Storks are nurtured here in a reserve and perch on chimneys everywhere. The village is crisscrossed by donkey carts and wagons, and behind every door lie entertaining demonstrations of the old ways. An off-season visit is a study in local architecture; in high season the place comes alive. Small restaurants, snack bars, a playground, and a few amusement rides are scattered about for breaks. Inexpensive lodging is available on-site. ☎ *03–89–74–44–74.* *69 frs.* *July–Aug., daily 9–7; June and Sept., daily 9–6; Apr.–May and Oct., daily 10–5; Nov.–Mar., daily 11–5.*

Murbach

5 km (3 mi) west of Guebwiller, 23 km (14 mi) northwest of Mulhouse.

In the tiny village of Murbach a vast rump of a church towers above the hillside. Only the east end remains of the church of **St-Léger,** once part of the most powerful abbey in Alsace. Roofs and towers create a geometric interplay of squares and triangles, lent rhythm and variety by those round-arched windows and arcades so loved by Romanesque architects. Note the tympanum above the door to the south transept: Its elongated lions, seen in profile, resemble stone images found more commonly in the Middle East.

Mulhouse

56 *23 km (14 mi) southeast of Guebwiller, 35 km (22 mi) south of Colmar.*

A pleasant if unremarkable industrial town, Mulhouse rates a visit for its superb car and train museums, as well as for its art museum.

Some 500 vintage and modern cars, dating from the steam-powered Jacquot of 1878 and spanning 100 different makes are housed at the **Musée National de l'Automobile.** ✉ *192 av. de Colmar,* ☎ *03–89–42–29–17.* 🎫 *57 frs.* ⏲ *Oct.–May, Wed.–Mon. 10–6; June–Sept., daily 10–6.*

A reconstructed Stephenson locomotive of 1846 sets the wheels rolling at the **Musée Français du Chemin de Fer** (National Train Museum). Rolling stock is spread over 12 tracks, including a vast array of steam trains and the BB 9004 electric train. ✉ *2 rue Alfred-de-Glehn,* ☎ *03–89–42–25–67.* 🎫 *44 frs.* ⏲ *Apr.–Sept., daily 9–6; Oct. and Mar., daily 9–5; Nov.–Feb., Tues.–Sun. 9–5.*

Dutch and Flemish masters of the 17th to 18th centuries—including Brueghel, Teniers, and Ruysdal—top the bill at the **Musée des Beaux-Arts,** complemented by French painters such as Boudin, Courbet, and Bouguereau. ✉ *4 pl. Guillaume-Tell,* ☎ *03–89–45–43–19.* 🎫 *20 frs.* ⏲ *Oct.–mid-June, Fri.–Mon. and Wed. 10–noon and 2–5, Thurs. 10–5; mid-June–Sept., Fri.-Mon. and Wed. 10–noon and 2–6, Thurs. 10–5.*

FRANCHE-COMTÉ

This area extends from Belfort to Besançon, then clockwise through the Jura—which has great expanses of quiet, untouched land with rivers, waterfalls, and cirques, and a challenging range of mountains where you can climb, ski, and enjoy the solitude—to Dole. From here it is an easy trip to Burgundy (☞ Chapter 9) and the Rhône Valley (☞ Chapter 10).

Belfort

57 *40 km (25 mi) southwest of Mulhouse, 146 km (90½ mi) southwest of Strasbourg.*

A beefy citadel and colossal stone lion bear witness to the distinguished military history of the stubborn warrior-town of Belfort. In the heart of town is a 36-foot-high **Lion** sculpted in red sandstone by Frédéric-Auguste Bartholdi, best known as the sculptor of the Statue of Liberty in New York. The lion was commissioned to celebrate Belfort's heroic resistance during the Franco-Prussian War (1870–71) when the town of Belfort, under the leadership of General Denfert-Rochereau, withstood a 103-day siege and surrendered only after the rest of France had capitulated. The Prussian leader Otto von Bismarck was so impressed by Belfort's plucky resistance that he granted Belfort independent status. Although Alsace was returned to France in 1918, Belfort maintained its special status—meaning that the *Territoire de Belfort* remains by far the smallest *département* (province) in France. ✉ *pl. des Bourgeois.* 🎫 *Climbing up to see Lion: 3 frs.*

Belfort's Lion sits proudly at the foot of Vauban's impregnable hilltop château, now home to the **Musée d'Art et d'Histoire** (Museum of Art and History), containing Vauban's 1687 scale model of the town, plus a detailed section on military history. There's also a collection of paintings and sculpture from the 16th through 19th centuries. From the ramparts you can look out over the old town, toward the Vosges Mountains to the north and the Jura to the south. ☏ *03–84–54–25–52.* *Château free, museum 11 frs (free Wed.).* *May–Sept., daily 10–7; Oct.–Apr., Wed.–Mon. 10–noon and 2–5.*

Dining and Lodging

$$ **Pot-au-Feu.** This rustic bistro, tucked in a 16th-century *cave* (cellar) at the foot of the citadel, serves good regional specialties and features—of course—a savory, long-simmered pot-au-feu. Two of the prix-fixe lunch menus include wine. ✉ *27 bis Grande-Rue,* ☏ *03–84–28–57–84. AE, MC, V. Closed Sun., and 2 wks in Aug. No lunch Sat. or Mon.*

$$ **Château Servin.** Set back from city streets in an intimate garden, this hyper-traditional hotel was built in 1885 and maintains that era's stuffy grandeur. Dark, polished woodwork, heavy floral carpets, fringe, gilt, and lace close in, whether in the velour-beswagged rooms or the stately restaurant. Chef Dominique Mathy creates classic menus, including sole soufflé in lobster sauce, fresh foie gras with poppy seeds, and hot cherry soufflé. The restaurant ($$$) is closed Sunday dinner and Friday. ✉ *9 rue du Général-Négrier, 90000,* ☏ *03–84–21–41–85,* FAX *03–84–57–05–57. 10 rooms with bath or shower. Restaurant. AE, DC, MC, V.*

Ronchamp

58 *21 km (13 mi) west of Belfort via N19.*

The little town of Ronchamp, in the windswept département of Haute-Saône, was once renowned for having France's deepest coal mine shaft (3,300 feet). The mine's huge chimney still towers above the valley, but Ronchamp is now the site of one of Europe's most famous postwar ★ buildings. The hilltop chapel of **Notre-Dame-du-Haut** was designed by Swiss-born French architect Le Corbusier in 1951 to replace a church destroyed during World War II. The chapel's curved, sloping white walls; small, irregularly placed windows; and unadorned slug-shape gray concrete roof are unique. Many consider it to be Le Corbusier's masterpiece. ☏ *03–84–20–65–13.* *10 frs.* *Mid-Mar.–Oct., daily 9–7; Nov.–mid-Mar., daily 9–4.*

Montbéliard

59 *16 km (10 mi) south of Belfort.*

Montbéliard is an industrial town that is home to the giant Peugeot automobile company and a stately castle. Only the two round towers of the **Château** remain from the heyday of the princes of Würtemberg who once ruled this Renaissance principality; its more classical 18th-century portions contain a museum devoted to insects, geological and archaeological finds, and local clocks and musical boxes. ✉ *rue du Château,* ☏ *03–81–99–22–61.* *Free.* *Wed.–Mon. 10–noon and 2–6.*

Across the rail line in the neighboring suburb of Sochaux, Peugeot's production methods and colorful history can be explored at the **Musée de l'Aventure Peugeot.** You can also tour the factory (children are not allowed). ✉ *carrefour de l'Europe,* ☏ *03–81–94–48–21.* *Museum 30 frs; factory tour free.* *Museum: daily 10–6; factory tours: 8:30 AM weekdays (to arrange,* ☏ *03–81–33–47–80; English-speaking guides are available).*

Besançon

60 *80 km (50 mi) southwest of Montbéliard, 238 km (147 mi) southwest of Strasbourg.*

The former capital of the Franche-Comté, Besançon is a graceful old, gray-stone city nestled in a vast bend of the River Doubs. Its defensive potential was quickly realized by Vauban, whose imposing citadel remains the town's architectural focal point. The town has long been a clock-making center and, more recently, was the birthplace of the rayon industry. Famous offspring include Auguste and Louis Lumière, the inventors of a motion-picture camera, and the poet Victor Hugo, born while his father was garrisoned here in 1802. Hugo is no local hero, though, having dismissed Besançon as an "old Spanish town," a reference to the lip service the town's inhabitants paid to the Austro-Spanish Habsburgs during medieval times.

A 75-minute **boat trip** along the River Doubs provides a good introduction to Besançon. Boats leave from Pont de la République and take in a lock and the 400-yard tunnel under the citadel. ☎ *03–81–68–13–25.* *43 frs.* ⏲ *July–early Sept., weekdays 10:30, 2:30, 4:30, weekends also at 6:15; May–June, weekends 2:30 and 4:30.*

Wander around the quayside to the **Musée des Beaux-Arts et d'Archéologie** (Museum of Fine Arts and Archaeology) to see its collection of tapestries, ceramics, and paintings by Bonnard, Renoir, and Courbet. There's also a section devoted to clocks and watches through the ages. ✉ *1 pl. de la Révolution,* ☎ *03–81–81–44–47.* *21 frs.* ⏲ *Wed.–Mon. 9:30–noon and 2–6.*

Grande-Rue, Besançon's oldest street, leads from the river toward the citadel, past fountains, wrought-iron railings, and stately 16th- to 18th-century mansions, the most stunning of which is the Renaissance **Palais Granvelle** (1540). Hugo was born at No. 140, the Lumière brothers just opposite.

The **Horloge Astronomique,** at the foot of the citadel, is a stupendous 19th-century astronomical clock with 62 dials and an array of automatons that spurt into action just before the hours are sounded. ✉ *2 rue du Chapitre,* ☎ *03–81–81–12–76.* *14 frs.* ⏲ *Tours hourly Wed.–Mon. 9:45–11:45 and 2:45–5:45; closed Wed. in winter.*

The **Citadelle** is perched on a rocky spur 350 feet above the town. From its triple ring of ramparts, now laid out as promenades and peppered with Vauban's original watchtowers, you can see the city and the countryside. The buildings contain a series of museums devoted to natural history, regional folklore, agricultural tools, and the French Resistance during World War II. There also are shops and restaurants. ☎ *03–81–65–07–44.* *Joint ticket with citadel and museums 50 frs.* ⏲ *Late Mar.–Sept., daily 9–7; Oct.–Mar., daily 10–5.*

Dining and Lodging

$$$ ✕ **Mungo Park.** This former warehouse on the banks of the River Doubs is now a bright, glassed-in restaurant. Locals and Parisians pile in to appreciate the inspired works of Jocelyne Choquart and Benoît Rotschi, who bring local ingredients into this century—Jura snails in horseradish cream; beef stew with barley and foie gras; and a sweet, hot dessert soup of walnuts, vin jaune, and nutmeg. ✉ *11 rue Jean-Petit,* ☎ *03–81–81–28–01. Reservations essential. MC, V. Closed Sun., 1 wk in Feb., 2 wks in Aug. No lunch Sat.*

$$ ★ ✕ **Poker d'As.** Carved-wood tables and cowbells counterbalanced by swagged tulle and porcelain capture the ethnic-chic of this landmark restaurant's cuisine: Earning kudos for his *cuisine du terroir* (regional cooking), chef Raymond Ferreux animates his upscale experiments with splashes of local color: Jura *morteau* (sausage) sautéed with artichokes and cèpes and pressed partridge with wild mushrooms. ✉ *14 square St-Amour,* ☏ *03–81–81–42–49. AE, DC, MC, V. Closed Mon., and late July–early Aug. No dinner Sun.*

$ ✕ **Bistrot du Jura.** In an intimate, downscale setting of checkered tiles and bentwood, sample home-cooked regional specialties herring with steamed potatoes or andouillette in Jura wine—a fine selection of which is served by the glass. The owner keeps proud standards but irregular hours; call in advance. ✉ *35 rue Charles-Nodier,* ☏ *03–81–82–03–48. V.*

$ ✕ **Quignon Comtois.** The dreadful setting—in a former shop cozied up with mail-order decor—is more than offset by earthy and delicious Franche-Comté cooking, served to loyal crowds of young locals. Try the simple fried carp, rich ham gratin with mushrooms, and Swiss-style *roëstis* (hash browns). Jura house wines are sold by the carafe. ✉ *10 rue G. Courbet,* ☏ *03–81–83–36–13. MC, V.*

$$$ ★ **Castan.** Just below the citadel, in a courtyard behind a tangle of ancient trees and crumbling Roman pillars, is this noble 17th- and 18th-century mansion that has become a chic *relais* (inn). The handful of rooms are atmospheric and exquisitely decorated. Regency moldings, period fabrics, luxurious baths, and a private collection of regional bibelots set the tone. ✉ *6 square Castan, 25000,* ☏ *03–81–65–02–00,* FAX *03–81–83–01–02. 8 rooms. Breakfast room, free parking. MC, V.*

$$ **Paris.** There are few decent hotels in the heart of Besançon. This one, though it is on main shopping streets, is a good bet. It's well run, unpretentious, and brightened by a tree-lined garden courtyard. ✉ *33 rue des Granges, 25000,* ☏ *03–81–81–36–56,* FAX *03–81–61–94–90. 55 rooms, 54 with bath or shower. Breakfast room. AE, DC, MC, V.*

$ **Granvelle.** Convenient to the citadel and set back from old-town streets, this modest, straightforward lodging has freshly decorated rooms, including some bargains without bathrooms. ✉ *13 rue du Général Lecourbe, 25000,* ☏ *03–81–81–33–92,* FAX *03–81–81–31–77. 30 rooms, 27 with bath. Breakfast room. DC, MC, V.*

Nightlife and the Arts

A **jazz festival** (☏ 03–80–83–39–09) takes place in July. An **international music festival** (☏ 03–81–80–73–26) is held in September.

Outdoor Activities and Sports

Rent canoes and kayaks from **Sport Nautique** (✉ 2 av. Chardonnet, ☏ 03–81–80–56–01) for 140–200 francs per day.

Ornans

61 *26 km (16 mi) south of Besançon.*

There are two reasons to visit the pretty village of Ornans: for the view of the steep-roof old houses that line the River Loue and to see the birthplace of Gustave Courbet (1819–77), the pioneering French Realist painter who influenced Édouard Manet. Gustave Courbet was an assertive, full-bearded radical who spent his last years in Swiss exile after toppling Napoléon's column on place Vendôme during the Paris Commune in 1871. The **Maison Natale de Courbet**—a rambling 18th-century mansion—hardly goes with his tempestuous image, and provides a sedate setting for souvenirs, documents, drawings, sculptures, and paintings. Courbet is best known for his *Burial at Ornans* (now in the Musée d'Orsay in Paris), with its procession of somber peasants. ✉ *pl. Robert-Fernier,* ☏ *03–81–62–23–30.* *20 frs; temporary exhibits 40 frs.* ⏲ *Apr.–June and*

Sept.–Oct., daily 10–noon and 2–6; Nov.–Mar., Wed.–Mon. 10–noon and 2–6.

OFF THE BEATEN PATH

SOURCE DE LA LOUE – From Ornans, take D67 down the steeply banked Loue Valley, through the picturesque villages of Vuillafans (with its 16th-century bridge and restored water mill), Lods, and Mouthier-Haute-Pierre, and turn right at La Main onto D41. Turn right again in Ouhans, and follow signs to the spectacular Source de la Loue, where the Loue River gushes from a cliff face, cascading past ruined water mills. To get to the source from the parking lot, take the stony path (for about 20 minutes). The trip from Ornans to the source is about 20 km (12 mi).

Montbenoît

62 *40 km (25 mi) southeast of Ornans.*

The tiny village of Montbenoît is dominated by its **Ancienne Abbaye.** Though it dates from the 11th century, the cloisters and chapter house were built 300 years later. Take time to study the superbly carved wooden choir stalls (1525–27), which often give a Renaissance interpretation of biblical tales. Samson, for instance, wears natty hose and a lace ruff collar as Delilah takes to his flowing locks with a pair of oversize scissors. ☎ *03–81–38–10–32.* 🎫 *15 frs.* ⏲ *Mon.–Sat. 9–noon and 2–6; Sun. 2–6. Guided tours with kitchen and refectory July–Aug. by request.*

Dining and Lodging

$$ ✕🏨 **France.** Swiss gourmets flock across the border, just two minutes away, to Villers-le-Lac, to savor chef Hugues Droz's lobster with morels and escargots in absinthe. Hugues's family runs the hotel and will happily book you a two-hour boat trip (40 francs) along the Gorges du Doubs. Breakfasts are large, but the rooms are somewhat noisy and the restaurant is closed Sunday evening and Monday. ✉ *8 pl. Maxime-Cupillard, 25130 Villers-le-Lac (24 km/15 mi northeast of Montbenoît),* ☎ *03–81–68–00–06,* FAX *03–81–68–09–22. 14 rooms with bath or shower. Restaurant. AE, DC, MC, V. Closed late Jan.*

Pontarlier

63 *14 km (9 mi) southwest of Montbenoît.*

Pontarlier, with its old streets, churches, and gateways, was once home to absinthe—a notorious anise-based aperitif, the forerunner of Ricard and Pernod. It was banned in 1915 for inducing alcoholism and even madness. The **Musée Municipal** has a section on the history of the *fée verte* (green fairy), as absinthe was called. Porcelain, pictures, and artifacts from local excavations are also on display. ✉ *2 pl. d'Arçon,* ☎ *03–81–46–73–68.* 🎫 *10 frs.* ⏲ *Weekdays 10–noon and 2–6, Sat. 2–6, Sun. 3–7.*

OFF THE BEATEN PATH

CHÂTEAU DE JOUX – Just south of Pontarlier via N57, this fortress perched on a steep hill glowers across the Jura landscape toward the Swiss border. Founded in the 11th century, it retains its round medieval towers, drawbridges, and 17th-century ramparts. The dungeon holds a sturdy collection of old guns and weapons (guided tours only; allow one hour). ☎ *03–81–69–47–95.* 🎫 *30 frs.* ⏲ *July–Aug., daily 9–6; Mar.–June and Sept., daily 10–11:30 and 2–4:30; Oct.–Mar., daily tours at 10, 11:15, 2, and 3:30.*

Syam

 *48 km (30 mi) southwest of Pontarlier: take D72/D471 to Champagnole then N5 south (toward Geneva) before bearing left on D127.*

Syam, nestled in the lush Ain Valley, forged into the limelight in the second decade of the 19th century as an ironworks center. The **Forges de Syam** (Syam Ironworks) was built in 1813; iron was hauled in by train, then dragged down to the riverside by oxen. Simple lodging was built on-site, now occupied by the nearly 50 people who still work here, making nails, locks, tools, and machinery. "Hot-rolling" and "hard drawing" techniques are explained at the museum (with video presentation). ☎ *03–84–51–61–00.* *12 frs.* *July–Aug., Wed.–Mon. 10–6; May–June and Sept., weekends 10–6.*

The founder of the forge, Alphonse Jobez, was clearly flushed with pride when he had himself build the **Château de Syam,** a sturdy, square, yellow-fronted neo-Palladian villa. Finished in 1818, this grandiose self-homage has outsized Ionic pilasters at each corner and, inside, a theatrical, colonnaded rotunda ringed with balconies and Pompeiian grotesques. Guided tours take you through restored rooms. ☎ *03–84–51–61–25.* *20 frs.* *July–Sept., Fri.–Mon. 2–6.*

OFF THE BEATEN PATH

CASCADES DU HÉRISSON – To get to the Hérisson waterfalls from Syam, take N5 south; turn right on D75 to Ilay; take D39 west (direction Doucier); then double back on the narrow, winding D326. It dead ends at the parking lot, from which it's a 10-minute, uphill walk to **L'Éventail,** the first waterfall, with its 210-foot drop. If you come after heavy rains, the noise is deafening, and the path is slippery. It's exhilarating but drenching, so dress accordingly. In summer you can usually progress beyond L'Éventail, along a rugged path past five more cascades, all the way to **Le Saut Girard,** 3 km (2 mi) away (allow three hours for the round-trip).

Baume-les-Messieurs

 *33 km (21 mi) west of Syam.*

A quaint old village in a breathtaking setting of cliffs and forests, Baume-les-Messieurs has a venerable medieval abbey and an underground network of caves. Its Romanesque stonework resonant with history, the 12th-century **Abbaye** has time-worn courtyards and a tenderly painted 16th-century Flemish altarpiece donated by the Belgian town of Ghent. ☎ *03–81–84–27–98.* *Abbey free.* *Daily 9–8 (church closed in winter).*

The **Grottes de Baume,** 2 km (1 mi) outside of town, consists of 650 yards of skillfully lit galleries 400 feet underground, containing a river, a lake, and weird-shape stalactites and stalagmites (the temperature is chilly, so take a sweater). The largest cave is more than 200 feet high, and classical music blasts out to heighten the dramatic effect. ✉ *Chalet de Guide,* ☎ *03–84–44–61–58.* *25 frs.* *Apr.–Sept., daily 9:30–noon and 2–6.*

Five kilometers (3 miles) outside of Baume-les-Messieurs (south on D4 then west on D71), is the **Belvedère des Roches de Baume.** The plummeting view of the ring of chalky cliffs hemming the village is spectacular; watch for signs.

Dining and Lodging

$–$$ ✕🏨 **Parenthèse.** Though its odd geometry and vivid color schemes deny its origins as a sturdy, rustic mansion, this ultramodern retreat in the tiny stone village of Chillé (southwest of Baume) pampers its guests with a pool and whirlpool baths. The ambitious, mid-priced restaurant features regional specialties with sophisticated twists: breast of Bresse chicken with morels and vin jaune, and saddle of rabbit in Macvin (the local aperitif). The restaurant is closed Sunday dinner and Monday. ✉ *111 Grande-Rue, 39570 Chillé (20 km/12 mi southwest of Baume, via D157 and Lons),* ☎ *03–84–47–55–44,* FAX *03–84–24–92–13. 31 rooms with bath or shower. Restaurant, grill, pool. MC, V.*

$ ★ ✕🏨 **Étape Gourmande.** In the abbey, under groin-vaulted stonework, lounge at weathered refractory tables or on the terrace overlooking the grounds while you indulge in sausages, omelets, and hearty salads. A lucky few can even climb up the spiral stone stair to vast beamed rooms (*chambres d'hôtes,* meaning there is no service staff except the owner) furnished casually with mismatched collectibles, electric kettles, and mini-refrigerators. Views defy description. A deli downstairs sells local picnic products and wine. ✉ *Abbaye de Baume-les-Messieurs, 39210,* ☎ *03–84–44–64–47. 3 rooms. Breakfast room, deli. MC, V.*

Outdoor Activities and Sports

Contact the **Poney Club des Chênes** (✉ 39110 Andelot, ☎ 03–84–51–45–97) for information about horseback riding in the area.

Château-Chalon

★ 66 *13 km (8 mi) north of Baume-les-Messieurs.*

The medieval village of Château-Chalon, perched on a rocky promontory high above vertiginous local vineyards, is renowned for its legendary vin jaune, said to keep for 200 years without losing its vigor. A charming place to sample its nutty, sherrylike flavor is opposite the 10th-century church of **St-Pierre,** on the tiny square where the Fruitière Vinicole runs generous tastings from an old cellar. Walk off any aftereffects with a stroll through the narrow, twisting streets. Though there's very little to "do" here, you could easily lose yourself for a day in its atmosphere: The restored stonework, restrained shop fronts, and archaic street signs help to keep out the 20th century.

OFF THE BEATEN PATH **CHÂTEAU D'ARLAY** – This 18th-century château, 8 km (5 mi) west of Château-Chalon, contains sumptuously carved regional furniture dating from the same period. The outstanding wine produced here can be sampled (and purchased) in the château's cellar (open Mon.–Sat. 8–noon and 2–6). Combine your visit with a walk around the magnificent park, with its grotto, medieval ruins, and alley of ancient *tilleuls* (basswood trees), and a stop at the **Volerie des Rapaces,** where (at 4 and 5 PM) trained eagles and other birds of prey perform wide-winged acrobatics overhead. ✉ *rue Haute-du-Bourg,* ☎ *03–84–85–04–22.* 🎟 *Château and volerie: 45 frs.* ⏲ *July–Aug., Mon.–Sun. 2–6. Volerie also open Apr.–Oct., Wed. and weekends 2–6.*

Arbois

67 *24 km (15 mi) north of Château-Chalon.*

The pretty wine market town of Arbois is worth a stop for its fine restaurant, Jean-Paul Jeûnet (☞ Dining and Lodging, *below*). It also has a museum dedicated to the vine and to Louis Pasteur (1822–95), the famous bacteriologist and father of pasteurization, who grew up in Arbois.

The **Maison de Pasteur,** Louis Pasteur's family home, is fully furnished in authentic style, containing many of his possessions. ✉ *83 rue de Courcelles,* ☎ *03–84–66–11–72.* *30 frs. Guided tours hourly June–Sept., daily 9:45–11:45 and 2:15–5:15; mid-Feb.–May and Oct., Fri.–Wed. at 10, 11, 2, 3, and 4.*

The Arbois vineyard is one of the finest in eastern France; to learn more about it, visit the **Musée de la Vigne et du Vin** and peruse its collection of tools and documents. ✉ *Château Pécauld,* ☎ *03–84–66–26–14.* *17 frs.* ⏲ *Feb.–Nov., Wed.–Mon. 10–noon and 2–6.*

A short excursion south along D469 will take you into the magnificent **Reculée des Planches,** a dramatic rocky valley created by glacial erosion and peppered with caves and waterfalls. *Caves 30 frs.* ⏲ *Apr.–Sept., daily 10–noon; Oct., Sat.–Thurs. 10–noon and 2–6.*

Continue along D469 from the Reculée des Planches to the beautiful, rocky **Cirque du Fer à Cheval** (Horseshoe Cirque), with its panoramic view of U-shape cliffs (10 minutes' walk from parking.) Watch for signs.

Dining and Lodging

$ ✕ **La Finette.** In a kitschy log-cabin setting, you can find hot, hearty local cooking at all hours: tripe in a casserole, sausage with lentils, and fondue. ✉ *22 av. Pasteur,* ☎ *03–84–66–06–78. MC, V.*

$$$ ★ ✕ **Jean-Paul Jeûnet.** This ancient stone convent, its massive beams enhanced with subtle lighting and contemporary art, is one of the most recognized eateries in the Jura. Chef Jeûnet's devotion to local flora and fauna has evolved into a bold, earthy, flavorful cuisine: crayfish sausage, prawns with heather flowers, and even sheeps' milk sorbet. The chef's father, once an award-winning sommelier, has established a worthy cellar. The restaurant is closed Tuesday and Wednesday. Rooms have pleasant modern decor and pretty pine furniture. ✉ *9 rue de l'Hôtel-de-Ville, 39600,* ☎ *03–84–66–05–67,* FAX *03–84–66–24–20. 17 rooms with bath or shower. Restaurant. DC, MC, V. Closed Dec.–Jan.*

$$ **Hôtel des Messageries.** This dignified, vine-covered inn on Arbois's main street has moderate rooms with flossy baroque decor and a warm public ambience enhanced by grand spaces full of old wood and stone. ✉ *2 rue des Courcelles, 39600,* ☎ *03–84–66–15–45,* FAX *03–84–37–41–09. 27 rooms with bath or shower. Breakfast room. MC, V. Closed Dec.–Jan.*

Outdoor Activities and Sports

Contact **Le Petit Cheval Blanc** (✉ 39800 Fay-en-Montagne, ☎ 03–84–85–32–07) for details on renting horses.

Salins-les-Bains

68 *14 km (9 mi) northwest of Arbois.*

If you want to learn about the salt industry in the area, head to Salins-les-Bains. **Les salines** (the saltworks), tucked away in the steep valley of the River Furieuse, functioned until 1962. Local salty water was pumped to the surface and then evaporated; it was a sticky, sweaty process that you can fully appreciate in the humid "heating room." ✉ *pl. des Salines,* ☎ *03–84–73–01–34.* *23 frs.* ⏲ *Easter–mid-Sept.; mid-Sept.–Nov. and Feb.–Easter guided tours at 10:30, 2:30, and 4.*

Arc-et-Senans

★ 69 *18 km (11 mi) north of Arbois.*

For a glimpse of the palatial pretensions of the erstwhile salt industry, explore Arc-et-Senans. The **Saline Royale** (Royal Saltworks), built 1774–79 by Claude-Nicolas Ledoux, is an extraordinary example of neoclassical industrial architecture. With their Palladian porticoes, rustication, and towering columns, the buildings—arranged in a gracious semicircle around sweeping lawns—display a grandeur worthy of the Romans. Originally they were intended to form part of a rationally planned, circular *ville idéale* (ideal town). ☎ *03–81–54–45–45.* 🎫 *35 frs.* 🕓 *July–Aug., daily 9–7; Apr.–June and Sept.–Oct., daily 9–noon and 2–6; Nov.–Mar., daily 10–noon and 2–5.*

Dole

70 *28 km (18 mi) northwest of Arc-et-Senans, 48 km (30 mi) southeast of Dijon, 48 km (30 mi) southwest of Besançon.*

The sturdy old hilltop town of Dole, where Louis Pasteur was born in 1822, climbs above the River Doubs. Visible above the rooftops for miles around is the muscular 250-foot tower of the 16th-century **Église Notre-Dame.** The warren of dank alleyways beneath the church invites exploration. Pasteur's birthplace, the **Maison Natale de Pasteur,** is now a museum, restored to its 1744 look, with original beams and waxed plank floors. It contains documents and mementos, plus the restored tanner's workshop of Pasteur's father who, like most of his neighbors, was a leather worker. ✉ *43 rue Pasteur,* ☎ *03–84–72–20–61.* 🎫 *20 frs.* 🕓 *July–Aug., Wed.–Mon. 10–6; Apr.–June and Sept.–Oct., Wed.–Sat. and Mon. 10–noon and 2–6, Sun. 2–6.*

Dining

$$ ★ ✕ **Les Templiers.** With its vaulted stone ceiling and pointed Gothic archways, this restaurant in a 16th-century building has an archetypal Old World feel enhanced by tapestry-upholstered high-back chairs and stained-glass windows. Chef Joël Césari's cuisine is a shade more nouvelle: Try the spicy carp tartare, the Bresse pigeon with caramelized radish, and the lemon shortbread. ✉ *35 Grande-Rue,* ☎ *03–84–82–78–78. AE, DC, MC, V. Closed Mon., and Nov.–Mar. No dinner Sun.*

ALSACE-LORRAINE AND FRANCHE-COMTÉ A TO Z

Arriving and Departing

By Car

The A4 toll expressway heads east from Paris to Strasbourg, via Verdun, Metz, and Saverne. It is met by A26, descending from the English Channel, at Reims. A31 links Metz to Nancy, continuing south to Burgundy and Lyon. The quickest route from Paris to Besançon and the Jura is on A6 (to Beaune) and then A36.

By Plane

Most international flights to Alsace land at Mulhouse-Basel airport on the Franco-Swiss border. There are also airports at Strasbourg, Metz-Nancy, Dole, and Mirecourt (Vittel/Épinal).

By Train

Mainline trains leave Paris (Gare de l'Est) every couple of hours for the four-hour, 504-km (315-mi) journey to Strasbourg. Some stop at Toul and all stop at Nancy, where there are connections for Épinal and

Gérardmer. Trains run three times daily from Paris to Verdun and more often to Metz (around three hours to each). Mainline trains stop at Mulhouse (four to five hours) en route to Basel. Three high-speed TGV (Trains à Grande Vitesse) leave Paris (Gare de Lyon) daily for Besançon (2½ to 3 hours).

Getting Around

By Car

N83/A35 connects Strasbourg, Colmar, and Mulhouse. A36 continues to Belfort and Besançon. A4, linking Paris to Strasbourg, passes through Lorraine via Metz, linking Lorraine and Alsace.

By Train

Several local trains a day run between Strasbourg and Mulhouse, stopping at Sélestat and Colmar. Several continue to Belfort and Besançon. Local trains link Besançon to Lons-le-Saunier, occasionally stopping at Arbois.

Contacts and Resources

Bed-and-Breakfast Information

Contact the **Service Tourisme** (✉ Chambre d'Agriculture, B.P. 417, 39016 Lons-le-Saunier) for its brochure on "Gîtes de France" in the Jura. The list includes both bed-and-breakfasts and houses for rent.

Car Rentals

Avis (✉ 7 pl. Flore, Besançon, ☎ 03–81–80–91–08), (✉ pl. de la Gare, Strasbourg, ☎ 03–88–32–30–44). **Europcar** (✉ 18 rue de Serre, Nancy, ☎ 03–83–37–57–24). **Hertz** (✉ 7 pl. Thiers, Nancy, ☎ 03–83–32–13–14).

Guided Tours

Aéroclub d'Alsace (☎ 03–88–34–00–98) arranges plane rides over Strasbourg and the Vosges from the Aérodrome du Polygone. **Tecnavia** (☎ 03–83–29–80–60) gives 15-minute helicopter tours of Nancy. Balloon trips are organized by **Air Adventures** of Arc-et-Senans (☎ 03–81–57–45–51).

Outdoor Activities and Sports

A guide to bicycling in the Lorraine is available from the **Comité Départemental de Cyclotourisme** (✉ 33 rue de la République, 54950 Laronxe). For information on biking in the Jura contact the **Comité Régional de Cyclotourisme VTT de Franche-Comté** (✉ 12 rue Charles-Dornier, 25000 Besançon, ☎ 03–81–52–17–13). A brochure on fishing, entitled "Pêche Gratuite," is available by writing to the **Comité Départemental du Tourisme** (✉ Hôtel du Département, 39021 Lons-le-Saunier). The **Comité Régional de Tourisme** (✉ 9 rue de Pontarlier, 25000 Besançon) provides full details on hiking in Franche-Comté. The **Fédération Jurassienne de Randonnée Pédestre** (✉ Hôtel du Département, BP652, 39021 Lons-le-Saunier) publishes a brochure on trails in the Jura. For a list of signposted trails in the Vosges foothills, contact the **Sélestat Tourist Office** (☞ *below*). For information on horseback riding in the area, contact the **Délégation Départementale de Tourisme Équestre** (✉ 4 rue des Violettes, 67201 Eckbolsheim, ☎ 03–88–77–39–64).

Travel Agencies

Wagons-Lits (✉ 30 pl. Kléber, Strasbourg, ☎ 03–88–32–16–34; 2 rue Raymond-Poincaré, Nancy, ☎ 03–83–35–06–97). **Havas Voyages** (✉ 23 rue de la Haute-Montée, Strasbourg, ☎ 03–88–32–99–77).

Visitor Information

The principal regional tourist offices are in **Strasbourg** (✉ 9 rue du Dôme, ☎ 03–88–21–01–02, and 17 pl. de la Cathédrale, ☎ 03–88–52–28–28). **Nancy** (✉ 14 pl. Stanislas, ☎ 03–83–35–22–41). **Besançon** (✉ 9 rue de Pontarlier, ☎ 03–81–83–50–47). In **Strasbourg,** there is also a city tourist office (✉ pl. de la Gare, ☎ 03–88–32–51–49). Other tourist offices: **Belfort** (✉ rue Jules-Vallès, ☎ 03–84–28–12–23). **Colmar** (✉ 4 rue Unterlinden, ☎ 03–89–20–68–92). **Guebwiller** (✉ 73 rue de la République, ☎ 03–89–76–10–63). **Lons-le-Saunier** (✉ 1 rue Louis-Pasteur, ☎ 03–84–24–65–01). **Metz** (✉ pl. d'Armes, ☎ 03–87–55–53–76). **Mulhouse** (✉ 9 av. du Maréchal-Foch, ☎ 03–89–45–68–31). **Obernai** (✉ 59 rue du Général-Gouraud, ☎ 03–88–95–64–13). **Saverne** (✉ Château des Rohan, ☎ 03–88–91–80–47). **Sélestat** (✉ 10 bd. Leclerc, ☎ 03–88–58–87–20). **Toul** (✉ Parvis de la Cathédrale, ☎ 03–83–64–11–69). **Verdun** (✉ pl. de la Nation, ☎ 03–29–86–14–18).

9 Burgundy

Beaune, Dijon, and Chablis Country

First and foremost are Burgundy's vineyards, producing complex and diverse wines, from the crisp white of Chablis to the rich reds of Côte de Nuits and Côte de Beaune. And then there is its history: the Roman ruins at Autun and the abbeys at Cluny and Vézelay, whose power still reverberates through the region in bare ruined choirs and echoing cloisters. In the midst of all this is the wonderfully varied Parc du Morvan, full of hikers and bicyclists, bird-watchers and botanists.

Updated by Nigel Fisher

For a region whose powerful medieval dukes ruled over large tracts of Western Europe and whose glamorous image is closely allied to its expensive and treasured wine, Burgundy (Bourgogne in French)—just southeast of Paris—can seem a surprisingly rustic backwater. Here "life in the fast lane" refers exclusively to the Paris-bound A6 expressway.

In the Middle Ages, Sens, Auxerre, and Troyes, in neighboring Champagne (but included here), came under the sway of the Paris-based Capetian kings, who erected mighty Gothic cathedrals in those towns. Burgundy's leading religious monuments, however, are the older, Romanesque basilica at Vézelay—once one of Christianity's most important centers of pilgrimage and today a tiny village hidden in the folds of rolling, verdant hills—and the ruined Abbey of Cluny—once a religious center as important as Vézelay.

Chablis is renowned for its excellent bone-dry white wine, although better value for the money can be found at St-Bris-le-Vineux and Irancy, south of Auxerre. The great red wine lands of Burgundy are farther east. Dijon, the province's only city, retains something of the opulence it acquired under the rich, powerful dukes of Burgundy who ruled in the late Middle Ages, but its latter-day reputation is essentially gastronomic.

Pleasures and Pastimes

Abbeys

From the sober beauty of splendid and well-preserved Fontenay and Pontigny to the romantic ruins of Cluny that is a ghost of its former glory, the abbeys of Burgundy are an evocative part of its history.

Dining

Dijon ranks with Lyon as one of the unofficial gastronomic capitals of France. Wealthy Parisian gourmets think nothing of driving three hours to sample the cuisine of Beaune's Jean Crotet or Vézelay's Marc Meneau. Game, freshwater trout, garlicky *jambon persillé* (ham flavored with parsley), goat cheese, coq au vin, snails, mustard, and mushrooms number among the region's specialties. Meat is often served in rich, wine-based sauces.

CATEGORY	COST*
$$$$	over 400 frs
$$$	250 frs–400 frs
$$	125 frs–250 frs
$	under 125 frs

**per person for a three-course meal, including tax (20.6%) and tip, but not wine*

Hiking

The Parc Naturel Régional du Morvan, with its rocky escarpments, hidden valleys, rushing streams, thick forests, and wooded hills is marvelous for hiking, especially in spring and fall.

Lodging

Burgundy is seldom deluged by tourists, so finding accommodations is not hard. But it is still wise to make advance reservations, especially in the wine country (from Dijon to Beaune). If you intend to visit Beaune for the Trois Glorieuses wine festival in November, make your hotel reservation several months in advance. Note that nearly all country hotels have restaurants, and you are usually expected to eat at them. Some towns have a large number of inexpensive hotels. In Dijon, you can find them around place Émile Zola; in Beaune, look around place Madeleine; in Auxerre, they're tucked away in the streets down from Cathédrale St-Étienne; in Tournus and Avallon, check out their old towns.

CATEGORY	COST*
$$$$	over 800 frs
$$$	550 frs–800 frs
$$	300 frs–550 frs
$	under 300 frs

**All prices are for a standard double room for two, including tax (20.6%) and service charge.*

Wine

The famous vineyards south of Dijon—the Côte de Nuits and Côte de Beaune—are among the world's most distinguished and picturesque. Don't expect to unearth many bargains here, but a good place for sampling is the Marché aux Vins in Beaune, an old town clustered around the patterned-tile roofs of its medieval Hôtel-Dieu (hospital). Less expensive Burgundies can be found between Chalon and Mâcon.

Exploring Burgundy

The best way to enter Burgundy is southeast from Paris—by car. First explore the northwest part of the region, from Sens to Autun, with a rewarding detour to the town of Troyes, in Champagne, and the Loire, in the west, around the Parc du Morvan. Go next to Burgundy's wine country, which begins at Dijon and stretches south down the Saône Valley through charming Beaune to Mâcon.

Great Itineraries

You could easily spend two weeks in Burgundy—visiting the sights, tasting the wine, and filling up on rich peasant food. If, however, you only have three days, you can see two of Burgundy's most interesting cities—Dijon and Beaune. With five days you can explore the northeast part of the region, from Sens to Beaune. Eight days will give you time to get to the Parc du Morvan and the Côte d'Or—home to Burgundy's finest vineyards.

Numbers in the text correspond to numbers in the margin and on the Burgundy, Troyes, and Dijon maps.

IF YOU HAVE 3 DAYS

Start with Burgundy's two most interesting cities—first, the age-old capital of Burgundy, **Dijon** ㉝–㊶, then, medieval **Beaune** ㊸. Between the two towns, visit the famous Burgundy vineyards around **Clos de Vougeot** ㊷.

IF YOU HAVE 5 DAYS

Make your first stop out of Paris the small town of **Sens** ①, with its vast cathedral and its 13th-century Palais Synodal. Then head for the serene abbey in **Pontigny** ⑮ and the Ancien Hôpital in **Tonnerre** ⑱. Spend the night in pretty **Chablis** ⑰ and sample the famous white wine. Begin day two with a visit to **Auxerre** ⑯ and its cathedral before going on to ancient **Clamecy** ㉙ and the world-famous basilica at **Vézelay** ㉚. Stay overnight in dramatic **Avallon** ㉛, with its medieval St-Lazarus church. By day three, get to **Dijon** ㉝–㊶ and stay two nights. On day five, take a short run down the wine-producing Côte d'Or to **Beaune** ㊸.

Burgundy

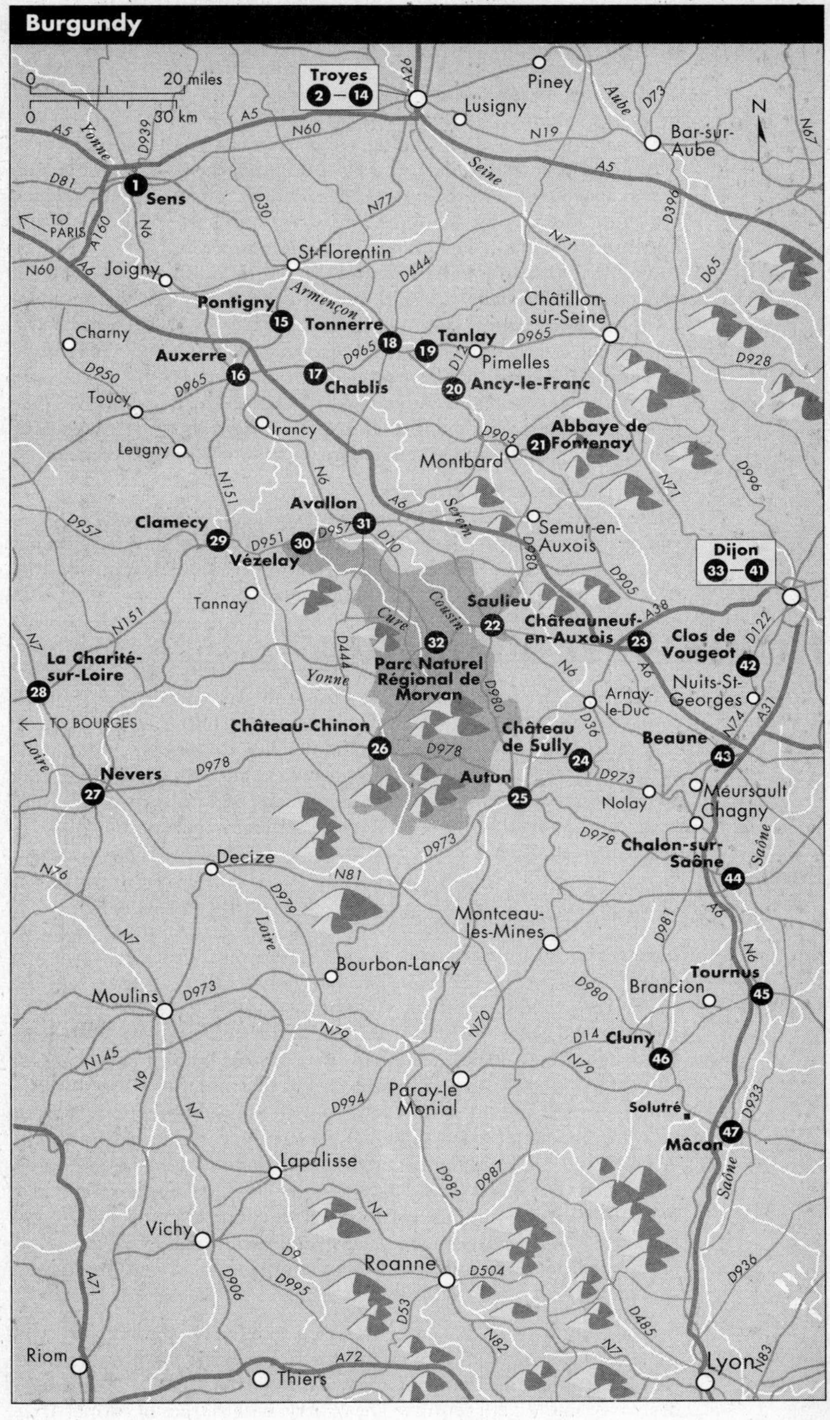

0 20 miles
0 30 km
Troyes 2–14
Piney
Lusigny
Bar-sur-Aube
Sens 1
TO PARIS
Joigny
St-Florentin
Pontigny 15
Tonnerre 18
Tanlay 19
Châtillon-sur-Seine
Charny
Auxerre 16
Chablis 17
Pimelles
Ancy-le-Franc 20
Toucy
Irancy
Abbaye de Fontenay 21
Leugny
Montbard
Avallon 31
Clamecy 29
Vézelay 30
Semur-en-Auxois
Dijon 33–41
Tannay
Saulieu 22
Châteauneuf-en-Auxois 23
Clos de Vougeot 42
32
La Charité-sur-Loire 28
Parc Naturel Régional de Morvan
Nuits-St-Georges
Arnay-le-Duc
TO BOURGES
Château-Chinon 26
Château de Sully 24
Beaune 43
Nevers 27
Autun 25
Nolay
Meursault
Chagny
Chalon-sur-Saône 44
Decize
Montceau-les-Mines
Bourbon-Lancy
Tournus 45
Brancion
Moulins
Cluny 46
Paray-le-Monial
Solutré
Mâcon 47
Lapalisse
Vichy
Roanne
Riom
Thiers
Lyon
Yonne
Seine
Aube
Armençon
Serein
Cousin
Cure
Loire
Saône

IF YOU HAVE 9 DAYS

Make **Troyes** ②–⑭, with its medieval pedestrian streets, your first stop. On day two head south to see **Tonnerre** ⑱, the Renaissance châteaux of **Tanlay** ⑲ and **Ancy-le-Franc** ⑳, and the Cistercian **Abbaye de Fontenay** ㉑. End the day in **Dijon** ㉝–㊶. Give yourself two days and nights in Dijon then go to **Beaune** ㊸ for another night. While you're in the vicinity, drive south down the Saône river to medieval **Tournus** ㊺ and the abbey of St-Philibert, as well as the ruined abbey of **Cluny** ㊻. The next day, drive north to see the cathedral and Roman remains in **Autun** ㉕, the **Château de Sully** ㉔, the hilltop town of **Châteauneuf-en-Auxois** ㉓, and the basilica in **Saulieu** ㉒; end up in **Avallon** ㉛. Spend day six driving through the **Parc Naturel Régional du Morvan** ㉜ and visiting the village of **Château-Chinon** ㉖, the imposing cathedral in **Nevers** ㉗, and the abbey-church in **La Charité-sur-Loire** ㉘, before returning to Avallon. Spend the next two days and nights around **Auxerre** ⑯, **Chablis** ⑰, or **Sens** ①. These make good bases for exploring unspoiled **Clamecy** ㉙, the vineyards around Chablis, the abbey in **Pontigny** ⑮, and the basilica in **Vézelay** ㉚.

When to Tour Burgundy

May in Burgundy is especially nice, as are September and October, when the sun is still warm on the shimmering golden trees and grapes are being harvested for the first time, scenting the air with anticipation. Many festivals take place around this time.

NORTHWEST BURGUNDY

From Paris, drive southeast into Burgundy on autoroute A6 (or, alternately, on A5 direct to Troyes, first sneaking into Champagne), before making a clockwise loop around the Parc du Morvan, visiting the small cities and ancient abbeys in the area. The towns and villages are largely preserved, with few industrial suburbs, and the surprisingly rural landscape seems to have remained the same for centuries.

Sens

❶ *112 km (70 mi) southeast of Paris on N6.*

It makes sense for Sens to be your first stop in Burgundy, since it is only 80 minutes by car from Paris on N6, a fast road that hugs the pretty Yonne Valley south of Fontainebleau. Sens was for centuries the ecclesiastical center of France and is still dominated by its **Cathédrale St-Étienne.** You can see the cathedral's 240-foot south tower from far away; the highway forges straight past it. The pompous 19th-century buildings that line this road can give you a false impression if you're in a hurry: The streets leading off it near the cathedral (notably rue Abelard and rue Jean-Cousin) are full of half-timber medieval houses, and within their midst sits the 13th-century church of St-Pierre-le-Rond, with its unusual wooden roof and 16th-century stained glass. On Monday, the cathedral square is crowded with stalls, while the colorful covered market throbs with people buying meat and produce. A smaller market is held on Friday mornings.

Begun around 1140, the cathedral used to have two towers; one was topped in 1532 by an elegant, though somewhat incongruous, Renaissance campanile that contains two monster bells, and the other was destroyed in the 19th century. The gallery, with statues of former archbishops of Sens, is a 19th-century addition, but the statue of St. Stephen, between the doors of the central portal, is thought to date from the late 12th century. The vast, harmonious interior is justly renowned for its stained-glass windows. The oldest (circa 1200) are in the north choir;

those in the south transept were manufactured in 1500 at nearby Troyes and include a much-admired *Tree of Jesse.* The cathedral treasury (access near the sacristy to the south of the choir) is one of the richest in France. It contains a collection of miters, ivories, and gold plates, together with the richly woven gold-and-silver robes of the archbishops of Sens and Thomas à Becket. Becket fled to Sens from England to escape the wrath of Henry II before returning to his cathedral in Canterbury where, in 1170, he was murdered. Stained-glass windows in the north of the chancel retrace his story. ✉ *pl. de la République,* ☏ *03–86–64–15–27. Admission to treasury included in ticket to Palais Synodal (*☞ below*).*

The 13th-century **Palais Synodal,** alongside Sens's cathedral, provides an encounter with Burgundy's multicolor tile roofs: From its courtyard, there is a fine view of the cathedral's Flamboyant Gothic south transept, constructed by master stonemason Martin Chambiges at the start of the 16th century. (Rose windows were his specialty, as you can appreciate here.) The Palais Synodal houses a museum with statues, mosaics, and tapestries, but its six grand windows and the vaulted Synodal Hall are the outstanding features. ☏ *03–86–64–46–27.* 🎫 *22 frs.* ⏲ *June–Sept., daily 10–noon and 2–6; Oct.–May, Wed. and weekends 10–noon and 2–6, Mon., Thurs., and Fri. 2–6.*

Dining and Lodging

$$–$$$ ★ ✗🏨 **Paris & Poste.** Owned for the last several decades by the Godard family, the modernized Paris & Poste, which began life as a post house in the 1700s, is a convenient and pleasant stopping point. Rooms are clean, bright, and airy. No. 42, facing the inner courtyard, is especially nice. Sumptuous breakfasts confirm the sense of well-being—further reinforced by a robust evening meal of roast duck or grilled salmon, served in the comfortable, traditional restaurant. ✉ *97 rue de la République, 89100,* ☏ *03–86–65–17–43,* FAX *03–86–64–48–45. 25 rooms. Restaurant. AE, DC, MC, V.*

$ ✗🏨 **Croix Blanche.** A five-minute walk from the cathedral will take you to this calm, straightforward hotel. Its two-room restaurant (plus veranda) provides three good-value menus, headed by turbot in crayfish sauce, salmon with sorrel, and beef with Roquefort (cheese) sauce. ✉ *9 rue Victor-Guichard, 89100,* ☏ *03–86–64–00–02,* FAX *03–86–65–29–19. 25 rooms with bath or shower. Restaurant. MC, V.*

$$$ 🏨 **Château de Prunoy.** Though it's a little out of the way, you may want to venture southwest to this vast château built by one of Louis XVI's finance ministers. Things can seem a little haphazard, but if you don't expect prompt service or mind Labradors running around—and have a sense of humor—you'll enjoy it. The comfortable rooms have idiosyncratic flair. One has a pair of carved, seven-foot-tall gilded wings guarding an 18th-century ivory-and-pearl-inlaid jewelry stand; another is designed as a Japanese tea house. Dinner is not especially grand—it's more a matter of convenience. ✉ *89120 Charny (40 km/25 mi southwest of Sens, 40 km/25 mi east of Auxerre on D950),* ☏ *03–86–63–66–91,* FAX *03–86–63–77–79. 19 rooms. Restaurant, pool, exercise room, meeting rooms. AE, DC, MC, V.*

Troyes

★ *64 km (40 mi) northeast of Sens, 179 km (111 mi) east of Paris.*

The inhabitants of Troyes would be insulted if you mistook them for Burgundians. Troyes is the capital of southern Champagne; as if to prove the point, its historic town center is shaped like a champagne cork, the rounded top enclosed by a loop of the Seine. Few, if any, French town centers contain so much to see and do. A web of enchanting pedestrian streets with timber-frame houses, magnificent churches, and fine museums and a wide choice of restaurants make it appealing. Consider buying a Museum Passport ticket from the tourist office (✉ 16 bd. Carnot, ☎ 03–25–82–62–70); it admits you to the four major museums for 60 francs—a 50% savings. The center of Troyes is divided by quai Dampierre, a broad, busy boulevard. On one side is the quiet cathedral quarter, on the other the more upbeat, commercial part.

Although Troyes is on the Seine, it is the capital of the Aube *départe-*
2 *ment* (province), run from the elegant **préfecture** (government building) that looks out across both the artificial lake, known as the Bassin de la Préfecture, and place de la Libération from behind its gleaming gilt-iron railings.

The best view from place de la Libération is undoubtedly that of the
3 **Cathédrale St-Pierre–St-Paul,** whose 200-foot tower peeps through the trees above the statue and old lamps of the central flower garden. (The tower is undergoing restoration until the end of 1998.) Note the incomplete one-tower facade; the small Renaissance campaniles on top of the tower; and the artistry of Martin Chambiges, who worked on Troyes's facade (with its characteristic large rose window) around the same time as he did the transept of Sens. At night, the floodlit features are thrown into dramatic relief. The cathedral's vast five-aisle interior, refreshingly light thanks to large windows and the near-whiteness of the local stone, dates mainly from the 13th century. Like Sens, it has renowned stained glass—fine examples of primitive 13th-century glass in the choir and richly colored 16th-century glass in the nave and facade rose window. The arcaded triforium above the pillars of the choir was one of the first in France to be glazed rather than filled with stone. Son-et-lumière shows are held in the cathedral at varying hours in summer; contact the tourist office for details. ✉ *pl. St-Pierre.* 🎟 *Free.* ⏲ *July–mid-Sept., daily 9–1 and 2–7; mid-Sept.–June, daily 10–noon and 2–6.*

4 Just south of Troyes's cathedral is the **Musée d'Art Moderne,** housed in the 16th- to 17th-century former Bishop's Palace. Its magnificent interior, with huge fireplaces, ceilings with carved wood beams, and a Renaissance staircase, plays host to the Levy Collection of modern art—drawings, sculpture, and nearly 400 paintings. ✉ *Palais Épiscopal, pl. St-Pierre,* ☎ *03–25–80–57–30.* 🎟 *30 frs.* ⏲ *Wed.–Mon. 11–6.*

Facing the cathedral square, the buildings of the former Abbaye St-Loup
5 now house the **Musée des Beaux-Arts et d'Archéologie** (Fine Arts and Archaeology Museum), often referred to as the Musée St-Loup. There are exhibits devoted to natural history, with impressive collections of birds and meteorites; local archaeological finds, especially gold-mounted 5th-century jewelry and a Gallo-Roman bronze statue of Apollo; medieval statuary and gargoyles; and paintings from the 15th to the 19th centuries, including works by Rubens, Anthony Van Dyck, Antoine Watteau, François Boucher, and Jacques-Louis David. ✉ *1 rue Chrétien-de-Troyes,* ☎ *03–25–42–33–33, ext. 35–92.* 🎟 *30 frs.* ⏲ *Wed.–Mon. 10–noon and 2–6.*

Where the rue de la Cité, packed with restaurants, joins quai Dampierre, it passes in front of the superb wrought-iron gates of the 18th-century
6 **Hôtel-Dieu** (hospital), topped with the blue-and-gold fleurs-de-lis emblems of the French monarchy. Around the corner is the entrance to the **pharmacie,** the former medical laboratory, the only part of the Hôtel-Dieu open to visitors. ✉ *quai des Comtes-de-Champagne,* ☎ *03–25–42–33–33, ext. 35–92.* 🎟 *20 frs.* ⏲ *Wed.–Mon. 10–noon and 2–6.*

Basilique St-Urbain, **7**
Cathédrale St-Pierre–St-Paul, **3**
Hôtel de Vaulvisant, **13**
Hôtel de Ville, **8**
Hôtel-Dieu, **6**
Maison de l'Outil, **11**
Musée d'Art Moderne, **4**
Musée des Beaux-Arts et d'Archéologie, **5**
préfecture, **2**
St-Jean, **9**
St-Nicolas, **14**
St-Pantaléon, **12**
Ste-Madeleine, **10**

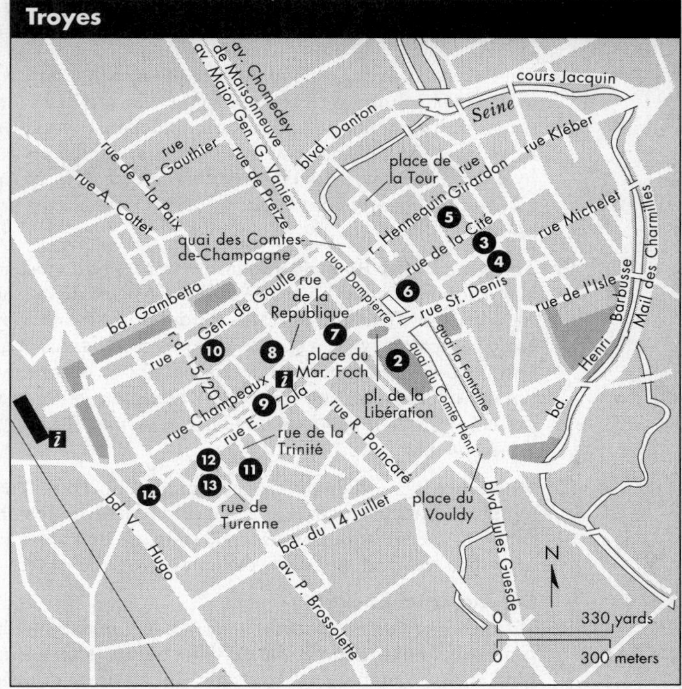

7 Southwest of quai Dampierre, on rue Clemenceau, is the **Basilique St-Urbain,** built between 1262 and 1286 by Pope Urban IV, who was born in Troyes. St-Urbain is one of the most remarkable churches in France, a perfect culmination of Gothic's quest to replace stone walls with stained glass. Huge windows, containing much of their original glass, ring the church, while the exterior bristles with the thrust-bearing flying buttresses that made this daring structure possible. ✉ *pl. Vernier.* 🎫 *Free.* ⏲ *July–mid-Sept., daily 10:30–5; mid-Sept.–June, daily 10–noon and 2–6.*

8 Place du Maréchal-Foch, the main square of central Troyes, is flanked by cafés, shops, and the delightful early 17th-century facade of the **Hôtel de Ville** (Town Hall). In summer, the square is filled from morning to night.

9 The clock tower of the church of **St-Jean,** is an unmistakable landmark. England's warrior king, Henry V, married Catherine of France in 1420 here. The church's tall 16th-century choir contrasts with the low earlier nave. ✉ *pl. du Marché au Pain.* 🎫 *Free.* ⏲ *July–mid-Sept., daily 10:30–5; mid-Sept.–June, daily 10–noon and 2–6.*

10 The church of **Ste-Madeleine,** the oldest in Troyes, is best known for its elaborate triple-arched stone rood screen separating the nave and the choir. Only six other such screens still remain in France—most were dismantled during the French Revolution—and this one was carved with panache by Jean Gailde between 1508 and 1517. ✉ *rue de la Madeleine.* 🎫 *Free.* ⏲ *July–mid-Sept., daily 10:30–5; mid-Sept.–June, daily 10–noon and 2–6.*

11 The private museum known as **Maison de l'Outil,** in the 16th-century Hôtel de Mauroy, contains a collection of paintings, models, and tools relevant to such traditional wood-related trades as carpentry, clog making, and barrel making. ⊠ *7 rue de la Trinité,* ☎ *03–25–73–28–26.* 🎫 *30 frs.* ⏲ *Daily 9–noon and 2–6.*

12 The 16th-century church of **St-Pantaléon,** which primarily serves the local Polish community, is close to the Maison de l'Outil, via Bordet. A number of fine stone statues, surmounted by canopies, cluster around its pillars. The tall, narrow walls are topped not by stone vaults but by a wooden roof, unusual for such a late church. ⊠ *rue de Turenne.* 🎫 *Free.* ⏲ *July–mid-Sept., daily 10:30–5; mid-Sept.–June, daily 10–noon and 2–6.*

13 The Renaissance **Hôtel de Vauluisant** houses two museums: the **Musée Historique** (History Museum) and the **Musée de la Bonneterie** (Textile Museum). The former traces the development of Troyes and southern Champagne, with a section devoted to religious art, and the latter outlines the history and manufacturing process of the town's traditional bonnet-making industry. ⊠ *4 rue Vauluisant,* ☎ *03–25–42–33–33, ext. 35–92.* 🎫 *Joint ticket for both museums 30 frs.* ⏲ *Wed.–Mon. 10–noon and 2–6.*

14 **St-Nicolas** is another of Troyes's many churches. You may not be tempted by its grimy exterior, but undaunted souls will be rewarded by the chance to scale a wide stone staircase up to an exuberantly decorated chapel and an unexpected view over the nave.

Dining and Lodging

$$$ ✕ **Valentino.** The restaurant is in an old, half-timber building on a pedestrian street next to the Hôtel de Ville, but its flowery interior makes a bold effort to mimic Art Deco chic. Tables are set outside in summer. Oysters are served as a complement to the menu's fish specialties—grilled crayfish with poppy seeds and Brittany lobster in a casserole flavored with ginger. ⊠ *11 cour de la Rencontre,* ☎ *03–25–73–14–14. Jacket and tie. AE, DC, MC, V. Closed Mon., and mid-Aug.–early Sept. No dinner Sun.*

$$$ 🏨 **Relais St-Jean.** This calm, stylish hotel, in the pedestrian zone near St-Jean, has fully equipped, good-size rooms. Service is personal—the staff knows guests by name. ⊠ *49 rue Paillot-de-Montabert, 10000,* ☎ *03–25–73–89–90,* FAX *03–25–73–88–60. 22 rooms. Bar, air-conditioning. AE, DC, MC, V. Closed mid-Dec.–early Jan.*

Shopping

If there is an ideal place for a shopping spree, it's Troyes. Many clothing manufacturers are just outside town, so prices in stores can be 50% cheaper than elsewhere in France. Rue des Bas-Trévois, rue Bégand, and rue Cartalon are good places to look.

Pontigny

15 *60 km (37 mi) south of Troyes, 56 km (35 mi) southeast of Sens.*

Pontigny can easily be mistaken for another drowsy, dusty village, but its once-proud abbey is as large as many cathedrals; in the 12th and 13th centuries, it sheltered three archbishops of Canterbury, including St. Thomas à Becket. The **Abbaye de Pontigny** was founded in 1114, but the current church was begun in 1150. The monks belonged to the Cistercian order, which, frowning on the opulence of the rival House of Cluny, fostered buildings of intense sobriety. Small, even-spaced windows render the abbey's silhouette monotonous, but inside, they serenely illuminate the tall, pale shafts of stone. The single tower, that of the facade, scrambles almost apologetically to roof level. The only ornament is provided by the late-17th-century wooden choir stalls, carved with garlands and angels. ☏ *03–86–47–54–99.* 🎫 *Free, 20 frs for a guided tour.* ⏲ *Daily 9–7, except during services.*

Auxerre

⓰ *21 km (13 mi) southwest of Pontigny, 58 km (36 mi) southeast of Sens.*

Auxerre is a small, peaceful town perched on a steep hill overlooking the River Yonne. The town's dominant feature is the **Cathédrale St-Etienne** rising majestically from the squat houses around it. The 13th-century choir, the oldest part of the edifice, contains its original stained glass, dominated by dazzling reds and blues. Beneath the choir, the frescoed 11th-century Romanesque crypt keeps company with the treasury, which features medieval enamels, manuscripts, and miniatures. ✉ *pl. St-Étienne,* ☏ *03–86–52–31–68.* 🎫 *Crypt and treasury: 8 frs each. The Passport Ticket (25 frs) gives entry to the crypt and treasury plus St-Germain* (☞ below). ⏲ *Easter–Nov., Mon.–Sat. 9–noon and 2–6, Sun. 2–6.*

Fanning out from Auxerre's main square, **place des Cordeliers** (just up from the cathedral), are a number of venerable streets lined with 16th-century houses worth exploring. North of place des Cordeliers is the town's most interesting church, the former **Abbaye de St-Germain,** which stands parallel to the cathedral some 300 yards away. The church's earliest section above ground is the 11th-century Romanesque bell tower, but the extensive underground crypt dates from the 9th century and contains its original frescoes. ✉ *pl. St-Germain,* ☏ *03–86–51–09–74.* 🎫 *20 frs. Guided tours of the crypt, Wed.–Mon. 9–11:30 and 2–5:30.*

Dining and Lodging

$$ ✕ **Jardin Gourmand.** As its name implies, this restaurant features a pretty garden where you can eat in summer; the interior, accented by light-color oak, is equally congenial. The cuisine is innovative but simple—ravioli and foie gras or the duck with black currants. Service is discreet. ✉ *56 bd. Vauban,* ☏ *03–86–51–53–52. MC, V. Closed Mon. No lunch Tues.*

$$$ ★ 🏨 **La Borde.** In their inn, a former granary of a manorial estate, southwest of Auxerre, the Duclos have four delightful, large rooms. You'll find exposed timbers, walls painted golden hues, and Indian rugs scattered on clay-tile floors. Furniture is kept to a minimum, except for a few antiques. Table d'hôte dinners (for just under 200 francs) are served in the huge kitchen and may include homemade terrine, roast leg of pork, cheese, and local Burgundy wine. Conversation is usually in English (the owners speak it fluently) since most guests come from the States. ✉ *89130 Leugny (20 km/12 mi southwest of Auxerre on D50 east of Toucy),* ☏ *03–86–47–64–28,* FAX *03–86–47–60–28. 4 rooms. No credit cards. Advance reservations essential.*

$$ 🏨 **Le Maxime.** This slightly old-fashioned, family-run hotel on the banks of the Yonne, a five-minute walk from the old town, is appealing if you like the personal touch. Rooms are individually decorated; reserve one with a river view. The bar, Le Cave de Bourgogne, with its exposed beams and copper pots, is a comfortable place for a drink. ✉ *2 quai de la Marine, 89000,* ☏ *03–86–52–14–19,* FAX *03–86–52–21–70. 25 rooms. Bar. AE, DC, MC, V. Closed late Dec.–late Jan.*

$–$$ 🏨 **Normandie.** The grand-looking vine-covered Normandie is in the center of Auxerre, a short walk from the cathedral. Rooms are unpretentious and clean and have such pleasantries as hair dryers in the bathroom. The garden is a pleasant place to relax. ✉ *41 bd. Vauban,*

89000, ☎ 03-86-52-57-80, FAX 03-86-51-54-33. 48 rooms with bath or shower. Bar, sauna, exercise room. AE, DC, MC, V.

Chablis

17 *16 km (10 mi) east of Auxerre, 74 km (45 mi) south of Troyes, 183 km (114 mi) southeast of Paris.*

The pretty little village of Chablis, famous for its white wine, nestles on the banks of the River Serein ("serene") and is protected by the massive, round, turreted towers of the Porte Noël gateway. Although "Chablis" in America has become a generic name for cheap white wine, not so in France: It's a fine, slightly oak-tasting wine of tremendous character, with the Premier Cru and Grand Cru wines standing head-to-head with the best French whites. Prices in the local shops tend to be inflated, so your best bet is to buy directly from a vineyard; keep in mind that most are closed Sunday.

Dining and Lodging

$$–$$$ ★ ✕ **Hostellerie des Clos.** The moderately priced, simple yet comfortable rooms at this inn have floral curtains and wicker tables with chairs. Come here for the food; it's the best in the region. Chef Michel Vignaud cooks superb cuisine: *sandre,* (white fish) served with a chicken-based sauce, casserole of hare, and *huîtres d'Isgny* (small oysters) in a dill and Chablis sauce. Desserts are equally splendid. ✉ *rue Jules-Rathier, 89800, ☎ 03-86-42-10-63, FAX 03-86-42-17-11. 26 rooms. Restaurant. AE, DC, MC, V.*

$ **Domaine de Montpierreux.** This private manor on a truffle farm south of Chablis has five immaculate rooms on its top floor. All are delightfully decorated in paisley fabrics and at least one piece of provincial antique furniture. The friendly owners help to make this a very comfortable base for exploring the area. Breakfast is served. ✉ *89290 Venoy (6 km/4 mi south of Chablis, 10 km/6 mi north of Auxerre on D965), ☎ 03-86-40-20-91, FAX 03-86-40-28-00. 5 rooms with bath or shower. No credit cards.*

Tonnerre

18 *16 km (10 mi) northeast of Chablis, 60 km (37 mi) south of Troyes.*

The small town of Tonnerre was mostly rebuilt after a devastating fire in 1556. Survey the 16th-century reconstruction and the Armançon Valley from the terrace of **St-Pierre** church. The chief attraction, the high-roofed **Ancien Hôpital,** or Hôtel Dieu, was built in 1293 and has survived the passing centuries—flames and all—largely intact. The main room, the **Grande Salle,** is 250 feet long and retains its oak ceiling; it was conceived as the hospital ward and after 1650 served as the parish church. The original hospital church leads off from the Grande Salle; in the adjoining **Chapelle du Revestière,** a dramatic 15th-century stone group represents the *Burial of Christ.* Look for good finds at the **Salon des Antiquaires,** held here on Toussaint weekend (second weekend in November). ✉ *rue du Prieuré, ☎ 03-86-54-33-00. 26 frs. ⏲ June–Sept., Wed.–Mon. 10–noon and 1–6; Apr.–May and Oct., weekends 1–6.*

Tanlay

19 *10 km (6 mi) east of Tonnerre, 45 km (28 mi) northeast of Auxerre.*

Tanlay is best known for its castle, the **Château de Tanlay.** Built around 1550, it is an example of the classical influence of the Renaissance. The vestibule, framed by wrought-iron railings, leads to a wood-paneled salon and dining room filled with period furniture. A graceful staircase climbs to the second floor with a frescoed gallery and ornate fireplaces. A small room in the tower above was used as a secret meeting place by Huguenot Protestants during the 1562–98 Wars of Religion; not the cupola with its fresco of scantily clad 16th-century religious personalities. ☎ *03–86–75–70–61.* *Guided tours only, 39 frs; grounds only, 15 frs.* ⏲ *Apr.–Nov. 11, Wed.–Mon. 9:30–11:30 and 2:15–5:15.*

Lodging

$ **Chez Batreau.** The lovely little farming village of Cuzy-le-Chatel, on a hillside close to Tanlay, is home to this inn in a walled garden. The large rooms are decorated with family furnishings and the beds sag a little. Nonetheless the rooms are good value for the money, especially the one at the end of the hall, whose exposed timbers and cross beams form a sort of loft. ✉ *89740 Cruzy-Le-Chatel,* ☎ *03–86–75–22-78. 4 rooms, 2 with bath. No credit cards.*

Ancy-le-Franc

20 *11 km (7 mi) southeast of Tanlay, 55 km (34 mi) northeast of Auxerre and north of Avallon.*

Ancy-le-Franc is famous for its Renaissance château. Built from Sebastiano Serlio's designs with interior decor by Primaticcio, both of whom worked at the court of François I (1515–47), the **Château de Ancy-le-Franc** has an Italian flavor. The plain, majestic exterior contrasts with the sumptuous rooms and apartments, many—particularly the magnificent Chambre des Arts—with carved or painted walls and ceilings and their original furniture. Such grandeur won the approval of Sun King Louis XIV, no less, who once stayed in the Salon Bleu. Adjoining the château is a small **Musée Automobile.** ✉ *pl. Clermont-Tonnerre,* ☎ *03–86–75–14–63.* *Château and musée: 42 frs.* ⏲ *Late Mar.–mid-Nov.; guided château tours at 10, 11, 2, 3, 4, 5, and (May–Sept.) 6.* *Musée Automobile: 20 frs.* ⏲ *10–5 or 6.*

Abbaye de Fontenay

★ 21 *50 km (31 mi) southeast of Tonnerre, 72 km (45 mi) east of Auxerre.*

Just east of Montbard is the Cistercian Abbaye de Fontenay, founded by St-Bernard in 1118. The same Cistercian criteria applied to Fontenay as to Pontigny (☞ *above*): no-frills architecture and an isolated site. By the end of the 12th century, the buildings were finished, and the abbey's community grew to some 300 monks. It prospered until the 16th century, when religious wars and administrative mayhem hastened its decline. Dissolved during the French Revolution, the abbey was used as a paper factory until 1906. Fortunately, the historic buildings emerged unscathed.

The abbey is surrounded by extensive gardens dotted with the fountains that gave it its name. The church's solemn interior is lit by windows in the facade and by a double row of three narrow windows, representing the Trinity, in the choir. A staircase in the south transept leads to the wood-roofed dormitory (spare a thought for the bleary-eyed monks, obliged to stagger down for services in the dead of night). The chapter house, flanked by a majestic arcade, and the scriptorium, where monks worked on their manuscripts, lead off from the adjoining cloisters. ✉ *Montbard,* ☎ *03–80–92–15–00.* *50 frs.* ⏲ *Daily 9–noon and 2–6; guided tours only on the hr mid-Mar.–mid-Nov. (every ½ hr July–Aug.).*

Saulieu

22 *49 km (30 mi) south of Fontenay, 62 km (37 mi) northwest of Beaune, 77 km (49 mi) west of Dijon.*

Saulieu's reputation belies its size: It is renowned for good food (Rabelais, that roly-poly 16th-century man of letters, extolled its gargantuan hospitality) and Christmas trees (a million are packed off from the area each year). The town's **Basilique de St-Andoche** is almost as old as that of Vézelay, though less imposing and much restored.

The **Musée François Pompon,** adjoining the basilica, is devoted, in part, to the work of animal-bronze sculptor Pompon (1855–1933), whose smooth, stylized creations seem contemporary but predate World War II. The museum also contains Gallo-Roman funeral stones, sacred art, and a room devoted to local gastronomic lore. ✉ *rue Sallier,* ☎ *03–80–64–19–51.* *22 frs.* ⏲ *Apr.–Sept., Wed.–Mon. 10–12:30 and 2–6 (until 5:30 Oct.–Mar.).*

Dining and Lodging

$$ ★ **Chez Camille.** Small, quiet, and friendly sum up this hotel in a 16th-century house with an exterior that looks so ordinary you might easily pass it by. Rooms have period furniture and original wooden beams. Ask for No. 22 or No. 23, the most dramatic, with a beamed ceiling that looks like spokes in a wheel. Traditional Burgundian fare—duck and boar are specialties—makes up the menu in the glass-roofed restaurant. ✉ *1 pl. Édouard-Herriot, 21230 Arnay-le-Duc (on N6 between Saulieu and Beaune),* ☎ *03–80–90–01–38,* FAX *03–80–90–04–64. 12 rooms. Restaurant. AE, DC, MC, V.*

Châteauneuf-en-Auxois

23 *48 km (30 mi) east of Saulieu, 35 km (22 mi) northwest of Beaune.*

The tiny hilltop town of Châteauneuf-en-Auxois catches your eye from autoroute A6. Turn off at the marked exit and take any one of the three narrow, winding roads up to the Middle Ages. The town's modest 15th-century church was the salvation for perhaps as many as 500 souls when the village was at its zenith.

The 12th-century **Château** (with some later modifications) still commands the same breadth of view over rolling farmland as far as the eye can see. It's open to the public on a limited basis. ☎ *03–80–49–21–89.* *21 frs.* ⏲ *Apr.–Sept., tours daily at 9:30, 10:30, 11:30, 2, 3, 4, and 5. Oct.–Mar., Thurs.–Mon. at 10, 11, 2, 3.*

Clustered behind the château are houses for ordinary folk, at least a score of them notable for their 14th- and 15th-century charm, where today just 63 people live. One of them, **M. Simon** (☎ 03–80–49–21–59), is so proud of his village that he gladly takes small groups on tours of the sights.

Dining and Lodging

$$ **Hostellerie du Château.** This hotel is in an ancient timbered building in the shadow of the castle. The restaurant serves classical Bourgogne fare—roasted *epoisses* (local cow's milk cheese) on a salad bed with walnuts, noisettes of lamb with thyme, and coq au vin. Rooms vary considerably—from small to much more commodious. The best have a view of the castle. ✉ *Châteauneuf-en-Auxois, 21320 Pouilly,* ☎ *03–80–49–22–00,* FAX *03–80–49–21–27. 17 rooms with bath or shower. Restaurant. Closed Nov.–mid-Mar.*

Château de Sully

24 *37 km (28 mi) south of Châteauneuf-en-Auxois, 33 km (20 mi) southeast of Saulieu.*

The turreted Renaissance Château de Sully stands in a stately park, surrounded by a moat. A monumental staircase leads to the north front and a broad terrace. Marshal MacMahon, president of France from 1873 to 1879, was born here in 1808. ☎ *03–85–82–10–27.* ⏲ *Château: 45-min guided tours June–Sept. (call for times). Grounds: daily 10–noon and 2–6.* 🎟 *Guided tours: 35 frs. Grounds: 15 frs.*

Autun

25 *9 km (6 mi) southwest of Sully, 41 km (25 mi) south of Saulieu, 49 km (30 mi) west of Beaune.*

Autun has been an important town since Roman times, as you can detect from the well-preserved archways, Porte St-André and Porte d'Arroux, and the Théâtre Romain, once the largest arena in Gaul. Julius Caesar even referred to Autun as the "sister and rival of Rome itself." Another famous warrior, Napoléon, studied here in 1779 at the military academy (now the Lycée Bonaparte).

★ Autun's principal monument is the **Cathédrale St-Lazarus,** built from 1120 to 1146 to house the relics of St. Lazarus; the main tower, spire, and upper reaches of the chancel were added in the late 15th century. The influx of medieval pilgrims accounts for the building's size (35 yards wide and nearly 80 yards long). Lazarus's tomb was dismantled in 1766 by canons who were believers in the rationalist credo of the Enlightenment. They also did their best to transform the Romanesque-Gothic cathedral into a Classical temple at the same time, adding pilasters and classical ornaments willy-nilly. Fortunately, some of the best Romanesque stonework, including the inspired nave capitals and the tympanum above the main door—a gracefully elongated *Last Judgment* sculpted by Gislebertus in the 1130s—emerged unscathed. Jean-Auguste Ingres's painting depicting the *Martyrdom of St-Symphorien* has been relegated to a dingy chapel in the north aisle of the nave. ✉ *pl. St-Louis.*

The **Musée Rolin,** across from the cathedral, contains several fine paintings from the Middle Ages and good examples of Burgundian sculpture, including a Gislebertus masterpiece, the *Temptation of Eve,* which originally topped one of the side doors of the cathedral. ✉ *pl. St-Louis,* ☎ *03–85–52–09–76.* 🎟 *18 frs.* ⏲ *Nov.–Mar., Mon. and Wed.–Sat. 10–noon and 2–6, Sun. 10–noon and 2–5; Apr.–Sept., Wed.–Mon. 9:30–noon and 1:30–6; Oct., Mon. and Wed.–Sat. 10–noon and 2–5, Sun. 10–noon and 2:30–5.*

The **Roman amphitheater** at the edge of town on the road to Chalon-sur-Saône is a historic spot for lunch. Pick up the makings in town and eat your picnic on the stepped seats where as many as 15,000 Gallo-Roman spectators sat two millennia ago. If you're in a classical mood, don't miss the **Juno Temple,** in a field at the other edge of town as you leave for Château-Chinon. Keep your eyes peeled to the right for the turnoff.

Dining and Lodging

$ ✕ **Chalet Bleu.** Solid, traditional French cuisine is served in a setting that resembles a converted conservatory. Foie gras and beef with shallots are trustworthy choices, but chef Philippe Bouché is creative with Bourgogne recipes, so be adventuresome. ✉ *3 rue Jeannin,* ☎ *03–85–86–27–30. AE, DC, MC, V. Closed Tues. No dinner Mon.*

$$ **St-Louis.** This comfortable hotel on a quiet street away from the traffic noise, dates from the 17th century; legend has it that Napoléon once slept here. The cozily decorated rooms have slightly faded charm. The hotel has a pleasant patio-garden and its own restaurant, La Rotonde. ✉ *6 rue de l'Arbalète, 71400,* ☎ *03–85–52–21–03,* FAX *03–85–86–32–54. 52 rooms with bath or shower. Restaurant. AE, DC, MC, V.*

Nightlife and the Arts

Autun's cathedral provides a stunning setting for **Musique en Morvan,** a classical music festival in July.

Château-Chinon

26 *37 km (23 mi) west of Autun, 58 km (36 mi) south of Avallon.*

Late President François Mitterrand was the former mayor of the small town of Château-Chinon, the capital of the Morvan. One of his legacies is the brash, colorful, and controversial **Niki de St-Phalle Fontaine,** in front of the Hôtel de Ville. The **Musée du Septennat** contains an astonishing variety of gifts Mitterrand received while president. ✉ *6 rue du Château,* ☎ *03–86–85–19–23.* *25 frs.* *May–Oct., daily 10–6; Nov.–Apr., weekends 10–6.*

The **Musée du Costume** has exhibits on the traditions of the Morvan. ✉ *16–18 rue St-Christophe,* ☎ *03–86–85–18–55.* *25 frs.* *Nov.–May, weekends 10–6; June and Sept.–Oct., daily 10–6; July and Aug., daily 10–7.*

Nevers

27 *64 km (40 mi) west of Château-Chinon, 119 km (74 mi) south of Auxerre, 239 km (149 mi) southeast of Paris.*

Burgundy's western outpost, Nevers, on the banks of the Loire, has been producing earthenware since the late 16th century. Promoted initially by Italian craftsmen, the industry suffered during the French Revolution, but three traditional manufacturers remain. An extensive selection of Nevers earthenware, retracing its stylistic development, can be admired at the **Musée Municipal.** *promenade des Remparts,* ☎ *03–86–68–45–62.* *10 frs.* *May–Sept., Wed.–Mon. 10–5:15; Oct.–Apr., 10–11:45 and 2–5:15.*

Part of Nevers's medieval walls extend behind the Municipal Museum, culminating in the intimidating gateway known as the **Porte du Croux** (built in 1393), which, thanks to its turrets and huge, sloping roof, resembles a small castle. The **Cathédrale** (✉ rue du Cloître-St-Cyr), with its 170-foot square tower and two apses, is an enormous building, constructed during several periods of the Middle Ages. The **Palais Ducal,** beyond the cathedral, has a sumptuous, large-windowed Renaissance facade but, unfortunately, is closed to the public.

Across a park that can be entered from the central place Carnot, a few hundred yards north of the Palais Ducal, is the **Couvent St-Gildard,** the convent where St. Bernadette of Lourdes (1844–79) spent the last 13 years of her life. A small museum contains mementos and outlines her life story (she claimed to have seen the Virgin several times in 1858 and was canonized in 1933). ✉ *rue St-Gildard,* ☎ *03–86–36–91–45.* *Free.* *Daily 10–5.*

Nightlife and the Arts

Musique en Nivernais, a classical music festival, takes place in September and October.

La Charité-sur-Loire

28 *24 km (15 mi) northwest of Nevers, 91 km (57 mi) south of Auxerre.*

La Charité-sur-Loire is best known for it's medieval church. Unlike those of Pontigny and Fontenay, the abbey church of **Ste-Croix-Notre-Dame** was dependent on Cluny; when it was consecrated by Pope Pascal II in 1107, it was the country's second largest church. Fire and neglect have taken their toll on the massive original edifice, and these days the church is cut in two, with the single-tower facade separated from the imposing choir and transept by pretty place Ste-Croix (where the nave used to be). A fine view of the church's exterior can be seen from square des Bénédictins, just off Grande-Rue.

Clamecy

29 *51 km (32 mi) northeast of La Charité-sur-Loire, 44 km (27 mi) south of Auxerre.*

Slow-moving Clamecy is not on many tourist itineraries, but its tumbling alleyways and untouched, ancient houses epitomize *La France Profonde.* The multishape roofs, dominated by the majestic square tower of the church of **St-Martin,** are best viewed from the banks of the Yonne River.

The river played a crucial role in Clamecy's development; trees from the nearby Morvan Forest were chopped down and floated to Paris in huge convoys. The history of this form of transport (*flottage*), which lasted until 1923, is detailed in the Musée Municipal (Town Museum), also known as the **Musée d'Art et d'Histoire Romain Rolland,** for native son Rolland, Nobel laureate for literature in 1915. Faïence and paintings from the 17th–19th centuries are also on display. ✉ *av. de la République,* ☏ *03–86–27–17–99.* 🎫 *15 frs.* ⏲ *Nov.–Easter, Mon. and Wed.–Sat. 10–noon and 3–6; Easter–Oct., Wed.–Mon. 10–noon and 2–6.*

In homage to the logs that were once floated downriver, *bûchette* (a log-shape, sugared-almond candy) has long been a favorite Clamecyçois. Sample it at **Avignon** (✉ 22 rue de la Monnaie, near steps leading to St-Martin), a pastry shop and tearoom.

Dining and Lodging

$$ ✕ **L'Angélus.** The cuisine here is as marvelous as the setting—opposite the collegiate church, in a wood-beamed medieval building. When young chef Thierry Lambelin escapes from the conservative eye of *patronne* Mafoy Danjean, the grande dame of Clamecy cuisine, he lets loose with such creations as perch in orange sauce and duck-and-chicken salad in raspberry vinegar. For lunch, the 59-franc *menu rapide* is an excellent value. ✉ *11 pl. St-Jean,* ☏ *03–86–27–23–25. AE, DC, MC, V. Closed Thurs. No dinner Wed.*

$ 🏨 **Boule d'Or.** This down-to-earth country hotel (not particularly comfortable but oh so cheap) is by the River Yonne. Ask for a room facing the river for lovely views of old Clamecy. The restaurant is housed in a former medieval chapel and serves good food from a duck terrine to roast pigeon at excellent prices. ✉ *5 pl. Bethléem, 58500,* ☏ *03–86–27–11–55,* FAX *03–86–24–47–02. 12 rooms with bath or shower. Restaurant. AE, MC, V.*

Vézelay

30 *24 km (15 mi) east of Clamecy, 51 km (32 mi) south of Auxerre, 13 km (8 mi) southwest of Avallon.*

The somewhat isolated, picturesque town of Vézelay is on a peak, with one main street, rue St-Etienne, climbing steeply to its summit and its medieval basilica. In summer, you'll have to leave your car at the bottom and walk up. Off-season, you can drive up and look for a spot to park in the square.

★ In the 11th and 12th centuries, the celebrated **Basilique Ste-Madeleine** was one of the focal points of Christendom. Pilgrims poured in to gasp at the relics of St. Mary Magdalene before setting off on the great trek to the shrine of St. James at Santiago de Compostela in northwest Spain. By the mid-13th century, the authenticity of St. Mary's relics was in doubt; others had been discovered in Provence. The basilica's decline continued until the French Revolution, when the basilica and adjoining monastery buildings were sold by the state. Only the basilica escaped demolition and was falling into ruin when ace restorer Viollet-le-Duc rode to the rescue in 1840 (he also restored the cathedrals of Laon and Amiens and Paris's Notre-Dame).

Today the basilica, under the patrimony of UNESCO, has recaptured its onetime glory and is considered to be France's most prestigious Romanesque showcase. Note the wonderful decoration in the nave, whose column capitals, imaginatively designed and superbly carved, represent miniature medieval men in all manner of situations. The basilica's exterior is best seen from the leafy terrace to the right of the facade. Opposite, a vast, verdant panorama encompasses lush valleys and rolling hills and hedgerows. In the forefront is the Flamboyant Gothic spire of St-Père-sous-Vézelay, a tiny village 3 km (2 mi) away that is the site of Marc Meneau's famed restaurant (☞ Dining and Lodging, *below*). *✉ pl. de la Basilique, ☎ 03–86–33–27–73. Free, but a donation of 15 frs is appreciated. ⏲ 8–8, except during offices Mon.–Sat. 12:15–1:15 and 5:15–7:15, and Sun. 10:30–12:30.*

Dining and Lodging

$$$$ ✕▣ **L'Espérance.** Chef Marc Meneau is not the most modest of men—his monogram appears everywhere—but he is renowned for his subtle, original cuisine: delicate lobster soup and scallops in lemon marmalade. The setting—by a stream and a large, statue-filled garden with Vézelay in the background—is delightful. The restaurant is closed Tuesday and lunch Wednesday; reservations are essential and a jacket required. Rooms are in different buildings and vary in price and style. *✉ 89450 Vézelay, ☎ 03–86–33–39–10, FAX 03–86–33–26–15. 40 rooms. Restaurant. AE, DC, MC, V. Closed Feb.*

$$$ ▣ **Résidence Hôtel Le Pontot.** With limited lodging in this isolated village, you would do well to book ahead, especially in this historic fortified house with sumptuous little rooms and a lovely garden. Another advantage is the hotel's location in the center of the village halfway up the hill. *✉ pl. du Pontot, 89450, ☎ 03–86–33–24–40. 10 rooms. DC, MC, V. Closed Nov.–Apr.*

Avallon

31 *13 km (8 mi) east of Vézelay, 97 km (60 mi) northeast of Nevers, 60 km (37 mi) southeast of Auxerre.*

Avallon is spectacularly situated on a promontory jutting over the Vallée du Cousin. The town's old streets and ramparts are pleasant places for strolling, before or after viewing the works of medieval stone carvers whose imaginations ran riot on the portals of the venerable church of **St-Lazarus.**

Dining and Lodging

$$ ✕ **Moulin des Ruats.** Once an old flour mill, the Moulin des Ruats became a family hotel in 1924 and is now a comfortable country inn. Rooms have pretty country-French decor; some have balconies overlooking the Cousin river. Choose from traditional dishes on the large menu as you look out over the river. The popular 230-franc menu includes a good Burgundian coq au vin. ✉ *Vallée du Cousin, 89200 (4 km/2 mi southwest of Avallon),* ☎ *03–86–34–07–14,* FAX *03–86–31–65–47. 26 rooms with bath or shower. Restaurant. AE, DC, MC, V. Closed Nov.–Feb.*

$–$$ ★ ✕ **Les Capucins.** On a peaceful square 10 minutes from the center, this intimate hotel has rooms in a range of prices. It is better known for its restaurant, however, which features four prix-fixe menus dominated by regional cooking—duck, trout in flaky pastry, and the very local *oeufs en meurette* (eggs poached in broth and red wine). There's a pleasing garden for breakfast and aperitifs, and small cozy rooms for a postprandial drink. ✉ *6 av. Paul-Doumer (also known as av. de la Gare), 89200,* ☎ *03–86–34–06–52,* FAX *03–86–34–58–47. 8 rooms, 7 with bath. AE, MC, V. Restaurant. AE, MC, V. Closed mid-Nov.–mid-Jan.*

Parc Naturel Régional du Morvan

32 *Take D944 out of Avallon and then turn left on D10 to Quarré-les-Tombes.*

The vast Parc du Morvan encompasses a 3,500-square-km (1,290-square-mi) chunk of Burgundy. A network of roads and *Grands Randonées* (GRs, or big trails) winds around the park's lush forests, photogenic lakes, wooded hills, idyllic farms, and tiny villages. Maps for specific trails are available from local tourist offices. Hiking in the Morvan is not strenuous, but it is enchanting: Every turn down a trail provides a new country scene. **Quarré-les-Tombes,** one of the best little villages peppering the park, is so named because of the empty prehistoric stone tombs discovered eerily arrayed in a ring around its church. Eight kilometers (5 miles) south of Quarré-les-Tombes is **Rocher de la Pérouse,** a mighty outcrop worth scrambling up for a view of the park and the Cure Valley.

WINE COUNTRY

East of the Parc du Morvan the low hills and woodland gradually open up and vineyards, clothing the contour of the land in orderly beauty, even in winter, appear on all sides. The vineyard's steeply banked hills stand in contrast to the region's characteristic gentle slopes. Burgundy's most famous vineyards run south from Dijon through Beaune to Mâcon along what has become known as the Côte d'Or.

Dijon

314 km (195 mi) southeast of Paris, 119 km (74 mi) east of Avallon.

Dijon, linked to Paris by expressway (A6/A38) and high-speed TGV (Train à Grande Vitesse), is the age-old capital of Burgundy. Throughout the Middle Ages, Burgundy was a duchy that led a separate existence from the rest of France, culminating in the rule of the four "Grand Dukes of the West" between 1364 and 1477. A number of monuments date from this period, including the Palais des Ducs (Ducal Palace), now largely converted into an art museum.

Dijon's fame and fortune outlasted its dukes, and the city continued to flourish under French rule from the 17th century on. It has remained the major city of Burgundy—the only one, in fact, with more than 100,000 inhabitants. Its site, on the major European north–south trade route and within striking distance of the Swiss and German borders, has helped maintain its economic importance. It's also a cultural center—a few of its 10 museums are mentioned below. And many of its gastronomic specialties are known worldwide: snails, mustard, and cassis (a black-currant liqueur often mixed with white wine—preferably Burgundy Aligoté—to make kir, the popular aperitif).

★ 33 The **Palais des Ducs** is Dijon's leading testimony to bygone splendor. The elegant, classical exterior of the former palace can best be admired from place de la Libération and cour d'Honneur. These days, it's home to one of France's major art museums, the **Musée des Beaux-Arts,** where the tombs of two of the aforementioned dukes—Philip the Bold and John the Fearless—are the center of a rich collection of medieval objects and Renaissance furniture. Among the paintings are works by Italian Old Masters and French 19th-century artists, such as Théodore Géricault and Gustave Courbet, and their Realist and Impressionist successors, notably Édouard Manet and Claude Monet. The **ducal kitchens** (circa 1435), with their six huge fireplaces, and the 14th-century **chapter house** catch the eye, as does the 15th-century **Salle des Gardes** (Guard Room), with its richly carved and colored tombs and late-14th-century altarpieces. ✉ *pl. de la Ste-Chapelle,* ☎ *03–80–74–52–70.* 🎟 *15 frs.* ⏲ *Wed.–Mon. 10–6.*

34 **Notre-Dame,** one of the city's oldest churches, stands out with its elegant towers, delicate nave stonework, 13th-century stained glass, and soaring chancel. ✉ *rue de la Préfecture.*

35 The church of **St-Michel,** to the east of the palace, takes us forward 300 years with its chunky Renaissance facade. ✉ *pl. St-Michel.*

36 The **Musée Magnin,** in a 17th-century mansion, showcases original furnishings and a variety of paintings from the 16th to the 19th centuries. ✉ *4 rue des Bons-Enfants,* ☎ *03–80–67–11–10.* 🎟 *15 frs.* ⏲ *June–Sept., Tues.–Sun. 10–6; Oct.–May, Tues.–Sun. 10–noon and 2–6.*

37 The **Cathédrale St-Bénigne** is comparatively austere; its chief glory is the 10th-century crypt—a forest of pillars surmounted by a rotunda. ✉ *pl. St-Bénigne.*

38 The **Musée Archéologique** (Archaeological Museum), housed in the former abbey buildings of St-Bénigne, traces the history of the region through archaeological discoveries. ✉ *5 rue du Dr-Maret,* ☎ *03–80–30–88–54.* 🎟 *11 frs.* ⏲ *June–Sept., Wed.–Mon. 9:30–6; Oct.–May, Wed.–Mon. 9–12 and 2–6.*

39 The **Musée d'Art Sacré,** devoted to religious art, has a collection of sculpture and altarpieces in the appropriate setting of a former church. ✉ *17 rue Ste-Anne,* ☎ *03–80–30–65–91.* 🎟 *8 frs.* ⏲ *Wed.–Mon. 9–noon and 2–6.*

40 The **Musée d'Histoire Naturelle** (Natural History Museum), sits behind the train station in an impressive botanical garden, the **Jardin de l'Arquebuse,** where it's pleasant to stroll amid the wide variety of trees and tropical flowers. ✉ *1 av. Albert I,* ☎ *03–80–76–82–76 museum, 03–80–76–82–84 gardens.* 🎟 *Museum 11 frs.* ⏲ *Museum: Wed.–Mon. 9–noon and 2–6; gardens: daily 7:30–6 (8 PM in summer).*

More links with Dijon's medieval past can be found west of the town center, just off the avenue Albert I beyond the train station. Keep an

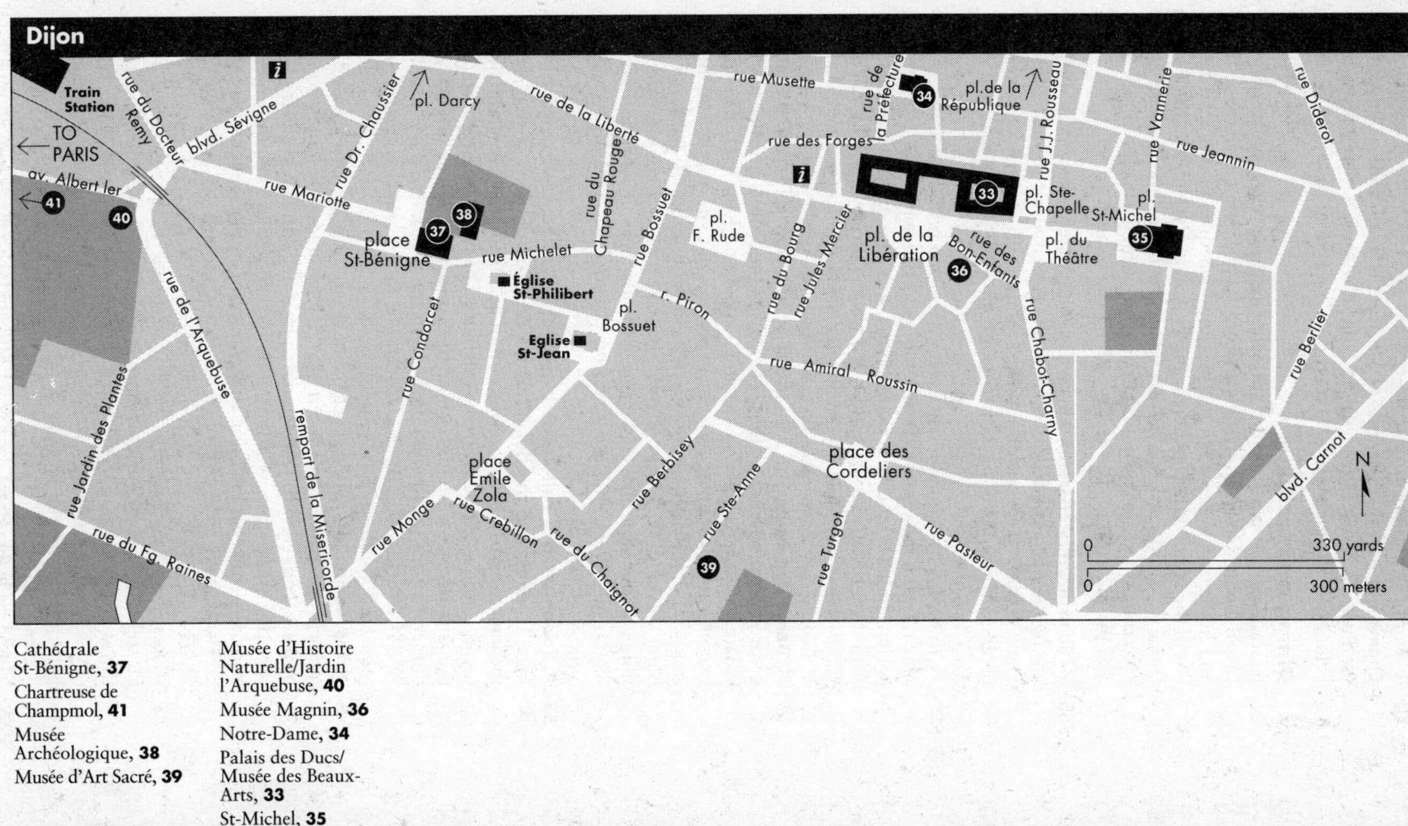

Cathédrale St-Bénigne, **37**

Chartreuse de Champmol, **41**

Musée Archéologique, **38**

Musée d'Art Sacré, **39**

Musée d'Histoire Naturelle/Jardin l'Arquebuse, **40**

Musée Magnin, **36**

Notre-Dame, **34**

Palais des Ducs/ Musée des Beaux-Arts, **33**

St-Michel, **35**

41 eye out for the exuberant 15th-century gateway to the **Chartreuse de Champmol**—all that remains of a former charter house. Next to it is the **Puits de Moïse**, the so-called Well of Moses, with six large, compellingly realistic medieval statues on a hexagonal base (1395–1405).

Dining and Lodging

Restaurants abound in Dijon but there are three very popular areas for casual dining. One is around place Darcy, a square that caters to all tastes and budgets: Choose from the bustling Concorde brasserie, the quiet bar of the Hôtel de la Cloche, the underground Caveau de la Porte Guillaume wine-and-snack bar, or—for your sweet tooth—the Pâtisserie Darcy. Two other areas for casual dining in the evening are place Émile Zola and the old market (Les Halles), along rue Bannelier.

$$$ ✕ **Central Grill Rôtisserie.** This grill room, attached to the Central Ibis (☞ *below*), is a good alternative to the gastronomic sophistication of Dijon. There's carpaccio and smoked salmon in addition to heavier *abats* (organ meats). ⊠ *3 pl. Grangier,* ☎ *03–80–30–44–00. AE, DC, MC, V. Closed Sun.*

$$–$$$ ✕ **Thibert.** The refined menu at this Art Deco restaurant changes regularly, but cabbage stuffed with snails, prawns with peas, truffles, and sorbets in black-and-white chocolate figure among the tours de force. And it represents remarkable value for the money. ⊠ *10 pl. Wilson,* ☎ *03–80–67–74–64. Reservations essential. Jacket and tie. AE, MC, V. Closed Sun., and early Jan. and Aug. No lunch Mon.*

$$ ✕ **Dame Aquitaine.** In a happy marriage between two of France's greatest gastronomic regions, chef Monique Saléra and her husband create a wonderful blend of regional cuisines. The foie gras and duck, in confit or with cèpes, come from Saléra's native Pau; the coq au vin, snails, and *lapin à la moutarde* (rabbit with mustard) from her husband's Burgundy. The moderate prix-fixe menus are good value; the dining room, in a medieval crypt, is atmospheric. ⊠ *23 pl. Boussuet,* ☎ *03–80–30–45–65. Reservations essential. AE, DC, MC, V. Closed Sun. No lunch Mon.*

$$ ★ ✕ **Toison d'Or.** A collection of superbly restored 16th-century buildings, belonging to the Burgundian Company of Wine Tasters, forms the backdrop to this fine restaurant. It is lavishly furnished and quaint (candlelight is de rigueur in the evening). The food is sophisticated: Try the langoustines with ginger, and the nougat and honey dessert. After dinner visit the small wine museum in the cellar. ⊠ *18 rue Ste-Anne,* ☎ *03–80–30–73–52. AE, DC, MC, V. Reservations essential. Jacket required. No dinner Sun.*

$ ✕ **Les Moules Zola.** For mussel lovers, this is the place. Mussels and only mussels—prepared a half dozen ways, from traditional *moules marinière* (mussels cooked with white wine) to mussels with Dijon mustard—are served. Large picture windows look over the square and the ambience is jovial—conversation hums to the music of empty shells clattering into bowls as diners plough through mounds of mussels. ⊠ *3 pl. Émile Zola,* ☎ *03–80–58–93–26. Reservations essential. MC, V.*

$ ✕ **Restaurant du Sauvage.** Full of atmosphere, the restaurant in the Hostellerie du Sauvage (☞ *below*) serves a range of grilled meats and fish at under 100 francs for a three-course, prix-fixe menu. A huge chimney wall with fireplaces on either side separates the bar from the dining room. ⊠ *64 rue Monge,* ☎ *03–80–41–31–21. MC, V.*

$$$$ 🏨 **Phillipe le Bon Hôtel.** This hotel, affiliated with the Toison d'Or restaurant (☞ *above*), has moderately priced, smallish, modern, L-shape rooms. The ones overlooking the courtyard garden are so wonderfully quiet that you'd never know you were sleeping in a provincial capital. ⊠ *18*

rue Ste-Anne, 21000, ☎ 03–80–30–73–52, FAX 03–80–30–95–51. 27 rooms with bath or shower. AE, DC, MC, V.

$$$ **Chapeau Rouge.** Off the maze of corridors within the venerable, thick stone walls of this hotel near the cathedral are rooms with old-fashioned furniture. Try to avoid the twin beds—they are narrow and short. The restaurant, renowned as a haven of classic regional cuisine, serves snails cooked in basil and stuffed pigeon. The staff and the owner, Patrick Lagrange, are attentive. ✉ *5 rue Michelet, 21000, ☎ 03–80–30–28–10, FAX 03–80–30–33–89. 29 rooms. Restaurant, bar. AE, DC, MC, V.*

$$ **Central Ibis.** This central, old, established hotel, now part of a national chain, offers comfort in excess of price. Rooms are ordinary yet clean. ✉ *3 pl. Grangier, 21000, ☎ 03–80–30–44–00, FAX 03–80–30–77–12. 90 rooms, 65 with bath, 25 with shower. Restaurant, air-conditioning. AE, DC, MC, V.*

$$ **Hôtel Wilson.** This hotel in a 17th-century post house is connected by a walkway to the Thibert restaurant (☞ *above*). Rooms are modern and comfortable. ✉ *1 rue Longvic 21000, ☎ 03–80–66–82–50, FAX 03–80–36–41–54. 27 rooms with bath or shower. AE, MC. V.*

$ **Hostellerie du Sauvage.** This small, quiet hotel in a courtyard off a busy street in the old quarter is a real find. Its old-fashioned rooms, though far from stylish, face the quiet courtyard. ✉ *64 rue Monge, 21000, ☎ 03–80–41–31–21, FAX 03–80–42–06–07. 23 rooms with bath or shower. Restaurant, bar, parking (fee). MC, V.*

Nightlife and the Arts

BARS AND CLUBS

L'An Fer (✉ 8 rue Pierre-Marceau, ☎ 03–80–70–03–69) caters to a slightly youngish clientele. **Bahia Brazil** (✉ 39 rue des Godrans, ☎ 03–80–30–90–19), a piano bar, is pleasant for a romantic drink. **L'Endroit** (✉ Centre Dauphine, ☎ 03–80–30–60–63) is a popular Dijon disco. For a rather sedate nightclub ambience, try **L'Iceberg** (✉ 47 rue Devosge, 03–80–72–41–41). **Le Messire** (✉ 3 rue Jules-Mercier, ☎ 03–80–30–16–40) attracts a middle-age crowd.

FESTIVALS

Dijon stages **L'Été Musical,** a music festival in June and July with a little bit of everything; the tourist office (☞ *below*) can supply the details. For three days in June you'll encounter **Arts in the Streets** (☎ 03–80–65–91–00 for information), an event where several hundred painters exhibit their work, . During the **Bell-Ringing Festival** in mid-August, all the churches' bells chime to their own tune. In September, Dijon puts on the **Festival International de Folklore.** November in Dijon is the time for the **International Gastronomy Fair.**

Shopping

The auction houses in Dijon are good places to prospect for antiques and works of art. Tempting food items—mustard, snails, and candy (including chocolate snails—escargots de Bourgogne) can easily be found in the heart of Dijon's pedestrian streets.

En Route A31 connects Dijon to Beaune, 40 km (25 mi) south. But if you prefer a leisurely route through the vineyards, chug along D122, past venerable properties such as Gevrey-Chambertin, Chambolle-Musigny, and Morey-St-Denis, to Clos de Vougeot.

Clos de Vougeot

42 *17 km (11 mi) south of Dijon.*

The reason to come to Vougeot is to see its medieval castle. The **Château du Clos de Vougeot** was constructed by Cistercian monks in the 12th century and completed during the Renaissance; it's famous as the seat of Burgundy's elite company of wine lovers, the Confrérie des Chevaliers du Tastevin, who gather here in November at the start of an annual three-day festival, Les Trois Glorieuses. You can admire the château's cellars, where ceremonies are held, and ogle the huge grape presses. ☎ *03–80–62–86–09.* *17 frs.* ⏲ *Apr.–Sept., weekdays and Sun. 9–7, Sat. 9–6:30; Oct.–Mar., weekdays and Sun. 9–11:30 and 2–5:30, Sat. 9–5.*

Dining and Lodging

$$$$ **Château de Gilly.** Formerly an abbey and a government-run cultural center, the château is now part of the Relais & Château chain. Vestiges of the abbey remain: painted ceilings and a vaulted wine cellar adorned with tapestries—today the dining room. Rooms are filled with good quality reproductions; size varies with price. The best, No. 46, has a sitting room and a view of the circular pool. The menu includes classical Bourgogne dishes—coq au vin and Charolais—and contemporary French cooking—coquilles St-Jacques on a bed of tomato puree. Refinement is demanded—cards are left in rooms requesting "an elegant form of dress" at dinner. ✉ *Gilly-les-Cîteaux, 21640,* ☎ *03–80–62–89–98,* FAX *03–80–62–82–34. 47 rooms. Restaurant, pool, 2 tennis courts, meeting rooms. AE, DC, MC, V.*

En Route Wine has been made in **Nuits-St-Georges,** south of Clos de Vougeot and north of Beaune since Roman times; its "dry, tonic, and generous qualities" were recommended to Louis XIV for medicinal use.

Beaune

43 *26 km (16 mi) south of Vougeot, 40 km (25 mi) south of Dijon, 315 km (197 mi) southeast of Paris.*

Despite the hordes of tourists, Beaune remains one of the most attractive French provincial towns. Some of the region's finest vineyards are ★ owned by the **Hospices de Beaune** (also known as the Hôtel Dieu), founded in 1443 as a hospital. A visit to the Hospices (across from the city's tourist office) is one of the highlights of a stay in Beaune; its gorgeous tiled roofs have become an icon of Burgundy, and in fact the same glowing colors and intricate patterns are seen throughout the region. The Hospices carried on its medical activities until 1971, its nurses still wearing their strange medieval uniforms, and its history is retraced in the museum, whose wide-ranging collections contain some weird and wonderful medical instruments of the 15th century. You can also see a collection of tapestries, including Rogier Van der Weyden's stirringly composed medieval Flemish masterpiece, *The Last Judgment.* A son-et-lumière show is presented every evening from April to mid-November. ✉ *rue de l'Hôtel-Dieu,* ☎ *03–80–24–45–00.* *32 frs.* ⏲ *Apr.–mid-Nov., daily 9–6:30; mid-Nov.–Mar., daily 9–11:30 and 2–5:30.*

A good series of tapestries, relating the life of the Virgin, can be admired in Beaune's main church, the 12th-century **Collégiale Notre-Dame.** ✉ *Just off av. de la République.*

There are few more delightful experiences than a visit to the candlelit cellars of the **Marché aux Vins.** Here—for the price of admission—you can taste as many of the regional wines as you wish, beginning with whites and fruity Beaujolais and ending with such big reds as Gevrey-Chambertin. The new collection of Grands Vins des Hospices de Beaune has now been added to the list. ✉ *7 rue Nicolas Rolin,* ☎ *03–80–22–27–69 or 03–80–22–25–68.* *Entry and tasting: 50* *frs.* ⏲ *Easter–3rd weekend in Nov., daily 9:30–noon and 2:30–6:30; late Nov.–Easter, daily 9:30–noon and 2:30–6.*

Dining and Lodging

$$ ✕ **Auberge St-Vincent.** The best thing about this restaurant is that it's opposite the Hospices. Not surprisingly, it pulls in as many tourists as locals. Though the cuisine and ambience are undistinguished, the grilled lobster tails flambéed with whiskey is quite a show. Service is attentive and the wine list lengthy, but order carefully, or the meal becomes expensive. Good choices are the *daurade* (sea bream) in a mille-feuille shell and the roast lamb. ✉ *pl. de la Halle,* ☎ *03–80–22–42–34. Reservations essential. AE, DC, MC, V.*

$$ ✕ **L'Écusson.** Don't be put off by its unprepossessing exterior. This is a comfortable, friendly, thick-carpeted restaurant with good value, prix-fixe menus. Showcased is chef Jean-Pierre Senelet's sure-footed culinary mastery in dishes like duck sweetbreads with ham and spinach, and rabbit terrine with tarragon. ✉ *pl. Malmédy,* ☎ *03–80–24–03–82. Reservations essential. AE, DC, MC, V. Closed Sun. and Feb.*

$–$$ ✕ **Le Gourmandin.** In the center of Beaune, this no-nonsense restaurant serves regional fare—beef Bourguignon and *tourte de canard* (duck pie)—and a good range of wines from small vineyards. The decor is simple, in the style of a 1930s café, with black and white table tops and art posters on the walls. Seating in front is tight. ✉ *8 pl. Carnot,* ☎ *03–80–24–07–88. Closed Wed., late Dec.–early Jan. No dinner Tues.*

$–$$ ★ ✕ **La Grilladine.** Chef Pierre Lenko's cuisine, though not elaborate, is good, hearty Burgundy fare: beef Bourguignon and oeufs en meurette. The prix-fixe menus are extremely reasonable. The ambience is warm and cheerful: rose-pink tablecloths, exposed stone walls, and an ancient beam supporting the ceiling. One room is for non-smokers. ✉ *17 rue Maufoux,* ☎ *03–80–22–22–36. Reservations essential. MC, V. Closed Mon., and end Nov.–mid-Dec.*

$$$$ ★ ✕🏨 **Hostellerie de Levernois.** The Crotet's marvelous hotel-restaurant gleams with light from its large picture windows. Rooms are traditionally furnished and have a comfortably elegant bourgeois feel; those in the modern building in the landscaped garden are done in natural wood and warm pastels. In the kitchen, Jean works with his son, Christophe, who has a more "nouvelle" approach. The combination makes for one of the most exciting dining rooms in Burgundy. Meals are occasions to be savored, but they are also expensive; menus begin at 380 francs (200 francs at lunch). ✉ *rte. de Verdun-sur-le-Doubs, Levernois, 21200, (10 km/6 mi east of Beaune),* ☎ *03–80–24–73–58,* FAX *03–80–22–78–00. 14 rooms. Restaurant. AE, DC, MC, V. Closed last 2 wks of Dec.*

$$$–$$$$ ✕🏨 **Lameloise.** This small hotel on the outskirts of Chagny, south of Beaune, may be the only Relais & Châteaux property to stock crayons for kids. But don't be misled: the clientele is well-heeled. Rooms are fresh and deluxe, with token rustic touches. Confident and consistent, chef-owner Jacques Lameloise cooks luxurious, but not stuffy dishes—scallops in black olive juice or veal kidney in shallot puree. ✉ *36 pl. d'Armes, 71150 Chagny (14 km/9 mi south of Beaune),* ☎ *03–85–87–08–85,* FAX *03–85–87–03–57. 8 rooms. Restaurant. AE, MC, V. Closed late Dec.–late Jan.*

$$ ✕🏨 **Central.** A well-run establishment with several modernized rooms, the Central lives up to its name. The stone-walled restaurant is cozy—some might say cramped—and the consistently good cuisine is popular with locals, who come to enjoy oeufs en meurette and coq au vin. Service is efficient, if a little hurried. The evening meal is obligatory in

July and August. ✉ *2 rue Victor-Millot, 21200,* ☎ *03–80–24–77–24,* FAX *03–80–22–30–40. 20 rooms with bath or shower. Restaurant. MC, V. Closed Dec.–Jan.*

$$$ ★ 🏨 **Le Cep.** A five-minute walk from the main square, Beaune's top hotel has large rooms tastefully furnished with antiques. It is a combination of several ancient town houses—the oldest circa 1547—whose courtyards have been made into a small garden. The ground-floor rooms have exposed wood beams. Choose one facing the courtyard, such as No. 303. Service is efficient, if a little curt, and can be harried when tour groups check in and out. ✉ *27 rue Maufoux, 21200,* ☎ *03–80–22–35–48,* FAX *03–80–22–76–80. 63 rooms with bath or shower. Restaurant. AE, DC, MC, V.*

$$$ 🏨 **La Poste.** The front rooms of this French provincial hotel look over ramparts and the rear ones look over vineyards. Inspect the room before accepting it—some (Room 205, for example) are not as good as others. The long, narrow restaurant breathes tradition. The setting compensates somewhat for the uninventive cuisine, as does the fabulous wine list. Service is briskly professional. ✉ *1 bd. Clemenceau, 21200,* ☎ *03–80–22–08–11,* FAX *03–80–24–19–71. 21 rooms, 9 suites.. Restaurant. AE, DC, MC, V. Closed winter.*

$$–$$$ 🏨 **Château de Chorey-les-Beaune.** To really soak up the flavor of the vineyards, stay at the Germain family's winery and B&B 1½ km (1 mi) north of Beaune. Guest rooms are up a circular, stone staircase; furnishings are from the attic. Though it's a bit rustic and casual, it's the kind of place where you can open the windows and let the country air, perfumed by grapes, waft in. A good breakfast is served, but no dinner; you may have a chance to try their wine before going out to eat in Beaune. ✉ *21200 Chorey-les-Beaune,* ☎ *03–80–22–06–05,* FAX *03–80–24–03–93. 7 rooms. Breakfast room. MC, V. Closed Dec.–Apr.*

$$ 🏨 **Hôtel de la Cloche.** In the heart of town, this hotel in a 15th-century residence has neatly furnished rooms decorated with care and attention by the owners, M. and Mme. Lamy, both of whom are always on hand to assist you. The best rooms, those with a full bath, are more expensive; the smaller, delightful attic rooms with a shower and separate toilet are less. Breakfast is served on the garden terrace in summer. ✉ *40–42 rue du Faubourg-Madeleine, 21200,* ☎ *03–80–24–66–33,* FAX *03–80–24–04–24. 22 rooms with bath or shower. Restaurant. MC, V.*

Nightlife and the Arts

In July, Beaune celebrates its annual **International Festival of Baroque Music,** which draws big stars of the music world. Beaune's famous wine festival, **Les Trois Glorieuses,** is held on the third Sunday in November at the Hospices.

Chalon-sur-Saône

44 *29 km (18 mi) south of Beaune, 127 km (79 mi) north of Lyon.*

Chalon-sur-Saône has its medieval heart near the **Église St-Vincent**—a former cathedral displaying a jumble of styles—close to the banks of the River Saône. This area was reconstructed to have an Old World charm, but the rest of Chalon is a modern, commercial, cosmopolitan city—the cultural and shopping center of southern Burgundy. Chalon is the birthplace of Nicéphore Niepce (1765–1833), whose early experiments, developed further by Jacques Daguerre, qualify him as the father of photography.

The **Musée Nicéphore Niepce,** occupying an 18th-century house overlooking the Saône, retraces the early history of photography and motion pictures with the help of some pioneering equipment. It also includes a selection of contemporary photographic work and a lunar camera used during the U.S. Apollo program. But the star of the museum is the primitive camera used to take the first photographs in 1816. ✉ *20 quai des Messageries,* ☎ *03–85–48–41–98.* 🎟 *10 frs (free Wed.).* ⏲ *Sept.–June, Wed.–Mon. 9:30–11:30 and 2:30–5:30; July–Aug., Wed.–Mon. 10–6.*

Dining and Lodging

$$–$$$ ★ **Moulin d'Hautrive.** In every room of this comfortable hotel—once a mill, built by Cistercian monks in the 12th century—in the country north of Chalon-sur-Saône and south of Beaune, you'll find blackened ancient beams. Rooms are filled with antiques and bric-a-brac. The restaurant's four-course, 240-franc menu may include sautéed foie gras, adequate *maigret de canard* (duck breast), and a delicious salad with *bleu bresse* (blue cheese). The restaurant is closed Monday and Tuesday. ✉ *Hameau de Chaublanc, 71350 St-Gervais-en-Vallière (28 km/17 mi from Chalon, 14 km/9 mi from Beaune),* ☎ *03–85–91–55–56,* FAX *03–85–91–89–65. 22 rooms. Restaurant, pool, tennis court. Closed Jan.*

$$ **St-Georges.** Close to the train station and town center, the friendly, white-walled St-Georges hotel is tastefully modernized and has many spacious rooms. Its cozy restaurant is known locally for its efficient service and menus of outstanding value. You can't go wrong with the duck in white pepper, foie gras with truffles, or roast pigeon. ✉ *32 av. Jean-Jaurès, 71100,* ☎ *03–85–48–27–05,* FAX *03–85–93–23–88. 48 rooms with bath or shower. Restaurant. AE, DC, MC, V.*

Tournus

45 *24 km (15 mi) south of Chalon-sur-Saône, 35 km (22 mi) north of Mâcon.*

Tournus, which retains much of the charm of the Middle Ages and the Renaissance, contains one of Burgundy's most spectacular and best-preserved Romanesque buildings. The abbey church of **St-Philibert,** despite its massiveness—unadorned cylindrical pillars more than 4 feet thick support the nave—is spacious and light. No effort was made to decorate or embellish the interior, whose sole hint of frivolity is the alternating red and white stones in the nave arches. The crypt and former abbey buildings, including the cloister and magnificent 12th-century refectory, can also be visited.

Dining and Lodging

$$ ★ **Aux Terrasses.** For a most enjoyable meal that takes advantage of the region's products at reasonable prices, try Chef Pariaut's light version of classic Burgundian cuisine: coq au vin, escargots in garlic butter, and *poulet Bresse* (chicken roasted with wine sauce). Desserts are simple but good. Many French, German, and Dutch travelers stop here for dinner and a night's rest. Rooms are reasonably large, comfortable, and each decorated differently in muted tones. ✉ *18 av. du 23-Janvier, 71700,* ☎ *03–85–51–01–74,* FAX *03–85–51–09–99. 30 rooms. Restaurant. MC, V. Closed early Jan.–early Feb.*

$$ **Le Rempart.** This hotel has adequate rooms that are modern, functional, and fresh in appearance. Double-glazed windows keep out traffic noise. At the "gastronomic" restaurant, prix-fixe dinners begin at 155 francs, and the cooking, though competently prepared by chef Daniel Rogie, doesn't live up to its reputation; you may wish to dine elsewhere. ✉ *2 av. Gambetta, 71700,* ☎ *03–85–51–10–56,* FAX *03–*

85–40–77–22. 32 rooms, 6 suites. Restaurant, bar, air-conditioning. AE, DC, MC, V.

$ ✕🏨 **Le Coq d'Or.** For inexpensive prix-fixe menus, this cheerful hotel-restaurant is just the spot. Many dishes are cooked on an open-hearth grill, and the exposed beams, peach tablecloths, and friendly service contribute to its cozy gaiety. The traditional fare is reliable, from onion soup and steak to poulet Bresse and fruit tarts. Rooms are bare-bones but clean. The best one is No. 8, at the quiet back of the building. ✉ *1 rue Pasteur, 71700,* ☎ *03–85–51–35–91. 6 rooms. Restaurant. MC, V.*

En Route The best way to reach Cluny from Tournus is to use picturesque D14. You'll pass the fortified hilltop town of **Brancion,** with its old castle and soaring keep before turning left at Cormatin.

Cluny

46 *33 km (20 mi) southwest of Tournus, 50 km (31 mi) south of Chalon-sur-Saône, 26 km (16 mi) northwest of Mâcon.*

The village of Cluny is famous for its medieval abbey, which was once the center of a vast Christian empire and is now a tourist mecca. Founded in the 10th century, the **Ancienne Abbaye** was the biggest church in Europe until the 16th century, when Michelangelo built St. Peter's in Rome. Cluny's medieval abbots were as powerful as popes; in 1098, Pope Urban II (himself a Cluniac) assured the head of his old abbey that Cluny was the "light of the world." That assertion, of dubious religious validity, has not stood the test of time, and today Cluny stands in ruins—a reminder of the limits of human grandeur.

The ruins nonetheless suggest the size and glory of the abbey at its zenith. Only the **Clocher de l'Eau-Bénite** (a majestic bell tower) and the right arms of the two transepts, climbing 100 feet above the ground, remain. The 13th-century **farinier** (flour mill), with its fine chestnut roof and collection of statues, can also be seen. The gardens contain an ancient lime tree, reputedly several hundred years old, named Abélard, after the controversial philosopher, who sought shelter at the abbey in 1142. A small **museum** displays religious paintings, sculptures rescued from demolished portions of the abbey, and the remains of the *bibliothèque des moines* (monks' library). ☎ *03–85–59–12–79.* 🎫 *33 frs, museum only: 15 frs.* ⏲ *Nov.–Mar., daily 10:30–11:30 and 2–4; Apr.–June, daily 9:30–noon and 2–6; July–Sept., daily 9–7; Oct., daily 10–noon and 2–5. Museum closed Tues.*

Dining and Lodging

$$–$$$ ✕🏨 **Bourgogne.** There's no better place to get into Cluny's medieval mood than the Bourgogne. The old-fashioned hotel building, dating from 1817, stands where other parts of the abbey used to be. There is a small garden and an atmospheric restaurant with sober pink decor and comfortable, if slightly stodgy, cuisine: foie gras, snails, and the more exotic fish with ginger. The evening meal is mandatory in July and August. ✉ *pl. de l'Abbaye, 71250,* ☎ *03–85–59–00–58,* FAX *03–85–59–03–73. 14 rooms. Restaurant. AE, DC, V. Closed mid-Nov.–early Mar.*

$–$$ ✕🏨 **Hôtel de l'Abbaye.** This modest hotel is five minutes' walk from the center of the village. The three rooms to the right of the dining room are the most recently decorated and the best value. The restaurant serves rich, hearty local fare that's less elaborate than at the Bourgogne, but better (according to the chef, who did his training there): Try the chicken fricassee in a white Mâcon sauce or the confit of rabbit. The prix-fixe menus are very reasonable. ✉ *av. Charles-de-Gaulle, 71250,*

☏ 03–85–59–11–14, FAX 03–85–59–09–76. 16 rooms, 9 with bath. Restaurant. MC, V. Closed Jan.–mid-Feb.

Nightlife and the Arts

The ruined abbey of Cluny forms the backdrop of the **Grandes Heures de Cluny** (☏ 03–85–59–05–34 for details), a classical music festival in August.

En Route On the road (D980/N79) between Cluny and Mâcon, stop just as you leave town to admire the giant rocky outcrop of **Solutré** on your right, towering above the vineyard of Pouilly-Fuissé, renowned for its white wine. Excavations around the Rock of Solutré have revealed the presence of prehistoric man—and prehistoric horse (so many horses, in fact, that one school of thought asserts that the poor beasts were driven over the top of the cliff to crash to their death below).

Mâcon

47 *25 km (16 mi) southeast of Cluny, 58 km (36 mi) south of Chalon-sur-Saône, 69 km (43 mi) north of Lyon.*

Mâcon is a bustling town, best known for its wine fair in May and for its pesky stone bridge across the Saône, whose low arches are a headache for the pilots of large river barges. The Romantic poet Alphonse de Lamartine (1790–1869) was born in Mâcon. The two octagonal towers of the ruined **Cathédrale de St-Vincent** loom over the wide quays along the river in the old part of town. The upper story of the **Maison du Bois,** an ancient timbered house near the cathedral, leans out over the street.

BURGUNDY A TO Z

Arriving and Departing

By Car

The A6 expressway heads southeast from Paris through Burgundy, passing Sens, Auxerre, Chablis, Avallon, Beaune, and Mâcon before continuing on to Lyon and the south. A38 leads from A6 to Dijon, 290 km (180 mi) southeast of Paris; the trip takes 2½ hours. If you have more time, take N6 to Sens, just 120 km (75 mi) southeast of Paris; then continue southeast.

By Plane

Dijon has Burgundy's only commercial passenger airport (☏ 03–80–67–67–67), which serves domestic flights on Air Inter between Paris and Lyon.

By Train

The TGV zip out of Paris (Gare de Lyon) to Dijon (75 minutes), Mâcon (100 minutes), and on to Lyon (2 hours). Trains run frequently, though the fastest Paris–Lyon trains do not stop at Dijon or go anywhere near it. A cross-country service links Dijon to Reims (320 km/200 mi) in 3½ hours. Sens is on a mainline route from Paris (45 minutes).

Getting Around

By Car

Burgundy is best visited by car because its meandering country roads invite leisurely exploration. A6 is the main autoroute through the region; N6 is a slower, prettier option. A38 provides a quick link between A6 and Dijon; A31 heads down from Dijon to Beaune (45 km/27 mi). Other smaller roads lead off the main routes to the little villages.

By Train

Train travel is unrewarding, especially since the infrequent cross-country trains chug along at the legendary speed of a Burgundian snail. You'll invariably have to change trains at La Roche-Migenne for Avallon, Auxerre, Clamecy, and Autun and at Dijon for Beaune.

Contacts and Resources

Car Rental

Avis (✉ 5 av. Foch, Dijon, ☎ 03–80–43–60–76). **Hertz** (✉ 18 bis av. Foch, Dijon, ☎ 03–80–43–55–22). **Europcar** (✉ 47 rue Guillaume-Tell, Dijon, ☎ 03–80–43–28–44).

Guided Tours

For general information on tours in Burgundy, write to the regional tourist office, the **Comité Régional du Tourisme** (✉ 12 bd. Brosses, 21000 Dijon). Tours of the old part of Beaune with a guide and a wine tasting at the city's oldest wine company can be arranged in advance through the **Beaune Tourist Office** (✉ rue de l'Hôtel-Dieu, ☎ 03–60–26–31–30).

Gastronomic weekends, including wine tastings, are organized by **Bourgogne Tour** (✉ 11 rue de la Liberté, 21000 Dijon, ☎ 03–80–30–49–49). Details about recommended bike routes and where to rent bicycles (train stations are a good bet) can be found at most **tourist offices. La Peurtantaine** (✉ Accueil Morvan Environment, École du Bourg, 71550 Anost, ☎ 03–85–82–77–74) arranges bicycle tours of Burgundy. In summer, **Air Escargot** (✉ 71150 Remigny, ☎ 03–85–87–12–30) arranges hot-air balloon rides over the countryside.

Travel Agencies

Air France (✉ 29 pl. Darcy, Dijon, ☎ 03–80–42–89–90). **Wagons-Lits** (✉ 8 av. du Maréchal-Foch, Dijon, ☎ 03–80–45–26–26).

Visitor Information

Principal regional tourist offices: **Dijon** (✉ 29 pl. Darcy, close to the cathedral, ☎ 03–80–45–15–84). **Auxerre** (✉ 1 quai de la République, ☎ 03–86–52–06–19). **Mâcon** (✉ 187 rue Carnot, ☎ 03–85–39–71–37). Addresses of other tourist offices in towns mentioned in this chapter: **Autun** (✉ 3 av. Charles-de-Gaulle, ☎ 03–85–52–20–34). **Avallon** (✉ 4 rue Bocquillot, ☎ 03–80–26–21–30). **Beaune** (✉ rue de l'Hôtel-Dieu, ☎ 03–80–26–31–30). **Clamecy** (✉ rue du Grand-Marché, ☎ 03–86–27–02–51). **Cluny** (✉ 6 rue Mercière, ☎ 03–85–59–05–34). **Sens** (✉ pl. Jean-Jaurès, ☎ 03–86–65–19–49). **Troyes** (✉ 16 bd. Carnot, ☎ 03–25–82–62–70 and rue Mignard, ☎ 03–25–73–36–88). **Vézelay** (✉ rue St-Pierre, ☎ 03–86–33–23–69).

10 Lyon and the Alps

Beaujolais and the Rhône Valley

In this diverse region, earthly pleasures have been perfected and chefs rival their Parisian counterparts. You can ski in the shadow of Mont Blanc, hike along trails over Alpine slopes, sail across Lake Annecy, and enjoy the urban sophistication and cultural treasures of Lyon. A visit to the Roman sites and medieval towns will remind you of other eras, and a trip along the Beaujolais Wine Road will show you what the region has to offer today.

Updated by Nigel Fisher

IT'S HARD TO PIN A NAME ON THIS PART of east-central France. The government solution, "Lyon-Rhône-Alpes," although hardly poetic, at least covers the features: grand Lyon, the broad Rhône valley, and the towering Alps on the Swiss-Italian frontiers. Despite the region's expressways and high-speed train lines, the pace is far from frenzied. The only city apart from Lyon is Grenoble, majestic in the foothills of the Alps.

Lyon has some of France's best cooking, best museums, and best theater. Small timeless villages dot the area—medieval hilltop retreats and tranquil valley communities. Roman ruins are found along the Rhône and remains of prehistoric man in the Alps, which themselves provide some of the world's best skiing, not to mention Western Europe's highest mountain, Mont Blanc.

Pleasures and Pastimes

Dining

Food lovers around the world celebrate Lyon's cuisine. Robust specialties like *saveloy* (sausage) and quenelles (poached fish dumplings) appear on tables in restaurants from elegant on down. Traditional *bouchons* (taverns) with homey wooden benches, zinc counters, and paper tablecloths serve salads, pork products like garlicky *rosette* sausage, and sturdy main courses such as tripe, veal stew, and andouillette (chitterling sausage). The Dombes is rich in game and fowl; the chicken is famous, especially *poulet de Bresse,* usually cooked with cream. Thrush, partridge, and hare star along the Rhône. Local cheeses include St-Marcellin, Roquefort, Beaufort, Tomme, and goat's-milk Cabecou. Privas has its marrons glacés, Montélimar its nougats. Alpine rivers and lakes teem with pike and trout. In the Alps, try a raclette, melted cheese over potatoes. Mountain herbs yield tangy, dark Suédois, sweet green Chartreuse, and bittersweet Suze (made from gentian).

CATEGORY	COST*
$$$$	over 400 frs
$$$	250 frs–400 frs
$$	125 frs–250 frs
$	under 125 frs

**per person for a three-course meal, including tax (20.6%) and tip but not wine*

Lodging

Hotels and inns abound. Many expect you to have your evening meal there, especially in summer. In winter, Alpine travelers must take *demi-pension,* with two meals, or *pension complète,* with three.

CATEGORY	COST*
$$$$	over 800 frs
$$$	550 frs–800 frs
$$	300 frs–550 frs
$	under 300 frs

**All prices are for a standard double room for two, including tax (20.6%) and service charge.*

Skiing

The famous ski venue is Chamonix. Chic, expensive Megève, Courcheval, and fashionable Méribel are also world-class. Val d'Isère is one of Europe's poshest. Nearby Tignes and novice-friendly Morzine are also good bets. L'Alpe d'Huez is near Grenoble, and Serre-Chevalier is linked by cable car to Briançon. The ski season lasts from December through April.

Exploring Lyon and the Alps

East-central France can be divided into two areas: the Alps and "not the Alps." The second group includes Lyon, the country's second city, a magnet for the surrounding region, including the vineyards of Beaujolais; and the area south of Lyon, dominated by the mighty Rhône as it flows toward the Mediterranean.

Great Itineraries

As you plan your trip, remember that you can whip along the autoroutes. But on smaller roads and in the Alps, don't make your daily itineraries too ambitious.

Numbers in the text correspond to numbers in the margin and on Lyon and the Alps and Lyon maps.

IF YOU HAVE 3 DAYS

Concentrate on **Lyon** ①–㉓, but take a day to head down the Rhône to see the Roman ruins in **Vienne** ㉚.

IF YOU HAVE 6 DAYS

Stay in **Lyon** ①–㉓ for two days. If you love wine, leave a day early to travel up the Saône valley, through the villages along the **Beaujolais Wine Road,** then head to **Bourg-en-Bresse** ㉗ or medieval **Pérouges** ㉙ for the night. On day three, make **Annecy** ㊷, with its medieval old town, your destination; be sure to drive around the lake to lovely **Talloires;** stay in either one. The next day, travel along the narrow roads that connect small villages via mountain passes in the Alps. Stop in the fashionable mountain resort town of **Megève** ㊻, before you relish the drive to elegant **Chambéry** ㊵. On day five, visit the abbey of **Grande Chartreuse** ㊴; then either go to **Grenoble** ㊳ to see the Grenoble Museum's fabulous collection or zip, via autoroute, to **Valence** ㉟ to view the old town's cathedral and art museum. The next day drive through the spectacular Gorges Ardèche, if you are heading for Provence, and stop in **Privas** ㊱. Or return to Lyon via **Montélimar** ㊲, with a stop along the way at **Vienne** ㉚ to see the Roman sites.

IF YOU HAVE 8 DAYS

Spend three days in **Lyon** ①–㉓ and another in **Bourg-en-Bresse** ㉗ or **Pérouges** ㉙. On day five, head south to **Vienne** ㉚, then continue on for an early lunch in **Serrières** ㉛ on the riverbank or in old **Annonay** ㉝. Go as far as **Valence** ㉟, after seeing the château in **Tournon** ㉞ and the panoramic views near **St-Romain-de-Lerp.** Rise early on day six and speed to **Grenoble** ㊳; visit the **Grande Chartreuse** ㊴ abbey before lunch. In the afternoon explore **Aix-les-Bains** ㊶ and Lac du Bourget or **Annecy** ㊷ and its lake; spend the night or, if you are short on time, stay near **Chambéry** ㊵. On day seven, wake early to drive to **Thonon-les-Bains** ㊸ on Lac Léman, then take D902 to **Chamonix** ㊺ for the day's high point—a cable car trip with staggering Mont Blanc views. The next day head deep into the Alps via **Albertville** ㊼, site of the 1992 Winter Olympics, stopping briefly in the resort town of **Bourg-St-Maurice** ㊽, on your way to tackle D902, the high Route de l'Iséran pass (closed November to June). Continue south on D902, past Valloire and more scenery to historic **Briançon** ㊾. From here, over the Alps to Gap, you can pick up the Route Napoléon and drop down to the Riviera.

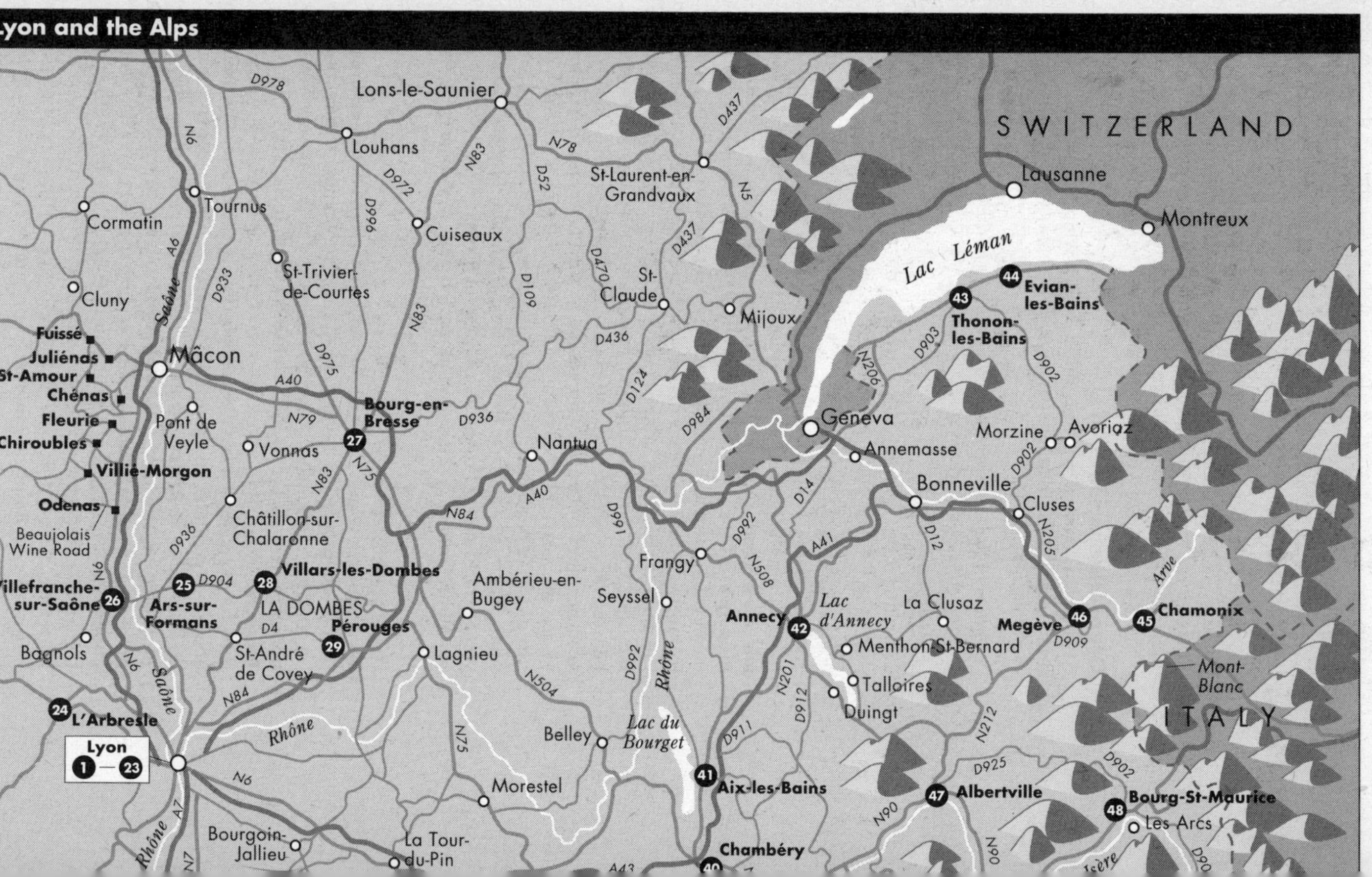
Lyon and the Alps
SWITZERLAND
ITALY
Lausanne
Montreux
Lac Léman
Evian-les-Bains
Thonon-les-Bains
Geneva
Annemasse
Morzine
Avoriaz
Bonneville
Cluses
Chamonix
Mont-Blanc
Megève
La Clusaz
Menthon-St-Bernard
Talloires
Duingt
Lac d'Annecy
Annecy
Albertville
Bourg-St-Maurice
Les Arcs
Aix-les-Bains
Chambéry
Lac du Bourget
Rhône
Arve
Isère
Frangy
Seyssel
Belley
Morestel
La Tour-du-Pin
Bourgoin-Jallieu
Lyon
Lagnieu
Ambérieu-en-Bugey
Nantua
St-Claude
Mijoux
St-Laurent-en-Grandvaux
Lons-le-Saunier
Louhans
Cuiseaux
St-Trivier-de-Courtes
Bourg-en-Bresse
Tournus
Cormatin
Cluny
Mâcon
Saône
Pont de Veyle
Vonnas
Châtillon-sur-Chalaronne
Villars-les-Dombes
LA DOMBES
Pérouges
St-André de Covey
Ars-sur-Formans
Villefranche-sur-Saône
Bagnols
L'Arbresle
Fuissé
Juliénas
St-Amour
Chénas
Fleurie
Chiroubles
Villié-Morgon
Odenas
Beaujolais Wine Road
A6
A7
A40
A41
A43
N5
N6
N7
N75
N78
N79
N83
N84
N90
N201
N205
N206
N212
N504
N508
D4
D12
D14
D52
D109
D124
D436
D437
D470
D902
D903
D904
D909
D911
D912
D925
D933
D936
D972
D975
D978
D984
D991
D992
D996
D90

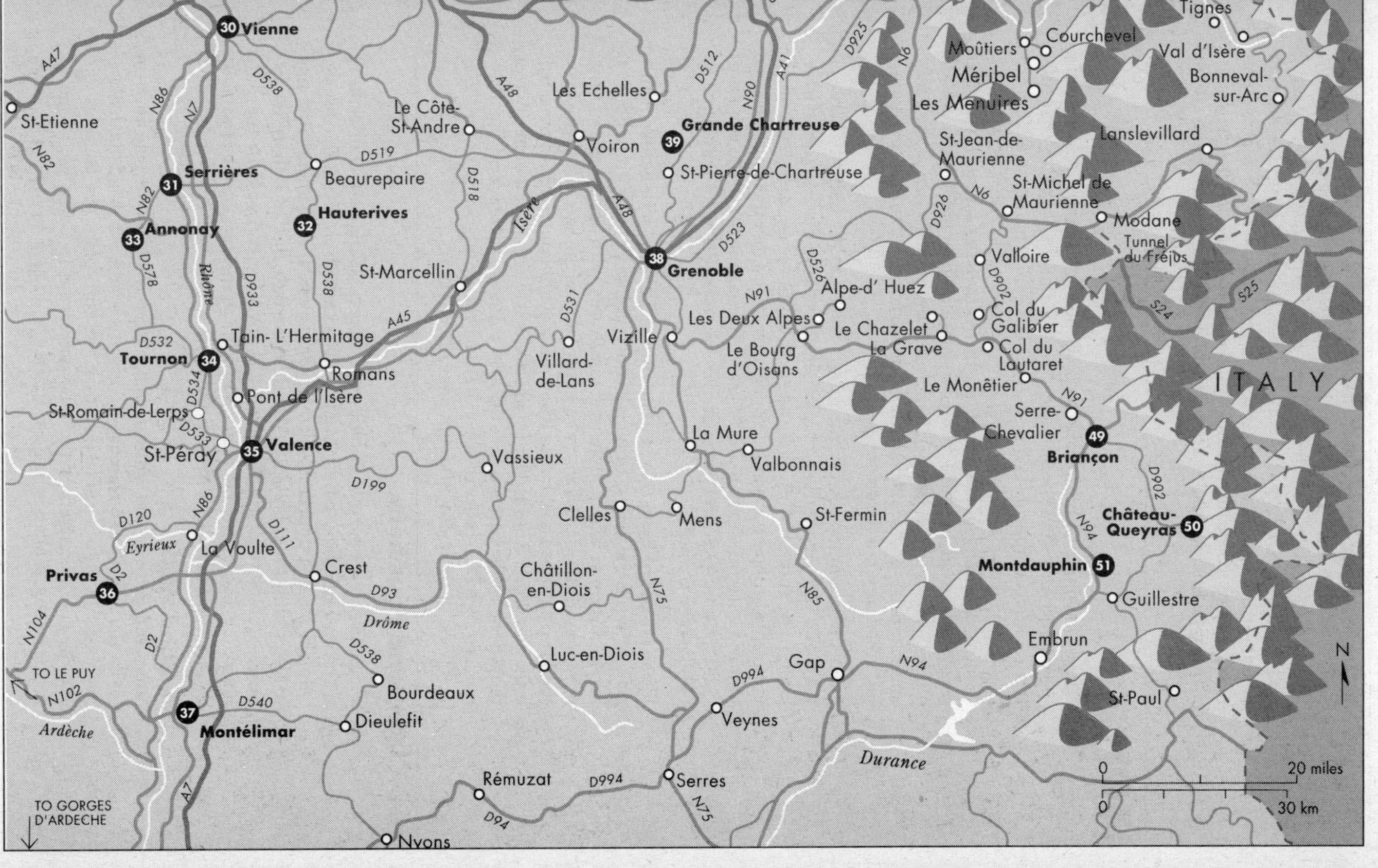
Vienne
30
St-Etienne
Le Côte-St-Andre
Les Echelles
Voiron
Grande Chartreuse
39
St-Pierre-de-Chartreuse
Moûtiers
Courchevel
Méribel
Les Menuires
Tignes
Val d'Isère
Bonneval-sur-Arc
Lanslevillard
St-Jean-de-Maurienne
St-Michel de Maurienne
Modane
Tunnel du Fréjus
Serrières
31
Beaurepaire
Hauterives
32
Annonay
33
Rhône
St-Marcellin
Isère
Grenoble
38
Valloire
Alpe-d' Huez
Col du Galibier
Col du Lautaret
Les Deux Alpes
Le Chazelet
La Grave
Le Bourg d'Oisans
Le Monêtier
ITALY
Tain- L'Hermitage
Tournon
34
Romans
Villard-de-Lans
Vizille
Pont de l'Isère
St-Romain-de-Lerps
St-Péray
Valence
35
Vassieux
La Mure
Valbonnais
Serre-Chevalier
Briançon
49
Clelles
Mens
St-Fermin
Château-Queyras
50
Eyrieux
La Voulte
Crest
Privas
36
Châtillon-en-Diois
Montdauphin
51
Guillestre
Drôme
Luc-en-Diois
Embrun
Gap
N
TO LE PUY
Bourdeaux
Veynes
St-Paul
Montélimar
37
Dieulefit
Ardèche
Durance
Rémuzat
Serres
0
20 miles
30 km
TO GORGES D'ARDECHE
Nyons
A47
A48
A41
A45
A7
N86
N7
N82
N90
N6
N91
N94
N85
N75
N104
N102
D538
D519
D518
D512
D925
D926
D523
D526
D902
D578
D933
D531
D532
D534
D533
D199
D120
D111
D93
D2
D540
D994
D94
S24
S25

When to Tour Lyon and the Alps

Summer is the time to hike, explore isolated villages, and ogle vistas in the Alps; in winter, the focus is snow and skiing. Avoid early spring and late autumn, when many hotels close. At lower altitudes, autumn is best—the lakes warm, the grape harvest underway. Winter is dreariest, despite the beauty in the crystal mist over the Rhône. Midsummer can be hot and sticky. Lyon, not at its best in August, has festivals in fall.

LYON

Lyon and Marseille both claim to be France's "second city." In terms of size and industrial importance, Marseille probably grabs that title. But for tourist appeal, Lyon, 462 km (287 mi) southeast of Paris, is the clear winner. It's easily accessible by car or by train. Its scale is human, with its historic buildings and quaint *traboules* (passageways under dwellings—used by the French Resistance during World War II to elude German street patrols). Its setting at the confluence of the Saône and Rhône is spectacular. And it has more good restaurants per square mile than any European city except Paris.

Lyon's development owes much to its riverside site halfway between Paris and the Mediterranean and within striking distance of Switzerland, Italy, and the Alps. Because Lyon has never endured hard times, untroubled content prevails. Lyonnais are proud that their city has been important for more than 2,000 years: Romans made it the capital of Gaul around 43 BC. Its name derives from the Roman Lugdunum, or "Hill of the Crow."

In the middle of Lyon is Presqu'île (Almost Island), a fingerlike peninsula between the rivers, only half a dozen blocks wide and about 10 km (6 mi) long, where modern Lyon throbs with shops, restaurants, museums, theaters, and an opera house. Across the Saône is Vieux Lyon (Old Lyon); above it is the old Roman district of Fourvière. To the north is the hilly Croix Rousse district, where you'll find more museums. Across the Rhône to the east is a mix of older residential areas and the ultramodern Part-Dieu office district. Consider taking advantage of the "Clés de Lyon," a three-day museum pass for 90 francs.

Vieux Lyon and Fourvière

Vieux Lyon has narrow cobblestone streets, 17th- and 18th-century mansions, small museums, and the city's cathedral. When the city developed as an important silk weaving town, Italian merchants and bankers built town houses in the area; the influence of Italian Renaissance architecture still dominates. Above Vieux Lyon, in the hilly Fourvière district, are the remains of Roman theaters and the Basilique de Notre-Dame, visible from all over the city.

A Good Walk

Start your walk armed with free maps from the Lyon tourist office on La Presqu'île's **place Bellecour** ①. Cross the square and head north along lively rue du Président-Herriot; turn left onto place des Jacobins and explore rue Mercière and the small streets off it. Cross the Saône on the passerelle du Palais du Justice (foot bridge); now you are in Vieux Lyon. Facing you is the old Palais de Justice. Turn right, then walk 200 yards along quai Romain Rolland to No. 36, where there is a traboule that leads to rue des Trois Maries. Take a right to get to small **place de la Baleine** ②. Exit the square on the left (north) side and go right on historic **rue St-Jean.** Head up to cobblestoned place du Change; on your left is the **Loge du Change** ③ church. Take rue Soufflot and turn left onto rue de Gadagne. The Hôtel de Gadagne is home to two museums: the **Musée Historique de Lyon** ④, with medieval sculpture and local artifacts, and the **Musée de la Marionnette,** a puppet museum.

Walk south along **rue du Boeuf,** which runs parallel to rue St-Jean. Just off tiny place du Petit-Collège, at No. 16 is the **Maison du Crible** ⑤, with its pink tower. Use the traboule at No. 1 rue du Boeuf to lead you to 24 rue St-Jean. Turn right and then left onto rue de la Bombarde to get to the **Jardin Archéologique** ⑥, a small garden with two excavated churches. Alongside the gardens is the solid **Cathédrale St-Jean** ⑦, itself an architectural history lesson. The *ficelle* (funicular railway) runs from the cathedral to the top of Colline de Fourvière (Fourvière Hill). Take the Montée de Fourvière to the **Théâtres Romains** ⑧, two ruined, Roman theaters. Overlooking the theaters is the semi-subterranean **Musée de la Civilisation Gallo-Romaine** ⑨, a repository for Roman finds. Continue up the hill and take the first right to the mock-Byzantine **Basilique de Notre-Dame-de-Fourvière** ⑩.

Return to Vieux Lyon via the Montée Nicolas-de-Lange, the stone staircase at the foot of the metal tower, the **Tour Métallique** ⑪. You will emerge alongside the St-Paul train station. Venture onto rue Juiverie, off place St-Paul, to see two splendid Renaissance mansions, the **Hôtel Paterin** ⑫ at No. 4 and the **Hôtel Bullioud** ⑬ at No. 8. On the northeast side of place St-Paul is the church of **St-Paul** ⑭. Behind the church, cross the river on the passarelle St-Vincent and take a left on quai St-Vincent; 200 yards along on the right is the **Jardin des Chartreux** ⑮, a small park. Cut through the park up to cours du Général Giraud, then turn right to place Rouville. Rue de l'Annonciade leads from the square to the **Jardin des Plantes** ⑯, botanical gardens.

TIMING

Spend the morning ambling around Vieux Lyon and Fourvière, then eat lunch in one of Vieux Lyon's many restaurants or have a picnic in the Jardin des Plantes. In the afternoon explore the Croix Rousse District (☞ *below*) and its many museums. Note that most museums are closed Monday.

Sights to See

10 **Basilique de Notre-Dame-de-Fourvière.** The pompous late-19th-century basilica, at the top of the ficelle, is, unfortunately, the symbol of Lyon. Its mock-Byzantine architecture and hilltop site make it a close cousin of Paris's Sacré-Coeur. Both were built to underline the might of the Roman Catholic Church after the Prussian defeat of France in 1870 gave rise to the birth of the anticlerical Third Republic. The excessive gilt, marble, and mosaics inside underscore that the church had wealth if not political clout. One of the few places in Lyon where you can't see the basilica is the adjacent terrace, whose panorama reveals the city, with the St-Jean cathedral in the foreground and the glass towers of the reconstructed Part-Dieu business complex glistening behind. For a yet more sweeping view, climb the 287 steps to the basilica observatory. ✉ *pl. de Fourvière.* ⊙ *Basilica: daily 8–noon and 2–6.* 🎟 *Observatory: 10 frs.* ⊙ *Easter–Oct., daily 10–noon and 2–6; Nov.–Easter, weekends 10–noon and 2–5.*

7 **Cathédrale St-Jean.** No soaring roof or lofty spires can be found here. Solid and determined—it withstood the sieges of time, revolution, and war—the cathedral's stumpy facade is stuck almost bashfully onto the nave. Although the mishmash inside has its moments—the fabulous 13th-century stained-glass windows in the choir and the varied window tracery and vaulting in the side chapels—the interior lacks drama and harmony. But it is an architectural history lesson. The cathedral

Basilique de Notre-Dame de Fourvière, **10**
Cathédrale St-Jean, **7**
Hôtel Bullioud, **13**
Hôtel de Ville, **19**
Hôtel Paterin, **12**
Jardin Archéologique, **6**
Jardin des Chartreux, **15**
Jardin des Plantes, **16**
Loge du Change, **3**
Maison des Canuts, **18**
Maison du Crible, **5**
Musée de la Civilisation Gallo-Romaine, **9**
Musée des Arts Décoratifs, **22**
Musée des Beaux-Arts, **20**
Musée Historique de Lyon/Musée de la Marionnette, **4**
Musée Historique des Tissus, **23**
Opéra de Lyon, **21**
Place de la Baleine, **2**
Place Bellecour, **1**
Place des Terreaux, **17**
St-Paul, **14**
Théâtres Romains, **8**
Tour Métallique, **11**

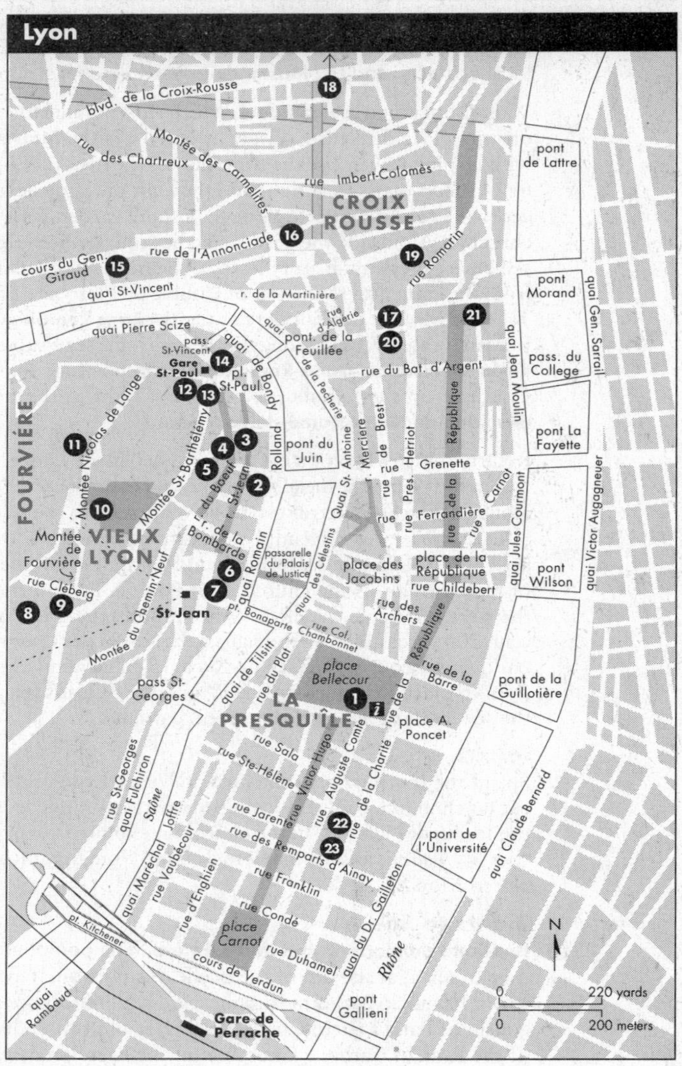

dates from the 12th century and the chancel is Romanesque, but construction continued over three centuries. The 14th-century astronomical clock, in the north transept, is a marvel of technology. It chimes a hymn to St-Jean on the hour at noon, 2, 3, and 4 PM as a screeching rooster and other automatons enact the Annunciation. To the right of the Cathédrale St-Jean stands the 12th-century **Manécanterie** (choir school). ✉ *70 rue St-Jean,* ☎ *04–78–92–82–29.*

13 **Hôtel Bullioud.** This Renaissance mansion, close to the Hôtel Paterin, is noted for its courtyard, with an ingenious gallery (1536) built by Philibert Delorme, one of France's earliest and most accomplished exponents of classical architecture. He worked at the Loire Valley châteaux of Fontainebleau and Chenonceau. ✉ *8 rue Juiverie, off pl. St-Paul.*

12 **Hôtel Paterin.** This splendid Renaissance mansion is one of many notable buildings in the area. ✉ *4 rue Juiverie, off pl. St-Paul.*

6 **Jardin Archéologique.** The Archaeological Garden contains the excavated ruins of two churches that succeeded one another on this spot. They were discovered after apartment buildings, built on the spot after the churches were destroyed in the Revolution, were undergoing repairs. When the apartment buildings were demolished the foundations of the churches were unearthed. One arch still remains and forms part of the ornamentation in the garden. ✉ *Entrance on rue de la Bombarde.*

15 **Jardin des Chartreux.** This garden is just one of several small, leafy parks in Lyon. It's a peaceful place to rest and eat a sandwich while admiring the splendid view of the river and Fourvière Hill. ✉ *Entrance on quai St-Vincent.*

16 **Jardin des Plantes.** The peaceful, luxurious Botanical Gardens contain remnants of the once-huge **Amphithéâtre des Trois Gauls,** built in AD 19. ✉ *Entrance on rue de la Tourette.* 🕓 *Dawn to dusk.*

3 **Loge du Change.** Germain Soufflot (architect of Paris's Panthéon) built this church in 1747. ✉ *pl. du Change.*

5 **Maison du Crible.** This 17th-century mansion is one of Lyon's oldest. In the courtyard you can glimpse a charming garden and the original Tour Rose—an elegant, pink tower. The higher the tower in those days, the greater the prestige; this one was owned by the tax collector. ✉ *16 rue du Boeuf (off tiny pl. du Petit-Collège).* 🎟 *25 frs.* 🕓 *Daily 10–noon and 2–6.*

9 **Musée de la Civilisation Gallo-Romaine.** Since 1933, systematic excavations have unearthed vestiges of Lyon's opulent Roman precursor. The statues, mosaics, vases, coins, and tombstones are excellently displayed at this semi-subterranean museum next to the Roman Theaters. The large bronze Table Claudienne is inscribed with part of Emperor Claudius's speech to the Roman Senate in AD 48, conferring senatorial rights on the Roman citizens of Gaul. ✉ *17 rue Clébert,* ☎ *04–78–25–94–68.* 🎟 *20 frs.* 🕓 *Wed.–Sun. 9:30–noon and 2–6.*

4 **Musée Historique de Lyon.** The Lyon Historical Museum is housed in the city's largest ensemble of Renaissance buildings, the Hôtel de Gadagne, built between the 14th and 16th centuries. Medieval sculpture, local furniture, pottery, paintings, and engravings are on display. Also housed here is the **Musée de la Marionnette** (Puppet Museum), tracing the history of marionettes beginning with Guignol and Madelon (Lyon's Punch and Judy, created by Laurent Mourguet in 1795). ✉ *1 pl. du Petit-Collège,* ☎ *04–78–42–03–61.* 🎟 *20 frs.* 🕓 *Wed.–Mon. 10:45–6 (until 8:30 Fri.).*

2 **Place de la Baleine.** This small square is lined with 17th-century houses once owned by those who became rich from the silk trade.

1 **Place Bellecour.** Shady, imposing place Bellecour is one of the largest squares in France and Lyon's fashionable center, midway between the Saône and the Rhône. Classical facades erected along its narrower sides in 1800 lend architectural interest. The large bronze equestrian Louis XIV, installed in 1828, is by local sculptor Jean Lemot. On the south side of the square is the **tourist office.**

Rue du Boeuf. At the corner of place Neuve St-Jean and rue du Boeuf is one of Old Lyon's most famous signs, portraying the bull for which the rue du Boeuf is named; it's by renowned French sculptor Jean de Bologne (1529–1608), trained in Renaissance Italy.

Rue St-Jean. Once Old Lyon's major thoroughfare, this street leads north from place de la Baleine to place du Change, where money changers operated during medieval trade fairs. Its elegant houses were largely built for illustrious Lyonnais bankers and silk merchants during the French Renaissance. No. 27 has an especially lovely courtyard. The houses once had just four stories; upper floors were added in the last century. Many area streets were named for their shops, still heralded by intricate iron signs.

14 **St-Paul.** The 12th-century church of St-Paul is noted for its octagonal lantern, its frieze of animal heads on the chancel, and its Flamboyant Gothic chapel. ✉ *pl. St-Paul.*

8 **Théâtres Romains.** Two ruined, semicircular Roman Theaters are tucked into the hillside, just down from the summit of Fourvière. The **Grand Théâtre,** the oldest Roman theater in France, was built in 15 BC to seat 10,000. The smaller **Odéon,** with its geometric flooring, was designed for music and poetry performances. Come in September for the Lyon International Arts Festival. ✉ *Colline Fourfière.* *Free.* *Daily 9–dusk.*

11 **Tour Métallique.** Beyond the Fourvière Basilica is this skeletal metal tower built in 1893 and now a television transmitter. The stone staircase, the **Montée Nicolas-de-Lange,** at the foot of the tower, is a direct but steep route from the basilica to the St-Paul train station. ✉ *Colline Fourvière.*

The Croix Rousse District

This hilly district north of the central place des Terreaux, flanked by the Jardins des Plantes on the west and the Rhône on the east, once resounded to the clanking of looms churning out the silk and cloth that made Lyon famous. By the 19th century, over 30,000 *canuts* (weavers) worked on looms on the upper floors of the houses. So tightly packed were the houses that the only way to transport fabrics was through the traboules, which had the additional advantage of protecting the cloth in bad weather.

A Good Walk

For an impromptu tour of the Croix Rousse District, walk along rue Imbert-Colomès. At No. 20, turn right through the traboule that leads to rue des Tables Claudiennes and right again across place Chardonnet. Take the passage Mermet alongside St-Polycarpe church, then turn left onto rue Leynaud. A traboule at No. 32 leads to the Montée St-Sébastien. Keep right, cross place Croix-Paquet, and take rue Romarin down to **place des Terreaux** ⑰. Armed with a detailed map, you could spend hours "trabouling" in the area, which is still busy with textile merchants despite the demise of the old-style cottage industry of silk weaving. In the very northern part of the Croix Rousse see old-time looms at the **Maison des Canuts** ⑱.

The sizable place des Terreaux has two notable buildings: On the north side is the **Hôtel de Ville** ⑲, the Town Hall; on the south side is the elegant **Musée des Beaux-Arts** ⑳, the art museum. To reach the barrel-vaulted **Opéra de Lyon** ㉑, walk west across place des Terreaux and through the ground floor of the Hôtel de Ville (go around if it's closed). For a look at Lyon's fashionable shops, walk down the pedestrian-only rue de la République and cross place Bellecour. Continue 300 yards further (now rue de la Charité) to the **Musée des Arts Décoratifs** ㉒, the Decorative Arts Museum. Next door is the **Musée Historique des Tissus** ㉓, the Fabric History Museum.

If you've seen all of Lyon's main cultural sights and want to indulge your children, take the métro from Perrache train station to Masséna, to the **Parc de la Tête d'Or.**

TIMING

The Croix Rousse District will probably take about an hour to meander through. The Musée des Beaux-Arts deserves at least two hours and the Musée des Arts Décoratifs and the Musée Historique des Tissus another couple of hours. You may want to leave these until the following day. Note that most museums are closed Monday and the Musée des Beaux-Arts is also closed Tuesday.

19 **Hôtel de Ville.** Architects Jules Hardouin-Mansart and Robert de Cotte redesigned the very impressive facade of the Town Hall after a 1674 fire. The rest of the building dates from the early 17th century. ✉ *pl. des Terreaux.*

18 **Maison des Canuts.** Despite the industrialization of silk and textile production, old-time "Jacquard" looms are still in action at this historical house in the Croix Rouge. The weavers are happy to show children how to operate a miniature loom. ✉ *12 rue d'Ivry,* ☎ *04–78–28–62–04.* *10 frs.* ⏲ *Weekdays 8:30–noon and 2–6:30, Sat. 9–noon and 2–6.*

★ 22 **Musée des Arts Décoratifs.** At the Decorative Arts Museum, housed in an 18th-century mansion, fine collections of silverware, furniture, objets d'art, porcelain, and tapestries are on display. ✉ *34 rue de la Charité,* ☎ *04–78–37–15–05.* *26 frs (joint ticket with the nearby Musée Historique des Tissus).* ⏲ *Tues.–Sun. 10–noon and 2–5:30.*

20 **Musée des Beaux-Arts.** The Fine Arts Museum is housed in the elegant 17th-century Palais St-Pierre, once a Benedictine abbey. It houses France's largest collection of art after the Louvre, including Rodin's *Walker,* Byzantine ivories, Etruscan statues, and Egyptian artifacts. Amid Old Master, Impressionist, and modern paintings are works by the tight-knit Lyon School, characterized by exquisitely rendered flowers and overbearing religious sentimentality. Note Louis Janmot's *Poem of the Soul,* immaculately painted visions that are by turns heavenly, hellish, and downright spooky. ✉ *Palais St-Pierre, 20 pl. des Terreaux,* ☎ *04–72–10–17–40.* *20 frs.* ⏲ *Wed.–Sun. 10:30–6.*

23 **Musée Historique des Tissus.** The Fabric History Museum has a fascinating exhibit of intricate carpets, tapestries, and silks, including Asian tapestries from as early as the 4th century, Turkish and Persian carpets from the 16th to the 18th centuries, and 18th-century Lyon silks. ✉ *34 rue de la Charité,* ☎ *04–78–37–15–05.* *26 frs (joint ticket with Musée des Arts Décoratifs).* ⏲ *Tues.–Sun. 10–noon and 2–5:30.*

21 **Opéra de Lyon.** The barrel-vaulted Lyon Opera, a reincarnation of a moribund 1831 building, was built in the early '90s at a cost of 478 million francs. It incorporates a columned exterior, soaring glass vaulting, neoclassical public spaces, and the latest backstage magic. High above, looking out between the heroic statues lined up along the parapet, is a small restaurant, Les Muses (☞ Dining and Lodging, *below*). ✉ *pl. de la Comédie,* ☎ *04–72–00–45–00 or 04–72–00–45–45 (tickets).*

Parc de la Tête d'Or. On the banks of the Rhône, this 300-acre park has a lake, pony rides, and a small zoo. It's ideal for an afternoon's outing with children. Take the métro from Perrache train station to Masséna. ✉ *pl. du Général Leclerc, quai Charles de Gaulle.* *Free.* ⏲ *Dawn to dusk.*

17 **Place des Terreaux.** The four majestic horses rearing up from a monumental 19th-century fountain in the middle of this large square are by Frédéric-Auguste Bartholdi, who also sculpted New York's Statue of Liberty. The two notable buildings sitting on either side are the Hôtel de Ville and the Musée des Beaux-Arts (☞ *above*).

Dining and Lodging

$$$$ ★ ✕ **Léon de Lyon.** Chef Jean-Paul Lacombe's innovative uses of the region's butter, cream, and foie gras puts this restaurant, in an old house, at the forefront of the city's gastronomic scene. Dishes such as fillet of veal with celery or leg of lamb with fava beans are memorable; suckling pig comes with foie gras, onions, and a truffle salad. Alcoves and wood paneling add charm. ✉ *1 rue Pléney,* ☎ *04–78–28–11–33. Reservations essential. Jacket required. MC, V. Closed most of Aug. No dinner Sun., no lunch Mon.*

$$$$ ✕ **Paul Bocuse.** In this culinary shrine north of Lyon in Collonges-au-Mont-d'Or, the grand dining room makes a fitting backdrop for the creations of star chef Paul Bocuse. Although he is often away, elegantly dressed food lovers throng here to feast on, say, truffle soup and sea bass. Book far in advance. ✉ *50 quai de la Plage, Collonges-au-Mont-d'Or,* ☎ *04–72–27–85–85. Reservations essential. Jacket and tie. AE, DC, MC, V.*

$$$–$$$$ ✕ **Orsi.** Pierre Orsi's lavish restaurant, a pink stucco wonder, sits by a tiny tree-lined square. All is festive among marble floors, brocade draperies, bronze nudes, and gilt-frame paintings. The foie gras ravioli with truffles, and the mesclun with goat cheese are hard acts to follow, though the sliced figs with pistachio ice cream hold their own. ✉ *3 pl. Kléber,* ☎ *04–79–89–57–68. Reservations essential. Jacket and tie. AE, V.*

$$ ✕ **Brasserie Georges.** This inexpensive brasserie at the end of rue de la Charité is one of the city's largest and oldest, founded in 1836 but now in a palatial Art Deco building. Meals range from hearty veal stew or sauerkraut and sausage to more refined fare. ✉ *30 cours de Verdun,* ☎ *04–72–56–54–54. MC, V.*

$$ ✕ **Café des Fédérations.** For 80 years this sawdust-strewn café with homey red-checked tablecloths has reigned as one of the city's friendliest spots. Raymond Fulchiron not only serves deftly prepared local classics like *boudin blanc* (white-meat sausage), but also chats with guests to make them feel at home. ✉ *8 rue du Major-Martin,* ☎ *04–78–28–26–00. AE, DC, MC, V. Closed weekends and Aug.*

$$ ★ ✕ **Les Muses.** High up under the glass vault of the Opéra de Lyon is this small restaurant run by Philippe Chavent. Look out the glass front between statues of the muses to the Hôtel de Ville. The nouvelle cuisine makes it hard to choose between salmon in butter sauce with watercress mousse and the 59-franc plat du jour, which may include chicken in tarragon cream with sautéed zucchini. ✉ *Opéra de Lyon,* ☎ *04–72–00–45–58. Reservations essential. AE, V.*

$$ ✕ **Le Vivarais.** Roger Duffaud's simple, tidy restaurant is an outstanding culinary value. Don't expect napkins folded into flower shapes—the excitement is on your plate, with dishes like *lièvre royale* (hare rolled and stuffed with truffles and pâté). ✉ *1 pl. du Dr-Gailleton,* ☎ *04–78–37–85–15. Reservations essential. MC, V. Closed Sun.*

$ ✕ **Brunet.** Tables are crammed together in this tiny bouchon where the decor is limited to past menus inscribed on mirrors and a few photographs. The food is good, traditional Lyonnais fare; besides the mandatory andouillette sausage and tripe, there is usually excellent roast pork on the 98-franc menu. On a busy night expect to be jostled—it's all part of the fun. ✉ *23 rue Claudia,* ☎ *04–78–37–44–31. Closed Sun. in summer; Sun. and Mon. in winter; and Aug. MC, V.*

$ ✕ **Hugon.** This typical, tiny bouchon with red-checked tablecloths is behind the Musée des Beaux-Arts. The owner drinks with patrons while Madame chops away in back. Go for a hunk of homemade pâté and stewed chicken in wine vinegar sauce or a plate of *ris de veau* (sweetbreads)—good, inexpensive food and plenty of it. ✉ *12 rue Pizay,* ☎ *04–78–28–10–94. Closed Sun. MC, V.*

$ ✕ **Le Jura.** The rows of tables, the mosaic tile floor, and the absence of anything pretty gives this place a men's club feel. The mustached owner, looking as if he stepped out of the turn-of-the-century prints on the walls, acts gruffly with a smile as his wife rushes around. The game and steak dishes are robust, as is the cassoulet *des escargots* (stew of beans, mutton, and snails). Desserts are mediocre, so order the cheese. ✉ *25 rue Tupin,* ☎ *04–78–42–20–57. Closed Sun. and Aug. MC, V.*

$ ✕ **Les Lyonnais.** This popular brasserie, decorated with local celebrities's photos, is particularly animated. The simple food—chicken simmered for hours in wine, meat stews, and grilled fish—is served on bare wood tables. A blackboard announces plats du jour, which are less expensive than the printed menu. ✉ *1 rue Tramassac,* ☎ *04–78–37–64–82. Closed Sun. MC, V.*

$$$$ ✕🏨 **La Tour Rose.** Philippe Chavent's silk-swathed Old Lyon hotel was created from several houses around a secret courtyard under a rose-washed tower; the glass-roof restaurant occupies a former chapel. Each room is named for an old silk factory and decorated in its goods; taffetas, plissés, and velvet cover walls, windows, and beds in daring, even startling style. Dinner is an occasion (and expensive at 450 francs a head). ✉ *22 rue du Boeuf, 69005,* ☎ *04–78–37–25–90,* FAX *04–78–42–26–02. 12 rooms. Restaurant, bar. AE, DC, MC, V.*

$$$$ ★ 🏨 **La Cour des Loges.** Young Lyonnais architects teamed with Italian designers to transform four Renaissance mansions into one of Lyon's most stylish hotels. It has an immense courtyard, spiral stone staircases, and exposed beams. Rooms range from fairly small to comfortably large and are either classic or contemporary in design. There is a cellar wine bar and a tapas bar. Concierge Gérard Ravet is not only a character, but he also knows Lyon inside out. ✉ *6 rue du Boeuf, 69005,* ☎ *04–78–42–75–75,* FAX *04–72–40–93–61. 63 rooms. Bar, breakfast room, indoor pool, hot tub, sauna, health club, library, meeting room. AE, DC, MC, V.*

$$$$ 🏨 **Villa Florentine.** High above the old town, near the Roman theater and basilica, this pristine hotel was once a convent, with beamed and vaulted ceilings, terraces everywhere, marvelous views, and a restaurant with refined cuisine. ✉ *25–27 Montée St-Barthélémy, 69005,* ☎ *04–72–56–56–56,* FAX *04–72–40–90–56. 16 rooms, 3 suites. Restaurant, bar, breakfast room, pool, meeting rooms. AE, DC, MC, V.*

$$$ 🏨 **Grande Hôtel Concorde.** In a 19th-century building off place de la République, this Belle Epoque hotel has high-ceilinged guest rooms with nondescript furniture and one unique piece. The staff is courteous and efficient. The restaurant has a very reasonable 78-franc lunch menu. ✉ *11 rue Grôlée, 69002,* ☎ *04–72–40–45–45,* FAX *04–78–37–52–55. 140 rooms. Restaurant, air-conditioning, meeting rooms. AE, DC, MC, V.*

$$$ 🏨 **Hôtel des Artistes.** This intimate hotel on an elegant square opposite the Théâtre des Célestins has long been popular among artists; black-and-white photographs of them adorn lobby walls. Rooms are smallish but modern and comfortable, and the friendly reception and great location appeal to all comers. ✉ *8 rue Gaspard-André, 69002,* ☎ *04–78–42–04–88,* FAX *04–78–42–93–76. 45 rooms. AE, MC, V.*

$$–$$$ 🏨 **Grand Hôtel des Beaux-Arts.** Half of the rooms at this hotel are "inspired worlds" where an artist has developed a theme through his paintings. In Room 309, for instance, the paintings of Carmelo Zagari are used to lead you into the world of the theater. Should you want a more conventional sleeping environment, other rooms are traditionally furnished. A buffet breakfast is served. ✉ *rue du Président Edouard-Her-*

riot, pl. des Jacobins, 69002, ☎ *78–38–09–50,* FAX *78–42–19–19. 80 rooms. AE, DC, MC, V.*

$ **Bed et Breakfast à Lyon.** This nonprofit agency can house you for one night or several: singles are 120–290 francs; doubles are 170–390 francs. ✉ *4 rue Joliot-Curie, 69005,* ☎ *04–72–57–99–22,* FAX *04–72–57–92–51. Agency open Mon.–Fri. 2 PM–6 PM.*

$ **Hôtel du Théâtre.** The friendliness and enthusiasm of the owner would be sufficient enough to recommend this small hotel, but its location and reasonable prices make it even more commendable. Rooms are simple but clean; those overlooking place des Célestins not only have a theatrical view but also a bathroom with a tub (330 francs). Those facing the side have a shower only. Breakfast is included. ✉ *10 rue de Savoie, 69002,* ☎ *04–78–42–33–32,* FAX *04–72–40–00–61. 24 rooms. MC, V.*

Nightlife and the Arts

Lyon is the region's liveliest arts center; check the weekly *Lyon-Poche,* published on Wednesday and sold at newsstands, for cultural events and goings-on at the dozens of discos, bars, and clubs.

For darts and pints, head to the **Albion Public House** (✉ 12 rue Ste-Catherine, 1er), where they even accept British pounds. The low-key, chic **L'Alibi** (✉ 13 quai Romain-Roland, 5e) has a laser show that complements the music. Romantics rendezvous at the **Bar de la Tour Rose** (✉ 22 rue du Boeuf, 5e). **Bouchon aux Vin** (✉ 64 rue Mercière, 2e) is a wine bar with 30-plus vintages. Computer jocks can head into cyberspace at **Le Chantier** (✉ 18–20 rue Ste-Catherine, 1er) while their friends listen to jazz and nibble on tapas. Caribbean and African music pulses at **Le Club des Îles** (✉ 1 Grande Rue des Feuillants, 1er). Hear live jazz in the stone-vaulted basement of **Hot Club** (✉ 26 rue Lanterne, 1er). A gay crowd can be found among the 1930s decor at **La Ruche** (✉ 22 rue Gentil, 2e). **Villa Florentine** (✉ 25 montée St-Barthélémy, 5e) is a quiet spot for a drink to the melody of a harp on Friday and Saturday.

Espace Gerson (✉ 1 pl. Gerson, ☎ 04–78–27–96–99) and **Café-Théâtre de L'Accessoire** (✉ 26 rue de l'Annonciade, ☎ 04–78–27–84–84) are two café-theaters where you can eat and drink while watching a revue.

Lyon's Société de Musique de Chambre performs at **Salle Molière** (✉ 18 quai Bondy, ☎ 04–78–28–03–11). The **Opéra de Lyon** (✉ 1 pl. de la Comédie, ☎ 04–72–00–45–45) presents plays, concerts, ballets, and opera from October to June.

Early fall sees the renowned **Biennale de la Danse** (even years). September is the time for the **Foire aux Tupiniers** (☎ 04–78–37–00–68), a pottery fair. October brings the **Festival Bach** (☎ 04–78–72–75–31). The **Biennale d'Art Contemporain** (☎ 04–78–30–50–66) is held odd years in October. The **Festival du Vieux Lyon** (☎ 04–78–42–39–04) is a musical festival in November and December. On December 8 (feast of the Immaculate Conception) lights go on city-wide for the marvelous **Fête de Lumière.**

Shopping

Lyon has the region's best; it is still the nation's silk-and-textiles capital, and all big-name designers have shops here. For chic clothing try the stores on rue du Président Edouard-Herriot and rue de la République in the center of town. Lyonnais designer **Clémentine** (✉ 18 rue Émile-Zola) is good for well-cut, tailored clothing. **Étincelle** (✉ 34 rue St-Jean) has trendy outfits for youngsters.

For antiques, wander down **rue Auguste-Comte** (from place Bellecour to Perrache). **Image en Cours** (☒ 26 rue du Boeuf) has superb engravings. **La Maison des Canuts** (☒ 10–12 rue d'Ivry, Croix Rousse) sells local textiles. Fabrics can be also found at the **Boutique des Soyeux Lyonnais** (☒ 3 rue du Boeuf). Look for Lyonnais puppets on **place du Change.**

Go to **Reynon** (☒ 13 rue des Archers) for charcuterie. **Pignol** (☒ 17 rue Émile-Zola) is good for meats and sandwich makings. For culinary variety, shop **Les Halles** (☒ 102 cours Lafayette). For chocolates, head to **Bernachon** (☒ 42 cours Franklin-Roosevelt); some say it is the best *chocolaterie* in France. **La Boîte à Dessert** (☒ 1 rue de l'Ancienne-Préfecture) makes luscious peach turnovers.

BEAUJOLAIS AND LA DOMBES

North of Lyon along the Saône are the vineyards of Beaujolais, a thrill for oenophiles. East of the Saône is the fertile lands of La Dombes where ornithologists flock to see the migratory bird life. North of La Dombes and east of the Beaujolais wine villages is Bourg-en-Bresse, home to a marvelous church and chicken that delights gourmets; it makes a good base after Lyon. South toward the Rhône, the great river of southern France, is the well-preserved medieval village of Pérouges.

L'Arbresle

24 *16 km (10 mi) northwest of Lyon.*

If you love modern architecture, don't miss Eveux, outside L'Arbresle. Here the stark, blocky Dominican convent of **Ste-Marie de la Tourette** protrudes over the hillside, resting on slender pillars that look like stilts and revealing the minimalist sensibilities of architect Le Corbusier, who designed it in 1957–59. ☎ *04–74–01–01–03.* 🎫 *20 frs.* ⏲ *July–Aug., daily 9–noon and 2–6; Sept.–June, weekends 2–6.*

Ars-sur-Formans

25 *30 km (19 mi) northeast of L'Arbresle; 36 km (22 mi) north of Lyon via A6, Villefranche exit.*

Each year 400,000 pilgrims invade this village (population 719) to honor the Curé d'Ars, Jean-Baptiste Vianney (1786–1859), patron saint of parish priests. Arriving in Ars in 1818, he was soon known as a charismatic confessor of unparalleled godliness and was famed as a "saint" well before his death in 1859 and canonization in 1925. The village church, enlarged to accommodate pilgrims, retains Vianney's confessional and embalmed body; his Saint's Day is August 4. Seventeen tableaux chart Vianney's life at the **Historial du St-Curé-d'Ars.** ☒ *Le Tonneau,* ☎ *04–74–00–70–22.* 🎫 *28 frs.* ⏲ *Apr.–Oct., daily 10–12:30 and 1:30–7; Nov.–Mar., weekends 2–6.*

Villefranche-sur-Saône

26 *6 km (4 mi) east of Ars-sur-Formans, 31 km (19 mi) north of Lyon.*

The lively industrial town of Villefranche-sur-Saône is the capital of the Beaujolais region and is known for its Vin Nouveau. This youthful, fruity, red wine, thanks to marketing hype, is eagerly gulped down every year around the world on the third Thursday of November (when it's officially released).

Dining and Lodging

$$$$ ✕🏨 **Château de Bagnols.** This exquisite, small medieval castle, southwest of Villefranche, began life in the 13th century. Period glassware,

fabrics, and porcelain were copied to complement the antique furniture. Adorning the walls are 17th- and 18th-century murals inspired by Lyon's textile industry. Wine tastings are held in the beautiful stone *cuvage* (wine-pressing room). A Continental breakfast is included in the astronomical rates. ✉ *69620 Bagnols (15 km/9 mi southwest of Villefranche on D38 to Tarare),* ☎ *04–74–71–40–00,* FAX *04–74–71–40–49. 12 rooms, 8 suites. Restaurant, library, meeting rooms. AE, DC, MC, V.*

Beaujolais Wine Road

16 km (10 mi) north of Villefranche-sur-Saône, 49 km (30 mi) north of Lyon.

Not all Beaujolais wine is promoted as *vin nouveau.* Wine classed as "Beaujolais Villages" is higher in alcohol and produced from a clearly defined region northwest of Villefranche. The Beaujolais Wine Road, a narrow strip just 23 km (14 mi) long, is home to nine deluxe Beaujolais wines known as *crus,* which rival the renowned wines of Burgundy. Most villages have a *cave* (communal cellar) or *coopérative,* where you can taste and buy.

In the southernmost and largest vineyard of the Beaujolais crus is **Odenas,** producing Brouilly, a soft, fruity wine best drunk young. In the vineyard's center is towering Mont Brouilly, a hill whose vines produce a tougher, firmer wine classified as Côte de Brouilly. From Odenas, take D68, via St-Lager to **Villié-Morgon,** in the heart of the Morgon vineyard; robust wines that age well are produced here. At **Monternot,** east of Villié-Morgon, you will find the 15th-century **Château de Corcelles,** noted for its Renaissance galleries, canopied courtyard well, and medieval carvings in its chapel. The guardroom is now an atmospheric tasting cellar. ✉ *Off D9 from Villié-Morgon.* ☎ *04–74–66–72–42.* ⏲ *Mon.–Sat. 10–noon and 2:30–6:30.*

From Villié-Morgon D68 wiggles north through several more wine villages. **Chiroubles** produces a rare, light wine that is best drunk young. **Fleurie**'s wines are elegant and flowery. Well-known **Chénas** is home to two crus: the robust, velvety, and expensive Moulin à Vent, and the fruity and underestimated Chénas. **Juliénas**'s wines are sturdy and of a deep color; sample them in the cellar of the town church (closed Tuesday and lunchtime), amid bacchanalian decor. **St-Amour,** west of Julienas, produces light but firm reds and a limited quantity of whites. The famous white Pouilly-Fuissé comes from the area around **Fuissé.**

Bourg-en-Bresse

27 *43 km (27 mi) east of St-Amour on N79; 65 km (40 mi) northeast of Lyon.*

Cheerful Bourg-en-Bresse is esteemed among gastronomes for its fowl, striking-looking chickens with plump white bodies and bright blue feet—the *poulet Bresse.* The town's southeasternmost district, Brou, is its most interesting, and the site of a striking church. This is a good place to stay before or after a trip along the Beaujolais Wine Road (☞ *above*).

The **Église de Brou,** a marvel of Flamboyant Gothic, is no longer in religious use. The church was built between 1506 and 1532 by Margaret of Austria in memory of her husband Philibert le Beau, duke of Savoy, and their finely sculpted tombs highlight the rich interior. Son et lumière shows—on Easter and Pentecost Sunday and Monday, and on Thursday, Saturday, and Sunday from May through September—are magical. Until 1999 a massive restoration of the roof is underway, bring-

ing it back to its 16th-century state. When it is done, it will have the same gorgeous, multicolor, intricate patterns found throughout Burgundy. The museum in the nearby **cloister** stands out for its paintings: 16th- and 17th-century Flemish and Dutch artists keep company with 17th- and 18th-century French and Italian masters, 19th-century artists of the Lyon School, Gustave Doré, and contemporary local painters. ✉ *63 bd. de Brou,* ☎ *04–74–45–39–00.* 🎫 *Church and museum: 32 frs.* ⏲ *Apr.–Sept., daily 9–noon and 2–6:30; Oct.–Mar., daily 9–noon and 2–5.*

Dining and Lodging

$$$ ★ ✕ **L'Auberge Bressane.** The location looking out on the Brou Church makes this modern, polished spot a good bet. Chef Jean-Pierre Vullin's preparations are not always consistent, but they are always interesting. Frogs' legs and Bresse chicken with morel mushroom cream sauce are specialties; try the *quenelles de brochet* (pike fish balls). Don't miss the house aperitif, a champagne cocktail with fresh strawberry puree. The wine list has 300 vintages. ✉ *166 bd. de Brou,* ☎ *04–74–22–22–68. Reservations essential. Jacket and tie. AE, DC, MC, V.*

$$–$$$ ✕ **La Petite Auberge.** This cozy flower-decked inn is in the countryside on the outskirts of town. Motherly Mme. Bertrand provides games for children. Chef Philippe Garnier has a subtle way with mullet (he grills it in saffron butter) and Bresse chicken (browned in tangy cider vinegar). ✉ *St-Just, rte. de Ceyzeriat,* ☎ *04–74–22–30–04. MC, V. Closed Jan. No dinner Mon.*

$$$$ ✕🏨 **Georges Blanc.** This simple 19th-century inn, full of beautiful rugs, grandfather clocks, and antique country furniture, makes a fine setting for Blanc's innovative preparations. Indulge in frogs' legs, wine from the extensive list, and the superb desserts. The restaurant is closed Wednesday and Thursday (except for dinner June–mid-September). The 30 guest rooms range from (relatively) simple to downright luxurious. It's worth the 19-km (12-mi) trip from Bourg-en-Bresse, but only if you have money to burn and want to eat in every luxury restaurant in France. ✉ *pl. du Marché, 01540 Vonnas,* ☎ *04–74–50–90–90,* FAX *04–74–50–08–80. 30 rooms. Restaurant, pool, 1 tennis court, helipad. AE, DC, MC, V. Reservations essential. Closed Jan.–mid-Feb.*

$$ ✕🏨 **Le France.** Le France is not memorable, but it is centrally located. Rooms are old-fashioned, though spacious. The staff is cheerful and helpful. The restaurant, under chef Jacques Guy, is considerably more innovative than the hotel; the regional cooking attracts many locals for lunch. ✉ *19 pl. Bernard, 01000,* ☎ *04–74–23–30–24,* FAX *04–74–23–69–90. 45 rooms with bath or shower. Restaurant. AE, DC, MC, V.*

Villars-les-Dombes

❷❽ *29 km (18 mi) south of Bourg-en-Bresse, 37 km (23 mi) north of Lyon.*

Villars-les-Dombes is the unofficial capital of La Dombes, an area once covered by a glacier. When the ice retreated, it left a network of lakes and ponds that draws anglers and bird-watchers today. The 56-acre **Parc des Oiseaux,** one of Europe's finest bird sanctuaries, is home to 400 species of birds (some 2,000 from five continents); 435 aviaries house species from waders to birds of prey; and tropical birds in vivid hues fill the indoor birdhouse. Allow two hours. ☎ *04–74–98–05–54.* 🎫 *35 frs.* ⏲ *Easter–Sept., daily 9–7:30; Oct.–Easter, daily 9–dusk.*

En Route N83 skirts the Dombes region's largest lake, the **Grand Étang de Birieux,** en route from Villars-les-Dombes to St-Andŕé de Covey.

Pérouges

★ 29 *21 km (13 mi) southeast of Villars-les-Dombes, 36 km (22 mi) northeast of Lyon.*

Wonderfully preserved (though a little too precious), hilltop Pérouges, with its medieval houses and narrow cobbled streets surrounded by ramparts, is just 200 yards across. Hand weavers brought it prosperity; the Industrial Revolution meant their downfall, and by the late 19th century, the population had dwindled from 1,500 to 12. Now the government has restored the most interesting houses; a potter, bookbinder, cabinetmaker, and weaver have given the town a new lease on life. A number of restaurants make Pérouges a good lunch stop.

Encircling the town is the **rue des Rondes;** from it there are fine views of the countryside and, on clear days, the Alps. Park your car by the main gateway, **Porte d'En-Haut,** alongside the 15th-century fortress-church. Rue du Prince, the town's main street, leads to the **Maison des Princes de Savoie,** which has a fine watchtower. **Place de la Halle,** a pretty square with great charm around the corner from the Maison des Princes de Savoie, is the site of a lime tree planted in 1792. The **Musée de Vieux Pérouges,** to one side of the place de la Halle, contains local artifacts and a reconstructed weaver's workshop. The medieval garden alongside has an array of rare medicinal plants. ✉ *pl. du Tilleul,* ☎ *04–74–61–00–88.* 🎫 *18 frs.* ⏲ *Daily 10–noon and 2–6. Closed Wed. and Thurs. morning Oct.–Apr.*

Dining and Lodging

$$$$ ★ ✕🏨 **Hostellerie du Vieux Pérouges.** Extraordinary even by French standards, this historic inn has antiques, glossy wood floors and tables, and gigantic stone hearths throughout. Rooms in the geranium-decked 15th-century manor are more spacious than those in the annex and have marble bathrooms and period furniture. In the restaurant, food is served on chunky pewter plates by waitresses in folk costume; the crayfish is particularly good. It is closed Thursday lunch and Wednesday, November to March. ✉ *pl. du Tilleul, 01800 Meximieux,* ☎ *04–74–61–00–88,* FAX *04–74–34–77–90. 28 rooms. Restaurant. V, MC.*

THE RHÔNE VALLEY

At Lyon, the Rhône, joined by the Saône, truly comes into its own, plummeting south in search of the Mediterranean. The river's progress is often spectacular, as steep vineyards conjure up vistas that are more readily associated with the river's Germanic cousin, the Rhine. All along the way, small-town vintners invite you to sample their wines. Roman towns like Vienne and Valence reflect the Rhône's importance as a trading route. To the west is the rugged, rustic Ardèche département (province), where time seems to have stood still.

Vienne

30 *27 km (17 mi) south of Lyon via A7.*

One of Roman Gaul's most important towns, Vienne became a religious and cultural center under its count-archbishops in the Middle Ages and retains historic charm, despite being a major road and train junction. The tourist office anchors cours Brillier in the leafy shadow of the Jardin Public (Public Gardens). A 26-franc "passport" available here admits you to all local monuments and museums.

On quai Jean-Jaurès, beside the Rhône, is the church of **St-Pierre.** Note the rectangular 12th-century Romanesque bell tower with its arcaded tiers. The lower church walls date from the 6th century. Although religious wars deprived the cathedral of **St-Maurice** of many statues, much original decoration is intact; the portals on the 15th-century facade are carved with Old Testament scenes. The cathedral was built between the 12th and 16th centuries, with later additions, such as the splendid 18th-century mausoleum, right of the altar. A frieze of the zodiac adorns the entrance to the vaulted passage that once led to the cloisters, but now opens onto place St-Paul.

Place du Palais is the site of the remains of the **Temple d'Auguste et de Livie** (Temple of Augustus and Livia), accessible via place St-Paul and rue Clémentine; they probably date, in part, from Vienne's earliest Roman settlements (1st century BC). The Corinthian columns were walled in during the 11th century, when the temple was used as a church; in 1833 Prosper Mérimée intervened to have the temple restored. The last vestige of the city's sizable Roman baths is a **Roman gateway** (⊠ rue Chantelouve) decorated with delicate friezes.

The **Théâtre Romain,** on rue de la Charité, is one of the largest in Gaul (143 yards across). It held 13,000 spectators and is only slightly smaller than Rome's Theater of Marcellus. Rubble buried Vienne's theater until 1922; 46 rows of seats, some marble flooring, and the frieze on the stage have been excavated. Concerts take place here in summer. ⊠ *7 rue du Cirque,* ☎ *04–74–85–39–23.* 🎫 *9 frs.* ⏲ *Apr.–mid-Oct., Wed.–Mon. 9:30–1 and 2–6; mid-Oct.–Mar., Wed.–Sat. 10–noon and 2–5, Sun. 1:30–5:30.*

Rue des Orfèvres (off rue de la Charité) is lined with Renaissance facades and distinguished by the church of **St-André-le-Bas,** once part of a powerful abbey. If possible, venture past the restoration now in progress, to see the finely sculpted 12th-century capitals (made of Roman stone) and the 17th-century wooden statue of St. Andrew. The cloisters are best during the music festival held here and at the cathedral from June to August. ⊠ *cour St-André,* ☎ *04–74–85–18–49.* 🎫 *9 frs.* ⏲ *Apr.–mid-Oct., Wed.–Mon. 9:30–1 and 2–6; mid-Oct.–Mar., Wed.–Sat. 10–noon and 2–5, Sun. 2–6.*

Across the Rhône from the town center is the excavated **Cité Gallo-Romaine,** where the Romans built spectacular villas. 🎫 *Free.* ⏲ *Daily.*

Dining

$$ ✕ **Le Bec Fin.** An inexpensive weekday menu makes this unpretentious eatery opposite the cathedral good for lunch and dinner. The steak and freshwater fish seldom disappoint and occasionally display a deft touch (turbot cooked with saffron). The dining room has an understated elegance. ⊠ *7 pl. St-Maurice,* ☎ *04–74–85–76–72. Reservations essential at dinner. Jacket required at dinner. MC, V. Closed Mon. No dinner Sun.*

Outdoor Activities and Sports

Rent horses at the **Centres Équestres** (⊠ Écuries du Couzon, La Petite Rente).

Serrières

31 *32 km (20 mi) south of Vienne, 59 km (37 mi) south of Lyon.*

River boats traditionally stop at little Serrières, on the Rhône's west bank. Life on the water is depicted at the **Musée des Mariniers du Rhône** (Boatmen's Museum), in the wooden-roofed Gothic chapel of St-Sornin. ☎ *04–75–34–01–26.* 🎫 *12 frs.* ⏲ *Apr.–Oct., weekends 3–6.*

Dining and Lodging

$$–$$$ ✕🏨 **Schaeffer.** In a sophisticated setting, chef Bernard Mathé dishes up inventive variants of traditional French dishes: smoked duck cutlet in lentil stew or lamb with eggplant in anchovy butter. The number of desserts is overwhelming, but pistachio cake with bitter chocolate is the clear winner. Reservations are essential and a jacket is required at the restaurant, which is closed Sunday night and Monday. Guest rooms are decorated in contemporary style. ✉ *quai Jules Roche, 07340,* ☎ *04–75–34–00–07,* FAX *04–75–34–08–79. 12 rooms. Restaurant. AE, DC, V. Closed 1st 3 wks Jan.*

Hauterives

32 *28 km (17 mi) east of Serrières, 40 km (25 mi) south of Vienne.*

Hauterives would be just another quaint village if not for the **Palais Idéal,** one of Western Europe's weirdest constructions. A fantasy constructed entirely of stones, it was the life work of a local postman, Ferdinand Cheval (1836–1924), haunted by visions of faraway mosques and temples. One of many wall inscriptions reads "1879–1912: 10,000 days, 93,000 hours, 33 years of toil." ☎ *04–75–68–81–19.* 🎫 *20 frs.* ⏲ *Daily 9–7 (9:30–5 in winter).*

Dining and Lodging

$$ ✕🏨 **Le Relais.** This comfortable, rustic inn is a stone's throw from the Palais Idéal. The good-size guest rooms have a country look, with chunky wooden desks and wicker chairs. The same warm, golden colors dominate the cozy restaurant, where you can enjoy roast partridge and delicately seasoned frogs' legs. Half board is mandatory in summer. ✉ *pl. de l'Église, 26390,* ☎ *04–75–68–81–12. 13 rooms. Restaurant. AE, DC, V. Closed Mon. and Jan.–Feb. No dinner Sun.*

Annonay

33 *44 km (27 mi) south of Vienne, 43 km (27 mi) southeast of St-Étienne.*

Prosperous Annonay, which grew up around the leather industry, is best known as the home of Joseph and Étienne Montgolfier, who, in 1783, invented the hot-air balloon (known in French as *une montgolfière*). The first flight was on June 4, 1783 in place des Cordeliers (although a commemorating obelisk is on avenue Marc-Seguin); the flight lasted a half hour and went to 6,500 feet. The narrow streets and passageways of central Annonay are full of character. Local history and folklore are evoked at the **Musée Vivarais César Filhol,** between the Mairie (Town Hall) and Notre-Dame church. ✉ *15 rue Béchetoille,* ☎ *04–75–67–67–93.* 🎫 *10 frs.* ⏲ *June–Aug., Tues.–Sun. 2–6; Sept.–May, Wed. and weekends 2–6.*

Tournon

34 *37 km (23 mi) southeast of Annonay, 59 km (37) mi) south of Vienne.*

Tournon is on the Rhône at the foot of granite hills. A hefty 15th- to 16th-century **Château** is its chief attraction. The castle's twin terraces have wonderful views of the old town, the river, and—towering above Tain-l'Hermitage across the Rhône—the steep vineyards that produce Hermitage wine, one of the region's most refined, and costly, reds. The museum of local history, in the château—the **Musée Rhodanien**—explores the life of Annonay-born engineer Marc Seguin (1786–1875), who built the first suspension bridge over the Rhône at Tournon in 1825 (demolished in 1965). ✉ *pl. Auguste-Faure,* ☎ *04–75–07–15–96.* 🎫 *15 frs.* ⏲ *June–Aug., Wed.–Mon. 10–noon and 2–6; Apr.–May and Sept.–Oct., Wed.–Mon. 2–6.*

A ride on one of France's last steam trains, the **Chemin de Fer du Vivarais,** makes an adventurous two-hour trip, 33 km (21 mi) along the narrow, rocky Doux Valley to Lamastre. Departures are from Tournon station. ☏ *04–78–28–83–34.* 🎫 *Round-trip: 150 frs.* ⏲ *June–Aug., daily 10 AM; May and Sept., weekends 10 AM.*

Dining and Lodging

$$ ✕ **Jean-Marc Reynaud.** Tain-l'Hermitage, across the Rhône from Tournon, is home to this fine restaurant with a comfortable, traditional dining room and a magnificent river view. The classic cuisine is brilliant; specialties include poached egg with foie gras, and pigeon fillet in black-currant sauce. ✉ *82 av. du Président-Roosevelt, Tain-l'Hermitage,* ☏ *04–75–08–07–96. AE, DC, MC, V. Closed Mon., Jan., and 1 wk in Aug. No dinner Sun.*

$$$ ✕🏨 **Michel Chabran.** This sophisticated hotel-restaurant is decidedly modern with its Danish-style furniture, floral displays, and airy picture windows overlooking the garden. The cuisine, such as grilled salmon in butter sauce, is imaginative and light. The restaurant is closed Sunday night and Monday, in winter. ✉ *29 av. du 45e Parallèle, 26600 Pont de l'Isère (on the east bank of the Rhône at Pont de l'Isère, 10 km/6 mi south of Tournon via N7 and 7 km/4 mi north of Valence),* ☏ *04–75–84–60–09,* FAX *04–75–84–59–65. 12 rooms. Restaurant. MC, V.*

En Route From Tournon's place Jean-Jaurès, slightly inland from the château, follow signs to narrow, twisting **Route Panoramique;** the views en route to the old village of St-Romain-de-Lerps are breathtaking. In good weather, the panorama at St-Romain includes 13 départements, Mont Blanc to the east, and arid Mont Ventoux to the south. D287 winds down to St-Péray and Valence; topping the **Montagne de Crussol,** 650 feet above the plain, is the ruined 12th-century **Château de Crussol.**

Valence

35 *17 km (11 mi) south of Tournon, 92 km (57 mi) west of Grenoble, 127 km (79 mi) north of Avignon.*

Largish Valence, the Drôme département capital, is the region's market center. Steep-curbed alleyways called *côtes* extend into the old town from the Rhône. At the center of the old town is the cathedral of **St-Apollinaire.** Although begun in the 12th century in the Romanesque style, it is not as old as it looks: Parts of it were rebuilt in the 17th century and the belfry in the 19th. The **Musée des Beaux-Arts,** next to the cathedral of St-Apollinaire, in the former 18th-century Bishops' Palace, displays local sculpture and furniture and 96 deft red-chalk drawings by landscapist Hubert Robert (1733–1808). ✉ *pl. des Ormeaux,* ☏ *04–75–79–20–80.* 🎫 *14 frs.* ⏲ *Mon.–Tues. and Thurs.–Fri. 2–6, Wed. and weekends 9–noon and 2–6.*

Dining and Lodging

$$$$ ★ ✕🏨 **Pic.** The Pic family are the undisputed kings among Drôme restaurateurs. Their food is subtle and original, such as the truffle-flavored *galettes* (pancakes) and asparagus with caviar. Comfortable, embroidered armchairs lend warmth to the carpeted peach dining room. In summer you can eat on the terrace. Reservations are essential and a jacket required at the restaurant, which is closed Sunday night and Wednesday. Three elegant guest rooms and two opulent suites are also available; book in advance. ✉ *285 av. Victor-Hugo, 26000,* ☏ *04–75–44–15–32,* FAX *04–75–40–96–03. 3 rooms, 2 suites. Restaurant. AE, DC, V. Closed Aug.*

En Route The best route between Valence and Privas is N8 on the right bank of the Rhône; after 16 km (10 mi) and just before La Voulte, turn onto attractive D120, which follows the Eyrieux Valley as far as Les Ollières-sur-Eyrieux; then turn south along D2, under the horse chestnut trees.

Privas

36 *41 km (25 mi) southwest of Valence.*

The capital of the spectacular Ardèche département, renowned for its caves and rocky gorges, Privas makes a good base for exploring the region. The tourist office, just off place Charles-de-Gaulle, can provide details. A Protestant stronghold during the 16th-century Wars of Religion, Privas was razed by Louis XIII in 1629, after 16 days of siege. The Pont Louis XIII over the River Ouvèze commemorates the town's return to royal good graces. It eventually became a peaceful administrative town, best known for the production of that French delicacy known as *marrons glacés* (candied chestnuts).

Dining

$–$$ ✕ **Lous Esclos.** This strikingly modern restaurant has more windows than walls—all overlooking the wild Ardèche landscape. The chef's masterpieces include goose and snail in flaky pastry—at prices that are too good to be true. ✉ *Alissas (5 km/3 mi southeast of Privas on D2),* ☏ *04–75–65–12–73. AE, V. Closed late-Dec.–mid-Jan.*

The Ardèche Valley

Aubenas is 30 km (18 mi) south of Privas on N104, 74 km (46 mi) northeast of Alés; Pont-St-Esprit is 43 km (27 mi) south of Montélimar, 45 km (28 mi) north of Avignon.

For the 120 km (75 mi) that the Ardèche River flows from its source to the Rhône, there is a spectacular variety of nature—basins of orchards, vertical cliffs, and spectacular gorges—plus medieval villages guarded by castles perched high up on rocky promontories. Make your base the small town of **Aubenas,** which has a thriving silk industry and a 12th-century castle (with later additions) that is now the town hall. The Ardèche River's source can be traced at the **Col de la Chavade** (1,266 meters/4,154 feet); take N102 west from Aubenas toward Mayres, 38 km (24 mi) upstream.

West of Aubenas on D104 and D579 is a 40-km (25-mi) stretch known as **La Valée Moyenne** (Middle Valley), where you'll find a number of small villages and a dramatic gorge. Pass through Rochecolombe and Balazuc to get to the small medieval village of **Voqümé.** Just before Ruoms, make a detour right on D245 for 3½ km (2 mi) en route to the tiny village of **Labesume:** The houses here are all built out of natural stone and, as if camouflaged, seem unnoticeable except for their balconies. Labesume is at the southern end of the **Gorges de la Beaume,** a 40-km (25-mi) gorge cut through by the Beaume River as it tumbles down from the Tanarque Massif to join the Ardèche River at Ruoms.

The last 58 km (35 mi) of the valley, from Vallon-Pont-d'Arc to Pont-St-Esprit, is particularly magnificent. Here you'll find another dramatic gorge, the 41-km-long (26-mi-long) **Gorges de l'Ardèche.** Route D290 runs from Vallon-Pont-d'Arc along the edge of the gorge on the side of the Gras Plâteau; stop periodically to look down. The most dramatic view of the gorge is from **Serre de Toure Belvedere,** about 11 km (7 mi) from Vallon, where you can peer down 750 feet to the river. Another 11 km (7 mi) along, the **Gournier Belevedere** permits a view of the river tumbling its way through the Gournier Toupine Rocks. All along the gorge are caverns and grottoes. The best is **Marzal Aven,** with its large variety of calcite formations. To reach it turn left onto D590 just after the Gournier Belevedere and drive about 5 km (3 mi); the entrance to the main cave is down 743 steps to the **Tomb Cave,** where translucent sheets of stalactites seem like shielding drapes to bear and deer bones. Spend a fascinating hour underground being guided through the fantastic caves; take a sweater, it can be chilly. *33 frs. Mid-Apr.–Sept., daily 9–6; mid-Mar.–mid-Apr. and Oct.–Nov., Sat. and Sun. 11, 3, and 5.*

Take one last look at the gorge at the **Ranc-Pointu Belvedere,** where the Le Louby River joins the Ardèche. Then the gorge ends and the countryside opens up to a fertile valley. Cross over the suspension bridge at **Pont-St-Esprit** and turn left on D941 to reach the Rhône and the north–south route A7 heading toward Montélimar.

Montélimar

37 *43 km (27 mi) north of Pont-St-Esprit, 35 km (22 mi) southeast of Privas, 83 km (52 mi) north of Avignon.*

Montélimar is the home of nougat, a chewy candy that can be bought at virtually every shop in town. The town got its name from the 12th- to 14th-century fortress of **Mont-Adhémar,** in a park surveying town and valley. *24 rue du Château, 04–75–01–07–85. 12 frs. Wed.–Mon. 9:30–11:30 and 2–5:30.*

Dining and Lodging

$$$ **Les Hospitaliers.** This tasteful, modern hotel with sweeping views is in tiny hilltop Le Poët-Laval, 22 km (14 mi) east of Montélimar. With its stone walls and red-tile roof, the hotel is perfect in its medieval setting. In cold weather, escape from the large but tacky rooms to the immense stone hearth in the sitting room. The airy restaurant serves local specialties; the thrush pâté with truffles is especially good. *Le Vieux Village, 26160 Le Poët-Laval, 04–75–46–22–32, FAX 04–75–46–49–99. 20 rooms. Restaurant, pool. AE, DC, MC, V. Closed mid-Nov.–Feb.*

Outdoor Activities and Sports

Horses can be rented from the **equestrian center** (Île Montmélian). A pleasant par-72 **golf course** is found at Château Le Monard (Montboucher-sur-Labron, Montélimar).

Shopping

Montélimar has more nougat shops than cafés; **Chabert et Guillot** (9 rue Charles-Chabert) is one of the best.

GRENOBLE AND THE ALPS

In winter, some of the world's best skiing is found in the Alps; in summer, chic spas, shimmering lakes, and hilltop trails come into their own. The Savoie and Haute-Savoie départements occupy the most impressive territory; Grenoble, in the Dauphiné, is the Alps' gateway and the area's only city. It's at the nexus of autoroutes from Marseille, Valence, Lyon, Geneva, and Turin.

Grenoble

38 *104 km (65 mi) southeast of Lyon, 138 km (86 mi) northeast of Montélimar.*

Cosmopolitan Grenoble's skyscrapers seem intimidating by homey French standards. But along with the city's nuclear research plant, they bear witness to the fierce local desire to move with the times. Grenoble is also home to a large university and is the birthplace of the great French novelist Stendhal. And all around are proud mountains, dramatic gorges, and hidden valleys.

A **cable car,** starting at quai St-Stéphane-Jay, on the north side of the River Isère, whisks you up to the hilltop and its **Fort de la Bastille,** with splendid views. *35 frs round-trip. Apr.–Oct., daily 9 AM–midnight; Nov.–Dec. and Feb.–Mar., daily 10–6.*

Rue Maurice-Gignoux is home to gardens, cafés, mansions, and a 17th-century convent that contains the **Musée Dauphinois,** a lively museum with local folk art. The "Premiers Alpins" exhibit explores the evolution of the Alps and its inhabitants. ✉ *30 rue Maurice-Gignoux,* ☎ *04–76–85–19–01. 15 frs, free Wed. Wed.–Mon. 9–noon and 2–6.*

The church of **St-Laurent,** near Musée Dauphinois, contains an atmospheric 6th-century crypt—one of the country's oldest Christian monuments—supported by a row of formidable marble pillars. ✉ *2 pl. St-Laurent,* ☎ *04–76–44–78–68. 15 frs. Wed.–Mon. 10–noon and 2–6.*

Place de Lavalette, on the south side of the river where most of Grenoble is concentrated, is the home to the **Musée de Grenoble,** the former Musée de Peinture et de Sculpture. Founded in 1796 and since enlarged, it is one of France's oldest museums and the first to concentrate on modern art (Picasso donated his *Femme Lisant* in 1921); a modern addition incorporates the medieval Tour de l'Isle, a Grenoble landmark. The collection includes 4,000 paintings and 5,500 drawings, including works from the Italian Renaissance, Rubens, Flemish still lifes, Zurburan, and Canaletto; Impressionists such as Renoir and Monet; and 20th-century works by Matisse (*Intérieur aux Aubergines),* Signac, Derain, Vlaminck, Magritte, Ernst, Miró, and Dubuffet. Modern sculpture adorns the gardens. ✉ *5 pl. de Lavalette,* ☎ *04–76–63–44–44. 25 frs. Wed. 11–10, Thurs.–Mon. 11–7.*

Dining and Lodging

$$–$$$ **Alpotel.** This reasonably priced chain hotel is modern and functional; comfortable rather than plush; and handily situated on a main boulevard a few minutes from the old town. The bustling restaurant's inventive menu has such delicacies as crab saveloy with cress, and poached salmon with pink butter. ✉ *12 bd. du Mal-Joffre, 38000,* ☎ *04–76–87–88–41,* FAX *04–76–47–58–42. 88 rooms with bath or shower. Restaurant, bar. AE, DC, MC, V.*

$$ **Château de la Commanderie.** The 13th-century building, in a southern suburb, has been owned by the same family for 200 years; ancestral portraits peer down on the grand salon. The 20th-century addition housing guest rooms needs work; some furnishings have seen better days. Still, rates are moderate and dining is a pleasure, and you may enjoy the juxtaposition of heirlooms—grandfather clocks alongside baroque blackamoors. Try the hot oysters coated with chopped watercress or venison fillet. The restaurant is closed weekends, except July and August. ✉ *17 av. D'Echirolles, 38320 Eybens,* ☎ *04–76–25–34–58,* FAX *04–76–24–07–31. 25 rooms. Restaurant, billiards, meeting rooms. AE, DC, MC, V.*

Nightlife and the Arts

The monthly *Grenoble-Spectacles* lists goings-on. **Le Joker** (✉ 1 Grande-Rue) is a youthful and lively disco. **La Soupe aux Choux** (✉ 7 rte. de Lyon) is the spot for jazz. **Cinq Jours de Jazz** is just that—five days of jazz—in February or March. In summer, classical fare characterizes the **Session Internationale de Grenoble-Isère.**

Outdoor Activities and Sports

The **Maison de La Randonée** (☒ 7 rue Voltaire, ☎ 04–76–51–76–00) has information on hiking around Grenoble.

En Route If you have time only for a brief glimpse of the Alps, take N91 out of Grenoble to Briançon, past the spectacular mountain scenery of L'Alpe d'Huez, Les Deux Alpes, and the Col du Galibier. Otherwise, take D512 north from Grenoble for 17 km (11 mi), fork left, and follow the small D57-D as far as you can (only a few miles) before leaving your car for the 30-minute climb to the top of the 6,000-foot Charmant Som peak. Your reward: a stimulating view over the Grande Chartreuse monastery to the north.

Grande Chartreuse

39 *23 km (14 mi) north of Grenoble.*

St-Bruno founded this 12-acre monastery in 1084; it later spawned 24 other charterhouses in Europe. Burned and rebuilt several times, it was stripped of possessions during the French Revolution, when the monks were expelled. On their return, they resumed making their sweet liqueur, Chartreuse, whose herb-based formulas are known today to only three monks. Today it is sold worldwide and is a main source of income for the monastery. Enclosed by wooded heights and limestone crags, the monastery is austere and serene. Although it is not open to visitors, you can see the road to it. Head north on D512 and fork left 8 km (5 mi) along D520-B just before St-Pierre-de-Chartreuse. The **Musée de La Correrie,** near the road to the monastery, has exhibits on monastic life and sells the monks' distillation. ☎ *04–76–88–60–45.* 🎟 *18 frs.* ⏲ *Easter–Oct., daily 9:30–noon and 2–6.*

Chartreuse is now also made in **Voiron,** 26 km (16 mi) west of St-Pierre-de-Chartreuse and 27 km (17 mi) northwest of Grenoble. Visit the distillery and enjoy a free tasting. ☒ *10 bd. Edgar-Kofler,* ☎ *04–76–05–81–77.* ⏲ *Daily except winter weekends, 8:30–11:30 and 2–5:30.*

Chambéry

40 *44 km (27 mi) northeast of Voiron, 40 km (25 mi) north of St-Pierre-de-Chartreuse, 55 km (34 mi) north of Grenoble.*

Elegant old Chambéry is the region's shopping hub. Townspeople congregate for coffee and people-watching on pedestrian **place St-Léger.** The town's highlight is the 14th-century **Château des Ducs de Savoie.** Its Gothic Ste-Chapelle has good stained glass and houses a replica of the Turin Shroud, once thought to have been Christ's burial wrappings, now known to have been a medieval hoax. ☒ *rue Basse du Château, no phone.* 🎟 *25 frs.* ⏲ *Guided tours May, June, and Sept., daily at 10:30 and 2:30; July and Aug., daily at 10:30, 2:30, 3:30, 4:30, and 5:30; Mar.–May and Oct.–Nov., Sat. at 2:15, Sun. at 3:30.*

Dining and Lodging

$$$$ ★ ✕🏨 **Château de Candie.** This rambling manor on a hill east of Chambéry makes a delightful base. M. Didier Lhostis, an avid antiques collector, spent four years renovating. Linger over a lavish breakfast in your large room—No. 106, a corner room with a view, has honey-gold beams, a grandfather clock, and a carved armoire. For dinner, chef Jean-Jacques's dishes include rabbit terrine with shallot compote and *escallope de fruits de mer* (seafood arranged in the shape of a lobster). ☒ *rue*

du Bois de Candie, 73000 Chambéry-le-Vieux (6 km/4 mi east of Chambéry), ☎ *04–79–96–63–00,* FAX *04–79–96–63–10. 20 rooms, 4 suites. Restaurant. AE, MC. V.*

Outdoor Activities and Sports

Horseback ride in the foothills of the Alps with a horse from the **Centre Équestre** (✉ Chenin des Bigornes, Voglans, ☎ 04–79–54–47–52).

Aix-les-Bains

41 *14 km (9 mi) north of Chambéry, 106 km (65 mi) east of Lyon.*

The family resort and spa town of Aix-les-Bains takes advantage of its position on the eastern side of Lac du Bourget, the largest natural fresh water lake in France, with a fashionable lakeshore esplanade. Although the lake is icy, you can sail, fish, play golf and tennis, or picnic on the 25 acres of parkland at the water's edge. On weekends it becomes horribly crowded. The main town of Aix is 3 km (2 mi) inland from the lake itself. Its sole reason for being is its thermal waters. Hundreds of small hotels line the streets and streams of visitors take to the baths each day. In the evening, they play the slot machines at the casino and attend tea dances.

The Roman Temple of Diana (2nd to 3rd centuries AD) now houses the **Musée Archéologique** (Archaeology Museum); enter via the tourist office on place Mollard. The ruins of the original Roman baths are underneath the present **Thermes Nationaux** (Thermal Baths), built in 1934. ⏲ *Guided tours only: Apr.–Oct., Mon.–Sat. at 3 PM; Nov.–Mar., Wed. at 3 PM.*

OFF THE BEATEN PATH **ABBAYE DE HAUTECOMBE** – Mass is celebrated with Gregorian chants at this picturesque spot, a half-hour boat ride from Aix-les-Bains. ☎ *04–79–54–26–12.* 🎫 *60 frs. Departures from the Grand Pont, Mar.–June and Sept.–Oct., daily at 2:30; July–Aug., daily at 9:30, 2, 2:30, 3, 3:30, and 4:30.*

Outdoor Activities and Sports

Some brave souls pursue water sports on the lake, but most swim in the local *piscine* or **pool** (✉ av. Daniel-Rops). The 18-hole **golf course** (✉ av. du Golf) is attractive.

En Route Fast A41 links Aix-les-Bains and Annecy. Prettier if longer: Go 24 km (15 mi) on D911; turn left onto D912 at La Charniaz to snake the 24 km (15 mi) north to Annecy next to the Montagne du Semnoz.

Annecy

42 *33 km (20 mi) north of Aix-les-Bains, 137 km (85 mi) east of Lyon, 43 km (27 mi) southwest of Geneva.*

Jewel-like Annecy is on crystal-clear Lac d'Annecy, surrounded by snow-tipped peaks. Though the canals, flower-decked bridges, and cobbled pedestrian streets are filled on market days, Tuesday and Friday, with shoppers and tourists, the town is still tranquil and invigorating. Does the River Thiou seem to flow the "wrong way" (out of the lake)? You're right: It drains the lake, feeding the town's canals. Most of the old town is now a pedestrian zone lined with half-timber houses. Most of the small restaurants are here, so you'll probably be back in the evening.

Meander through the old town, starting on the small island in the River Thiou, at the 12th-century **Palais de l'Isle,** once home to courts of law and a prison, now a landmark and one of France's most photographed sites. It houses the Musée d'Histoire d'Annecy (Museum of Annecy) and organizes visits to the old prisons and cultural exhibitions. ☎ *04–50–33–87–30.* *20 frs.* *June–Sept., Wed.–Mon. 10–6; Oct.–May, Wed.–Mon. 10–12 and 2–6.*

From the towers of the medieval **Château d'Annecy,** high on a hill opposite the Palais, there are good views of the lake. This mighty castle of four towers (the oldest is from the 12th century) has a stout defensive outer wall and an inner courtyard whose several dwellings reflect different eras of Annecy history (covered in a small permanent exhibit on site). ☎ *04–50–33–87–31.* *30 frs.* *June–Sept., Wed.–Mon. 10–6; Oct.–May, Wed.–Mon. 10–12 and 2–6.*

A drive around Lake Annecy—or at least along its eastern shore—is a must; set aside a half day for the 40-km (25-mi) drive. Picturesque **Talloires,** on the eastern side, has hotels and restaurants. Keep an eye open for the privately owned medieval **Château de Duingt.** You can tour the **Château de Menthon-St-Bernard.** ☎ *04–50–6–12–05.* *28 frs.* *Tours every afternoon July and Aug.; open Thurs. and weekend afternoons only in May, June, and Sept.*

Dining and Lodging

$ ✕ **Le Petit Zinc.** Near the Pont-Morens bridge in the old quarter, this cozy, beamed bistro serves reasonably-priced lunches. Locals throng for the cheese croquettes and salad, roast pork, and good carafes of wine—so show up early. ✉ *11 rue du Pont-Moren,* ☎ *04–50–51–12–93. No credit cards.*

$$$$ ✕ **Impérial Palace.** Though the Palace, across the lake from the town center, is Annecy's leading hotel, it lacks character. In contrast to its Belle Epoque exterior, the spacious, high-ceilinged guest rooms are done in the subdued colors so loved by contemporary designers. The better rooms face the public gardens on the lake; waking up to breakfast on the terrace is a great way to start the day. Service is professional, but you pay for it. Fine cuisine is served in the stylish La Voile (jacket and tie required); Le Jackpot Café in the casino is acceptable and less costly. ✉ *32 av. Albigny, 74000,* ☎ *04–50–09–30–00,* FAX *04–50–09–33–33. 98 rooms. 2 restaurants, casino. AE, DC, MC, V.*

$$$$ ✕ **Père Bise.** This deluxe inn on the lake has a leafy veranda, fine views, and a classy restaurant (with less-than-perfect service). Chef Sophie Bise's grilled lobster with spicy tomato and her puff pastry with potatoes, foie gras, and truffles are memorable. You'll also find a superb wine list and the famous *marjolaine,* a multilayer chocolate-and-nut cake. Alas, some of the non-air-conditioned rooms are stuffy and the better ones are very expensive. ✉ *rte. du Port, 74290 Talloires,* ☎ *04–50–60–72–01,* FAX *04–50–60–73–05. 25 rooms, 9 suites. Restaurant. AE, DC, MC, V. Closed Dec.–Mar.*

$$ ★ **Hôtel du Palais de l'Isle.** Steps away from the lake, in the heart of old Annecy, is this delightful small hotel. Without destroying the buiding's antiquity, the rooms have a cheery, contemporary look and Starck furnishings; some have a view of the Palais de l'Isle. Room rates reflect the size of the room. Breakfast is served. Though the area is pedestrian only, you can drive up to unload luggage. ✉ *13 rue Perrière, 74000,* ☎ *04–50–45–86–87,* FAX *04–50–51–87–15. 26 rooms. MC, V.*

Outdoor Activities and Sports

Bikes can be rented at the **train station** (✉ pl. de la Gare). Mountain bikes are available from **Sports Passion** (✉ 3 av. du Parmelan, ☎ 04–50–51–46–28) and **Loca Sports** (✉ 37 av. de Loverchy, ☎ 04–50–45–44–33).

Thonon-les-Bains

43 *74 km (46 mi) east of Annecy, 37 km (23 mi) northeast of Geneva.*

Most of the south side of Lake Geneva (Lac Léman in French) is French, not Swiss, and is popular for its thermal waters. Thonon-les-Bains, a fashionable summer resort, primarily draws Geneva residents.

Evian-les-Bains

44 *9 km (6 mi) east of Thonon-les-Bains, 83 km (52 mi) east of Annecy.*

People stay in chic Evian-les-Bains as much to be seen as for the creature comforts and spa facilities of its deluxe hotels. In late afternoon, they promenade along the lake—a constitutional that precedes formal dinner parties.

En Route Many Alpine **ski resorts** lie south of Lake Geneva, accessible via riverside D902: **Morzine; Avoriaz,** accessible via Thonon-les-Bains and by cable car (or D338) from Morzine; and **Cluses.** From Cluses, take N205 left along the Arve Valley to get to Chamonix.

Chamonix

45 *96 km (60 mi) south of Thonon-les-Bains, 94 km (58 mi) east of Annecy, 83 km (51 mi) southeast of Geneva.*

Chamonix is the oldest and biggest of the French winter-sports resort towns. It was the site of the first Winter Olympics, held in 1924. The world's highest cable car soars 12,000 feet up the Aiguille du Midi, for positively staggering views of 15,700-foot **Mont Blanc,** Europe's loftiest peak. Be prepared for a lengthy wait, both going up and coming down—and wear warm clothing. *185 frs round-trip. May–Sept., daily 8–4:45; Oct.–Apr., daily 8–3:45.*

Dining and Lodging

$$$ **Albert I & Milan.** At the town's best-value quality hotel, rooms are furnished with elegant reproductions and most have balconies. The dining room has stupendous Mont Blanc views, while Pierre Carrier's cuisine scales heights of invention; try the oysters fried with asparagus. ✉ *119 impasse du Montenvers, 74400,* ☎ *04–50–53–05–09,* FAX *04–50–55–95–48. 17 rooms, 12 suites. Restaurant, pool, hot tub, sauna. AE, DC, MC, V. Closed 2 wks mid-May.*

Outdoor Activities and Sports

Contact the **Chamonix Tourist Office** (☞ Lyon and the Alps A to Z, *below*) for information on skiing in the area. The 18-hole **Chamonix Public Course** (✉ rte. de Tines, Les Praz de Chamonix) has Mont Blanc for a background.

Megève

46 *35 km (22 mi) west of Chamonix, 69 km (43 mi) southeast of Geneva.*

Idyllic Alpine Megève is not only a major ski resort, but also a chic winter watering hole that draws royalty, celebrities, and big wallets from all over the world. In summer it's popular with golfers. From Megève, the drive along D909 to Albertville is through one of the prettiest little gorges in the Alps.

Dining and Lodging

$$$$ ★ **Chalet-Hôtel du Mont d'Arbois.** This rustic but quietly sophisticated mountain roost overlooking Megève is run by Nadine de Rothschild. Its well-appointed rooms have fine views and are decorated with antiques; down comforters cover the beds. It also has the best restau-

rant in town, with delicious spit-roasted meats and fish (try salmon in red-wine sauce). The superb wine list features many bottles from the Rothschilds' Bordeaux vineyards. ✉ *447 chemin Rocaille, 74120,* ☎ *04–50–21–25–03,* FAX *04–50–21–24–79. 20 rooms, 1 suite. Restaurant, pool, sauna, 18-hole golf course, tennis courts. AE, DC, MC, V. Closed Apr.–mid-June, Oct.–mid-Dec.*

Outdoor Activities and Sports

For information about skiing in the area contact the tourist office (☞ Lyon and the Alps A to Z, *below*). In summer, play at the 18-hole **Megève Golf Course** (✉ Mont d'Arbois).

Albertville

47 *32 km (20 mi) southwest of Megève, 80 km (50 mi) northeast of Grenoble.*

Albertville, in the Arly Valley, was the site of the 1992 Winter Olympics. To the south are two other serious ski resorts, where many of the Olympic competitions were held. As a result, you'll find some of France's most up-to-date ski facilities in the area, though Albertville itself is more of a transit town to the slopes around it than a resort.

Courchevel, at the base of a vast north-facing Alpine amphitheater whose snows last long into spring, started out as a rustic Savoyard village; it's now oh-so-chic, comprised of a quartet of planned ski villages named for their metric elevation. **Méribel,** with Courchevel, is part of the Les Trois Vallées (Three Valleys) area, with **Val Thorens** and **Les Menuires.**

Bourg-St-Maurice

48 *53 km (33 mi) east of Albertville on the spectacular D925 (becomes D902), 76 km (47 mi) south of Chamonix.*

In winter, Bourg-St-Maurice, in the Isère Valley, is a bustling ski station. In summer, it is a popular base for hiking, mountain biking, and kayaking along the Isère. **Les Arcs** ski resort is 11 km (7 mi) up the mountain peaks that rise up more than 3,000 meters (9,900 feet) from Bourg-St-Maurice. **Tignes,** another major ski resort, is 20 km (12 mi) beyond Les Arcs via D902. **Val d'Isère,** a favorite ski resort among the rich and famous, is 31 km (19 mi) from Bourg-St-Maurice. An extensive network of chairlifts and cable cars connect Tignes and Val d'Isère with other, smaller resorts—**La Daille, Les Boisses,** and **Les Brévières.**

Outdoor Activities and Sports

A map of hiking trails and information about skiing in Les Arcs is available at the **Bourg-St-Maurice Tourist Office** (pl. de la Gare, ☎ 04–79–07–04–92), across from the train station. The **Le Lac Tourist Office** (☎ 04–79–06–50–09) in Tignes can help you organize all kinds of sporting activities in the area. Mountain bikes can be rented from **Cyclo Minoret** (✉ 66 av. Général Leclerc, ☎ 04–79–07–70–16). **L'Espace Killy** (☎ 04–79–06–00–35) encompasses Val d'Isère and Tignes, with over 100 lifts and endless skiing possibilities.

En Route From Val d'Isère to Bonneval-sur-Arc (at 9,084 feet the country's highest mountain pass, accessible only between July and late October), take the **Route de l'Iséran,** D902, for some magnificent views. From Bonneval-sur-Arc, continue on D902 to **Lanslevillard,** which is tucked in beneath an old church on a rocky outcrop; soon after the town D902 broadens into N6. Further along N6 is Modane, and just beyond, the 13-km (9-mi) **Tunnel du Fréjus,** which leads to Italy. At St-Michel de Maurienne, pick up D902 south, now called the **Route du Galibier.** Usually closed November to May, it twists between France and Italy in rugged grandeur, passing through the busy ski village of **Valloire.** Enjoy the spectacular views along the Route du Galibier as you wind up the barren **Col du Galibier,** one of the French Alps' highest passes. A short walk to the 8,900-foot summit (follow signs) yields a panorama of the southern Alps. Just afterward, stop to admire a monument to Henri Desgranges, founder of the Tour de France bike race, and spare a thought for the hapless cyclists who pedal up here each July. Eight kilometers (5 miles) past the Col du Galibier, before N91, is 6,750-foot **Col du Lautaret,** alive with wildflowers in summer.

Briançon

★ 49 *117 km (73 mi) southeast of Grenoble, 52 km (32 mi) south of Valloire.*

Altitudinous Briançon combines historic appeal with direct access to the Serre-Chevalier ski complex, accessible via cable car from the lower town. The old town, referred to as the **Ville Haute** (Upper Town) or Briançon-Vauban, was remodeled by Vauban from 1692 onward. His three-tiered defensive outworks proved their worth in 1815 by keeping marauding Austro-Sardinian troops at bay in the aftermath of Waterloo. The **Porte Pignerol** is one of the town's four gateways.

Since the area is famed for its sunny microclimate (300 days of rays a year), it's not surprising that both towers of the early 18th-century **Collégiale Notre-Dame** have a sundial; it's accessible via avenue Vauban, to the right after you enter the old town through Porte Pignerol. There are two more sundials on bustling **place d'Armes,** which leads to the Ville Haute's main street. **Grande Gargouille,** also called Grande Rue, has a gutter down the middle. Admire the fine doorway at No. 64, built in 1714, and the **Fontaine François I,** whose spouts whimsically take the shape of elephants' heads. Rue du Pont-Asfeld, off Grande Rue, leads past the Chapelle des Pénitents and the **Église des Cordeliers** (down stone stairs), renowned for its 15th-century frescoes. The daring **Pont d'Asfeld** (Asfeld Bridge), at the end of rue du Pont-Asfeld, straddles the River Durance. Admire the view, then head along chemin de Rond, beneath the citadel, back to Porte Pignerol.

Lodging

$$ **Vauban.** Despite its name, this hotel is in a modern, unpretentious, comfortable, and convenient building—300 yards from the train station and a 10-minute walk from the Ville Haute. Many rooms have balconies. The best face south on the fourth floor. ✉ *13 av. du Général-de-Gaulle, 05100,* ☎ *04–92–21–12–11,* FAX *04–92–50–58–20. 44 rooms, 26 with bath, 12 with shower. Restaurant, bar. MC, V. Closed early Nov.–Dec.*

Château-Queyras

50 *29 km (18 mi) south of Briançon.*

Château-Queyras is perched on a hilltop above the Guil Valley. A **fort** has stood here since the 14th century. Cross the drawbridge to visit the casemates, courtyard, and 14th-century keep. *18 frs.* ⌚ *Mid-June–early Sept., Wed.–Mon. 10–7.*

En Route From Château-Queyras, drive south on D902 along the crystal-clear River Guil, beneath pine-covered slopes and the jagged Combe du Queyras.

Montdauphin

51 *15 km (9 mi) southwest of Château-Queyras, 36 km (22 mi) south of Briançon.*

Montdauphin sits on a barren promontory at 3,400 feet. Vauban chose this strategic site for a new citadel and used local pink stone to build a fortified town from scratch. He intended to attract a community, but only soldiers lived here until 1980, when artisans and craftsmen moved in. The 18th-century **Arsenal** outlines Montdauphin's construction—it took nearly a century. Other highlights include the **Poudrière** (powder mill), with its vaulted upper chamber and larch-beam ground floor; the airy **church**, and the huge beamed roof of the **Caserne Rochambeau** (barracks). ☎ *04–92–45–17–80 for guided tours.*

LYON AND THE ALPS A TO Z

Arriving and Departing

By Car

A6 speeds south from Paris to Lyon (463 km/287 mi). The Tunnel de Fourvière, which cuts through Lyon, is a classic hazard, and at peak times you may sit for hours. From Marseille, Lyon is 313 km (194 mi) north on A7.

By Plane

The international airport is in **Satolas** (☎ 04–72–22–72–21 for flight information), 26 km (16 mi) east of Lyon. **Air Inter, British Airways,** and many other major carriers have connecting services from Paris into Lyon-Satolas. Air Inter also flies between Paris and Grenoble. Frequent **shuttle buses** run from the airport to the center of Lyon between 5 AM and 9 PM, and for the train station 6 AM and 11 PM; journey time is 35–45 minutes; the fare is 45 francs. There's also a bus from Satolas to Grenoble; journey time is just over an hour, and the fare is 120 francs.

By Train

The high-speed TGV (Trains à Grande Vitesse) to Lyon leaves from Paris (Gare de Lyon) hourly and arrives in just two hours. There are also six TGVs daily between Charles de Gaulle airport near Paris and Lyon. The TGV also has less frequent service to Grenoble and villages in the Alps.

Getting Around

By Bus

Buses cover the entire region, but Lyon and Grenoble are the two main bus stations for long distance (national and international) routes. From these towns, buses go to the smaller towns.

By Car

Regional roads are fast and well maintained, though smaller mountainous routes can be difficult to navigate, and high passes may be closed in winter.

By Plane

There are domestic airports at Grenoble, Valence, Annecy, Chambéry, and Aix-les-Bains.

By Subway

Lyon's good subway system serves both of the city's train stations. A single ticket costs 7.50 francs, and a 10-ticket book 65 francs. A day pass for bus and métro is 23.50 francs (available from bus drivers and the automated machines in the métro).

By Taxi

Lyon Espace Affairés (☎ 04–78–39–26–11) runs a fleet of well-kept taxi-vans in the city.

By Train

Major rail junctions include Grenoble, Annecy, Valence, Chambéry, and Lyon with frequent train service to other points. Albertville is the rail station for continuing by bus up into the Alps to the ski resorts of Val d'Isère, Courchevel, and Megève.

Contacts and Resources

Car Rental

Avis (✉ 1 av. du Docteur-Desfrançois, Chambéry, ☎ 04–79–33–58–54; and Aéroport de Lyon-Satolas, ☎ 04–72–22–75–25). **Hertz** (✉ 16 rue Émile-Gueymard, Grenoble, ☎ 04–76–43–12–92; and 11 rue Pasteur, Valence, ☎ 04–75–44–39–45).

Guided Tours

The **Lyon Tourist Office** (✉ pl. Bellecour, ☎ 04–78–42–25–75) organizes walking tours of the city in English, as well as minibus tours. To survey Lyon by air, contact the **Aéro-Club du Rhône et du Sud-Est** (✉ Aéroport de Lyon-Bron, 69500 Bron, ☎ 04–78–26–83–97). **Navig-Inter** (✉ 13 bis quai Rambaud, 69002 Lyon, ☎ 04–78–42–96–81) arranges daily boat trips along the Saône and Rhône Rivers. **Philibert** (✉ 24 av. Barthélémy-Thimonier, B.P. 16, 69300 Caluire, ☎ 04–72–23–10–56, FAX 04–72–27–00–97) runs bus tours of the region from April to October.

Travel Agencies

American Express (✉ 6 rue Childebert, 69002 Lyon, ☎ 04–78–37–40–69). **Wagons-Lits** (✉ 76 rue des Alliés, 38100 Grenoble, ☎ 04–76–40–47–78; 48 bd. Vauban, 26000 Valence, ☎ 04–75–42–02–04).

Visitor Information

Contact the **Comité Régional du Tourisme Rhône-Alpes** (✉ 78 rte. de Paris, 69260 Charbonnières-les-Bains, ☎ 04–72–59–21–59) for Lyon and the Alps. The **Maison du Tourisme** (✉ 14 rue de la République, B.P. 227, 38019 Grenoble, ☎ 04–76–42–41–41) deals with the Isère département and the area around Grenoble.

Local tourist offices for towns mentioned in this chapter include: **Annecy** (✉ Centre Bonlieu, 1 rue Jean-Jaurès, ☎ 04–50–45–00–33). **Briançon** (✉ 1 pl. du Temple, ☎ 04–92–21–08–50). **Bourg-en-Bresse** (✉ 6 av. d'Alsace-Lorraine, ☎ 04–74–22–49–40). **Chambéry** (✉ 24 bd. de la Colonne, ☎ 04–79–33–42–47). **Chamonix** (✉ 85 pl. du Triangle de l'Amitié, ☎ 04–50–53–00–24). **Courchevel** (✉ La Croisette, ☎ 04–79–08–00–29). **Evian-les-Bains** (✉ pl. d'Allinges, ☎ 04–50–75–04–26). **Grenoble** (✉ 14 rue de la République, ☎ 04–76–42–41–41; ✉ Train station, ☎ 04–76–54–34–36). **Lyon** (✉ pl. Bellecour, ☎ 04–78–42–25–75; ✉ av. Adolphe Max, near cathedral, ☎ 04–78–42–25–75; ✉ Perrache train station). **Megève** (✉ rue Monseigneur Conseil, ☎ 04–50–21–27–28). **Montélimar** (✉ av. Rochemaure, ☎ 04–75–01–00–20). **Privas** (✉ 3 rue Elie-Reynier, ☎ 04–75–64–33–35). **Valence** (✉ parvis de la gare, ☎ 04–75–44–90–40). **Vienne** (✉ cours Brillier, ☎ 04–74–85–12–62).

11 The Massif Central and the Auvergne

The Parc National des Volcans, Rocamadour, and the Gorges du Tarn

Metropolitan pleasures are scarce in the Massif Central and the Auvergne, but wide-open spaces, volcanic peaks, and gorges abound. This is a land of early to bed and early to rise, of hearty meals, and of delight in nature. The thrill of unblemished countryside and the awe of spectacular panoramas are reminders of our basic relationship to the earth.

Updated by Nigel Fisher

WINDSWEPT PLAINS, SNOWCAPPED mountains, volcanic plateaus, deep ravines, and thick forests are at the heart of the Massif Central and the Auvergne, France's geographic center. To outsiders this isolated and insular land is forbidding; even for inhabitants, it has made life hard. In the old days, it is said, people trained their dogs to lie on top of them for warmth; dangers, real and imagined, lurked everywhere.

The region has been a battleground since the dawn of history: Romans versus Arvernes (the original Celtic settlers); Gauls versus Visigoths; Charlemagne versus Saracens; the Duke of Dakotan versus Frankish kings Pépin I and II; English Plantagenets versus French kings in the Hundred Years' War; the dukes of Bourbon versus Francis I; and Huguenots versus Catholics in the Wars of Religion. By the Revolution, the Auvergnois had had enough; they kept to themselves and managed to escape most of of the Revolution's excesses. In World War II, Nazi puppet Pétain set up a figurehead French government at Vichy, and thus the region was spared from bombing. Though embroiled in tumultuous history, the people of the Massif Central and the Auvergne have never been part of courtly France. Their heritage is the rugged geography.

Pleasures and Pastimes

Dining

Food in the Massif Central and the Auvergne is fuel for the body; fine dining it is not. But there are a few regional specialties: *aligot* (puree of potatoes with Tomme de Cantal cheese and garlic), *cousinat* (chestnut soup), *sanflorin* (fried pork and herbs in pastry), and *salmis de colvert Cévenole* (wild duck sautéed in red wine and onions). Several well-known cheeses are also made here: Roquefort, creamy Bleu d'Auvergne, Gaperon with garlic, and the delightfully nutty St-Nectaire. In summer, bakers turn *myrtilles* (blueberries) into pies and tarts.

CATEGORY	COST*
$$$$	over 400 frs
$$$	250 frs–400 frs
$$	125 frs–250 frs
$	under 125 frs

**per person for a three-course meal, including tax (20.6%) and tip but not wine*

Lodging

Because the region was difficult to get to for so long, you won't find a large selection of accommodations. The larger towns generally have modest hotels; the villages have small inns; a few châteaux dot the countryside. In July and August rates are higher and rooms are at a premium, so be sure to make reservations in advance. Many hotels are closed from November to March.

CATEGORY	COST*
$$$$	over 800 frs
$$$	550 frs–800 frs
$$	300 frs–550 frs
$	under 300 frs

**All prices are for a standard double room for two, including tax (20.6%) and service charge.*

Outdoor Activities and Sports

Few tourists venture up to the region's volcanic peaks or along its gorges, making the Massif Central a great alternative to the Alps for outdoor adventures. Bicycling and mountain biking (known as VTT, *vélo touts terrains*) over the hills and along country roads is a good way to see the region. Bikes can be rented at train stations in most towns. For serious hiking or ardent ambling strike out along the extensive network of trails that crisscross the large Parc National des Volcans and follow the Gorges du Tarn. For gentler hiking from village to village and valley to valley follow the Monts du Cantal.

Exploring the Massif Central and the Auvergne

France's heartland offers dramatic untouched terrain, quiet medieval villages, imposing castles, and few large towns: Clermont-Ferrand (population 150,000), in the center of the region, is the major metropolis; elegant, infamous Vichy and industrial St-Etienne are two other cities. The expansive Parc National des Volcans, the grand Gorges du Tarn, and the magnificent Cévennes mountains, crisscrossed with canyons, are favorite destinations of nature lovers.

Great Itineraries

The size of the Massif Central makes it infeasible to see everything in one trip. With 10 days, however, you can cover much of the region by car, if you don't mind a lot of driving. In three days you can see the land of the Bourbon kings, from Bourges to Moulins, and drive through the Parc National des Volcans as far as Orcival before heading west to the Dordogne River or east to the Rhône Valley.

Numbers in the text correspond to numbers in the margin and on The Massif Central and the Auvergne map.

IF YOU HAVE 3 DAYS

Begin your first day in **Bourges** ①, the former, short-lived capital of France. Spend the night nearby at the Château de la Commanderie. On day two, explore Bourbonnais country, with stops in **Bourbon-l'Archambault** ③ and **Souvigny** ④. Head to medieval **Moulins** ⑤ for the night. On day three, drive through the **Parc National des Volcans** to see the natural wonder, the **Puy-de-Dôme** ⑬, then visit the Romanesque church in **Orcival** ⑭.

IF YOU HAVE 10 DAYS

Have lunch in **Bourges** ①, then head to the Château de la Commanderie in nearby St-Amand-Montrand for the night. The second day explore **Bourbon-l'Archambault** ③, **Souvigny** ④, and **Moulins** ⑤, home of the Bourbons. On day three, pass through **Vichy** ⑦ on your way to **Thiers** ⑧; stop in **Roanne** ⑨ for the night and try to dine at the superb Troisgros restaurant. The following day drive south to **Le Puy-en-Velay** ⑪ and on to **Millau** ㉛; stay overnight there or in one of the towns closer to the **Gorges du Tarn** ㉜. The next day explore the Tarn Gorge, then drive through the Corniches des Cévennes to **Anduze** ㉞. On day six retrace your steps by winding through the **Gorges de la Jonte** ㉟ back to Millau, then head south to the impressive **Cirque de Navacelles** ㊳. Stop in the cheese-producing caves at **Roquefort-sur-Soulzon** ㉚ on your way to beautiful **Plaisance** ㉙; have a fantastic dinner at Les Magnolias. The following day head to **Rodez** ㉘ to see its pink sandstone cathedral, en route to the basilica in **Conques** ㉗. By nightfall get to **Cahors** ㉔ on the Lot River. Explore Cahors and **St-Cirq-Lapopie** ㉕ on the morning of day eight; in the afternoon drive to **Rocamadour** ㉓, the wondrous pilgrim village carved into a rock face. On day nine work your way northeast to medieval **Salers** ⑲. Spend the last day traveling through the **Parc National des Volcans** around the **Puy-de-Dôme** ⑬ on your way to **Clermont-Ferrand** ⑫.

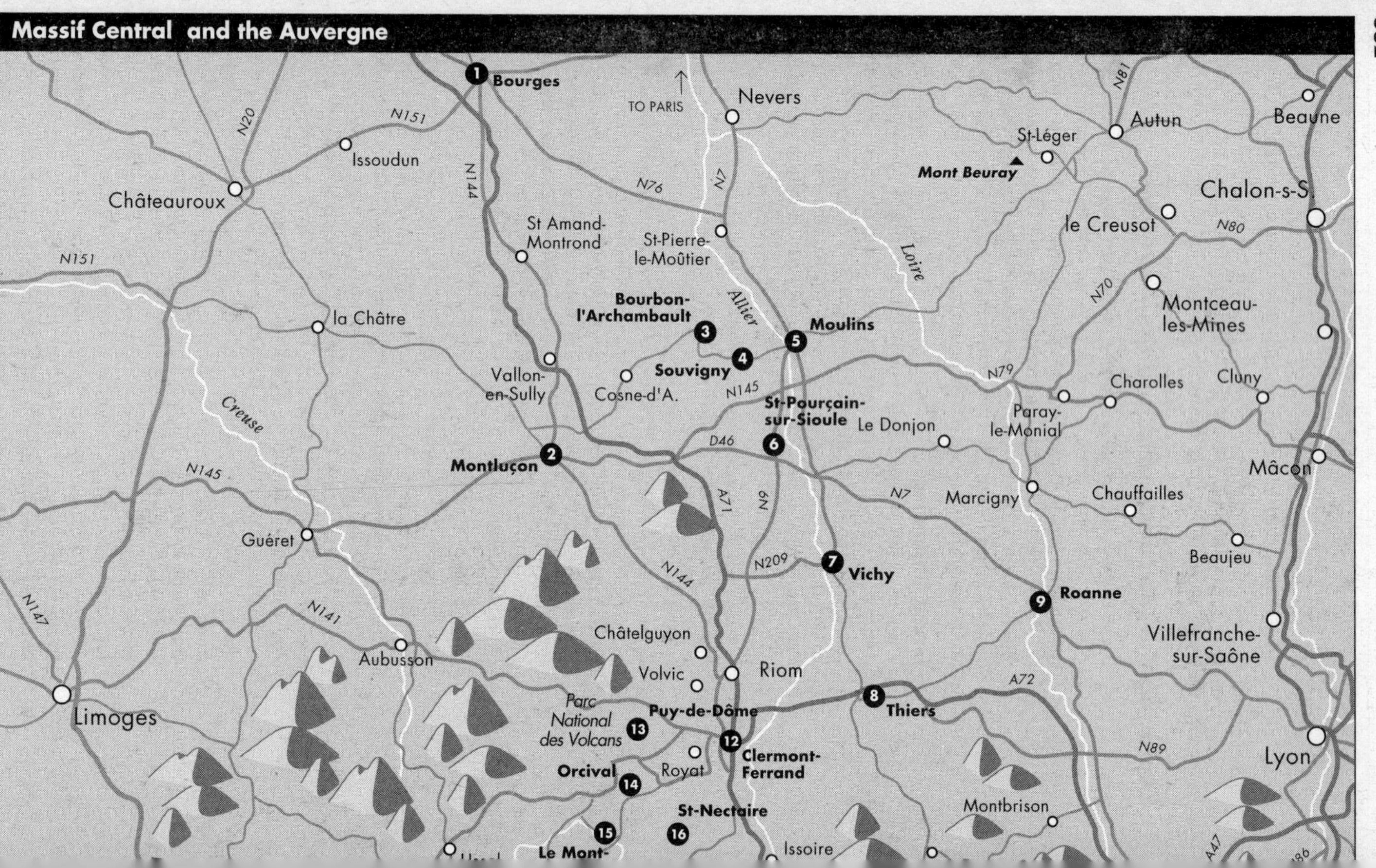
Massif Central and the Auvergne
Bourges
TO PARIS
Nevers
N20
N151
Issoudun
Châteauroux
N144
N76
N7
St Amand-Montrond
St-Pierre-le-Moûtier
N151
la Châtre
Bourbon-l'Archambault
Allier
Moulins
Souvigny
Vallon-en-Sully
Cosne-d'A.
N145
St-Pourçain-sur-Sioule
Le Donjon
Creuse
D46
Montluçon
N145
Guéret
A71
N9
N7
Marcigny
N209
Vichy
N144
Roanne
N147
N141
Châtelguyon
Aubusson
Volvic
Riom
Limoges
Parc National des Volcans
Puy-de-Dôme
Thiers
Clermont-Ferrand
Orcival
Royat
St-Nectaire
Le Mont-
Issoire
Montbrison
Loire
Mont Beuray
St-Léger
N81
Autun
Beaune
Chalon-s-S.
le Creusot
N80
N70
Montceau-les-Mines
N79
Charolles
Cluny
Paray-le-Monial
Mâcon
Chauffailles
Beaujeu
Villefranche-sur-Saône
A72
N89
Lyon
A47
1
2
3
4
5
6
7
8
9
12
13
14
15
16

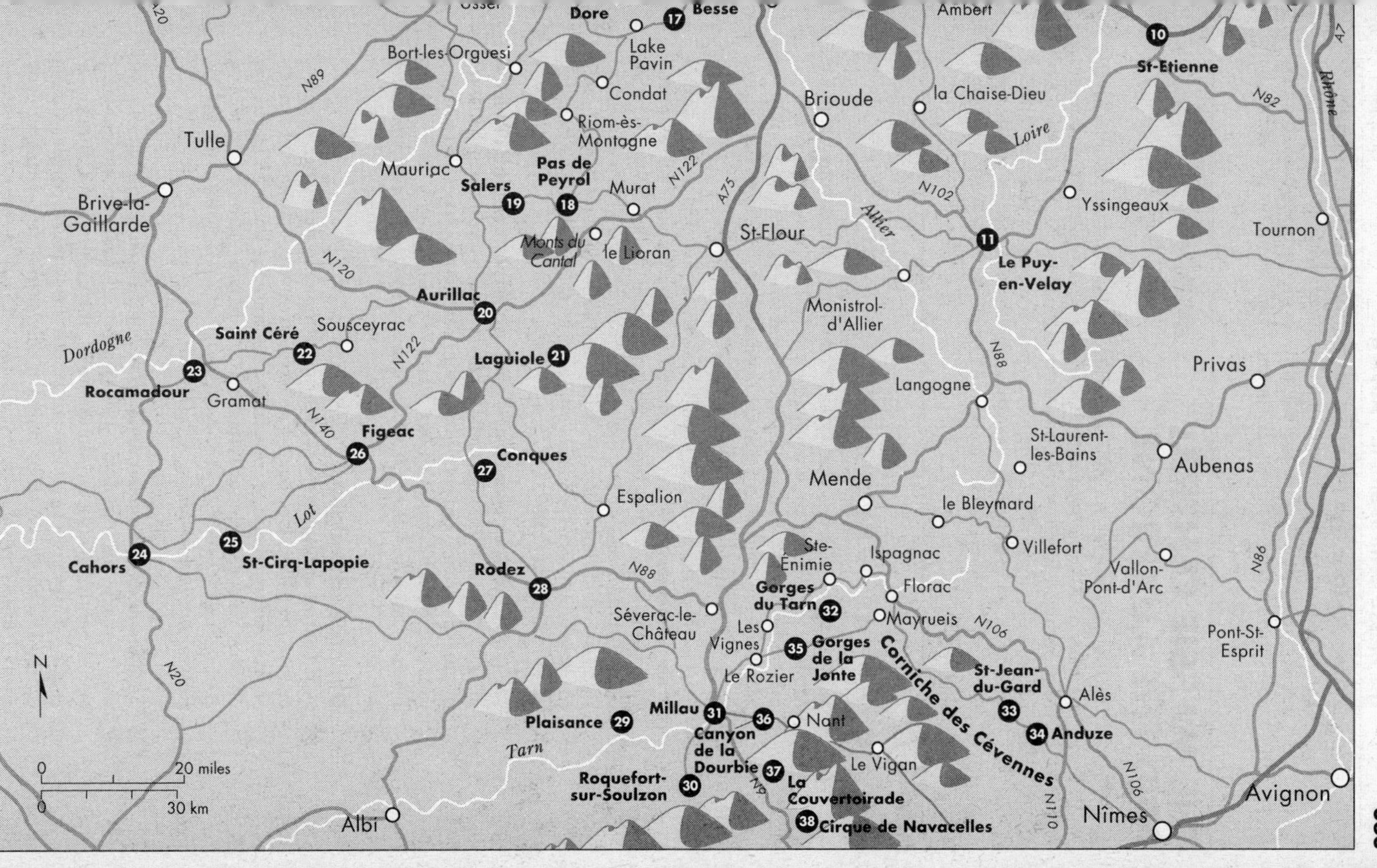

Dore
17 Besse
Ambert
10 St-Etienne
A7
Rhône
Bort-les-Orgues
Lake Pavin
Condat
Riom-ès-Montagne
Brioude
la Chaise-Dieu
Loire
N82
N89
Tulle
Mauriac
Pas de Peyrol
Salers 19
18
Murat
N122
A75
N102
Yssingeaux
Tournon
Brive-la-Gaillarde
Monts du Cantal
le Lioran
St-Flour
Allier
11 Le Puy-en-Velay
N120
Aurillac 20
Monistrol-d'Allier
Saint Céré 22
Sousceyrac
N122
Dordogne
Laguiole 21
N88
Privas
23 Rocamadour
Gramat
Langogne
N140
Figeac 26
27 Conques
St-Laurent-les-Bains
Aubenas
Mende
Espalion
le Bleymard
Lot
25 St-Cirq-Lapopie
24 Cahors
Villefort
Ste-Enimie
Ispagnac
Vallon-Pont-d'Arc
N86
Rodez 28
N88
Florac
Gorges du Tarn 32
Séverac-le-Château
Mayrueis
N106
Pont-St-Esprit
Les Vignes
35 Gorges de la Jonte
Corniche des Cévennes
St-Jean-du-Gard 33
N
N20
Le Rozier
Alès
Plaisance 29
Millau 31
36
Nant
34 Anduze
Tarn
Canyon de la Dourbie 37
Le Vigan
N106
0
20 miles
0
30 km
Roquefort-sur-Soulzon 30
N9
La Couvertoirade
Avignon
Albi
38 Cirque de Navacelles
N110
Nîmes

When to Tour the Massif Central and the Auvergne

Fall, when the sun is still warm on the shimmering, golden trees, and early spring (May), when the wildflowers are in bloom, are the best times to visit central France. In summer it's hot and the sky is cloudy; in winter it's cold.

THE MASSIF CENTRAL AND THE AUVERGNE

The Massif Central is roughly demarcated by Burgundy, the Rhône River, Languedoc-Roussillon, and the Dordogne River valley. From Bourges to Montluçon the area is known as the Bourbonnais, for the dynasty of kings that it spawned. The Auvergne—the core of central France—stretches from Montluçon to Aurillac and is characterized by *puys* (craggy lava peaks). Along the Dordogne and Lot rivers, to the west, is the Dordogne region.

Bourges

❶ *243 km (151 mi) south of Paris.*

Find your way to Bourges, and you'll find yourself at the center of France. Modern times have largely passed it by, and the result is a preserved market town with medieval cathedral and streets. Pedestrian-only rue Mirabeau and rue Coursarlon are lined with timber-frame houses and are particularly charming places to stroll and shop.

★ Approaching the town you'll see the towers of the 13th-century **Cathédrale St-Etienne.** The central portal is a masterpiece of sculpture: Cherubim, angels, saints, and prophets cluster in the archway. The interior is unlike that of any other Gothic cathedral. The height of the side aisles that flank the nave is an astonishing 65 feet—high enough to allow windows to be placed above the level of the second side aisles. ✉ *Off rue Porte Jaune.*

The **Palais Jacques-Coeur** is one of the most luxurious Gothic dwellings in France. Notice its vaulted chapel, the wooden ceilings covered with original paintings, and the dining room with its tapestries and massive fireplace. ✉ *rue Jacques-Coeur,* ☎ *02–48–24–06–87.* 🎫 *31 frs.* ⏲ *Daily 9–noon and 2–6. 45-min guided tours only, begin 15 mins after the hr.*

Dining and Lodging

$$ ✕🏨 **Central et Angleterre.** This efficient hotel in the center of town, close to the palace, is popular with business travelers. Rooms have modern conveniences, and the restaurant, decorated in Louis XVI style, has prix-fixe menus starting at 120 francs. ✉ *1 pl. des Quatre-Piliers, 18000 Bourges,* ☎ *02–48–24–68–51,* FAX *02–48–65–21–41. 31 rooms. Restaurant, bar, minibars. AE, DC, MC, V.*

$$$ ★ 🏨 **Château de la Commanderie.** You won't regret going out of your way to reach this impressive 11th-century château. Rooms are large and elegantly furnished. Join the hosts, the Comte and Comtesse de Jouffrey-Gonsans, for an aperitif before meals in the paneled dining room. The food is well-prepared family fare—often with perfectly aged Charolais beef. ✉ *Farges-Allichamps, 18200 St-Amand-Montrond (44 km/27 mi south of Bourges on N144),* ☎ *02–48–61–04–19,* FAX *02–48–61–01–84. 7 rooms, 1 suite. Restaurant. MC, V.*

Montluçon

2 *94 km (58 mi) south of Bourges.*

Montluçon is best known for its Bourbon castle in its old quarter, where small 16th- and 17th-century houses line the streets. Built during the Hundred Years' War, the **Château de Montluçon** is remarkably well preserved. The **Musée du Vieux Château** (Old Castle Museum) includes a historical account of the hurdy-gurdy, a traditional stringed instrument. ☎ *04–70–05–00–06.* *15 frs.* ⏲ *Tues.–Sun. 10–noon and 2:30–6.*

En Route On the way to Bourbon-l'Archambault pass through the delightful rural town of **Cosne-d'Allier** (exit 10 off A71 to D94 east), where locals come to market.

Bourbon-l'Archambault

3 *48 km (58 mi) northeast of Montluçon.*

During the 17th, 18th, and 19th centuries, Bourbon-l'Archambault was a ritzy thermal spa. Talleyrand, France's powerful foreign minister, took the waters here. But the fleeting fancy for fashionable spas left the town a little less noble. Still, the weathered buildings and the ruined 14th-century **Château**—once the quarters of the noble tourists—still have an appealing faded glory. ✉ *rue du Château.* ⏲ *Mid-Apr.–mid-Oct., daily 2–6.*

Souvigny

4 *14 km (9 mi) southeast of Bourbon-l'Archambault.*

Small, picturesque Souvigny is dominated by its surprisingly large church. Built in the 11th, 12th, and 15th centuries of pale golden stone, the **Prieuré St-Pierre** appears light compared to most Auvergne buildings, which are made out of volcanic stone. This village was the financial base of the Bourbon fortunes, solid enough to enable them to establish a royal dynasty.

Dining

$ ★ ✕ **Auberge des Tilleuls.** In an old town house on a small square near the priory, this restaurant serves innovative cuisine at exceptional prices. In the small dining room, a pair of old oil paintings humorously depicts village scenes. Try the hearty beef casserole with its rich, zesty sauce. ✉ *pl. St-Eloi,* ☎ *04–70–43–60–70. MC, V. Closed Mon.*

Moulins

5 *12 km (7 mi) east of Souvigny, 291 km (182 mi) south of Paris, 98 km (61 mi) southeast of Bourges.*

Once the capital of the dukes of Bourbon, Moulins has a compact, medieval center, dominated by its cathedral. The oldest part (1474–1507) of the **Cathédrale Notre-Dame** (✉ rue de Paris), in Flamboyant Gothic style, is known for its stained-glass windows. In the 15th century such windows served as picture books for illiterate peasants, enabling them to follow the story of the crusades of Louis IX. The cathedral's other medieval treasure is the triptych of the Maître de Moulins, painted toward the end of the 15th century. Notice that the Virgin is not as richly clothed as the Duke and Duchess of Bourbon, who commissioned the painting! The town's belfry, known as the **Jacquemart** (✉ pl. de l'Hôtel), was built in 1232 and rebuilt in 1946 after having ignited during a fireworks display. The **Musée du Folklore,** in a 15th-century mansion next door to the Jacquemart, is filled with costumes, farming implements, and other reminders of Moulins's past. ✉ *pl. de l'Hôtel,* ☎ *04–70–44–39–03.* *10 frs.* ⊙ *Tues.–Sun. 9:30–noon and 2–5:30.*

Dining and Lodging

$$$ ★ ✕ **Hôtel de Paris-Jacquemart.** This family-owned hotel, just a block from the town's medieval quarter, is a genuine delight—traditional France at its best. Service is efficient and welcoming. Rooms are suitably large, with high ceilings and 19th-century antiques. The menus—between 170 and 230 francs—might include *paillette d'homard* (lobster in thin pastry wafers and rich sauce) and a chariot of pastries. ✉ *21 rue de Paris, 03000 Moulins,* ☎ *04–70–44–00–58,* FAX *04–70–34–05–39. 28 rooms. Restaurant. AE, DC, MC, V.*

St-Pourçain-sur-Sioule

❻ *31 km (19 mi) south of Moulins, 27 km (18 mi) northwest of Vichy.*

Most of the region's wine comes from the attractive little village of St-Pourçain-sur-Sioule—one of the oldest viticulture centers in France. The wine, which varies considerably in quality and price, is generally not found in other parts of France and is often a good value.

Lodging

$$$ **Château de Boussac.** Although the turrets and moat suggest its defensive past, this château is fully modernized. The property is a working Charolais cattle farm and is sublimely quiet. Guest rooms are furnished with antiques. In the evening, have an aperitif with the Marquis and Marquise de Longueil before the table d'hôte dinner (advance arrangements required). Lovely breakfasts are served in rooms. ✉ *Target, 03140 Chantelle (10 km/6 mi from St-Pourçain on D987),* ☎ *04–70–40–63–20,* FAX *04–70–40–60–03. 4 rooms. MC, V. Closed Dec.–Mar.*

Vichy

❼ *30 km (19 mi) south of St-Pourçain-sur-Sioule, 54 km (33 mi) north of Clermont-Ferrand, 349 km (216 mi) south of Paris.*

Vichy is the most elegant city in the Auvergne. And yet it does not have the depth of character you'd expect from a town whose mineral waters attracted the Romans and, later, Paris haute society. Nobles such as the Marquise de Sévigné and the Duchess of Angoulême started the trend, then the arrival of Napoléon III and the railroad attracted the middle classes.

When France fell to the Germans in 1940 and the country was divided under direct and indirect German control, the Pétain government moved to Vichy. Hotels served as embassies and ministries. After the war, the puppet government left a stain of infamy on the city. Today Vichy is trying to overcome its past, as well as the perception that it's only a place for retirement. A stretch of the River Allier is being transformed into a lake and large conference facilities and thermal baths are being built. Although there are no old, famous buildings to admire, the city has a mosquelike Thermal Establishment and a Grand Casino with an opera house. The area around the Parc des Sources is also pleasant.

Dining and Lodging

$$ ✕ **L'Alambic.** Chef-owner Jean-Jacques Barbot is a master with local produce. He grills fish from nearby streams with endives and an anise-based sauce, and bakes his *sandre* (white fish) with a mustard coating. Be sure to try his lentil salad made with the famous, tiny *lentilles de Puy.* ✉ *8 rue Nicolas-Larbaud,* ☎ *04–70–59–12–71. MC, V. Closed early Mar., early Sept., and Mon. No lunch Tues.*

$$ **Hôtel Averna.** This hotel in an 18th-century building in the center of town provides excellent value for the money. Rooms are modest but functional; bathrooms are clean. *12 rue Debrest, 03200 Vichy, 04–70–31–31–19, FAX 04–70–97–86–43. 26 rooms. AE, DC, MC, V. Closed mid-Dec.–Jan.*

Thiers

8 *34 km (21 mi) south of Vichy, 47 km (29 mi) northeast of Clermont-Ferrand.*

Built on a steep hill, Thiers is a slightly grimy, but nonetheless fascinating, 18th- and 19th-century town that is famous for its cutlery. It supplies 70% of France's cutting needs, producing everything from table knives to daggers. In the old days, while the River Durolle turned the massive grindstones, craftsmen would lie on planks over the icy water to hone their blades on the stone. Today's factories use less exotic methods, but the tourist office gives demonstrations of the old way (as well as maps and information). Be prepared for stiff walking—the streets run only up and down!

Follow rue Conchette, then rue Bourg to appealing place du Pirou. On place du Pirou, look for the 15th-century, half-timber **Maison du Pirou.** At No. 11 rue de Pirou is the **Maison des Sept Péchés Capitaux** (House of the Seven Deadly Sins)—look at the carvings on the ends of the beams and you'll know why. On rue de la Coutellerie you'll find old knife-making workshops and the 15th-century **Maison des Coutelliers,** a small museum and workshop with demonstrations of five centuries of knife-making. *58 rue de la Coutellerie, 04–73–80–58–86. 15 frs. May–Oct., daily 9–noon and 2–5; Nov.–Apr., weekdays 2–6.*

Roanne

9 *59 km (37 mi) east of Thiers, 87 km (54 mi) west of Lyon, 98 km (61 mi) southeast of Moulins, 389 km (243 mi) south of Paris.*

The thriving, industrial city of Roanne is on everyone's itinerary for one reason—the world-famous Troisgros restaurant.

Dining and Lodging

$$$$ ★ **Troisgros.** One of the most revered restaurants in France serves a seven-course feast, the Menu dans la Tradition (540 francs), which might include lightly sautéed foie gras with grilled groundnuts, frogs'-leg lasagna, regional cheeses, and fantastic desserts. The surprisingly ordinary dining room has comfortable chairs and big windows. Service is at your table before you know you need it. The high-design guest rooms are luxurious and comfortable. *pl. Jean Troisgros (across from train station), 42300, 04–77–71–66–97, FAX 04–77–70–39–77. 13 rooms. Restaurant. AE, DC, MC, V.*

St-Etienne

10 *84 km (52 mi) south of Roanne, 147 km (91 mi) southeast of Clermont-Ferrand, 56 km (35 mi) southwest of Lyon.*

The former mining city of St-Etienne (population 200,000) is better known for its soccer team than for its attractions. But it does have a good museum. And in June of 1998, the city will host rounds of the World Cup soccer competition.

St-Etienne's fine **Musée d'Art et d'Industrie** has paintings (Rubens, Whistler, Monet) as well as exhibits on local industry. *2 pl. Louis-*

Comte, ☎ *04–77–33–04–85.* 🎫 *Free.* ⏲ *Wed. 2–5, Thurs.–Mon. 10–noon and 2–5.*

OFF THE BEATEN PATH

LA CHAISE-DIEU – "The Chair of God" abbey, about 40 km (25 mi) north of Le Puy-en-Velay via N102 and D906, has splendid red-and-black frescoes of the *Danse Macabre* (Death dancing with the nobility, bourgeoisie, and peasants).

Le Puy-en-Velay

11 *76 km (47 mi) southwest of St-Etienne.*

Le Puy-en-Velay is a stunning sight, built up on the puys that rise from the fertile valley like pyramids. These solidified-lava peaks are crowned with man-made monuments: on the lowest, a statue of St. Joseph and the Infant Jesus; on the highest, the 11th-century chapel of St-Michel; on another, a huge statue of the Virgin. Most spectacular of the monuments is the Romanesque cathedral, **Notre-Dame-du-Puy,** built of polychrome lava and balanced atop the fourth narrow pinnacle, reachable only by a long flight of steps.

Clermont-Ferrand

12 *130 km (80 mi) northwest of Le Puy-en-Velay, 40 km (24 mi) west of Thiers, 400 km (248 mi) south of Paris, 178 km (110 mi) west of Lyon.*

Known to historians as the hometown of Vercingétorix, who rallied the Arvernes to defeat Julius Caesar in 52 BC and who is immortalized in Astérix comic books, Clermont-Ferrand is the only large city in the Auvergne. A bustling, modern commercial center that is the Michelin tire company's headquarters, Clermont-Ferrand probably won't draw you for more than a few hours. But the city is an ideal transfer point to the rest of the Auvergne. The town has some good museums and a small old quarter dominated by its cathedral.

The monolithic **Cathédrale Notre-Dame-de-l'Assomption** (✉ pl. de la Victoire) was built of a special black volcanic stone that enabled the pillars to be thinner and the interior to soar to greater heights than ever before. Built 200 years earlier out of yellow sandstone, the Romanesque **Notre-Dame-du-Port** (✉ rue du Port) has an entirely different feel than the cathedral. Note the raised choir with carved capitals that illustrate such tales as the struggle of virtue and vice, and the fall of Adam and Eve.

Housed in a former Ursuline convent, the **Musée des Beaux-Arts** has a beautifully designed exhibit on the history of painting and sculpture. ✉ *pl. Louis-Deteix,* ☎ *04–73–23–08–49.* 🎫 *21 frs.* ⏲ *Tues.–Sun. 11–7.*

The **Musée du Ranquet** houses an assortment of artifacts, from ancient musical instruments to the world's first calculating machine, invented in the 17th century by native son Blaise Pascal. ✉ *34 rue des Gras,* ☎ *04–73–37–38–63.* 🎫 *12 frs.* ⏲ *Tues.–Sat. 10–noon and 2–6 (until 5 in winter), Sun. 2–5.*

Dining and Lodging

$$$ ★ ✕ **Bernard Audrieux.** Chef Bernard Audrieux cooks deceptively simple dishes such as salmon with truffle sauce or *escalope de foie chaud de canard* (sliced hot duck liver). The restaurant has tasteful decor—cream-color walls, white linens, well-spaced tables. All this elegance contrasts with its dowdy location in a Clermont-Ferrand suburb. ✉ *rte. de la Baroque (3 km/2 mi northwest of Clermont-Ferrand on*

D641A), ☎ 04–73–37–00–26. AE, DC, MC, V. Closed Sun.; mid-July–mid-Aug. No lunch Sat.

$$ **Hôtel de Lyon.** Convenience is the chief attribute of this down-to-earth hotel in the center of town. Rooms are clean and service is perfunctory but efficient. *✉ 16 pl. de Jaude, 63000 Clermont-Ferrand, ☎ 04–73–93–32–55, FAX 04–73–93–54–33. 32 rooms. Restaurant. MC, V.*

The Puy-de-Dôme and the Parc National des Volcans

★ 13 *18 km (11 mi) west of Royat on D68, 24 km (15 mi) west of Clermont-Ferrand.*

Stretching 150 km (90 mi) from north to south, the Parc National des Volcans contains 80 or so dormant volcanoes, with all kinds of craters, dikes, domes, prismatic lava flows, caldera cones, and basaltic plateaus. The volanoes are (relatively) young; the most recent is only 6,000 to 8,000 years old, which explains why their shapes are so well preserved.

At 1,465 meters (4,806 feet), the Puy-de-Dôme is the highest volcano in the Mont-Dôme range. The Romans built a temple to Mercury here; the ruins of the temple were uncovered in 1872. The number of tourists, especially in July and August, is tremendous—Puy-de-Dôme is one of the three most visited sights in France. Give yourself the best part of the day here, and bring your walking shoes so that you can follow the trails up to magnificent panoramas. For those set on a bird's-eye view, parasailing, hot-air ballooning, and hang-gliding can be arranged. *20 frs per automobile. Mar. and Nov., daily 8–6; Apr. and Oct., daily 8–8; May–Sept., daily 7–10 PM; Dec., weekends 7–5:30.*

Orcival

14 *13 km (8 mi) southwest of Puy-de-Dôme, 22 km (14 mi) southwest of Clermont-Ferrand.*

Mont-Dôme was a major hurdle for pilgrims making the long walk to Santiago de Compostela in Spain. To house them, five major sanctuaries—St-Austremoine d'Issoire, Notre-Dame du Port, Notre-Dame d'Orcival, St-Nectaire, and St-Saturnin—were erected in the 12th century. Orcival's **Notre-Dame** (1146–1178) was the most famous of these vaulted Romanesque hospices. Step inside to inspect a most unusual statue of the Virgin carrying an adult-looking child.

En Route From Orcival take D27, which joins D983, for a beautiful ride over the **Col de Guery** pass at 1,268 meters (4,160 feet).

Le Mont-Dore

15 *19 km (12 mi) south of Orcival.*

Le Mont-Dore, on the Dordogne River at the head of the sheltered Chaudefour Valley, was once a Roman spa town. Today there are still hot springs, though the town now derives much of its income as a convenient, although not particularly attractive, summer and winter resort town. There are trails radiating from the town center, a *télépherique* (cable car) to the peaks, and mostly intermediate slopes leading down.

Dining and Lodging

$ ✕ **Le Boeuf dans l'Assiette.** This restaurant provides simple fare for ravenous skiers and hikers. With a three-course menu and a bottle of St-Pourçain wine, two people can replenish their energy for less than 175 francs. *✉ 9 av. Michel-Bertrand, ☎ 04–73–65–01–23. MC, V.*

$$ ★ **Château de Bassignac.** This sturdy, fortified 16th-century manor has just four rooms, decorated with an assortment of family antiques. Bassignac is still a working farm, but the Bessons leave that aspect of business to their children. M. Besson is an artist who often gives painting classes; Mme. Besson acts like everyone's mother. In the evening, sit before the fire mellowing with a class of Armagnac. In winter, the château is only open by advance arrangement. ✉ *Brousse, 15240 Bassignac (on edge of village, 14 km/9 mi southwest of Bort-les-Orgues on D922),* ☎ FAX *04–71–40–82–82. 4 rooms. Fishing.*

St-Nectaire

16 *16 km (10 mi) east of Le Mont-Dore, 44 km (27 mi) southwest of Clermont-Ferrand.*

In the upper part of the village of St-Nectaire is a Romanesque hospice—you may want to give thanks after the drive over the passes. But your true reward will be when you try St-Nectaire's superb, soft, nutty-tasting cheese, which has been made since the 3rd century.

Besse and Lake Pavin

17 *6 km (4 mi) east of St-Nectaire.*

Besse, like many of the other small, old farming villages in the mountainous Mont-Dôme region, has become a popular winter-sports and summer hiking center. If you are here on Monday, go to the cheese market—the Auvergne's wheel of life. A favorite excursion from Besse is to nearby Lake Pavin, a perfectly symmetrical caldera lake. Anglers come here to fish for mammoth-size trout called *omble chevalier*—delicious in the hands of a good chef.

En Route The route south from Besse is splendid if you take D978 through the **Monts du Cantal** and Condat and Riom-les-Montagnes. The route becomes even more dramatic when, at Riom, D62 leads to the **Pas de Peyrol.** West from Besse, D680 heads through the **Cirque de Falgoux,** whose twists and turns will require all your attention.

Pas de Peyrol

18 *38 km (23 mi) south of Besse.*

At nearly 1,600 meters (5,249 feet), the Pas de Peyrol is the Auvergne's highest pass. Leave your car in the parking lot and take the 30-minute ★ walk to the summit of **Puy Mary.** The views are tremendous: Thirteen valleys radiate from the mountain, funneling their streams into some of France's major rivers.

Salers

★ 19 *11 km (7 mi) west of Pas de Peyrol, 20 km (12 mi) south of Mauriac, 43 km (25 mi) north of Aurillac.*

Perched above the Maronne Valley, medieval Salers is filled with tourists. But the town cannot fail to seduce you, too. Feeling isolated in the country, the people of Salers built protective ramparts and, subsequently, won the right to govern themselves. Many of the 15th- and 16th-century houses, built of black lava stone, remain and are filled with boutiques and small restaurants. Once an important cattle-market town, farming now plays a smaller role than tourism—though you still may be woken up by the sound of cowbells. On market days, **Grande Place,** in the heart of the village, is very busy.

South of Salers, the valley ridges are so beautiful that you could spend a day or two exploring the tiny, winding roads. The ***cols*** (mountain passes) are high enough (plus or minus 3,000 feet) to have snow in the winter, but they are really quite gentle and they provide a good view of the comely valleys below. Find your way to the small *hameaux* (hamlets) of **Fontanges,** with its tiny chapel hollowed out of a limestone bluff on which stands a white Madonna. The sweet hillside village of **Tournemire** and its **Château Anjony** are also worth a visit. *Château: ☎ 04–71–40–23–22. 25 frs. Mar.–mid-Nov., Mon.–Sat. 2–5:30.*

Dining and Lodging

$$–$$$ **Château de la Vigne.** Rebuilt in the 15th century, this château on a hillcrest still retains elements of its past as an 8th-century Merovingian castle and then a medieval fortress. The Parc National des Volcans is visible in the distance. Family coats of arms and stained-glass windows decorate the best guest room, the large Chambre Troubadour; it is said that Jean-Jacques Rousseau stayed here in 1767. Otherwise, furnishings are sparse and bathrooms makeshift. Dinner (reservations required) with owners Mme. and M. du Fayet de la Tour is served in the splendid dining room. Regional foods are used and the aperitifs include local dandelion wine. ✉ *15700 Ally,* ☎ FAX *04–71–69–00–20. 4 rooms. No credit cards. Closed mid-Oct.–late Mar.*

$$–$$$ **Hostellerie de la Maronne.** In a tranquil valley, this converted 19th-century farmhouse has well-kept, modern rooms (some with balconies). Furnishings, however, are department-store variety. The lounge and bar are pleasant, but the most care has been put into the dining room and the glassed-in kitchen. Dinner provides an opportunity to savor the best Salers beef, though the cuisine is not worth a special trip. ✉ *Le Treil, 15140 St-Martin-Valmeroux,* ☎ *04–71–69–20–33,* FAX *04–71–69–28–22. 17 rooms. Bar, lobby lounge, restaurant. Closed All Saints' Day–Easter. MC, V.*

$$ **Hôtel des Remparts.** From its position atop the ramparts, this hotel has spectacular panoramic views. Rooms are simple and functional. The management likes to quote half-pension rates, which you should resist if you are staying for more than one night. ✉ *esplanade de Barrouze, 15410 Salers,* ☎ *04–71–40–70–33,* FAX *04–71–40–75–32. 18 rooms. Restaurant. MC, V. Closed late-Oct.–late-Dec.*

Aurillac

20 *42 km (26 mi) south of Salers, 157 km (97 mi) southwest of Clermont-Ferrand.*

The prefecture and market town of Aurillac, at the edge of the Monts du Cantal, bustles by day and becomes a sleepy country village by night. The oldest part of town—a small area—has an old cheese market, ancient houses, and narrow streets that twist along the banks of the River Jordanne. Locals and tourists alike spend their days at the cafés on the **place du Palais-de-Justice,** the main square. Stop by the **tourist office** here for a free walking-tour map—well worth following.

At the **Musée d'Art et d'Archéologie,** remains of a Gallo-Roman temple and various religious objects are on display. A unique collection of umbrellas from the past three centuries—about half of all French umbrellas are made in Aurillac—is also housed here. ✉ *Centre Pierre Mendès-France, 37 rue des Carmes,* ☎ *04–71–45–46–10. 15 frs. Apr.–Oct., Tues.–Sun. 10–noon and 2–6 (daily July and Aug.).*

On the south side of Aurillac is the **National Stud Farm of Aurillac.** The stables accommodate 22 stallions from standardbreds to Arabians. ☎

04–71–64–19–61. 20 frs. (guided tours only). Mid-July–mid-Sept. (tours at 10, 11, 2, 3, 4, and 5).

Dining and Lodging

$$ **Poivre & Sel.** This intimate, friendly bistro serves a refined version of Auvergne fare. It is a good place to try Salers beef, as well as other regional dishes such as *salmis de colvert Cévenole* (ragout of game). ✉ *4 rte. du 14-Juillet,* ☎ *04–71–64–20–20. MC, V. Closed Mon.*

$ **Le Bistro.** For genuine Auvergne grub come to this little bistro with Formica tables and a long bar. Two fine regional specialties served here are *truffade* (sautéed potato slices covered with melted cheese) and *choux farcis* (stuffed cabbage). ✉ *23 rue Gambetta,* ☎ *04–71–48–01–04. Reservations not accepted. MC, V.*

$$ **Grand Hôtel de Bordeaux.** There are advantages to this Best Western hotel—its central location and its private garage. Rooms are compact but clean, functional, and adequate. ✉ *2 av. de la République, 15000 Aurillac,* ☎ *04–71–48–01–84,* FAX *04–71–48–49–93. 33 rooms. Bar. AE, DC, MC, V.*

Laguiole

21 *85 km (53 mi) southeast of Aurillac, 56 km (35 mi) north of Rodez.*

On the high basalt plateau, Laguiole is more than 3,000 feet above sea level. Locals claim that their home is nature at its purest. In winter, the wind roars across the land, piling up snow on ski trails; in summer, the sun scorches the land; in spring and fall, the angled sunlight dances on the granite outcroppings. The town is known for its hardy breed of Aubrac cattle, for its distinctive cheese made from unpasteurized cows' milk, flavored by the varied local flora, and for its spring-hinged pocket knife. You can visit the factory, the **Societé Forge de Laguiole** (☎ 05–65–48–43–34), where the slightly curved handle and a long blade knives are made; buy one here or in town.

Dining and Lodging

$$$$ **Michel Bras.** Despite the flowery prose used by the Bras to describe their contemporary hotel-restaurant, it does not really "mold itself perfectly to the countryside," but stands on a promontory like a spaceship about to be launched. Others have described it as a glass barn with wooden sheds alongside. To be fair, the rooms *are* full of light, creature comforts are everywhere, and the views of the granite outcrops are haunting. But the main draw is Michel Bras's unique creations—foie gras with apricots and honey vinegar, and asparagus with truffle vinaigrette—as well as his more classic Aubrac beef and wild boar dishes. ✉ *rte. de l'Aubrac, 12210 Laguiole,* ☎ *05–65–44–32–24,* FAX *05–65–48–47–02. 15 rooms. Restaurant. Closed Nov.–Mar. AE, DC, MC, V.*

$$ **Grand Hôtel Auguy.** An excellent alternative to the high-price Michel Bras, the Auguy has basic rooms with just enough space for a bed, a desk, and a couple of armchairs. Ask for one of the quieter rooms, away from the street. Owner Isabelle Auguy is a creative cook who uses her grandparents' rustic recipes, giving them a lighter touch. Her foie gras salad is a delight, as are the Aubrac beef and the fresh trout. ✉ *2 allée de l'Amicale, 12210 Laguiole,* ☎ *04–65–44–31–11,* FAX *04–65–51–50–81. 30 rooms. Restaurant, bar, lobby lounge. MC, V.*

St-Céré

22 *65 km (40 mi) west of Aurillac, 28 km (17 mi) east of Rocamadour.*

A small, medieval village on the Bave River, a tributary of the Dordogne, St-Céré is an ideal base for exploring the area. Overlooking its ancient houses are the ruins of the Château de St-Laurent-les-Tours, whose two partially restored keeps date from the 12th and 15th centuries. During World War II, the town was a center for the Resistance. Two km (1 mi) west is the 16th-century Château du Montal, worth checking out.

Dining and Lodging

$ ★ ✕🏨 **Ferme de la Rivière.** Make yourself at home at this charming farmhouse on the edge of the beautiful village of Autoire, just outside St-Céré. Rooms have ancient, exposed beams and gabled ceilings. Rates are extremely reasonable at 200 francs for two, including breakfast, and an extra 85 francs per person for an excellent table d'hôte dinner. ✉ *Autoire, 46400 St-Céré,* ☎ *05–65–38–18–01. No credit cards.*

En Route Between St-Céré and Rocamadour, along D673, is the **Causses de Gramat,** an extensive limestone plateau where stubbly trees claw the white-gray earth.

Rocamadour

★ 23 *28 km (17 mi) west of St-Céré.*

Rocamadour is a medieval village that seems to defy the laws of gravity; it surges out of a cliff 465 meters (1,500 feet) above the Alzou River gorge. The town got its name after the discovery in 1166 of the 1,000-year-old body of St-Amadour "quite whole." It was moved to the cathedral, where it began to work miracles. Pilgrims flocked to the site, climbing the 216 steps to the church on their knees. Making the climb on foot is sufficient reminder of the medieval penchant for agonizing penance; today an elevator lifts weary souls. The village is especially mobbed with pilgrims and tourists in summer. Cars are not allowed; park in a lot below the town or in L'Hospitalet, 1.5 km (1 mi) away.

The staircase and elevator up to the **Cité Religieuse** start from place de la Carreta; if you walk, pause at the landing 141 steps up to admire the fort. Once up, you'll see tiny place St-Amadour and its seven sanctuaries: the basilica of St-Sauveur opposite the staircase; the St-Amadour crypt under the basilica; the chapel of Notre-Dame to the left; the chapels of John the Baptist, St-Blaise, and Ste-Anne to the right; and the Romanesque chapel of St-Michel, built into an overhanging cliff. St-Michel's two 12th-century frescoes—depicting the Annunciation and the Visitation—have survived in superb condition. ✉ *Centre d'Accueil Notre-Dame.* ⏲ *Guided tours Mon.–Sat. 9–5; tips at visitors' discretion. English-speaking guide available.*

The village itself, though very touristy, is full of beautifully restored medieval houses. One of the finest is the 15th-century **Hôtel de Ville,** near the Porte Salmon, which houses the tourist office and an excellent collection of tapestries. 🎫 *Free.* ⏲ *Mon.–Sat. 10–noon and 3–8.*

Dining and Lodging

$$ ✕🏨 **Le Beau Site.** This is the best of the few old town hotels. The charm of the ancient beams, exposed stone, and open hearth in the foyer ends as you climb the stairs; rooms are modern and functional. The dining room overlooks the canyon and, best of all, you can park inside Rocamadour if you stay here. ✉ *Cité Médiévale, 46500,* ☎ *05–65–33–63–08,* FAX *05–65–33–65–23. 55 rooms with bath or shower. Restaurant. MC, V. Closed mid-Dec.–mid-Jan.*

Cahors

24 *56 km (35 mi) south of Rocamadour.*

Once an opulent Gallo-Roman town, Cahors, sitting snugly within a loop of the River Lot, is famous for its tannic red wine, known to the Romans as black wine. Many of the small estates in the area have tastings. The town's finest sight is the **Pont Valentré,** a bridge, with elegant towers, that is a spellbinding feat of medieval engineering. Look out for the fortresslike **Cathédrale St-Etienne** (✉ off rue du Mar Joffre) with its cupolas. Its cloisters connect to the courtyard of the archdeaconry, which is awash with Renaissance decoration and thronged with visitors who come for the art exhibits.

Dining and Lodging

$ ✕ **Le Coq & la Pendule.** This small, bustling, café-restaurant, on a pedestrian street near the cathedral, serves homey French cooking in a down-to-earth setting. ✉ *10 rue St-James,* ☎ *05–65–35–28–84. No credit cards.*

$$$–$$$$ ✕🏨 **Château de Mercuès.** Just outside Cahors, this hotel in the former home of the Counts of Cahors has older rooms in baronial splendor, as well as boring, modern ones. One of the best rooms is Tour, with a unique ceiling that slides back to expose the shaft of the turret. Duck, lamb, and truffles reign in the restaurant, but the high prices lead you to expect more creativity than is produced. ✉ *46090 Mercuès (6 km/4 mi west of Cahors on the road to Villeneuve-sur-Lot),* ☎ *05–65–20–00–01,* FAX *05–65–20–05–72. 25 rooms, 9 suites. Restaurant, pool, 2 tennis courts, helipad. AE, DC, MC, V. Closed Nov.–mid-Mar.*

$$ ✕🏨 **Terminus.** Only a two-minute walk from the train station, this small, ivy-covered hotel is deep in the heart of truffle country. The young owners go out of their way to assist guests. The restaurant, La Balandre, is the town's best. The decor is mainly Roaring Twenties; besides truffles exceptional cod *brandade* (mousse) is served. The restaurant is closed for two weeks in February, one week in June, and Sunday dinner. ✉ *5 av. Charles-de-Freycinet, 46000 Cahors,* ☎ *05–65–35–24–50,* FAX *05–65–37–95–93. 31 rooms. Restaurant. AE, MC, V.*

St-Cirq-Lapopie

25 *25 km (16 mi) east of Cahors: take D653 in the direction of Figeac; after 8 km (5 mi) turn right on D662 and continue along the Lot River until a sign directs you over a one-lane bridge.*

The beautiful, 13th-century village of St-Cirq-Lapopie (pronounced san-*sare*) is on a rocky spur 262 feet up, with nothing but a vertical drop to the Lot River below. Filled with artisans' workshops, and not yet renovated à la Disney, the town has so many dramatic views that you may end up spending several hours here. A mostly ruined château can be reached by a stiff walk along the path that starts near the Hôtel de Ville. Stop by the tourist office in the center of town for information.

Figeac

26 *43 km (27 mi) northwest of St-Cirq-Lapopie.*

The old town of Figeac, which has a lively Saturday-morning market, was a stopping point for pilgrims heading toward Santiago de Compostela. Many of the 13th, 14th, and 15th centuries houses in the old part of town have been carefully restored; note their octagonal chimneys and *soleilhos* (open attics used for drying flowers and wood). The elegant, 13th-century **Hôtel de la Monnaie,** a block from the River Célé, is a characteristic old Figeac house. It was probably used as a money-changing office in the middle ages, today it houses the **tourist office** and a museum of relics. ✉ *pl. Vival,* ☎ *05–65–34–06–25.* 🎫 *Free.*

⏲ *July–Aug., daily 10–noon and 2:30–6:30; Sept.–June, Mon.–Sat. 3–5.*

Jean-François Champollion (1790–1830), one of the first men to decipher Egyptian hieroglyphics, was born in Figeac. The **Musée Champollion** (leave place Vival on rue 11-Novembre, take the first left, and follow it as it veers right) contains a casting of the Rosetta stone, discovered in the Nile River delta, which Champollion used to decode Pharaonic dialect. ✉ *5 impasse Champollion,* ☎ *05–65–34–66–18.* 🎟 *22 frs.* ⏲ *May–Sept., Tues.–Sat. 10–noon and 2:30–6:30.*

Dining and Lodging

$$$$ ✕🏨 **Château du Viguier du Roy.** Everything—the tower, the cloister, the gardens, the wooden beams, the tapestries, and the canopied beds—in this medieval palace, once the residence of the king's *viguier* (representative), has been painstakingly restored. Rooms throughout are regal. The restaurant, La dinée du Viguier, is excellent. ✉ *rue Droite, 46100 Figeac,* ☎ *05–65–50–05–05,* FAX *05–65–50–06–06. 17 rooms, 3 suites. Restaurant. AE, DC, MC, V. Closed early–mid-Dec., early Jan.–Feb.*

$$–$$$ ✕🏨 **Ferme Auberge Domaine des Villedieu.** This lovely farmhouse, partly dating from the 16th century, is lovingly run by the Villedieus. Cozy rooms in outbuildings, cassoulet in front of the fire in a bubbling earthenware casserole, and homemade foie gras. ✉ *rte. D13, Vallée du Célé, Boussac 46100 (10 km/6 mi from Figeac),* ☎ *05–65–40–06–63,* FAX *05–65–40–09–22. 4 rooms. AE, DC, MC, V.*

En Route Leave Figeac on the road to Rodez and take D52, a small road on your left: It leads through the beautiful Lot Valley to D901, which goes to Conques.

Conques

27 *44 km (27 mi) east of Figeac.*

The pretty, red-ocher houses of Conques harmonize perfectly with the surrounding rocky gorge. The village was home to a Benedictine abbey whose outstanding Romanesque church was one of the principal stopping points on the pilgrimage route between Le Puy-de-Dôme and Santiago de Compostela.

Begun in the early 11th century, the abbey church of **Ste-Foy** had its heyday in the 12th and 13th centuries, after which the flood of pilgrims and their revenue dried up. The two centuries of success were due to the purloined relics of St. Faith (Ste-Foy), a 13-year-old Christian girl who was martyred in 303 in Agen, where her remains were jealousy guarded. A monk from Conques venerated them so highly that he traveled to Agen, joined the community of St. Faith, and won their trust. After 10 years they put him in charge of guarding the saint's relics, whereupon he stole them and brought them back to Conques. Devastated by Huguenot hordes, the church languished until the 19th century, when the writer Prosper Mérimée raised the money to salvage it. Ste-Foy clings to a hill so steep that even driving and walking—let alone building—are precarious. The church's interior is high and dignified; the ambulatory was given a lot of wear by medieval pilgrims, who admired the church's most precious relic, a 10th-century wooden statue of Ste-Foy encrusted with gold and precious stones. You can see it in the treasury, off the recently restored cloister.

The **Musée Docteur Joseph-Fau** (Trésor II), opposite the pilgrims' fountain near Ste-Foy, houses a collection of furniture, statues, tapestries, and sculpture. *22 frs. Sept.–June, Mon.–Sat. 9–noon and 2–6, Sun. 2–6; July–Aug., Mon.–Sat. 9–noon and 2–7, Sun. 2–7.*

Rodez

28 *39 km (24 mi) south of Conques.*

Rodez, capital of the Aveyron, stands on a windswept hill. At its center is the pink sandstone **Cathédrale Notre-Dame** (13th–15th centuries). Its bulk is lightened by decorative upper stories, completed in the 17th century, and by the magnificent 285-foot bell tower. The renovated **Cité Quartier,** once ruled by medieval bishops, lies behind the cathedral. On tiny place de l'Olmet, just off place du Bourg, is the 16th-century **Maison d'Armagnac,** a fine Renaissance mansion with a courtyard and an ornate facade covered with medallion emblems of the Counts of Rodez. The extensively modernized **Musée Denys Puech,** an art museum, is just east of the wide boulevard that circles the old town. *pl. Clemenceau, 05–65–42–70–64. 17 frs. Mon. 2–8, Wed.–Sat. 10–noon and 3–7, Sun. 3–7.*

Dining and Lodging

$–$$ ★ **La Diligence.** Expect to hear more about talented chef Joel Delmas. Of special note are his succulent mille-feuille of lamb kidneys and his superb banana coconut tart. Equally impressive are the prices: Prix-fixe lunches start at 89 francs. Dinner is not served on Tuesday or Wednesday. Rooms, furnished in modern style, are not luxurious, but they are adequate and modestly priced. *12000 Marcillac-Vallon (10 km/6 mi northwest of Rodez), 05–65–72–60–20. 6 rooms. Restaurant. MC, V. Closed Jan., 1st 2 wks of Sept.*

En Route If you are traveling from Rodez to Millau and have time, skip N88 and take the shorter and prettier route D28, off N88.

Plaisance

29 *71 km (44 mi) south of Rodez, 70 km (43 mi) west of Millau.*

Plaisance is typical of many of the villages tucked into the Tarn Valley and the rolling, wooded hills that serve as watersheds for the Tarn River. In this relatively undiscovered part of France, Take a day to hike along the many trails that traverse the verdant hills.

Dining and Lodging

$$ ★ **Les Magnolias.** Rustic charm and sophisticated cooking at this 14th-century inn are orchestrated by jocular owner Francis Roussel. Sample his foie gras, and Roussel is only too happy to divulge his trade secrets. He has a flair for finding tastes that complement one another: grilled cheese in duck bouillon, for example, and perch in red wine sauce. The ambience is wonderfully medieval, with oak beams and stone staircases. Rooms are simple and slightly eclectic. *12550 Plaisance, 05–65–99–77–34, FAX 05–65–99–70–57. 6 rooms with bath or shower. Restaurant. AE, MC, V. Closed mid-Nov.–mid-Mar.*

Roquefort-sur-Soulzon

30 *24 km (15 mi) south of Millau.*

So widely sought after is Roquefort cheese that the milk from local sheep is not enough—30% of it now comes from the Pyrénées and Corsica. Foul play, you may say, but what makes Roquefort is not the milk but the place it is stored—in the seven levels of the caves at Roquefort-sur-Soulzon, home to the *Penicillium glaucum roquefortii.* The caves are between 7°C (45°F) and 9°C (48°F), the temperature that the Penicillium likes, year-round. These happy bacteria float through the air inoculating the cheeses for three months. Take a sweater. *☎ 05–65–58–59–58. 🎟 Guided tour: 15 frs. ⏲ July–Aug., daily 9:30–6; Sept.–June, daily 9:30–11:30 and 2–5.*

Millau

31 *66 km (41 mi) southeast of Rodez, 70 km (43 mi) east of Plaisance, 248 km (154 mi) south of Clermont-Ferrand.*

Millau is primarily a good jumping-off point for exploring the magnificent gorges (☞ *below*) that cut through the limestone *causses* (plateaus). Give yourself time to wander through the old quarter, especially around place du Maréchal-Foch, with its 800-year-old arcades. Browse through the shops on place des Mandarous and place de la Tine for leather goods, by-products of all those sheep producing milk for Roquefort cheese. In Roman times, Millau produced pottery and sent its vases as far afield as Scotland. Some of these artifacts, collected from the nearby archaeological site, are on display at the **Musée de Millau.** *✉ Hôtel de Pégayrolles, pl. Foch, ☎ 05–65–59–01–08. 🎟 22 frs. ⏲ Apr.–Sept., Mon.–Sat. 10–noon and 2–6; Oct.–Mar., Mon.–Sat. 10–noon and 2–6.*

Dining and Lodging

$$ ✕🏨 **Château de Creissels.** This hotel, in an ancient 12th-century fort, has rooms furnished in simple country style, as well as more modern decor. Dinner is served in the vaulted cellar with a medieval atmosphere. *✉ rte. de Ste-Affrique, 12100 Millau (3 km/2 mi outside of town on D992), ☎ 05–65–60–31–79, FAX 05–65–61–24–63. 31 rooms, 26 with bath or shower. Restaurant. MC, V. Closed mid-Dec.–Feb. 10.*

Outdoor Activities and Sports

Mountain bikes, a good way to explore the gorges, can be rented from **William Orts** (✉ 21 bd. de l'Ayrolle, ☎ 05–65–61–14–29).

Gorges du Tarn

★ 32 *Extends from Le Rozier (16 km/10 mi northeast of Millau) to Florac, 75 km (47 mi) northeast.*

Though not as awesome as the Grand Canyon, the Gorges du Tarn (Tarn Gorge) is beautiful and dramatic. Route D907 leads into its mouth and runs along it, 600 meters (1,968 feet) below the cliff top. Beginning at **Le Rozier,** the Tarn River, flowing out of the gorge, is joined by the Jonte, coming from the Gorges de la Jonte (☞ *below*). Follow D907B to **Les Vignes,** where the gorge opens into a little valley. Take D995 to the top, along some challenging switchbacks, and follow signs for **Point Sublime,** where you'll find views that justify the name. After Les Vignes, the gorge becomes the most dramatic, with sheer cliffs and rock face dappled with grays, whites, and blues. In summer you can take a boat through this stretch; a bus takes you to the embarkation point.

At the **Cirque des Baumes,** just before the village of La Malène, the cliffs form a natural amphitheater. Continue on to **Les Détroits,** the gorge's narrowest section, where the tumbling waters squeeze through. After passing La Malène, note the 15th-century **Château de la Caze,** with its imposing array of turrets. Beyond, just before the village of St-Chély-du-Tarn, is the **Cirque de Pournadoires** and, catercorner, another, larger natural amphitheater. On summer nights it is the site of a son-et-lumière show. But don't make a point of seeing it: The gorge looks far more beautiful under natural light.

Ste-Enimie, the gorge's major town, is mired in summer by a flood of tourists. In its little church, ceramic tiles tell the 7th-century legend of Ste-Enimie, the beautiful sister of the Frankish king. When she was about to marry, she fell ill with leprosy and was scorned by her suitor. On the advice of an angel she was cured at the fountain of Burle, where she then founded a convent. Its ruins can still be seen, as can the fountain. From Ste-Enimie, the road winds through the valley, opening out just before the small market town of **Florac.**

Dining and Lodging

$ ✕🏨 **Le Vallon.** Locals are drawn year-round by the simple, yet good, fare at this restaurant-inn in the touristy town of Ispagnac, along the gorge. For 85 francs you get four courses, which might include an omelet, a salad, a casserole, and some cheese. Rooms are simple, clean, and inexpensive. ✉ *rte. D907B, 48320 Ispagnac,* ☎ *04–66–44–21–24. 24 rooms, most with bath. Restaurant, bar. MC, V.*

En Route Between Florac and St-Jean-du-Gard, the **Corniches des Cévennes** road winds its way through spectacular scenery. Follow D907 from Florac, then take a left on D983 toward St-Laurent-de-Trèves. From here the road ascends the Col du Rey, high above the valley.

St-Jean-du-Gard

33 *53 km (33 mi) southeast of Florac.*

In the old days, bolts of silk made their way from St-Jean-du-Gard, on the Gardon River, to Paris couture houses. But hard times came to the town with silk imports. Now most of what is left of the silk industry is represented by the **Musée des Vallées Cévenoles.** ✉ *95 Grand Rue,* ☎ *04–66–85–10–48.* 🎫 *12 frs.* ⏲ *June–Sept., Tues.–Sat. 9–noon and 2–5, Sun. 2–5.*

Anduze

34 *7 km (4 mi) southeast of St-Jean-du-Gard.*

Once a Huguenot stronghold, this pretty village had such mighty bulwarks that Louis XIII left it alone and sacked nearby Alès instead. The peace treaty stipulated that Anduze's fortifications be torn down; now only the 14th-century Tour d'Horloge (Clock Tower) remains.

Dining and Lodging

$$–$$$ ★ ✕🏨 **La Ranquet.** The hilly, wooded setting, the comfortable, spacious rooms, and top-ranking chef Annie Majourel are all reasons to come here. Majourel's menus (two moderately priced) change monthly, but you can expect such delightful dishes as roast wild boar and orange praline mousse. Be sure to visit the herb garden: It a delightful education, and it explains why Annie's cooking is so aromatic. The restaurant is closed Tuesday and Wednesday in winter. ✉ *rte. de St-Hippolyte, 30140 Tornac (6 km/4 mi southwest of Anduze),* ☎ *04–66–77–51–63,* FAX *04–66–77–55–62. 10 rooms. Restaurant, piano bar, air-conditioning, pool. Closed mid-Nov.–Dec. 25; Feb.*

Gorges de la Jonte

35 *Extends from Meyrueis (35 km/22 mi southwest of Florac) 21 km/13 mi west to Le Rozier (16 km/10 mi northeast of Millau).*

The splendid Gorges de la Jonte is narrower than the Gorges du Tarn (☞ *above*), thus easier to see across and into. At its depths is the Jonte River. Start from the village of **Meyrueis,** where the gorge is broad. Within a short distance, the gorge narrows, and the eroded limestone cliffs form strange pinnacle shapes. Stop for a snack in **Les Douzes,** then proceed to the deepest part of the gorge. The road winds along the cliff side. Past **Truel**—a cluster of houses clinging to the cliff face—is a lookout where, for a moment, the view opens to reveal two levels of cliff—Les Terrasses de Truel—then closes again before Le Rozier.

Dining and Lodging

$$ ★ ✕🏨 **Château d'Ayres.** The spacious guest rooms are furnished with antiques and public rooms resemble those in a country house. Family recipes such as cèpe quiche, and homemade terrine of foie gras are fine fare after a day's exploring. This is a good base for exploring the Jonte and Tarn gorges. ✉ *rte. d'Ayres, 48150 Meyrueis,* ☎ *04–66–45–60–10,* FAX *04–66–45–62–26. 24 rooms, 3 suites. Restaurant, pool, tennis court, horseback riding. AE, DC, MC, V. Closed mid-Nov.–late Mar.*

Canyon de la Dourbie

36 *Extends from Millau 40 km (25 mi) southeast to Nant.*

The most peaceful of the gorges ending in Millau is the Canyon de la Dourbie. Though it has its share of limestone cliffs and eroded rocks, the gorge's verdant, meadow-covered downstream section is the most interesting. Follow the gorge to the hilltop village of **St-Véran** and the ruined castle once owned by the Marquis de Montcalm, defender of the Battle of Québec. Further on, where the Trévezel joins the Dourbie, beautiful **Cantobre** clings as if by magic to the cliff. Its tiny houses are prized and even its name says it is extraordinary: Cantobre, from *quant obra,* means "what a masterpiece." Past Cantobre is a fertile valley and the pleasant town of **Nant,** which contains a marvelous, arcaded 14th-century covered market and the plain but beautiful church of St-Pierre, built in 1135.

Dining and Lodging

$ ✕🏨 **Hôtel des Voyageurs.** A very reasonable 78-franc menu, including, perhaps, a country terrine, confit of duck, fresh mountain trout, and cheese or dessert is served here. The winter dining room is austere; the cool, vaulted summer dining room looks out on a vine-covered terrace. Ask for a room overlooking the lively square and don't expect *House & Garden* decor—many rooms have linoleum floors. ✉ *pl. St-Jacques, 12230 Nant,* ☎ *05–65–62–26–88,* FAX *05–65–62–15–64. 11 rooms, 6 with shower. Restaurant. Closed Jan. and Feb. MC, V.*

La Couvertoirade

37 *18 km (11 mi) south of Nant, 25 km (16 mi) west of Le Vigan, 33 km (21 mi) southeast of Millau.*

This perfectly intact medieval village was home to the Knights Templar in the 12th century and later the Knights of St. John, who built the encircling ramparts about 1450. Now classified as one of France's most beautiful villages, it is home to a few craftsmen. Wander through town and look at the pretty stone houses, then visit the fortress, the church, and a small historical museum. 🎟 *15 frs for fortress, church, museum.* ⏲ *Daily 10–noon and 2–4.*

Cirque de Navacelles

38 *18 km (5 mi) east of La Couvertoirade, 19 km (12 mi) southwest of Le Vigan, 68 km (42 mi) southeast of Millau. Take D158 south from Alzon (halfway between La Couvertoirade and Le Vigan) to Blandas, then D713.*

The River Vis, cutting its way for aeons between the Causse de Blandas and the Causse du Larzac, produced a small wonder, the Cirque de Navacelles, in an abandoned meander. From a viewpoint along the road you can see where, long ago, the river looped around a little hill and later took a short cut through the neck of the loop. Within the loop is the village of **Navacelles.** Follow the road down through a series of hairpins to the valley floor (⅓ of the way down there is a place to park and take a 3-km/2-mi hike to the river along a marked, sometimes steep, trail). Or take route D130 up the far side of the canyon to the village of **La Baume-Auriol,** for more remarkable views. Route N9 leads back to Millau or south to Montpellier.

THE MASSIF CENTRAL AND THE AUVERGNE A TO Z

Arriving and Departing

By Car

Take A10 from Paris to Orléans, then A71 into the center of France. From Paris, Bourges is 229 km (137 mi) and Clermont-Ferrand is 378 km (243 mi). Coming from Lyon, it takes less than 90 minutes to drive the 179 km (111 mi) on A72 to Clermont-Ferrand. Entry into the Auvergne from the south (☞ Chapter 15) is mostly on small, curving, national roads, though A71 will eventually link Montpellier with Clermont-Ferrand through Millau; portions of the autoroute are already completed and open to vehicles.

By Plane

The major airport for the region, at Clermont-Ferrand (☎ 04–73–62–71–00), has regularly scheduled flights to Paris (Orly), Bordeaux, Dijon, Lyon, Marseille, Nantes, Nice, and Toulouse on **Air France** and **Air Inter** and direct international flights to Geneva, Milan, and London on **Air France, British Airways,** and **Swissair. TAT** (Transport Aérien Transrégional) flies from Paris's Orly airport to Rodez (☎ 01–42–79–05–05 reservations in Paris; ☎ 05–65–42–20–30 in Rodez).

By Train

The fastest way from Paris (Gare de Lyon) to Clermont-Ferrand, the capital of the Auvergne, is on the high-speed TGV (Train à Grande Vitesse) via Lyon, where you change for the regular train to Clermont-Ferrand (☎ 04–73–92–50–50). Regular SNCF trains also go from Paris to Bourges and Clermont-Ferrand and from Nîmes to Clermont-Ferrand.

Getting Around

By Car

There is really only one way to explore the region, and that is by car. Although national highways will get you from one place to another fairly expediently, the region's beauty is best discovered on the regional roads that twist through the mountains and along the gorges.

Contacts and Resources

Car Rental

Avis (✉ 57 rue Bonnabaud, Clermont-Ferrand, ☎ 04–73–93–39–90; Clermont-Ferrand airport, ☎ 04–73–91–18–08). **Europcar** (✉ rue Emile-Loubet, ☎ 04–73–92–70–26; Clermont-Ferrand airport, ☎ 04–73–92–70–26 at the airport). **Hertz** (✉ 71 av. de l'Union Soviétique, Clermont-Ferrand, ☏ 04–73–92–36–10; Clermont-Ferrand airport, ☏ 04–73–62–71–93).

Guided Tours

Rafting trips of the Gorges du Tarn can be arranged through **Service Loisirs** (✉ Haute-Loire, ☏ 05–61–09–20–80) or **Association Le Merlet** (✉ rte. de Nîmes, St-Jean du Gard, ☏ 04–66–85–18–19). From April to November float through the skies above the volcanoes in a balloon; contact **Objectif** (✉ 43 av. Julien, 63011 Clermont-Ferrand, ☏ 04–73–35–32–01).

Travel Agencies

Centre Auvergne Tourisme (✉ 9 rue Ballainvilliers, 63000 Clermont-Ferrand, ☏ 04–73–90–10–20). **Voyagers Maisonneuve** (✉ 24 rue Georges-Clemenceau, 63000 Clermont-Ferrand, ☏ 04–73–93–16–72).

Visitor Information

Main regional tourist office: **Comité Régional du Tourisme** (✉ 43 av. Julien, 63011 Clermont-Ferrand, ☏ 04–73–93–04–03). Local tourist offices: **Allier** (✉ pl. de l'Hôtel de Ville, 03000 Moulins, ☏ 04–70–44–14–14). **Aveyron** (✉ pl. Maréchal-Foch, 12000 Rodez, ☏ 05–65–68–02–27). **Cantal** (✉ 28 av. Gambetta, 15018 Aurillac, ☏ 04–71–09–91–43). **Haute-Loire** (✉ 12 bd. Phillipe-Jourde, 43012 Le Puy-en-Velay, ☏ 04–71–09–66–66). **Lot** (✉ pl. Françoise Mitterrand, 46000 Cahors, ☏ 05–65–35–09–56). **Lozère** (✉ 14 bd. Henri-Bourrillon, 48000 Mende, ☏ 04–66–65–60–00). **Puy-de-Dôme** (✉ 26 rue St-Esprit, 63000 Clermont-Ferrand, ☏ 04–73–42–21–21).

12 Provence

Nîmes, Arles, Avignon, and Marseille

Provence means dazzling light and rugged, rocky countryside interspersed with vineyards, fields of lavender, and olive groves. The Romans staked their first claim here and left riches behind; van Gogh and Cézanne taught us to see it through their eyes; then Peter Mayle bought a house and the world was not far behind. From Montpellier to Toulon, from Orange to the sea, this ancient, alluring land is still seducing visitors.

Updated by Nigel Fisher

AS YOU APPROACH PROVENCE, there is a magical moment when the north is finally left behind: Cypresses and red-tile roofs appear; you hear the screech of the cicadas and catch the scent of wild thyme and lavender. Even on the modern highway, oleanders flower on the central strip against a backdrop of harsh, brightly lit landscapes that inspired the paintings of Paul Cézanne and Vincent van Gogh.

Provence lies in the south of France, bordered by Italy to the east and the blue waters of the Mediterranean. The Romans called it Provincia—the Province—for it was the first part of Gaul they occupied. Roman remains litter the ground in well-preserved profusion. The theater and triumphal arch at Orange, the amphitheater at Nîmes, and the aqueduct at Pont-du-Gard are considered the best of their kind.

Provençal life continues at an old-fashioned pace. Hot afternoons tend to mean siestas, with signs of life discernible only as the shadows under the *platanes* (plane trees) start to lengthen and lethargic locals saunter out to play *boules* (the French version of bocce) and drink long, cooling *pastis,* an anise-based aperitif. The famous mistral—a fierce, cold wind that races through the Rhône Valley—is another feature of Provence. Thankfully, clear blue skies usually follow in its wake.

The Rhône, the great river of southern France, splits in two at Arles, 24 km (15 mi) before reaching the Mediterranean: The Petit Rhône crosses the marshy region known as the Camargue on its way to Stes-Maries-de-la-Mer, while the Grand Rhône heads off to Fos, an industrial port just along the coast from Marseille. North of Marseille lies Aix-en-Provence, whose old-time elegance reflects its former role as regional capital. We've extended Provence's traditional boundaries westward slightly into Languedoc, to include historic Nîmes and the dynamic university town of Montpellier.

Pleasures and Pastimes

Bullfighting

Provence's most popular summer spectator sport is bullfighting, both Spanish-style or the kinder *courses libres,* where the bulls have star billing and are often regarded as local heroes (they always live to fight another day). Spectacles are held in the Roman arenas in Arles and Nîmes and in surrounding villages.

Dining

In the old days, Provençal cooking was based on olive oil, fruit, and vegetables; garlic and wild herbs improved the scant meat dishes. The current gastronomic scene is a far cry from this frugality: Parisian chefs have created internationally renowned restaurants to satisfy demanding palates. Still, there's a lot to be said for simple Provençal food—pastis, that pale green, anise-based aperitif; *tapenade,* a delicious paste of capers, anchovies, olives, oil; *aïoli,* a garlicky mayonnaise; and grilled lamb and beef with a chilled bottle of rosé. Locals like to end their meal with a round of goat cheese and fruit. In Marseille, bouillabaisse is a specialty. But beware: The high-priced versions use fresh fish and can be delicious, but cheaper ones are often of dubious origins. Steer clear of the cheap fish restaurants, many with brisk ladies out front who deliver throaty sales pitches.

CATEGORY	COST*
$$$$	over 400 frs
$$$	250 frs–400 frs
$$	125 frs–250 frs
$	under 125 frs

**per person for a three-course meal, including tax (20.6%) and tip but not wine*

Lodging

Accommodations in this oft-visited part of France range from luxurious villas to elegantly converted *mas* (farmhouses) to modest city-center hotels. Service is often less than prompt, a casualty of the sweltering summer heat. Reservations are essential for much of the year and many hotels are closed in winter.

CATEGORY	COST*
$$$$	over 800 frs
$$$	550 frs–800 frs
$$	300 frs–550 frs
$	under 300 frs

**All prices are for a standard double room for two, including tax (20.6%) and service charge.*

Outdoor Activities and Sports

Provence provides a plethora of outdoor activities. You can sail and windsurf at La Grande Motte, Stes-Maries-de-la-Mer, Martigues (near Marseille), Cassis, Hyères-Plage, and the Îles de Porquerolles, in the south; ride through the Camargue on a horse rented from a local stable; tool around the Bouches-du-Rhône on a bike rented from the train station; or hike along blazed trails in the Luberon Mountains or Les Calanques.

Exploring Provence

Provence falls easily into three areas. The Camargue is at the heart of the first, though you might venture briefly into Languedoc to see the fine old towns of Nîmes, famed for its Roman arena, and Montpellier, known for its university, before wheeling back to visit the Roman remains at Arles and St-Rémy. In the second area, which falls within the boundaries of the Vaucluse, begin at Avignon and head north to Orange and Vaison-la-Romaine; the main natural feature here is Mont Ventoux, towering above the surrounding plains. The third area encompasses Aix-en-Provence, then stretches south to Marseille and east along the coast to Toulon.

Great Itineraries

The popular book entitled *A Year in Provence* dictates just that, but even a year might not be long enough to soak up all the charm of this captivating region. In three days you can see most of the major Roman towns: Nîmes, Arles, and Avignon; with seven days you can easily add Montpellier, Orange, and Aix-en-Provence; with 10 days you can cover all the important towns, add Marseille and the hill towns in the Luberon mountains, and relax on a Mediterranean *plage* (beach). The following are suggested itineraries for seeing the area; another option is to make one place your base and take day trips from there.

Numbers in the text correspond to numbers in the margin and on the Provence, Nîmes, Avignon, and Marseille maps.

IF YOU HAVE 3 DAYS

Begin your trip at the **Pont du Gard** ①, the 2,000-year-old Roman aqueduct, then head for **Nîmes** ②–⑪ to see the Arènes and the Maison Carrée. Try to make the 30-minute drive to the former Roman city of

Arles ⑰ before the 5 PM rush hour. Hopefully, you'll have an hour or two to explore the city. Spend the next morning in Arles, then drive, after lunch, through the countryside, stopping in medieval **Les Baux-de-Provence** ⑲ and the castle in **Tarascon** ㉑; stay overnight in **St-Rémy-de-Provence** ⑳. On your last day go to the walled city of **Avignon** ㉒–㉙ to see the famous Palais des Papes.

IF YOU HAVE 7 DAYS

Visit **Orange** ㉛ on your first day before stopping to see the **Pont du Gard** ①. Spend the night and the next morning in **Nîmes** ②–⑪. In the afternoon, drive to the fortified town of **Aigues-Mortes** ⑮ and make a slight detour through the Camargue to **Arles** ⑰. The next morning, explore Arles's Roman remains. Try to get to **Les Baux-de-Provence** ⑲ by lunchtime, then continue to **St-Rémy-de-Provence** ⑳ to explore Roman ruins and see where van Gogh painted. On day four, wend your way via **Tarascon** ㉑ to **Avignon** ㉒–㉙. The following day, head through **L'Isle-sur-la-Sorgue** ㉟ and **Gordes** ㊲, in the Luberon Mountains, on your way south to **Aix-en-Provence** ㊵; spend two nights and a day there visiting the marvelous 18th-century mansions and museums.

IF YOU HAVE 10 DAYS

Stay in **Avignon** ㉒–㉙ your first two nights, making trips to **Orange** ㉛, **Vaison-la-Romaine** ㉜, and **Mont Ventoux** ㉝. On your third day stop at the **Pont du Gard** ① on your way to **Nîmes** ②–⑪ for the afternoon and night. The fourth day head to the university town of **Montpellier** ⑫, then east past the resort town of **La Grande Motte** ⑭ to medieval **Aigues-Mortes** ⑮. Plan on several hours to explore the Camargue and visit the fortresslike church at **Stes-Maries-de-la-Mer** ⑯. By nightfall, be in the Roman city of **Arles** ⑰. Spend the morning of day five sightseeing in Arles, then make the short drive to **St-Rémy-de-Provence** ⑳ for the night by way of **Les Baux-de-Provence** ⑲ and **Tarascon** ㉑. On the sixth day, head to the Luberon Mountains; visit **L'Isle-sur-la-Sorgue** ㉟ and stay overnight in **Gordes** ㊲ or **Venasque** ㉞. Make **Aix-en-Provence** ㊵ your destination on days seven and eight. Aim for **Marseille** ㊶–㊽ on your ninth and tenth days—it may seem drab at first, but it has its own vitality.

When to Tour Provence

Spring and fall are the best months to experience the dazzling light, rugged rocky countryside, fields of lavender, and fruitful vineyards of Provence. In summer, it gets very hot and very crowded on the beaches. Still, if you are interested in seeing the bullfights, this is the time to come. Winter has some nice days, but it often rains.

NÎMES AND THE CAMARGUE

Though Roman remains are found throughout Provence, their presence is strongest where the rivers meander their way to the sea on the region's western flank: the beautiful aqueduct at Pont du Gard, the arenas at Nîmes and Arles, and the excavations at St-Rémy de Provence. Within this area are strange landscapes: the arid outcrops around Les Baux-de-Provence and the marshy wilderness of the Camargue. Formed by the sprawling Rhône delta and extending over 800 sq km (300 sq mi), the Camargue is an area of endless horizons, vast pools, low flat plains, innumerable species of migrating birds, and sturdy, free-roaming gray horses. The entire terrain is flat and not many feet above sea level, so occasionally the river bursts its banks and floods the entire region.

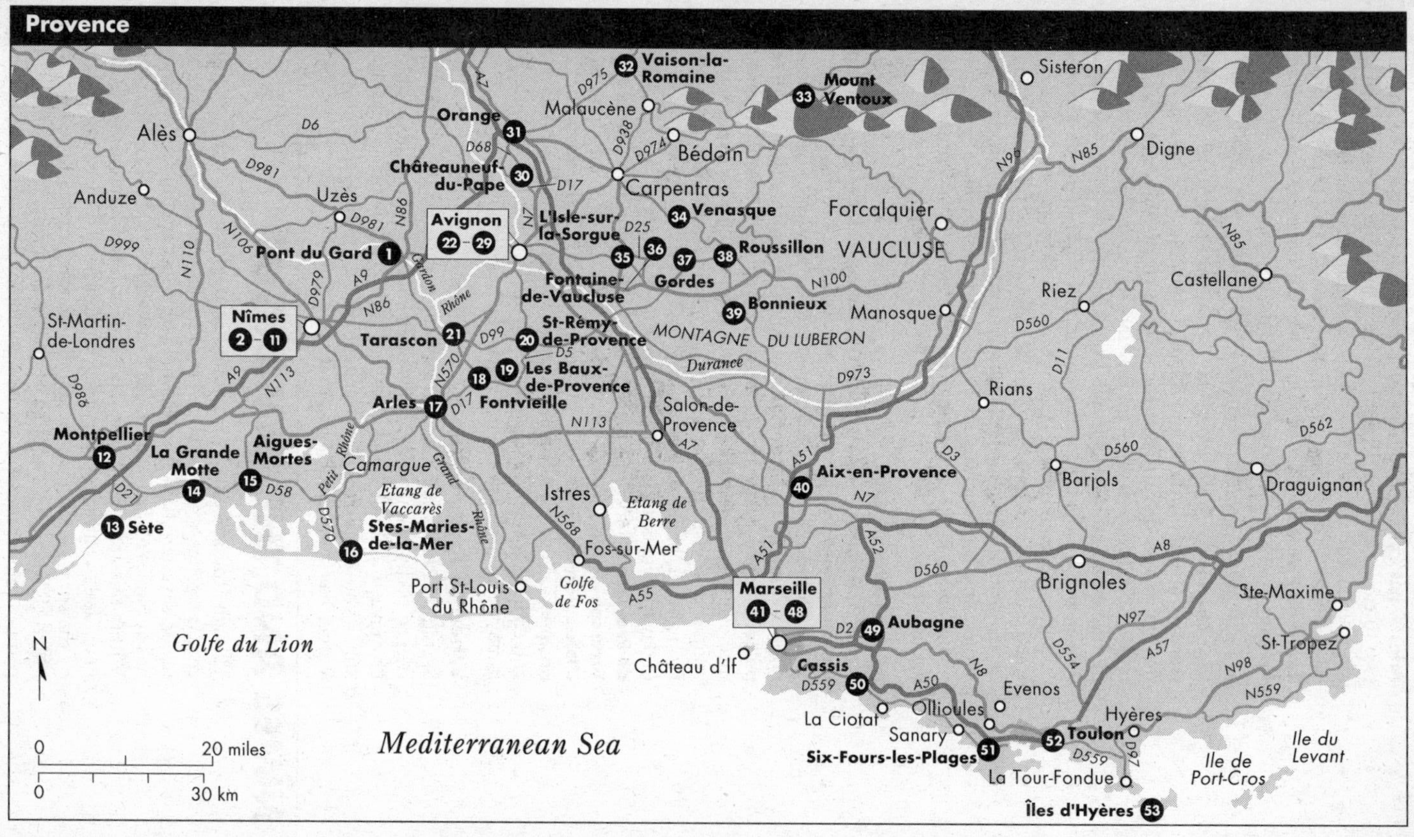
Provence
32 Vaison-la-Romaine
33 Mount Ventoux
Sisteron
Alès
Malaucène
Orange 31
Bédoin
Digne
Châteauneuf-du-Pape 30
Carpentras
Anduze
Uzès
Avignon 22 – 29
L'Isle-sur-la-Sorgue
34 Venasque
Forcalquier
Pont du Gard 1
35
36
37
38 Roussillon
VAUCLUSE
Fontaine-de-Vaucluse
Gordes
Castellane
Riez
39 Bonnieux
Manosque
St-Martin-de-Londres
Nîmes 2 – 11
Tarascon 21
20 St-Rémy-de-Provence
MONTAGNE DU LUBERON
Durance
18
19 Les Baux-de-Provence
Fontvieille
Rians
Arles 17
Salon-de-Provence
Montpellier 12
La Grande Motte 14
Aigues-Mortes 15
Camargue
Petit Rhône
Grand Rhône
Rhône
Gardon
40 Aix-en-Provence
Barjols
Draguignan
Etang de Vaccarès
Istres
Etang de Berre
13 Sète
Stes-Maries-de-la-Mer 16
Fos-sur-Mer
Brignoles
Port St-Louis du Rhône
Golfe de Fos
Marseille 41 – 48
49 Aubagne
Ste-Maxime
St-Tropez
Golfe du Lion
Château d'If
Cassis 50
Evenos
La Ciotat
Ollioules
Hyères
Sanary
52 Toulon
Six-Fours-les-Plages 51
Ile du Levant
Ile de Port-Cros
La Tour-Fondue
Îles d'Hyères 53
Mediterranean Sea
N
0 20 miles
0 30 km
A7
A8
A9
A50
A51
A52
A55
A57
N7
N8
N85
N86
N96
N97
N98
N100
N106
N110
N113
N559
N568
N570
D2
D3
D5
D6
D11
D17
D21
D25
D58
D68
D97
D99
D554
D559
D560
D562
D570
D938
D974
D973
D975
D979
D981
D986
D999

Pont du Gard

★ ❶ *22 km (13 mi) southwest of Avignon, 37 km (23 mi) southwest of Orange, 48 km (30 mi) north of Arles.*

No other sight in Provence can rival the Pont du Gard, this *pont* (bridge) midway between Avignon and Nîmes (off the N86 highway) that symbolically links the 20th century to the area's Roman past. A huge, three-tier aqueduct, erected 2,000 years ago as part of a 48-km (30-mi) canal supplying water to Roman Nîmes, the Pont du Gard is astonishingly well preserved. Its setting, spanning a rocky gorge 150 feet above the River Gardon, is nothing less than spectacular. There is no entry fee or guide, though parking is 15 francs, and at certain times you can have it all to yourself: Early morning is best. Gauge the full majesty of the Pont du Gard by walking along the top.

Nîmes

20 km (13 mi) southwest of the Pont du Gard, 43 km (26 mi) south of Avignon, 121 km (74 mi) west of Marseille, 711 km (427 mi) south of Paris.

Few towns have preserved such visible links with their Roman past: Nemausus, as Nîmes was then known, grew to prominence during the reign of Caesar Augustus (27 BC–AD 14) and still has the Arènes, temple, and watchtower. A 60-franc "passport," available from the tourist office, admits you to all the town's museums and monuments and is valid for three days.

★ ❷ Start out at the **Arènes** (Roman amphitheater) which is more than 140 yards long and 110 yards wide, with a seating capacity of 21,000. After a checkered history—it was transformed into a fortress by the Visigoths and used for housing in medieval times—the amphitheater has been restored almost to its original look. An inflatable roof covers it in winter, when various exhibits and shows occupy the space, and bullfights and tennis tournaments are held here in summer. A smaller version of the Colosseum in Rome, this is considered the world's best-preserved Roman amphitheater. ⊠ *bd. Victor-Hugo,* ☎ *04–66–67–29–11.* 🎟 *24 frs; joint ticket to Arènes and Tour Magne 32 frs.* ⏲ *May–Mar., daily 9–noon and 2–6. Apr. guided visits only.*

❸ At the **Musée des Beaux-Arts** (Fine Arts Museum), a few blocks south of the Arènes, you can admire a vast Roman mosaic; the marriage ceremony depicted provides intriguing insights into the Roman aristocratic lifestyle. Old Master paintings (by Nicolas Poussin, Pieter Brueghel, Peter Paul Rubens) and sculpture (by Auguste Rodin) form the mainstay of the collection. ⊠ *rue de la Cité-Foulc,* ☎ *04–66–67–38–21.* 🎟 *24 frs.* ⏲ *Tues.–Sat. 11–6.*

❹ The **Musée Archéologique et d'Histoire Naturelle** (Museum of Archaeology and Natural History), a few blocks northeast of the Arènes, is rich in local archaeological finds, mainly statues, busts, friezes, tools, glass, coins, and pottery. ⊠ *bd. de l'Amiral-Courbet,* ☎ *04–66–67–25–57.* 🎟 *24 frs.* ⏲ *Tues.–Sun. 11–6.*

❺ The uninspired 19th-century reconstruction of the **Cathédrale Notre-Dame et St-Castor** is of less interest than either the surrounding streets or the Museum of Old Nîmes. ⊠ *pl. Aux Herbes.*

❻ The **Musée du Vieux Nîmes** (Museum of Old Nîmes), opposite the cathedral in the 17th-century Bishop's Palace, has embroidered garments in exotic and vibrant displays. Nîmes used to be a cloth-manufacturing center and lent its name to what has become one of the world's most

Arènes, **2**
Cathédral Notre-Dame et St-Castor, **5**
Jardin de la Fontaine, **9**
Maison Carrée, **7**
Musée Archéologique et d'Histoire Naturelle, **4**
Musée d'Art Contemporain, **8**
Musée des Beaux-Arts, **3**
Musée du Vieux Nîmes, **6**
Temple de Diane, **10**
Tour Magne, **11**

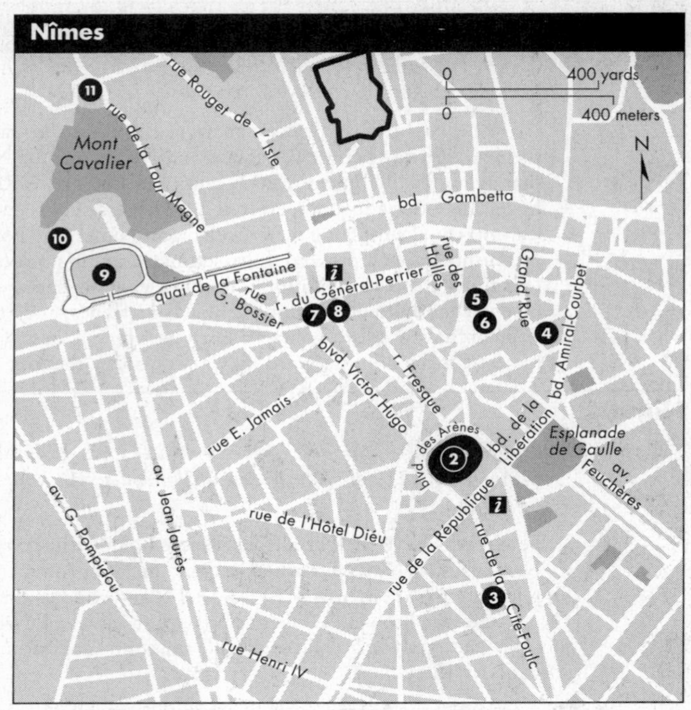

popular fabrics—denim (*de Nîmes*—from Nîmes). ✉ *pl. aux Herbes,* ☎ *04–66–36–00–64.* 🎫 *24 frs.* 🕐 *Tues.–Sun. 11–6.*

★ 7 Despite its name, which means "square house," the **Maison Carrée** is an oblong Roman temple, dating from the 1st century AD. Today the building holds exhibitions. The exquisite carvings along the cornice and on the Corinthian capitals rank as some of the finest in Roman architecture. Thomas Jefferson admired the Maison Carrée's chaste lines of columns so much that he had them copied for the Virginia state capitol in Richmond. ✉ *bd. Victor-Hugo,* ☎ *04–66–67–29–11.* 🎫 *Free.* 🕐 *May–Oct., daily 9–7; Nov.–Apr., daily 9–6.*

8 The swanky, glass-fronted **Musée d'Art Contemporain,** often called the Carrée d'Art (it's directly opposite the Maison Carrée), showcases international painting and sculpture from 1960 onward. ✉ *pl. de la Maison Carrée,* ☎ *04–66–76–35–35.* 🎫 *22 frs.* 🕐 *Tues.–Sun. 11–6.*

9 The **Jardin de la Fontaine,** an elaborate, formal garden, was landscaped on the site of the Roman baths in the 18th century, when the Source de Nemausus, a once-sacred spring, was channeled into pools and a canal.

Just northwest of the Jardin de la Fontaine you'll see the shattered Roman
10 ruin known as the **Temple de Diane,** which dates from the 2nd century BC. The temple's function is unknown, though it is thought to be part of a larger Roman complex that is still unexcavated. In the Middle Ages, Benedictine nuns occupied the building before it was converted into a church. Destruction came in the Wars of Religion.

11 At the far end of the Jardin de la Fontaine is the **Tour Magne**—a stumpy pre-Roman tower that was probably used as a lookout post. Despite having lost 30 feet during the course of time, it still provides fine views of Nîmes for anyone energetic enough to climb the 140 steps

up. ✉ *quai de la Fontaine,* ☎ *04–66–67–29–11.* 🎫 *Tour Magne: 12 frs; joint ticket with Arènes 32 frs.* ⏲ *May.–Oct., daily 9–7; Nov.–Apr., daily 9–12:30 and 1:30–6.*

Dining and Lodging

$$–$$$ ✕ **L'Enclos de la Fontaine.** Nîmes's most fashionable restaurant is in the Impérator hotel (☞ *below*). Chef Jean-Michel Nigon provides such inventive dishes as iced, dill-perfumed langoustine soup. The prix-fixe lunch menus are bargains. ✉ *15 rue Gaston-Boissier,* ☎ *04–66–21–90–30. AE, DC, MC, V.*

$ ★ ✕ **Nicolas.** You'll hear the noise of this homey place before you open the door. A friendly, frazzled staff serves up delicious *bourride* (fish soup) and other local specialties—all at unbelievably low prices. ✉ *1 rue Poise,* ☎ *04–66–67–50–47. AE, MC, V. Closed Mon., 1st 2 wks in July, and mid-Dec.–1st wk in Jan. No lunch Sat.*

$$–$$$ ★ 🏨 **Impérator.** This little palace-hotel, part of the Concorde hotel group, has been tastefully modernized, though most rooms retain a Provençal feel. ✉ *15 rue Gaston-Boissier, 30900,* ☎ *04–66–21–90–30,* FAX *04–66–67–70–25. 62 rooms. Restaurant. AE, DC, MC, V.*

$$ 🏨 **Lisita.** This cozy hotel, just a stone's throw from the Arènes, is a favored haunt of Spanish matadors whenever they're in town for a bullfight. Rooms are on the small side, but some have a view of the plane trees lining the street; most are tastefully decorated with regional furniture. The humorous owner speaks French and Spanish, but not English. Classic French fish and meat dishes are served in the restaurant. ✉ *2 bis bd. des Arènes, 30000,* ☎ *04–66–67–66–20,* FAX *04–66–76–22–30. 30 rooms with bath or shower. Restaurant. AE, DC, MC, V.*

$ 🏨 **48 Grand'rue.** This B&B in the small town of Calvisson, 20 minutes from Nîmes, is run by a painter and an art historian whose ravishing taste informs every room. The 15th-century architecture—circular stone staircase, interior courtyard, and vaulted dining room—help, too. Breakfast is included, parking is not (30 francs); dinner can be arranged for an extra 75 francs. You can also get instruction in painting or drawing in one-week courses from April to October. ✉ *48 Grand'rue, 30420 Calvisson (20 km/12 mi east of Nîmes),* ☎ *04–66–01–23–91,* FAX *04–66–01–42–19. 5 rooms with bath or shower. No credit cards.*

Outdoor Activities and Sports

Aquatropic (✉ 39 rue de la Hostellerie, ☎ 04–66–38–31–00) is an indoor swimming pool with a difference: Wave machines, slides, water cannons, and bubble baths add to the fun for kids and adults alike. It's open weekdays 10–8 and weekends 10–7, for a cost of 35 francs.

Shopping

The **flower market** (✉ bd. Jean-Jaurès) takes place Monday mornings.

Montpellier

12 *50 km (30 mi) southwest of Nîmes, 94 km (58 mi) southwest of Avignon, 152 km (91 mi) north of Perpignan.*

Montpellier is a comparatively young town, a mere 1,000 years old; no Romans settled here. Ever since medieval times, its reputation has been linked to its university, which was founded in the 14th century. Its medical school in particular was so highly esteemed in the 16th century that the great writer François Rabelais left his native Loire Valley to take his doctorate here. Nowadays, the student population of 20,000 helps keep Montpellier young.

The 17th-century town center has been improved by an imaginative urban planning program, and several streets and squares are banned to cars. The heart of Montpellier is **place de la Comédie,** a wide square with cafés and terraces laid out before the handsome 19th-century facade of the civic theater. Boulevard Sarrail leads north from place de la Comédie, past the leafy Esplanade with its rows of plane trees, to the **Musée Fabre.** The museum's collection of art highlights important works by Gustave Courbet (notably *Bonjour Monsieur Courbet*) and Eugène Delacroix (*Femmes d'Alger*), as well as paintings by Frédéric Bazille—whose death during the Franco-Prussian War deprived Impressionism of one of its earliest exponents. ✉ *37 bd. Sarrail,* ☎ *04-67-14-83-00.* 🎫 *20 frs.* ⏲ *Tues.-Fri. 9-5:30, weekends 9:30-5.*

In the heart of old Montpellier—a maze of crooked, bustling streets ideal for shopping and strolling—rue Foch strikes a more disciplined note, slicing straight east to west, to the pride of Montpellier, the **promenade du Peyrou.** An equestrian statue of Louis XIV rides triumphant and carved friezes and columns mask a water tower at the far end of this long, broad, tree-shaded terrace with majestic steps. Water used to arrive along the St-Clément aqueduct, an imposing two-tier structure; locals still cluster beneath its arches to play boules.

Boulevard Henri IV runs north from the promenade du Peyrou to France's oldest botanical garden, the **Jardin des Plantes,** planted by order of Henri IV in 1593. An exceptional range of plants, flowers, and trees grows here. 🎫 *Free.* ⏲ *Gardens Mon.-Sat. 9-noon and 2-5. Greenhouses weekdays 9-noon and 2-5, Sat. 9-noon.*

Within walking distance of Old Montpellier is the **Antigone** district, a fine example of innovative urban planning. Not so long ago Montpellier was in the doldrums, but with the effort of city planners and local industries, the city transformed itself into a hub of economic activity. The Antigone district, designed by the Catalan architect, Ricard Borfill, is a product of these changes. The area is a vast, harmonious, 100-acre complex with neoclassical elements. Here you'll find plazas, esplanades, shops, restaurants, and low-income housing. Note the attention to detail, from pediments to pilasters to street lamps, all constructed out of stone-color, pre-stressed concrete. Be sure to visit **place du Nombre d'Or**—symmetrically composed of curves—and the 1-km-long (½-mi-long) vista that stretches down a mall of cypress trees to the glass-fronted **Hôtel du Région.**

Dining and Lodging

$$$ ✕ **La Closerie.** Chef Jean-Luc Rabanel serves regional dishes like mullet with olives or lamb with thyme, accompanied by a good selection of local, fruity wines in this restaurant in the Métropole hotel. ✉ *3 rue du Clos-René, 34000,* ☎ *04-67-58-11-22. AE, DC, MC, V.*

$$-$$$ ★ ✕ **Le Chandelier.** The only complaints here concern the prices à la carte; the service is impeccable, the trendy pink decor is more than acceptable, and Gilbert Furlan's inventive cuisine is delicious. Try his chilled artichoke and rabbit soup or sea bass with crushed olives. Cinnamon-honey ice cream makes a fine end to your meal. ✉ *267 av. Léon Blum,* ☎ *04-67-92-61-62. Reservations essential. AE, DC, MC, V. Closed part of Feb., 1st 2 wks in Aug., and Sun. No lunch Mon.*

$$ ✕ **Petit Jardin.** As the name implies, there is a leafy garden, as well as a flower-bedecked dining room. Owner Roland Heilmann has made a rapid name for himself with such regional dishes as bourride and the *piperade* omelet with king-size prawns. ✉ *20 rue Jean-Jacques-Rousseau,* ☎ *04-67-60-78-78. Reservations essential. AE, DC, MC, V. Closed Mon. and Jan.-Mar. No dinner Sun.*

$–$$ ✕ **Le César.** In the heart of the Antigone district, this lunch spot is ideal on a sunny day when you can sit outside. Inside, the brasserie-style ambience is also pleasant. Choose from typical regional cuisine—*bouillinade* (a local version of bouillabaisse) or tuna with red wine and shallot based sauce—on the à la carte menu. Or order the 70-franc *menu rapide* (two-course menu) or the 100-franc, four-course meal. ✉ *pl. du Nombre d'Or,* ☎ *04–67–64–87–87. MC, V.*

$–$$ ✕ **Le Restaurant de Teroir.** This restaurant is in the headquarters of the Syndicat des Vignerons Côteaux du Languedoc—the folks who ensure that the region's wines are up to standard—so you can bet that wine is an important part of the menu. The lunch menu du jour—not the best in the area, but certainly good—may comprise mussels in butter sauce, grilled *daurade* (sea bream), and pasta simmered in octopus ink. Meals are served in the pleasant, stone-vaulted cellar or on the terrace. After, visit the Maison du Vin, where the syndicat's best wines are sold at good prices. ✉ *Mas de Saporta, Lattes (from downtown Montpellier follow signs to des Prés D'Arènes; the restaurant is near the Montpellier Sud interchange of autoroute A9),* ☎ *04–67–06–04–40. MC, V. Closed Sun. No dinner Sat.*

$$$ **Métropole.** This venerable 19th-century hotel, halfway between the train station and the city center, was entirely renovated. Though it lost some of its old charm, it still retains a mixture of the old (paneled ceilings and friezes) with the new (furnishings). The staff tries hard—sometimes too hard—to please. ✉ *3 rue du Clos-René, 34000,* ☎ *04–67–58–11–22,* FAX *04–67–92–13–02. 92 rooms. Restaurant, bar. AE, DC, MC, V.*

$$ **Le Guilhem.** In the heart of the historic district, this superb, small hotel has tastefully furnished, small rooms; many look onto the garden. All is quiet, except for the ringing bell at the nearby cathedral. Owners M. and Mme. Charpentier are superb hosts. ✉ *18 rue Jean-Jacques Rousseau, 34000,* ☎ *04–67–52–90–90,* FAX *04–67–60–67–67. 33 rooms with bath or shower. Parking (fee). MC, V.*

Nightlife and the Arts

In the center of town, **Le Petit Negresco** (✉ 6 pl. Jean Jaurès, ☎ 04–67–66–02–10) has tapas and live music. Many of the lively discos, such as **La Croisière** (✉ Espace Latipolia, rte. de Palavas, ☎ 04–67–64–19–52) and **Gyssertin** (✉ à Calade, rte. de Palavas, ☎ 04–67–22–45–82) are in Lattes, on the south side of Montpellier. Concerts are performed at the 19th-century **Théâtre des Treize Vents** (✉ allée Jules-Milhau, ☎ 04–67–58–08–13).

Sète

13 *29 km (18 mi) south of Montpellier.*

In Sète you can get a breath of salt air, have a delightful seafood lunch, and swim in the Mediterranean along the 15 km (9 mi) of sandy beaches that stretch to the Cap d'Agde. The old town is built on a limestone outcrop, Mont St-Clair, which was once an island, but is now linked to the mainland by two narrow sand spits. Head first for the town center and the **Vieux Port** (Old Port) where colorful fishing boats auction off their catches. Running north from the harbor is the **Canal de Sète,** full of moored fishing and tourist boats ready to take you on a tour of the harbor or even on a day trip to Aigues-Mortes. **La Marine,** the quayside street, is lined with seafood restaurants. And be sure to take a trip up **Mont St-Clair** (574 feet) for panoramic views of Sète, the lagoons, and, on a clear day, the distant Pyrénées to the southwest and the Alps to the east.

OFF THE BEATEN PATH **ABBAYE DE VALMAGNE** – Just outside the village of Villeveyrac, 20 km (12 mi) from Sète, is the Valmagne Abbey. Not many individuals own an abbey, but the Baron de Gaudert d'Allaines does—as well as its vineyard. The abbey was established in 1138 under the Benedictine Order, but transferred its allegiance to the Cistercians two decades later. It prospered until the Wars of Religion when one of the abbots joined the Protestant camp and came back in the dead of night to hack to death all the other brothers. After the Revolution, the abbey was sold off and became the property of the Gaudert d'Allaines's family. Eight generations later, they decided to restore the abbey, whose church, some 83 meters in length and 23 meters in height, had been used to store mammoth wine casks (one holds 40,000 liters). The wine is now stored in a nearby building, but the casks remain. The most delightful part of the abbey is its cloisters, with its golden stonework, Tuscany Gardens, and beautiful fountain enclosed by filigreed stone (this abbey is one of the few to have an intact fountain). The guided tour of the abbey ends in the wine tasting room and wine shop, where the purchase of a bottle or two could benefit your next picnic. ✉ *rte. D5.* 🎫 *25 frs.* ⏲ *Apr.–Nov., Mon.–Sat. 10–noon and 2–4.*

Dining

$$ ✕ **La Palangrotte.** Don't miss out on Alain Gémignani's subtly prepared seafood creations. His specialty, the *rémoulade* (a mixture with spicy sauce) of marinated fresh salmon with shrimp, fillet of grouper, and a confit of vegetables, is particularly good. Lunch menus begin at 110 francs, but the 150-franc menu has the best choices. Decor is contemporary. ✉ *39 quai de la Marine,* ☏ *04–67–74–80–25. Closed Mon. No dinner Sun. AE, DC, MC, V.*

$ ✕ **La Racasse.** This place has one of the best value prix-fixe menus along this restaurant-filled street. Sea scallops, oysters, and turbot in white wine sauce are some of the local favorites. ✉ *27 quai de la Marine,* ☏ *04–67–74–38–46. MC, V.*

La Grande Motte

⓮ *20 km (12 mi) east of Montpellier, 87 km (54 mi) north of Beziers, 45 km (28 mi) south of Nîmes.*

The arid, rocky landscape of the Midi region of Languedoc begins to change as you head southeast from Montpellier along the coast on D21, en route to the Camargue, past pools and lagoons, to La Grande Motte. The town is the most lavish—and, some would say, ugliest—of a string of new resort towns built along the coast. The mosquitoes that once infested this watery area have finally been vanquished, and tourists have taken their place. La Grande Motte was only a glint in an architect's eye back in the late 1960s; since then, its arresting pyramidal apartment blocks have influenced several French resorts.

Dining

$$ ✕ **Alexandre-Amirauté.** Tons of oysters are cultivated in the nearby *étangs* (lagoons); you can sample them in the elegant surrounds of Louis XV furnishings while gazing out over the Mediterranean. Other dishes include a splendid array of seafood. ✉ *345 esplanade Maurice-Justin,* ☏ *04–67–56–63–63. Closed Mon. No dinner Sun. AE, MC, V.*

Aigues-Mortes

⓯ *13 km (8 mi) east of La Grande Motte, 41 km (25 mi) east of Nîmes, 48 km (30 mi) southwest of Arles.*

Created at the behest of Louis IX (St-Louis) in the 13th century, Aigues-Mortes is an astonishing relic of early town planning. Medieval streets are usually crooked; at Aigues-Mortes, however, a grid plan was adopted, hemmed in by sturdy walls sprouting towers at regular intervals. The town was originally a port, and Louis used it as a base for his Crusades to the Holy Land. The sea has long since receded, though, and Aigues-Mortes's size and importance have gone away with it. In the center of the old city is the elegant place St-Louis, with restaurants galore. Here, it seems, every tourist gathers around midday to plunk down at a sidewalk table and relish the atmosphere during the mandatory two-hour lunch break.

Unlike most of the medieval buildings, the **fortifications** remain intact. Walk along the top of the city ramparts and admire some remarkable views across the town and salt marshes. You can also explore the powerful Tour de Constance, originally designed as a fortress-keep and used in the 18th century as a prison for Protestants who refused to convert to official state Catholicism. One such unfortunate, Marie Durand, languished here for 38 years. Abraham Mazel was luckier. He spent 10 months chiseling a hole in the wall, while his companions sang psalms to distract the jailers. The ruse worked: Mazel and 16 others escaped. ☎ *04–66–53–61–55.* 🎫 *28 frs.* ⏲ *Tower and ramparts Apr.–Oct., daily 9–7; Nov.–Mar., 9:30–noon and 2–5:30.*

Stes-Maries-de-la-Mer

16 *32 km (20 mi) southeast of Aigues-Mortes, 129 km (80 mi) west of Marseille, 39 km (24 mi) south of Arles.*

Stes-Maries-de-la-Mer is a commercialized resort town, frequented mainly by British tourists in search of the Camargue's principal sandy beach, 4 km (2½ mi) of dunes and flat sand. Even if you just have a day, the beach makes a great picnic spot. Park in the lots on the east side of town or along the road to the west.

The town's tiny, dark fortress-church houses caskets containing relics of the "Holy Maries" after whom the town is named. Legend has it that Mary Jacobi (the sister of the Virgin), Mary Magdalene, Mary Salome (mother of the apostles James and John), and their black servant Sarah were washed up here around AD 40 after being abandoned at sea. Their adopted town rapidly became a site of pilgrimage, the most important site for Gypsies. Sarah was adopted as their patron saint, and to this day, Gypsies from all over the world make pilgrimages to Stes-Maries in late May and late October, while guitar-strumming pseudo-gypsies serenade tourists throughout the summer.

To the north of Stes-Maries-de-la-Mer, in the center of the Camargue, is the 30-acre **Parc Ornithologique,** itself part of the vast Réserve Nationale centered on the Étang de Vaccarès. It is a protected environment for vegetation and wildlife: Birds from northern Europe and Siberia spend the winter here, while flamingos flock here in summer. ☎ *04–90–97–82–62.* 🎫 *35 frs.* ⏲ *Mar.–Oct., daily 8–dusk; Nov.–Feb., daily 9–dusk.*

Arles

17 *38 km (24 mi) north of Stes-Maries-de-la-Mer, 92 km (57 mi) northwest of Marseille, 36 km (22 mi) south of Avignon, 31 km (19 mi) east of Nîmes.*

The first inhabitants of Arles were probably the Greeks, who arrived from Marseille in the 6th century BC. The Romans, however, left a stronger mark, constructing the theater and amphitheater that remain the biggest tourist attractions. Arles used to be a thriving port before the Mediterranean receded over what is now the Camargue. It was also the site of the southernmost bridge over the Rhône, and became a commercial crossroads; merchants from as far afield as Arabia, Assyria, and Africa would linger here to do business on their way from Rome to Spain or northern Europe.

The Dutch painter Vincent van Gogh produced much of his best work—and chopped off his ear—in Arles during a frenzied 15-month spell (1888–89) just before his suicide at 37. Unfortunately, the houses he lived in are no longer standing—they were destroyed during World War II—but part of one of his most famous subjects remains: the **Pont de Trinquetaille,** across the Rhône. Van Gogh's rendering of the bridge, painted in 1888, was auctioned a century later for $20 million. Local art museums can't compete with that type of bidding—which is one reason none of van Gogh's works are displayed there. Another is that Arles failed to appreciate him; he was jeered at and eventually packed off to the nearest lunatic asylum in St-Rémy (☞ *below*). The city has since softened and now you'll find signs with reproductions of famous van Gogh paintings at the spots where he set up his easel.

Before van Gogh was embraced by Arles, the city chose to name the local museum, the **Musée Réattu,** after Jacques Réattu, a local painter of dazzling mediocrity. His works fill three rooms, van Gogh's none. But there are modern drawings and paintings by Pablo Picasso, Fernand Léger, and Maurice de Vlaminck, as well as a notable photography section. ✉ *rue du Grand-Prieuré,* ☎ *04–90–49–37–58.* 🎫 *15 frs; joint ticket to all monuments and museums in Arles: 55 frs.* ⏲ *June–Sept., daily 9:30–7; Nov.–Mar., daily 10–12:30 and 2–5; Apr.–May and Oct., daily 9:30–12:30 and 2–6.*

★ Reminders of Roman society are found at the ruins of the **Palais Constantin,** on the site of the **Thermes de la Trouille,** Provence's largest Roman baths. ✉ *rue Dominique-Maisto.* 🎫 *12 frs; joint ticket 55 frs as above.* ⏲ *June–Sept., daily 9:30–7; Nov.–Mar., daily 10–12:30 and 2–5; Apr.–May and Oct., daily 9:30–12:30 and 2–6.*

The most notable Roman sight is the 26,000-capacity **Arènes,** built in the 1st century AD for circuses and gladiator combats. The amphitheater is 150 yards long and as wide as a football field, with each of its two stories composed of 60 arches; the original top tier has long since crumbled, and the three square towers were added in the Middle Ages. Climb to the upper story for some satisfying views. Despite its age, the amphitheater still sees a lot of action, mainly Sunday afternoon bullfights. ✉ *Rond-Point des Arènes,* ☎ *04–90–96–03–70.* 🎫 *15 frs; join ticket 55 frs as above.* ⏲ *June–Sept., daily 8:30–7; Nov.–Mar., daily 9–noon and 2–4:30; Apr.–May and Oct., daily 9–12:30 and 2–6:30.*

The bits of marble column scattered around the grassy enclosure of ★ the diminished remains of the **Théâtre Antique** (Roman Theater), just 100 yards from the Arènes, hint poignantly at the theater's onetime grandeur. The capacity may have shrunk from 7,000 to a few hundred, but the orchestra pit and a few tiers of seats are still used for the city's Music and Drama Festival each July. ✉ *rue du Cloître,* ☎ *04–90–96–93–30 for ticket information.* 🎫 *15 frs; joint ticket 55 frs as above.* ⏲ *June–Sept., daily 8:30–7; Nov.–Mar., daily 9–noon and 2–4:30; Apr.–May and Oct., daily 9–12:30 and 2–6:30.*

The church of **St-Trophime,** on place de la République in the center of Arles, dates mainly from the 11th and 12th centuries; subsequent additions have not spoiled its architectural harmony. Take time to admire the accomplished 12th-century sculptures flanking the main portal, featuring the *Last Judgment,* the apostles, the Nativity, and various saints. There are other well-crafted sculptures in the cloisters. ✉ *rue de l'Hôtel-de-Ville,* ☎ *04–90–49–36–36.* 🎫 *Cloisters 15 frs; joint ticket 55 frs as above.* ⏲ *June–Sept., daily 8:30–7; Nov.–Mar., daily 9–noon and 2–4:30; Apr.–May and Oct., daily 9–12:30 and 2–6:30.*

Housed in a former church next to the 17th-century Hôtel de Ville (Town Hall), opposite the church of St-Trophime, the **Musée d'Art Païen** (Museum of Pagan Art) contains Roman statues, busts, mosaics, and a white marble sarcophagus. You'll also see a copy of the famous statue the *Venus of Arles;* Sun King Louis XIV waltzed off to the Louvre with the original. ✉ *pl. de la République.* 🎫 *12 frs; joint ticket 55 frs as above.* ⏲ *June–Sept., daily 8:30–7; Nov.–Mar., daily 9–noon and 2–4:30; Apr.–May and Oct., 9–12:30 and 2–6:30.*

The **Musée d'Art Chrétien** (Museum of Christian Art) has a magnificent collection of sculpted marble sarcophagi, second only to the Vatican's, that date from the 4th century. Though the building is a former 17th-century Jesuit chapel, it was built on a Roman foundations. Downstairs, you can explore a vast Roman double gallery built in the 1st century BC as a grain store and see part of the great Roman sewer built two centuries later. ✉ *rue Balze.* 🎫 *12 frs; joint ticket 55 frs as above.* ⏲ *June–Sept., daily 8:30–7; Nov.–Mar., daily 9–noon and 2–4:30; Apr.–May and Oct., daily 9–12:30 and 2–6:30.*

The **Muséon Arlaten,** an old-fashioned folklore museum, is housed in a 16th-century mansion next door to the Musée d'Art Chrétien. The charming displays of costumes and headdresses, puppets, and waxworks were lovingly assembled by that great 19th-century Provençal poet Frédéric Mistral. ✉ *29 rue de la République,* ☎ *04–90–96–08–23.* 🎫 *15 frs; joint ticket 55 frs as above.* ⏲ *June–Sept., daily 8:30–7; Nov.–Mar., Tues.–Sun. 9–noon and 2–4:30; Apr.–May and Oct., Tues.–Sun. 9–12:30 and 2–6:30.*

The fountains in the **Jardin d'Hiver** (Winter Garden), the public garden at the east end of the boulevard des Luces, figure in several of van Gogh's paintings.

The **Alyscamps** starts at the allée des Sarcophages, on the southeast side of town. This was a prestigious burial site from Roman times through the Middle Ages. A host of important finds have been excavated here, many of which are exhibited in the town's museums. Empty tombs and sarcophagi line the allée des Sarcophages, creating a gloomy atmosphere in dull weather. ☎ *04–90–49–36–87.* 🎫 *12 frs.* ⏲ *Daily 9–5.*

On the south side of town (across highway N113), by the Rhone, is the **Musée de l'Arles Antique** (Museum of Ancient Arles). Many of the historical artifacts excavated in Arles are displayed here. If you haven't understood why Arles is referred to as the "Petite Rome des Gaules," you will after a visit here: Most of the 1,300 objects in the museum are of Roman origin. ✉ *Presque'île du Cirque Romain,* ☎ *04–90–19–88–89.* 🎫 *25 frs.* ⏲ *Apr.–Sept., daily 9–8; Oct.–Mar., daily 10–8.*

Dining and Lodging

$$$ ✕ **Lou Marquès.** Chef Pascal Renaud pleases with nouvelle cuisine and traditional Provençal dishes in his fashionable restaurant in the Jules César hotel (☞ *below*). Try the cod with lentils and fresh cream. ✉ *bd. des Lices, 13200,* ☎ *04–90–93–43–20. AE, DC, MC, V.*

$$ ✕ **Le Vaccarès.** In the footsteps of his father and grandfather, chef Bernard Dumas serves classic Provençal dishes. Try his mussels dressed in herbs and garlic. The dining-room decor is as elegant as the cuisine. ✉ *11* *rue Favorin,* ☎ *04-90-96-06-17. Reservations essential. MC, V. Closed mid-Jan.–mid-Feb. and Mon. No dinner Sun.*

$ ✕ **Le Constantin.** For 89 francs you get three substantial courses at this tiny, inexpensive restaurant. The meal might include homemade terrines, grilled tuna, steaks with *pommes frites* (french fries), and a dessert to fill any remaining corners. The atmosphere is set by exposed brick walls, cheerful waitresses, and red-checkered tablecloths. ✉ *rue Dominique Maiso,* ☎ *04-90-96-59-33. MC, V. Closed Wed.*

$$$ ★ **Arlatan.** Follow the signposts from place du Forum to the picturesque street where you'll find this 15th-century house, the former home of the counts of Arlatan, built on the site of a 4th-century basilica (tiled flooring dating from this period is visible below glass casing). Antiques, pretty fabrics, and tapestries lend it a gracious atmosphere. There is a lovely garden and a private bar. ✉ *26 rue du Sauvage, 13200,* ☎ *04-90-93-56-66,* FAX *04-90-49-68-45. 51 rooms. Bar. AE, DC, MC, V.*

$$$ **Château de Vergières.** Down an avenue of trees on an 800-acre estate, you'll find this small 18th-century château filled with family portraits, antique furniture, and bric-a-brac. It's a guest house where you can (with advance arrangements) dine with the family on an excellent dinner and stay overnight. The large rooms have high ceilings and wood floors. The pool, surrounded by aromatic plants, suits the relaxed; more active guests are offered maps and guides to wildlife in the Camargue. ✉ *La Dynamite, 13310 St-Martin de Crau (15 km/9 mi southeast of Arles),* ☎ *04-90-47-17-16,* FAX *04-90-47-38-30. 6 rooms. Pool. No credit cards.*

$$$ **Jules César.** This elegant hotel was originally a Carmelite convent. Rooms, on the small side, are tastefully decorated with antiques; many overlook the 17th-century cloisters. The peaceful Provençal garden is a splendid place for dinner; breakfast is served in the cloisters. ✉ *bd. des Lices, 13200,* ☎ *04-90-93-43-20,* FAX *04-90-93-33-47. 55 rooms. Restaurant, pool. AE, DC, MC, V. Closed Nov.–late Dec.*

$ **Hôtel Calendal.** The cheery Provençal colors of this small hotel next to the Arènes reflect the spirit of the hotel and its staff, most of whom speak English. Rooms overlook the amphitheater and the courtyard garden; some sleep four. Light meals are served in the tearoom. ✉ *22 pl. du Docteur Pomme, 13200,* ☎ *04-90-96-11-89,* FAX *04-90-96-05-84. 27 rooms. Restaurant, air-conditioning. AE, MC, V.*

$ **Hôtel Gauguin.** The rooms, painted in fresh yellows and blues, are small, but so is the price. Full bathrooms are a little more. Ask for a room in front, looking onto the square. The welcoming owner, Mme. Dugand, is happy to try her English. ✉ *5 pl. Voltaire, 13200,* ☎ *04-90-96-14-35. 18 rooms, 7 with shared WCs, 11 with shower. MC, V.*

Nightlife and the Arts

The **International Photography Festival** takes place in July at the Théâtre Antique (✉ rue de la Calade/rue du Cloître).

Shopping

Delicately patterned Provençal print fabrics can be found at Arles's **Souleiado** (✉ 18 bd. des Lices). Fruit, vegetables, and household goods are sold at the **market** on Wednesday at boulevard des Lice and boulevard Clémenceau and on Saturday morning at boulevard Émile Combes.

Fontvieille

18 *10 km (6 mi) east of Arles: Take N570 toward Avignon, and almost immediately turn right on D17:*

The striking village of Fontvieille, among the limestone hills, is best known as the home of writer Alphonse Daudet. In the well-preserved, charming **Moulin de Daudet** (windmill), just up D33 on a hill in the outskirts of the village, 19th-century writer Alphonse Daudet dreamed up his short stories, *Lettres de Mon Moulin*. Inside there's a small museum devoted to Daudet, and you can walk upstairs to see the original milling system. ☎ *04–90–54–60–78.* 🎫 *10 frs.* ⏲ *Apr.–Oct., daily 9–noon and 2–7; Nov.–Dec. and Feb.–Mar., daily 10–noon.*

Les Baux-de-Provence

★ ⓳ *18 km (11 mi) northeast of Arles, 29 km (18 mi) south of Avignon, 8 km (5 mi) east of Fontvieille.*

Perched on a mighty spur of rock high above the surrounding countryside with its vines, olive trees, and quarries, Les Baux-de-Provence is an amazing place. The mineral bauxite was discovered here in 1821. Half of Les Baux is composed of tiny climbing streets and ancient stone houses inhabited, for the most part, by local craftsmen. The other half, the Ville Morte (Dead Town), is a mass of medieval ruins, vestiges of Les Baux's glorious past, when the town had 6,000 inhabitants and the defensive impregnability of its rocky site far outweighed its isolation and poor access. Cars must be left in the parking lot (18 francs) at the entrance to the village.

The 16th-century **Hôtel des Porcelets,** close to the 12th-century church of **St-Vincent** (where local shepherds continue an age-old tradition of herding their lambs to midnight mass at Christmas), features some 18th-century frescoes and a small but choice collection of contemporary art. ✉ *pl. Hervain,* ☎ *04–90–54–36–99.* 🎫 *34 frs; joint ticket with Musée Lapidaire and Ville Morte.* ⏲ *Easter–Oct., daily 9–noon and 2–6.*

Enter the **Ville Morte** (Dead Town) through the 14th-century Tour-de-Brau on rue Neuve. The tower houses the **Musée Lapidaire,** displaying locally excavated sculptures and ceramics. You can wander at will amid the rocks and ruins of the Dead Town. A 13th-century castle stands at one end of the cliff top and, at the other, the **Tour Paravelle** and the **Monument Charloun Rieu.** From here, you can enjoy a magnificent view of Arles and the Camargue as far as Stes-Maries-de-la-Mer. ✉ *La Citadelle,* ☎ *04–90–54–37–37.* 🎫 *34 frs; joint ticket with Musée Lapidaire and Ville Morte.* ⏲ *Daily 9:15–6:15.*

One kilometer (½ mile) north of Les Baux, off D27, is the **Cathédrale d'Images,** where the majestic setting of the old bauxite quarries, with their towering rock faces and stone pillars, is used as a colossal screen for nature-themed films (Jacques Cousteau gets frequent billing). ✉ *rte. de Maillane,* ☎ *04–90–54–38–65.* 🎫 *40 frs.* ⏲ *Mid-Feb.–mid-Nov., daily 10–6. Some special exhibitions are held mid-Dec.–mid-Jan.*

Dining and Lodging

$$$$ ✕🏨 **L'Oustau de la Baumanière.** Sheltered on three sides by rocky cliffs below the village of Les Baux, this hotel, with its formal terrace and large swimming pool, has the air of a Roman palazzo. Chef Jean-André Charial's signature, sublime dish is ravioli *de truffes aux poireaux* (stuffed with truffles and leeks). Make reservations and note that the restaurant is closed Wednesday. A few drawbacks: the staff can be reserved and repairs are sometimes delayed. But rooms are beautifully furnished with a mix of antiques. Those in the main house convey grandeur—enormous chimneys, sumptuous fabrics, and solid armoires. Three kilometers (2 miles) away are 15 less-formal rooms and, in a third, small, vine-covered building, three more simple but charming ones. ✉ *Val d'Enfer, 13520,* ☎ *04–90–54–33–07,* FAX *04–90–54–40–46. 25 rooms. Restaurant, pool, 2 tennis courts, horseback riding. AE, DC, MC, V. Closed late Jan.–early Mar.*

St-Rémy-de-Provence

★ 20 *8 km (5 mi) north of Les Baux, 24 km (15 mi) east of Arles, 19 km (12 mi) south of Avignon.*

The small, market town of St-Rémy-de-Provence was an important trading post in the 6th century BC. The Phocaeans enlarged the town with Greek-style houses. But disaster struck when the invading Teutons ravaged the country in the latter part of the 1st century BC. Peace was not secured until the Roman general Marius drove the invaders out defeating them at the battle of St-Victoire in 102 BC—a famous date in the history of the taming of southern Gaul. St-Rémy, known as Glanum to the Romans, was rebuilt and it is the architectural remains from these Roman days that has placed the town on the cultural map. Temples, baths, forum, and houses have been excavated, while the Mausoleum and Arc Municipal (Triumphal Arch) will welcome you as you enter the town. After the Romans left, the town was rebuilt under the auspices of the Abbaye de St-Remi of Rheims. Today it is a quintessential Provençal town with fountains in its squares and tree-lined streets. No wonder Vincent van Gogh chose to spend a year (1889) here at the asylum to ease his mental anguish. Consider making it your base for exploring the area.

The Roman **Mausolée** (Mausoleum) was erected around AD 100; the four bas-reliefs around its base, depicting ancient battle scenes, are stunningly preserved. The mausoleum is composed of four archways topped by a circular colonnade. The nearby **Arc Municipal** is a few decades older and has suffered heavily; the upper half has crumbled away, although you can still make out some of the stone carvings.

Excavations of **Glanum** began in 1921, and a 10th of the original Roman town has now been unearthed. The remains, spread over 300 yards along what was once the Aurelian Way between Arles and Milan, are less spectacular than the arch and mausoleum, but you can still see that they were once temples, fountains, gateways, baths, houses, and a forum. ☎ *04–90–92–23–79.* *32 frs.* *Apr.–Sept., daily 9–noon and 2–6; Oct.–Mar., daily 9:30–noon and 2–5.*

Many of the finds—statues, pottery, and jewelry—can also be examined at the town museum, **Le Musée Archéologique,** in the center of St-Rémy. ✉ *Hôtel de Sade, rue Parage,* ☎ *04–90–92–64–04.* *15 frs.* *June–Sept., daily 9–noon and 2–6; Apr.–May and Oct., weekends 10–noon, weekdays 3–6; closed Nov.–Mar.*

The 12th-century **Monastère de St-Paul-de-Mausolée,** the asylum where van Gogh spent a year resting and painting, is a short walk from Glanum. Still a psychiatric hospital, only the 12th-century church with an 18th-century facade, the Romanesque cloisters, and the small gift shop (with works of art by patients for sale) are open to the public. Along the paths between the monastery and Glanum, there are signs with reproductions of van Gogh's paintings at the spots where he is believed to have worked on several masterpieces, including *Starry Night.* ☎ *04–90–92–77–00.* *May–Sept., daily 8–7; Oct.–Apr., daily 8–5.*

Dining and Lodging

$$$–$$$$ **Vallon de Valrugues.** This luxurious villa is fast making a name for itself. From rooms you can see the rocky Alpilles hills and the olive groves. Chef Joël Guillet, who learned his trade at the famous Négresco in Nice, specializes in imaginative regional dishes like sea bass with calamari, pigeon roasted in lavender honey, and fruit desserts. ✉ *chemin Canto-Cigalo, 13210,* ☎ *04–90–92–04–40,* FAX *04–90–92–44–01. 34 rooms, 17 suites. Restaurant, pool, hot tub, sauna. AE, MC, V.*

$$$ **Château des Alpilles.** This lavishly appointed 19th-century château lords over a fine park off D31. Statesmen and aristocrats stayed here; today the crowd is as sophisticated. The best of classic luxury—plush carpeting and polished wood furniture—is found in rooms. Many are equipped with kitchenettes. ✉ *Ancienne rte. du Grès, 13210,* ☎ *04–90–92–03–33,* FAX *04–90–92–45–17. 15 rooms, 4 suites. Kitchenettes, pool, sauna, 2 tennis courts. AE, DC, MC, V. Closed mid-Nov.–mid-Dec. and Jan.–mid-Mar.*

$$$ **Mas de Cornud.** Welcoming ex-pat owners David and Nito Carpitras have turned their classic Provençal farmhouse, just outside St-Rémy, into a private inn (make reservations in advance). The house and the large rooms are filled with French country furniture and objects from around the world. Table d'hôte dinners, cooking classes, and tours can be arranged. Breakfast is included. ✉ *rte. de Mas-Blanc, 13210,* ☎ *04–90–92–39–32,* FAX *04–90–92–55–99. 4 rooms. Pool. No credit cards. Closed Jan.–Feb.*

Tarascon

21 *16 km (10 mi) west of St-Rémy, 17 km (11 mi) north of Arles, 25 km (15 mi) east of Nîmes.*

The mythical Tarasque, a monster that would emerge from the Rhône to gobble up children and cattle, came from Tarascon. Luckily, Saint Martha, who washed up at Stes-Maries-de-la-Mer, allegedly tamed the beast with a sprinkle of holy water, after which the inhabitants slashed it to pieces. This dramatic event is celebrated on the last Sunday in June with a parade and immortalized by Alphonse Daudet in his tales of a folk hero known to all French schoolchildren as Tartarin de Tarascon.

One of the highlights of a visit to Tarascon is its formidable 12th-century **Château,** intended to protect the town from any beast or man that might be tempted to emulate the Tarasque's fiendish deeds. The castle's massive stone walls, towering 150 feet above the rocky banks of the Rhône, are among the most daunting in France, so it's not surprising that the castle was used as a prison for centuries. Since 1926, however, the chapels, vaulted royal apartments, and stone carvings of the interior have been restored to less-intimidating glory. ☎ *04–90–91–01–93.* *28 frs.* *July–Aug., daily 9–7; Sept.–June, daily 9–noon and 2–6 (Oct.–Mar., 2–5).*

Dining and Lodging

$$ **St-Jean.** A dozen cozy, spacious, rustic rooms are hidden behind the austere facade. Regional dishes, including steak with shallot butter and salad niçoise, are served in the wood-beam dining room. ✉ *24 bd. Victor-Hugo, 13150,* ☎ *04–90–91–13–87,* FAX *04–90–91–32–42. 12 rooms with shower or bath. Restaurant. AE, DC, MC, V. Closed mid-Dec.–mid-Jan.*

THE VAUCLUSE

Though the Roman presence is still evident in this region, especially in Orange and at Vaison-la-Romaine, Avignon's more recent history revolves around its being the seat of the papacy in the 14th century. The outstanding geographic feature of this hilly landscape with stubbly trees is Mont Ventoux, but it's the small villages in the Luberon mountains—Venasque, Gordes, Roussillon—that will win your heart.

Avignon

24 km (15 mi) northeast of Tarascon, 82 km (51 mi) northwest of Aix-en-Provence, 95 km (59 mi) northwest of Marseille, 224 km (140 mi) south of Lyon.

A warren of medieval alleys nestling behind a protective ring of stocky towers, Avignon is possibly best known for its Pont d'Avignon, the St-Bénezet bridge, which many will remember singing about during their nursery-rhyme days. No one dances across the bridge these days, however; it was amputated in midstream in the 17th century, when a storm washed half of it away. Still, Avignon has lots to offer, starting with the Palais des Papes (Papal Palace), where seven exiled popes camped between 1309 and 1377 after fleeing from the corruption of Rome. Avignon remained papal property until 1791, and elegant mansions bear witness to the town's 18th-century prosperity. From the tourist office (✉ 41 cours Jean-Jaurès), rue de la République, Avignon's main street, leads past shops and cafés to place de l'Horloge and place du Palais.

★ 22 The colossal **Palais des Papes** (Papal Palace) creates a disconcertingly fortresslike impression, underlined by the austerity of its interior decor; most of the furnishings were dispersed during the French Revolution. Some imagination is required to picture it in medieval splendor, awash with color and with worldly clerics enjoying what the 14th-century Italian poet Petrarch called "licentious banquets." On close inspection, two different styles of building emerge at the palace: the severe **Palais Vieux** (Old Palace), built between 1334 and 1342 by Pope Benedict XII, a member of the Cistercian order, which frowned on frivolity, and the more decorative **Palais Nouveau** (New Palace), built in the following decade by the arty, lavish-living Pope Clement VI. The Great Court, where visitors arrive, links the two.

The main rooms of the Palais Vieux are the **Consistory** (Council Hall), decorated with some excellent 14th-century frescoes by Simone Martini; the **Chapelle St-Jean** (original frescoes by Matteo Giovanetti); the **Grand Tinel,** or Salle des Festins, with a majestic vaulted roof and a series of 18th-century Gobelin tapestries; the **Chapelle St-Martial** (more Matteo frescoes); the **Chambre du Cerf,** with a richly decorated ceiling, murals featuring a stag hunt, and a delightful view of Avignon; the **Chambre de Parement** (papal antechamber); and the **Chambre à Coucher** (papal bedchamber). The principal attractions of the Palais Nouveau are the **Grande Audience,** a magnificent two-nave hall on the ground floor, and, upstairs, the **Chapelle Clémentine,** where the college of cardinals gathered to elect the new pope. ✉ *pl. du Palais,* ☎ *04–90–27–50–73.* 🎟 *35 frs.* ⏲ *Apr.–Oct., daily 9–7; Nov.–Mar., daily 9–12:45 and 2–6.*

23 Avignon's 12th-century **Cathédrale,** not far from the Palais des Papes,
24 contains the Gothic tomb of Pope John XII. From the **Rocher des**
Doms, a large, attractive garden just east of the cathedral, you can get
a look at Avignon and the Rhône. The first bridge to span the Rhône
25 at Avignon is the celebrated **Pont St-Bénezet**—built, according to legend, by a local shepherd named Bénezet in the 12th century. Though
only half of the original 900 yards remains, it's worth strolling along,
for the views and to visit the tiny **Chapelle St-Nicolas** that juts out over
the river. ☎ *04–90–85–60–16.* 🎟 *15 frs.* ⏲ *Apr.–Sept., daily 9–6:30;*
Oct.–Mar., Tues.–Sun. 9–1 and 2–5.

Cathédral, **23**
Le Cloître des Arts, **29**
Musée Calvet, **28**
Musée Lapidaire, **27**
Palais des Papes, **22**
Petit Palais, **26**
Pont St-Bénezet, **25**
Rocher des Doms, **24**

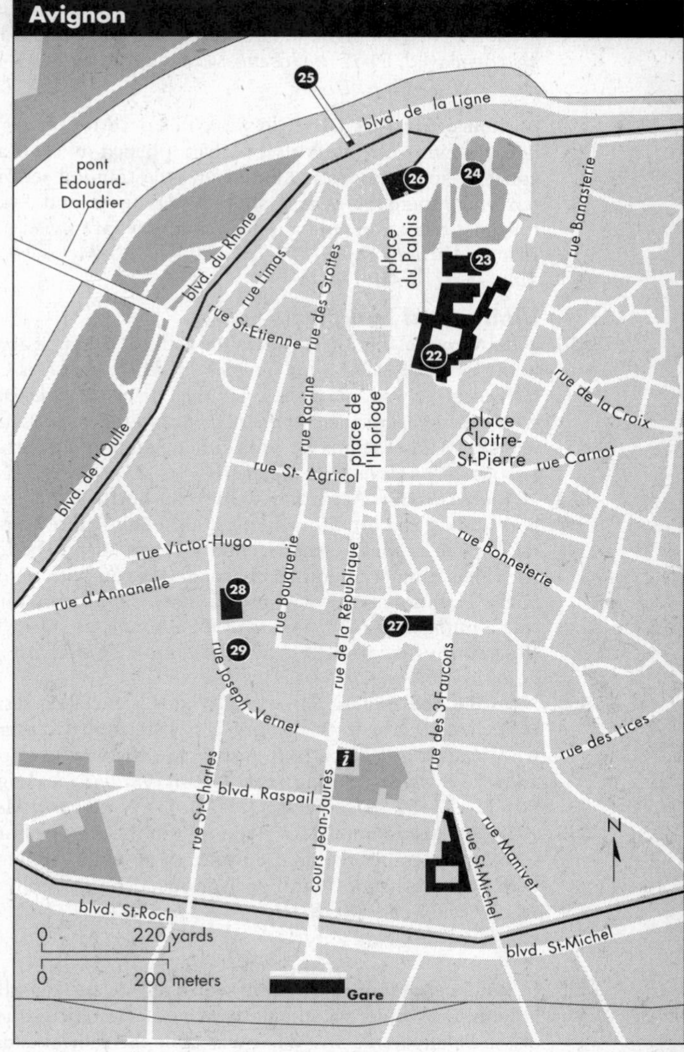

26 The medieval **Petit Palais** (Little Palace), between Pont St-Bénezet and the Rocher des Doms garden, was once home to cardinals and archbishops. Nowadays it contains an outstanding collection of Old Masters, led by the Italian schools of Venice, Siena, and Florence (note Sandro Botticelli's *Virgin and Child*). ✉ *21 pl. du Palais,* ☎ *04–90–86–44–58.* 🎫 *20 frs.* ⏲ *Wed.–Mon. 9:30–noon and 2–6.*

Venture into the narrow, winding, shop-lined streets of old Avignon, south of the Papal Palace, to get to a sturdy 17th-century Baroque chapel
27 fronted by an imposing facade and housing the **Musée Lapidaire.** On display are a variety of archaeological finds—including the remains of Avignon's Arc de Triomphe. ✉ *27 rue de la République,* ☎ *04–90–85–75–38.* 🎫 *10 frs.* ⏲ *Wed.–Mon. 10–noon and 2–6.*

28 An 18th-century town house is home to the **Musée Calvet.** It features an extensive collection of mainly French paintings from the 16th century on, including works by Théodore Géricault, Camille Corot,

Édouard Manet, Raoul Dufy, Maurice de Vlaminck, and the Italian artist Amedeo Modigliani. Greek, Roman, and Etruscan statuettes are also displayed. ✉ *65 rue Joseph-Vernet,* ☎ *04–90–86–33–84.* 🎫 *30 frs.* ⏲ *Wed.–Mon. 10–6.*

29 **Le Cloître des Arts** (Art Cloister), in an 18th-century building two doors down from the Musée Calvet, opened in 1966 as a venue for concerts and expositions. Enhancing the tranquil setting is the cloister, where there is a pottery shop, a restaurant, and a tearoom—ideal for quiet relaxation and a quick read on what to visit next. ✉ *83 rue Joseph-Vernet,* ☎ *04–90–82–70–60.* ⏲ *Mon. 10 AM–7:30 PM; Tues.–Sat. 10 AM–12 AM.*

Dining and Lodging

$$$$ ✕ **La Mirande.** Tapestries warm the walls of the large airy dining room in the Hôtel de la Mirande (☞ *below*), where chef Eric Coisel presents his deceptively simple dishes. Try the terrine *de gibier au foie gras* (of wild boar liver) or the *crepinette de faisan* (pheasant sausage). In winter, Chef Coisel teams up with other Avignon chefs to give cooking lessons. ✉ *pl. de la Mirande,* ☎ *04–90–85–93–93. AE, DC, MC, V.*

$$$ ★ ✕ **Hiély-Lucullus.** According to most authorities, this restaurant numbers among the top 50 in France, although André Chaussy has now taken over as chef for the legendary Pierre Hiély. The upstairs dining room has a quiet, dignified charm and is run with aplomb by Mme. Hiély. Traditional delicacies include crayfish tails in scrambled eggs inside a puff-pastry. ✉ *5 rue de la République,* ☎ *04–90–86–17–07. Reservations essential. AE, V. Closed most of Jan., last 2 wks in June, and Mon. No lunch Tues.*

$$$ ✕ **Jardin des Frênes.** The specialty at this excellent restaurant in the Hostellerie les Frênes (☞ *below*) is stylish country cuisine. The pigeon with black truffles in a puff-pastry case is always a good bet. ✉ *645 av. des Vertes-Rives, Montfavet (5 km/3 mi outside Avignon),* ☎ *04–90–31–17–93. AE, DC, MC, V. Closed Nov.–early Mar.*

$$$ ✕ **La Vieille Fontaine.** This restaurant in the Europe hotel (☞ *below*) serves respectable regional cuisine. In summer, enjoy your chicken with wild mushrooms or duck liver outside in the stone courtyard. ✉ *12 pl. Crillon, 84000,* ☎ *04–90–82–66–92. AE, DC, MC, V. Closed Sat. lunch and Sun.*

$$$$ ★ 🏨 **Hôtel de la Mirande.** Avignon's most refined and beautifully furnished hotel is in a former papal palace on a quiet cobbled square at the foot of the Palais des Papes. What was once the central courtyard is now an enclosed, skylit lounge. Rooms are decorated with antiques. ✉ *pl. de la Mirande, 84000,* ☎ *04–90–85–93–93,* FAX *04–90–86–26–85. 19 rooms, 1 suite. Restaurant, bar. AE, DC, MC, V.*

$$$ 🏨 **Cloître St-Louis.** Although close to Avignon's train station, this stately hotel stands calm within its sturdy 17th-century walls. The early Baroque building, erected by the Jesuits in 1611, was a theological school and later a hospital before it became a hotel at the beginning of the decade. Some rooms have exposed beams; most on the top floor have sloping ceilings. ✉ *20 rue du Portail-Boquier, 84000,* ☎ *04–90–27–55–55,* FAX *04–90–82–24–01. 80 rooms. Restaurant, bar, pool. AE, DC, MC, V.*

$$$ 🏨 **Europe.** This 16th-century town house became a hotel in Napoléonic times. The great man himself was one of the very first customers; since then, everyone from crowned heads of state to Robert and Elizabeth Browning has stayed here. The spacious guest rooms are filled with period furniture and have lavish bathrooms. ✉ *12 pl. Crillon, 84000,* ☎ *04–90–82–66–92,* FAX *04–90–85–43–66. 47 rooms. Restaurant. AE, DC, MC, V.*

$$$ **Hostellerie les Frênes.** This luxurious hotel in a country house has gardens to ramble in, splashing fountains, and individually decorated rooms in styles ranging from subtle modern to art deco. ✉ *645 av. des Vertes-Rives, 84140 Montfavet (5 km/3 mi outside Avignon),* ☎ *04–90–31–17–93,* FAX *04–90–23–95–03. 15 rooms. Restaurant, pool, sauna. AE, DC, MC, V. Closed Nov.–early Mar.*

$ **Hôtel Colbert.** This very reasonably priced hotel is 50 yards from the tourist office. Rooms are small, but air-conditioned. ✉ *7 rue Agricol Perdiquier, 84000,* ☎ *04–90–86–20–20. 15 rooms, most with shower. Air-conditioning. No credit cards.*

Nightlife and the Arts

The prestigious **International Music and Drama Festival,** held the last three weeks of July, is centered in the Grand Courtyard of the Palais des Papes (✉ pl. du Palais, ☎ 04–90–82–67–08). Cabaret fans should try **Les Ambassadeurs** (✉ 27 rue Bancasse).

Outdoor Activities and Sports

Barthelasse (✉ chemin du Mont Blanc, ☎ 04–90–85–83–48) rents horses to experienced equestrians and gives riding lessons to children.

Châteauneuf-du-Pape

30 *18 km (11 mi) north of Avignon, 23 km (14 mi) west of Carpentras.*

The hillside village of Châteauneuf-du-Pape was founded in the 14th century. The popes who lived here knew their wine: The vineyard here is still regarded as the best of the southern Rhône, even though the vines are embedded less in soil than in stones and pebbles. Several producers stage tastings in the village and sell distinctive wine bottles emblazoned with the crossed-key papal crest.

Dining

$ ✕ **La Mule du Pape.** Test the local wines, dine heartily on regional fare, and enjoy a cheerful lunch at this good place. ✉ *2 rue de la République,* ☎ *04–90–83–79–22. MC, V. Closed Tues.*

Orange

31 *10 km (6 mi) north of Châteauneuf-du-Pape, 31 km (19 mi) north of Avignon, 193 km (121 mi) south of Lyon.*

Orange is a small, pleasant town that sinks into total siesta somnolence during hot afternoons, but at other times buzzes with visitors keen on admiring its Roman remains.

★ The magnificent, semicircular **Théâtre Antique,** in the center of town, is the best-preserved remains of a theater from the ancient world. It was built just before the birth of Christ, to the same dimensions as that of Arles. Orange's theater, however, has a mighty screen wall and steeply climbing terraces carved into the hillside. Seven thousand spectators can crowd in; the acoustics are superb. This is the only Roman theater that still possesses its original Imperial statue, of Caesar Augustus—one of the tallest in existence—which stands, 12 feet tall, in the middle of the screen. ✉ *pl. des Frères-Mounet,* ☎ *04–90–34–70–88.* *30 frs; joint ticket with Musée Municipal.* ⏲ *Apr.–Oct., daily 9–6:30; Nov.–Mar., daily 9–noon and 1:30–5.*

The **Parc de la Colline St-Eutrope,** the banked garden behind the Théâtre Antique, yields a fine view of the theater and of the 6,000-foot Mont Ventoux to the east.

The venerable **Arc de Triomphe**—a 70-foot central arch flanked by two smaller ones, the whole topped by a massive entablature—towered over the old Via Agrippa between Arles and Lyon and was probably built around AD 25 in honor of the Gallic Wars. The carvings on the north side depict the legionnaires' battles with the Gauls and Caesar's naval showdown with the ships of Marseille. Today the arch presides over a busy traffic circle.

Dining and Lodging

$$–$$$ ★ ✕ **Le Pigraillet.** One of Orange's best lunch spots is Le Pigraillet, on the chemin Colline St-Eutrope at the far end of the gardens. You may want to eat in the garden, but most diners seek shelter from the mistral in the glassed-in terrace. The modern cuisine includes crab ravioli and duck breast in the muscat wine of nearby Beaumes-de-Venise. ✉ *chemin de la Colline St-Eutrope,* ☎ *04–90–34–44–25. Reservations essential. MC, V. Closed Jan.–Feb. and Mon.*

$$ 🏨 **Arène.** This stylish old hotel, on a shady square lined with plane trees, prides itself on attentive service and large, air-conditioned rooms. ✉ *pl. de Langes, 84100,* ☎ *04–90–34–10–95,* FAX *04–90–34–91–62. 30 rooms with bath or shower. Air-conditioning. AE, DC, MC, V. Closed Nov.–mid-Dec.*

Nightlife and the Arts

The **International Opera Festival** takes place the last two weeks of July in the Théâtre Antique (✉ pl. des Frères-Mounet).

Shopping

Fruit, herbs, honey, and truffles can be purchased at the **market** (✉ cours Aristide-Briand) on Thursday morning. Provençal print fabrics can be found at Orange's **Souleiado** (✉ 5 rue Joseph-Vernet).

Vaison-la-Romaine

32 *27 km (17 mi) northeast of Orange, 30 km (19 mi) northeast of Avignon.*

Vaison-la-Romaine, as its name suggests, was once a Roman town. The ruins are more extensive, though less spectacular than Orange's; they can be found on either side of the avenue du Général-de-Gaulle. Parts of houses, villas, a basilica, and a theater have been unearthed; interesting finds are housed in the small **Musée Archéologique Théo Desplans.** With its lush lawns and colorful flower beds, the entire site suggests a historical garden. ☎ *04–90–36–02–11.* 🎫 *Ruins and museum 35 frs.* ⏲ *June–Sept., daily 10–12:30 and 2:30–5:45 (6:45 June–Aug.); Oct.–May 10–noon and 2–4:30.*

Before leaving Vaison, pause to admire the 2,000-year-old **Pont Romain** (Roman Bridge) over the River Ouvèze and venture briefly into the medieval town across the river.

Dining and Lodging

$$ ✕🏨 **Le Beffroi.** This hotel in a 16th-century mansion, with a 17th-century annex, is on a hill in the old town. The spacious, comfortable rooms are filled with old furniture; the best have views of the gardens. The restaurant serves a wonderful lamb terrine with apples, saddle of hare, and *dorade* (sea bream) baked in its own juices; it is closed from late December to early March and for lunch during the week. ✉ *rue de l'Évêché, 84110,* ☎ *04–90–36–04–71,* FAX *04–90–36–24–78. 20 rooms, some with bath or shower. Restaurant, free parking. AE, DC, MC, V. Closed mid-Feb.–mid-Mar. and mid-Nov.–mid-Dec.*

$$ 🏨 **Évêché.** Stay in one of the Verdiers's four rooms in this turreted, 17th-century former bishop's palace in the medieval part of town. The

warm welcome and the rustic charm—exposed beams and wooden bedsteads—has garnered a loyal following among travelers who prefer character to modern luxury. Breakfast is served on a terrace overlooking the Ouvèze Valley; this is the time to try out your French as the Verdiers's English is rudimentary. Advance reservations are essential. ✉ *rue de l'Évêché, 84110,* ☎ *04–90–36–13–46,* FAX *04–90–36–32–43. 2 rooms with bath, 2 rooms with shower. No credit cards.*

Mont Ventoux

33 *16 km (10 mi) southeast of Vaison-la-Romaine.*

A huge mountain that looms above the surrounding plains, Mont Ventoux is known reverentially as "Le" Ventoux. Weather conditions on this whalelike bulk can vary dramatically: In summer, few places in France experience such scorching heat; in winter, the Ventoux's snow-topped peak recalls the Alps. Its arid heights sometimes provide a grueling setting for the Tour de France cycling race; British bicyclist Tommy Simpson collapsed and died under the Ventoux's pitiless sun in 1967. D974 winds its way from Malaucène up to the summit, 6,250 feet above sea level. Stay on D974 as it doubles back around the southern slopes, then runs from Bédoin toward Carpentras.

Venasque

34 *36 km (23 mi) southeast of Mont Ventoux, 16 km (12 mi) north of Gordes, 12 km (7 mi) southeast of Carpentras, 35 km (22 mi) northeast of Avignon.*

Once the capital of Comtat Venaissin, the large agricultural region east of Avignon, Venasque now only has a population of less than 675 inhabitants. The village, tucked inside fortified walls, stands proudly on a hill overlooking the Carpentras Plain. The ambience is wonderfully medieval and tranquil—enough to enjoy in itself—but be sure to pop into the **Notre-Dame** church, one of France's oldest buildings, to see the baptistry dating from the 6th century and remodeled in the 11th.

Dining and Lodging

$$$ ✕▣ **Auberge La Fontaine.** This ancient, renovated house has eight small apartments with eclectic furnishings. One is ultramodern; the others are more traditional. The hotel abuts other village buildings, so there are no views. On the first floor is a small lounge and restaurant serving four-course dinners; on the ground floor is a bistro for light meals. It makes an ideal base for exploring the region. ✉ *84210 Venasque,* ☎ *04–90–66–02–96,* FAX *04–90–66–13–14. 8 apartments. Restaurant, kitchenettes. MC, V.*

L'Isle-sur-la-Sorgue

35 *18 km (11 mi) south of Malaucène, 41 km (25 mi) southeast of Orange, 26 km (16 mi) east of Avignon.*

At L'Isle-sur-la-Sorgue the River Sorgue splits into a number of channels. The river once turned the waterwheels of the town's silk factories. Silkworms were cultivated locally, one reason for the profusion of mulberry trees in the region. Some of the waterwheels are still in place, and you can admire them as you stroll along the banks of the river. The richly decorated 17th-century church, the **Collégiale Notre-Dame-des-Anges,** is also of interest. Follow the signs to Le Partage des Eaux, where the rivers meet—the small park here is perfect for picnicking.

Dining

$ ✕ **Lou Nego Chin.** Among the several restaurants along the river, many locals lunch here. Tables are across the (quiet) street, on a wooden deck on the river. Ask for a table at the edge, so you can watch the ducks cavorting, and order the inexpensive house wine and the 60-franc menu du jour, which consists of a salad and a main dish—usually lamb chops or grilled fish. Depending on what is available, you may or may not forgo dessert (an additional 30 francs): the profiterole is delicious and big enough for two. ✉ *12 quai Jean Jaurès,* ☎ *04–90–20–88–03. MC, V. Closed Sun.*

Fontaine-de-Vaucluse

36 *8 km (5 mi) east of L'Isle-sur-la-Sorgue, 33 km (20 mi) east of Avignon.*

The "fountain" in Fontaine-de-Vaucluse is the site of the River Sorgue's emergence from underground imprisonment: Water shoots up from a cavern as the emerald-green river cascades at the foot of steep cliffs. This is the picture in springtime or after heavy rains; with summer's drought and crowds, the scene may be less spectacular.

Dining and Lodging

$$ ✕🏨 **Le Parc.** This old-fashioned hotel with a terrace overlooking the River Sorgue is in the heart of the village. The restaurant serves a good choice of prix-fixe menus; specialties range from pasta with foie gras to duckling with berries. Rooms are a little musty and furnishings tired, but those facing the garden are wonderfully quiet. ✉ *rue de Bourgades, 84800,* ☎ *04–90–20–31–57,* FAX *04–90–20–27–03. 12 rooms with bath or shower. Restaurant. AE, DC, MC, V. Closed Wed. and Jan.–mid-Feb.*

Gordes

37 *16 km (10 mi) southeast of Fontaine-de-Vaucluse, 35 km (22 mi) east of Avignon.*

Gordes is only a short distance from Fontaine-de-Vaucluse, but you'll have to wind your way south, east, and then north on D100-A, D100, D2, and D15 to skirt the impassable hillside. The golden-stone village is perched dramatically on its own hill. On the summit is the Renaissance **Château,** with its collection of mind-stretching, geometric-pattern paintings by 20th-century Hungarian-French artist Victor Vasarely. ☎ *04–90–72–02–89.* 🎫 *25 frs.* ⏲ *Wed.–Mon. 10–noon and 2–6.*

In a wild valley some 4 km (2 mi) north of Gordes (via D177) is the beautiful 12th-century **Abbaye de Sénanque.** In 1969 its Cistercian monks moved to the island of St-Honorat, off the shore of Cannes, and the admirably preserved buildings here are now a cultural center that presents concerts and exhibitions. The dormitory, refectory, church, and chapter house can be visited, along with an odd museum devoted to the Sahara's Tuareg nomads. ☎ *04–90–72–05–72.* 🎫 *20 frs.* ⏲ *Mar.–Oct., Mon.–Sat. 10–noon and 2–6, Sun. 2–6; Nov.–Feb., weekdays 2–5, weekends 2–6.*

Dining and Lodging

$$$ ✕ **Comptoir du Victuailler.** You'll find only 10 tables at this tiny restaurant where elegantly simple meals—using only the freshest local capon, guinea fowl, asparagus, artichokes, and truffles—are served. The fruit sorbets are a revelation. ✉ *pl. du Château,* ☎ *04–90–72–01–31. Reservations essential. MC, V. Closed mid-Nov.–mid-Dec., mid-Jan.–mid-Mar., and Wed. Sept.–May. No dinner Tues.*

$$$ **Domaine de l'Enclos.** Small, private stone cottages with panoramic views make up this charming hotel just outside Gordes. The simple exteriors suggest a rustic interior, but furnishings are modern, functional, and utilitarian. Opt for the demi-pension for a one-night stay; this is a good value, whereas paying for the rooms and meals separately makes the hotel over-priced. The restaurant's menu of good nouvelle dishes varies with the season; if it's available, try the excellent aromatic duck. ✉ *rte. de Sénanque, 84220,* ☎ *04–90–72–08–22,* FAX *04–90–72–03–03. 14 rooms. Restaurant, pool, tennis court. AE, DC, MC, V.*

$$–$$$ **Les Romarins.** At this small inn you can gaze across the valley at Gordes while you breakfast on a sheltered terrace in the morning sun. Rooms are clean, well-lighted, and feel spacious—ask for either No. 1, in the main building, from whose white-curtained windows you can see forever, or the room with a terrace in the atelier. Warm Oriental rugs, antique furniture around the fireplace in the sitting room, and a swimming pool add to your contentment. ✉ *rte. de Sénanque, 84220,* ☎ *04–90–72–12–13,* FAX *04–90–72–13–13. 10 rooms with bath or shower. Pool. AE, MC, V.*

Roussillon

38 *10 km (6 mi) east of Gordes, 45 km (28 mi) east of Avignon.*

Roussillon is a picturesque hilltop village whose houses are built with a distinctive orange and pink stone. This is ocher country, and local quarrying has slashed the cliffs into bizarre shapes. If you are short of time, the view of the village is better than the sights in it.

Bonnieux

39 *11 km (7 mi) south of Roussillon, 45 km (28 mi) north of Aix-en-Provence.*

Bonnieux is one of several wondrous villages in the Vaucluse. Wander around, then climb to the terrace of the old church (not to be confused with the big 19th-century Église Neuve, in the lower part of the village) for a sweeping view of Gordes, Roussillon, and the ruined château of Lacoste, once home to the notorious marquis de Sade.

AIX-EN-PROVENCE AND THE MEDITERRANEAN COAST

The southeastern part of this area of Provence, on the edge of the Cote d'Azur, is dominated by two major towns: Aix-en-Provence, considered the capital of Provence and the most cultural town in the region; and Marseille, a vibrant port that combines seediness and fashion, decrepit buildings, and modern architecture. For a breathtaking experience of the dramatic contrast between the azure Mediterranean sea and the rocky, olive tree–filled hills, take a trip along the coast from Marseille to Toulon and make an excursion to the Îles d'Hyères.

Aix-en-Provence

★ 40 *48 km (29 mi) southeast of Bonnieux, 82 km (51 mi) southeast of Avignon, 176 km (109 mi) west of Nice, 759 km (474 mi) south of Paris.*

Many villages, but few towns, are as well preserved as the traditional capital of Provence: elegant Aix-en-Provence. The Romans were drawn here by the presence of thermal springs; the name Aix originates from Aquae Sextiae (Waters of Sextius) in honor of the consul who reputedly founded the town in 122 BC. Twenty years later, a vast army of

Germanic invaders were defeated by General Marius at a neighboring mountain, known ever since as the Montagne Ste-Victoire. Marius remains a popular local first name to this day.

Aix-en-Provence numbers two of France's most creative geniuses among its sons: the Postimpressionist Paul Cézanne (1839–1906), many of whose paintings feature the nearby countryside, especially Montagne Ste-Victoire (though Cézanne would not recognize it now, after the forest fire that ravaged its slopes in 1990); and the novelist Émile Zola (1840–1902), who, in several of his works, described Aix ("Plassans") and his boyhood friendship with Cézanne.

The celebrated **cours Mirabeau,** flanked with intertwining plane trees, is the town's nerve center, a graceful, lively avenue with the feel of a toned-down, intimate Champs-Elysées. It divides Old Aix into two, with narrow medieval streets to the north and sophisticated, haughty 18th-century mansions to the south. Begin your visit at the west end of cours Mirabeau; the **tourist office** is close by (✉ 2 place du Général-de-Gaulle). Halfway down is the Fontaine des Neuf Canons (Fountain of the Nine Cannons), dating from 1691, and farther along is the Fontaine d'Eau Thermale (Thermal Water), built in 1734. South of cours Mirabeau the streets are straight and rationally planned, flanked with symmetrical mansions imbued with classical elegance. Rue du Quatre-Septembre, three-quarters of the way down cours Mirabeau, leads to the splendid **Fontaine des Quatre Dauphins** (✉ pl. des Quatre Dauphins), where sculpted dolphins play in a fountain erected in 1667.

The **Musée d'Histoire Naturelle** is in the sumptuous **Hôtel Boyer d'Eguilles,** erected in 1675 and worth a visit itself for its fine woodwork, sculpture, and murals. The highlight of the museum is its rare collection of dinosaur eggs, accompanied by life-size models of the dinosaurs that roamed locally 65 million years ago. To get here from cours Mirabeau, turn left down rue Clemenceau to place St-Honoré, with another small fountain, then make a left again onto rue Espariat. Also notice on rue Espariat the sculpted facade of the **Hôtel d'Albertas** (built in 1707) at No. 10. ✉ *6 rue Espariat,* ☎ *04–42–26–23–67.* 🎫 *15 frs.* ⏲ *Mon.–Sat. 10–noon and 2–6, Sun. 2–6.*

To get to the **Hôtel de Ville** (✉ pl. de l'Hôtel de Ville), wend your way down rue Aude, north off rue Esperiat, lined with ancient town houses. Pause to admire its 17th-century iron gates and balcony and the 16th-century Tour de l'Horloge (former town belfry) alongside. Then stop for a coffee in one of the square's many cafés.

Though the **Cathédrale St-Sauveur** (✉ rue de la Roque), just north of the Hôtel de Ville, is a mishmash of styles that lack harmony, and has an interior that feels gloomy and dilapidated, it contains a remarkable 15th-century triptych by Nicolas Froment. Entitled *Triptyque du Buisson Ardent* (*Burning Bush Triptych*), it depicts King René (duke of Anjou, count of Provence, and titular king of Sicily) and Queen Joan kneeling beside the Virgin. Ask the sacristan to spotlight it for you (he'll expect a tip) and to remove the protective shutters from the ornate 16th-century carvings on the cathedral portals. Afterward, wander into the tranquil Romanesque cloisters next door to admire the carved pillars and slender colonnades.

The highlight of the **Musée des Tapisseries** (Tapestry Museum), in the **Archevêché** (Archbishop's Palace) adjacent to the cathedral, is a magnificent suite of 17 tapestries made in Beauvais that date, like the palace itself, from the 17th and 18th centuries. Nine woven panels illustrate the adventures of Don Quixote. ✉ *28 pl. des Martyrs de la*

Résistance, ☏ *04–42–23–09–91.* 🎫 *14 frs.* ⏲ *Wed.–Mon. 10–noon and 2–5:45.*

No major paintings are on display at the **Atelier Paul Cézanne,** but the great man's studio remains as he left it at the time of his death in 1906, scattered with his pipe, clothing, and other personal possessions, many of which he painted in his still lifes. Cézanne's pioneering work, with its interest in angular forms, paved the way for the Cubist style of the early 20th century. To get to his studio from the town center, take rue de la Roque north to the broad, leafy boulevard that encircles Old Aix. Head up avenue Pasteur, opposite, then turn right onto avenue Paul-Cézanne. Fans of Cézanne can pick up a map of his "footsteps" at the tourist office: Gold studs in the pavement chronicle where the painter worked, went to school, and got married. ✉ *9 av. Paul-Cézanne,* ☏ *04–42–21–06–53.* 🎫 *15 frs.* ⏲ *Wed.–Mon. 10–noon and 2–5.*

The **Musée Granet,** south of the cours Mirabeau, is named after another of Aix's artistic sons: François Granet (1775–1849), whose works are good examples of the formal, at times sentimental, style of art popular during the first half of the 19th century. Cézanne is also represented here with several oils and watercolors, as are European painters from the 16th to the 19th century and archaeological finds from Egypt, Greece, and the Roman Empire. ✉ *13 rue Cardinale, pl. St-Jean de Malte,* ☏ *04–42–38–14–70.* 🎫 *18 frs.* ⏲ *Wed.–Mon. 10–noon and 2–6.*

Dining and Lodging

$$$ ★ ✕ **Le Clos de la Violette.** Aix's best restaurant is in a residential district north of the old town. Chef Jean-Marc Banzo uses local ingredients in his nouvelle and traditional recipes, such as *saumon vapeur* (aromatic steamed salmon), and oyster and calamari salad. Enjoy his fine dishes under the chestnut trees or in the airy pink-and-blue dining room. The moderately-priced weekday lunch menu is well worth the trek. ✉ *10 av. de la Violette,* ☏ *04–42–23–30–71. Jacket required. AE, MC, V. Closed Sun., early Nov., and most of Mar. No lunch Mon.*

$$ ✕ **Les Bacchanales.** This small, intimate establishment in the old quarter of Aix is worth tracking down. From the 130-franc menu, sample the *marbré de lapereau* (stuffed baby rabbit) or the salmon with a light tomato sauce. For dessert, the *tarte aux pommes soufflés* (apple tart soufflé) is particularly good. ✉ *10 rue de la Couronne,* ☏ *04–42–27–21–06. MC, V. Closed Wed. No lunch Thurs.*

$ ✕ **Le Bistro Latin.** Whether you sit up or downstairs, the tables are tight, but the effect is friendly. The 98-franc *menu du marché* (what the chef bought from the market that day) might include excellent *maigret de canard* (duck) in a light cream sauce or flavorful lamb casserole. For an appetizer, hope that the tiny morsels of lamb in puff pastry showered in beurre blanc is available. ✉ *18 rue de la Couronne,* ☏ *04–42–38–22–88. Closed Sun. No lunch Mon. MC, V.*

$ ✕ **Domaine de Chasse des Puits de Rians.** In a rural area not far from Aix, this joint venture of two Provençal farmers is characterized by hearty country food, wine flowing from the flagon, the camaraderie of shared tables, and joyful repartee. After checking the blackboard you might start with warm goat cheese salad, followed by *jambon de sanglier* (boar haunch) roasted on a spit outside. The dining room is like a huge working-man's bar, with a bare stone floor and plain wood tables with well-used checkered tablecloths. A truly baronial hall, off the main room, is used for big groups. ✉ *Rians (40 km/25 mi northeast of Aix-en-Provence),* ☏ *04–74–80–58–77. No credit cards. Closed Mon.*

$$$ ✕🏨 **Relais Ste-Victoire.** The main reason to stay at this country inn is to dine on chef Jugy-Berges's modern Provençal cooking—eggs poached with truffles, delicately flavored roast partridge, and *tarte au châtaigne* (chestnut tart). The restaurant is closed Sunday dinner and Monday. Rooms are more than adequate: Tile floors shine, fabrics cover the walls, and glass doors lead onto private balconies. But the single beds joined by one bedspread can slip apart and romantics end up on the floor. ✉ *13100 Beaurecueil (15 km/9 mi east of Aix),* ☎ *04–42–66–94–98,* FAX *04–42–66–85–96. 10 rooms. Restaurant, pool. AE, DC, MC, V. Closed 1st wk Jan., 1 wk Feb., and 1 wk Nov. (call in advance for exact dates).*

$$$$ 🏨 **Le Pigonnet.** A 10-minute walk from the cours Mirabeau brings you to this refined, family-run hotel. Here in the wonderful gardens Cézanne caught distant Mont Ste-Victoire on canvas. The high-ceilinged rooms are furnished with family heirlooms and Provençal armoires; the slightly higher-priced ones look out over the garden. La Riviera restaurant is happily more traditional than nouvelle; local meats and game are served, as well as fish from the Mediterranean. ✉ *5 av. du Pigonnet, 13090,* ☎ *04–42–59–02–90,* FAX *04–42–59–47–77. 53 rooms with bath or shower. Restaurant, pool, meeting rooms. AE, DC, MC, V.*

$$$$ ★ 🏨 **Villa Gallici.** On a slight rise just outside town, this Relais & Châteaux hotel breathes country fragrance. The terrace and the garden with swimming pool are shaded by hundred-year-old cypress trees. Rooms have separate sitting areas; fabric with green and rust chinoiserie covers the walls and the floor-to-ceiling windows. The hotel's dining room (closed Friday, October to May) serves food that is well prepared, though not particularly special. More elaborate meals are served at Le Clos de la Violette, 100 yards away (closed Sunday). ✉ *av. de la Violette, 13100,* ☎ *04–42–23–29–23,* FAX *04–42–96–30–45. 15 rooms, 4 suites. Restaurant, pool. AE, DC, MC, V.*

$$$ 🏨 **Mercure-Paul Cézanne.** Mlle. Rossotie runs this efficient hotel a block off cours Mirabeau. Antiques and ornate furnishings are scattered throughout the public areas and the rooms. A small lounge off the lobby is a comfortable spot to meet up with friends. Though the rooms are small, they are a good value. ✉ *40 av. Victor-Hugo, 13100,* ☎ *04–42–26–34–73,* FAX *04–42–27–20–95. 56 rooms. AE, DC, MC, V.*

$$–$$$ 🏨 **Nègre-Coste.** A cours Mirabeau location makes this hotel both a convenient and atmospheric choice. The elegant 18th-century town house has been completely modernized but features luxurious Old World decor in the guest rooms and public areas. The views of cours Mirabeau and the sunlight make the front rooms worth the extra bit of noise (kept to a minimum by double-glazed windows). This place is very popular, so make reservations far in advance. ✉ *33 cours Mirabeau, 13100,* ☎ *04–42–27–74–22,* FAX *04–42–26–80–93. 37 rooms. AE, DC, MC, V.*

Nightlife and the Arts

Le Scat Club (✉ 11 rue de la Verrerie) is a good spot for jazz. Those who thrive on roulette and blackjack go to the **Casino Municipal d'Aix Thermal** (✉ 2 bis av. Napoléon-Bonaparte, ☎ 04–42–26–30–33), open from 3 PM to 2 AM.

Opera and classical concerts are performed throughout the year at the 18th-century **Théâtre Municipal** (✉ 17 rue de l'Opéra, ☎ 04–42–38–44–71). The **Festival International des Arts et Musique,** with first-class opera, symphonic concerts, and chamber music, flourishes from mid-July to mid-August; its principal venue is the Théâtre de l'Archevêché (✉ pl. des Martyrs-de-la-Résistance). The **Festival International de Danse** (✉ espace Gambetta, cours Gambetta, ☎ 04–42–96–05–01), known as Danse à Aix, features modern and jazz dance in July. Tickets go on sale two weeks before the show and can be purchased at the tourist office.

Outdoor Activities and Sports

The tourist office has information on hiking or bicycling up **Mont Ste-Victoire. Golf International du Château de l'Arc** (✉ Fuveau, 20 km/32 mi from Aix, ☎ 04–42–53–28–38) is an 18-hole course open to the public. **Sellerie Lou Mazet** (✉ Lançon-de-Provence, 27 km/17 mi from Aix off N113, ☎ 04–90–42–89–38) arranges horseback excursions of the Camargue for 250 to 400 francs a day.

Shopping

Deliciously fragrant soaps and *calissons d'Aix,* ingeniously sculpted marzipan figures, are two specialties of Aix. One thousand different models of *santons,* the colorful painted clay figures traditionally placed around a Christmas crib, can be found at **Santons Fouque** (✉ 65 cours Gambetta). **Makaire** (✉ 2 rue Thiers, near place du Palais, ☎ 04–42–38–19–63) has very nice stationary, fountain pens, and books. **Riederer** (✉ 6 rue Thiers, ☎ 04–42–38–19–69) makes irresistible chocolates and pastries. Lovely blooms of all sorts are found at the **flower market** (✉ pl. de l'Hôtel-de-Ville) on Tuesday, Thursday, and Saturday mornings. A **produce market** takes place on place Richel every morning and place des Prêcheurs on Tuesday, Thursday, and Saturday mornings. An **antiques market** is held on Tuesday, Thursday, and Saturday mornings on the place de Verdun.

Marseille

31 km (19 mi) south of Aix-en-Provence, 188 km (117 mi) west of Nice, 772 km (483 mi) south of Paris.

Marseille, the Mediterranean's largest port, is not crowded with tourist goodies, nor is its reputation as a big dirty city entirely unjustified, but it still has more going for it than many realize: a craggy mountain hinterland that provides a spectacular backdrop, superb coastal views of nearby islands, and the sights and smells of a Mediterranean melting pot where different peoples have mingled for centuries—ever since the Phocaean Greeks invaded in around 600 BC. The most recent immigrants come from North Africa. The large city is divided into 16 *arrondissements* (districts). An efficient bus and métro system can get you around.

At the heart of Marseille is the **Vieux Port,** an intimate, picturesque old harbor packed with fishing boats and pleasure craft, and the sizable, ugly industrial docks next to it. For 4 francs round-trip or 2.50 francs one-way you can cross the harbor on a ferry that runs every few minutes. Restaurants line the quays, and fishwives spout incomprehensible Provençal insults as they serve gleaming fresh sardines each morning. The Marseillais can be an irascible lot: Louis XIV built the Fort St-Nicolas, at the entry of the Vieux Port, with the guns facing inland to keep the citizens in order. The famous, chaotic Marseille **fish market** is held here every day. A short way down the quay (as you look out to sea) is the elegant 17th-century **Hôtel de Ville.**

Running east from the Vieux Port is the legendary **La Canebière**—known as the "Can O' Beer" to sailors from around the world—where stately mansions recall faded glory. Many an operetta has been inspired by the avenue and it was still talked about by Legionnaires in the late 1950s, though by then what was left of the action could only be found in the Quartier de Panier. The avenue has been on the decline in recent years,

Basilique St-Victor, **44**
Cathédrale de la Major, **42**
Jardin des Vestiges, **47**
Musée des Beaux-Arts, **48**
Musée de la Marine, **46**
Musée de la Vieille-Charité, **43**
Musée du Vieux Marseille, **41**
Notre-Dame de la Garde, **45**

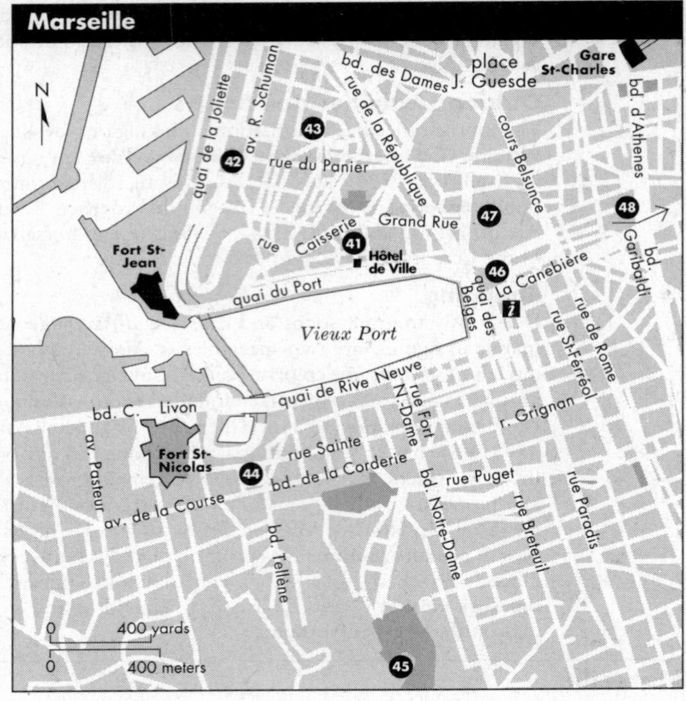

but cafés and restaurants continue to provide an upbeat pulse. The **tourist office** is at No. 4.

Costumes, engravings, and paintings depicting 18th-century Marseille
41 are on display at the **Musée du Vieux Marseille** (Museum of Old Marseille), housed in the Maison Diamantée, a 16th-century mansion with an elaborate interior staircase just behind the town hall. After renovations, the museum is scheduled to reopen at a yet undetermined date in 1998. ✉ *rue de la Prison,* ☎ *04–91–55–10–19.* 🎫 *12 frs.* ⏲ *Tues.–Sun. 11–6 in summer; 10–5 in winter.*

42 Marseille's pompous, striped neo-Byzantine **Cathédrale de la Major** is a few blocks from the Vieux Port. Its various domes look utterly incongruous against the backdrop of industrial docks. If, however, you climb up rue du Panier behind the city police station, or *archevêché* (archbishop's seat), as it is irreverently known, the cathedral's silhouette, facing out over the Mediterranean, acquires fresh significance as a symbol of Marseille's role as gateway to the Levant. ✉ *esplanade de la Tourette.*

The grid of narrow, tumbledown streets leading off rue du Panier is called simply **le Panier.** There is a claustrophobic feel here, heightened by the lines of washing strung from window to window, sometimes blotting out the sky; you can taste some of the dowdy, Naples-like essence of Marseille. Apart from the colorful, sleazy ambience, le Panier is worth visiting for the elegantly restored 17th-century hospice now housing a
43 museum, the **Musée de la Vieille-Charité.** Excellent art exhibitions are held here, and the architecture—a shallow-domed chapel in the middle of an arcaded, three-story courtyard—displays subtlety lacking in the cathedral. ✉ *2 rue de la Charité,* ☎ *04–91–56–28–38.* 🎫 *12 frs (25 frs for exhibitions).* ⏲ *Tues.–Sun. 11–6 in summer; 10–5 in winter.*

44 The **Basilique St-Victor,** on the south side of the Vieux Port, stands in the shadow of the Fort St-Nicolas (which can't be visited). With its powerful tower and thick-set walls, the basilica itself resembles a fortress; it has one of southern France's oldest doorways (circa 1140), a 13th-century nave, and a 14th-century chancel and transept. Downstairs, you'll find the murky 5th-century underground crypt, with its collection of ancient sarcophagi. ✉ *rue Sainte.* *10 frs to enter crypt.* ⏲ *Daily 8:30–6:30.*

A brisk 1-km (½-mi) walk up boulevard Tellène from the Vieux Port, followed by a trudge up a steep flight of steps, will take you to the foot
45 of **Notre-Dame de la Garde.** This church, a flashy 19th-century cousin of the Sacré-Coeur in Paris and Fourvière in Lyon, features a similar hilltop location. The expansive view stretches from the hinterland mountains to the sea via the Cité Radieuse, a controversial 1950s housing project by architect Le Corbusier. The church's interior is generously endowed with bombastic murals, mosaics, and marble. At the top of the tower, the great gilded statue of the Virgin stands sentinel over the Vieux Port, 500 feet below. If you are not up to the hike, Bus 60 from the port is an easy way out. ✉ *pl. du Colonel-Edon,* ☎ *04–91–13–40–80.* ⏲ *Daily 7:30–5:30 in winter; 7 AM–7:30 PM in summer.*

46 The **Musée de la Marine** (Nautical Museum) is housed in the big, white **Palais de la Bourse** (Stock Exchange). It gives a history of the port and has an interesting display of model ships. ✉ *Palais de la Bourse, La Canebière,* ☎ *04–91–39–33–33.* *12 frs.* ⏲ *Wed.–Mon. 10–noon and 2–6.*

47 The **Jardin des Vestiges,** a public park behind the Palais de Bourse, contains the excavated ruins of Greek and Roman fortifications and foundations. Here you will find the little **Musée d'Histoire de Marseille** (Marseille History Museum), featuring exhibits related to the town's history. One of the highlights is a 60-foot Roman boat. ✉ *Centre Bourse,* ☎ *04–91–90–42–22.* *15 frs.* ⏲ *Mon.–Sat. noon–7.*

48 The **Musée des Beaux-Arts,** in the imposing **Palais Longchamp,** was built in 1860 by Henri Espérandieu (1829–74), the architect of Notre-Dame de la Garde. The Fine Art Museum's collection of paintings and sculptures includes works by 18th-century Italian artist Giovanni Battista Tiepolo, Rubens, and French caricaturist and painter Honoré Daumier. ✉ *bd. Longchamp,* ☎ *04–91–62–21–17.* *12 frs.* ⏲ *Tues.–Sun. 11–6 in summer, 10–5 in winter.*

Marseille is no seaside resort, but a scenic 5-km (3-mi) coast road—**corniche du Président-J.-F.-Kennedy**—links the Vieux Port to the newly created Prado beaches in the swanky parts of southern Marseille. There are breathtaking views across the sea toward the rocky Frioul islands, which can be visited by boat.

Ferries leave the Vieux Port hourly in summer and frequently in winter to visit the Château d'If and the Frioul islands; the trip takes 90 minutes and the cost is 45 francs to Château d'If or Frioul and 70 francs to both. The very name of **Château d'If,** the castle where political prisoners were held captive down the ages, speaks of romance and derring-do. Alexandre Dumas condemned his fictional hero, the count of Monte Cristo, to be shut up in a cell here, before the wily count made his celebrated escape through a hole in the wall. Contrary to legend, the man in the iron mask, whose cell is still being shown, was not actually imprisoned here. ☎ *04–91–59–02–30.* *23 frs.* ⏲ *Apr.–Sept., daily 8:30–7; Oct.–Mar., Tues.–Sun. 9–5:30.*

Dining and Lodging

$$$ ✕ **Chez Fonfon.** The Marseillais come here for the best bouillabaisse in the world, and past diners lured by the top-quality seafood have included John Wayne and Nikita Khrushchev. You'll also find rock fish soup, grilled lobster, and octopus with oil and vinegar and truffles. Chef Alphonse Mounier, known as "Fonfon," is thinking of retiring, but a successor is being trained to his rigorous standards. The great sea views come gratis. ✉ *140 rue du Vallon des Auffes,* ☎ *04–91–52–14–38. Reservations essential. AE, DC, MC, V. Closed Oct., Dec. 25–Jan. 1. No dinner Sun.*

$$ ★ ✕ **Chez Madie.** Every morning Madie Minassian, the colorful *patronne,* bustles along the quayside to trade insults with the fishwives and scour their catch for the freshest specimens. They swiftly end up in her bouillabaisse, fish soup, and *favouilles* sauce (made with tiny local crabs). ✉ *138 quai du Port,* ☎ *04–91–90–40–87. AE, DC, MC, V. Closed Mon. and most of Aug. No dinner Sun.*

$$ ✕ **Dar Djerba.** This is one of the best North African restaurants scattered throughout Marseille, specializing in couscous of all kinds (with lamb, chicken, or even quail) as well as Arab coffees and pastries. ✉ *15 cours Julien,* ☎ *04–91–48–55–36. Reservations essential in summer. DC, MC, V.*

$$$ ★ ✕▣ **Le Petit Nice.** Only the smallest of signs marks the turnoff from the corniche to the rocky promontory 1½ km (1 mi) from the Vieux Port where you'll find the Passédat's small enclave. Gérald is renowned for his regional recipes, with a lighter, creative touch, served in the many-windowed dining room. The menu focuses on seafood like grilled *coquilles St-Jacques* (scallops) with baby artichokes, though game is available in late fall. The restaurant is closed Saturday lunch and Sunday, off season. Rooms have smooth stone floors, rich, rare woods, and almost no doors or walls; most have sea views. ✉ *anse de Maldormé, corniche J.-F.-Kennedy, 13007,* ☎ *04–91–59–25–92,* FAX *04–91–59–28–08. 15 rooms. Restaurant, pool. AE, DC, MC, V.*

$$$ ✕▣ **Sofitel.** Mainly because of its idyllic views, the Sofitel has more appeal than most modern chain hotels. Rooms with a balcony are more expensive, but the pleasure of breakfast in the morning sunshine is worth the splurge. The top-floor restaurant, Les Trois Forts, has stunning panoramic views and delicious Provençal fare; the red mullet with pepper is superb. ✉ *36 bd. Charles-Livon, 13007,* ☎ *04–91–15–59–00,* FAX *04–91–15–59–50. 130 rooms, 3 suites. Restaurant, pool. AE, DC, MC, V.*

$$$ ★ ▣ **Mercure Vieux Port.** Charming Old World opulence characterizes this hotel in a totally modernized 200-year-old coaching inn on the Vieux Port. Wood paneling, fine paintings, genuine antique furniture, and exceptional service enhance a stay at the hotel. The best rooms look out onto the port. ✉ *4 rue Beauvau, 13001,* ☎ *04–91–54–91–00 (800/223–9868 U.S. reservations; 0171/621–1962 in the U.K.),* FAX *04–91–54–15–76. 71 rooms. Bar, breakfast room. AE, DC, MC, V.*

$$ ▣ **Climat.** There is nothing remarkable about this chain hotel, a block from the Vieux Port (though there are no views). But it is clean, reasonably priced, and very convenient. Rooms are functional and have good-sized beds and a small desk. ✉ *6 rue Beauvau, 13001,* ☎ *04–91–33–02–33,* FAX *04–91–33–21–34. 49 rooms with bath or shower. Air-conditioning. AE, DC, MC, V.*

Nightlife and the Arts

Marseille's nightlife lasts into the wee hours of the morning. The under-40-year set be-bops at the temple of jazz, **Le Orleans** (✉ 1 quai de Rive Neuve, ☎ 04–91–54–71–09). **Le Passport** (✉ 26 cours d'Estienne d'Orves, ☎ 04–91–33–71–55) serves tequila frappée and other drinks on its terrace until 4 AM. **Le Pelle Mele** (✉ 45 pl. aux Huiles, ☎ 04–91–54–85–26) has a piano bar and, on special nights, jazz combos. **Le Trolleybus** (✉ 24 quai de Rive Neuve, ☎ 04–91–54–30–45) has concerts, three dance "grottoes," and the most alternative feel of all the clubs. In July the large **Festival Marseille Méditerranée** celebrates the city's rich Mediterranean heritage with concerts and exhibits.

Shopping

Leading south from La Canebière, the busy rue Paradis, rue St-Ferréol, and rue de Rome are good spots to shop. **Four des Navettes** (✉ 136 rue Sainte, ☎ 04–91–33–32–12), up the street from the basilica, is a bakery where orange-spice, shuttle-shape *navette* loaves have been made for more than 200 years.

Outdoor Activities and Sports

Though Marseille is not know for its seashore, the city does have numerous beaches—most are shingle, some are made of sand and grass. The best, however, are found in *les calanques,* picturesque coves along the coastline between Marseille and Cassis (☞ *below*). The sandy **Prado beaches** cover 90 acres and offer activities from windsurfing to kite flying. Bus 83 or Bus 19 will take you there. **Plage des Catalans,** on Anse des Catalans in the city area, is the most popular beach, but there is an admission charge. To get there, take Bus 83 or Line 1 on the métro from the Vieux Port. You can also find your own little beach on the **Îsles de Frioul,** reached from the Château d'If. Sailboats can be rented from **Midi Nautisme** (✉ 13 pl. aux Huiles, ☎ 04–91–54–86–09).

Aubagne

49 *16 km (10 mi) east of Marseille, 36 km (22 mi) south of Aix-en-Provence.*

Aubagne is the headquarters of the French Foreign Legion (to get there, take a left off D2 onto D44A just before Aubagne). The legion was created in 1831 and accepts recruits from all nations, no questions asked. The discipline and camaraderie instilled among its motley team of adventurers, criminals, and mercenaries has helped the legion forge a reputation for exceptional valor—a reputation romanticized by songs and films in which sweaty deeds of heroism are performed under the desert sun. The **Musée du Képi Blanc,** named after the distinctive white caps of the *légionnaires,* does its best to polish the image by way of medals, uniforms, weapons, and photographs. ✉ *Caserne Viénot,* ☎ *04–42–03–03–20.* *Free.* ⏲ *June–Sept., Tues.–Sun. 9–noon and 2–5; Oct.–May, Wed. and weekends 9–noon.*

The Wild West has invaded Provence at the **O. K. Corral,** a huge amusement park with roller coasters, Ferris wheels, and rootin' tootin' cowboy shows. The less than authentic flavor is more Gallic than *Gunsmoke,* but children love it nonetheless. ✉ *11 km (7 mi) west of Aubagne on N8, just beyond Cuges-les-Pins,* ☎ *04–42–73–80–05.* *78 frs.* ⏲ *June, daily 10:30–6:30; July–Aug., daily 10:30–7:30; Apr.–May and Sept.–Oct., Wed. and weekends 10:30–6:30.*

Cassis

50 *11 km (7 mi) south of Aubagne, 30 km (19 mi) east of Marseille, 42 km (26 mi) west of Toulon.*

Cafés, restaurants, and seafood shops cluster around the harbor and three beaches in the fishing village of Cassis, at the foot of Europe's highest cliff, the 1,300-foot Cap Canaille. Boats leave the harbor from quai St-Pierre to the neighboring calanques, the lovely coves in long creeks that weave their way between towering white-stone cliffs. The most spectacular and the farthest of the three calanques visited by boat is En-Vau. Take the boat there and walk back along the scenic footpath.

En Route From Cassis, a daring clifftop road runs along the top of Cap Canaille to the shipbuilding base of **La Ciotat,** 13 km (8 mi) away. From La Ciotat, follow D559 for 19 km (12 mi), through Bandol, to **Sanary,** whose old streets and picturesque seafront invite exploration.

Six-Fours-les-Plages

51 *28 km (17 mi) east of Cassis, 58 km (36 mi) east of Marseille.*

Six-Fours-les-Plages on the dramatic Cap Sicié peninsula is a sprawling town of limited interest, though three nearby sites deserve a visit. The **Fort of Six-Fours,** at the top of a steep hill, is a military base closed to the public, but the views from here across the Bay of Toulon are stupendous; follow the signs from town. The former parish church of **St-Pierre,** near the fort, features a Romanesque nave and a rich medieval altarpiece by Louis Bréa. Archaeological digs to the right of the entrance have revealed Roman walls on the site.

Just north of Six-Fours (take D63 and turn left following signs marked MONUMENT HISTORIQUE) is the small stone chapel of **Notre-Dame de Pépiole,** hemmed in by pines and cypresses. It is one of the oldest Christian buildings in France, dating from the 5th century. The simple interior has survived the years in remarkably good shape, although the colorful stained glass that fills the tiny windows is modern—composed mainly of broken bottles! ⏲ *Most afternoons.*

En Route A right on D616, around the **Cap Sicié** (Cape Sicié) will take you to more fine panoramas and a colossal view across the Bay of Toulon. For another scenic route, take D11 to Ollioules, 5 km (3 mi), then follow N8 (direction Le Beausset) through a 5-km (3-mi) route that twists its scenic way beneath the awesome chalky rock faces of the spectacular **Gorge d'Ollioules.** A right on D462 will take you to the village of **Evenos,** a patchwork of inhabited and ruined houses dominated by an abandoned cliff-top castle.

Toulon

52 *16 km (10 mi) east of Six-Fours, 42 km (26 mi) east of Cassis, 64 km (40 mi) east of Marseille.*

Toulon is France's leading Mediterranean naval base. Leave your car in the underground parking lot at place de la Liberté, head along boulevard de Strasbourg, and turn right after the theater into rue Berthelot. It leads into the pedestrian-only streets that constitutes the heart of old Toulon. Shops and colorful stalls make it an attractive area by day, but avoid it at night.

Avenue de la République, an ugly array of concrete apartment blocks, runs parallel to the waterfront, where yachts and pleasure boats—some available for trips to the Îles d'Hyères or around the bay—add bright splashes of color. At the western edge of the quay is the **Musée Naval,** with large models of ships, figureheads, paintings, and other items related to Toulon's maritime history. ✉ *pl. Monsenergue,* ☎ *04–94–02–02–01.* 🎫 *22 frs.* ⏲ *Wed.–Mon. 9–noon and 2–5.*

Mighty hills surround Toulon. **Mont Faron,** at 1,600 feet, is the highest of all. Either drive to the top, taking the circular route du Faron in either direction, or make the six-minute ascent by cable car from boulevard de l'Amiral Jean-Vence. ☎ *04–94–92–68–25.* ⏲ *Daily 9:15–noon and 2:15–6; closed Mon., Sept.–May.*

Dining

$ ✕ **La Ferme.** Good-value menus and a cozy setting make this little home-style eatery a sensible choice for lunch. The 85-franc three-course menu usually has a fish terrine or mussels appetizer, followed by pork, steak, or a fillet of sole, and ends with a dessert. ✉ *6 pl. Louis-Blanc,* ☎ *04–94–42–69–77. Closed Sun. and Aug. MC, V.*

Outdoor Activities and Sports

On a sunny day set out for a game at **Golf de Valcros** (✉ La Londe–Les Maures, 37 km/23 mi east of Toulouse, ☎ 04–94–66–81–02). Sailboats and sail boards can be rented from **Wanako Centre du Nautisme** (✉ av. du Dr-Robin, Hyères, 19 km/12 mi east of Toulouse, ☎ 04–94–57–77–20), starting at 300 francs a day.

Shopping

The celebrated **fish, fruit, and household-goods market** (✉ cours Lafayette) takes place near the harbor Monday through Saturday mornings.

Îles d'Hyères

53 *Boats leave frequently from La Tour-Fondue, at the tip of the narrow Giens peninsula (every half hour in July and Aug., every 60 or 90 mins at other times) for the Île de Porquerolles. Boats for Île de Port-Cros and Île du Levant leave from Hyères-Plages and, farther along, from Port-de-Miramar and Le Lavandou.*

Îles d'Hyèress is an archipelago that spans some 32 km (20 mi) and consists of three main islands—**Porquerolles, Port-Cros,** and **Le Levant.** The boat trip from La Tour-Fondue to Île de Porquerolles, the largest island, takes 20 minutes and costs 70 francs round-trip. The island's village has several small hotels and restaurants, but the main reason to come here is to escape the modern world. Filmmakers love the island and use it as a handy base for shooting tropical or South Sea Island–type scenery. You can stroll across it, from the harbor to *le phare* (the lighthouse), in about 90 minutes, or head east among luxuriant flowers and thick woods. Île de Port-Cros, a national park, has delightful, well-marked hiking trails. Île du Levant is long and rocky and much less interesting; the French Navy owns part of it, and most of the rest is a nudist camp.

Dining and Lodging

$$$ ★ ✕🏨 **Mas du Langoustier.** This luxurious hideout lies amid some stunningly lush terrain at the westernmost point of Île de Porquerolles, 3 km (2 mi) from the harbor. Mme. Richard will pick you up. Rooms are delightful and the views superb. You must eat here if you stay overnight (no hardship). Chef Michel Sarran uses a delicate touch with his seafood dishes, such as fresh sardines in ginger accompanied by the rare island rosé. ✉ *pointe du Langoustier, 83400 Île de Porquerolles,* ☎ *04–94–58–30–09,* FAX *04–94–58–36–02. 55 rooms. Restaurant, tennis court, beach, billiards. AE, DC, MC, V. Closed Nov.–Apr.*

PROVENCE A TO Z

Arriving and Departing

By Car

The A6/A7 expressway (toll road) from Paris, known as the Autoroute du Soleil—the Expressway of the Sun—takes you straight to Provence, whereupon it divides at Orange, 659 km (412 mi) from Paris; the trip can be done in a fast five hours or so.

By Plane

Marseille and Montpellier are served by frequent flights from Paris and London, and daily flights from Paris arrive at the smaller airport at Nîmes. Flights take about an hour. There are direct flights in the summer from the United States to Nice, 160 km (100 mi) from Aix-en-Provence.

By Train

Avignon is less than four hours from Paris (Gare de Lyon) by the high-speed TGV (Trains à Grande Vitesse). Add another hour for Marseille and Montpellier.

Getting Around

By Bicycle

Bikes can be rented from the train stations in Aix-en-Provence, Arles, Avignon, Marseille, Montpellier, Nîmes, and Orange; the cost is about 40 francs per day. Contact the **Comité Départemental de Cyclotourisme** (⊠ les Passadoires, 84420 Piolenc) for a list of scenic bike paths in Provence.

By Bus

A moderately good network of bus services links places not served, or badly served, by the railway. If you plan to explore Provence by bus, Avignon is the best base. The town is well served by local buses, and excursion buses and boat trips down the Rhône start from here.

By Car

After route A7 divides at Orange, A9 heads west to Nîmes and Montpellier (765 km/475 mi from Paris), and continues into the Pyrénées and across the Spanish border. Route A7 continues southeast from Orange to Marseille on the coast (1,100 km/680 mi from Paris), while A8 goes to Aix-en-Provence (with a spur to Toulon) and then to the Riviera and Italy.

By Train

After the main line divides at Avignon, the westbound link heads to Nîmes, Montpellier (less than five hours from Paris by TGV), and points west. The southeast-bound link takes in Marseille (also under five hours from Paris by TGV), Toulon, and the Riviera. There are also frequent, daily, local trains to other towns.

Contacts and Resources

Car Rental

Avis (⊠ Gare SNCF, av. Paulin Talbot, Arles, ☏ 04–90–96–82–42; 1800 av. Maréchal Juin, Nîmes, ☏ 04–66–29–05–33; 11 cours Gambetta, Aix-en-Provence, ☏ 04–42–21–64–16; 267 bd. National, Marseille, ☏ 04–91–50–70–11). **Budget** (⊠ 40 bd. de Plombières, Marseille, ☏ 04–91–64–40–03; Marignane Airport, Marseille, ☏ 04–42–14–24–55). **Europcar** (⊠ 2 bis av. Victor-Hugo, Arles, ☏ 04–90–93–23–24; 27 av. St-Ruf, Avignon, ☏ 04–90–82–49–85; 68 cours Aristide Briand, Orange, ☏ 04–90–51–67–53; Airport, Montpellier,

☎ 04–67–99–82–00). **Hertz** (✉ Parking des Gares, 18 rue Jules-Ferry, Montpellier, ☎ 04–67–58–65–18; 5 bd. de Prague, Nîmes, ☎ 04–66–76–25–91; Marignane Airport, Marseille, ☎ 04–42–14–32–70).

Guided Tours

The regional tourist offices' "52 Week" program pools 52 tours organized by various agencies, allowing you to choose from myriad tours throughout the year, including wine tasting, sailing, hang gliding, golfing, gastronomy, and cultural exploration. Contact **Loisirs-Acceuil** (✉ Domaine de Vergon, 13370 Mallemort, ☎ 04–90–59–18–05) for details. In addition, local tourist offices can arrange many tours, ranging from one-hour guided walks to excursions that take a week or longer by bus, bicycle, horseback, or foot.

The **Aix-en-Provence Office du Tourisme** (✉ 2 pl. du Général de Gaulle, ☎ 04–42–16–11–61) gives city tours in English, July–September. The **Arles Office du Tourisme** (✉ 35 pl. de la République, ☎ 04–90–18–41–22) employs 15 guide-lecturers who run tours of the town and region. The **Comité Départemental du Tourisme** (✉ 13 Roux de Brignoles, 13006 Marseille, ☎ 04–91–13–84–13) arranges bus tours of the area. **S.A.A.F.** (✉ 110 bd. des Dames, 13002 Marseille, ☎ 04–91–91–10–91) organizes a two-day tour of Marseille and Avignon.

The **Association de Tourisme Équestre** (✉ chemin St-Julien, 30133 Les Angles, ☎ 04–90–25–38–91) can give you information about horseback riding tours. The **Marseille Office Municipal du Tourisme** features a six-day guided tour on horseback. **Cheval Nomade** (✉ col du Pointu, Bonnieux, ☎ 04–90–74–40–48) specializes in tours by horseback.

Outdoor Activities and Sports

For a list of trails and outfitters, contact the **Comité Départemental de la Randonnée Pédestre** (✉ 307 av. Foch, Orange, ☎ 04–90–51–14–86). The **Comité Régional du Tourisme du Languedoc-Roussillon** (☞ *below*) publishes a brochure on golf courses in the area and sells a pass good for 14 different courses.

Travel Agencies

Wagons-Lits (✉ 2 rue Olivier, Avignon, ☎ 04–90–82–20–56; 225 av. du Prado, Marseille, ☎ 04–91–79–30–80; 3 rue des Cordeliers, Aix-en-Provence, ☎ 04–42–96–31–88). **Midi-Libre Voyages** (✉ 40 bd. Victor-Hugo, Nîmes, ☎ 04–66–67–45–34).

Visitor Information

Provence's regional tourist offices accept written inquiries only. The **Comité Régional du Tourisme du Languedoc-Roussillon** (✉ 20 rue de la République, 34000 Montpellier, ☎ 04–67–22–81–00) provides information on all towns west of the Rhône River. The remainder of towns covered in this chapter are handled by the **Comité Régional du Tourisme de Provence-Alpes-Côte d'Azur** (✉ 14 rue Ste-Barbe, Espace Colbert, 13001 Marseille, ☎ 04–91–39–38–00) and the **Chambre Départementale de Tourisme de Vaucluse** (✉ la Balance, pl. Campana, B.P. 147, 84008 Avignon, ☎ 04–90–86–43–42). Local tourist offices for major towns covered in this chapter are as follows: **Aix-en-Provence** (✉ 2 pl. du Général-de-Gaulle, ☎ 04–42–16–11–61). **Arles** (✉ esplanade Charles-de-Gaulle, ☎ 04–90–18–41–20). **Avignon** (✉ 41 cours Jean-Jaurès, ☎ 04–90–82–65–11). **Marseille** (✉ 4 La Canebière, ☎ 04–91–13–89–00). **Montpellier** (✉ pl. René-Devic, ☎ 04–67–58–67–58). **Nîmes** (✉ 6 rue Auguste, ☎ 04–66–67–29–11). **Toulon** (✉ pl. des Riaux, ☎ 04–94–18–53–00).

13 The Riviera

St-Tropez to Monaco

The fabled Riviera is France's open door to the color and emotion of southern Europe and the Mediterranean. Without the Pyrénées or the Alps blocking the way, it's an easy slide into Monaco and Italy, across the border. The distinct light and feeling here have not only attracted movie stars, but have also inspired artists, from Renoir to Matisse to Picasso, who came to live in the medieval hill town of Vence, the beaches and tiny streets of St-Tropez, and the ochre and pastel hues of old Nice.

Updated by
Nigel Fisher

THE RIVIERA CONJURES UP IMAGES of fabulous yachts and villas, movie stars and palaces, and budding starlets sunning themselves on ribbons of golden sand. But the truth is that most beaches, at least east of Cannes, are small and pebbly, and that, in summer, hordes of visitors are stuffed into concrete high-rises and roadside campsites—on weekends it can take two hours to drive the last 10 km (6 mi) into St-Tropez. Yes, the film stars are here—but in their private villas. When the merely wealthy come, they come off-season, in the spring and fall.

That said, we can still recommend the Riviera, even in summer, as long as you're selective about the places you visit. Inland are fortified medieval towns perched on mountaintops, high above the sea. The light that Renoir and Matisse came to capture is as magical here as ever (it pays to get up early to see it) and fields of roses and lavender still send their heady perfume up to these fortified towns, where craftspeople make and sell their wares, as did their predecessors in the Middle Ages.

It's impossible to be bored along the Riviera. You can try a different beach or restaurant every day. When you've had enough sun, you can visit pottery towns like Vallauris, where Picasso worked, or the perfumeries at Grasse. You can drive along dizzying gorges, almost as deep as the Grand Canyon. You can disco or gamble the night away in Monte Carlo and shop in Cannes or Nice. And only minutes from the beaches are some of the world's most famous modern art museums.

Pleasures and Pastimes

Beaches

If you like your beaches sandy, stick to those between St-Tropez and Antibes; most of the others are pebbly, though Menton and Monaco have imported vast tons of sand to spread around their shores. Private beaches are everywhere. You'll have to pay to use them (between 80 and 140 francs a day), but they usually have a café or restaurant, cabanas and showers, mattresses and umbrellas, and a parade of people in stylish swimwear.

Dining

Though prices often scale Parisian heights, the Riviera shares its cuisine with Provence—vegetable and fish dishes prepared with vivid seasonings. The most famous is bouillabaisse, a fish stew. Local fish is scarce, however, so dishes like *loup flambé* (sea bass with fennel and anise liqueur), braised tuna, and even fresh sardines are priced accordingly. *Estocaficada* (fish stew with garlic and olives) is a Nice specialty as is *pan bagna* (salad in a bun) and *poulpe à la niçoise* (octopus in tomato sauce). With Italy so close, it's no surprise that many menus feature such specialties as ravioli, potato gnocchi, vegetable *soupe au pistou* (a seasoned, aromatic soup), and *pissaladière* (a version of pizza with olives, anchovies, and onions). Anise-flavored pastis is the Riviera's number one drink.

CATEGORY	COST*
$$$$	over 500 frs
$$$	250 frs–500 frs
$$	150 frs–250 frs
$	under 150 frs

**per person for a three-course meal, including tax (20.6%) and tip but not wine*

Lodging

Hotels on the Riviera can push opulence to the sublime—or the ridiculous. Pastel colors, gilt, and plush are the decorators' staples in the hotels catering to the beau monde. The glamour comes hand in hand with hefty price tags, however, and although inexpensive hotels do exist, they're found mainly on dull outskirts of big centers and in less fashionable "family" resort towns. But less expensive inns can also be found in the hilltop villages above the coast.

CATEGORY	COST*
$$$$	over 1,000 frs
$$$	600 frs–1,000 frs
$$	300 frs–600 frs
$	under 300 frs

**All prices are for a standard double room for two, including tax (20.6%) and service charge.*

Exploring the Riviera

Also known as the Côte d'Azur, the French Riviera stretches for 120 km (75 mi) along the Mediterranean coastline, from St-Tropez to the Italian border. It's best to begin exploring the region on the western end at St-Tropez. Make Cannes and Antibes your next targets, then head inland to the medieval *villages perchés* (hilltop villages) of Grasse, Vence, and St-Paul-de-Vence. Lastly, visit the area to the east that includes Cagnes, Nice, and Monaco.

Great Itineraries

The towns along the Mediterranean are quite close together—Antibes is practically a suburb of Cannes and St-Paul-de-Vence is just a 10-minute drive inland from Nice—so you can see many places in a short amount of time (the only problem is that you may want to stay forever). If you have limited time, it is possible, even advisable, to rush along the coast and see it all.

Numbers in the text and in the margins correspond to numbers on the Riviera: St-Tropez to Cannes; the Riviera: Cannes to Menton; Nice; and Monaco maps.

IF YOU HAVE 3 DAYS

Start in **St-Tropez** ①. In the afternoon, loop through the ancient villages of **Ramatuelle** ② and **Gassin** ③. Then drive along the Corniche de l'Esterel through **Fréjus** ⑥, an old Roman town, and **La Napoule** ⑨, with a stop, if you have time, at the Château de La Napoule Art Foundation. Get to world-famous **Cannes** ⑩ by evening. On day two explore Cannes and then drive to **Antibes** ⑬. The perfume-producing town of **Grasse** ⑰ is just 20 minutes inland; from there you can drive through the country on your way to the medieval hilltop villages of **Vence** ⑳ and **St-Paul-de-Vence** ㉑ for the night. The next day head to **Cagnes-sur-Mer** ㉒ to see the Renoir museum, then go to the faded but graceful city of **Nice** ㉔–㊶.

IF YOU HAVE 5 DAYS

Follow the three-day tour at a more relaxed pace, spending a night in both **St-Tropez** ① and **Antibes** ⑬ and stopping in the medieval town of **Eze** ㊻ on your way to Monte Carlo.

IF YOU HAVE 7 DAYS

Follow the five-day itinerary, with lunch in **Cagnes-sur-Mer** ㉒ on your way to **Nice** ㉔–㊶ for a night and day. On the sixth day, drive along the Moyenne Corniche, stopping in **Eze** ㊻, then heading on to **Monaco** ㊼–(54) for the night. On day seven visit **Roquebrune** (55) and

Menton 56. Extra days would give you time to drive inland along the Corniche Sublime (D71), overlooking the spectacular Grand Canyon du Verdon.

When to Tour the Riviera

October, May, and June are optimal times to be on the Riviera. Summer is too hot and too crowded, unless you want to be part of the banks of sunbathers watching each other on the beach. From early November through Easter, many of the most famous places are closed. But the ones that do stay open off-season are guaranteed to be good.

ST-TROPEZ, CANNES, AND ANTIBES

The *caps* (capes) of St-Tropez and Antibes look across the Corniche de l'Esterel at each other with little but the Îles de Lérins between them. The 60 km (37 mi) of towns, beaches, and the small but vibrant city of Cannes comprise an intense combination of riches that have made this coast into one of France's most sought-after destinations.

St-Tropez

1 *73 km (45 mi) east of Toulon and southwest of Cannes, 878 km (549 mi) southeast of Paris.*

Old money never came to St-Tropez, but Brigitte Bardot did—with her director Roger Vadim in 1956 to film *And God Created Woman.* The town has never been the same since. Actually, the village was first "discovered" by the writer Guy de Maupassant (1850–93) and again, later, by the French painter Paul Signac (1863–1935), who came in 1892 and brought his friends—Matisse, Pierre Bonnard, and others. The writer Colette moved into a villa here between the two world wars and contributed to its notoriety. What attracted them was the pure, radiant light and the colors of the landscape.

Anything associated with the distant past almost seems absurd in St-Tropez. Still, the place has a history that predates the invention of the bikini, and people have been finding reasons to come here for centuries. First, in AD 68 there was a Roman soldier from Pisa named Torpes who was beheaded for professing his Christian faith in the presence of the emperor Nero. The headless body was put in a boat between a dog and a cock and sent drifting out to sea. The body eventually floated ashore, perfectly preserved, still watched over by the two animals. The buried remains became a place of pilgrimage, which by the 4th century was called St-Tropez. In the late 15th century, under the Genovese, St-Tropez became a small independent republic. Since then, people—and celebrities—have come for the sun and the sea. In summer, the population swells from 7,000 to 64,000.

Off-season is the time to come, but even in summer there are reasons to stay. The soft, sandy beaches are the best on the coast. Take an early morning stroll along the harbor or down the narrow medieval streets—the rest of the town will still be sleeping—and you'll see just how pretty St-Tropez is, with its tiny squares and rich, pastel-color houses. There are trendy boutiques and many cafés with colored awnings. Five minutes from town, you'll be in a green world of vineyards, fields, and mountains crowned with medieval villages. Perhaps it's the soft light, perhaps the rich fields and faded pastels, but nowhere else along the coast will you experience so completely the magic of the Riviera.

Walk along the harbor, filled with pleasure boats, and along the breakwater, to the **Musée de l'Annonciade,** a church converted into a major art museum. The collection of Impressionist paintings is filled with views

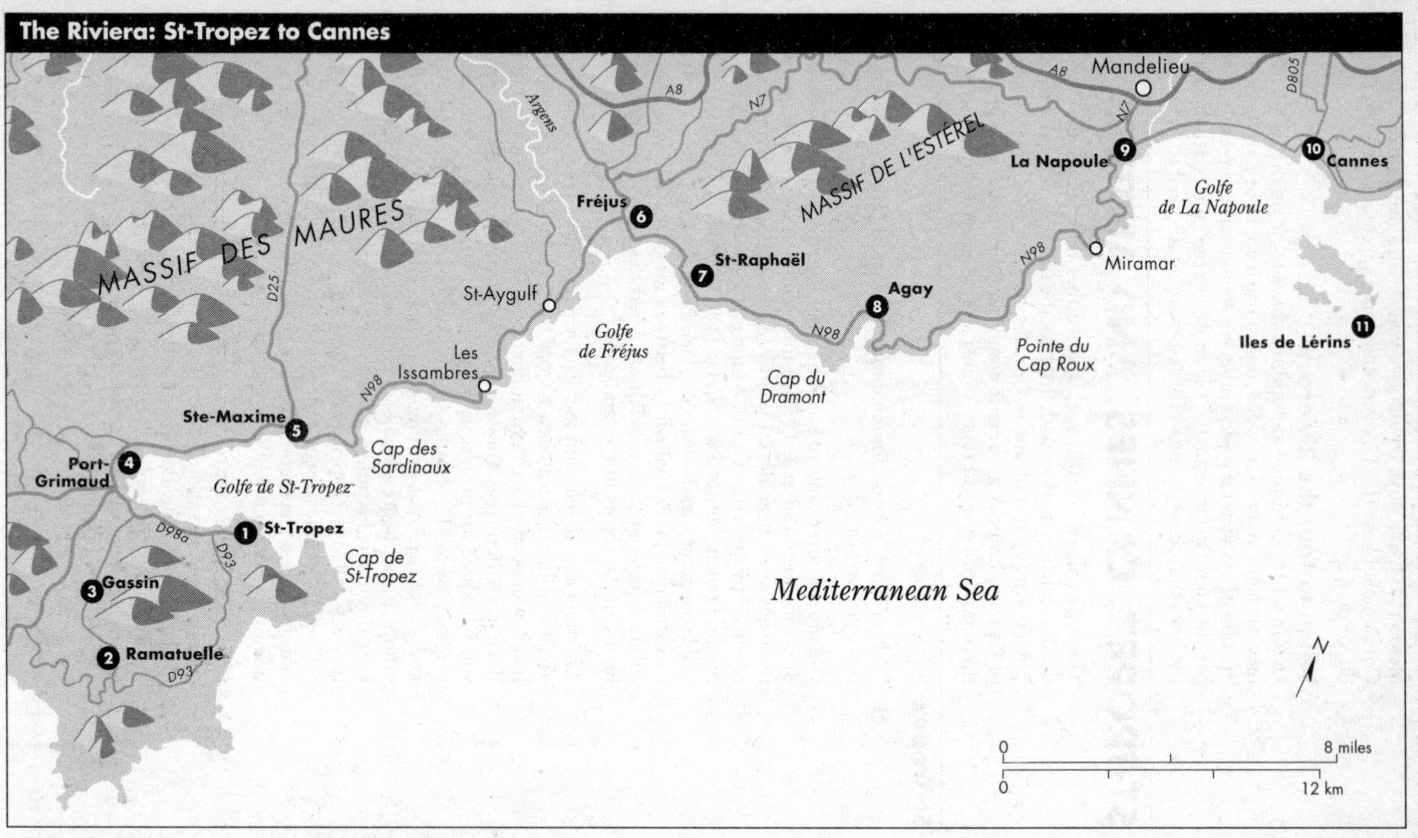
The Riviera: St-Tropez to Cannes
MASSIF DES MAURES
MASSIF DE L'ESTÉREL
Mediterranean Sea
1 St-Tropez
2 Ramatuelle
3 Gassin
4 Port-Grimaud
5 Ste-Maxime
6 Fréjus
7 St-Raphaël
8 Agay
9 La Napoule
10 Cannes
11 Iles de Lérins
Mandelieu
Miramar
St-Aygulf
Les Issambres
Golfe de St-Tropez
Cap de St-Tropez
Cap des Sardinaux
Golfe de Fréjus
Cap du Dramont
Pointe du Cap Roux
Golfe de La Napoule
Argens
A8
N7
N98
D25
D93
D98a
D805
N
0
8 miles
0
12 km

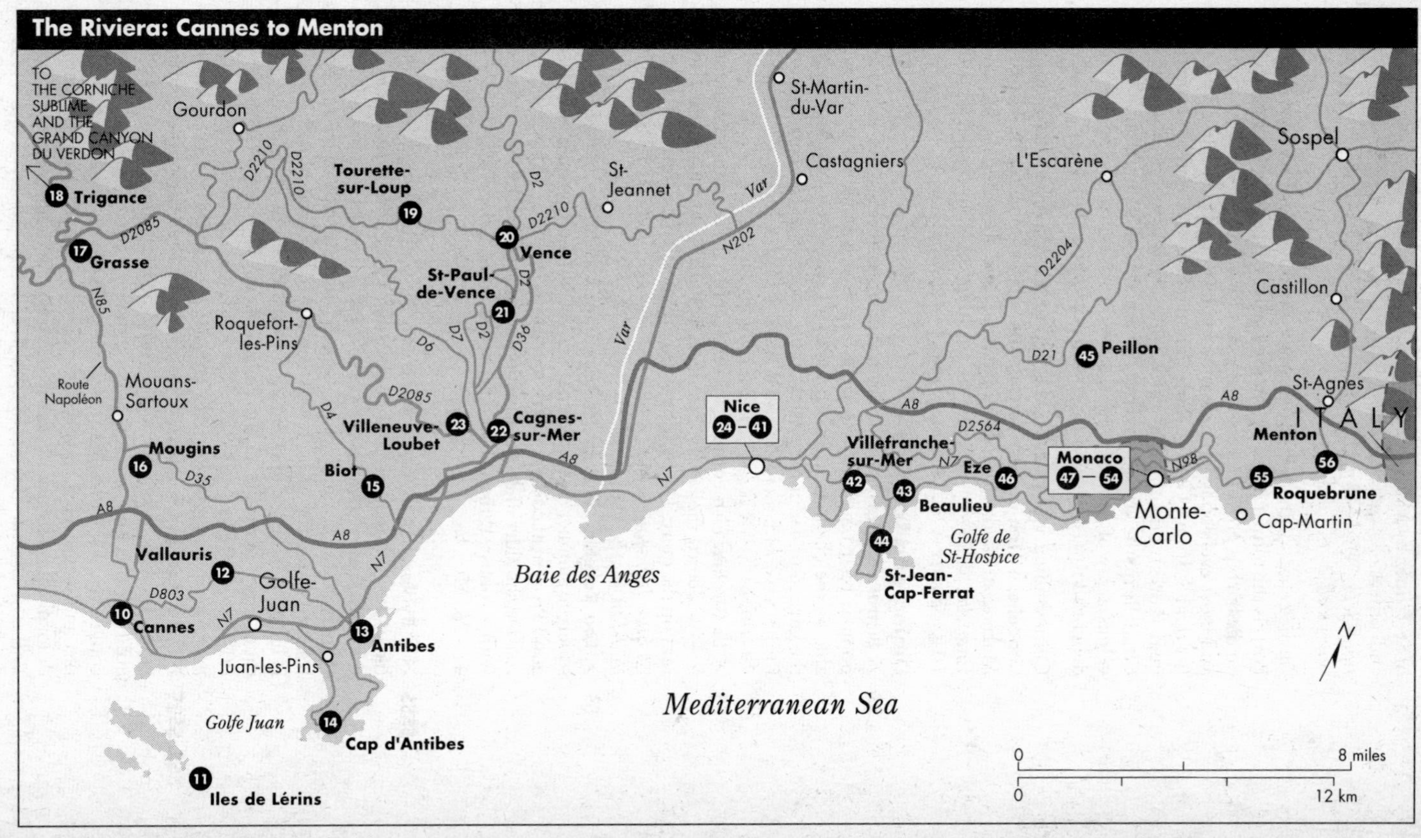
The Riviera: Cannes to Menton
TO
THE CORNICHE
SUBLIME
AND THE
GRAND CANYON
DU VERDON
18 Trigance
17 Grasse
Gourdon
D2210
D2085
N85
Route
Napoléon
Mouans-
Sartoux
16 Mougins
D35
A8
Vallauris
12
D803
10 Cannes
N7
Golfe-
Juan
Juan-les-Pins
Golfe Juan
11 Iles de Lérins
14 Cap d'Antibes
13 Antibes
Roquefort-
les-Pins
D4
Biot 15
Tourette-
sur-Loup 19
20 Vence
D2
St-Paul-
de-Vence 21
D7
D6
D36
D2085
Villeneuve-
Loubet 23
22 Cagnes-
sur-Mer
St-
Jeannet
Var
N202
St-Martin-
du-Var
Castagniers
Nice
24 – 41
Baie des Anges
Villefranche-
sur-Mer 42
43 Beaulieu
44 St-Jean-
Cap-Ferrat
Golfe de
St-Hospice
Eze 46
D2564
Monaco
47 – 54
Monte-
Carlo
N98
L'Escarène
D2204
D21
45 Peillon
Sospel
Castillon
St-Agnes
ITALY
Menton
55
56
Roquebrune
Cap-Martin
Mediterranean Sea
N
0
8 miles
0
12 km

of St-Tropez by Matisse, Bonnard, Paul Signac, Maurice de Vlaminck, and others. ✉ *quai de l'Épi,* ☎ *04–94–97–04–01.* 🎟 *25 frs.* ⏲ *June–Sept., Wed.–Mon. 10–noon and 3–7; Oct.–May, Wed.–Mon. 10–noon and 2–6.*

At the center of the half-moon quay surrounding the **Vieux Port** (Old Port) is the **tourist office** (✉ on the corner of rue de la Citadelle). Cafés on the harbor provide dress-circle seats for admiring the St-Tropez scene and most everybody at some time hangs out at places like **Le Gorille** (✉ quai Suffren), **Café de Paris** (✉ quai Suffren), and **Sénéquier's** (✉ quai Jaurès). Less than 20 yards from the tourist office up rue de la Citadelle on the left is a covered **fish market**—it's small, but has a marvelous array of *fruits de mer* (seafood). Pass through the market to a delightful tiny square with produce stalls and shops.

Commanding views across the bay to Ste-Maxime are found at the **Citadelle,** a 16th-century fortress. Its keep is home to the **Musée de la Marine,** stocked with marine paintings and ship models. ✉ *rue de la Citadelle,* ☎ *04–94–97–59–43.* 🎟 *30 frs.* ⏲ *Nov.–Easter, Wed.–Mon. 10–5; Easter–Oct., 10–noon and 2–4:30.*

Dining and Lodging

$$ ✕ **Bistrot des Lices.** You'll find a mix of celebrities and locals at this popular bistro, where interesting food is served by a staff as fashionable as the clientele. Bronzed men and glamorous women lounge in the garden or eat in the pastel dining room. The barman is renowned for his way with a cocktail shaker. ✉ *3 pl. des Lices,* ☎ *04–94–97–29–00. MC, V. Closed Jan.–Mar., Nov.–Dec. 25.*

$$ ✕ **Le Girelier.** Fish enthusiasts—especially those with a taste for garlic—will enjoy the hearty, heavily spiced dishes at this bustling restaurant on the quay. The fish soup and the giant shrimp are local favorites. ✉ *quai Jean-Jaurès,* ☎ *04–94–97–03–87. AE, DC, MC, V. Closed mid-Jan.–early Mar.*

$$ ✕ **Lou Revelen.** This smart restaurant has tables outside in a tiny square in summer and an open fire in the dining room in winter. It serves good Provençal cooking, with menus beginning at 125 francs. Try the roasted shoulder of rabbit with thyme and a wide selection of fish, many with a robust, tomato-based sauce. ✉ *bd. d'Aumale,* ☎ *04–94–97–41–76. MC, V.*

$$$$ ✕🏨 **Byblos.** The Byblos resembles a Provençal village, with cottage-like suites grouped around courtyards. Inside, the atmosphere is distinctly Casbah, with lots of heavy damask, a leopard-skin bar, and Persian carpets on the dining room ceiling. If you can't afford to stay here, at least go to use the pool (for a steep fee). The restaurant, Les Arcades, is lucky to have the talented Philippe Audibert as chef; his grilled sardines are memorable. ✉ *av. Paul Signac, 83990,* ☎ *04–94–56–68–00,* FAX *04–94–56–68–01. 58 rooms, 48 suites. Restaurant, pool, exercise room, nightclub. AE, DC, MC, V. Closed mid-Oct.–mid-Mar.*

$$$–$$$$ ✕🏨 **Le Mas de Chastelas.** This pink-toned old farmhouse, offset by white shutters, was once a silkworm farm. Inside, white walls, modern furniture, and sculpture by the owner's sister combine to create a cool retreat. The restaurant is usually filled with a mélange of celebrities and well-heeled travelers, attracted by chef Patrick Cartier's traditional regional cuisine, such as asparagus with sea urchins. ✉ *quartier Bertaud, Grande Bastide, 83580 Gassin,* ☎ *04–94–56–09–11,* FAX *04–94–56–11–56. 15 rooms, 12 duplexes. Restaurant, pool. AE, DC, MC, V. Closed Nov.–Easter.*

$$$ ★ **Ermitage.** This hotel near the heart of St-Tropez has old-fashioned charm. The rooms' white walls are offset by strong primary colors on the beds and windows; ask for one overlooking the garden and the town. The friendly bar always seems open and owner Annie Bolloreis is more than willing to chat (in English) on the virtues and vices of her hometown. ✉ *av. Paul-Signac, 83990,* ☎ *04–94–97–52–33,* FAX *04–94–97–10–43. 28 rooms. Bar. AE, DC, MC, V.*

$–$$ **Lou Cagnard.** This in-town farmhouse is one of the few inexpensive hotels in St-Tropez, just a two-minute walk from place des Lices, so book well ahead. Don't expect great style or comfort, but the rooms are clean and not too cramped. ✉ *18 av. Paul-Roussel, 83990,* ☎ *04–94–97–04–24.* FAX *04–94–97–09–44. 19 rooms. AE, DC, MC, V. Closed Nov.–Dec. 25.*

Nightlife and the Arts

St-Tropez's major concert hall, which doubles as a cinema, is the **Salle de la Renaissance** (✉ pl. des Lices, ☎ 04–94–97–48–16). The hottest night spot in St-Tropez is **Les Caves du Roy** in the Byblos Hotel (✉ av. Paul-Signac); the decor is stunningly vulgar, but the *très chic* clientele doesn't seem to mind. Look your best if you want to get in.

Outdoor Activities and Sports

The best ***plages*** (beaches) are scattered along a 5-km (3-mi) stretch reached by the route des Plages (beach road); the most fashionable are **Moorea, Tahiti Plage,** and **Club 55.** You'll see lots of topless bathers; some beaches allow total nudity. Those beaches close to town—**Plage des Greniers** and the **Bouillabaisse**—are great for families, but French vacationers snub them, preferring the 10-km (6-mi) sandy crescent at **Les Salins** and **Pampellone,** 3 km (2 mi) from town. **Sailboats** can be rented from **Sportmer** (✉ 8 pl. Blanqui). **Bicycles** are an ideal way to get to the beach; try **M. Mas** (✉ rte. des Tamaris, ☎ 04–94–97–00–60) or **Holiday Bikes** (✉ R.N. 98, ☎ 04–94–79–87–75).

Shopping

Rue Sibilli is a street with all kinds of trendy boutiques. **Soleido** (✉ av. du 8-mai-1945) sells very French printed fabrics and clothes. **Georget** (✉ 11 rue Allard) has delicious handmade chocolates. Vegetables, fruit, and daily games of *boules* are found at the **produce market** (✉ pl. Carnot) on Tuesday and Saturday. The **clothing and antiques market** (✉ pl. des Lices) takes place on Tuesday and Saturday.

Ramatuelle

❷ *12 km (7 mi) southwest of St-Tropez.*

The old market town of Ramatuelle is a 20-minute drive south of St-Tropez through fields and vineyards. The ancient houses are huddled together on the slope of a rocky spur 440 feet above the sea and the central square has a 17th-century church and a huge 300-year-old elm. Surrounding the square are narrow, twisting streets with medieval archways and vaulted passages.

En Route From Ramatuelle, the ride through vineyards and woods to the hilltop village of Gassin is lovely and takes you over the highest point of the peninsula (1,070 feet).

Gassin

❸ *7 km (4 mi) north of Ramatuelle.*

The hilltop village of Gassin, with its venerable old houses and 12th-century Romanesque church, has managed to maintain its medieval appearance. When it gets really hot at the beaches, people come up here to have a drink and contemplate the view and the vineyards.

Port-Grimaud

❹ *6 km (3 mi) north of Gassin.*

On your way along the coast, stop at Port-Grimaud, a modern architect's idea of a Provençal fishing village-cum-Venice, built into the gulf for the yachting crowd—each house with its own mooring. Particularly appealing are the harmonious pastel colors, which have weathered nicely, and the graceful bridges over the canals.

Ste-Maxime

❺ *8 km (5 mi) east of Port-Grimaud, 33 km (20 mi) east of St-Tropez.*

Lively Ste-Maxime, across the gulf from St-Tropez, is a family resort with fine sandy beaches. Surrounded by the red mountains of the Massif des Maures, the town has the same relaxed feeling and creature comforts as its neighbor across the water, but is less expensive.

En Route The coastline between Ste-Maxime and Cannes consists of a succession of bays and beaches. Minor resorts—curious mixtures of lush villas, campsites, and fast-food stands—have sprung up wherever nature permits.

Fréjus

❻ *19 km (12 mi) northeast of St-Maxime, 52 km (32 mi) northeast of St-Tropez.*

Fréjus was founded by Julius Caesar as Forum Julii in 49 BC, and it is thought that the Roman city grew to 40,000 people—10,000 more than the population today. The Roman remains are unspectacular, and consist of part of the theater, an arena, an aqueduct, and city walls. In the heart of town is the **Cathédrale** (✉ pl Formigé). Though it dates from the 10th century, its richly worked choir stalls belong to the 15th century. The baptistry alongside it, square on the outside and octagonal inside, is thought to date from AD 400, making it one of France's oldest buildings. The cloisters have an unusual combination of round and pointed arches.

En Route The rugged **Massif de l'Estérel,** between Fréjus and Cannes, is a hiker's joy. Made up of volcanic rocks (porphyry) carved by the sea into dreamlike shapes, the harshness of the landscape is softened by patches of lavender, cane apple, and gorse. Take N7, the mountain route to the north, or stay on the N98 coast road past tiny rust-color beaches and sheer rock faces plunging into the sea.

St-Raphaël

❼ *4 km (2 mi) east of Fréjus.*

St-Raphaël, next door to Fréjus, is a family resort town with sandy beaches, marinas, an 18-hole course at Golf de l'Esterel (☏ 04–94–82–47–88), and a casino (☏ 04–94–95–10–54). It is best known as the railway stop for St-Tropez. It was here that the Allied forces landed in their offensive against the Germans in August 1944.

Agay

8 *10 km (6 mi) east of St-Raphaël.*

Agay has the best protected anchorage along the Esterel coast and was once used as a deep-water anchorage by traders from ancient Greece. It was near here that writer Antoine de St-Exupéry (*The Little Prince*) was shot down in July 1944, having just flown over his family castle on his last mission.

La Napoule

9 *24 km (15 mi) northeast of Agay, 10 km (6 mi) southwest of Cannes.*

La Napoule forms a unit with the older, inland village of Mandelieu. The village explodes with color during the Fête du Mimosa in February and has extensive sports facilities. Art lovers will want to stop at the **Château de La Napoule Art Foundation** to see the eccentric work of the American sculptor Henry Clews. A cynic and reputed sadist, Clews had, as one critic remarked, a knowledge of anatomy worthy of Michelangelo and the bizarre imagination of Edgar Allen Poe. ✉ *av. Henry-Clews,* ☎ *04–93–49–95–05.* 🎫 *30 frs. Guided visits Mar.–Nov., Wed.–Mon. at 3, 4, and 5; Dec.–Feb., at 3 and 4.*

Dining and Lodging

$$$ 🏨 **Le Domaine d'Olival.** There's not the slightest hint of mass production at this charming hotel, with rooms that were individually designed by the architect-owner. It's small, so make reservations far in advance. Rooms have balconies. Some suites sleep six, which brings the price down to $$. ✉ *778 av. de la Mer, 06210,* ☎ *04–93–49–31–00,* FAX *04–92–97–69–28. 18 apartments. Air-conditioning, kitchenettes, tennis court. AE, DC, MC, V. Closed Nov.–mid-Jan.*

$$$ ✕🏨 **Royal Hôtel Casino.** With plenty of marble, plush, and gilt, this is a pocket edition of the Loews at Monte Carlo. Rooms have balconies and sea views and are decorated in pink and blue, with blond wood furniture. Those overlooking the main road can be noisy. Diners at the restaurant can gaze out over a floodlit swimming pool and deliberate among such textbook delicacies as caviar, lobster, and champagne. Unfortunately, the preparation is relatively uninspiring for the price. ✉ *605 av. Général-de-Gaulle, 06210,* ☎ *04–92–97–70–00,* FAX *04–93–49–51–50. 211 rooms. 2 restaurants, bar, pool, sauna, 18-hole golf course, 2 tennis courts, cabaret, casino, travel services. AE, DC, MC, V.*

Outdoor Activities and Sports

Ask for the **"Star du Siècle"** brochure at the tourist office for details about canoeing, bicycling, riding, climbing, rambling, hang gliding, and rafting. There are also facilities for boating, golfing, horseback riding, and tennis, and eight beaches with waterskiing, jet-skiing, deep-sea diving, and windsurfing. **Club Nautique de L'Esterel** (✉ port de la Rague, ☎ 04–93–49–74–33) gives deep-sea diving lessons to anyone over age eight. The **Plongée International Center** (✉ port Cannes Marina, ☎ 04–93–49–01–01) rents diving gear. Boats and other water sports equipment can be rented from **Maison de la Mer** (✉ av. du Général de Gaulle). For windsurfing equipment try **Sillages** (✉ av. Henry-Clews). The **Poney Club du Soleil** (✉ Domaine de Barbossi, 3 mi/2 km inland from Mandelieu-La Napoule on N7) rents horses and gives lessons to children and adults. The **Riviera Golf Club** (✉ av. des Amazones, ☎ 04–92–97–67–67) is open to the public.

Cannes

⑩ *73 km (45 mi) northeast of St-Tropez, 33 km (21 mi) southwest of Nice, 908 km (567 mi) southeast of Paris.*

Cosmopolitan, sophisticated, smart—these are words that describe the most lively and flourishing town on the Riviera. Cannes is a resort town—unlike Nice, which is a city—that exists only for the pleasure of its guests. It's a tasteful and expensive breeding ground for the upscale, a sybaritic heaven for those who believe that life is short and sin has something to do with the absence of a tan.

★ Alongside the narrow beach runs a broad, elegant promenade bordered by palm trees and flowers, known as **La Croisette.** All along the promenade are cafés, boutiques, and luxury hotels. Speedboats and water-skiers glide by; little waves lick the beach, lined with prostrate bodies. Behind the promenade lies the town, and beyond, the hills with the villas of the very rich. At one end of La Croisette is the **Palm Beach Casino** and a modern harbor for some of the most luxurious yachts in the world. As you walk in this direction you'll pass the **Parc de la Roserie,** where some 14,000 roses nod their heads in the wind. At the other end of La Croisette is the modern **Palais des Festivals** (Festival Hall), the sight of the famous Cannes film festival. Just past the Festival Hall is **place du Général de Gaulle** and the **Vieux Port** where pleasure boats are moored.

Behind the Vieux Port, on **allées de la Liberté,** is a tree-shaded area, where flowers are sold in the morning, boules is played in the afternoon, and a flea market is held on Saturday. Stop for restoration at one of the outdoor kiosks; the **Kiosque des Sports** is the best. The **Hôtel de Ville** (Town Hall), an ornate structure with an elegant stairway, is on rue Félix Faure. Parallel to this street is **rue Meynadier,** Cannes's old main street, lined with 18th-century houses that are now boutiques and specialty food shops. **Rue Louis Blanc,** off rue Meynadier, is home to the colorful Forville vegetable and general produce market. Continue along the street to get to the **Église Miséricorde,** with its tiny bell tower.

To get to **Le Suquet,** known as *le berceau* (the cradle) of Cannes, take a right turn off rue Félix Faure onto rue St-Antoine and continue spiraling up through rue du Suquet to the top of a 60-meter (197-foot) hill. In the 12th-century tower overlooking the rooftops of Cannes you'll find the **Musée de la Castre,** filled with Provençal paintings, ethnological artifacts, and medieval archaeological finds. ✉ *pl. de la Castre,* ☎ *04–93–39–17–49.* 🎫 *15 frs.* ⏲ *Daily 10–noon and 2–6.*

Dining and Lodging

$$ ✕ **Chez Astoux.** For seafood, this stands out among the other restaurants on the block. The ambience is simple but elegant, both on the terrace and inside. Locals go to the restaurant and seafood stall next door, Astoux & Brun, for their own kitchens and pockets. ✉ *43 rue Félix-Faure,* ☎ *04–93–39–06–22. AE, DC, MC, V.*

$$ ✕ **La Mère Besson.** Locals come to this quiet family restaurant, for its authentic Provençal fare. Go on Friday for the *aïoli,* a heaped platter of fish, seafood, and vegetables in a thick garlic mayonnaise. The *lapin farci* (stuffed rabbit) is equally superb. The decor is classically simple. ✉ *13 rue des Frères-Pradignac,* ☎ *04–93–39–59–24. AE, DC, MC, V. Closed Sun. No lunch Sat.*

$ ★ ✕ **Au Bec Fin.** Devoted regulars will attest to the quality of this cheerful, family-run bistro near the train station, distinguished by its spirited local clientele and homey food. The prix-fixe menus are a fantastic value; *choucroute* (sauerkraut and sausage) and fish are often the main dishes, or try fish with fennel or salade niçoise. ✉ *12 rue du 24-Août,* ☎ *04–93–38–35–86. AE, DC, MC, V. Closed Sun., and mid-Dec.–mid-Jan. No dinner Sat.*

$$$$ ✕🏨 **Gray d'Albion.** This striking contemporary hotel is the last word in state-of-the-art luxury. Its white facade is austere; inside, the atmosphere is ultra-sophisticated. Rooms are fitted with slick, modern accessories. Comfort is the key word, making up for the lack of sea views. There are a number of restaurants; the Royal Gray is one of Cannes's most fashionable; it's closed Sunday, Monday, and February. ✉ *38 rue des Serbes, 06400,* ☎ *04–92–99–79–79,* FAX *04–93–99–26–10. 174 rooms. 3 restaurants, beach, dance club. AE, DC, MC, V.*

$$$$ ✕🏨 **Majestic.** Unlike the other "palaces" that line La Croisette, this one has a more discreet, less blatantly luxurious charm. Rooms are spacious and traditional in decor. Service is impeccable. The restaurant serves excellent and reasonably priced fare all year. ✉ *14 bd. de la Croisette, 06400,* ☎ *04–92–98–77–00,* FAX *04–93–38–97–90. 262 rooms, 25 apartments. Air-conditioning, pool, 18-hole golf course, 5 tennis courts, parking (fee). AE, DC, MC, V. Closed early Nov.–mid-Dec.*

$$$$ ★ ✕🏨 **Martinez.** The Art Deco Martinez still manages to retain an atmosphere of indulgence. Rooms are decorated in cool blues and salmons, with wood furniture. One of the hotel's biggest assets is the Palme d'Or restaurant, where chef Christian Willer draws lavish praise for his modern, Mediterranean cuisine; it's closed Monday and Tuesday lunch, mid-November to mid-December, and February. ✉ *73 bd. de la Croisette, 06400,* ☎ *04–92–98–73–00,* FAX *04–93–39–67–82. 418 rooms, 12 apartments. 3 restaurants, bar, pool, 7 tennis courts, beach. Closed mid-Nov.–mid-Jan. AE, DC, MC, V.*

$$$$ ✕🏨 **Noga Hilton.** On the site of the old Palais des Festivals, the Noga has "*Palais Croisette*" unashamedly emblazoned on its gleaming white-and-glass facade. Service and comfort are as you'd expect from the luxury Hilton chain. Chef Jean-Yves Méraud oversees the hotel's four restaurants, including a Caviar House, a round-the-clock brasserie, a beach diner across the road, and the upscale, Italian La Scala. ✉ *50 bd. de la Croisette, 06400,* ☎ *04–92–99–70–00,* FAX *04–92–99–70–11. 229 rooms, 45 suites. 4 restaurants, 3 bars, pool, health club, beach. AE, DC, MC, V.*

$$$ 🏨 **Le Fouquet's.** If you're looking for a comfortable base from which to explore in a quiet residential neighborhood, this is the place. The ambience is welcoming—from the brightly lit archway, plants, and mirrors to the large rooms, decorated in warm shades and decked out with lots of French flounce. ✉ *2 Rond-Point Duboys-d'Angers, 06400,* ☎ *04–93–38–75–81,* FAX *04–92–98–03–39. 10 rooms. AE, DC, MC, V. Closed Nov.–Dec.*

$$ 🏨 **Le Mondial.** A three-minute walk from the beach takes you to this six-story hotel, a haven of unpretentious lodging. Many rooms have sea views and most have small terraces, though the hotel is in the heart of the commercial center, 250 yards from the train station. ✉ *77 rue d'Antibes, 06400,* ☎ *04–93–68–70–00,* FAX *04–93–99–39–11. No credit cards. Closed Nov.*

$–$$ 🏨 **Beverly.** Halfway between the train station and La Croisette is one of the best-value little hotels in central Cannes. The quieter rooms (some with small balconies) are at the back. ✉ *14 rue Hoche, 06400,* ☎ *04–93–39–10–66,* FAX *04–92–98–65–63. 19 rooms, 16 with shower. AE, MC, V. Closed Dec.*

$–$$ 🏨 **Touring Hôtel.** This simple but elegant little hotel, in an ancient town house, is just five minutes from the beach and two minutes from the train station. The place retains a distinct Old World flavor thanks to its high ceilings, solid furnishings, floor-to-ceiling windows, and small balconies. ✉ *11 rue Hoche, 06400,* ☎ *04–93–38–34–40,* FAX *04–93–38–73–34. 30 rooms. AE, DC, MC, V.*

Nightlife and the Arts

The Riviera's cultural calendar is splashy and star-studded, and never more so than during the **International Film Festival** in May. The film screenings are not open to the public, so unless you have a pass, your star-studded glimpses will be on the streets or in restaurants. One of the top night spots all year round is **Studio-Circus** (✉ 48 bd. de la République, ☎ 04–93–38–32–15). **Jimmy's** (✉ Palais des Festivals, ☎ 04–93–38–12–11) admits celebrities, stars, and starlets, but not necessarily everyone else; the cabaret shows are legendary. For insomniacs and gamblers, there are a number of **casinos:** the famous **Casino Croisette** (✉ Palais des Festivals, ☎ 04–93–38–12–11), **Carlton Intercontinental Casino** (✉ 58 bd. de la Croisette, ☎ 04–93–06–40–06), the **Noga Hilton Casino** (☞ *above*), and the **Palm Beach Casino** (✉ Palm Beach).

Outdoor Activities and Sports

Most of the **beaches** along La Croisette are owned by hotels and/or restaurants, and you must pay for a chair or mat to use them; one of the most fashionable is the **Hôtel Carlton Intercontinental's** (☞ *above*). You can easily recognize public beaches by the crowds. Other fee beaches include the **Martinez hotel's,** which has the largest strip in Cannes, **Long Beach,** and **Rado Plage.** Rent **sailboats** from the **Yacht Club de Cannes** (✉ Palm Beach Port) or **Camper & Nicholson's** (✉ Port Canto). Get **windsurfing equipment** from **Le Club Nautique La Croisette** (✉ plage Pointe Palm-Beach) or the **Centre Nautique Municipal** (✉ 9 rue Esprit-Violet). **Bicycles** can be rented from the train station (✉ pl. de la Gare); tool around town or take a scenic ride to Cap Ferrat along the coast road. **Golf courses** in town include **Golf de Biot** (✉ La Bastide du Roy, ☎ 04–93–65–08–48) and **Golf Cannes-Mandelieu** (✉ rte. du Golf, ☎ 04–93–49–55–39).

Shopping

The same chic designer labels that you find in Paris (Chanel, Yves Saint-Laurent, Christian Dior, etc.) can be found for similar prices in Cannes on La Croisette, Rond-Point Duboys-d'Angers, rue des Belges, and rue des Serbes. Sweet tooths head to **Schwartz** (✉ 75 bd. de la République), which is renowned for its candy and macaroons. Almost anything, from strings of garlic to secondhand gravy boats, can be found at the **market** (✉ allées de la Liberté) every Saturday. On the first and third Saturday of each month, an array of old books, posters, and postcards are on sale at the **Marché du Livre Ancien et des Vieux Papiers** (✉ pl. de la Justice).

Îles de Lérins

⓫ *15–30-min boat ride from Cannes Harbor.*

You may want to take a day trip to the peaceful Îles de Lérins (Lerin Islands) off the coast of Cannes to escape the crowds. The ferry (☎ 04–93–39–11–82) leaves from Cannes's harbor (near the Palais des Festivals) approximately every hour. It's a 15-minute, 50-franc trip to **Ste-Marguerite,** an island of wooded hills and a tiny main street lined with fishermen's houses; and a 30-minute, 55-franc trip to the wilder and quieter **St-Honorat,** named for the monk who started a monastery on the island. A ticket to both islands is 60 francs.

Vallauris

12 *5 km (3 mi) north of Cannes on D803, 6 km (4 mi) west of Antibes.*

Ceramics are on sale throughout the pottery-making center of Vallauris, and several workshops can be visited. Picasso spurred a resurgence of activity when he settled here in 1947 and created some whimsically beautiful pieces. The fresco in the tunnel-like medieval chapel of the former priory—now the **Musée National Picasso**—was done by the great man himself. ✉ *pl. de la Libération,* ☎ *04–93–64–18–05.* 🎫 *15 frs.* 🕘 *Mid-Dec.–Oct., Wed.–Mon. 10–noon and 2–6 (until 5 in winter).*

Antibes

13 *11 km (7 mi) northeast of Cannes.*

Founded as a Greek trading port in the 4th century BC, Antibes is now a resort town, fishing port, and, until recently, an important rose-growing center. Antibes officially forms one town (dubbed "Juan-tibes") with the newer, Juan-les-Pins to the south, where beach and nightlife attract a younger and less affluent crowd. In summer, the mood is especially frenetic. **Avenue de l'Amiral-Grasse** runs along the seafront from the harbor to the marketplace, a colorful sight most mornings. The church of the **Immaculate Conception,** on the avenue, has intricately carved portals (dating from 1710) and a 1515 altarpiece by Nice artist Louis Bréa (circa 1455–1523).

★ The **Château Grimaldi,** built in the 12th century by the ruling family of Monaco and extensively rebuilt in the 16th century, is reached by steps near the church of the Immaculate Conception. Tear yourself away from the sunbaked terrace overlooking the sea to go inside the **Musée Picasso.** Roman remains are on exhibit, but the works of Picasso—who occupied the château during his most cheerful and energetic period—hold center stage. ✉ *pl. du Château,* ☎ *04–93–34–91–91.* 🎫 *25 frs.* 🕘 *Dec.–Oct., Wed.–Mon. 10–noon and 2–6 (3–7 July–Sept.).*

St-André Bastion, constructed by the military engineer Sébastien de Vauban in the late 17th century, is home to the **Musée Archéologique.** Here 4,000 years of local history are illustrated. ✉ *av. de l'Amiral-Grasse,* ☎ *04–93–34–48–01.* 🎫 *15 frs.* 🕘 *Dec.–Oct., weekdays 9–noon and 2–6.*

Marineland is only a short distance from Antibes: Take N7 north, then head left at La Brague onto D4. ✉ *309 rue Mozart,* ☎ *04–93–33–49–49.* 🎫 *93 frs.* 🕘 *Apr.–Oct., daily 10–9; Nov.–Mar., daily 10–6; 1st performance at 2:30.*

The **Jungle des Papillons,** opposite Marineland, hosts a fluttering "Butterfly Ballet" that must be seen to be believed. You are requested to wear colored clothing because this stimulates the butterflies into a wing-flapping frenzy. ✉ *309 av. de Mozart,* ☎ *04–93–33–55–77.* 🎫 *30 frs.* 🕘 *Daily 10–5.*

If you want a change of venue, ferries leave from Juan-les-Pins to the **Îles de Lérins** (☞ *above*) hourly in summer.

Dining and Lodging

$$–$$$ ✕ **La Bonne Auberge.** Chef Philippe Rostang creates such specialties as lamb in thyme with kidneys, lobster ravioli, and airy soufflés on his seasonal menus. The dining room is a flower-filled haven of exposed beams, dim lantern lighting, and rose-color walls; huge glass windows allow diners a view of the inspired work in the kitchen. ✉ *quartier de la Brague,* ☎ *04–93–33–36–65. Jacket required.* AE, MC, V. Closed

Mon. (except for dinner mid-Apr.–Sept.), and mid-Nov.–mid-Dec. No lunch Wed. July–Aug.

$$ ★ ✕ **Le Brûlot.** This bistro is one of the busiest in Antibes. Burly Chef Christian Blancheri horses anything from suckling pigs to apple pies in and out of his roaring wood oven, and it's all delicious. The decor is rustic and chaotic and the seating so close it's almost unavoidable to become part of one large unruly mob at this popular spot. ✉ *3 rue Frédéric Isnard,* ☎ *04–93–34–17–76. MC, V. Closed Sun., late Dec.–mid-Jan., last 3 wks of Aug. No lunch Mon.*

$$$$ ★ ✕ 🏨 **Juana.** This luxuriously renovated '30s hotel, near the casino and a couple of blocks from the beach, is run by the second generation of the Barrache family. Service is attentive and rooms are large and individually decorated with creature comforts in mind. Pine trees tower over the grounds and the white marble pool. Chef Christian Morisset wins praise for his fine seafood at La Terrasse, one of the best restaurants on the Côte d'Azur. ✉ *av. Georges-Gallice, 06160 Juan-les-Pins,* ☎ *04–93–61–08–70,* FAX *04–93–61–76–60. 45 rooms. Restaurant, bar, pool. AE, MC, V. Closed late Oct.–mid-Apr.*

$$–$$$ ✕ 🏨 **Auberge de l'Esterel.** The affable Denis Latouche runs the best moderately priced restaurant in Juan-les-Pins, lending a nouvelle twist to local dishes; try the monkfish and, for dessert, the lemon tart. The secluded garden is a romantic setting for dinner under the stars. Rooms are in the small, attached hotel. ✉ *21 rue des Îles, 06160 Juan-les-Pins,* ☎ *04–93–61–74–11. 15 rooms, 6 with bath. Restaurant. MC, V. Closed mid-Nov.–mid-Dec., part of Feb., and Mon. No dinner Sun.*

$$ ✕ 🏨 **Auberge Provençale.** The six rooms in this one-time abbey, complete with exposed beams, canopied beds, and lovely antique furniture, seem out of a romantic Victor Hugo novel. The dining room and the covered garden are decorated with the same impeccable taste; the menu features fresh seafood, duck grilled over wood coals, and excellent bouillabaisse. The restaurant is closed Monday and Tuesday lunch. ✉ *61 pl. Nationale, 06600,* ☎ *04–93–34–13–24,* FAX *04–93–34–89–88. 6 rooms. Restaurant. AE, DC, MC, V.*

$$ 🏨 **Le Mas Djoliba.** There are only 14 rooms in this converted Provençal farmhouse. The salon features an airy bamboo-shoot motif, while the rooms, painted in a range of pastel shades, have antique furnishings. Choose between views of the park or the sea. ✉ *29 av. de Provence, 06600,* ☎ *04–93–34–02–48,* FAX *04–93–34–05–81. 14 rooms. Restaurant. AE, DC, MC, V. Closed Jan.*

Nightlife and the Arts

The **Eden Casino** (✉ bd. Baudoin, Juan-les-Pins, ☎ 04–92–93–71–71) draws a young crowd. For raging till dawn, **La Siesta** (✉ rte. du Bord de Mer, ☎ 04–93–33–01–18) is an enormous setup, with dance floors, bars, and roulette; it's only open in summer.

Outdoor Activities and Sports

Bicycles can be rented from **Juan Midi Location** (✉ 93 bd. Wilson, ☎ 04–92–93–05–06) and **Holiday Bikes** (✉ 93 bd. Wilson, ☎ 04–93–61–51–51).

Cap d'Antibes

★ 14 *2 km (1 mi) from Antibes.*

The Cap d'Antibes peninsula is rich and residential, with beaches, views, and large villas hidden in luxurious vegetation. You gain some appreciation of the wealth in this area when you pass by the Hôtel du Cap Eden Roc on boulevard Kennedy as you cross from Juan-les-Pins onto the peninsula. Barely 3 km long by 1½ km wide (2 mi long by 1 mi wide), it is perfect for a day's outing from Antibes.

Take a walk along the **Sentier des Douaniers,** the customs officers' path. At Pointe Bacon there is a striking view of the Baie des Anges (Bay of Angels) toward Nice. Climb up to the **Plateau de la Garoupe** for a sweeping view inland over the Esterel massif and the Alps. The Sanctuaire de la Garoupe (Sailors' Chapel) has a 14th-century icon, a statue of Our Lady of Safe Homecoming, and numerous frescoes and votive offerings. The ***phare*** (lighthouse) on the Plateau de la Garoupe has a powerful beam that carries more than 64 km (40 mi) out to sea. ✉ *Plateau de la Garoupe.* 🎫 *Free.* ⏲ *Nov.–Mar., daily 10:30–12:30 and 2:30–5; Apr.–Oct., daily 10:30–12:30 and 2–7:30.*

The lovely **Jardin Thuret** was established by botanist Gustave Thuret (1817–75) in 1856 as France's first garden for subtropical plants and trees; it is now run by the Ministry of Agriculture. ✉ *bd. du Cap.* 🎫 *Free.* ⏲ *Weekdays 8–12:30 and 2–5:30.*

At the southwest tip of the peninsula, opposite the luxurious Grand Hôtel du Cap d'Antibes, is the **Musée Naval et Napoléonien,** a former battery, where you can spend an interesting hour scanning Napoleonic proclamations and viewing scale models of oceangoing ships. ✉ *Batterie du Grillon, av. Kennedy,* ☎ *04–93–61–45–32.* 🎫 *20 frs.* ⏲ *Apr.–Sept., weekdays 10–noon and 3–7, Sat. 10–noon; Oct.–Mar., weekdays 9:30–noon and 2:15–4, Sat. 9:30–noon.*

Dining and Lodging

$$$–$$$$ ★ ✕ **Restaurant de Bacon.** At the Riviera's top spot for bouillabaisse and fish the prices generally match the quality, except for the bargain 250-franc lunch and dinner menus. The Sordellos have owned Bacon since 1948, and don't regard a fish as fresh unless it's still twitching. Ask for a table outside on the terrace overlooking the old port and the bay. ✉ *bd. de Bacon,* ☎ *04–93–61–50–02. Reservations essential. Jacket required. AE, DC, MC, V. Closed Mon. and mid-Nov.–Jan.*

$$ 🏨 **Manoir Castel Garoupe Axa.** This old inn is known locally as Motel Axa, after owner Madame Axa. She speaks little English, but smiles and a minimal grasp of French will do. Not deluxe by any means, it's a friendly place and only two minutes from the beach. Rooms have balconies with countryside views. Breakfast is served. ✉ *959 bd. de la Garoupe, 06600,* ☎ *04–93–61–36–51,* FAX *04–93–67–74–88. 27 rooms. Kitchenettes, pool, tennis court. MC, V. Closed early Nov.–mid-Mar.*

Biot

⓯ *4 km (3 mi) northeast of Antibes on N7 and D4, 11 km (7 mi) northeast of Cannes, 22 km (14 mi) southwest of Nice.*

The picturesque old village of Biot is known for its mimosa and roses, grown for flower markets all over the country, as well as for its blown glass and its most famous citizen, artist Fernand Léger (1881–1955). Léger lived in Biot until his death, and hundreds of his paintings, ceramics, and tapestries are on display at the strikingly designed **Musée National Fernand Léger.** Léger's stylistic evolution is traced from his early flirtation with cubism to his ultimate preference for flat expanses of primary color and shades of gray, separated by thick black lines. ✉ *chemin du Val de Pomme,* ☎ *04–93–65–63–61.* 🎫 *32 frs.* ⏲ *Apr.–Oct., Wed.–Mon. 10–noon and 2–6; Nov.–Mar., Wed.–Mon. 10–noon and 2–5.*

At the **Verrerie de Biot** (glassworks) you can observe the glassblowers at work. ✉ *5 chemin des Combes,* ☎ *04–93–65–05–85.* ⏲ *Mon.–Sat. 9–6:30, Sun. 10:30–1 and 2:30–6:30.*

CANNES TO MENTON

Begin in the medieval hill towns of Provence, then dip down through Nice and Monaco to balmy Menton (close to the Italian border). The eastern part of the Riviera has an extraordinary range of sights, from the Grand Canyon du Verdon to the casinos at Monte Carlo.

Mougins

16 *8 km (5 mi) north of Cannes, 12 km (7 mi) northwest of Antibes, 32 km (20 mi) southwest of Nice.*

From quaint, fortified, hilltop Mougins, with its cluster of ancient houses dating from the 15th century, you can see Cannes and the Golfe de Napoule. The **Notre-Dame-de-Vie** hermitage and the **Chapelle St-Barthelmy** with its 17th-century bell tower roofed in colored tiles are the village's most interesting sights. Unfortunately, Mougin's popularity means that you have to park at the bottom of the hill and hike into the old village, which is a little hard to find behind the new houses and shopping centers that form Cannes's suburban sprawl. Don't be misled by signs for Mougins-le-Haut, a huge real-estate development that has become a village in its own right.

Dining and Lodging

$$$$ ★ ✕🏨 **Moulin de Mougins.** Housed in a 16th-century olive mill is a small inn and one of the country's top restaurants. Chef Roger Vergé's repertoire of traditional and innovative cuisine changes seasonally. The intimate beamed dining rooms, with oil paintings, plants, and porcelain tableware, are perfect for world-class fare. In summer, dine outside under the awnings. Reservations are essential for the restaurant, which is closed Monday and Thursday for lunch. Rooms are elegantly rustic; the apartments are small. ✉ *Notre-Dame-de-Vie, 06250,* ☎ *04–93–75–78–24,* FAX *04–93–90–18–55. 3 rooms, 2 apartments. Restaurant. AE, DC, MC, V. Closed Feb.–Mar.*

Grasse

17 *10 km (6 mi) northwest of Mougins, 17 km (10½ mi) northwest of Cannes, 22 km (14 mi) northwest of Antibes, 42 km (25 mi) southwest of Nice.*

If touring a perfume factory in a tacky modern town is your idea of pleasure, by all means visit Grasse. If you had visited four centuries ago, when the town specialized in leather, you would have come for gloves. In the 16th century, when scented gloves became the rage, the town began cultivating flowers and distilling essences. That was the beginning of the perfume industry. Today some three-fourths of the world's essences are made here from wild lavender, jasmine, violets, daffodils, and other sweet-smelling flowers. Five thousand producers supply some 20 factories and six cooperatives. If you've ever wondered why perfume is so expensive, consider that it takes 10,000 flowers to produce 2.2 pounds of jasmine petals and that nearly one ton of petals is needed to distill 1½ quarts of essence. Sophisticated Parisian perfumers mix Grasse essences into their own secret formulas; perfumes made and sold in Grasse are considerably less subtle. You can, of course, buy Parisian perfumes in Grasse at Parisian prices.

Several **perfume houses** welcome visitors—daily 9–noon and 2–6, free—for a whiff of their products and an explanation of how the perfumes are made: Galimard (✉ 73 rte. de Cannes, ☎ 04–93–09–20–00); Molinard (✉ 60 bd. Victor-Hugo, ☎ 04–93–36–01–62); and Fragonard (✉ 20 bd. Fragonard, ☎ 04–93–36–44–65), which is conveniently central and has its own museum. At the **Musée International de la Parfumerie,** the International Perfume Museum, the history and manufacturing process of perfume is explained. Old machinery, pots, and flasks can be admired; toiletry, cosmetics, and makeup accessories are on display. ✉ *8 pl. du Cours,* ☎ *04–93–36–80–20.* 🎫 *14 frs.* ⏲ *Oct.–May, daily 10–noon and 2–5; June–Sept., daily 10–7.*

The artist Jean-Honoré Fragonard (1732–1806) was born in Grasse, and many of his pictures, etchings, drawings, and sketches—plus others by his son Alexandre-Evariste and his grandson Théophile—are hung in the 17th-century **Musée Fragonard.** ✉ *23 bd. Fragonard,* ☎ *04–93–36–01–61.* 🎫 *10 frs.* ⏲ *Wed.–Sun. 10–noon and 2–5.*

The **Musée d'Art et d'Histoire de Provence,** 150 yards away from the Musée Fragonard, in an 18th-century mansion, houses a collection of china and Provençal furniture, folk art, and tools. ✉ *2 rue Mirabeau,* ☎ *04–93–36–01–61.* 🎫 *10 frs.* ⏲ *Apr.–Oct., Mon.–Sat. 10–noon and 2–6; Nov.–Mar., Mon.–Sat. 10–noon and 2–5.*

Lodging

$$ 🏨 **Panorama.** This tidy modern hotel has a pleasant, helpful staff and well-appointed rooms. Some have sunny balconies overlooking Cannes and the sea; these are air-conditioned and more expensive. But breakfast in the morning sun can't be beat. Many of the rooms at the back don't have a view and only have a shower. ✉ *2 pl. Cours, 06130,* ☎ *04–93–36–80–80,* FAX *04–93–36–92–04. 36 rooms with bath or shower. MC, V.*

Route Napoléon

176 km (110 mi) from Grasse to Sisteron.

One of the most famous and panoramic roads in France is the Route Napoléon, taken by Napoléon Bonaparte in 1815 after his escape from imprisonment on the Mediterranean island of Elba. Napoléon landed at Golfe-Juan, near Cannes, on March 1, and forged northwest to Grasse and through dramatic, hilly countryside to Castellane, Digne, and Sisteron. In Napoléon's day, most of this road (now N85) was little more than a winding dirt track. Commemorative plaques bearing the imperial eagle stud the route, inspired by Napoléon's remark that, "The eagle will fly from steeple to steeple until it reaches the towers of Notre-Dame." That prediction came true. Napoléon covered the 176 km (110 mi) from the coast to Sisteron in just four days, romped north through Grenoble and Burgundy, and entered Paris in triumph on May 20.

Except for the occasional inn with the name Napoléon, there are no historical buildings or monuments, bar the plaques. It is the panoramic views as the road winds its way up into the Alps that makes this route so worth traveling. Unless you are heading north to Grenoble, you can easily make a circular day trip along the Route Napoléon, starting from the coast at Grasse. Without stopping, you could reach Sisteron in 90 minutes, so take your time and stop for a picnic along the way. Sisteron, which is guarded by a medieval citadel perched 1,650 feet above the river, is the gateway between Provence and Dauphine. It is also famous for its lamb, the best according to Provençal chefs. At Sisteron, pick up autoroute A51 down to Aix-en-Provence (☞ Chapter 12), then join autoroute A6 to return to the Riviera.

The Corniche Sublime and the Grand Canyon du Verdon

From Grasse, take the Route Napoléon (N85), turn left after 43 km (27 mi) on D21, which becomes D71 at Comps-sur-Artuby.

The Route Napoléon leads to another spectacular road—the Corniche Sublime (D71), which runs along the south side of the Grand Canyon du Verdon, France's answer to the Grand Canyon. The Corniche Sublime is not a road for anyone who is afraid of heights. The narrow lane—just wide enough for two cars to scrape by—snakes its way for 40 km (25 mi), along the cliffside, 3,000 feet above the gorge and the tiny River Verdon. At times the river disappears from view beneath the sheer rock face. At the far end of the gorge you'll arrive at the sparkling blue Lac de Ste-Croix, where you may want to stop for a picnic and a walk.

Trigance

18 *72 km (45 mi) north of Grasse.*

Trigance, a tiny village of stone houses and some 60 souls, is arranged in rampartlike rings around the château. The **Chapelle St-Roch** stands sentinel to the labyrinth of narrow alleys winding to the ancient bell tower and the church of **St-Michel.**

Dining and Lodging

$$–$$$ ✕▣ **Château de Trigance.** Not much remains of the 9th-century original, except for the barrel vaulting in the lounge and dining room. Hospitable owner Monsieur Thomas has spent the last decade reconstructing the castle. The setting, on top of a bluff above a small village, gives commanding views of the surrounding hills. Rooms are comfortable and pleasantly simple. The dining atmosphere is wonderful; the culinary art, average. ✉ *83840 Trigance,* ☏ *04–94–76–91–18,* FAX *04–94–85–68–99. 8 rooms, 2 apartments. Restaurant, helipad. AE, DC, MC, V. Closed early Nov.–mid-Mar.*

Tourrettes-sur-Loup

19 *20 km (12 mi) east of Grasse via D2085 and D2210, 20 km (12 mi) west of Nice.*

The outer houses of Tourrettes form a rampart on a rocky plateau, 1,300 feet above a valley full of violets. The town is much less commercialized than many others in the area; its shops are filled not with postcards and scented soaps but with the work of dedicated artisans. A rough stone path takes you on a circular route around the rim of the town, past their workshops: Ask the local tourist office for a map that locates each of the shops. Also worth visiting is the single-nave 14th-century church with its notable wooden altar.

Vence

20 *5 km (3 mi) east of Tourrettes-sur-Loup, 22 km (13 mi) north of Nice.*

When you arrive in Vence, leave your car on avenue Foch and climb up to the **Vieille Ville** (Old Town), the medieval town. It is a maze of narrow streets with a central square, the place du Peyra. The beauty of this area is that there are real shops—great wine stores, *fromageries* (cheese shops), and *charcuteries* (butcher shops)—aside from touristy restaurants.

The Romans were the first to settle on the 1,000-foot hill. Rising above the medieval ramparts and traffic-free streets of the Old Town is the **Cathédrale.** It was built on the site of a temple to Mars between the 11th and 18th centuries, using Roman stones with inscribed dates of AD 239. Of special note is a Marc Chagall mosaic of Moses in the bulrushes and the ornate 15th-century wooden choir stalls. ✉ *pl. Clemenceau.*

On the outskirts of Vence is the **Chapelle du Rosaire,** a small chapel decorated with beguiling simplicity and clarity by Matisse between 1947 and 1951. The walls, floor, and ceiling are gleaming white and there are small stained-glass windows in cool greens and blues. "Despite its imperfections I think it is my masterpiece . . . the result of a lifetime devoted to the search for truth," wrote Matisse, who designed and dedicated the chapel when he was in his eighties and nearly blind. ✉ *av. Henri-Matisse,* ☎ *04–93–58–03–26.* *Free.* ⌚ *Tues. and Thurs. 10–11:30 and 2–5:30.*

Dining and Lodging

$ ✕ **Le Passe Muraille.** Food at Patrick and Michele Louasse's little restaurant is well-prepared and occasionally innovative. Excellent Sisteron lamb and fresh seafood from Nice are often on the menu. In both the ground floor and stone-arched cellar dining rooms, tables are tight. Patrick's true love is music (he graduated from the Paris conservatory) and Michele has a marvelous voice, so as the evening winds down, he plays and she sings. ✉ *2 rue du Peyra.* ☎ *04–93–58–10–21. Closed Mon. No lunch. MC, V.*

$$$$ ✕ **Château St-Martin.** The secluded, elite St-Martin stands on the site of a Templar castle, surrounded by tall, shady trees. Rooms are exquisitely decorated with antiques and brocade; those in the tower are smaller and less expensive. The excellent restaurant serves Provençal-inspired dishes. ✉ *rte. de Coursegoules, 06140,* ☎ *04–93–58–02–02,* FAX *04–93–24–08–91. 25 rooms. Restaurant, pool, 2 tennis courts. AE, DC, MC, V. Closed mid-Oct.–early May.*

$$ ★ **La Roseraie.** Although there's no rose garden, a giant magnolia spreads its venerable branches over the terrace. The delightful owners, M. and Mme. Ganier, speak excellent English and are quick to help. Mme. Ganier has marvelously decorated the rooms with antiques and warm fabrics; No 2, with its ochre walls and wrought-iron bed, is particularly special; all have sunny southern exposure. Super breakfasts are served on the terrace. ✉ *51 av. Henri-Giraud, 06140,* ☎ *04–93–58–02–20,* FAX *04–93–58–99–31. 12 rooms. Pool. AE, MC, V. Closed Jan.*

St-Paul-de-Vence

21 *4 km (2½ mi) south of Vence on D2; 18 km (11 mi) north of Nice.*

St-Paul-de-Vence is a perfectly preserved medieval town. Not even the hordes of tourists—to which the village now caters—can destroy its ancient charm. You can walk the narrow, cobbled streets in perhaps 15 minutes, but you'll probably need another hour to visit the shops. Your best bet is to come in the late afternoon, when the tour buses are gone, and enjoy a drink among the Klees and Picassos in the Colombe d'Or (☞ Dining and Lodging, *below*). Be sure to stop into the remarkable 12th-century Gothic church. The treasury is rich in 12th- to 15th-century pieces, including processional crosses, reliquaries, and an enamel Virgin and Child.

★ Many people come here just to see the **Fondation Maeght** (founded in 1964 by art dealer Aimé Maeght), one of the world's most famous small modern art museums. Monumental sculptures are scattered around its pine tree park, and a courtyard full of Alberto Giacometti's creations separates the two museum buildings. The rooms inside showcase the works of Miró, Braque, Kandinsky, Bonnard, Matisse, and others. ☎ *04–93–32–81–63.* 🎫 *45 frs.* ⏲ *July–Sept., daily 10–7; Oct.–June, daily 10–12:30 and 2:30–6.*

Dining and Lodging

$$$ ★ ✕🏨 **Colombe d'Or.** Although you'll have to pay for your room or meal with cash or credit cards, Picasso, Klee, Dufy, Utrillo—all friends of the former owner—paid to stay and eat at this country-feeling inn with the paintings that now decorate the walls. The restaurant has a very good reputation. The Colombe d'Or is certainly on the tourist trail, but many of those who stay are rich and famous—if that's any consolation. ✉ *pl. Général-de-Gaulle, 06570,* ☎ *04–93–32–80–02,* FAX *04–93–32–77–78. 24 rooms. Restaurant, pool. AE, DC, MC, V. Closed mid-Nov.–late Dec.*

$$ ✕🏨 **Les Ramparts.** This simple, rustic inn built into the town ramparts is a handy alternative if you feel less than compelled to blow a lot of francs for a night's sleep and don't mind tiny rooms. Excellent Provençal cuisine is served in the restaurant. The corner table in the dining porch is one of the finest perches in Provence. ✉ *72 rue Grande, 06570,* ☎ *04–93–32–09–88. 16 rooms. Restaurant. AE, DC, MC, V. Closed late Nov.–late Dec.*

Cagnes-sur-Mer

22 *6 km (4 mi) south of St-Paul-de-Vence on D2.*

An attractive castle and a Renoir museum make Cagnes-sur-Mer worth a visit. The **Château,** once a medieval fortress, is perched on a hilltop within the walls of Haut-de-Cagnes. Much of its Renaissance decoration—frescoes, plasterwork, and fireplaces—remains intact, and the third floor hosts an art gallery devoted to Mediterranean artists, including Chagall and Raoul Dufy. ✉ *pl. Grimaldi,* ☎ *04–93–20–85–57.* 🎫 *20 frs.* ⏲ *Easter–mid-Oct., daily 10–noon and 2:30–7; mid-Oct.–Easter, Wed.–Mon. 10–noon and 2–5.*

Painter Auguste Renoir (1841–1919) spent the last 12 years of his life at Cagnes and his home has been preserved as the **Musée Renoir.** See his studio, as well as some of his work and a bronze statue of Venus nestled amid the fruit trees in the colorful garden. ✉ *av. des Collettes,* ☎ *04–93–20–61–07.* 🎫 *22 frs.* ⏲ *June–Oct., daily 10–noon and 2–6; Nov.–May, Wed.–Mon. 10–noon and 2–5.*

Villeneuve-Loubet

23 *1½ km (1 mi) west of Cagnes-sur-Mer.*

The tiny village of Villeneuve-Loubet is best known for its gourmet shrine, the **Fondation Escoffier,** a museum dedicated to Auguste Escoffier (1846–1935), one of Europe's top chefs. As kitchen overlord at the London Carlton and the Paris Ritz, he invented, among other dishes, peach melba. The museum, in the house where he was born, displays some elaborate creations in sugar and marzipan and a collection of 15,000 lip-smacking menus. ✉ *3 rue Escoffier,* ☎ *04–93–20–80–51.* 🎫 *15 frs.* ⏲ *Dec.–Oct., Tues.–Sun. 2–6.*

Nice

12 km (7 mi) northeast of Cagnes-sur-Mer on N7; 960 km (600 mi) southeast of Paris.

The congested road from Cagnes to Nice at the wrong time of day or year can be enough to put you off the Riviera for life. Tedious concrete constructions assault the eye; the railroad on one side and the stony shore on the other offer scant respite. Soon, however, you'll arrive at the Queen of the Riviera—Nice. Less glamorous, less sophisticated, and less expensive than Cannes, Nice is also older and more weathered. A big, sprawling city of 350,000 people—five times as many as Cannes—it has a life and vitality that survive when tourists pack their bags and go home.

Nice is worth a visit, but should you stay here? On the negative side, its beaches are cramped and pebbly, though that's true for much of the Riviera. It's congested with traffic and many of its hotels are run-down. On the positive side, Nice is likely to have hotel space, at prices you can afford. If you are using public transportation, it's a convenient base from which to explore the coast, Monte Carlo, and the medieval towns in the interior. It has its share of first-class restaurants, nightclubs, and shops, and an evening stroll through the old town or along the promenade des Anglais is something to savor.

We suggest that you divide your visit to Nice into three short walks,
24 using the arcaded **place Masséna,** the city's main square, as your starting point. You may wish to buy a museum pass (available at any of the museums) if you plan on seeing more than five municipally owned museums. Individual admission to municipal museums is 25 francs; the pass is 125 francs.

From place Masséna, head west through the fountains and gardens of
25 the **Jardin Albert I** to the promenade des Anglais, built, as the name indicates, by the English community in 1824. Traffic on this multilane highway can be heavy, but once you have crossed to the seafront, there are fine views, across private beaches, of the Baie des Anges.

26 The **Palais Masséna,** just off the promenade des Anglais, is a museum concerned principally with the Napoleonic era and, in particular, with the life of local-born general André Masséna (1756–1817). Bonaparte rewarded the general for his heroic exploits during the Italian campaign with the sonorous sobriquet *L'Enfant Chéri de la Victoire* (the Cherished Child of Victory). Sections of the museum evoke the history of Nice and its carnival; there are also some fine Renaissance paintings. ✉ *65 rue de France,* ☎ *04–93–88–11–34.* 🎫 *Free.* ⏲ *Dec.–Oct., Tues.–Sun. 10–noon and 2–5 (3–6 May–Sept.).*

Head west along rue de France, then turn right up avenue des Baumettes
27 to the **Musée des Beaux-Arts Jules-Chéret,** Nice's fine-arts museum, built in 1878 as a palatial mansion for a Russian princess. The rich collection of paintings includes works by Auguste Renoir, Edgar Degas, Claude Monet, and Raoul Dufy; sculptures by Auguste Rodin; and ceramics by Pablo Picasso. Jules Chéret (1836–1932) is best known for his Belle Epoque posters; several of his oils, pastels, and tapestries can be admired here. ✉ *33 av. des Baumettes,* ☎ *04–93–44–53–72.* 🎫 *25 frs.* ⏲ *May–Sept., Tues.–Sun. 10–noon and 3–6; Oct. and Dec.–Apr., Tues.–Sun. 10–noon and 2–5.*

28 To get to the **Russian Orthodox Cathedral** from the north side of place Masséna, take avenue Jean-Médecin, Nice's main shopping street, to avenue Thiers: Take a left (west), pass the train station, turn right on boulevard Gambetta, then make the first left onto boulevard du Tzare-

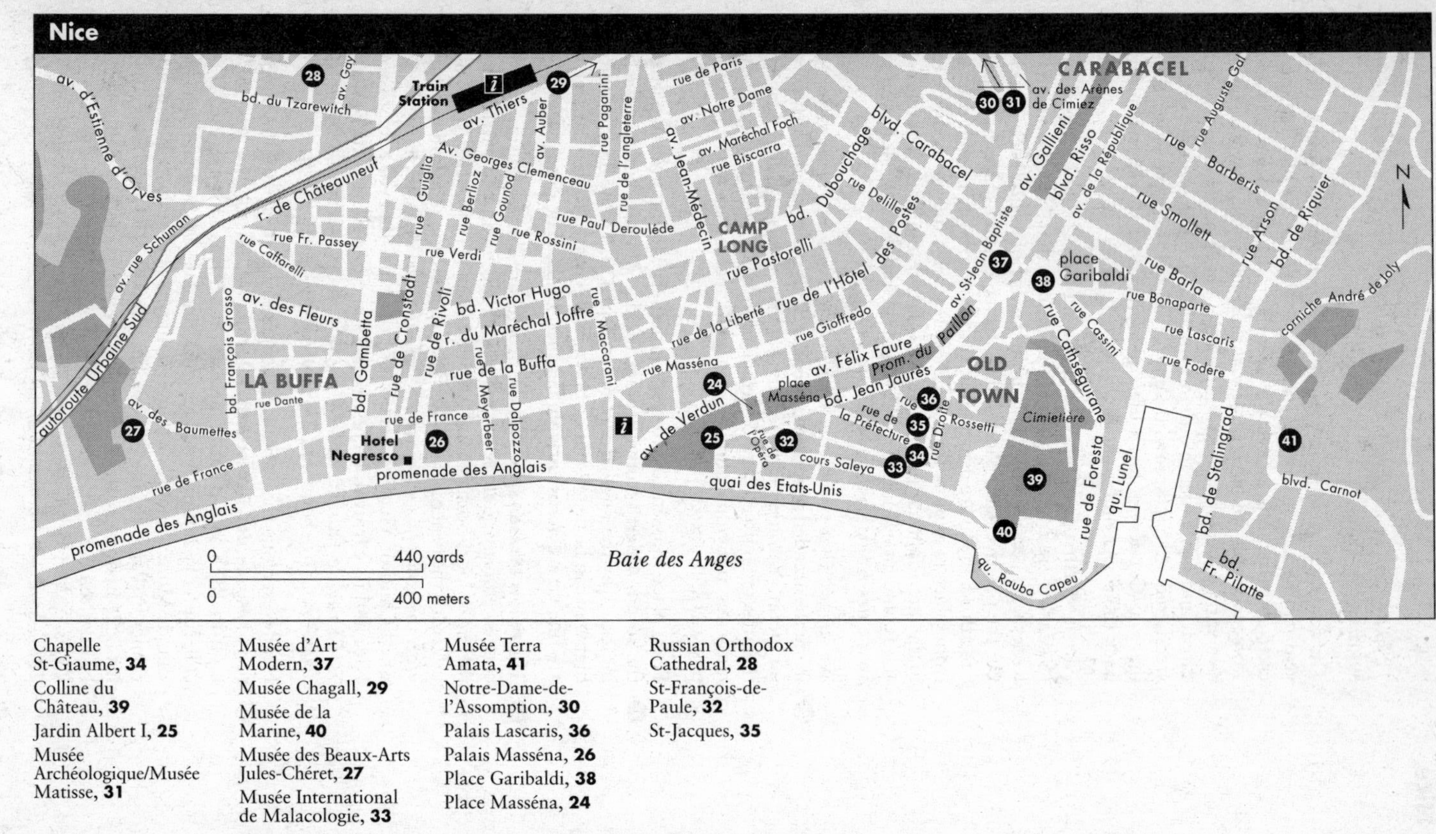

Chapelle St-Giaume, **34**
Colline du Château, **39**
Jardin Albert I, **25**
Musée Archéologique/Musée Matisse, **31**
Musée d'Art Modern, **37**
Musée Chagall, **29**
Musée de la Marine, **40**
Musée des Beaux-Arts Jules-Chéret, **27**
Musée International de Malacologie, **33**
Musée Terra Amata, **41**
Notre-Dame-de-l'Assomption, **30**
Palais Lascaris, **36**
Palais Masséna, **26**
Place Garibaldi, **38**
Place Masséna, **24**
Russian Orthodox Cathedral, **28**
St-François-de-Paule, **32**
St-Jacques, **35**

witch. As the name of the street suggests, the Russian Orthodox Cathedral—a famously unorthodox Nice landmark, with its colorful ceramics, onion domes, and icon-filled interior—is right around the corner. It was built largely with money from Czar Nicholas II (early this century, the Riviera was popular with Russian top brass, too). But within six years of its 1912 grand opening, Czar Nicholas and the "Czarevitch"—his son Alexis—were dead and the Romanov dynasty overthrown. ⊠ *bd. du Tzarewitch.*

29 The **Musée Chagall,** on the northeast side of the train station (head up avenue Thiers, then take a left onto avenue Malausséna, cross the railway tracks, and take the first right), was built to show off the paintings of Marc Chagall (1887–1985) in natural light. The Old Testament is the primary subject of the works, which include 17 huge canvases, 195 preliminary sketches, several sculptures, and nearly 40 gouaches. ⊠ *av. du Dr-Ménard,* ☎ *04–93–81–75–75.* 🎫 *28 frs.* 🕐 *July–Sept., Wed.–Mon. 10–7; Oct.–June, Wed.–Mon. 10–12:30 and 2–5:30.*

Boulevard de Cimiez, just east of the Chagall Museum, runs northeast to the residential quarter of Nice—the hilltop site of **Cimiez,** occupied by the Romans 2,000 years ago. The foundations of the Roman town can be seen, along with vestiges of the arena, which is less spectacular than those at Arles or Nîmes but still in use (notably for a summer jazz
30 festival). The Franciscan monastery of **Notre-Dame-de-l'Assomption,** in Cimiez, has some outstanding late-medieval religious pictures; guided tours include the small museum and an audiovisual show on the life and work of the Franciscans. ⊠ *pl. du Monastère,* ☎ *04–93–81–00–04.* 🎫 *Free.* 🕐 *Mon.–Sat. 10–noon and 3–6.*

31 A 17th-century Italian villa amid the Roman remains houses the **Musée Matisse** and the **Musée Archéologique.** The Matisse Museum has a collection of paintings and bronzes by Henri Matisse (1869–1954), illustrating the different stages of his career. The Archaeology Museum contains a plethora of ancient objects. ⊠ *164 av. des Arènes-de-Cimiez. Musée Matisse:* ☎ *04–93–81–08–08.* 🎫 *25 frs.* 🕐 *Apr.–Oct. daily 10–6; Nov.–Mar. daily 10–5. Musée Archéologique:* ☎ *04–93–81–59–57.* 🎫 *Free.* 🕐 *Dec.–Oct., Tues.–Sat. 10–noon and 2–5, Sun. 2–5.*

★ **Vieux Nice** (Old Nice), on the eastern side of the city, is one of the delights of the Riviera. Cars are forbidden on streets that are so narrow that their buildings crowd out the sky. The winding alleyways are lined with faded 17th- and 18th-century buildings. Flowers cascade from window boxes on soft-pastel-color walls. **Cours Saleya** is one of the main thoroughfares and the sight of a colorful morning market. Head
32 west on cours Saleya to reach the 18th-century church of **St-François-de-Paule** (⊠ rue St-François-de-Paule), renowned for its ornate Baroque interior and sculpted decoration. Head east on cours Saleya to get to
33 the **Musée International de Malacologie,** with its collection of seashells from all over the world (some for sale) and a small aquarium of Mediterranean sea life. ⊠ *3 cours Saleya,* ☎ *04–93–85–18–44.* 🎫 *25 frs.* 🕐 *Dec.–Oct., Tues.–Sat. 10:30–1 and 2–6.*

34 The **Chapelle St-Giaume** (⊠ rue la Poissonnerie), one block north of the cours Saleya, is also known as the Chapelle de l'Annonciation and, to make it more confusing, referred to by locals as the Chapelle du St-Rita. Stop in to admire its gleaming Baroque interior and grand al-
35 tarpieces. **St-Jacques** (⊠ rue de Jésus), around the corner from St-Giaume, features an explosion of painted angels and scenes from the life of St. James on the ceiling. Built in the 17th century along the lines of the Gesù Church in Rome, it became a popular place for notable families to sponsor small chapels on either side of the barrel-vaulted nave.

36 The elegant **Palais Lascaris,** just north of St-Jacques, was built in the mid-17th century in the Genovese style for the Count of Vintimiglia whose family had supported the emperors of Nicaea in Asia Minor during the 13th century. It is decorated with paintings and tapestries and has a particularly grand staircase and a reconstructed 18th-century pharmacy. ✉ *15 rue Droite.* 🎫 *25 frs.* ⏲ *Dec.–Oct., Tues.–Sun. 9:30–noon and 2–6.*

37 The state-of-the-art **Musée d'Art Modern** has four marble-fronted towers overlooking a sculpture-laden concourse. Its collection of French and international abstract and figurative art from the late 1950s onward is outstanding. ✉ *promenade des Arts,* ☎ *04–93–62–61–62.* 🎫 *25 frs.* ⏲ *Wed.–Mon. 11–6, Fri. 11–10.*

38 **Place Garibaldi,** east of the Modern Art Museum, was built in the 18th century in Piedmont style with yellow ochre stone. It used to be the northern edge of the city; now it is a symbol separating Vieux Nice and the new city sprawling inland. The statue in the center of the square is of Giuseppe Garibaldi, one of the principal authors of the Italian revolution of 1860 and a friend of France. On the south side is the **Chapelle du St-Sepulchre,** a Baroque 18th-century building under the auspices of the religious order, Les Penitents Bleus.

39 Dominating Vieux Nice is the **Colline du Château** (Castle Hill), a romantic cliff fortified many centuries before Christ. It's fun to explore the ruins of the 6th-century castle and the surrounding garden. The
40 small **Musée de la Marine** (Naval Museum) is in the 16th-century **Tour Bellanda** (tower). It contains models, instruments, and documents charting the history of the port of Nice. The elevator between the tower and the quay operates daily 9 to 7 in summer and 2 to 6 in winter. ✉ *rue du Château,* ☎ *04–93–80–47–61.* 🎫 *25 frs.* ⏲ *June–Sept., Wed.–Mon. 10–noon and 2–7; Oct.–mid-Nov. and Jan.–May, Wed.–Mon. 10–noon and 2–5.*

41 Relics of a local settlement that was active 400,000 years ago are in the **Musée Terra Amata.** Recorded commentaries in English and films explain the lifestyle of prehistoric dwellers. ✉ *25 bd. Carnot,* ☎ *04–93–55–59–93.* 🎫 *25 frs.* ⏲ *Oct.–mid-Sept., Tues.–Sun. 9–noon and 2–6.*

OFF THE BEATEN PATH

CORSICA – If you have a day or two to spare, a high-speed ferry will whisk you to Corsica (☞ Chapter 14) for less than 300 francs: 2½ hours to Calvi or 3½ hours to Bastia. These ferries, operated by SNCM Ferryterranée (☎ 04–36–67–95–00), depart from Nice twice a day.

Dining and Lodging

$$$$ ✕ **L'Ane Rouge.** In the Vieux Port, this restaurant has been famous for generations as *the* place to go to for fish and seafood. Celebrities frequent the place, so if that whets your appetite, give it a try. The reputation of chef Michel Devilliers, who prepped at Troisgrois, is beyond question. But the feeling here is too serious and too expensive despite the fine cuisine. ✉ *7 quai des Deux-Emmanuel,* ☎ *04–93–89–49–63. Reservations essential. AE, DC, MC, V. Closed Wed. in winter.*

$$ ✕ **Grand Café de Turin.** This booming spot on place Garibaldi is one of Nice's top shellfish emporiums. Eat on the terrace or under the arcaded porticoes of the square. Brown bread and a dozen oysters is a standard order. Ask for *fines de claires,* especially good Atlantic-bred oysters. ✉ *5 pl. Garibaldi,* ☎ *04–93–62–29–52. AE, DC, MC, V. Closed June.*

$$ ✕ **L'Olivier.** Franck Musso bakes his own bread and serves up sturdy Provençal dishes (fish soup, snail ravioli) and homemade desserts, while his brother Christian provides guests with a chirpy welcome to the small, cozy dining room that locals love. ✉ *2 pl. Garibaldi,* ☎ *04–93–26–89–09. Reservations essential. AE, MC, V. Closed Sun., and Aug. No lunch Mon.*

$–$$ ★ ✕ **La Cambuse.** This little bistro on the cours Saleya next to the lovely Chapelle de la Miséricorde is a winner. Aptly named for a ship's storeroom, this sunny place serves fresh seafood and wonderful steamed vegetable dishes on elevated platters to save space on the tables. The resulting proximity of diners and dinner can only be described as erotic. ✉ *5 cours Saleya,* ☎ *04–93–80–12–31. MC, V. Closed Sun.*

$ ✕ **Le Tire Bouchon.** In the heart of Vieux Nice, this small, popular restaurant is made to seem wider by mirrors on the wall. It serves good simple fare at very reasonable prices. The salade niçoise is an obvious choice; less obvious is the salad with smoked duck. Other dishes include curries, entrecôte, and grilled fish. ✉ *19 rue de la Préfecture,* ☎ *04–63–92–63–64. MC, V. Closed Sun.*

$$$$ ✕🏨 **Elysée Palace.** This glass-fronted hotel is close to the seafront and rooms have views of the Mediterranean. The interior is spacious and ultramodern, with plenty of marble. The restaurant is a sound bet for nouvelle cuisine, enjoyed amid contemporary art. ✉ *59 Promenade des Anglais (entrance at 117 rue de France), 06000,* ☎ *04–93–86–06–06,* FAX *04–93–44–50–40. 143 rooms. Restaurant, bar, pool, sauna, health club. AE, DC, MC, V.*

$$$$ ✕🏨 **Negresco.** Henri Negresco wanted to out-Ritz all the Ritzes when he built this place. There were eight kings at the opening ceremony in 1912, grouped on the 560,000-franc gold Aubusson carpet beneath the 1-ton crystal chandelier. No two rooms are the same, though each floor has its own motif based on an epoch from the 16th to the 20th century. Chef Dominique Le Stanc has made the restaurant one of France's finest—it is also one of the most expensive. The brasserie, decorated with carousel horses, serves lighter, less expensive fare. ✉ *37 promenade des Anglais, 06000,* ☎ *04–93–16–64–00,* FAX *04–93–88–35–68. 148 rooms. 2 restaurants, bar, beach.*

$$$–$$$$ ★ ✕🏨 **Beau Rivage.** Occupying an imposing late-19th-century town house near the cours Saleya, this hotel is just a few steps from the best parts of old Nice and the beach. Rooms are decorated in soothing pastels. The hotel's fine restaurant, Le Relais, is expertly directed by the affable Armand. Try the hot goat cheese salad. ✉ *24 rue St-François-de-Paule, 06000,* ☎ *04–93–80–80–70,* FAX *04–93–80–55–77. 106 rooms. Restaurant, beach. AE, DC, MC, V.*

$$ 🏨 **Florence.** This old-yet-modernized hotel, just off rue Jean-Médecin (Nice's major shopping street), is recommended for friendly service, comfort (air-conditioning), and style (marble bathrooms). ✉ *3 rue Paul-Déroulède, 06000,* ☎ *04–93–88–46–87,* FAX *04–93–88–43–65. 56 rooms with bath or shower. Air-Conditioning. AE, DC, MC, V.*

$$ 🏨 **Mirabeau.** This stylishly renovated hotel lies 200 yards from the train station on busy avenue Malausséna, a good 15-minute walk from the beach. Plants, flowers, and leather armchairs brighten up the lobby-breakfast area; rooms, with floral-pattern quilts and functional modern furniture, vary in size. Nos. 206 and 406 are especially pleasant. The owners are extremely friendly and always ready to assist. ✉ *15 av. Malausséna, 06000,* ☎ *04–93–88–33–67,* FAX *04–93–16–14–08. 42 rooms with shower. Bar, air-conditioning. AE, MC, V.*

$ ★ **Hôtel Felix.** On popular, pedestrian rue Masséna and a block from the beach, this tiny hotel is owned by a hard-working couple (both fluent in English) who make guests feel welcome. It is also Nice's best bargain. Other hotels often charge extra for everything, but not the Felix; if you are there for a while and need some laundry done, for instance, the owners will do it with their own. Rooms are compact, but neat and bright, so they don't feel as small. There's also TV with CNN. ✉ *41 rue Masséna, 06000,* ☎ *04–93–88–67–73,* FAX *04–93–16–15–78. 14 rooms with shower or bath. Air-conditioning. AE, DC, MC, V.*

$ **La Mer.** This small hotel is close to Vieux Nice and the seafront. Though rooms are spartan (and carpets sometimes frayed), the location and prices are good, and the staff is generally pleasant. Ask for a room away from the square to be sure of a quiet night. ✉ *4 pl. Masséna, 06000,* ☎ *04–93–92–09–10,* FAX *04–93–85–00–64. 12 rooms with bath or shower. AE, MC, V.*

Nightlife and the Arts

After dark the trendy **Offshore** (✉ 29 rue Alphonse-Karr) comes alive; dress sharply to get past the doorman. If you don't make it into the Offshore, try the young, lively **Bin's Discothèque** (✉ 71 bd. Jean-Béhra). Not much more needs to be said about the **casino** (✉ Promenade des Anglais) other than it is expensive and sophisticated.

The **jazz festival,** held in July, draws international performers from around the world. The **Théâtre de Verdure** (✉ Jardin Albert I, ☎ 04–93–82–38–68) is another spot for jazz and pop; concerts relocate to the **Arènes de Cimiez** in summer. Classical music and ballet performances take place at the **Acropolis** (✉ Palais des Congrès, Esplanade John F. Kennedy, ☎ 04–93–92–80–00). The season at the **Nice Opéra** (✉ 4 rue St-François-de-Paul, ☎ 04–93–85–67–31) extends from September to June.

The **Théâtre Municipal Francis-Gag** (✉ 4 rue St-Joseph, ☎ 04–93–62–00–03) is the place for drama. Plays are also performed at the **Théâtre de Nice** (✉ promenade des Arts, ☎ 04–93–13–90–90).

Outdoor Activities and Sports

Nice's **beaches** extend along the Baie des Anges. Ruhl Plage is one of the most popular, with a good restaurant and facilities for waterskiing, windsurfing, and children's swimming lessons. Neptune Plage has all that plus a sauna.

Rent **bicycles** from the train station (✉ 17 av. Thiers, ☎ 04–36–35–35–35), then take the coast road to Cap d'Antibes or ride through the hills to Villefranche-sur-Mer. In winter, **skiing** is the sport of choice: Nice is just 97 km (60 mi) from Valberg (4,600 feet), Auron (5,250 feet), and Isola (6,500 feet) in the Alps.

Shopping

The main shopping street, **avenue Jean-Médecin,** runs inland from place Masséna; all needs and most tastes are catered to in its big department stores (Nouvelles Galeries, Prisunic, and the split-level Étoile mall). **Soleido** sells lovely clothes in very French print fabrics (✉ 1 bis rue du Paradis). Olive oil by the gallon, in cans sporting colorful, old-fashioned labels, is sold at tiny **Alziari** (✉ 14 rue St-François-de-Paule); from November to April you can visit Alziari's "oil mill" (✉ 318 bd. de la Madeleine). **Henri Auer** (✉ 7 rue St-François-de-Paule) has a good selection of crystallized fruit, a Nice specialty. Seafood of all kinds is sold at the **fish market** (✉ pl. St-François). The **flea market** (✉ pl. Robilante) by the Old Port is held Tuesday through Saturday and every first

Sunday of the month. The daily **flower market** (✉ cours Saleya) features all kinds of plants and mounds of fruits and vegetables.

En Route There are three scenic roads at various heights above the coast between Nice and Monte Carlo, a distance of about 19 km (12 mi). All are called "corniches"—literally, a projecting molding along the top of a building or wall. The **Basse** (lower) **Corniche** is the busiest and slowest route because it passes through all the coastal towns. The **Moyenne** (middle) **Corniche** is high enough for views and close enough for details. It passes the perched village of Eze. The **Grande** (upper) **Corniche** winds some 1,300 to 1,600 feet above the sea, giving sweeping views of the coast. It follows the Via Aurelia, the great Roman military road that brought Roman legions from Italy to Gaul (France). In 1806 Napoléon rebuilt the road and sent Gallic troops into Italy. The best advice is to take the Moyenne Corniche one way and the Grande Corniche the other. The view from the upper route is best in the early morning or evening.

Villefranche-sur-Mer

42 *4 km (2½ mi) east of Nice on the Basse Corniche (N98).*

Be sure to include Villefranche on a tour of Cap Ferrat; it is the least commercialized of the Riviera's old fishing ports. With its steep narrow streets—one, rue Obscure, is actually a tunnel winding down to the sea—the town is a miniature version of old Marseille. It is also a stage set of brightly colored houses. The 17th-century church of **St-Michel** (✉ pl. Poullan), in the center of the old town, has a strikingly realistic Christ carved of boxwood by an unknown convict.

The **Cocteau Chapel,** also known as **St-Pierre-des-Pêcheurs,** near the port, is a small Romanesque chapel that was once used for storing fishing nets and was decorated by French writer and painter Jean Cocteau in 1957. Walk through the flames of the Apocalypse (represented by staring eyes on either side of the door) and enter a room filled with frescoes of St. Peter, Gypsies, and the women of Villefranche. ✉ *pl. Pollanais.* 🎫 *15 frs.* ⏲ *May–Oct., Tues.–Sun. 9–noon and 2:30–7; Dec.–Apr., Tues.–Sun. 9:30–noon and 2:30–5.*

Guarding Villefranche is the **Citadelle,** built in 1557 on the site of a smaller fort. On the orders of the Sun King, Louis XIV, the Citadel was partially demolished along with the other defenses of the county of Nice. Much of the fort still remains, though, with its imposing walls, which house the **Town Hall** and the **Fondation Musée Volyi** with its collection of contemporary sculpture. ✉ *Citadelle de Villefranche,* ☎ *04–93–76–61–00. Museum:* 🎫 *15 frs.* ⏲ *Daily 10–noon and 3–7.*

Lodging

$$$ 🏨 **Hôtel Welcome.** When Villefranche was fashionably exclusive, writer Somerset Maugham stayed in one of the low-ceilinged *chambres bâteaux* (boat rooms) on the top floor. These romantic rooms (especially No. 56) with private balconies feel as if they are cabins in a grand old liner. Most guests prefer the lighter, more traditionally furnished rooms with bay views. Prices reflect the hotel's superb location on the quai in the old village (two rooms have views of both the bay and the harbor) rather than luxury. But this is the only place in the old village you would want to stay. ✉ *quai Courbet, 06230,* ☎ *04–93–76–76–93,* FAX *04–93–01–88–81. Restaurant. Closed mid-Nov.–mid-Dec. MC, V.*

Beaulieu

43 *6 km (4 mi) east of Villefranche-sur-Mer, 10 km (6 mi) east of Nice.*

Beaulieu was a turn-of-the-century high society haunt and you can still get a flavor for how things used to be if you walk along the promenade, sometimes called Petite Afrique (Little Africa) because of its magnificent palm trees.

In the early part of the century, a rich amateur archaeologist named Théodore Reinach asked an Italian architect to build an authentic Greek house for him here. The **Villa Kérylos** is a faithful reproduction, made from cool Carrara marble, alabaster, and rare fruitwoods. The furniture, of wood inlaid with ivory, bronze, and leather, was copied from drawings of Greek interiors found on ancient vases and mosaics. ✉ *rue Gustave-Eiffel,* ☎ *04–93–01–01–44.* 🎫 *40 frs.* ⏲ *July–Aug., weekdays 3–7, weekends 10:30–12:30 and 3–7; Sept.–June, Tues.–Fri. 2–5:30, weekends 10:30–12:30 and 2–5:30.*

St-Jean-Cap-Ferrat

44 *1 km (½ mi) south of Beaulieu on D25.*

The lush peninsula of St-Jean-Cap-Ferrat has 17 acres of gardens, as well as a richly varied art museum. The **Musée Ephrussi de Rothschild** reflects the sensibilities of its former owner, Madame Ephrussi de Rothschild, sister of Baron Edouard de Rothschild. An insatiable collector, she surrounded herself with an eclectic but tasteful collection of Impressionist paintings, Louis XIII furniture, rare Sèvres porcelain, and objets d'art from the Far East. The remarkable gardens provide a mini–world tour: Provençal-, Japanese-, Spanish-, and Florentine-style gardens surround the centerpiece, a garden shaped in the form of a boat. ✉ *Villa Île-de-France,* ☎ *04–93–01–33–09.* 🎫 *38 frs. Guided tours 17 frs extra.* ⏲ *June–Sept., daily 10–6; Oct.–May, weekdays 2–6, weekends 10–6.*

Peillon

45 *19 km (12 mi) northeast of Nice on D2204 to D21, then right up the mountain.*

Of all the perched villages along the Riviera, the fortified medieval town of Peillon, on a craggy mountaintop more than 1,000 feet above the sea, is the most spectacular and the least spoiled. Unchanged since the Middle Ages, the village has only a few narrow streets and many steps and covered alleys. There's really nothing to do here but look—which is why the tour buses stay away, leaving Peillon uncommercialized for the 50 families who live there—including professionals summering away from Paris and artists who want to escape the craziness of the world below. Visit the Chapelle des Pénitents Blancs (Chapel of the White Penitents)—the key is available at the Auberge de la Madone (☞ *below*).

Dining and Lodging

$$ ✕🏨 **Auberge de la Madone.** Above a tiny square at the edge of town, this charming inn serves a lunch of regional cuisine on its wide veranda. Rooms have exposed beams; some have terraces and fabulous views, from which you can daydream of the damsels and knights who dwelt in Peillon. ✉ *06440 Peillon Village,* ☎ *03–93–79–91–17,* FAX *03–93–79–99–36. 19 rooms. Restaurant. Closed mid-Oct.–mid-Dec., and early Jan.–late Jan. MC, V.*

Eze

46 *2 km (1 mi) east of Beaulieu, 12 km (7 mi) east of Nice, 8 km (5 mi) west of Monte Carlo.*

Almost every tour from Nice to Monaco includes a visit to the medieval hill town of Eze, perched on a rocky spur near the Moyenne Corniche, some 1,300 feet above the sea. (Don't confuse Eze with the beach town of Eze-sur-Mer, which is down by the water on the Basse Corniche. If you arrive by train from Nice, there is a shuttle bus, in summer, between Eze-sur-Mer and Eze Village.) Although Eze has its share of serious craftspeople, most of its vendors cater to the crowds of tourists.

Enter the town through the fortified 14th-century gate and wander down the narrow, cobbled streets with vaulted passageways and stairs. The church is from the 18th century, but the small **Chapelle des Pénitents Blancs** dates from 1306 and contains a 13th-century gilded wooden Spanish Christ and some notable 16th-century paintings. Touristy and crafts shops line the streets leading to the ruins of the castle, which has a scenic belvedere.

Near the top of the village is the **Jardin Exotique,** a garden with exotic flowers and cacti. It's worth the admission price, but it's not as nice as the one in Monte Carlo. ✉ *rue du Château,* ☎ *04–93–41–10–30.* 🎫 *12 frs.* ⏲ *June–Sept., 9–8; Oct.–May, 9–noon and 2–5.*

If you're not going to Grasse (☞ *above*), consider visiting a branch of a Grasse perfumery, **La Parfumerie Fragonard,** in front of the public gardens. ✉ *Moyenne Corniche,* ☎ *04–93–41–05–05.* 🎫 *free.* ⏲ *Daily 8:30–6:30.*

Dining and Lodging

$$$$ ★ ✕🏨 **Château de la Chèvre d'Or.** A member of the Relais & Châteaux group, this hotel comprises a number of ancient houses whose mellow stone walls are set off by terra-cotta pots brimming with geraniums. Rooms are small and decorated with antiques; ask for No. 9. Views from the poolside terrace are sensational. The bar is in a medieval room with stone walls and Louis XIII furniture. The restaurant is dignified, but pricey. Swallow the price and you can enjoy beautifully presented cuisine, scented, as chef Mazot likes to say, with the perfumes of Provence. ✉ *rue du Barri, 06360,* ☎ *04–93–41–12–12,* FAX *04–93–41–06–72. 28 rooms. Restaurant, bar, café, pool. AE, DC, MC, V. Closed mid-Nov.–early Mar.*

Monaco

8 km (5 mi) east of Eze on the Moyenne Corniche, 20 km (12 mi) east of Nice.

The Principality of Monaco covers just 473 acres and would fit comfortably inside New York's Central Park or a family farm in Iowa. Its 5,000 citizens would fill only a small fraction of the seats in Yankee Stadium. Note that when calling Monaco from France or elsewhere, you must first dial the country code, 377.

The present ruler, Prince Rainier III, traces his ancestry to Otto Canella, who was born in 1070. The Grimaldi dynasty began with Otto's great-great-great-grandson, Francesco Grimaldi, also known as Frank the Rogue. Expelled from Genoa, Frank and his cronies disguised themselves as monks and seized, in 1297, the fortified medieval town known today as the Rock. Except for a short break under Napoléon, the Grimaldis have been here ever since, which makes them the oldest reigning family in Europe. On the Grimaldi coat of arms are two monks

Casino, **47**
Cathédrale, **51**
Jardin Exotique, **53**
Loew's Casino, **48**
Musée National, **49**
Musée Océanographique, **52**
Museum of Prehistoric Anthropology, **54**
Palais du Prince, **50**

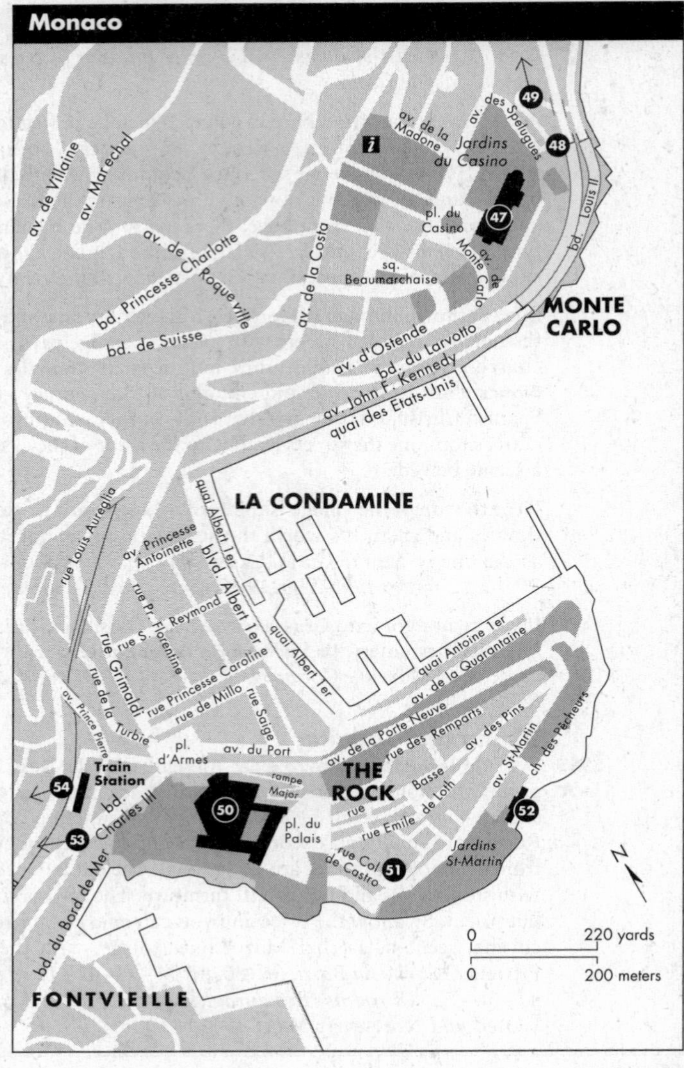

holding swords (look up and you'll see them above the main door as you enter the palace).

Back in the 1850s, a Grimaldi named Charles III made a decision that turned the Rock into a giant blue chip. Needing revenues but not wanting to impose additional taxes on his subjects, he contracted with a company to open a gambling facility. The first spin of the roulette wheel was on December 14, 1856. There was no easy way to reach Monaco then—no carriage roads or railroads—so no one came. Between March 15 and March 20, 1857, one person entered the casino—and won two francs. In 1868, however, the railroad reached Monaco, filled with wheezing Englishmen who came to escape the London fog. The effects were immediate. Profits were so great that Charles eventually abolished all direct taxes.

Almost overnight, a threadbare principality became an elegant watering hole for European society. Dukes (and their mistresses) and duchesses (and their gigolos) danced and dined their way through a world of spinning roulette wheels and bubbling champagne—preening themselves for nights at the opera, where such artists as Vaslav Nijinsky, Sarah Bernhardt, and Enrico Caruso came to perform.

Monte Carlo—the modern gambling town with elegant shops, man-made beaches, high-rise hotels, and a few Belle Epoque hotels—is actually only one of four parts of Monaco. The second part is Old Monaco, the medieval town on the Rock, 200 feet above the sea. It's here that Prince Rainier lives. The third area is La Condamine, the commercial harbor area with apartments and businesses. Fontvieille, the fourth area of Monaco, is an industrial district on 20 acres of reclaimed land.

Start at the **tourist office** (✉ av. de la Costa), just north of the casino gardens. Ask for the useful English booklet *Getting Around in the Principality* to give you an idea about which buses you can use. For what to see and where to find it, request the booklet *Monaco's Tourist Attractions.*

★ 47 Place du Casino is the center of Monte Carlo and the **casino** is a must-see, even if you don't bet a sou. You may find it fun to count the Jaguars and Rolls-Royces parked outside and breathe on the windows of shops selling Yves Saint-Laurent dresses and fabulous jewels. Into the gold-leaf splendor of the casino, where fortunes have been won and shirts have been lost, the hopeful traipse from tour buses to tempt fate at slot machines beneath the gilt-edged rococo ceiling. The main gambling hall, once called the European Room, has been renamed the **American Room** and fitted with 150 one-armed bandits from Chicago. Adjoining it is the **Pink Salon,** now a bar where unclad nymphs float about on the ceiling smoking cigarillos. The **Salles Privées** (Private Rooms) are for high rollers. ✉ *pl. du Casino.* ⏲ *noon–the last die is thrown. Jacket and tie in the back rooms, which open at 4* PM. *Bring your passport (under-21s not admitted).*

In the true spirit of the town, it seems that the **Opéra,** with its 18-ton gilt-bronze chandelier, is part of the casino complex. The designer, Charles Garnier, also built the Paris Opera. ✉ *pl. du Casino.*

48 The serious gamblers, some say, play at **Loews Casino.** It opens weekdays at 4 PM and weekends at 1 PM. You may want to try parking here, since parking near the old casino is almost impossible.

From place des Moulins there is an escalator down to the Larvotto beach
49 complex, artfully created with imported sand, and the **Musée National,** housed in a Garnier villa within a rose garden. This museum has a beguiling collection of 18th- and 19th-century dolls and mechanical automatons. ✉ *17 av. Princesse Grace,* ☎ *93–30–91–26.* 🎟 *28 frs.* ⏲ *Daily Easter–Aug., 10–6:30; Sept.–Easter, 10–12:15 and 2:30–6:30.*

50 Prince Rainier spends much of the year in his grand Italianate **Palais du Prince** on the Rock. The changing of the guard takes place here each morning at 11:55, and the State Apartments can be visited in summer. ☎ *93–25–18–31.* 🎟 *35 frs. Joint ticket with Musée Napoléon 40 frs.* ⏲ *June–Oct., daily 9:30–6:30.*

One wing of the palace, open throughout the year, is taken up by the **Musée Napoléon,** filled with Napoleonic souvenirs and documents related to Monaco's history. ☎ *93–25–18–31.* 🎟 *25 frs. Joint ticket with palace apartments as above.* ⏲ *Tues.–Sun. 9:30–6:30.*

51 The **Cathédrale,** a short stroll though the medieval alleyways near the Napoléon museum, is a neo-Romanesque monstrosity (1875–84), with several important paintings of the Nice school. ✉ *rue Col de Castro.*

52 One of Monaco's most outstanding showpieces, the **Musée Océanographique,** is an important research institute headed by celebrated underwater explorer and filmmaker Jacques Cousteau (his films are shown in the museum cinema). Prince Rainier's great-grandfather Albert I (1848–1922), an accomplished marine biologist, founded the institute in 1910. It now has two exploration ships, laboratories, and a staff of 60 scientists. Nonscientific visitors may wish to go straight to the well-arranged and generously stocked aquarium in the basement. Other floors are devoted to Prince Albert's collection of seashells and whale skeletons and to Cousteau's diving equipment. For a fine view and a restorative drink, take the elevator to the roof terrace. ✉ *av. St-Martin,* ☏ *93–15–36–00.* 🎫 *70 frs.* ⏲ *July–Aug., daily 9–8; Sept.–June, daily 9:30–7 (6 in winter).*

53 Six hundred varieties of cacti and succulents cling to a sheer rock face at the **Jardin Exotique** (Tropical Gardens), a brisk half-hour walk west from the palace. ✉ *bd. du Jardin Exotique,* ☏ *93–30–33–65.*

54 The **Museum of Prehistoric Anthropology,** on the grounds of the tropical gardens, contains bones, tools, and other artifacts. Shapes of the stalactites and stalagmites in the cavernous grotto (entered from the gardens) resemble the cacti outside. ✉ *bd. du Jardin Exotique,* ☏ *93–15–80–06.* 🎫 *39 frs.* ⏲ *Daily 9–7 (dusk in winter).*

Dining and Lodging

$$$$ ★ ✕ **Louis XV.** This restaurant, in the Hôtel de Paris (☞ *below*), stuns with royal decor and superb food made by chef Alain Ducasse, one of Europe's most celebrated chefs. Ducasse often refers to his deceptively simple style as "country cooking." Using the sensual flavors of Provence and northern Italy and nothing but the finest produce, he creates dishes such as braised baby pigeon with duck foie gras and milk-fed lamb stuffed with a mixture fragrant with black olives. ✉ *Hôtel de Paris, pl. du Casino,* ☏ *92–16–30–01. Closed Tues. and Wed. (except dinner July–Aug.), mid-Feb.–early Mar., and late Nov.–late Dec.*

$$–$$$ ✕ **Port.** Harbor views from the terrace and top-notch Italian food make the Port a good choice. The large, varied menu includes shrimp, lasagna, fettuccine, and fish risotto. ✉ *quai Albert-I,* ☏ *93–50–77–21. AE, DC, MC, V. Closed Mon. and Nov.*

$–$$ ★ ✕ **Polpetta.** This popular little trattoria is close enough to the Italian border to pass for the real McCoy. If it's on the menu, go for the vegetable soupe au pistou and the *risotto al porcini* (risotto with wild mushrooms). ✉ *2 rue Paradis,* ☏ *93–50–67–84. Reservations essential in summer. MC, V. Closed Feb. No lunch Tues. or Sat.*

$ ✕ **Le Bistrot.** At this restaurant, which is popular with locals and tourists alike at lunch, you can sit outside and watch the activities of the port, sit inside at banquettes, or just have a drink at the bar. The menu du jour of 60 francs might include grilled sardines or a small entrecôte steak. ✉ *21 bd. Albert-I,* ☏ *93–30–26–88. Closed Sun. MC, V.*

$$$$ ✕🏨 **Hermitage.** Even if you're not staying, come to see the glass-dome Art Nouveau vestibule and the white-stucco rococo corridor leading to the lavish dining room, where pink marble columns hold up a gilded, frescoed ceiling. The adjacent terrace has a tinkling pianist in summer and a view of the harbor. Rooms are comfortable but far less stylish; not all face the sea—and these are priced accordingly. The hotel is one block west of the casino. ✉ *sq. Beaumarchais, BP 277, 98005,* ☏ *92–16–40–00,* FAX *93–50–47–12. 216 rooms, 25 apartments. Restaurant, bar, pool. AE, DC, MC, V.*

$$$$ ✕🏨 **Hôtel de Paris.** This hotel has one of the most prestigious addresses, and you pay for it at every turn. The hotel exudes the ambience of an era in which kings and grand dukes were regulars, though the hallways and public areas are not as striking as you might expect. The spacious, yellow-painted rooms have high ceilings, floral-patterned curtains, and white, wood furniture; from some you can see the sea or the casino. Dinner is served in the superb Louis XV (☞ *above*); breakfast (a Continental runs 140 francs) is served on the terrace in Le Côte Jardin; and Mediterranean-style cuisine is served in Le Grill. ✉ *pl. du Casino, 98000,* ☎ *92–16–30–00,* FAX *92–16–38–49. 143 rooms, 41 suites, and 19 junior suites. 4 restaurants, 1 indoor and 1 outdoor pool, spa. AE, DC, MC, V.*

$$$$ ✕ **Loews.** Big, brash, and more than a touch vulgar, Loews has a plush extravagance on a scale Donald Trump would envy. Contemporary rooms are decorated in ice cream shades. Celebrities mix with sheikhs in the bars, casino, and restaurants. Diehard football fans can watch the Super Bowl by satellite; those in search of live entertainment can head for the Folie Russe cabaret. ✉ *12 av. des Spélugues, 98000,* ☎ *93–50–65–00,* FAX *93–30–01–57. 650 rooms, 69 apartments. 3 restaurants, pool, hot tub, health club, casino. AE, DC, MC, V.*

$$ **Alexandra.** Shades of the Belle Epoque linger in this comfortable hotel's spacious lobby and airy rooms; tan and rose colors dominate the newer ones. If you're willing to do without a private bath, you can save 150 francs. The friendly proprietress, Madame Larouquie, makes foreign visitors feel right at home. ✉ *35 bd. Princesse-Charlotte, 98000,* ☎ *93–50–63–13,* FAX *92–16–06–48. 55 rooms, 46 with bath. Air-conditioning. AE, DC, MC, V.*

Nightlife and the Arts

There's no need to go to bed before dawn in Monte Carlo when you can go to the **casino** (✉ pl. du Casino). **Jimmy's** (✉ pl. du Casino Sept.–June, av. Princesse Grace July–Oct.) is another fun spot. If you can't get in to Jimmy's, try the neighboring, chic, and slightly younger **Parady's** (✉ av. Princesse Grace). The **Living Room** (✉ 7 av. des Spélugues) is a popular, crowded bar open year-round. **Tiffany's** (✉ 3 av. des Spélugues) is another year-round hot spot. **Harry's** piano bar (✉ 19 av. Charles-III) often attracts good jazz singers.

Monte Carlo's spring arts festival, **Printemps des Arts,** takes place from early April to mid-May and includes the world's top ballet, operatic, symphonic, and chamber performers. The **Théâtre Princesse Grace** (✉ 12 av. d'Ostende, ☎ 93–25–32–27) stages a number of plays during the spring festival; off-season, there's usually a new show each week. Year-round, ballet and classical music can be seen at the **Salle Garnier** (✉ pl. du Casino, ☎ 93–50–76–54).

Outdoor Activities and Sports

The best **beaches** in Monte Carlo are Plage Monte Carlo and Plage du Larvotto, the public beach. Both are off avenue Princesse Grace and both have a variety of water sports facilities. Diving equipment can be rented from the **Under Water Diving Club** (✉ quai des Sanbarbani, ☎ 92–05–91–78). Sailboats are available at the **Monaco Yacht Club** (✉ 16 quai Antoine I, ☎ 93–30–63–63). The 18-hole **Golf de Monte Carlo** (✉ rte. du Mont-Agel, 06329 La Turbie, ☎ 93–41–09–11) is open to the public. The **Monte Carlo Tennis Tournament** is held during the Spring Arts Festival. When the tennis stops, the racing begins: The **Grand Prix de Monaco** (☎ 93–15–26–00 for information) takes place in mid-May.

Roquebrune

55 *5 km (3 mi) east of Monaco.*

The hilltop village of Roquebrune has a Carolingian castle, medieval houses, covered steps, and narrow streets. The adjacent Cap Martin peninsula is colonized by wealthy villa dwellers. Near the tip, on avenue Winston-Churchill, is the start of a coastal path—promenade Le Corbusier—that leads to Monte Carlo in 1½ hours.

Menton

56 *9 km (5½ mi) east of Monaco.*

Next door to Roquebrune is Menton, a comparatively quiet resort town with the warmest climate on the Riviera. Lemon trees flourish here, as do senior citizens, enticed by a long strand of beaches. Menton likes to call itself the Pearl of the Riviera—beautiful, respectable, and not grossly expensive.

Walk eastward from the casino along promenade du Soleil to the harbor where there is a small 17th-century fort housing the **Musée Cocteau.** Writer, artist, and filmmaker Jean Cocteau (1889–1963) once worked here. The museum has a fantastic array of his paintings, drawings, stage sets, and a large mosaic. ✉ *Bastion du Port, 111 quai Napoléon-III,* ☎ *04–93–57–72–30.* 🎫 *Free.* ⏲ *Apr.–Oct., Wed.–Sun. 10–noon and 2–6; Nov.–Mar., Wed.–Sun. 10–noon and 3–6.*

The quaint **Vieille Ville** above the jetty has an Italian feel to it. The church of **St-Michel** (✉ rue St-Michel) has an ornate Baroque interior and altarpiece of St-Michel slaying a dragon. Chamber music concerts take place in the square on summer nights. Walk up through the old town to get to the **Vieux Cimetière** (Old Cemetery) and a magnificent view of the old town and coast. Here lie Victorian foreigners who hoped (in vain, as the dates on the tombstones reveal) that Menton's balmy climate would reverse the ravages of tuberculosis.

In the center of town is the **Hôtel de Ville.** The room in which civil marriage ceremonies are conducted has vibrant allegorical frescoes by Cocteau; a tape in English helps to interpret them. ✉ *17 av. de la République.* 🎫 *5 frs.* ⏲ *Weekdays 8:30–12:30 and 1:30–5.*

On the west side of town is the **Palais Carnolès,** an 18th-century villa once used as a summer retreat by the princes of Monaco. The gardens are beautiful, and the collection of European paintings (13th to 18th century) is extensive. ✉ *3 av. de la Madone,* ☎ *04–93–35–49–71.* 🎫 *Free.* ⏲ *Wed.–Sun. 10–noon and 2–6.*

Dining and Lodging

$$ ✕🏨 **Londres.** This small, central hotel is close to the beach and the casino. Rooms are plain but clean. The restaurant serves solid, traditional French cuisine; in summer, meals are served in the small garden. The restaurant is closed Wednesday. ✉ *15 av. Carnot, BP 73, 06502,* ☎ *04–93–35–74–62,* FAX *04–93–41–77–78. 26 rooms with shower or bath. Restaurant, bar. AE, MC, V.*

Nightlife and the Arts

The **casino** (✉ promenade de Soleil) has the usual slot machines and roulette tables, as well as top-class cabaret in its Club 06. In August a **Chamber Music Festival** takes place in the church of St-Michel. The **September Music Festival,** at the Palais d'Europe (✉ av. Boyer), also focuses on chamber music.

THE RIVIERA A TO Z

Arriving and Departing

By Car

If you're traveling from Paris by car, you can avoid a lengthy drive by taking the overnight motor-rail (*train-auto-couchette*) service to Nice, which departs from Paris (Gare de Bercy). Otherwise, leave Paris by A6 (becoming A7 after Lyon), which continues down to Avignon. Here A8 branches off east toward Italy, with convenient exit/entry points for all major towns (except St-Tropez, which is some 30 km/19 mi south on a minor road branching off A8). Driving nonstop from Paris to Nice takes about eight hours; if you are driving from Provence (such as Aix-en-Provence) to Nice, allow 90 minutes.

By Plane

The area's only international airport is the **Aéroport Nice–Côte d'Azur** in Nice (☎ 04–93–21–30–12). Air France and Air Inter have many flights to Paris daily. Air Corse Méditerranée has flights to Corsica.

By Train

The high-speed TGV (Trains à Grande Vitesse) from Paris (Gare de Lyon) to Nice takes about seven hours. Regular SNCF trains from Paris to Nice take more than 10 hours, so reserve a *couchette* (an overnight sleeping car). Frequent daily local trains run along the coast from Nice to Menton. For Monaco, take a connecting train out of Nice; the trip takes 30 to 40 minutes.

Getting Around

By Bus

Local buses cover a network of routes along the Riviera and stop at many out-of-the-way places that can't be reached by train. Timetables are available from tourist offices, train stations, and local bus depots (*gares routières*).

By Car

If you prefer to avoid the slower, albeit spectacularly scenic, coastal roads (especially in summer), opt for the Italy-bound A8. While trains are convenient along the coast, it is really only with a car that you can appreciate the beauty of the inland hills and villages.

By Train

The train is a practical and inexpensive way of getting around the Riviera and stops at dozens of stations. Pick up a schedule at any of the local train stations to plan your times, but don't worry too much about missing a train as they run frequently during the day. Nice's train station (✉ av. Thiers, ☎ 04–93–87–50–50) serves all lines along the Riviera. Note that the pretty Nice–Digne line is not run by the SNCF but by the Chemin de Fer de Provence (✉ Gare du Sud, 33 av. Malausséna, Nice, ☎ 04–93–88–28–56).

Contacts and Resources

Car Rental

Avis (✉ 9 av. d'Ostende, Monaco, ☎ 04–93–30–17–53; and av. du 8-Mai-1945, St-Tropez, ☎ 04–94–97–03–10). **Europcar** (✉ 9 av. Thiers, Menton, ☎ 04–93–28–21–80). **Hertz** (✉ 147 rue d'Antibes, Cannes, ☎ 04–93–99–04–20; and 12 av. de Suède, Nice, ☎ 04–93–87–11–87).

Guided Tours

Any tourist office will produce a sheaf of suggestions on gourmandizing, golfing, and walking tours, among others. **Novatour** (✉ 9 rue de Lille, 06400 Cannes, ☏ 04–93–69–47–47) arranges tailor-made packages, though museum tours are a specialty. **Santa Azur** (✉ 11 av. Jean-Médecin, 06000 Nice, ☏ 04–93–85–46–81, FAX 04–93–87–90–08) organizes a variety of bus tours (most starting from the bus station, or gare routière, on Promenade du Paillon in Nice; but sometimes with pickups in Menton, Cannes, or Antibes). **Joe's Sight-Seeing** (✉ 12 ave. de Verdun, 06000 Nice, ☏ 04–93–88–97–11, FAX 04–93–82–44–93) organizes full- or half-day minibus tours for up to eight passengers, with English-speaking driver-guides; a 10% discount on normal prices is promised to Fodor's readers. **Gallus Excursions 80** (✉ 24 quai Lunel, 06000 Nice, ☏ 04–93–55–33–33) runs enjoyable daylong jaunts by boat to the Îles de Lérins; the cost is about 175 francs.

Travel Agencies

American Express (✉ 8 rue des Belges, Cannes, ☏ 04–93–38–15–87; 11 promenade des Anglais, Nice, ☏ 04–93–16–53–53). **Wagons-Lits** (✉ 2 av. Monte Carlo, Monaco, ☏ 04–93–25–01–05).

Visitor Information

The Riviera's regional tourist office is the **Comité Régional du Tourisme de Riviera-Côte d'Azur** (✉ 55 promenade des Anglais, 06000 Nice; written inquiries only). Local tourist offices in major towns covered in this chapter are as follows: **Antibes** (✉ 11 pl. Général-de-Gaulle, ☏ 04–92–90–53–00). **Cannes** (✉ Palais des Festivals, 1 La Croisette, ☏ 04–93–39–24–53). **Fréjus** (✉ 325 rue Jean-Jaurès, ☏ 04–94–17–19–19). **Grasse** (✉ 22 cours Honoré-Cresp, ☏ 04–93–36–03–56). **Juan-les-Pins** (✉ 51 bd. Charles-Guillaumont, ☏ 04–93–61–04–98). **La Napoule** (✉ 272 av. Henry-Clews, ☏ 04–93–49–95–31). **Menton** (✉ Palais de l'Europe, av. Boyer, ☏ 04–93–57–57–00). **Monte Carlo** (✉ 2a bd. des Moulins, ☏ 92–16–61–66). **Nice** (✉ av. Thiers, ☏ 04–93–87–07–07). **St-Tropez** (✉ quai Jean-Jaurès, ☏ 04–94–97–45–21). **Vence** (✉ pl. du Grand-Jardin, ☏ 04–93–58–06–38).

14 Corsica

This Mediterranean "mountain in the sea," off the coast of Monaco, is known for its striking, unspoiled scenery and its rich, cultural treasures. Visit the port city of Bastia, explore a chestnut forest, climb to Corte's citadel, and laze on a beach in Calvi. Or admire the cliffs of Bonifacio, see Napoléon's birthplace, listen to traditional folk music, and delight in fine yet simple Corsican cuisine.

Updated by George Semler

ANCIENT MEDITERRANEAN PORTS, artistic and archaeological treasures, crystalline waters, granite peaks, and pine forests, make Corsica one of France's most beautiful regions. For thousands of years, its natural resources and strategic location, 168 km (105 mi) south of Monaco and just 81 km (50 mi) west of Italy, have made Corsica a prize hotly contested by many Mediterranean civilizations. You can still see vestiges of those invaders—the city-state of Genoa ruled Corsica for more than 200 years, leaving behind impressive citadels and bridges and a network of nearly 100 medieval watchtowers that still encircle the island. The Italian influence is also apparent in village architecture and in the Corsican language, a combination of Italian, Tuscan dialect, and Latin.

Although it's only 215 km (133 mi) long and 81 km (50 mi) wide, Corsica seems much larger—partly because rugged, mountainous terrain makes for slow traveling and partly because the landscape and the culture varies so much from one "micro-region" to another. Much of Corsica that is not wooded or cultivated is covered with a dense thicket of undergrowth called the *maquis.* The maquis is made up of a variety of sweet-smelling plants including lavender, myrtle, and heather that gave Corsica one of its nicknames, "the perfumed isle." The maquis is also famous for harboring a motley crew of fugitives. In Corsica, you didn't head for the hills, you headed for the maquis.

There has always been a black legend associated with the island, stemming mainly from a tradition of apparent lawlessness and deeply entrenched clannishness. As justice from "the Continent," whether France or Italy, was usually slow and often unsatisfying, Corsican clans frequently fought each other in blood feuds of revenge. The term "vendetta" is, in fact, Corsica's prime contribution to world lexicography.

Corsica is especially famous as the birthplace of Napoléon Bonaparte. Although he never returned to the island after beginning his military career, you can visit his family's home in Ajaccio. Perhaps better suited to the island's individualist character is Corsica's real national hero, Pasquale Paoli, who framed the world's first constitution for the independent Corsican republic in 1755 and whose ideas significantly influenced the French Revolution as well as the founding fathers of the United States.

Pleasures and Pastimes

Architecture and Archaeology

Corsica is superbly endowed with cultural riches ranging from megalithic monuments to Roman ruins to baroque churches to Genoan bridges. Forts, mills, bell towers, tombs, *bergeries* (shepherd's huts), mountain refuges, and traditional farmhouses also provide feasts for the eyes.

Dining

Authentic Corsican fare based on free-range livestock, game (especially wild boar), herbs, and wild mushrooms is best found in the tiny villages of the mountainous interior between October and April. *Civets* (meat stews) feature prominently on menus, as do many versions of the prototypical, hearty Corsican soup, (alternately known as *soupe paysanne, soupe corse,* or *soupe de montagne*) made from herbs and vegetables simmered for hours with a ham bone. Seafood dishes are available on the coast: Particularly good is *aziminu,* a rich bouillabaisse. Everywhere you'll find all kinds of *charcuterie* (pork products): *Lonzu* (shoulder), *coppa* (fillet), and *figatelli* (liver sausage) are standard cuts, along with *prisuttu* (cured ham).

Corsican cheeses include *Brocciu* (pronounced *bro*-cho), similar to ricotta and used in omelettes, *fiadone* (cheesecake), *fritelli* (chestnut-flour doughnuts), and as stuffing for trout or rabbit; *bastelicaccia,* a soft, creamy sheep cheese; and *sartenais,* a harder and sharper cheese. Many of the most powerful cheeses are simply designated as *brebis* (sheep) or *chèvre* (goat). Chestnuts and chestnut flour also play an important part in Corsican gastronomy: In *castagna* (chestnut in Corsican), a cake; *panetta,* a kind of bread; *canistrelli,* dry cookies; *beignets* (fried dough), often made of chestnut flour; *pulenta,* a doughy chestnut-flour bread; and *pietra,* chestnut beer. Be sure to try some of Corsica's fine wines: Orenga de Gaffory or Gentile, from the Patrimonio vineyards; Domaine Peraldi Clos du Cardinal from Ajaccio; and Fiumicicoli from Sartène.

CATEGORY	COST*
$$$$	over 350 frs
$$$	250 frs–350 frs
$$	125 frs–250 frs
$	under 125 frs

**per person for a three-course meal, including tax (20.6%) and tip but not wine*

Lodging

The amount of building around Porto-Vecchio in the 1950s was so horrifying to Corsicans that they resolved to avoid excessive tourist-driven development. Instead, *fermes-auberges* (farmhouse-inns) are being restored at a rapid clip and tastefully designed new hotels are being built. During the peak season (July to mid-September) prices are higher and some hotels insist that you have breakfast and dinner. The best seaside hotels are priced only marginally lower than in the Riviera, but lodging in the interior villages remains substantially cheaper. Off-season, good prices can be found all over.

CATEGORY	COST*
$$$$	over 750 frs
$$$	400 frs–750 frs
$$	250 frs–400 frs
$	under 250 frs

**All prices are for a standard double room for two, including tax (20.6%) and service charge.*

Outdoor Activities

From the wild, undeveloped strands of Cap Corse (Cape Corsica) to the Riviera-like tourist beaches near Calvi and Propriano, the island's coastline offers astonishing variety. In summer, during the *canicule* (literally, "dog days") Corsicans take to the rivers, always cooler than the Mediterranean. Others take on the rugged GR 20 (Grande Randonnée 20): Considered one of Europe's greatest hiking trails, it requires 70 to 100 hours to complete. Planned in stages from one mountain refuge to another, the well-marked GR 20 is the ultimate way to see Corsica. If you are traveling by car, short probes along the GR 20 are easily feasible. Check with tourist offices and/or bookstores for guides.

Exploring Corsica

Both leaving Marseille (on the excellent SNCM *Ferryterranée,* which also departs from Toulon and Nice) in the sunset and arriving in Ajaccio as the sun rises are among the finest moments of any trip to Corsica. Napoléon claimed he could identify the fragrance of the Corsican maquis from 162 km (100 mi) away at sea; approaching the island by airplane seems like heresy. The northern half of the island (Haute Corse) is generally wilder than the southern half (Corse du Sud), which is hotter and more barren. On the other hand, southern Corsica's archaeological sites at Filitosa and Pianu de Levie, the Col de Bavella and its majestic laricio pine forest, and the towns of Sartène and Bonifacio all rank indisputably among the island's finest treasures. The least interesting part of the island is the coast between Porto-Vecchio and Bastia; the prettiest route is the one around Cap Corse. If you spend too much time at sea level, you'll miss the dramatic heights for which the island is famous. Also be sure to brush up on your French before you go outside the main towns—the port city of Bastia and the French capital, Ajaccio (pronounced ah-*jack*-sio)—it's difficult to find people who speak English.

Great Itineraries

Three days is barely sufficient time to visit Corsica's three main cities and some of the island's prettiest scenery. In five days you can cover most of Haute Corse and in 10 days it is possible, though not necessarily advisable, to see the whole island: The danger is of spending too much time car-bound. One approach is to settle in Corte, near the island's center, sallying forth each day to different attractions.

Numbers in the text correspond to numbers in the margin and on the Corsica and Ajaccio maps.

IF YOU HAVE 3 DAYS

Ajaccio ①–⑦ is a good place to start. A two-hour drive over the Vizzavona pass to **Corte** ⑮ will place you at the island's historical heart for the night. Explore the **Restonica gorges** and Corte the next day. On day three, drive through the chestnut-covered **La Castagniccia** region, visiting the small villages along the way. Find your way out of La Castagniccia via Folelli, stopping for lunch in **Murato** ㉝. Save the afternoon and evening for exploring **Bastia** ㊴, before shipping out for the mainland.

IF YOU HAVE 5 DAYS

Follow the three-day itinerary, but spend the fourth and fifth nights in or near **Bastia** ㊴. Tour Cap Corse on day four, starting out on the eastern side, stopping for lunch in the fishing port of **Centuri** ㊲, and visiting **Nonza** ㊱, **St-Florent** ㉞, and the **Patrimonio** ㉟ vineyards before driving up over the Col de Teghime (if possible at sunset). Spend day five exploring Bastia, then head back to the mainland.

IF YOU HAVE 10 DAYS

Start in **Ajaccio** ①–⑦ and reach the megalithic site at **Filitosa** ⑨ by noon. Have a late lunch in **Sartène** ⑩ and drive into **Bonifacio** ⑪ as the sun sets into the sea. The next day, get to the Laricio pine forest near the **Col de Bavella** ⑬ to see or even a walk to the famous granite peaks. Tiny D268 comes out on the east coast at N198, which will take you up to **Aléria** ⑭ and into **Corte** ⑮ on N200. Make Corte your base: Devote day three to Corte and the Restonica gorges; day four to the **Asco Valley;** day five to the small villages in **La Castagniccia.** On day six, take **La Scala di Santa Regina** road through the Aitone Forest. Spend the night in **Ota** ㉒. Pass through the Scandola Natural Reserve on day seven, reaching the Riviera-like **Calvi** ㉕ by evening. Go to the beach in Calvi on day eight. In the evening drive through La Balagne to **L'Île Rousse** ㉛ and medieval **Lama** ㉜. On the ninth day drive around Cap Corse and spend the night in **Erbalunga** ㊳, in **Bastia** ㊴, or in **San Martino di Lota** ㊵. On the morning of day ten, hike up to the Bocca di Santo Lunardo or go to the beach at Erbalunga; in the afternoon explore Bastia, then head back to the mainland.

Corsica

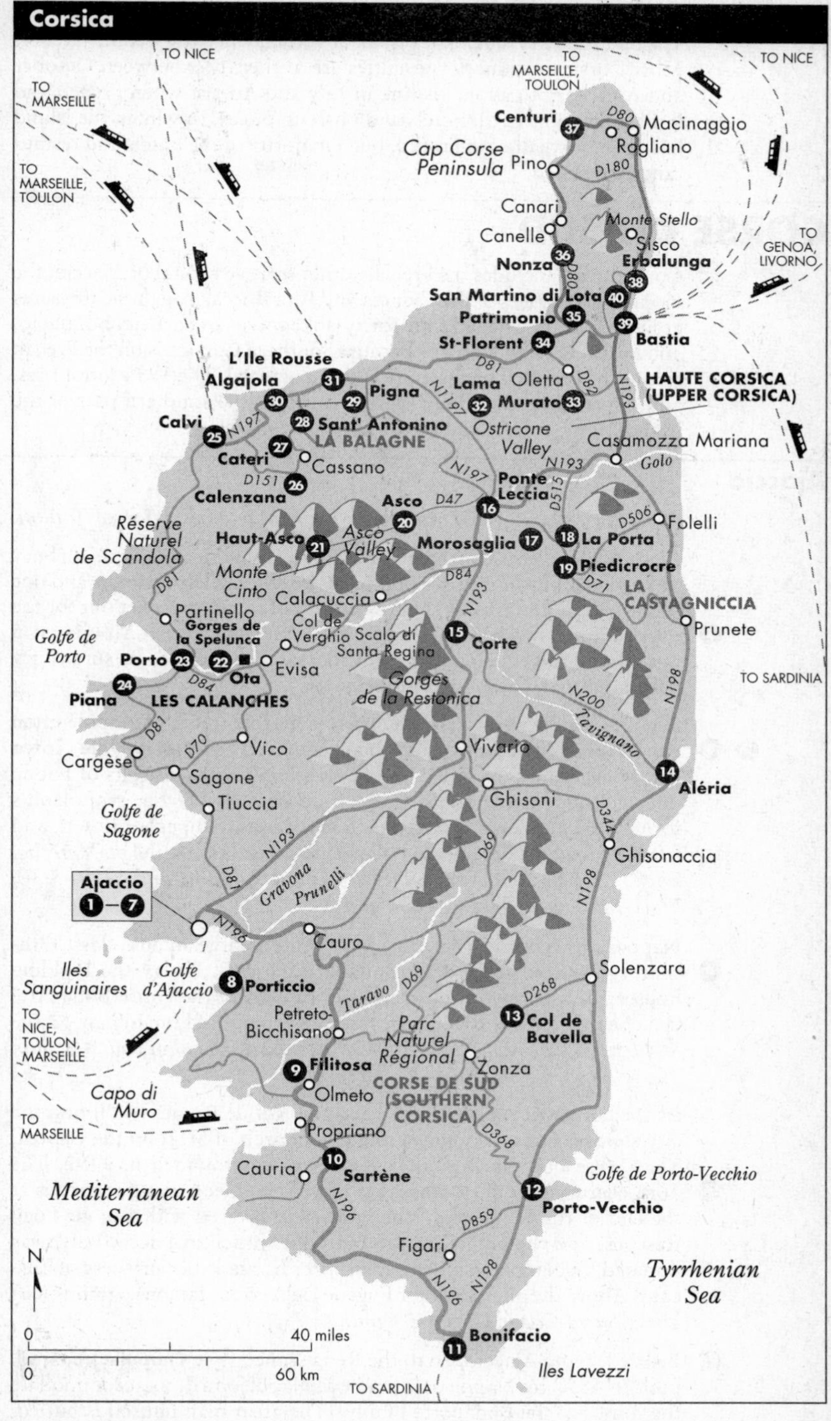
TO NICE
TO MARSEILLE
TO MARSEILLE, TOULON
TO MARSEILLE, TOULON
TO NICE
TO GENOA, LIVORNO
Centuri
Macinaggio
Rogliano
Cap Corse Peninsula
Pino
Canari
Monte Stello
Canelle
Sisco
Nonza
Erbalunga
San Martino di Lota
Patrimonio
Bastia
St-Florent
L'Ile Rousse
Algajola
Pigna
Lama
Oletta
Murato
HAUTE CORSICA (UPPER CORSICA)
Calvi
Sant' Antonino
LA BALAGNE
Ostricone Valley
Casamozza Mariana
Cateri
Cassano
Golo
Calenzana
Ponte Leccia
Asco
Folelli
Réserve Naturel de Scandola
Haut-Asco
Asco Valley
Morosaglia
La Porta
Monte Cinto
Piedicrocre
LA CASTAGNICCIA
Calacuccia
Partinello
Gorges de la Spelunca
Col de Verghio
Scala di Santa Regina
Corte
Prunete
Golfe de Porto
Porto
Ota
Evisa
Gorges de la Restonica
TO SARDINIA
Piana
LES CALANCHES
Tavignano
Vico
Vivario
Cargèse
Sagone
Aléria
Ghisoni
Tiuccia
Golfe de Sagone
Ghisonaccia
Ajaccio
Gravona
Prunelli
Cauro
Solenzara
Iles Sanguinaires
Golfe d'Ajaccio
Porticcio
Taravo
TO NICE, TOULON, MARSEILLE
Petreto-Bicchisano
Parc Naturel Régional
Col de Bavella
Zonza
Filitosa
Olmeto
CORSE DE SUD (SOUTHERN CORSICA)
Capo di Muro
TO MARSEILLE
Propriano
Cauria
Sartène
Golfe de Porto-Vecchio
Mediterranean Sea
Porto-Vecchio
Figari
Tyrrhenian Sea
Bonifacio
Iles Lavezzi
TO SARDINIA
N
0
40 miles
0
60 km

When to Tour Corsica

The best time to visit Corsica is fall or spring, when the weather is cool. Most Corsican culinary specialties are at their best between October and April. Try to avoid visiting in July and August when French and Italian vacationers fill hotels and push up prices. In winter, the island has the best weather in France, but a majority of the hotels and restaurants are closed.

CORSE DU SUD

Corse du Sud includes the French administrative capital of Ajaccio, the mountainous zones of the Cinarca and Alta Rocca, megalithic treasures at Filitosa and Levie, and the fortresslike towns of Sartène, Bonifacio, and Porto-Vecchio. Perhaps because Southern Corsica is on the French side of the island, it seems more Continentalized. The 1994 forest fires, and the resulting flooding, scarred much of the southern part of the island, though the maquis is quickly growing back.

Ajaccio

40 mins by plane, 5–10 hrs by ferry from Marseilles, Nice, or Toulon.

Ajaccio, Napoléon's birthplace and Corsica's modern capital, is a busy town with a bustling port, voluptuous beaches, ancient streets and one of the best collections of paintings south of the Louvre. Set out for the
1 **city market,** a lovely square where every morning except Monday you can admire the enticing array of produce and seafood. Be sure to try the traditional, chestnut-flour beignets.

Rows of stately palm trees lead up to a marble statue of Napoléon on
2 3 **Place Maréchal Foch,** the city's main square. The **Hôtel de Ville** (Town Hall) has an Empire-style Grand Salon hung with portraits of a long line of Bonapartes. You'll find a fine bust of Letizia, Napoléon's formidable mother, a bronze death mask of the emperor himself, and a frescoed ceiling that portrays Napoléon's meteoric rise. ⊠ *pl. Maréchal Foch.* 🎟 *7 frs.* ⏲ *Apr.–Oct., weekdays 9–noon and 2:30–5:30; Nov.–Mar., weekdays 9–noon and 2–5.*

Napoléon was born on August 15, 1769 in the large, middle-class, 18th-
4 century **Maison Bonaparte** (Bonaparte House). Today the building houses a museum with portraits and cameos of the entire Bonaparte clan. Search out the two family trees woven out of human hair. ⊠ *rue St-Charles.* 🎟 *20 frs.* ⏲ *Mon. 2–5, Tues.–Sat. 10–noon and 2–5, Sun. 10–noon.*

At the corner of rue St-Charles and rue Roi de Rome, you'll find the city's **oldest houses,** opposite the tiny church of **St. John the Baptist.** They were built shortly after the town was founded in 1492. The
5 16th-century baroque **Cathédrale** where Napoléon was baptized is at the end of rue St-Charles. The interior is covered with trompe l'oeil frescoes, and the high altar, from an old church in Lucca, Italy, was donated by Napoléon's sister Eliza after he made her princess of Tuscany. Above the altar, look for Eugène Delacroix's famous painting *Virgin of Sacré Coeur.* ⊠ *rue F.-Conti.*

6 Before leaving Ajaccio, go to the Renaissance-style **Chapelle Impérial,** built in 1857 by Napoléon's nephew, Napoléon III, to accommodate the tombs of the Bonaparte family. (The great man himself is buried, however, in the Hôtel des Invalides in Paris.) A Coptic crucifix taken from Egypt during the general's 1798 campaign hangs over the main altar. ⊠ *50 rue Fesch.* 🎟 *10 frs.* ⏲ *Tues.–Sat. 10–12:30 and 3–7.*

Cathédral, **5**
Chapelle Impérial, **6**
city market, **1**
Hôtel de Ville, **3**
Maison Bonaparte, **4**
Musée Fesch, **7**
Place Maréchal Foch, **2**

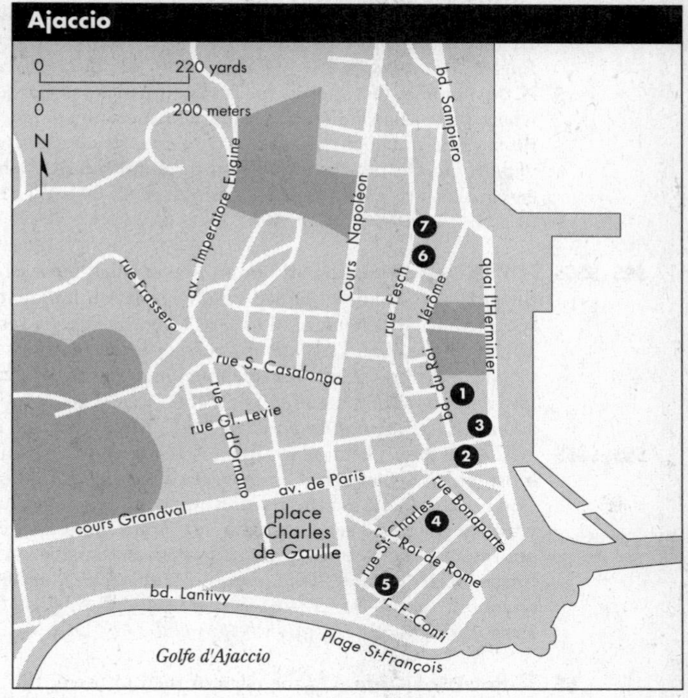

★ **7** The **Musée Fesch** houses what is considered the best collection of Italian masters Botticelli, Canaletto, and De Tura outside Florence and Paris—part of a collection of 30,000 paintings bought at bargain prices following the French revolution by Napoléon's uncle, Cardinal Fesch, the archbishop of Lyon. ✉ *50 rue Fesch,* ☎ *04–95–21–48–17.* 🎫 *25 frs.* ⏲ *Apr.–Oct., Wed.–Mon. 9:30–noon and 3–6:30 (also in July and Aug., Tues.–Sat. 9–midnight); Nov.–Mar., Wed.–Mon. 9:30–noon and 2:30–6.*

After visiting the old quarter, make your way down to the plage St-François and stop at the **Café Fesch** for coffee while you contemplate the Golfe d'Ajaccio.

Dining and Lodging

$$–$$$ ✕ **A La Funtana.** A fountain greets diners at the door of this gourmet restaurant, named for a popular Corsican folk song. Fresh flowers and Oriental carpets are the only touch of decoration in the simple white dining room. The house specialty is homemade foie gras; other dishes worth sampling include *morilles* (morels) in foie gras and homemade sorbets. ✉ *7 rue Notre-Dame,* ☎ *04–95–21–78–04. AE, DC, MC, V. Closed June, Sun., Mon.*

$$ ★ ✕ **Auberge de Prunelli.** This cheerful riverside inn overlooking the Prunelli River has an excellent 175-franc five-course menu. Dine on brocciu omelets, trout, roast lamb, and figatelli sausage. ✉ *Pisciatellu (about 11 km/7 mi south of Ajaccio just off N196; look for the turn-off onto D55B just before crossing the river),* ☎ *04–95–20–02–75. Reservations essential. No credit cards. Closed Tues. and Oct.–Nov.*

$$ ✕ **Le Maximilien.** This stylish spot across from the cathedral is one of the hottest places for dinner. Chef-owner Serge Alain Gros serves Continental cuisine to a smart crowd interested in something more than local cooking. The cassoulet *périgord* (with duck, sausage, and white beans) and the *lotte au foie gras de canard* (burbot with goose liver) are interesting combinations of maritime and upland products. ✉ *rue Eugene Macchini,* ☎ *04–95–51–36–39. AE, DC, MC, V. Closed Mon.*

$ ✕ **Da Mamma.** Just after 13 rue Fesch, turn into passage de la Guinghetta where there is a small shady square of the same name. Under a leafy rubber tree you might, in season, try a *civet de sanglier* (wild boar stew) with *trompettes de la mort* (wild mushrooms) served in a bubbling earthenware casserole. ✉ *2 passage Guingetta,* ☎ *04–95–21–39–44. AE, MC, V. No lunch Sun. or Mon. Feb.–Oct.*

$$$–$$$$ ✕🏨 **La Dolce Vita.** Spread out on flower-filled terraces at the edge of the gulf of Ajaccio, La Dolce Vita has a lavish Italianate decor and a spectacular swimming pool overlooking the sea. Its restaurant ranks as one of the island's best for gourmet interpretations of traditional Corsican dishes. ✉ *rte. des Îles Sanguinaires, 20000 (8 km/5 mi from the center of town),* ☎ *04–95–52–00–93,* FAX *04–95–52–07–15. 32 rooms. Restaurant, bar, pool. AE, DC, MC, V. Closed Nov.–Easter.*

$$$–$$$$ ✕🏨 **Eden Roc.** The modern Eden Roc overlooks the gulf in Ajaccio's most exclusive suburb. Gardens surround the swimming pool and a tiny beach lies across the road. Rooms are large and luxurious, each with a terrace and sea view. The restaurant, no longer considered the gourmet haven it once was, nevertheless remains one of Ajaccio's finest. ✉ *rte. des Îles Sanguinaires, 20000 (8 km/5 mi from the center of town),* ☎ *04–95–52–01–47,* FAX *04–95–52–05–03. 45 rooms. Restaurant, piano bar, pool, health club. AE, DC, MC, V.*

$$ 🏨 **Hotel San Carlu.** On the edge of the old town, this friendly hotel overlooking the ramparts and the sea is ideal for exploring Ajaccio. Rooms are clean and comfortable; those on the gulf side on the third floor even have morning sunshine streaming across the bed. ✉ *8 bd. Danielle Casanova, 20000,* ☎ *04–95–21–13–84,* FAX *04–95–21–09–99. 40 rooms. AE, DC, MC, V.*

Nightlife and the Arts

Hear traditional Corsican music at **Le Pavillon Bleu** (✉ 54 cours Grandval). Have a drink to the tinkling of a piano at **Le Brazil Café** (✉ 28 cours Grandval). **Ricanto** (✉ plage Ricanto) has a transvestite revue. **Le Weekend Discothèque** (✉ rte. des Îles Sanguinaires) is the spot for dancing.

The **Fête de la Miséricorde** (Feast of Our Lady of Mercy) on March 18 features the Procession de la Madunnuccia, Ajaccio's patron saint. In May Ajaccio celebrates during its festive **carnival.** In July you can attend the classical **International Music Meeting.** A major **festival** takes place on August 15th, Napoléon's birthday.

Outdoor Activities and Sports

Bicycles can be rented from **Corsica Loisirs** (✉ 3 Montée St-Jean). Horseback riding is ideal along the former mule paths; both the **Centre de Randonnées de St-Georges** (✉ Domaine de Campiccioli, rte. de Vigna Piana, ☎ 04–95–25–34–83) and the **Poney-Club d'Ajaccio** (✉ Campo dell' Oro, ☎ 04–95–23–03–10) rent horses and organize outings. For fishing, swimming, underwater diving, kayaking, or windsurfing, **Les Dauphins** (✉ rte. des Sanguinaires, plage de Barbicaja, ☎ 04–95–52–07–78) and the **Club des Calanques** (✉ Hôtel des Calanques, rte. des Sanguinaires, ☎ 04–95–21–39–65) are the places to go. For sailing, contact the **Tahiti Nautic Club d'Ajaccio** (✉ plage du Ricanto, ☎ 04–95–20–05–95).

Shopping

Paese Nostru (✉ passage Guinguetta) sells Corsican crafts of all kinds. **U Tilaghju** (✉ rue Forcioli Conti), one of several artisan shops near the cathedral, has an impressive collection of ceramics. **Librairie la Marge** (✉ 7 rue Emmanuelle Arène) is much more than a bookstore. Specializing in books about the island, it is a hub of Corsican identity. It also has an excellent selection of Corsican music, as well as poetry readings and performances.

Porticcio

8 *17 km (10½ mi) south of Ajaccio on N196.*

Across the Prunelli River from Ajaccio, amidst quiet, pastoral scenery, is the capital's fancy suburb and luxurious beach resort town, Porticcio.

Dining and Lodging

$$$–$$$$ ★ **Le Maquis.** The evocatively named Maquis ranks as one of the island's (and Europe's) finest *hôtels de charme.* The quaint, ivy-covered building reaches down to a private beach. Rooms have views of the sea or the hills. At the candlelit restaurant, with ancient beams and wicker chairs, the food is a blend of traditional and nouvelle: Fish tartare, scrambled eggs with truffles, and fresh tagliatelles. ✉ *D55, 20166 Porticcio,* ☎ *04–95–25–05–55,* FAX *04–95–25–11–70. 27 rooms. Restaurant, outdoor pool, indoor pool, tennis court, beach. AE, DC, MC, V.*

Outdoor Activities and Sports

Bikes are a great way to explore the beach; **Avis** (✉ Hôtel Marina Viva) rents them. Kids love **Aqua Cyrné Gliss,** a water park with water slides and swimming pools. ☎ *04–95–25–17–48.* *67 frs.* ⏲ *Mid-June–mid-Sept., daily 10:30–7, plus 2 evenings a wk (usually Tues. and Fri.).*

Filitosa

9 *71 km (43 mi) southeast of Ajaccio off N196.*

Filitosa is the site of Corsica's largest grouping of megalithic menhir statues. Bizarre, life-size stone figures of ancient warriors rise up mysteriously from the undulating terrain, many with human faces that have been eroded and flattened with time. A small museum on the site houses archaeological finds, including the menhir known as Scalsa Murta, whose delicately carved spine and rib cage make it difficult to believe the statue dates from some 3,000 years BC. Be sure to buy the excellent guidebook in English (30 francs) by experts Cesari and Acquaviva. You can study it over a snack at the pleasant museum café. *Contact the Centre Préhistorique Filitosa,* ☎ *04–95–74–00–91, for information.* *Guided tours in English 25 frs.* ⏲ *June–Aug., daily 8–7.*

Sartène

10 *27 km (16 mi) southeast of Filitosa on N196.*

The hillside town of Sartène was called the "most Corsican of all Corsican towns" by French novelist Prosper Mérimée. Dorothy Carrington described it as one of the least changed places on Corsica. Founded in the 16th century, Sartène has survived pirate raids and bloody feuding among the town's families. The word "vendetta" is believed to have originated here as the result of a 19th-century family feud so serious that French troops were brought in as a peace-keeping buffer force. Centuries of fighting have left the town with a somewhat eerie and menacing atmosphere. Perhaps adding to this is the annual Good Friday *catenacciu* procession in which an anonymous sinner, dragging ankle chains, lugs a heavy cross through the village streets.

The most interesting part of town is **Vieux Sartène** (Old Sartène), surrounded by ancient ramparts. Start at the place de la Libération, the main square. To one side is the **Hôtel de Ville,** the former Genoese governor's palace. For a taste of the Middle Ages, slip through the tunnel in the town hall to place du Maggiu and the old quarter of **Santa Anna,** a somber warren of narrow, cobbled streets lined with granite houses. Scarcely 100 yards from the Hôtel de Ville, down a steep and winding street, a 12th-century **watchtower** stands out in sharp contrast to the modern apartment buildings behind.

Sartène is the center for research into Corsica's prehistory, due to its proximity to Pianu de Levie and the region's riches in dolmens and megalithic statues. For a look at some of the island's best prehistoric relics, stop by the **Musée Départemental de la Préhistoire Corse** (Departmental Museum of Corsican Prehistory) in the town's former prison. ✉ *rue Croce,* ☎ *04–95–77–01–09.* 🎫 *15 frs.* ⏲ *Apr.–Oct., Mon.–Sat. 10–noon and 2–6; Nov.–Mar., weekdays 10–noon and 2–5.*

Dining

$$ ✕ **Auberge de Santa Barbara.** This excellent restaurant is just 1 km (½ mi) north of Sartène. Known as one of the best half dozen or so practitioners of authentic Corsican cuisine on the island, Giselle Lovighi also serves innovative seafood specialties such as shrimp soufflée or crayfish salad. ✉ *Alzone, Sartène,* ☎ *04–95–77–09–06. MC, V. Closed Mon., Nov.–Easter.*

Outdoor Activities and Sports

In nearby Propriano, north of Sartène, horses can be rented from the **Ferme Équestre de Baracci** (Propriano, ☎ 04–95–76–08–02). Another way to see the area is to hike along the **Tra Mare a Mare** (Sea-to-Sea Trail) from Propriano to Porto-Vecchio. Watch for roadside information points with maps and suggested itineraries.

Bonifacio

★ ⓫ *54 km (33 mi) southeast of Sartène on N196.*

The ancient fortress town of Bonifacio occupies a spectacular clifftop setting above a harbor carved from limestone cliffs. It is just 13 km (8 mi) from Sardinia, and local speech is heavily influenced by the accent and idiom of the neighboring Italian island. Established in the 12th century as Genoa's first Corsican stronghold, Bonifacio remained Genoese through centuries of battles and sieges. As you wander the narrow streets of the **Haute Ville** (Upper Village), inside the walls of the citadel, think of Homer's *Odyssey.* It was here, in the harbor, that Classics scholars have placed the catastrophic encounter between Ulysses's fleet and the vicious Laestrygonians who hurled boulders down from the cliffs.

From the place d'Armes at the city gate, enter the **Bastion of the Standard**; you can still see the system of weights and pulleys used to pull up the drawbridge. The former garrison now houses life-size dioramas of Bonifacio's history. 🎫 *20 frs.* ⏲ *June 15–Sept. 15, daily 9–7.*

In the center of the maze of cobbled streets that make up the citadel you'll find the 12th-century church of **Ste-Marie-Majeure,** with buttresses attaching it to surrounding houses. Inside the church, note the Renaissance baptismal font, carved in bas-relief, and the 3rd-century white marble Roman sarcophagus. Walk around the back to see the loggia, which is built above a huge cistern that contained water for use in times of siege, as were the circular silos throughout the town.

From Bonifacio, you can take a **boat trip** to the **Dragon Grottoes** and **Venus's Bath** (the trip takes one hour on boats that set out every 15 minutes during July and August) or the **Lavezzi Islands** (boats leave from outside Hôtel La Caravelle, ☎ 04–95–75–05–93).

Dining and Lodging

$$ ★ ✕ **U Ceppu.** This rustic, barn-size restaurant, just outside of Bonifacio, features grilled meats and seafood prepared in the dining room on a big open hearth—smoked salmon and wild boar stew. Picture windows look out on lobster pots bobbing in the bay and sprinkled on the beach. ✉ *l'Auberge de Santa Manza (about 5 km/3 mi east of Bonifacio on the road to Santa Manza beach),* ☎ *04–95–73–02–34. AE, MC, V. No lunch Mon.–Sat.*

$–$$ ★ ✕ **Les 4 Vents.** This friendly restaurant is popular with the yachting crowd and with families. In winter, the kitchen serves up Alsace specialties like sauerkraut and sausages, but in summer it concentrates on barbecued fish and meats, as well as typical Corsican dishes. ✉ *29 quai Bando di Ferro,* ☎ *04–95–73–07–50. No credit cards. Closed Tues.*

$ ✕ **Restaurant du Pêcheur.** People often line the sidewalk waiting to dine at this tiny, most authentic seafood spot in town. True to its name, the restaurant is run by fishermen who serve the catch of the day straight from the sea. There's no written menu, so ask what's available. ✉ *14 rue Doria,* ☎ *04–95–73–12–56. Reservations not accepted. MC, V. Closed Nov.–Easter.*

$$$–$$$$ 🏨 **Hôtel le Genovese.** This small, personal hotel is built into the ramparts of the upper town's citadel. Rooms glow with peach fabric wall coverings; those upstairs have superb views—the best thing about the hotel. ✉ *quartier de Citadelle, Haute Ville 20169,* ☎ *04–95–73–12–34,* FAX *04–95–73–09–03. 14 rooms. Bar. AE, DC, MC, V.*

Nightlife and the Arts

Party until dawn at **Le Fa Dièse** (✉ 10 rue Portone). Or drive out to **Amnesia** (✉ km 10 on the Porto-Vecchio road), the disco of choice.

The **Fête Millénaire de Bonifacio,** Bonifacio's celebration of the thousandth anniversary of its founding, has been held in late August for the last two years and is threatening to become an annual event, with concerts, processions, and street dances.

Outdoor Activities and Sports

The area around Bonifacio is ideal for water sports; contact **Club Atoll** (✉ B.P. 3, ☎ 04–95–73–02–83). The best golf course on Corsica (and one of the best in the Mediterranean), a 6,130-meter par 72 gem designed by Robert Trent Jones, is at **Sperone** (✉ Domaine de Sperone, ☎ 04–95–73–17–13) just east of Bonifacio.

Shopping

Pierres de Cade (✉ Haute Ville) has a good selection of beautiful objects carved from Corsica's rich chestnut and juniper trees.

Porto-Vecchio

⓬ *27 km (16 mi) north of Bonifacio on N198.*

The old walled town of Porto-Vecchio has become synonymous throughout Corsica with mass tourism dominated by tour operators from Italy. Nevertheless, the town features a network of medieval streets now largely given over to bistros, boutiques, and cafés, and the Gulf of Porto-Vecchio is lined with beautiful beaches. The exquisite Grand Hôtel de Cala Rossa (☞ *below*) is worth a visit whether you are staying or not.

Dining and Lodging

$$–$$$$ ★ ✕🏨 **Grand Hôtel de Cala Rossa.** One of Corsica's finest, this mansion-hotel, close to the beach, showcases modern design at its best. Nothing

jars, from the curves of the heavy white walls to the contemporary paintings. The luxurious rooms vary greatly in price. Corsican-style nouvelle dishes are featured in the restaurant; you can't go wrong with the roast kid or the fresh-mint omelet. ✉ *Cala Rossa, 20137 (8 km/5 mi north of Porto-Vecchio),* ☎ *04–95–71–61–51,* FAX *04–95–71–60–11. 50 rooms. Restaurant, 1 tennis court. AE, DC, MC, V. Closed Nov.–Apr.*

$$–$$$ ✕🏨 **Moby Dick.** This sophisticated modern hotel in blue and white is virtually surrounded by water and sandy beaches, which can be seen from rooms. The restaurant serves a good-value buffet lunch and both a "normal" and *gastronomique* (gargantuan) menu at dinner. The crayfish is delicious. ✉ *baie de Santa Giulia, 20137 (8 km/5 mi south of town),* ☎ *04–95–70–43–23,* FAX *04–95–70–01–54. 44 rooms. Restaurant. AE, DC, MC, V. Closed Nov.–Apr.*

En Route Porto-Vecchio backs onto Corsica's largest cork oak forest, **L'Ospédale.** An excursion across the forest on D368, climbing 49 km (30 mi) to the mountain pass of **Col de Bavella,** is one of the island's most memorable excursions and should under no circumstances be missed in favor of the flat, straight road up the east coast.

Col de Bavella

⓭ *50 km (31 mi) northeast of Porto-Vecchio on D368 and D268.*

The granite peaks known as the Aiguilles de Bavella ("needles of Bavella") tower some 6,562 feet overhead as you reach the *col* (pass). Hiking trails are well marked. The narrow but mostly well-paved roadway will take you back to the coast along the Solenzara River. If you stop and look carefully, you may be able to see wild Corsican trout dining on aquatic insects.

Dining

$ ✕ **Le Refuge.** Near the top of the spectacular drive from Porto-Vecchio to the Col de Bavella, follow signs for Le Refuge, an inexpensive little hikers' inn. A lunch of Corsican mountain fare by a roaring fire will be more than welcome. ✉ *Cartalavonu (2 km/1½ mi off D368 to the left),* ☎ *04–95–70–00–39.*

Aléria

⓮ *32 km (20 mi) north of Solenzara on N198, 70 km (63 mi) north of Porto-Vecchio.*

Just before the village are the ruins of the Roman city of Aléria. On a pine-studded plateau you'll see the carefully restored 16th-century **Fort de Matra,** which houses the **Musée Jérôme Carcopino.** On display are pottery and tools found on the site, as well as Etruscan, Greek, and Roman artifacts dating from as far back as 500 BC. 🎫 *15 frs.* ⏲ *Apr.–Oct., daily 8–noon and 2–7; Nov.–Mar., Mon.–Sat. 8–noon and 2–5.*

Dining and Lodging

$$ ✕ **Chez Mathieu.** This beach-side restaurant is open year round and specializes in very fresh *loup* (sea bass) and dorade. In summer, dinner on the beach at sunset before driving back up into the mountains at Corte can give you—aside from the fresh fish—a sense of Corsica's unique geographical diversity. ✉ *Plage Padulone,* ☎ *04–95–57–12–03. AE, MC, V.*

Outdoor Activities and Sports

Aléria's **beach** stretches north from the mouth of the Tavignano River and gets increasingly wilder the farther you go. It's a fine place for surf casting, swimming, or sailing. **Camping-Bungalows Marina d'Aléria** (✉ at the intersection of N200 and the beach, ☎ 04–95–57–01–42) rents different kinds of nautical equipment.

Shopping

For antique ceramic reproductions try the shops near the entrance to the Roman ruins.

HAUTE CORSE

Haute Corse (Upper Corsica) encompasses the northeastern end of the island, and is, indeed, higher in mean altitude than Corse-du-Sud, topped by the 2,706-meter (8,876-feet) Monte Cinto. Most Corsica enthusiasts agree that Haute Corse is richer in what is most Corsican about this "mountain in the sea": highland forests, remote villages, hidden cultural gems, and alpine lakes and streams. In the center of Haute Corse is the city of Corte, Corsica's heart and soul. To the east is the forested region of La Castagniccia, named for the abundance of *châtaignes* (chestnuts or castagna). It is one of the most colorful parts of Corsica, especially in the fall when leaves and chestnuts cover the ground. Driving through the forest's tiny roadways, you'll find villages with stunning baroque churches and houses still roofed in traditional blue-gray slate. To the north is Cap Corse: The 105-km (65-mi) drive along the coastal route D80, from the town of Patrimonio to the city of Bastia, will take you three hours (four with lunch in Centuri and five with a run up the Col de Ste-Lucie). The road is better on the east coast, and there are fewer reasons to stop.

Corte

15 *48 km (30 mi) northwest of Aléria on N200, 83 km (51 mi) northeast of Ajaccio, 70 km (43 mi) southwest of Bastia.*

Among spectacular cliffs and gorges at the confluence of the Tavignano, Restonica, and Orta rivers, Corte is the spiritual heart and soul of Corsica. Capital of Pasquale Paoli's government from 1755 to 1769, it was also where Paoli established the Corsican University in 1765. Closed by the victorious French in 1769, the university, always a symbol of Corsican identity, was reopened in 1981.

To reach the upper town and the 15th-century château looking over the rivers, walk up the cobblestone ramp from place Pasquale-Paoli. Stop in lovely **place Gaffori** at one of the cafés or restaurants. Note the bullet-pocked house where the Corsican hero Gian Pietro Gaffori and his wife, Faustina, held off the Genoans in 1750.

★ The **Citadelle,** a Vauban-style fortress (1769–78), is built around the original, 15th-century fortification at the highest point of the cliff, with the river below. It contains the **Musée de la Corse,** a museum dedicated to the island's history and ethnography. ☎ *04–95–61–00–61.* 🎫 *20 frs.* ⏲ *Weekdays 9–6.*

The **Palais National,** just outside the citadel and above place Gaffori, is the ancient residence of Genoa's representatives in Corsica and was the seat of the Corsican parliament from 1755 to 1769. The building is now part of the Corsican university at Corte. ✉ *pl. du Poilu.* ⏲ *Weekdays 2–6.*

For an unforgettable view of the river junction and the Genoan bridge below, the citadel's tiny watchtower above and the mountains behind, walk left along the citadel wall to the **Belvedere.**

Leave the Haute Ville and go through the **Quartier de Chiostra.** Follow the cobblestone path (as you look down) to the right from the Belvedere, bearing right and across at the **St-Théophile chapel.** Coming into the tiny square on your left, don't miss the flying stone staircase on the opposite wall, or the prehistoric fertility goddess carved into the wall to the left next to the pottery artisans shop. After leaving this little space, continue downhill and you will rejoin the ramp leading into place Pasquale-Paoli.

A nice excursion from Corte is a day at the **Gorges de la Restonica.** Drive up the Restonica valley and leave your car at the end of the road. A two-hour climb will take you to **Lac de Mélo,** a trout-filled mountain lake, 1,700 meters (6,528) feet above sea level, surrounded by a circle of craggy granite peaks. Another, more strenuous hour up takes you to the usually snow-bordered, **Lac de Capitello.** Information on trails is available from the tourist office (☞ Corsica A to Z, *below*) or the Parc Naturel Régional (☞ *below*). At the top of the drivable part of the Restonica Gorge, in the stone shepherds' huts at the **Bergeries de Grotelle,** light meals are served.

Dining and Lodging

$$ ★ ✕▣ **Auberge de la Restonica–Hôtel Dominique Colonna.** Over the crystalline Restonica River, this cozy inn—known for its fine, nouvelle Corsican cuisine—has rooms in the hunting lodge, the original building, and the modern new annex across the parking lot. Owner Dominique "Dumé" Colonna, one of France's great soccer stars, drops by from time to time. ✉ *Vallée de la Restonica, 20250,* ☎ *04–95–46–20–13 auberge; 04–95–61–05–45 hotel,* FAX *04–95–61–03–91; 04–95–46–09–58 restaurant. 35 rooms. Restaurant. AE, DC, MC, V.*

Outdoor Activities and Sports

In summer, you can get information on hiking and trail maps from the local office of the **Parc Naturel Régional de la Corse** (☞ Corsica A to Z, *below*), on the road about halfway between Corte and the Auberge de la Restonica.

Ponte Leccia

16 *24 km (15 mi) north of Corte on N193, 14 km (9 mi) northeast of Morosaglia, 24 km (15 mi) north of Corte.*

Ponte Leccia is the entry point to La Castagniccia: take D71 southeast into the forest. A rail and road crossing with gas stations and a supermarket, the town has little else to recommend it.

Morosaglia

17 *14 km (9 mi) southeast of Ponte Leccia, 9 km (5 mi) east of La Porta.*

The town of Morosaglia is the birthplace of Pasquale Paoli. Letters, portraits, and memorabilia from Paoli's life are on display at the **Maison de Pasquale Paoli.**

La Porta

18 *9 km (5 mi) west of Morosaglia, 14½ km (9 mi) north of Piedicroce on D515.*

As the name of the village suggests, La Porta is the doorway to La Castagniccia. The **St-Jean-Baptiste** church is widely accepted as the crowning glory of Corsican baroque art. The bright ochre facade and the five-story bell tower are feasts for the eyes, as are the paintings inside.

Dining

$$ ✕ **L'Ampugnani–Chez Elisabeth.** This excellent restaurant is known throughout Corsica as one of the top gourmet experiences in La Castagniccia. Specializing in *cuisine de terroir* (local country cooking), Elisabeth reinvents the leg of lamb with herbs from the surrounding hills and brings new meaning to the notion of *figatellu* (liver sausage). ✉ *La Porta,* ☎ *04–95–39–22–00. MC, V. Reservations essential. Closed Mon. Oct.–Easter.*

Piedicroce

⓳ *14 km (9 mi) south of La Porta on D515, 66 km (40 mi) south of Bastia.*

Piedicroce's panoramic view of La Castagniccia is superb. Be sure to stop in the vividly painted baroque church of **St-Pierre-et-St-Paul,** one of the finest of its type in the area. The nearby mineral springs of **Orezza,** reputed to have miraculous powers, and the trout-rich **Fium Alto stream** are two other reasons to come here. Follow signs for **Folelli** (37 km/22 mi north) or Bastia (66 km/40 mi north), to exit La Castagniccia.

Dining and Lodging

$$ ✕ **U Fragnu.** Having exited La Castagniccia at Folelli, head north to this place for some exquisite cuisine du terroir. The Garelli family has cooked for the French premier as representatives of Corsican gastronomy and Mme. Garelli is a specialist in *soupe de berger* (shepherd's soup)—a recipe restored after much research. ✉ *rte. de Vescovato, Venzolasca (7 km/4 mi north of Folelli on N198, then 2 km/1 mi up D37),* ☎ *04–95–36–62–33. Reservations essential. No credit cards. No lunch Thurs.–Sat. Nov.–Mar.*

$$ ★ ✕🏨 **Le Refuge.** Rooms at this hotel–restaurant are suspended over the valley of the Fium Alto stream. A handy midway point in the labyrinthine Castagniccia, it is a good place to stop for a Corsican beer, a superb meal based on the Rafalli family's home-processed charcuterie, and a night's sleep in the small but cozy quarters. ✉ *20229 Piedicroce,* ☎ *04–95–35–82–65,* FAX *04–95–35–84–42. 20 rooms. Restaurant. MC, V. Closed Nov.*

Asco

⓴ *22 km (13 mi) west of Ponte Leccia: 2 km (1 mi) north of Ponte Leccia, D147 turns off N197 toward the village of Asco, 16 km (10 mi) away.*

The Asco Valley runs west to an awe-inspiring barrier of mountains crowned by **Monte Cinto,** rising to 8,795 feet, the highest point in Corsica. As you travel, the maquis-covered valley gives way to a sheer granite gorge hung with sweet-smelling juniper. This is certainly a drive well worth making in daylight, although if your time is short you can see it on the way down the next day.

The valley is studded with beehives, and honey and cheese abound in Asco's shops. Don't miss the Genoan bridge below Asco, or even better, a swim in the river. Above Asco the granite gorge becomes a cool pine forest, perfect for hiking. Follow the road for another 12 km (7 mi) past the village, ending at the top against a wall of mountains.

Haut-Asco

㉑ *13 km (8 mi) west of Asco.*

Haut-Asco is the starting point for the eight- to nine-hour walk to atop Monte Cinto and back down again. From the top, on a clear day, you can see the entire island and even the Appennines on the Italian mainland. Clouds and mist gather after about 10 AM, however, particularly in summer. For this reason a 4 AM start is recommended. Questions can be answered at Le Chalet (☞ *below*).

Dining and Lodging

$ ✕🏨 **Le Chalet.** This tidy hideaway at the very top of the island has an impeccable restaurant serving Corsican cuisine. Walls are covered with photographs of famous mountaineers. Along with the 22 private rooms there is also a hiker's dormitory, a bar, and a store selling supplies to trekkers, who use the chalet as a way station from the GR 20. ✉ *Haut-Asco, 20276,* ☎ *04–95–47–85–84,* FAX *04–95–30–25–59. 22 rooms, dormitory with shared bath. Restaurant, bar, shop. MC, V. Closed early Nov.–early May.*

Outdoor Activities and Sports

For information about hiking up Monte Cinto, contact the **Parc Naturel Régional de la Corse** (☞ Corsica A to Z, *below*). From at least December to April, Corsica's upper reaches are snowed in and there is both alpine and cross-country skiing; consult the **Club Alpin Français** (☎ 04–95–22–73–81) in Ajaccio.

La Scala di Santa Regina

★ *9 km (5 mi) south of Ponte Leccia, D84 leaves N193, starts up the Golo River, and turns into La Scala di Santa Regina.*

This road, known as La Scala di Santa Regina (Stairway of the Holy Queen), is one of the most spectacular on the island. It's also one of the most difficult to navigate, especially in winter. The route follows the twisty path of the Golo River, which has carved its way through layers of red granite, forming dramatic gorges and waterfalls. Be prepared for herds of animals to cross the road. Follow the road to the **Col de Verghio** (mountain pass) where there are superb views of Tafunatu, the legendary perforated mountain, and Monte Cinto. On the way up, you'll pass through the **Valdo Niello Forest,** Corsica's most important woodlands, filled with pines and beeches. The col is considered the border between Haute-Corse and Corse-du-Sud. As you descend through the **Forêt d'Aitone,** note how well manicured it is—the pigs, goats, and sheep running rampant through the tall Laricio pines keep it this way. As you pass the village of Evisa, with its orange roofs, look across the impressive **Gorges de Spelunca** to see the hill village of Ota. A small road on the right will take you across the gorge, where there's an ancient Genoese-built bridge.

Ota

22 *16 km (10 mi) northwest of Evisa on La Scala di Santa Regina.*

The tiny village of Ota, overlooking the Gorges de Spelunca, has traditional stone houses that seem to be suspended on the mountainside, an amazing view of the surrounding mountains, and a number of trailheads. It's an excellent base for hiking in the area.

Dining and Lodging

$ ✕🏨 **Chez Fèlix.** This homey place serves as dining room, taxi stand, and town hall. Cheerful owner Marinette Ceccaldi cooks up heaping portions of Corsican specialties ranging from wild boar to chestnut-flour beignets. Suites are decorated with curios and antiques, each with a balcony overlooking the gorge; rooms are comfortable and rustic.

The hotel has a van that will transport you out to hiking routes. ✉ *pl. de la Fontaine, 20150,* ☎ *04–95–26–12–92. 10 suites. Restaurant, bar, kitchenettes. No credit cards.*

Porto and Les Calanches

23 *5 km (3 mi) west of Ota, 30 km (19 mi) south of Calvi.*

The flashy resort town of Porto doesn't have much character, but its setting on the crystalline Golfe de Porto, surrounded by massive pink granite mountains, is superb. Activity focuses on the small port where there is a boardwalk with restaurants and hotels. A short hike from the boardwalk will bring you to a 16th-century Genoese tower that overlooks the bay. Boat excursions leave daily for the Réserve Naturel de Scandola (☞ *below*).

Detour south of Porto on D81 to get to Les Calanches, jagged outcroppings of red rock considered among the most extraordinary natural sites in France. There are arches and stelae, standing rock formations that seem to have faces and distorted animal shapes.

Piana

★ 24 *11 km (7 mi) south of Porto, 71 km (44 mi) north of Ajaccio.*

Piana overlooks Les Calanches and the Golfe de Porto. Explore the crooked streets of the old town and climb up to the old fortress at the top of Capo Rosso to admire the craggy rocks that jut out from the water.

Dining and Lodging

$$ ✕🏨 **Les Roches Rouges.** On the hillside just below the Capo Rosso, this rambling old mansion has a distinctive British flavor. Don't be misled by the crumbling facade; the current owners are still renovating. Most rooms are monastic, but the irrepressible owner, Mady, and the hotel's stunning location make the hotel a winner. The vast Imperial-style restaurant is classified as a historic monument; go for the fish soup or grilled lobster. ✉ *rte. de Porto, 20115 Piana,* ☎ *04–95–27–81–81. 20 rooms. Restaurant. AE, DC, MC, V. Closed Nov.–Mar.*

$$–$$$ 🏨 **Capo Rosso.** The Capo Rosso sits high in the hills overlooking the gulf, just yards from Les Calanches. The views—whether seen from your room, the outdoor pool, or the restaurant's terrace—are dramatic. Unfortunately, the modern rooms are functional rather than charming. ✉ *20115 Piana,* ☎ *04–95–27–82–40,* FAX *04–95–27–80–00. 70 rooms. Restaurant. AE, DC, MC, V. Closed mid-Oct.–Easter.*

Calvi

25 *92 km (58 mi) north of Piana, 159 km (100 mi) north of Ajaccio.*

Calvi, Corsica's slice of the Riviera, has been described by Dorothy Carrington as "an oasis of pleasure on an otherwise austere island." Calvi grew rich by supplying products to Genoa; its citizens remained loyal supporters of Genoa long after the rest of the island declared independence. Calvi also claims to be the birthplace of Christopher Columbus. During the 18th century the town endured assaults from Corsican nationalists, including celebrated patriot Pasquale Paoli. Today, Calvi sees a summertime invasion of tourists, drawn to the 6 km (4 mi) stretch of sandy white beach, the citadel, and the booming night life.

The Genoese **Citadelle,** perched on a rocky promontory at the tip of the bay, competes with the beach as a major attraction. An inscription above the drawbridge, *Civitas Calvi semper fidelis,* "The citizens of Calvi always faithful," reflects the town's unswerving allegiance to Genoa. At the welcome center, just inside the gates, you can see a video on the city's history, and take a guided tour in English (three times a day) or a self-guided walking tour. ✉ *Up the hill off av. de l'Uruguay,* ☎ *04–95–65–36–74.* *Guided tour and video show 50 frs.* *Tour: 10 AM, 4:30, and 6:30, Easter–early Oct.*

Stop in at the 13th-century church of **St-Jean-Baptiste;** it contains an interesting Renaissance baptismal font. Look up to see the rows of pews screened by grillwork: The chaste young women of Calvi's upper classes sat here. ✉ *pl. d'Armes.*

OFF THE BEATEN PATH

GOLFE DE GIROLATA AND RÉSERVE NATUREL DE SCANDOLA – North of Porto are the Gulf of Girolata and the Scandola Natural Reserve, a dazzling sanctuary of maquis and underwater park where all hunting, fishing, and camping is prohibited. Founded in 1975, Scandola is managed by the Parc Naturel Régional and is inhabited by dolphins, falcons, ospreys, and many other strains of flora and fauna that have thrived here protected for the last 20 years. Only accessible by boat, excursions leave Calvi and Porto daily at 9 AM from April through October.

Dining and Lodging

$$$ ★ ✕ **Chez Tao.** At Chez Tao, a mandatory stop on almost everyone's itinerary, you can rub elbows with the town's glitterati in the ocher-color 16th-century vaults that look out over the bay. Seafood is what everyone eats, but food plays second fiddle to the atmosphere, which includes Corsican folk singing and Tao's charismatic son on the piano until the wee hours. ✉ *pl. de la Citadelle,* ☎ *04–95–65–00–73. AE, DC, MC, V. Closed mid-Sept.–Easter.*

$$$ ✕ **L'Île de Beauté.** One of Calvi's most celebrated restaurants, it has been pulling in crowds since 1929. Metal suns adorn the walls of the dining room, where the menu features a range of seafood and upland dishes ranging from lobster fricassee to wild boar stew. ✉ *quai Landry,* ☎ *04–95–65–00–46. AE, DC, MC, V. Closed Oct.–Apr. No lunch Wed.*

$–$$ ✕ **U San Carlu.** Good, classic Corsican and French cooking at reasonable prices makes U San Carlu a favorite. The brick-vaulted dining room is in a 16th-century building that was once a hospital. In summer, you can eat outdoors on the palm-shaded patio. Specialties include steak in Roquefort and prawns flamed in brandy and an excellent daily menu. ✉ *10 pl. St-Charles,* ☎ *04–95–65–92–20. AE, DC, MC, V. Closed Wed. mid-Oct.–mid-May. No dinner Tues.*

$ ✕ **Le Poème.** Drop in at Martine Abitbol's friendly restaurant in the citadel for Corsican cuisine or tea. (There is also a Le Poème in Manhattan's SoHo.) ✉ *9 rue Ste-Antoine,* ☎ *04–95–65–23–85. Closed mid-Oct.–June. No credit cards.*

$$$ ★ ✕ **Le Signoria.** This 17th-century country manor and annex have homey bedrooms and large bathrooms. From the pool and patio there are panoramic views of the mountains and the bay. The renowned restaurant serves imaginative, regional cuisine. It is closed for lunch, except for weekends from July through August. ✉ *rte. de la Forêt de Bonifato, 20260 (about 5 km/3 mi from Calvi),* ☎ *04–95–65–23–73,* FAX *04–95–65–33–20. 10 rooms. Restaurant, bar, pool, Turkish bath. AE, MC, V. Closed Nov.–Easter.*

$$$$ **La Villa.** On a hill with marvelous views of the town and the citadel, this Relais & Châteaux hotel feels like a modern Italian villa. The architecture leans heavily toward arched loggias and wrought iron; fountains, paintings, and sculpture abound. Rooms are large and have terra-cotta floors and balconies. The canopied dining area overlooks the pool, surrounded by a fragrant garden. ✉ *chemin de Notre Dame de la Serra, 20260,* ☎ *04–95–65–10–10,* FAX *04–95–65–10–50. 25 rooms. Restaurant, bar, pool, beauty salon, Turkish bath. AE, DC, MC, V. Closed Jan.–Mar.*

$$ 🏨 **Le Magnolia.** Rooms in this cozy hotel between the church and the marketplace are named after French literary figures: "Verlaine" overlooks rooftops to the port. Cupids and cherubs perch over beds. The restaurant is in the garden under a giant magnolia tree. ✉ *pl. du Marché,* ☎ *04–95–65–19–16,* FAX *04–95–65–34–52. DC, MC, V. Closed Jan.–Feb.*

Nightlife and the Arts

The in spot at night is the cabaret-restaurant **Chez Tao** (✉ pl. de la Citadelle). **La Camargue,** on the outskirts of town, is the big dance club; a free *navette* (shuttle bus) cruises downtown Calvi until dawn collecting and returning clubgoers.

The **Calvi Jazz Festival** takes place in mid-June. **Rencontres Polyphoniques,** an international choral festival, is held in mid-September. **Festiventu,** a celebration of wind-powered sports, musical instruments, and scientific artifacts, happens in late October.

Outdoor Activities and Sports

The **GR 20** begins near Calvi and follows the watershed line on the crests of the mountains, northwest–southeast to Ste-Lucie de Porto-Vecchio. Contact the tourist office (☞ Corsica A to Z, *below*) for information. For watersports, diving, boating information, and equipment rental, contact **Calvi Nautique Club** (✉ Port de Plaisance, ☎ 04–95–65–10–65). The **Centre Équestre de Calvi** (✉ rte. de Pietramaggiore, ☎ 04–95–65–22–22) arranges tours on horseback.

Shopping

The major shopping streets are rue Clemenceau and boulevard Wilson. Look for pottery, for which the region is known. Corsican knives are another specialty item, as are regional charcuterie, cheeses, and jams.

Calenzana

26 *13 km (8 mi) from Calvi: head east on N197 for 5 km (3 mi), then south on D151.*

Leave the Calvi region via the rose-color hill towns of La Balagne, known as the garden of Corsica. This remained a feudal society right up until the French Revolution. Calenzana, once a hideout for Corsica's notorious bandits, lies among the olive groves. The 11th-century church of **Ste-Restitute,** about 1 km (½ mi) beyond town, has an altar backed by medieval frescoes depicting the life of St. Restitute. Legend has it that the saint was martyred here in the 3rd century, and when the people of the town began building a church on another site, the stone blocks were moved here each night by two huge white bulls. Apparently, this happened several times before the townsfolk finally got the divine message and changed building sites.

En Route From Calenzana, serpentine D151 winds around hillsides dotted with picturesque villages. Most are surrounded by walls and have the same layout: a central area surrounded by short streets leading out like the spokes of a wheel, ending with a final house built into the village walls.

Cateri

27 *18 km (11 mi) north of Calenzana on D151.*

The cheese-making center of Cateri (or Catteri, as it is often spelled), in La Balagne, is known for its unique bell tower facade, a scrolled and pilastered pediment that is a miniature replica of Notre-Dame-des-Anges, of which it is part.

Dining

$ ✕ **Restaurant A Lataria.** This little spot just beyond the crossroads of Cateri has a flower-filled terrace with views of the village and the sea. The Corsican and Mediterranean fare, such as paella and brocciu lasagna, is a good value. ✉ *Cateri,* ☎ *04–95–61–71–44. Reservations essential off-season. Closed Oct.–May.*

Sant'Antonino

28 *7 km (4 mi) north of Cateri on D13, then across the gorge.*

The medieval stone village of Sant'Antonino, believed to date from the 9th century, is one of the oldest still-inhabited places on the island.

Pigna

29 *7 km (4 mi) northeast of Sant'Antonino on D151.*

The unusual village of Pigna is dedicated to bringing back traditional Corsican music and crafts. Here you can listen to folk songs in cafés, visit workshops, and buy handmade musical instruments. The Casa Musicale (☞ *below*), a concert hall, auberge, and restaurant, is at the center of it all. During the first half of July, the Casa Musicale hosts a Festivoce (singing festival) of vocalists and a capella groups.

Dining and Lodging

$ ✕🏨 **Casa Musicale.** This unique spot has traditional local cuisine, music of all kinds—often authentic Corsican polyphonic singing—and a lovely view over La Balagne down to Calvi. Rooms are simple but elegant, with whitewashed walls and rustic furniture. ✉ *Pigna 20220,* ☎ *04–95–61–77–31,* FAX *04–95–61–77–81. 7 rooms that sleep 2, 3, or 4. MC, V. Closed Mon., Jan.–Feb.*

Shopping

Casa di l'Artigiani sells a wide range of local crafts, from jam and honey to handknitted sweaters and musical instruments.

Algajola

30 *8 km (5 mi) east of Pigna, 10 km (6 mi) southwest of L'Île Rousse on N197.*

Built in the 16th century, the village of Algajola is another ancient fortress, the last and smallest of the seven citadel towns built by the Genoese on Corsica's shores. A low-key and friendly resort, its perfect crescent beach attracts crowds.

Dining and Lodging

$$ ✕🏨 **L'Ondine.** Nestled into the rocks at the edge of a sandy cove, L'Ondine is part of a pleasantly landscaped village of single-story, beige stucco buildings. The dining room, serving typical Corsican maritime cuisine, commands a million-dollar view of the beach and Algajola. ✉ *7 rue à Marina, Algajola 20220,* ☎ *04–95–60–70–02,* FAX *04–95–60–60–36. 55 rooms. Restaurant, bar, pool. MC, V. Closed late Oct.–late Mar.*

L'Île Rousse

31 *10 km (6 mi) northeast of Algajola, 37 km (22 mi) southwest of St-Florent.*

L'Île Rousse, named for the mass of reddish rock now connected to the town by a causeway, is a favorite spot of French vacationers who come to bask in its Riviera-like atmosphere. A small two-car train runs from here along the coast to Calvi, delivering sun worshipers to beaches not accessible by road.

Dining and Lodging

$$ ✕🏨 **A Pasturella.** This picturesque hotel has simple rooms with modern furnishings and geranium-filled window boxes; most overlook the mountains. The well-known restaurant specializes in seafood and Corsican dishes. Though it's unusual, rates are not higher in July and August. ✉ *Monticello, 20220 (5 km/3 mi outside of L'Île Rousse),* ☎ *04–95–60–05–65,* FAX *04–95–60–21–78. 14 rooms. Restaurant, bar. AE, MC, V. Closed mid-Nov.–mid-Dec.*

Outdoor Activities and Sports

Two of the best **beaches** in the area are the **Plage d'Ostriconi,** at the mouth of the Ostriconi River (20 km/13 mi north of town) and the wilder and much-frequented by nudists **Plage Saleccia,** used in the 1960s filming of *The Longest Day.*

Shopping

Baked goods, local wines, and herbs from the maquis can be bought at the **market** (✉ pl. Paoli).

Lama

32 *15 km (9 mi) southeast of L'Île Rousse, 57 km (24 mi) north of Corte.*

The charmingly restored medieval village of Lama is only 10 minutes up the Ostriconi valley and is a handy place to spend a night on your way to Cap Corse. Everyone from the mayor to the local children works to accommodate visitors; people say hello in the streets and seem to know where you are staying. Once a prosperous olive-growing town, the village was nearly deserted after a 1971 fire destroyed 35,000 olive trees in one afternoon. Carefully cultivated tourism has put Lama back on the map.

Dining and Lodging

$$ ✕ **U Campu Latinu.** Skillfully built into an ancient bergerie using old stone and drywall construction, this flower-festooned restaurant overlooks Lama, the sea, and the mountains. Try an omelet or lasagna prepared with mint and brocciu or lamb grilled over coals with maquis herbs. ✉ *Lama,* ☎ *04–95–48–23–83. DC, MC, V. Closed Sept.–June.*

$$–$$$ ✕🏨 **Ferme Équestre de L'Ostriconi.** Pierre-Jean and Christine Costa will make you a part of this place, whether on horseback, on a wild boar hunt, or by showing you Lama's hidden corners and secret spots. Open year-round, this lively restaurant is the happening place in town. ✉ *Lama 20218,* ☎ *04–95–48–22–99,* FAX *04–95–48–21–49. 50 cottages. Kitchenettes. DC, MC, V.*

Outdoor Activities and Sports

Riding along the old mule trails on horseback is an excellent way to see the countryside; contact **Ferme Équestre de L'Ostriconi** (☞ *above*).

Murato

33 *15 km (9 mi) west of Lama, 12 km (7 mi) south of Bastia: Take N193 to D82 to D305 at Rutalli.*

The village of Murato has two excellent restaurants and an extraordinary 12th-century Pisan church. The polychrome, green and white marble **Église Mosaïque de San Michele** overlooks the Golfe de St-Florent and sometimes even the mainland.

Dining

$$ ★ ✕ **Le Ferme Campo di Monte.** The Julliards prepare some of Corsica's best, most authentic fare at this lovely 350-year-old farmhouse. Be sure to try the *storzapreti* (brocciu croquettes). ✉ *D305 Rutali-Murato,* ☎ *04–95–37–64–60. Reservations essential. AE, DC, MC, V. Closed weekdays Sept.–June.*

St-Florent

34 *28 km (17 mi) northeast of the exit for Lama on D81, 46 km (28½ mi) northeast of L'Île Rousse.*

St-Florent is a postcard-perfect village nestled into the crook of the Golfe de St-Florent between the rich Nebbio Valley and the desert of Agriates. The town has a crumbling citadel and a popular yacht basin ringed by shops and restaurants. Be sure to seek out the interesting Romanesque **Santa Maria Assunta,** just outside the village. Standing in isolated splendor among the vineyards, this 12th-century limestone church is one of only two Pisan churches remaining on the island. The facade and interior columns support a menagerie of sculpted human faces, snakes, snails, and mythical animals. ✉ *rue Agostino Giustiniani.*

Dining

$$$ ✕ **La Rascasse.** This fine restaurant overlooking the port is known for its excellent fish stews and fresh seafood dishes. Try to get an upstairs table for a better view of the gulf. The *civet de lotte* (stewed sea bass) and the warm scallop salad are especially good. ✉ *esplanade du Port,* ☎ *04–37–06–99. AE, DC, MC, V. Closed Mon. Apr.–June, Sept.*

Patrimonio

35 *5 km (3 mi) northeast of St-Florent, 18 km (11 mi) west of Bastia.*

Patrimonio lies at the base of the Cap Corse peninsula, among acres of vineyards that produces some of Corsica's best red wine. The Antoine Arena vineyards are gaining ground steadily, but the **Orenga de Gaffory** label is the most famous. Tours of the vineyard and art gallery can be arranged. ☎ *04–95–37–11–38.* ⏲ *Weekdays 9–noon and 3–6.*

Nightlife and the Arts

The **Nuits de la Guitare** music festival during the third week of July is one of Corsica's top musical events, featuring blues, jazz, and flamenco guitarists from all over the world.

Outdoor Activities and Sports

One of the most spectacular mountain **hiking** routes in Corsica follows the crest of Cap Corse over the 1,307-meter (4,287-feet) Monte Stello, from which you can see hills of Tuscany and Provence. Contact the Parc Naturel Régional de la Corse (☞ Corsica A to Z, *below*) for details.

Nonza

36 *14 km (9 mi) north of Patrimonio, 8 km (5 mi) south of Canelle.*

On your way along Cap Corse, be sure to stop in Nonza. This vertiginous crag seems impossibly high over its famous black beach, the legacy of a former asbestos mine down the coast at Canari. The beach is accessible only by 600 steps leading down from Nonza, and no doubt this is the reason it's usually deserted. The chapel is dedicated to the martyred Ste-Julie, whose severed breasts became the double fountain, known as the *Fontaine aux Mamelles* (Fountain of Mammaries) on the way down to the beach. The spectacular, gravity defying tower was constructed by Pasquale Paoli in 1760. Its squared corners made it easier to defend, as famed Captain Casella proved in 1768 when he stood off 1200 French troops.

Dining and Lodging

$$ ✕🏨 **Auberge Patrizi.** On a shady terrace in the center of town, this place serves excellent Corsican cuisine in a lively setting. There are also rooms—small and a little close to the road—with spectacular views. ✉ *pl. du Village, 20217,* ☎ *04–95–37–82–16. 13 rooms. AE, MC, V. Closed Nov.–Mar.*

Centuri

37 *55 km (34 mi) north of Patrimonio, 41 km (25 mi) north of Nonza.*

Centuri is a good place to stop for lunch on your way around Cap Corse. Watch for the arrival of the fishing boats at the end of the afternoon; the town is known as Cap Corse's top fishing port.

Dining and Lodging

$$$ ✕🏨 **Le Vieux Moulin.** If you're after Old World charm and authentic Corsican flavor, this is the place. The main house was built in 1870 as a private residence; the eight-room annex is more recent but no less inviting, with bougainvillea cascading from its balconies. Boat rides and fishing trips can be arranged, and there are tennis courts and golf nearby. The restaurant specializes in seafood: Try the bouillabaisse. ✉ *Centuri Port, 20238,* ☎ *04–95–35–60–15,* FAX *04–95–35–60–24. 14 rooms. Restaurant. AE, DC, MC, V. Closed Nov.–Mar.*

En Route From Centuri, continue along the D80 coastal road to the **belvedere** near the Moulin Mattei windmill at Col de Serra, on the tip of the peninsula. As you round the tip, you can see some of Corsica's 90 **Genoan watchtowers,** as well as the Giraglia island with its lighthouse. Take D253 north to reach the fishing village of **Barcaggio.** A long sandy beach extends east from the village, ending in a path leading to the 16th-century Tour D'Agnello. The **Finocchiarola islands,** a protected aviary reserve visitable by boat from Macinaggio, are visible off the northeast corner of the peninsula. As you head down the east coast of Cap Corse on D80, you might want to make a detour on D180 through the **Col de Ste-Lucie** to the Tour de Sénèque, home of the Roman philosopher and writer after he was exiled for seducing the niece of Emperor Claudius. Farther south on D80, a drive up D32 to the town of **Sisco** will take you to within a 2-km (1-mi) walk of the Romanesque church of San Michele, built in 1030.

Erbalunga

38 *40 km (25 mi) southeast of Centuri, 10 km (6 mi) north of Bastia.*

Erbalunga is one of the most charming villages on Cap Corse's east coast, with stone houses sloping gently down to a Genoan tower built into a rock ledge. Probably as a result of Erbalunga's aesthetic grace, though possibly because it was French poet Paul Valéry's ancestral home, a colony of artists settled here in the '20s.

Lodging

$$–$$$ ★ **Castel Brando.** This 19th-century mansion has dark green shutters and terra-cotta tiles. The large rooms are furnished with country-style antiques and dried flowers. The large pool and the terrace, where breakfast is served, is in the garden. ✉ *B.P. 20 Erbalunga, 20222,* ☎ *04–95–30–10–30,* FAX *04–95–33–98–18. 16 rooms. Air-conditioning, kitchenettes, pool. AE, MC, V. Closed late Oct.–Apr.*

Bastia

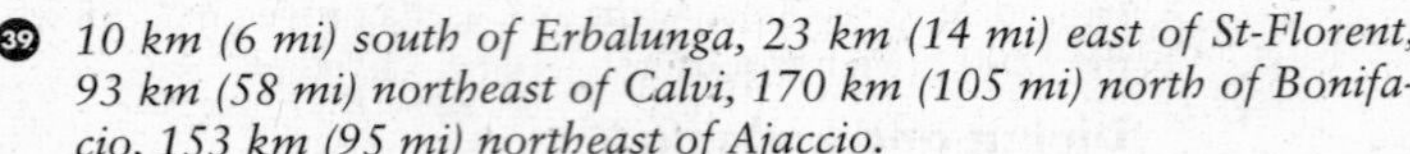

39 *10 km (6 mi) south of Erbalunga, 23 km (14 mi) east of St-Florent, 93 km (58 mi) northeast of Calvi, 170 km (105 mi) north of Bonifacio, 153 km (95 mi) northeast of Ajaccio.*

Bastia's name comes from the *bastaglia,* or fortress, which the Genoese built here in the 14th century as a stronghold against rebellious islanders and potential invaders. Today, the city is Corsica's business center and largest town. Despite sprawling suburbs, the center of Bastia retains the timeless, salty flavor of an ancient Mediterranean port.

The **Terra Vecchia** (Old Town) is small enough to be explored on foot. Start at the wide, palm-filled **place St-Nicolas** bordered on one side by the sea and on the other by two blocks of cafés that stretch out along boulevard **Général de Gaulle.** These cafés with their tables spilling into the square are the hub of Bastia's social life.

Head south on boulevard de Gaulle, which becomes rue Napoléon, and in two blocks on the left you will see the **Church of the Conception** occupying a pebble-studded square. Step inside to admire the church's ornate 18th-century interior, although the lighting is poor and you'll need a bright day to see much. The walls are covered with a riot of wood carvings, gold, and marble, and the ceiling is painted with vibrant frescoes. ✉ *rue Napoléon.*

The **place du Marché,** the market square, open every morning except Monday, is behind the church. The warren of tiny streets that make up the old fishermen's quarter begins at the far side of the square.

To the south is the picturesque **Vieux Port** (Old Port), along quai des Martyrs de la Libération, dominated by the hilltop citadel. The harbor, lined with excellent seafood restaurants, is home to million-dollar yachts, but you can still find many bright red-and-blue fishing boats and tangles of old nets and lines. A walk around the port takes you to **Terra Nova** (New Town), a maze of not-so-new streets and houses at the base of the 15th-century fortress. Climb the stairs to the top for a sweeping view of the Italian islands of Capraia, Elba, and Montecristo.

Stop in at the **Genoese Governor's Palace,** whose vaulted, colonnaded galleries now house the **Corsican Ethnographic Museum,** with collections detailing the island's history. Look for the 18th-century rebel flag with the black head and white headband. Behind the ancient defense tower, a tiny stairway leads past the *Casablanca,* a French submarine used by the Resistance. The swastikas on the turret are from downed Nazi aircraft. ✉ *pl. du Donjon,* ☎ *04–95–31–09–12.* 🎫 *18 frs.* ⏲ *Weekdays 9–noon and 2–6, weekends 10–noon and 2–5.*

A network of cobbled alleyways rambles across the citadel to the 15th-century **Cathédrale Ste-Marie.** Inside, classic Baroque abounds in an explosion of gilt decoration. The 18th-century silver statue of the Assumption is paraded at the head of a religious procession every August 15th. ✉ *rue Notre-Dame.*

The sumptuous Baroque style of the **Chapelle Ste-Croix,** behind the cathedral, makes it look more like a theater than a church. The chapel owes its names to a blackened oak crucifix, "Christ of the Miracles," discovered by fishermen at sea in 1428 and venerated to this day by Bastia's fishing community.

Dining and Lodging

$$–$$$ ★ ✕ **Lavezzi.** Enjoy the view of the old port as you choose from a host of fish and seafood specials. The cuisine is traditional Corsican; try the crèpes au brocciu or, in winter, the duck breast in honey and olives. ✉ *8 rue St-Jean,* ☎ *04–95–31–05–73. Reservations essential. AE, DC, MC, V. Closed Sun. and Feb.–Mar.*

$$ ✕ **La Voûte.** Kids come here for the pizza cooked in a wood-fire oven, while their parents dip into excellent fish and steaks at these former stables. Vaulted brick ceilings, exposed stone, and indirect lighting add an authentic Corsican atmosphere. The smoked salmon and the ravioli in cream of sea urchins are superb. ✉ *6 bis rue Luce de Casabianca,* ☎ *04–95–32–27–82. AE, MC, V. Closed Sun.*

$$$ **Pietracap.** Perched on a hillside five minutes north of Bastia, Pietracap is a strikingly modern hotel nestled into a fragrant garden. The large rooms have stark, white modern furnishings and balconies. The lobby and hallways are decorated with bold canvases painted by the amiable owner's brother. ✉ *20 rte. de San Martino di Lota, Pietranera-Bastia, 20200,* ☎ *04–95–31–64–63,* FAX *04–95–31–39–00. 42 rooms. Bar, pool, bicycles. AE, DC, MC, V. Closed mid-Dec.–early Mar.*

$$ **Posta Vecchia.** The greatest feature of this hotel in an old building is its quai-side location in town. The unpretentious rooms have floral wallpaper and wood-beam ceilings; some are small. Ask for one in the main house facing the port. ✉ *quai des Martyrs, 20200,* ☎ *04–95–32–32–38.* FAX *04–95–32–14–05. 49 rooms. AE, DC, MC, V.*

Nightlife and the Arts

For a night of traditional Corsican music, head to **U-Fanale** (✉ Vieux Port). Musicians fill the lively patio of the **Pub Chez Assunta** (✉ pl. Fontaine Nueve 4) on most summer nights. **L'Alba** (✉ 22 quai des Martyrs) is a piano bar for an older crowd. A younger set gathers at **Mayflower** (✉ port de Plaisance) to hear loud rock and roll.

One of Corsica's major carnivals, the **Fête du Christ Noir** (Feast of the Black Christ), dedicated to Bastia's most important religious icon, takes place on the third of May. A **Film Festival** is held every November. The **International Music Festival** takes place in early December.

Outdoor Activities and Sports

Rent bikes from **Locacycles** (✉ 40 rue César-Campinchi). Gallop along the coast on a horse from the **Société Hippique Urbaine de Bastia La Marana** (☎ 04–95–33–53–08 or 04–95–30–37–62). Golf at the 9-hole **Bastia Golf Club** (✉ Castellarèse, rte. de l'aéroport, Borgo, 12 km/7 mi south of Bastia, ☎ 04–95–38–33–99).

Shopping

Casa di l'Artigiani (✉ 5 rue des Terrasses) has a wide selection of local crafts. The **Mattei Cap Corse** store (✉ pl. St-Nicolas) sells the Mattei family's special Cap Corse liqueur. At the **market** (✉ pl. du Marché, behind St-Jean-Baptiste) everything from local cheeses to charcuterie to myrtle liqueur is sold on weekday mornings.

San Martino di Lota

40 *12 km (7 mi) north of Bastia.*

Just 20 minutes from downtown Bastia, the turnoff to the perched village of San Martino di Lota winds through thick vegetation as the flat blue expanse of the Tyrrhenian Sea spreads out below. A hike up the **Bocca di Santo Lunardo** above the village is a great way to develop a ravenous appetite: It's a six- to eight-hour round-trip trek with fantastic views of Cap Corse, the Tyrrhenian, and the Tuscan hills.

Dining and Lodging

$$ ✕🏨 **La Corniche.** The Anziani family runs this excellent hotel–restaurant serving Corsican fare—*cabri aux herbes du maquis* (roast kid in herbs from the maquis) and wild boar terrine. The restaurant is closed Sunday dinner and Monday from October–April. Rooms have panoramic views of the Tyrrhenian. ✉ *San Martino di Lota, 20200,* ☏ *04–95–31–40–98,* FAX *04–95–32–37–69. 18 rooms. Restaurant. AE, DC, MC, V. Closed late Dec.–late Jan.*

CORSICA A TO Z

Arriving and Departing

By Ferry

Regular car-ferries run from Marseille, Nice, and Toulon to Ajaccio, Bastia, Calvi, L'Île Rousse, and Propriano. These crossings take from 5 to 10 hours, with sleeping cabins available. Packages including the crossing with a car, onboard cabin, and hotel in Corsica are available from SNCM. **SNCM** (✉ Société Nationale Maritime Corse-Méditerranée, Paris, ☏ 01–49–24–24–24; Marseille, ☏ 04–91–56–30–30; Nice, ☏ 04–93–13–66–99; Toulon, ☏ 04–94–16–66–66; Ajaccio, ☏ 04–95–29–66–99; Bastia, ☏ 04–95–54–66–88; Calvi, ☏ 04–95–65–01–38; L'Île Rousse, ☏ 04–95–60–09–56). **CMN** (✉ Compagnie Méridionale de Navigation, Ajaccio, ☏ 04–95–21–20–34; Bastia, ☏ 04–95–31–63–38).

Connections from the Italian mainland are run by: **Corsica Ferries** (Bastia, ☏ 04–95–32–95–95; Genoa, Italy, ☏ 010–59–33–01). **Moby Lines** (Bastia, ☏ 04–95–31–46–29; Bonifacio, ☏ 04–95–73–00–29; Genoa, ☏ 010–20–56–51). Sardinia can be reached by ferry from Bastia or Bonifacio on: **Navarma Lines** (✉ 4 rue Luce-de-Casablanca, 20200 Bastia, ☏ 04–95–31–46–29 or at the port in Bonifacio, ☏ 04–95–73–00–29). **Saremar** (✉ Gare Maritime, 20169 Bonifacio, ☏ 04–95–73–06–75).

By Plane

Corsica has four major airports: Ajaccio, Bastia, Calvi, and Figari. **Air Inter** (☏ 04–95–29–45–45 Ajaccio; ☏ 01–45–46–90–00 Paris) has daily service connecting Paris and Lyon with Ajaccio, Bastia, and Calvi. **Delta Airlines** (☏ 800/241–4141) connects with Air Inter for flights from the United States to Corsica from May to October. **TAT** (✉ Transport Aérian Transrégional, toll free in France, ☏ 05–05–50–05; ☏ 04–95–71–01–20 Figari) flies to Figari from Paris. **Compagnie Corse Méditérranée** (☏ 04–95–29–05–00 Ajaccio) connects Ajaccio and Bastia to Nice and Marseille, with several flights a day.

The airports at Ajaccio and Bastia run regular **shuttle bus** services to and from town. At Figari, a bus meets all incoming flights and will take passengers as far as Bonifacio and Porto-Vecchio for about 100 francs. If you arrive at Calvi, take a taxi into the town center for about 100 francs.

Getting Around

By Bus

The local bus network is geared to residents who take it to school and work. At least two buses a day connect all the southern towns with Ajaccio, while northern towns are connected by bus to Bastia.

By Car

Though driving is undoubtedly the best way to explore the island's scenic stretches, note that winding, mountainous roads and uneven surfaces can actually double or triple your expected travel time. The Michelin 1/200,000 map No. 90 is essential. Be prepared for spelling anomalies, many of which are simply Corsican instead of French. Drive defensively: Drivers circulate at terrifying speeds.

By Plane

Airlines with inter-island flights are: **Air Balagne** (☎ 04–95–65–02–97). **ATM** (Air Transport Méditérranée, ☎ 04–95–76–04–99). **Kyrnair** (☎ 04–95–20–52–29).

By Train

The main line of Corsica's simple rail network runs from Ajaccio, in the west, to Corte, in the central valley, then divides at Ponte Leccia. From here, one line continues to L'Île Rousse and Calvi in the north and the other to Bastia in the northeast. Another daily service runs four times daily between Ajaccio and Bastia. In summer, a small train connects Calvi and L'Île Rousse, stopping at numerous beaches and resorts (for information: ☎ 04–95–23–11–03, Ajaccio; ☎ 04–95–32–60–06, Bastia; ☎ 04–95–65–00–61, Calvi; ☎ 04–15–46–00–87, Corte).

Contacts and Resources

Car Rental

Avis Ollandini (✉ Ajaccio airport, ☎ 04–95–23–25–14). **Europcar** (✉ 1 rue du Nouveau Port, Bastia, ☎ 04–95–31–59–29). **Hertz** (✉ Ajaccio airport, ☎ 04–95–22–14–84; 8 cours Grandval, Ajaccio, ☎ 04–95–21–70–94; square St-Victor, Bastia, ☎ 04–95–31–14–24; quai du Commerce, Bonifacio, ☎ 04–95–73–02–47; 2 rue Maréchal Joffre, Calvi, ☎ 04–95–65–06–64) serves the entire island with 18 offices at all the airports, harbors, and major towns. Be sure to reserve at least two weeks in advance in July and August.

Guided Tours

Much of Corsica's most spectacular scenery is best viewed from the water. **Colombo Line** (✉ quai Landry, ☎ 04–95–65–32–10) and **Promenades en Mer** (✉ Porto Marine, ☎ 04–95–26–15–16) in Calvi organize whole-day tours in glass-bottom boats of Girolata, the Scandola nature reserve, and the Golfe de Porto. **Promenades en Mer** (✉ Port de l'Amirauté 20000 Ajaccio, ☎ 04–95–23–23–38) in Ajaccio organizes daily trips (at 9 AM and 2 PM) to the Îles Sanguinaires. **Vedettes Christina** (☎ 04–95–73–14–69) and **Vedettes Méditérranée** (☎ 04–95–73–07–71) arrange outings from Bonifacio to the Îles Lavezzi, Les Calanches, and Les Grottes.

Canoeing, kayaking, and rafting are popular pastimes on the inland mountain rivers in the area; for details, write the **Association Municipale de Ponte-Leccia** (✉ 20218 Ponte Leccia). Two- and three-day guided hikes through the mountains and lake region are organized by the **Associu di Muntagnoli Corsi** (✉ quartier Pentaniedda, 20122 Quenza, ☎ 04–95–78–64–05).

Ollandini (✉ 1 rte. d'Alata, Ajaccio, ☎ 04–95–21–10–12) arranges whole- and half- day bus tours of the island leaving from Ajaccio. **Kyrnair** (☎ 04–95–20–52–29) and **ATM** (☎ 04–95–76–04–99) arrange sightseeing tours by plane.

Travel Agencies

Corse Itineraries (✉ 32 cours Napoléon, Ajaccio, ☎ 04–95–51–01–10, FAX 04–45–21–52–30). **Corse Voyages** (✉ Immeuble Les Remparts, bd. Wilson, Calvi, ☎ 04–95–65–26–71). **Cyrnea Tourisme** (✉ 9 av. Xavier-Luciani, Corte, ☎ 04–95–46–24–62, FAX 04–95–46–11–22). **Kallistour** (✉ 6 av. Maréchal-Sebastiani, Bastia, ☎ 04–95–31–71–49, FAX 04–95–32–35–73).

Visitor Information

The **Agence du Tourisme de la Corse** (✉ 17 bd. Roi-Jérome, 20000 Ajaccio, ☎ 04–95–51–77–77) can provide information about the whole island. The **Parc Naturel Régional de la Corse** (✉ 2 rue Sergent Casalonga; mailing address BP 417, 2184, Ajaccio; ☎ 04–95–51–79–10), Corsica's wildlife and natural resource management authority, controlling well over a third of the island, can provide trail maps, booklets, and a wide range of information. Local tourist offices are: **Ajaccio** (✉ Hôtel de Ville, pl. Foch, ☎ 04–95–21–53–39). **Bastia** (✉ pl. St-Nicholas, ☎ 04–95–31–00–89). **Bonifacio** (✉ rue des Deux Moulins, ☎ 04–95–73–11–88). **Calvi** (✉ port de Plaisance, ☎ 04–95–65–16–67). **Corte** (✉ La Citadelle, ☎ 04–95–46–24–20). **Sartène** (✉ rue Borgo, ☎ 04–95–77–15–40).

15 Toulouse, the Midi-Pyrénées, and Roussillon

The Midi-Pyrénées and Roussillon form the main body of France's traditional southwestern Languedoc region. Languedoc, named for the local medieval language, Langue d'Oc (literally, "language of yes") possesses some of France's finest and most varied treasures: cosmopolitan Toulouse, the wild peaks of the Pyrénées, and colorful Mediterranean fishing villages. A cultural capital at the end of the last millennium, Toulouse is still one of France's liveliest and loveliest cities.

Updated by George Semler

THE MIDI-PYRÉNÉES IS FRANCE'S largest region, spreading over 75,000 sq km (28,500 sq mi) from the Dordogne in the north to the Spanish border along the Pyrénées in the south. Mountains, lakes, rivers, and arid limestone plateaus lend the region extreme natural variety. This is the perfect spot for nature lovers, sports enthusiasts, and gastronomes alike.

The Pyrénées, Western Europe's highest mountain range after the Alps, give birth to the Garonne, the great Atlantic-bound river of Toulouse and Bordeaux. The Garonne is joined by the Rivers Aveyron and Tarn (as well as by the Lot and the Célée to the north), flowing east to west, all of which carve out steep gorges and wide green valleys. The Pyrénées and their foothills are richly endowed with lakes, glacial ponds, brooks, streams, thermal springs, and Roman spas.

Toulouse is an upbeat university center with a rhythm more redolent of Spain (two hours' drive away) than of the drowsy French provinces. The city is known as the Ville Rose (Pink City) because of the ruddy glow of its redbrick buildings. The Canal du Midi, built in the 17th century, passes through Toulouse and continues east, near the medieval walls of Carcassonne, on its way from the Atlantic to the Mediterranean.

Other highlights range from the picturesque hilltop village of Cordes to the religious mecca of Lourdes to the natural wonder of the Pyrenean Cirque de Gavarnie. There are two outstanding art museums: the Musée Ingres at Montauban, devoted to one of France's most accomplished pre-Impressionist painters, and the Musée Toulouse-Lautrec at Albi, with its unique collection of works by the leading observer of Belle Epoque cabaret.

Roussillon—between Narbonne and the Spanish border—is easy to reach from Toulouse. Perpignan, its capital, has a bustling, Iberian feel. There are strong linguistic and historic ties with Catalonia: The area was ceded to France as recently as 1659. The streets of even the smallest towns display the Catalan colors of *sang et or* (blood and gold).

Pleasures and Pastimes

Dining

The region is known for rich and strongly seasoned cooking: Garlic and goose fat are generously used. Be sure to try some of the renowned foie gras and confit *de canard* (of duck). The most famous regional dish is cassoulet, a succulent white-bean stew with confit *d'oie* (of goose) or confit de canard, spicy sausage, pork, and sometimes lamb. Cheaper specialties include *garbure,* mixed vegetables served as a broth or puree; *farci du lauragais,* a kind of pork pancake; and *gigot de sept heures,* a leg of lamb cooked for seven hours. Finish your meal with a glass of Armagnac, distilled throughout the Gers *département* (province). You'll see signs for *dégustation* (tasting) just about everywhere.

CATEGORY	COST*
$$$$	over 400 frs
$$$	250 frs–400 frs
$$	125 frs–250 frs
$	under 125 frs

**per person for a three-course meal, including tax (20.6%) and tip but not wine*

Lodging

Hotels range from Mediterranean modern to Middle Ages baronial; most are small and cozy rather than luxurious. Toulouse has the usual range of big-city hotels; make reservations well in advance if you plan to visit in spring or fall.

CATEGORY	COST*
$$$$	over 800 frs
$$$	550 frs–800 frs
$$	300 frs–550 frs
$	under 300 frs

**All prices are for a standard double room, including tax (20.6%) and service charge.*

Outdoor Activities and Sports

More than 3,200 km (1,987 mi) of marked hiking trails traverse the Midi-Pyrénées. The Pyrénées Orientales (eastern Pyrénées) between Foix and Prades offer great walks, though sturdy legs come in handy. The rough waters of the Tarn and Aveyron gorges are perfect for canoeing and kayaking; the peaceful River Quercy is better for a gentler trip. Skiing—downhill or cross-country—is excellent in the Pyrénées, with over two dozen ski resorts along the central and eastern part of the range. There are also equestrian tours, fishing opportunities, and several superb golf courses.

Exploring the Midi-Pyrénées

This region can be divided into four areas. The first covers Toulouse, a lively city imbued with culture and history. The second encompasses the area to the north and west of Toulouse, including Albi, the Lot valley, Montauban, and verdant Gascony—the Gers département. The third stretches into the Hautes Pyrénées (High Pyrénées) to the south. The fourth extends east into Roussillon at Carcassonne, up through the Ariège and through the Pyrénées Orientales to the Mediterranean before swinging north through Perpignan and Narbonne.

Great Itineraries

Getting to know the large Midi-Pyrénées and Roussillon regions would take several weeks or even years. But it is possible to sample their finest offerings in three to ten days, if that's all you have.

Numbers in the text correspond to numbers in the margin and on The Midi-Pyrénées and Roussillon and Toulouse maps.

IF YOU HAVE 3 DAYS

Bask in the rich rose color of **Toulouse** ①–㉓ for a day, then head to **Cordes** ㉕, a fortified medieval village. Make Toulouse-Lautrec's hometown, **Albi** ㉔, your home for the night: Locals argue that it's a deeper rose hue than Toulouse—you can decide. On day three, explore the medieval citadel at **Carcassonne** ㊳.

IF YOU HAVE 7 DAYS

Spend the first day and a half in **Toulouse** ①–㉓, then drive west to **Auch** ㉛, the capital of the Gers département. Next head north to **Condom** ㉙, in the Armagnac region, for a taste of the famous brandy. On your way to the cloisters at **Moissac** ㉗, roam around the old Roman town of **Lectoure** ㉘. On day three, study up on the university town of **Montauban** ㉖ before stepping back in time in medieval **Cordes** ㉕. Spend the night at **Albi** ㉔ or at the delightful inn in nearby Plaisance (☞ Chapter 11). Go south to **Carcassonne** ㊳ for more medieval history, on the fourth day, before going to **Mirepoix** ㊴, near the castle town of **Foix** ㊵, for the night. The next day drive into the Pyrénées, passing through **Tarascon-sur-Ariège** ㊶ to see the Grotte de Niaux, the mountain resort of **Font-Romeu** ㊸, and the Vauban fortress town of **Mont-Louis** ㊺. Spend the night in nearby **Eyne** ㊹ before con-

Midi-Pyrénées and Roussillon

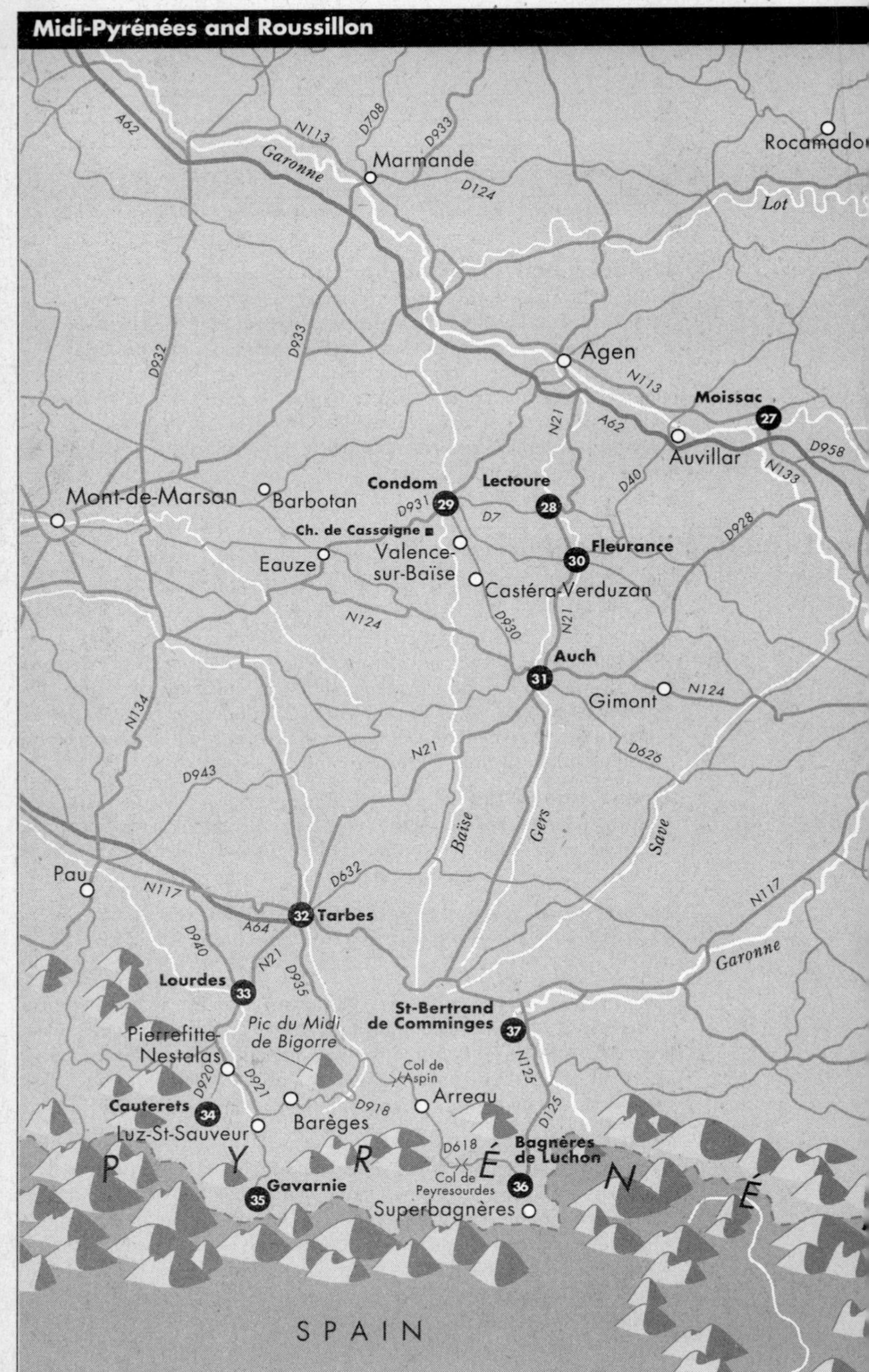

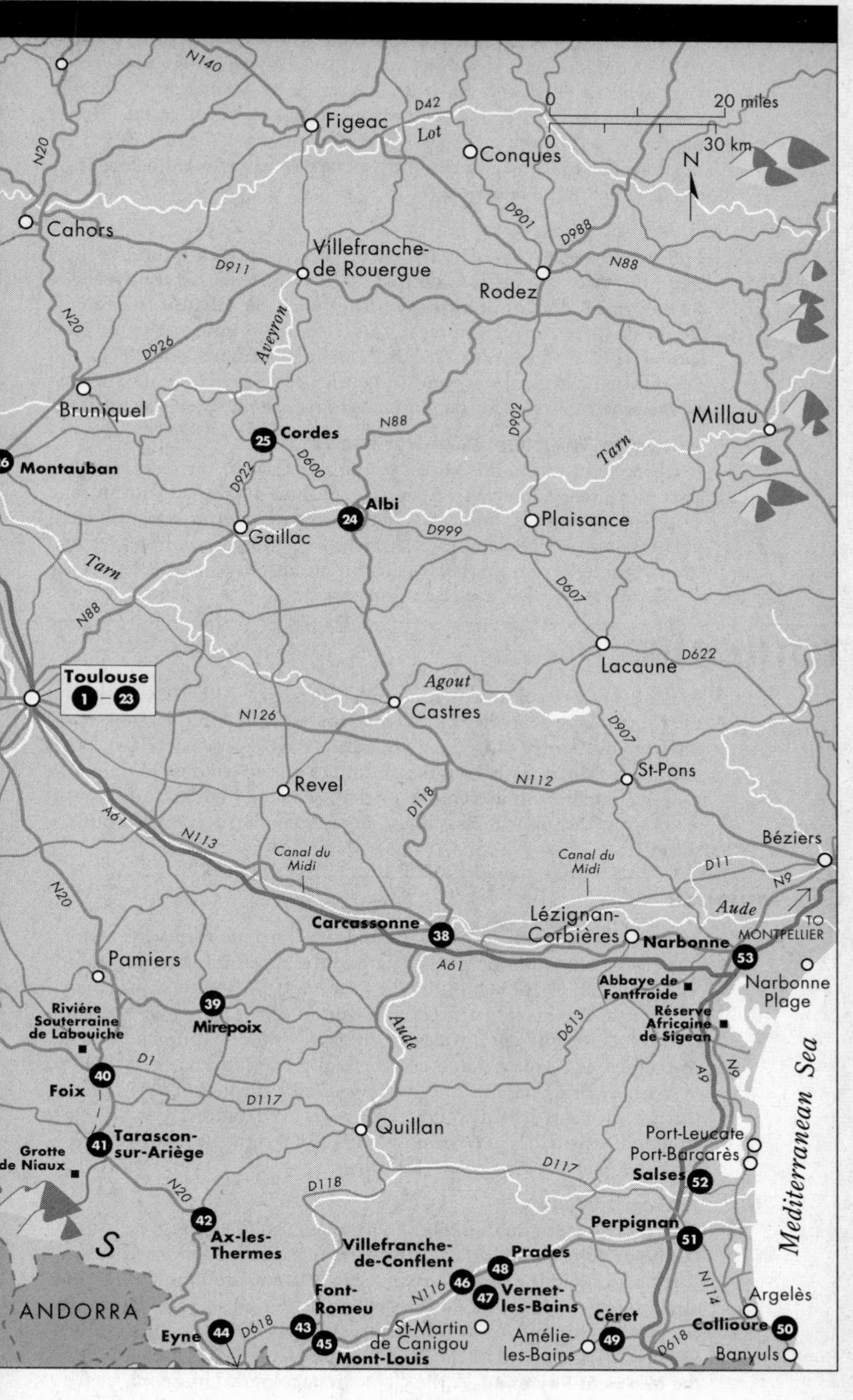

0
20 miles
0
30 km
N
Figeac
Conques
Lot
D42
N140
N20
Cahors
Villefranche-de Rouergue
Rodez
D911
D901
D988
N88
Aveyron
D926
Bruniquel
Millau
25 Cordes
N88
D902
Tarn
6 Montauban
D922
D600
24 Albi
Plaisance
Gaillac
D999
Tarn
D607
N88
Lacaune
D622
Toulouse
1 – 23
Agout
Castres
N126
D907
St-Pons
N112
Revel
D118
A61
N113
Canal du Midi
Canal du Midi
Béziers
D11
N9
N20
Aude
Carcassonne 38
Lézignan-Corbières
Narbonne 53
TO MONTPELLIER
A61
Pamiers
Abbaye de Fontfroide
Narbonne Plage
39 Mirepoix
Rivière Souterraine de Labouiche
Réserve Africaine de Sigean
Aude
D613
D1
40 Foix
A9
N9
Mediterranean Sea
D117
Quillan
41 Tarascon-sur-Ariège
Grotte de Niaux
Port-Leucate
Port-Barcarès
D117
Salses 52
D118
N20
42 Ax-les-Thermes
Perpignan 51
S
Villefranche-de-Conflent
48 Prades
N116
46
47 Vernet-les-Bains
N114
Font-Romeu
Argelès
ANDORRA
St-Martin de Canigou
Céret
Collioure 50
Eyne 44
D618
43
45 Mont-Louis
Amélie-les-Bains
49
D618
Banyuls

tinuing east out of the Pyrénées toward the Mediterranean. Stop in the fortified town of **Villefranche-de-Conflent** ㊻ and the Abbaye de St-Martin-de-Canigou. Pass through the spa town of **Vernet-les-Bains** ㊼ on your way to **Prades** ㊽ and the Abbaye de St-Michel-de-Cuxa, and **Céret** ㊾. Spend the sixth night in Roussillon's historic capital, **Perpignan** 51 or the fishing village of **Collioure** ㊿. On the final day, drive north to **Salses** 52, where Hannibal once passed through, before leaving this region at **Narbonne** 53.

IF YOU HAVE 10 DAYS

Follow the seven-day itinerary, except head south early on the third day, after two days in **Toulouse** ①–㉓, to the towns in the Pyrénées: **St-Bertrand de Comminges** ㊲, **Bagnères de Luchon** ㊱, and **Gavarnie** ㉟. Spend night three in Gavarnie before going on to (or past) **Cauterets** ㉞ and **Lourdes** ㉝. Drive through **Tarbes** ㉜, **Auch** ㉛, and **Condom** ㉙, with stops as time and curiosity dictate. Stay the night in **Moissac** ㉗. From Moissac, continue following the seven-day itinerary.

When to Tour the Midi-Pyrénées

If you want to ski in the Midi-Pyrénées, December through March is the time to visit. Otherwise, April through June and September through October are the best months. Many towns host music and arts festivals in summer. November and early December are often wet and dreary, though more of the architecture is visible when the leaves are down and the air has a medieval mystery.

TOULOUSE

Make the rose-brick city of Toulouse, capital of the Midi-Pyrénées and the fourth largest city in France, your first destination. Just 96 km (60 mi) from the border with Spain, Toulouse's flavor is cosmopolitan, loose, and lively. The sidewalks and restaurants pulse well past midnight as tourists mingle with immigrant workers, college students, and technicians from the giant Airbus aviation complex headquartered outside the city.

Old Toulouse

The area between the boulevards and the Garonne forms the historic nucleus of Toulouse. Originally part of Roman Gaul, later capital for Visigoths and Carolingians, by the year AD 1000 Toulouse was one of the artistic and literary centers of medieval Europe. Despite the 13th-century defeat by the lords of northern France, Toulouse quickly reemerged as a cultural and commercial power and has remained so ever since. The religious and civil structures throughout this part of town bear witness to this illustrious past, even as the city's booming student life provides a dynamic present. This is the heart of Toulouse, with the place du Capitole at its center.

A Good Walk

Start on the **place du Capitole** ①, stopping into the donjon next to the **Capitole/Hôtel de Ville** ②, where there is a tourist office with maps. Rue du Taur, off the square, leads to **Notre-Dame du Taur** ③. Continue along rue du Taur to the **Ancien Collège de Périgord** ④, to see the oldest part of the medieval university. The emblematic church of **St-Sernin** ⑤ is at the end of rue du Taur on place St-Sernin. Next door is the **Musée St-Raymond** ⑥, the city's archaeological museum.

Leave place St-Sernin and cut out along rue Bellegarde to the boulevard de Strasbourg, where the open air vegetable and produce market is held. Take the boulevard to rue Victor Hugo and the **Marché Victor**

Hugo ⑦, the large market halls. Find your way back to place du Capitole, cross the square, and take rue Gambetta to rue Lakanal; a right will take you to the **Église des Jacobins** ⑧, one of Toulouse's greatest structures.

Back on rue Gambetta, to your right, is the opulent **Hôtel de Bernuy** ⑨. Cut through rue J. Suau to **place de la Daurade** ⑩. **Notre-Dame de la Daurade** ⑪ is the church on your left. After a pause here, continue up the quai de Tounis past the sculpted facade of the École des Beaux-Arts toward the **Pont Neuf** ⑫. Turn left on rue de Metz, continuing down to the **Hôtel d'Assézat** ⑬, home to the **Fondation Bemberg** and its excellent collection of paintings. If you are interested in religious art, pop over to the **Musée des Augustins** ⑭.

Take a left on rue des Changes, once part of the Roman road that sliced through Toulouse from north to south; today it's a chic pedestrian shopping area. Stop to admire the **Hôtel d'Astorg** ⑮ at No. 16, the **Hôtel d'Arnault Brucelles** ⑯ at No. 19, and the **Hôtel Delpech** ⑰ at No. 20. Continue along rue des Changes to the intersection with rue de Temponières. Note the handsome wood and brick building on the far right corner, and the faux-granite at the near left, complete with painted lines between the "stones" and trompe l'oeil windows bricked in and painted, a reminder of the legendary window tax all good citizens struggled to avoid. The next street to the left, rue Tripière, loops through place du May onto rue du May, which leads to the **Musée du Vieux Toulouse** ⑱ housed in the Hôtel Dumay (sic) at No. 7. Continue past the Le Bol Bu tearoom and the small Renaissance doorway at No. 16 to rejoin what was rue des Changes, now rue St-Rome. Turn left and have a look at (and a whiff of) the delicious Berdoncle dry goods store at No. 38. Then continue back to place du Capitole.

TIMING

This walk covers some 3 km (2 mi) and should take from three to four hours depending on how long you spend at each sight. Places close punctually at noon, so it is essential that you get an early start. Or, better yet, take a long lunch, too, continuing on again after 2 PM when places reopen.

Sights to See

4 **Ancien Collège de Périgord.** The wooden structure of the Old Périgord College, on the street side of the courtyard, is the oldest remnant of the 14th-century residential college. ✉ *56–58 rue du Taur.*

2 **Capitole/Hôtel de Ville.** The 18th-century Capitole (Capital) is home of the Hôtel de Ville (Town Hall) and the city's highly regarded opera company. The reception rooms are open when not in use for official functions or weddings. Halfway up the **Grand Escalier** (Grand Staircase) hangs a large painting of the *Jeux Floraux* (Floral Games), organized by a literary society created in 1324 to promote the local language, Langue d'Oc. The festival continues to this day: Poets give public readings here each May, the best are awarded silver- and gold-plated violets, one of the emblems of Toulouse.

At the top of the stairs is the **Salle Gervaise**, a hall used for weddings, beneath a series of paintings inspired by the theme of love and marriage. The mural at the far end of the room portrays the Isle of Cythères, where Venus received her lovers, alluding to the French euphemism for getting married: *embarquer pour Cythères* (to embark or shove off for Cythères). Four more giant paintings in the **Salle Henri-Martin,** named for the artist (1860–1943), show the passing seasons set against the eternal Garonne. Look for Jean Jaurès, one of France's greatest socialists (1859–1914), in *Les Rêveurs* (The Dreamers); he's wearing a boater

Ancien Collège de Périgord, **4**
Capitole/Hôtel de Ville, **2**
Cathédrale St-Étienne, **19**
Église des Jacobins, **8**
Hôtel d'Arnault Brucelle, **16**
Hôtel d'Assézat, **13**
Hôtel d'Astorg, **15**
Hôtel de Bernuy, **9**
Hôtel de Clary, **22**
Hôtel Delpech, **17**
Marché Victor Hugo, **7**
Musée des Augustins, **14**
Musée Paul Dupuy, **20**
Musée St-Raymond, **6**
Musée du Vieux Toulouse, **18**
Muséum d'Histoire Naturelle, **21**
Notre-Dame de la Dalbade, **23**
Notre-Dame de la Daurade, **11**
Notre-Dame du Taur, **3**
Place du Capitole, **1**
Place de la Daurade, **10**
Pont Neuf, **12**
St-Sernin, **5**

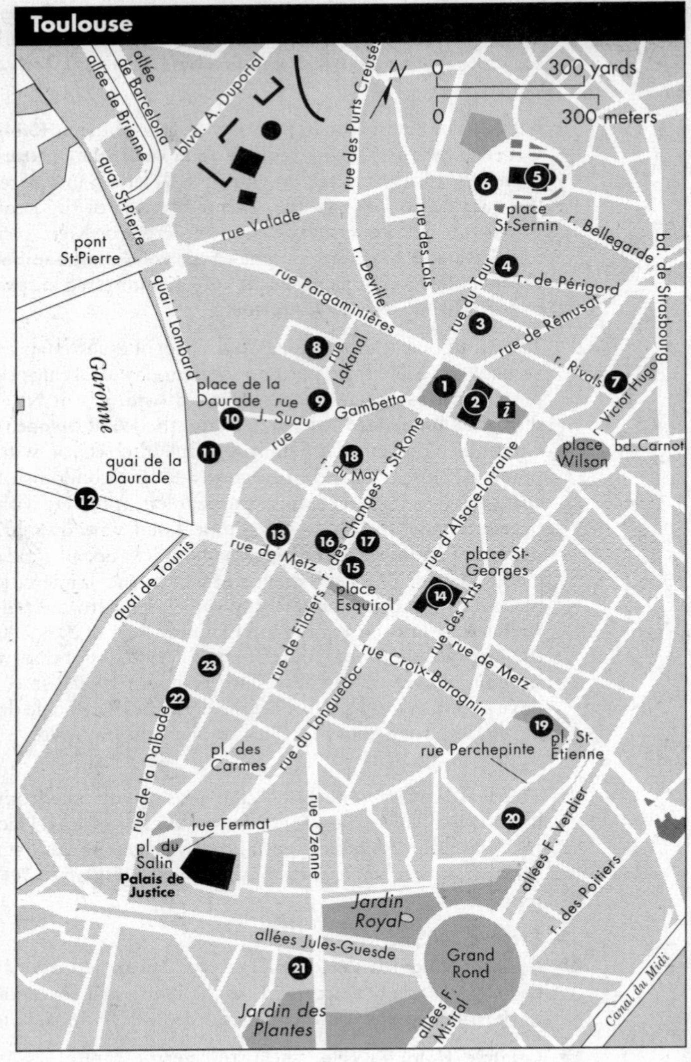

and a beige coat. At the far left end of the elegant **Salle des Illustres** is a large painting of a fortress under siege, portraying the women of Toulouse killing Simon de Montfort, leader of the Albigensian crusade against the Cathars, during the siege of Toulouse in 1218. ✉ *pl. du Capitole,* ☏ *05–61–11–34–12.* 🎫 *Free.* ⏲ *Weekdays 8:30–5, weekends 10–6.*

❽ **Église des Jacobins.** An extraordinary structure built in the 1230s for the Dominicans (dubbed Jacobins in 1217 for their Parisian base in Rue St-Jacques), this church has two rows of columns running the length of the nave—a standard feature of Dominican churches. The column farthest from the entrance is one of the world's two or three finest examples of palm-tree vaulting. The original refectory is used for temporary art exhibitions. In summer, the cloister hosts piano concerts ("Piano Jacobins"). ✉ *rue Lakanal.*

⓭ **Hôtel d'Assézat/Fondation Bemberg.** Built in 1555 by Toulouse's top Renaissance architect, Nicolas Bachelier, this mansion, considered the city's most elegant, has arcades and ornately carved doorways. It is now home of the Fondation Bemberg, an exceptional collection of paintings ranging from Tiepolo to Toulouse-Lautrec. Climb to the top of the tower for splendid views over the city's rooftops. ⊠ *rue de Metz.* 🎫 *Free.* 🕗 *Daily 10–noon and 2–6.*

16 **Hôtel d'Arnault Brucelles.** One of Toulouse's tallest and best towers can be found at this 16th-century mansion. ⊠ *19 rue des Changes.*

15 **Hôtel d'Astorg.** This 16th-century mansion is notable for its lovely wooden stairways and galleries, and for its top floor *mirande,* a wood-ceilinged observation deck. ⊠ *16 rue des Changes.*

9 **Hôtel de Bernuy.** Now part of a school, this mansion, around the corner from the Église des Jacobins, was built for Jean de Bernuy in the 16th century when Toulouse was at its most prosperous. De Bernuy, a merchant, made his fortune exporting dye, and his wealth is reflected in the use of stone, a costly material in this region of brick, and by the octagonal stair tower, the highest in the city. You may wander freely around the courtyard. ⊠ *rue Gambetta.*

17 **Hôtel Delpech.** Distinguishing this mansion is the biblical inscriptions in Latin carved in stone under the windows. ⊠ *20 rue des Changes.*

7 **Marché Victor Hugo.** This hangarlike indoor market is always a refreshing stop. Consider eating lunch at one of the seven upstairs restaurants. Chez Attila, just to the left at the top of the stairs, is the best of them. ⊠ *pl. Victor Hugo.*

14 **Musée des Augustins.** Housed in a medieval Augustinian convent, the museum uses the sacristy, chapter house, and cloisters for displaying an outstanding array of Romanesque sculpture and religious paintings. ⊠ *rue de Metz,* ☎ *05–61–23–55–07.* 🎫 *10 frs (free Sun.).* 🕗 *Wed. 10–9, Thurs.–Mon. 10–5.*

6 **Musée St-Raymond.** The city's archaeological museum, next to the basilica of St-Sernin, has an extensive collection of imperial Roman busts, as well as ancient coins, vases, and jewelry. ⊠ *pl. St-Sernin,* ☎ *05–61–22–21–85.* 🎫 *10 frs.* 🕗 *Mon., Wed.–Sat. 8–noon and 2–6; Sun. noon–6.*

18 **Musée du Vieux Toulouse.** The Museum of Old Toulouse is worthwhile for the building itself as much as for its collection of Toulouse memorabilia, paintings, sculptures, and documents. Be sure to note the ground floor fireplace and wooden ceiling. ⊠ *7 rue du May,* ☎ *05–61–13–97–24.* 🎫 *10 frs.* 🕗 *June–Sept., Mon.–Sat. 3–6.*

11 **Notre-Dame de la Daurade.** Overlooking the River Garonne is this 18th-century church. The name Daurade comes from *doré* (gilt), referring to the golden reflection given off by the mosaics decorating the 5th-century temple to the Virgin Mary that once stood on this site. ⊠ *pl. de la Daurade.*

3 **Notre-Dame du Taur.** Built on the spot where St-Saturnin (or Sernin), the martyred bishop of Toulouse, was dragged to his death in AD 257 by a rampaging bull, this church is famous for its *cloche-mur,* or wall tower. The wall looks like an extension of the facade and has inspired many similar versions throughout the region. ⊠ *rue du Taur.*

1 **Place du Capitole.** A vast, open square lined with shops and cafés in the city center, it is a good spot for getting your bearings. There is a parking lot underneath.

10 **Place de la Daurade.** This is one of Toulouse's nicest squares. Check out the quay-side walks suggested at the top of the ramp down to the

Garonne and note the Restaurant-Péniche (barge) moored along the quay. The Café des Artistes is almost obligatory. Opposite the church suspended over the Garonne you'll find a romantic view of the Pont Neuf.

⓬ **Pont Neuf.** The graceful span of the Pont Neuf (New Bridge) opened to traffic in 1632. It leads your eye to the Château d'Eau, a 19th-century water tower at the far end, now used for photography exhibits. The remains of the old bridge—one arch and the lighter-color outline on the brick wall of the Hôtel Dieu (hospital)—are visible across the river. The 16th-century hospital was used for pilgrims on their way to Santiago de Compostela. Just over the bridge, on a clear day in winter, the snowcapped peaks of the Pyrénées are visible in the distance, said to be a sign of imminent rain.

★ ❺ **St-Sernin.** Toulouse's most famous landmark and the world's largest Romanesque church once belonged to a Benedictine abbey, built in the 11th century to house pilgrims on their way to Santiago de Compostela in Spain. When illuminated at night, St-Sernin's five-tier octagonal tower glows red against the sky. Not all the tiers are the same: The first three, with their rounded windows, are Romanesque; the upper two, with their pointed Gothic windows, were added around 1300. ✉ *rue du Taur,* ☎ *05–61–21–70–18.* *Crypt 10 frs.* ⏲ *Daily 10–11:30 and 2:30–5:30.*

South of rue de Metz

South of rue de Metz, the St-Étienne Cathedral and the antiques district, along rue Perchepinte, are amid streets that are lined with some of the city's finest town houses.

A Good Walk

From the **Cathédrale St-Étienne** ⑲ walk down rue Fermat to rue Perchepinte. The street, lined with 18th-century houses, makes up the antiques district. At place Perchepinte cut across to rue de la Pleau. At No. 13 is the **Musée Paul Dupuy** ⑳, a museum of medieval arts. Take a right on rue Ozenne and note No. 9, the 15th-century Hôtel de Dahus. To get to the **Muséum d'Histoire Naturelle** ㉑, go the other direction on rue Ozenne. If you choose, instead, to continue on from No. 9, you'll come to rue du Languedoc: Look at No. 36, the 15th- and 16th-century mansion Hôtel du Vieux Raisin, with its unusual octagonal tower. Across the street is the Marché des Carmes, a market worth a stop. Continue back down rue du Languedoc to place du Salin, where farmers sell homemade foie gras on market mornings. Rue de la Dalbade, parallel to the Garonne, leads past one stately facade after another. The finest is No. 25, the **Hôtel de Clary** ㉒. Continue up the street to the church of **Notre-Dame de la Dalbade** ㉓.

TIMING

This walk will take you two or three hours. Note that the market is only open in the morning.

Sights to See

⓳ **Cathédrale St-Étienne.** The cathedral was erected in stages between the 13th and 17th centuries, though the nave and choir languished unfinished because of a lack of funds. A fine collection of 16th- and 17th-century tapestries traces the life of St-Étienne. Fronting the cathedral is the city's oldest fountain, dating from the 16th century. ✉ *pl. St-Étienne.*

㉒ **Hôtel de Clary.** This mansion, known as the Hôtel de Pierre because of its unusual solid *pierre* (stone) construction—at the time considered a sign of great wealth—is one of the finest 17th- and 18th-century mansions on the street. The ornately sculpted stone facade was built in 1608 by parliamentary president François de Clary. ✉ *25 rue de la Daurade.*

20 **Musée Paul Dupuy.** This museum, dedicated to medieval applied arts, is housed in the Hôtel Pierre Besson, a 16th-century mansion. ✉ *13 rue de la Pleau,* ☎ *06–61–22–21–82.* *15 frs.* ⏲ *Wed. 10–9, Thurs.–Mon. 10–5.*

21 **Muséum d'Histoire Naturelle.** The Natural History Museum, surrounded by gardens, has a varied collection of stuffed birds and prehistoric exhibits. ✉ *35 allée Jules-Guesde,* ☎ *05–61–52–00–14.* *8 frs.* ⏲ *Wed.–Mon. 10–5.*

23 **Notre-Dame de la Dalbade.** Originally called Sancta Maria de Ecclesia Alba in Langue d'Oc (Ste-Marie de l'Église Blanche in French, or Holy Mary of the White Church), the name of the church evolved into "de albata" and later Dalbade. One of its outstanding features today is the colorful 19th-century ceramic tympanum over the Renaissance door. ✉ *pl. de la Dalbade.*

Dining and Lodging

$$$$ ✕ **Jardins de l'Opéra.** One of the most fashionable restaurants in town is in the Grand Hôtel de l'Opéra (☞ *below*). Intimate dining rooms and a covered terrace around a little pond make for undeniable, if slightly over-formal, charm. The food is a successful mix of innovation and traditional Gascon fare: for example, ravioli stuffed with foie gras. ✉ *1 pl. du Capitole,* ☎ *05–61–21–82–66. Reservations essential. AE, DC, MC, V.*

$$–$$$ ✕ **Au Pois Gourmand.** This wood and brick garden restaurant over the Garonne is one of Toulouse's latest revelations. Chef Jean-Claude Plazzotta is making such a name for himself that there is no guarantee he'll still be there when you arrive, but here's hoping. Hot foie gras, spices, and wild mushrooms are just some of the stellar ingredients in his dishes. ✉ *3 rue Emi Heybrard,* ☎ *05–61–31–95–95. AE, DC, MC, V. Closed Sun. No lunch Sat.*

$$–$$$ ✕ **La Corde.** This little hideaway is worth taking the time to find. Built into a lovely 15th-century corner tower hidden in the courtyard of the 16th-century Hôtel Bolé, La Corde claims the distinction of being the oldest restaurant in Toulouse. Try the *effiloché de canard aux pêches* (shredded duck with caramelized peach). ✉ *4 rue Jules Chalande,* ☎ *05–61–29–09–43. AE, DC, MC, V. Closed Sun. No lunch Mon.*

$$ ✕ **Chez Emi.** There are two dining rooms at this restaurant: The ground floor has a seafood menu that changes daily; if it's available, have the turbot in ginger. Upstairs is a cozy hideaway for those who want a more traditional taste of Toulouse: cassoulet, *magret de canard* (duck breast), and other sturdy choices. ✉ *13 pl. St-Georges,* ☎ *05–61–21–05–56. Reservations essential. AE, DC, MC, V. Closed last wk in Aug., Sun., and Mon.*

$$$$ ★ **Grand Hôtel de l'Opéra.** This downtown doyen has an Old World feeling. The comfortably plush rooms are decorated in traditional style and soothing pastels, yet lack none of the usual modern conveniences. The three restaurants have a range of cuisine, from provincial bistro to international gourmet to Indian curry. ✉ *1 pl. du Capitole, 31000,* ☎ *05–61–21–82–66,* FAX *05–61–23–41–04. 49 rooms. 3 restaurants, café, pool, health club. AE, DC, MC, V.*

$$$ **Château de Garrevaques.** Equidistant (50 km/31 mi) from Carcassonne, Toulouse, and Albi, this castle makes a great base. Built in 1470 and rebuilt in the early 19th century, the château is on 8 acres of parkland. Mme. Combes is a helpful hostess, the château's 15th generation, and will guide you through the family heirlooms and antiques. Continental breakfast is included in the room rates. The table d'hôte dinner costs extra and is plain family fare. ✉ *81700 Garrevaques (5 km/3 mi northwest of Revel),* ☎ *05–63–75–04–54,* FAX *05–63–70–26–44. 7 rooms and 2 suites. Pool, tennis court, billiards. AE, MC, V. Advance reservations are required.*

$$$ ★ **Hôtel des Beaux-Arts.** In the thick of the most Toulousain part of town, over the Pont Neuf and next to the Hôtel d'Assézat, this cozy place has small but tastefully decorated rooms; the best have a tiny breakfast terrace overlooking the Garonne. The management is attentive. ✉ *1 pl. du Pont-Neuf, 31000,* ☎ *05–61–23–40–50,* FAX *05–61–22–02–27. 20 rooms. Breakfast room. AE, DC, MC, V.*

$–$$ **Hôtel Albert I.** The building is rather ordinary and the reception area is just functional, but rooms are cheerful and as spacious as you can expect from a hotel in the heart of Toulouse. The extremely personable owner, Mme. Hilaire, is on hand for a chat and to give suggestions on where to dine and shop. A Continental breakfast is served. ✉ *8 rue Rivals, 31000,* ☎ *05–61–21–17–91,* FAX *05–61–21–09–64. 46 rooms. Breakfast room. MC, V.*

Nightlife and the Arts

Toulouse's classical, lyrical, and chamber music orchestras; dramatic arts center; and ballet are all listed as national companies—no mean feat in this arts-oriented country. For a schedule of current programs, contact the city tourist office. If you want to stay up late—and they do in Toulouse—a complete list of clubs and discos can be found in the weekly *Toulouse Pratique,* available at any newsstand.

Any night of carousing should begin at **Père Louis** (✉ 45 rue des Tourneurs), an old-fashioned winery (and restaurant) with barrels for tables and vintage photographs. **Bar Basque** (✉ 7 pl. St-Pierre) is one of the many good bars around place St-Pierre. **Bagamoyo** (✉ 27 rue des Couteliers) is a lively place for a nocturnal snack of simple but delicious African fare. Brazilian guitarists play at **La Bonita** (✉ 112 Grand-Rue St-Michel). For jazz try **Le Café des Allées** (✉ 64 allée Charles-de-Fitte), a hothouse for local musicians. **Café Le Griot** (✉ 34 rue des Blanchers) features a number of American duos and trios. At **El Mexicano** (✉ 37 rue de l'Industrie) a tight crush of people inhale tequila and three-inch steaks. **La Péniche** (✉ Canal de Brienne, 90 allée de Barcelone) is a local gay bar. **Puerto Habana** (✉ 12 port St-Étienne) is the place for salsa. The **St-André** (✉ 39 rue St-Rome), open 7 PM to dawn (closed Sunday), is the place for onion soup in the wee hours. Local glitterati and theater stars go to **L'Ubu** (✉ 16 rue St-Rome), the city's top night spot for 20 years.

The main theaters in Toulouse are the **Théâtre du Capitole** (✉ pl. du Capitole, ☎ 05–61–23–21–35); the **Théâtre de la Digue** (✉ 3 rue de la Digue, ☎ 05–61–42–97–79); the **Théâtre du Taur** (✉ 69 rue du Taur, ☎ 05–61–21–77–13); the **Halle Aux Grains** (✉ pl. Dupuy, ☎ 05–61–63–18–65); and the **Théâtre Daniel Sorano** (✉ 35 allée Jules Guesde, ☎ 05–61–25–66–87). So many opera singers sing at the **Théâtre du Capitole** and the **Halle aux Grains** that the city is known as the *capitale du bel canto.* The opera season lasts from October until late May, with occasional summer presentations. A wide variety of dance companies perform in Toulouse: The **Ballet du Capitole** stages classical ballets. **Ballet-Théâtre Joseph Russilo** and **Compagnie Jean-Marc Matos** put on modern dance concerts. The **Centre National Choré-**

graphique de Toulouse welcomes international companies each year in the St-Cyprien quarter.

Outdoor Activities and Sports

Toulouse is just 100 km (60 mi) from the nearest peaks. For information about hiking, ski touring, mountain refuges, and just about anything having to do with the Pyrénées, check with the **Pyrénées Club** (✉ 29 rue du Taur, ☎ 05–61–21–11–44). There are two good 18-hole golf courses near Toulouse: **Golf Club de Toulouse** (✉ Vieille Toulouse, ☎ 05–61–73–45–48) and **Golf Club de Toulouse Palmola** (✉ rte. d'Albi, ☎ 05–61–84–20–50). If you want to go horseback riding, contact **Poney City** (✉ St-Paul, 40 km/25 mi east of Toulouse, ☎ 05–63–42–06–45).

Shopping

Toulouse is a chic design outlet for clothing and artifacts of all kinds. Rue St-Rome, rue des Changes, and rue d'Alsace-Lorraine are all good places for browsing through shops and small boutiques.

ALBI AND THE GERS

Along the banks of the Tarn to the northeast of Toulouse is Albi, Toulouse's rival in rose colors. West from Albi, along the river, the land opens up to the rural Gers département, home of the heady liqueur Armagnac and heart of the former dukedom of Gascony. It's studded with châteaux—from simple medieval fortresses to ambitious classical residences—and tiny, isolated villages.

Albi

★ 24 *75 km (47 mi) northeast of Toulouse.*

Toulouse-Lautrec's native Albi is a well preserved and busy provincial market town. In its heyday, Albi was a major center for Cathars, members of a dualistic and ascetic religious movement critical of the hierarchical and worldly ways of the Catholic Church. Pick up a copy of the excellent visitor's booklet (in English) from the tourist office, and follow the walking tours—of the old city, the old ramparts, and the banks of the River Tarn.

The huge **Cathédrale Ste-Cécile,** with its intimidating clifflike walls, resembles a cross between a castle and an ocean liner. It was constructed as a symbol of the church's return to power after the 13th-century crusade that wiped out the Cathars. The interior is an astonishingly ornate reply to the massive austerity of the outer walls. Maestro Donnelli and a team of 16th-century Italian artists covered every possible surface with religious scenes and brightly colored patterns. The most striking fresco is a 15th-century depiction of the Last Judgment on the west wall. ✉ *pl. Ste-Cécile.*

★ The **Palais de la Berbie,** between the cathedral and the Pont Vieux (Old Bridge), was built in 1265 as a defensive fortress. The gardens were André Le Nôtre, known for the Versailles gardens. In 1905, the fortress became a museum, the **Musée Toulouse-Lautrec,** honoring Albi's most famous son: Belle Epoque painter Henri de Toulouse-Lautrec (1864–1901). Toulouse-Lautrec left Albi for Paris in 1882 and soon became famous for his colorful and tumultuous evocations of the bohemian glamour in and around Montmartre. Despite his aristocratic origins (Lautrec is a town not far from Toulouse), Henri cut a far-from-noble figure. He was less than 5 feet tall (due to a genetic bone deficiency) and pursued a decadent life that led to an early grave. With over 1000 of the artist's works, the Albi exhibit is the country's largest Toulouse-Lautrec collection. ✉ *Just off pl. Ste-Cécile,* ☎ *05–63–49–48–70.* *25 frs, gardens free.* ⏲ *May–Sept., daily 10–noon and 2–6; Oct.–Apr., Wed.–Mon. 10–noon and 2–5.*

After visiting the Palais Berbie, stroll around old town. Leaving the palace behind you, walk to the 11th- to 15th-century college and cloister of **St-Salvy** (✉ rue St-Cécile). Next, visit Albi's finest restored traditional house, the **Maison du Vieil Albi** (✉ on the corner of rue de la Croix-Blanche and Puech-Bérenguer). Real fans of Toulouse-Lautrec will want to see his birthplace, the **Maison Natale de Toulouse-Lautrec** (✉ 14 rue Henri de Toulouse-Lautrec). Rue de l'Hôtel de Ville, two streets west of the Maison Natale, leads past the Mairie (Town Hall), with its hanging globes of flowers, to Albi's main square, **place du Vigan.** Take a break in one of the two main cafés, Le Pontie or Le Vigan.

Dining and Lodging

$$$ ✕ **Le Moulin de la Mothe.** This one-time mill on the banks of the Tarn is neatly tucked in to the river and the lush vegetation around it. Chef-owner Michel Pellaprat specializes in inventive cooking based on high-quality local products. ✉ *rue de Lamothe,* ☎ *05–63–60–38–15. AE, MC, V. Closed Wed. and Sun. dinner Sept.–June.*

$$ ✕ **Le Jardin des Quatre Saisons.** There are two reasons for this restaurant's excellent reputation: value and fish. Owner-chef Georges Bermond's house specialties include mussels baked with leeks and *suprême de sandre* (a freshwater fish similar to a pickerel cooked in wine). ✉ *19 bd. de Strasbourg,* ☎ *05–63–60–77–76. AE, MC, V. Closed Mon.*

$$$–$$$$ ✕🏨 **La Réserve.** A 5-acre park surrounds this modern, hacienda-style building with arched windows, terraces, and a garden that stretches to the river. Guest rooms are spacious, but those in the main building have the most charm, with elegant reproduction furniture and lots of pretty knickknacks. The restaurant (closed from November to April) serves tempting local specialties; the salmon with grapefruit is a good bet. ✉ *rte. de Cordes, 81000 Fonvialane (5 km/3 mi outside town),* ☎ *05–63–60–80–80,* FAX *05–63–47–63–60. 24 rooms. Restaurant, pool, tennis court. AE, DC, MC, V.*

$$–$$$ ✕🏨 **Hostellerie St-Antoine.** Founded in 1734, this is one of the oldest hostelries in France. It's in the center of town, but it's quiet. Modern renovations have made it eminently comfortable. Room 30 has a pleasing view of the garden; its pristine white furnishings create a spacious atmosphere. The superb restaurant serves classical cuisine—rich and delicious foie gras de canard and saddle of hare with a foie gras based sauce. ✉ *15 rue St-Antoine, 81000,* ☎ *05–63–54–04–60,* FAX *05–63–47–10–47. 50 rooms. Restaurant, parking (fee). AE, DC, MC, V.*

$$ ✕🏨 **Hôtel Chiffre.** This centrally located town house has impeccably decorated rooms that overlook a cozy garden retreat. The restaurant, the Bateau Ivre, run by chef Michel Gouty, is one of Albi's finest. ✉ *50 rue Séré-de-Rivières, 81000,* ☎ *05–63–54–04–60,* FAX *05–63–47–20–61. 40 rooms. Restaurant. AE, DC, MC, V.*

$$–$$$ 🏨 **La Pérouse.** This tastefully decorated enclave with its secluded swimming pool is centrally located and supremely quiet and intimate. Rooms are comfortable and the garden is a lush and shady spot to rest between sorties in and around Albi. ✉ *21 pl. Lapérouse,* ☎ *05–63–54–69–22,* FAX *05–63–38–03–69. 22 rooms. Pool, tennis court. AE, DC, MC, V.*

$$ **Le George V.** This little in-town bed-and-breakfast is near the cathedral and the train station. Each room is unique. The garden is a handy retreat in summer. ✉ *29 av. Maréchal Joffre,* ☎ *05–63–54–24–16,* FAX *05–63–49–90–78. 9 rooms. Pool, tennis court. AE, DC, MC, V.*

$$ **Mercure Albi Bastides.** This converted 18th-century *vermicellerie* (noodle mill), across the river from the old center of Albi, has rooms that are functional and modern, if somewhat cramped. The views of the Tarn and the Pont Vieux are spectacular. The hotel restaurant is a stylish place to try chef Gérard Belbèze's regional specialties and his Toulouse-Lautrec menu. ✉ *41 rue Porta, 81000,* ☎ *05–63–47–66–66,* FAX *05–63–46–18–40; 800/637–2873 U.S. reservations; 0181/741–3100 U.K. reservations. 56 rooms. Restaurant, free parking. AE, DC, MC, V.*

Outdoor Activities and Sports

Eighteen-hole golf courses can be found at **Golf d'Albi** (✉ Château de Lasbordes, ☎ 05–63–54–98–07) and **Golf de Florentin** (✉ Le Bosc, Florentin, 28 km/17 mi from Albi, ☎ 05–63–55–20–50).

Shopping

Around **place Ste-Cécile** there are numerous shops for clothing, books, music, and antiques. Don't miss **L'Artisan Chocolatier** (✉ 4 rue Docteur Camboulives, on pl. du Vigan, ☎ 05–63–38–95–33), Michael Belin's famous emporium. The finest foie gras in town is found at **Albi Foie Gras** (✉ 29 rue Mariès, ☎ 05–63–38–21–23). There are many **markets** in Albi: A produce market takes place Tuesday through Sunday in the market halls near the cathedral; another produce market is held on Sunday morning at place Ste-Cécile; and a flea and antiques market happens in the Halle du Castelviel (✉ pl. du Castelviel) Saturday morning.

Cordes

★ ㉕ *25 km (15 mi) northwest of Albi, 80 km (50 mi) northeast of Toulouse.*

The picture-book hilltop village of Cordes, built in 1222 by Count Raymond VII of Toulouse, is one of the most impressively preserved *bastides* (fortified medieval town built to a strict grid plan) in all of France. When mists steal up from the Cérou Valley and enshroud the hillside, Cordes appears to hover in midair, hence its tacky nickname, Cordes-sur-Ciel (Cordes-on-Sky/Heaven). Many of the restored medieval houses are occupied by artisans and craftsmen; the best crafts shops are found along the main street, Grande-Rue. The village's venerable covered market, supported by 24 octagonal stone pillars, is also noteworthy, as is the nearby well, which is more than 300 feet deep.

Dining and Lodging

$$$ ★ **Le Grand Ecuyer.** The dramatic hilltop setting of this hotel suits it well—it is a perfectly preserved medieval mansion. Rooms have period furnishings; the best, Planol, Horizon, and Ciel, have grand views of the rolling countryside. Yves Thuriès is one of the region's best chefs and chocolatiers; sample his salmon and sole twist in vanilla puree or the guinea fowl supreme in pastry. Menus begin at 180 francs and culminate in a 520-franc, seven-course, gourmet extravaganza. ✉ *rue Voltaire, 81170,* ☎ *05–63–56–01–03,* FAX *05–63–56–16–99. 13 rooms. Restaurant. AE, DC, MC, V. Closed mid-Oct.–early Apr.*

$$ ★ **L'Hostellerie du Vieux Cordes.** This magnificent 13th-century house has a lovely courtyard, shaded by a 200-year-old wisteria and dotted with tiny white tables. Guest rooms are richly decorated but not nearly as opulent as the vast crimson dining rooms. Bernard Lafuente, Yves Thuriès's brother-in-law, is an accomplished chef. There

are no fixed menus; each dish costs 40 francs. It's closed Monday from November to Easter and in January. ✉ *rue St-Michel, 81170,* ☎ *05–63–56–00–12,* FAX *05–63–56–02–47. 21 rooms. Restaurant. AE, DC, MC, V. Closed Jan.*

Montauban

26 *59 km (37 mi) west of Cordes, 52 km (32 mi) north of Toulouse.*

Montauban is best known as the birthplace of the great painter Jean Auguste Dominique Ingres (1780–1867) and is home to a superb collection of his works. Ingres was the last of the great French classicists, who favored line over color and took much of their subject matter from the antique world. Ingres's sour personality and (for some) his arid painting style, with its worship of line and draftsmanship, led many contemporaries to ridicule his work. These days, he is undergoing a considerable revival; looking at his works, with their quasiphotographic realism, it's easy to see why.

The **Musée Ingres** is housed in the sturdy brick 17th-century Bishop's Palace overlooking the River Tarn. Ingres has the second floor to himself; note the contrast between his love of myth (*Ossian's Dream*) and his deadpan, uncompromising portraiture (*Madame Gonse*). Most of the paintings are from Ingres's excellent private collection, ranging from his followers (Théodore Chassériau) and precursors (Jacques-Louis David) to Old Masters. ✉ *pl. Bourdelle,* ☎ *05–63–63–18–04.* *16 frs.* *July–Aug., Mon.–Sat. 9:30–noon and 1:30–6, Sun. 1:30–6; Sept.–June, Tues.–Sat. 10–noon and 2–6.*

Moissac

27 *29 km (18 mi) west of Montauban, 72 km (45 mi) north of Toulouse.*

Moissac has wonderful cloisters and one of the region's most remarkable abbey churches. Little is left of the original 7th-century ★ **Abbaye St-Pierre,** and religious wars laid waste its 11th-century replacement. Today's abbey, dating mostly from the 15th century, narrowly escaped demolition in this century when the Bordeaux-Sète railroad was rerouted within feet of the cloisters, sparing the precious columns around the arcades. Each of the 76 capitals has a unique pattern of animals, geometric motifs, and religious or historical scenes. The highlight of the abbey church is the 12th-century south portal, topped with carvings illustrating the Apocalypse. The **Musée des Arts et Traditions Populaires** contains regional treasures and a room of local costumes. ✉ *6 bis rue de l'Abbaye,* ☎ *05–63–04–03–08.* *Cloisters and museum 24 frs.* *Tues.–Sun. 9–noon and 2–5 (until 6 Apr.–June and Sept.; until 7 in July and Aug.).*

Lodging

$$–$$$ **Château St-Roch.** This neo-Renaissance château, with turrets and spirals, is an eye-stopper. Guest rooms are huge, with coffered ceilings and French doors leading onto terraces. Other rooms are on display to visitors for 25 francs. Two drawbacks: The barracklike bar and the dining room, in a separate modern building. The food is just acceptable, so consider eating elsewhere. On the plus side, breakfasts—brought to your room—include good coffee and fresh bread. English is not spoken, but a few words of French will get you by. ✉ *82340 Le Pin (19 km/12 mi west of Moissac; 5 km/3 mi east of Auvillar),* ☎ *05–63–95–95–22,* FAX *05–63–94–85–54. 15 rooms. Restaurant, bar. MC, V. Closed Nov.–Mar.*

Lectoure

57 km (35 mi) southwest of Moissac, 94 km (58 mi) northwest of Toulouse.

Once a Roman city and a fortified Gallic town, Lectoure stands on a promontory above the Gers Valley in the heart of the former dukedom of Gascony. Although Lectoure was ravaged in 1473, when Louis XI attacked its fortress and established direct royal rule by killing the last count of Armagnac, there's still plenty to see in its old arched streets, such as the 13th-century **Fontaine Diane** (Diana's Fountain) on rue Fontélie and the 15th-century **Cathédrale St-Gervais et St-Protais** (park in front of the tourist office).

The **Musée Municipal,** near the cathedral, is installed in the vaulted cellars of the former **Palais Épiscopal** (Bishop's Palace), now the town hall. Its collection contains a dramatic group of 20 pagan altars, discovered in 1640 under the choir of the cathedral. These altars feature Latin inscriptions and heads of the sacrificed bulls (or rams). ✉ *Hôtel de Ville,* ☎ *05–62–68–70–22.* 🎟 *25 frs.* ⏲ *Daily 9–noon and 2–6.*

Condom

24 km (15 mi) west of Lectoure on D7, 123 km (76 mi) northwest of Toulouse.

A town of seven churches, Condom is in the heart of Ténarèze, one of the three regions that produces Armagnac. Condom's location on the River Baïse made it an excellent base for exporting the local brandy to Bordeaux and Bayonne on the Atlantic coast. The musty **Musée de l'Armagnac,** in an 18th-century annex of the former Bishop's Palace in the town center, details the production process. Armagnac is distilled only once (unlike cognac, which is distilled twice); you can inspect the copper alembics. ✉ *2 rue Jules-Ferry,* ☎ *05–62–28–31–41.* 🎟 *10 frs.* ⏲ *June–Sept., Tues.–Sun. 10–noon and 2–6; Oct.–May, Tues.–Sat. 10–noon and 2–4.*

Six kilometers (4 miles) southwest of Condom on D931/D208 is the **Château de Cassaigne,** once the country residence of the bishops of Condom. The vineyards surrounding this 13th-century manor were originally cultivated for wine, with only the unconsumed leftovers distilled to make brandy. By the 17th century, the English were importing Armagnac in large quantities; ever since, brandy production has been the château's main raison d'être. You can visit the château's 17th-century cellars, where the Armagnac is stored in oak barrels that give it an amber color, and the 16th-century vaulted kitchen, where you can taste and buy brandy. There's also a small museum. ☎ *05–62–28–04–02.* 🎟 *Free.* ⏲ *Mar.–mid-Oct., daily 9–noon and 2–7; mid-Oct.–Feb., Mon.–Sat. 9–noon and 2–6:30.*

OFF THE BEATEN PATH

ABBAYE DE FLARAN – Find your way from Condom to the 12th-century Flaran Abbey, just over 4 km (2½ mi) away from the Château de Cassaigne, on D142. In 1971 regional authorities took over the abbey, renovated it, and converted the guests' quarters into a cultural center for temporary exhibits. The abbey was built by Cistercian monks under St-Bernard; the monks' rooms on the second floor, overlooking the cloisters, remain largely unchanged. Have a look at the impressive sacristy, with its ribbed arches resting on one central column. ✉ *Valence-sur-Baïse,* ☎ *05–62–28–50–19.* 🎟 *22 frs.* ⏲ *July–Aug., daily 9:30–7; Sept.–June, Wed.–Mon. 9:30–noon and 2–6.*

Dining and Lodging

$$$ ✕ **La Bastide Gasconne.** In Barbotan-les-Thermes, west of Condom, this sumptuously decorated 18th-century manor near an immense lake houses a fine hotel-restaurant. M. Hubert cheerfully presides over the magnificent, wood-beam dining room and dishes up exceptional nouvelle cuisine; try the fresh foie gras cooked in muslin. Cognac or Armagnac and coffee by the open hearth make a suitably grand finale. Rooms feature quaint-chic touches. Reservations are essential in the restaurant and a jacket and tie are required. ✉ *rue des Thermes, 32150 Barbotan-les-Thermes (36 km/21 mi west of Condom),* ☎ *05–62–08–31–31,* FAX *05–62–08–31–53. 22 rooms. Restaurant, pool. AE, DC, MC, V. Closed Nov.–Mar.*

$$ ✕ **Hôtel des Trois Lys.** You can recognize this hotel in the heart of Condom by its 18th-century facade. Most of the furnishings are Empire reproductions. The high-ceiling guest rooms vary in size; the smaller ones are a little cramped. The bar is open for evening aperitifs, and in summer, breakfast is served on the terrace overlooking the pool. ✉ *38 rue Gambetta, 32100,* ☎ *05–62–28–33–33,* FAX *05–62–28–41–85. 10 rooms. Bar, pool. AE, DC, MC, V.*

Fleurance

30 *30 km (19 mi) east of Condom, 83 km (51 mi) northwest of Toulouse.*

Fleurance is one of several bastide towns in the Armagnac region with a regimented street plan. Particularly notable is the Gothic **St-Laurent** church, with three stained-glass windows by Arnaud de Moles, whose most famous windows are in Auch (☞ *below*).

Auch

31 *24 km (15 mi) south of Fleurance, 79 km (40 mi) west of Toulouse.*

Auch, the capital of the Gers département, is best known for its stunning Gothic cathedral. The **Cathédrale Ste-Marie,** in the center of town, dates from the 15th and 16th centuries. Most of the stained-glass windows in the choir were done by Arnaud de Moles; they portray biblical figures and handsome pagan sibyls, or prophetesses. The oak choir stalls are carved with more than 1,500 figures, both biblical and mythological; they took 50 years to complete. In June, classical music concerts are held here. ✉ *pl. Salinis.* *6 frs.* ⏲ *Daily 8–noon and 2–6.*

Cross place Salinis to the terrace overlooking the River Gers. A monumental flight of 232 steps leads down to the riverbank. Halfway down is the statue of D'Artagnan, the musketeer immortalized by Alexandre Dumas. Although Dumas set the action of his historical drama *The Three Musketeers* in the 1620s, the true D'Artagnan—Charles de Batz—was born in 1620, probably at Castlemore near Lupiac, and didn't become a musketeer until 1645.

On the other side of the cathedral, behind the former Archbishop's Palace (now the Préfecture), is the **Musée des Jacobins,** with a fine collection of Latin-American art and pre-Columbian pottery. The museum also contains Gallo-Roman relics; look for the white-marble epitaph dedicated by a grief-stricken mistress to her dog Myia. ✉ *rue Daumesnil,* ☎ *05–62–05–74–79.* *12 frs.* ⏲ *May–Oct., Tues.–Sun. 10–noon and 2–6; Nov.–Apr., Tues.–Sat. 10–noon and 2–4.*

Dining and Lodging

$$$ ★ ✕ **France.** Despite the building's sober facade, the ambience at this celebrated restaurant is as warm as at any corner bistro, with a bit of extra plush thrown in for good measure. Renowned chef André Daguin

creates traditional Gascon cuisine with a masterly touch; his best dishes include cod in flaky pastry with a whipped liver sauce and magret de canard. Save room for dessert—chocolates in *banyuls* (warmed wine). Be sure to make reservations and avoid Sunday dinner, Monday, and January, when the restaurant is closed. The charmingly decorated guest rooms have exposed wood beams. Ask about two-day, off-season packages. ✉ *pl. de la Libération, 32000,* ☎ *05–62–61–71–71,* FAX *05–62–61–71–81. 29 rooms. Restaurant. AE, DC, MC, V.*

$–$$ ✕🏨 **Ténarèze.** This hotel-restaurant is in the spa town of Castéra-Verduzan, northwest of Auch. Rooms are traditionally decorated, with heavy velvet draperies and lace trim. The unpretentious restaurant, Le Florida, is completely upstaged by chef Bernard Ramounéda's creative flair: Try his foie gras with grapes, apples, or gooseberries and a glass of Sauternes and opt for the reasonable, prix-fixe menus. The restaurant is closed Sunday dinner, Monday, and February; reservations are essential and a jacket and tie are required. ✉ *Castéra-Verduzan (25 km/15 mi northwest of Auch on D390),* ☎ *05–62–68–10–22,* FAX *05–62–68–14–69. 24 rooms, 13 with bath. Restaurant. AE, DC, MC, V. Closed late Oct.–early Apr.*

Shopping

Caves de l'Hôtel de France (✉ rue d'Étigny) has a wide selection of Armagnac.

THE HAUTES PYRÉNÉES

A little over 162 km (100 mi) southwest of Toulouse, the Pyrénées divide the Iberian Peninsula from the European continent and provide the natural border with Spain. Except for the religious pilgrimage at Lourdes, the major spectacle in this area is nature: wooded hills sliced by gorges give way to majestic and often treeless mountaintops.

Tarbes

32 *75 km (45 mi) southeast of Auch, 152 km (94 mi) southwest of Toulouse, 214 km (133 mi) southeast of Bordeaux.*

Your point of entry into the Hautes Pyrénées will probably be Tarbes. Stop in the **tourist office** (✉ 3 cours Gambetta, ☎ 05–62–51–30–31) for information, brochures, and maps of the region. The city is the commercial and administrative center of the Pyrénées region and of no particular tourist interest. But you might enjoy a stroll around the pretty **Jardin Massey** amid the abundance of summer flowers.

Lourdes

33 *19 km (12 mi) southwest of Tarbes.*

Each year some 5 million pilgrims flock to Lourdes, many in quest of a miraculous cure for sickness or disability. Whether it's worth seeing is another question. The area surrounding the famous churches and grotto is woefully lacking in beauty. Out of season, the acres of nearly empty parking lots echo. Shops are shuttered and restaurants are closed. In season, a milling throng jostles to get a glimpse of the grotto lurking behind a forest of votive candles.

The history of this Catholic mecca is relatively recent. In February 1858, Bernadette Soubirous, a 14-year-old miller's daughter, claimed the Virgin Mary had appeared to her in the **Grotte de Massabielle** near the River Gave de Pau. During the night, Bernadette dug at the ground in the grotto, releasing a gush of water from a spot where no spring existed. From then on, pilgrims thronged the Massabielle rock in response to the water's supposed healing powers. But church authorities reacted skeptically. It took four years of inquiry for the miracle to be authenticated by Rome and a sanctuary erected over the grotto. In 1864 the first organized procession was held. Today there are six official annual pilgrimages, the most important on August 15.

In 1958 Lourdes celebrated the centenary of Bernadette Soubirous's visions by constructing the world's largest underground church, the **Basilique St-Pie X.** The basilica looks more like a parking lot than a church, but it can accommodate 20,000 people—more than the permanent population of the entire town.

Two other **basilicas** stand above St-Pie X: the neo-Byzantine **Basilique Rosaire** (1889) and the tall, white basilica of **Basilique Supérieure** (1871). Both are open throughout the day, but their spiritual function far outweighs their aesthetic appeal.

The **Pavillon Notre-Dame,** across from St-Pie X, houses the **Musée Bernadette,** with mementos of Bernadette's life and an illustrated history of the pilgrimages. In the basement is the **Musée d'Art Sacré du Gemmail.** *Gemmail* is a modern approach to the stained-glass technique involving the assembly of broken glass. ✉ *72 rue de la Grotte,* ☎ *05–62–94–13–15.* *Free.* *July–Nov., daily 9:30–11:45 and 2:30–6:15; Dec.–June, Wed.–Mon. 9:30–11:45 and 2:30–5:45.*

Just across the river is the **Moulin des Boly,** where Bernadette was born on January 7, 1844. You can also visit the **Cachot,** a shabby little room where she and her family lived. ✉ *Moulin des Boly: 12 rue Bernadette-Soubirous.* *Free.* *Easter–mid-Oct., daily 9:30–11:45 and 2:30–5:45. Cachot: 15 rue des Petits-Fossés,* ☎ *05–62–94–51–30.* *Free.* *Easter–mid-Oct., daily 9:30–11:45 and 2:30–5:30; mid-Oct.–Easter, daily 2:30–5:30.*

The **Château** on the hill above town can be reached on foot or by escalator. In the 17th and 18th centuries, the castle was used as a prison; now it contains the **Musée Pyrénéen,** one of France's best provincial museums, devoted to the region's popular customs and arts. ✉ *25 rue du Fort,* ☎ *05–62–94–02–04.* *30 frs.* *Easter–mid-Oct., daily 9–noon and 2–7 (last admission at 6); mid-Oct.–Easter, Wed.–Mon. 9–noon and 2–7.*

Dining and Lodging

$$ **Hôtel Albert/La Taverne de Bigorre.** The Moreau family's popular establishment serves traditional French mountain cooking such as garbure (the hearty country soup). Rooms are clean and comfortable, with a personal touch that is very welcome in Lourdes. ✉ *21 pl. du Champ Commun, 65100,* ☎ *05–62–94–75–00,* FAX *05–62–94–78–45. 27 rooms. Restaurant. AE, DC, MC, V. Closed mid-Nov.–mid-Dec., Jan.*

Cauterets

34 *30 km (19 mi) south of Lourdes, 49 km (30 mi) south of Tarbes.*

Cauterets is a spa-resort town deep in the mountains, where you can sometimes ski until May. Ever since Roman times, Cauterets's thermal springs have been revered as a miracle cure for female sterility. Virile novelist Victor Hugo (1802–85) womanized here, and Lady Aurore Dudevant—better known as the writer George Sand (1804–76)—discovered her feminism.

En Route South from Cauterets is the Pont d'Espagne, where steep-twisting D920 peters out. Continue on foot or by chairlift to the plateau and a view over the bright blue **Lac de Gaube,** fed by the river of the same name. Return via Cauterets to Pierrefitte-Nestalas and turn right on D921 and the Gorge de Luz to Gavarnie.

Gavarnie

35 *30 km (19 mi) south of Cauterets on D921, 50 km (31 mi) south of Lourdes.*

The village of Gavarnie is a good base for exploring the mountains in the region. For starters, it is at the foot of the **Cirque de Gavarnie,** one of the world's most remarkable examples of glacial erosion and a daunting challenge to mountaineers. Horses and donkeys, rented in the village, can take you partway into the mountains. When the upper snows melt, numerous streams whoosh down from the cliffs to form spectacular waterfalls; the greatest of them—the **Grande Cascade**—drops nearly 1,400 feet.

Dining and Lodging

$$ ✕ **Hôtel Astazou.** Mme. Gaby's traditional cuisine, prepared with the freshest produce, is impeccable, as are the modest yet comfortable rooms. Stone, wood, and plenty of glass are the main architectural ingredients; the views of the surrounding peaks, including the eponymous 3,000-meter (9,842-foot) Astazou are both inspiring and intimidating. ✉ *Village de Gavarnie, 65120,* ☎ *05–62–92–48–07,* FAX *05–62–92–40–79. 13 rooms. Restaurant. MC, V.*

En Route The dramatic mountain scenery is impressive all along D921 from Gavarnie as far as Luz-St-Sauveur and then, if you turn right, along D918 all the way to **Arreau.** The road passes through the lively little spa town of **Barèges** and under the brow of the mighty **Pic du Midi de Bigorre,** towering nearly 10,000 feet above the **Col du Tourmalet** pass. **Luz-St-Sauveur** is technically just 29 km (18 mi) from Arreau, but 61 km (38 mi) along the tortuous twists of the D918. The finest views—and the sharpest curves—are found toward the **Col d'Aspin** pass. Another spectacular road is D618 from Arreau traveling over the **Col de Peyresourde** to Bagnères de Luchon.

Bagnères de Luchon

36 *150 km (93 mi) east of Gavarnie.*

The largest and most fashionable Pyrenean spa is Bagnères de Luchon (simply known as Luchon), at the head of a lush valley. The Romans considered Luchon to rank second as a spa only to Naples. Thermal waters here cater to the vocal cords: Opera singers, lawyers, and politicians hoarse from electoral promises all pile in.

OFF THE BEATEN PATH **SUPERBAGNÈRES** – Above Luchon is the ski resort of Superbagnères, reached by a serpentine road (D46). On the way up, admire the breathtaking views of the Maladeta Mountains across the border in Spain.

St-Bertrand de Comminges

37 *32 km (20 mi) north of Bagnères de Luchon, 57 km (35 mi) southeast of Tarbes, 107 km (66 mi) southwest of Toulouse.*

A Roman road led directly from Luchon to St-Bertrand de Comminges (then a huge town of 60,000). This delightful village, whose inhabitants number just 500 today, is dwarfed beneath the imposing (mostly) 12th-century **Cathédrale Ste-Marie.** Old houses, sloping alleyways, and crafts shops add to the charm.

ROUSSILLON

Draw a line from Toulouse and Narbonne, on the Mediterranean—the area to the south, long part of the Catalonia-dominated House of Aragón, is known as Roussillon. Rolling plains sweep along the northern border, the Pyrénées line the southern end, and craggy hills, divided by gorges, lie in between. On the eastern side is the Mediterranean and the Côte Vermeille (Yellow Coast).

Carcassonne

38 *88 km (55 mi) southeast of Toulouse, 105 km (65 mi) south of Albi.*

On a hill overlooking lush green countryside and the River Aude, Carcassonne is a storybook medieval town with the longest walls in Europe. The circle of towers and battlements is said to be the setting for Charles Perrault's *Puss in Boots.* The town is divided into two parts by the river—La Cité, the fortified upper town, and the rest, the lower, newer city, known simply as Carcassonne. Unless you are staying at a hotel in the upper town, private vehicles are not permitted; park in the lot (15 francs) across the road from the drawbridge. Be aware that the train station is in the lower town, and that means a cab ride or a 45-minute walk up to the old city. Plan on spending at least a couple of hours exploring the walls and peering over the battlements across sun-drenched plains toward the distant Pyrénées.

The earliest sections of the wall, built by the Romans in the 1st century AD, were later enlarged by the Visigoths in the 5th century. During the 13th century, Louis IX (St-Louis) and his son Philip the Bold strengthened the fortifications and gave Carcassonne much of its present-day appearance. Still, in 1835, the Historic Monument Inspector (and poet) Prosper Mérimée was appalled by the dilapidated state of the walls, and by 1844 Viollet-le-Duc was at work restoring them. Once inside the walls of the upper town, 20th-century tourism takes over. The streets are lined with souvenir shops, crafts boutiques, and restaurants. Staying overnight within the ancient walls lets you savor the timeless atmosphere after the visitors are gone.

The 12th-century **Château Comtal** is the last inner bastion of Carcassonne. It has a drawbridge and a museum, the **Musée Lapidaire,** home to stone sculptures found in the area. ☎ *04–68–25–01–66.* 🎫 *32 frs.* ⏲ *June–Sept., daily 9–6; Oct–May, daily 9–noon and 2–5.*

The Ville Basse, built between the River Aude and the Canal du Midi, is less captivating. You may, however, wish to visit the **Musée des Beaux-Arts,** which houses a fine collection of porcelain, 17th- and 18th-century Flemish paintings, and works by local artists—including some stirring battle scenes by Jacques Gamelin (1738–1803). ✉ *rue Verdun,* ☎ *04–68–72–47–22.* 🎫 *Free.* ⏲ *Mon.–Sat. 10–noon and 2–5.*

Dining and Lodging

$$ ✕ **Le Languedoc.** Under chef Didier Faugeras's culinary direction, this restaurant in Carcassonne serves up a light version of the region's specialties, from confit to game. While the food may be less than commanding, the service is enthusiastic. ✉ *32 allée d'Iéna,* ☎ *04–68–25–22–17. Closed mid-Dec.–mid-Jan.; Sun.–Mon. Sept.–June.*

$$$$ ✕🏨 **La Cité.** Enter the ivy-covered building and you'll be surrounded by the kind of luxurious creature comforts the ascetic Cathars would have decried. Have afternoon tea in the library or in the garden. Change for dinner in your spacious, high-ceilinged room (No. 21 is a good choice), then have an aperitif in the bar. Though the cuisine and

service does not always live up to the promise (or price) of the setting, a new chef is taking over as this goes to press. ✉ *pl. de l'Église, 11000 La Cité de Carcassonne,* ☎ *04–68–25–03–34,* FAX *04–68–71–50–15. 23 rooms, 3 suites. Restaurant, pool. AE, DC, MC, V. Closed Jan.–mid-Feb.*

$$$$ ✕🏨 **Domaine d'Auriac.** Former rugby player Bernard Rigaudis and family maintain a countrified atmosphere in this 19th-century manor house southwest of Carcassonne. Room prices vary according to the size and view; the largest look out over the magnificent park and vineyards. In the dining room, festooned with copper pots, traditional Languedoc cuisine is served. This Relais & Châteaux property tends to charge even more than top dollar—a superior room runs more than 1,500 francs and a good after-dinner brandy can cost 400 francs. ✉ *rte. de St-Hilaire, 11330 Auriac (4 km/2½ mi southwest of Carcassonne),* ☎ *04–68–25–72–22,* FAX *04–68–47–35–54. 28 rooms. Restaurant, air-conditioning, pool, 18-hole golf course, tennis court. AE, MC, V. Closed last 2 wks of Feb., last 2 wks of Nov., 1st wk of Dec.*

$$ 🏨 **Hôtel Montségur.** With its Carcassonne location, this hotel is especially convenient. Rooms on the first two floors feature Louis XV and Louis XVI furniture, some of it genuine, while those above are more romantic, with gilt-iron bedsteads set under the sloping oak beams. ✉ *27 allée d'Iéna, 11000,* ☎ *04–68–25–31–41,* FAX *04–68–47–13–22. 21 rooms. Restaurant. DC, MC, V. Closed mid-Dec.–mid-Jan.*

Nightlife and the Arts

Carcassonne hosts a major **arts festival** in July, featuring dance, theater, classical music, and jazz; for details, contact the Théâtre Municipal (✉ B.P. 236 rue Courtejaire, 11005, ☎ 04–68–25–33–13; ☎ 04–68–77–71–26 reservations).

Mirepoix

39 *48 km (29 mi) southwest of Carcassonne, 88 km (53 mi) southeast of Toulouse.*

This 13th-century walled town is built around its lovely, medieval main square, place Général-Leclerc, surrounded by 13th- to 15th-century houses with timber *couverts* forming arcades or porticoes. A good time to come is during Mirepoix's medieval festival, the third weekend in July.

Dining and Lodging

$$$ ★ ✕🏨 **Château de Camon.** If you are within a 160-km (100-mi) radius, make a point of staying in this medieval castle in Camon, 8 km (5 mi) southeast of Mirepoix. Furnishings in most guest rooms are 18th- and 19th-century. The astonishing overall scheme, with red velvet and tassels, seems suitable either for a Louis XVI resort or an elite bordello, depending on your perspective. A table d'hôte dinner (by reservation only) is served in the family dining room. Consider yourself an honored guest in this private house. ✉ *09500 Mirepoix (35 km/22 mi northeast of Foix),* ☎ *05–61–68–28–28,* FAX *05–61–68–81–56. 9 rooms. Dining room. MC, V. Closed end Nov.–mid-Mar.*

Foix

40 *35 km (22 mi) from Mirepoix, 84 km (52 mi) south of Toulouse, 16 km (10 mi) north of Tarascon-sur-Ariège, 138 km (86 mi) west of Perpignan.*

Nestled in the Ariège Valley is Foix, capital of the Ariège département. Notice the swanky 19th-century administrative buildings to the south of avenue Fauré, the town's major thoroughfare. The **Château de Foix,** sitting impregnably on a promontory above the town and river, has three enormous towers that reach skyward like sentinels. The castle museum details regional history and archaeological finds. ✉ *rue Mercadal,* ☎ *05–61–65–56–05.* 🎫 *20 frs.* ⏲ *Daily 10–noon and 2–5:30.*

A 5-km (3-mi) drive northwest from Foix along D1 leads to the **Rivière Souterraine de Labouiche,** a mysterious underground river whose waters have tunneled a 5-km (3-mi) gallery through the limestone. The 75-minute boat trip covers a 1½-km (1-mi) stretch, past weirdly shaped, subtly lit stalactites and stalagmites, ending with a subterranean waterfall. Dry land is 230 feet overhead. ☎ *05–61–65–04–11.* 🎫 *38 frs.* ⏲ *mid–late June, early–mid-Sept., daily 10–noon and 2–5; July–Aug., daily 9–6; Apr.–May, daily 2–5.*

Dining and Lodging

$ ✕🏨 **Audoye-Lons.** This former post house in the town center has comfortable, modernized rooms that vary in size. The restaurant is reasonably priced and overlooks the Ariège river; it is closed Saturday in winter. ✉ *4 pl. Georges-Duthil, 09000,* ☎ *05–61–65–52–44,* FAX *05–61–02–68–18. 35 rooms, 24 with bath or shower. Restaurant. AE, DC, MC, V. Closed mid-Dec.–mid-Jan.*

Outdoor Activities and Sports

The rivers and mountain lakes here are excellent trout habitat. Beginner and advanced fishing courses are run by **Loisirs Accueil** (✉ Service Pêche, 14 rue Lazéma, 09000, ☎ 05–61–65–01–15).

Tarascon-sur-Ariège

41 *16 km (10 mi) south of Foix.*

Tarascon is best known for its superb, extensive grotto, with its collection of prehistoric art second only to Lascaux (☞ Chapter 16). As you enter Tarascon, veer left along D8 to the **Grotte de Niaux,** which contains scores of red-and-black Magdalenian rock paintings done in charcoal and iron oxide. Stylized horses, goats, deer, and bison, dating from about 20,000 BC, gallop around a naturally circular underground gallery (known as the Salon Noir or Black Room) 1 km (½ mi) inside the entrance. Now that the famous caves at Lascaux in the Dordogne can be seen only in reproduction, this is the finest assembly of prehistoric art open to the public anywhere in France. ☎ *05–61–05–88–37 (guided tours only; call ahead for reservations and to check schedule).* 🎫 *40 frs.* ⏲ *July–Sept., tours daily every 45 mins 8:30–11:30 and 1:30–5:15; Oct.–June, tours daily at 11, 3, and 4:30.*

Ax-les-Thermes

42 *26 km (15 mi) southeast of Tarascon-sur-Ariège.*

A summer and winter resort town, Ax-les-Thermes has over 80 mineral springs. Alpine ski stations at Ax-Bonascre and Ascou-Pailhères and nordic areas at Plateau de Beille and Domaine de Chioula along with Ax's thermal hot springs are an unbeatable winter combination. Crisscrossing the surrounding heights are 400 km (248 mi) of trails.

Font-Romeu

43 *75 km (45 mi) southeast of Ax-les-Thermes, 87 km (54 mi) southeast of Tarascon-sur-Ariège.*

Font-Romeu first became a high-altitude vacation spot in 1920. French Olympians trained here for the Mexico City games of 1968. Excellent indoor and outdoor sports facilities include ski lifts, an ice rink, a riding school, a swimming pool, tennis courts, and a golf course.

Dining and Lodging

$–$$ ✕🏨 **Carlit.** This modern resort hotel is the traditional Font-Romeu haven. The staff will arrange a ski instructor or mountain guide for you or organize a minibus excursion to nearby Spain and Andorra. Popular with French families on vacation in the mountains, prices are highest in ski season and midsummer. The restaurant serves hearty mountain fare (demi-pension is mandatory during peak periods). ✉ *av. du Dr-Capelle, 66120,* ☏ *04–68–30–80–30,* FAX *04–68–30–80–68. 58 rooms with bath or shower. Restaurant, bar, brasserie, pool. MC, V. Closed Nov.–mid-Dec.*

Eyne

44 *12 km (7 mi) southeast of Font-Romeu.*

Eyne, with a grand total of no (zero) in-town commercial establishments—not a café, not a bakery—is one of the purest villages remaining in the broad Pyrenean valley of the Cerdagne. Eyne also has a nationally classified botanical park, the **Vall d'Eyne,** where Atlantic and Mediterranean weather systems and vegetation converge. In the park are archaeological walks to menhirs and Neolithic dolmens, and a ski station uphill.

Dining and Lodging

$$ ✕🏨 **Cal Pai.** This 17th-century country farmhouse is a *gîte d'étape* (way station for hikers and skiers) with table d'hôtes (communal table) of uncommon design and quality. The impeccable taste of owner-builder-manager-chefs Françoise and Jean-Pierre—in both decoration and cuisine—makes this an unforgettable place. ✉ *Eyne Village,* ☏ *04–68–04–06–96. 12 rooms with shared bath. Dining room. MC, V. Reservations essential.*

Mont-Louis

45 *5 km (3 mi) east of Eyne, 30 km (18 mi) west of Villefranche-de-Conflent.*

This fortified village, at 1,600 meters (5,200 feet)—France's highest—was set up as a border stronghold by Vauban in 1679 and commands views over the Cerdagne valley to the west, the Capcir to the north, and the Conflent to the east. The ramparts and the citadel, never attacked, are perfectly preserved. The solar oven, the only one in France in commercial use, is a key attraction.

Dining and Lodging

$$ ✕🏨 **Lou Rouballou.** Widely recommended as the best value and top cuisine in Mont-Louis, Pierre and Christiane Duval's tiny flower-covered hideaway is the place to go. Rooms are simple, small, and cozy. The cuisine is rich in sauces based on Pyrenean herbs, wild mushrooms, and game. Try the *civet d'isard* (mountain-goat stew). Reservations are essential. ✉ *rue des Écoles Laïques, 66210,* ☏ *04–68–04–23–26,* FAX *04–68–04–14–09. 14 rooms, 7 with bath. MC, V. Closed May, Oct.–Dec.*

Villefranche-de-Conflent

46 *30 km (18 mi) east of Mont-Louis, 6 km (4 mi) west of Prades.*

Named for its location at the confluence of the Têt and Cady rivers, this village combines elements of an 11th-century fortress with Vauban improvements from the 17th century. Cross the tiny St-Pierre bridge over the Têt and use the pink marble "stairway of a thousand steps" to climb up to Fort-Liberia for views of the village, the Canigou, and the valleys east to Prade.

Dining and Lodging

$$$ ✕ **Auberge St-Paul.** One of the best known tables in the area, this warm stone-surrounded refuge is known for its fine Catalan cuisine. Try the *truite à la llosa* (trout on slate slabs) or the civet d'isard. ✉ *7 pl. de l'Église,* ☎ *04–68–96–30–95. Reservations essential. MC, V. Closed Mon.*

$$ ✕▣ **Auberge du Cèdre.** This comfortable little place over the river commands fine views of the fortress. Rooms are small but cozy. Pyrenean and Catalan specialties are served on a little glassed-in porch suspended over the Têt. Reservations are essential at the restaurant; call before you go to make sure it's open. ✉ *Domaine Ste-Eulalie, 66500,* ☎ *04–68–96–37–37. 10 rooms. Restaurant. AE, DC, MC, V.*

Vernet-les-Bains

47 *12 km (7 mi) west of Prades, 55 km (34 mi) west of Perpignan.*

English writer Rudyard Kipling came to take the waters in Vernet-les-Bains, a long-established spa town. The hilltop village church is dwarfed by the imposing Mont Canigou behind. Even higher up is the medieval abbey. Leave your car in Casteil, 2 km (1¼ mi) farther, and complete the journey to the **Abbaye St-Martin du Canigou** on foot. Brace yourself for the steep half-hour climb; the abbey is perched on a triangular promontory at an altitude of nearly 3,600 feet. Although the abbey was diligently restored by the bishop of Perpignan early this century, part of the cloisters, along with the higher (and larger) of the two churches, date from the 11th century. The lower church, dedicated to Notre-Dame-sous-Terre, is even older. Rising above is a stocky, battlemented bell tower. ☎ *04–68–05–50–03.* 🎫 *15 frs.* ⏲ *Daily 10–12:30 and 2:30–5.*

Prades

48 *6 km (4 mi) east of Villefranche-de-Conflent, 43 km (27 mi) west of Perpignan.*

Once home to Catalan cellist Pablo Casals, the market town of Prades is famous for its annual summer music festival. Founded by Casals in ★ 1950, the festival is held at the medieval **Abbaye de St-Michel de Cuxa,** 3 km (2 mi) south of town on D27. One of the gems of the Pyrénées, the abbey's sturdy, crenellated, four-story bell tower is visible from afar. If the remains of the cloisters here seem familiar, it may be because you have seen the missing pieces at New York City's Cloisters museum; they were purchased by American sculptor George Grey Barnard in 1907 and subsequently by the Metropolitan Museum in 1925. The 10th-century pre-Romanesque church is a superb aesthetic and acoustical venue for the summer cello concerts.

Céret

49 *68 km (41 mi) southeast of Prades, 35 km (21 mi) west of Collioure.*

Picasso, Braque, Juan Gris, and many other artists found this small Pyrenean town surrounded by cherry orchards irresistible at the beginning of this century. Others, such as Chagall in the late '20s, followed. The result is a museum, the **Musée d'Art Moderne,** housing an extraordinary collection of paintings by these 20th-century masters. ✉ *8 bis Maréchal Joffre,* ☎ *04–68–87–27–76.* ⏲ *May–Sept., Wed.–Mon. 10–6.*

After visiting the Modern Art Museum, stroll through pretty **Vieux Céret** (Old Céret): find your way through the place des Neufs Jets (Nine Fountains Square), around the church, and out to the lovely fortified Porte de France gateway. Then walk over the single-arched Vieux Pont (Old Bridge).

Dining

$$$ ★ ✕ **Les Feuillants.** Widely known as one of the top restaurants in the area, this elegant place combines cuisine, wine, and traditional design in another manifestation of Céret's superb and surprising artistic endowment. Marie Louise and Didier Banyols, sommelier and chef respectively, produce spectacular fare, such as *rouelles de homard Bretagne au Banyuls et châtaignes* (sliced Brittany lobster in sweet wine and chestnuts). ✉ *1 bd. La Fayette,* ☎ *04–68–87–37–88. AE, DC, MC, V. No lunch Sat.*

Collioure

50 *35 km (21 mi) east of Céret, 27 km (17 mi) southeast of Perpignan.*

This pretty seaside fishing village with a sheltered natural harbor has become a summer magnet for tourists and should be strenuously avoided in July and August. Painters such as Henri Matisse, André Derain, Henri Martin, and Georges Braque—dubbed "Fauves" for their "savage" approach to color and form—were among the early discoverers of Collioure. The view they admired remains largely unchanged today: To the north, the rocky Ilot St-Vincent juts out into the sea, a modern lighthouse at its tip, while inland, the Albères range rises to connect the Pyrénées with the Mediterranean.

Near the old Quartier du Mouré is the 17th-century church of **Notre-Dame-des-Anges** (✉ pl. de l'Église). It has exuberantly carved altarpieces and a pink-domed bell tower that doubled as the original lighthouse. A slender jetty divides the Boramar beach, beneath the church, from the small landing area at the foot of the **Château Royal,** a 15th-century castle remodeled by Vauban 200 years later. ☎ *04–68–82–06–43.* 🎟 *20 frs.* ⏲ *Mar.–Oct., daily 10–noon and 2–5.*

Dining and Lodging

$$–$$$ ✕🏨 **Relais des Trois Mas.** Overlooking Collioure from the cliffs south of town, this hotel has small rooms but interestingly furnished rooms—headboards, for example, are made from antique Spanish doors. Rooms are named for painters whose work appears on the bathroom tiles. The views are spectacular. Below is a pebbled beach, though you may prefer the small pool (hewn from rock) or the huge Jacuzzi. Dine at the restaurant, La Balette, on the terrace or in one of the two small dining rooms looking over the harbor. ✉ *rte. de Port-Vendres, 66190,* ☎ *04–68–82–05–07,* FAX *04–68–82–38–08. 19 rooms, 4 suites. Restaurant, pool, exercise room. AE, DC, MC, V. Closed mid-Nov.–mid-Dec.*

$$ ★ ✕🏨 **Les Templiers.** Universally considered the "soul" of Collioure, no visit is complete without a stop here. Owner Jojo Pous, son of the force behind Collioure's art colony, has over 2,500 original works hanging from every nook and cranny. The bar itself is a work of art, curved like the hull of a skiff and ending with a wood sculpture of a mermaid suckling an infant sailor. The mostly Catalan cuisine is excellent, and the rooms overlooking the château cozy. ✉ *quai de l'Amirauté, 66190,* ☎ *04–68–98–31–10,* FAX *04–68–98–01–24. 43 rooms with bath or*

shower. Restaurant, bar-café. AE, DC, MC, V. Closed early Jan.–early Feb.

Perpignan

51 *16 km (10 mi) south of Salses, 64 km (40 mi) south of Narbonne.*

During medieval times, Perpignan was the second city of Catalonia (after Barcelona), before falling to Louis XIII's French army in 1642. The Spanish influence is evident in Perpignan's leading monument, the fortified **Palais des Rois de Majorque** (King of Majorca Palace) begun in the 14th century by James II of Majorca. Highlights here are the majestic **Cour d'Honneur** (Courtyard of Honor), the two-tier Flamboyant Gothic chapel of **Ste-Croix**, and the **Grande Salle** (Great Hall) with its monumental fireplaces. ✉ *rue des Archers,* ☎ *04–68–34–48–29.* *10 frs.* *Daily 9–5.*

The center of town is marked by the medieval monument, the 14th-century **Le Castillet**, with its tall, crenellated twin towers. Originally this hulking brick building was the main gate to the city, later it was used as a prison. Now the **Casa Pairal**, a museum devoted to Catalan art and traditions, is housed here. ✉ *pl. de Verdun,* ☎ *04–68–35–42–05.* *Free.* *Wed.–Mon. 9–noon and 2–6.*

The **promenade des Plantanes,** across boulevard Wilson from Le Castillet, is a cheerful place to stroll among flowers, plane trees, and fountains. To see more interesting medieval buildings, walk along the streets—the **Petite Rue des Fabriques d'En Nabot** is the best—near Le Castillet and the adjacent place de la Loge, the town's nerve center. Note the frilly wrought-iron campanile and dramatic medieval crucifix on the **Cathédrale St-Jean** (✉ pl. Gambetta). The **Loge de Mer** (✉ rue de la Loge), a graceful 14th-century building, was once the chamber of commerce for maritime trade. The 15th-century **Palais de la Députation** (✉ rue de la Loge) was once the seat of the permanent deputy or representative of the Catalan Corts (Parliament). The massive arched entryway is typical of the Catalonian or House of Aragon civil design of that period.

Dining and Lodging

$$$–$$$$ ✕ **Chapon Fin.** The local bourgeoisie pours into this excellent restaurant in the Park hotel (☞ *below*) to sample the subtle, understated cuisine. Three prix-fixe menus showcase authentic Mediterranean food. ✉ *18 bd. Jean-Bourrat,* ☎ *04–68–35–14–14. AE, DC, MC, V. Closed Sun. No lunch Mon.*

$$ ★ ✕ **La Casa Sansa.** This very Catalan, very popular restaurant serves fine regional specialties in an atmosphere thick with tastefully designed local color. Paintings crowd the walls with Roussillon themes. ✉ *2 rue Fabrique d'en Nadal,* ☎ *04–68–34–21–84. Reservations essential. AE, DC, MC, V. Closed Sun. No lunch Mon.*

$$$ ★ **Park.** This family-run hotel enjoys ironclad prestige in Perpignan. Don't be deceived by the undistinguished facade; although some rooms are small, most are luxurious, soundproof, and air-conditioned. ✉ *18 bd. Jean-Bourrat, 66000,* ☎ *04–68–35–14–14,* FAX *04–68–35–48–18. 67 rooms with bath or shower. Restaurant. AE, DC, MC, V.*

$–$$ **Hôtel de la Poste et de la Perdrix.** If you're looking for an inexpensive place with old French charm in the center of town next to Le Castillet, don't miss this little spot. Rooms, like the hotel, are simple and poetic, as opposed to overcomfortable and prosaic. The cuisine is Catalan. ✉ *6 rue Fabriques Nabot, 66000,* ☎ *04–68–34–42–53,* FAX

04–68–34–58–20. 38 rooms with bath or shower. Restaurant. AE, DC, MC, V.

Shopping

Rue des Marchands, near Le Castillet, is thick with chic shops. **Maison Quinta** (✉ rue Louis Blanc) is a top design and architectural artifacts store. Excellent local ceramics can be found at the picturesque **Sant Vicens crafts center** (✉ rue Sant Vicens, off D22 east of the town center).

Salses

52 *16 km (10 mi) north of Perpignan, 48 km (30 mi) south of Narbonne.*

Salses has a history of sieges. Hannibal stormed through the town with his elephants on his way to the Alps in 218 BC, though no trace of his passage remains. The colossal and well-preserved **Fort de Salses,** built by Ferdinand of Aragon in 1497 and equipped for 300 horses and 1,000 soldiers, fell to the French under Cardinal Richelieu in 1642 after a three-year siege. Bulky round towers ring the rectangular inner fort, while the five-story keep, with its narrow corridors and small-scale drawbridges, was designed to keep the fort's governor safe to the last. ☎ *04–68–38–60–13.* 🎫 *25 frs.* ⏲ *July–Aug., daily 9–6; Sept.–June, daily 9:30–11:30 and 2–5:30 (until 4 Nov.–Easter).*

Narbonne

53 *64 km (40 mi) north of Perpignan, 60 km (37 mi) east of Carcassonne, 94 km (58 mi) south of Montpellier.*

In Roman times bustling, industrial Narbonne was the second-largest town in Gaul (after Lyon) and an important port, though today little remains of its Roman past. Until the sea receded during the Middle Ages, Narbonne prospered. The town's former wealth is evinced in the 14th-century **Cathédral St-Just;** its vaults rise 133 feet from the floor, making it the tallest cathedral in southern France. Only Beauvais and Amiens, in Picardy, are taller, and as at Beauvais, the nave at Narbonne was never built. ✉ *rue Armand-Gauthier.*

Richly sculpted cloisters link the cathedral to the former **Palais des Archevêques** (Archbishops' Palace), now home to the museums of archaeology, art, and history. Note the enormous palace kitchen and the late-13th-century keep, the **Donjon Gilles-Aycelin;** climb the 180 steps to the top for a view of the region and the town. ✉ *Palais des Archevêques,* ☎ *04–68–90–30–30.* 🎫 *25 frs (includes all town museums).* ⏲ *May–Sept., daily 9–noon and 2–6; Oct.–Apr., Tues.–Sun. 10–noon and 2–5:30.*

On the south side of the Canal de la Robine is the **Musée Lapidaire** (Sculpture Museum), housed in the handsome, 13th-century former church of **Notre-Dame de la Mourguié.** Classical busts, ancient sarcophagi, lintels, and Gallo-Roman inscriptions await you. ✉ *pl. Lamourguier,* ☎ *04–68–65–53–58.* 🎫 *25 frs (includes all town museums).* ⏲ *May–Sept., daily 9–noon and 2–6; Oct.–Apr., Tues.–Sun. 10–noon and 2–5:30.*

For the nearest decent beach, follow pretty D168 as it winds its way over the Montagne de la Clape to **Narbonne-Plage,** 15 km (9 mi) away. Just up the coast at St-Pierre-sur-Mer is the curious **Gouffre de l'Oeil-Doux,** an inland lake fed by seawater.

Some 3000 wild animals roam freely in the 500-acre, pond-studded **Réserve Africaine de Sigean,** 15 km (9 mi) south of Narbonne. The reserve was designed by France's leading game expert, the vicomte de La Panouse, who is best known for cross-breeding lions and tigers. ☎ *04–68–48–20–20.* 💶 *100 frs.* ⏲ *Daily 9–6:30 (until 5 in winter).*

OFF THE BEATEN PATH

ABBAYE DE FONTFROIDE – Roughly 11 km (7 mi) southwest of Narbonne is the Fontfroide Abbey, one of the largest and best preserved in France. Founded in 1093, it is surrounded by cypress trees—the type of setting beloved of Cistercian monks. Pope Benedict XII was abbot here from 1311 to 1317, and the finest monastic buildings—including the church, flower-bedecked cloisters, chapter house, and dormitory—date from his time. Especially noteworthy is the rose garden, with 2,000 bushes. ✉ *Head west from Narbonne on N113 and turn left 5 km (3 mi) from town center onto D613; 7 km (4½ mi) farther is a sign for the abbey down a small road to the left.* ☎ *04–68–45–11–08.* 💶 *Guided tours only: 32 frs.* ⏲ *Daily 10–noon and 2–5:30; tours every 45 mins in summer, hourly in winter; closed weekday mornings in winter.*

Dining and Lodging

$$$ ✕🏨 **Le Relais du Val d'Orbieu.** Good hotels are scarce in Narbonne. The most commodious, though a bit overpriced, is this hostelry west of town. Owner Jean-Pierre Gonsalvez speaks English and is extremely helpful. Designed around a courtyard, most rooms are reached through covered arcades; the better ones are pleasantly simple, with bare tile floors and large French windows leading onto terraces; the standard ones (100 francs less) are slightly smaller and do not have terraces or views. The dining room lacks intimacy, but the wine list has good local wines at reasonable prices. ✉ *D24, 11200 Ornaisons (14 km/8 mi west of Narbonne),* ☎ *04–68–27–10–27,* FAX *04–68–27–52–44. 20 rooms. Restaurant, pool, tennis court. AE, DC, MC, V.*

$$ ✕🏨 **Languedoc.** In this old-fashioned, turn-of-the-century hotel downtown, the smallish rooms vary in style and comfort; a full bath is an extra 100 francs. La Coupole restaurant serves inexpensive regional dishes with menus starting at 90 francs; it is closed Sunday dinner and Monday. ✉ *22 bd. Gambetta, 11100,* ☎ *04–68–65–14–74,* FAX *04–68–65–81–48. 38 rooms, 34 with bath or shower, 2 suites. Restaurant, piano bar. AE, DC, MC, V.*

TOULOUSE, THE MIDI-PYRÉNÉES, AND ROUSSILLON A TO Z

Arriving and Departing

By Car

The fastest route from Paris to Toulouse (700 km/435 mi southwest) is via Bordeaux on A10, then A62; journey time is about nine hours. If you choose to head south over the Pyrénées to Barcelona, the Tunnel du Puymorens saves a half hour of switchbacks between Hospitalet and Porta, but in good weather and with time to spare, the drive over the Puymorens pass is spectacular. Plan on taking three hours between Toulouse and Font-Romeu and another three to Barcelona. The fastest route from Toulouse to Barcelona (three to four hours) is via Carcassonne and Perpignan on A61 and A9, becoming A7 at Le Perthus.

By Plane

All international flights arrive at Toulouse's **Blagnac Airport,** a 20-minute drive from the center of town. Regular **Air France** flights link Toulouse with most European capitals. **Air Inter** runs as many as 30 flights a day during the week between Paris and Toulouse (for reservations, ☎ 01–

45–39–25–25 Paris; ☎ 05–61–71–11–10 Toulouse). There are also four flights daily from Paris to Perpignan. **TAT** (Transport Aérien Transrégional) has direct flights from Paris's Orly Airport to Rodez (for reservations, ☎ 01–42–79–05–05 Paris; ☎ 05–65–42–20–30 Rodez).

Airport shuttles run regularly (every half hour between 8:15 AM and 8:45 PM) from the airport to the bus station in Toulouse (fare 20 francs) and also at 9:20, 10, and 10:45 PM. From Toulouse bus station to the airport, buses leave at 5:30 AM, 6, 7, 7:30, and then every half hour until 8:30 PM.

By Train

Trains for the southwest leave from Paris (Gare d'Austerlitz). There are direct trains to Toulouse (six to seven hours), Carcassonne (seven to eight hours), and Montauban (six hours). For Rodez (seven to eight hours), change in Brive, and for Auch (over eight hours), in Toulouse. Seven trains leave Paris (Gare de Lyon) daily for Narbonne (six hours) and Perpignan (seven hours); a change at Montpellier is often necessary. Note that at least one high-speed TGV (Train à Grande Vitesse) per day leaves Paris (Gare Montparnasse) for Toulouse; journey time is five hours.

Getting Around

By Car

The A62 expressway slices through the region on its way to the coast at Narbonne, where A9 heads south to Perpignan. At Toulouse, where A62 becomes A61, various highways fan out in all directions: N117 to Pau, N20 to Montauban and Cahors, and N88 to Albi and Rodez.

By Plane

From Toulouse's Blagnac Airport, you can pick up an **Air Inter** flight to Tarbes, near Lourdes (☎ 05–61–71–11–10 for information).

By Train

The French rail network in the southwest provides regular services to all towns.

Contacts and Resources

Car Rental

Avis (✉ pl. de la Gare, Lourdes, ☎ 05–62–34–26–76; 13 bd. Conflent, Perpignan, ☎ 04–68–34–26–71; Blagnac Airport, Toulouse, ☎ 05–61–30–04–94). **Hertz** (✉ pl. Lagarrasic, Auch, ☎ 05–62–05–26–26; 5 av. Chamier, Montauban, ☎ 05–63–20–29–00).

Guided Tours

Contact the **Toulouse Tourist Office** (✉ Donjon du Capitole, ☎ 05–61–11–02–22) for information about walking tours and bus tours in and around Toulouse. The **Comité Régional du Tourisme** (✉ CRT, 54 bd. de l'Endouchure, 31200 Toulouse, ☎ 05–61–13–55–55) has a brochure, "1,001 Escapes in the Midi-Pyrénées," with descriptions of weekends and short organized package vacations.

Music Festivals

There are 50 music festivals a year in smaller towns throughout the region; the Comité Régional du Tourisme (CRT) and larger tourist offices can provide a list of dates and addresses, or contact the **Délégation Musicale Régionale** (✉ 56 rue du Taur, 31080 Toulouse, ☎ 05–61–29–21–00).

Outdoor Activities and Sports

For information on canoeing or kayaking, contact the **Ligue de Canoë-Kayak** (✉ 16 rue Guillemin-Tarayre, 31000 Toulouse, ☎ 05–61–62–65–05). For information on hiking or horseback riding, contact the **Comité de Randonnées Midi-Pyrénées** (✉ CORAMIP, 14 rue Bayard, 31000 Toulouse, ☎ 05–61–99–44–00). Local tourist offices have detailed maps of more than 3,220 km (2,000 mi) of marked trails. The **Comité Regional du Tourisme du Languedoc-Roussillon** (✉ 20 rue de la République, 24000, Montpellier, ☎ 04–67–22–81–00) publishes a brochure on golf courses in the area and sells a pass good for 14 different courses.

Travel Agencies

American Express (✉ Office Catholique de Voyages, 14 chaussée du Bourg, Lourdes, ☎ 05–62–94–40–84). **Havas** (✉ 73 rue d'Alsace-Lorraine, Toulouse, ☎ 05–61–23–16–35). **Wagons-Lits** (✉ Voyages Dépêche, 42 bis rue d'Alsace-Lorraine, Toulouse, ☎ 05–62–15–42–70).

Visitor Information

The regional tourist office for the Midi-Pyrénées is the **Comité Régional du Tourisme** (✉ CRT, 54 bd. de l'Endouchure, 31200 Toulouse, ☎ 05–61–13–55–55). For Roussillon, contact the **Comité Départemental de Tourisme** (✉ quai de Lattre de Tassigny, 66000 Perpignan, ☎ 04–68–34–29–94). Local tourist offices are as follows: **Albi** (✉ pl. Ste-Cécile, ☎ 05–63–49–48–80). **Auch** (✉ 1 rue Dessoles, ☎ 05–62–05–22–89). **Carcassonne** (✉ 15 bd. Camille-Pelletan, ☎ 04–68–25–07–04). **Lourdes** (✉ pl. Peyramale, ☎ 05–62–94–15–64). **Montauban** (✉ 2 rue du Collège, ☎ 05–63–63–60–60). **Narbonne** (✉ pl. Roger-Salengro, ☎ 04–68–65–15–60). **Pau** (✉ pl. Royale, ☎ 05–59–27–27–08). **Perpignan** (✉ pl. Armand-Lanoux, ☎ 04–68–35–98–70). **Rodez** (✉ pl. du Mal-Foch, ☎ 05–65–68–02–27). **Toulouse** (✉ Donjon du Capitole, ☎ 05–61–11–02–22).

16 The Atlantic Coast

Bordeaux, Biarritz, and the Atlantic Pyrénées

Let the vast beaches near Biarritz, the waterways of "Green Venice," and the Basque villages in the Pyrénées draw you to the Atlantic Coast region. See castles and châteaux recalling medieval battles and Romanesque abbeys and cathedrals echoing with history. Sip splendid wine with oysters in Bordeaux, savor Périgord truffles and foie gras, and dine heartily on confit de canard in the Dordogne.

Updated by Nigel Fisher and George Semler

IF THERE'S A FORMULA FOR ENJOYING the Atlantic Coast of France and its hinterland, it should include cultural exploration, wine tasting, eating oysters, and relaxing by the sea. Swaths of sandy beaches line the coast: Well-heeled resorts, like Biarritz, are thronged with glistening bodies baking in the sun, but if you prefer solitude, you won't have any trouble discovering vast, underpopulated stretches.

For three centuries during the Middle Ages, this region was a battlefield in the wars between the French and the English. Castles and châteaux stud the area—those at Biron, Hautefort, and Beynac are among the best. Robust Romanesque architecture is more characteristic of this area than the airy Gothic style found elsewhere in France: Poitiers showcases the best examples, notably Notre-Dame-la-Grande, with its richly worked facade, though Romanesque style can also be admired at nearby St-Savin abbey and at Angoulême and Périgueux.

The elegant 18th-century city of Bordeaux is synonymous with the wine trade: The vineyards of Médoc, Sauternes, Graves, Entre-Deux-Mers, and St-Émilion are all within a short drive. In the Gironde *département* (province) around Bordeaux, the great Landes pine forest extends south. North of Bordeaux lies the Marais Poitevin, whose marshy network of rivers and canals is nicknamed "Green Venice." Along the Spanish border rise the Atlantic Pyrénées, with their trout streams, pilgrimage churches, and Basque villages.

Pleasures and Pastimes

Beaches and Water Sports

French families go for their annual vacations all along the coast, especially around Arcachon, but most foreign visitors head for the beaches between Biarritz and St-Jean-de-Luz. Biarritz is the French surfing capital, though some say the rolling Atlantic waves south of Arcachon are even better.

Bullfighting

Bullfights are a major preoccupation along the Pyrénées in Basque country. Dax, Mont-de-Marsan, and Bayonne all hold bullfights; in summer, you can't miss the colorful posters announcing the fights.

Dining

Truffles, foie gras, walnuts, plums, trout, eel, oysters, and myriad succulent species of mushrooms jostle for attention on restaurant menus. The hearty food of the Dordogne, the rich agricultural produce of the Landes, the succulent seafood caught in the Atlantic off La Rochelle, and the Basque cooking in the south makes for diversified tables. Béarn, around Pau, is famous for richly marinated *civets* (stews) made with *palombes* (wood pigeon) or *isnard* (wild goat). The versatile wines of Bordeaux make fine accompaniments to most regional dishes, but don't overlook their less prestigious cousins (Bergerac, Pécharmant, Fiefs Vendéens, Monbazillac, Charentes). Cognac is de rigueur at the end of a meal.

CATEGORY	COST*
$$$$	over 400 frs
$$$	250 frs–400 frs
$$	125 frs–250 frs
$	under 125 frs

**per person for a three-course meal, including tax (20.6%) and tip but not wine*

Hiking

To truly appreciate the Basque Pyrénées' beauty, you need to get out of the car and hike along the gorges and into the mountains. Trail maps are available from tourist offices.

Lodging

Vacationers flock to La Rochelle, Royan, Arcachon, Biarritz, and the nearby islands of Ré and Oléron, and for miles around, hotels are booked solid months in advance. Farther inland the situation is easier, but there aren't as many places to stay. Advance booking is particularly recommended in Bordeaux and in Périgord; the few towns' hotels fill up quickly in midsummer. Many country or small-town hotels expect you to have at least one dinner there, and, if you can have two meals a day with lodging and stay several nights, it will save you money. Prices off-season (Oct.–May) often drop as much as 20%.

CATEGORY	COST*
$$$$	over 800 frs
$$$	550 frs–800 frs
$$	300 frs–550 frs
$	under 300 frs

**All prices are for a standard double room for two, including tax (20.6%) and service charge.*

Pelota

The ancestral ball game of pelota, from the medieval *jeux de paume* (hand games, or, literally "palm" games), is a fundamental part of rural Basque culture. A Basque village without a *fronton* (backboard and pelota court) is as unimaginable as an American town without a baseball diamond. Players always wear white, but you'll see different versions of pelota being played.

Exploring the Atlantic Coast

The Atlantic Coast region encompasses much of southwestern France and can be divided into four areas. To the north is rural Poitou-Charentes, stretching from St-Savin through the canals around Poitiers to the seacoast town of La Rochelle and back, again, through Cognac country and Limoges. South of Poitou-Charentes are the medieval villages, cliff-top châteaux, and prehistoric sites of the Dordogne and Périgord. The vineyards surrounding Bordeaux form the basis of the third area, which continues south through sand dunes and forested scenery to the coastal resort of Biarritz. The fourth area covers the Basque Pyrénées on the Spanish border.

Great Itineraries

To see all of the Atlantic Coast in one trip would be overly ambitious, so you need to be selective about where you go. If you love the beach and the outdoors, head south to Biarritz and the Atlantic Pyrénées. If you're a gourmet, go straight to Bordeaux and Eugénie-les-Bains. If you like to roam around the countryside, explore the Dordogne. Following are some suggested itineraries.

Numbers in the text correspond to numbers in the margin and on the Atlantic Coast and Bordeaux maps.

IF YOU HAVE 4 DAYS

Begin in **Poitiers** ①, known for its Romanesque cathedral and an easy hour's drive from the Loire Valley—add another hour if you are coming from Paris. Try to get to **Cognac** ⑬ or **Jarnac** ⑭ by afternoon, so that you have time to visit a *chais,* a wine and spirit store. The following day enter the Dordogne region via hilltop **Angoulême** ⑮ and quaint **Brantôme** ⑲. Rest up in **Hautefort** ⑱ or the medieval market town of **Sarla-la-Canéda** ㉓. The next day follow the Dordogne river to **La Roque-Gageac** ㉕, huddled beneath a towering gray cliff—make it your base for exploring the castle at **Beynac** ㉔, the fortified medieval village of **Monpazier** ㉗, the hilltop château in **Biron** ㉘, the cave paintings at the **Grotte de Lascaux,** or the Musée Nationale de Préhistoire in **Les Eyzies-de-Tayac** ㉑. On the fourth day eat lunch in medieval **St-Émilion** ㉜ and end the day in **Bordeaux** ㉝–㊴.

IF YOU HAVE 6 DAYS

Follow the four-day itinerary to **Bordeaux** ㉝–㊴. On the fifth day, visit the Médoc vineyards near Bordeaux or the beaches around **Arcachon** ㊷, then return to Bordeaux for another night. The next morning, head north to **Soulac-sur-Mer** ㊵ and travel over the Gironde to **Royan** ⑪, then drive up to **La Rochelle** ⑦, stopping for lunch in **Brouage** ⑨. On day six, explore the Marais Poitevin from **Coulon** ⑤ and the archaeology and fine arts museums in **Niort** ④.

IF YOU HAVE 9 DAYS

Follow the four-day itinerary to **Bordeaux** ㉝–㊴. On your fifth day visit the Médoc vineyards near Bordeaux or the beaches around **Arcachon** ㊶, then return to Bordeaux for another night. On day six either head south through the Sauternes wine country en route to **Eugénie-les-Bains** ㊸ and the Atlantic Pyrénées, or go north to **Saintes** ⑫ and the towns along the Atlantic Coast. This itinerary takes you south to the mountains. On your seventh day stop in the elegant town of **Pau** ㊼, then drive on to the Basque village of **Ste-Engrâce** ㊿ and the Gorges de Kakouetta, just beyond; spend the night in a cozy **Larrau** (51) inn. The next morning, continue through the mountains; have lunch in **St-Jean-Pied-de-Port** (53) before making your way to the coast at **Bayonne** ㊹. Stay the night and following day in **Biarritz** ㊺ or **St-Jean-de-Luz** ㊻ on the Spanish border.

When to Tour the Atlantic Coast

Spring and autumn are the best times to visit—there aren't as many tourists and the weather is still nice. The *vendanges* (grape harvests) usually begin about mid-September in the Bordelais (though you can't visit the wineries at this time). Harvests begin two weeks later in the Cognac region to the north, famed for its brandy. If you want to enjoy the beaches, you're going to have to bear with the hordes of vacationers in late July and August. But you can also see a bullfight in Dax, Mont-de-Marsan, or Bayonne at this time. Many hotels close from the end of October through March.

POITOU-CHARENTES

Occupying the northern part of the Atlantic Coast region, Poitou-Charentes extends from St-Savin to the coastal towns of La Rochelle and Brouage and back through the Cognac region to Limoges. Between La Rochelle and Poitiers is the Marais Poitevin, the marshy area known as Green Venice for its crisscrossing small canals.

Poitiers

102 km (63 mi) southwest of Tours, 132 km (82 mi) southeast of Angers, 120 km (75 mi) northwest of Limoges, 339 km (212 mi) southwest of Paris.

Thanks to its majestic hilltop setting above the River Clain and its position halfway along the Bordeaux–Paris trade route, Poitiers became an important commercial, religious, and university town in the Mid-

The Atlantic Coast

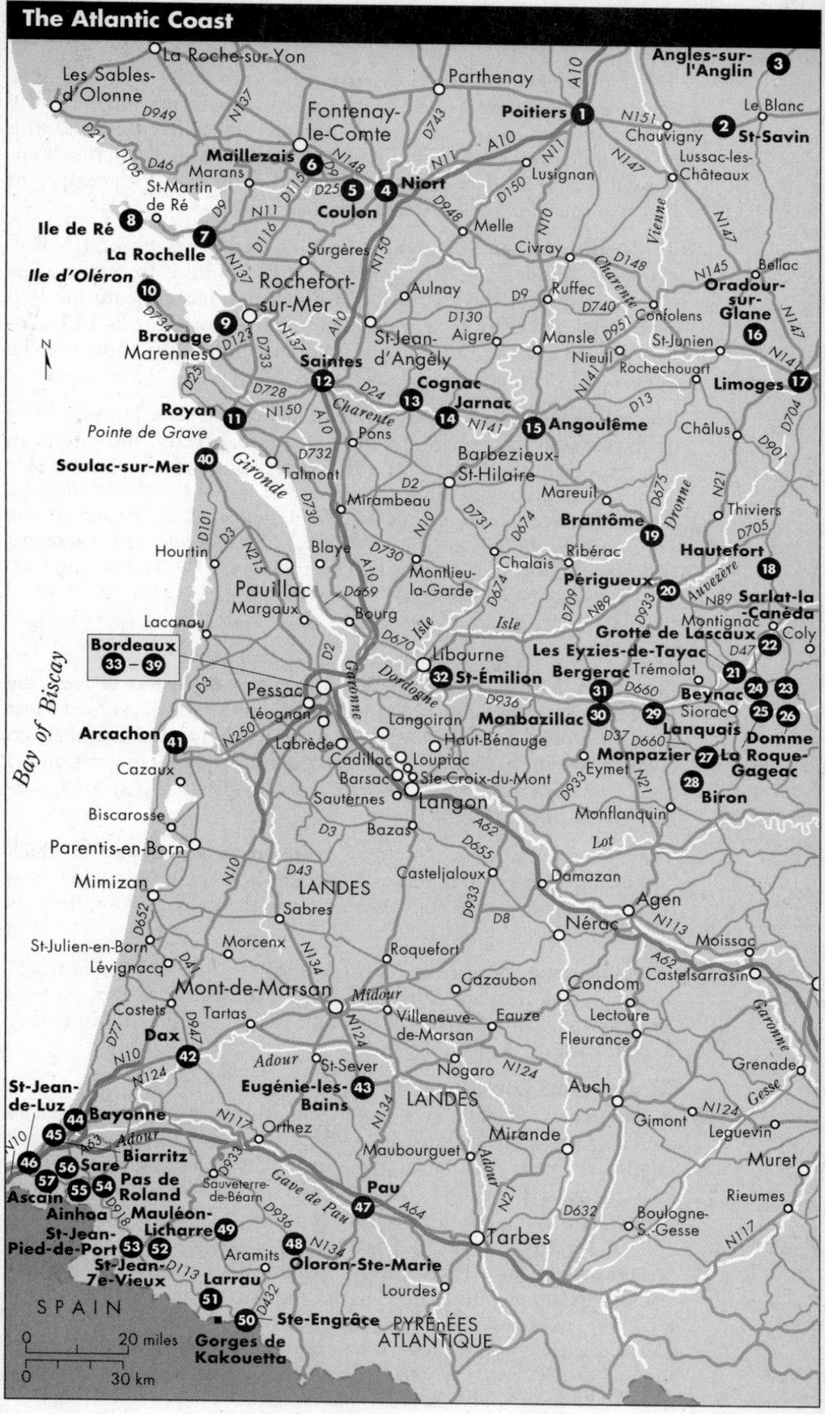

dle Ages. Life quieted down after the 17th century, but tranquillity has resulted in excellent architectural preservation.

The church of **Notre-Dame-la-Grande,** in the town center, is an impressive example of the Romanesque architecture so common in western France. Its 12th-century facade is framed by rounded arches and decorated with a multitude of bas-reliefs and sculptures while its dark interior is enlivened with reproduction murals painted in the mid-19th century to brighten the church. ✉ *rue des Cordeliers.*

The **Cathédrale de St-Pierre,** a few hundred yards beyond Notre-Dame-la-Grande, was built during the 12th to the 14th century. The largest church in Poitiers, it has a distinctive facade featuring two asymmetrical towers. The imposing interior is noted for its 13th-century stained glass and 13th-century wooden choir stalls, thought to be the oldest in France. ✉ *pl. de la Cathédrale.*

The **Musée Ste-Croix,** in a modern building off rue Jean-Jaurès, houses archaeological discoveries, traditional regional crafts, and European paintings from the 15th to the 19th century of good, though not outstanding, quality. The museum is part of a triad that includes the **Musée Chièvre-Croix** and the **Musée Hypogée.** ✉ *Ste-Croix: 61 rue St-Simplicien,* ☎ *05–49–41–07–53.* 🎫 *15 frs (includes the museums of Chièvre-Croix and Hypogée). Chièvre-Croix: rue Victor Hugo,* ☎ *05–49–41–42–21. Hypogée: 44 rue du Père de la Croix,* ☎ *05–49–01–68–85.* ⏲ *All museums Tues.–Sun. 10–noon and 1–5 (2–6 on weekends).*

Next to the Musée Ste-Croix is the 4th-century **Baptistère St-Jean,** the oldest Christian building in France. Its heavy stone bulk, some 12 feet beneath ground level, includes a rectangular baptismal chamber; go inside to see the octagonal basin, for baptism by total immersion. ✉ *rue Jean-Jaurès.* 🎫 *4 frs.* ⏲ *Summer, daily 10–12:30 and 2–4:30; winter, Thurs.–Tues. 2–4:30.*

The oldest of Poitiers's churches is **St-Hilaire-le-Grand,** part of which dates from the early 11th century. The semicircular, mosaic-floor choir rises high above the level of the nave, and there are striking frescoes and finely carved capitals. ✉ *rue St-Hilaire.*

At **Futuroscope** experience futuristic thrills via "simulated seating" (which moves, tilts, and jolts) and interactive cinema. ✉ *Poitiers (exit 18 off A10),* ☎ *05–49–49–31–10.* 🎫 *132 frs.* ⏲ *Mid-Feb.–Nov., daily 9–6; July–Aug., 9–8.*

Dining and Lodging

$$ ✕ **Maxime.** Reasonable prix-fixe menus and chef Christian Rougier's cooking have made Maxime a crowd-pleaser. Enjoy foie gras and duck salad in the pastel dining room featuring '30s-style frescoes. ✉ *4 rue St-Nicolas,* ☎ *05–49–41–09–55. Reservations essential. AE, MC, V. Closed Sat., Sun., and most of July and Aug.*

$$ **Europe.** An early 19th-century building with a modern extension houses this unpretentious hotel in the middle of town. Because it is off the main street and has a forecourt, rooms are quiet. There is also a pleasant garden in the back for an afternoon tea or an evening aperitif. ✉ *39 rue Carnot, 86000,* ☎ *05–49–88–12–00,* FAX *05–49–88–97–30. 88 rooms with bath or shower. MC, V.*

Nightlife and the Arts

For a night of dancing, head to **Black House** (✉ 195 av. du 8-mai-1945). **La Grand'Goule** (✉ 46 rue du Pigeon-Blanc) is a split-level disco with good ambience. At **Le Théâtre St-Nationale de Poitiers** (✉ 1 pl. du

Maréchal-Leclerc, ☎ 05–49–41–28–33) mainly French works are performed.

Shopping

La Boutique du Pâtisserie (✉ North side of pl. M. Leclerc) sells Poitiers's famous nougat.

St-Savin

❷ *40 km (25 mi) east of Poitiers.*

The tiny village of St-Savin is famous for its impressively large medieval abbey. Inside the 11th-century **Abbaye de St-Savin,** carved monsters run riot on the column capitals and well-preserved paintings, dating from the building's construction, decorate the walls. Swaying folds of cloth and enormous hands lend life to the biblical figures.

Angles-sur-l'Anglin

❸ *16 km (10 mi) north of St-Savin, 49 km (30 mi) east of Poitiers, 30 km (18 mi) southeast of Châtellerault.*

Well-preserved bas-reliefs carved 15,000 years ago during the Magdalenian period have been found in the ancient village of Angles-sur-l'Anglin. The most exciting find is a 175-foot frieze made up mostly of animal sculptures—including bison and deer—and three female torsos. To prevent the originals from being damaged by overexposure, only scholars are permitted to study them. But by late 1998 or early 1999 an exact replica will be on display—not at the original site along the Anglin River, but in the cliffs below the château that has guarded the village since the 12th century.

The village got its name because it was occupied by the English (Angles) for a long period during the Hundred Years War. Even without the age-old sculptures, which will probably bring an influx of tourists, the village is worth a stop. Be sure to walk up the path that the English soldiers did 600 years ago: You'll see their footsteps, weighed down by the suits of armor, hollowed into the stones.

Dining and Lodging

$$ ✕🏨 **Lion d'Or.** Native son Guillaume Thoreau and his English wife, Heather, own this hotel-restaurant. Though some might find the place too fussily French, it is very comfortable. The largest room, "Cardinal la Balue," has exposed gable beams and sleeps up to four. Other rooms—especially on the second floor—are smaller, but equally charming. In the grand dining room, enjoy traditional, regional cuisine such as *gigot pour sept heures* (lamb cooked for seven hours with herbs and vegetables)—not a culinary masterpiece, but wholesome, honest food. ✉ *4 rue d'Enfer, 86260,* ☎ *05–49–48–32–53,* FAX *05–49–84–02–28. 11 rooms with bath or shower. Restaurant. MC. V.*

Niort

❹ *72 km (45 mi) southwest of Poitiers, 145 km (90 mi) southeast of Nantes.*

Niort is a complacent, middle-class town best known as the capital of the French insurance business. But the remains of its medieval fortress and its two museums—archaeology and fine arts—make it worth a stop. All that is left of the Plantagenet Castle built at the end of the 12th century by English kings Henry II and Richard the Lionhearted is the massive **donjon,** with its two square towers dominating the River Sèvre. Inside there is a museum with an extensive collection of arms and local costumes. ✉ *rue Duguesclin,* ☎ *05–49–28–14–28.* 🎫 *20* *frs.* ⏲ *Apr.–Oct., Wed.–Mon. 9–noon and 2–6; Nov.–Mar., Wed.–Mon. 9–noon and 2–5.*

Just off rue Victor-Hugo is the old town hall, a triangular building completed in 1535. It now houses the **Musée du Pilori,** with a collection of local archaeological finds and Renaissance artifacts. The highlight is an ebony chest encrusted with gold and silver. ✉ *Just off rue Victor-Hugo,* ☏ *05–49–28–51–73.* 🎫 *15 frs.* ⏲ *Apr.–Oct., Wed.–Mon. 9–noon and 2–6; Nov.–Mar., Wed.–Mon. 9–noon and 2–5.*

On rue St-Jean, the oldest street in Niort, is the **Musée des Beaux-Arts** (Fine Arts Museum), where tapestries, gold and enamelware, and 17th- to 18th-century paintings are on display. ✉ *rue St-Jean,* ☏ *05–49–24–97–84.* 🎫 *21 frs.* ⏲ *Wed.–Mon. 9–noon and 2–6.*

In Echiré, north of Niort, the **Laiterie Co-Opérative** (Cooperative Dairy) makes some of the best butter in the world.

Coulon and the Marais Poitevin

★ ❺ *11 km (7 mi) west of Niort.*

Coulon is the best base for exploring the Marais Poitevin—France's "Green Venice"—an extraordinary region of canals and lush fields. Willow, ash, and alder trees line the rivers and canals of the Marais; artichokes, onions, melons, and garlic are grown in the fields alongside. The only way to explore the Marais proper is by rowboat—or, more typically, on a *pigouille* (a flat, narrow boat maneuvered with a long pole), which you can find in Coulon. They cost about 90 francs per hour per boat, maximum six persons, or you can hire a boat with a guide (for 45 minutes at 120 francs). If your French is decent, you'll get an earful of local lore as well as a ride. The town also has a lovely medieval church and a delightful, privately-run folk museum, the **Musée Maraichin** (✉ rue de l'Église). There are no regular hours: Just show up and see if it's open; donations are accepted.

Dining and Lodging

$–$$ ✕🏨 **Au Marais.** The Merrière's small, waterside inn and restaurant is delightful. Light, regional fare, with prix-fixe menus of 95 francs and 150 francs, is served in the restaurant (closed Sunday dinner and Monday). Sample the succulent mussels in dill sauce or the veal chops in Madeira sauce, and, for dessert, the crunchy crème brûlée. Rooms are plain, yet clean and reasonably priced. ✉ *48 quai Louis-Tardy, 79510,* ☏ *05–49–35–90–43,* FAX *05–49–35–81–98. 11 rooms. Restaurant. MC, V. Closed mid-Nov.–mid-Mar.*

Outdoor Activities and Sports

One of the best ways to explore the area is by bicycle (a detailed map is advisable), rented from **La Ribellale** (✉ pl. de l'Église, ☏ 05–49–35–90–88).

Maillezais

❻ *13 km (8 mi) northwest of Coulon, 29 km (18 mi) west of Niort.*

In the countryside northwest of Coulon, there is little but the occasional pretty village—Maillezais is one of these. The main reason to come here is to see the ruins of its abbey. Maillezais used to be a bishop's seat and a powerful Benedictine monastery, but all that remains of the **Abbaye de Maillezais** are the 14th-century cloister and refectory, the 11th-century porch, and the 15th-century transept. ☏ *05–51–00–70–11.* 🎫 *16 frs.* ⏲ *Nov.–Mar., Fri.–Wed. 9–12:30 and 2–6; Apr.–Oct., daily 9–8.*

En Route Between Maillezais and the Atlantic Coast, the **Marais Mouillé** (Wet Marsh) gradually dries up and a flat, barren, eerie landscape appears: the **Marais Desséché** (Dried-Out Marsh). To get to the coast from Maillezais, head south along D15, then turn right after La Ronde onto narrow D262, which hugs the straight banks of the Canal de la Branche as far as Marans, once a thriving seaport but now linked to the sea only by canal. D105 sneaks seaward from Marans. At the first major crossroad, 8 km (5 mi) past Marans, turn left along D9 toward La Rochelle, 16 km (10 mi) away.

La Rochelle

7 *44 km (27 mi) southwest of Maillezais, 56 km (35 mi) west of Coulon, 475 km (297 mi) southwest of Paris.*

La Rochelle is an appealing old town, a vibrant collection of the old and the new. Its ancient streets are off of its harbor, the picturesque Vieux Port. Standing sentinel on either side of the port are two fortresslike 14th-century **tours** (towers) known as **Tour de la Chaîne** (to the right) and **Tour St-Nicolas** (to the left)—climb to the top for a view of the bay toward the Île d'Aix. *18 frs for each tower. Mid-Feb.–mid-Nov., daily 10–noon and 2–6; mid-Nov.–mid-Feb., daily 2–6.*

From the towers, follow the western wall of the Vieux Port to cours des Dames, a spacious avenue lined with sturdy trees and 18th-century houses. It leads to the **Porte de la Grosse Horloge** (Big Clock Gate), a massive stone gate marking the entrance to the narrow, bustling streets of the old town. From the gate, head down rue du Palais and onto rue Gargoulleau: Halfway down on the left is the 18th-century Bishop's Palace, now the **Musée des Beaux-Arts.** ✉ *rue Gargoulleau,* ☎ *05–46–41–46–50. 18 frs. Wed.–Sat. and Mon. 10:30–12:30 and 1:30–6; Sun. 3–6.*

The **Musée d'Histoire Naturelle** (Museum of Natural History) is housed in an elegant mansion and contains extensive collections of rocks, coral, and shell work. Other items range from a tribal idol from Easter Island to a giraffe (now stuffed) given as a gift to King Charles X (reigned 1824–30). ✉ *28 rue Albert I,* ☎ *05–46–41–18–25. 18 frs. Apr.–Oct., Tues.–Sun. 10–noon and 2–6; Nov.–Mar., Tues.–Sat. 10–noon and 2–5, Sun. 2–5.*

Not far from the Bishop's Palace is an 18th-century building containing the **Musée du Nouveau-Monde** (New World Museum). Old maps, engravings, watercolors, and even wallpaper evoke the commercial links between La Rochelle and the New World. ✉ *10 rue Fleuriau,* ☎ *05–46–41–46–50. 18 frs. Wed.–Mon. 10:30–12:30 and 1:30–6, Sun. 3–6.*

In summer, boats operated by Ré Croisières leave La Rochelle harbor daily for cruises to the nearby **îles** (islands): **Île de Ré, Île d'Aix,** and **Fort Dayard.** ✉ *Buy tickets from Agence de la Rochelle, Bessin d'Échouage, Vieux Port,* ☎ *05–07–65–43–42 or 05–46–09–39–00. Round-trip: Île de Ré, 72 frs; Île d'Aix and Fort Dayard, 90 frs.*

Dining and Lodging

$–$$ ✕ **André.** The salty decor is somewhat excessive—fishing nets and posters of ocean liners—but the food and service have so much gusto that you'll be caught up in the mood, especially if you order the monumental seafood platter and wash it down with white Charentes wine. ✉ *5 rue St-Jean,* ☎ *05–46–41–28–24. AE, DC, MC, V.*

$–$$ ✕ **Les Quatre Sergents.** On this street in the north side of the Vieux Port, where good restaurants abound, this place serves delightful, traditional seafood with distinctive sauces. Plants grow in every nook and cranny, shielding one table from another—it's like dining in a winter garden. ✉ *49 rue St-Jean Perrot,* ☎ *05–46–41–35–80. AE, DC, MC, V. Closed Mon. No dinner Sun.*

$ ✕ **Pub Lutece.** More of a brasserie than a pub, this cheerful spot with brass rails and comfortable banquettes serves good, inexpensive food from mussels to confit *de canard* (of duck). Conversation and bustle are as much the reason for coming as the wholesome fare. ✉ *1 rue Bletterie,* ☎ *05–46–41–40–80. MC, V.*

$$ **Hôtel de la Monnaie.** This 17th-century house by the Vieux Port has a wonderful lobby and cobblestone courtyard. Rooms are less inspiring; the quietest overlook the courtyard. Bathrooms have a tub and hand-held shower. Free parking is available adjacent to the hotel, a definite plus since it's only a few minutes' walk to the harbor and town. ✉ *3 rue de la Monnaie, 17000,* ☎ *05–46–50–65–65,* FAX *05–46–50–63–19. 32 rooms, 4 suites. AE, DC, MC, V.*

$$ ★ **33 Thiers.** Amiable Mme. Iribe, who speaks English fluently and has a wealth of local knowledge, owns this inn in a private town house. With advance notice, she will prepare a splendid dinner made from fresh market products. You're likely to eat in the kitchen and, if you want, pick up some cooking tips (Mme. Iribe teaches cooking classes). Rooms are large and wonderfully furnished, expressing the owner's idiosyncrasies: The Mexican Room is gaily decorated with cheerful colors; the Blue Room is also a delight. ✉ *33 rue Thiers, 17000,* ☎ *05–46–41–62–23,* FAX *05–46–41–10–76. 8 rooms. Dining room. MC, V.*

$$ **Tour de Nesle.** This 19th-century hotel is around the corner from quai Valin. Rooms are a bit cramped, but up-to-date; some have a view across the canal. Breakfast is served. ✉ *2 quai Louis-Durand, 17000,* ☎ *05–46–41–30–72,* FAX *05–46–41–95–17. 28 rooms with shower or bath. Breakfast room. MC, V.*

Nightlife and the Arts

Held over Pentecost, La Rochelle's major festival, the **Fêtes de la Mer,** is a festival inspired by the sea.

Outdoor Activities and Sports

A good way to get around town is on a bicycle; rent one from the **Centre de Location Agrée** (✉ 48 rue St-Jean, ☎ 05–46–41–84–32).

Shopping

La Rochelle will impress you as more than a port town if you are here on a Wednesday or Saturday for the **market** in the old town.

En Route Thirty-two kilometers (20 miles) south of La Rochelle on N137, on the way to Brouage, is **Rochefort-sur-Mer,** home to the 400-yard-long Corderie Royale—a rope-making factory built for Louis XIV's fleet in 1666.

Île de Ré

8 *22 km (14 mi) west of La Rochelle.*

A bridge (round-trip toll is 110 francs) curves across from La Rochelle to the cheerful island of Île de Ré, just 26 km (16 mi) long and never more than 6 km (4 mi) wide. Vineyards sweep over the eastern part of the island while oyster beds straddle the shallow waters to the west. The first village on the north coast reached from the mainland is **La Flotte.** The rectangular harbor hiding tiny fishing boats is surrounded by sturdy houses ready to stand against Atlantic winds. Ten kilometers (6 miles) further on is the largest village on the island, **St-Martin de Ré** (population 3,000). It has a lively harbor and a citadel built by ace military architect Sébastien de Vauban in 1681. Many of its streets also date from the 17th century, and the villagers' low, white houses are typical of that period. **Ars,** a smaller village 10 km (6 mi) farther west, has a black-and-white church spire and cute harbor. If you go all the way to the northwestern end of Île de Ré, be sure to climb up the **Phare de la Baleine** (Baleine Lighthouse) for sweeping views of the Atlantic. At the foot of it is the Café de la Phare, which has a surprising Art Deco setting full of arty '30s lamps and serves a good *poutargue,* a local specialty made from smoked cod roe and served with shallots and sour cream.

Dining and Lodging

$$$ ✕🏨 **Le Richelieu.** Eat chef Dominique Bourgeois's seafood while gazing at the ocean. Let tuna in lemon butter spark your taste buds for excellent grilled turbot in beurre blanc and superb wine. Guest rooms are innocuously furnished, but have all the amenities, from bathrobes to balconies. A separate building houses masseurs, beauticians, and thalassotherapy equipment. A beach fronts the hotel, but it's better for strolling than lounging. ✉ *44 av. de la Plage, 17630 La Flotte-en-Ré,* ☎ *05–46–09–60–70,* FAX *05–46–09–50–59. 45 rooms. Restaurant, pool, beauty salon, massage, 2 tennis courts. AE, DC, MC, V. Closed early Jan.–mid-Feb.*

Brouage

❾ *42 km (26 mi) south of La Rochelle.*

The ancient town of Brouage's 17th-century walls loom sullenly above deserted marshland. Samuel de Champlain, who founded Quebec in 1608, was born in Brouage—then a major port. Stroll around the walls and gaze across the marsh toward the sea—now more than 3 km (2 mi) away—and then visit the village church to learn more of Champlain's tale. Then muse on the fate of Louis XIV's sweetheart, Marie Mancini, who retired here in 1659 after learning that her regal suitor had wed the Infanta of Spain for reasons of state.

Dining and Lodging

$ ✕🏨 **Brouage.** This cheerful hotel-restaurant on the main street doubles as the village bar. Meals are top-value and include such regional specialties as oysters, *bouchots* (tiny mussels), and eel fricassee. Only lunch is served, except from mid-July to mid-August, when dinner is available; the restaurant is closed Monday. Rooms are small and have contemporary fabrics, a nice change from the ubiquitous chintz. Unfortunately, the owner may sell this auberge; we can only hope a new owner will not make any changes. ✉ *rue de Québec, 17320 Hiers-Brouage,* ☎ *05–46–85–03–06. 8 rooms with bath or shower. MC, V.*

Île d'Oléron

❿ *36 km (22 mi) northwest of Brouage, 78 km southwest of La Rochelle. From Brouage, head toward Marennes, turning right onto D26 and crossing a modern 3-km (2-mi) bridge to the island.*

Sand dunes ring the Île d'Oléron (Oléron Island) to the north and west. Oyster beds line the eastern shores, notably along the **Route des Huîtres** (Oyster Road), north of the **Château d'Oléron,** a ruined 17th-century castle.

Royan

11 *45 km (28 mi) southeast of Île d'Oléron: once back on the mainland take D25 across the Baie de la Seudre; 40 km (25 mi) west of Saintes.*

Royan is a commercialized resort town that was rebuilt—largely in concrete—after being destroyed by Nazi bombing in 1945. Its vast seafront is packed to the gills in summer, although there are prettier beaches just north (Pontaillac and St-Palais). A car ferry (follow signs to the BAC) plows across the Gironde estuary to the Médoc peninsula from Royan Harbor several times daily. The Royan skyline is dominated by the tower of the **Église Notre-Dame,** an enormous concrete church with a breathtaking oval interior; the huge, unsupported sweep of its curved ceiling is a technical tour de force.

En Route Down the coast from Royan along D25 is the pleasant resort town of **St-Georges-de-Didonne.** Continuing south will lead you through a landscape of pine forest and chalky grottoes to **Meschers** and Les Grottes de Matata, where you can sip tea or eat ice cream on a flower-bedecked terrace overlooking the estuary, from June–September. From Meschers, head south to **Talmont,** an unspoiled village renowned for its gently proportioned 12th-century church jutting out over the waters on a rocky promontory.

Saintes

12 *40 km (25 mi) east of Royan, 40 km (25 mi) southeast of Rochefort, 138 km (86 mi) southwest of Poitiers.*

On the banks of the River Charente, Saintes is a city of stately serenity, littered with religious edifices and Roman ruins dating back to the 1st century. Saintes owes its development to the salt marshes that first attracted the Romans to the area some 2,000 years ago. The Romans left their mark with the impressive **Arènes** (amphitheater). There are several better-preserved examples in France, but few as old. You'll find it to the south of the town center, close to the river off cours Reverseaux. The **Arc de Germanicus** built in AD 19, just across the bridge from the town center to the right, is another grand Roman vestige.

Climbing above the red roofs of the old town is the **Cathédrale St-Pierre,** which seems to stagger beneath the weight of its stocky tower. Engineering caution foiled plans for the traditional pointed spire, so the tower was given a shallow dome—incongruous, perhaps, but distinctive. The austere 16th-century interior is lined with circular pillars of formidable circumference. The narrow pedestrian streets clustered around the cathedral contrast with the broad boulevards that slice through the town and over the river. ✉ *pl. du Synode.*

Saintes's ecclesiastical pride and joy is the **Abbaye aux Dames,** consecrated in 1047. The abbey church is fronted by an exquisite, intricately carved, arcaded facade. Although the Romanesque choir remains largely in its original form, the rest of the interior is less harmonious since the abbey fell on hard times after the death of the last abbess—the 30th—in 1792. It was a prison, then a barracks, and now it is a cultural center for expositions. Opposite the abbey portals the brasserie has inexpensive lunch menus (60 and 100 francs). ✉ *rue G. Martel,* ☎ *05–46–97–48–48.* ⏲ *June–Sept., daily 10–12:30 and 2–7; Oct.–May, Wed. and Sat. 10–12:30 and 2–7, Mon., Tues., Thurs., Fri., and Sun. 2–7. Closed Dec. 4–Jan. 3.*

Dining and Lodging

$$$ ✕🏨 **Relais du Bois.** Rooms in this hotel vary; some have contemporary furnishings, others traditional; some are miniduplexes with loft

beds, others are small and have fold-down beds (one is named "Count de Montecristo's Prison Cell"); many have separate sitting areas. Service is enthusiastic because the staff has input in running the hotel. The restaurant looks out over the gardens and a lake. Specialties from the Charente region and seafood become eye-catching creations in the hands of chef Jérôme Emery. ✉ *rue de Royan, Cours Genet, 17100,* ☎ *05–46–93–50–99,* FAX *05–46–93–34–93. 27 rooms, 3 suites. Restaurant, bar, indoor pool, croquet, meeting rooms. MC, V.*

$$–$$$ ★ ✕ **Moulin de Marcouze.** You, too, can feast like a brandy baron—if you make the 30-minute drive from Saintes to Mosnac. Dominique Bouchet has transformed this old mill into a sophisticated restaurant. The style is understated: spacious layout, artwork, and food that is innovative but not flashy (sautéed sole fillet or duck pie with truffles). At midday, local executives come for power lunches; dinner is more peaceful. The restaurant is closed February, and Tuesday and Wednesday off-season. ✉ *rte. de St-Georges, 17240 Mosnac (33 km/20 mi south of Saintes, 34 km/21 mi southwest of Cognac),* ☎ *05–46–70–46–16,* FAX *05–46–70–48–14. 10 rooms. Restaurant, pool, helipad. AE, DC, MC, V. Closed Feb., 1 wk in Nov.*

Nightlife and the Arts

Le Vaudeville (✉ 13 quai de la République) has a homey English atmosphere and a tongue-tingling array of old whiskeys.

Cognac

⓭ *27 km (17 mi) southeast of Saintes, 146 km (91 mi) southwest of Poitiers, 119 km (74 mi) northeast of Bordeaux.*

The black-walled town of Cognac seems an unlikely hometown for one of the world's most successful drink trades. You may be disappointed initially by the town's unpretentious appearance, but, like the drink, it tends to grow on you. Cognac owed its early development to the transport of salt and wine along the River Charente. When 16th-century Dutch merchants discovered that the local wine was both tastier and easier to transport if distilled, the town became the heart of the brandy industry. Most cognac houses organize visits of their premises and chais. Wherever you decide to go, you will literally soak up the atmosphere of cognac; 3% of the precious cask-bound liquid evaporates every year! This has two consequences: Each chais smells delicious, and a small, black mushroom, which feeds on cognac's alcoholic fumes, forms on walls throughout the town.

The leading monument in Cognac is the former **Château de Cognac,** now on the premises of Otard Cognac. Volatile Renaissance monarch François I was born here in 1494. The remaining buildings are something of a hodgepodge, though the stocky towers recall the site's fortified origins. The tour of Otard Cognac combines its own propaganda with historical comment on the drink itself. At the end you get to sample free cognac, and you can buy some at vastly reduced prices. ☎ *05–45–82–40–00.* 🎫 *Free. Guided tours daily on the hr 10–noon and 2–5 (except Sun. Oct.–May).*

Hennessy, along the banks of the Corinth and easily recognized by the company's emblem—an ax-wielding arm carved in stone—includes in its tour a cheerful jaunt across the Corinth in old-fashioned boats. ✉ *rue Richonne,* ☎ *05–45–35–72–72.* ⏲ *June–Sept., Mon.–Sat. 9–5:30; Oct.–May, weekdays 9–11 and 1:30–5:30.*

Martell gives the most polished guided tour of the Cognac houses and its chais are perhaps more picturesque than Hennessy's. ✉ *pl. Édouard Martell,* ☎ *05–45–36–33–33.* ⏲ *July–Aug., weekdays 9–5, week-*

ends 10–4:30; June and Sept., weekdays 9–11 and 1:30–5; Oct.–May, weekdays 9–11 and 2–5.

Rue Saulnier, alongside the Hennessy premises, is the most atmospheric of the somber, sloping, cobbled streets that compose the core of Cognac, dominated by the tower of **St-Léger,** a church with a notably large Flamboyant Gothic rose window.

Busy boulevard Denfert-Rochereau twines around the old town, passing the town hall and the neighboring **Musée du Cognac.** ✉ *48 bd. Denfert-Rochereau,* ☎ *05–45–32–07–25.* 🎫 *15 frs.* ⏲ *June–Sept., Wed.–Mon. 10–noon and 2–5:30; Oct.–May, Wed.–Mon. 2–5:30.*

Dining and Lodging

$$ ★ ✕🏨 **Pigeons Blancs.** White Pigeons, a modernized coaching inn on spacious grounds 1½ km (1 mi) from the center of Cognac, has been owned by the same family since the 17th century. Each room is different: No. 32 has a gabled ceiling supported by an ancient beam and a skylight. The major draw, though, is chef Jacques Tachet's cuisine: Try his milk-fed lamb with *jus d'ail doux* (sweet garlic) or grilled escargots. The three-course, prix-fixe menu is a find at 155 francs. You can arrange to have two meals per day with your room rate. ✉ *110 rue Jules-Brisson (rte. de St-Jean Anjou), 16100,* ☎ *05–45–82–16–36,* FAX *05–45–82–29–29. 6 rooms. Restaurant. AE, DC, MC, V. Closed 1st ½ of Jan.*

Nightlife and the Arts

Le Bas Roc (✉ av. de la Dordogne) is the place to party every night. Each September Cognac hosts a **crime film festival.**

Outdoor Activities and Sports

Hit the greens at Cognac's **golf course** (☎ 05–45–32–18–17); fees range from 300 francs in peak season to 200 francs off-season.

Shopping

A bottle of old cognac makes a fine souvenir; try **La Cognathèque** (✉ 10 pl. Jean-Monnet) in Cognac itself, though you can sometimes find the same item infinitely cheaper at a local producer.

Jarnac

⑭ *16 km (10 mi) east of Cognac, 110 km (68 mi) north of Bordeaux.*

The village of Jarnac is primarily know as the birthplace of late President François Mitterrand, though several excellent cognac firms are found up the Charente River. **Hine** (✉ quai de l'Orangerie, ☎ 05–45–81–11–38), one of Jarnac's cognac firms, organizes visits of its riverbank premises. **Courvoisier** (✉ pl. du Château, ☎ 05–45–35–55–55), in a bombastic redbrick factory, gives tours of its premises and its chais.

Dining and Lodging

$ ★ ✕🏨 **Maison Karina.** Co-owner Niki Legon is an English woman who describes herself as a cupboard cook: she starts with a recipe then looks into her cupboard to see what to add. The result is that no dish is ever the same, be it canard *à la pineau* (with pineau) or *côte de porc* (pork chops). Rooms have exposed beams and walls. You'll not find cognac from Cognac in the cozy bar, but from Jarnac and from some excellent lesser known houses such as Louis Royet. ✉ *Bois-Faucon, 16200 Sigogne (off D736 and 8 km/5 mi north of Jarnac),* ☎ *05–45–36–26–26,* FAX *05–45–81–10–93. 7 rooms and 2 suites, all with bath or shower. Restaurant, bar, pool, 18-hole golf course, 1 tennis court, horseback riding. MC, V.*

Angoulême

15 *26 km (16 mi) east of Jarnac, 108 km (67 mi) south of Poitiers, 130 km (81 mi) southeast of La Rochelle.*

Angoulême is divided, like many other French towns, between an old, picturesque section perched around a hilltop cathedral and a modern, industrial part sprawling along the valley and railroad below (don't let the outskirts deter you). The 19th-century novelist Honoré de Balzac is one of the town's adopted sons; Balzac described Angoulême in his meaty novel, *Lost Illusions.* In the **Ville Haute** (Upper Town), known as "le plateau," there are stunning views from the ramparts and a warren of quaint old streets around the Hôtel de Ville (Town Hall).

The 12th-century **Cathédrale d'Angoulême** bears little resemblance to the majority of its French counterparts because of the cupolas topping each of its three bays, a style popular in the southwest. The cathedral was partly destroyed by Calvinists in 1562, then restored in a heavy-handed manner in 1634 and 1866. Its main attraction is the magnificent Romanesque facade, whose layers of rounded arches boast 70 stone statues and bas-reliefs illustrating the Last Judgment. ✉ *pl. St-Pierre.*

Dining and Lodging

$ ✕ **La Tour des Valois.** This restaurant diagonally across from the market has a good choice of regional food. Sample one of the veal dishes—the one using the local mustard from Jarnac is particularly good—and the locally made foie gras. ✉ *7 rue Massillon,* ☎ *05–45–95–91–76. Reservations not accepted. MC, V. Closed Sun. No lunch Sat.*

$$$ ✕🏨 **Château de Nieuil.** Approach this former hunting lodge—a huge château with towers—down an avenue of trees opening onto a circular lawn. Rooms vary: Some have traditional furnishings and pastel blue fabric; others have a *petit salon* (small sitting area) or a garden view. Unfortunately, the reception area is small. The formidable dining room has a large stone fireplace with sculpted family crests and a multifaceted chandelier. Enjoy superb lamb (a regional specialty) or escallop of milk-fed veal with grapes. The wine list is impressive, but you need to search for an affordable bottle. ✉ *16270 Nieuil (off N141 between Angoulême and Limoges),* ☎ *05–45–71–36–38,* FAX *05–45–71–46–45. 14 rooms and 3 suites. Restaurant, pool, tennis court, fishing, helipad. AE, DC, MC, V. Closed Nov.–Mar.*

$$ 🏨 **Mercure Hôtel de France.** On the fringe of the Ville Haute, across from the covered market, this hotel has a traditional air. From the garden there are fine views of the city. Rooms are decorated in light blues with striped curtains and bedspreads. Solid, unpretentious regional cuisine is served in the restaurant, closed lunch Sunday, and all day Sunday from September to May. The staff is professional and accustomed to speaking English. ✉ *1 pl. des Halles, 16000,* ☎ *05–45–95–47–95,* FAX *05–45–92–02–70;* ☎ *0181/741–3100 in the U.K., 800/637–2873 in the U.S. 90 rooms. Restaurant, bar. AE, DC, V.*

Oradour-sur-Glane

16 *78 km (48 mi) northeast of Angoulême on N141, 25 km (16 mi) northwest of Limoges on N141.*

The village of Oradour-sur-Glane stands as a reminder of war's inhumanity. No one knows why the Germans stormed the village on the night of June 10, 1944, herded the men into a barn, the women and children into the church, and killed them. Some believe they mistook it for another town, reputed to harbor the Resistance. Nevertheless,

642 people, including 205 children, were murdered. Ten villagers survived by hiding under the corpses. A new town was established with the same name 1 km (½ mi) away, leaving this village as it was on that evening. *Donation of 30 frs to visit the village. Daily 9–sunset.*

Limoges

17 *20 km (12 mi) east of Oradour-sur-Glane, 102 km (63 mi) east of Angoulême, 120 km (75 mi) southeast of Poiters, 94 km (58 mi) northeast of Périgueux.*

Limoges, the economic capital of western France, is famous for its porcelain. Every other shop, especially on rue Jean-Jaurès, rue du Clocher, rue du Consulat, and rue St-Michel, seems to sell it. You can get a good overview of what is produced by the factories at the **Limoges-Castel Demonstration Center.** *Pavillon de la Porcelaine, 40 av. John-Kennedy, Zone Industrielle Magré, 05–55–30–21–86. Mid-Apr.–mid-Oct., daily 8:30–6; mid-Oct.–mid-Apr., Mon.–Sat. 8:30–6.*

The best porcelain made over the last two centuries is on display at the **Musée National Adrien-Dubouché.** It also has a good technical section introducing the process that gave rise to the four principal ceramic groups: terra-cotta, glazed earthenware, stoneware, and porcelain. *pl. Winston-Churchill, 05–55–77–45–58. 20 frs. Wed.–Mon. 10–noon and 1:30–5:15.*

At the **Musée Municipal de l'Évêché** (Town Museum in the 18th-century Bishop's Palace), there's an extensive array of ceramics—from the 12th to the 20th century—and an archaeological section on Limoges Roman history. Look out, too, for the few works of Renoir. Limoges was his birthplace. *pl. de la Cathédrale, 05–55–45–61–75. Free. Wed.–Mon. 10–11:45 and 2–6 (to 5 PM Oct.–June).*

The **Cathédrale St-Étienne,** across from the Musée Municipal de l'Évêché, was begun in 1273 and closely resembles the cathedrals of Narbonne and Clermont-Ferrand, with their extremely high vaults—the trademark of architect Jean Deschamps. *pl. de la Cathédrale.*

DORDOGNE AND PÉRIGORD

Stretching east from Hautefort to Blaye, along the Dordogne, Isle, Dronne, and Auvezère rivers, this region's rolling hills and valleys are full of romantic riverside châteaux, small medieval villages, and prehistoric sites. You may want to spend a week exploring the small country roads and having picnic lunches on the riverbanks.

Hautefort

18 *86 km (53 mi) south of Limoges, 32 km (20 mi) north of Sarlat, 99 km (61 mi) northeast of Périgueux.*

The only reason to come to Hautefort is to see its castle, which presents a disarmingly arrogant face to the world. The skyline of the **Château de Hautefort** bristles with high roofs, domes, chimneys, and cupolas. The square-lined Renaissance left wing clashes with the muscular, round towers of the right wing, as the only surviving section of the original medieval castle—the gateway and drawbridge—referees in the middle. Adorning the inside are 17th-century furniture and tapestries. *05–53–50–51–23. 26 frs. Easter–Nov., daily 2–6; Dec.–Easter, Sun. 2–6.*

Dining and Lodging

$$ ★ ✕ 🏨 **Manoir d'Hautegente.** This old ivy-covered manor is in a pastoral setting with a lily pond, sheep in a paddock, and a 13th-century windmill. Inside, the simple rooms have beige, patterned fabric wallpaper and colorful curtains that match the bedspreads. Regional fare, such as homemade foie gras, is given a balanced lightness in the hands of the chef. ✉ *24120 Coly (6 km/4 mi south of Hautefort, 26 km/16 mi north of Sarlat),* ☎ *05–53–51–68–03,* FAX *05–53–50–38–52. 10 rooms. Restaurant, pool. MC, V. Closed Nov.*

Brantôme

⓳ *27 km (17 mi) north of Périgueux, 60 km (37 mi) southeast of Angoulême.*

The beautiful old town of Brantôme, with its abbey, village square, small streets, and bridges across the sparkling waters of the River Dronne will either be your entry to or exit from the Dordogne. It deserves a stop, even if you just take a walk along the river. At night, the abbey is floodlit and the reflecting light on the river adds to the romance of the stars.

Outside of Brantôme, on the Angoulême road, is the **Château de Mareuil.** The 14th–15th-century fortified castle with a moat is a magnificent place, which M. and Mme. Montebello call home. Though the château has been in the Montebello family for generations (the Duke of Montebello, Marshal Lannes, took part in the coup d'état that brought Napoléon to power and then became one of the Corsican's ablest generals), M. Montebello is only beginning to win the battle of restoring his ancestral home (with the help of government grants). Be sure to see the Gothic chapel with ribbed vaulting inside the left tower, the prisons, and the living quarters. ✉ *Mareuil-sur-Belle,* ☎ *05–53–60–74–13.* 🎫 *15 frs.* ⏲ *Wed.–Mon. 2–4:30.*

Dining and Lodging

$$$ ✕ 🏨 **Château de Vieux Mareuil.** This modern, courtyard-style manor is built on the foundations of an ancient farmhouse. Most rooms are contemporary and tasteful, with spacious bathrooms and small terraces. High ceilings, thick stone walls, and exposed beams make Tour 1, in the old part of the building, particularly special. Nouvelle cuisine is served in two small dining rooms; the *cabecon* (local goat cheese) salad and the *navarin* (ragout) of lamb are delicious. ✉ *rte. d'Angoulême-Périgueux, 24340 Vieux Mareuil (15 km/9 mi north of Brantôme),* ☎ *05–53–60–77–15,* FAX *05–53–56–49–33. 14 rooms, 2 suites. Restaurant, pool. MC, V. Closed Sept.–Apr.*

$$ 🏨 **Château Laborie.** In the countryside 5 minutes north of Brantôme is this château, a step above your usual B&B. A long avenue of *tilleuls* (linden trees) leads to the impressive facade. Turrets and a moat, now dry, suggest times when guests were not welcome. Not so today. Mme. Duseau is an amiable hostess who chats with guests and offers advice on where to dine (one of these suggestions, the Terrace des Jardins, is well below par). Rooms, furnished with hand-me-down antiques, are comfortable, if a little stilted, though two rooms on the first floor are warmer and have less bourgeois pretense. ✉ *24530 Champagnac-de Belair,* ☎ *05–53–54–22–99,* FAX *05–53–08–53–78. 5 rooms with bath or shower. Breakfast room, pool. No credit cards. Closed early Nov.–Easter.*

Périgueux

20 *99 km (61 mi) west of Hautefort, 128 km (79 mi) northeast of Bordeaux, 94 km (58 mi) southwest of Limoges.*

Périgueux is best known for its weird-looking cathedral. Finished in 1173, the **Cathédrale St-Front** might be on loan from Istanbul, given its shallow, scale-pattern domes and elongated, conical cupolas sprouting from the roof like baby minarets. You may be struck by similarities with the Byzantine-style Sacré-Coeur in Paris; that's no coincidence—architect Paul Abadie (1812–84) worked on both. ✉ *pl. de la Clautre.*

Les Eyzies-de-Tayac

21 *45 km (28 mi) southeast of Périgueux.*

Many signs of prehistoric man have been discovered in the vicinity of Les Eyzies; a number of excavated caves and grottoes, some with wall paintings, are open for public viewing. At the **Musée Nationale de Préhistoire,** in a Renaissance château, you can examine many artifacts, including primitive sculpture, furniture, and tools. You can also get ideas about excavation sights to visit in the region at the museum. ☎ *05–53–06–97–03.* 🎫 *22 frs.* ⏲ *Apr.–Oct., Wed.–Mon. 9:30–noon and 2–6; Nov.–Mar., Wed.–Mon. 9:30–noon and 2–5.*

About 10 km (6 mi) from Les Eyzies is the ruined **Château de Cammarque.** In a picturesque valley, the site has been home to three epochs: prehistory cave man; troglodytes; and knights of the Middle Ages. Though the paintings of early man are not on view, the caves of the trogs may be visited. Above these caves, burrowed into the rock face, the walls and towers of the château soar. The castle was left to the ruins of time for four centuries, but recently its owner, the Comte de Cammarque, has begun a large-scale preservation project to open the castle and trog dwellings to the public. At press time (1997), work was not yet finished, though with sturdy legs and no hint of vertigo you can clamber around the ruins. 🎫 *Undetermined at press time (1997).* ⏲ *May–Oct., daily 10–4.*

Dining and Lodging

$$$–$$$$ ★ ✕🏨 **Le Vieux Logis.** A member of the Relais & Châteaux group, this rambling old stone house at the edge of Tremolat is one of the best hotels in Dordogne. The warmly decorated rooms vary in size; most face the well-tended garden and a rushing brook. One favorite, No. 22, has a terra-cotta tile floor, exposed beams, stone walls, and a suitelike bathroom. For dinner, the five-course Menu Vieux Logis (240 francs) might include the chef's forte, pigeon terrine, salad with veal knuckles, and duck sautéed with olives. The restaurant is closed Tuesday from mid-January through May. ✉ *24510 Tremolat (8 km/5 mi west of Les Eyzies-de-Tayac),* ☎ *05–53–22–80–06,* FAX *05–53–22–84–89. 19 rooms and 3 suites. Restaurant, pool. AE, DC, MC, V.*

$$$ ✕🏨 **Le Centenaire.** Although it is a stylish, modern, comfortable hotel, Le Centenaire is known first as a restaurant. Chef Roland Mazère adds flair to the preparation of local specialties: risotto with truffles, and snails with ravioli and gazpacho. The dining room, with its gold-color stone and wooden beams, retains local character. The restaurant is closed Tuesday lunch; a jacket is required. Rooms, especially at the lower end of the price scale, are pretty small. ✉ *24620 Les Eyzies-de-Tayac,* ☎ *05–53–06–97–18,* FAX *05–53–06–92–41. 21 rooms. Restaurant, pool, sauna, health club. MC, V. Closed Nov.–Mar.*

Grotte de Lascaux

22 *18 km (11 mi) northeast of Les Eyzies-de-Tayac.*

The famous Grotte de Lascaux, or Lascaux Caves, in the Vézère Valley, contains hundreds of mesmerizing prehistoric wall paintings—thought to be at least 20,000 years old. They were discovered by chance in 1940. Although the caves have been sealed off to prevent irreparable damage, two of the galleries and many of the paintings have been reproduced in vivid detail in the Lascaux 2 exhibition center nearby. ☎ *05–53–51–95–03.* *50 frs.* *Tues.–Sun. 10–noon and 2–5:30.*

Sarlat-la-Canéda

★ 23 *20 km (12 mi) southeast of Les Eyzies-de-Tayac.*

Another Dordogne gem is the small town of Sarlat-la-Canéda, which is hectic during the weekly Saturday market—all the geese on sale are proof of the local addiction to foie gras. To do justice to the town's golden-stone splendor, wander through its medieval streets, aided by the tourist office's walking map.

Of particular note is rue de la Liberté, which leads to **place du Peyrou,** occupied on one corner by the pointed-gable Renaissance house where writer-orator Étienne de la Boétie (1530–63) was born. The elaborate turret-topped tower of the **Cathédrale St-Sacerdos** (✉ pl. du Peyrou), begun in the 12th century, is the oldest part of the building and, along with the choir, all that remains of the original Romanesque cathedral. The sloping garden behind the cathedral, the **Cour de l'Évêché,** contains a strange, conical tower known as the Lanterne des Morts (Lantern of the Dead), which was occasionally used as a funeral chapel.

Rue d'Albusse, adjoining the garden behind the cathedral, and rue de la Salamandre are narrow, twisty streets that head to place de la Liberté and the 17th-century **Hôtel de Ville.** Opposite the town hall is the rickety former church of **Ste-Marie,** overlooking place des Oies. Ste-Marie points the way to Sarlat's most interesting street, **rue des Consuls.** Among its medieval buildings are the Hôtel Plamon, with broad windows that resemble those of a Gothic church, and, opposite, the 15th-century Hôtel de Vassal.

Musée-Aquarium shows the fish found in the local rivers: salmon, eel, pike, perch, trout, and even sturgeon, rarely seen outside the Caspian Sea. ✉ *3 rue du Commandant-Marátuel,* ☎ *05–53–59–44–58.* *32 frs.* *June–mid-Sept., daily 10–7; mid-Sept.–Oct. and Apr.–May, daily 10–noon and 2–6.*

Dining and Lodging

$$$–$$$$ **Château de la Treyne.** Part of the Relais & Châteaux chain, this small hotel east of Sarlat serenely guards the Dordogne River, as it has since the 14th century. Dinner is served in a delightful paneled room with old portraits and a roaring fire. Spacious rooms are traditionally furnished with 19th-century paintings and country antiques. During high season, you are expected to dine at the hotel. ✉ *46200 Lacave (40 km/25 mi east of Sarlat),* ☎ *05–65–32–66–66,* FAX *05–65–37–06–57. 14 rooms. Restaurant, pool, sauna, tennis court. MC, V. Closed mid-Nov.–Easter.*

$–$$ ★ **Hôtels St-Albert et Montaigne.** The Garrigou family has two hotels on this delightful square in the center of town. The Montaigne is in a manor. Ask for lovely Room 33, with exposed beams. The St-Albert has varying size, simply furnished rooms. Hearty regional fare is served in the restaurant. Over dinner, discuss your next day's itinerary with M. Garrigou: He not only knows the region well, he is also the town's backroom politician. The restaurant is closed Sunday dinner and Monday from November to mid-April. ✉ *10 pl. Pasteur, 24200,* ☎ *05–53–31–55–55,* FAX *05–53–59–19–99. 56 rooms, 6 suites, all with bath or shower. Restaurant. AE, MC, V. Closed Nov.–mid-Apr.*

En Route From Sarlat to Les Eyzies-de-Tayac, on twisty D47, you'll pass the elegant **Château de Puymartin** (☎ 05–53–59–29–97); it's open April–October, daily 10–noon; admission is 32 francs.

Beynac

24 *11 km (7 mi) south of Sarlat-la-Canéda, 63 km (39 mi) east of Bergerac.*

The main reason to visit Beynac is to see its medieval castle. Daringly perched atop a sheer cliff face beside an abrupt bend in the Dordogne, the 13th-century **Château de Beynac** has unforgettable, muscular architecture and staggering views from its battlements. ☎ *05–53–29–50–40.* *32 frs.* *Mar.–mid-Nov., daily 10–noon and 2–5; July and Aug., daily 10–7.*

Dining and Lodging

$$$ **Château Regagnac.** M. and Mme. Pardoux's 16th-century manor house is hidden in the wooded hills south of Beynac. Guest rooms are filled with homey collectibles. But most outstanding is dinner (advance reservations necessary): a nine-course meal that might include homemade foie gras, baked pike with herb stuffing, and *maigret de canard* (duck's breast)—in the banquet hall decorated with shields. Breakfast, too, is superb. M. Pardoux speaks excellent English (he was seconded to the British Army during the war) and his military bearing makes an amusing counterpoint to Mme.'s warmth. ✉ *Montferrand-Cadouin, 24440 Beaumont (25 km/15 mi south of Beynac),* ☎ *05–53–63–27–02. 5 rooms. MC, V.*

$$ **Auberge du Noyer.** This inn, in a small, 18th-century building 5 km (3 mi) outside La Bugue (west of Beynac), is owned by two ex-pats. The comfortable rooms, decorated in provincial style, are in the main building or in the former barn (avoid the ground-floor barn rooms: you can hear the upstairs plumbing). The good four-course prix-fixe dinner menu is made up of soup, a starter, a main dish, such as maigret de canard or fresh trout, and cheese or dessert. ✉ *Le Reclaud-de-Bouny-Bas, 24260 Le Bugue,* ☎ *05–53–07–11–73,* FAX *05–53–54–57–44. 10 rooms. Restaurant, pool. MC, V. Closed Nov.–Mar.*

La Roque-Gageac

25 *12 km (7 mi) northwest of Sarlat-le-Canéda, 37 km (23 mi) northeast of Monpazier.*

A short distance up the Dordogne from Beynac, huddled beneath a towering gray cliff, is La Roque-Gageac, one of the best-restored villages in the Dordogne Valley. Crafts shops line its low, narrow streets, dominated by the outlines of the 19th-century mock-medieval **Château de Malartrie** and the **Manoir de Tarde,** with its cylindrical turret.

Dining and Lodging

$$ **La Plume d'Oie.** This small inn overlooks the river and the limestone cliffs. Rooms, decorated in light fabrics and wicker furniture, vary in size and price. La Plume d'Oie's major raison d'être, however, is the stone-walled restaurant at which you are expected to have at least one meal. Chef-owner Marc-Pierre Walker prepares classical regional cuisine: fillet of beef cooked in red wine and ragout of foie gras. The restaurant is closed Monday. ✉ *24250 La Roque-Gageac,* ☎ *05–53–29–57–05,* FAX *05–53–31–04–81. 4 rooms with bath or shower. Restaurant, minibars. MC, V. Closed late Nov.–mid-Dec. and Feb.*

Domme

26 *6 km (4 mi) east of La Roque-Gageac.*

The historic cliff-top village of Domme lies across the Dordogne from La Roque-Gageac. It is famous for its *grottes* (caves), where prehistoric bison and rhinoceros bones have been discovered. You can visit the 500-yard-long illuminated galleries, lined with stalagmites and stalactites. ✉ *Entrance on pl. de la Halle.* 🎫 *28 frs.* ⏲ *Apr.–Sept., daily 9:30–noon and 2–6; Mar. and Oct., daily 2–6.*

Dining and Lodging

$$ ✕🏨 **L'Esplanade.** Make sure your room looks over the Dordogne—it's the expansive view that makes this hotel special. Rooms are small but modern, and the staff speaks English. Salmon and trout top the menu; dining à la carte can be pricey. The restaurant is closed Sunday dinner and Monday off-season. ✉ *24250 Domme,* ☎ *05–53–28–31–41,* FAX *05–53–28–49–92. 19 rooms with bath or shower. AE, MC, V. Closed mid-Nov.–mid-Feb.*

Monpazier

27 *37 km (23 mi) southwest of La Roque-Gageac, 45 km (28 mi) southeast of Bergerac.*

On the south bank of the Dordogne is the tiny town of Monpazier, one of France's best-preserved *bastides* (fortified medieval towns with regimented street plans). It was built in ocher-color stone by English king Edward I in 1284 to protect the southern flank of his French possessions. The bastide features three stone gateways (of an original six), a large central square, and the church of **St-Dominique,** housing 35 carved wooden choir stalls and a would-be relic of the True Cross. Opposite the church is the finest medieval building in town, the **Maison du Chapître** (Chapter House), once used as a barn for storing grain. Its wood-beam roof is constructed of chestnut to repel web-spinning spiders.

En Route If you travel northeast along D53 from Monpazier you'll pass by the **Château des Milandes,** once owned by the American-born cabaret star of Roaring '20s Paris, Josephine Baker. It's open May–October, daily 9:30–11:30 and 2–6. D53 then goes by the ruined castle of **Castlenaud,** open May–November, daily 10–7.

Biron

28 *8 km (5 mi) south of Monpazier.*

Stop in Biron to see its hilltop castle. Highlights of a visit to the **Château de Biron,** which, along with the keep, square tower, and chapel, date from the Middle Ages, include monumental staircases and the kitchen with its huge stone slabs. The classical buildings were completed in 1730. English Romantic poet Lord Byron (1788–1824) is claimed as a distant descendant of the Gontaut-Biron family, who lived here for 14 generations. ☎ *05–53–63–13–39.* 🎫 *22 frs.* ⏲ *Feb.–June and Sept.–Nov., Wed.–Mon. 9–11:30 and 2–6; July–Aug., daily 9–11:30 and 2–6.*

Lanquais

29 *20 km (12 mi) north of Monpazier.*

The small village of Lanquais is another château town (across the Dordogne river you can see the looming towers of yet another castle, the Château Baneuil). The interior of the turreted **Château de Lanquais** (15th–17th centuries) is richly furnished with majestic Italian fireplaces on loan from the Louvre. ☎ *05–53–61–24–24.* *18 frs.* *Apr.–Oct., Fri.–Wed. 9:30–noon and 2:30–7.*

Monbazillac

30 *37 km (23 mi) west of Monpazier, 8 km (5 mi) south of Bergerac on D13.*

Vineyards producing one of the region's best-known wines surround the town of Monbazillac and its wine-producing castle. The squat corner towers of the beautifully proportioned 16th-century gray-stone **Château de Monbazillac** pay tribute to the fortress tradition of the Middle Ages but its large windows and sloping roofs reveal the Renaissance influence. Regional furniture and an ornate, early 17th-century bedchamber enliven the interior. A wine tasting is provided at the end of your tour to tempt you into buying a case or two. ☎ *05–53–57–06–38.* *32 frs.* *Daily 10–noon and 2–4:15. Closed Jan.10–mid-Feb.*

Bergerac

31 *3 km (2 mi) north of Monbazillac, 57 km (35 mi) west of St-Émilion on D936, 47 km (29 mi) south of Périgueux.*

Bergerac is a quiet town with ancient half-timber houses and narrow alleys. Most of the time the town is quite subdued, though it comes alive with its Saturday market. Always robust, however, are the regional Bergerac wines, including Monbazillac, a sweet wine made from overripe grapes that enjoyed an international reputation long before its Bordeaux rival, Sauternes. Guided walking tours of its old town, lasting 90 minutes and costing 22 francs, leave from the **tourist office** (☎ 05–53–57–03–11). You can also take an hour-long cruise on the Dordogne for 35 francs: Check with the tourist office or the cruise company (☎ 05–53–24–58–80).

The **Couvent des Récollets,** a former convent, is also in the wine business. The convent's stone-and-brick buildings range in date from the 12th to the 17th century and include galleries, a large, vaulted cellar, and a cloister, where the **Maison du Vin** dishes out information on—and samples of—local wines. ✉ *pl. de la Myrpe,* ☎ *05–53–63–57–57.* *25 frs.* *July–Aug., daily tours every hr 10:30–11:30 and 1:30–5:30; mid-May–June and Sept.–mid-Oct., Tues.–Sat. at 3:30 and 4:30.*

Not only are there vineyards in the region, but there are also tobacco plantations. Learn about this local industry from its American origins to its spread worldwide at the **Musée du Tabac** (Tobacco Museum), a museum housed in the haughty 17th-century Maison Peyrarède near the quayside. ✉ *10 rue de l'Ancien-Pont,* ☎ *05–53–63–04–13.* *15 frs.* *Tues.–Fri. 10–noon and 2–6, Sat. 10–noon and 2–5, Sun. 2:30–6:30.*

Dining and Lodging

$$ ✕ **Hôtel Bordeaux.** One of the better hotels in town, the Bordeaux has contemporary furnishings and neat rooms. Request one on the gar-

den-courtyard or No. 22, which is slightly more spacious. Though you're not obliged to eat at the restaurant, it's difficult to refuse the marinated salmon in anisette and lime or the pan-fried escallop de foie gras. Owner M. Maury speaks fluent English. ✉ *38 pl. Gambetta, 24100,* ☎ *05–53–57–12–83,* FAX *05–53–57–72–14. 40 rooms. Restaurant, bar, pool. AE, DC, MC, V. Closed mid-Dec.–Jan.*

$$ ★ ✕🏨 **La Petite Auberge.** Head south to Razac d'Eymet to find this modernized, old country house. Rooms are tidy and cozy; for an extra 100 francs you might be tempted to stay in No. 7, the spacious ground-floor suite with a fireplace and kitchenette. Locals come to dine on the light version of Périgord cooking, particularly confit de canard, foie gras, and walnut tart, as well as vegetarian dishes. The restaurant is closed Sunday and Monday from September to June. ✉ *24500 Razac d'Eymet (4 km/2 mi east of D933, before the town of Eymet),* ☎ *05–53–24–69–27,* FAX *05–53–61–02–63. 7 rooms and 2 suites. Restaurant, pool. MC, V.*

St-Émilion

★ 32 *56 km (35 mi) west of Bergerac, 41 km (9 mi) east of Bordeaux.*

Suddenly, the sun-fired flatlands of the Pomerol vineyards break into hills and send you tumbling into St-Émilion. This jewel of a town has old buildings of golden stone, ruined town walls, well-kept ramparts offering pleasing views, and a church hewn into a cliff. Sloping vineyards invade from all sides, as do tourists.

The medieval streets are filled with wine stores (local wines reach maturity earlier than other Bordeaux reds and offer better value for the money), crafts shops, and bakeries selling macaroons, a local specialty. Tours of the pretty St-Émilion vineyards—Château Petrus and Cheval Blanc, among others—including wine tastings, are organized by the tourist office, the **Syndicat d'Initiative** (the association that ensures that the region's wines are up to standard; ✉ pl. des Créneaux, ☎ 05–57–24–72–03), as are train rides through the vineyards.

A stroll along the 13th-century ramparts takes you to the **Château du Roi** (Royal Castle), built by occupying sovereign Henry III of England (1216–72). 🎫 *28 frs.* ⏲ *Daily 9:30–12:30 and 2–6:30.*

From the ramparts of the castle, steps lead down to **place du Marché,** a wooded square where cafés remain open late into the balmy summer night. Beware of the inflated prices at the café tables. The **Église Monolithe,** lining one side of the place du Marché, is one of France's largest underground churches, hewn out of the rock face between the 9th and 12th centuries. 🎫 *34 frs.* ⏲ *Tours leave every 45 mins, 10 AM–5 PM, from the tourist office and cover the church, the citadel, the Catacombes, and the Grotte de l'Ermitage.*

Just south of the town walls is the **Château Ausone,** an estate that is ranked with Cheval Blanc as producing the finest wine of St-Émilion.

Dining and Lodging

$$ ✕ **Chez Germaine.** Family cooking and regional dishes are featured at this central St-Émilion eatery. The candlelit upstairs dining room and the terrace are both pleasant places to enjoy the reasonably priced set menus. Grilled meats and fish are house specialties; for dessert, go for the almond macaroons. ✉ *pl. du Clocher,* ☎ *05–57–24–70–88. DC, V. Closed Sun., Mon., and mid-Dec.–mid-Jan.*

$$$$ ✕🏨 **Grand Barrail.** This turn-of-the-century estate outside St-Émilion has been converted into a luxury hotel, albeit a little stiff and Germanic.

Rooms are unusually large for a French hotel and are smartly furnished; about half are in the former stables. The talented young chef serves traditional regional fare in the small dining room. St-Émilions constitute at least 60% of the impressive wine list. ✉ *rte. de Libourne, 33330 (4 km/2½ mi northwest of St-Émilion),* ☎ *05–57–55–37–00,* FAX *05–57–55–37–49. 28 rooms. Restaurant, pool. AE, DC, MC, V.*

$$$ ★ ✕🏨 **Hostellerie de Plaisance.** Across from the tourist office in the upper part of town is this sought-after hotel. Rooms are furnished in warm, appealing style; the Descault Room has an excellent view of the vineyards. Dinner matches the St-Émilion wines; if you are not staying here, make this your number-one choice for a leisurely lunch or dinner. The restaurant tends to be overbooked, so be ready to be turned away or fight for your rights. ✉ *pl. du Clocher, 33330,* ☎ *05–57–24–72–35,* FAX *05–57–74–41–11. 12 rooms. Restaurant. AE, DC, MC, V. Closed Dec., Jan.*

$$ ✕🏨 **Auberge de la Commanderie.** This two-story, 19th-century hotel with a garden and a view of the vineyards is close to the ramparts. Rooms are small but clean and individually decorated. The attractive restaurant is often frequented by non-guests and has a good selection of local wines; it's closed Tuesday, except in July and August. ✉ *rue des Cordeliers, 33300,* ☎ *05–57–24–70–19,* FAX *05–57–74–44–53. 15 rooms with bath or shower. Restaurant. MC, V. Closed late Dec.–Feb.*

$$$ 🏨 **Château Lamothe.** St-Émilion's hotels are mostly in-and-out tourist stops and Bordeaux's lack charm; a delightful alternative is this private manor house halfway between both. The large guest rooms have big four-poster beds with soft cotton sheets. You may find the decor a little too frilly, but rooms are very comfortable. Invariably the friendly hosts, M. and Mme. Bastide, will join you for an aperitif or a sumptuous breakfast. M. Bastide speaks English and is extremely helpful with suggestions. ✉ *33450 St-Suplice et Cameyrac (25 km/16 mi northeast of St-Émilion, 20 km/12 mi west of Bordeaux),* ☎ *05–56–30–82–16,* FAX *05–56–30–88–33. 3 rooms. MC, V. Advance reservations essential.*

BORDEAUX TO BIARRITZ

This area extends south from Bordeaux, the commercial and cultural center of southwest France, through renowned vineyards, the great Landes pine forest, and the Atlantic Coast from Arcachon to Biarritz. Long ago, the region was part sandy desert—a result of the alarming inland advance of drifting sands along the coast—and part marshy wilderness, whose eccentric inhabitants sported sheepskin jackets and stomped around on stilts (some still do, though mainly for the benefit of tourists). At the start of the 19th century, efforts were made to stop the sandy invasion by planting a front line of sturdy beach grass and pine trees: The resulting forest made the area what it is today.

Bordeaux

579 km (360 mi) southwest of Paris, 245 km (152 mi) west of Toulouse, 253 km (157 mi) southwest of Poitiers, 190 km (118 mi) northeast of Biarritz.

Bordeaux, the capital of southwest France and the region's largest city, has tried to diversify its tourist appeal—its May music festival is a major crowd puller—but the city remains synonymous with the wine trade. Wine shippers have long based their headquarters along the banks of the Garonne and vineyards extend on all sides: Graves and pretty Sauternes to the south; flat, dusty Médoc to the west and north; and

Pomerol and St-Émilion to the east. Stylish châteaux loom above the most famous vineyards, but much of the wine-making area is unimpressive, with little sign of the extraordinary regional affluence it promotes.

An aura of 18th-century elegance permeates downtown Bordeaux, where fine shops invite exploration. To the south of the city center are the old docklands, targeted for renewal, but still a bit shady. As a whole, Bordeaux is a less exuberant city than most others in France. To get a feel for the historic port of Bordeaux, take the 90-minute boat tour, weekdays from the Embarcadères des Quinconces at around 3; the cost is 56 francs. In June of 1998 the city will host a number of matches of the World Cup soccer competition; contact the tourist office (✉ 12 cours du XXX-Juillet, ☎ 05–56–48–04–61) for information.

33 For a view of the picturesque quayside, stroll across the **Pont de Pierre** that spans the Garonne; built by Napoléon at the start of the 19th century, the bridge makes spectacular viewing itself. Two blocks from the riverbank, along cours Chapeau-Rouge, is the city's leading 18th-cen-
34 tury monument: the **Grand Théâtre,** designed by architect Victor Louis and built between 1773 and 1780. Its elegant exterior is ringed by graceful Corinthian columns, and the majestic foyer, with its two-winged staircase and cupola, inspired Charles Garnier's design for the Paris Opéra. The theater-hall has a frescoed ceiling, a shimmering chandelier composed of 14,000 Bohemian crystals, and, it is said, perfect acoustics. ✉ *pl. de la Comédie,* ☎ *05–57–81–90–81. Contact the tourist office for guided tours.* 🎫 *32 frs.*

The tree-lined allées de Tourny and cours du 30-Juillet reel off from
35 the Grand Théâtre. At the start of the cours du 30-Juillet is the **CIVB,** headquarters of the Bordeaux wine trade, where information can be had and samples tasted; you can make purchases at the **Vinothèque,** opposite. At the far end of the cours is the **esplanade des Quinconces,** a vast square overlooking the Garonne. One kilometer (½ mile) north
36 of the esplanade is the ambitious **Cité Mondiale du Vin,** part office block, part shopping mall, and part cultural center, all focusing on the world of wine. ✉ *Entry at 25 quai des Chartrons.*

37 Just a block in from the river is **place de la Bourse,** an important 18th-century landmark. A provincial reply to Paris's celebrated place Vendôme, the square (built 1730–55) features airy, large-windowed buildings designed by the era's most esteemed architect, Jacques-Ange Gabriel.

38 Narrow streets wend their way from the river to the **Cathédrale St-André.** This hefty edifice isn't one of France's better Gothic cathedrals, but the soaring 14th-century chancel makes an interesting contrast with the earlier, more severe nave. Excellent—albeit grimy—stone carvings adorn the facade. ✉ *pl. Pey-Berland.*

39 The **Musée des Beaux-Arts,** across the tidy gardens behind the luxurious Hôtel de Ville, has a notable collection of works spanning the 15th–20th centuries, with important paintings by Paolo Veronese (*Apostle's Head*), Camille Corot (*Bath of Diana*), and Odilon Redon (*Chariot of Apollo*), and sculptures by Auguste Rodin. ✉ *20 cours d'Albret,* ☎ *05–56–10–17–17.* 🎫 *18 frs.* ⏲ *Wed.–Mon. 10–6.*

To see one of the region's most famous wine-producing châteaux, follow N250 southwest from central Bordeaux (direction Arcachon) for 3 km (2 mi) to the district of Pessac: **Haut-Brion,** producer of the only non-Médoc wine to be ranked a *premier cru* (the most elite wine classification). The white, classical château surveys the celebrated pebbly

Cathédrale St-André, **38**
Cité Mondiale du Vin, **36**
CIVB, **35**
Grand Théâtre, **34**
Musée des Beaux-Arts, **39**
Place de la Bourse, **37**
Pont de Pierre, **33**

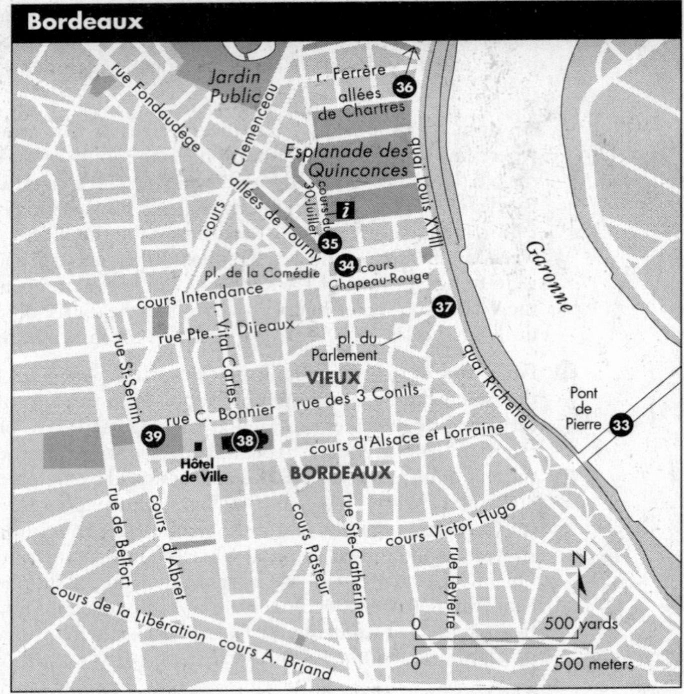

soil. The wines produced at **La Mission-Haut Brion,** across the road, are almost as sought after.

Dining and Lodging

Old Bordeaux has many small restaurants, particularly around the 18th-century place du Parlement: bustling L'Ombrière (No. 14), with fairly priced steaks; La Ténarèze (No. 18), for rich dishes from Gascony; and expensive Chez Philippe (No. 1), one of the city's top fish restaurants. What is lacking are charming hotels. You may want to consider staying outside of Bordeaux, at the Château Lamothe in St-Sulpice et Cameyrac, 20 km (12 mi) east of the city (☞ St-Émilion Lodging, *above*), for instance.

$$ ★ ✕ **Clavel St-Jean.** The sister restaurant to a city-center establishment of the same name is one of the few places in town where you can sample claret by the glass. The squeaky-clean modern-rustic decor and varied cuisine (including ravioli stuffed with lobster and duck with orange and chocolate sauces) make this an excellent choice. ✉ *44 rue Charles-Domercq,* ☎ *05–56–92–91–52. MC, V. Closed Sun. and 1st ½ of Aug. No lunch Sat.*

$$ ★ ✕ **Vieux Bordeaux.** This lively, much-acclaimed nouvelle cuisine haunt lies on the fringe of the old town. Chef Michel Bordage's menu is short but of high quality, complemented by three 165-franc prix-fixe menus. His fish dishes are particularly tasty, such as the grilled *bar* (bass) on a peppery galette of crab. ✉ *27 rue Buhan,* ☎ *05–56–52–94–36. AE, MC, V. Closed Sun., Aug., and 1 wk in Feb. No lunch Sat.*

$–$$ ✕ **Gravelier.** Anne-Marie, daughter of Pierre Troisgros of Roanne, married Yves Gravelier, and they combined their culinary talents. In sparse decor, full of light and openness, imaginative cuisine is served: fillets of *rouget* (red mullet) with foie gras and pigeon pot pie with Chinese cabbage. The 95-franc lunch menu is a good deal. ✉ *114 cours*

Verdun, ☎ *05–56–48–17–15. AE, DC. MC, V. Closed Sun. and 1st 2 wks in Aug. No lunch Sat.*

$ ✕ **La Cafetière.** On a small street a block and a half from place du Parlement, La Cafetière has only half a dozen tables in an intimate, cozy atmosphere. The salads are enormous, the confit de canard tasty. ✉ *14 rue des Faussets,* ☎ *05–56–51–66–55. MC. V. Closed Sun.*

$$$ ✕🏨 **Burdigala.** Of the three luxury hotels in Bordeaux, Burdigala (Latin for Bordeaux) is the only one within walking distance of the center of town. The modern exterior is extremely unappealing, but the inside is comfortable. The soundproof rooms are smart and neat; no. 416 is especially quiet and sunny. Deluxe rooms have marble bathrooms with whirlpool baths. The Jardin du Burdigala restaurant serves nouvelle haute cuisine. ✉ *115 rue Georges-Bonnac, 33000,* ☎ *05–56–90–16–16,* FAX *05–56–93–15–06. 76 rooms and 7 suites. Restaurant, meeting rooms. AE, DC, MC, V.*

$$$ ✕🏨 **Hôtel Ste-Catherine.** This fashionable hotel is in a 19th-century building in the old part of town. Service is limited, but the reception staff is helpful. The compact rooms are decorated with light floral fabrics. Beautifully presented, light nouvelle cuisine is served in the dining room with 12th-century vaulted ceilings. The street is reserved for pedestrians until 8 PM, so if you come by car, approach the hotel along the side street, rue de Parlement. ✉ *22 rue du Ste-Catherine, 33000,* ☎ *05–56–81–95–12,* FAX *05–56–44–50–51. 83 rooms and 3 suites. Restaurant, piano bar. AE, DC, MC, V.*

$$–$$$ 🏨 **Le Bayonne.** Rooms in this hotel in an 18th-century building in the heart of town have standard furnishings. Where Le Bayonne stands out is in its relative newness, its excellent location, and the freshness of its rooms. A simple breakfast is served. ✉ *15 cours de l'Intendance (enter from the small rue Martignace, off the street), 33000,* ☎ *05–56–48–00–88,* FAX *05–56–52–03–79. 36 rooms. Breakfast room. AE, DC, MC, V.*

$–$$ 🏨 **Hôtel des Quatre Soeurs.** This inexpensive gem, more of a rooming house than a hotel, near the Grand Théâtre has well-kept rooms of varying sizes and prices. In the adjoining café you may be treated to classical music on many afternoons. The owner, Mme. Defalque, is pleasant and helpful. ✉ *6 cours du 30-Juillet, 33000,* ☎ *05–56–48–16–00,* FAX *05–54–01–04–28. 35 rooms with bath or shower. Bar, café. MC, V.*

Nightlife and the Arts

Les Argentiers (✉ 7 rue Teulère), a respected and long-established Bordeaux hangout, is the place for jazz. **L'Aztécal** (✉ 61 rue du Pas-St-Georges) is a comfortable bar. **Cabaret Andalucia** (✉ 7 quai Bacalan) is a happening spot. **Le Chat-Bleu** (✉ 122 quai Bacalan) is a late-night venue for rock music, complete with videos. Dance the night away at **Sénéchal** (✉ 57 bis quai de Paludate).

The **Grand Théâtre** (✉ pl. de la Comédie, ☎ 05–56–90–91–60) puts on performances of French plays and occasionally operas. Bordeaux's **International Musical May** is a leading event on France's cultural calendar for classical concerts.

Shopping

Between the cathedral and the Grand Théâtre are numerous pedestrian streets where stylish shops abound. For an exceptional selection of cheeses, go to **Jean d'Alos** (✉ 4 rue Montesquieu). **Vinothèque** (✉ 8 cours du 30-Juillet) sells top-ranking Bordeaux wines. The **Maison de**

Tourisme et du Vin (✉ on the route du Médoc in Pauillac, north of Bordeaux) has a vast selection of claret.

Vineyards Around Bordeaux

Oenophiles will want to tour the vineyards around Bordeaux, but for others this might be boring. Bear in mind that though vineyards refer to themselves as châteaux, it does not mean a noble building stands on the property. Most of the better vineyards like you to make an appointment, with the implication and expectation that a purchase will be made. Excursions to the Sauternes, Graves, and Médoc regions can be made as day trips from Bordeaux.

The vineyards of the **Graves** region, so called because of its gravelly soil, encircles western Bordeaux and is the region's most historic appellation; a lightish red wine known as Claret (origin of the word claret, which means red Bordeaux) was esteemed by English occupiers during the Middle Ages. White wine—both dry and sweet—is also produced, some of the best at the tiny Domaine de Chevalier in **Léognan,** 10 km (6 mi) southwest of Bordeaux.

Nothing in the tiny village of **Sauternes,** 48 km (30 mi) southeast of Bordeaux, would tell you that mind-boggling wealth lurks amid the picturesque vine-laden slopes and hollows. The grubby village has a wine shop where bottles of the celebrated Château d'Yquem gather dust on rickety shelves, next to handwritten price tags demanding 1,000 francs (about $200) and more. Making Sauternes is a tricky business. Autumn mists that steal up the valleys promote a form of rot called *pourriture noble,* which sucks moisture out of the grapes, leaving a high proportion of sugar.

Not all grapes achieve the required degree of over-ripeness simultaneously; up to seven successive harvests are undertaken at **Château d'Yquem,** a little more than 1½ km (1 mi) north of Sauternes, to assure the optimum selection. This painstaking attention to detail, added to a centuries-old reputation and soil ideally suited to making sweet white wine, enables bottles of d'Yquem to obtain prices more appropriate to liquid gold. If you do splurge on a recent vintage, you may as well lock it away; Château d'Yquem needs to wait a good 10 years before coming into its own and will reward decades of patience.

Other **vineyards** produce excellent sweet wines, some at a fraction of the cost of prestigious Sauternes. From Sauternes, take D8 to Langon, cross the Garonne, and head north up the attractive D10, sandwiched between the river and the vineyards of **Ste-Croix-du-Mont, Loupiac,** and **Cadillac** in picturesque villages.

Near the ruins of the **Château de Haut-Bénauge,** 10 km (6 mi) north of Sauternes, a different style of wine is produced. The vines here are too far from the Garonne to benefit from the rising early morning damp of the river valley; their grapes prove more suitable for excellent dry white.

North of Bordeaux, the route de Médoc wine road (D2) heads toward **Médoc,** a strange, dusty region. Even the vines in Médoc look dusty, and so does the ugly town of **Margaux,** the area's unofficial capital, 27 km (17 mi) from Bordeaux. Yet the small, arid communes and châteaux of Haut-Médoc feature such venerable names as Margaux, St-Julien, Pauillac, and St-Estèphe. **Château Margaux,** an elegant, coolly restrained classical building of 1802, and three wineries at **Pauillac**—Lafite-Rothschild, Latour, and Mouton-Rothschild—are recognized as producers of premiers crus, their wines qualifying with Graves's

Haut-Brion as Bordeaux's top five reds. Of all the towns and villages in the Médoc region, **Pauillac** is the nicest; you may want to stroll along the riverfront and stop for refreshments at one of the restaurants. Should you wish to cross the Gironde, there is a ferry from Lamarque to Blaye four times a day for 86 francs per car and 24 francs per passenger.

Soulac-sur-Mer

40 *68 km (42 mi) northwest of Margaux on D2 and N215, 95 km (59 mi) northwest of Bordeaux.*

Soulac-sur-Mer is the last town on the route du Médoc before the ocean. Soulac's 12th-century basilica of **Notre-Dame de la Fin-des-Terres** deserves to have an outlandish history, given its name—Our Lady of the Ends of the Earth—and it does. By 1800 it had been almost completely embedded in drifting sands and was dug out and restored only 100 years ago. At the tip of the peninsula is **Pointe de Grave** and just south of it is the site of an American memorial commemorating the landing of U.S. troops in 1917. From Soulac-sur-Mer you can take a **ferry** across the Gironde to Royan; it runs four times daily and costs 132 francs per car and 35 francs per passenger.

Arcachon

41 *64 km (40 mi) west of Bordeaux.*

Arcachon became a resort town in the 1850s when the new railroad connected it with Bordeaux. These days, Arcachon is a lively, busy boating center, with three jetties protruding over its sandy beaches. From boulevard de la Mer, there are good views toward Cap Ferret, across the narrow straits that mark the divide between bay and ocean.

The town is at the southernmost tip of a chain of **lacs** (lakes) connected by streams and canals. The largest is the 19-km-long (12-mi-long) **Lac d'Hourtin-Carcans.** The small town of **Hourtin,** with a marina and 460-yard jetty, stands on its northernmost shore. In the center of this chain is the smaller **Lac de Lacanau,** which teems with pike, perch, and eel and is linked by the **Canal de Lège** to the **Bassin d'Arcachon.** The bay is renowned both for its variety of migratory birds and for its excellent oysters, clustered around the **Île aux Oiseaux,** a small island in the middle.

Nightlife and the Arts

Festivities are on-going at Arcachon's **casino** (✉ 163 bd. de la Plage). Arcachon's major festival, celebrating the sea, is the **Fêtes de la Mer,** held in mid-August.

Outdoor Activities and Sports

Both Arcachon and Lacanau, to the north, have 18-hole **golf courses** (Archachon, ☎ 05–56–54–44–00; Lacanau, ☎ 05–56–26–35–50). The **Aquacity** (✉ ff N250 south of Arcachon, ☎ 05–56–66–39–39) complex has water slides, a wave machine, and a heated swimming pool; it's open 9 AM–9 PM and costs 80 francs.

Shopping

La Maison des Produits Régionaux, in the Cestras complex on N250 outside Arcachon, sells a comprehensive selection of local products including oysters, foie gras, and preserves.

En Route A small lake, 13 km (8 mi) south of Arcachon, the **Étang de Cazaux,** marks the boundary between the Gironde and Landes départements. **Mimizan,** on the southern shore of the Étang d'Aureilhan (the next lake along the coast), was swamped in roving sand during the 18th century; sand still surrounds its ruined Benedictine abbey. From Mimizan, take D652 down to St-Julien-en-Born, then D41 to the old village of **Lévignacq,** with its fortified church and low houses that are typical of the region.

Dax

42 *143 km (89 mi) south of Arcachon, 145 km (90 mi) south of Bordeaux.*

Known in Roman times as Aquae Tarbellicae, Dax has been famous for 2,000 years for its thermal springs. The daughter of Caesar Augustus came here to soothe her aches and pains and was the first in a long line of seasonal guests whose numbers have swollen to 50,000 each year. Steaming water gushes out of the lion-headed Néhé fountain in the center of town. Take a walk through the parks and gardens and along the banks of the River Adour. Fine sculpture and 11th-century bas-reliefs can be seen at the church of **St-Paul-les-Dax** and the classical-style cathedral of **Notre-Dame,** but people generally come to Dax for the waters. Unless you plan to do so, you may not want to make the stop.

Eugénie-les-Bains

43 *68 km (42 mi) east of Dax, 140 km (87 mi) south of Bordeaux.*

Eugénie-les-Bains's heyday was a century ago when Empress Eugénie popularized it with her visits and, in gratitude for her patronage, the villagers changed the name of the town. The village was forgotten until Michel and Christine Guérard brought it back to life by recreating one of the most fashionable thermal retreats in France. The spa has 13 therapeutic treatments for everything from weight loss to rheumatism. Two springs are certified by the French Ministry of Health, "l'Impératrice" and the "Christine-Marie," whose 102°F waters come from nearly 1300 feet below the earth's surface.

Dining and Lodging

$$ ✕ **La Ferme aux Grives.** The Guérards delightfully re-created an old coaching inn barn, where the bounty of nature is the theme. A banquet table is laid out with vegetables and breads, darkened beams give a rich hue, and hunting paintings cover the walls. The three-course 170-franc menu may include a vinaigrette of grilled pears over locally cured ham, milk-fed lamb roasted in a pastry shell, and a huge meringue with Chantilly sauce. ✉ *Eugénie-les-Bains,* ☏ *05–58–51–19–08. MC, V. Closed Jan.–mid-Feb.*

$$$$ ★ ✕▣ **Les Prés d'Eugénie.** People come from all over to enjoy chef Michel Guérard's superb *tourte sauvagine de Garenne et du canard au foie gras* (marinate wild rabbit and duck baked with foie gras in pastry) and taste-bud tingling *coquilles St-Jacques* (scallops). Service is attentive, but the number of waiters is almost excessive. Grandeur prevails in the public areas of the 19th-century main house. Rooms are formal, though not outstandingly designed. High ceilings, antique furniture, and wicker chairs give them an uncluttered look. Those in the former 18th-century convent have an understated luxury. ✉ *40320 Eugénie-les-Bains,* ☏ *05–58–05–06–07,* FAX *05–58–51–13–59,* ☏ *05–58–05–05–05 (restaurant reservations). 44 rooms. Restaurant, pool, 9-hole golf course, 2 tennis courts, exercise room. AE, DC, MC, V.*

Bayonne

44 *48 km (30 mi) southwest of Dax, 184 km (114 mi) south of Bordeaux, 295 km (183 mi) west of Toulouse.*

Bayonne is the gateway to Basque country, a territory stretching across the Pyrénées to Bilbao in Spain. It stands at the confluence of the Adour and Nive rivers; the port of Bayonne extends along the valley to the sea 5 km (3 mi) away. You could easily spend an enjoyable few hours here, admiring the town's 13th-century cathedral, cloisters, old houses, and 17th-century ramparts, and visiting the museum. The airy, modernized **Musée Bonnat** houses a notable collection of 19th-century paintings. ✉ *5 rue Jacques-Lafitte,* ☎ *05–59–59–08–52.* *15 frs.* *Wed.–Mon. 10–noon and 2:30–6:30.*

En Route If you can arrange it, drive from Bayonne to Pau (one hour on the highway) in the late afternoon or early evening. As you go east, the views of the Pyrenean peaks to the south, illuminated by the sun sinking behind you, are unforgettable.

Biarritz

45 *7 km (4 mi) south of Bayonne, 190 km (118 mi) southwest of Bordeaux, 50 km (31 mi) north of San Sebastian.*

Biarritz rose to prominence in the 19th century when upstart emperor Napoléon III took to spending his holidays here on the prompting of his Spanish wife, Eugénie. Although not as stylish as it once was, the town is making a comeback with a new casino and a new convention center. The narrow streets around the cozy 16th-century church of **St-Martin** are delightful to stroll and, together with the harbor of **Port des Pêcheurs,** are a tantalizing glimpse of the Biarritz of old. The beaches, too, still attract crowds—particularly the fine, sandy beaches of **Grande Plage** and the neighboring **Plage Miramar,** both amid craggy natural beauty.

Dining and Lodging

$$ ✕ **Les Platanes.** Chef-owner Arnaud Daguin specializes in adapting country recipes and giving them a lighter touch. Be sure to try his foie gras, which he gets from his hometown in Gers. The decor of the restaurant, in an old Basque town house, is comfortably formal. ✉ *32 av. Beau-Soleil,* ☎ *05–59–23–13–68. Jacket and tie. MC, V. Closed Mon. No lunch Tues.*

$ ✕ **Grill Eugénie.** For a substantial lunch, head to this place in the Hôtel Florida. The three- and four-course, prix-fixe menus might include mussels in a dill sauce, crab and avocado salad, or trout in white wine. The traditional cooking, if not inspired, is a good value. ✉ *5 pl. Ste-Eugénie,* ☎ *05–59–24–01–76. MC, V.*

$$$$ ★ ✕ **Palais.** This majestic redbrick hotel, with immense driveway, lawns, and semicircular dining room, exudes a stylish, opulent, aristocratic air that stops short of decadence. Empress Eugénie, wife of Napoléon III, left her mark here a century ago. Chef Jean-Marie Gautier creates deft, innovative fare. Informal lunch is served on the terrace facing the curved pool above the Atlantic. Rooms are spacious; the 2,000-franc ones facing the ocean are especially grand. ✉ *1 av. de l'Impératrice, 64200,* ☎ *05–59–24–09–40,* FAX *05–59–41–67–99. 134 rooms and 20 suites. 3 restaurants, 2 bars, pool, sauna. AE, DC, MC, V. Annual winter closing varies.*

$$$ ★ ✕ **Café de Paris.** Although a moderately priced menu is available, most of chef Pierre Laporte's specialties at this elegant restaurant can

only be ordered à la carte—and you pay handsomely for the privilege. Sample the *ris de veau* (calf's sweetbreads), or the fish served with an imaginative nouvelle touch. The reasonably priced wine list is strong on Bordeaux. The restaurant is closed Sunday dinner and Monday, except July–September and January–April. Rooms are luxurious and have ocean views. ✉ *5 pl. Bellevue, 64200,* ☎ *05–59–24–19–53,* FAX *05–59–24–18–20. 19 rooms. Restaurant. AE, DC, V. Closed Feb.–Mar.*

$$–$$$ ✕🏨 **Windsor.** Built in the 1920s, this hotel is close to the casino and beach. The restaurant serves a variety of dishes, including terrine de foie gras with Armagnac, and ravioli stuffed with crab. Rooms are modern and cozy; those with sea views cost about twice as much as those facing the inner courtyard. ✉ *19 bd. du Général-de-Gaulle, 64200,* ☎ *05–59–24–08–52,* FAX *05–59–24–98–90. 49 rooms. Restaurant. AE, MC, V. Closed Jan.–mid-Mar.*

Nightlife and the Arts

A comfortable hangout both day and night is the small **Le Queen's Bar** (✉ 25 pl. Clémenceau, ☎ 05–59–24–70–65) where the young at heart gather in the evening and the not-so-shy take the mike to do karaoke. To keep your connections in cyberspace, the **Internet&Café** (✉ 5 rue Jauerry, ☎ 05–59–24–03–31) behind the post office provides the link. At the **Casino de Biarritz** (✉ 1 av. Edouard VII, ☎ 05–59–22–77–77) you can wrestle with the one-armed bandit, play blackjack, or, alternatively, lose some pounds at the Flamingo disco.

Outdoor Activities and Sports

Pelota, a Basque specialty, is played on Wednesday and Saturday at 9 PM in July, August, and September, at the **Parc des Sports d'Aguilera** (☎ 05–59–23–91–09). **Golf de Biarritz** (2 av. Edith-Cavell, ☎ 05–59–03–71–80) has an 18-hotel par 69 course. **Côte Basque Surf Training** (✉ 10 rue Larrepunte, ☎ 05–59–23–15–31) gives body-boarding and surfing lessons. The **Freedom Surf Shop** (✉ 2 av. de la Reine Victoria, ☎ 05–59–38–40–25) gives surfing lessons and rents equipment. **Désertours Aventure** (✉ 65 av. Maréchal Juin, ☎ 05–59–41–22–02) arranges rafting trips on the Nive river and four-wheel drive trips through the Atlantic Pyrénées.

St-Jean-de-Luz

★ 46 *26 km (16 mi) southwest of Bordeaux, 24 km (18 mi) east of San Sebastian.*

Along the coast between Biarritz and the Spanish border, St-Jean-de-Luz deserves a visit, for its old streets, curious church, colorful harbor, and elegant beach. The tree-lined **place Louis-XIV,** alongside the Hôtel de Ville with its narrow courtyard and dainty statue of Louis XIV on horseback, is the hub of the town. The church of **St-Jean-Baptiste** has unusual wooden galleries that line the walls to create a theaterlike effect. ✉ *pl. des Corsaires.*

Of particular note is the **Maison de l'Infante,** between the harbor and the bay, where Maria Teresa of Spain stayed prior to her wedding to the Sun King. The four-square mansion now houses the Musée Grévin, which contains worthy 17th-century furnishings and period costumes. ✉ *quai de l'Infante,* ☎ *05–59–51–24–88.* 🎫 *33 frs.* ⏲ *Apr.–Oct., 10:30–noon and 2–6:30; Nov.–Mar., by appointment.*

Dining and Lodging

$$$ ✕ **La Coupole.** In this semicircular gourmet restaurant in the Grand hotel (☞ *below*) look out at the bay while feasting on Chef Patrice Demangel's excellent regional specialties: confit of lobster, baby lamb from the Pyrénées, and a luscious dessert of three chocolate flowers in a vanilla

sauce. ✉ *43 bd. Thiers,* ☎ *05–59–26–35–36. AE, DC, MC, V. Closed late Oct.–early Apr.*

$ ✕ **Chez Pablo.** This place is a local institution. The simple, home-style menu is based on what the fishing fleet caught that morning. Long tables covered with red and white tablecloths, benches, and plastered walls make for a casual meal. There is also a room laid out with cutlery and glasses, but this is for regulars. ✉ *rue M. Etcheto,* ☎ *05–56–26–37–81. No credit cards. Closed Sun.*

$$$ **Grand.** Although it is the town's leading hotel, it is not as grand as you might expect—rooms have seen better days. But a major plus is that it is on the bay. ✉ *43 bd. Thiers, 64500,* ☎ *05–59–26–35–36,* FAX *05–59–51–19–91. 43 rooms, 3 suites. Restaurant. AE, DC, MC, V. Closed late Oct.–early Apr.*

$$$ **Lehen Tokia.** Two rooms in this bed-and-breakfast have marvelous views of the bay. All are filled with a hodgepodge of home-style furnishings; the Amethyst Room has a queen-size brass bed with two single mattresses (that part in the night), mismatched night stands, and a bookcase with English and French books. But all in all, it's comfortable, despite the price (this is an expensive town). ✉ *chemin Achotarreta, 64500 Ciboure (1½ km/1 mi southwest of St-Jean-de-Luz),* ☎ *05–59–47–18–16,* FAX *05–59–47–38–04. 6 rooms with bath or shower. Breakfast room, pool. MC, V.*

THE ATLANTIC PYRÉNÉES

Along the border between France and Spain rise the Atlantic Pyrénées, with their trout streams, pilgrimage churches, and hilltop villages. As you travel southeast from Bayonne, the Basque language will begin to appear on road signs, alongside French.

Pau

47 *106 km (63 mi) east of Bayonne and Biarritz.*

The busy and elegant town of Pau is the historic capital of Béarn, a state annexed to France in 1620. Pau was "discovered" in 1815 by British officers returning from the Peninsular War in Spain, and it soon became a prominent winter resort town. Fifty years later, English-speaking inhabitants made up one-third of Pau's population. They started the Pont-Long steeplechase, still one of the most challenging in Europe, in 1841; created France's first golf course here, in 1856; and introduced fox hunting to the region.

Pau's regal past is commemorated at the **Château,** begun in the 14th century by Gaston Phoebus, the flamboyant count of Béarn. The building was transformed into a Renaissance palace in the 16th century by Marguerite d'Angoulême, sister of François I. Marguerite's grandson, the future King Henri IV, was born in the château in 1553. Temporary exhibits connected to Henri's life and times are staged regularly. His cradle, a giant turtle shell, is on exhibit in his bedroom, one of the sumptuous, tapestry-lined royal apartments. ✉ *rue du Château,* ☎ *05–59–82–38–00.* *26 frs, Sun. 14 frs.* ⏲ *Apr.–Oct., daily 9:30–11:30 and 2–5:45; Nov.–Mar., daily 9:30–11:30 and 2–4:30.*

The **Musée Béarnais,** on the fourth floor of the château, gives an overview of the region, encompassing everything from fauna to furniture to festival costumes. There is a reconstructed Béarn house and displays of local crafts. ☎ *05–59–27–07–36.* *8 frs.* ⏲ *Apr.–Oct., daily 9:30–12:30 and 2:30–6:30; Nov.–Mar., daily 9:30–12:30 and 2:30–5:30.*

Dining and Lodging

$$–$$$ ✕ **Gousse d'Ail.** In the Hédas district, the deep mid-city canyon in the oldest part of Pau, this lovely hideaway is tucked under the stairway at the end of the street. Traditional Béarn and international cuisine are served. Have the maigret de canard cooked over coals. ✉ *12 rue du Hédas,* ☎ *05–59–27–31–55,* FAX *05–59–06–10–53. MC, V. Closed Sun. No lunch Sat.*

$$ 🏨 **Hôtel de Gramont.** Within sight of the château gardens, the Gramont is a convenient base for exploring Pau. Ask for one of the *chambres mansardés* (dormered bedrooms) under the eaves. ✉ *3 pl. de Gramont, 64000,* ☎ *05–59–27–84–04,* FAX *05–59–27–62–23. 36 rooms. Breakfast room. AE, DC, MC, V.*

Nightlife and the Arts

During the music and arts **Festival de Pau** there are events almost every evening, nearly all of them gratis, mid-July–late-August.

Oloron-Ste-Marie

48 *33 km (20½ mi) southwest of Pau on N134.*

Oloron-Ste-Marie straddles the confluence of the *gave* (mountain torrent) d'Aspe and the gave d'Ossau. Trout and even the occasional Atlantic salmon can be spotted when the sun is out. Originally an Iberian and later a Roman military outpost, the town was made a stronghold by the viscounts of Béarn in the 11th century.

The **quartier Ste-Croix** occupies the once fortified point between the two rivers and is the most interesting part of town. The fortresslike church of **Ste-Croix**, with its Moorish-influenced cupola, the two Renaissance buildings nearby, and the 14th-century **Tour Grède** (Grède Tower) are the main attractions. A walk around the **promenade Bellevue** along the ramparts below the west side of the church will give you a view down the Aspe Valley and into the mountains behind.

Dining and Lodging

$–$$ ✕ **Le Biscondau.** This establishment serves one of the best *garbures* (a hearty peasant vegetable soup) in Oloron. The view over the gave d'Ossau is at its best from the terrace in summer. ✉ *7 rue de la Filature,* ☎ *05–59–39–06–15. DC, MC, V. Closed Mon.*

$ ✕ **Le Corn Henric.** Eat here for a look into a real Béarn kitchen. M. and Mme. Claverie serve excellent *pipérade,* a hearty dish of ham, peppers, and beans. ✉ *10 pl. de la Résistance.* ☎ *05–59–39–03–59. No credit cards.*

$ 🏨 **Chambre d'Hôtes Paris.** This bed-and-breakfast in Féas, run by Christian and Marie-France Paris, is a bargain, especially if you like fly-fishing. Christian, a registered guide, knows every trout in the Barétous by name. ✉ *64570 Féas (7½ km/5 mi past Oloron-Ste-Marie),* ☎ *05–59–39–01–10. 3 rooms. Closed late Dec.–early Jan. No credit cards.*

Outdoor Activities and Sports

If you're interested in fly-fishing, take D919 from Oloron-Ste-Marie along the Vert River to the nearby town of **Féas.** The gentle Vert Valley with its meadow brook, well populated with trout, is a great place to fish.

En Route To the west of Oloron-Ste-Marie is the **Soule,** the smallest Basque province, where nearly all the inhabitants speak Euskera (Basque), a non-Indo-European language of mysterious origins. The Soule is in the

Barétous region, an undulating and moist transitional zone between the Basque country and Béarn, characterized by rolling green hills and corn fields. To begin exploring the Soule, take D936 from Oloron-Ste-Marie northwest toward Sauveterre de Béarn; after 12 km (7 mi) turn left on D25. **L'Hôpital-St-Blaise,** the first village on D25, has a 12th-century church, another example of the Hispano-Moorish influence, which is rare north of the Pyrénées. From Sauveterre de Béarn, head to Mauléon-Licharre.

Mauléon-Licharre

49 *26 km (16 mi) south of Sauveterre de Béarn, 29 km (18 mi) west of Oloron-Ste-Marie.*

Mauléon-Licharre, the capital of the Soule, is on the banks of the Saison. Stop to see the 16th-century **Hôtel de Maytie** (also known as the Château d'Andurain), the 17th-century **Hôtel de Montréal,** and the remains of a 12th-century fortress.

En Route Heading south from Mauléon-Licharre on D918 you'll come to the rustic 11th-century **Chapelle St-Jean-de-Berraute,** built by the Order of Malta for pilgrims on the way to Santiago de Compostela. Three kilometers (2 miles) beyond the chapel St-Jean is **Gotein,** with its characteristic *clocher-calvaire,* a three-peaked bell tower, designed as an evocation of Calvary. Trois Villes, Tardets, and Lanneare are the last three villages you'll pass before reaching **Aramits,** capital of the Barétous region. From Aramits, take D918/D932 in the direction of **Arette,** which was rebuilt after a 1967 earthquake leveled most of the town. Continue south and upward into the Pyrénées, 22 km (14 mi), through increasingly spectacular scenery to the ski station of **Arette-Pierre-St-Martin.** Just short of Arette-Pierre-St-Martin, make a hairpin right turn onto D113 to Ste-Engrâce.

Ste-Engrâce

50 *37 km (23 mi) southwest of Oloron-Ste-Marie, 100 km (62 mi) southwest of Pau.*

Ste-Engrâce, a village still largely populated by Basque shepherds, was once an important medieval pilgrimage site. Pilgrims on the way to Santiago de Compostela flocked to Ste-Engrâce's especially haunting 11th-century **church** to venerate the arm of Sancta Gracia, a young Portuguese noblewoman martyred around the year 300. In 1569, pillaging Calvinists removed the cherished relic. Sancta Gracia's right-hand ring finger was then sent from Zaragoza, the scene of her martyrdom. The church has an asymmetrical, slanting roof, reminiscent of the typical *maison Basque* (Basque house) and its gray stone seen against the green hills and fields behind seems to communicate unusual emotion. The rich ornamentation of the church interior is a surprising contrast to the stark exterior. The town remains an important crossroads for pilgrims traveling west to Santiago and trans-Pyrenean trekkers going east across the "dragon's back."

Just beyond Ste-Engrâce is the **Gorges de Kakouetta,** a famous canyon cut through the limestone cliffs by the Uhaitxa river, one of the wonders of the Pyrénées. At times as narrow as 12 feet across, the gorges are more than 700 feet deep. Stairways are cut into the rock, and hanging bridges span the watercourse. A waterfall and a grotto mark the end of the climb, a two-hour walk round-trip. This hike is recommended only during low-water conditions, normally between June and October. Good hiking shoes are indispensable.

Eleven kilometers (6 miles) from the Gorges de Kakouetta on D113, a left turn at the junction of the Uhaitxa and Larrau rivers will take you to the **Crevasses d'Holçarté,** another spectacular natural phenomenon. The highlight of the 90-minute round-trip hike is a spectacular bridge that hangs 561 feet above the rocky stream bed.

Lodging

$ **Auberge Elichalt.** This cozy hikers' inn has 50 beds in varying conditions, all good. There are double rooms, dormitory beds, and an apartment for rent, all in the shadow of the church. M. and Mme. Burguburu ("town's end" in Basque) can recommend hikes into the mountains. ✉ *64560 Ste-Engrâce,* ☎ *05–59–28–61–63. 5 double rooms with bath, 1 apartment for 5 with bath, 40 dormitory beds with shared bath. No credit cards.*

Larrau

51 *20 km (12 mi) west of Ste-Engrâce, 42 km (26 mi) southwest of Oloron-Ste-Marie.*

Larrau, west of the Gorges de Kakouetta, is a cozy way station on the road over the Larrau pass into Spain. It is known for its 19th-century forges.

Dining and Lodging

$$–$$$ ★ **Hôtel Etxemaïté.** This country inn with spectacular views is one of the area's most exquisite spots. In the dining room, which seems suspended over the garden, there are several *susulia,* a Basque combination chair and table designed to allow two people to sit and dine comfortably by the fire. The Basque cooking is excellent: the terrine *de poule au foie gras* (of hen and duck liver) is just one of many good choices. The restaurant is closed Sunday dinner and Monday from mid-November to mid-May. ✉ *rte. D26, 64560 Larrau,* ☎ *05–59–28–61–45,* FAX *05–59–28–72–71. 16 rooms. DC, MC, V. Closed mid–late Jan.*

En Route The road between Larrau and St-Jean-Pied-de-Port twists through mountain passes (Col de Bagargui and Col de Burdinkurutzeta) up into the limestone massif and the vast Iraty forest to the south, and out over the Arbailles forest and the sweeping Basque hills to the north. The Iraty forest, one of Europe's largest stands of beech, provided masts for the Spanish and French fleets up through the 18th century.

St-Jean-le-Vieux

52 *41 km (24 mi) northwest of Larrau, 5 km (3 mi) east of St-Jean-Pied-de-Port, at the junction of D933 and D19.*

St-Jean-le-Vieux is a village, like many others, along the road out of the Soule. There are adorable farmhouses and chapels—even sometimes matching sister chapels such as the twin buildings in Bascassan and Alciette, a not uncommon phenomenon in the Basque country.

St-Jean-Pied-de-Port

53 *46 km (28 mi) west of Larrau, 54 km (33 mi) east of Biarritz.*

St-Jean-Pied-de-Port, a fortified town on the Nive river, got its name from its position at the foot (*pied*) of the *port* (mountain pass) of Roncevaux (Roncesvalles). The pass was the setting for *La Chanson de Roland* (*The Song of Roland*), the 11th-century epic poem considered the real beginning of French literature. The bustling town center, a major stop for pilgrims en route to Santiago de Compostela, seems, after a tour through the Soule, like a frenzied metropolitan center—even in winter. In summer, especially around the time of Pamplona's San Fermin blowout (the running of the bulls, July 7–14), the place is filled to the gills and is somewhere between exciting and unbearable.

Walk into the old section through the Porte de France just behind and to the left of the tourist office, climb the steps on the left up to the walkway circling the ramparts, and walk around to the stone stairway down to the rue de l'Église. The street leads down to the magnificent doorway of **Notre-Dame-du-Bout-du-Pont** (Our Lady of the End of the Bridge), a characteristic Basque three-tier structure: men above, women below, and the choir loft above that. Walk out on the bridge, the **Pont Notre-Dame,** near the church of Notre-Dame-du-Bout-du-Pont, and watch the wild trout in the Nive, which is also a scheduled Atlantic salmon stream. Fishing is *défendu* (forbidden) in town. Follow the left bank upstream to get to another wooden bridge. Cross there and then walk around and back through town, crossing back to the left bank on the main road. At the **Relais de la Nive** (hanging over the river at the north end of the bridge in the center of town), admire the reflection of the Notre-Dame bridge upstream and watch the trout working in the current as you sip your coffee.

Take **rue de la Citadelle,** running from the square in front of the church, to see the Arcanzola house at No. 32 (1510), the Maison des Évêques (Bishops' House) at No. 39, and the famous Prison des Évêques next door. Rue de la Citadelle leads to the **Citadelle** up above, a classic Vauban fortress, now occupied by a school.

Dining and Lodging

$$–$$$ ✕ **Chez Arbillaga.** Tucked inside the citadel ramparts, this lively bistro is a sound choice for lunch or dinner. The food represents what the Basques do best: simple cooking of excellent quality, such as *agneau de lait à la broche* (roast lamb) in winter or coquilles St-Jacques *au lard fumé* (in smoked lard) in summer. ✉ *8 rue de l'Église,* ☎ *05–59–37–06–44. MC, V. Closed 1st 2 wks of June and Oct., and Wed. Jan.–May.*

$$$ ✕🏨 **Les Pyrénées.** In this inn is the best restaurant in town, specializing in nouvelle Basque cuisine, such as ravioli and prawns with caviar sauce or the hot wild-mushroom terrine. Rooms are modern and vary in size; four have balconies. ✉ *19 pl. du Général-de-Gaulle, 64220,* ☎ *05–59–37–01–01,* FAX *05–59–37–18–97. 18 rooms and 2 apartments. Restaurant, pool. AE, DC, MC, V. Closed last 3 wks of Jan., late Nov.–late Dec.*

$$ ✕🏨 **Central Hôtel.** This family-run hotel and restaurant over the Nive offers the best quality for price in town. The owners speak Basque, Spanish, French, English, and some German as well, so communicating is no problem. Trout for breakfast can be literally (though illegally) caught from the rooms over the river. There is a wonderful, 200-year-old, handmade oak staircase. The cuisine is superb: Try the maigret de canard. ✉ *1 pl. Charles-de-Gaule, 64220,* ☎ *05–59–37–00–22,* FAX *05–59–37–27–79. 14 rooms. Restaurant. AE, DC, MC, V. Closed mid-Dec.–early Mar.*

Pas de Roland

54 *30 km (18 mi) northwest of St-Jean-Pied-de-Port along the Nive on D918; follow signs for Itxassou and proceed past the town up to the pass.*

Legend has it that it was at the Pas de Roland where Roland, to allow Charlemagne's troops to pass, cut a breach through a boulder with his mystical sword Durandal, in the process leaving his footprint in the rock. The evidence remains.

Dining and Lodging

$$ ✕🏨 **Hôtel du Mont Roland.** Just upstream of the Pas de Roland, this rustic little inn is a good place for a meal or a night. Home-grown native trout are available from the hotel's private pool, or have the pipérade *basquaise au jambon* (basque vegetable stew with ham). Rooms are simple but clean and cozy. ✉ *Laxîa, 64250 Itxassou,* ☎ *05–59–29–75–23. 9 rooms with showers and sinks, WC in the hall. Restaurant. MC, V. Closed Jan.*

En Route From the Pas de Roland, if you're heading to Ainhoa, backtrack as far as D118 near Espelette and follow signs for the town.

Ainhoa

55 *31 km (19 mi) northwest of St-Jean-Pied-de-Port, 22 km (14 mi) southeast of St-Jean-de-Luz.*

The classical Basque village of Ainhoa is one of the prettiest towns in France. The streets are lined with one beautiful house after another, complete with whitewashed walls, flower-filled balconies, brightly painted shutters, and carved master beams. The church of **Notre-Dame de l'Assomption** is another three-tier beauty, with carved railings and woodwork.

Lodging

$$ 🏨 **Hôtel Ohantzea.** Across from the church, this classical Basque house, with a beautiful facade and garden, was originally a 17th-century farm. The original antiques and the many paintings by artists who traded them for lodging, all make this comfortable space as much of a museum as a hotel. Ask for a room with a balcony overlooking the garden. ✉ *rue Principale, 64250,* ☎ *05–59–29–90–50. 9 rooms. MC, V. Closed Dec.–Jan.*

Sare

56 *1 km (½ mi) southwest of Ainhoa on D118; take the first left.*

The tiny village of Sare is one of the most beautiful in France. Shady streets, a large fronton (for pelota), and a lovely three-tier church are among its chief assets.

Up the Sare valley is the panoramic Col de Lizarrieta and the **Grottes de Sare,** where you can take a guided tour (in five languages) for 1 km (⅔ mi) underground and see a sound-and-light show. ☎ *05–59–54–21–88.* 🎟 *30 frs. Closed Jan.–mid-Feb.*

West of Sare on D4, at the Col de St-Ignace, take the **Petit Train de la Rhune,** a tiny wood-paneled cogwheel train that reaches the dizzying speed of 8 kph (5 mph) while climbing up La Rhune peak. The views of the Bay of Biscay, the Pyrénées, and the grassy hills of the Basque farmland are wonderful. 🎟 *45 frs.* ⏲ *Round-trip (1 hr): Easter vacation and May–June, daily 10 and 3; July–Sept., daily every 35 mins.*

Ascain

57 *15 km (9 mi) west of Ainhoa, 7 km (4 mi) east of St-Jean-de-Luz.*

Ascain, with its Roman bridge, three-tier church, and arcaded bell tower, is the last town before the Nivelle River leads to St-Jean-de-Luz (☞ *above*) and the sea.

THE ATLANTIC COAST A TO Z

Arriving and Departing

By Car

As the capital of southwest France, Bordeaux has superb transport links with Paris, Spain, and even the Mediterranean (A62 expressway via Toulouse). The A10 Paris–Bordeaux expressway passes close to Poitiers, Niort (exit 23 for La Rochelle), and Saintes before continuing toward Spain as A63.

By Plane

There are frequent daily flights from Bordeaux, Biarritz, and the domestic airport at Limoges to Paris on Air Inter (☎ 05–59–33–34–35), and to London on Air France. Air Inter also flies to Pau.

By Train

The super-fast TGV (Trains à Grande Vitesse) Atlantique service linking Paris (Gare Montparnasse) to Bordeaux—584 km (365 mi) in three hours—stops at Poitiers (change for Niort, La Rochelle, and Rochefort) and Angoulême (change for Jarnac, Cognac, and Saintes). The TGV covers the 800 km (500 mi) from Paris to Biarritz in 4–5½ hours. A train links Bordeaux to Lyon (8 hours) and Nice (10 hours) via Toulouse.

Getting Around

By Car

The fast (130 kph/80 mph) N137 connects La Rochelle with Saintes via Rochefort; Angoulême is linked to Bordeaux and Poitiers by N10; and D936 runs along the Dordogne Valley to Bergerac.

By Train

Bordeaux is the region's major train hub (☞ Arriving and Departing By Train, *above*). Trains run regularly from Bordeaux to Bergerac (80 minutes), with occasional stops at St-Émilion, and, three times daily, to Sarlat (nearly 3 hours). Poitiers is the connecting point for Niort, La Rochelle, and Rochefort; Angoulême is the connecting point for Jarnac, Cognac, and Saintes.

Contacts and Resources

Car Rental

Avis (✉ 59 rue Peyronnet, Bordeaux, ☎ 05–56–92–69–38; 133 bd. du Grand-Cerf, Poitiers, ☎ 05–49–58–13–00; and 166 bd. Joffre, La Rochelle, ☎ 05–46–41–13–55). **Hertz** (✉ pl. de la Gare, Bergerac, ☎ 05–53–57–19–27; and 107 bd. du Grand-Cerf, Poitiers, ☎ 05–49–58–24–24).

Guided Tours

Horizons Européens (✉ France Tourisme, 3 rue d'Alger, 75001 Paris, ☎ 01–42–60–31–25) organizes a seven-day bus tour of Dordogne and Périgord, leaving from Paris.

Travel Agencies

American Express (✉ 14 cours de l'Intendance, Bordeaux, ☎ 05–56–81–70–02). **Wagons-Lits** (✉ 43 rue Porte-Dijeaux, Bordeaux, ☎ 05–56–52–92–70).

Visitor Information

Suggestions about wine tours and tastings, as well as information on local and regional sights, are available at the **Bordeaux Office de Tourisme** (✉ 12 cours du 30-Juillet, ☎ 05–56–00–66–00), which also provides a round-the-clock answering service in English. The addresses of other tourist offices in towns mentioned in this chapter are as follows: **Angoulême** (✉ 2 pl. St-Pierre, ☎ 05–45–95–16–84). **Bergerac** (✉ 97 rue Neuve d'Argenson, ☎ 05–53–57–03–11). **Biarritz** (✉ 1 sq. Ixelles, ☎ 05–59–24–20–24). **Cognac** (✉ 16 rue du XIV-Juillet, ☎ 05–45–82–10–71). **Niort** (✉ rue Ernest-Pérochon, ☎ 05–49–24–18–79). **Pau** (✉ pl. Royale, ☎ 05–59–27–27–08). **Poitiers** (✉ 15 rue Carnot, ☎ 05–49–41–58–22). **La Rochelle** (✉ pl. de la Petite-Sirène, ☎ 05–46–41–14–68). **St-Émilion** (✉ pl. du Clocher, ☎ 05–57–24–72–03). **St-Jean-de-Luz** (✉ pl. Foch, ☎ 05–59–26–03–16). **St-Jean-Pied-de-Port** (✉ 14 pl. Charles-de-Gaulle, ☎ 05–59–37–03–57). **Saintes** (✉ 62 cours National, ☎ 05–46–74–23–82). **Sarlat** (✉ pl. de la Liberté, ☎ 05–53–59–27–67).

17 Portraits of France

France at a Glance: A Chronology

The Art of French Cooking

An Introduction to French Wine

A Survey of French Architecture

Books and Videos

FRANCE AT A GLANCE: A CHRONOLOGY

ca. 3500 BC Megalithic stone complexes erected at Carnac, Brittany.

ca. 1500 BC Lascaux cave paintings executed (Dordogne, southwest France).

ca. 600 BC Greek colonists found Marseille.

after 500 BC Celts appear in France.

58–51 BC Julius Caesar conquers Gaul; writes up the war in *De Bello Gallico.*

52 BC Lutetia, later to become Paris, is built by the Gallo-Romans.

46 BC Roman amphitheater built at Arles.

14 BC The Pont du Gard aqueduct at Nîmes is erected.

AD 406 Invasion by the Vandals (Germanic tribes).

451 Attila invades and is defeated at Châlons.

The Merovingian Dynasty

486–511 Clovis, king of the Franks (481–511), defeats the Roman governor of Gaul and founds the Merovingian Dynasty. Great monasteries, such as those at Tours, Limoges, and Chartres, become centers of culture.

497 Franks convert to Christianity.

567 The Frankish kingdom is divided into three parts—the eastern countries (Austrasia), later to become Belgium and Germany; the western countries (Neustria), later to become France; and Burgundy.

The Carolingian Dynasty

768–78 Charlemagne (768–814) becomes king of the Franks (768); conquers northern Italy (774); and is defeated by the Moors at Roncesvalles, Spain, after which he consolidates the Pyrénées border (778).

800 The pope crowns Charlemagne Holy Roman Emperor in Rome. Charlemagne expands the French kingdom far beyond its present borders and establishes a center for learning at his capital, Aix-la-Chapelle (Aachen, in present-day Germany).

814–987 Death of Charlemagne. The Carolingian line continues through a dozen or so monarchs, with a batch called Charles (the Bald, the Fat, the Simple) and a sprinkling of Louises. Under the Treaty of Verdun (843), the empire is divided in two—the eastern half becoming Germany, the western half France.

The Capetian Dynasty

987 Hugh Capet (987–996) is made king of France and establishes the principle of hereditary rule for his descendants. Settled conditions and the increased power of the church see the flowering of Romanesque architecture in the cathedrals of Autun and Angoulême.

1066 Norman conquest of England by William the Conqueror (1028–87).

1067 Work begins on the Romanesque Bayeux Tapestry, celebrating the Norman Conquest.

ca. 1100 First universities in Europe include one in Paris. Development of European vernacular verse: *Chanson de Roland.*

1140 The Gothic style of architecture first appears at St-Denis and later becomes fully developed at the cathedrals of Chartres, Reims, Amiens, and Paris's Notre-Dame.

ca. 1150 Struggle between the Anglo-Norman kings (Angevin Empire) and the French; when Eleanor of Aquitaine switches husbands (from Louis VII of France to Henry II of England), her extensive lands pass to English rule.

1257 The Sorbonne University is founded in Paris.

1270 Louis IX (1226–70), the only French king to achieve sainthood, dies in Tunis on the seventh and last Crusade.

1302–07 Philippe IV the Fair (1285–1314) calls together the first States-General, predecessor to the French Parliament. He disbands the Knights Templars to gain their wealth (1307).

1309 Pope, under pressure, leaves a corrupt and disorderly Rome for Avignon in southern France, seat of the papacy for nearly 70 years.

The Valois Dynasty

1337–1453 Hundred Years' War between France and England: fighting for control of those areas of France gained by the English crown following the marriage of Eleanor of Aquitaine and Henry II.

1348–50 The Black Death rages in France.

1428–31 Joan of Arc (1412–31), the Maid of Orléans, sparks the revival of French fortunes in the Hundred Years' War but is captured by the English and burned at the stake at Rouen.

1434 Johannes Gutenberg invents the printing press in Strasbourg, Alsace.

1453 France finally defeats England, terminating the Hundred Years' War and English claims to the French throne.

1475 Burgundy at the height of its power under Charles the Bald.

1494 Italian wars: beginning of Franco-Hapsburg struggle for hegemony in Europe.

1515–47 Reign of François I, who imports Italian artists, including Leonardo da Vinci (1452–1519), and brings the Renaissance to France. The château of Fontainebleau is begun (1528).

1558 France captures Calais, England's last territory on French soil.

1562–98 Wars of Religion: Catholics versus Huguenots (French Protestants).

The Bourbon Dynasty

1589 The first Bourbon king, Henri IV (1589–1610), is a Protestant who converts to Catholicism and achieves peace in France. He signs the Edict of Nantes, giving limited freedom of worship to Protestants. The development of Renaissance Paris begins.

ca. 1610 Scientific revolution in Europe begins, marked by the discoveries of mathematician and philosopher René Descartes (1596–1650).

1643–1715 Reign of Louis XIV, the Sun King, a monarch who builds the Baroque power base of Versailles and presents Europe with a glorious view of France. With his first minister, Colbert, Louis makes France, by force of arms, the most powerful nation-state in

Europe. He persecutes the Huguenots, who emigrate in great numbers, nearly ruining the French economy.

1660 Classical period of French culture: dramatists Pierre Corneille (1606–84), Jean-Baptiste Molière (1622–73), and Jean Racine (1639–99), and painter Nicolas Poussin (1594–1665).

ca. 1715 Rococo art and decoration develop in Parisian boudoirs and salons, typified by the painter Antoine Watteau (1684–1721) and, later, François Boucher (1703–70) and Jean-Honoré Fragonard (1732–1806).

1700–onward Writer and pedagogue François-Marien Voltaire (1694–1778) is a central figure in the French Enlightenment, along with Jean-Jacques Rousseau (1712–78) and Denis Diderot (1713–84), who, in 1751, compiles the first modern encyclopedia. The ideals of the Enlightenment—for reason and scientific method and against social and political injustices—pave the way for the French Revolution. In the arts, painter Jacques-Louis David (1748–1825) reinforces revolutionary creeds in his neoclassical works.

1756–63 The Seven Years' War results in France's losing most of its overseas possessions and in England becoming a world power.

1776 The French assist in the American War of Independence. Ideals of liberty cross the Atlantic with the returning troops to reinforce new social concepts.

The French Revolution

1789–1804 The Bastille is stormed on July 14, 1789. Following upon early Republican ideals comes the Reign of Terror and the administration of the Directory under Robespierre. There are widespread political executions—Louis XVI and Marie Antoinette are guillotined in 1793. Reaction sets in, and the instigators of the Terror are themselves executed (1794). Napoléon Bonaparte enters the champion of the Directory (1795–99) and is installed as First Consul during the Consulate (1799–1804).

The First Empire

1804 Napoléon crowns himself emperor of France at Notre-Dame in the presence of the pope.

1805–12 Napoléon conquers most of Europe. The Napoleonic Age is marked by a neoclassical artistic style called Empire as well as by the rise of Romanticism—characterized by such writers as François-Auguste-René de Chateaubriand (1768–1848) and Marie-Henri Stendhal (1783–1842), and the painters Eugène Delacroix (1798–1863) and Théodore Géricault (1791–1824)—which is to dominate the arts of the 19th century.

1812–14 Winter cold and Russian determination defeat Napoléon outside Moscow. The emperor abdicates and is transported to Elba.

Restoration of the Bourbons

1814–15 Louis XVIII, brother of the executed Louis XVI, regains the throne after the Congress of Vienna settles peace terms.

1815 The Hundred Days: Napoléon returns from Elba and musters an army on his march to the capital, but lacks national support. He is defeated at Waterloo (June 18) and exiled to the island of St-Helena in the south Atlantic.

1821 Napoléon dies in exile.

1830 Bourbon king Charles X, locked into a pre-Revolutionary state of mind, abdicates. A brief upheaval (Three Glorious Days) brings Louis-Philippe, the Citizen King, to the throne.

1840 Napoléon's remains are brought back to Paris.

1846–48 Severe industrial and farming depression contributes to Louis-Philippe's abdication (1848).

Second Republic and Second Empire

1848–52 Louis-Napoléon (nephew and step-grandson of Napoléon I) is elected president of the short-lived Second Republic. He makes a successful attempt to assume supreme power and is declared emperor of France, taking the title Napoléon III.

ca. 1850 The ensuing period is characterized in the arts by the emergence of realist painters—Jean-François Millet (1814–75), Honoré Daumier (1808–79), Gustave Courbet (1819–77)—and late-Romantic writers—Victor Hugo (1802–85), Honoré de Balzac (1799–1850), and Charles Baudelaire (1821–87).

1863 Napoléon III inaugurates the Salon des Refusés in response to critical opinion. It includes work by Édouard Manet (1832–83), Claude Monet (1840–1926), and Paul Cézanne (1839–1906) and is commonly regarded as the birthplace of Impressionism and of modern art in general.

The Third Republic

1870–71 The Franco-Prussian War sees Paris besieged by and fall to the Germans. Napoléon III takes refuge in England. France loses Alsace and Lorraine to Prussia before the peace treaty is signed.

1871–1914 Before World War I, France expands its industries and builds vast colonial empires in North Africa and Southeast Asia. Sculptor Auguste Rodin (1840–1917), composers Maurice Ravel (1875–1937) and Claude Debussy (1862–1918), and poets such as Stéphane Mallarmé (1842–98) and Paul Verlaine (1844–96) set the stage for Modernism.

1870s Emergence of the Impressionist school of painting: Claude Monet, Auguste Renoir (1841–1919), Camille Pissarro (1830–1903), and Edgar Degas (1834–1917).

1889 The Eiffel Tower is built for the Paris World Exhibition. Centennial of the French Revolution.

1894–1906 Franco-Russian Alliance (1894). Dreyfus affair: The spy trial and its anti-Semitic backlash shock France.

1900 Paris holds World Exposition.

1904 The Entente Cordiale: England and France become firm allies.

1914–18 During World War I, France fights with the Allies, opposing Germany, Austria-Hungary, and Turkey. Germany invades France; most of the big battles (Vimy Ridge, Verdun, Somme, Marne) are fought in trenches in northern France. French casualties exceed 5 million. With the Treaty of Versailles (1919), France regains Alsace and Lorraine and attempts to exact financial and economic reparations from Germany.

1918–39 Between wars, Paris attracts artists and writers, including Americans Ernest Hemingway (1899–1961) and Gertrude Stein (1874–1946). France nourishes major artistic and philosophical movements: Constructivism, Dadaism, Surrealism, and Existentialism.

1939–45 At the beginning of World War II, France sides with the Allies until invaded and defeated by Germany in 1940. The French government, under Marshal Philippe Pétain (1856–1951), moves to Vichy and cooperates with the Nazis. French overseas colonies split between allegiance to the legal government of Vichy and declaration for the Free French Resistance, led (from London) by General Charles de Gaulle (1890–1970).

1944 D-Day, June 6: The Allies land on the beaches of Normandy and successfully invade France. Additional Allied forces land in Provence. Paris is liberated in August 1944, and France declares full allegiance to the Allies.

1944–46 A provisional government takes power under General de Gaulle; American aid assists French recovery.

The Fourth Republic

1946 France adopts a new constitution; French women gain the right to vote.

1946–54 In the Indo-Chinese War, France is unable to regain control of its colonies in Southeast Asia. The 1954 Geneva Agreement establishes two governments in Vietnam: one in the north, under the Communist leader Ho Chi Minh, and one in the south, under the emperor Bao Dai. U.S. involvement eventually leads to French withdrawal.

1954–62 The Algerian War leads to Algeria's independence from France. Other French African colonies gain independence.

1957 The Treaty of Rome establishes the European Economic Community (now known as the European Union—EU) with France as one of its members.

The Fifth Republic

1958–69 De Gaulle is the first president under a new constitution; he resigns in 1969, a year after widespread disturbances begun by student riots in Paris.

1976 The first supersonic transatlantic passenger service begins with the Anglo-French Concorde.

1981 François Mitterrand (1916–1996) is elected the first Socialist president of France since World War II.

1988 Mitterrand is elected for a second term.

1990 TGV (*Trains à Grande Vitesse*) clocks a world record—515 kph (322 mph)—on a practice run. Channel Tunnel link-up between France and England begins.

1993 After nine years of painstaking renovations by I. M. Pei, American-Chinese architect, the Richelieu Wing of the Louvre is opened to the public, doubling the museum's exhibition space.

1994 The Channel Tunnel (or Chunnel) opens; trains link London to Paris in three hours.

1995 Jacques Chirac, mayor of Paris, is elected president. Paris becomes the focus of extremist terrorist bomb attacks and is crippled by one of the country's worst strikes in history.

1997 Inauguration of the world's largest library, the Bibliothèque Nationale François-Mitterrand, in Paris. President Jacques Chirac calls early elections, a Socialist coalition win a majority, and Lionel Jospin is appointed prime minister.

1998 France hosts month long Soccer World Cup, with final on July 12 at giant new stadium, the Stade de France, in St-Denis near Paris.

THE ART OF FRENCH COOKING

BORN BRITISH, naturalized American, I am an unabashed chauvinist about French food. To wander through a French open market, the vegetables overflowing from their crates, the fruits cascading in casual heaps on the counter, is a sensual pleasure. To linger outside a bakery in the early morning, watching the fresh breads and croissants being lined up in regimental rows, must awaken the most fickle appetite. Just to read the menu posted outside a modest café alerts the imagination to pleasures to come.

Best of all, the French are happy to share their enthusiasm for good food with others. There are more good restaurants and eating places in France than in any other European country; the streets are lined with delicatessens, butchers, cheese shops, bakeries, and pastry shops. And I have yet to find a Frenchman, cantankerous though he may be, who does not warm to anyone who shows an interest in his national passion for wines and fine cuisine.

Fine cuisine does not necessarily mean fancy cuisine. Masters though French chefs are of the soufflé and the butter sauce, the salmon in aspic, and the strawberry *feuilleté,* such delicacies are reserved for celebration. Everyday fare is much more likely to be roast chicken, steak and *frites,* omelet, or pork chop. Bread, eaten without butter, is mandatory at main meals, while the bottle of mineral water is almost as common as wine.

Where the French do score is in the variety and quality of their ingredients. Part of the credit must go to climate and geography—just look at the length of the French coastline and the part seafood plays in the cooking of Normandy, Brittany, and Provence. Count the number of rivers with fertile valleys for cattle and crops. Olives and fruit flourish in the Mediterranean sun, while the region from southwest of Paris running up north to the Belgian border is one of the great breadbaskets of Europe.

No one but the French identifies three basic styles of cuisine—classical, nouvelle, and regional. No other European nation pays so much attention to menus and recipes.

Most sophisticated are the sauces and soufflés, the *mousselines* and *macédoines* of classical cuisine. Starting in the 17th century, successive generations of chefs have lovingly documented their dishes, developing an intellectual discipline from what is an essentially practical art. As a style, classical cuisine is now outmoded, but its techniques form the basis of rigorous professional training in French cooking. In some measure, all other styles of cooking are based on its principles.

Nouvelle cuisine, for instance, is directly descended from the classics. Launched with great fanfare over 20 years ago, it takes a fresh, lighter approach, with simpler sauces and a colorful view of presentation. First-course salads, often with hot additions of shellfish, chicken liver, or bacon, have become routine. For a while, cooks experimented with such way out combinations as vanilla with lobster and chicken with raspberries, but now new-style cooking has settled down, establishing its own classics. Typical are *maigrets de canard* (boned duck breast) sautéed like steak and served with a brown sauce of wine or green peppercorns, and pot-au-feu made of fish rather than the usual beef.

Cooks have recently made a refreshing return toward country-style cooking. Indeed, many cooks never left it, for classical and nouvelle cuisines are almost exclusively the concern of professionals. However, regional dishes are cooked by everyone—chefs, housewives, grandma, and the café on the corner.

The city of Lyon exemplifies the best of regional cuisine. They feature such local specialties as poached eggs in *meurette* (red-wine sauce), quenelles (fish dumplings) in crayfish sauce, sausage with pistachios, and chocolate gâteau (cake). The Lyonnais hotly dispute Paris's title of gastronomic capital of France, pointing to the number of prestigious restaurants in their city. What is more, some of the world's finest wines are produced only 90 miles north, in Burgundy.

Lyon may represent the best of French regional cooking, but there's plenty to look for elsewhere. Compare the sole of Normandy, cooked with mussels in cream sauce, with the sea bass of Provence, flamed with dried fennel or baked with tomatoes and thyme. Contrast the butter cakes of Brittany with the yeast breads of Alsace, the braised endive of Picardy with the gratin of cardoons (a type of artichoke) found in the south.

Authentic regional specialties are based on local products. They have a character that may depend on climate (cream cakes survive in Normandy but not in Provence) or geography (each mountain area has its own dried sausages and hams). History brought spice bread to Dijon, legacy of the days when the dukes of Burgundy controlled Flanders and the spice trade. Ethnic heritage explains ravioli around Nice on the Italian border, waffles in the north near Belgium, and dumplings close to Germany. Modern ethnic influences show up in cities, with many an Arab pastry shop started by Algerian immigrants and many a restaurant run by Vietnamese.

Fundamental to French existence is the baker, the *boulanger.* From medieval times, legislation has governed the weight and content of loaves of bread, with stringent penalties for such crimes as adulteration with sand or sawdust. Today the government pegs the price of white bread, and you'll find the famous long loaves a bargain compared with the price of brioche, croissants, or loaves of whole wheat (*pain complet*), rye (*pain de seigle*), and bran (*pain de son*). White bread can be bought as thin *flûtes* to slice for soup; as baguettes; or as the common, thicker loaves known simply as *pains.*

Since french bread stays fresh for only a few hours, it is baked in the morning for midday and baked again in the afternoon. A baker's day starts at 4 AM to give the dough time to rise. Sadly, there is a lack of recruits, so more and more French bread is being produced industrially, without the right nutty flavor and chew to the crisp crust. The clue to bread baked on the spot is the heady smell of fermenting yeast, so sniff out a neighborhood bakery before you buy.

IF BREAD IS THE STAFF of French life, pastry is the sugar icing. The window of a city pastry shop (in the country, bakery and pastry shop are often combined) is a wonderland of éclairs and meringues, madeleines, and puff pastry, spun sugar, and caramel. You'll find pies laden with seasonal fruit, nut cakes, and chocolate cakes, plus the baker's specialty, for he is certain to have one. Survey them with a sharp eye; they should be small (good ingredients are expensive) and impeccably alike in color and size (the sign of an expert craftsman). Last, the window should not be overflowing; because of the high cost, the temptation to cram the shelves with leftovers from the day before is strong.

The charcuterie is almost as French an institution as the bakery. *Chair cuite* means "cooked meat," and a charcuterie is a kind of delicatessen, specializing in pâtés, terrines, ham, and sausages. A charcuterie also sells long-lasting salads, such as cucumber, tomato, or grated carrot vinaigrette and root celery (celeriac) *rémoulade* (with mustard mayonnaise). Cooked "dishes of the day" may include coq au vin and *choucroute alsacienne* (sauerkraut with smoked pork hock). Often you'll also find such condiments as pickles, plus a modest selection of wines, cheeses, and desserts—rice pudding or baked apple, for example. Only bread is needed to complete the meal, and you're set for the world's best picnic!

French cheese deserves, and gets, close attention. Choosing a cheese is as delicate a matter as deciding on the right wine. In a good cheese shop you will be welcome to sample any of the cut cheeses, and assistants will gladly offer advice. One cardinal rule is to look for *fromage fermier* (farmhouse cheese), a rough equivalent of château-bottled wine. If the label says *lait cru* (raw milk)—even better; only when milk is unpasteurized does the flavor of some cheeses, Camembert, for example, develop properly. Try to keep a cheese cool without refrigeration and eat it as soon as you can. Delicate soft cheeses like Brie can become overripe within a matter of hours, one reason it is rare to find a wide-ranging selection of cheeses in a restaurant.

MANY OTHER KINDS of specialty stores exist, often for local products. In Dijon, for instance, you'll find shops selling mustards in ornamental pots; in Gascony (near Bordeaux), it's foie gras and canned confit (preserved duck or goose). But the most famous concentration of food shops in the world must be clustered around the place de la Madeleine in Paris. On one corner stands Fauchon, dean of luxury food emporiums. Just across the square stands Hédiard, specializing in spices, rare fruits, and preserves.

The Madeleine crossroads may be unique, but with a bit of persistence, a more modest version can be found in most French towns in the weekly market, often held in a picturesque open hall that may be centuries old. Markets start early, typically around 8 AM, and often disband at noon. In Paris, street markets continue to thrive in almost every quarter, and although the main wholesale market of Les Halles has moved to the suburbs, the area around the rue Coquillière is still worth exploring for its maze of truffle vendors, game purveyors, and professional kitchen-equipment outlets.

French markets are still dominated by the season—there is little or no sign of frozen produce and meats. The first baby lamb heralds Christmas, little chickens arrive around Easter, together with kid and asparagus. Autumn excitement comes with game—venison, pheasant, and wild boar. Even cheeses look and taste different according to the time of year.

If you're an early riser, there's a long wait until lunch, for snacks are not a French habit. The structure of a meal, its timing, and its content are taken seriously. The "grazing" phenomenon of minimeals snatched here and there throughout the day is almost unheard of, and snacks are regarded as spoiling the appetite, not to mention being nutritionally unsound.

Still, the French light breakfast can come as no surprise; its unbeatable wake-up combination of croissant, brioche, or crusty roll with coffee has swept much of the world. Traditionally, the coffee comes as café au lait, milky and steaming in a wide two-handled bowl for dipping the bread.

At noon you'll be rewarded by what, for most Frenchmen, remains the main meal of the day. In much of the country, everything stops for two hours; children return from school, and museums and businesses lock their doors. The pattern is much the same in large provincial cities. Restaurants, bistros, and cafés are crammed with diners, most of whom eat at least two and often three or more courses.

Lunch keeps french adults going until evening, but you may want to follow the example of schoolchildren, who are allowed a treat on the way home. Often it is a *pain au chocolat* (chocolate croissant). By 8 PM, you'll be ready for dinner and one of the greatest pleasures France has to offer.

The choice of restaurants in France is a feast in itself. At least once during your trip you may want to indulge in an outstanding occasion. But restaurants are just the beginning. You can also eat out in cafés, bistros, brasseries, fast-food outlets (they, too, have reached France), or auberges, which range from staid country inns to sybaritic hideaways.

Simplest is the café (where the espresso machine is king), offering drinks and such snacks as *croque monsieur* (toasted ham and cheese sandwich), *oeuf au plat* (baked eggs), *le hot dog,* and foot-long sandwiches of French bread. Larger-city cafés serve hot meals, such dishes as onion soup and braised beef with vegetables, consumed on marble-topped tables to a background of cheerful banter. Like English pubs, French cafés are a way of life, a focal point for gossip and dominoes in practically every village.

The bistro, once interchangeable with the café, has recently taken a fashionable turn. In cities, instead of sawdust on the floor and a zinc-topped counter, you may find that a bistro is designer-decorated, serving new-style cuisine to a trendy, chattering crowd. If you're lucky the food will be as witty and colorful as the clientele.

With few exceptions, brasseries remain unchanged—great bustling places with white-aproned waiters and hearty food. Go to them for oysters on the half shell and fine seafood, garlic snails, *boudin* (black pudding), sauerkraut, and vast ice cream desserts. Originally a brasserie brewed beer, and since many brewers came from

Alsace on the borders of Germany, the cooking reflects their origins.

Training is an important factor in maintaining the standards of French cooking. Professional chefs begin their three-year apprenticeship at age 16, starting in baking, pastry, or cuisine and later branching out into such specialties as aspic work and sugar sculpture. To be a *chocolatier* is a career in itself. Much more than a manual trade, cooking in France aspires to being an art, and its exponents achieve celebrity status. Each decade has its stars, their rise and fall a constant source of eager speculation in the press and at the table.

The importance placed on food in France is echoed by the number of gastronomic societies, from the Chevaliers du Tastevin to the Chaîne des Rôtisseurs and the Confrérie des Cordons Bleus, to mention only three. The French believe that good eating, at whatever level, is an art that merits considerable time and attention. They have done the hard work, and, as a traveler, you can reap the benefits.

— Anne Willan

Anne Willan is president and founder of the *École de Cuisine La Varenne* in Paris. Her food column in the *Washington Post* is widely syndicated and her books include *French Regional Cooking* and *La Varenne's Cooking Course.*

AN INTRODUCTION TO FRENCH WINE

ALTHOUGH FRANCE marginally trails Italy as the largest wine-producing country in the world, the reputation of French wines is second to none. That's partly because of luck—the exceptional variety of France's soils and climate—and partly because of 2,000 years of know-how. Few understand better than the French which grapes produce the best wines and where.

The credentials of French wines have been internationally established since at least 1787, when Thomas Jefferson went down to Bordeaux and splurged on bottles of 1784 Château Yquem and Château Margaux, for prices that were, he reported, "indeed dear." Jefferson knew his wines: In 1855, both Yquem and Margaux were officially classified among Bordeaux's top five. In 1986, Jefferson's unopened bottle of Yquem rated $56,000 at auction. The Margaux—of which Jefferson boasted "there cannot be a better bottle of Bordeaux" (in fact, it was a half bottle)—was sold for $30,000 in 1987.

With such eminent roots, it is no surprise that the United States is the richest export market for French wines, along with Great Britain. France, like Italy, produces about 20% of the world's wine—more than double that of Spain and Russia and four times as much as the United States. Nearly a quarter of a million people in France make and sell wine. Many more produce it for their own consumption.

Bordeaux's reputation dates from the Middle Ages. From 1152 to 1453, along with much of what is now western France, Bordeaux belonged to England. The light red wine then produced was known as *clairet*, the origin of our word "claret." Champagne, on the other hand, has existed as we know it only since 1700, when—thanks to the introduction of strong bottles, cork stoppers, and the blending of wines from different vineyards—its sparkle was first captured by a blind monk, Dom Pérignon. The abbey at Hautvillers, where he lived, is a pilgrimage site for champagne aficionados. So is the monster oak barrel languishing in the Épernay cellars of the Mercier firm: It has a mind-boggling capacity of 200,000 bottles, and 24 thirsty oxen spent three weeks carting it to the Paris Exhibition in 1889.

Such publicity coups have brought champagne fame, fortune—and problems. Like cognac (a brandy produced in a strictly defined area north of Bordeaux), its name is illegally exploited worldwide by would-be imitators. Producers of the real McCoy fight such fraud in international law courts, but it is a hapless struggle. It has proved easier for French authorities to attack fraud in their own backyard. Thomas Jefferson, who cagily noted that his expensive wines were "bought on the spot and therefore genuine," would have enjoyed perusing today's legal texts. Their bureaucratic aridity may be of no succor to the thirsty tourist, but their role is essential in ensuring that the wine in your glass is precisely what the bottle says it is.

Prominently printed on any self-respecting French wine label is the term Appellation d'Origine Contrôlée (often abbreviated AC). Such wines have to meet stringent requirements. Yield, production methods, and geographic limits are meticulously controlled, as are the varieties of grapes that are permitted (sometimes one, sometimes several—no fewer than 13 types of grapes can be used at Châteauneuf-du-Pape), and the requisite degree of alcohol (all wines must respect a minimum, ranging from 8.5% for the sunless, sharp white Gros Plant Nantais to 13% for sweet whites like Sauternes). AC wines now account for nearly a third of production, a figure that has doubled in 20 years.

The next category, Vin Délimité de Qualité Supérieure (VDQS), accounts for about 10% of French wines. It is a sort of second division for wines that may be promoted to the AC category if they prove their mettle and show signs of steady improvement. Then come the Vins de Pays, regional titles with fewer restrictions, that account for about 15% of production. The simplest classification is Vin de Table, a poor relation in terms of price, if not necessarily quality.

Each bottle tells a tale. Usually the fancier it is, the more it has to hide. Beware of garish labels. Also, note where the wine was bottled: If it was not bottled on the spot (*mise en bouteille à la propriété/au domaine/au château*) or at least by a local merchant (often the case with burgundies), it should be treated with suspicion.

Napoléon, incidentally, was partial to unblended burgundy and, in a fit of alcoholic lucidity, once revealed the secret of his military genius: "No wine—no soldiers!" The English took the rival view of battle before wine: General Palmer celebrated victory over Napoléon at Waterloo by galloping down to Margaux and founding Château Palmer.

The vineyards of Margaux are among the ugliest in France, lost amid the flat, dusty plains of Médoc. Bordeaux is better represented at historic St-Émilion, with its cascading cobbled streets, or at Sauternes, where the noble rot (a tiny mushroom that sucks water from the grapes, leaving them sweeter) steals up the riverbanks as autumn mists vanish in the summer skies. From the chilly hills of Champagne in the north to the sun-pelted slopes of the southern Midi, vines cover France. Steep-banked terraces tower above the River Rhône. The vineyards of Alsace sway and ripple into the foothills of the Vosges. Chalky cliffs, cellars, and caves line the softly lit Loire Valley.

Names of wines can be as charming as the scenery. The Loire Valley yields Vin de Pays du Jardin de la France—Country Wine from the Garden of France. Entre-Deux-Mers quaintly translates as Between Two Seas (actually the Garonne and Dordogne rivers). It's difficult to resist flowery Fleurie, lovable St-Amour, sober Bouzy, or—if you overindulge—an early Graves.

More than a hundred different types of grapes exist in France. Some sound delicious. Try wrapping your tongue around Mourvèdre, Bourboulenc, Gewürztraminer, or Sciacarello. Visualize a bunch of Barbarossa ("red beard"), Folle Blanche ("crazy white"), or Fer ("iron"). Some names are confusing: The Auxerrois grape is used at Cahors, not near Auxerre; the Beaunois is used near Auxerre, not near Beaune; the St-Émilion is used for making cognac, not St-Émilion; while the Melon de Bourgogne has nothing to do with melons or burgundy (it's a white grape grown near the Atlantic coast).

YOU CAN BUY local wines from a cooperative (which handles wines from a number of local growers) or from an individual producer. Although the big champagne houses in Reims and Épernay organize slick, informative visits, the leading Bordeaux châteaux don't—partly because the Bordelais are notoriously reserved, mainly because they have no need to seduce passersby: Bulk orders account for 99% of their sales. You can obtain parsimonious gulps of second-string clarets at the Maison du Vin on the cours du XXX Juillet in central Bordeaux, but, unfortunately, there is nothing to match the Marché aux Vins in the Burgundian town of Beaune, where a string of fine burgundies can be sampled for a modest sum.

Different occasions warrant different wines. If you're buying wine for a picnic, go for something simple, such as a rosé or fruity red (Beaujolais or Gamay de Touraine). Full-bodied reds from the hottest regions of France are likely to knock you out if you drink them at lunchtime. Beware of restaurant wine lists designed to beef up the price of your meal, and always go for the house wine rather than a vague description such as "Bordeaux" or "Côtes du Rhône"; if there's no year or precise origin, don't expect quality. If wine is made locally, try it; you may not come across it elsewhere, and regional cuisine is invariably tailored to regional wines.

The harvests, or *vendanges,* begin in September and can last into December. In Sauternes, the grapes have to rot before being picked, and at Château Yquem, up to seven successive manual harvests may be required, with each grape inspected individually and picked only after achieving the right degree of maturity (by which time it looks a foul, shriveled mess). The year's biggest celebration, however, is the appearance of Beaujolais Nouveau on the third Thursday of November. Wine villages pay tribute to their patron saint on January 22, St. Vincent's Day.

Other wines to look out for include two from the Jura region of eastern France. Vin Jaune, also made from grapes picked late, is kept in oak barrels for six years or longer while yeasts form on the surface; the result is a wine (with a unique, nutty flavor sometimes likened to sherry) that can last for more than a hundred years. The grapes that produce the strong, amber-color Vin de Paille are left for two months on straw mats while the juice is drawn out and the sugar concentration intensifies.

CHAMPAGNE OFFERS tiny quantities of wine without a fizz. Still reds and whites made near Reims are known as Côteaux Champenois while, far to the south, there is even a still pink, Rosé des Riceys: rare, delicious, and expensive. Neither the truly black wine of Cahors nor the sweet white Jurançon of the Pyrénées is easy to find, unlike the sand wines (Vins de Sable) of Provence, which are made from vines that creep right down to the beach. There are even vines in and around Paris, at Suresnes and Montmartre, where the harvest is celebrated behind the basilica of Sacré-Coeur on the first weekend of October; unfortunately, the resultant wine is often undrinkable.

Don't be a prisoner of fashion. Marketing men have convinced the British that Muscadet is *the* dry white, while Americans jostle for Pouilly-Fumé and Sancerre—fine wines, certainly, but in overhyped demand and therefore of poor value. Try instead to ferret out unfamiliar, peasanty wines, concocted by authentic local characters. If you hunt around, you may meet someone like Marcel.

Marcel makes illegal wines out of illegal vines in a lost corner of Burgundy that is off both the beaten track and the straight and narrow. People say—maps and guidebooks, anyway—there aren't any vines in Marcel's bit of Burgundy. We ambled over the Canal du Nivernais and scrambled up a hill. The hill became a street and the street a village square. There was a large sign on the square saying LOCAL WINE. It was 12:15. The wine merchant was closed for lunch. Till 3. We sidled hopefully into a bar. "Local wine? Not here. Try Gaston by the church."

Gaston sold it, all right, and sloshed some into cracked glass beakers. We stared solemnly at the wine, and all the flat-hatted old men playing cards in the corner stared solemnly at us. We shared impressions. Unexpected. Perky but pale. Seemed friendly, but you never know.

Gaston leaned confidentially forward, stroked his mustache, and asked, "Want some more?" Yes. "Try that fellow there who's just gone out." Which fellow? "Marcel," said Gaston, adding helpfully, "The one in the flat hat."

Eventually—many country roads and twisty bends later—we tracked Marcel down. Who were we? We'd come about the wine. What wine? His wine. Marcel looked suspicious. His *excellent* wine. Marcel mellowed and got out the key to his cellar. We clattered down the slimy steps, taste buds tingling. Marcel grabbed a bottle. The wine's freshness came soaring through the dinge. Its sunniness pierced the murk. Marcel tossed back a glass and belched.

We murmured a few clichés of admiration. Marcel downed another glass, receded into the darkest, dirtiest depths of his cellar and rummaged under a heap of jerricans. Out popped a bottle as black as ink. Marcel squirted some into a glass, dashed it back and said, "Let's finish the bottle!"

Drinking this thick, cloying illegality was like being half-strangled in a velvet curtain. We fought our way free and staggered to the car with a crate. Marcel turned his back on us, brandished his francs triumphantly, and watered his garden in celebration.

— Simon Hewitt

A SURVEY OF FRENCH ARCHITECTURE

DESPITE THE RAVAGES OF wars throughout the centuries, France retains examples of nearly every historic and regional style.

Each region has its own characteristics. The dark red brick of the north stands in contrast to the pink brick of Toulouse, as does the white, chalky stone of the Cognac and Champagne regions when compared with the pink sandstone of the Vosges. Roofs vary as well, from the steep slopes of Alsace to the flat, orange-tiled expanses of the Midi and the colorful slate patterns of Burgundy.

Medieval black-and-white timber-frame houses survive in towns north of the Loire, such as Troyes, Dinan, Rennes, and the Petite France sector of Strasbourg. Castles perch grandly on cliffs throughout the southwest; hilltop villages survey the vineyards and olive groves of Provence in the southeast. Grim gateways repel strangers in the Charente region, whereas flower-strewn balconies welcome them to Alsace. Flemish belfries and Spanish gables flourish in the north, while the Germans, armed with their heavy Gothic-Renaissance style, transformed parts of Strasbourg into a Gallic Berlin.

Although the cave paintings at Lascaux in the Dordogne and the freestanding *menhirs* of Brittany prove that Frenchmen (or their ancestors) have created and constructed since prehistoric times, the first great builders were the Romans. Their efforts—mostly in ruins—are found throughout France, especially in the south. The amphitheaters of Nîmes and Arles, the theater of Orange, and the Pont du Gard aqueduct are masterpieces equal to anything in Italy. Autun, Saintes, and Reims boast proud Roman arches, and even the sprawling cities of Lyon and Paris house Roman remains.

With occasional exceptions, such as the 5th-century chapel at La Pépiole, near Toulon, the next architectural style of note was the Carolingian, in the 9th and 10th centuries. Surviving examples include the Basse-Oeuvre at Beauvais and the octagonal abbey church of Ottmarsheim in Alsace. The massive Romanesque style that succeeded Carolingian differed in various ways—with its stone (as opposed to wood) ceilings or vaults, its introduction of windows high up the walls, and its preference for stone sculpture over such superficial ornament as mosaic and painting. Many 10th- and 11th-century Romanesque buildings survive in Burgundy, Alsace, the Auvergne, and western France, notably Poitiers, with the intricately carved west front of the church of Notre-Dame-la-Grande.

The airier Gothic of the great French cathedrals built between the 12th and 16th centuries represented a fundamental departure from Romanesque. The most obvious visual change: pointed arches replaced round ones. Just as important, though, was a new vaulting structure based on intersecting ribbed vaults, which sprang across the roof from column to column. Outward thrust was borne by flying buttresses, slender arches linking the outer walls to freestanding columns, often topped by spiky pinnacles. Whereas Romanesque architecture had thick, blocky walls with little room for window space, Gothic architecture, technically more sophisticated, replaced stone with stained glass.

Most medieval churches were built in the form of a cross, often topped by a tower in Romanesque churches. The nave, divided into bays (the spaces between columns) and flanked on either side by aisles, formed the main body of the church, with the east end, known as the chancel, containing the choir and altar. Many Gothic churches also have a number of small chapels behind the high altar, forming an outline known as the *chevet,* or apse.

Romanesque and gothic churches are divided into three or four distinct vertical sections, like strata. Forestlike rows of pillars, topped by carved capitals, spring from the ground either to a gallery or triforium (an arcade of small columns and arches, originally of stone, later filled with glass), then to a clerestory (row of windows) above. The Romanesque facade was intended as an ornate screen and was sometimes fronted by a large porch (or narthex). The tympanum, a large sculpted panel above the central doorway (usually representing Christ in Judgment or Glory), was retained in the Gothic facade, which also featured huge portals, a circular rose window, a statue gallery, and lofty towers. Other towers, over the crossing or alongside the transepts, gradually lost favor: The stone bulls on top of the many-towered cathedral of Laon mourn a dying breed.

POINTED ARCHES and ribbed vaults were first used during the 1130s at Sens and St-Denis—home of Abbot Suger, the leading political figure of the day. Within a decade, local bishops had followed Suger's lead, and huge Gothic cathedrals were under way at Noyon, Senlis, and Laon. As France expanded during the early Middle Ages from its Parisian epicenter, Gothic went with it. But the Gothic style did not displace the Romanesque overnight. Many Romanesque churches survive as crypts beneath later buildings (as at Dijon Cathedral, for example). Similarly, Romanesque naves were conserved at Mont-St-Michel, Vézelay, and Le Mans despite the addition of new Gothic chancels. At Strasbourg Cathedral, the reverse is true and a Romanesque chancel survives.

As the Gothic style evolved, less and less stone was used, and churches became delicate, almost skeletal. Paris's Ste-Chapelle is the most famous example, though as a stained-glass showcase, its scale doesn't match that of Metz Cathedral or St-Urbain in Troyes. The circular rose window spans through the Middle Ages like a leitmotif, evolving from 13th-century geometric splendor at St-Denis and Notre-Dame in Paris to a petal-like fluidity during the first half of the 16th century.

Height was another Gothic quest. Roofs soared higher and higher—until that at Beauvais Cathedral came crashing down in 1284. Notre-Dame of Paris is 106 feet high, but later cathedrals are even taller: Chartres climbs 114 feet; Bourges 120; Reims 124; Amiens 137; and Beauvais an ill-fated 153.

The Chambiges family, last in a long line of medieval master masons and star glaziers, played a major role in the development of the Flamboyant style. When the bishop of Beauvais was planning a grandiose transept he sent for Martin Chambiges, tempting him away from Sens and keeping him jealously at Beauvais for 30 years. Some see in the flamelike Flamboyant style the last neurotic shrieks of Gothic decadence. But while its decorative profusion smacks of sculptural self-indulgence (St-Pierre in Caen is a good example), there are some admirable Flamboyant churches—take St-Séverin (Paris) and St-Nicolas de Port near Nancy.

In the 16th century, Gothic architecture was subject to the influx of Renaissance ideas, given official encouragement when François I (1515–47) invited Italian painters and architects Il Rosso, Primaticcio, and Leonardo da Vinci to his court. Renaissance architecture, marked by a stylistic return to ancient Rome, existed side by side with Gothic throughout the 16th century. In a number of Paris churches you will see classical columns and ornaments superimposed on Gothic structures (St-Étienne-du-Mont, St-Gervais, and St-Eustache are the best examples). While Gothic was essentially an ecclesiastical style, the chief creations of Renaissance architecture were the châteaux of noblemen, princes, and kings. In the Loire Valley, medieval castles (like Chinon) gradually yielded to ideals of comfort and luxury (like Cheverny). Along the way, Renaissance proportion and daintiness were mingled with medieval massiveness, as at Azay-le-Rideau and Amboise.

To contrast the Renaissance style with the Baroque, its successor, compare the pink-brick arcades of the place des Vosges in Paris (1612) with the grand, solemn stonework of the place Vendôme, built in 1685 across town. A similar difference can be observed between the intimate château of Fontainebleau (mid-16th century) and the immense palace of Versailles (late 17th century).

Baroque imbued the classical style with drama and a sense of movement: Take a look at Mansart's dome surging above Paris's Hôtel des Invalides, or the powerful rhythms of Charles Perrault's Louvre facade. Yet only in northern France, under the temporary influence of Spanish occupiers, did Latin exuberance find an outlet, typified in the soaring curls on the colossal belfry of St-Amand-les-Eaux near Lille. The overblown fantasies of Baroque in Italy, Spain, southern Germany, and Austria—wild curves, broken outlines, and sculptural overkill—were held firmly in check by the French love of discipline. Whole towns survive to remind us: The rigid plan and identical houses of Richelieu, south of Chinon, are restrained and austere.

The 18th century saw several major provincial building programs in the neoclassical style—a more literal, toned-down interpretation of antique precedent. The state rooms of Strasbourg's Château des Rohan, the charming place Stanislas in Nancy, and the Grand Théâtre and place de la Bourse in Bordeaux are top examples. Baroque, however, continued to dominate church building until the early 19th century (witness the cathedrals of Nancy and Arras). Many clerics commissioned architects to dress up Gothic buildings in classical apparel, sticking pilasters on columns or transforming pointed arches into rounded ones. Louis XIV set the tone by remodeling the choir of Notre-Dame in Paris in 1708, but Autun Cathedral—revamped throughout—is the most extreme example of such architectural rethink.

Napoléon ushered in the 19th century with the Arc de Triomphe, which remained unfinished for 20 years—typifying the hesitations of a century bereft of original ideas. Iron made its appearance—most obviously at the Eiffel Tower, most frequently accompanied by glass in train stations and covered markets.

The 19th century bequeathed us Paris as we know it, with Baron Haussmann carving boulevards through the city. Luckily, Haussmann's seven-story buildings have proved sufficiently large and imposing to withstand the rapacious onslaughts of modern developers, and central Paris has remained unchanged for 100 years. But it's not surprising that the showpiece of Haussmann's Paris, the Opéra, is a pompous jumble of styles.

THINGS PERKED UP in the 20th century. While such Paris landmarks as the Grand and Petit Palais and opulent town halls throughout the country were faithful to conservative taste, Émile Gallé and Hector Guimard led an artistic revolution known as Art Nouveau, with sinuous, nature-based forms. The Paris métro, ornamented by iron railings and canopies, is the most familiar example. A reaction occurred in the straighter lines of Art Deco, which first turned up at the Théâtre des Champs-Elysées in 1913. At the same time, the French developed a taste for reinforced concrete that they have never lost. Its most imaginative exponent was Swiss-born Le Corbusier, an architectural Picasso whose best work (like the chapel at Ronchamp in eastern France) obeys few established rules.

In the first half of the 20th century, much energy was spent repairing the damage of two world wars: Many towns had to be rebuilt almost from scratch. The result at its worst was bland and hurried (Amiens, Reims), at its best spacious, rational, and monumentally austere (Le Havre). Official buildings—like town halls and train stations—number among the most significant buildings of the period.

The most visited postwar building in France is Paris's futuristic Pompidou Center. Its pipes and workings are on the outside, ensuring that the interior is uncluttered to a fault. Paris's latter-day skyscrapers have—with the exception of the Tour Montparnasse—been banished to the city outskirts, notably La Défense. There, since 1989, the giant glass and concrete arch known as La Tête Défense has cemented a vista that stretches along the avenue de la Grande Armée, past the Arc de Triomphe, down the Champs-Elysées, across the place de la Concorde, and over the Tuileries to the gleaming glass pyramid of the Louvre.

— Simon Hewitt

BOOKS AND VIDEOS

THE BEST INTRODUCTION to modern France, surveying social, political, and economic developments, is John Ardagh's *France Today* (Penguin). A witty, but less complete, survey of the country and its people is Theodore Zeldin's *The French* (Pantheon); Joseph T. Carroll's *The French—How They Live and Work* (David & Charles) is in a similar vein. Another entry on the list is Richard Bernstein's *Fragile Glory* (Knopf). An immensely popular, if slightly satiric, introduction to French country life is provided by Peter Mayle's two autobiographical books on Provence, *A Year in Provence* and *Toujours Provence* (Knopf).

Nancy Mitford's readable *The Sun King* (Crown) covers the regal grandeur of the 17th century, while Alfred Cobban's workmanlike *History of Modern France* (Pelican) describes trends and events from the death of Louis XIV up to 1962. For a history of Paris from the Revolution to the Belle Epoque, try Johannes Willms's *Paris: Capital of Europe* (Holmes & Meier). For modern French history, particularly the Vichy Era, good bets are Paul Webster's *Pétain's Crime* (Macmillan), and Robert Paxton's *Vichy France* (Knopf) and *Vichy & the Jews* (Shocken). Architecture buffs should read Henri Focillon's thoughtfully illustrated *The Art of the West* (Cornell University Press), a scholarly study of Romanesque and Gothic architecture.

Historian and archaeologist Dorothy Carrington's well-documented *Granite Island: A Portrait of Corsica,* gives a thoughtful insight into the islanders' archaic beliefs, infamous vendettas, and complicated internal politics.

As for books about French wine and cuisine, Patricia Wells's *The Food Lover's Guide to Paris* and *The Food Lover's Guide to France* (Workman Publishing) provide a great beginning. One wine book, Eunice Fried's *Burgundy, the Country, the Wines, the People* (Harper & Row), gives a good account of Burgundy, while Nicholas Faith's *The Winemasters* (Hamish Hamilton) offers a full history of Bordeaux's ups and downs. Steven Spurrier's pocket-size *French Country Wines* (Putnam) is unusually thorough in its treatment of lesser-known wines, often representing good value. Alexis Lichine's *Guide to Wines and Vineyards of France* (Knopf) is still the classic wine guide. A. J. Leibling's *Between Meals* (Modern Library) provides a more entertaining look at the fine art of eating in France.

Charles Dickens in *A Tale of Two Cities* (Bantam), George Orwell in *Down and Out in Paris and London* (Penguin), Ernest Hemingway, notably in *A Moveable Feast* (Scribner), F. Scott Fitzgerald in *Tender is the Night* (Scribner), and Gertrude Stein in *Paris, France* are just some of the authors who have written about Paris in English. The novels of Émile Zola—*La Curée, L'Assommoir, Nana,* and *La Débâcle* (Penguin)—are situated mostly in Provence or in Paris, emerging from mid-19th-century reconstruction amid backstreet squalor and brash glamour.

Several good thrillers set in France are *Assignment in Brittany* (Fawcett), by Helen MacInnes; Pierre Salinger's *The Dossier* (Doubleday); Philip Loraine's *Death Wishes* (St. Martins); and *Most Secret* (Amereon), by Nevil Shute.

If you want to see France on film before you go, consider renting one of the following films: *A Sunday in the Country* (1984), Bertrand Tavernier's story of a day in the life of an elderly painter on his country estate; *Everyone Says I Love You* (1996), a Woody Allen musical with Paris as a backdrop; *Jean de Florette* (1986) or *My Father's Glory* (1990), Claude Berri's and Yves Robert's views of rural Provençal life; *My Favorite Season* (1993), André Techiné's family drama set in southwest France; *Mr. Hulot's Holiday* (1953), Jacques Tati's classic comedy on the beach in Brittany; *Ready to Wear* (1994), Robert Altman's send-up of the fashion industry in Paris; *Return of Martin Guerre* (1982), Daniel Vigne's vision of 16th-century village life; *To Catch a Thief* (1955), Alfred Hitchcock's mystery on the French Riviera with Grace Kelly and Cary Grant.

FRENCH VOCABULARY

One of the trickiest French sounds to pronounce is the nasal final *n* sound (whether or not the *n* is actually the last letter of the word). You should try to pronounce it as a sort of nasal grunt—as in "huh." The vowel that precedes the *n* will govern the vowel sound of the word, and in this list we precede the final *n* with an *h* to remind you to be nasal.

Another problem sound is the ubiquitous but untransliterable *eu,* as in *bleu* (blue) or *deux* (two), and the very similar sound in *je* (I), *ce* (this), and *de* (of). The closest equivalent might be the vowel sound in "put," but rounded.

Words and Phrases

Basics

English	French	Pronunciation
Yes/no	Oui/non	wee/nohn
Please	S'il vous plaît	seel voo **play**
Thank you	Merci	mair-**see**
You're welcome	De rien	deh ree-**ehn**
That's all right	Il n'y a pas de quoi	eel nee ah pah de **kwah**
Excuse me, sorry	Pardon	pahr-**dohn**
Sorry!	Désolé(e)	day-zoh-**lay**
Good morning/ afternoon	Bonjour	bohn-**zhoor**
Good evening	Bonsoir	bohn-**swahr**
Goodbye	Au revoir	o ruh-**vwahr**
Mr. (Sir)	Monsieur	muh-**syuh**
Mrs. (Ma'am)	Madame	ma-**dam**
Miss	Mademoiselle	mad-mwa-**zel**
Pleased to meet you	Enchanté(e)	ohn-shahn-**tay**
How are you?	Comment ça va?	kuh-mahn-sa-**va**
Very well, thanks	Très bien, merci	tray bee-ehn, mair-**see**
And you?	Et vous?	ay **voo**?

Numbers

English	French	Pronunciation
one	un	uhn
two	deux	deuh
three	trois	twah
four	quatre	**kaht**-ruh
five	cinq	sank
six	six	seess
seven	sept	set
eight	huit	wheat
nine	neuf	nuff
ten	dix	deess
eleven	onze	ohnz
twelve	douze	dooz

thirteen	treize	trehz
fourteen	quatorze	kah-**torz**
fifteen	quinze	kanz
sixteen	seize	sez
seventeen	dix-sept	deez-**set**
eighteen	dix-huit	deez-**wheat**
nineteen	dix-neuf	deez-**nuff**
twenty	vingt	vehn
twenty-one	vingt-et-un	vehnt-ay-**uhn**
thirty	trente	trahnt
forty	quarante	ka-**rahnt**
fifty	cinquante	sang-**kahnt**
sixty	soixante	swa-**sahnt**
seventy	soixante-dix	swa-sahnt-**deess**
eighty	quatre-vingts	kaht-ruh-**vehn**
ninety	quatre-vingt-dix	kaht-ruh-vehn-**deess**
one-hundred	cent	sahn
one-thousand	mille	meel

Colors

black	noir	nwahr
blue	bleu	bleuh
brown	brun/marron	bruhn/mar-**rohn**
green	vert	vair
orange	orange	o-**rahnj**
pink	rose	rose
red	rouge	rooje
violet	violette	vee-o-**let**
white	blanc	blahnk
yellow	jaune	zhone

Days of the Week

Sunday	dimanche	**dee**-mahnsh
Monday	lundi	**luhn**-dee
Tuesday	mardi	**mahr**-dee
Wednesday	mercredi	**mair**-kruh-dee
Thursday	jeudi	**zhuh**-dee
Friday	vendredi	**vawn**-druh-dee
Saturday	samedi	**sahm**-dee

Months

January	janvier	**zhahn**-vee-ay
February	février	**feh**-vree-ay
March	mars	marce
April	avril	a-**vreel**
May	mai	meh
June	juin	zhwehn
July	juillet	**zhwee**-ay
August	août	oot
September	septembre	sep-**tahm**-bruh
October	octobre	awk-**to**-bruh
November	novembre	no-**vahm**-bruh
December	décembre	day-**sahm**-bruh

Useful Phrases

Do you speak . . . English?	Parlez-vous . . . anglais?	par-lay **voo** **ahn**-glay
I don't speak . . . French	Je ne parle pas . . . français	zhuh nuh parl **pah** frahn-**say**
I don't understand	Je ne comprends pas	zhuh nuh kohm-prahn **pah**
I understand	Je comprends	zhuh kohm-**prahn**
I don't know	Je ne sais pas	zhuh nuh say **pah**
I'm American/ British	Je suis américain/ anglais	zhuh sweez a-may-ree-**kehn**/ahn-**glay**
What's your name?	Comment vous appelez-vous?	ko-mahn voo za-pell-ay-**voo**
My name is . . .	Je m'appelle . . .	zhuh ma-**pell** . . .
What time is it?	Quelle heure est-il?	kel air eh-**teel**
How?	Comment?	ko-**mahn**
When?	Quand?	kahn
Yesterday	Hier	yair
Today	Aujourd'hui	o-zhoor-**dwee**
Tomorrow	Demain	duh-**mehn**
This morning/ afternoon	Ce matin/cet après-midi	suh ma-**tehn**/set ah-pray-mee-**dee**
Tonight	Ce soir	suh **swahr**
What?	Quoi?	kwah
What is it?	Qu'est-ce que c'est?	kess-kuh-**say**
Why?	Pourquoi?	**poor**-kwa
Who?	Qui?	kee
Where is . . .	Où se trouve . . .	oo suh **troov**
the train station?	la gare?	la gar
the subway? station?	la station de? métro?	la sta-**syon** duh may-**tro**
the bus stop?	l'arrêt de bus?	la-**ray** duh **booss**
the airport?	l'aérogare?	lay-ro-**gar**
the post office?	la poste?	la post
the bank?	la banque?	la bahnk
the hotel?	l'hôtel?	lo-**tel**
the store?	le magasin?	luh ma-ga-**zehn**
the cashier?	la caisse?	la **kess**
the museum?	le musée?	luh mew-**zay**
the hospital?	l'hôpital?	lo-pee-**tahl**
the elevator?	l'ascenseur?	la-sahn-**seuhr**
the telephone?	le téléphone?	luh tay-lay-**phone**
Where are the rest rooms?	Où sont les toilettes?	oo sohn lay twah-**let**
Here/there	Ici/là	ee-**see**/la
Left/right	A gauche/à droite	a goash/a drwaht
Straight ahead	Tout droit	too drwah

Is it near/far?	C'est près/loin?	say pray/lwehn
I'd like . . .	Je voudrais . . .	zhuh voo-**dray**
a room	une chambre	ewn **shahm**-bruh
the key	la clé	la clay
a newspaper	un journal	uhn zhoor-**nahl**
a stamp	un timbre	uhn **tam**-bruh
I'd like to buy . . .	Je voudrais acheter . . .	zhuh voo-**dray** **ahsh**-tay
a cigar	un cigare	uhn see-**gar**
cigarettes	des cigarettes	day see-ga-**ret**
matches	des allumettes	days a-loo-**met**
dictionary	un dictionnaire	uhn deek-see-oh-**nare**
soap	du savon	dew sah-**vohn**
city map	un plan de ville	uhn plahn de **veel**
road map	une carte routière	ewn cart roo-tee-**air**
magazine	une revue	ewn reh-**vu**
envelopes	des enveloppes	dayz ahn-veh-**lope**
writing paper	du papier à lettres	dew pa-pee-**ay** a **let**-ruh
airmail writing paper	du papier avion	dew pa-pee-**ay** a-vee-**ohn**
postcard	une carte postale	ewn cart pos-**tal**
How much is it?	C'est combien?	say comb-bee-**ehn**
It's expensive/cheap	C'est cher/pas cher	say share/pa share
A little/a lot	Un peu/beaucoup	uhn peuh/bo-**koo**
More/less	Plus/moins	plu/mwehn
Enough/too (much)	Assez/trop	a-say/tro
I am ill/sick	Je suis malade	zhuh swee ma-**lahd**
Call a . . . doctor	Appelez un . . . médecin	a-play uhn mayd-**sehn**
Help!	Au secours!	o suh-**koor**
Stop!	Arrêtez!	a-reh-**tay**
Fire!	Au feu!	o fuh
Caution!/Look out!	Attention!	a-tahn-see-**ohn**

Dining Out

A bottle of . . .	une bouteille de . . .	ewn boo-**tay** duh
A cup of . . .	une tasse de . . .	ewn **tass** duh
A glass of . . .	un verre de . . .	uhn **vair** duh
Ashtray	un cendrier	uhn sahn-dree-**ay**
Bill/check	l'addition	la-dee-see-**ohn**
Bread	du pain	dew pan
Breakfast	le petit-déjeuner	luh puh-**tee** day-zhuh-**nay**
Butter	du beurre	dew burr
Cheers!	A votre santé!	ah vo-truh sahn-**tay**
Cocktail/aperitif	un apéritif	uhn ah-pay-ree-**teef**

Dinner	le dîner	luh dee-**nay**
Special of the day	le plat du jour	luh plah dew **zhoor**
Enjoy!	Bon appétit!	bohn a-pay-**tee**
Fixed-price menu	le menu	luh may-**new**
Fork	une fourchette	ewn four-**shet**
I am diabetic	Je suis diabétique	zhuh swee dee-ah-bay-**teek**
I am on a diet	Je suis au régime	zhuh sweez oray-**jeem**
I am vegetarian	Je suis végé-tarien(ne)	zhuh swee vay-zhay-ta-ree-**en**
I cannot eat . . .	Je ne peux pas manger de . . .	zhuh nuh **puh** pah mahn-**jay** deh
I'd like to order	Je voudrais commander	zhuh voo-**dray** ko-mahn-**day**
I'm hungry/thirsty	J'ai faim/soif	zhay fahm/swahf
Is service/the tip included?	Le service est-il compris?	luh sair-**veess** ay-teel com-**pree**
It's good/bad	C'est bon/mauvais	say bohn/mo-**vay**
It's hot/cold	C'est chaud/froid	say sho/frwah
Knife	un couteau	uhn koo-**toe**
Lunch	le déjeuner	luh day-zhuh-**nay**
Menu	la carte	la cart
Napkin	une serviette	ewn sair-vee-**et**
Pepper	du poivre	dew **pwah**-vruh
Plate	une assiette	ewn a-see-**et**
Please give me . . .	Merci de me donner . . .	Mair-**see** deh meh doe-**nay**
Salt	du sel	dew sell
Spoon	une cuillère	ewn kwee-**air**
Sugar	du sucre	dew **sook**-ruh
Waiter!/Waitress!	Monsieur!/ Mademoiselle!	muh-**syuh**/ mad-mwa-**zel**
Wine list	la carte des vins	la **cart** day van

MENU GUIDE

General Dining

French	English
Entrée	Appetizer/Starter
Garniture au choix	Choice of vegetable side
Selon arrivage	When available
Supplément/En sus	Extra charge
Sur commande	Made to order

Breakfast

French	English
Confiture	Jam
Miel	Honey
Oeuf à la coque	Boiled egg
Oeufs au bacon	Bacon and eggs
Oeufs sur le plat	Fried eggs
Oeufs brouillés	Scrambled eggs
Tartine	Bread with butter or jam

Appetizers/Starters

French	English
Anchois	Anchovies
Andouille(tte)	Chitterling sausage
Assiette de charcuterie	Assorted pork products
Crudités	Mixed raw vegetable salad
Escargots	Snails
Jambon	Ham
Jambonneau	Cured pig's knuckle
Pâté	Liver puree blended with meat
Quenelles	Light dumplings
Saucisson	Dried sausage
Terrine	Pâté in an earthenware pot

Soups

French	English
Bisque	Shellfish soup
Bouillabaisse	Fish and seafood stew
Julienne	Vegetable soup
Potage/Soupe	Soup
Potage parmentier	Thick potato soup
Pot-au-feu	Stew of meat and vegetables
Soupe du jour	Soup of the day
Soupe à l'oignon gratinée	French onion soup
Soupe au pistou	Provençal vegetable soup
Velouté de . . .	Cream of . . .
Vichyssoise	Cold leek and potato cream soup

Fish and Seafood

French	English
Bar	Bass
Bourride	Fish stew from Marseilles
Brandade de morue	Creamed salt cod
Brochet	Pike
Cabillaud/Morue	Fresh cod
Calmar	Squid
Coquilles St-Jacques	Scallops
Crabe	Crab
Crevettes	Shrimp
Daurade	Sea bream

Écrevisses	Prawns/crayfish
Harengs	Herring
Homard	Lobster
Huîtres	Oysters
Langouste	Spiny lobster
Langoustine	Prawn/lobster
Lotte	Monkfish
Lotte de mer	Angler
Loup	Catfish
Maquereau	Mackerel
Matelote	Fish stew in wine
Moules	Mussels
Palourdes	Clams
Perche	Perch
Poulpe	Octopus
Raie	Skate
Rascasse	Scorpion-fish
Rouget	Red mullet
Saumon	Salmon
Thon	Tuna
Truite	Trout

Meat

Agneau	Lamb
Ballotine	Boned, stuffed, and rolled
Blanquette de veau	Veal stew with a white-sauce base
Boeuf	Beef
Boeuf à la Bourguignonne	Beef stew
Boudin blanc	Sausage made with white meat
Boudin noir	Sausage made with pig's blood
Boulettes de viande	Meatballs
Brochette	Kabob
Cassoulet	Casserole of white beans, meat
Cervelle	Brains
Châteaubriand	Double fillet steak
Côtelettes	Chops
Choucroute garnie	Sausages and cured pork served with sauerkraut
Côte de boeuf	T-bone steak
Côte	Rib
Cuisses de grenouilles	Frogs' legs
Entrecôte	Rib or rib-eye steak
Épaule	Shoulder
Escalope	Cutlet
Foie	Liver
Gigot	Leg
Langue	Tongue
Médaillon	Tenderloin steak
Pavé	Thick slice of boned beef
Pieds de cochon	Pig's feet
Porc	Pork
Ragoût	Stew
Ris de veau	Veal sweetbreads
Rognons	Kidneys
Saucisses	Sausages
Selle	Saddle

Tournedos	Tenderloin of T-bone steak
Veau	Veal
Viande	Meat

Methods of Preparation

À point	Medium
À l'étouffée	Stewed
Au four	Baked
Bien cuit	Well-done
Bleu	Very rare
Bouilli	Boiled
Braisé	Braised
Frit	Fried
Grillé	Grilled
Rôti	Roast
Saignant	Rare
Sauté/poêlée	Sautéed

Game and Poultry

Blanc de volaille	Chicken breast
Caille	Quail
Canard/caneton	Duck/duckling
Cerf/chevreuil	Venison (red/roe)
Coq au vin	Chicken stewed in red wine
Dinde/dindonneau	Turkey/young turkey
Faisan	Pheasant
Lapin	Rabbit
Lièvre	Wild hare
Oie	Goose
Pigeon/pigeonneau	Pigeon/squab
Pintade/pintadeau	Guinea fowl/young guinea fowl
Poularde	Fattened pullet
Poulet/Pouissin	Chicken/Spring chicken
Sanglier/marcassin	Wild boar/young wild boar
Volaille	Fowl

Vegetables

Artichaut	Artichoke
Asperge	Asparagus
Aubergine	Eggplant
Carottes	Carrots
Champignons	Mushrooms
Chou-fleur	Cauliflower
Chou (rouge)	Cabbage (red)
Choux de Bruxelles	Brussels sprouts
Courgette	Zucchini
Cresson	Watercress
Épinard	Spinach
Haricots blancs/verts	White kidney/green beans
Laitue	Lettuce
Lentilles	Lentils
Maïs	Corn
Oignons	Onions
Petits pois	Peas
Poireaux	Leeks
Poivrons	Peppers

Pomme de terre	Potato
Pommes frites	French fries
Tomates	Tomatoes

Sauces and Preparations

Béarnaise	Vinegar, egg yolks, white wine, shallots, tarragon
Béchamel	White sauce
Bordelaise	Mushrooms, red wine, shallots, beef marrow
Bourguignon	Red wine, herbs
Chasseur	Wine, mushrooms, shallots
Diable	Hot pepper
Forestière	Mushrooms
Hollandaise	Egg yolks, butter, vinegar
Indienne	Curry
Madère	With Madeira wine
Marinière	White wine, mussel broth, egg yolks
Meunière	Brown butter, parsley, lemon juice
Périgueux	With goose or duck liver puree and truffles
Poivrade	Pepper sauce
Provençale	Onions, tomatoes, garlic

Fruits and Nuts

Abricot	Apricot
Amandes	Almonds
Ananas	Pineapple
Cacahouètes	Peanuts
Cassis	Black currants
Cerises	Cherries
Citron/citron vert	Lemon/lime
Figues	Figs
Fraises	Strawberries
Framboises	Raspberries
Fruits secs	Dried fruit
Groseilles	Red currants
Marrons	Chestnuts
Melon	Melon
Mûres	Blackberries
Noisettes	Hazelnuts
Noix de coco	Coconut
Noix	Walnuts
Pamplemousse	Grapefruit
Pêche	Peach
Poire	Pear
Pomme	Apple
Pruneaux	Prunes
Prunes	Plums
Raisins blancs/noirs	Grapes green/purple
Raisins secs	Raisins

Desserts

Coupe (glacée)	Sundae
Crêpe	Thin pancake
Crème brûlée	Custard with caramelized topping

Crème caramel	Caramel-coated custard
Crème Chantilly	Whipped cream
Gâteau au chocolat	Chocolate cake
Glace	Ice cream
Mousse au chocolat	Chocolate mousse
Sabayon	Egg-and-wine-based custard
Tarte aux pommes	Apple pie
Tarte tatin	Caramelized apple tart
Tourte	Layer cake

Alcoholic Drinks

À l'eau	With water
Avec des glaçons	On the rocks
Kir	Chilled white wine mixed with black-currant syrup
Bière	Beer
blonde/brune	Light/dark
Calvados	Apple brandy from Normandy
Eau-de-vie	Brandy
Liqueur	Cordial
Poire William	Pear brandy
Porto	Port
Vin	Wine
sec	*dry/neat*
brut	*very dry*
léger	*light*
doux	*sweet*
rouge	*red*
rosé	*rosé*
mousseux	*sparkling*
blanc	*white*

Nonalcoholic Drinks

Café	Coffee
noir	*black*
crème	*with steamed milk/cream*
au lait	*with steamed milk*
décaféiné	*caffeine-free*
express	espresso
Chocolat chaud	Hot chocolate
Eau minérale	Mineral water
gazeuse/non gazeuse	*carbonated/still*
Jus de . . .	. . . juice
Lait	Milk
Limonade	Lemonade
Thé	Tea
au lait/au citron	*with milk/lemon*
glacé	*Iced tea*
Tisane	Herb tea

INDEX